You're Busy so We're Bite-Sized

- ✓ Complete Each Lesson in 30-45 minutes
- ✓ Video, Text, Assessment in Each Lesson
- ✓ Mobile App that Syncs Automatically with the Online Course
- ✓ Always Know Exactly Where You Stand
- ✓ Lesson Progress and Mastery Metrics

Your Plan to Pass is Waiting

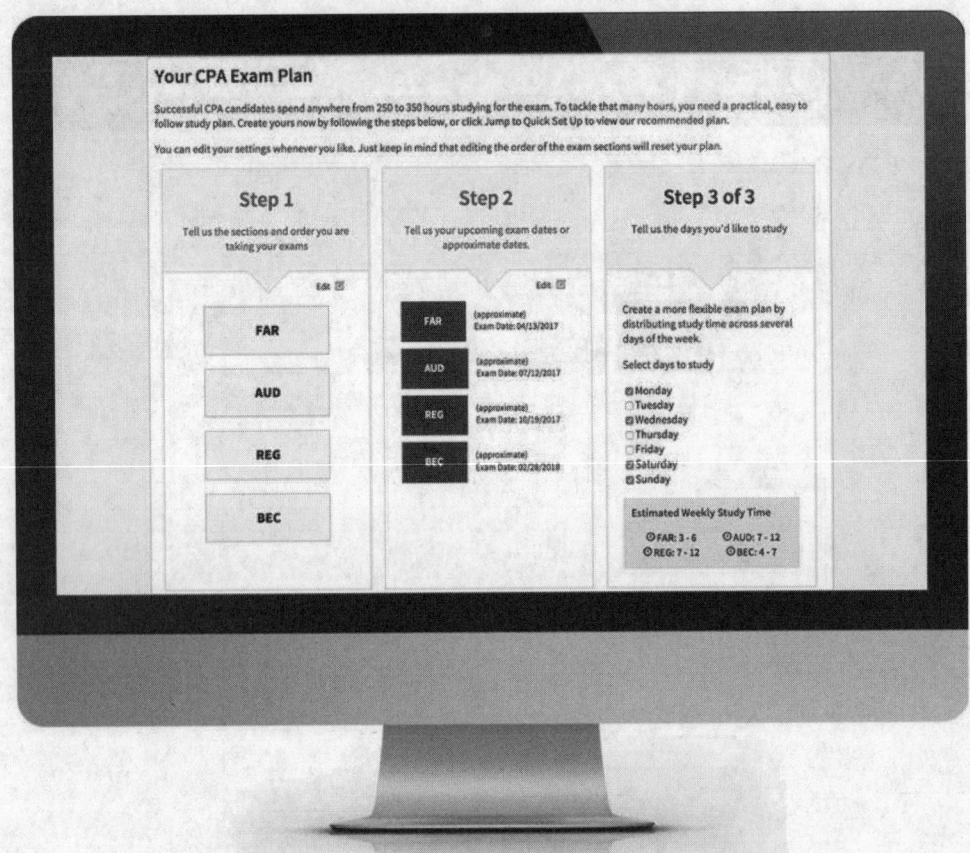

If you fail to plan, then plan to fail. Wiley's Exam Planner is at the heart of why 9 out of 10 pass using our system.

- ✔ **Enter Your Exam Date**
- ✔ **Enter Your Weekly Study Hours**
- ✔ **See 700 Lessons Scheduled to the Day**

You Can Do This!

"

The Wiley CPAexcel comprehensive study materials are truly exceptional. Being able to listen to the video lectures and having access to the professor mentoring made the learning process a little more interactive and effective.

— Merike H, Arlington, VA

I used Wiley CPAexcel exclusively and was able to pass all four sections on the first try. The material they provide is very thorough and helped me to feel confident on exam day. The iPhone app was great and allowed me to go through practice questions at any time.

— Aaron J, New Canaan, CT

I passed all four sections of the CPA Exam on my first attempt and feel that Wiley CPAexcel contributed a great deal to my success. Wiley CPAexcel's Bite-Sized Lessons break the voluminous CPA Exam material into small, manageable pieces.

— Jason R, Emporia, KS

The video lectures, study texts, and various tools available enabled me to efficiently and effectively focus on weak areas in my review.

— Chris O, Tamuning, Guam

"

efficientlearning.com/resources

Wiley CPAexcel® Review

STUDY
GUIDE

APRIL 2017

Wiley CPAexcel® Exam Review

STUDY GUIDE

APRIL 2017

FINANCIAL ACCOUNTING AND REPORTING

Craig Bain, Ph.D., CPA
Charles J. Davis, Ph.D., CPA
Donald R. Deis Jr., Ph.D., CPA, CFE
Pam Smith, Ph.D., CPA, MBA

Wiley Efficient Learning™

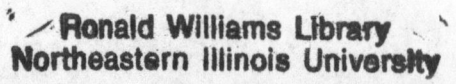

Contents

Contents

Contents

Contents

Contents

About the Authors

CPAexcel® content is authored by a team of accounting professors and CPA Exam experts from top accounting colleges such as the University of Texas at Austin (frequently ranked the #1 accounting school in the country), California State University–Sacramento, Northern Illinois University (frequently ranked in the top 10 in its peer group and top 20 overall), and the University of North Alabama.

Professor Craig Bain
CPAexcel® Author, Mentor, and Video Lecturer
Ph.D., CPA
Northern Arizona University, Franke College of Business, Professor and Accounting Area Coordinator

Professor Allen H. Bizzell
CPAexcel® Author, Mentor, and Video Lecturer
Ph.D., CPA (inactive)
Former Associate Dean and Accounting Faculty, University of Texas (Retired)
Associate Professor, Department of Accounting, Texas State University (Retired)

Professor Gregory Carnes
CPAexcel® Author and Video Lecturer
Ph.D., CPA
Raburn Eminent Scholar of Accounting, University of North Alabama
Former Dean, College of Business, Lipscomb University.
Former Chair, Department of Accountancy, Northern Illinois University

Professor B. Douglas Clinton
CPAexcel® Author and Video Lecturer
Ph.D., CPA, CMA
Alta Via Consulting Professor of Management Accountancy, Department of Accountancy, Northern Illinois University

Professor Charles J. Davis
CPAexcel® Author and Video Lecturer
Ph.D., CPA
Professor of Accounting, Department of Accounting, College of Business Administration, California State University—Sacramento

Professor Donald R. Deis Jr.
CPAexcel® Author and Video Lecturer
Ph.D., CPA, CFE
TAMUS Regents Professor and Ennis & Virginia Joslin Endowed Chair in Accounting, College of Business,
    Texas A&M University—Corpus Christi
Former Director, School of Accountancy, University of Missouri—Columbia
Former Professor and Director, Accounting
Ph.D. Program, Louisiana State University—Baton Rouge

Professor Emeritus Marianne M. Jennings
CPAexcel® Author and Video Lecturer
J.D.
Professor of Legal and Ethical Studies, W.P. Carey School of Business, Arizona State University

Professor Robert A. Prentice
CPAexcel® Author and Video Lecturer
J.D.
Ed and Molly Smith Centennial Professor In Business Law and Distinguished Teaching Professor, J.D., McCombs School of Business, University of Texas—Austin

Professor Pam Smith
CPAexcel® Author and Video Lecturer
Ph.D., MBA, CPA
KPMG Professor of Accountancy, Department of Accountancy, Northern Illinois University

Professor Dan N. Stone

CPAexcel® Author and Video Lecturer

Ph.D., MPA, CPA (inactive)

Gatton Endowed Chair, Von Allmen School of Accountancy, University of Kentucky

Professor Donald Tidrick

CPAexcel® Author and Video Lecturer

Ph.D., CPA, CMA, CIA

Deloitte Professor of Accountancy, Northern Illinois University

Former Associate Chairman of the Department of Accounting, Director of Professional Program in Accounting and Director
of the CPA Review Course, University of Texas at Austin

About the Financial Accounting Professors

Dr. Craig Bain received his Ph.D. at Texas A & M University in 1983 and has held faculty positions at Boise State University and Northern Arizona University. He has performed research in accounting, accounting information systems, and financial accounting. Professor Bain has taught accounting both on the undergraduate and continuing education levels. He is also an experienced Certified Public Accountant.

Dr. Charles Davis is currently Professor of Accounting in the College of Business Administration, California State University—Sacramento. His main teaching interest is financial reporting. He has taught in several educational and professional development programs including calculus for MBA students, CPA review courses, seminars for international groups from Russia, Turkmenistan, Latvia, and technical lectures in financial reporting for accounting professionals.

Professor Davis's work has been published in several domestic and international academic and professional journals in the area of accounting and healthcare finance. In addition, Dr. Davis is a coauthor of *Intermediate Accounting,* published by McGraw-Hill (2002), a mainstream accounting text used by many universities in the U.S. and internationally. Professor Davis also has written several online accounting educational packages and has reviewed 12 academic accounting texts.

Professor Davis has been involved in many consulting engagements in the area of financial reporting, real estate feasibility, EDP auditing and accounting systems, and has "Big Eight" accounting experience (now the "Big Four"). He is the recipient of teaching awards at California State University–Sacramento and the University of Illinois.

Dr. Donald R. Deis Jr. is Texas A&M University Regents Professor and the Ennis & Virginia Joslin Endowed Chair in Accounting within the College of Business at Texas A&M University—Corpus Christi. Prior to joining TAMUCC, Dr. Deis was the Joseph A. Silvoso Distinguished Director of the School of Accountancy at the University of Missouri-Columbia and was Ernst & Young Endowed Research Professor and Director of the Accounting Ph.D. Program at Louisiana State University—Baton Rouge. His primary research focus is on the quality of audits provided by public accounting firms, fraud, corporate governance, and the privatization of government services.

Dr. Pam Smith is KPMG Professor of Accountancy at Northern Illinois University. She has won more than a dozen teaching awards at all levels: department, college, university, state, and international. Dr. Smith is a leader in the creation and operation of NIU's nationally ranked ethics program, BELIEF (Building Ethical Leaders using an Integrated Ethics Framework). She is co-author of NIU's *Building Ethical Leaders* handbook. Her primary teaching and research interests are in financial reporting, mergers and acquisitions, risk management, and ethical business practices.

Welcome to Financial Accounting and Reporting

I. **Business Enterprise Accounting and Reporting**

   A. Business enterprise accounting and reporting relates to for-profit enterprises in the Financial Accounting and Reporting (FAR) section of the CPA Exam. The CPA Exam focuses on the accounting and reporting represented on the four major financial statements: balance sheet, income statement, statement of cash flows, and the statement of changes in equity. A very large amount of information is presented in FAR, but it all basically boils down to three functions:

     1. Recognition

     2. Measurement

     3. Disclosure

   B. One of the most important threads running through the CPA Exam is the framework of concepts from which the FASB develops GAAP. This framework provides the theoretical underpinnings for all GAAP. The framework concepts are:

     1. Primary qualitative characteristics—Relevance and faithful representation;

     2. Enhancing qualitative characteristics—Comparability, verifiability, timeliness and understandability;

     3. Assumptions—Entity, going concern, time period and unit of measure;

     4. Principles—Historical cost, revenue recognition, matching and full disclosure;

     5. Constraint cost benefit.

     Each of these concepts is covered in the material.

   C. If you really understand these concepts, you then have a basis for figuring out specific questions in areas you may not have studied completely. Trust your training and your gut instinct when answering the questions. Basing your response on the framework will serve you well.

   D. All the areas and topics in the AICPA Content Specifications for FAR are covered in the study text. Generally, the topics are presented in the study text in the same sequence as they are presented in the Content Specification. However, in a few cases, the order of presentation for some items is different than in the specifications.

     1. The Content Specifications provide a complete list of matters subject to being tested on the exam, but the topics are not intended to be presented in a logical sequence for learning purposes.

     2. Therefore, a few topics have been rearranged in the study text to present them in a more logical sequence for learning purposes.

   E. In covering the material, you should spend more time on the areas most difficult for you. These may come from the following list of topics which are common on the exam:

     1. Financial Statements, including the statement of cash flows

     2. Revenue recognition

     3. Financial instruments, including investments, bonds and derivatives

     4. Stock options and earnings per share (EPS)

     5. Pensions

     6. Leases

     7. Income tax accounting

     8. Inventories

9. Accounting changes

10. Business combinations

11. Consolidated financial statements

F. For each topic, outline the main GAAP (what is recognized and when, how much, and are there additional important disclosures). Concentrate on journal entries. If you know how to record the relevant journal entries and understand how they affect the financial statements, you are 85% there.

G. Don't ignore topics you feel are really challenging. You learned it once, so you can refresh your mind more easily than you think. Remember dollar value LIFO for example—if you have covered this in your classes, you can "relearn" it quickly.

H. International Financial Reporting Standards (IFRS) are also covered throughout the study materials. Significant differences between U.S. GAAP and (IFRS) are tested. Review the significant differences that are presented at the end of all relevant lessons of the study text. Focus on differences related to recognition and measurement.

I. Finally, when you study and review, don't just read passively. There is so much to remember as you study:

1. Continually assess whether you understand the material.

2. Take notes in your own words on aspects that you find difficult to remember.

3. For the more complex material, jot down the main procedures and reasons for the procedure.

4. Periodically go back over your notes and you will find that the amount of material that seems most challenging begins to dwindle.

J. We are confident that you will succeed if you spend sufficient quality time studying the material and practicing the questions. Please let us know if you feel there are areas where the material needs improving. Thank you.

   ~ Professors Charles Davis and Pam Smith

II. Governmental and Not-for-Profit Enterprises

A. The governmental and not-for-profit (GNP) topics are traditionally covered in a governmental accounting course. If you took a governmental accounting course, you should find the questions to be fairly easy. Do not worry if you did not take such a course because the questions lean toward basic governmental and nonprofit accounting and financial reporting, which can be learned with a modest amount of effort.

B. Accounting and reporting for governmental entities

1. Governmental accounting concepts

   a. Measurement focus and basis of accounting

   b. Fund accounting concepts and application

   c. Budgetary process

2. Format and content of governmental financial statements

   a. Government-wide financial statements

   b. Governmental funds financial statements

   c. Conversion from fund to government-wide financial statements

   d. Proprietary fund financial statements

   e. Fiduciary fund financial statements

   f. Notes to financial statements

      g. Required supplementary information, including management's discussion and analysis

      h. Comprehensive annual financial report (CAFR)

3. Financial reporting entity including blended and discrete component units

4. Typical items and specific types of transactions and events: recognition, measurement, valuation and presentation in governmental entity financial statements in conformity with GAAP

      a. Net position and its three categories:

          i. Net investment in capital assets

          ii. Restricted

          iii. Unrestricted

      b. Capital assets and infrastructure

      c. Transfers

      d. Other financing sources and uses

      e. Fund balance and its five types:

          i. Nonspendable

          ii. Restricted

          iii. Committed

          iv. Assigned

          v. Unassigned

      f. Nonexchange revenues

      g. Expenditures

      h. Special Items

      i. Encumbrances

      j. Deferred outflows of resources and deferred inflows of resources

5. Accounting and financial reporting for governmental not-for-profit organizations (e.g., public colleges and universities and healthcare organizations)

C. Accounting and reporting for not-for-profit entities

1. Financial Statements

      a. Statement of financial position

      b. Statement of activities

      c. Statement of cash flows

      d. Statement of functional expenses (for VHWO)

2. Typical items and specific types of transactions and events: recognition, measurement, valuation and presentation in governmental entity financial statements in conformity with GAAP

      a. Support, revenues, and contributions

      b. Types of restrictions on resources:

          i. Temporarily restricted as to time

          ii. Temporarily restricted as to purpose or use

          iii. Permanently restricted (e.g., an endowment)

          iv. Unrestricted

    c. Three types of net assets

        i. Unrestricted

        ii. Temporarily restricted

        iii. Permanently restricted

    d. Expenses, including depreciation and functional expenses

    e. Investments

    f. Recent developments

    g. Accounting for not-for-profit college and universities and healthcare organizations

D. It is important to remember that the Governmental Accounting Standards Board (GASB) establishes accounting and reporting standards for state and local governmental entities. The Financial Accounting Standards Board (FASB) establishes accounting and reporting standards for not-for-profit (nongovernmental) entities. Be on the lookout for questions related to hospitals or universities since governmental hospitals and universities follow GASB standards while nongovernmental (not-for-profit) hospitals and universities follow FASB standards. It is possible that you will see task-based questions that will require you to search the FASB standards to answer not-for-profit questions.

E. In the governmental area, it is very important to have a good understanding of each of the types of funds used. You must know the basis of accounting for each fund type and the purpose of each fund. You should also have a good understanding of both government-wide financial statements (GASB Statement No. 34) and fund-level financial statements. If you took a governmental accounting course in the past, be careful with questions about fund balance since GASB Statement No. 54 completely changed all of the categories of fund balance and the word *reserve* no longer appears the fund balance section of combining and individual fund financial statements for governmental fund types. At the government-wide financial statement level and for proprietary and fiduciary fund financial statements, GASB Statement No. 63 changed *net assets* to *net position*. This change was made to accommodate two new financial statement elements: (1) deferred outflows of resources and (2) deferred inflows of resources.

F. In the not-for-profit area, you should expect questions about when to recognize a contribution as revenue and how to account for contributions that have restrictions related to purpose or time. You should also expect questions about promises to give that include a condition and what to do in those situations.

G. With practice, you should be able to master GNP questions. In my governmental accounting classes, I give a pretest on the first day with 20 typical GNP CPA Exam-style questions and a posttest at the end. Since GNP accounting is "different," the pretest result is usually less than 20% correct. The posttest is usually 85 to 90% correct. You should see similar results.

~ Professor Deis

Conceptual Framework and
Financial Reporting

Financial Accounting Standards Board (FASB)

Role and Standard-Setting Process

FASB and Standard Setting

This lesson presents an overview of the standard-setting process in the United States.

After studying this lesson, you should be able to:

1. Describe the role of the Financial Accounting Standards Board.
2. Describe the primary purpose of financial reporting.
3. List the three aspects of financial reporting addressed by GAAP.
4. Identify the major organizations in U.S. accounting standards.

I. **Introduction**

    A. Financial accounting and reporting is concerned with providing relevant information to all users of the financial statements: investors, creditors, competitors, employees, and regulatory bodies. Financial statement information is used to make informed decisions regarding allocation of resources. A common use is whether to invest in a firm or to lend money to it.

    B. Financial information is disseminated in many forms including news releases, prospectuses for future securities offerings, filings with the Securities and Exchange Commission (SEC), and annual reports to shareholders. Financial statements are the culmination of the accounting process and represent the most comprehensive financial information disclosures made by firms. The footnotes and other textual and tabular information provide supplementary information and help to explain the amounts disclosed in those statements.

II. **Generally Accepted Accounting Principles (GAAP)**

Definition
Generally Accepted Accounting Principles (GAAP): The rules of financial reporting for business enterprises. GAAP are also called *accounting standards*.

    A. **What GAAP Addresses**—GAAP is a set of reporting rules to address three aspects of financial reporting:

        1. **Recognition**—A recognized item is recorded in an account and ultimately affects the financial statements.

Note
Recognition is an accounting concept that indicates that the item is recorded on the financial statements. In contrast, *realization* is an economic concept that indicates that cash is paid or received. GAAP focuses on accrual accounting and therefore is concerned with recognition more than with realization.

        2. **Measurement**—Concerns the dollar amount assigned to an item.

        3. **Disclosure**—Many unrecognized amounts are reported in the footnotes to complete the portrayal of the firm's financial position and performance.

    B. GAAP affects what is disclosed in financial statements and in what amount. For example, GAAP requires that many assets be reported at their historical cost, rather than at current market value.

Without a relatively uniform set of GAAP, business entities would be free to report whatever amounts they desired.

III. Organizations Involved in Developing Accounting Standards

A. **Financial Accounting Standards Board (FASB)**—The FASB is currently the standard-setting body in the United States.

B. The **Securities and Exchange Commission (SEC)** is the federal government agency that administers the securities laws of the United States. These laws affect firms that issue debt and equity securities to the public. Such firms register with the SEC and are called *registrants*. The financial statements of these firms must be filed with the SEC and must be audited by independent third parties (CPA firms).

C. Congress granted the SEC the authority to establish GAAP for the firms within its jurisdiction (publicly traded firms) but generally has ceded this authority to a private sector body (currently, the FASB). In a few instances, the SEC has exercised its right to reverse or modify an accounting standard adopted by the private sector body. The SEC also has pressured the FASB to establish certain principles more quickly.

D. The FASB considers the potential reaction of the SEC to its proposed standards. The SEC frequently responds to the FASB's initial "exposure" draft providing useful commentary for the final pronouncement.

E. The **American Institute of Certified Public Accountants (AICPA)** is the national professional organization for practicing CPAs and has had a great impact on accounting principles over the years. The mission of the AICPA is to provide its members with resources, information, and leadership so that they may in turn provide valuable services for the benefit of their clients, employers, and the general public.

F. In 1939, the AICPA appointed its Committee on Accounting Procedure (CAP), the first private sector body charged with the responsibility of promulgating GAAP. CAP issued 51 Accounting Research Bulletins (ARBs). To the extent that an ARB has not been rescinded or superseded, it constitutes GAAP.

G. In 1959, the AICPA created the Accounting Principles Board (APB), another committee, to take over the work of CAP. The APB is the second private sector group designated to formulate GAAP. Members were required to be CPAs. The APB issued 31 opinions, many of which remain as GAAP, in whole or in part.

H. In 1971, the AICPA appointed the Wheat Committee, which recommended the formation of yet another private sector body—the FASB—to take over the reins from the APB. In 1973, the FASB assumed the role of standard setter for the accounting profession. The FASB is not affiliated with the AICPA.

I. The **FASB** is one of three parts of the current accounting standard-setting mechanism in the United States. The other two are the Financial Accounting Foundation (FAF)—the parent body, and the Financial Accounting Standards Advisory Council (FASAC):

1. FAF—Appoints the members of the FASB and its advisory councils, ensures adequate funding for the FASB, and exercises oversight over the FASB. Funding sources include fees levied on publicly traded firms under the Sarbanes-Oxley Act, contributions, and publication sales. The trustees of the FAF are appointed from organizations with an interest in accounting standards.

2. FASB—Establishes financial accounting standards for business entities. The FASB is an independent body, subject only to the FAF.

3. FASAC—Provides guidance on major policy issues, project priorities, and the formation of task forces.

J. The FASB is the current private-sector body that establishes GAAP for business entities. **The mission of the FASB** (in brief) is to:

1. Improve the usefulness of financial reporting

2. Maintain current accounting standards

3. Promptly address deficiencies in accounting standards

> **Note**
> *The FASB operated with seven Board members from its inception in 1973 until 2008 when the Board was reduced to five members. The Board membership increased back to seven in early 2011. The FAF Chairman, Jack Brennan, gave this rationale for the change: "Returning the Board to the seven-member structure will enhance the FASB's investment in the convergence agenda with the International Accounting Standards Board (IASB), while addressing the unprecedented challenges facing the American capital markets in the months and years ahead."*

    4. Promote international convergence of accounting standards

    5. Improve the common understanding of the nature and purposes of information in financial reports

K. Facts in Brief about the FASB

    1. Seven full-time members with renewable (for one additional term) and staggered 5-year terms

    2. Subject to FAF policies and oversight

    3. Members cannot have employment or investment ties with other entities.

    4. Members need not be CPAs although typically the public accounting profession is represented; also the preparer (reporting firm) and investor communities are represented.

L. In promulgating GAAP, the FASB applies the following principles:

    1. Accounting standards should be unbiased and not favor any particular industry; standards are for the benefit of financial statement users;

    3. The needs and views of the economic community should be considered; the views of the accounting profession should not take precedence;

    4. The process of developing standards should be open to the public and allow due process to provide opportunity for interested parties to make their views known;

    5. The benefits of accounting standards should exceed their cost.

M. The FASB Uses the Following Process when Issuing an Accounting Standard—The FASB:

    1. Considers whether to add a project to its agenda, in consultation with the FAF—the FASB receives many requests from its constituencies including the SEC, auditing firms, investors, and reporting firms to address new financial reporting issues and clarify existing standards

    2. Conducts research on the topic and issues a Discussion Memorandum detailing the issues surrounding the topic; the FASB's conceptual framework plays a role in this process by providing a theoretical structure for guiding the development of a specific standard

    3. Holds public hearings on the topic

    4. Evaluates the research and comments from interested parties and issues an Exposure Draft—the initial accounting standard

    5. Solicits additional comments, modifies the Exposure Draft if needed

    6. Finalizes the new accounting guidance and approves with a majority vote (four of seven affirmative votes)

    7. Issues an Accounting Standards Update (ASU). The section on FASB Codification discusses the nature of an ASU in greater detail

N. FASB's Emerging Issues Task Force (EITF)—This group was formed to consider emerging reporting issues and to accelerate the process of establishing rulings on such issues. In this sense, the EITF acts as a "filter" for the FASB, enabling the FASB to focus on more pervasive issues. When a consensus of the 15 members is reached on an issue, no further action by the FASB is required. EITF pronouncements are included in GAAP. If the EITF is unable to reach a consensus, the FASB may become involved, ultimately revising an existing standard or adopting a new one.

IV. The Political Nature of the Accounting Standard-Setting Process

    A. Parties, Preferences, and Outcomes—The parties interested in the outcome of the standard-setting process may have opposing preferences and interests. Firm managers (referred to as "preparers" or "preparer firms") often prefer standards with lower compliance costs and that tend to portray their firms in a more positive light (higher earnings and assets, lower liabilities).

    B. Financial statement users, on the other hand, prefer unbiased, transparent reporting. They want the facts. Investors also want conservative reporting-disclosure of less positive results under conditions of uncertainty or where the firm has a choice of reporting alternatives under GAAP. The FASB has pledged to adopt unbiased accounting standards, and thus has the interests of financial statement users in mind when developing accounting standards.

C. The FASB considers its conceptual framework, the collection of Statements of Financial Accounting Concepts (SFACs), a "constitution" or underlying set of theoretical concepts in its deliberations. However, the FASB does not create GAAP in a vacuum. Historically, the Board has been very responsive to the views of affected parties through its due diligence process and actively solicits public comment before adopting a final accounting standard.

D. User groups (e.g., industry associations, financial institutions) influence the outcome of FASB standards by:

    1. Making their views public through the financial press

    2. Providing input during the due process procedure

    3. Putting pressure on the SEC directly to change a proposed standard, or through the U.S. Congress

E. The Board is careful to pay attention to this type of input, particularly when it helps clarify the issues. However, although the FASB has pledged to be unbiased rather than promulgate standards favoring a particular reporting position or industry, it has admitted to responding to pressure from interested parties.

F. For example, negative *economic consequences* is often the argument of an interested party. Economic consequences refers to the effect of a proposed standard on a firm's financial statements. A common argument against a proposed standard is that it will cause earnings to decline, thus reducing the firm's ability to raise capital. Although some observers believe that the FASB should not be sensitive to the views of reporting firms, there have been some spectacular cases in which the FASB has delayed an accounting standard or even reversed itself in light of the concerns reporting firms have had about the "economic consequences" of a proposed standard.

V. Enforcement of GAAP

A. Methods of Enforcement

    1. Accounting standards are not laws; they are not determined by legislatures but rather by private sector bodies. They are *generally accepted*. GAAP are a type of regulation, imposed on the economic system by its constituents. Without GAAP, the economy and capital markets as we know them would not work. Investors need to have confidence in the numbers they receive. Without some kind of common language, the system could not function. Corruption would become much more prevalent than it is today.

    2. However, the private-sector bodies that contribute to the formulation of GAAP have no enforcement authority. Rather, there are economic sanctions for firms not complying with GAAP. These sanctions include increased difficulty in raising debt and equity capital.

    3. The SEC, however, does have the authority to penalize firms and managers subject to its jurisdiction when financial statements do not comply with GAAP. Public companies are violating the securities laws if they publish financial statements that materially depart from GAAP.

    4. The SEC sends a *deficiency* letter to a registrant when an accounting irregularity is found. If the firm disagrees, the SEC may issue a "stop order" preventing trading in the firm's securities until the disagreement is resolved. Outright violations of the securities laws may result in criminal sanctions against managers, or fines against the company.

    5. The enactment of the Sarbanes-Oxley Act of 2002 significantly affects the enforcement procedures relating to audits of public companies, and penalties for noncompliance with GAAP. The Auditing section of CPAexcel® covers the implications of this Act in depth.

Accrual Accounting

This lesson presents an overview of GAAP and the basic theory of accrual accounting.

After studying this lesson, you should be able to:

1. List the components of an external financial report.

2. Define accruals and deferrals and give examples of each.

3. Reconcile cash basis income to accrual basis income.

4. Reconcile accrual basis income to cash basis income.

I. Introduction

A. Financial accounting is, like most types of accounting, a service activity.

B. The provision of information is accomplished through the issuance of a General Purpose External Financial Report. That is, the financial report issued by business enterprises, is a general-purpose one intended for all external users. External users of financial reports do not have access to the internal records of businesses and thus are dependent on the information in the report. The report is a "general-purpose" report because it is designed to meet the information needs of a broad class of users (mainly investors and creditors), rather than a predefined specific use report.

C. **External Financial Report**—The general-purpose external financial report (also called the annual report) is prepared by applying Generally Accepted Accounting Principles (GAAP). The general-purpose external financial report has the following key components.

   1. Income Statement

   2. Statement of Comprehensive Income

   3. Balance Sheet

   4. Statement of Changes in Owners' Equity

   5. Statement of Cash Flows

   6. Footnote Disclosures and supplementary schedules

   7. Auditor's Opinion

D. **GAAP**—The composition of GAAP includes principles, methods, and procedures that are generally accepted by the accounting profession. The majority of GAAP includes the pronouncements issued by the Committee on Accounting Procedure (CAP), the Accounting Principles Board (APB), and the Financial Accounting Standards Board (FASB). The FASB Codification is the sole authoritative source for such GAAP and includes guidance from the above sources. For publicly traded entities, the SEC has additional reporting guidelines.

E. **Authoritative GAAP**

   1. **Codification**

      a. The FASB Accounting Standards Codification is the sole source of authoritative U.S. GAAP for nongovernmental entities, except for SEC guidance. All guidance in the Codification carries the same level of authority (one level of GAAP). There is no longer a hierarchy of GAAP.

      b. Accounting and financial reporting practices not included in the Codification are nonauthoritative.

      c. The Codification does not change GAAP but rather provides accounting standards in a newly structured electronic form. The Codification is a compilation and reorganization of existing GAAP before the Codification, with updates being added as they are promulgated. The individual accounting-standard form of presentation is not used in the Codification. Rather, material is organized by major area and topic. Basis for conclusions, appendices and other ancillary content are included in the Codification only if the material is considered essential to the understanding and application of GAAP.

    d. Some accounting standards have allowed entities to apply the provisions of superseded standards for transactions that have an ongoing effect on an entity's statements. Such superseded guidance continues to be authoritative but is not included in the Codification. Examples include pooling of interests and pension transition obligations.

    e. The Codification does not include guidance for non-GAAP matters including:

        i. Other Comprehensive Basis of Accounting

        ii. Cash Basis

        iii. Income Tax Basis

        iv. Regulatory Accounting Principles

2. No specified GAAP

    a. If guidance for a transaction or event is not specified in the Codification, authoritative GAAP for similar transactions or events should be considered before considering nonauthoritative GAAP. Sources of nonauthoritative guidance include widely recognized and prevalent practices, FASB Concepts Statements, AICPA Issues Papers, IFRS, and others. There is no implied hierarchy for these sources.

        i. The guidance for similar transactions or events is not followed if that guidance either prohibits the application of the guidance to the particular transaction or event, or indicates that the accounting treatment not be applied by analogy.

3. SEC guidance

    a. Authoritative GAAP include relevant SEC rules and interpretative releases (applicable only to publicly traded firms). The Codification includes relevant portions of SEC content but does not contain the entire text of relevant SEC rules, regulations, interpretive releases and staff guidance. For example, the Codification does not include SEC content related to Management's Discussion and Analysis and other items appearing outside the financial statements. The Codification does not replace or affect guidance issued by the SEC and is provided on a convenience basis.

    b. An adjacent lesson provides additional details on the structure and use of the Codification.

II. Accrual Basis of Accounting

    A. GAAP, and therefore the financial statements, reflect the accrual basis of accounting rather than the cash basis of accounting. Both U.S. and international GAAP reflect the accrual basis of accounting.

    B. Under the accrual basis, revenues are recognized when earned, regardless of the period of cash collection.

    C. Expenses are recognized when incurred, regardless of the period of cash payment.

    D. The accrual basis of accounting is preferred over the cash basis of accounting because it reflects a better association of revenues and expenses with the appropriate accounting period. The accrual basis of accounting recognizes all resource changes when they occur. The cash basis of accounting limits the recognition of resource changes to cash flows.

Example

A firm sells $40,000 worth of goods during the year, and collects $30,000 on the resulting accounts receivable. There is no uncertainty regarding the collection of the remaining $10,000. Under the accrual basis, $40,000 of revenues would be recognized for the year; under the cash basis, only $30,000 would be recognized. The next year, when the remaining $10,000 of cash is collected, the cash basis would recognize $10,000 of revenue. The accrual basis would recognize no additional revenue. The accrual basis provides a more comprehensive measurement of the change in value of the firm resulting from income producing activities for a period because it does not limit the recognition of resource changes to the cash flows for that period. Accrual accounting much more fully reflects the economic substance of transactions.

E. Accrual basis accounting recognizes and reports the **economic activities** of the firm in the period the activity was **incurred**, regardless of when the cash activity takes place. The table below depicts the possible scenarios and the terminology related to timing differences. In essence, cash can precede or follow an economic transaction. The economic transaction is one that generates revenue or expense.

The table displays a common theme for **accruals** and **deferrals**:

- When the economic event occurs, first you create an accrual account. (You are accruing the cash owed or to be paid as an asset or liability.)

- When the cash activity occurs, first you create a **deferral** account. (You are deferring the recognition of an expense or revenue as an asset or liability.)

Transaction	Event	Account created	Examples
Revenue	Cash received before revenue earned	Deferred revenue— liability	Rent, subscriptions, gift certificates
	Revenue earned before cash received	Accrued asset—asset	Sales on account, interest, rent
Expense	Cash paid before expense incurred	Deferred expense—asset	Prepaid insurance, supplies, rent, PP&E
	Expense incurred before cash paid	Accrued expense— liability	Salaries, wages, interest, taxes

Using the payment and receipt of $100 for rent, the entries made by the renter and rentee are shown below.

	Landlord (Rentee)	Tenant (Renter)
CASH RECEIVED THEN RENT EARNED		
Dec. entries: Rent paid December 31	Cash 100 Unearned 100 Rent (liability) (Rent revenue is deferred)	Prepaid 100 Rent (asset) Cash 100 (Rent expense is deferred)
Jan. entries: January rent earned	Unearned 100 Rent Rent revenue 100	Rent 100 expense Prepaid 100 Rent

RENT EARNED THEN CASH RECEIVED		

Dec. entries:
December rent paid on January 1
	Accrued Rent Revenue (asset) 100
	   Rent revenue 100
	(Rent revenue is accrued)
		Rent expense 100
		   Accrued Rent Expense (liability) 100
		(Rent expense is accrued)

Jan. entries:
December rent collected
	Cash 100
	   Accrued Rent Revenue 100
		Accrued Rent Expense 100
		   Cash 100

Important points to note. The revenue and expense are recorded in the period the economic event occurred (e.g., using the space). The accrual and deferral accounts are simply holding the revenue or expense amounts on the balance sheet until they can be recognized on the income statement.

Example

Assume Mayer Corporation had $28,000 of revenue in the first year of operations, $6,000 was on account and $22,000 was paid in cash. Mayer Corporation incurred operation expenses of $15,800, $12,000 was paid in cash and $3,800 was owed on account at year-end. In addition, Mayer Corporation prepaid $2,400 for insurance that will not be used until the next year.

Below are an Income Statement, Balance Sheet and Statement of Cash Flows under the cash basis and accrual basis of accounting. Note that the ending cash balance is exactly the same under both cash and accrual basis. The difference is the *timing* of the receipt and payment of cash.

Cash Basis

Income Statement		Balance Sheet	
Sales	$22,000	Cash	**$7,600**
Op Exp	(12,000)		
Ins Exp	(2,400)		
Total	$7,600		

Statement of Cash Flows—Direct Method

Operating Activities		
Sales		$22,000
Operating expense	(12,000)	
Insurance expense	(2,400)	
		(14,400)
Total Cash Flow from Operating Activities		**$7,600**

Note: Δ = change in the account balance.

Example
Continuation:

Below are an Income Statement, Balance Sheet and Statement of Cash Flows under the accrual basis of accounting.

Accrual Basis

Income Statement		Balance Sheet	
Sales	$28,000	Cash	$7,600
Op Exps	(15,800)	Acct Rec	6,000
		Prepaid	2,400
			$16,000
		Acct Pay	3,800
		Equity	12,200
Total	$12,200		$16,000

Statement of Cash Flows—Indirect Method

Operating Activities

Net Income		$12,200
ΔAccounts Receivable	(6,000)	
ΔPrepaid Expenses	(2,400)	
ΔAccounts Payable	3,800	
Total Cash Flow from Operating Activities		**$7,600**

Example
J&L Pecans maintain accounting records on an accrual basis. In 20X6 J&L decided to convert to cash basis accounting. During 20X5 J&L reported $95,178 of net income. On January 1, 20X5 and December 31, 20X5 J&L had the following amounts.

	January	December
Accounts receivable	9,250	15,927
Unearned revenue	2,840	4,111
Accrued expenses	3,435	2,108
Prepaid expense	1,917	3,232

Conversion of J&L's income from accrual basis to cash basis can be viewed various ways. The simplest way is to use the accounting equation. Starting with the accounting equation, we follow simple algebra to isolate the change in cash. (Note: Δ = change in account value.)

1) $A = L + E$
2) $\Delta A = \Delta L + \Delta E$
3) $\Delta cash + \Delta other\ assets = \Delta L + \Delta E$
4) $\Delta cash = \Delta L + \Delta E - \Delta other\ assets$

1) is the accounting equation; 2) is the change in all of the variables in the accounting equation (still an equality); 3) is separating the changes in cash from the changes in all other assets; and 4) is isolating cash on the left side of the equation. Using equation 4) we can convert J&L Pecans from accrual to cash:

Conversion of Accrual Basis to Cash Basis
For the Year 20X5

Net income on an accrual basis	$95,178
Subtract increase in accounts receivable ($9,250 – $15, 927)	(6,677)
Add increase in unearned service revenue ($2,840 – $4,111)	1,271
Subtract decrease in accrued expense ($3,435 – $2,108)	(1,327)
Subtract increase in prepaid expenses ($1,917 – $3,232)	(1,315)
Net income on an cash basis	$87,130

If you are asked to change from cash to accrual, you can still use the accounting equation formula, but the signs would be opposite those used in the conversion from accrual to cash.

Conversion of Cash Basis to Accrual Basis
For the Year 20X5

Net income on a cash basis	$87,130
Add increase in accounts receivable ($9,250 – $15, 927)	6,677
Subtract increase in unearned service revenue ($2,840 – $4,111)	(1,271)
Add decrease in accrued expense ($3,435 – $2,108)	1,327
Add increase in prepaid expenses ($1,917 – $3,232)	1,315
Net income on an accrual basis	$95,178

Financial Statements

This lesson presents a summary of the three primary financial statements.

After studying this lesson, you should be able to:

1. Describe the form and content of the income statement.

2. Describe the form and content of the balance sheet.

3. Describe the form and content of the statement of cash flows.

I. **Summary of the Primary Financial Statements**—Here we present an overall summary of the basic financial statements. Later lessons will cover each statement in more depth.

A. **Income Statement—Statement of Profit or Loss**

1. The income statement measures the performance of the firm for the period. It is dated for the entire period (e.g., for the year ended December 31, 20xX).

2. The income statement is prepared by applying the all-inclusive approach. That is, almost all revenues, expenses, gains, and losses are shown on the income statement and are included in the calculation of net income. A major exception here is prior period adjustments, which are the effects of corrections of errors affecting prior year net income. Prior period adjustments are shown on the Statement of Retained Earnings as adjustments to the beginning balance of retained earnings in the year the error is discovered.

3. There are other items that would appear to be income items but are not reflected in net income. These include unrealized gains and losses on investments in securities available-for-sale, certain pension cost adjustments, and foreign currency translation adjustments. These items are included in *comprehensive income*, which now is a required disclosure. However, except for items included in *comprehensive income* but not also in net income, prior period adjustments, and a few other items, the reporting of net income in the income statement reflects an all-inclusive approach.

B. **Statement of Comprehensive Income**

1. The statement of comprehensive income reports all non-owner changes in equity over a period of time—the same time period as the income statement. This statement is also dated for the year ended December 31, 20xX.

2. The statement of comprehensive income includes net income (or loss) and the items included in comprehensive income that are not part of net income. Those items include:

   a. Unrealized gains and losses on available-for-sale securities

   b. Adjustments in the calculation of the pension liability

   c. Foreign currency translation adjustments

   d. Deferrals of certain gains or losses on hedge accounting.

C. **Balance Sheet—Statement of financial position**

1. The balance sheet discloses the resources of the firm at a point in time. It is dated as of a specific date (e.g., December 31, 20xX).

2. The balance sheet is formally referred to as the Statement of Financial Position, but balance sheet is the more commonly used term. A business enterprise discloses its economic resources (assets) and the manner of financing the acquisition of those resources (creditors, owners' contributions, and prior year's earnings) in the balance sheet.

3. **Formats for presentation**

   a. The presentation format for a balance sheet is typically one of two formats: the account format or the report format.

   b. In the account format, the assets are shown on the left side of the page, and the liabilities and owners' equity are shown on the right side. This format emphasizes the balance sheet equation: A=L+OE.

Account Format at	
Debits	**Credits**
<u>Assets</u>	Liabilities
	<u>Stockholders' Equity</u>

   c. In the report format, which is the most popular form, the three categories of accounts are listed from top to bottom, as in a report, with assets always shown first.

Report Format at
<u>Assets</u>
Liabilities
<u>Stockholders' Equity</u>

4. **Classification of accounts**

   a. Regardless of balance sheet format, assets, liabilities, and equities are presented on the balance sheet in a prescribed order, which is summarized below.

      i. **Assets** are presented in order of decreasing liquidity. The most liquid assets (such as cash) are shown first, and less liquid assets are shown last (such as property, plant, and equipment).

      ii. **Liabilities** are shown in order of maturity. Current liabilities are presented first and then long-term liabilities are presented.

      iii. **Owners' Equity** (also referred to as Shareholders', Stockholders', or Shareowners' Equity) items are shown in order of permanence.

   Example
   For a corporation, the contributed capital accounts are shown first and retained earnings are typically shown as the final item in Stockholders' Equity. Retained earnings are thought to be less permanent due to the fact that dividends are a distribution of earnings.

5. **Balance sheet presentation**

   a. Balance sheet presentation reflects the classification of assets and liabilities. The classification criteria used for each is indicated below and is affected by the firm's operating cycle. The operating cycle of a firm is the period of time required to purchase or produce inventory, sell the inventory, and collect cash from the resulting receivables. For most firms, the operating cycle is significantly less than one year. For firms in some industries, such as construction, the operating cycle is longer than one year.

b. **Current assets**—Assets that are in the form of cash, or will be converted into cash, or consumed within one year or the operating cycle of the business, whichever is longer.

Example
Cash, accounts receivable, short-term investments, inventory, and prepaid assets are current assets.

c. **Current liabilities**—Liabilities that are due in the upcoming year or in the operating cycle of the business, whichever is longer, and that will be met through the transfer of a current asset or the creation of another current liability. Both criteria must be met in order for a liability to be classified as current.

Example
Accounts payable, wages payable, income tax payable, unearned revenues, and warranty liability are current liabilities. (For the last two items, only the portion to be extinguished within one year of the balance sheet would be classified as current.) Also, the current portion of long-term debt is classified as current; it is the amount of debt previously classified as long-term that is now due within one year of the balance sheet date.

d. **Long-term assets and long-term liabilities**—These are defined by exclusion. All assets that do not meet the criteria necessary to be classified as current are classified as long-term assets. Likewise, all liabilities that do not meet the criteria necessary to be classified as current are classified as long-term liabilities.

Example
Long-term investments, plant assets, certain deferred charges, and intangible assets are non-current assets. Notes and bonds payable and mortgages payable are long-term liabilities.

6. **Valuation and measurement**

a. Balance Sheet Valuation is summarized below but will be emphasized more in the coverage of individual balance sheet items. The point here is that the meaning of the dollar amount of an item listed in the balance sheet depends on the account being measured.

b. Several different measurement bases are currently used in the balance sheet. For example, an account receivable listed at $10,000 does not necessarily mean the same thing as $10,000 listed for an intangible asset.

Note
CPA Exam questions tend to emphasize sections of the balance sheet. For example, a question might focus on the property, plant, and equipment section of the balance sheet or on the long-term liability section of the balance sheet. As we cover the individual items presented on the balance sheet, these problems will be a primary focus.

Account Type	Measurement Basis
Property, Plant and Equipment, Intangibles	Historical Cost and Depreciated/Amortized Historical Cost
Receivables	Net Realizable Value
Inventory	Lower of Cost or Market
Investments in Marketable Securities	Market Value
Liabilities	Present Value
Owners' Equity	Historical Value of Cash Inflows and Residual Valuation

D. Statement of Stockholders' Equity—The statement of stockholders' equity (sometimes referred to as shareholders' equity) presents the changes in the owners' equity over a period of time—the same time period as the income statement. Like the income statement, this statement is dates for the year ended (e.g., December 31, 20xX). This statement presents the changes in contributed capital, additional paid-in capital, and retained earnings. These changes arise from the purchase and sale of shares of the entities stock, the changes in comprehensive income, and the payment of dividends.

E. Statement of Cash Flows

1. The statement of cash flows is the third of the three major financial statements required to be reported. It describes the major changes in cash by meaningful category. Like the income statement, it is dated for the entire period (e.g., for the year ended December 31, 20xX).

2. The purpose of the Statement of Cash Flows is to explain the change in cash and cash equivalents that has occurred during the past accounting year. Cash equivalents are short-term investments that:

   a. Are convertible into a known and fixed amount of cash; *and*

   b. Have an original maturity to the purchaser of three months or less.

Example
A US treasury obligation purchased when there are three months or less remaining to maturity is a cash equivalent. Investments in stocks are not cash equivalents because they have no maturity value and are not convertible into a specific unchanging amount of cash.

3. In reviewing the statement of cash flows, it is important to remember the articulation between the balance sheet and the statement of cash flows. If the statement of cash flows employs a pure cash definition of funds, the first asset listed on the balance sheet will be cash. If the statement of cash flows employs a broader definition of funds (cash and cash equivalents), the first asset listed on the balance sheet will be Cash and Cash Equivalents.

4. The presentation of cash flows in the statement of cash flows follows a classification system established by the FASB. Cash flows are classified into three categories: operating, investing, and financing.

    a. **Operating**—Those cash flows related to transactions that flow through the income statement.

Example
Operating cash inflows include receipts from customers and interest. Cash outflows include payments to suppliers, to employers, and to taxing authorities.

    b. **Investing**—Cash flows related to the acquisition and disposal of long-term assets and investments (other than cash equivalents and trading securities; these are operating).

Example
Investing cash outflows include purchases of plant assets and investments. Cash inflows include proceeds from the sale of these items.

    c. **Financing**—Cash flows related to the liabilities and owners' equity sections of the balance sheet.

Example
Financing cash inflows include issuing debt and equity securities. Cash outflows include retirement of debt and equity securities, and dividend payments.

Financial Accounting Standards Codification

This lesson presents the Financial Accounting Standards Codification.

After studying this lesson, you should be able to:

1. Describe the goals and purpose of the Codification.

2. Identify the main areas of the Codification.

3. Illustrate how you would research using the Codification.

I. Financial Accounting Standards Codification

Caution: It is important that you practice using the Codification before the CPA Exam so that you do not waste valuable time struggling with the interface during the exam. The Codification website has several useful tutorials for first-time users.

A. **Goals of the Codification**—The FASB Codification Research System is the online, real-time database by which users access the Codification. The Codification system became effective on July 1, 2009. The online nature of the Codification and its internal structure were designed to achieve the following goals:

1. Simplify the structure and accessibility of authoritative GAAP.

2. Provide all authoritative literature in a single location.

3. Reduce the time and effort required to research an accounting issue.

4. Reduce the risk of noncompliance with GAAP.

5. Facilitate updating of accounting standards.

6. Assist the FASB with research and convergence (IFRS) efforts.

B. **Updating the Codification**

1. Changes to authoritative GAAP are accomplished through FASB Accounting Standards Updates (ASU), including amendments to SEC content. No longer will separate FASB Statements or other documents be separately published. ASUs are designated chronologically by year. For example, ASU 2014-12 refers to the twelfth ASU issued by the FASB in 2014.

2. An ASU is a separate document posted on the FASB website and incorporated in the Codification. The ASU will (1) summarize the key aspects of the update, (2) detail how the Codification will change, and (3) explain the basis for the update. ASUs are not authoritative—ASUs are a vehicle to update the codification and are not permanent in their own right, but a way to amend the codification. When changes to the codification happen, the FASB updates the Codification and issues the ASU simultaneously.

3. During the transition period for an ASU to become effective, the Codification shows the new guidance as "Pending Text." When the new guidance is effective, the previous guidance (if any) is deleted and the new guidance takes its place.

4. Although updates no longer use the old FASB numbering system, the Codification provides access to the original standards used in creating the Codification.

5. The Codification provides links enabling users to provide feedback, which then is directly transmitted to the FASB.

C. **Codification Structure**

1. **Overall structure**—Accounting guidance within the Codification has the following structure:

Areas—Topics—Subtopics—Sections—Subsections—Paragraphs

a. Each area has at least one topic. Within a topic, there are subtopics. Within subtopics, there are sections, and so forth. The topic, subtopic, and section levels reflect the structure used by international accounting standards.

2. **Areas**—The highest level in the Codification is the area, of which there are nine, each with a specific numeric identifier:

a. General principles (100)

b. Presentation (200) (does not address recognition or measurement)

c. Assets (300)

d. Liabilities (400)

e. Equity (500)

f. Revenue (600)

g. Expenses (700)

h. Broad transactions (800) (transactions involving more than one area such as interest, and subsequent events)

i. Industry (900) (special industry accounting)

3. **Topics**—There are approximately 90 topics across the nine areas. For example, all asset topics are within 300–399. The number of topics varies by area, depending on the content within each area. For example, 310 is the receivables topic, within the Asset area.

4. **Subtopics**—There is at least one subtopic within each topic. The "overall" subtopic appears within each topic. The number of subtopics within a topic varies by area, again depending on content. Each carries a numeric identifier. The "overall" subtopic contains the "big picture" level guidance for a topic. The other subtopics provide additional specific guidance and exceptions. For example, 310-40 is the Troubled-Debt Restructurings by Creditors subtopic within the Receivables topic, which is within the Asset area.

5. **Sections**—Each subtopic has the following 16 sections with the associated numeric identifier:

00	Status
05	Overview and Background
10	Objectives
15	Scope and Scope Exceptions
20	Glossary
25	Recognition
30	Initial Measurement
35	Subsequent Measurement
40	Derecognition
45	Other Presentation Matters
50	Disclosure
55	Implementation Guidance and Illustrations
60	Relationships
65	Transition and Open Effective Date Information
70	Grandfathered Guidance
75	XBRL Definitions

a. The listing of sections is uniform across all subtopics, unless no material exists for a section within a particular subtopic. For example, 310-40-35 is the Subsequent Measurement section within the Troubled-Debt Restructurings by Creditors subtopic within the Receivables topic, which is within the Asset area.

b. The section level is the primary research level because the accounting guidance in the form of paragraphs resides within the sections.

c. For SEC guidance, the same section numbering system is used with the addition of the letter *S* preceding the section number.

6. **Subsections**—In some cases, a section is divided into subsections to facilitate the exposition. These are not numbered.

7. **Paragraphs**

a. The actual accounting standard material is provided in paragraphs within sections or subsections. For example, 310-40-35-2 is paragraph 2, Troubled-Debt Restructuring, within the General subsection within the Subsequent Measurement section within the Troubled-Debt Restructurings by Creditors subtopic within the Receivables topic, which is within the Asset area.

b. Paragraphs follow a hierarchical structure allowing lower level paragraphs to be associated with higher-level paragraphs within a group, similar to threads in an online discussion group. Greater-than symbols (>, >>, >>>) are used for nesting paragraphs.

c. Paragraph numbers do not change over time. New paragraphs will use a letter extension.

d. Entities are encouraged to use purely verbal references to Topic levels within the Codification for the footnotes to their financial statements because FASB standard numbers are no longer used. For example, to refer to requirements concerning interest capitalization, the footnote would refer to "as required by the Interest Topic of the FASB Accounting Standards Codification."

e. The Codification standardized certain terms. For example, the Codification uses the term "entity" rather than "firm" or "company" and thus uses the term "intra-entity" rather than "intercompany". Moreover, the word "shall" is used for required treatments, rather than "should," "must," or other terms.

8. **Industry**

a. Area 900 holds industry topics and contains only the guidance that is not otherwise applicable in the other eight areas. For consistency, the topics within the industry area are structured the same way as in the other areas. Agriculture is industry topic 905 for example. Within that topic, the receivables subtopic is listed and numbered as Agriculture —Receivables: 905-310.

b. The general area topics include relevant guidance referenced to specific industries. Thus, the Codification is cross-referenced.

D. **Researching the Codification**

1. The Codification provides four different ways for researching an issue:

a. Browse the structure (illustrated above) in the menu provided.

b. Search by key word(s); this mode allows narrowing of a search both by related term and by major area within the Codification structure.

c. Enter the specific Codification location (using the numerical system within the Codification); this is designed for users who know their topic and section of interest.

d. Search by previous GAAP standard number (e.g., by FAS 13).

2. In addition, the Codification allows users to aggregate findings by similar content. For example, all Status sections for a topic can be accessed and joined without separately accessing the Status section for each subtopic.

3. Moreover, information can be combined. For example, all content in a subsection may be viewed in one document without having to separately access each individual section.

E. What is Excluded from the Codification?

4. The Codification does not include accounting guidance related to:

   a. Other Comprehensive basis of accounting

   b. Cash basis accounting

   c. Income tax basis accounting

   d. Regulatory accounting principles (e.g., insurance)

   e. Governmental accounting standards

Conceptual Framework of Financial Reporting by Business Enterprises

Objectives and Qualitative Characteristics

This lesson presents an overview of the conceptual framework related to the objectives of financial reporting and the qualitative characteristics of accounting information.

After studying this lesson, you should be able to:

1. Describe the objective of financial reporting.

2. Describe the qualitative characteristics of accounting information.

3. List the primary qualitative characteristics of accounting information.

4. List the enhancing qualitative characteristics of accounting information.

I. **Conceptual Framework Outline**

   A. The FASB's Statements of Financial Accounting Concepts, as amended, comprise the conceptual framework for financial accounting. The framework does not constitute GAAP but rather provides consistent direction for the development of specific GAAP. The conceptual framework is a "constitution" for developing specific GAAP.

   B. A listing of the parts of the conceptual framework follows. This outline lists the major subsections of the framework in a progression leading from definitions and general concepts to specific accounting principles, the ultimate purpose of the framework.

      1. Objective of financial reporting

      2. Qualitative characteristics of accounting information

      3. Accounting assumptions

      4. Basic accounting principles

      5. Cost constraint

      6. Elements of financial statements

II. **Objective of Financial Reporting**

   A. The objective of general-purpose financial reporting is to provide information about the entity useful to current and future investors and creditors in making decisions as capital providers.

   B. Useful information includes information about:

      1. The amount, timing, and uncertainty of an entity's cash flows;

      2. Ability of the entity to generate future net cash inflows;

      3. An entity's economic resources (assets) and claims to those resources (liabilities) that provides insight into the entity's financial strengths and weaknesses, and its liquidity and solvency;

      4. The effectiveness with which management has met its stewardship responsibilities;

      5. The effect of transactions and other events that change an entity's economic resources and the claims to those resources.

III. Qualitative Characteristics of Accounting Information

A. For financial statement information to be useful, it should have several qualitative characteristics. There are two primary characteristics and four enhancing characteristics, each of which has subcomponents. The following diagram shows the primary and enhancing characteristics and their components, as contributing to the objective of financial reporting.

Objective of Financial Reporting: Decision Usefulness

Primary Qualitative Characteristics

1. Relevance	**2.** Faithful representation
a. Predictive value	**a.** Completeness
b. Confirmatory value	**b.** Neutrality
c. Materiality	**c.** Free from error

Enhancing Qualitative Characteristics

1. Comparability
2. Verifiability
3. Timeliness
4. Understandability

B. Primary Characteristics (Relevance, Faithful Representation)—For information to be useful for decision-making, it must be both relevant and a faithful representation of the economic phenomena that it represents.

1. **Relevance (primary characteristic)**—Information is relevant if it makes a difference to decision makers in their role as capital providers. Information is relevant when it has predictive value, confirmatory value, or both.

   a. **Predictive value**—Information has predictive value if it assists capital providers in forming expectations about future events.

   b. **Confirmatory value**—Information has confirmatory value if it confirms or changes past (or present) expectations based on previous evaluations. For example, if reported earnings for a period bear out market expectations, then it has confirmatory value.

   c. **Materiality**—Information that is material will impact a user's decision. Materiality is somewhat pervasive throughout the objectives of financial reporting in the sense that the financial statements should present material information because it is decision useful. The FASB believes that materiality is an entity specific attribute and that material information is relevant to the decision maker. Therefore, materiality is an attribute of relevance.

2. **Faithful representation (primary characteristic)**—Information faithfully represents an economic condition or situation when the reported measure and the condition or situation are in agreement. Financial information that faithfully represents an economic phenomenon portrays the economic substance of the phenomenon. Information is representationally faithful when it is complete, neutral, and free from material error. Faithful representation replaces reliability as a primary qualitative characteristic.

Example
If a firm reports gross plant assets of $100,000, the firm must actually have purchased that much in plant assets and be currently using them in operations.

    a. Completeness: Information is complete if it includes all data necessary to be faithfully representative.

    b. Neutral: Information is neutral when it is free from any bias intended to attain a prespecified result, or to encourage or discourage certain behavior.

Example
Firms may be reluctant to report losses. Neutrality requires that losses, if they are probable and estimable, be reported regardless of any possible effect on the firm.

    c. Free from error: Information is free from error if there are no omissions or errors.

C. Enhancing Characteristics—These are complementary to the primary characteristics and enhance the decision usefulness of financial reporting information that is relevant and faithfully represented.

    1. Comparability—The quality of information that enables users to identify similarities and differences between sets of information. Consistency in application of recognition and measurement methods over time enhances comparability.

    2. Verifiability—Information is verifiable if different knowledgeable and independent observers could reach similar conclusions based on the information.

    3. Timeliness—Information is timely if it is received in time to make a difference to the decision maker. Timeliness can also enhance the faithful representation of information.

    4. Understandability—Information is understandable if the user comprehends it within the decision context at hand. Users are assumed to have a reasonable understanding of business and accounting and are willing to study the information with reasonable diligence.

D. Relevance and Faithful Representation May Conflict—In such cases, a trade-off is made favoring one or the other.

Examples
    1. Relevance over faithful representation. The pervasive use of accounting estimates (depreciation, bad debt expense, pension estimates) is an example of emphasizing relevance over faithful representation. Firms are providing estimates, rather than certain amounts. Reasonable approximations, although they cannot be perfectly reliable, are preferred by financial statement users to either (1) perfect information issued too late to make a difference, or (2) no information at all.

    2. Faithful representation over relevance. In the opinion of many, the use of historical cost as a valuation base is an example of emphasizing faithful representation over relevance. Historical cost is very reliable because it is based on objectively verifiable past information. However, historical cost is considered to be less current and, therefore, less relevant than market value.

Note
Candidates should be able to identify the components of relevance and faithful representation. It helps to remember that there are three components to both qualities.

Assumptions and Accounting Principles

This lesson presents an overview of accounting assumptions and principles in the related conceptual framework.

After studying this lesson, you should be able to:

1. List and describe the principles in the conceptual framework.

2. List and describe the assumptions in the conceptual framework.

I. **Accounting Assumptions**

   A. **Entity Assumption**—We assume there is a separate accounting entity for each business organization.

 Example
The owners and the corporation are separate. The owners own shares in the corporation; they do not own the assets of the firm. The corporation owns the assets. The financial statements represent the corporation, not the owners. A firm cannot own itself. Treasury shares are not assets to the firm—no one owns treasury shares. A firm can sue and be sued. If a firm is sued, the owners are not liable.

   B. **Going-Concern Assumption**

   1. In the absence of information to the contrary, a business is assumed to have an indefinite life, that is, it will continue to be a going concern. Therefore, we do not show items at their liquidation or exit values.

   2. This assumption, also called the continuity assumption, supports the historical cost principle for many assets. Income measurement is based on historical cost of assets because assets provide value through use, rather than disposal. Thus, net income is the difference between revenue and the historical cost of assets used in generating that revenue. Without the going-concern principle, historical cost would not be an appropriate valuation basis.

 **Example**
Prepaid assets, such as prepaid rent, would not be assets without the assumption of continuity.

   C. **Unit-of-Measure Assumption**—Assets, liabilities, equities, revenues, expenses, gains, losses, and cash flows are measured in terms of the monetary unit of the country in which the business is operated. Price level changes cause the application of this assumption to weaken the relevance of certain disclosures.

 **Example**
The amounts of all assets are added together even though amounts recorded at different times represent different purchasing power levels.

   1. **Capital maintenance and departures from the unit of measure assumption**

      a. The concept of capital maintenance is related to the unit of measure assumption. Capital is said to be maintained when the firm has positive earnings for the year, assuming no changes in price levels. When a firm has income, it has recognized revenue sufficient to replace all the resources used in generating that revenue (return *of* capital), and has resources left over in addition (income, which is return *on* capital). That income could be distributed as dividends without eroding the net assets (capital) existing at the beginning of the year. GAAP is based on the concept of "financial" capital maintenance. As long as dividends do not exceed earnings, and earnings is not negative, financial capital has been maintained.

b. An alternative concept of capital maintenance is *physical* capital maintenance. This concept holds that earnings cannot be recognized until the firm has provided for the physical capital used up during the period. To measure the capital used up, changes in price level must be considered.

> **Example**
> A firm uses up $5,000 worth of supplies in providing its service during the year, but to replace those supplies for use next year, $5,500 will have to be paid (10% increase in specific price of supplies). The *financial* capital maintenance model uses the $5,000 cost of supplies as the measure of revenue needed to maintain capital. If revenue for the current period is $5,000 and the firm had no other expenses, earnings would be zero and capital would just be maintained. The *physical* capital model would require revenue of $5,500 for capital to be maintained.
>
> GAAP does not require adjustments for price level changes and thus applies the *financial* capital maintenance concept in financial reports.

D. **Time Period Assumption**—The indefinite life of a business is broken into smaller time frames, typically a year, for evaluation purposes and reporting purposes. For accounting information to be relevant, it must be timely. The reliability of the information often must be sacrificed to provide relevant disclosures. The use of estimates is required for timely reporting but also implies a possible loss of reliability.

II. **Accounting Principles**

A. **Measurement**—At the time of origination, assets and liabilities are recorded at the market value of the item on the date of acquisition, usually the cash equivalent. This origination value is referred to as historical cost. For many assets and liabilities, this value is not changed even though market value changes. Other assets, such as plant assets and intangibles, are disclosed at historical cost less accumulated depreciation or amortization. Given the going-concern assumption, revaluation to market value is inappropriate for plant assets, because the value of these assets is derived through use, rather than from disposal.

B. There are measurement attributes other than historical costs that are used to represent items reported on the financial statements. Below is a brief summary and example of each measurement attribute.

1. **Net realizable value**—This value is used to approximate liquidation value or selling price. It is the net value to be received after the costs of sale are deducted from the current market value

   a. Example: Lower cost or market for inventory valuation uses NRV.

2. **Current replacement cost**—This value represents how much you would have to pay to replace an asset. Current replacement cost would represent current market value from the buyer's perspective.

   a. Example: Replacement cost is also used in inventory valuation.

3. **Fair value**—This value is also referred to as current market value. It is the price that would be received to sell an asset (or the price to settle a liability) in an orderly transaction from the perspective of a market participant at the measurement date (see the fair value lessons for further discussion of fair value).

   a. Example: Current market value (or fair value) is used to value trading and available-for-sale securities.

4. **Amortized cost**—This value is historical cost less the accumulated amortization or depreciation of the asset.

   a. Example: Buildings and equipment are reported at historical cost less accumulated depreciation.

5. **Net present value**—This is the value determined from discounting the expected future cash flows.

   a. Example: The discounted future cash flows are used in many capital budgeting decisions.

C. **Revenue Recognition Principle**—This principle addresses three important issues related to revenues. Below is a general view of revenue—see the revenue recognition lessons for more details.

   1. **Revenue Defined**—*What* revenue is: Revenue refers to increases in assets or the extinguishment of liabilities stemming from the delivery of goods or the provision of services—that is, the main activities of the firm.

   2. **When to Recognize Revenue**—Revenues are recognized when the entity completes its performance obligation to a customer and the revenue is earned and realized (or realizable). The performance obligation is completed when the goods or services are delivered (revenue is earned) and cash or promise of cash is received (realized). In general, there are five steps to allocate the components of revenue.

      a. Identify the contract with the customer (promise to deliver a good or service).

      b. Identify if there is more than one performance obligation.

      c. Determine the transaction price.

      d. Allocate the transaction price to the separate performance obligations (if there is more than one performance obligation).

      e. Recognize revenue when each performance obligation is satisfied.

   3. **Measure Revenue**—*How* to measure revenue: Revenues are measured at the cash equivalent amount of the good or service provided.

 **Example**
A contract is entered into with the customer to deliver an automobile and provide a warranty on the parts associated with the automobile.

There are two separate performance obligations: Deliver the automobile and provide parts if needed.

Determine the price of the automobile without the warranty or the price that the warranty is sold for separate from the automobile.

Allocate the transaction price to the separate performance obligations.

Recognize revenue when each performance obligation is satisfied. With respect to the automobile, revenue would be recognized upon delivery; with respect to the warranty, the revenue would be recognized over the warranty period.

D. **Expense Recognition Principle**—This principle addresses when to recognize expenses and is sometimes referred to as the matching principle.

   1. The matching principle says: *Recognize expenses only when expenditures help to produce revenues.* Revenues are recognized when earned and realized or realizable; the related expenses are recognized, and the revenues and expenses are "matched" to determine net income or loss.

   2. Expenses that are directly related to revenues can be readily matched with revenues they help produce.

3. Cost of goods sold and sales commissions are expenses that are directly associated and, therefore, matched with revenue. Other expenses are allocated based on the time period of benefit provided. Depreciation and amortization are examples. Such expenses are not directly matched with revenues. Still other expenses are recognized in the period incurred when there is no determinable relationship between expenditures and revenues. Advertising costs are an example.

E. **Full Disclosure Principle**—Financial statements should present all information needed by an informed reader to make an economic decision. This principle is sometimes referred to as the adequate disclosure principle.

Example
An aircraft manufacturer enters into a contract to build 200 airplanes for an airline company. As of the balance sheet date, production has not begun. Thus, there is no recognition of this contract in the accounts. However, a footnote should explain the financial aspects of the contract. This information is potentially of greater interest than many items recognized in the accounts.

Constraints and Present Value

This lesson presents an overview of accounting assumptions and principles in the related conceptual framework.

After studying this lesson, you should be able to:

1. List and describe the constraints in the conceptual framework.

2. Describe how cash flow and present value are used in accounting measurements.

I. **Cost Constraint**

    A. The cost constraint on GAAP limits recognition and disclosure if the cost of providing the information exceeds its benefit. Firms may not omit disclosures if they are material and mandated by GAAP.

> **Example**
> A firm would not report its entire inventory subsidiary ledger in the footnotes or financial statements. The reporting of total inventory cost is sufficient. Reporting more detailed information is not worth the cost of doing so.

    B. **Note: Conservatism**—Conservatism (also called prudence) is the reporting of less optimistic amounts (lower income, net assets) under conditions of uncertainty or when GAAP provides a choice from among recognition or measurement methods.

        1. Conservatism is a guideline that is used to limit the reporting of aggressive accounting information. Conservatism is used to avoid misleading internal and external users of the financial statements.

        2. If estimates of an outcome are not equally likely, the preferred approach is to report the most likely estimate, rather than the more conservative estimate, if the latter is less likely.

        3. It should be noted that overly conservative estimates can be misleading and cause over reporting in subsequent periods.

> **Examples**
> 1. Conservatism usually arises when there is uncertainty and management must make estimates. The allowance for uncollectible accounts receivable is an estimate, but an overly conservative accrual of the allowance in the current year will lead to lower net income and assets in the current period, but would over report income in subsequent years.
>
> 2. When estimating a contingent liability that arises from a lawsuit, often legal counsel provides a range of outcomes, for example $500,000—$1,000,000 loss. Accruing the most conservative loss in the current period, $1,000,000, will result in a gain in the subsequent period when the loss is settled for an amount less than $1,000,000, for example $800,000.

DR: Contingent Liability	$1,000,000	
CR: Cash		$800,000
CR: Gain on settlement of contingent liability		200,000

II. **Financial Statements, Recognition Criteria, Elements**

    A. A full set of financial statements should include the following:

        1. Financial Position at year-end (balance sheet)

        2. Earnings for the year (income statement)

3. Comprehensive Income for the year—total nonowner changes (statement of comprehensive income)

4. Cash Flows during the year (statement of cash flows)

5. Investments by and Distributions to Owners during the year (statement of owner's equity)

B. **Recognition and Measurement Criteria**—In relation to measurement and recognition of items in a financial report, the following criteria must be met:

   1. **Definition**—The definition of a financial statement element is met.

   2. **Measurability**—There is an attribute to be measured, such as historical cost.

   3. **Relevance**—The information to be presented in the financial report is capable of influencing decisions. The information is timely, has predictive ability, provides feedback value, and is material.

   4. **Faithful Representation**—The information is complete, neutral and free from material error.

C. **Elements of Financial Statements**—Ten elements that appear in a financial report.

   1. **Assets**—Resources that have probable future benefits to the firm, controlled by management, resulting from past transactions. Note the three aspects of this definition.

   2. **Liabilities**—Probable future sacrifices of economic benefits arising from present obligations of an entity to transfer assets or provide services to other entities as a result of past transactions or events.

   3. **Equity**—Residual interest in the firm's assets, also known as net assets. Equity is primarily comprised of past investor contributions and retained earnings.

   4. **Investments by Owners**—Increases in net assets of an entity from transfers to it by existing owners or parties seeking ownership interest

   5. **Distributions to Owners**—Decreases in net assets of an entity from the transfer of assets, provision of services, or incurrence of liabilities by the enterprise to owners

   6. **Comprehensive Income**—Accounting income (transaction based) plus certain holding gains and losses and other items. It includes all changes in equity other than investments by owners and distributions to owners.

   7. **Revenues**—Increases in assets or settlements of liabilities of an entity by providing goods or services

   8. **Expenses**—Decreases in assets or incurrences of liabilities of an entity by providing goods or services. Expenses provide a benefit to the firm

   9. **Gains**—Increases in equity or net assets from peripheral or incidental transactions

   10. **Losses**—Decreases in equity or net assets from peripheral or incidental transactions. Losses provide no benefit to the firm.

III. **Using Cash Flow Information and Present Value in Accounting Measurements**—The concepts statement addresses the use of present-value measurements. Like all concepts statements, it does not constitute GAAP but is used in the development of GAAP.

A. **Measurement Issues**

   1. This Statement addresses only measurement issues, not recognition. The statement applies to initial recognition, fresh-start measurements, and amortization techniques based on future cash flows. A fresh-start measurement establishes a new carrying value after an initial recognition and is unrelated to previous amounts (e.g., mark-to-market accounting and recognition of asset impairments).

   2. If the fair value of an asset or liability is available, there is no need to use present-value measurement. If not, present value is often the best available technique to estimate what fair value would be if it existed in the situation.

B. Present Value Measure—When a present-value measure is used:

1. The result should be as close as possible to fair value if such a value could be obtained.

2. The expected cash flow approach is preferred, because present-value measurements should reflect the uncertainties inherent in the estimated cash flows.

C. Capture Economic Differences—A present value measurement that fully captures the economic differences between various estimates of future cash flows would include the following:

1. An estimate of future cash flows

2. Expectations about variations in amount or timing of those cash flows

3. Time value of money as measured by the risk-free rate of interest

4. The price for bearing the uncertainty inherent in the asset or liability

5. Any other relevant factors

D. Two Approaches—The statement contrasts two approaches to computing present value:

1. **The traditional approach** (referred to as discounted cash flows) incorporates factors 2–5 above in the discount rate and uses a single most-likely cash flow in the computation. The traditional approach uses the interest rate to capture all the uncertainties and risks inherent in a cash flow measure. This is the approach that continues to be applied in some present value applications in financial accounting.

2. **The expected cash flow approach** uses a risk-free rate as the discount rate. That is, factors 2–5 are incorporated into the risk-adjusted expected cash flow and the discount factor is the risk-free rate.

> **Note**
> *The risk and uncertainty is incorporated into either the discount rate or the cash flows—not both!*

E. Expected Cash Flow Approach—The expected cash flow approach uses expectations about all possible cash flows instead of a single most-likely cash flow. Both uncertainty as to timing and amount can be incorporated into the calculation. The Board believes that the expected cash flow approach is likely to provide a better estimate of fair value than a single value because it directly incorporates the uncertainty in estimated future cash flows.

Examples

1. (Example of uncertain amount) The amount of a cash flow may vary as follows: $200, $400, or $600 with probabilities of 10%, 60%, and 30%, respectively. The expected cash flow is $440 = $200(.10) + $400(.60) + $600(.30). The expected cash flow approach uses a range of cash flows with probabilities attached. Thus, the uncertainties of the cash flows themselves are reflected in the distribution of cash flows. Calculation of the present value is determined by using the probability weight cash flows discounted using the risk-free rate.

2. (Example of uncertain timing) A $100 cash flow might be received in 1, 2, or 3 years with probabilities of 10%, 60%, and 30%, respectively. Assuming an interest rate of 5%, the expected present value = $100(pv1, .05, 1)(.10) + $100(pv1, .05, 2)(.60) + $100(pv1, .05, 3)(.30). [(pv1, .05, 1) is the symbol for the present-value of a single payment of $1, due in 1 year discounted at 5%.] Calculation of the present value is determined by using the probability weight cash flows discounted using the risk free rate.

---

1. Different rates of interest may also be used in each of the single present value terms to reflect different risk for the different timing of cash flow.

F. The expected cash flow approach has been incorporated into Accounting for Asset Retirement Obligations.

Fair Value Framework

Fair Value Framework—Introduction and Definitions

This lesson introduces fair value framework for accounting. The framework includes the definition of fair value, the techniques for measuring fair value whenever it is used in accounting, and disclosures required when fair value is used. This lesson describes the need for a fair value framework and the application of the framework in practice. This lesson also defines fair value and describes the individual components of the definition. In addition, the special conditions that apply separately to assets, to liabilities, and to shareholders' equity are presented.

After studying this lesson, you should be able to:

1. Define fair value for accounting purposes.

2. Describe the individual components of the fair value definition and how each component impacts the application of the definition.

3. Demonstrate the application of the fair value definition to assets, liabilities, and shareholders' equity and to a net portfolio of assets and liabilities.

4. Explain when a practical expedient can be used to determine fair value.

I. **Introduction**—The use of fair value to measure and report financial statement items is required or permitted by a number of GAAP pronouncements (ASCs). Some of those pronouncements, however, provide somewhat different definitions of "fair value" and provide only limited guidance in the determination of fair value for GAAP purposes. As a consequence, in the past, inconsistencies have occurred in how fair value is measured in practice. ASC 820 provides a framework for how to measure fair value to achieve increased consistency and comparability in fair value measurements and expanded disclosure when fair value measurements are used.

> **Note**
> *As a result of the joint efforts of the IASB and the FASB, there are no significant differences between U.S. GAAP and IFRS related to the meaning of fair value, its measurement or required disclosures. According to ASU 2011-04: "The Boards (FASB and IASB) worked together to ensure that fair value has the same meaning in U.S. GAAP and in IFRSs and that their respective fair value measurement and disclosure requirements are the same (except for minor differences in wording and style)."*

    A. **Objectives**—In order to accomplish the objectives of ASC 820, it provides the following:

        1. A definition of fair value for GAAP purposes;

        2. A framework for measuring (determining) fair value for accounting purposes;

        3. A set of required disclosures about fair value measurement when it is used.

II. **Fair Value Defined**

> **Definition**
> *Fair Value:* The price that would be received to sell an asset or paid to transfer a liability in an orderly transaction between market participants at the measurement date.

In order to fully understand and apply this definition, several components of the definition need to be described further:

    1. Fair value is a market-based measurement, not an entity-specific measurement.

    2. The determination of fair value is for a particular asset or liability (or equity item), which may be either a stand-alone asset or liability (e.g., a financial instrument or a nonfinancial operating asset) or a group

> **Note**
> *The fair value definition focuses on **how** to measure fair value not **when** to measure fair value.*

of assets/liabilities (e.g., a reporting unit or business). Fair value determination should consider the attributes (e.g., condition, location, restriction on asset use or sale, etc.) of the specific asset or liability being measured.

3. The transaction to sell the asset or transfer the liability is a hypothetical transaction at the measurement date that would occur under current market conditions; it is not a transaction that would occur in a forced liquidation or distress sale.

4. Even when there is no observable market to provide pricing information about the sale of an asset or the transfer of a liability at the measurement date, a fair value measurement assumes that a transaction takes place at that date.

5. The assumed transaction establishes a basis for estimating the price to sell the asset or transfer the liability.

6. The hypothetical transaction to sell the asset or transfer the liability is assumed to occur in the principal market or, alternatively, in the absence of a principal market, the most advantageous market for the asset or liability, to which the entity has access, after taking into account transaction costs and transportation costs.

   a. The **principal market** is the one with the greatest volume and level of activity for the asset or liability within which the reporting entity could sell the asset or transfer the liability.

   b. The **most advantageous market** is the one in which the reporting entity could sell the asset at a price that maximizes the amount that would be received for the asset or that minimizes the amount that would be paid to transfer the liability.

7. The price determined in the principal or most advantageous market should not be adjusted for transaction costs—incremental direct cost to sell the asset or transfer the liability—which do not measure a characteristic of the asset or liability. However, cost incurred to transport the asset or liability to its principal or most advantageous market (the location characteristic of an asset) would be used to adjust fair value for measurement purposes.

> **Note**
> *Notice that although transaction and transportation costs are taken into account in determining the most advantageous market, transaction costs are not used (i.e., not deducted from the asset market price or added to the liability transfer cost) in determining the fair value of an asset or liability in the most advantageous market.*

8. Market participants, as used in the definition, are buyers and sellers of the asset or liability that are:

   a. Independent of the reporting entity

   b. Acting in their economic best interest

   c. Knowledgeable of the asset or liability and the transaction involved

   d. Able and willing, but not compelled, to transact for the asset or liability

III. Application of Definition to Assets, Liabilities, and Shareholders' Equity

A. Application to Assets

1. The determination of fair value of a nonfinancial asset assumes the highest and best use of the asset by market participants, even if the intended use of the asset by the reporting entity is different; the concept of *highest and best use* does not apply to measuring the fair value of financial assets (or liabilities).

2. The highest and best use must take into account what is physically possible, legally permissible and financially feasible at the measurement date.

3. The highest and best use of an asset may be:

   a. **In use**—Maximum value to market participants would occur through its use in combination with other assets as a group; *or*

   b. **In exchange**—Maximum value to market participants would occur principally on a stand-alone basis (i.e., the price that would be received in a current transaction to sell the [single] asset).

B. Application to Liabilities

1. The determination of fair value of a liability assumes that the liability is transferred to a market participant at the measurement date; it is not settled or canceled.

    a. The liability to the counterparty (i.e., the party to whom the obligation is due) is assumed to continue after the hypothetical transaction.

    b. Nonperformance risk relating to the liability is assumed to be the same after the hypothetical transaction as before the transaction.

2. The determination of fair value of a liability should consider the effects of the reporting entity's credit risk (or credit standing) on the fair value of the liability in each period for which the liability is measured at fair value; a third-party credit enhancement should not be considered.

3. A separate input or an adjustment to other inputs to account for a restriction that prevents the transfer of liabilities should not be made in measuring fair value.

4. When a quoted price for the transfer of an identical or similar liability is not available, and the identical liability is held by another party as an asset, the liability should be measured from the perspective of the party that holds the item as an asset.

C. Application to Shareholders' Equity

1. The requirements for the determination of fair value apply to instruments classified in shareholders' equity that are measured at fair value (e.g., equity interest issued as consideration in a business combination).

2. The measurement assumes the instrument is transferred to a market participant at the measurement date and is measured from the perspective of a market participant that holds the instrument as an asset.

3. A separate input or an adjustment to other inputs to account for a restriction that prevents the transfer of a shareholder equity instrument should not be made in measuring the fair value.

4. When a quoted price for the transfer of an identical or similar shareholders' equity instrument is not available and the identical instrument is held by another party as an asset, the instrument should be measured from the perspective of the party that holds the item as an asset.

D. Application to Net Financial Assets and Financial Liabilities

1. An exception to the requirement that fair value of qualified financial assets and financial liabilities be measured separately is permitted when a reporting entity manages risk associated with a portfolio of financial instruments on a net exposure basis, rather than on a gross exposure basis.

2. An entity that holds financial assets and financial liabilities and manages those instruments on the basis of their net risk exposure may measure the fair value of those financial assets and financial liabilities at:

    a. The price that would be received to sell a NET asset position for a particular risk, or

    b. The price that would be paid to transfer a NET liability position for a particular risk.

IV. Applicability—The content of ASC 820 is for items that uses fair value measurement either as required or as permitted by GAAP, except in very limited situations. Specifically, the guidance of ASC 820 does **not** apply to:

A. Accounting principles that address share-based payment transactions

B. ASCs that require or permit measurements that are similar to fair value but that are not intended to measure fair value, including:

1. Accounting principles that permit measurements that are determined using vendor-specific objective evidence of fair value; *or*

    2. Accounting principles that address fair value measurement for purposes of inventory pricing.

C. Accounting principles that address fair value measurements for purposes of lease classification or measurement

D. ASCs that permit practicability exceptions to fair value measurement (see below)

E. Pervasive Applicability—Other than the exceptions noted above, the content of ASC 820 must be followed when fair value measurement is used, either as required or permitted by other pronouncements.

V. Practical Expedient Exception—ASU 820 allows a company to use a "practical expedient" to measure the fair value of an investment that does not have a quoted market price but reports a net asset value per share (NAV). These investment vehicles are often referred to as alternative investments. Examples are hedge funds, private equity funds, real estate funds, venture capital funds, common/collective funds, and offshore funds.

For example, a private equity fund (PE) may invest in start-up companies, rare archeological artifacts, artwork, and real estate. The PE fund most likely reports the investment in these items at fair value or investment value. The PE fund may report NAV to the investors; if the PE fund meets the criteria as an alternative investment, the investor can use NAV as a practical expedient to measure fair value. The following diagram shows the structure of an alternative investment.

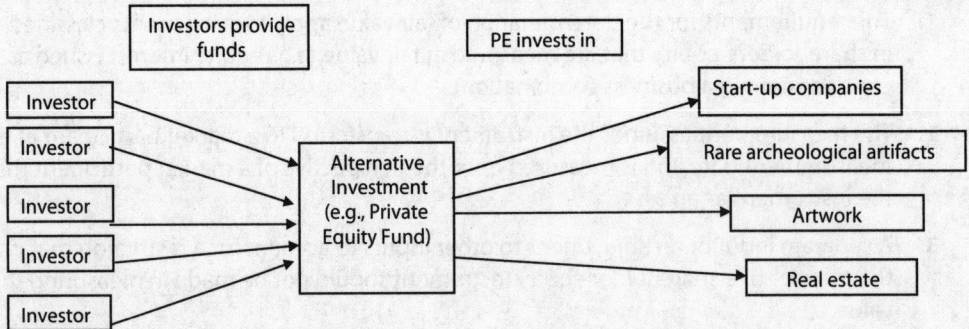

A. Alternative investments must meet the criteria in order to use NAV as the practical expedient:

    1. Does not have a "readily determinable fair value."

    2. The investment meets the criteria for an investment company as stipulated in ASC 940-10-15-2 or does not meet the criteria to be an investment company but follows industry practice and issues financial statements consistent with the measurement principles for an investment company.

B. Classification in the Fair Value Hierarchy. The investor is not allowed to "look through" the alternative investment fund and classify the investment in the fair value hierarchy according to the investments made by the PE fund. The investor owns a share of the PE fund, not a share of the start-up company or the real estate.

    1. Alternative investments that are reported at NAV as a practical expedient are NOT categorized in the fair value hierarchy (Level 1, 2, or 3) but are separately reported in the footnotes with disclosures that indicate that NAV is being used and these disclosures must reconcile to the amounts reported on the balance sheet.

    2. Companies that use NAV as a practical expedient for measuring fair value must disclose sufficient information so that financial statement users understand the nature and the risks of the investment. The disclosure must include information about the terms and conditions in which the company can redeem its investments.

C. There are other instances where practical expedient is allowed. An entity is allowed to use a practical expedient in other circumstances, such as in the valuation of benefit plans or for a private company's measurement of share-based payments.

Recognition and Measurement

The measurement of fair value is based on an exit price—that is, the amount that would be received to sell an asset or paid to transfer a liability. In some cases, that amount will be the same amount as an entry price, but not in all cases. This lesson discusses the relationship between an exit price and an entry price and identifies those situations where the prices may be different amounts.

After studying this lesson, you should be able to:

1. Describe the nature of an entry price and an exit price and distinguish between the two.

2. Choose which technique or approach would be used to determine fair value.

3. Identify when the fair value option can be applied.

4. Apply the definition of fair value to specific accounts or transactions.

I. **Fair Value Determination**—When an asset is acquired or a liability is assumed in an actual transaction, the price paid to acquire the asset or the price received to assume the liability (the *transaction price*) is an entry price—the price paid when an asset or liability is initially recognized, which may or may not be fair value. Fair value of an asset or a liability is the price that would be received to sell an asset or paid to transfer a liability—an exit price.

   A. Conceptually, an entry price and an exit price are different.

   B. In many cases, the entry price (transaction price) and the exit price (fair value) will be the same at the date of initial recognition of an asset or liability and, therefore, constitute the fair value of the asset or liability at that date.

   C. In some cases, however, the entry (transaction) price may not be the exit price and therefore not be fair value at the date of initial recognition of an asset or liability. For example, the transaction price might not be fair value (exit price) if:

      1. The transaction is between related parties;

      2. The transaction takes place when the seller is under duress (e.g., in a liquidation sale);

      3. The unit of account for the transaction price is different from the unit of account that would be used to measure the asset or liability at fair value. For example, if the asset or liability measured at fair value is part of a business in a business combination, there are unstated rights associated with an asset that are measured separately, or the quoted price includes transaction costs, such as with oil; *or*

      4. The market in which the transaction price takes place is different from the principal market (or most advantageous market).

   D. If an entity is required or permitted to measure an asset or liability initially at fair value and the transaction price at initial recognition differs from fair value, a gain or loss is recognized in earnings at initial recognition of the asset or liability (unless otherwise required by GAAP for that item).

      1. The asset or liability would be recorded at fair value.

      2. The difference between the transaction (entry) price and the recorded fair value (exit price) would be recognized as a loss or gain in the period of initial recognition.

II. **Measurement Techniques**

   A. **Valuation Techniques/Approaches**—In the determination of fair value for GAAP purposes, three valuation techniques or approaches could be used:

      1. **Market approach**—This approach uses prices and other relevant information generated by market transactions involving assets or liabilities that are identical or comparable to those being valued.

2. **Income approach**—This approach converts future amounts to a single present amount. Discounting future cash flows would be an income approach to determining fair value.

3. **Cost approach**—This approach uses the amount that currently would be required to replace the service capacity of an asset (i.e., current replacement cost), adjusting for obsolescence.

B. **Valuation Technique/Approach Selection**—Which approach (or approaches) is appropriate to measure fair value will depend on the circumstances, including the availability of sufficient data for the respective approaches, and will maximize the use of relevant observable inputs and minimize the use of unobservable inputs.

1. In some cases, a single valuation technique will be appropriate (e.g., using quoted prices in an active market for identical assets or liabilities).

2. In some cases, multiple valuation techniques will be appropriate (e.g., when valuing an entire business).

   a. When multiple valuation techniques are used, the different results should be evaluated and weighted.

   b. When multiple valuation techniques are used, professional judgment will be required to select the fair value from within the range of alternative values that is most representative in the circumstances.

3. Under all valuation techniques, the valuation must take into account appropriate risk adjustments, including a risk premium for uncertainty.

C. **Consistent Application of Approach/Technique**

1. Valuation techniques used to measure fair value should be consistently applied.

2. A change in valuation technique or its application is appropriate if the change will result in a more representative fair value.

   a. A change in valuation technique or application may be appropriate, for example, if new markets develop, new information becomes available, previous information is no longer available, or valuation techniques improve.

   b. Changes in fair value resulting from changes in valuation techniques or applications are treated as changes in accounting estimates.

III. **Fair Value Option**

A. An entity can apply the fair value option to an eligible item only on the date when one of the following events occurs (an election date):

1. When the item is first recognized;

2. When an eligible firm commitment is established;

3. Specialized accounting for an item ceases to exist;

4. An investment becomes subject to equity method accounting (but is not consolidated) or to a VIE that is no longer consolidated; *or*

5. An event that requires the item to be measured at fair value, such as a business combination or significant modifications to debt instruments.

B. Entities that elect to use the fair value measurement (referred to as the fair value option) for eligible financial assets and financial liabilities must adhere to certain requirements. Those requirements include:

1. The fair value option may be applied on an instrument-by-instrument basis, with limited exceptions.

    a. The fair value option may be elected for a single eligible item without electing it for other identical items with the following exceptions:

        i. If multiple advances are made to one borrower as part of a single contract and the individual advances lose their identity, the fair value option must be applied to all advances under the contract;

        ii. If the fair value option is applied to an investment that would otherwise be accounted for under the equity method of accounting, it must be applied to all of the investor's financial interests, both equity and debt, in that entity; *or*

        iii. If the fair value option is applied to an eligible insurance/reinsurance contract, it must be applied to all claims/obligations and features/coverages under the contract.

    b. The fair value option does not have to be applied to all instruments issued or acquired in a single transaction (except as noted in 1, above). The fair value option may be applied to some of the individual instruments issued or acquired (e.g., shares of stock or bonds) in a single transaction, but not to other individual instruments issued or acquired in that transaction.

2. The fair value option is irrevocable unless and until a new election date for the specific item occurs.

3. The fair value option is applied only to an entire instrument and not to only specific risks, specific cash flows, or portions of an instrument.

4. If the fair value option is elected for held-to-maturity securities, those securities will be treated and reported as trading securities.

    a. Gains and losses resulting from change in fair value will not be reported in other comprehensive income.

    b. Gains and losses resulting from changes in fair value will be reported in current income.

IV. Instruments Not Eligible for Fair Value Option—Entities may NOT use fair value to measure and report the following financial assets and financial liabilities:

A. An investment in a subsidiary that is to be consolidated

B. An interest in a variable interest entity that is to be consolidated

C. Employers' and plans' obligations (or assets) for pension benefits, other postretirement benefits, postemployment benefits, and other employee-oriented plans

D. Financial assets and liabilities recognized under lease accounting

E. Demand deposit liabilities of financial institutions

F. Financial instruments that are classified by the issuer as a component of shareholders' equity

Inputs and Hierarchy

When determining fair value, many assumptions and sources of data may be used. In some cases, only limited assumptions and data may be required—for example, when quoted prices in an active market are appropriate and available. In other cases, however, a number of assumptions and a variety of data may be needed to develop a fair value measure. This lesson identifies the kinds of inputs that may be used and the relative importance of each.

After studying this lesson, you should be able to:

1. Distinguish between observable and unobservable inputs in determining fair value.

2. Describe the three levels of the fair value hierarchy and give examples of each.

3. Categorize valuation inputs and/or results into the three levels of the fair value hierarchy.

I. **Inputs**—Inputs refer to the various assumptions that market participants would use in determining fair value, including assumptions about the risk inherent in using a particular valuation technique, as well as the risk inherent in using various inputs (data, assumptions, etc.) with each valuation technique.

    A. Inputs used may be

        1. **Observable**—Inputs used in pricing an asset, liability, or equity item that are developed based on market data obtained from sources independent of the reporting entity; *or*

        2. **Unobservable**—Inputs that reflect the reporting entity's own assumptions used in pricing the asset, liability, or equity item that are developed based on the best information available in the circumstances.

    B. Valuation techniques used to measure fair value should maximize the use of observable inputs and minimize the use of unobservable inputs.

II. **Fair Value Hierarchy**—The fair value hierarchy (provided in ASC 820) prioritizes or ranks the inputs to valuation techniques used to measure fair value into three levels:

    A. **Level 1**—Inputs in this, the highest level, are unadjusted quoted prices in active markets for assets or liabilities (or equity items) identical to those being valued that the entity can obtain at the measurement date.

        1. Quoted prices in an active market provide the most reliable evidence of fair value and, except in unusual circumstances, should be used to measure fair value when available.

        2. Quoted prices should not be adjusted because the entity holds a sizable position in the asset or liability relative to the trading volume in the market (often referred to as the "blockage factor").

        3. Adjustments to quoted prices generally result in a fair value measurement categorized in a lower level of the fair value hierarchy (i.e., Level 2 or 3).

    B. **Level 2**—Inputs in this level are observable for assets or liabilities (or equity items), either directly or indirectly, other than quoted prices described in Level 1, above.

        1. This level includes:

            a. Quoted prices for similar assets or liabilities in active markets;

            b. Quoted prices for identical or similar assets or liabilities in markets that are not active markets in which there are few relevant transactions, prices are not current or vary substantially, or for which little information is publicly available;

            c. Inputs, other than quoted prices, that are observable for the assets or liabilities being valued, including, for example, interest rates, yield curves, implied volatilities and credit spreads; *and*

            d. Inputs that are derived principally from, or corroborated by, observable market date by correlation or other means (referred to as "market-corroborated inputs").

2. Depending on factors specific to the asset or liability being valued, these inputs may need to be adjusted when applied to the asset or liability for factors such as: condition, location, and the level of activity in the relevant market.

3. When market participants would apply a premium or discount related to a characteristic of an asset or liability being valued (e.g., a control premium), an entity should apply the premium or discount in measuring fair value.

4. If significant unobservable inputs are used to adjust observable inputs, the resulting measurement may be categorized in Level 3.

C. **Level 3**—Inputs in this, the lowest level, are unobservable for the assets or liabilities (or equity items) being valued and should be used to determine fair value only to the extent observable inputs are not available.

1. Unobservable inputs should reflect the entity's assumptions about what market participants would assume and should be developed based on the best information available in the circumstances, which might include the entity's own data.

2. The reporting entity should not ignore information available about market participants' assumptions and should adjust its own data if information indicated that market participants would use different assumptions.

3. When market participants would apply a premium or discount related to a characteristic of the asset or liability being valued (e.g., a control premium), an entity should apply the premium or discount in measuring fair value.

4. When a valuation technique uses unobservable inputs to determine fair value subsequent to initial recognition and fair value at initial recognition is the transaction price, the valuation technique should be calibrated (adjusted) at initial recognition so that the results of the valuation technique equals the transaction price.

Note

If net asset value (NAV) is used as a practical expedient to determine fair value, NAV is not reported within the fair value hierarchy but rather is separately disclosed in the footnotes of the financial statements. See the "Fair Value Framework—Introduction and Definitions" lesson on for more discussion on use of practical expedients.

Disclosure Requirements

Any time fair value measurement is used, whether as required by GAAP or as permitted by GAAP, specific disclosures are required when financial statements are issued. This lesson identifies the most important of those disclosures.

After studying this lesson, you should be able to:

1. Describe significant disclosures required for assets, liabilities, and equity items measured at fair value on a recurring basis.

2. Describe significant disclosures required for assets, liabilities, and equity items measured at fair value on a nonrecurring basis.

3. Describe the significant disclosure requirements for the election of the fair value option applied to assets, liabilities, and equity items.

I. **Disclosures Required**—GAAP requires the following disclosures when fair value measurement is used, either as required or permitted by other accounting pronouncements.

II. **For Assets and Liabilities That Are Measured at Fair Value on a Recurring Basis**—In periods subsequent to initial recognition (e.g., investments in trading securities measured on a recurring basis) the reporting entity must disclose the following information in the statement of financial position (balance sheet) for each interim and annual period for each major category of asset and liability:

   A. The fair value measurements at the reporting date

   B. Segregated into each of the three levels within the fair value hierarchy

   C. Transfers into each level and transfers out of each level disclosed and discussed separately, with the amounts of any transfers between Level 1 and Level 2, the reasons for such transfers, and the policy for determining when those transfers occur disclosed separately

   D. For Levels 2 and 3, a description of the valuation techniques and inputs used to measure fair value and a discussion of changes in valuation techniques during the period, if any

   E. For fair value measurements in Level 3, unobservable inputs, a reconciliation of the beginning and ending balances, separately presenting changes during the period attributable to the following:

      1. Total gains or losses recognized, showing separately those included in earnings and those included in other comprehensive income, and the line item(s) in which they are recognized in the respective statements

      2. Purchases, sales, issuances, and settlements, disclosed separately

      3. Transfer in and/or out of Level 3 disclosed separately, the reasons for such transfers, and the policy for determining when those transfers occur

   F. For fair value measurements in Level 3:

      1. A description of the valuation process used

      2. Quantitative information about the unobservable inputs used

      3. A narrative description of the sensitivity of the fair value measurement to changes in unobservable inputs

   G. The amount of total gains or losses for the period that are attributable to the change in unrealized gains or losses relating to assets and liabilities still held at the reporting date and a description of where those unrealized amounts are reported in the Income Statement.

   H. For nonfinancial assets, disclose if highest and best use differs from current use and why.

III. For Assets and Liabilities That Are Measured at Fair Value on a Nonrecurring Basis—In periods subsequent to initial recognition (e.g., an asset impairment that is not measured on a recurring basis) the reporting entity must disclose the following information in the statement of financial position (balance sheet) for each major category of asset and liability:

A. The fair value measurements at the reporting date and the reasons for the measurement

B. Segregated into each of the three levels of the fair value hierarchy

C. For Levels 2 and 3, a description of the valuation techniques and inputs used to measure fair value and a discussion of changes in valuation techniques during the period, if any

D. For fair value measurements in Level 3, unobservable inputs, a description of the valuation process used and quantitative information about the unobservable inputs used

E. For nonfinancial assets, disclose if highest and best use differs from current use and why

IV. Other Disclosure Issues

A. The quantitative disclosures required above must be presented using a tabular format (examples are provided in ASC 820-10-55-100 through 820-10-55-107).

B. Reporting entities are encouraged, but not required, to combine the fair value information disclosures under this ACS with fair value information disclosures required by other accounting pronouncements.

C. If net asset value (NAV) is used as a practical expedient to determine fair value, NAV is not reported within the fair value hierarchy but rather is separately disclosed in the footnotes of the financial statements. See the "Fair Value Framework—Introduction and Definitions" for more discussion on use of practical expedients.

    1. Alternative investments that are reported at NAV as a practical expedient are NOT categorized in the fair value hierarchy (Level 1, 2, or 3) but are separately reported in the footnotes with disclosures that indicate that NAV is being used and these disclosures must reconcile to the amounts reported on the balance sheet.

    2. Companies that use NAV as a practical expedient for measuring fair value must disclose sufficient information so that financial statement users understand the nature and the risks of the investment. The disclosure must include information about the terms and conditions in which the company can redeem its investments.

V. Disclosure Related to the Fair Value Options

A. Fair Value Option Disclosures Objectives—Disclosures required when the fair value option is elected are intended to accomplish the following objectives:

    1. The disclosures are intended to facilitate comparisons:

        a. Between entities that choose different measurement methods for similar assets and liabilities, and

        b. Between assets and liabilities in the financial statements of a single entity that selects different measurement methods for similar assets and liabilities.

    2. The disclosure requirements are expected to result in the following:

        a. Information to enable users of financial statements to understand management's reasons for electing or partially electing the fair value option

        b. Information to enable users to understand how changes in fair value affect earnings for a period

        c. Provide the same kind/amount of information about certain items that would have been disclosed if the fair value option had not been elected for the items

        d. Information to enable users to understand the differences between fair values and contractual cash flows for certain items

3. To achieve these objectives and outcomes, required disclosures must be provided in both interim and annual financial statements.

4. The disclosures, as outlined below, do not replace disclosure requirements in other existing GAAP pronouncements, including other pronouncements that require fair value measurement use and disclosures.

B. **Required Disclosures for Interim and Annual Statements of Financial Position (Balance Sheet)**—As of each date for which a Statement of Financial Position (Balance Sheet) is presented, the following must be disclosed:

1. Management's reasons for electing a fair value option for each eligible item or group of similar eligible items

2. If the fair value option is elected for some, but not all, eligible items within a group of similar eligible items:

    a. A description of those similar items and the reasons for partial election

    b. Information to enable users to understand how the group of similar items relates to individual line items on the Statement of Financial Position

3. For each line item in the Statement of Financial Position that includes an item or items for which the fair value option has been elected:

    a. Information to enable users to understand how each line item in the statement relates to major categories of assets and liabilities

    b. The aggregate carrying amount of items included in each line item in the statement that are not eligible for the fair value option, if any

4. The difference between the aggregate fair value and the aggregate unpaid principal balance of:

    a. Loans and long-term receivables that have contractual principal amounts and for which the fair value option is used

    b. Long-term-debt instruments that have contractual principal amounts and for which the fair value option has been elected

5. For loans held as assets for which the fair value option has been elected:

    a. The aggregate fair value of loans that are 90 days or more past due

    b. If the entity's policy is to recognize interest income separately from other changes in fair value, the aggregate fair value of loans in nonaccrual status (i.e., loans for which interest income is not accrued)

    c. The difference between the aggregate fair value and the aggregate unpaid principal balance for loans that are 90 days or more past due, are in nonaccrual status, or both

6. For investments that would have been accounted for under the equity method if the entity had not chosen to apply the fair value option, the information required by ASC 323, *The Equity Method of Accounting for Investments*, including:

    a. The name of each investee and the percentage ownership of its common stock

    b. The accounting policies of the investor with respect to investments in common stock

C. **Required Disclosures for Interim and Annual Income Statements**—For each period for which an Income Statement is presented, the following must be disclosed about items for which the fair value option has been elected:

1. For each line item in the Statement of Financial Position (Balance Sheet), the amount of gains and losses from fair value changes included in earnings for the period and in which line in the Income Statement those gains/losses are reported

2. A description of how interest and dividends are measured and where they are reported in the Income Statement

3. For loans and other receivables held as assets:

    a. The estimated amount of gains and losses included in earnings for the period attributable to changes in instrument-specific credit risk, *and*

    b. How those gains and losses were determined.

4. For liabilities with fair values that have been significantly affected during the reporting period by changes in the instrument-specific credit risk:

    a. The estimated amount of gains and losses from fair value changes included in earnings that are attributable to changes in the instrument-specific credit risk

    b. How the gains and losses were determined

    c. Qualitative information about the reasons for those changes

D. Other Disclosure Requirements

1. In annual reports only, the methods and significant assumptions used to estimate fair value (of items for which the fair value option has been elected) must be disclosed.

2. If an entity elects the fair value option at the time an investment becomes subject to the equity method of accounting or when it ceases to consolidate a subsidiary, it must disclose:

    a. Information about the nature of the event, *and*

    b. Where the effect on earnings shows in the Income Statement.

International Financial Reporting Standards (IFRS)

IASB Accounting Standards

This lesson provides a general introduction to the International Accounting Standards Board (IASB) and to International Financial Reporting Standards (IFRS).

After studying this lesson, you should be able to:

1. Identify the authoritative guidance for international accounting standards.
2. Describe the standard-setting process for the International Accounting Standards Board (IASB).
3. Identify major differences between U.S. GAAP and IFRS.

I. International Accounting Pronouncements

A. IFRS has become a globally recognized basis for financial accounting and reporting. The IFRS Foundation's independent standard-setting body is the IASB. IFRS is now the primary or alternate basis of financial accounting and reporting in more than 100 countries. IFRS are authoritative guidance for preparation of general-purpose financial statements of all entities that use IFRS for their primary financial reporting basis.

B. The International Accounting Standards Committee (IASC) issued International Accounting Standards (IAS) from 1973 to 2001. In addition, the IASC created a Standing Interpretations Committee (SIC) that provided further interpretive guidance on accounting issues not addressed in the standards. In 2001, the International Accounting Standards Board (IASB) replaced the IASC. The IASB adopted the existing International Accounting Standards (IAS) and interpretations issued by the Standing Interpretations Committee (SIC). Since 2001, the IASB is responsible for issuing International Financial Reporting Standards (IFRS), and the IFRS Interpretations Committee (IFRIC) is responsible for issuing interpretations of the standards. Therefore, the current international accounting guidelines are contained in the IAS and IFRS pronouncements. Together with SIC and IFRIC interpretations, International Financial Reporting Standards comprise all existing standards and interpretations of the IASB and its predecessor. This means that when one refers to IFRS, one refers to pronouncements of all of the guidance described.

C. It is often said that U.S. GAAP employs a rules-based approach. In other words, the standards are usually explicit as to precise rules that must be followed for recognition, measurement, and financial statement presentation. IFRS, in contrast, is considered a principles-based approach because it attempts to set general principles for recognition, measurement, and reporting and allows professional judgment in applying these principles. This principles-based approach should focus on a true and fair view or a fair representation of the financial information.

II. Accounting Standard Convergence

A. **Convergence** refers to the working relationship between the FASB and the IASB to develop compatible, high-quality accounting standards. **Adoption** in the United States refers to the SEC requirement for publicly traded companies to implement the IFRS accounting standards—the latter of which has *not* occurred.

B. In 2002, the FASB and the IASB agreed to work toward convergence in the accounting standards. Therefore, you will find some IFRS accounting treatments identical, some similar, and others different from U.S. GAAP. An effective study strategy is to study U.S. GAAP and then learn the significant differences between U.S. GAAP and IFRS. This compare/contrast strategy will help you to remember which method is U.S. GAAP and which method is IFRS. As you study, take note of the differences in the following areas:

1. **Vocabulary or definition differences**—Although the concepts of U.S. GAAP and IFRS may be similar, vocabulary and definitions are often somewhat different.

2. **Recognition and measurement differences**—Differences may exist in when and how an item is recognized in the financial statements. Alternative methods may be acceptable in U.S. GAAP whereas only one method may be allowed for IFRS (or vice versa). In some instances, either IFRS or U.S. GAAP may not require an item to be recognized in the financial statements. In addition, the amount recognized (measurement of the item) may be different in the two sets of standards.

3. **Presentation and disclosure differences**—**Presentation** refers to the presentation of items on the financial statements, whereas **disclosure** refers to the additional information contained in the notes to financial statements. Again, differences exist as to whether an item must be presented in the financial statements or disclosed in the footnotes, as well as the types of information that must be disclosed.

III. IASB Standard-Setting Process

A. The IFRS standards-setting due process is similar to the FASB's and entails six stages:

1. Set agenda.

2. Plan project.

3. Develop and publish a discussion paper.

4. Develop and publish an exposure draft.

5. Develop and publish a standard.

6. Address unanticipated issues after the standard is issued.

B. IFRS differs in history and level of development as compared with U.S. GAAP. U.S. GAAP is precise and provides conservative guidance, whereas IFRS allows for subjectivity in many areas and provides general qualitative guidance. The resulting standards are significantly different in size.

1. The volume of IFRS (about 3,000 pages) is substantially less than U.S. GAAP (about 17,000 pages).

C. The International Organization of Securities Commissions (IOSCO) is a global cooperative body made up of national securities regulatory agencies. The IOSCO is the recognized international standard setter for securities markets. In an agreement between the IASC and the IOSCO, it was agreed to endorse the use of international accounting standards for cross-border listings on stock exchanges. The international standards were formally endorsed in 2000.

D. IFRS pronouncements address recognition, measurement, presentation, and disclosure matters related to transactions and events (items) that affect the entity and are therefore reported in the financial statements. The same is true with U.S. GAAP, albeit in considerably more detail. Because IFRS serves a much broader constituency than U.S. GAAP, there are certain reporting matters that may be modified or otherwise enhanced by other national SEC-type agencies and/or exchanges where foreign securities are traded. For example, in Europe, the European Union (EU) Parliament has established its own modifications and enhancements to IFRS, even though IFRS has already been adopted for all EU member states for publicly traded entities.

IV. High-Level Overview of Major Differences in U.S. GAAP and IFRS—The table below highlights the major accounting differences between U.S. GAAP and IFRS. Differences are discussed in more detail in the applicable lessons.

U.S. GAAP	IFRS

Financial Statement Presentation

U.S. GAAP	IFRS
No specific requirement regarding comparative information	Requires comparative information for prior year
Subsequent events evaluated through the financial statement issuance date	Subsequent events evaluated through financial statement **authorization** to be issued date

Consolidated Financial Statements

U.S. GAAP	IFRS
No exemption from consolidating subsidiaries in general purpose financial statements	Under certain restrictive situations a subsidiary (normally required to be consolidated) may be exempt from the requirement.
Noncontrolling interest measured at fair value including goodwill	Noncontrolling interest may be measured either at fair value including goodwill or the proportionate share of the value of the identifiable assets and liabilities of the acquiree excluding goodwill.
Fair value option allowed for equity method investments and joint ventures	Fair value option prohibited for equity method investments and joint ventures

Current Assets and Current Liabilities

U.S. GAAP	IFRS
Short-term obligations expected to be refinanced can be classified as noncurrent if the entity has the intent and ability to refinance	Short-term obligations expected to be refinanced can be classified as noncurrent only if the entity has entered into an agreement to refinance prior to the balance sheet date
Contingencies that are probable (>70%) and can be reasonably estimated are accrued.	Contingencies that are probable (> 50%) and measurable are considered provisions and accrued.
For contingencies, accrue minimum in a range if no amount is more likely than another.	For contingencies, accrue the midpoint in a range if no amount is more likely than another.

Inventory

U.S. GAAP	IFRS
LIFO cost flow assumption is an acceptable method.	The LIFO cost flow assumption is not allowed.
Any impairment write-downs create a new cost basis; previously recognized impairment losses are not reversed.	Previously recognized impairment losses are reversed.

Fixed Assets

U.S. GAAP	IFRS
Revaluation not permitted	Revaluation of assets is permitted as an election for an entire class of assets but must be done consistently.
No separate accounting for investment property	Separate accounting is prescribed for investment property versus property, plant, and equipment.
Unless the assets are "held for sale" they are valued using the cost model.	Investment property may be measured at fair value.
Allowable borrowing cost capitalization is calculated using a weighted-average accumulated expenditure times a borrowing rate.	Allowable borrowing cost capitalization is calculated using actual borrowing costs less any earnings on investments of the borrowing.
Biological assets are not a separate category.	Biological assets are a separate category and not included in property, plant, and equipment.

There is no requirement to account for separate components of an asset.

If the major components of an asset have significantly different patterns of consumption or economic benefits, the entity must allocate the costs to the major components and depreciate them separately.

Two-step impairment approach

One-step impairment approach

Impairment is a function of fair value and carrying value.

Impairment is a function of the recoverable amount and carrying value.

Impairment losses are not reversed.

Impairment losses may be reversed in future periods.

Intangible Assets

Unless specific ASC guidance exists (e.g. software), development costs are expensed.

Development costs may be capitalized if specific criteria are met.

Revaluation is not permitted.

Revaluation of intangible assets other than goodwill is permitted although uncommon.

Goodwill impairment may be qualitatively assessed to determine if two-step impairment test is necessary.

One-step impairment test for goodwill must be performed.

Impairment loss is a function of carrying value and fair value.

Impairment loss is a function of carrying value and the recoverable amount.

Impairment losses are not reversed.

Impairment losses, except those related to goodwill, may be reversed.

Financial Investments

Impairment testing is completed relative to fair value.

Impairment testing is completed relative to recoverable amount.

When impairment is recognized through the income statement, a new cost basis is established and such losses cannot be reversed.

Impairment losses in available-for-sale investments may be reversed in future periods.

Revenue Recognition

Construction contracts are accounted for using the percentage-of-completion method if certain criteria are met. Otherwise the completed-contract method is used.

Construction contracts are accounted for using the percentage-of-completion method if certain criteria are met. Otherwise, revenue recognition is limited to the costs incurred. The completed-contract method is not allowed.

Leases

Operating leased assets are never recorded on the balance sheet.

Assets held by lessee under operating leases may be capitalized on the balance sheet if they meet certain requirements.

A lease for land and building that transfers ownership to the lessee or contains a bargain purchase option would be classified as a capital lease regardless of the relative value of the land. If the fair value of the land at inception represents 25% or more of the total fair value, the lessee must consider the components separately when evaluating the lease.

When land and buildings are leased, elements of the lease are considered separately when evaluating the lease unless the amount for the land element is immaterial.

Pensions

Actuarial gains and losses are recognized through the corridor approach or recognized as they occur.

Prior service cost is initially deferred in other comprehensive income and recognized using the future years of service method or average remaining service period method.

Actuarial gains and losses must be recognized in other comprehensive income immediately.

Prior service cost is recognized immediately in income.

Income Taxes

Deferred tax assets are recognized in full but valuation allowances reduce them to the amount that is more likely than not to be realized.

Deferred tax assets are recognized only to the extent it is probable that they will be realized.

IASB Framework

This lesson presents an overview of the International Accounting Standards Board (IASB) conceptual framework.

After studying this lesson, you should be able to:

1. Identify the purpose of the IASB's conceptual framework.

2. Identify the IASB framework objectives, qualitative characteristics and constraints.

I. Background

A. The IASB's *Framework for the Preparation and Presentation of Financial Statements* (Framework) is similar to the FASB's Concepts Statements although much shorter in length. Like the FASB's, the IASB Framework does not constitute GAAP (exception, see below) but, rather, provides the basis for development of specific GAAP on a consistent basis. The IASB Framework is intended to apply to the financial statements of all entities, public or private.

    1. In rare cases, where the IASB Framework is in conflict with an accounting standard for compelling practical reasons, the standard is used as the guidance.

    2. In cases where no applicable accounting exists, the IASB Framework may be considered as guidance for GAAP (see International GAAP hierarchy in the preceding lesson).

B. Purposes of the IASB Framework

    1. To assist the Board in developing new IASs and reviewing existing IASs (the Framework was written when the IASC was the body promulgating standards. "IASs" here may be more loosely interpreted to include IASs, IFRSs, SICs, and IFRICs).

    2. To assist the Board in promoting harmonization of standards by providing a basis for reducing the number of alternative accounting treatments permitted by IASs

    3. To assist national standard-setting bodies in developing standards

    4. To assist preparers in applying IASs and dealing with topics not yet covered by IASs

    5. To assist auditors in forming an opinion as to whether financial statements conform with IASs

    6. To assist users in interpreting financial statements prepared in conformity with IASs

    7. To provide information for parties interested in the work of the IASC (now IASB)

C. General-Purpose Financial Statements. The Framework is concerned with general-purpose financial statements (similar to the FASB Concepts Statements), directed to provide financial information to a wide variety of users. *Financial statements* include (1) balance sheet, (2) income statement, (3) statement of changes in financial position (note that a later IAS requires a statement of cash flows), (4) notes and supplementary material. Excluded from the purview are directors' and management reports and the like.

D. One of the more involved joint convergence projects is the development of a common conceptual framework. This project's purpose is to develop a framework that will be the underlying conceptual support for future principles-based internally consistent accounting standards for the most useful financial reporting.

    1. The joint framework project is divided into eight phases or chapters with the goal of providing the framework in a single document:

        a. Objective and qualitative characteristics

        b. Elements and recognition

        c. Measurement

        d. Reporting entity

    e. Presentation and disclosure

    f. Framework for a GAAP hierarchy

    g. Applicability to the not-for-profit sector

    h. Remaining issues

2. In September 2010 the first phase of the joint convergence project was completed. As such, the **objectives, qualitative characteristics,** and **constraints** sections discussed in previous FASB Conceptual Framework lessons apply to the IASB framework as well. The two constraints (materiality and cost effectiveness) also are included in Phase (a). The material from Phase (a) is not repeated here. Please refer back to the FASB Conceptual Framework lessons.

3. The portions of the original IASB Framework not yet modified by the joint IASB-FASB project are provided in this lesson. You will notice considerable similarity with the FASB framework.

4. The objective of financial reporting under the IASB Framework is similar to the FASB: to aid in the decision-making of the financial statement user. The Framework states (para. 12): "The objective of financial statements is to provide information about the financial position, performance and changes in financial position of an entity that is useful to a wide range of users in making economic decisions."

E. Although the IASB Framework contains information similar to the Statement of Financial Accounting Concepts by the US Financial Accounting Standards Board (FASB), several important differences exist.

1. Some terms and definitions are different.

2. The elements of financial statements are not identical.

3. Candidates should become familiar with these subtle differences in the two sets of concepts.

II. Elements of Financial Statements

A. The definitions of elements are at the center of the standard setting-process for the IASB. The Framework defines income and expenses in terms of assets and liabilities.

B. Differences—The IASB Framework lists only five elements: assets, liabilities, equity, income, and expense. The FASB Framework lists 10 elements: assets, liabilities, equity, investment by owners, distributions to owners, comprehensive income, revenues, expenses, gains, and losses. The IASB Framework does not include as elements the following items appearing in the FASB Framework's list of elements: investments by owners, distributions to owners, comprehensive income, gains, and losses. However, specific IFRSs address these elements within the context of the specific standard.

C. An item is recognized as an element if it meets one of the element definitions below **and** also meets the following two recognition criteria: (1) it is probable that a future economic benefit associated with the item will flow to or from the entity, and (2) the item has a cost or value that can be measured with reliability. In addition, the *substance over form* principle must be considered (e.g., accounting for income taxes and for capital leases).

1. Where only one or no criterion is met, note disclosure may be required.

2. The Framework does not provide specific guidance on how to measure whether future benefits are "probable" although several international accounting standards include specific guidance pertaining to the relevant standard.

3. Similarly, there is no concrete guidance on reliable measurement, which often requires making a reasonable estimate. The framework contains little guidance on specific measurement bases noting that several are available with historical cost the most common, often being combined with other bases.

> **Note**
> *The vocabulary differences regarding the elements of financial statements are subtle but important. With U.S. GAAP, the term "income" is not a financial statement element. Rather, the term is used to describe a calculation of some type (e.g., income from continuing operations, net income) or to designate a specific type of income, such as interest income. However, with IFRS, the term "income" is a financial statement element, and the items that are considered "income" are revenues and gains. IFRS uses the term "profit" where U.S. GAAP uses the term "net income."*

4. Failure to recognize in the financial statements an item satisfying the recognition criteria and one of the element definitions is not cured by disclosure in the notes.

5. Offsetting in financial statements is not allowed unless the procedure reflects the underlying substance of related events or transactions, or where permitted by an accounting standard.

D. **Assets**—Currently, the IASB Framework definition is as follows (para. 49 a): "An asset is a resource controlled by the entity as a result of past events and from which future economic benefits are expected to flow to the entity."

E. **Liabilities**—Currently, the IASB Framework definition is as follows (para. 49 b): "A liability is a present obligation of the entity arising from past events, the settlement of which is expected to result in an outflow from the entity of resources embodying future benefits."

F. **Equity**—Currently, the IASB Framework definition is as follows (para. 49 c): "Equity is the residual interest in the asset after subtracting liabilities. Several sub-categories of equity are mentioned including funds contributed by shareholders, retained earnings, and reserves representing appropriations or capital maintenance adjustments."

G. **Income**—Income represents increases in economic benefits deriving from increases in assets or decreases in liabilities that result in increases in equity (other than those related to contributions from shareholders).

1. Income may be realized or unrealized. Income includes both revenues (arising from ordinary activities) and gains. Gains are not treated as separate elements because they also may be due to ordinary activities, as well as from activities not in the ordinary course of business. Gains are usually reported separately from revenues.

   a. **Difference**—The IASB Framework element is *income*, which includes both revenues and gains, whereas the FASB Framework treats *revenue* and *gains* as separate elements.

H. **Expenses**—Expenses represent decreases in economic benefits deriving from decreases in assets or increases in liabilities that result in decreases in equity (other than those related to distributions to shareholders).

1. Expenses may be realized or unrealized. An expense is recognized immediately for expenditures producing no future economic benefit qualifying as an asset.

2. Expenses result from ordinary activities. Losses also may result from ordinary activities and thus are not treated as separate elements. Losses may also arise from activities not in the ordinary course of business. Losses are usually reported separately from expenses.

   a. **Difference**—The IASB Framework *expense* element includes losses whereas the FASB Framework treats *expenses* and *losses* as separate elements.

3. The Framework defines income and expenses in terms of assets and liabilities. As such, the Framework cautions that applying the matching principle should not result in recognizing items that do not meet the definition of assets and liabilities.

   a. **Difference**—The FASB Framework has no such prohibition.

III. **Assumptions**

A. In the IASB Framework, there are only two underlying assumptions: (1) that the financial statements are prepared on the accrual basis and (2) that the entity is a going concern. The meaning is the same as in the FASB Framework.

1. **Difference**—Accrual accounting considers an assumption in the IASB Framework but not in the FASB Framework.

B. Neither assumption needs to be stated as such in the notes. When material uncertainties exist as to the continuation of the entity, or when it is clear that the going-concern assumption does not apply resulting in a different basis of reporting, the entity should disclose this information.

C. The IASB Framework does discuss economic entity, monetary unit, and periodicity as underlying concepts for the preparation of financial statements but not as formal assumptions. Along with going concern, these three assumptions comprise the four FASB Framework assumptions.

IFRS for SMEs

Unlike U.S. GAAP, International Financial Reporting Standards (IFRS) include a set of accounting and reporting standards specifically intended for use by small and medium-sized entities. These standards, known as *IFRS for SMEs*, are intended for use primarily by private entities and are a modification and simplification of the complete set of IFRS. For U.S. entities that qualify, IFRS for SMEs can be used as a U.S. GAAP-basis for the preparation of general-purpose financial statements. This lesson provides an overview of IFRS for SMEs, including which entities may use those standards and the major differences between those standards and other, more extensive, reporting standards.

After studying this lesson, you should be able to:

1. Describe the major aspects of IFRS for SMEs.

2. Identify entities that are eligible to use IFRS for SMEs as the basis for preparing financial statements.

I. **International Financial Reporting Standards (IFRS)**—Issued by the International Accounting Standards Board (IASB), do not contain a concept comparable to "other comprehensive basis of accounting" (OCBOA), nor do they address the issue of personal financial statements. Therefore, there are no international standards for preparing financial statements under either of these bases of accounting.

    A. **IFRS Small and Medium-Sized Entities**

        1. Millions of companies worldwide can, and are, using *IFRS for Small and Medium Sized Enterprises* (IFRS for SMEs). In many of these countries (but not the United States) incorporated companies are required to have audited financial statements regardless of whether they are a public company with publicly traded equity or debt.

        2. The IASB issued IFRS for SMEs in 2009. The IFRS for SMEs pronouncement is a modification and simplification of the full IFRS and is designed to be used primarily by private companies. Although simplified, it is still based on the IFRS conceptual framework. As set forth in IFRS for SMEs, the objectives of financial statements of small or medium sized entities are:

            a. To provide information about the financial position, performance and cash flows of an entity that is useful for economic decision-making by a broad range of users who are not in a position to demand reports tailored to meet their particular information needs (i.e., general-purpose financial statements for external users); *and*

            b. To show the results of the stewardship of management—that is, the accountability of management for the resources entrusted to it.

        3. IFRS for SMEs are not an *other comprehensive basis of accounting* but rather are a form of generally accepted accounting principles (GAAP) for U.S. entities and can be used by qualified U.S. companies as the basis for preparing financial statements. Thus, an entity that does not have to follow either standard U.S. GAAP or the full IFRS may elect to prepare general-purpose financial statements under the requirements of IFRS for SMEs.

    B. **Eligibility for and Election of IFRS for SMEs**

        1. IFRS for SMEs may be used by entities that **do not have** *public accountability*. Under the standard, the following kinds of entities would have public accountability and, therefore, **would be precluded from** using IFRS for SMEs:

            a. Entities that are required to file financial statements with a securities commission or other regulatory body for the purpose of issuing instruments in a public market, such as equity or debt securities.

    b. Entities that hold assets in a fiduciary capacity for a broad group of outsiders, including:

        i. Banks;

        ii. Insurance companies;

        iii. Brokers and dealers in securities;

        iv. Pension funds;

        v. Mutual funds.

    c. In addition, IFRS for SMEs are not intended for use by not-for-profit or governmental entities.

C. Characteristics of Financial Statements under IFRS for SMEs

    1. Unlike OCBOA, IFRS for SMEs is based on the accrual basis of accounting, just as is standard U.S. GAAP. However, IFRS for SMEs is both less complicated and less voluminous than U.S. GAAP. Some of that simplification is reflected in the following key areas where IFRS for SMEs differs from U.S. GAAP:

        a. Accounting for financial assets and financial liabilities makes greater use of cost.

        b. The use of the cost method to account for investments over which the investor has significant influence is permitted; the equity method also is permitted, but not required.

        c. Inventories must be valued using FIFO or weighted-average cost; LIFO inventory valuation is prohibited.

        d. Capitalization of interest incurred during construction of an asset is not required.

        e. When the major components of an item of property, plant, or equipment have different patterns of consumption, depreciation must be based on a components approach.

        f. Goodwill and other intangible assets are amortized and assumed to have a limited life and, if the life cannot be estimated, a 10-year period must be used for amortization purposes.

        g. Impairment of goodwill is assessed using a one-step process, rather than a two-step process.

        h. A simplified approach to temporary differences is used for income tax accounting.

        i. If certain criteria are met, reversal of impairment charges is allowed, including for financial assets.

        j. Only certain hedge types are allowed and conditions for the use of hedge accounting for those types are less restrictive.

        k. There is no requirement for earnings per share or segment disclosures.

        l. Disclosure requirements are simplified in several areas, including:

            i. Financial instruments;

            ii. Leases;

            iii. Pensions.

    2. The attractiveness of IFRS for SMEs is further enhanced by the fact that the IASB has limited the revision of the standards to once every three years rather than the more or less continuous revisions made to US GAAP and full IFRS.

D. Summary

    1. A U.S. entity that is not **required** to follow either U.S. GAAP or full IFRS in the preparation of its financial statements may use one of four bases of accounting:

        a. Use, on an elective basis, U.S. GAAP;

        b. Use, on an elective basis, full IFRS;

c. Use an Other Comprehensive Basis of Accounting;

d. Use IFRS for SMEs.

2. Each of these bases would be considered the application of generally accepted accounting principles and a U.S. CPA could audit the resulting statements. An audit report of financial statements based on IFRS for SMEs might say something like the following: "These statements fairly present the financial position, results of operations, and cash flows in conformity with the International Financial Reporting Standards for Small and Medium Sized Enterprises."

IFRS—General-Purpose Financial Statements

This lesson presents the major differences in the reporting of the general-purpose financial statements under IFRS: balance sheet (statement of financial position), income statement, statement of comprehensive income, statement of shareholders' equity, and the statement of cash flows.

After studying this lesson, you should be able to:

1. Describe the presentation and content of the IFRS financial statements.

2. Identify major differences in the reporting of the general-purpose financial statements under IFRS.

I. **IFRS: Balance Sheet—Statement of Financial Position**

   A. **IFRS Financial Statements**

   1. The objective of financial statements is to provide information about the financial position, financial performance, and cash flows of an entity that is useful to a wide range of users in making economic decisions. The financial information included in the financial statements along with the note disclosures assist users of financial statements in predicting the entity's future cash flows and, in particular, their timing and certainty.

   2. Financial statements should *present fairly* the financial position, financial performance and cash flows of an entity.

   3. A complete set of financial statements includes

      a. Statement of financial position (balance sheet);

      b. Statement of comprehensive income;

      c. Statement of changes in equity;

      d. Statement of cash flows;

      e. Notes; *and*

      f. Statement of financial position at the beginning of the earliest comparative period for which an entity applies an accounting policy retrospectively or makes a retrospective restatement of items in its financial statements, or when it reclassifies items in its financial statements.

   4. The financial statements and notes must be clearly identified, including the following information:

      a. Name of the reporting entity

      b. Whether the statements are consolidated or of an individual entity

      c. The date of the end of the reporting period or period covered

      d. The presentation currency

      e. The level of rounding (e.g., amounts in millions)

   5. Frequency of reporting—At a minimum, a complete set of financial reports at least annually, including comparative information.

   B. **General Considerations for the Statement of Financial Position**

   1. Both IFRS and U.S. accounting standards require a classified statement of financial position (commonly called a balance sheet in the United States) to be reported. Each IFRS statement of financial position must present two classifications: current and noncurrent. (The definitions of these terms are presented later in this lesson.) IFRS specifies a minimum listing of accounts that must be presented whereas U.S. GAAP does not have such specification, although SEC registrants must follow SEC guidelines that require specific line items.

   2. IFRS requires more detailed note disclosures for various statements of financial position items, compared with U.S. GAAP. Under IFRS, the financial statements themselves are quite clean,

meaning typical U.S. GAAP parenthetical disclosures such as wording "net of depreciation," "net of allowance for uncollectibles," and "at lower of cost or market" do not appear on IFRS financial statements but are disclosed in the notes to the financial statements.

3. IFRS does not require specific formatting of statement of financial position information. For example, both horizontal and vertical formats are acceptable. Firms may change the order of accounts, the title of the statements (e.g., Balance Sheet is acceptable instead of the formal name, Statement of Financial Position) and the level of detail to provide the most useful information.

4. Typically, the ordering of the statement of financial position items for U.S. GAAP balance sheets starts with current items. Since IFRS does not have any recommended format, many countries use their customary formats, including presenting the items in reverse order, reporting noncurrent items before current items. In addition, within categories, the ordering may be the opposite of U.S. GAAP ordering, that is, from less liquid to more liquid, but this is simply a local format and not one required by IFRS.

C. IFRS Statement of Financial Position Format

1. A typical layout for an IFRS Statement of Financial Position follows. (Note: This order is commonly found in British or former British countries.)

Assets
Noncurrent assets
Property, plant and equipment
Intangible assets
Investments
Total noncurrent assets
Current assets
Inventories
Trade receivables
Cash and cash equivalents
Total current assets
Total assets
Equity
Equity attributable to owners of the parent
Share capital
Retained earnings
Noncontrolling interest
Total equity
Noncurrent liabilities
Long-term borrowings
Deferred income taxes
Total noncurrent liabilities
Current Liabilities
Trade payables
Short-term borrowings
Current tax payable
Total current liabilities
Total liabilities
Total equity and liabilities

2. The above presentation of the statement of financial position emphasizes the long-run perspective. Within assets and liabilities, first displayed are the infrastructure assets that provide the long-term physical structure of operating capacity and the means of obtaining the long-term financing of those assets.

3. Other variations include (a) reporting net assets (total assets less total liabilities), (b) reporting current assets and liabilities in one section labeling the difference as working capital or net current assets, and (c) ordering by liquidity where the entire statement of financial position is listed in order of liquidity, within assets and liabilities.

D. Required Statement of Financial Position Items (Where Present for an Entity)

Property, plant and equipment

Investment property

Intangible assets

Financial assets

Investments accounted for using the equity method

Biological assets

Inventories

Trade and other receivables

Cash and cash equivalents

Noncurrent assets held for sale

Trade and other payables

Provisions—liabilities of uncertain timing or amount

Financial liabilities

Liabilities and assets for current tax

Deferred tax liabilities and deferred tax assets (can be classified noncurrent only)

Liabilities included in the disposal groups classified as held for sale

Noncontrolling interests presented within equity

Issued capital and reserves attributable to the owners of the parent

1. The requirements may not apply to interim financial statements, if the entity reports interim financial reports according to IAS 34, *Interim Financial Reporting*. Those interim reports are more condensed.

2. U.S. GAAP discourages the use of the term "reserve," which is a category found within equity and liabilities under IFRS. IFRS permits this term. Examples include reserves arising from revaluation of plant assets, foreign currency translation, and recognition of expenses before they are legally due. Note that wherever the term reserve is used, it represents a specific purpose, and not simply *general* reserves that might be used to smooth earnings.

E. Definition of Current Assets and Current Liabilities

1. The definitions of current assets and liabilities for IFRS are worded slightly differently from those definitions under U.S. GAAP, but the result of their application will generally yield the same results.

2. An asset is classified *current* if it meets one of the following criteria:

   a. It is expected to be realized in, or is intended for sale or consumption in, the entity's normal operating cycle.

   b. It is primarily held for the purpose of being traded.

   c. It is expected to be realized within 12 months after the reporting period.

   d. It is cash or a cash equivalent unless it is restricted from being exchanged or used to settle a liability for at least 12 months after the reporting period.

   e. All assets not meeting any one of the above criteria are classified as noncurrent, being the default classification.

3. A liability is classified current if it meets one of the following criteria:

   a. It is expected to be settled in the entity's normal operating cycle;

   b. It is held primarily for the purpose of being traded;

   c. It is due to be settled within 12 months after the reporting period; *or*

   d. The entity does not have an unconditional right to defer settlement of the liability for at least 12 months after the reporting period.

   e. All liabilities not meeting any one of the above criteria are classified as noncurrent, being the default classification.

II. IFRS—Income Statement

A. General Considerations for the Income Statement

1. As with the statement of financial position, IFRS requires certain line items to be disclosed on the face of the income statement (see B. below). Other than certain earnings per share disclosures, U.S. GAAP standards have no such requirement.

2. In the United States, it is generally accepted that either a single-step or a multiple-step format be used and the bottom portion of the income statement is prescribed by U.S. GAAP. However, specific IFRS standards do mandate that additional line items, headings, or subtotals depending on whether a firm is reporting a pertinent item be disclosed separately.

3. IFRS and U.S. GAAP does **not** allow the reporting of income statement items as extraordinary (U.S. GAAP eliminated reporting of extraordinary items effective 2015).

4. Some of the IFRS terminology is also different from the U.S. GAAP counterpart. U.S. statements refer to the bottom line as *net income* or *net loss*. For IFRS statements, that net amount is called *profit or loss for the period*. It appears as a subtotal in the single statement option above or as the bottom line in the income statement under the two-statement option. As another example, the term *turnover* is used for *sales* by some firms in their IFRS income statements, even though IFRS uses the term *Revenue*. This is usually a cultural difference, as British companies refer to *Revenue* as *Turnover*.

5. U.S. GAAP allows alternative measures of performance to be reported on the face of the income statement. Examples include earnings before interest, taxes, depreciation and amortization. Such reporting in the income statement is not included in the illustrative examples that are part of IAS 1, *Presentation of Financial Statements*.

B. Specific Items to be Reported in the IFRS Income Statement—The following items are required to be reported on the face of the statement of comprehensive income (under either option above), subject to materiality constraints and the nature of the business. Material items should be presented separately either on the face of the income statement or in the footnotes.

Revenue

Finance costs

Share of the profit or loss of associates under the equity method

Tax expense

A single amount comprising the total of (1) after-tax profit or loss on discontinued operations and (2) after-tax gain or loss on disposal of discontinued operations

Profit or loss

Each component of other comprehensive income (discussed in a later lesson)

Share of other comprehensive income of associates under the equity method

Total comprehensive income

C. Expense Classifications

1. IFRS requires firms to analyze expenses either by (a) function or (b) nature of the expense. If a firm uses the functional system, the firm must disclose the additional information on the nature of expenses. This disclosure is usually in the notes. In the U.S. GAAP there is no such requirement although SEC registrants must report expenses by function.

   a. The *function* of expense reporting focuses on the activity to which the expense relates. Examples include cost of sales, distribution costs, and administrative expenses.

   b. The *nature* of expense reporting focuses on the type of expense. Examples include changes in inventories of finished goods and work in progress, raw materials and consumables used, employee benefit expense, depreciation and amortization expense.

2. The expense classification and disclosure may be presented either on the face of the income statement or in the notes.

3. Example of function of expense presentation in an income statement:

Revenue

Cost of sales

Gross profit

Other income

Less:

   Distribution costs

   Administrative expenses

   Other expenses

Profit before tax

4. Example of nature of expense presentation in an income statement:

Revenue

Other income

Less:

  Change in inventories of finished goods and work in progress

  Raw materials and consumables used

  Employee benefits expense

  Depreciation and amortization expense

  Other expenses

    Total expenses

Profit before tax

5. Reporting by expense function is more prevalent in IFRS financial reports.

III. IFRS—Statement of Comprehensive Income

A. Per Share Measures—Comprehensive income per share is not prohibited under IFRS but is prohibited under U.S. GAAP.

B. A Fifth Other Comprehensive Income (OCI) Item

1. International accounting standards allow firms to revalue plant assets and intangibles to fair value (details in a later lesson). U.S. standards prohibit this practice. Under international standards, if the revaluation results in an increase in the value of the asset, the increase is called a revaluation surplus and is reported in other comprehensive income. This surplus is a fifth OCI item, in addition to the four under U.S. standards. The revaluation surplus can never be reclassified to affect net income. Once a firm has chosen to revalue assets, those revaluations cannot affect net income. See the lesson on fixed assets for more discussion of IFRS revaluation of fixed assets.

IV. IFRS—Statement of Shareholders' Equity

A. The IFRS and U.S. GAAP statements are quite similar. Under U.S. GAAP the statement of shareholders' equity can be presented in the footnotes; under IFRS, it must be presented as a separate statement.

V. IFRS—Statement of Cash Flows

A. The differences between IFRS and U.S. GAAP relate to the classification of items as operating, investing, or financing activities. The next table presents the major classification differences.

Item	U.S. GAAP	IFRS
Interest paid	Operating only	Operating or financing
Interest received	Operating only	Operating or investing
Taxes paid	Operating only	Operating—In financing or investing if specifically identified with an item
Dividends received	Operating only	Operating or investing
Dividends paid	Financing only	Operating or financing
Cash and cash equivalents	Bank overdrafts not allowed	May include bank overdrafts

VI. IFRS—Footnotes

    A. **Footnotes**—Footnotes, including the summary of significant accounting policies, are considered an integral part of a complete set of financial statements and thus are required for all entities reporting under international accounting standards.

    B. International standards suggest the following order of footnote presentation:

        1. Statement of compliance with IFRS;

        2. Summary of significant accounting policies; *and*

        3. Supporting information for financial statement items.

    C. The summary of significant accounting policies should include:

        1. Judgments and key assumptions made in applying those policies;

        2. Measurement bases used for recognition (e.g., historical cost, fair value); *and*

        3. Information enabling an assessment of the estimation uncertainty that could result in a material adjustment to the balances of assets and liabilities, which are point estimates in many cases.

    D. Footnotes concerning financial statement items should be disclosed in the order of those financial statement items, which, in turn, should be cross-referenced to any related footnote.

    E. Also to be included in the notes:

        1. The amount of dividends proposed or declared before the statements were authorized for issue (U.S. standards do not require disclosure of proposed dividends); *and*

        2. Additional information enabling an assessment of the firm's objectives, policies and processes for managing capital.

VII. Disclosures for the Effect of Changing Prices

    A. The international accounting experience with reporting the effects of changing prices is similar to that of the United States. Initially entities were required to disclose the impact of changing prices on their results of operations and financial position. Firms could apply either general price level adjustments (inflation), or current replacement cost (specific prices). These requirements were withdrawn as inflation became less of a problem, although they are encouraged.

    B. **Hyperinflationary Economies**—However, a significant difference between US and international standards is the latter's requirement that firms operating in economies with very substantial inflation are required to provide disclosure of the impact of inflation.

    C. This requirement specifically requires financial statements to be restated to reflect the current general price level. The restated statements are to be presented as the primary statements. International standards discourage reporting of the pre-restated financial statements. At present, very few such economies are experiencing hyperinflation (defined roughly as 100% or more over three years), and therefore this requirement does not affect many firms.

General-Purpose Financial Statements

Balance Sheet/Statement of Financial Position

This lesson presents an overview of the balance sheet.

After studying this lesson, you should be able to:

1. Identify the measurement bases used to measure the items on the Balance Sheet.

2. Distinguish between a current and noncurrent asset or liability.

3. Prepare a Balance Sheet.

I. **The Balance Sheet**

A. **Background on the Balance Sheet**

1. The statement of financial position is another name for the balance sheet.

2. It is the only statement dated as of a point in time. The title consists of three lines:

> ABC Company
>
> Balance Sheet
>
> As of December 31, 20X4

3. Only asset, liability, and owners' equity accounts are represented (and related contra (−) and adjunct (+) accounts) and as such the balance sheet reports the entity's financial position at a point in time.

4. Total assets = total liabilities + owners' equity.

5. Many different measurement (valuation) bases are represented—total assets of $10 million is not really $10 million of the types of same dollars. Most reported account balances do not represent current market value.

6. The balance sheet provides information useful in assessing the entity's financial strengths and weaknesses, especially risk (relative proportion of debt to equity, for example), and the allocation of assets.

7. A classified balance sheet distinguishes current and noncurrent assets and liabilities which helps users assess liquidity.

8. Account balances reflect only the transaction-based U.S. GAAP recognition and measurement system. A transaction or event is required for recognition of all items. The balance sheet does not report all assets of the firm, only the assets acquired through a transaction. For example, internally generated goodwill is not recorded (recognized), and the recorded value of other intangibles such as trademarks may be significantly less than their current value.

B. **Factors Limiting the Interpretation of Balance Sheet Information**

1. Assets and liabilities are acquired at different times and are not affected in the same way by inflation and specific price-level changes. This causes the recorded value of these accounts to be different from their current or real value and makes comparisons difficult.

2. Several different measurement bases are used (historical cost, depreciated historical cost, market (fair) value, realizable value, present value) which compromises the comparability characteristic of accounting information.

3. Consolidation of subsidiaries compounds the difficulties with interpretation of account balances when the parent and subsidiaries use different accounting methods.

4. The value of many assets is derived primarily through use (exceptions are investments, receivables); this value may differ considerably from book value and market value. How does the user really interpret book value when book value and market value are different?

C. **Measurement Bases for Balance Sheet Valuation**—Because so many different measurement bases are represented in the balance sheet, the totals for assets and liabilities are difficult to interpret and compare across firms.

Definition
Measurement Base: The attribute of an account being measured and reported

1. **Historical cost or other historical value**—Some accounts are measured and reported at a fixed, unchanging historical amount. Examples include land, some investments, cash, prepaids, many current liabilities, contributed capital accounts, and treasury stock.

2. **Depreciated, amortized, or depleted historical cost**—Other accounts reflect the remaining portion of a fixed unchanging historical amount. In some cases, the original cost or other relevant amount is maintained in one account, with a contra or adjunct account being subtracted from or added to that account for the purpose of reporting net book value (carrying value). Examples include property, plant and equipment; intangibles; natural resources.

3. **Market value, a type of current value**—Examples include investments in marketable securities (stocks and bonds) for which the holding firm does not have significant influence and does not intend to hold to maturity (in the case of bonds). *Fair value*, often used synonymously with *market value*, is the selling price for assets and amount currently required to retire a liability. These are *exit* values rather than *entry* values.

4. **Net realizable value**—This is another type of current value but one that is less in amount than the historical value. Net realizable value is the amount the firm expects to receive from the sale or collection of the item. Examples include accounts receivable and inventories.

5. **Present value**—The present value of a future cash flow is its discounted value. This is the primary measurement basis for noncurrent debt (mainly bonds and long-term notes). The present value is the measure of current sacrifice when extinguishing the debt at the balance sheet date.

6. **Aggregate of more than one valuation basis**—Retained earnings-net income reflects all measurement bases through revenue and expense recognition.

D. **Classification of Assets and Liabilities**—Assets and liabilities are classified as current or noncurrent. U.S. GAAP defines only current items; the noncurrent classification represents items that are not classified as current. The purpose of this classification is to distinguish items that will affect the firm's liquidity in the near term (one year) from those that will not. Classification helps financial statement users assess the ability of a firm to pay its debts in the near future. Owners' equity accounts are not classified because they do not represent resources or obligations.

1. **Current asset (CA)**

   a. An asset expected to be realized in cash or to be consumed or sold during the normal operating cycle, or within one year of the balance sheet date, whichever is longer.

   b. The operating cycle is the period of time from purchasing inventory to paying for the payable incurred on inventory purchase to the sale of goods to the collection of receivable and then to purchasing inventory all over again.

   c. For most firms the operating cycle is less than one year, but some firms, such as construction and engineering companies, have operating cycles exceeding one year. Construction in process, an inventory account found in construction firms' balance sheets, is a current asset even though the constructed asset may require several years to complete.

2. **Current liability (CL)**

   a. A liability expected to be extinguished through the use of current assets or by the incurrence of other current liabilities.

   b. The *incurrence of other CL* part of the definition means that CL that are continuously refinanced (rolled over) by replacing them with other CL due later (but within one year of the balance sheet date) must still be classified as CL, even though no CA will be used to extinguish them in the year after the balance sheet date.

Example

A note payable due 3/1/x2 is expected to be refinanced continuously on a 4-month basis, each time substituting a new 4-month note for the old. This note should be classified as a CL in the 12/31/x1 balance sheet because there is no certainty that the firm will not use CA in the next year to pay off the debt. The debtor firm cannot control the creditor who may decide not to refinance. Interest rates may increase substantially changing the strategy of the debtor firm. However, if the new note is due later than 12/31/x2 then the original note is classified as NCL.

Only if the firm refinances an otherwise current liability with a noncurrent liability before the balance sheet is issued (or is available to be issued) can the original liability be reclassified as noncurrent. *Refinance* here includes:

- Replacing the liability with a new liability that is due one year from the balance sheet date

- Entering into an irrevocable agreement to do so with a capable creditor

- Issuing stock to extinguish the debt

---

3. **Noncurrent assets (NCA) and noncurrent liabilities (NCL)**—Defined by default as assets and liabilities that are not current. The current/noncurrent distinction is important because firms would rather report more CA and less CL to appear more liquid and less risky in the short run. There is great incentive to move CLs into the NCL category, for example.

4. **Ratios for liquidity**

   a. Current ratio = CA/CL. This ratio is frequently used as a measure of liquidity. Many analysts use a minimum value of 2 when evaluating firms because the extra CA provides a buffer for uncertainty, and CA includes inventories and prepaids that are not considered very liquid.

   b. Quick or acid-test ratio = (cash + short term investments + AR)/CL. This ratio provides a more rigorous test of liquidity.

   c. Effect of transactions on ratios.

> **Exam Tip**
> The CPA Exam may ask the effect of certain transactions on ratios. Analyze the effect by determining whether the numerator or denominator has experienced the greater percentage change.

Example

Assume the current ratio exceeds 1. What is the effect on the current ratio of paying an account payable? Answer: Both CA (cash) and CL (accts pay) decrease by the same amount. The ratio increases because the denominator falls by a greater percentage.

E. **Balance Sheet Account Types by Category**

   1. For balance sheet reporting, assets and liabilities are typically reported in order from most liquid to least liquid. For example, current assets begin with cash and cash equivalents, then short-term investments, receivables, inventories and finally prepaids.

2. **Current assets**

   a. Cash, cash equivalents, short-term investments, accounts receivable, other receivables, inventories, prepaids

   b. Cash is the only account for which the following are the same:

      i. Nominal value

      ii. Market value

      iii. Realizable value

      iv. Present value

      v. Future value

3. **Noncurrent assets**

   a. Long-term investments, property, plant and equipment, intangibles, "other" assets (including long-term prepaids)

   b. Goodwill is by far the largest intangible in terms of dollar amount for many firms and equals the excess of the purchase price paid for another business over the market value of its net assets. Only when a firm is purchased by another is goodwill recognized in the balance sheet of the purchaser. Internally, generated goodwill is expensed.

4. **Current liabilities**—Accounts payable, accrued liabilities, unearned revenue, income tax payable, notes payable, current portion of long-term debt (the portion due within one year of the balance sheet date)

5. **Noncurrent liabilities**—Notes payable, bonds payable, lease liabilities, pension liabilities, postretirement healthcare liabilities, deferred taxes. (Although this item can appear in all four possible classifications (i.e., CA, NCA, CL, and NCL), the NCL category is by far the largest.)

6. **Owners' equity—two main types**

   a. Contributed capital (common stock, preferred stock, contributed capital in excess of par), treasury stock (a contra account)

   b. Retained earnings (total net income to date less total dividends to date)

F. **Reporting Within the Balance Sheet**—The use of contra accounts (−) and "adjunct" accounts (+); valuation accounts.

1. **Contra and adjunct accounts**

   a. Accounts can be accompanied by contra and adjunct accounts

   b. A contra account has a balance opposite that of the associated account in terms of debit and credit. Contras can be debit or credit balances, and can be considered valuation accounts or merely accumulations of items such as depreciation and amortization over time

   c. An adjunct account has a balance that is the same as that of the associated account in terms of debit and credit. An adjunct can have either a debit or a credit balance. An adjunct account is added whereas a contra is subtracted

2. **Valuation accounts**

   a. A valuation account is one used to increase or decrease the book value of an item to a measure of current value.

   b. Not all contra or adjunct accounts are valuation accounts, but all valuation accounts are contras or adjuncts.

3. Examples

Examples

1. Accumulated depreciation is a contra account to property, plant, and equipment but is not a valuation account because net book value in this case is not equal to market value.

Property, plant, and equipment	$40,000	(cost)
Accumulated depreciation	(5,000)	
Net book value	$35,000	(undepreciated cost)

2. Allowance for uncollectible accounts is a contra account to accounts receivable and is a valuation account because net accounts receivable is an approximation to net realizable value, a measure of current value.

Accounts receivable	$60,000	(sales value)
Allowance for doubtful accounts	(8,000)	
Net book value	$52,000	(net realizable value)

3. Valuation allowance for investments in marketable securities can be a contra or adjunct account and is a valuation account because it decreases or increases the net book value of the investment to current market value. The account is a contra if the market value is less than original cost, and is an adjunct if the market value exceeds original cost.

Investments in marketable securities	$30,000	(cost)
Valuation allowance	4,000	
Market value	$34,000	(market value)

4. Bond premium and discount are adjunct and contra accounts respectively but are not valuation accounts because the net bond liability is generally not equal to market value.

Bonds payable	$100,000	(face value)
Bond premium	3,000	
Net bond liability	$103,000	(net carrying value)

G. The Balance Sheet and Firm Valuation

1. The total owners' equity of most publicly traded firms (also known as net assets or A − L) is significantly less than the market value of the firm because investors place a higher value on firms that include the investors' expectation of future earnings. Firms are usually worth much more than the sum of their individual net assets, even at market value.

2. There are three important valuations for a firm:

   a. **Total OE or net assets**—This is the amount determined by current U.S. GAAP and is found in the balance sheet;

   b. **Market value of net identifiable assets**—The amount of cash that would remain after selling all identifiable assets (including identifiable intangibles) and paying off all liabilities. This amount is also called the firm's "split up" or liquidation value. To determine this amount, the firm must have its assets appraised;

   c. **Total value of the firm**—Its *market capitalization*—that is, the total value of the firm's outstanding stock. For publicly traded firms, this value can be found on Internet financial sites.

3. Identifiable assets and liabilities with market values different from their book values cause the difference between total OE and the market value of net identifiable assets. Examples include investments and natural resources.

4. The difference between a firm's market capitalization and the market value of net identifiable assets is goodwill—an amount that cannot be identified with any individual recorded asset. However, goodwill is recorded for accounting purposes only when one firm purchases all or a controlling interest of another firm.

H. **Market Capitalization**—The market capitalization is generally many times recorded OE in amount. The purpose of the balance sheet is not to provide a firm's market value, but rather to provide information that is a starting point for valuing a firm and assessing its riskiness. The relative investment in plant assets, natural resources, investments, and in affiliated companies, along with the ratio of debt to equity provides investors with valuable information about the financial structure and direction of the firm. The trend in balance sheet values over time also provides useful information.

1. In addition, the balance sheet is largely historical, and is limited to transactions that have already taken place. It is not the responsibility of financial statements to provide current value. Rather, current value is a constantly changing amount based on investors' perceptions in the market at the time. In sum, the information in the balance sheet and other financial statement information is an input to market valuation, not the other way around. Stock prices react to changes in financial statement information and other information.

I. **Debt Disclosures**—These are perhaps the most important items found in the balance sheet, dollar for dollar. They indicate a quantifiable financial risk faced by the firm in the future.

J. **Control and Subsidiary Accounts**

1. The accounts reside in the ledger. The general ledger contains all accounts to be used in preparing the balance sheet. Some of these accounts are called **control** accounts because they report the aggregate balance of several subsidiary accounts.

Example
The accounts receivable (AR) control account balance (in the general ledger) is the sum of the subsidiary AR account balances. For example, a firm has 100 subsidiary AR accounts, each one for a different customer. The sum of the 100 subsidiary AR balances equals the balance in the control AR account balance, which is reported on the balance sheet.

2. Control and subsidiary accounts are used for any account that consists of many individual accounts. Inventory, plant assets (property, plant, and equipment) and accounts payable are examples.

3. A chart of accounts typically assigns account numbers to accounts for use in computerized information systems. For example, assets may be assigned numbers 100–199, liabilities 200–250, etc. Cash might be assigned the number 100, with AR control assigned number 104. Each account in the AR subsidiary ledger then could be numbered 104-1, 104-2, etc.

K. **Accounting Cycle Review**

1. The periodic accounting process leading to the preparation of financial statements is called the accounting cycle. The cycle steps used by a firm are specific to the information technology applied. The following is a representative list, in chronological order.

   a. Analyze relevant source documents (e.g., sales invoices) and record journal entries in a journal, a temporary listing of accounts affected and the amount by which they are to be changed by transaction, event, or adjustment.

b. Post (distribute) the information from the journal to the accounts in the ledger, on a periodic basis. Only after posting, the account balances are updated.

c. Record adjusting journal entries at the end of the accounting period. These journal entries record changes in resources and obligations not signaled by a new transaction or event. Examples include accrual of wages expense from the last payday to the end of the fiscal period, expiration of prepaids, and recognition of estimated expenses such as depreciation and warranty expense. These journal entries are also posted to the accounts.

d. Prepare trial balances. Some firms prepare a trial balance, which is a test of the equality of the sum of debit account balances and credit account balances, before and after adjusting journal entries. A trial balance is a quick test for the presence of an error in recording or posting.

e. Prepare the income statement, balance sheet, and statement of cash flows (often in that order). The first two are prepared directly from the ledger accounts or trial balance; the cash flow statement requires additional analysis.

f. Close the temporary account balances (revenues, expenses, gains, losses) setting them to zero, and transfer the net income amount to retained earnings.

2. Throughout the accounting cycle, U.S. GAAP is applied primarily at the two journal entry steps (1 and 3), and in preparing the financial statements and note disclosures. Otherwise, the cycle is largely mechanical and usually not performed manually.

L. Special Journals

1. Similar to the control-subsidiary account distinction for ledger accounts, firms may use special journals, and a general journal. High volume similar transactions are recorded in special journals (e.g., the sales journal) with very infrequent transactions being recorded in the general journal. Special journals facilitate the review and control of similar transactions (all sales, all cash receipts etc.).

2. Advantages of special journals

a. Special journals simplify the recording of journal entries because each recording affects the same accounts each time. Your check register is an example; it is a cash receipts/payments journal. Each entry you make always affects cash, and you need only write into the register the other item affected (e.g., utility bill).

b. The number of postings also is reduced because only the sum of the changes in the special journal accounts for the period need to be posted to the respective accounts.

c. Separation of duties for improved internal control is fostered with the use of special journals. Only particular individuals may be authorized to access the sales journal for example, but not the cash receipts journal, or the general journal.

3. Sales journal as an example of a special journal—A sales journal for a firm might record all cash and credit sales and have the following six columns:

Date	Customer	Invoice #	DR Cash	DR AR	CR Sales

Each line entered into the journal is a complete journal entry. Cash sales use all columns except for the DR AR column, and credit sales use all columns except for the DR Cash column. Special journals dispense with the *flush left* formatting for debits and *indenting right* for credits.

4. Periodic posting is as follows:

a. Sum of the DR Cash column for a period is posted to the cash account;

b. Sum of the DR AR column for a period is posted to the AR control account while each individual amount in that column is posted to the appropriate AR subsidiary account;

c. Sum of the CR Sales account is posted to the sales account.

5. Posting is usually performed within the computerized system and is mechanical from the user's point of view. Posting references enables cross-referencing between journal and ledger. For example, the posting to the AR control account from the special journal might indicate the location of the total from the sales journal within the information system.

Income Statement

This lesson presents an overview of the balance sheet.

After studying this lesson, you should be able to:

1. List and define the components of the Income Statement.

2. Identify the difference between economic income and accounting income.

3. Prepare an Income Statement.

I. Background

A. Definitions of Revenues, Expenses, Gains, and Losses

Definitions

Revenues: Revenues represent increases in net assets or settlements of liabilities by providing goods and services. Revenues are related to the company's primary business operations.

Expenses: Expenses represent decreases in net assets or incurred liabilities through the provision of goods or services. Expenses are related to the company's primary business operations. Expenses provide benefit to the firm. Losses do not.

Gains: Gains represent increases in equity or net assets from peripheral or incidental transactions.

Losses: Losses represent decreases in equity or net assets from peripheral or incidental transactions. Losses do not provide value or benefit to the firm.

B. All-Inclusive versus Current Operating Performance Views of the Income Statement

1. **All-inclusive income statement**—The current income statement under GAAP is mostly an all-inclusive one in which essentially all revenues, expenses, gains, and losses are shown on the income statement and included in the net income calculation.

   a. **Exceptions**—There are exceptions to all-inclusive income statements.

      i. **Prior-period adjustments**—Prior-period adjustments are shown on the Statement of Retained Earnings and are the correction of accounting errors affecting income of prior years.

      ii. **Other comprehensive income items (OCI)**

         1. Foreign currency translation adjustments

         2. Unrealized holding gains and losses on securities available for sale

         3. Pension and other postretirement benefit plan cost adjustments

         4. Certain deferred derivative gains and losses

      iii. The OCI items above are disclosed in the statement of comprehensive income discussed in a later lesson. The different income amounts for a period are related as follows:

Net Income + Other Comprehensive Income = Comprehensive Income

      iv. Retrospective changes in accounting principle affecting income. These are treated as direct adjustments to retained earnings.

2. Current operating performance income statement

    a. At the other end of the spectrum is the current operating performance approach to income statement preparation, which would limit the income statement to normal, recurring items.

    b. Many other items would be run through owners' equity and thus escape the attention of financial statement users who rely more heavily on the income statement.

    c. Due to enhanced opportunities to manipulate net income, the all-inclusive approach was selected over the current operating approach for income statement presentation purposes.

C. Concepts of Income—The accountant and economist have different ways to measure income. There are many different ways to approach the problem. GAAP takes an objective, arm's-length transaction approach to measurement and recognition.

1. Definition

Definition

Accounting Income: Revenues less expenses plus gains less losses.

---

    a. That is, accounting income reflects recorded transactions, events, and adjustments.

    b. For many assets and liabilities, changes in market value are not recognized until substantiated by a transaction between willing parties.

    c. Investments with readily determinable market values are an exception. These investments (trading securities, securities available for sale) are reported at market value. Moreover, inventories are written down to lower of cost or market.

2. Definition

Definition

Economic Income: The change in the net worth of a business enterprise during an accounting period.

---

    a. The net worth of a business enterprise is described as the fair value (FV) of net assets (rather than total owners' equity per GAAP).

    b. Thus, the FV of a business on December 31 of a given year is compared with the FV of the business on January 1 of that year to determine economic income.

    c. Net income for the period would include all changes in FV of assets and liabilities during the period.

    d. Any investments by owners would be added and any dividends paid or treasury stock purchased would be subtracted, when making this calculation.

Fair Value of Net Assets at Jan. 1	+	Net Income for the Period (including increases in FV)	+	Owner Investments	−	Dividends and Stock Repurchases	=	Fair Value at Dec. 31

    e. The use of fair values and other price level changes takes into account the changes in the value of the firm's assets and liabilities and goes beyond the recording of transactions. However, because GAAP is concerned with reliability of information, transaction-based reporting is the current model used.

II. **Structure of the Statement**

A. **Continuing Operations and Other Items of Income**—The income statement is divided roughly into two portions.

   1. **Top portion**—The top portion includes routinely occurring items and other items that are appropriately included in income from continuing operations.

     a. The subtotal income from continuing operations is used by investors as a broad measure of operating income.

     b. GAAP does not prescribe the specific format in which information should be presented in the top portion of the Income Statement.

     c. Income from continuing operations includes all income items other than those in the bottom portion of the income statement.

   2. **Bottom portion**—The bottom portion includes items that are specifically defined by GAAP as being unrelated to continuing operations.

     a. These items are not representative of the firm's ability to generate income and are unique items that will not be repeated. They are, however, components of total income.

     b. GAAP is very specific about the measurement and presentation of items in the bottom portion. For example, there is very specific guidance on the presentation and measurement of discontinued operations.

     c. Discontinued operations are required to be presented at the bottom portion of the income statement. Discontinued operations are major components of an entity that are either sold or planned to be sold and thus are no longer part of continuing operations.

B. **Sample Income Statement**—A generalized income statement appears next.

> **ABX Company**
>
> **Income Statement**
>
> **For the Year Ended December 31, 20X0**
>
>   Net sales
> − Cost of goods sold
> = Gross margin
> − Operating expenses
> + Miscellaneous revenues and gains
> − Miscellaneous expenses and losses
> ± Unusual or infrequent items
> = Income from continuing operations before tax
> − Less income tax expense
> = Income from Continuing Operations
> ± Income from Discontinued Operations (net of tax)
> = Net income

C. **Presentation Requirements**—There is no prescribed way of displaying the items above income from continuing operations. For example, some firms provide a subtotal called "operating income," which appears before miscellaneous items, but such disclosure is not mandated by GAAP.

D. Presentation Order—Below income from continuing operations, the prescribed presentation is the order as shown above.

E. Income Tax Expense—Income tax expense is attributable only to income from continuing operations. The tax effects of items below continuing operations are shown along with the item itself in a process called "intraperiod tax allocation."

F. Multiple Disclosures

1. The total income tax effect for a given year is accomplished through multiple disclosures. The items for which intraperiod tax allocation is applied include:

    a. Discontinued operations

    b. Other comprehensive income items

    c. Adjustment for retroactive accounting principle changes

    d. Prior-period adjustments

2. The first item is reported in the income statement; the third is reported in a special OE account called accumulated other comprehensive income, and the last two are reported in the retained earnings statement.

Example
Intraperiod tax allocation and discontinued operations disclosure. A loss on discontinued operations before tax is $12,000, and the associated tax rate is 30%. The disclosure in the income statement below continuing operations would appear as:

Less discontinued operations, net of $3,600 tax savings........$8,400

G. Intraperiod Tax Allocation—Pertains to the tax effects for only one year. It is the allocation of the total tax consequence for that year among income from continuing operations, and the four items listed above. This process contrasts with *interperiod* tax allocation, which records a period's total tax consequence in current taxes payable and deferred tax accounts. Interperiod tax allocation is a much more extensive process and is covered in another lesson.

III. Unusual or Infrequent Income Items

A. GAAP requires that unusual or infrequent items be separately reported if material, as a component of income from continuing operations. Note that there is no longer a category for "extraordinary items" at the bottom of the income statement. Any unusual or infrequent items (such as an impairment loss) is show as a component of income from continuing operations.

IV. Formats Leading to Income from Continuing Operations—Income from continuing operations includes the revenues, expenses, gains, and losses that are normal and recurring. In addition to including those items that are specifically related to primary business operations, income from continuing operations also includes those revenues, expenses, gains, and losses that are the result of incidental or peripheral activities. The presentation of income from continuing operations follows one of two formats, the single-step format or the multiple-step format. Note the required per share disclosures shown at the bottom of the income statements. Earnings per share are discussed in detail in later lessons.

A. Formats in Practice

1. Two formats have become accepted in practice: single-step and multiple step statements. There are many variants of each.

    a. Both formats provide the same information although the multiple-step format provides more subtotals and organization.

    b. Income from continuing operations and net income are the same amounts regardless of the format used.

    c. The format differences affect only the ordering in calculating income from continuing operations.

2. The presentation below income from continuing operations is mandated by U.S. GAAP and is the same regardless of how the top portion is presented.

B. **Single-Step Format**—The single-step format involves a presentation of income from continuing operations that is largely based on a single comparison. Total revenues and gains are compared with total expenses and losses in the single-step format. A single-step illustration for the Wolf Company follows.

Wolf Company		
Income Statement		
For the Year Ended December 31, 20xX		
Revenues and Gains:		
Net Sales	$1,000,000	
Rent Revenue	10,000	
Investment Revenue	20,000	
Gain on Sale of Operational Assets	30,000	1,060,000
Expenses and Losses:		
Cost of Goods Sold	400,000	
Distribution Expenses	10,000	
General and Administrative Expenses	20,000	
Depreciation Expense	30,000	
Interest Expense	10,000	
Loss on Sale of Investments	20,000	(490,000)
Unusual or Infrequent Gains and Losses:		
Casualty Loss	(100,000)	
Gain on Sale of Real Estate	200,000	100,000
Pretax Income from Continuing Operations		670,000
Income Tax Expense		(201,000)
Income from Continuing Operations		469,000
Income from Discontinued Operations		
Results of Operations (less income tax expense of $30,000)	70,000	
Loss on Disposal of Business Segment (less income tax savings of 60,000)	(140,000)	(70,000)
Net Income		$399,000
Earnings per Share:		
Income from Continuing Operations		4.69
Income from Discontinued Operations		(.70)
Net Income		$3.99

C. **Multiple-Step Format**—The multiple-step format involves a presentation of income from continuing operations that includes multiple comparisons of revenues, expenses, gains, and losses. In doing so, the reader is provided with the operating margin of the company, which is the excess of operating revenues over operating expenses. In other words, these revenues and expenses are directly tied to the company's primary business operations. Beyond the operating margin, the incidental or peripheral gains and losses are shown in the presentation of income from continuing operations. Next is a multiple-step illustration for the Wolf Company.

Wolf Company

Income Statement

For the Year Ended December 31, 20xX

Sales Revenue	$1,100,000	
Less Sales Returns and Allowances	(100,000)	
Net Sales		1,000,000
Cost of Goods Sold		(400,000)
Gross Margin		600,000
Operating Expenses:		
Distribution Expenses	10,000	
General and Administrative Expenses	20,000	
Depreciation Expense	30,000	(60,000)
Operating Margin		540,000
Other Revenues and Gains:		
Rent Revenue	10,000	
Investment Revenue	20,000	
Gain on Sale of Operational Assets	30,000	60,000
Other Expenses and Losses:		
Interest Expense	10,000	
Loss on Sale of Investments	20,000	(30,000)
Unusual or Infrequent Gains and Losses:		
Casualty Loss	(100,000)	
Gain on Sale of Real Estate	200,000	100,000
Pretax Income from Continuing Operations		670,000
Income Tax Expense		(201,000)
Income from Continuing Operations		469,000
Income from Discontinued Operations:		
Results of Operations (less income tax expense of $30,000)	70,000	
Loss on Disposal of Business Segment (less income tax savings of $60,000)	(140,000)	(70,000)
Net Income		$399,000
Earnings Per Share:		
Income from Continuing Operations		4.69
Income from Discontinued Operations		(.70)
Net Income		$3.99

Statement of Comprehensive Income

This lesson presents a discussion of the Statement of Comprehensive Income.

After studying this lesson, you should be able to:

1. Define comprehensive income.

2. List the components of other comprehensive income.

3. Prepare a Statement of Comprehensive Income.

4. Identify the reporting alternatives for comprehensive income.

I. **Background**—Topic 220 has aligned the U.S. GAAP presentation of Comprehensive Income with IFRS. That is, comprehensive income is presented either in a separate statement or in the Statement of Income, which is consistent with what is required by IFRS.

    A. U.S. GAAP requires the disclosure of comprehensive income in a financial report in one of two ways:

        1. Single statement of comprehensive income—This alternative presents the components of profit or loss (net income) within this single statement leading to net income as a subtotal. Displaying the other comprehensive income items leads to total comprehensive income.

        2. Two statements—A separate income statement is presented (and as such it becomes part of a complete set of financial statements) immediately before the statement of comprehensive income. The net income amount resulting from the first statement is used as the beginning amount for the second statement, which then reports the other comprehensive income items leading to comprehensive income.

    B. The companies choosing the two-statement approach have the option to begin the second statement with or without net income.

    C. Net income is not replaced by comprehensive income. The purpose of requiring the reporting of comprehensive income is to report the net change in equity (other than from transactions with owners) in a single amount and to provide a more complete picture of the total earnings of the firm for a period. This reporting contributes to the objective of reporting an "all inclusive" income amount.

II. **Comprehensive Income Defined**

    A. Comprehensive income was designed to report the change in net assets during the period from all sources other than from transactions with owners acting as owners. There are two components of comprehensive income:

        1. Net income; *and*

        2. "Other" comprehensive income.

        3. It is the second category that causes comprehensive income to differ from net income. "Other" comprehensive income items are not currently recognized in net income. They are recorded directly as increases or decreases in owners' equity.

Definition
Comprehensive income: The sum of (1) net income, and (2) other comprehensive income.
$CI = NI + OCI$

III. **"Other" Comprehensive Income Items (OCI)**

    A. The following items are items included in the second category above, that is, they are included in comprehensive income but not in income:

1. Unrealized gains and losses on securities available for sale (AFS);

2. Unrecognized pension and postretirement benefit cost and gains. Currently, GAAP does not recognize all changes in these liabilities and assets immediately in income. Rather, some are recognized in other comprehensive income;

3. Foreign currency translation adjustments are changes in the value of foreign currency and accounts measured in foreign currency;

4. Certain deferred gains and losses from derivatives.

B. OCI items are typically reported net of tax. Alternatively, firms may report each item on a pretax basis with the net aggregate income tax effect reported as a separate item.

C. Comprehensive income does not include the following:

1. Retrospective effects of changes in accounting principle

2. Prior-period adjustments

D. The above two items are both reported as adjustments to retained earnings. Therefore, comprehensive income accounts for most but not all nonowner changes in owners' equity.

IV. Reporting Comprehensive Income—The following two examples of formats for reporting comprehensive income use assumed values.

Example
Separate Statement of Comprehensive Income:

ABX Inc.

Statement of Comprehensive Income

For the Year Ended December 31, 20X7

Net income		$24,000
Other comprehensive income, net of tax		
Net unrealized holding loss on AFS	($7,000)	
Unrealized pension cost adjustment	(2,000)	
Other comprehensive income		(9,000)
Comprehensive income		$15,000

Comprehensive income is the sum of net income and other comprehensive income.

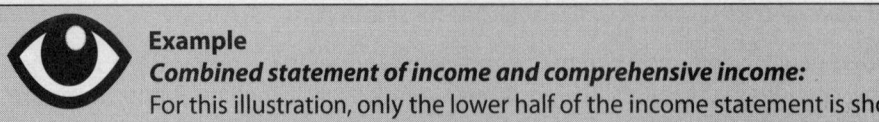

Example
Combined statement of income and comprehensive income:
For this illustration, only the lower half of the income statement is shown.

ABX Inc.

Statement of Income and Comprehensive Income

For the Year Ended December 31, 20X7

Income from continuing operations		$14,000
Discontinued Operations, net of tax		10,000
Net income		$24,000
Other comprehensive income, net of tax		
Net unrealized holding loss on AFS	($7,000)	
Unrealized pension cost adjustment	(2,000)	
Other comprehensive income		(9,000)
Comprehensive income		$15,000

Comprehensive income is the sum of net income and other comprehensive income.

V. Accumulated Other Comprehensive Income (AOCI)

A. Accumulated other comprehensive income (AOCI) is the amount carried over from the previous period, and then either increased or decreased during the current period. This total is the running total of other comprehensive income items through the balance sheet date. Irrespective of the reporting option chosen for comprehensive income, U.S. GAAP requires that the total of other comprehensive income be separately displayed in the owners' equity section of the balance sheet in an account with a title such as AOCI. AOCI is an owners' equity (OE) account.

B. In addition, the accumulated balances of each individual component of OCI must be reported. This information can appear in the balance sheet, statement of owners' equity, or footnotes. This disclosure allows the user to understand the changes in individual components of other comprehensive income.

C. Both net income and OCI items occur each year and together yield comprehensive income. Net income is closed to retained earnings and OCI is closed to AOCI each year. Both retained earnings and AOCI are OE accounts.

D. Think of OCI as a separate but parallel "income" track, along with net income. "Net income is to retained earnings as OCI is to AOCI."

E. An item recognized in OCI one year may be recognized in net income in a later year. To avoid double counting in OE, the OCI item from the previous year is removed from AOCI. This is called a reclassification adjustment. The entity must disclose the reclassification adjustments and the effect of the reclassification adjustment on NI and OCI.

Example
A firm recognizes a $5,000 unrealized gain on an AFS investment in year 1 OCI. In year 2, the AFS investment is sold for a $5,000 gain (recognized in net income causing retained earnings to increase by $5,000). At the end of year 2, the $5,000 unrealized gain from year 1 in AOCI is removed by reducing AOCI by $5,000 (the reclassification adjustment). The gain in OCI is "reclassified" as a gain recognized in net income. Without the reclassification adjustment, total OE would count the $5,000 twice. Reclassification adjustments are reported in the footnotes.

Statement of Changes in Equity

This lesson presents an overview of the Statement of Changes in Equity.

After studying this lesson, you should be able to:

1. Identify the components included in the Statement of Owners' Equity.

2. Construct a Statement of Owners' Equity.

I. **Background**

    A. Firms are required to report the changes in their owners'-equity (OE) accounts for the period. Supplementary schedules or footnotes may be used, but often large firms report the Statement of Changes in Equity to meet this requirement.

        1. Other titles for this statement include Statement of Changes in Owners' Equity, Owners' Equity Statement, Statement of Shareholders' Equity, and Statement of Owners' Equity. Some firms prefer to only report a separate statement of retained earnings and report the other changes in the notes.

        2. In addition to the changes in OE accounts for the period, firms must also report the changes in the number of shares of equity securities. This information is the counterpart to some of the account changes in the statement of changes in equity, but measured in shares. Some firms report the share information in a column adjacent to the changes in the relevant accounts measured in dollars.

    B. The Statement of Changes in Equity effectively expands the OE section of the balance sheet by listing all the changes in those accounts, explaining how the beginning balance increased or decreased in deriving the ending balance. Reporting investments by owners and distributions to owners are important aspects of this disclosure. The statement is dated like the Income Statement and Statement of Cash Flows—for a period.

    C. The format of the statement varies.

II. **Format of the Statement**—The most common formats encountered are the vertical and horizontal formats.

III. **Vertical Format**—In this format, each OE account is reported in a separate column of a spreadsheet-type document. The following is an example of this format for a single period.

Business Enterprises, Inc.

Statement of Changes in Equity

For the Year Ended December 31, 20X2

	Common Stock	Contributed Capital in Excess of Par	Accumulated Other Comprehensive Income	Retained Earnings	Treasury Stock	Total OE
Balance, 1/1/x2	$40,000	$180,000	$20,000	$230,000	($30,000)	$440,000
Issued stock	5,000	30,000				35,000
Issued stock dividend	2,000	11,000		(13,000)		
Purchased treasury stock					(20,000)	(20,000)
Declared cash dividend				(25,000)		(25,000)
Net income				90,000		90,000
Other comprehensive income			(6,000)			(6,000)
Balance, 12/31/x2	$47,000	$221,000	$14,000	$282,000	($50,000)	$514,000

A. Each column reconciles the beginning and ending account balance for one account by disclosing all the changes in the account during the period. Total OE is also shown as a column. This format allows a check of accuracy by comparing total OE computed as (1) the sum of each transaction affecting OE, and (2) the sum of individual OE account balances.

B. In most cases, each event causing a change in OE requires at least two entries per row (more than one column affected). The total OE column is usually but not always affected. The stock dividend, for example, has no effect on total OE. Later lessons review the underlying accounting leading to the line items in this statement. Both net income (from the income statement) and cash dividends declared are entered into the retained-earnings column and total-OE column and have opposite effects. Treasury stock is a contra-OE account, a direct reduction to owners' equity.

C. The statement of comprehensive income is presented either in a separate statement or in a combined statement with net income. The firm is not required to report the components of other comprehensive income in this statement. However, accumulated other comprehensive income totals are reported.

D. Nonetheless, accumulated other comprehensive income (AOCI) has its own column. Recall that AOCI is the running total of all other comprehensive income (OCI) items. Any firm with AOCI will report it in the statement of changes in equity, regardless of its policy concerning reporting the statement of comprehensive income.

IV. **Horizontal Format**—Alternatively, the statement can be presented in horizontal format. Each account is explained from beginning balance to ending balance in one set of rows, one account schedule on top of another. The first two accounts for this format are shown as follows:

Common stock, 1/1/x2	$40,000	
Issued stock	5,000	
Issued stock dividend	2,000	
Common stock, 12/31/x2		47,000
Contributed capital in excess of par, 1/1/x2	180,000	
Issued stock	30,000	
Issued stock dividend	11,000	
Contributed capital in excess of par, 1/1/x2		$221,000

   A. After all the remaining accounts are entered, the totals of each account (to the left of each account schedule) add to total OE.

V. Comparative Statements—SEC registrants report three years of OE statements, as is the case with the income statement and statement of cash flows. The current year statement is shown comparatively with the statement for the previous two years. Again, either the vertical or the horizontal format is used for presentation.

   A. The comparative multiyear display for the vertical format for single year statements results in the statements of three years stacked one on top of the other. This type of display, thus, is vertical within each year and horizontal across years.

   B. The comparative multiyear display for the horizontal format for single year statements adds two more sets of columns, one for each year shown comparatively. This type of display, thus, is horizontal within each year and vertical across years.

VI. Other Columns—Other columns found in the statement of changes in equity include:

> Preferred stock
>
> Contributed capital in excess of par, preferred
>
> Contributed capital from treasury stock
>
> Equity attributable to noncontrolling interests (minority interest)
>
> Equity attributable to the shareholders of the parent (the reporting company). The sum of this total and for minority interest yields the total OE of the reporting company.

VII. Other events—Other events reported in the statement of changes in equity (and columns affected) include:

> Retrospective change in accounting principle affecting prior earnings (retained earnings and total OE)
>
> Restatement of income statement for an error affecting prior earnings—prior period adjustment (retained earnings and total OE)
>
> Contributed capital from conversion of bonds (contributed capital and total OE)
>
> Contributed capital from stock options and stock award plans (contributed capital and total OE)

   A. The first two items above explain how the beginning retained earnings balance is affected by retroactive application of an accounting policy or error correction.

Statement of Cash Flows

Sources and Uses of Cash

This section describes the primary purposes of a Statement of Cash Flows. This section also provides an overview of the content and format of the Statement of Cash Flows. Because the concept of cash may include other highly liquid items called "cash equivalents," such equivalents are defined and examples given. Next, the major sections of the Statement are identified. A graphic model summarizes the relationship between cash as it appears on Balance Sheets and the Statement of Cash Flows. This model facilitates an understanding of the general purpose and format of the Statement of Cash Flows.

After studying this lesson, you should be able to:

1. Describe the purpose of a Statement of Cash Flows.

2. Define cash and cash equivalents.

3. List the categories included in a Statement of Cash Flows.

I. **Statement of Cash Flows—Requirements and Purpose**

   A. **Statement Requirement**—A Statement of Cash Flows (SCF) is required for all business enterprises that report both financial position (Balance Sheet) and results of operations (Income Statement) for a period.

      1. The SCF is a basic financial statement like the Income Statement and Balance Sheet.

      2. A SCF is not required for certain investment-type entities (e.g., employee benefit plan entities).

   B. **Statement Purposes**

      1. The basic purpose of the SCF is to provide information about the cash receipts and cash payments for an entity to help investors, creditors, and others assess:

         a. Past ability to generate and control cash inflows and cash outflows

         b. Probable future ability to generate cash inflows sufficient to meet future obligations and pay dividends

         c. The likely need for external borrowing

      2. The SCF also provides information about investing and financing activities that do not involve cash inflows (receipts) or outflows (payment) (e.g., acquiring a major long-term asset by incurring a liability).

   C. The SCF must exactly explain the change in cash (and cash equivalents) between the beginning and end of the reporting period on the Balance Sheet.

      1. **Cash equivalents are**

         a. Short-term, highly liquid investments;

         b. Readily convertible to known amounts of cash; and

         c. Sufficiently close to maturity so that the risk of changes in value due to changes in interest rate is insignificant.

      2. Investments are usually considered cash equivalents only when their original maturity is three months or less (e.g., treasury bills, money market funds). Investments in equity securities could not be cash equivalents because they are not convertible to a known amount of cash.

 **Example**
A T-bill purchased when there are only three months left in its term is a cash equivalent. But a T-bill purchased when there are four months left to its term does not become a cash equivalent after holding it one month.

3. The entity should disclose its policy for designating cash equivalents. A change in policy for designating cash equivalents is a change in accounting principle.

D. Information Reported

1. The SCF must report information in the following categories:

   a. Net Cash inflow or outflow from Operating Activities

   b. Net Cash inflow or outflow from Investing Activities

   c. Net Cash inflow or outflow from Financing Activities

   d. Effects of Foreign Currency Translation

   e. Reconciliation of net cash inflows/outflows (sum of the items listed above) with the reported change in cash and cash equivalents on the Balance Sheet

   f. Noncash Investing and Financing Activities

E. SCF Graphic Presentation—See the following illustration.

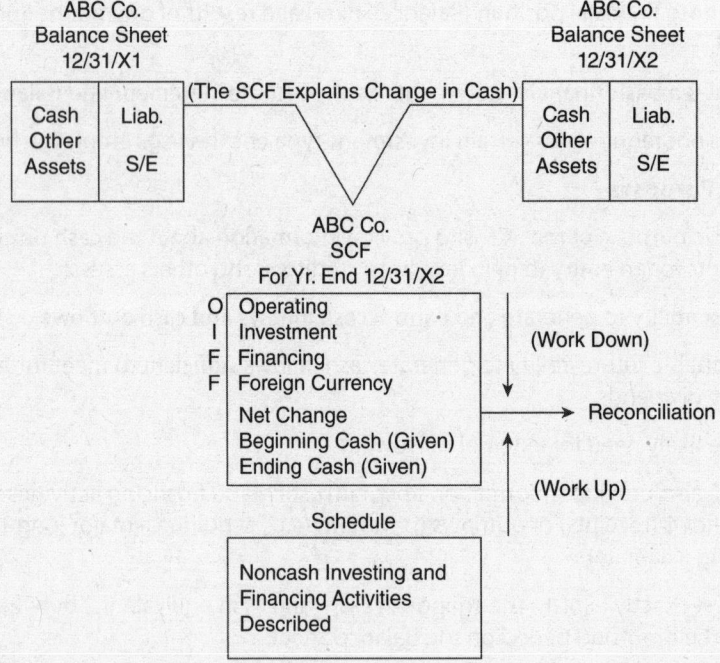

F. Comments on SCF Presentation

1. The categories used to explain the net change in cash and equivalents (operating, investing, financing, and foreign currency) should be presented in the order shown and can be remembered as OIFF ("Oh If"—I could only remember).

2. The categories used to explain the net change in cash (and equivalents) include items of both inflow (receipts) and outflow (payments).

3. The beginning and ending cash (and cash equivalents) are given on the balance sheets for the ends of the prior and current periods.

4. The change in cash (and equivalents) is a known amount, the difference between the beginning and ending cash (and equivalents), and can be plugged into the statement.

5. The OIFF elements must exactly explain the known amount of change in cash (and equivalents).

6. The new cash flow derived from the OIFF elements (working down) equals the derived change in cash (and equivalents) (working up).

G. The disclosure of noncash investing and financing activities must be on a separate schedule or other presentation, not on the face of the SCF.

II. Two Formats Allowed by GAAP

A. As discussed in detail later, the Statement of Cash Flows can be presented using either the direct or the indirect format.

B. The only difference between the two is in the operating activity section of the statement. The direct method reports the actual operating cash flows in the operating section. The indirect method reports the reconciliation of net income and net operating cash flow in the operating section. Both lead to the same subtotal: net operating cash flow. The following diagram shows the differences and similarities between the approaches.

	Direct Method	Indirect Method
Operating Activities:	Operating Cash Flows	Reconciliation
Investing Activities:	Investing Cash Flows	Investing Cash Flows
Financing Activities:	Financing Cash Flows	Financing Cash Flows

C. The direct method reports the reconciliation in a separate schedule.

D. Only the operating-activities section is different between the formats. Most firms use the indirect method.

Operating, Investing, and Financing Activities

This section presents the possible sources of cash inflows and outflows from operating, investing, and financing activities that are reported on the Statement of Cash Flows (SCF). This lesson also presents the requirements for disclosure of investing and financing activities that do not involve cash inflow or outflow. In addition, the implications of foreign currency conversion are described and illustrated.

After studying this lesson, you should be able to:

1. Identify the items included in operating, investing, and financing activities on the Statement of Cash Flows.

2. Describe the disclosures needed for noncash investing and financing activities.

3. Describe the implications of foreign currency conversion on the Statement of Cash Flows.

4. Prepare a Statement of Cash Flows using the direct method.

I. **Cash Flows from Operating Activities**—This category reports cash inflows and cash outflows that relate to items that enter into the determination of net income.

A. The major cash flow items in this category are the following:

Inflows (Cash Received)	Outflows (Cash Paid)
From Customers	To Suppliers (Goods/Services)
Dividends (from Investment)	To Employees (Payroll)
Interest received	Interest paid
	Income taxes

B. Any cash inflow or cash outflow not properly classified as from investing or financing would be included as from operating activities (e.g., collection of a lawsuit settlement).

C. The net of the above items constitutes Net Cash Flow from Operating Activities, and can be positive or negative.

D. The items that make up Cash Flow from Operating Activities may be presented in the SCF using one of two possible approaches:

1. **Direct approach**—Presents operating cash flow by classes of sources and uses.

2. **Indirect approach**—Presents operating cash flow by adjusting accrual net income to operating cash flow (called the reconciliation of net income and net operating cash flow).

E. The association of cash flows with income is one of the hallmarks of operating cash flows. Notice that interest paid and received and dividends received are all operating cash flows, but dividends paid is a financing cash flow. The first three flows are associated with income statement items (interest expense and revenue, dividend revenue), but dividends paid is not an income item; rather, it is a direct reduction in retained earnings. Dividends paid are a distribution of income.

F. These alternative approaches to presenting cash flows from operation are covered later. Firms use either the direct method or the indirect method. The direct method shows both

1. The operating cash flows by classes of sources and uses; *and*

2. The reconciliation of net income and net operating cash flow. The indirect method shows only the reconciliation of net income and net operating cash flow. The indirect method therefore does not report the actual operating cash flows.

II. Cash Flows from Investing Activities—This category reports cash inflows and cash outflows that relate to "investment in" and disposal of noncash assets.

    A. The major cash flow items in this category are:

Inflows (Cash Received)	Outflows (Cash Paid)
Sale of Long-Term Assets	Purchase of Long-Term Assets
Collection of Loan Principal	Lending (to others)
Disposal of Debt and Equity Securities (of others, e.g., Held-to-Maturity and Available-for-Sale Classifications)	Investment in Debt and Equity Securities (of others, e.g., Held-to-Maturity and Available-for-Sale Classifications)
Sale of Other Productive Assets (e.g., Patent; but not Inventory)	Purchase of Other Productive Assets (e.g., Patent; but not Inventory)

    B. Investment in and disposal of debt and equity securities of other entities includes those classified as Held to Maturity and Available for Sale.

    C. Firms classify cash flows from purchases, sales, and maturities of investments in trading securities based on the intended purpose of the investment. If the firm plans to hold the securities only for a short time, then the related cash flows are classified as operating. If the intent of holding is other than for short-term speculation, then the related cash flows are classified as investing.

    D. The net of above items constitutes Net Cash Flow from Investing Activities, and can be positive or negative.

    E. The items that make up Cash Flow from Investing Activities are presented in the same manner, regardless of whether the direct or indirect approach is used to present Cash Flow from Operating Activities.

III. Cash Flows from Financing Activities—This category reports cash inflows and cash outflows that relate to how the entity is financed.

    A. The major cash flow items in this category are the following:

Inflows (Cash Received)	Outflows (Cash Paid)
Sale of (Own) Stock	Repurchase Own (Treasury) Stock
Proceeds from Borrowing (Bonds, Notes, etc.)	Paying Back Lenders (Principal Only)
	Payment of Dividends

    B. The net of above items constitutes Net Cash Flow from Financing Activities, and can be positive or negative.

    C. The items that make up Cash Flow from Financing Activities are presented in the same manner, regardless of whether the direct or indirect approach is used to present Cash Flow from Operating Activities.

IV. Effects on Cash of Foreign Currency Translation—This category reports the effect on the change in cash (between the beginning and the end of the period) that results from changes in currency exchange rates.

   A. Companies that have transactions in foreign currencies or convert financial statements expressed in a foreign currency to statements expressed in dollars may incur a change in the dollar value of cash simply as a result of exchange-rate changes.

> **Note**
> *See the "Import Transaction" and "Export Transaction" lessons for a complete description of foreign currency transactions and translation.*

 **Example**
A foreign subsidiary has a (nondollar) cash balance that does not change during 20X2 of €100,000. The (spot) exchange rates were:

12/31/X1: €1 = $ .10

12/31/X2: €1 = $ .11

The dollar value of cash for US reporting would be:

12/31/X1 (€100,000 × .10)	$10,000
12/31/X2 (€100,000 × .11)	$11,000
Net Increase in Cash	$ 1,000

   B. Changes in cash caused by changes in exchange rates must be shown "as part of the reconciliation of the change in cash and cash equivalents during the period."

   1. Foreign currency transactions that occur during the period and affect cash flow should be converted to their dollar equivalent using (1) the exchange rate in effect at the date of each transaction or (2) an average exchange rate for the period, if not materially different from the specific rates in effect on the dates of the transactions.

   2. Cash balances held in foreign currency at period end should be converted to dollars using the spot (current) exchange rate at the date of the Balance Sheet.

   C. The net of the above items constitutes Net Effect (on Cash) of Foreign Currency Translation.

   D. The items that make up Net Effect of Foreign Currency Translation are presented in the same manner, regardless of whether the direct or indirect approach is used to present Cash Flow from Operating Activities.

V. Reconciliation of Change in Cash—This category reconciles the net effect of operating, investing, financing cash flows, and the net effect of foreign currency translation with the difference between cash (and equivalents) at the beginning and end of the period.

   A. The items in this category are:

> Net Increase (or Decrease) in Cash and Equivalents (during X2)
>
> + Beginning Cash and Equivalents (1/1/X2)
>
> = Ending Cash and Equivalents (12/31/X2)

B. The beginning and ending Cash and Equivalents are given on the respective (1/1/X2 and 12/31/X2) Balance Sheets.

C. The difference between beginning and ending Cash and Equivalents = the net change (increase or decrease) in Cash and Equivalents (working up).

D. The net change in Cash and Equivalents is the amount that must be exactly explained by the Operating, Investing, Financing, and Foreign Currency categories (working down).

VI. Noncash Investing and Financing Activities—This category reports significant investing and financing activities that occur, at least in part, without affecting (going through) cash.

A. Noncash activities must be presented in related disclosures (e.g., schedule or footnote).

B. If an Investing or Financing Activity involves part cash and part noncash, the cash portion should be a part of (on the face of) the SCF; the noncash portion should be disclosed in Noncash Investing and Financing Activities.

 **Example**
A $100,000 note payable is settled by a cash payment of $60,000 and issuing stock with a fair value of $40,000.

The cash portion ($60,000) would be a financing cash outflow.

The noncash portion ($40,000) would be disclosed as a noncash financing activity in the Schedule of Noncash Investing and Financing Activities.

Operating Cash Flows—Indirect Method

This lesson presents the indirect method of presenting Net Cash Flow from Operating Activities. Whether the direct or the indirect method is used, the Net Cash Flow from Operating Activities and the remainder of the body of the Statement of Cash Flows will be the same. The nature and content of the Statement of Cash Flows is summarized in a hypothetical statement, which includes the alternative presentations of cash flow from operating activities. The various sources and uses of cash shown in each section are assumed but are representative of a typical statement.

After studying this lesson, you should be able to:

1. Prepare the operating activities on the Statement of Cash Flows using the direct method.

2. Prepare the operating section on the Statement of Cash Flows using the direct method.

3. Prepare a complete Statement of Cash Flows.

I. **Methods**

    A. The Net Cash Flow from Operating Activities section of the Statement of Cash Flows (SCF) may be presented using either:

        1. The direct method (approach); *or*

        2. The indirect method (approach).

II. **Similarities in Methods**—The other major sections (Net Cash Flow from Investing Activities, Net Cash Flow from Financing Activities, and the reconciliation with net change in cash) will be the same, regardless of whether the direct or the indirect method is used. However, the additional disclosures will be different for the two methods, as described below.

III. **Graphic Representation of Presentation Alternatives**

Direct Method		Indirect Method
Statement		
Components of Cash Flows from Operating Activities (subtotal is same)	<—Different—>	Components of Cash Flows from Operating Activities (subtotal is same)
Cash Flows from Investing Activities	<—Same—>	Cash Flows from Investing Activities
Cash Flows from Financing Activities	<—Same—>	Cash Flows from Financing Activities
Effect of Foreign Currency Translation	<—Same—>	Effect of Foreign Currency Translation
Reconciliation with Cash Change	<—Same—>	Reconciliation with Cash Change
Additional Disclosures		
Noncash Investing and Financing	<—Same—>	Noncash Investing and Financing
Reconcile Cash Flows from Operating Activities with Net Income in supporting schedule	<—(N/A)—>	(In Body of Statement)
(N/A—In Body of Statement)	<—(N/A)—>	Payments for Interest
(N/A—In Body of Statement)	<—(N/A)—>	Payments for Income Tax

IV. **Body of the SCF**—Note that even though the presentation of the *components* of the Cash Flows from Operating Activities is different when using the direct or indirect method. The *total* Cash Flows from Operations will be the same. In addition, the content in the sections on cash flows from Investing and Financing activities will also be the same for the two methods.

V. **Direct Method of Presenting Cash Flow from Operating Activities)**—The direct method reports the components of Cash Flow from Operating Activities as individual items of gross receipts of cash (from revenue activities) and gross payments of cash (from expenses incurred).

   A. **Operating Activities**—To derive net cash provided by operating activities using the direct method each item in the income statement is adjusted from an accrual basis to cash basis.

      1. Under GAAP, the income statement is prepared on the accrual basis, which recognizes accruals and deferrals. Therefore, the items of revenue and expense do not necessarily reflect cash received and cash paid. Income Statement items affected by accrual accounting must be adjusted to reflect the actual cash generated or used.

      2. **Key point:** The effects of accrual accounting (e.g., Receivables, Payables) used to measure net income have to be reversed out to get cash flows.

   B. **Direct Method Disclosure of Operating Cash Flows**

      1. Under the direct method of presenting Cash Flows from Operating Activities, the section should separate cash flows for the following elements of operations:

         a. Collections from customers

         b. Collections for interest and dividends (on loans made and investments)

         c. Collections from other operating sources

         d. Payments to employees

         e. Payments to suppliers

         f. Payments for operating expenses

         g. Payments for interest (on debt)

         h. Payments for income taxes

         i. Payments for other operating uses

      2. The difference between these collections and payments is Cash Flow from Operating Activities.

   C. **Procedures for Converting from Accrual Basis to Cash Basis**—In order to convert revenue and expense items on the accrual based income statement to the amount of cash they generated or used, the effects of accruals and deferrals must be taken out. The following subsections describe and illustrate the conversion process for the major types of items including cash collected from customers, cash payments to suppliers, and cash payments for (any) operating expense:

      1. **Collection from customers**—Revenues on an income statement may include accruals (revenue earned but not collected) and exclude deferrals (cash collected but revenue not earned). To derive cash actually collected from customers, these accruals/deferrals must be reversed.

Example

Assume the following information is from the Income Statement (20X2) and Balance Sheets (20X1 and 20X2) of ABC Co.:

Revenue (sales—20X2)	$900,000
Accounts Receivable 12/31/X1	60,000
Accounts Receivable 12/31/X2	75,000
Net Increase—20X2	$15,000
Unearned Revenue 12/31/X1	–0–
Unearned Revenue 12/31/X2	25,000
Net Increase—20X2	$25,000

Schedule Calculation of Cash Collected from Customers—20X2

Revenues	900,000
Deduct: Increase in Receivables	–15,000*
Add: Increase in Unearned Revenue	25,000**
Cash Collected from Customers	$910,000

*Since Receivables increased by $15,000, that amount was recognized as revenue (Debit A/R; Credit. Revenue), but was not collected yet. (A decrease in Receivables would increase cash collected).

**Since Unearned Revenues increased by $25,000, that amount was collected (Debit Cash; Credit Unearned Revenue) but was not reported in revenues yet. (A decrease in Unearned Revenue would decrease cash collected.)

Entry Calculation of Cash Collected from Customer—20X2

DR: Increase in Receivables (given)	$ 15,000	
DR: Cash (Amount to Balance)	910,000	
CR: Increase in Unearned Revenue (given)		$ 25,000
CR: Revenues (given)		900,000

2. **Cash payments to suppliers**—Cost of Goods Sold on an income statement may include changes in inventory and/or changes in accounts payable. To determine cash actually paid to suppliers for purchases, these changes must be taken into account.

Example
The following information is from the Income Statement (20X2) and the Balance Sheets (20X1 and 20X2) of ABC Co.:

Cost of Goods Sold	$ 400,000
Inventory (12/31/X1)	100,000
Inventory (12/31/X2)	120,000
Net Increase—20X2	20,000
Accounts Payable 12/31/X1	80,000
Accounts Payable 12/31/X2	90,000
Net Increase—20X2	$10,000

Schedule Calculation of Cash Paid to Suppliers—20X2

Cost of Goods Sold—20X2	$ 400,000
Add: Increase in Inventory	20,000*
Total Purchases	420,000
Deduct: Increase in Accts. Payable	10,000**
Cash Payments to Suppliers	$410,000

*Since Inventory increased, more goods were purchased than were in Cost of Goods Sold. (A decrease in Inventory would reduce purchases).

**Since Accounts Payable increased by $10,000, that amount of purchases (DR. Purchases; CR. Accounts Payable) was not paid for yet. (A decrease in Accounts Payable would increase cash paid.)

Entry Calculation of Cash Paid to Suppliers

DR: Cost of Goods Sold (given)	$400,000	
CR: Increase in Inventory (given)	20,000	
CR: Increase in Accts. Payable (given)		$ 10,000
DR: Cash paid to Suppliers (amt. to bal.)		410,000

3. **Cash payments for operating expenses**—Expenses on an income statement may include accruals (expenses incurred but not paid) and/or deferrals (cash paid but expense not incurred). To derive cash actually paid for operating expenses these accruals/deferrals must be reversed.

   a. The required adjustments, as described above, and the example that follows apply to all types of expenses, even though the example uses General Operating Expense (I/S) and Prepaid Expense (B/S) items. The same analysis would apply to Selling, General and Administrative Expenses, Interest Expense, or Income Tax Expense.

Example

Assume the following information is from the Income Statement (20X2) and Balance Sheets (20X1 and 20X2) of ABC Co.

Operating Expenses—200X	$ 150,000
Prepaid Expenses 12/31/X1	10,000
Prepaid Expenses 12/31/X2	5,000
Net Decrease—200X	5,000
Operating Expense Payable 12/31/X1	20,000
Operating Expense Payable 12/31/X2	35,000
Net Increase—200X	$15,000

Schedule Calculation of Cash Paid for Operating Expenses—200X

Operating Expense—200X	150,000
Deduct: Decrease in Prepaid Expense	5,000*
Subtotal	145,000
Deduct: Increase in Expenses Payable	15,000**
Cash Payments for Operating Expenses	$130,000

*Since Prepaid Expense decreased, Operating Expenses included $5,000 paid for (prepaid) in a prior period, not paid for in the current period. (An increase in Prepaid Expense would increase cash paid.)

**Since Operating Expenses Payable increased by $15,000, that amount of expenses (Debit—Operating Expenses; Credit—Expense Payable) was not paid for yet. (A decrease in Expense Payable would increase cash paid.)

Entry Calculation of Cash Paid for Operating Expenses—X2

DR: Operating Expenses (given)	$150,000	
CR: Decrease in Prepaid Expense (given)		$ 5,000
CR: Increase in Expense Payable (given)		15,000
CR: Cash Paid for Operating Expenses (amount to balance)		130,000

4. **Cash payments for other types of expenses**—The calculation methodology used to derive cash flow from operating expenses (in the examples above) can be used for other types of expenses (e.g., interest, income taxes, etc.)

D. Presentation of Cash Flow from Operating Activities—Direct Method—Using the cash flow values developed in the prior examples and assuming cash outflows for payments to employees, interest expense, and income tax expense, the Cash Flow from Operating Activities under the Direct Method would be presented as follows:

Cash Flow from Operating Activities		
Cash Collected from Customers (per above)		$910,000
Cash Payments:		
To Suppliers (per above)	$410,000	
To Employees (assumed)	50,000	
For Operating Expense (per above)	130,000	
For Interest (assumed)	20,000	
For Income Taxes (assumed)	40,000	
Total Cash Payments		650,000
Net Cash Provided by Operating Activities		$260,000

E. Reconciliation of Net Cash Flow from Operating Activities with Net Income—If the direct method is used to present Net Cash Flow from Operating Activities, a separate schedule must be provided which reconciles cash flow with Net Income.

1. The reconciliation shows the adjustments to Net Income necessary to arrive at Cash Flow from Operating Activities.

2. The schedule that presents the reconciliation is identical to the Cash Flow from Operating Activities section in the Statement of Cash Flows presented using the indirect method.

3. **Reconciliation presentation:** Using values developed above and assuming other adjustments that will be covered in the indirect method, the reconciliation would be presented as follows:

Net Income		$110,000
Adjustment to Reconcile Net Income to Net Cash provided by Operating Activities:		
Depreciation Expense (assumed)*	$150,000	
Loss on Equipment Sale (assumed)*	5,000	
Undistributed Equity Revenue (assumed)*	(28,000)	
Amortization of Premium on Bond Investment (assumed)*	3,000	
Increase in Accounts Receivable (above)	(15,000)	
Increase in Inventory (above)	(20,000)	
Decrease in Prepaid Expense (above)	5,000	
Increase in Accounts Payable (above)	10,000	
Increase in Expense Payable (above)	15,000	
Increase in Unearned Revenues (above)*	25,000	
Total Adjustments		150,000
Net Cash Provided by Operating Activities		$260,000

Note: Items marked with an asterisk (*) are assumed at this point to illustrate a complete reconciliation of net income and cash flow from operating activities. The analysis of each of these items and the calculation of each amount is shown in the following section covering the indirect method of deriving Net Cash Provided by Operating Activities.

VI. Indirect Method (of Presenting Cash Flow from Operating Activities)—The indirect method of presenting Cash Flow from Operating Activities begins with Net Income (accrual basis) and adjusts for items that entered into computing Net Income, but did not affect cash by the same amount.

A. **Accruals and Deferrals**—As previously discussed, under GAAP, net income is based on using accrual accounting, which recognizes accruals and deferrals. In addition, certain items used in determining net income do not reflect the correct related cash flow (e.g., losses and gains). Therefore, net income does not reflect net cash flow from operations. Using the indirect method, net income is adjusted to derive net cash flow from operating activities by:

1. Adding back noncash charges (reductions) included in deriving Net Income; *and*

2. Subtracting out noncash credits (increases) included in deriving Net Income.

B. **Indirect Method Disclosure of Operating Cash Flow**—Under the Indirect Method, the Net Income must be adjusted by the following types of Add Backs and Subtract Outs to get Cash Flow from Operating Activities:

1. **Add back (to Net Income):** These items were deducted in getting net income but did not cause cash to be used:

   a. Depreciation Expense

   b. Amortization Expense

   c. Depletion Expense

   d. Losses (from sale of assets, etc.)

   e. Loss under equity method of accounting for Investments

   f. Amortization of Premium on Bond Investment

   g. Amortization of Discount on Bonds Payable

   h. Decreases in current assets (accounts receivable, inventory, prepaid assets, etc.)

   i. Increases in Current Liabilities (accounts payable, deferred taxes, etc.)

   j. Increase in Unearned Revenue

2. **Subtract out (of Net Income):** These items were added in getting net income, but did not cause cash to be received:

   a. Gains (from sale of assets, etc.)

   b. Amortization of Discount on Bond Investment

   c. Amortization of Premium on Bond Payable

   d. Undistributed income under equity method of accounting for Investments

   e. Increases in Current Assets (accounts receivable, inventory, prepaid assets, etc.)

   f. Decreases in Current Liabilities (accounts payable, deferred taxes, etc.)

   g. Decrease in Unearned Revenue

3. Net income adjusted by the foregoing items is Cash Flow from Operating Activities.

C. **Procedures for adjusting Net Income for noncash debits and credits**—In order to convert Net Income to the net amount of cash generated or used by operations, the noncash debits must be added back and the noncash credits subtracted. The following subsections describe and illustrate the adjustment process for the major types of add backs and subtract outs.

> **Note**
> *Look for items with an income effect different from their effect on operating cash flow. These are the reconciling items.*

1. **Depreciation/amortization/depletion expenses**—These are noncash expenses that must be added back to Net Income (by the amount recognized as an expense).

   a. If the amount of expense is not provided, it can be derived from the balance sheet and related information, if given.

   b. Calculation of the unknown expense can be done using a Schedule or a T-Account approach.

 **Example**

Assume the following information is from the Balance Sheets (20X1 and 20X2) and additional disclosures of ABC Co.:

Accumulated Depreciation (A/D) 12/31/X1 $400,000

Accumulated Depreciation (A/D) 12/31/X2   500,000

Net Increase—20X2 $100,000

Additional Information: Equipment with a book value of $25,000 (cost = $75,000 and accumulated depreciation = $50,000) was sold for $30,000.

T-Account Calculation of Expense

Accumulated Depreciation

	400,000
50,000	150,000 (forced)
	500,000

$150,000 should be added back to Net Income.

---

2. **Losses/gains**

   a. These are noncash deductions or additions in computing net income that must be added back to or subtracted from Net Income (by the amount recognized as a loss or gain).

   b. If the amount of a loss or gain is not provided, it can be derived from the balance sheet and related information, if given.

Example
(Assumes a loss) Assume the following information is from the additional disclosures of ABC Co.:

Additional Disclosure: During 20X2, Equipment with a cost of $75,000 and accumulated depreciation of $50,000 was sold for $20,000.

Schedule Calculation of Loss

Sale Price		$20,000	
Less: Cost	$75,000		
A/D	50,000		
Book Value		25,000	
Loss on Sale		$ 5,000	

$5,000 should be added back to Net Income.

3. **Equity method adjustments**

   a. An investor that uses the equity method to account for an investment must recognize its share of the investee's net income or net loss in the period it is reported by the investee, regardless of whether any dividends are paid by the investee. Therefore, the investor would make the following entries:

   i. Investee reports Net Income, Investor entry:

   > DR: Investment in Investee (asset)
   >   CR: Investment (Equity) Revenue

   ii. Investee reports Net Loss, Investor entry:

   > DR: Investment (Equity) Loss
   >   CR: Investment in Investee (asset)

   b. In either case, the investor has increased (with revenue) or decreased (with loss) its net income without any related cash flow.

   c. If the investee paid a cash dividend during the period, the Investor entry would be:

   > DR: Cash
   >   CR: Investment in Investee (asset)

   d. Therefore, under the equity method, only cash dividends received from the investee cause a cash flow. The adjustments to net income to get cash flow would be:

   i. If a loss, add back the amount of the loss.

   ii. If an income (revenue), subtract out the amount recognized as revenue that was not received as cash dividends.

Example

Assume ABC Company owns 40% of XYZ Company and appropriately accounts for its investment using the equity method. During 19X2, XYZ had net income of $100,000 and paid cash dividends of $30,000.

Schedule Calculation of Amount to Subtract

	XYZ Co.	ABC Co.
Net Income $100,000 × .40 =		$40,000
Less: Cash Dividend 30,000 × .40 =		12,000
ABC Revenue NOT Received as Cash		$28,000

$28,000 should be subtracted from Net Income.

4. **Amortization of bond premiums/discounts**—Bond Premiums and Discounts, whether related to an investment in bonds or the issuing of bonds, originate at the time the bonds are bought or sold. The subsequent amortization of a premium or discount will enter into net income (through interest income or interest expense), but will not generate or use cash. Therefore, the effects of premium or discount amortization must be added back to or subtracted from net income. Two illustrations are given:

   a. **Amortization of premium on bond investment**—When bonds are purchased for more than maturity value, a premium results.

      i. The related entry would be:

      DR: Investment in Bonds (at face value)
      DR: Premium on Bond Investment
          CR: Cash

      ii. The cash outflow would be recognized in the period the investment is made as a component of Cash Flow from Investing Activities.

      iii. The subsequent amortization of the premium would be recorded by a periodic entry:

      DR: Interest Income
          CR: Premium on Bond Investment

         1. The debit to Interest Income reduces the amount of net income, but does not use cash.

      iv. The amount of amortization should be added back to Net Income.

      v. If the bonds had been acquired at less than maturity value, the resulting amortization of the discount would have to be subtracted from Net Income.

b. **Amortization of discount on bonds payable**—When bonds are issued for less than maturity value, a discount results.

    i. The related entry would be:

> DR: Cash
> DR: Discount on Bonds Payable
>   CR: Bonds Payable

    ii. The cash inflow would be recognized in the period the bonds were sold as a component of Cash Flow from Financing Activities.

    iii. The subsequent amortization of the discount would be recorded by a periodic entry:

> DR: Interest Expense
>   CR: Discount on Bonds Payable

        a. The debit to interest expense reduces the amount of net income but does not use cash.

    iv. The amount of amortization should be added back to Net Income.

    v. If the bonds had been issued (sold) at more than maturity value, the resulting amortization of the premium would have to be subtracted from Net Income.

5. **Increases and decreases in current assets and current liabilities**—Increases and decreases in current assets and current liabilities reflect differences between the amount of revenue or expense recognized for net income and the amount of cash received or paid. Two examples illustrate the relevant points:

a. **Increase in accounts receivable**

    i. When sales are made on account, the related entry would be:

> DR: Assets Receivable
>   CR: Sales

    ii. The sales amount (credit) enters into Net Income, but unless the account receivable is collected within the same period there is no increase in cash. Therefore, net income would have to be decreased by the amount of the uncollected account receivable.

    iii. The aggregate change in accounts receivable will have the same effect on net income as shown above. Therefore, the amount of the aggregate change in receivables (and other current assets) must be used to adjust net income to get the related cash flows.

    iv. Illustration Facts: Assume ABC Company's Accounts Receivable balances for 20X1 and 20X2 were:

Accounts Receivable 12/31/X1	$60,000
Accounts Receivable 12/31/X2	75,000
Net Increase—20X2	$15,000

v. Because Accounts Receivable increased by $15,000, sales of that amount are included in Net Income, but the cash has not been collected. Therefore, $15,000 should be subtracted from Net Income.

vi. If Accounts Receivable had decreased, more cash would have been collected than sales recognized for the period. Therefore, the amount of decrease would have been added to Net Income to get the related cash flow.

vii. Increases and decreases in other current assets would be treated in the same manner.

b. Increase in accounts payable

i. When purchases are made on account, the related entry would be:

> DR: Purchases (or other asset)
> CR: Account Payable

ii. The purchase account (debit) enters into net income, but unless the accounts payable is paid within the same period there is no decrease in cash. Therefore, net income would have to be increased by the amount of the unpaid account payable.

iii. The aggregate change in accounts payable will have the same effect on net income as shown above. Therefore, the amount of the aggregate change in payables (and other current liabilities) must be used to adjust net income to get the related cash flows.

iv. Illustration facts: Assume ABC Company's Accounts Payable balances for 20X1 and 20X2 were:

Accounts Payable 12/31/X1	$80,000
Accounts Payable 12/31/X2	90,000
Increase—20X2	$10,000

v. Because Accounts Payable increased by $10,000, an expense (including possibly COGS) is included in net income, but the cash has not been paid. Therefore, $10,000 would be added to Net Income.

vi. If Accounts Payable had decreased, more cash would have been paid than expenses recognized for the period. Therefore, the amount of decrease would have to be deducted from net income to determine the related cash flow.

vii. Increases and decreases in other current liabilities would be treated in the same manner.

6. Increases and decreases in unearned revenues—Increases and decreases in unearned revenues reflect differences between the amount of revenue recognized for net income and the amount of cash received. Therefore, the amount of these increases or decreases must be added back to or subtracted from net income to get the related cash flow. The following example illustrates the required adjustment:

a. Illustration facts: Assume the following information is from the Balance Sheets (X1 and X2) of ABC Co.:

Unearned Revenue 12/31/X1	$ –0–
Unearned Revenue 12/31/X2	25,000
Increase—X2	$25,000

b. The increase occurred as a result of ABC making one or more of the following entries:

> DR: Cash
>
> > CR: Unearned Revenues

c. The debit to cash increased cash flow, but the credit to unearned revenue did not enter into net income. Therefore, net income understates cash flow for the period.

d. The amount of increases in unearned revenues must be added back to net income to determine cash flow.

e. If unearned revenue had decreased, it would have caused an increase in net income (DR: Unearned Revenue; CR: Revenues) without generating a related cash flow. Therefore, the amount of a decrease in Unearned Revenue must be subtracted from net income to determine the related cash flow.

D. Presentation of Cash Flow from Operating Activities—Indirect Method—Using the cash flow values developed in prior illustrations, including those developed under the direct method, the Cash Flow from Operating Activities under the indirect method would be presented as follows:

Cash Flow From Operating Activities		
Net Income (given)		$110,000
Adjustments to Reconcile Net Income to Net Cash provided by Operating Activities:		
Depreciation Expense (above)	$150,000	
Loss on Equipment Sale (above)	5,000	
Undistributed Equity Revenue (above)	(28,000)	
Amortization of Premium on Bond Investment (assumed)	3,000	
Increase in Accounts Receivable (above)	(15,000)	
Increase in Inventory (direct method)*	(20,000)	
Decrease in Prepaid Expenses (direct method)*	5,000	
Increase in Accounts Payable (above)	10,000	
Increase in Expenses Payable (direct method)*	15,000	
Increase in Unearned Revenues (above)	25,000	
Total Adjustments		$150,000
Net Cash Provided by Operating Activities		$260,000

(*Note: Items marked with an asterisk (*) were developed in the illustration of the direct method. Under the indirect method, the adjustment for Inventory and Prepaid expenses would have been developed the same way the change in accounts receivable was developed. The adjustment for Expenses Payable would have been developed the same way the change in Accounts Payable was developed.

VII. Direct/Indirect Comparison—The direct method and the indirect method are alternative ways of developing and presenting Cash Flow from Operating Activities. The most significant aspects of the two methods are:

A. The direct method presents cash flows in terms of the specific sources from which cash was received (inflows) and to which cash was paid (outflows).

B. The indirect method develops cash flows by adjusting net income, and does not (necessarily) identify the specific sources of cash inflows or outflows.

C. Under either method, the Cash Flow from Operating Activities will be the same amount.

D. Under either method, the other major sections of the Statement of Cash Flows—Investing, Financing, Foreign Currency effects, and the Reconciliation of the Change in Cash—**will be the same.**

E. The direct method is preferred (by the FASB).

F. Both methods require disclosure of the "Noncash Investing and Financing."

G. The direct method requires an additional schedule to reconcile net income to Cash Flow from Operating Activities.

H. The indirect method requires an additional disclosure of the amount (of cash) paid for interest and dividends.

VIII. Summary Illustration of a Statement of Cash Flows—A complete Statement of Cash Flows would take the following form:

ABC Company

Statement of Cash Flows

For the Year Ended December 31, 20X2

Cash Flows from Operating Activities:

Direct Method

Cash Collected From:

Customers

Dividends

Etc.

Cash Payments To:

Suppliers

Employees

Interest

Increase in Current Assets

Indirect Method

Net Income

Add: Noncash Expenses

Losses

Decreases in Current Assets

Etc.

Deduct: Noncash Revenues

Gains

Increase in Current Assets

Increase in Current Assets

—>Net Cash Provided By Operating Activities<—

Cash Flows from Investing Activities

Cash Received from:

    Sale of Equipment

    Collection of Loan

    Etc.

Cash Paid to:

    Purchase Equipment

    Loan to (other)

    Investment in (other)

    Etc.

Net Cash Provided by Investing Activities

Cash Flows from Financing Activities

Cash Received from:

    Sale of Own Stock

    Proceeds from Borrowing

    Etc.

Cash Paid to:

    Repaying Debt

    Paying Dividends

    Etc.

Net Cash Provided by Financing Activities

Cash Effects of Foreign Currency Translation:

    Add: Increase in Cash Due to Foreign Currency Translation

    Deduct: Decrease in Cash Due to Foreign Currency Translation

    Net Effect of Foreign Currency Translation

Net Change in Cash (and Cash Equivalents)

Beginning Cash (and Cash Equivalents) 1/1/X2

Ending Cash (and Cash Equivalents) 12/31/X2

Additional Disclosures:

Noncash Investing and Financing Activities

Direct Method	*Indirect Method*
Reconcile Cash Flows from Operating Activities to Net Income	Cash Paid for Interest
	Cash Paid for Income Taxes

Notes to Financial Statements

Notes to Financial Statements

> This lesson presents a discussion of the notes to the financial statements.
>
> **After studying this lesson, you should be able to:**
>
> **1.** Describe the reason for footnote disclosures.
>
> **2.** List the major disclosures required in the footnotes.

I. Notes to the Financial Statements

    A. Financial Report Disclosures—To achieve the objectives of the full disclosure principle, the three primary financial statements are supplemented by footnote disclosures and disclosures that appear in related schedules. Summaries of the major required financial report disclosures follow.

        1. Summary of significant accounting policies—The first footnote is typically a summary of significant accounting policies—the principles and methods chosen by management where GAAP allows a choice. Such disclosure is required. Users' understanding of financial statement amounts is greatly facilitated by knowing the methods used in preparing the statements. This footnote usually includes information about the following:

            a. The chosen depreciation method

            b. The chosen method of valuing inventory

            c. The securities classified as cash and cash equivalents

            d. The basis for consolidation:

                i. Amortization policies

                ii. Revenue recognition policies

        2. This summary must include information about all significant accounting policies but is not required in interim statements if the policies have not changed.

        3. Related party transactions—Companies must disclose the following information:

            a. The nature of the relationship between the related entities (Related parties include a parent and its subsidiaries, a firm and its principal owners and management and members of their immediate families, a firm and its equity-method investees, and others.)

            b. A description of all related-party transactions for the accounting years in which an income statement is presented in the financial report

            c. The dollar amounts of the related-party transactions for the accounting years in which an income statement is presented in the financial report

            d. In relation to related parties, any receivables or payables from or to related parties as of the date of each balance sheet presented in the financial report

    B. Noncurrent Liability Disclosures—Companies are required to disclose the following information about liabilities:

        1. Combined aggregate amount of maturities on borrowings for each of the five years following the balance sheet

        2. Sinking fund requirements

3. The aggregate amount of payments for unconditional obligations to purchase fixed or minimum amounts of goods or services

4. The fair value of each financial debt instrument in the financial statements or in the notes

5. The nature of the firm's liabilities, interest rates, maturity dates, conversion options, assets pledged as collateral, and restrictions

C. **Capital Structure Disclosures**—Companies are required to provide the following information related to capital structure:

1. **Rights and privileges** of outstanding securities

2. The **number of shares issued** during the annual fiscal period and any subsequent interim period presented

3. **Liquidation preference** of preferred stock

4. If the liquidation value of preferred stock is considerably in excess of par value or stated value of preferred stock, this information should be disclosed in the equity section of the balance sheet.

5. **Other preferred stock disclosures**—The following information can be disclosed in the footnotes or in the equity section of the balance sheet:

   a. Aggregate or per-share amounts at which preferred stock can be called or is subject to redemption through sinking fund operations

   b. Aggregate or per-share amounts of arrearages for cumulative preferred stock

6. **Redeemable preferred stock**—For each of the five years following the balance sheet date, the amount of redemption requirements for all types of redeemable capital stock must be disclosed in the notes to the financial statements.

D. **Errors and Irregularities**—A later lesson discusses the accounting for these items.

1. Errors are unintentional.

2. Irregularities are intentional.

3. Both require footnote disclosure. If prior-year income is affected, a prior-period adjustment is recorded that corrects the beginning balance of retained earnings and any other accounts affected in the year of discovery.

E. **Illegal Acts**—Examples include illegal contributions and bribes. The Foreign Corrupt Practices Act was passed by the US Congress to discourage such acts. The nature and impact of illegal acts on the financial statements should be disclosed fully in the notes.

II. **Management's Discussion and Analysis (MD&A)**—This is a narrative written by management and, although not considered part of the footnotes, is nonetheless an important disclosure supplementing the financial statements.

A. Publicly held firms are required to include the MD&A in the annual report. It provides management's discussion about the operations of the firm, its liquidity, and capital resources.

B. Additional discussion involves management's view of the firm's financial condition, changes in financial condition, and results of operations through analysis of the financial statements. Explanations of the reasons for major changes in financial performance and financial position are examples. Discussion of the effects of significant and unusual events provides further insight.

C. Forward-looking information is provided that is not reflected in the financial statements. This includes management's general prognosis about future sales, effects of competition, and expected effects of general macroeconomic conditions. An example is a discussion of the effect of inflation or specific price-level changes on future sales and earnings. Another is a discussion of the possible effects of uncertainties on the firm's financial statements.

III. Disclosures for the Effects of Changing Prices

A. Background

1. During times of price instability, financial reporting can be distorted, especially for items measured using historical cost. Both the balance sheet and income statement items (e.g., depreciation expense) are affected. Both inflation (general price-levels) and specific price changes affect the interpretation of reported amounts.

> **Note**
> *It is expected that the remaining material in this subtopic will have a lower probability of being tested than other material in this lesson.*

2. In the past, large firms were required to provide extensive footnote disclosure about the effects of price changes on the financial statements. Because inflation has subsided, there currently is no such requirement although disclosure of information on the effects of changing prices continues to be encouraged.

3. The remaining material in this subtopic provides a summary of price level changes.

B. General Price-Level Changes

> **Definitions**
> *Inflation:* The increase in general prices for a period of time; deflation is the decrease in general prices. When inflation is 4%, there has been a 4% increase in the general price level index.
>
> *General Prices:* A market basket of items that the typical consumer purchases.

1. The Bureau of Labor Statistics publishes the CPI-U (Consumer Price Index for All Urban Consumers), which is an index reflecting the aggregate increase in the price of many goods and services used by individuals. It is one measure of inflation commonly quoted in the financial press. If inflation is 2% for an annual period, then the CPI-U has increased 2% for the year.

> **Definition**
> *Nominal Dollars:* Measurements in the price level in effect at a transaction date. These measurements are not adjusted for inflation.

2. Financial statement amounts are measured in nominal dollars. If a firm purchased equipment and paid $10,000, that transaction is measured and reported in nominal dollars at $10,000. Price level changes are ignored.

> **Definition**
> *Constant Dollars:* Measurements in the general price level as of a specific date. Constant dollar measurements reflect an adjustment for inflation and allow comparisons using dollars with the same purchasing power.

3. If equipment is purchased for $10,000 when the general price level index is 100, the constant dollar measurement for that equipment when the general price level index is 120 at a later date is $12,000 ($10,000 × 120/100). If the price of equipment had kept pace with inflation, the firm would have to spend $12,000 now to obtain the equipment it purchased for $10,000 on a previous date.

> **Note**
> In the adjustment ratio above (120/100), the numerator is the price level for the date on which the constant dollar measurement is desired. The denominator is the price level in effect on the date the transaction occurred.

a. Constant dollar adjustments allow comparisons of dollar amounts for transactions occurring on different dates. The effect of inflation is stripped away leaving "real" dollar measurements.

C. Specific Price Changes

Definition
Specific Price Change: The change in the price of a specific good or service over a period of time.

1. If the price of crude oil increased from $17 to $18 per barrel, then the specific price level of oil increased 5.9% ($18 – $17)/$17.

2. **Restrictions**—Specific price changes refer only to specific goods and services and are not necessarily correlated with inflation (general price level increase) although frequently they are.

Examples
1. The price of potato chips increased 3% during a period in which inflation was 2%. The specific price of potato chips moved in the same direction as inflation but the rate of increase was higher.

2. The price of computer chips has steadily declined over the last several years even though there has been moderate inflation. The specific price of computer chips has moved in a direction opposite that of inflation.

D. Effects of General Changes

Definition
Purchasing Power: The purchasing power of an asset is the amount of goods and services that can be obtained by transferring the asset to another party.

1. During inflation, the purchasing power of an asset having a fixed unchangeable value decreases.

Example
The purchasing power of a $10 bill decreases during periods of inflation because the amount of goods and services that the bill can purchase declines. (There was a time that going to a movie cost $1.00. Now it costs as much as $8.00 for a movie. A dollar does not go as far as it used to.)

E. Monetary and Nonmonetary Items

E. Monetary and Nonmonetary Items—Assets and liabilities are categorized as (1) monetary or (2) nonmonetary, depending on whether the item has a fixed unchangeable value.

1. **Monetary items**—The specific price of monetary items cannot change. A $50 bill is always "worth" $50. An account receivable recorded at $3,000 is a monetary item because the claim the creditor has on the debtor is fixed at $3,000.

   a. Examples of monetary items—Cash, most receivables, accounts payable, all liabilities payable in fixed dollar amounts, and certain investments in debt securities.

2. **Nonmonetary items**—The specific price of nonmonetary items can change. The value of an item of inventory purchased for $300 can change before it is sold. The item of inventory does not command a fixed value.

   a. Examples of nonmonetary items—Inventory, plant assets, investments in equity securities, unearned rent, and other liabilities payable in goods and services

F. Purchasing Power Gains and Losses—The change in the purchasing power of an item due to a change in the general price level is measured only for monetary items because the specific price of nonmonetary items can change. During inflation, the amount of goods a $10 bill can purchase definitely decreases but the same cannot necessarily be said for an item of inventory originally costing $10. The value of the inventory item may increase with inflation but the value of the $10 bill cannot increase.

1. **Purchasing power gain**—A purchasing power gain results from holding monetary assets during deflationary times or having monetary liabilities during inflationary times.

Example
A firm owes $4,000 on a note due in one year. If inflation is 10% during that year (beginning price level of 100, ending price level of 110), the purchasing power of the dollars paid at the end of the year is 10% less than the dollars borrowed. Thus, the firm has a purchasing power gain because the firm is paying 10% less in purchasing power to extinguish the debt than it received from the creditor. (This is why interest rates increase with inflation, to compensate the creditor for the loss in purchasing power during the term of the borrowing.)

Amount of debt required at 12/31, for the firm to be in the same purchasing power position it was in at 1/1:

$4,000(110/100) =	$ 4,400
Amount of debt actually owed at 12/31:	$(4,000)
Purchasing power gain	$ 400

If the debt increased to $4,400 by year-end, the firm would be in the same purchasing power situation as it was at the beginning of the year.

But it actually owes only $4,000. Therefore, the firm is $400 ahead in purchasing power at 12/31.

2. **Purchasing power loss**—A purchasing power loss results from holding monetary assets during inflationary times or having monetary liabilities during deflationary times.

Example
A firm has a cash balance of $4,000 at the beginning of the year. If inflation is 10% during the year (beginning price level of 100, ending price level of 110), and the firm has had no change in its cash balance, the value of the dollars held at year's end is 10% less in terms of purchasing power. Thus, the firm has a purchasing power loss because the firm has 10% less in purchasing power than it had at the beginning of the year.

Amount of cash required at 12/31 to be in the same purchasing power position it was in at 1/1:

$4,000(110/100) =	$ 4,400
Amount of cash actually held at 12/31:	$(4,000)
Purchasing power loss	$ 400

The firm's $4,000 cash will buy $400 less in goods and services at year-end compared with the amount it could buy at the beginning of the year.

3. **Computation** of purchasing power gain or loss with both monetary assets and liabilities.

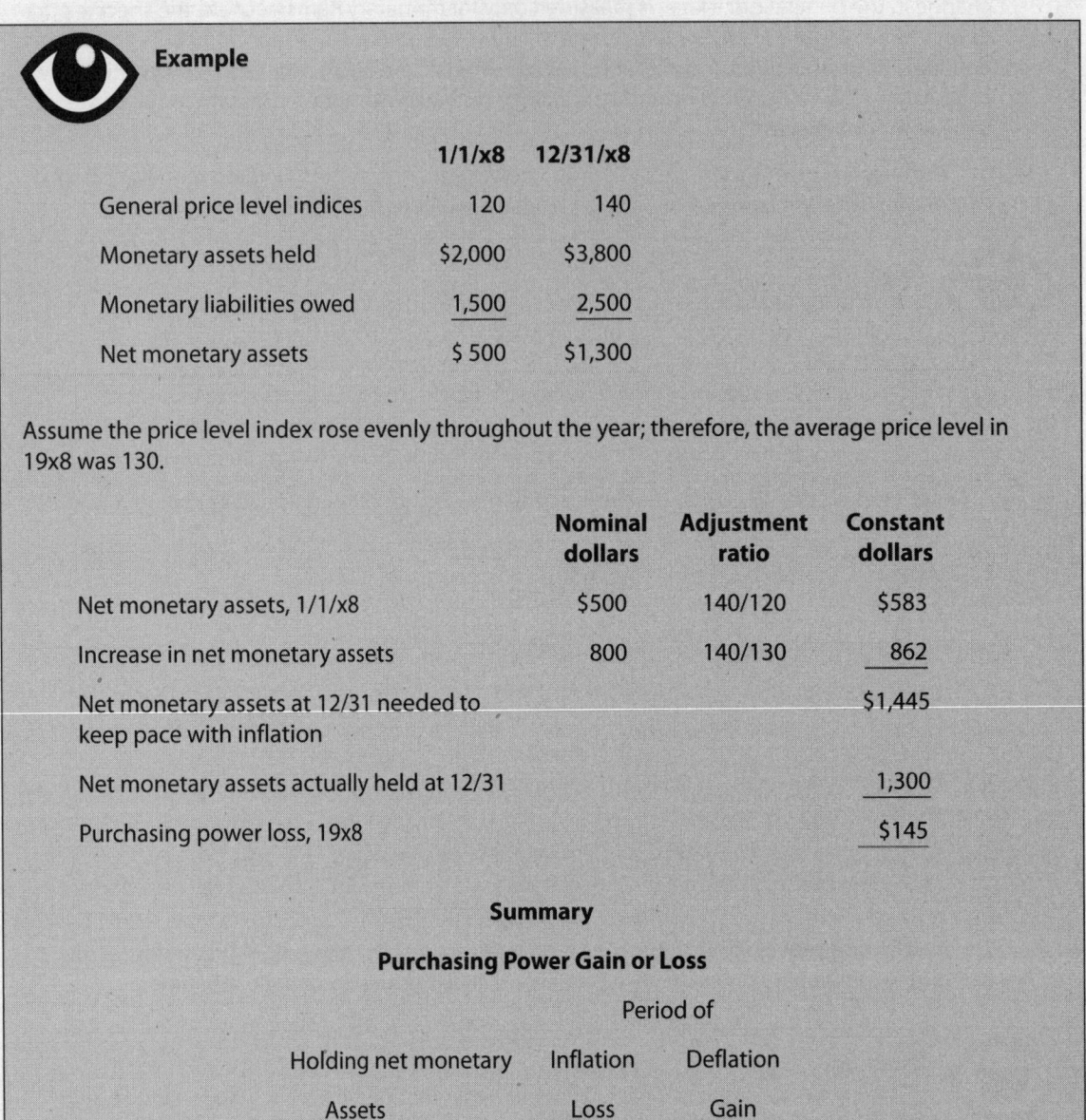

Example

	1/1/x8	12/31/x8
General price level indices	120	140
Monetary assets held	$2,000	$3,800
Monetary liabilities owed	1,500	2,500
Net monetary assets	$ 500	$1,300

Assume the price level index rose evenly throughout the year; therefore, the average price level in 19x8 was 130.

	Nominal dollars	Adjustment ratio	Constant dollars
Net monetary assets, 1/1/x8	$500	140/120	$583
Increase in net monetary assets	800	140/130	862
Net monetary assets at 12/31 needed to keep pace with inflation			$1,445
Net monetary assets actually held at 12/31			1,300
Purchasing power loss, 19x8			$145

Summary

Purchasing Power Gain or Loss

	Period of	
Holding net monetary	Inflation	Deflation
Assets	Loss	Gain
Liabilities	Gain	Loss

Risks and Uncertainties

This lesson addresses the required disclosures by firms of the risks and uncertainties they face.

After studying this lesson, you should be able to:

1. Identify the five areas of required disclosure.

2. Describe the main disclosure requirements within the five areas.

3. Define and describe the four concentrations within the significant concentration areas of disclosure.

4. Explain the scope of the required disclosures and the kinds of risks and uncertainties that are required to be disclosed.

I. **Background**

   A. Information about the risks and uncertainties faced by the firm enhances the ability of financial statement users to predict the future cash flows and operations of the firm. GAAP requires certain information about risks and uncertainties to be disclosed. The applicable accounting standard provides for selectivity whereby specified criteria are used to screen all the possible risks so that the required disclosures are limited to matters that materially affect a particular entity.

   B. The disclosures are primarily concerned with risks and uncertainties that could materially affect financial statement amounts within one year of the date the financial statements are issued (the near term).

   C. The required disclosures involve the following sources of risk and uncertainty. Each is discussed in more detail later in this lesson.

      1. Nature of the entity's operations

      2. Use of estimates in financial statements

      3. Certain significant estimates

      4. Current vulnerability due to significant concentrations in certain aspects of operations

      5. The entity's ability to exist as a going concern

   D. The five areas are not mutually exclusive; rather, there may be some overlap.

   E. The requirements of the standard apply to annual and complete interim statements but not to condensed or summarized interim statements. The disclosure requirements only apply to the current year's statements in comparative financial statements.

   F. The requirements apply only to those included in the standard and not to risks and uncertainties related to:

      1. Management or key personnel

      2. Proposed changes in government regulations

      3. Proposed changes in accounting principles

      4. Deficiencies in internal control

      5. Possible effects of acts of God, war, sudden catastrophe

II. **Nature of Operations**

   A. Different types of businesses have different risks. Knowledge of the firm's (1) products and services, (2) geographical locations and (3) principal markets will assist users in assessing risks concerning the firm's operations. For example, identification of competition and vulnerability to technological change are aided with this knowledge.

B. Financial statements and notes are required to include a description of the major products or services of the firm, and its principal markets and their locations. If the firm operates in more than one type of business, the relative importance of the operations in each business is disclosed, along with the basis of this determination (based on assets, revenues, or earnings for example).

C. These disclosures are not required to be on a quantified basis; relative importance can be described in such terms as major, intermediate, minor, and other similar ways.

III. Use of Estimates

A. The firm must communicate that: (1) use of estimates is inescapable in preparing financial statements that conform with GAAP, (2) the use of estimates results in approximate amounts, not certainty, and (3) estimates involve assumptions about future events.

B. The degree to which estimates can be relied upon is affected by many factors including whether the business and economic environment is stable or unstable at the time. This area of disclosure reminds users that they should not place an unwarranted degree of reliability on the reported amounts in financial statements.

IV. Certain Significant Estimates

A. When estimates used to value assets, liabilities, or contingencies are subject to a reasonable possibility of material change, disclosures may be required. Disclosure about an estimate is required when information available before the financial statements are issued or are available to be issued indicates that the following two criteria are met:

    1. It is at least reasonably possible that an estimate will change in the near term;

    2. The effect of the change would be material.

        a. Materiality is based on the effect of using the new estimate on the financial statements.

B. The disclosures must include:

    1. The nature of the uncertainty that may cause an estimate to change and a statement that it is at least reasonably possible that a change in an estimate will occur in the near term. If the estimate concerns a loss contingency, the disclosure must also include an estimate of the possible loss or range of loss, or state that such an estimate cannot be made.

    2. The estimated effect of the change as of the date of the financial statements must be disclosed.

C. If the criteria above are not met because the firm uses a risk-reduction technique, the disclosures are encouraged but not required.

D. The following are examples of assets and liabilities, related revenues and expenses, and disclosures of gain or loss contingencies that may be particularly sensitive to change in the near term:

    1. Inventory subject to obsolescence

    2. Equipment subject to technological obsolescence

    3. Deferred tax asset valuation allowances

    4. Capitalized software costs

    5. Environmental remediation obligations

    6. Litigation obligations

    7. Obligations for defined benefit pension plans and other postemployment benefits

V. Significant Concentrations

A. Susceptibility to risk and uncertainty increases when diversification is lacking – when the firm has concentrations in various aspects of its business. Examples of concentrations include excessive reliance on one customer, having one product or service account for most of the firm's revenues, and reliance on one or a small number of suppliers.

B. The standard is concerned with "severe impacts" caused by concentrations. A severe impact is a significant financially disruptive effect on the normal functioning of the firm, where "severe" is greater than material but less than catastrophic. Bankruptcy is considered catastrophic for example.

C. The standard applies only to the following defined set of four concentrations, rather than all possible concentrations.

    1. Concentrations in the volume of business with a particular customer, supplier, lender, grantor, or contributor. The loss of the relationship is an example of an event that could cause a severe impact. The standard states that it is always at least reasonably possible to lose such a customer, grantor or contributor although the impact may not be severe.

    2. Concentrations in revenue from specific products, services, or fund-raising sources. A price or demand change could cause a severe impact.

    3. Concentrations in specific sources (suppliers) of services, materials, labor, licenses or other rights used in operations. Losses of a key supplier or a patent are examples of events that could cause a severe impact.

    4. Concentrations in the market or geographic area of operations. The standard states that it is always at least reasonably possible that operations located outside the firm's home country will be disrupted in the near term.

D. Disclosure of a concentration is required if all the following criteria are met. These concentrations are called *disclosable concentrations*.

    1. The concentration exists at the balance sheet date;

    2. The entity is vulnerable to the risk of a near-term severe impact because of a concentration;

    3. It is at least reasonably possible that events capable of causing a severe impact will occur in the near term. (Note: Reasonably possible is less than probable.)

E. For disclosable concentrations (those meeting the above criteria), the following is to be disclosed:

    1. Information adequate to inform users about the nature of the risk associated with the concentration

    2. For concentrations of labor (one of the four listed concentrations, see above) subject to collective bargaining agreements, the firm must disclose (a) the percentage of the labor force covered by the agreement, and (b) the percentage of the labor force covered the agreement that will expire within one year.

    3. For concentrations of operations located outside of the entity's home country (one of the four listed concentrations, see above), the firm also must disclose the carrying amounts of net assets and the geographic areas in which they are located.

VI. Management's Going-Concern Assessment

A. Management must assess the entity's ability to continue as a going concern. Management's assessment should be based on facts and circumstances that are "known or reasonably knowable" as of the date the financial statements are issued. Note this assessment is not as of the balance sheet date, but rather should include information up to the date that the financial statements are issued.

B. There is uncertainty regarding the entity's ability to meet maturing obligations if there is "substantial doubt" that the entity cannot meet its obligations as they become due. Substantial doubt means that it is probable that the entity will be unable to meet its obligations. Probable is the threshold associated with contingencies and is broadly interpreted to mean greater than 70% or 80% probably that the event will occur.

C. Both quantitative and qualitative information should be considered when assessing the entity's ability to meet its obligations. The *look-forward* period for this assessment is one year from the issuance of the financial statements. Per ASU 2014-15, the following information should be taken into consideration:

1. **The company's current financial condition**—Including its current liquid resources (e.g., available cash or available access to credit).

2. **Conditional and unconditional obligations**—Due or anticipated in the next year (whether or not they are recognized in the financial statements).

3. **Funds necessary to maintain operations**—Considering the company's current financial condition, obligations, and other expected cash flows in the next year.

4. **Other conditions**—That could adversely affect the company's ability to meet its obligations in the next year (when considered in conjunction with the above). For example: Negative financial trends (e.g., recurring operating losses, working capital deficiencies, or negative operating cash flows).

   a. Other indications of financial difficulties (e.g., default on loans, denial of supplier credit, a need to restructure debt or seek new debt, noncompliance with statutory capital requirements, or a need to dispose of substantial assets)

   b. Internal matters (e.g., labor difficulties, substantial dependence on the success of a project, uneconomic long-term commitments, or a need to significantly revise operations)

   c. External matters (e.g., significant litigation, loss of a key customer, franchise, license, patent or supplier, or an uninsured natural disaster)

D. Disclosures are required only when conditions give rise to substantial doubt about the entity's going concern. No disclosures are required if there is no going concern uncertainties. If the substantial doubt is alleviated because management developed a plan to mitigate the effects of the uncertainties, the disclosures are still needed and the disclosures would include a description of management's plans to alleviate the substantial doubt. Disclosures include:

1. The principal conditions that give rise to the uncertainties

2. Management's evaluation of these conditions (essentially management's response to the factors found in C. above

3. Management's plans to alleviate the substantial doubt

VII. U.S. GAAP–IFRS Differences

A. International standards require some of the same disclosures regarding risks and uncertainties as for U.S. standards but the international requirements are less voluminous and the two sets of requirements are not exactly parallel.

B. Entities are encouraged (but not required) to present, outside the financial statements, a review by management describing the entity's financial performance and position, and the main uncertainties faced by the entity. This section of the standard does not provide detail regarding required disclosures in the risk and uncertainty area.

C. Entities are required to disclose judgments, other than those involving estimates, that management made in applying the firm's accounting policies.

D. Also required are disclosures about the assumptions made about the future, and major sources of estimation uncertainty that have a significant risk of requiring material adjustment to the carrying amounts of assets and liabilities within the coming year. An exception is assets and liabilities measured at fair value based on observed market prices because such changes are attributable to market forces.

1. The above disclosures are to be presented in such a way that users of the statements understand the judgments made by management and about other sources of estimation uncertainty. Examples include:

    a. The nature of the assumption or other estimation uncertainty

    b. The sensitivity of carrying amounts to assumptions and estimates, and an explanation for their sensitivity

    c. How the uncertainty is expected to be resolved and the range of reasonably possible carrying values of the assets and liabilities affected, within the next year

    d. If the uncertainty remains unresolved, a description of the changes made to past assumptions concerning the affected assets and liabilities

2. If it is impracticable to determine the effects of an assumption or another source of estimation uncertainty, the entity discloses that it is reasonably possible for outcomes to require a material adjustment to the carrying amount of the asset or liability affected.

Subsequent Events

This lesson presents the accounting and reporting for subsequent events.

After studying this lesson, you should be able to:

1. Define a subsequent event.

2. Distinguish between subsequent events that require recognition or disclosure on the financial statements.

3. Provide the key disclosure requirements for subsequent events.

4. Identify the key differences between IFRS and U.S. GAAP for subsequent events.

I. **Subsequent Events**

   A. **Definition and Examples**

Definition

Subsequent Events: Events or transactions that have a material effect on the financial statements. Subsequent events occur *after* the date of the financial statements but *before* the statements are issued or are available to be issued.

      1. **Examples**

         a. Examples include lawsuits, changes in corporate structure, issuances of debt and equity securities, major acquisitions, and significant gains and losses.

         b. Although the financial statement date is the "closing date" for reporting, users of financial statements typically read the disclosures as if they are current as of the date of issue. Furthermore, the full disclosure principle mandates that all relevant information be disclosed.

      2. **Two categories**—There are two categories of subsequent events, each requiring different accounting treatment:

         a. The condition leading to the subsequent event **existed** at the balance sheet date;

         b. The condition leading to the subsequent event **did not exist** at the balance sheet date-the condition arose after the balance sheet date.

   B. **Subsequent Events—Conditions Existed at the Balance Sheet Date**—The financial statements should reflect all information regarding these events up to the balance sheet date. This category of subsequent events requires recognition in the financial statements and includes all events that provide evidence about conditions existing at the balance sheet date including estimates used in the process of preparing the statements. Footnotes may be included to supplement and explain the recognition.

Examples

1. A major customer's financial situation has been deteriorating during the reporting year (20X4), with bankruptcy being declared early in 20X5. As a result, a receivable from that customer is deemed worthless after the 20X4 balance sheet date but before the issuance of the financial statements. The loss from the write-off of the receivable should be recognized in 20X4 income, and the 20X4 balance sheet should reflect the write-off because the condition leading to the bankruptcy existed at the balance sheet date.

2. Information is discovered early in 20X5 indicating that the total useful life of certain plant assets will be significantly less than originally estimated due to obsolescence. This condition developed gradually during 20X4. The useful lives of the affected assets should be re-estimated and depreciation expense for 20X4 should reflect those revised estimates.

C. Subsequent Events—Conditions Did Not Exist at the Balance Sheet Date—This category of subsequent event requires only footnote disclosure of events that have material effects on the financial statements. The footnote disclosures include a description of the nature of the event and an estimate of the financial effect, or a statement that an estimate cannot be made. Recognition is inappropriate because the condition existed after the balance sheet date

> **Examples**
>
> **1.** A major customer declared bankruptcy as a result of a casualty in early 20X5. As a result, a receivable from that customer is deemed worthless after the 20X4 balance sheet date but before the issuance of the financial statements. The loss from the worthless receivable is disclosed in the footnotes, but recognition is postponed until the 20X5 statements, because the casualty occurred after 20X4.

2. A firm completes a large issuance of bonds early in 20X5, before the issuance of the 20X4 statements. The footnotes to the 20X4 statements should disclose the relevant information about the issuance, but recognition is postponed until the 20X5 statements.

D. Period of evaluation for subsequent events

1. The period during which to evaluate subsequent events is the period between the balance sheet date, and either:

    a. The date the financial statements are **issued**—when they are widely distributed (e.g., filed with the SEC) for general use, *or*

    b. The date the financial statements are **available to be issued**—when they are complete, comply with GAAP, and have all the approvals necessary for issuance.

2. Public entities or any entities that widely distribute their financial statements use the *issued* date.

3. All other entities use the **available to be issued date**. These entities are not required to evaluate subsequent events after the point of availability. However, a non-SEC filer must also disclose the date through which the subsequent events were evaluated and whether that date is the date the financial statements are issued or available to be issued.

E. Related Situations—The recognition and disclosure requirements for subsequent events apply to both annual and interim financial statements but do not apply to subsequent events or transactions that are governed by other applicable GAAP.

1. **Contingent liabilities**

    a. The examples presented here are addressed in detail in other lessons. Here we present an overview as it relates to subsequent events.

    b. The reporting principles for contingent liabilities are similar to those of subsequent events and in some cases overlap. However, for recognized contingencies (those that are probable and estimable as of the balance sheet date), the event confirming the loss, reduction in asset, or recognition of liability need not take place before the issuance of the financial statements.

    c. For example, a firm recognizes warranty expense and a warranty liability at the end of 20X4 on sales recognized in 20X4 because warranty claims are probable and the amount to service the claims is estimable. The condition giving rise to the expense and liability existed at the balance sheet date (the obligation to service the claims and the probable nature of the claims), but the warranty claims need not occur before the issuance of the balance sheet in order for the liability to be recognized at the end of 20X4.

    d. In addition, for contingent liabilities, the quality that distinguishes recognition from footnote disclosure only is the likelihood of the future event and whether the economic sacrifice is estimable. Thus, although the situation appears to be similar to subsequent events accounting, a specific accounting principle governs this accounting.

    d. Gain contingencies are not recognized, although it could be argued that the conditions giving rise to the gain existed before the balance sheet date.

2. **Refinancing current debt**

   a. The examples present here are addressed in detail in other lessons; here we present an overview as it relates to subsequent events.

   b. A firm can reclassify a current liability as noncurrent if it accomplishes one of the following after the balance sheet date but before the financial statements are issued:

      i. Issue stock to extinguish the debt;

      ii. Refinance the current liability with a non-current liability; *or*

      iii. Enter into an irrevocable agreement to refinance the current liability with a noncurrent liability.

   c. The recognition (change in classification to noncurrent) takes place during the subsequent event period, but it can be argued that the decision was made to effect the reclassification after the balance sheet date. Thus, although the situation appears to be similar to subsequent events accounting, a specific accounting principle governs this accounting.

   d. Stock dividends and splits after the balance sheet date are treated as if they occurred as of the balance sheet date. Although it could be argued that because the dividend or split should not be recognized because it took place after the balance sheet date, a specific accounting principle requires recognition.

II. **Subsequent Events and IFRS**

   A. Under U.S. GAAP, the cut-off date for subsequent events is when the financial statements are issued or available to be issued. Under IFRS, the cut-off date for subsequent events is the date the financial statements are considered authorized for issuance.

   B. IFRS does not require adjustment to the balance sheet for share splits or reverse splits occurring after the reporting date but before the financial statements are issued.

   C. IFRS does not consider refinancing, amendments or waivers when determining the classification of debt as current or noncurrent. U.S. GAAP permits the entity to consider these items when determining the current or noncurrent classification of debt.

Evaluating Financial Statements

Ratios—Liquidity/Solvency and Operational

This lesson presents financial statement ratios for liquidity/solvency and operational analysis.

After studying this lesson, you should be able to:

1. Calculate and interpret liquidity and solvency ratios.

2. Calculate and interpret operational ratios.

I. **Background**

> **Definition**
> *Financial Statement Ratio Analysis:* The development of quantitative relationships between various elements of a firm's financial statements.

A. Ratio analysis enables comparisons across firms, especially within the same industry, and facilitates identifying operating and financial strengths and weaknesses of a firm.

B. The names given to ratios frequently indicate the nature of the quantitative analysis needed to develop the ratios.

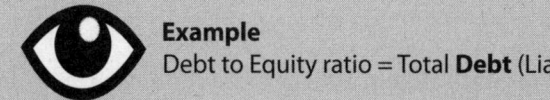

Example
Debt to Equity ratio = Total **Debt** (Liabilities) / Owner's **Equity**

C. Ratios can be grouped according to the major purpose or type of measure being analyzed. The major purposes or types of measures being analyzed are:

1. Liquidity/Solvency

2. Operational Activity

3. Profitability

4. Equity/Investment Leverage

D. Below is a diagram of the "big picture" of all ratios. This overview helps put the dozens of individual ratios into perspective and helps "see" how the balance sheet / income statement relationships tie together. This diagram also makes it easy to see the difference between ROA and ROE. **Return on Assets** (ROA)—measures operating performance *independent* of financing. **Return on Equity** (ROE)—explicitly *includes* the amount and cost of financing.

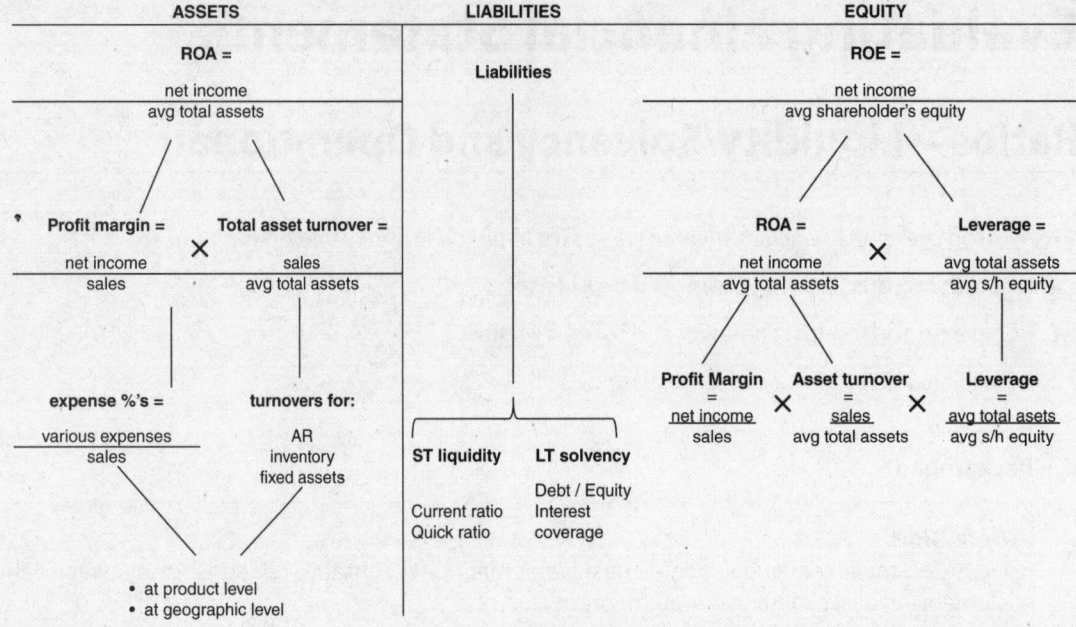

II. Liquidity/Solvency Ratios

A. Major liquidity measures

> **Definition**
>
> *Liquidity Ratios (also known as Solvency Ratios):* Measure the ability of the firm to pay its obligations as they become due.

1. **Working capital:** Measures the extent to which current assets exceed current liabilities and, thus, are uncommitted in the short term. It is expressed as:

> Working Capital = Current Assets – Current Liability
>
> Working Capital Ratio = Current Assets / Current Liabilities
>
> The more common name of this ratio is "current ratio."

2. Measures the quantitative relationship between current assets and current liabilities in terms of the "number of times" current assets can cover current liabilities.

   a. Is a widely used measure of the firm's ability to pay its current liabilities

   b. Changes in Current Assets and/or Current Liabilities have determinable effects on the Working Capital Ratio (WCR):

> WCR = Current Assets / Current Liabilities
>
> An increase in current assets (alone) increases the WCR.
>
> A decrease in current assets (alone) decreases the WCR.
>
> An increase in current liabilities (alone) decreases the WCR.
>
> A decrease in current liabilities (alone) increases the WCR.
>
> If the WCR equals 1.00, equal increases or equal decreases in current assets and liabilities will not change the WCR; it will remain 1.00.

    c. If the WCR **exceeds** 1.00:

        i. Equal increases in current assets and liabilities decrease the WCR.

> WCR = CA 20,000 / CL 10,000 = 2
>
> WCR = (CA 20,000 + 10,000) / (CL 10,000 + 10,000) = 30,000 / 20,000 = 1.5

        ii. Equal decreases in current assets and liabilities increase the WCR.

> WCR = CA 30,000 / CL 20,000 = 1.5
>
> WCR = CA 20,000 / CL 10,000 = 2

    d. If the WCR is **less than** 1.00:

        i. equal increases in current assets and liabilities increase the WCR.

> WCR = CA 10,000 / CA 20,000 = .50
>
> WCR = (CA 10,000 + 10,000) / (CA 20,000 + 10,000) = 20,000 / 30,000 = .66

        ii. Equal decreases in current assets and liabilities decreases the WCR.

> WCR = 20,000 / 30,000 = .66
>
> WCR = 10,000 / 20,000 = .50

3. The **acid-test ratio** measures the quantitative relationship between highly liquid assets and current liabilities in terms of the "number of times" that cash and assets that can be converted quickly to cash cover current liabilities:

> Acid-Test Ratio (also known as Quick Ratio) = (Cash + (Net) Receivables + Marketable Securities) / Current Liabilities

4. The **securities defensive-interval ratio** measures the quantitative relationship between highly liquid assets and the average daily use of cash in terms of the number of days that cash and assets can be quickly converted to support operating costs

> Securities Defensive-Interval Ratio = (Cash + (Net) Receivables + Marketable Securities) / Average Daily Cash Expenditures

5. The **times interest earned ratio** measures the ability of current earnings to cover interest payments for a period.

> Times Interest Earned Ratio = (Net Income + Interest Expense + Income Tax) / Interest Expense

6. The **times preferred dividend earned ratio** measures the ability of current earnings to cover preferred dividends for a period.

> Times Preferred Dividend Earned Ratio = Net Income / Annual Preferred Dividend Obligation

III. Operational Activity Ratios—These measure the efficiency with which a firm carries out its operating activities.

    A. Accounts receivable turnover measures the number of times that accounts receivable turnover (are incurred and collected) during a period. Indicates the quality of credit policies (and the resulting receivables) and the efficiency of collection procedures.

> Accounts Receivable Turnover = (Net) Credit Sales / Average (Net) Accounts Receivable (e.g., Beginning + Ending/2)

    B. Number of days' sales in average receivables measures the average number of days required to collect receivables; it is a measure of the average age or receivables.

> Number of Days' Sales in Average Receivables = (300 or 360 or 365 (or other measure of business days in a year)) / Accounts Receivable Turnover (computed above)

    C. Inventory turnover measures the number of times that inventory turnover (is acquired and sold or used) during a period. Indicates over or under stocking of inventory or obsolete inventory.

> Inventory Turnover = Cost of Goods Sold / Average Inventory (e.g., Beginning + Ending/2)

    D. Number of days' supply in inventory measures the number of days inventory is held before it is sold or used. Indicates the efficiency of general inventory management.

> Number of Days' Supply in Inventory = (300 or 360 or 365 (or other measure of business days in a year)) / Inventory Turnover (computed above)

    E. Operating number of cycle measures the average length of time to invest cash in inventory, convert the inventory to receivables, and collect the receivables; it measures the time to go from cash back to cash.

> Operating Number of Cycle = Days in Operating = Number of Days' Sale in A/R + Length Cycle Number of Days' Supply in Inventory

Ratios—Profitability and Equity

> This lesson presents financial statement ratios for profitability and equity analysis.
>
> **After studying this lesson, you should be able to:**
>
> 1. Calculate and interpret profitability ratios.
>
> 2. Calculate and interpret equity ratios.

I. Background

> **Definition**
> *Financial Statement Ratio Analysis:* The development of quantitative relationships between various elements of a firm's financial statements.

   A. Ratio analysis enables comparisons across firms, especially within the same industry, and facilitates identifying operating and financial strengths and weaknesses of a firm.

   B. The names given to ratios frequently indicate the nature of the quantitative analysis needed to develop the ratios.

> **Example**
> Debt to Equity ratio = Total **Debt** (Liabilities) / Owner's **Equity**

   C. Ratios can be grouped according to the major purpose or type of measure being analyzed. The major purposes or types of measures being analyzed are:

      1. Liquidity/solvency

      2. Operational activity

      3. Profitability

      4. Equity/investment leverage

II. Profitability Ratios—These measure aspects of a firm's operating (income/loss) results on a relative basis.

   A. Profit margin (on sales) measures the net profitability on sales (revenue).

> Profit Margin (on Sales) = Net Income / (Net) Sales

   B. Return on total assets measures the rate of return on total assets and indicates the efficiency with which invested resources (assets) are used.

> Return on Total Assets = (Net Income + (add back) Interest Expense (net of tax effect)) / Average Total Assets

   C. Return on common stockholders' equity measures the rate of return (earnings) on common stockholders' investment.

> Return on Common Stockholders' Equity = (Net Income—Preferred Dividend (obligation for the period only)) / Average Common Stockholders' Equity (e.g., (Beginning + Ending)/2)

D. Return on owners' (all stockholders') equity measures the rate of return (earnings) on all stockholders' investment.

> Return on Owners' (all Stockholders') Equity = Net Income / Average Stockholders' Equity (e.g., (Beginning + Ending)/2)

E. Earnings per share (EPS—basic formula) measures the income earned per (average) share of common stock. Indicates ability to pay dividends to common shareholders.

> Earnings Per Share (EPS—Basic Formula) = (Net Income—Preferred Dividends (obligation for the period only)) / Weighted Average Number of Shares Outstanding

F. The price-earnings (P/E) ratio measures the price of a share of common stock relative to its latest earnings per share. Indicates a measure of how the market values the stock, especially when compared with other stocks.

> Price-Earnings Ratio (P/E Ratio) = Market Price for a Common Share / Earnings per (Common) Share (EPS)

G. Common Stock Dividends Pay Out Ratio

> Total Basis = Cash Dividends to Common Shareholders / Net Income to Common Shareholder

H. Per share basis measures the extent (percentage) of earnings distributed to common shareholders.

> Per Share Basis = Cash Dividends per Common Share / Earnings per Common Share

I. Common stock yield measures the rate of return (yield) per share of common stock.

> Common Stock Yield = Dividend per Common Share / Market Price per Common Share

III. Equity/Investment Leverage Ratios—These provide measures of relative sources of equity and equity value.

A. The **debt to equity ratio** measures relative amounts of assets provided by creditors and shareholders.

> Debt to Equity Ratio = Total Liabilities / Total Shareholders' Equity

B. The **owners' equity ratio** measures the proportion of assets provided by shareholders.

> Owners' Equity Ratio = Shareholders' Equity / Total Assets

C. The **debt ratio** measures the proportion of assets provided by creditors. Indicates the extent of leverage in funding the entity.

> Debt Ratio = Total Liabilities / Total Assets

D. **Book value per common stock** measures the per share amount of common shareholders' claim to assets. (See the section on this ratio in the owner's equity module for more details.)

Book Value per Common Stock = Common Shareholders' Equity / Number of Outstanding Common Shares

E. **Book value per preferred share** measures the per share amount of preferred shareholders' claim to assets.

Book Value per Preferred Share = Preferred Shareholders' Equity (including dividends in arrears) / Number of Outstanding Preferred Stocks

Consolidated Financial Statements

Introduction to Consolidated Financial Statements

This lesson presents the criteria for consolidated financial statements, the exceptions to those criteria, and an overview to the consolidating process.

After studying this lesson, you should be able to:

1. Identify the alternative accounting methods that a parent may use to carry an investment in a subsidiary on its books.

2. Describe the effects of the alternative accounting methods on the consolidating process and on the consolidated statements.

3. Describe when consolidated financial statements are required under U.S. GAAP (and when they are not appropriate) .

4. Describe the information needed in order to prepare consolidated financial statements.

5. Describe where the consolidating process is carried out.

6. List the basic sequence of steps used in carrying out the consolidating process.

7. Identify the specific circumstances that affect how the consolidating process is carried out.

I. **Background**

  A. Consolidated financial statements are required when one entity has effective control over another entity.

    1. Controlling interest is usually present when an entity (investor/parent) has a greater than 50% ownership (directly or indirectly) of another entity (investee/subsidiary) and, therefore, can direct the activities of the investee/subsidiary; or

    2. Control is also evident when an entity (variable-interest holder) is the principal beneficiary of a variable-interest entity.

  B. In either of the foregoing cases, the entities are separate legal entities, but are under common economic control.

    1. The shareholders of the parent entity control that entity, which, in turn, has control of the subsidiary entity.

    2. The shareholders of the variable-interest holder entity control that entity, which, in turn, has control of the variable-interest entity.

  C. Because the entities are under common economic control, GAAP requires consolidated financial statements.

    1. **Consolidated financial statements** present the financial information of two or more separate legal entities, usually a parent company and one or more of its subsidiaries, as though they were a single economic entity (remember the economic entity concept from the conceptual framework).

    2. The **consolidating process** is the sequence of steps or activities carried out in order to combine the financial information of two or more entities. The consolidating process results in consolidated financial statements.

D. The process of presenting consolidated financial statements can be represented graphically in the following way:

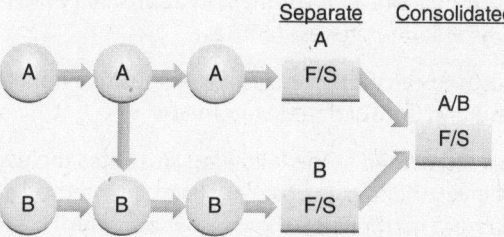

II. Justification—The preparation and presentation of consolidated financial statements is justified based on:

A. The presumption that consolidated statements are more meaningful than separate financial statements.

   1. "There is a presumption that consolidated statements are more meaningful than separate statements and that they are usually necessary for a fair presentation when one of the entities in the group directly or indirectly has a controlling financial interest in the other entities" (ASC 810-10-1).

B. The supposition that economic substance (common controlling interest) take precedence over legal form (separate legal entities).

III. Exceptions—There are certain limited exceptions to when an entity must consolidate another entity. Those exceptions include:

A. If an investor/parent has majority ownership of an investee/subsidiary (> 50% of the voting stock of the investee), but is prevented from exercising that majority ownership to control the financial and operating policies or activities of the subsidiary, it will not consolidate the subsidiary. Effective control may be lacking (even for a majority owned subsidiary) when it is:

   1. A foreign subsidiary largely controlled by the foreign government through prohibition on paying dividends, control of day-to-day operations, or other impediments to control.

   2. A domestic subsidiary in bankruptcy and under the control of the courts.

B. Certain entities are precluded from consolidating controlled entities by industry-specific guidelines, including:

   1. Registered investment companies.

   2. Brokers/dealers in securities.

C. A variable-interest (investment) or subsidiary (unconsolidated subsidiary) that is not included in consolidated statements would be reported as an "Investment" by the interest-holder/investor.

   1. The variable-interest investment would be measured as the entity's claim to the net asset value of the variable-interest entity.

   2. The unconsolidated subsidiary investment would be measured using either fair value or the equity method of accounting, depending on the extent of influence that can be exercise over the subsidiary by the parent.

IV. Parent's Accounting for a Subsidiary to be Consolidated

A. A Parent records a subsidiary **on its books** as an *investment* (in Subsidiary).

B. Subsequently, a Parent may carry an *investment* in a subsidiary that will be consolidated **on its books** using:

   1. Cost method;

   2. Equity method;

   3. Any other method it chooses.

V. A Parent Must Report Entities Under Its Control in Consolidated Statements

    A. The method a parent uses to carry an *investment* in a subsidiary on its books (cost, equity, or other) **will affect only** the consolidating process (entries).

    B. The method a Parent uses to carry an *investment* in a subsidiary on its books (cost, equity, or other) **will not affect** final resulting Consolidated Statements.

    C. Consolidating Process Illustrated—The following illustrates the use of alternative methods by a parent to carry its investment in a subsidiary (the cost method and the equity method) and the effects of those different methods on the consolidating process (different) and on the final consolidated statements (the same).

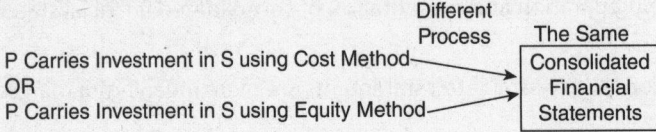

VI. Information Requirements—In order to consolidate the financial statements of two or more entities, certain specific information is needed, including:

    A. Financial statements (or adjusted trial balances) of the separate affiliated entities to be consolidated

    B. Data as of the date of a business combination (i.e., acquisition date):

        1. Book values of assets acquired and liabilities assumed as of the acquisition date

        2. Fair values of assets acquired and liabilities assumed as of the acquisition date

        3. Fair value of any noncontrolling interest in the acquired entity as of the acquisition date

        4. Fair value of any equity interest in the acquired entity owned by the parent prior to the acquisition date

    C. Intercompany (i.e., between the companies being consolidated) transaction data (for the operating period) and intercompany balances (as of period end)

VII. Consolidating Process

    A. The consolidating process is carried out on a consolidating worksheet, not on the books of any entity.

        1. The basic information for the worksheet comes from the account balances of the separate entities.

        2. The consolidating process is primarily concerned with adjusting and eliminating those balances to develop information that would report the separate entities as though they were a single entity.

        3. The consolidating process and the results of that process are not recorded on the books of any of the affiliated entities.

        4. The result of the consolidating process is the full set of consolidated financial statements.

    B. The basic sequence of steps in carrying out the consolidating process are (each of these requirements is covered in detail in the following lessons):

        1. Record trial balances—Record account titles and balances of the separate entities on the consolidating worksheet from the adjusted trial balances, separate statements, or other sources.

        2. Record adjusting entries—Develop and post to the worksheet consolidating adjusting entries, if any.

        3. Record eliminating entries—Develop and post to the worksheet consolidating eliminating entries; these entries are likely to include:

            a. Investment eliminating entry (always required)

            b. Intercompany receivables/payables elimination(s)

      c. Intercompany revenue/expense elimination(s)

      d. Intercompany profit elimination(s)

   4. Complete consolidating worksheet.

   5. Prepare formal consolidated financial statements from worksheet.

VIII. Factors Effecting the Consolidation Process—Although the general process is the same for carrying out all consolidating processes, the specific adjustments, eliminations and related amounts depend on the specific circumstances. The following alternatives will affect the specific adjustments and eliminations made during the consolidating process:

   A. Whether the consolidating process is being carried out at the date of the business combination or at a subsequent date

   B. Whether the parent owns 100% (all) of the voting stock of a subsidiary or less than 100% of the voting stock

   C. Whether on its books the parent carries its investment in a subsidiary using the cost or equity method of accounting

   D. Whether transactions between the affiliated entities (parent and its subsidiaries) originate with the parent or with a subsidiary

Consolidating Process

Consolidation at Acquisition

This lesson discusses the preparation of consolidated financial statements immediately following a business combination or following an operating period that occurs after the combination. This lesson describes and illustrates the specific requirements of the consolidating process carried out immediately following the acquisition of a subsidiary by a parent.

After studying this lesson, you should be able to:

1. Describe the characteristics of consolidated financial statements immediately following a business combination.

2. Prepare consolidated financial statements immediately following a business combination, including:

   - Calculate consolidated balances on the consolidated balance sheet.
   - Understand consolidating investment eliminating entries.
   - Understand intercompany receivable/payable eliminating entries.

3. Describe the effects that the method a parent uses to carry an investment (on its books) in a subsidiary has on the investment balance that must be eliminated in the consolidating process.

I. **Business Combinations**—A business combination must be accounted for using the acquisition method of accounting. Immediately following an acquisition the consolidated balance sheet will be different from the parent's (acquiring entity's) financial statements. If an income statement, statement of cash flows, or statement of retained earnings were prepared at the date of acquisition, it would represent information of the parent company only because there will not yet have been any activity including the subsidiary.

II. **Consolidated Balance Sheet**—At the date of the combination, a consolidated balance sheet will "combine" the assets, liabilities, and shareholder claims (majority and noncontrolling, if any) of the parent and its newly acquired subsidiary(ies).

III. **Consolidated Income Statement/Retained Earnings Statement/Cash Flow Statement**—At the date of combination, a consolidated income statement, statement of retained earnings, or statement of cash flow would be the same as the statements of the parent entity.

   A. Under the acquisition method of accounting for the combination, the operating results of the acquired entity up to the date of the combination is part of what the parent paid for in the cost of the investment in the subsidiary.

   B. There has not yet been an operating period (and operating results) during which the Subsidiary was controlled by the parent. Therefore, the consolidated income statement, retained earnings statement, and cash flow statement will be the same as the parent's at the date of the combination.

IV. **Carrying Investment in Subsidiary**—At the date of combination, the method the parent will use to account for the investment in the subsidiary (cost, equity or other) is not a consideration—that is, there is no "carrying" period yet.

V. **Overview**—The following example will depict the information needed to answer questions regarding the date of acquisition.

 **Example**
P (Passing) purchased 100% of S (Score) for $200,000 on January 1, year 1. The book value equals the fair value of all of S's assets and liabilities except for equipment, which had an FMV of $100,000 (the carrying value was $80,000). Any excess purchase price is attributed to goodwill. P owes S $10,000 and S has a receivable from P of $10,000.

The decomposition of the purchase price is:

Decompose the purchase price

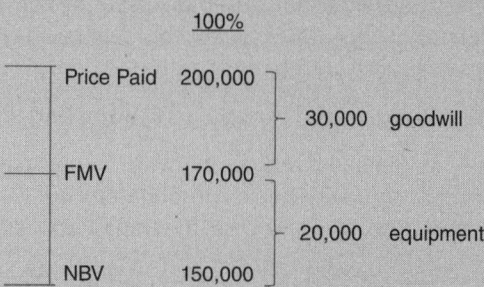

Below are the balance sheets of P and S immediately after the acquisition. The far right-hand columns represent the *consolidated entity* as of **January 1, year 1** (the date of the acquisition).

	Passing		Score		ELIM	CONSOLIDATED	
	Debit	Credit	Debit	Credit		Debit	Credit
Current Assets	80,000		30,000			**100,000**[1]	
Inventory	150,000		350,000			**500,000**	
Equipment (Net)	430,000		80,000			**530,000**[2]	
Investment in Score	200,000					**0**	
Goodwill						**30,000**	
Current Liabilities		150,000		110,000			**250,000**[3]
Long-Term Debt		460,000		200,000			**660,000**
Common Stock		200,000		140,000			**200,000**[4]
Retained Earnings		50,000		10,000			**50,000**[4]
Totals	810,000	810,000	460,000	460,000		**1,160,000**	**1,160,000**

[1]**P's current assets**   80,000
S's current assets   30,000
Less interco AR   (10,000)
Consolidated current assets   100,000

[2]**P's equipment**   430,000
S's equipment   80,000
Plus FMV adjust   20,000
Consolidated equipment   530,000

[3]**P's current liabilities**   150,000
S's current liabilities   110,000
Less interco AP   (10,000)
Consolidated current liabilities   250,000

[4]**Only P's**

VI. Focus on the end result (the consolidated balances) for most of the CPA Exam questions. If you need to complete an entire consolidating worksheet, knowing how to derive the ending balances will help you get to consolidated totals. If you want a refresher on the process of consolidation (or have never studied consolidation in your course work) then you will want to review the following description of the steps to consolidation.

VII. Process Steps to Follow—The steps to be followed in deriving consolidated financial statements from the separate trial balances or statements of the separate companies are:

A. Record Trial Balances—Record Account titles and balances on worksheet from trial balance, separate financial statements, or other sources of the separate companies that are to be consolidated. (In simulations on recent CPA Exams this data has been provided in the form of a preprinted worksheet.)

B. Adjusting Entries—Identify and record consolidating **adjusting** entries required, if any:

1. **Adjusting entries**—Are needed if one company (to be consolidated) has recorded a transaction with another company (to be consolidated), but the receiving company has not recorded the transaction. In such a case, the transaction is "in-transit" to the receiving company.

2. **Examples are**

    a. Payment of accounts payable by one company at year-end, but not yet received/recognized by the other company

    b. Dividend declared by one company (e.g., subsidiary) at year-end, but not yet recognized by the receiving company (e.g., parent)

3. **Rule**—The rule for handling *in-transit* intercompany transactions is to make an adjusting entry on the consolidating worksheet to complete the transaction as though it had been received by the receiving company (i.e., as though the transaction were completed on both sets of books).

    a. **Example**—At the time P acquired S, S had recorded a payment of $5,000 to P on an Accounts Payable; the payment was still in transit (i.e., P had not yet received the payment). What entry would be made **on the consolidating worksheet immediately after the combination** as an adjusting entry?

DR: Cash	$5,000	
CR: Accounts Receivable		$5,000

4. **Posting of adjusting entries**—The effects of adjusting entries are eventually posted to the appropriate separate company books as a result of actual completion of the in-transit transaction.

C. Eliminating Entries—Identify and record balance sheet eliminating entries: The common balance sheet eliminating entries at the date of combination are:

1. **Investment elimination entry**—All consolidations **require** an investment elimination entry to eliminate investment in the subsidiary account (brought on to the consolidating worksheet (W/S) by the parent) against the subsidiary's shareholders' equity (brought on to the W/S by the subsidiary).

    a. **Avoids double counting**—This elimination avoids *double counting* that would otherwise result on the consolidated B/S—that is, counting the asset *investment* (from the parent) and the assets and liabilities (from the subsidiary) to which the Investment gives the parent a claim.

b. Entry when parent owns 100% of subsidiary—Sample investment elimination (on the consolidating worksheet) when there is no noncontrolling interest (formerly *minority interest*) in the subsidiary:

DR: Common Stock (of subsidiary)

    Additional Paid-in Cap (of subsidiary)

    Retained Earnings (of subsidiary)

    Identifiable Assets (of subsidiary to FV, as needed)

    Goodwill (if Investment cost > FV of subsidiary's NA)

CR: Identifiable Liabilities (of subsidiary to FV, as needed)

    Investment in subsidiary (from parent's books)

    i. In the sample entry, identifiable assets (liabilities) would be debited (credited) if the fair value of identifiable assets (liabilities) is greater than the book value of identifiable assets (liabilities) at the acquisition date.

        1. This debit or credit would be to specific assets or liabilities (for example: inventory, equipment, land, or accounts payable, etc.) to adjust them to fair value (on the worksheet) at the date of the business combination.

        2. If depreciable assets are increased (debited), at the date of acquisition no assessment of impairment is required. (But, at the end of every subsequent period, additional depreciation expense must be taken on the consolidating worksheet).

        3. If the identifiable assets or liabilities had a fair value less than book value, the specific assets or liabilities would be written down to fair value (on the worksheet).

    ii. In the sample entry, goodwill would be debited if the Investment value is greater than the FV of net identifiable assets.

        1. Recall from a prior lesson that *investment value* is the fair value of consideration paid by the acquirer (parent) to acquire the subsidiary plus the fair value of the noncontrolling interest at the acquisition date.

        2. If goodwill is recognized (debited), at the date of acquisition no assessment of impairment is required. (But, at the end of every subsequent period, goodwill must be assessed for impairment; it is not amortized.)

    iii. Allocation assuming fair value exceeds book value of the net identifiable assets at the date of acquisition and that the investment value exceed the fair value of the net (identifiable) assets.

c. Entry when parent owns less than 100% of subsidiary—Sample investment elimination entry (on the consolidating worksheet) when there is a noncontrolling interest in the subsidiary.

    i. Subsidiary's shareholder equity not owned by the parent (either directly or indirectly) belongs to the noncontrolling interest.

    ii. It is the **noncontrolling interest (minority) claim** to consolidate net assets attributable to the subsidiary, which includes the subsidiary's net assets at fair value and the full fair value of any goodwill recognized on the acquisition.

iii. Sample entry

> DR: Common Stock (of subsidiary)
>
> Add'l Paid-in Cap (of subsidiary)
>
> Retained Earnings (of subsidiary)
>
> Identifiable Assets (of subsidiary to FV, as needed)
>
> Goodwill (if Investment value > FV of subsidiary's NA)
>
> CR: Identifiable Liabilities (of subsidiary to FV, as needed)
>
> Investment in subsidiary (from parent's books)
>
> Noncontrolling Interest (% claim to consolidated net assets attributable to the subsidiary)

iv. The noncontrolling interest account—Will show on the consolidated balance sheet as a separate item within shareholders' equity.

2. **Intercompany receivables/payables eliminations**—Receivables and payables between companies being consolidated must be eliminated to the extent the amounts are intercompany (between the companies).

   a. **Examples** and the amount to eliminate are:

      i. **Accounts receivable/account payable (100%)**—All intercompany receivables and payables between the affiliated firms that exist at the date of the combination must be eliminated.

         1. **Illustration facts**—Assume that at the date Company P acquired controlling interest of Company S in a legal acquisition, Company S owed Company P $10,000 for services it had received from Company P. Therefore, the separate companies would bring onto the consolidating worksheet the following balances:

> Company P / Receivable from S = $ 10,000
>
> Company S / Payable to Company P = $ 10,000

         2. **Eliminating entry**—On the consolidating worksheet, the following eliminating entry would be made:

> DR: Payable to P $10,000
>
> CR: Receivable from S $10,000

         3. **Consequence**—As a consequence of the eliminating entry, on the consolidating worksheet (and the consolidated financial statements) there will be no receivable/payable between Companies P and S shown; it is as though they are a single entry.

      ii. **Interest**—Interest receivable/interest payable (100%): If an intercompany receivable/payable was for interest, an entry similar to the one above would be made for 100% of the intercompany balance.

iii. **Dividends**—Dividends receivable/dividends payable (intercompany %): dividends receivable and dividends payable between the affiliated firms that exist at the date of the combination must be eliminated.

    1. **Illustration facts**—Assume that at the date Company P acquired controlling interest of Company S in a legal acquisition, Company S had a $100,000 dividends payable balance on its books and that Company P owned 5% of Company S just prior to acquiring controlling interest. As a consequence, 5% of Company S's dividends payable is a dividends receivable to Company P. The separate companies would bring onto the consolidating worksheet the following balances:

> Company P / Dividends Receivable (from Co. S) = $5,000
>
> Company S / Dividends Payable = $100,000

    2. **Eliminating entry**—On the consolidating worksheet the following eliminating entry would be made:

> DR: Dividends Payable $5,000
>
>   CR: Dividends Receivable $5,000

    3. **Consequence**—As a consequence of the eliminating entry, on the consolidating worksheet (and the consolidated financial statements) Company P's dividends receivable will have been eliminated and Company S's dividends payable will have been reduced to $95,000, the amount due to nonaffiliates. Note that only the intercompany (between P and S) portion of the dividend is eliminated.

iv. **Bonds**—Investment in bonds/bonds payable (intercompany %): Bonds issued by one affiliate (bonds payable) and held by another affiliate (investment in bonds) at the date of the combination must be eliminated against each other.

    1. **Illustration facts**—Assume that at the date Company P acquired controlling interest of Company S in a legal acquisition, Company P already held $100,000 of Company S's bonds, which it had acquired at par ($100,000). Company S had total bonds payable of $1,000,000. Therefore, the separate companies would bring onto the consolidating worksheet the following balances:

> Company P / Investment in S Bonds = $100,000
>
> Company S / Bonds Payable (at par) = $1,000,000

    2. **Eliminating entry**—On the consolidating worksheet the following eliminating entry would be made:

> DR: Bonds Payable $100,000
>
>   CR: Investment in Bonds $100,000

    3. **Consequence**—As a consequence of the eliminating entry, on the consolidating worksheet (and the consolidated financial statements) Company P's investment in Company S's bonds will have been eliminated and Company S's bonds

payable will have been reduced to $900,000, the amount due to nonaffiliates. Note that only the intercompany (between P and S) portion of the bonds is eliminated.

4. **Other eliminations**—If either the investment in bonds or the bonds payable accounts had a related premium or discount, these amounts would have been eliminated as well and would have resulted in a gain or loss depending on the nature of the premium or discount (debit or credit). (Eliminating intercompany bonds with premiums or discounts is covered in the following section dealing with the consolidating process following the date of acquisition.)

VIII. Complete Worksheet—After the separate company account balances and the adjusting and eliminating entries have been posted to the worksheet, it can be complete, mostly by "adding" across and down.

IX. Formal Consolidated Statements—Prepare formal consolidated statements: Once the worksheet is completed, it is the basis for preparing the formal consolidated financial statements.

Consolidation Subsequent to Acquisition

On its books, a parent may carry an investment in a subsidiary to be consolidated using any accounting method it desires because the investment will be eliminated in the consolidating process. The method a parent uses will affect the entries for the investment eliminating entry made on the worksheet in the consolidating process but will not affect the final consolidated statements—they will be the same regardless of the method used by the parent to carry the investment on its books. Although the parent can use any method it chooses to carry the investment, the two traditional methods are the cost method and the equity method. (Those are the only methods assumed on the CPA Exam.) This lesson covers the consolidating process when the parent uses the cost method.

After studying this lesson, you should be able to:

1. Describe the characteristics of the cost method of accounting for an investment.

2. Describe the necessary treatment of the consolidating worksheet when a parent uses the cost method to account for an investment in a subsidiary.

3. Record the adjusting (reciprocity) entry and the investment-eliminating entry on the consolidating worksheet when a parent uses the cost method to account for an investment in a subsidiary.

4. Record other eliminating entries that may be necessary on the consolidating worksheet as a direct result of the investment-eliminating entry.

I. **Consolidation After Acquisition**—After the date of acquisition, the parent company (P) will account for its Investment in S using either the equity method or cost method. Remember that P's stand-alone financial statements are not GAAP compliant because P must consolidate all subsidiaries under its control. In order to consolidate P and S, you must first understand how P accounted for the Investment in S, because upon consolidation the Investment in S is eliminated.

II. **If P uses the Equity Method**—If the equity method is used to carry the investment in the subsidiary, the parent:

   A. *Does* adjust on its books the carrying value of its investment in the subsidiary to reflect:

   1. The parent's share of the subsidiary's income or loss.

   > DR: Investment in Subsidiary
   >   CR: Income from Equity Investment

   2. The parent's share of dividends declared by the subsidiary.

   > DR: Dividends Receivable/Cash
   >   CR: Investment in Subsidiary

   3. The amortization (e.g., "depreciation") of any difference between the FV of identifiable assets (but not goodwill) and the book value of those assets. Example entry (assuming FV > BV):

   > DR: Income from Equity Investment
   >   CR: Investment in Subsidiary

   4. This entry reduces the income recognized from the subsidiary (and the related investment increase) by the amount of "depreciation" the parent must recognize on its fair value greater than book value. Below are the T-accounts on P's books with respect to the equity method accounting for S.

Equity Method Accounting

Investment in S		Income from Equity Investment in S	
Initial investment	P's share of S's dividends	Depreciation/ amortization of purchase price differential	P's % share of S's NI
P's % share of S's NI	Depreciation/ amortization of purchase price differential		
Ending Balance			Ending Balance

Example

P (Passing) purchased 100% of S (Score) for $200,000 on January 1, 20X2. On that date the book value equaled the fair value of all of S's assets and liabilities except for equipment, which had an FMV of $100,000. Any additional excess purchase price is attributed to goodwill. The equipment has a remaining life of four years.

Below, we show the decomposition of the price paid for S and reconstruct the T-accounts for the equity method accounting recorded by P. Understanding the components of the purchase price and the equity method accounting aids understanding of the consolidation.

The decomposition of the purchase price is as follows:

Decompose the Purchase Price

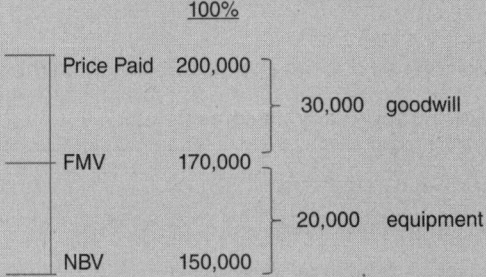

$\underline{100\%}$

Price Paid	200,000	
		30,000 goodwill
FMV	170,000	
		20,000 equipment
NBV	150,000	

T- Account
Equity Method Accounting

Investment in S		Income from Investment in S	
Cost 200,000	0 dividends		50,000—P's share of S's NI
		Depreciation of equipment 5,000	
P's % S's NI 50,000	5,000 depreciation of equipment		
Ending Balance 245,000		45,000	

The consolidating worksheet presents the trial balance of P and S and the Consolidated balances as follows. The consolidating worksheet does not reflect the eliminating entries in the consolidation process. Rather our focus is on the end result after consolidation. The footnotes below show how certain balances were derived.

	Passing		Score		ELIM	CONSOLIDATED	
	Debit	Credit	Debit	Credit		Debit	Credit
Current Assets	80,000		30,000			**110,000**	
Inventory	150,000		350,000			**500,000**	
Equipment (net)	430,000		80,000			**525,000**[1]	
Investment in Score	245,000					**0**	
Goodwill	0		0			**30,000**[2]	
Current Liabilities		150,000		110,000			**260,000**[3]
Long-Term Debt		255,000		150,000			**405,000**
Common Stock		200,000		140,000			**200,000**[4]
Retained Earnings		50,000		10,000			**50,000**
Sales		500,000		75,000			**575,000**
Income from S		45,000					**0**
Expenses	295,000		25,000			**325,000**[3]	
Totals	1,200,000	1,200,000	485,000	485,000		**1,490,000**	**1,490,000**

[1]**P's Equipment**   430,000

S's Equipment   80,000

FMV adjustment   20,000

Depreciation of FMV adj   (5,000)

Total   525,000

[2]**Goodwill**   30,000

Impairment   0

Total   30,000

[3]**P's Expenses**   295,000

S's Expenses   25,000

Depreciation of FMV adj   5,000

Total   325,000

[4]**Only P's**

NOTE: Push-down accounting would require that S record the fair market revaluations on the general ledger on the date of acquisition. Push down accounting is required for SEC Registrants with 100% owned subsidiaries. Push-down accounting essentially "pushes down" the revaluations on to the general ledger of S so that the revaluations are not allocated during the consolidation process. In the example above, the push-down accounting entry made by S would be:

Equipment   20,000

Goodwill   30,000

    Revaluation Capital (an equity account) 50,000

Upon consolidation the revaluation capital account would be eliminated.

III. If P Uses the Cost Method to Account for the Investment in S—In this case the parent:

    A. DOES NOT adjust on its books **the carrying value of its investment in the subsidiary** to reflect:

        1. The parent's share of the subsidiary's income or loss;

        2. The parent's share of dividends **declared by** the subsidiary;

        3. The "depreciation"/amortization of any difference between the fair value of the subsidiary's identifiable net assets and the book value of the subsidiary's identifiable net assets.

    B. DOES recognize its share of dividends declared by the subsidiary **as dividend income** (not as an adjustment to the investment account).

        1. Example entry

> DR: Dividends Receivable/Cash
>   CR: Dividend Income

IV. Investment Elimination—The investment elimination entry is made to eliminate the adjusted Investment account (as of the beginning of year) against the subsidiary Shareholders' Equity (as of the beginning of year).

    A. Sample entry assuming the parent owns 100% of the subsidiary:

> DR: C/S (of subsidiary)
>   Additional Paid-in Capital (of subsidiary)
>   R/E (of subsidiary including change since acquisition)
>   Identifiable Assets (of subsidiary to FV at acquisition, as needed)
>   Goodwill (If Investment > FV of subsidiary's NA at acquisition)
>   CR: Identifiable Liabilities (of subsidiary to FV at acquisition, as needed)
>   Investment in subsidiary

    B. The effects of this entry on the worksheet are to:

        1. Eliminate the investment account of the parent (as of the beginning of the year) against the shareholder equity accounts of the subsidiary (as of the beginning of the year);

        2. Adjust identifiable assets and liabilities of the subsidiary to fair value as of the date of the business combination;

        3. Recognize goodwill, if any, as of the date of the business combination. Goodwill would be recognized at the original amount by which the investment value > FV of identifiable net assets acquired.

V. Fair Value of Subsidiary's Identifiable Assets/Liabilities Different than Book Value—When the fair value of the subsidiary's identifiable assets and/or liabilities are different than the book value at the date of acquisition, depreciation/amortization must be recognized on the worksheet for any amount of Identifiable Assets recognized by the Investment elimination (above).

    A. Recall that the extent to which the parent's investment (and the fair value of noncontrolling interest, if any) as of the acquisition date is greater than the book value of subsidiary's identifiable net assets at the acquisition date is not identified on the separate books.

1. Any difference is implicit in the acquisition date difference between the Investment on the parent's books (plus the noncontrolling interest, if any) and the Shareholders' Equity on the subsidiary's books (which is also the book value of the subsidiary's net assets).

2. It is only when the two values (P's Investment + any noncontrolling interest and S's Shareholders' Equity) are brought together in the Investment elimination entry on the worksheet that the difference becomes explicit. The subsidiary's identifiable assets and liabilities are adjusted to fair value on the worksheet and, if the investment value is different than the resulting net asset value, goodwill (or a bargain purchase gain) is recognized. Any adjustment (increase or decrease) to depreciable or amortizable assets on the worksheet will result in the need for an adjustment (increase or decrease) to depreciation or amortization expense on the worksheet.

B. When the subsidiary's assets are written up to fair value (in the investment elimination entry, for example) it is as though the parent and noncontrolling interest, if any, paid more for the assets than the subsidiary paid for them. Therefore, additional depreciation or amortization must be taken.

C. **Sample Entry on Worksheet (at End of 1st Period)**—Assuming depreciable and amortizable assets were written up as part of the investment eliminating entry:

> DR: Depreciation Expense
>   Amortization Expense
>   CR: Accumulated Depreciation
>   Intangible Assets (Not Goodwill!)

D. **Sample Entry on Worksheet (at End of Subsequent Periods)**—Assuming depreciable and amortizable assets were written up as part of the investment eliminating entry:

> DR: Retained Earnings P – Beginning*
>   Depreciation Expense**
>   Amortization Expense**
>   CR: Accumulated Depreciation***
>   Intangible Assets (Not Goodwill!)***

*For expense recognized in prior year(s) on consolidating worksheet(s)

**For current year expense

***For cumulative prior and current amounts

E. If at acquisition the fair value of the subsidiary's identifiable net assets was greater than the parent's investment (plus the fair value of the noncontrolling interest, if any), a bargain purchase would have resulted.

1. In this case, the bargain purchase amount would have been recognized by the parent as a gain in the period of the business combination.

2. At the end of the period of the business combination, the bargain purchase gain would have been closed to the parent's Retained Earnings, and would be included in that Retained Earnings in all subsequent periods.

Consolidation Less than 100% Ownership

In many instances the Parent company purchases less than 100% of the subsidiary. When P owns more than 50% of S, P will consolidate S to create consolidated statements. The percentage of S not owned by P is reflected in the consolidated financial statements as Noncontrolling Interest (NCI). On the balance sheet NCI is presented in the equity section of the consolidated balance sheet. On the income statement NCI is presented as Income to NCI—a reduction of consolidated net income.

After studying this lesson, you should be able to:

1. Allocate the purchase price for less than a 100% acquisition.

2. Calculate the components of the balance sheet and income statement that would be represented on the consolidated statements with less than a 100% acquisition.

3. Calculate the amount of income to the noncontrolling interest that would be represented on the consolidated income statement.

4. Calculate the amount of equity attributed to the noncontrolling interest on the consolidated balance sheet.

I. **Noncontrolling Interest (NCI)**—If the parent does not own 100% of the subsidiary, the Noncontrolling Interest must be determined and recognized in the consolidated statements.

   A. **Consolidated Income Statement**

      1. For each operating period, the noncontrolling interest percentage claim to consolidated net income will be shown as a separate line item on the consolidated income statement. This account is usually shown as Income to Noncontrolling Interest.

      2. The noncontrolling interest claim to consolidated net income is the noncontrolling interest percentage share of the subsidiary's reported net income, plus (minus) its percentage share of depreciation/amortization expense on fair value in excess of (less than) book value and its percentage share of any other revenues/expenses or gains/losses attributable to the subsidiary recognized on the consolidating worksheet.

   B. **Consolidated Balance Sheet**

      1. On each consolidated balance sheet, the noncontrolling interest will be recognized as a separate line item (e.g., Noncontrolling Interest Equity) in the Shareholders' Equity section.

      2. The amount of the noncontrolling equity interest is the noncontrolling percentage claim to the subsidiary's book value at the acquisition date, plus (minus) its claim to the unamortized difference between fair values and book values at acquisition, plus its claim to goodwill recognized at acquisition, minus its share of any goodwill/impairment /losses.

II. **Determining NCI Equity**

   A. Determining the value of the NCI Equity reported by the consolidated entity can be done via calculation. NCI Equity is represented on the consolidated financial statements and is created during the consolidation process. This account does not exist on the individual financial statements of P or S. The CPA Exam frequently will ask you to provide the value of the NCI Equity or the Income that should be allocated to the NCI. Here we show you how to calculate theses values, it is also important because the calculation shows the conceptual relationship between S's NBV and the amount of S's NBV that is allocated to the noncontrolling interest. NCI Equity is the NBV of S that is allocated to the noncontrolling interest and is represented on the consolidated balance sheet.

   B. First determine the NBV of S as of the date of consolidation. Add to S's NBV the 100% purchase price differential less 100% of any depreciation/amortization or goodwill impairment. Multiply the S's adjusted NBV by the NCI % to arrive at NCI Equity. NCI Equity represents the amount of S's NBV allocated to the non-controlling shareholders of S including any FMV adjustments from the date of acquisition.

Calculation of NCI Equity	End of Year
S's Net Book Value	$
Plus 100% of the differential	
Less: Goodwill impairment loss	
Less: Depreciation / amortization of differential	$
S's adjusted NBV	$
NCI % ownership of S	%
NCI Equity	$

C. Often CPA Exam questions will not provide enough information to complete the above calculation. In these cases you can also calculate ending NCI Equity by "rolling forward" the beginning NCI Equity using the following calculation.

Calculation of NCI Equity	End of Year
NCI Equity at the beginning of the year*	$
Plus: NCI % of S's Net Income	
Less: NCI % of S's dividends	
Less: NCI % of Goodwill impairment loss	$
Less: NCI %Depreciation / amortization of differential	$
NCI Equity at the end of the year	$

*Make sure you use the full fair value of the beginning NCI equity. That is, make sure this number includes the NCI share of any fair market revaluations and goodwill from the date of the acquisition.

III. Determining Income to NCI

A. The portion of S's net income that is allocated to the NCI is created during the consolidation process and can be calculated. 100% of S's revenues and expenses are represented on the consolidated income statement. The NCI portion of S's net income that is not available for distribution to the shareholders of P must be subtracted out of total net income.

B. To calculate income to the NCI, start with S's net income and adjust it for the depreciation and/or amortization of the purchase price differential from the date of acquisition. You will also subtract any goodwill impairment loss that occurred during the current year. Once you have S's net income adjusted for the amounts related to the purchase price differential, multiply by the NCI percentage ownership and this will give you the amount of income to the NCI.

Calculation of Income to NCI	End of Year
S's Net Income	$
Less: Depreciation / amortization of differential	$
Less: Goodwill impairment loss	$
S's adjusted Net Income	$
NCI % ownership of S	%
Income to Noncontrolling Interest	$

Example

P (Passing) purchased 80% of S (Score) for $200,000 on January 1, 20X2. On that date the full value of the Noncontrolling interest is $50,000. The book value equaled the fair value of all of S's assets and liabilities except for equipment, which had an FMV of $100,000 (the carrying value of the equipment is $80,000). Any additional excess purchase price is attributed to goodwill. The equipment has a remaining life of four years. During 20X2 S reported net income of $50,000 and did not pay dividends.

Below is the decomposition of the value of S allocated between the controlling and noncontrolling interest. In addition we have reconstructed the T-accounts for the equity method accounting that would have been recorded by P during the year. Understanding the components of the equity method accounting, and tying the ending balances of these T-accounts to the consolidation worksheet, is useful in understanding the consolidations process.

The decomposition of the purchase price is:

	100%	80%	20%
Total	250	200	50
Goodwill	80	64	16
FMV	170	136	34
Equip	20	16	4 (4 yr life)
BV	150	120	30

Below are the equity-method accounts:

Equity-Method Accounting

Investment in S		Income from Equity Investment	
Cost 200,000	0 dividends		40,000 P's share of S's NI
		Depreciation of equip 4,000	
P's % of S's NI 40,000	4,000 depreciation equip		
Ending Balance 236,000			36,000

Below is the consolidation worksheet with the trial balance of P and S on December 31, 20X2. The *consolidated entity* as of **December 31, 20X2,** is presented in the final two columns. The focus here is **not** the consolidation process. That is, the focus is not on completion of eliminating entries. The focus is on the ending balances reported by the consolidated entity. The footnotes below the worksheet show the computations to derive the ending balances.

	Passing		Score		Elimination	CONSOLIDATED	
	Debit	Credit	Debit	Credit		Debit	Credit
Current Assets	80,000		30,000			**110,000**	
Inventory	150,000		350,000			**500,000**	
Equipment (net)	430,000		80,000			**525,000**[1]	
Investment in S	236,000					**0**	
Goodwill	0	0				**80,000**[2]	
Current Liabilities		150,000		110,000			**260,000**[3]
Long-Term Debt		260,000		150,000			**410,000**
NCI Equity	0	0					**59,000**[3]
Common Stock		200,000		140,000			**200,000**[4]
Retained Earnings		50,000		10,000			**50,000**
Sales		500,000		75,000			**575,000**
Income from S		36,000					**0**
Expenses	300,000		25,000			**330,000**[5]	
Income to NCI	0	0				**9,000**[4]	
Totals	1,196,000	1,196,000	485,000	485,000		**1,554,000**	**1,554,000**

[1]**Equipment**

P's equipment	430,000
S's equipment	80,000
FMV adjustment	20,000
Depreciation	(5,000)
Total	525,000

[2]**Goodwill**

Beg. balance	80,000
Impairment	(0)
Total	80,000

[3]**NCI Equity**

Book Value of S*	200,000
FMV adjustment	100,000
Depreciation	(5,000)
Total	295,000
NCI %	x .20
NCI Equity	59,000

*Note: S's ending Net Book Value (NBV) is beginning NBV plus Net Income less Dividends. In this example beginning NBV $150,000 (140,000 CS + 10,000 RE) plus NI (75,000 Sales − 25,000 Expenses) = Ending NBV $200,000.

[4]Income to NCI

S's NI	50,000
FMV Depreciation	(5,000)
	45,000
NCI %	x .20
Income to NCI	9,000

[5]Expenses

P's expenses	300,000
S's expenses	25,000
Depreciation	5,000
Total	330,000

Intercompany (I/C) Transactions and Balances

Intercompany I/C Transactions and Balances— Introduction

Transactions between entities that are to be consolidated are referred to as *intercompany transactions*, or *transactions between affiliated companies*. To the extent the entities being consolidated have intercompany transactions, or account balances that resulted from intercompany transactions, those transactions or balances have to be eliminated in the consolidating process. This lesson provides an overview of the elimination of intercompany transactions in the consolidating process.

After studying this lesson, you should be able to:

1. Describe the conceptual basis for the elimination of intercompany transactions.

2. Identify the primary types of intercompany transactions and balances that will need to be eliminated in preparing consolidated financial statements.

3. Record the entries required on the consolidating worksheet to eliminate intercompany receivables/payables and revenues/expenses.

4. Describe how intercompany receivables/payables and intercompany revenues/expenses come about.

I. **Conceptual Basis**

   A. From the perspective of the **separate legal entities**, transactions between them, and the related gains/losses and changes in account balances, should be recognized on their separate books. Even if the parent owns less than 100% of the subsidiary (but more than 50% as required for consolidation)—the entire amount of the intercompany transaction must be eliminated.

   B. For **consolidated financial statements** purposes the separate entities are treated as a single economic entity. As a consequence, only transactions with nonaffiliates should be recognized in consolidating financial statements.

   C. The results of transactions with other entities to be included in the consolidated financial statements must be eliminated, including the results of:

      1. Transactions between a parent and its subsidiaries

      2. Transactions between affiliated subsidiaries

   D. The kinds of transactions (and their related consequences) that must be eliminated, and those not to be eliminated, can be illustrated as follows:

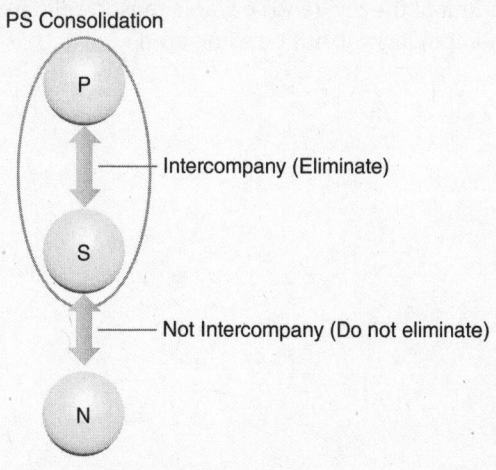

II. Intercompany Items

A. The primary types of intercompany transactions and related intercompany balances are:

1. Receivable/payables
2. Revenues/expenses
3. Inventory
4. Fixed assets
5. Bonds

III. I/C Receivables and Payables

A. Recall that intercompany receivables and payables result from one affiliated company providing goods or services to another affiliated company and permitting the buying affiliated to "charge" the amount owed.

Example

Assume that, during the period, Company P, the parent company, provided services to its subsidiary, Company S, and that Company S owed Company P $10,000 for those services at the end of the period. Each company would bring the following account balances onto the consolidating worksheet:

Company P / Receivable from S = $10,000 (DR)

Company S / Payable to P = $10,000 (CR)

On the consolidating worksheet the following eliminating entry would be required so that no intercompany receivable or payable will show on the consolidated financial statements:

DR: Payable to P	$10,000	
CR: Receivable from S		$10,000

B. Typical intercompany accounts receivable/accounts payable and the amount of each to eliminate are:

1. (Trade) Accounts Receivable/Accounts Payable (100%): The full amount of the intercompany receivable and intercompany payable must be eliminated.

2. Loan Receivable/Loan Payable

3. Interest Receivable/Interest Receivable (100%)

4. Dividends Receivable (100%)/Dividends Payable (Intercompany %): Note that only the intercompany amount of the dividends payable must be eliminated. Any dividend payable to noncontrolling shareholders will not be eliminated.

IV. I/C Revenues and Expenses

A. Recall that intercompany revenues and expenses result from one affiliated company providing services for a fee to another affiliated company.

Example

Assume that, during the period, Company P, the parent company, provided services to its subsidiary, Company S for $10,000. Each company would bring the following account balances onto the consolidating worksheet:

Company P / I/C Revenue (from S) = $10,000 (DR)

Company S / I/C Expense (to P) = $10,000 (CR)

On the consolidating worksheet the following eliminating entry would be required so that no intercompany revenue or expense will show on the consolidated financial statements:

DR:	I/C Revenue (from S)	$10,000
	CR: I/C Expense (to P)	$10,000

B. The full amount (100%) of intercompany revenues and expenses must be eliminated, even if the original transaction occurred at no profit to the "selling" affiliate.

C. Typical intercompany revenues and expenses and the amount of each to eliminate are:

1. Management Services Expense/Management Services Revenue (100%)

2. Interest Expense/Interest Revenue (100%)

Intercompany (I/C) Inventory Transactions

When one affiliated entity sells inventory (finished goods, raw materials, etc.) to another affiliated entity, an intercompany inventory transaction has occurred. Intercompany transactions need to be eliminated and the account balances adjusted to the values as if the transaction did not occur. This lesson identifies the accounts that will be affected, and describes and illustrates the eliminations that are needed on the consolidating worksheet.

After studying this lesson, you should be able to:

1. Identify the accounts affected by intercompany inventory transactions.

2. Record intercompany bond eliminations on a consolidating worksheet under the various circumstances identified above.

3. Analyze facts and calculate the amounts needed to be eliminated for intercompany inventory transactions under various circumstances, including the following:

    *   When intercompany inventory transactions occur at cost,

    *   When intercompany inventory transactions occur at more (or less) than cost,

    *   When intercompany balances are in ending inventory and/or in beginning inventory,

    *   When intercompany sales are made by a parent (to a subsidiary) or by a subsidiary (to a parent), and

    *   When intercompany sales by a subsidiary are from a 100% owned subsidiary or less than 100% owned subsidiary.

I. Objective

A. ALL intercompany transactions *must be removed (eliminated)* as if the transaction never occurred. You cannot have a transaction with YOURSELF! Transactions of the consolidated entity are ONLY those with outside third parties.

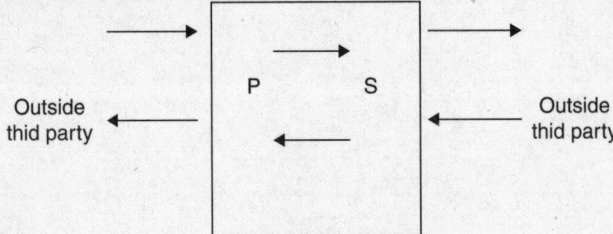

II. Terms and Concepts

A. Intercompany Transactions—Include buying, selling, and transfers. They also include the profits or losses and the outstanding balances that result from these transactions.

    1. A **downstream** transaction is when the parent sells to the subsidiary. Any intercompany profit that results from the sale will be on the books of the parent.

    2. An **upstream** transaction is when the subsidiary sells to the parent. Any intercompany profit that results from the sale will be on the books of the subsidiary.

    3. A transaction may also be between two subsidiaries with a common parent, or any other combination of tiering the transaction.

III. Accounts Affected—Intercompany inventory transactions affect the following accounts:

A. Sales/Cost of Goods Sold—The level of sales and cost of goods sold (COGS) (of the selling affiliate) are overstated because for consolidated purposes it is as though no sale occurred and, therefore, the effects of the sale should be eliminated.

B. Inventory—Any intercompany profit (or loss) in the ending inventory of the buying affiliate overstates (or understates) the carrying value of that inventory for consolidated purposes and should be eliminated.

IV. Tool to use to help you organize information and answer questions:

Diagram:

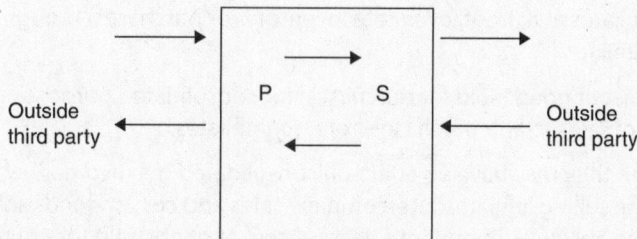

Tables to organize data:

	Should be	What is		Difference
		P	S	
Sales				
COGS				
Inventory				

V. Example Application Using Tools

Example

P purchased inventory for $16,000, and sold it to S for $20,000 (Gross profit = 20% = 4,000 / 20,000).

S purchased inventory for $20,000 and sold it to P for $38,000 (Gross profit = 47.4% = 18,000 / 38,000)

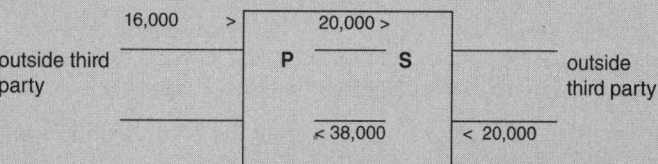

Downstream:

	Should be	What is		Difference
		P	S	
Sales	0	20,000	0	20,000 DR
COGS	0	16,000	0	16,000 CR
Inventory	16,000	0	20,000	4,000 CR

Upstream:

	Should be	What is		Difference
		P	S	
Sales	0	0	38,000	38,000 DR
COGS	0	0	20,000	20,000 CR
Inventory	20,000	38,000	0	18,000 CR

A. The following sections of this lesson present a step-by-step walk-through of the elimination of intercompany inventory transactions. Use the method/technique that works best for you!

VI. Elimination of Intercompany Sales/COGS

A. For **consolidated purposes,** sales by one affiliate to another affiliate will overstate sales and cost of goods sold brought onto the worksheet by the selling affiliate and, if the inventory was sold between the affiliates at a profit, overstate inventory (or purchases) brought onto the worksheet by the buying affiliate.

1. Sales and cost of goods sold (or purchases) for consolidated purposes should consist only of the effects of sales to and purchases from nonaffiliates.

2. Even though they may have no effect on consolidated net income (because the sale was at cost to the selling affiliate), intercompany sales and cost of goods sold (or purchases) overstate the absolute amount of sales and cost of goods sold (or purchases) for consolidated purposes and, therefore, must be eliminated against each other to prevent incorrect values for ratios and other analytical purposes.

B. **Illustration—I/C Sale with NO Profit**—Assume Company P sold inventory that cost it $8,000 to its 100% owned subsidiary, Company S, for $8,000 cash (P to S = a downstream sale). Entries made by the respective companies on their books would be:

Company P

DR: Cash	$8,000	
CR: Sale		$8,000
DR: COGS	$8,000	
CR: Inventory		$8,000

Company S

| DR: Inventory | $8,000 | |
| CR: Cash | | $8,000 |

1. Because Company P sold the goods at its cost, there is no intercompany profit in the sales, cost of goods sold or in the inventory held by Company S.

2. All the resulting balances are brought on to the consolidating worksheet by the separate companies at year's end.

C. **Eliminating Entry**—Even though the intercompany sale resulted in no net profit or loss, on the consolidating worksheet, the following eliminating entry would be made to eliminate (only) the intercompany sale/COGS. (The eliminating entry for intercompany profit and profit in ending inventory will be illustrated in the following subsection.)

	Should be	What is		Difference
		P	S	
Sales	0	8,000	0	8,000 DR
COGS	0	8,000	0	8,000 CR
Inventory	8,000	0	8,000	0

| DR: Sales | $8,000 | |
| CR: COGS | | $8,000 |

1. This elimination is a reversal of the original intercompany sale and COGS.

2. As a consequence of this eliminating entry, on the consolidating worksheet (and consolidated financial statements) no sales or COGS results from transactions between the affiliated companies; it is as though they never occurred.

3. The same kind of eliminating entry (i.e., same DR and CR at the amount of intercompany sale) would be made if all the intercompany inventory had been resold by the buying affiliate to nonaffiliates during the period of intercompany sale.

VII. IC Sales with Profit/Loss—Elimination of intercompany inventory profit (or loss) in ending inventory:

  A. Ending Inventory Value—Profit (or loss) recognized on an intercompany sale that is related to inventory **that has not been resold** (to a non-affiliate) by the buying affiliate, will also overstate (or understate) the carrying value of the remaining intercompany ending inventory (as brought onto the worksheet by the buying affiliate).

  B. Illustration Facts—Assume Company P sold inventory that cost it $8,000 to its 100% owned subsidiary, Company S, for $12,000 cash (P to S = a downstream sale). Entries made by the respective companies on their books would be:

Company P		
DR: Cash	$12,000	
CR: Sale		$12,000
DR: COGS	$8,000	
CR: Inventory		$8,000
Company S		
DR: Inventory	$12,000	
CR: Cash		$12,000

    1. Because Company P sold the goods to Company S at more than its (P's) cost, the inventory carrying value to Company S includes an intercompany profit that must be eliminated for consolidated purposes.

    2. All the resulting balances are brought on to the consolidating worksheet by the separate companies at year's end.

  C. Eliminating Entry—On the consolidating worksheet, the following eliminating entries (or combined entry) would be made to simultaneously eliminate the intercompany sales, intercompany cost of goods sold, and intercompany profit in ending inventory (i.e., intercompany inventory not resold.)

    1. **Illustration #1**—Assume from the example that 100% (all) of the intercompany inventory is still in the buying affiliate's inventory (on hand) at year end:

Company P Sales Price (to Co. S)	$12,000
Company P COGS (from nonaffiliate)	8,000
Intercompany Profit (all on hand)	$ 4,000

    2. Entries to eliminate intercompany sales/COGS and profit in ending inventory:

DR: Sales (I/S)	$12,000	
CR: COGS (I/S)		$12,000
DR: COGS (I/S)	$4,000	
CR: Inventory (B/S)		$4,000

a. In the first entry, the debit to sales and credit to COGS have the effect of eliminating (reversing) the intercompany amounts brought onto the worksheet by the selling affiliate.

b. In the second entry, the debit to COGS (an I/S account) reduces consolidated net income by $4,000 (the unrealized profit in intercompany inventory) and the credit to Inventory eliminates the intercompany profit of $4,000 from ending inventory brought onto the worksheet by the buying affiliate.

c. The two eliminating entries shown above could be (and often are) combined into a single entry, as follows:

	Should be	What is		Difference
		P	S	
Sales	0	12,000	0	12,000 DR
COGS	0	8,000	0	8,000 CR
Inventory	8,000	0	12,000	4,000 CR

DR: Sales (I/S)	$12,000	
CR: COGS (Inventory—I/S)		$8,000
CR: Inventory (B/S)		$4,000

d. As a consequence of the eliminating entries (or entry), no intercompany sales or COGS are recognized from the intercompany transaction and the inventory would be reported at its cost from a nonaffiliate, $8,000.

3. Illustration #2—Assume from the example above that 50% (half) of the intercompany inventory has been resold and, therefore, only 50% is still in the buying affiliates inventory (on-hand) at year-end. S sold the inventory for $10,000:

Company P Sales Price (to Co. S)	$12,000
Company P COGS (from nonaffiliate)	8,000
Total Intercompany Profit	$ 4,000
% of Intercompany Inventory on hand	x .50
Intercompany Profit to eliminate	$ 2,000

4. Entries to eliminate intercompany sale/COGS and profit in ending inventory:

DR: Sales (I/S)	$12,000	
CR: COGS (Inventory—I/S)		$12,000
DR: COGS (I/S)	$2,000	
CR: Inventory (B/S)		$2,000

a. In the first entry, the debit to sales and credit to COGS have the effects of eliminating (reversing) the intercompany amounts brought onto the worksheet by the selling affiliate.

b. In the second entry, the debit to COGS (an I/S account) reduces consolidated net income by $2,000 (the unrealized profit in ending inventory) and the credit to Inventory eliminates from the remaining ending inventory the intercompany profit of $2,000 brought onto the worksheet by the buying affiliate.

c. No intercompany profit-eliminating entry is required for the goods that have already been resold and therefore, are not in ending inventory.

d. The two eliminating entries present above could be (and often are) combined into a single entry:

	Should be	What is P	What is S	Difference
Sales	10,000	12,000	10,000	12,000 DR
COGS	4,000	8,000	6,000	10,000 CR
Inventory	4,000	0	6,000	2,000 CR

DR: Sales (I/S) $12,000
   CR: COGS (I/S)(+$2,000 − $12,000) $10,000
   CR: Inventory (B/S) $2,000

e. The correctness of the above entries can be confirmed by looking at the resulting balances on the consolidating worksheet after the eliminating entries are recorded:

i. Intercompany sales are $0 (zero).

ii. Cost of goods sold is : DR. $8,000 (P) + $6,000 (S) + $2,000 (E) − CR. $12,000 (E) = $4,000, the cost from a nonaffiliated of 1/2 the inventory now sold (1/2 × $8,000 = $4,000).

1. The $8,000 in COGS is the cost to P from a nonaffiliated recognized when it sold the inventory to S.

2. The $6,000 in COGS is 1/2 the $12,000 cost to S of the inventory acquired from P and recognized as COGS when it sold half the goods to nonaffiliates.

3. The $2,000 and $12,000 are the eliminating entries (E) posted to COGS.

Note
S's selling price to an outside third party will always be the amount reported on the consolidated statements. So if you are not given the selling price to the third party, it doesn't matter, because the selling price you want to eliminate is just the price from P to S.

VIII. Sale by Subsidiary to Parent—Intercompany Inventory Sale by subsidiary to parent: The prior illustrations assumed that the sale was made by the parent company to a subsidiary—a downstream sale. If a subsidiary sells to its parent, the transaction is an upstream sale. The intercompany elimination for upstream sales depends, in part, on the parent's percentage ownership of the subsidiary.

A. Parent owns 100% of the subsidiary

1. Eliminate sales/COGS—All the intercompany sale/COGS would be eliminated as above. It is a mere reversal of the original intercompany sale and cost of goods sold.

2. Profit elimination—All the intercompany profit and profit in ending inventory carrying value would be eliminated as above and would reduce the parent's claim to net income and asset (inventory) carrying value, since there are no noncontrolling claims to the subsidiary.

B. Parent Owns Less than 100% of the Subsidiary—If You Have a Worksheet Without Income Statement—If the elimination occurs on a consolidating worksheet that does not include an income statement (i.e., only a balance sheet is provided), the elimination would be allocated on the worksheet between the parent and the noncontrolling shareholders' interest in proportion to their respective ownership percentages.

1. Eliminate sale/COGS—All the intercompany sale/COGS would be eliminated as above. It is a mere reversal of the original intercompany sale and cost of goods sold.

2. **Profit elimination**—All the intercompany profit and the profit in ending inventory would be eliminated, but the profit elimination would be allocated between the parent and the noncontrolling shareholders' interest in proportion to their respective ownership percentages as part of the allocation of net income.

   a. **Worksheet with income statement**—If the elimination occurs on a consolidating worksheet that includes an income statement, the elimination would be the same as presented above to eliminate intercompany profit in ending inventory:

   > DR: COGS (I/S)
   >
   >   CR: Inventory (B/S)

      i. Eliminating entry on worksheet with balance sheet only. Assume that P owns 80% and noncontrolling interest owns 20% of the subsidiary.

   > DR: Retained Earnings—P $3,200
   > DR: Noncontrolling Interest   800
   >   CR: Inventory (B/S) $4,000

      ii. The debits reduce Company P's consolidated retained earnings ($3,200) and noncontrolling interest ($800); the credit eliminates the profit in ending inventory ($4,000), all on the consolidated balance sheet.

C. **Illustration facts**—Assume Company P owns 80% of its subsidiary, Company S. Company S sold inventory that cost it $8,000 to Company P for $12,000 cash (an upstream sale). All the inventory is still held by Company P at year's end. The elimination of intercompany profit in ending inventory would be allocated as follows:

   > Parent   .80 X $4,000 = $3,200
   > Noncontrolling Interest .20 X $4,000 =   800
   > Total Profit Eliminated $ 4,000

D. Eliminating entry on worksheet with balance sheet only:

   > DR: Retained Earnings—P $3,200
   > DR: Noncontrolling Interest   800
   >   CR: Inventory (B/S) $4,000

E. The debits reduce Company P's consolidated retained earnings ($3,200) and noncontrolling interest ($800); the credit eliminates the profit in ending inventory ($4,000), all on the consolidated balance sheet.

IX. Eliminate Profit/Loss in Beginning Inventory—Elimination of intercompany inventory profit (or loss) in beginning inventory:

A. Profit/Loss Remain—Because the intercompany inventory profit (or loss) eliminated from ending inventory (illustrated above) occurs ONLY on the consolidating worksheet, the intercompany profit (or loss) will remain:

1. On the books of the selling affiliate as an element of profit (or loss) closed to its retained earnings;

2. On the books of the buying affiliate as an overstatement (or understatement) of its beginning inventory for the subsequent period.

B. Eliminate on Worksheet—The intercompany profit (or loss) in retained earnings and beginning inventory will be brought onto the consolidating worksheet of the subsequent period by the selling and buying affiliate, respectively, and must be eliminated on the worksheet.

C. Eliminating Entry—On the subsequent consolidating worksheet, the following eliminating entry would be made to simultaneously eliminate the intercompany profit in (beginning) retained earnings (of the selling affiliate) and the overstatement of the beginning inventory (of the buying affiliate):

> DR: Retained Earnings
>   CR: Inventory—Beginning (I/S)

1. If a loss in intercompany inventory had been eliminated in the prior period, the debit and credit would be reversed.

2. The amount of intercompany profit (or loss) in retained earnings and beginning inventory to be eliminated is the same amount as eliminated in the ending inventory of the prior period.

3. The debit to retained earnings eliminates the intercompany profit recognized in the prior period on the books of the selling affiliate and brought on to the worksheet of the current period in its (selling affiliates) retained earnings; the credit to beginning inventory as reported on the worksheet income statement eliminates the intercompany profit in the beginning inventory shown on the books of the buying affiliate and brought on to the worksheet of the current period.

4. The credit to beginning inventory on the consolidating worksheet causes a reduction in beginning inventory in the income statement section of the worksheet that reduces cost of goods sold as follows (using assumed amounts, including intercompany profit in beginning inventory of $20,000):

		Without Elimination		With Elimination
	Begin Inventory	$120,000	<————>	$100,000
+	Purchases	100,000		100,000
=	Available for Sale	$220,000		$200,000
−	Ending Inventory	50,000		50,000
=	Cost of Goods Sold	$170,000		$150,000

a. The credit to beginning inventory in the income statement section (and the resulting reduction in cost of goods sold) causes the intercompany profit eliminated (deferred) in the prior period to be treated as though it is confirmed (recognized) in the subsequent period.

b. If the intercompany inventory on hand at the beginning of the period is not sold to a nonaffiliate as of the end of the period, the related intercompany profit will be eliminated (deferred) again as part of the elimination of intercompany profit in ending inventory of that period.

Intercompany (I/C) Fixed Asset Transactions

When one affiliated entity sells fixed assets to another affiliated entity, an intercompany fixed asset transaction has occurred. This transaction needs to be eliminated and the account balances brought to the balances as if the transaction had not occurred. This lesson identifies the accounts that will be affected and illustrates the adjustments or eliminations that will be needed on the consolidating worksheet.

After studying this lesson, you should be able to:

1. Analyze facts and calculate the amounts needed to be eliminated for intercompany fixed-asset transactions under various circumstances, including:

   - For the effects of intercompany fixed-asset transactions in the period of the transfer and on posttransfer depreciation expense and accumulated depreciation,

   - When intercompany fixed-asset sales are made by a parent (to a subsidiary) or by a subsidiary (to a parent), and

   - When intercompany fixed asset sales by a subsidiary are from a 100% owned subsidiary or less than 100% owned subsidiary.

2. Record intercompany fixed-asset eliminations on a consolidating worksheet under the various circumstances identified above.

3. Identify the accounts affected by intercompany fixed-asset transactions.

I. Objective

A. **ALL** intercompany transactions **must be removed (eliminated)** as if the transaction never occurred. You cannot have a transaction with YOURSELF! Transactions of the consolidated entity are ONLY those with outside third parties.

B. Transfer of a depreciable or nondepreciable asset between parent and subsidiary for anything other than original cost must be stated on the consolidated trial balance as if the transfer had not occurred.

II. Accounts Affected—Intercompany fixed asset transactions affect the following accounts:

A. **Fixed Asset**—Any gain (or loss) recognized by the selling affiliate will cause the cost to the buying affiliate to overstate (or understate) the carrying value of the asset for consolidated purposes and must be corrected so that the asset is reported at original cost from a nonaffiliate.

B. **Accumulated Depreciation**—The sale of the fixed asset will cause the selling affiliate to write off its accumulated depreciation (on the asset sold), which will understate accumulated depreciation for consolidated purposes; the accumulated depreciation should be reinstated.

C. **Depreciation Expense/Accumulated Depreciation**—Any gain (or loss) included in the cost to the buying affiliate will cause subsequent depreciation taken by the buying affiliate and brought onto the consolidating worksheet to overstate (or understate) depreciation expense and accumulated depreciation for consolidated purposes in each subsequent period; these elements must be adjusted.

D. Tools to use to help you organize information and answer questions:

   1. Diagrams:

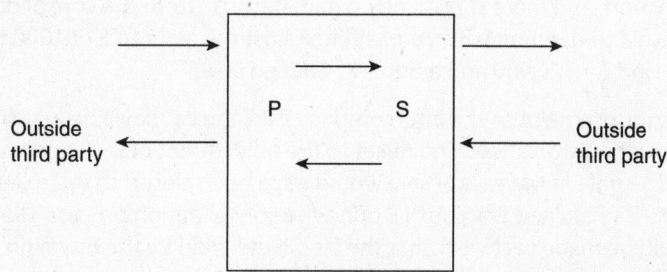

159

2. Tables to organize data:

	Should be	What is	Difference
Equipment			
Accum Depr			
Depr Expense			
Gain on Sale			

E. Nondepreciable Assets

1. Suppose on December 31, P sold land to S for $150,000. The land originally cost P $130,000. S still holds the land.

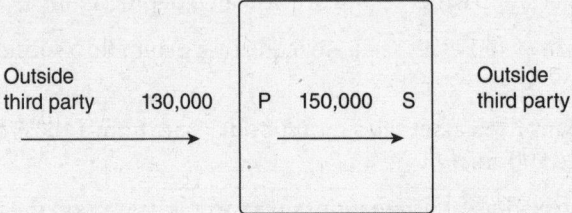

2. To understand the transaction, it helps to first evaluate the journal entries each company made at the date of the sale. Here are the entries that P and S would have made on December 31.

> On P's Books
>
> DR: Cash   150,000
>
>   CR: Land   130,000
>
>   Gain on Sale   20,000
>
> On S's Books
>
> DR: Land   150,000
>
>   CR: Cash   150,000

3. To help keep straight what the consolidated amount should be, prepare a table that compares the original asset basis to the intercompany asset basis.

	Should be	What is	Difference
Land	130,000	150,000	20,000 CR
Gain on Sale	0	20,000	20,000 DR

4. If this transaction had never occurred, Land "Should be" $130,000 on the consolidated financial; therefore, $130,000 is in the "Should be" column. Because of the intercompany transaction, the Land "Is" recorded on S's books at $150,000. P recorded a gain as a result of this transaction, and there should be no gain because from the consolidated perspective you cannot have a transaction with yourself! To adjust the asset to $130,000 the eliminating entry is a credit land for $20,000 and a debit to Gain on sale.

5. In the years subsequent to the intercompany sale, the Land will be adjusted each year on the consolidating worksheet. The offset to the adjustment of the Land will be to Retained Earnings. The gain in the year of sale would have been closed to the seller's Retained Earnings (in this case P's Retained Earnings). During the consolidation process, the following eliminating entry would be made each year that the land is still held by the buyer (in this case S).

DR: Retained Earnings	20,000	
CR: Land		20,000

III. Depreciable Assets

A. Now suppose on December 31, P sold equipment to S for $7,000, and the equipment originally cost $9,000. The equipment had an original life of 10 years and P held the equipment for 3 years before the sale to S.

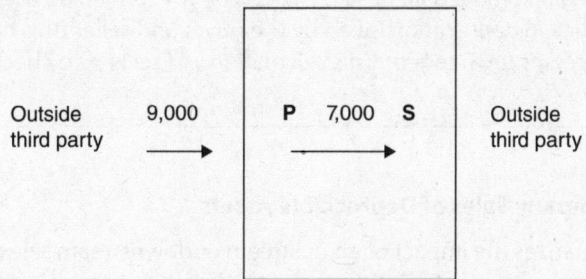

B. To understand the transaction, it helps to first evaluate the journal entries each company made at the date of the sale. Here are the entries that P and S would have made on December 31.

Original cost to P	9,000	NBV	6,300
Less AD (900 × 3 yrs)	(2,700)	Selling Price	7,000
NBV	6,300	Gain on Sale	700

On P's Books

DR: Depreciation Expense	900	
CR: Accumulated Depreciation		900
DR: Cash	7,000	
Accumulated Depreciation	2,700	
CR: Equipment		9,000
Gain on Sale		700

On S's Books

DR: Equipment	7,000	
CR: Cash		7,000

	Should be	What is	Difference
Equipment	9,000	7,000	2,000 DR
Accum Depr	2,700	0	2,700 CR
Depr Expense	900	900	0
Gain on Sale	0	700	700 DR

1. The eliminating entry in year 1 is the "difference" column:

Equipment	2,000	
Gain on Sale	700	
Accumulated Depreciation		2,700

2. The table for year 2 would appear as follows:

	Should be	What is	Difference
Equipment	9,000	7,000	2,000 DR
Accum Depr	3,600	1,000	2,600 CR
Depr Expense	900	1,000	100 CR
Retained Earnings	–	–	700 DR

Note: The intercompany gain on the date of sale, divided by the remaining useful live of the asset, will always equal the difference in deprecation taken by the buyer and seller (this holds true only if the useful life of the asset remains unchanged). This calculation will serve as a check figure for the should be/Is/Difference table.

IV. Summary of Intercompany Sales of Depreciable Assets

The table below summarizes the impact of an upstream or downstream sale on various calculations and on the consolidating entries in both the year of the intercompany sale and the years after the intercompany sale. The first column shows the impact on the calculation of Consolidated Net Income (CNI), Income to the Controlling Interest (CI), and Income to the Noncontrolling Interest (NCI). The second column shows the impact on the calculation of the Noncontrolling Interest Equity (NCI Equity). The third column shows the impact on the consolidating entries.

CY = Current year: PY = Prior Year: NI = Net Income: EOY = End of year:

A. Downstream (P sells to S):

	Calculation of CNI, CI, NCI	Calculation of NCI Equity	Consolidating Entries
Year of sale	1. Adjust P's independent NI for CY gain or loss 2. Adjust P's independent NI for CY depreciation adjustment (if sale is not at EOY)	N/A	Eliminate intercompany gain or loss, adjust asset basis, accumulated depreciation, and depreciation expense
Years after sale	Adjust P's independent NI for CY depreciation adjustment	N/A	Eliminate prior-year intercompany gain or loss through investment in S, adjust asset basis, accumulated depreciation, and depreciation expense

B. Upstream (S sells to P)

	Calculation of CNI, CI, NCI	Calculation of NCI Equity	Consolidating Entries
Year of sale	1. Adjust S's independent NI for CY gain or loss 2. Adjust S's independent NI for CY depreciation adjustment (if sale is not at EOY)	1. Adjust S's NBV for CY gain or loss 2. Adjust S's NBV for CY depreciation adjustment (if sale is not at EOY)	Eliminate intercompany gain or loss, adjust asset basis, accumulated depreciation, and depreciation expense

Years after sale	Adjust S's independent NI for CY depreciation adjustment	1. Adjust S's NBV for PY gain or loss 2. Adjust S's NBV for PY **PLUS** CY depreciation adjustment	Eliminate prior-year intercompany gain or loss through **investment in S and NCI Equity**, adjust asset basis, accumulated depreciation, and depreciation expense

C. The following sections of this lesson present a step-by-step walk through of the elimination of intercompany inventory transactions. Use the method/technique that works best for you.

V. **Elimination of Intercompany Gain (or Loss) and Reinstatement of Accumulated Depreciation—In Year of Intercompany Transactions**

A. **Illustration Facts**—Assume that on January 2, 20X1 Company P sold a depreciable fixed asset to its 100% owned subsidiary, Company S, for $30,000 cash (P to S = a downstream sale). At the time of the sale, the asset had the following values on Company P's books:

Original Cost	$40,000
Accumulated Depreciation	15,000
Net Book Value	$25,000

1. The asset net book value had an original expected life of 8 years, no expected residual value, and is being depreciated using the straight-line method. Entries made by the respective companies on their books to record the intercompany sale would be:

Company P

DR:	Cash	$30,000
DR:	Accumulated Depreciation	15,000
	CR: Fixed Asset	$40,000
	CR: Gain on Sale	5,000

Company S

DR:	Fixed Asset	$30,000
	CR: Cash	$30,000

2. All the resulting balances are brought onto the consolidating worksheet by the separate companies at year's end.

B. **Eliminating Entry**—On the consolidating worksheet, the following eliminating entry would be made to simultaneously eliminate the intercompany gain, reinstate the carrying value of the asset to its cost to the parent from a nonaffiliate, and reinstate the accumulated depreciation: (The eliminating entry for overstated depreciation expense and accumulated depreciation taken by the purchasing subsidiary will be illustrated in the following section.)

DR:	Fixed Asset	$10,000
DR:	Gain on Sale	5,000
	CR: Accumulated Depreciation	$15,000

1. This eliminating entry on the consolidating worksheet will:

    a. Reestablish the fixed asset to its original cost from a nonaffiliate—$40,000

    b. Eliminate the gain of $5,000 brought onto the consolidating worksheet by the selling affiliate—Company P

    c. Reestablish the accumulated depreciation as of the date of the intercompany sale to the amount based on original cost—$15,000

2. As a consequence of this eliminating entry, on the consolidating worksheet (and consolidated financial statements) the intercompany gain will have been eliminated and the fixed asset and related accumulated depreciation will be reported at amounts based on original cost from a non-affiliate.

VI. Elimination of Overstated (or Understated) Depreciation Expense and Accumulated Depreciation

A. **Illustration Facts** (continued from above): Company S would record on its books the depreciable fixed asset purchased from its Parent at $30,000. It elects to continue to use straight-line depreciation with no expected residual value over the remaining 5 years of the asset life. Therefore, each year Company S would record depreciation expense of $6,000 ($30,000/5 yrs.) as follows:

DR: Depreciation Expense $6,000
    CR: Accumulated Depreciation $6,000

1. These amounts would be brought onto the consolidating worksheet by Company S.

B. **Analysis of Facts**—On the books of the selling affiliate (prior to the intercompany sale) the asset had a book value of $25,000 (cost $40,000—accumulated depreciation $15,000 = $25,000), which would have been depreciated at the rate of $5,000 per year ($25,000/5 yrs.).

1. Because the purchase price to the buying affiliate included a $5,000 intercompany profit (Cost $30,000 – BV $25,000 = $5,000) the buying affiliate will recognize depreciation expense on its books (and brought onto the worksheet) of $6,000 per year ($30,000/5 yrs.).

2. The extra $1,000 per year is attributable to the intercompany profit ($5,000) depreciated over 5 years. In summary, an analysis for each year shows:

Depreciation after the intercompany transaction   = $6,000
Depreciation based on original cost   = 5,000
Excess depreciation expenses (per year)   = $1,000

3. The excess depreciation expense (and related accumulated depreciation) must be eliminated on the consolidating worksheet.

C. **Eliminating Entry**—On the consolidating worksheet the following eliminating entry would be made to reduce the depreciation expense and the related accumulated depreciation:

DR: Accumulated Depreciation $1,000
    CR: Depreciation Expense $1,000

1. This eliminating entry on the consolidating worksheet will:

    a. Reduce the depreciation expense recognized to the amount ($5,000) based on the original cost from a nonaffiliate;

    b. Reduce the accumulated depreciation to the amount ($5,000, for the first year) based on the original cost from a nonaffiliate.

  2. As a consequence of the eliminating entry, (net) depreciation expense for consolidated purposes will be $5,000 ($6,000 – $1,000) and accumulated depreciation will be $20,000 ($15,000 reinstated as part of the gain elimination above + $5,000 net depreciation recognized for the current period). The correctness of the accumulated depreciation is confirmed by:

> Original Cost $40,000/8 years Life = $5,000 per Year x 4 Years since Acquisition of the Asset = $20,000.

VII. Elimination in Years Subsequent to Intercompany Transaction—Elimination of Intercompany Gain (or loss) and Adjustment of Asset and Accumulated Depreciation—In Years Subsequent to Intercompany Transaction:

  A. Effects/Eliminations—Because the elimination made at the end of one period is recorded only on the consolidating worksheet (and not on the entity books), in years subsequent to the intercompany sale the following affects and eliminations apply:

    1. The gain (or loss) on the sale of fixed assets recognized by the selling affiliate will have been closed through net income to retained earnings. Therefore, the unconfirmed portion of the gain (or loss) will have to be eliminated from retained earnings brought onto the worksheet by the selling affiliate.

    2. The cost of the asset as recorded by the buying affiliate will continue to misstate the cost from a nonaffiliate. Therefore, the asset value brought onto the worksheet by the buying affiliate will have to be adjusted to its cost from a nonaffiliate; the amount of the adjustment will remain the same and will have to be made for as long as the asset remains on the books of the buying affiliate.

    3. The accumulated depreciation on the buying affiliate's books will continue to be misstated (by a decreasing amount) until the asset is fully depreciated because it does not include the accumulated depreciation written off by the selling affiliate. Therefore, accumulated depreciation related to the intercompany fixed asset will have to be adjusted each period until the asset is fully depreciated.

  B. Correct Depreciation Expense—Because the buying affiliate has the asset on its books at its cost from the selling affiliate, the annual depreciation expense (and related accumulated depreciation) recognized will be misstated for consolidated purposes because it will include depreciation on the intercompany gain (or loss). Therefore, the depreciation expense for the period brought onto the consolidating worksheet by the buying affiliate will have to be corrected to eliminate the depreciation related to the intercompany gain or loss.

  C. Illustration Facts (continued from above): As a result of entries made on the books of the affiliated companies P and S during the prior period in which the intercompany fixed-asset transaction occurred and the depreciation expense taken for the current period, the following account balances will be brought onto the worksheet at the end of the second period:

Company P (Selling Affiliate)	
Retained Earnings (Original Intercompany Gain)	$ 5,000
Company S (Buying Affiliate)	
Fixed Assets	$30,000
Accumulated Depreciation ($30,000/5 yrs. = $6,000 × 2 yrs)	$12,000
Depreciation Expense (current year only)	$ 6,000

1. Each of these account balances is analyzed below.

D. Analysis of Facts—The following should be noted about the account balances (above) brought onto the consolidated worksheet:

1. Retained earnings of the selling affiliate contain the $5,000 intercompany gain recognized on the sale of the asset to the buying affiliate. At the end of the second period, $1,000 of the intercompany gain will have been confirmed as a result of the depreciation on the intercompany gain taken during the first period. Therefore, the unconfirmed intercompany gain in retained earnings to be eliminated on the consolidating worksheet at the end of the second year is $4,000.

2. Fixed assets of the buying affiliate are reported at its cost, $30,000. The original cost from a nonaffiliate was $40,000. Therefore, the fixed assets will have to be written up $10,000 on the consolidating worksheet. This write up of $10,000 will increase the assets' reported value for consolidated purposes to $40,000, its original cost from a nonaffiliate.

3. Accumulated depreciation of the buying affiliate, $12,000, consists of two years depreciation on the intercompany asset at $6,000 per year ($30,000 cost/5 year remaining life = $6,000). The $12,000 includes $2,000 of depreciation expense related to the intercompany gain, $1,000 each for the prior year and the current year end which have the following affects:

    a. The depreciation of the gain related to the prior period ($1,000) reduces the amount of accumulated depreciation written off by the selling affiliate. Recall that Company P, the selling affiliate, wrote off $15,000 in accumulated depreciation when it sold the fixed asset to the buying affiliate.

    b. The $1,000 in excess depreciation taken by the buying affiliate (on the $5,000 gain) during the prior period reinstates $1,000 of the $15,000 written off by the selling affiliate. Thus, at the end of the second year only $14,000 needs to be reinstated.

    c. The depreciation of the gain related to the current period ($1,000) must be reversed in order to report depreciation expense for the current period at $5,000. (See next item.)

4. Depreciation expense for the current period of $6,000 ($30,000/5 years) will have been recognized by the buying affiliate on its books and brought onto the consolidating worksheet. That $6,000 includes $1,000 depreciation ($5,000 gain/5 years) on the gain recognized by the selling affiliate and must be eliminated for consolidated purposes. Therefore, depreciation expense (and related accumulated depreciation) brought to the worksheet by the buying affiliate must be reversed by $1,000.

E. Eliminating Entries—On the consolidating worksheet at the end of the second period the following entries would be made:

1. To simultaneously eliminate the unconfirmed gain in retained earnings, reinstate the carrying value of the asset to its original cost to the parent and reinstate the accumulated depreciation:

DR:	Retained Earnings	$4,000	
DR:	Fixed Asset	10,000	
	CR: Accumulated Depreciation		$14,000

2. To reduce the depreciation expense and related accumulated depreciation for the current period:

DR:	Accumulated Depreciation	$1,000	
	CR: Depreciation Expense		$1,000

3. The two entries could be made as a single entry:

DR: Retained Earnings	$4,000	
DR: Fixed Asset	10,000	
CR: Accumulated Depreciation		$13,000
CR: Depreciation Expense		1,000

4. The effects of the eliminated entries (or entry) for consolidating purposes will be to:

   a. Reestablish the fixed asset to its original cost from a non-affiliate—$40,000.

   b. Eliminate the unconfirmed intercompany gain in retained earnings—$4,000.

   c. Reduce depreciation expense recognized for the period to the amount based on original cost from a non-affiliate—$5,000.

   d. Reestablish accumulated depreciation to the amount based on depreciation of original cost—$25,000—as follows:

Brought onto worksheet	$12,000
Reinstatement on worksheet	13,000
Total Accumulated Depreciation	$25,000

   e. Proof:

Written off by selling affiliate	$15,000
Two years additional depreciation	10,000
(Cost $40,000/8 years) × 5 years =	$25,000

5. **Remaining Three-Year Period**—The eliminating entries made above will continue to be made as part of the consolidating process for the remaining three year estimated life of the fixed asset:

   a. The following elements of the eliminations will not change during the three-year period:

      i. The amount of addition to fixed asset remains $10,000.

      ii. The amount of depreciation expense eliminated remains $1,000.

   b. The following elements of the elimination will change:

      i. The amount of unconfirmed intercompany profit in retained earnings to be eliminated will decrease by $1,000 each year.

      ii. The amount of accumulated depreciation to be reinstated will decrease by $1,000 each year.

c. The eliminating entries for each of the remaining three years would be:

		Year 6	Year 7	Year 8
DR:	Retained Earnings	$ 3,000	$ 2,000	$ 1,000
DR:	Fixed Asset	10,000	10,000	10,000
	CR: Accumulated Depre.	$12,000	$11,000	$10,000
	CR: Depreciation Exp.	1,000	1,000	1,000

d. If the asset is retained beyond the 8th year, the following eliminating entry will be required until the asset is disposed:

DR:	Fixed Asset	$10,000
	CR: Accumulated Depreciation	$10,000

VIII. Sale By Subsidiary to Parent—Intercompany fixed asset by subsidiary to parent: The prior illustration assumed that the sale was made by the parent company to a subsidiary—a downstream sale. If a subsidiary sells to its parent the transaction is an upstream sale. The intercompany elimination for upstream sales depends, in part, on the parent's percentage ownership of the subsidiary.

A. Parent Owns 100% of the Subsidiary

1. The worksheet eliminating entries made when the parent **owns 100%** of a subsidiary, which sells fixed assets to the parent are the same as those made when the parent sells fixed assets to the subsidiary; there is no noncontrolling interest in the subsidiary.

2. All of the intercompany gain (or loss), net asset adjustment and subsequent depreciation expense adjustment would affect the parent's claim to net income and net asset carrying value.

B. Parent Owns Less than 100% of the Subsidiary

1. The worksheet eliminating entries made when the parent **owns less than 100%** of a subsidiary that sells fixed assets to the parent are the same as those made when the parent sells fixed assets to the subsidiary, but the gain (or loss) eliminated, the net asset adjustment and the subsequent depreciation expense adjustment would be allocated between the parent and the noncontrolling shareholders' interest in proportion to their respective ownership percentages. Those entries are repeated below as a means of review and to show the allocations necessary when a less than 100% owned subsidiary sells fixed assets to its parent.

2. **Worksheet with Income Statement**—If the elimination occurs on a consolidating worksheet that includes an income statement, the eliminations assuming an intercompany gain would be:

    a. For Period of Intercompany Sale

DR:	Fixed Asset
DR:	Gain on Sale
	CR: Accumulated Depreciation

b. To reestablish the fixed asset to its original cost, eliminate the intercompany gain, and reestablish accumulated depreciation written off by the selling affiliate. The debit to the gain will reduce the amount of income that will be allocated between the parent and the noncontrolling shareholders (interest) in proportion to their respective ownership percentages.

> DR: Accumulated Depreciation
>   CR: Depreciation Expense

c. To eliminate the depreciation expense (and related accumulated depreciation) taken by the buying affiliate on the intercompany gain. The credit to depreciation expense will increase the amount of income that will be allocated between the parent and the noncontrolling shareholders' interest in proportion to their respective ownership percentages.

d. For periods subsequent to intercompany sale

> DR: Fixed Assets
> DR: Retained Earnings—S
>   CR: Accumulated Depreciation

e. To reestablish the fixed asset to its original cost, eliminate the *un*confirmed portion of the intercompany gain in retained earnings and reestablish accumulated depreciation to the amount based on depreciation of original cost. The debit to fixed asset will remain constant; the debit to retained earnings and the credit to accumulated depreciation will decrease each year as a portion of the intercompany gain is confirmed.

f. The debit to retained earnings of S, the selling affiliate, will reduce the sub's retained earnings by the amount of the **un**confirmed profit.

> DR: Accumulated Depreciation
>   CR: Depreciation Expense

g. To eliminate the depreciation expense (and related accumulated depreciation) taken by the buying affiliate on the intercompany gain. The credit to depreciation expense will increase income that will be allocated between the parent and noncontrolling interest.

3. Worksheet without income statement—If the elimination occurs on a consolidating worksheet that does not include an income statement (i.e., only a balance sheet is provided), the eliminations would be allocated on the worksheet between the parent and the noncontrolling shareholders' interest in proportion to their respective ownership percentages. The eliminating entries each year, assuming a gain, would be:

> DR: Fixed Assets
> DR: Retained Earnings—S
>   CR: Accumulated Depreciation
> DR: Accumulated Depreciation
>   CR: Retained Earnings—P

a. The debit to retained earnings of S replaces a debit to gain because there is only a balance sheet. Otherwise, the purpose and effect of each debit and credit is the same as previously described.

Intercompany (I/C) Bond Transactions

When one affiliated entity owns the bonds issued by another affiliated entity, an intercompany bond transaction has occurred, and those bonds are intercompany bonds. Such transactions will result in the need to adjust and/or eliminate a number of account balances brought on to the consolidating worksheet by the separate entities. This lesson identifies the accounts that will be affected, and illustrates the adjustments or eliminations that will be needed on the consolidating worksheet.

After studying this lesson, you should be able to:

1. Identify the accounts affected by intercompany bond transactions.

2. Analyze facts and calculate the amounts needed to be eliminated for intercompany bond transactions under various circumstances, including:

   - When intercompany bonds have premiums or discounts associated with either the intercompany bond investment or bond liability.

   - When intercompany bonds are issued by a parent (and held by a subsidiary) or issued by a subsidiary (and held by a parent).

   - When intercompany bonds are issued by a subsidiary that is a 100% owned subsidiary or less than 100% owned subsidiary.

3. Record intercompany bond eliminations on a consolidating worksheet under the various circumstances identified above.

I. **Intercompany Bonds**—Occur when one affiliate owns the bonds issued by another affiliate.

II. **Intercompany Bonds May Result from**

    A. Bonds issued by one company are held by another company at the time the two companies become affiliated as a result of a business combination.

    B. One affiliate acquires the bonds issued by another affiliate (after the two companies are already affiliated as a result of a business combination).

III. **Intercompany Bond Consequences**

    A. When one affiliate acquires the bonds of another affiliate, for consolidated purposes it is as though the bonds have been retired; they have been constructively retired for consolidated purposes.

    B. Therefore, on the consolidating worksheet the bonds payable (and related accounts) brought on by the issuing company must be eliminated against the investment in bonds (and related accounts) brought on by the buying affiliate.

IV. **Accounts Affected**—Intercompany bonds affect the following accounts brought onto the consolidating worksheet by the separate companies:

    A. **Bonds Payable**—To the extent the bonds are held by an affiliate, the bonds have been constructively retired and the liability must be eliminated against the investment in the bonds held by an affiliate (in IV C, below)

    B. **Premium or Discount on Bonds Payable**—Any premium (issue price > face value of bonds) or discount (issue price < face value) related to bonds payable that are constructively retired must also be eliminated.

1. Since the face value of the bonds payable will be exactly eliminated against the face value of the bond investment, any premium or discount on bonds payable that is eliminated will result in a gain or loss on constructive retirement.

   a. Elimination of a Premium on Bonds Payable = Gain (on constructive retirement)

   b. Elimination of a Discount on Bonds Payable = Loss (on constructive retirement)

C. **Investment in Bonds**—Any investment in the bonds of an affiliate has been constructively retired and the asset must be eliminated against the owned portion of the bonds payable of the affiliate (in IVS A, above).

D. **Premium or Discount on Investment in Bonds**—Any premium (cost > face value of bonds) or discount (cost < face value) on the bond investment being eliminated also must be eliminated. Since the face value of the bond investment will be exactly eliminated against the face value of the bonds liability, any premium or discount on the bond investment that is eliminated will result in a loss or gain on constructive retirement:

   1. Elimination of a Premium on Investment in Bonds = Loss (on constructive retirement)

   2. Elimination of a Discount on Investment in Bonds = Gain (on constructive retirement)

E. **Interest Income/Interest Expense**—Any interest income recognized by the affiliate with the investment in intercompany bonds and the interest expense related to the intercompany bonds recognized by the issuing affiliate must be eliminated. Since for consolidated purposes the bonds are considered retired at the time they became intercompany, no subsequent interest income or interest expense can be recognized for consolidated purposes;

F. **Interest Receivable/Interest Payable**—Any intercompany interest receivables and interest payable resulting from intercompany bonds must be eliminated against each other.

V. **Elimination of Intercompany Bonds and Related Premiums/Discounts—At Date Bonds Become Intercompany**

   A. **Illustration Facts**—Assume that on January 1, 20X1 Company P had the following account balances related to its 10% bonds.

Bonds Payable (face amount)	$100,000
Premium on Bonds Payable	3,000

   B. The bonds have a three-year remaining life and pay interest annually on December 31.

   C. On January 1, 20X1 P's subsidiary, Company S, acquired all of P's bonds in the market for $106,000 ($100,000 face amount plus a $6,000 premium). Entries and related account balances on the books of the respective companies would be:

Company P (account balances)	
Bonds Payable	$100,000
Premium on Bonds Payable	3,000
Carrying Value	$103,000

Company S (entry)

Investment in P Bonds (face)	$100,000*	
Premium on Investment in P Bonds	6,000*	
Cash		$106,000

*These two debits likely would be combined in practice.

D. **Analysis of Intercompany Bond Facts**—At the time Company S acquired its parent's bonds, the bonds became intercompany and for consolidated purposes will be treated as if they are retired.

    1. The constructive retirement of the bond investment ($100,000) against the bond liability ($100,000) will necessitate the elimination of the related premiums on the investment and on the liability.

    2. The elimination of the related premiums will result in recognition of a $3,000 loss on constructive retirement for consolidated purposes, calculated as:

Premium on Bonds Payable (Credit)	= $3,000	Gain
Premium on Investment Bonds (Debit)	= $6,000	Loss
Net Loss on Constructive Retirement	= $3,000	Loss

E. **Eliminating Entry**—If an eliminating entry was made on a consolidating worksheet immediately following the intercompany bond transaction, the entry would be:

DR:	Bonds Payable	$100,000	
	Premium on Bonds Payable	3,000	
	Loss (on Constructive Retirement)	3,000	
	CR: Investment in Bonds Payable		$100,000
	Premium on Investment in Bonds		6,000

    1. The loss (or gain) is attributable to the company that issued the bonds, Company P in this illustration.

VI. **Book Transactions Subsequent to Intercompany Bonds Relationship**—Although the intercompany bonds are constructively retired and eliminated for consolidated purposes, the bond liability and the bond investment will continue to exist on the books of the separate companies.

A. As a consequence, the companies will make the following entries on their separate books for each of the three years' remaining life of the bonds:

Company P

Interest Expense	$10,000	
Interest Payable/Cash		$10,000

(Annual interest @ $100,000 × .10)

Premium on Bonds Payable	$ 1,000	
Interest Expense		$ 1,000

(Annual amortization @ $3,000/3 years)

Company S

Interest Receivable/Cash	$10,000	
Interest Income		$10,000

(Annual interest @ $100,000 × .10)

Interest Income	$ 2,000	
Premium on Investment in Bonds		$ 2,000

(Annual amortization @ $6,000/3 years)

B. Although the above bond-related entries will be recorded on the books of the separate companies, for consolidated purposes the bonds were constructively retired at the date the bonds became intercompany owned.

C. Therefore, the effects of the bond-related entries that apply after the bonds become intercompany must be eliminated for consolidated purposes.

VII. Elimination—Year End—Elimination of Intercompany Bonds and Related Accounts—At End of Year of Intercompany Bond Transaction.

A. Illustration Facts (continued from above): As a result of the transactions described above, at the end of 20X1, (the year in which the bonds became intercompany), the following account balances would exist on the books of the separate companies and be brought onto the consolidating worksheet:

Company P

Bonds Payable (face amount)	$100,000 (CR)
Premium on Bonds Payable ($3,000 – $1,000)	2,000 (CR)
Interest Expense ($10,000 – $1,000)	9,000 (DR)

Company S

Investment in P Bonds (face amount)	$100,000 (DR)
Premium on Bonds Investment ($6,000 – $2,000)	4,000 (DR)
Interest Income ($10,000 – $2,000)	8,000 (CR)

B. Eliminating Entry—The following eliminating entry would be made on the consolidating worksheet at the end of the period in which the bonds become intercompany bonds:

DR: Bonds Payable	$100,000	
Premium on Bonds Payable	2,000	
Interest Income	8,000	
Loss on Constructive Retirement	3,000	
CR: Investment in P Bonds		$100,000
Premium on Bond Investment		4,000
Interest Expense		9,000

C. Recall, this eliminating entry is required because for consolidated purposes the bonds must be treated as though they were retired at the time they became intercompany. Therefore, all subsequent balances and effects must be eliminated. The eliminating entry accomplishes the following:

1. Eliminates the intercompany liability and investment ($100,000)

2. Eliminates the non-amortized premiums on the liability ($2,000) and on the investment ($4,000)

3. Eliminates the net interest income recognized by Company S, the owner of the bonds (interest received $10,000 minus $2,000 premium amortization = $8,000)

4. Eliminates the net interest expense recognized by Company P, the issuing affiliate (interest paid $10,000 minus $1,000 premium amortization = $9,000)

5. Recognizes for consolidated purposes the $3,000 loss on the constructive retirement of the bonds

VIII. Elimination—Subsequent Years

Elimination of intercompany bonds and related accounts—in years subsequent to intercompany transaction.

A. Gain/Loss

1. The gain or loss on constructive retirement of intercompany bonds is determined as the net amount of premium(s) and/or discount(s) related to the bonds when they become intercompany and is recognized at the date (in the period) in which the bonds become intercompany.

2. However, as shown above, the separate companies will continue to carry on their books and amortize the premium and/or discount. At the end of each period, the effects of such amortization will be to recognize on the separate company books a portion (by the amount being amortized for the period) of the gain or loss already recognized for consolidated purposes (at the time the bonds became intercompany).

3. Therefore, in subsequent periods the amount needed to be recognized in eliminating entries for consolidated purposes that has not been recognized on the separate books will decrease each period. When the premium and/or discount related to intercompany bonds is fully amortized on the separate books (i.e., at maturity), the separate books will have recognized the total gain or loss recognized for consolidated purposes when the bonds became intercompany.

B. Illustration Facts (continued from above): The following illustration shows the effects on the separate company books of amortizing the premiums from the facts in the above illustration:

	I/C Date 1/1/X1	X1 Amortize Net Income Affect +/−	Balance 12/31/ X1	X2 Amortize Net Income Affect +/−	Balance 12/31/X2
Co. P Prem. on B/P (CR)	$3,000	(+1,000)	2,000	(+1,000)	1,000
Co. S Prem. on B/I (DR)	$6,000	(−2,000)	4,000	(−2,000)	2,000
Net (DR)	$3,000	(−1,000)	2,000	(−1,000)	1,000
Consolidated Loss	$3,000				

1. **Net value**—Note that the net value of the premiums at the date the bonds became intercompany, $3,000, is the amount of loss recognized at that time for consolidated purposes.

2. **Subsequent year**—Each subsequent year the amortization taken on the books of the separate companies causes $1,000 (net) of the $3,000 to be recognized on the books of the companies. The books are "catching up" a portion of the $3,000 already recognized for consolidated purposes.

3. Therefore, in subsequent periods the amount of gain or loss needed to be recognized for consolidated purposes will decrease.

4. **Account balances**—As a result of transactions by the separate companies during 20X1 and 20X2 (including the closing of accounts at the end of 20X1), at the end of 20X2 the following account balances would exist on the books of the separate companies and be brought onto the consolidating worksheet:

Company P

Bonds Payable (face amount)	$100,000 (CR)
Premium on Bonds Payable	1,000 (CR)
Interest Expense ($10,000 − $1,000)	9,000 (DR)

Company S

Investment in P Bonds (face amount)	$100,000 (DR)
Premium on Bonds Investment ($6,000 − $2,000 − $2,000)	2,000 (DR)
Interest Income ($10,000 − $2,000)	8,000 (CR)

C. Eliminating Entry—The following eliminating entry would be made on the consolidating worksheet at the end of 20X2, the period after the one in which the bonds became intercompany bonds:

DR: Bonds Payable	$100,000	
Premium on Bonds Payable	1,000	
Interest Income	8,000	
Retained Earnings—P	2,000	
CR: Investment in P Bonds		$100,000
Premium on Bond Investment		2,000
Interest Expense		9,000

D. This entry is the same as for the prior year except:

1. The amount of the premiums has decreased by the amounts of amortization taken in the second year;

2. The debit to Retained Earnings replaces the debit to Loss because the loss occurred in the prior period for consolidated purposes. The amount of the debit to Retained Earnings ($2,000) is $1,000 less than the debit to the loss in the prior period ($3,000) because $1,000 of the loss—the net amortization for the first period—has now been closed to retained earnings on the separate books;

3. A similar entry would be made on the consolidating worksheet at the end of 20X3, except the premiums will have been fully eliminated on the separate books (thus, no eliminating entry will be required for them) and the debit to retained earnings will be $1,000, the amount not yet recognized in the retained earnings of the separate companies through amortization of the premiums.

IX. Bonds Issued by Subsidiary—Intercompany bond Issued by a subsidiary: The prior illustration assumed that the bonds were issued by the parent and acquired by a subsidiary. If a subsidiary issues bonds, which are subsequently acquired by the parent, the consolidating eliminations will depend, in part, on the parent's percentage ownership of the subsidiary.

A. Parent Owns 100% of the Subsidiary

1. The worksheet eliminating entries made when the parent owns 100% of a subsidiary, which has its bonds reacquired by its parent, are the same as those made when the parent was the issuer.

2. The gain or loss on constructive retirement will be attributable to the issuing subsidiary, but the full amount will effect the parent's claim to net income since there is no noncontrolling interest in the subsidiary.

3. The eliminating entry in years subsequent to the bonds becoming intercompany will debit (loss) or credit (gain) the retained earnings of the subsidiary, rather than the parent, but the consolidated income and retained earnings effects will be the same.

B. Parent Owns < 100% of the Subsidiary

1. The worksheet eliminating entries made when the parent owns < 100% of a subsidiary, which has its bonds reacquired by its parent, are essentially the same as those made when the parent was the issuer, but the gain or loss on constructive retirement would be allocated between the parent and the noncontrolling shareholders' interest in proportion to their respective ownership on the consolidated income statement and balance sheet. Those entries are repeated below as a means of review and to show the allocations necessary when the subsidiary issues the bonds.

2. **Worksheet with Income Statement**—If the elimination occurs on a consolidating worksheet that includes an income statement, the elimination assuming a discount on the bond issue, a premium on the bond investment, and a net loss on the constructive retirement would be:

   a. **For period of intercompany bond transaction**

> DR: Bonds Payable
>
>   Loss on Constructive Retirement
>
> CR: Investment in Intercompany Bonds
>
>   Discount on Bonds Payable
>
>   Premium on Investment in Bonds

   b. To eliminate the intercompany bond liability and bond investment, related premium and discount, and recognize the resulting loss on constructive retirement. Since the loss is attributable to the issuer, the subsidiary's net income will be reduced which will reduce its contribution to consolidated net income. The amount of the loss attributable to noncontrolling shareholders will be allocated to that interest when the share of consolidated net income attributable to noncontrolling interest is allocated to those shareholders on the consolidated income statement.

   c. **For periods subsequent to the intercompany bond transaction**

> DR: Bonds Payable
>
>   Retained Earnings—S
>
> CR: Investment in Intercompany Bonds
>
>   Discount on Bonds Payable
>
>   Premium on Investment in Bonds

   d. This entry is the same as that made in the period following the intercompany bond transaction, except that retained earnings of the subsidiary is debited rather than loss because the loss occurred in a prior period. The debit will reduce retained earnings of the subsidiary, which will be allocated between the parent and the noncontrolling shareholders' interest in proportion to their respective ownership percentages.

3. **Worksheet without income statement**—If the elimination occurs on a consolidating worksheet that does not include an income statement (i.e., only a balance sheet is provided) the eliminations would be allocated on the worksheet between the parent and the noncontrolling shareholders' interest in proportion to their respective ownership percentages. The eliminating entry each year, assuming a discount on the bond issue, a premium on the bonds investment, and a net loss on constructive retirement, would be:

> DR: Bonds Payable
>
>   Retained Earnings—S
>
> CR: Investment in Intercompany Bonds
>
>   Discount on Bonds Payable
>
>   Premium on Investment in Bonds

4. This debit to retained earnings of S replaces a debit to loss because there is only a balance sheet. Otherwise, the purpose and effect of each debit and credit is the same as previously described.

IFRS—Consolidations

This lesson presents the significant differences in the accounting for consolidations under IFRS versus U.S. GAAP.

After studying this lesson, you should be able to:

1. Identify the major differences in the accounting for consolidations under IFRS versus U.S. GAAP.

I. Consolidations—U.S. GAAP–IFRS Differences

U.S. GAAP	IFRS
Control defined as > 50% ownership	Control can be obtained with > 50% ownership in certain circumstances i.e., potential rights, right to appoint key personnel, or decision making rights.
Defines variable interest entities	Does not define variable interest entities, but does have similar concept with special purpose entities
Accounting policies do not have to align.	Accounting policies have to align.
Accounting periods can be up to three months apart.	Accounting periods should have the same end date, if not adjust for transactions during gap period.
Noncontrolling interest is assigned their percentage of goodwill from the acquisition premium (purchase price differential).	Parent has a choice at acquisition whether or not to either assign goodwill to NCI.

A. Control Concept Differences

1. **U.S. GAAP**—Under U.S. GAAP, generally, the entity (investor) that owns, directly or indirectly, greater than 50% of the voting shares of another entity (investee) is considered to have control of that entity and, generally, would be required to consolidate the investee. If the investee entity is a variable interest entity, the controlling entity is the one that is the primary beneficiary of the variable interest entity. (Simply put, a variable interest entity [VIE] is an investee in which the investor holds controlling interest that is not based on holding a majority of the voting rights in the entity. They are a form of special purpose entity [SPE]. Both VIEs and SPEs are covered in a later lesson.)

2. **IFRS**

   a. Under IFRS No. 10, just as under U.S. GAAP, the ability of one entity (investor) to control another entity (investee) requires that the controlled entity be consolidated with the investor. However, under IFRS the definition and determination of control specifies that control can be achieved even when an investor holds less than 50% of the voting rights.

   b. Under IFRS, one entity (investor) controls another entity (investee) when the investor has:

      i. Power over an investee through existing rights that give it the ability to direct the activities that significantly affect the investee's returns; and

      ii. Exposure, or rights, to variable returns from its involvement with the investee; and

      iii. The ability to use its power over the investee to affect the amount of the investor's return.

   c. Under IFRS, power over an investee arises from rights of the investor, which may include:

        i. Voting rights (the critical criteria under U.S. GAAP)

        ii. Potential voting rights (e.g., convertible instruments, stock options, etc.)

        iii. Rights to appoint key personnel of the investee

        iv. Decision-making rights under a management agreement

    d. Under IFRS, an exposure, or a right, to variable returns from its involvement with an investee, which may be either positive, negative, or both, might include, for example:

        i. Dividends

        ii. Remuneration

        iii. Other returns or benefits not available to other stakeholders (e.g., economies of scale, cost savings, access to scarce resources or proprietary information, synergies, etc.)

3. Thus, under IFRS, the standard for determining control is broader than under U.S. GAAP. The IFRS standard applies regardless of the form of the investee entity, including to structured entities (what would be designated as SPEs or VIEs under U.S. GAAP) and the determination that control exists may occur in a greater number of relational circumstances than under U.S. GAAP. For example, under IFRS control may be deemed to exist in the following circumstances (which would not be considered control for consolidation purposes under U.S. GAAP):

    a. An investor has control over more than 50% of the voting rights by virtue of an agreement with other investors.

    b. An investor has the ability to govern the financial and operating policies of the entity under a statute or an agreement.

    c. An investor can appoint or remove the majority of the members of the board of directors.

    d. An investor can cast the majority of votes at a meeting of the board of directors.

B. Variable-Interest Entities/Special-Purpose Entities—IFRS does not address variable-interest entities or control of such entities, but it does address special-purpose entities, a similar entity concept.

1. A special-purpose entity (SPE), as the term implies, is a separate legal entity (or other entity) established to fulfill a narrow, specific or temporary purpose, generally with the intent of isolating the establishing firm from risk and assigning responsibility for risk through the use of agreements and other instruments.

2. Most, but not all, special-purpose entities will be variable-interest entities. Therefore, they have the same general characteristics as VIEs and, under IFRS, are treated similar to the treatment of VIEs under U.S. GAAP.

3. IFRS establishes that an entity may control a special-purpose entity (SPE), even when it owns little or none of the SPE's equity.

4. Under IFRS, the determination of control would be based on an analysis of all the relevant facts and circumstances, including the design of the entity and the risk and reward relationship between the entities.

5. Where the substance of the relationship indicates that an entity controls an SPE, the SPE should be consolidated by the controlling entity.

Note

In rare circumstances, under IFRS an investor may have the ability to control another entity with 50% or less of its voting ownership when it has significant ownership and other ownership is widely dispersed and not organized. Such a determination would have to be made on a case-by-case basis taking into account all relevant facts and circumstances.

C. Accounting Policy and Period Requirements

1. **Accounting policy requirement**—Under U.S. GAAP, a parent and its subsidiaries do not have to follow the same accounting policies in order to be consolidated. Different accounting policies can be used by different affiliated entities as long as all policies used are U.S. GAAP. Under IFRS, however, consolidated statements have to be prepared using the same accounting policies by all affiliated entities for like transactions and events. Thus, under IFRS, if a subsidiary used an accounting policy different than that employed by the parent, for consolidating purposes the subsidiary's accounts affected by the different policy would have to be adjusted prior to consolidation.

2. **Accounting period requirement**—Under U.S. GAAP, the fiscal reporting period of a parent and its subsidiaries may be up to three months different. Significant transactions or events that occur during the gap require only disclosure in the consolidated statements; no adjustment to accounts or amounts is required. Under IFRS, however, the financial information of a parent and its subsidiaries should be as of the same period-ending date, unless it is impracticable to do so. In any case, the difference between the parent ending date and the subsidiary ending date cannot be more than three months. Further, significant transactions or events that occur during the gap must be reflected in adjustments to the accounts/amounts used for consolidating purposes.

D. Noncontrolling Interest Valuation

1. One of the most significant differences between U.S. GAAP and IFRS in accounting for business combinations is in the possible measurement of noncontrolling interest (NCI) because of the goodwill allocated to NCI.

   a. U.S. GAAP requires that any noncontrolling interest be measured at full fair value, including the goodwill attributable to the noncontrolling interest.

   b. IFRS gives the acquirer a choice between two options for measuring noncontrolling interest in the acquiree; those options are to measure noncontrolling interest using either:

      i. Full fair value of the NCI, including goodwill attributable to noncontrolling interest, or

      ii. Proportional share of fair value of the fair value, excluding goodwill attributable to the noncontrolling interest.

   c. Example of allocation of full fair value versus proportional share of noncontrolling interest (NCI)

      i. Note: The primary purpose of these examples is to illustrate the difference between allocating goodwill to NCI. Eliminating entries are given to show how the different measures result in different amounts of goodwill and noncontrolling interest. The preparation of eliminating entries is covered in detail in other sections on consolidated statements.

Example

Facts: Torco, Inc., acquired 70% of Teeco, Inc. for $900 cash. The fair value of the 30% noncontrolling interest was determined to be $400. Therefore, the total fair value of Teeco at the date of the business combination is $900 + $400 = $1,300. The fair value of Teeco's identifiable net assets are $1,000.

1. Full Fair Value calculation (which is U.S. GAAP and one [of two] options under IFRS)

Total Fair Value ($900 + $400)	$1,300
Fair Value of Identifiable Net Assets (given)	1,000
Total Goodwill	$ 300
Goodwill Allocated to Torco $900 – (.70 x $1,000) = $900 – $700 =	(200)
Goodwill Allocated to NCI	100
Total Noncontrolling Interest (given)	400

	100%	Parent share 70%	NCI share 30%
Total (FV of entity)	1,300	900	400
Goodwill	300	200	100
FMV Net Assets	1,000	700	300

Entries:

Investment

DR:	Investment in Subsidiary Teeco	$ 900	
	CR: Cash		$ 900

Investment Elimination (Summary)

DR:	Teeco Shareholder' Equity/Net Assets	$1,000	
	Goodwill	300	
	CR: Investment in Subsidiary Teeco		$ 900
	Noncontrolling Interest		400

2. Proportional Share of Fair Value calculation—which is not U.S. GAAP, but is one (of two) options under IFRS

Total Fair Value ($900 + $400)	$1,300
Fair Value of Identifiable Net Assets (given)	1,000
Goodwill Recognized – Torco only $900 – (.70 x $1,000) = $900 – $700 =	200
Goodwill Allocated to NCI	-0-
Goodwill Allocated to Torco	(200)
Total Noncontrolling Interest (given)	300

	100%	Parent share 70%	NCI share 30%
Total (FV of entity)	1,300	900	400
Goodwill		200	0
FMV Net Assets	1,000	700	300

Entries:

Investment

DR: Investment in Subsidiary Teeco $ 900
      CR: Cash $ 900

Investment Elimination (Summary)

DR: Investment in Subsidiary Teeco $1,000
      Goodwill   200
      CR: Investment in Subsidiary Teeco $ 900
           Noncontrolling Interest   300

Comments on Noncontrolling Interest Valuation

1) Under IFRS, the acquirer can elect to allocate the proportional share goodwill on a business combination-by-business combination basis; it does not have to use the same basis for all combinations.

2) The net effect of the alternative valuations of NCI is in the amount of goodwill recognized. Under the full fair value approach, the goodwill attributable to the NCI is derived and allocated to NCI. Under the proportional share of fair value approach, only the goodwill paid for by the acquirer is recognized; no goodwill is derived for or allocated to NCI.

Combined Financial Statements

Sometimes there is a need to aggregate the financial information of two or more affiliated entities, but the preparation of consolidated financial statements is not appropriate because none of the affiliated entities controls (is the parent) of the other firms. In such circumstances, the preparation of combined financial statements may be appropriate. This lesson is concerned with the concept and preparation of combined financial statements.

After studying this lesson, you should be able to:

1. Identify when combined financial statements are appropriate.

2. Describe how combined financial statements are prepared.

I. **Basis for Combined Financial Statements**—Like consolidated financial statements, combined financial statements are the product of bringing together the financial statements of two or more related firms. However, the circumstances when combined financial statements (as opposed to consolidated financial statements) would be appropriate, as well as the process of combining financial statements (as opposed to consolidating financial statements), are somewhat different.

    A. Consolidated financial statements are justified only when the controlling financial interest of the firms being consolidated rests directly or indirectly with one of the firms (a "parent") to be included in the consolidation.

    B. There are circumstances when there is not a parent company, or when a parent does not have effective control of subsidiaries, but bringing together (combining) the financial statements of two or more related firms would be more meaningful than their separate financial statements.

    C. Combined financial statements (as distinguished from consolidated statements) would be appropriate when:

        1. **Common control:** One individual (not a corporation) owns a controlling interest in two or more businesses that have related operations;

        2. **Common management:** Two or more businesses are under common management;

        3. **Unconsolidated subsidiaries:** A parent lacks effective control over two or more subsidiaries (unconsolidated subsidiaries) for which it wishes to show summary results.

II. **Process for Combining Financial Statements**—The process of preparing combined financial statements is similar to the process of consolidating financial statements.

    A. **Intercompany Items**—Intercompany transactions and balances (i.e., between the companies being combined) are eliminated, including:

        1. Intercompany receivables and payables

        2. Intercompany revenues and expenses

        3. Intercompany gains and losses

        4. Intercompany ownership and related equity—The carrying value of an investment in a company to be combined is eliminated against an equal amount of equity of that company; thus, there are no differences (between the debit and credit) to be allocated.

B. Any other "unusual" matters would be treated in the same manner as in consolidated financial statements, including:

1. Minority ownership in any combined company

2. Foreign operations

3. Income taxes

4. Different fiscal periods

C. Unlike consolidated financial statements, the resulting combined financial statements do not represent the financial position, results of operations, or cash flows of a single controlling entity but, rather, the aggregate results of the combined companies after eliminating intercompany account activity and balances.

Variable Interest Entities (VIEs)

Consolidated financial statements may be required in certain other circumstances where one entity has control over another entity through means other than equity ownership. This control usually occurs through a variable interest in another entity. This lesson identifies a variable interest entity (VIE) and when the VIE should be consolidated financial statement with the primary beneficiary.

After studying this lesson, you should be able to:

1. Understand the concept of variable-interest entities (VIEs) and when VIEs must be consolidated.

2. Identify a primary beneficiary and when the VIE should be consolidated.

I. **Eligibility for Consolidated Financial Statements**—Whether an entity (e.g., an investee), in which another entity (e.g., an investor) has an interest, must be consolidated depends on the nature of the relationship between entities. GAAP establishes a two-step (or two-tier) process for determining whether the relationship requires an entity to be consolidated with another entity. The entity being considered for consolidation must be assessed to determine (1) if it is a variable-interest entity (VIE) and, if so, the primary beneficiary of the VIE, and (2) if the entity is not a VIE, whether an investor has equity ownership that enables it to exercise control of the investee.

II. **Variable-Interest Entity Assessment**—Each entity that is considered for consolidation must first be evaluated to determine if it is a variable-interest entity (VIE) and, if it is, which other entity is its primary beneficiary.

   A. A VIE is a legal entity, which by design either:

   1. Cannot finance its activities without additional subordinated financial support (i.e., its expected losses exceed its total equity investment at risk), or

   2. Its equity holders, as a group, do not have the direct or indirect ability to make decisions about the VIE's activities.

   B. Structurally, a VIE may be a legal trust, partnership, joint venture, limited company or corporation.

   1. Typically, a VIE is established by another entity or entities (the sponsors) to carry out a well-defined, limited business purpose, with the sponsor(s)—also the variable-interest holders—providing most resources to the VIE, often in the form of loans or loan guarantees.

   2. The activities of and decision-making in a VIE are governed largely by the agreement that establishes the entity and generally resides with the variable-interest holders; nonsponsor equity owners may play little role in the operation of the entity.

   3. The risks and rewards associated with the VIE are largely attributable to the variable-interest holders, not the equity owners who may bear little risk and receive only a small rate of return.

   4. The value of the VIE to the variable-interest holders depends on (varies with) the success of the VIE; the variable-interest holders' interest increases if the net asset value of the VIE increases or decreases if the net asset value of the VIE decreases.

   C. In summary, even though the equity investors in a VIE are its legal owners, because of contractual or other arrangements, they play little role in the operation of the entity and carry little risk or receive little benefit from ownership; those risks and benefits accrue to the variable-interest holders (usually also the sponsors). Thus, a VIE is an entity in which another entity has a controlling interest achieved by a means other than holding a majority of the voting rights.

   D. An entity with a variable interest in a VIE must qualitatively assess whether it is the primary beneficiary of the VIE; if so, it is deemed to have a controlling financial interest in the VIE.

E. An entity will be considered the primary beneficiary of a VIE if it meets both of the following conditions:

    1. It has the power to direct activities of the VIE that most significantly impact the VIEs economic performance (called the power criterion), and

    2. It has the obligation to absorb losses from or right to receive benefits of the VIE that potentially could be significant to the VIE (called the losses/benefits or risks/rewards criterion).

F. Only one entity (e.g., sponsor), if any, will be the primary beneficiary of a VIE.

G. An entity that is determined to be the primary beneficiary of a VIE (an, therefore, has a controlling financial interest) will consolidate the financial statements of the VIE.

H. An entity that is determined to be the primary beneficiary of a VIE and, therefore, consolidates its financial statements, must assess whether it continues to be the primary beneficiary on an ongoing basis.

III. Voting Interest Assessment—If an entity being considered for consolidation (e.g., an investee) is not a variable-interest entity, it would be assessed to determine whether an investor has majority ownership of its voting securities and, if so, that nothing prevents the investor from exercising his or her control of the operating and financial activities of the investee.

A. Controlling ownership of an investee by an investor results from a business combination carried out in the form of a legal acquisition.

    1. A business combination carried out as a legal merger or legal consolidation results in only one remaining firm. Financial statements are prepared for that single firm; there are no sets of financial statements to consolidate.

    2. A business combination carried out as a legal acquisition results in one legal entity (the parent) having majority ownership, either directly or indirectly, of the other legal entity (the subsidiary). Each firm is a separate legal (and accounting) entity, but under the common control of the parent shareholder.

    3. In form, the parent and subsidiary are separate legal entities; in substance, they are a single "economic entity." If the parent can exercise its majority ownership to control the operating and financial activities of the subsidiary, consolidated parent-subsidiary financial statements must be the primary form of financial reporting for the entities.

B. A majority owned (> 50% of voting stock, controlled either directly or indirectly) subsidiary must be consolidated with its parent unless the parent lacks the ability to exercise its majority ownership to control the operating and financial activities of the subsidiary (i.e., the parent lacks effective control of the subsidiary).

    1. Effective control may be lacking due to:

        a. Foreign subsidiary being largely controlled by the foreign government through:

            i. Prohibition on paying dividends

            ii. Control of day-to-day operations

        b. Domestic subsidiary in bankruptcy and under the control of the courts.

C. Unless a parent lacks effective control of a subsidiary, the subsidiary's financial statements must be consolidated with parent's financial statements for public reporting.

D. If a majority-owned subsidiary is not consolidated because the investor lacks effective control (for one of the reasons given above), the subsidiary is an "unconsolidated subsidiary."

    1. An unconsolidated subsidiary would be reported as an "Investment" asset by the parent.

    2. The parent would account for its investment in an unconsolidated subsidiary using either fair value or the equity method, depending on the extent of influence that it can exercise over the investee.

Exit or Disposal Activities and Discontinued Operations

This lesson presents the accounting and reporting for exit or disposal activities and discontinued operations.

After studying this lesson, you should be able to:

1. Calculate the gain or loss on the disposal or involuntary conversion of a plant asset.

2. Complete the journal entry to record the disposal or involuntary conversion of a plant asset.

3. Complete the financial statement presentation of a discontinued operation.

4. Define what is meant by a *component of an entity*.

5. Calculate the gain or loss on a discontinued operation.

I. The following categories capture the types of exit or disposal activities: 1) those disposals that occur in the normal course of business that are disposals of individually insignificant assets, 2) disposals that meet the criteria of a discontinued operation, and 3) individually significant disposals that do not meet the criteria of a discontinued operation. Each category is discussed further below.

II. **Exit or Disposal Activity in the Ordinary Course of Business**

   A. A company may voluntarily sell, dispose, or abandon plant assets that are individually insignificant to the operations of the business. These disposals occur and are not the primary source of revenue for the entity, but are incidental to operations. In the case of fire, flood, or other event, the plant asset may be destroyed involuntarily. In either case, the asset must be depreciated up to the date of the disposal. The first thing that must be done before recording an exit or disposal activity is to record depreciation.

   B. Sale of a plant asset requires removing the asset and accumulated depreciation, recording the receipt of cash, and recognition of the gain or loss on the sale. When the cash received from the sale exceeds the assets net book value (asset cost – accumulated depreciation), then a gain is recognized. When the cash received is less than the assets net book value, then a loss is recognized. The gain or loss on the disposal of an asset is reported on the income statement with other items from customary business activities.

 **Example**
Assume Shelby Company purchased a plant asset for $20,000 with a 10-year life on January 1, 20X0. On July 1, 20X8, Shelby Company sold the plant asset for $5,000. The entries for the sale of the plant asset are as follows:

| Depreciation expense | $1,000 | |
| Accumulated depreciation | | $1,000 |

(to record 6 months of depreciation in the year of sale—(20,000/10 years) × 6/12)

Cash	$5,000	
Accumulated depreciation	$17,000*	
Plant Asset		$20,000
Gain on sale of plant asset		$ 2,000

(to record the gain on the sale of the plant asset)

*((20,000/10 years) × 8.5 years held) = 17,000)

C. If the asset is abandoned or there is an involuntary conversion because the asset is destroyed, then no cash is received and the gain or loss equals the net book value of the asset on the date of the abandonment or conversion. The loss on abandonment or conversion is an ordinary loss and part of continuing operations on the income statement. The next section presents the accounting and reporting for discontinued operations.

III. Discontinued Operations

A. A discontinued operation is when a component or group of components of an entity are 1) disposed for by sale or other than sale, or classified as held-for-sale, and 2) the disposal "represents a strategic shift that has (or will have) a major effect on an entity's operation and financial results." (ASU 2014-08) A strategic shift includes the disposal of a major geographical area, a major line of business, a major equity method investment, or other major parts of the entity.

B. **Comparative Financial Statements**—The income of a discontinued operation, and any gain or loss from its disposal, are separated from income from continuing operations, for **all periods presented**, even though in previous periods the income from the segment was part of continuing operations. This requirement enhances the consistency of comparative financial statements. Discontinued operations are shown below income from continuing operations in the income statement. Earnings per share is presented for discontinued operations on the face of the income statement.

1. **Income statement:** The gain or loss from the discontinued operation is presented on the face of the income statement as income (loss) from discontinued operation (net of tax). In contrast, gains or losses from the disposal that does not qualify as a discontinued operation is included in income from continuing operations.

Example
The income of Old, a reporting unit of Car, Inc., is $20 and $5 for years 6 and 7. Total Car income is $100 each year. In year 7 Old is discontinued and put up for sale. Year 7's comparative income statement shows the change in reporting for year 6.

	Year 6	Year 7
Income from continuing operations	$80	$95
Discontinued operation	$20	$5
Net income	$100	$100

The year 6 income statement published in year 6 included Old's income of $20 in income from continuing operations because in that year Old was part of the continuing operations of Car, Inc. However, in year 7, that is no longer the case and Old's results are separated from income from continuing operations for both years presented.

2. **Balance sheet:** All assets and liabilities of the discontinued operation for all comparative periods are presented separately on the balance sheet. These assets and liabilities cannot be presented as a net single amount; rather the gross amount of assets and liabilities must be shown.

IV. Two Values to Report—The following are separately disclosed and computed in the income statement below income from continuing operations:

A. **Income**—Income from the discontinued operation (DOP) for the portion of the year to disposal (or if disposal occurs in a later year, income for the entire year).

B. Gain or Loss—On disposal of the operation.

1. The gain or loss is the net proceeds from sale of the component less book value of the component's net assets. Net proceeds are equal to the gross amount received on sale less the cost to dispose of the assets. Thus, the cost to dispose increases a loss and decreases a gain.

Example
Disposal loss or gain calculation:

Component data:

Assets net of applicable depreciation	$400
Liabilities	$150
Amount received on sale	$220
Cost to sell	$20

Book value of net assets = $400 − $150 = $250. Proceeds = $220 − $20 = $200. Loss on disposal = $250 − $200 = $50.

C. All items reported for discontinued operations are net of tax (after tax).

D. The measurements for the DOP disposal loss is the same as for individual impaired assets held for disposal (impairment is covered in a different lesson). The only difference is the location on the income statement the gain or loss is reported. The gain or loss recognized for individual assets is included in income from continuing operations whereas the gain or loss from DOP is reported as *discontinued operations* below income from continuing operations.

E. Gain on Disposal—Actual gains on disposal (when the decision to discontinue the operation and the disposal occur in the same period) are recognized but estimated gains are not. A gain occurs when the net proceeds from the sale of the component exceed the BV (book value) of the net assets of the component.

F. Loss on Disposal—When the BV of the net assets of the component exceeds the component's fair value less cost of disposal at year-end, then the component assets are written down to fair value less cost of disposal. The latter amount (fair value less cost of disposal) is estimated at the end of the year, and the loss is recognized even though disposal or sale has not taken place.

G. If the disposal takes place in the year the decision is made, then the disposal loss reported is the actual amount.

H. If the actual disposal loss is different from the estimated loss recognized previously, then in the period of disposal the difference is recognized as a gain or loss.

Example
If the previously recognized estimated loss was $40,000 and the actual loss in the year of disposal was $30,000, then in the year of disposal a $10,000 gain is recognized and reported in the DOP section of the income statement.

I. The disposal loss or gain is a separate line item in the DOP section of the income statement in addition to the separate operating income of the component during the period. Alternatively, the two amounts can be netted with footnote disclosure showing them both. The assets are separated from the others in the BS when disposal takes place after the decision to eliminate the component.

Example

In year 3, a firm decided to discontinue an operation (DOP) that qualifies for separate DOP reporting. The operation's operating income was $60 in year 2 and negative $20 in year 3 (operating loss). For simplicity, assume the firm shows only two years comparatively. At the end of year 3 the BV of the component's net assets is $400. The fair value of the component is $250, and the firm expects to incur $20 of direct incremental cost to dispose of the component in year 4. Income from continuing operations for year 2 reported in year 2 was $300. Income from continuing operations in year 3 is $320. All amounts are after-tax.

The latter portion of the comparative income statement:

		Year 3	Year 2
Income from continuing operations		$320	$240
Income from DOP	(20)		60
Loss on disposal of DOP	(170)*	(190)	
Net income		$130	$300

*$170 = $400 BV − ($250 fair value − $20 cost to sell)

All amounts shown above are after tax.

Note that income from continuing operations for year 2 reported in the year 2 income statement was $300. For comparative purposes, the components year 2 income is separated from income from continuing operations. The assets of this component are also reported on a separate line on the balance sheet.

J. After the disposal of an operation is completed, there may be adjustments to amounts previously reported in the DOP section of the income statement. These adjustments might stem from resolution of contingencies, settlement of pension obligations, and others that occur after disposal. Such adjustments are reported in the DOP section of the income statement in the year they occur.

V. **Disclosures**—There are several disclosure requirements for both (1) disposals that meet the criteria for a discontinued operation and (2) individually significant disposals that do not meet these criteria.

A. For disposal of an individually significant component that does not meet the definition of a discontinued operation, the entity must disclose pretax profit or loss reported in the income statement for the period in which the disposal group is sold or is classified as held for sale.

B. For a disposal that meets the criteria of a discontinued operation the entity must disclose the following (ASU 2014-08):

1. Fact and circumstances leading to the disposal and reasons for the strategic shift and the effect of the strategic shift on operations

2. For the initial period in which the disposal group is classified as held for sale and for all prior periods presented in the statement of financial position, a reconciliation of (1) total assets and total liabilities of the discontinued operation that are classified as held for sale in the notes to the financial statements to (2) total assets and total liabilities of the disposal group classified as held for sale that are presented separately on the balance sheet

3. Operating and investing cash flows for the periods for which the discontinued operation's results of operations are reported in the income statement

4. Depreciation and amortization, capital expenditures, and significant operating and investing noncash items for the periods for which the discontinued operation's results of operations are reported in the income statement

5. Entities that have significant continuing involvement with a discontinued operation after the disposal date must provide additional disclosures regarding the nature of activities, including cash flows from or to the discontinued operation.

VI. Discontinued Operations and IFRS

A. IFRS identifies a component of an entity similarly to U.S. GAAP. The main difference is that U.S. GAAP has more disclosure requirements than IFRS.

Public Company Reporting Topics (SEC, EPS, Interim, and Segment)

U.S. Securities and Exchange Commission (SEC)

SEC—Role and Standard-Setting Process

After studying this lesson, you should be able to:

1. Recognize that there are mandatory exemptions from first time adoption as well as voluntary exceptions.

2. Describe the components of SEC's organizational structure.

3. Describe the SEC's role in the standard setting process.

4. List the main pronouncements issued by the SEC.

I. **Introduction**

   A. The SEC is a federal agency created by Congress after the 1929 stock market crash. It administers the U.S. securities laws, most notably the Securities Act of 1933 and the Securities Exchange Act of 1934. The SEC requires registrants (those publicly held companies under its purview) to adhere to U.S. GAAP when reporting financial statements, except those non-U.S.-domiciled companies who may report using IFRS without a reconciliation to U.S. GAAP (see discussion below).

   B. Although the SEC has the legal authority to prescribe accounting standards for publicly traded corporations, it continues to believe that standard setting should remain in the private sector, subject to its oversight. The SEC often agrees with the FASB's accounting standards, while communicating its preferences in comments on FASB Exposure Drafts and other documents. In a few cases, the SEC has rejected a FASB standard and in others has applied pressure to have a standard or proposed standard modified, or to come to a decision more quickly.

II. **The SEC's Main Purposes**

   A. "The mission of the U.S. Securities and Exchange Commission is to protect investors, maintain fair, orderly, and efficient markets, and facilitate capital information" (http://www.sec.gov/about/whatwedo.shtml). An important component of the mission is ease and access to information that is relevant to the decision maker. (Remember that relevance is a primary characteristic in the FASB's conceptual framework!)

   B. The SEC regulates the issuance of securities by publicly traded companies and regulation of the trading of those securities on secondary markets. The SEC's intent is to ensure that there is adequate information in the public domain before firms issue securities and before those securities are subsequently traded. Some of the most critical information used by the participants in the marketplace is the financial information provided by the registrant. This is why the SEC is so involved with financial reporting and accounting standards.

   C. The SEC's IDEA (Interactive Data Electronic Applications) database replaced the SEC's EDGAR (Electronic Data Gathering, Analysis and Retrieval System) database to facilitate the reporting of financial statement information in XBRL (Extensible Business Reporting Language) format, which tags accounting data according to a taxonomy allowing users to quickly prepare any type of report they wish. The purpose of IDEA is to increase the efficiency of the securities markets by providing timely and accessible data.

   D. The global economy has called for the need for one high-level, comprehensive set of accounting standards. The SEC has been the champion and driver in the United States to converge GAAP and

IFRS. In 2005, SEC and top European Union officials agreed to a roadmap toward convergence between U.S. GAAP and IFRS.

E. In 2008, the SEC began accepting the financial statements of foreign private issuers prepared in compliance with IFRS without reconciliation to U.S. GAAP. This is a significant step toward acknowledging the IFRSs as issued by IASB. The reconciliation (complete on Form 20-F) was considered to be an unnecessary requirement if the goal was one set of high-quality standards. In addition, the cost of completing the reconciliation was viewed as a deterrent for foreign issuers to access the U.S. capital markets. Eliminating the requirement will hopefully encourage more foreign businesses to list their securities in the United States.

    1. A foreign private issuer is any foreign issuer other than a foreign government, *except* an issuer that meets the following conditions (Rule 205, Securities Act 1933):

        a. More than 50% of the outstanding voting securities are directly or indirectly owned by residents of the United States and

        b. Any of the following:

            i. The majority of its executive officers or directors are U.S. citizens or residents.

            ii. More than 50% of the assets of the issuer are located in the United States.

            iii. The business of the issuer is administered principally in the United States.

F. When the SEC determines that a firm has reported in such a way that GAAP has been violated, it sends a deficiency letter to the firm. If not resolved, the SEC can then stop the trading of the firm's securities. If warranted the Department of Justice becomes involved and criminal charges for violations of the securities laws are filed.

> **Note**
> *Although the SEC can prescribe accounting standards, it has delegated that task to the private sector (currently the FASB). However, the SEC maintains the enforcement power for all publicly traded companies to assure compliance with U.S. GAAP.*

III. SEC Organizational Structure

A. The SEC is a member of the International Organization of Securities Commissions (IOSCO), which consists of more than 100 securities regulatory agencies or exchanges across the globe.

B. The SEC has five commissioners appointed by the president of the United States and five divisions (collectively referred to as "the commission").

    1. **The Division of Corporation Finance**—This division oversees the compliance with the securities acts and examines all filings made by publicly held companies. All filings go to this division.

    2. **The Division of Enforcement**—When there is a violation of a securities law (except the Public Utility Holding Company Act), this division completes the investigation and takes appropriate actions. This division makes recommendations to the Justice Department concerning any punishments or potential criminal prosecution.

    3. **The Division of Trading and Markets**—This division oversees the secondary markets, exchanges, brokers, and dealers.

    4. **The Division of Investment Management**—This division oversees the investment advisers and investment companies under the Investment Company Act of 1940 and the Investment Advisers Act of 1940.

    5. **Division of Economic and Risk Analysis**—This division was created in 2009 in response to the credit market crisis. The purpose of the division is to integrate financial economics and data analytics into the core mission of the SEC (www.sec.gov).

C. The Office of the Chief Accountant of the SEC is the most important office for standard setting. This office houses the technical expertise on accounting principles, auditing standards and financial disclosure requirements. This office also issues position papers for the SEC to consider and is the link between the SEC and the accounting profession. The Office of the Chief Accountant has oversight of the FASB and AICPA and is the voice of the SEC regarding standard-setting issues.

D. Laws Administered by the SEC

1. The Securities Acts of 1933 and 1934

2. The Public Utility Holding Company Act of 1935

3. Trust Indenture Act of 1939

4. Investment Company Act of 1940

5. Investment Advisors' Act of 1940

6. Securities Investor Protection Act of 1970

7. Sarbanes-Oxley Act of 2002

IV. Participation in Standard Setting

A. Even though the SEC delegates the creation of accounting standards to the private sector, the SEC frequently comments on accounting and auditing issues. The SEC communicates through an array of venues. SEC pronouncements, along with the FASB Accounting Standards Codification, comprise authoritative U.S. GAAP. Public companies must adhere to SEC pronouncements as well as U.S. GAAP; private companies do not have to adhere to SEC pronouncements. The main pronouncements published by the SEC are listed next.

1. **Financial Reporting Releases (FRR)**—These are formal pronouncements and are the highest-ranking authoritative source of accounting for public companies.

2. **Staff Accounting Bulletins (SAB)**—These provide the SEC's current position on technical issues. Although SABs are not formal pronouncements (in the sense that they have not gone through any due process), they still are of importance to financial statement preparers, because they reflect the staff's current thinking on various technical issues.

Example

An example is SAB 104 on revenue recognition. This SAB was adopted in response to concerns about premature recognition of revenue.

This SAB was issued to reduce the degree to which management could decide the timing and amount of revenue recognition. It lays out very specific principles affecting revenue recognition. It primarily addresses abuses by start-up and growing firms involved in complex transactions. Key provisions are:

Revenue should not be recognized before both legal and economic ownership of goods has passed to the buyer. Fees charged at the beginning of a revenue-generating arrangement should be recognized over the term of the arrangement. An annual fee is not fully earned until the seller has provided its service for the year.

In terms of the earned criterion, on the sale of products, the SEC presumes that the sale is not earned unless title has passed and the customer assumes the risks and rewards of ownership. In addition, in some cases, acceptance by the firm after installation is a required part of the earned criterion.

In terms of the realizability criterion, the SEC requires that the price is fixed or determinable and there must be persuasive evidence that an arrangement exists. This means that if the ordinary practice of a provider is to obtain a signed contract, then a signed contract must be obtained or revenue cannot be recognized (even if the work is done and the client has verbally accepted the work and paid for the good or service.)

B. **Accounting and Auditing Enforcement Releases (AAER)**—These report the enforcement actions that have been taken against accountants, brokers, or others.

Example

AAER No. 1585 against WorldCom on its massive accounting fraud—this was the mechanism to publicly report that the SEC was taking action against WorldCom.

SEC Reporting Requirements

After studying this lesson, you should be able to:

1. Identify the main reporting requirements for the 1933 and 1934 Securities Acts.

2. Identify the forms used for registration of securities and subsequent reporting.

3. Identify the content that should be contained in these forms.

I. Introduction

A. The 1933 Securities Act requires publicly traded firms offering securities for sale to the public in primary and secondary markets to file a registration statement, and to provide each investor with a proxy statement before each shareholders' meeting.

B. The 1934 Securities Act regulates the trading of securities after they are issued and provides the requirements for periodic reporting and disclosures.

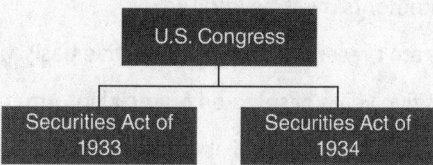

C. The formal SEC rules are found in the Code of Federal Regulations. All publicly traded companies (either public equity or public debt) must comply with the securities regulations. The governing regulations are Regulation S-X and Regulation S-K.

1. Regulation **S-X** governs the form and content of financial statements and **financial** statement disclosures. These include:

   a. Income statement

   b. Balance sheet

   c. Changes in shareholders equity

   d. Cash flow statement

   e. Footnotes to financial statements

   f. Qualification of accountants (independence rules)

2. Regulation **S-K** governs the form and content of **nonfinancial** statement disclosures. These disclosures are the content of the 10-K outside of the financial statements (remember that "S-K" governs the "10-K" nonfinancial statement content). The nonfinancial statement disclosures are

   a. Description of the business

   b. Description of stockholder matters

   c. Management's discussion and analysis (MD&A)

   d. Changes in and disagreements with accountants

   e. Information on directors and management

Definition of a Security: Section 2.1 of the 1933 Act defines a security as: "Any note, stock, treasury stock, bond, debenture, evidence of indebtedness, certificate of interest, or participation in any profit-sharing agreement, collateral trust certificate, reorganization certificate or subscription, transferable share, investment contract, voting trust certificate, certificate of deposit for a security, fractional undivided interest in oil, gas, or other mineral rights, or in general, any interest or instrument commonly known as a *security*, or any certificate of interest or participation in, temporary or interim certificate for, receipt of, guarantee of, or warrant or right to subscribe to or to purchase any of the foregoing."

II. Initial Registration of Securities—The Securities Act of 1933

A. A company that wants to sell debt or stock in interstate offerings to the general public is required to register those securities with the SEC. Registration requires extensive disclosures about the company, management, and the intended use of the proceeds from the issue. The intent of the securities laws is, in part, to regulate the disclosure of financial information by firms issuing publicly traded securities.

B. Form S-1 is the basic registration form for new securities and it includes a list of required disclosures. The financial information includes a balance sheet dated within 90 days of the filing. Part 1 on Form S-1 is the prospectus that is supplied to each potential purchaser of the security.

    1. A prospectus describes the issuing company, the business operations and risks, the financial statements, and the expected use of the proceeds. The basic financial statements requirements are:

        a. Two years of balance sheets

        b. Three years of income statements, statements of cash flow, and statements of shareholders' equity

        c. The financial statements must be audited.

        d. Prior statements are presented on a comparative basis.

        e. The SEC requires five years of selected financial information.

    2. Part 2 of Form S-1 includes information about the cost of issuing and distributing the security, more detailed information about the directors and officers and additional financial statement schedules.

C. Small registrations, under a certain monetary threshold or number of purchasers are considered to be private placements and are exempt from certain disclosures.

D. The offering process is diagrammed below:

> Issuer -> Underwriter -> Dealer -> Public

    1. The underwriter provides marking and distribution of the securities. The underwriter is often contractually obligated to sell the securities under one of the following arrangements:

        a. Firm commitment—The underwriter purchases the entire issue at a fixed price.

        b. Best efforts—The underwriter sells as many shares as possible.

       c. All or none—If the underwriter is unable to sell all (or a significant portion) then the issue may be canceled.

    2. Once the stock is issued, it may be traded over the counter by dealers or on an organized exchange.

III. Subsequent Reporting of Securities—The Securities Exchange Act of 1934

A. The 1934 Securities Exchange Act enacted reporting requirements for the purpose of fully disclosing relevant information about publicly traded firms. The SEC's reporting principles for information in the reports are found in Regulation S-X, Financial Reporting Releases (FRRs), and Staff Accounting Bulletins (SAB). Regulation S-X helps reduce redundancy in reporting by allowing for integrated disclosures whereby a company may satisfy certain Form 10-K disclosure requirements by referencing its shareholder annual report as long as that report includes the required disclosures. The following is a list of the most common required forms:

    1. Annual filing—Form 10-K

    2. Quarterly filing—Form 10-Q

    3. Report significant events affecting the company—Form 8-K

    4. Proxy Statement—The report by which management requests the right to vote through proxy for shareholders at meetings

B. Filing Deadlines. Filing deadlines depend on the size of the company. Company size is as follows:

1. **Large accelerated filer**—A company with worldwide market value of outstanding voting and nonvoting common equity held by nonaffiliates of $700 million or more;

2. **Accelerated filer**—A company with worldwide market value of outstanding voting and nonvoting common equity held by nonaffiliates that is $75 million or more but less than $700 million;

3. **Nonaccelerated filer**—A company with worldwide market value of outstanding voting and nonvoting common equity held by nonaffiliates less than $75 million.

Filing deadlines for filing after the reporting date are as follows		
Filer	10-K	10-Q
Large accelerated filer	60 days after fiscal year end	40 days after quarter end
Accelerated filer	75 days after fiscal year end	40 days after quarter end
Nonaccelerated filer	90 days after fiscal year end	45 days after quarter end

C. Form 10-K is the required vehicle for reporting annual financial information to the SEC. The 10-K is separated into four parts. The content of each part is outlined in the following chart:

Part I

1. Description of the business
    A. Risk factors
    B. Unresolved staff comments
2. Description of properties
3. Legal proceedings involving the company
4. Submission of matters to a vote of stockholders

Part II

5. Market price of common stock, dividends & stockholder matters
6. Selected financial data
7. Management's Discussion and Analysis (MD&A) of financial condition and results of operations
    A. Quantitative and qualitative disclosures about market risk
8. Financial statements and supplementary financial information
9. Change in disagreements with accountants on accounting and financial disclosure
    A. Controls and procedures

Part III

10. Directors and officers
11. Executive compensation and transactions with executives
12. Security ownership by certain beneficial owners and by management
13. Certain relationships and related-party transactions
14. Principal accountant fees and services

Part IV

15. Exhibits; signatures; certification

1. The SEC requires the Management's Discussion and Analysis (MD&A) to be included in its reporting and, as such, provides a discussion of important aspects of the firm from the viewpoint of management. This report covers the firm's financial condition, changes in financial condition, results of operations, liquidity, capital resources and operations, identifies trends and significant events and uncertainties. The discussion also includes information about the effects of inflation and changing prices in nonquantitative form, and explanation of significant or unusual events and uncertainties and their effect or expected effect on the firm's financial performance. Also, the firm's important accounting policies are discussed in the MD&A.

   a. Forward-looking or prospective information is included for the purpose of assessing future cash flows. Prospective information is useful to the financial statement user because it promotes understanding of events, circumstances, trends, and uncertainties when there are material trends and uncertainties. When material, prospective information is required to aid the analysis of long and short-term liquidity, capital resources, material changes in a line item on the financial statements, and any preliminary merger negotiations.

   b. Prospective information should be prepared in accordance with GAAP, using information that is consistent with the plans of the entity, and with due professional care so as not to mislead the user of the financial statements. Prospective financial statements should disclose information as to the purpose of the statements, assumptions, and significant accounting policies.

2. In general, SEC registrants must disclose more information to the SEC than in the annual reports to shareholders. For off-balance-sheet financing relationships, the SEC requires firms to disclose all contractual liabilities and contingent liabilities, whether they are recognized in the accounts.

D. Form 10-Q reports the quarterly information to the SEC within 45 days (nonaccelerated filer) of the end of the quarter. (Only the first three quarters are reported because the 10-K reports the annual information.) Large companies designated as accelerated filers must file within 40 days. Disclosures are less extensive than in the 10-K and include information for the specific quarter and year-to-date information.

   1. The quarterly report is intended to provide investors with an update since the last annual report. The 10-Q is not required to be audited, but must be reviewed by the independent auditor.

   2. The financial statements presented are:

      a. Balance sheet for the quarter and prior fiscal year end

      b. Quarterly and year-to-date income statements for this quarter and the same period in the previous year

      c. Cumulative year-to-date statements of cash flow for the current and prior fiscal years

E. Form 8-K reports significant events affecting the company such as material impairment, bankruptcy, entry or termination of a definitive agreement, changes in the registrant's CPA, changes in control etc. These are all events that the public shareholder should be aware of, as the events are significant enough to influence decisions.

F. Proxy statements are materials sent to the shareholders for vote. Proxy materials can address things such as election of directors, changes in the corporate charter, issuance of new securities, plans for a major business combination etc. Frequently these items are voted on during the shareholders annual meeting, but sometimes these matters need to be addressed during interim periods, in which case the proxy materials regarding the issue must be circulated.

IV. Corporate Governance

A. The Foreign Corrupt Practices Act of 1977 prohibits bribes of foreign governmental or political officials for the purpose of securing contracts or business. It requires publicly held companies to maintain an adequate system of internal control.

B. The Sarbanes-Oxley Act of 2002 (SOX) contains provisions to enhance corporate governance and to mitigate financial accounting abuses. A few of the significant provisions related to financial reporting are presented below.

1. The SEC requires registrants to have annual audits of their financial statements. The auditing firm must be registered with the Public Company Accounting Oversight Board (PCAOB), a private-sector organization created by the 2002 Sarbanes-Oxley Act (the SEC has oversight authority for the PCAOB). The PCAOB provides oversight of registered auditing firms.

2. Auditors are prohibited from providing nonaudit services to audit clients.

3. Audit committees are required to be composed of nonmanagement members of the board of directors, and the chair has to have financial experience.

4. Annual filing must include a management's report on the internal controls. This report must attest to the existence and effectiveness of the company's internal controls over corporate reporting.

5. There are Increased penalties for fraud and white-collar crime. Willfully failing to maintain audit records for five years is a felony. Criminal charges can be brought against corporate officers who fail to certify financial reports or who willfully certify statements they know do not comply with SOX.

Earnings per Share

Introduction to Earnings per Share

This is the first of three lessons on earnings per share (EPS). This lesson provides the basic and diluted EPS calculations as well as the disclosure requirements.

After studying this lesson, you should be able to:

1. Complete a calculation of basic EPS.

2. Complete a calculation of diluted EPS.

3. Identify the disclosure requirements for EPS.

I. **Earnings per Share**—Only public entities are required to present earnings per share (EPS). Nonpublic entities often choose to present EPS, but are not required to do so. There are two EPS figures that firms disclose: basic and diluted. Basic EPS is the EPS based only on actual transactions for the year. Diluted EPS is a "worst-case" figure reflecting the potential dilution of stock options and convertible securities. EPS allows comparisons of performance for firms of any size.

II. **EPS Background**

A. EPS is computed only for common stock. It represents the amount of earnings on a per-share basis. If EPS were $4, this means that $4 of dividends could have been paid, on average, to each share of common stock outstanding during the year, from earnings in that year. It does not mean the firm is obligated to pay that much, or that it will pay that much. Also, actual common stock dividends paid do not reduce EPS.

B. There are **two different EPS figures**, each of which is reported for several intermediate subtotals in addition to net income.

> **Definitions**
> *Basic EPS (BEPS):* Includes only actual common shares outstanding.
>
> *Diluted EPS (DEPS):* Includes securities that may become common stock in the future, such as convertible stock and stock options, in addition to actual shares of common outstanding.

1. The securities that may become common stock in the future are called potential common stock (PCS) or potentially dilutive securities. If a firm has no PCS then only BEPS is reported.

C. **Disclosure of EPS—ASC 260** provides guidance on the disclosure of earnings per share information on the face of the income statement. This guidance is provided for companies with a simple capital structure and for those companies with a complex capital structure.

1. **Simple capital structure**—A simple capital structure is one in which the corporation only has common stock outstanding or one in which the corporation has common stock and nonconvertible preferred stock outstanding.

   a. **Formula**—If the corporation only has common stock outstanding, the Basic Earnings per Share (BEPS) is calculated by the formula shown below.

   > BEPS = (Net Income) / (Weighted Average Common Shares Outstanding)

   b. **Formula**—If the company has common stock and nonconvertible preferred stock outstanding, the Basic Earnings per Share is calculated by the formulas shown below.

> BEPS = (Net Income Available to Common) / (Weighted Average Common Shares Outstanding)
>
> BEPS = (Net Income – Preferred Stock Dividend) / (Weighted Average Common Shares Outstanding)

2. **Complex capital structure**

   a. A complex capital structure typically includes common stock, along with equity contracts and convertible securities. These securities may become common stock in the future and thus must be included in an EPS figure so that users can assess the impact of these potential changes on EPS.

   b. A company with a complex capital structure is required to disclose the Basic Earnings per Share and the Diluted Earnings per Share. This is called dual EPS reporting.

   > **Note**
   > *The potential common stock may affect both the numerator and denominator.*

      i. **Formula**—The Diluted Earnings per Share is calculated by the formula shown below, which includes the effects of potential common stock (PCS).

> DEPS = (Net Income Available to Common Adjusted for Effects of PCS) / (Weighted Average Common Shares Plus Shares Issuable from PCS)

> **Example**
> A convertible bond is a PCS. Under certain conditions, discussed below, they are assumed converted into common stock. If they were actually converted, no interest would be paid and net income (numerator of DEPS) would increase. Likewise, the common shares from conversion would have been outstanding, thus increasing the denominator of DEPS.

III. **Disclosure Requirements**

   A. EPS amounts (all after tax) must be disclosed for the following line items in the income statement:

	Simple Capital Structure (No PCS)	Complex Capital Structure (PCS Present)
On the face of the Income Statement		
1. Income from Continuing Operations	BEPS	BEPS and DEPS
2. Net Income	BEPS	BEPS and DEPS
Either on the face of the Income Statement or in Footnotes		
3. Discontinued Operations	BEPS	BEPS and DEPS

B. BEPS and DEPS for the first two amounts must be shown with equal prominence. The terms basic EPS and diluted EPS are not required terms. Earnings per share, and earnings per share-assuming dilution, are also acceptable.

C. Elaboration

1. As the previous table shows, the maximum EPS disclosures in a simple capital structure is three BEPS amounts and in a complex capital structure the maximum disclosure is three BEPS and three DEPS (or six total EPS amounts).

2. Financial statement users wishing to compute EPS for intermediate subtotals such as income before discontinued operations may do so with the required disclosures.

3. If BEPS and DEPS are equal, both are reported so that users know there are PCS but there was no material dilutive effect.

IV. Basic EPS—A Closer Look

A. Effect of Preferred Stock (numerator of BEPS)

> BEPS = (Net Income Available to Common) / Weighted Average Shares Outstanding
>
> BEPS = (Net Income – Preferred Stock Dividends) / Weighted Average Shares Outstanding

B. Preferred Stock Cumulative/Not

1. The amount of preferred stock dividends subtracted in the numerator of BEPS depends on whether the preferred stock is cumulative or not, and if not, on the amount declared in the period.

2. **Amount Subtracted Table**—Amount of Preferred Dividend Subtracted in EPS Numerator:

Study Tip
Most preferred stock is cumulative.

	Cumulative Preferred	Noncumulative Preferred
Current-period dividends declared	1 full year's dividends	Amount declared
Current-period dividends not declared	1 full year's dividends	None

3. *Cumulative* means that if a year's preferred dividend is not paid (skipped), no other dividends may be paid before the skipped dividends (dividends in arrears) are paid. Regardless of whether dividends are declared on cumulative preferred stock, one full year's dividends is subtracted from the numerator of BEPS because no common dividends can be paid on these earnings before the preferred dividends are declared. This also means that in a year in which dividends in arrears from a previous year are paid in addition to the current year dividend, still only one year is subtracted from the current-year BEPS numerator because BEPS in the previous year has already been reduced by the skipped dividends.

4. **Noncumulative preferred stock**—Receives dividends only if declared. Skipped dividends are never paid.

5. **Tax Effect**—There is no tax effect to consider for preferred stock dividends because dividends paid are not deductible for tax purposes.

6. **Examples**—A firm has had 1,000 shares of 7%, $100 preferred stock outstanding for several years. The annual dividend on the preferred is $7,000 = .07($100)(1,000). Year 4 is the current year.

a. The preferred stock is cumulative and there are no dividends in arrears. $7,000 is subtracted from income in computing BEPS whether or not the dividend is declared in Year 4. Even if only a partial dividend (say $4,000) is paid, the full $7,000 is subtracted.

b. The preferred stock is cumulative and there are two years' dividends in arrears. $7,000 is subtracted from income in computing BEPS whether or not the dividend is declared, and regardless of the amount declared.

c. The preferred stock is noncumulative. No dividends are declared in Year 4. There is no subtraction in computing Year 4 BEPS.

d. The preferred stock is noncumulative and $2,000 of dividends is declared in Year 4. Subtract $2,000 only.

e. The preferred stock is noncumulative, three years' dividends have been skipped, and $2,000 of dividends is declared in Year 4. Subtract $2,000 only.

Note
In all these cases, it is the amount of dividends declared that matters, not the amount paid.

Basic Earnings per Share

This is the second of three lessons on earnings per share (EPS). This lesson explains the calculation of weighted average shares outstanding used in the calculation of EPS.

After studying this lesson, you should be able to:

1. Complete a calculation of weighted average shares outstanding when there is stock issuance, repurchase, dividends, and splits.

I. **Weighted Average (WA) Computation (Denominator of BEPS)**

   A. The denominator of BEPS is the weighted average (WA) shares outstanding during the period (not the number outstanding at the end of the period unless there has been no change in the number of shares outstanding all year). Treasury shares purchased during the period reduce the WA. The reason for weighting the shares is that shares outstanding a longer portion of the year represent capital investment that has been working longer for the firm than shares outstanding a shorter portion of the year. The numerator of EPS is income, an amount representing the entire year. The income earned on the capital investment must be related to the period for which the investment was used by the firm.

   B. The calculation weights each change in shares for the portion of the period the new shares are outstanding (add), or for the period the shares were not outstanding as in the case of a purchase of treasury shares (subtract).

	# Shares
Shares outstanding January 1	2,000
Issue shares April 1	1,200
Purchase shares for treasury October 1	400
Issue shares December 1	120
Issue shares December 31	200

The WA shares outstanding (denominator of BEPS) =

$$2,000(12/12) + 1,200(9/12) - 400(3/12) + 120(1/12) = 2,810$$

   1. **Explanation**—The April 1 issuance caused 1,200 shares to be issued. These shares were outstanding 9 months. This is equivalent to 900 shares being outstanding the entire year. The shares issued December 31 were not outstanding for any period of time during the year and are not included in the WA. If the firm had no preferred stock and net income was $5,620 for the period, BEPS would be $2.00 ($5,620/2,810).

II. **Share Adjustments**—Stock dividends and splits are adjustments to the number of shares outstanding for all investors holding stocks.

   A. **Two for One Stock Split**—A 10% stock dividend gives an investor holding 1,000 shares an additional 100 shares. Each investor maintains the percentage of the firm previously owned. There are 10% more shares outstanding but each share is worth proportionately less. A two-for-one stock split doubles the number of shares outstanding but the value of each share is halved. These are not substantive changes in shares outstanding the way a new stock issuance is. They bring no resources into the firm.

   B. **General Rule WA Calculation**—All stock dividends and splits are assumed to have been outstanding since the inception of the firm. Apply the percentage of the stock dividend or the factor in a split (factor = 3 in a three-for-one split) to all changes in outstanding stock occurring before the stock dividend or split.

Example
Assume the data from the previous example, with the addition of a stock split and dividend:

Shares outstanding January 1	2,000
Issue shares April 1	1,200
Two-for-one stock split May 1	
Purchase shares for treasury October 1	400
30% stock dividend November 1	
Issue shares December 1	120
Issue shares December 31	200

The WA shares outstanding (denominator of BEPS) =

$$\{[2{,}000(12/12) + 1{,}200(9/12)]2 - 400(3/12)\}1.30 + 120(1/12)$$

$$= 7{,}420$$

The factor of 2 for the two-for-one split is applied to the shares outstanding at the beginning of the year and the April 1 issuance. The 30% stock dividend is likewise applied to all changes before it. The factor used is 1.30 because the 30% stock dividend increases the shares already outstanding on that date by 30%.

    C. Adjust for EPS—If a stock dividend or split occurs between the balance sheet date and issuance of the balance sheet, all share amounts are adjusted for EPS purposes.

III. Contingent Shares

    A. Shares that are issuable for little or no cash consideration upon satisfaction of certain conditions are contingent shares. They are considered outstanding as of the date the conditions have been met.

    B. Weighting Fraction Period—The weighting is for the fraction of the period the conditions were met.

Example
If 2,400 shares are issuable contingent on a particular performance measure that is met by the firm on August 1, then even though the shares may not be issued until the next period, 1,000 shares are included in the WA for BEPS for the current period ($2{,}400 \times 5/12$).

    C. Contingency—If the contingency is a future earnings level, no contingent shares are included in the WA of BEPS because the contingency cannot be met until a future period. The same holds for a current-period earnings level because the contingency cannot be met until the last day of the year.

IV. Illustration of BEPS Reporting

Example

All amounts after-tax:

		Common stock:
Income from continuing operations	$40,000	Shares outstanding Jan.1: 10,000
Discontinued operations (net)	(10,000)	Issued 2,000 shares May 1
		Issued 20% stock dividend June 14
		Purchased 1,000 treasury shares July 1
Net income	$42,000	

The firm has 1,000 shares of 4%, $100 par cumulative preferred stock. No dividends were declared on the preferred stock in this year.

WA shares = $[10,000 + 2,000(8/12)]1.2 - 1,000(6/12) = 13,100$. This value is used for all EPS figures.

Annual preferred dividend requirement: $1,000($100)(.04) = $4,000$

Presentation of EPS:

Income from continuing operations: ($40,000 − $4,000)/13,100	$2.75
Discontinued operations: ($10,000/13,100)	(.76)
Net income ($30,000 − $4,000)/13,100 (rounded)	$1.99

Note

Only income from continuing operations and net income subtract the preferred dividends from the numerator. The discontinued operations are not income amounts but rather individual components on a per-share basis.

V. Additional Example—The following example is provided for additional practice. You should verify the calculations for practice.

Example
This example shows an alternative way to compute the weighted average shares. The Simple Company is located in Knoxville, Tennessee and has an accounting year that ends on December 31 of each year. A modified income statement for the 20X7 accounting year is presented below.

Income from Continuing Operations	$1,500,000
Discontinued Operations (less Income Tax Expense of $90,000)	210,000
Net Income	$1,710,000

The tax rate for 20X7 was 30%.

The capital structure of the Simple Company includes common stock and nonconvertible, cumulative, preferred stock. Relevant information related to these securities is shown below.

Common Stock, Par Value of $1

Common Shares Outstanding on January 1, 20X7	270,000	Shares
Sold Common Shares on September 1, 20X7	18,000	Shares
Common Shares Outstanding on December 31, 20X7	288,000	Shares

Non-Convertible, Cumulative, 6% Preferred Stock, Par Value of $20
Preferred Shares Outstanding throughout the year 7,500 Shares

Requirement: Determine the earnings per-share disclosure for the 20X7 accounting year.

Preferred Stock Dividend: $7,500 \times \$20 \times 6\% = \$9,000$

Weighted Average of Common Shares Outstanding:

Shares		Months	
270,000	$\times$	8	2,160,000
288,000	$\times$	4	1,152,000
		12	3,312,000

$3,312,000/12 = 276,000$ Shares*

Basic Earnings Per Share Calculation:

Income from Continuing Operations	($1,500,000 − $9,000)/276,000	=	$5.40
Discontinued Operations	$210,000/276,000	=	0.76
Net Income	($1,710,000 − $9,000)/276,000	=	$6.16

*This agrees with the calculation method shown in the previous discussion: 270,000 + 18,000(4/12) = 276,000

Diluted Earnings per Share

This is the third of three lessons on earnings per share (EPS). This lesson presents how to incorporate potentially dilutive securities into the diluted EPS calculation.

After studying this lesson, you should be able to:

1. Calculate the potentially dilutive effect of convertible preferred stock on basic EPS.

2. Calculate the potentially dilutive effect of stock options and warrants using the *treasury stock method* on basic EPS.

3. Calculate the potentially dilutive effect of multiple dilutive securities on basic EPS.

I. Diluted EPS—This measure takes into consideration the effect of all potentially dilutive common shares outstanding during the period. It is an imaginary calculation based on events that have not happened as of the balance sheet date. The diluted EPS number is valuable to the financial statement user as it reflects the effects of securities that may become common stock in the future.

II. Background

> **Definition**
> *Diluted EPS (DEPS):* Reflects the maximum dilution or **lowest value of EPS** that is possible given the firm's outstanding securities at the balance sheet date.

    A. Effect PCS into BEPS—DEPS incorporates the effect of potential common stock (PCS). PCS are securities that can become common stock in the future and are incorporated into BEPS. There may be both numerator and denominator effects. BEPS is used as the benchmark value into which the numerator and denominator changes stemming from PCS are incorporated. Thus, DEPS equals BEPS adjusted by the effects of PCS.

III. How Potential Common Stock Affects EPS

> **Note**
> An important thing to remember is that PCS is not common stock at the balance sheet date. They are assumed to be exercised (stock options and warrants) or converted (convertible preferred stock and bonds) as of the beginning of the year (or date of issuance if later). Upon assumed exercise or conversion, the numerator and denominator effects are computed, and are considered for incorporation into EPS.

> **Example**
> A firm has 10, 8%, $1,000 convertible bonds outstanding the entire period. Each bond is convertible into 20 shares of common stock. The tax rate is 30%. At the beginning of the period, the bonds are assumed converted. The result is that interest of $560 after tax would not have been paid $(10)(\$1,000)(.08)(1 - .30)$. That is the numerator effect. The denominator effect is the 200 shares of common stock that would be issued on conversion $(10)(20)$.

IV. Dilution and Antidilution

    A. Diluted PCS—Only dilutive PCS are incorporated into DEPS.

        1. Explanation—This means when we add the numerator effect of a PCS to the numerator of BEPS, and the denominator effect to the denominator of BEPS, the result is a lower EPS number. A dilutive PCS means that DEPS is lower than BEPS as a result of assumed conversion or exercise of the PCS.

B. **An antidilutive PCS** (one that increases EPS when it is added into BEPS) is ignored for purposes of computing DEPS.

C. **Control Number**—For purposes of testing for dilution and antidilution, the control number is income from continuing operations.

Example

1. BEPS = $1,000/2,000 = $.50. A potential common stock is assumed converted and the numerator and denominator effects are $200 and 500, respectively. DEPS = ($1,000 + $200)/(2,000 + 500) = $.48. The numerator and denominator effects are added to the numerator and denominator of BEPS. In this case, the PCS is dilutive because DEPS is lower than BEPS. BEPS would be reported at $.50 and DEPS would be reported at $.48.

BEPS = $1,000/2,000 = $.50. A potential common stock is assumed converted and the numerator and denominator effects are $200 and 300, respectively. DEPS = ($1,000 + $200)/(2,000 + 300) = $.52. In this case, the PCS is antidilutive because DEPS is higher than BEPS. The PCS is not entered into BEPS. BEPS = DEPS in this case.

2. Income from continuing operations is $1,200 and the WA shares outstanding is 2,400. A loss from discontinued operations of $200 is also reported, resulting in net income of $1,000. The firm has a PCS with no numerator effect but a denominator effect of 200 (200 shares issuable on exercise).

Income from continuing operations	BEPS	DEPS
$1,200/2,400 =	$.50	
$1,200/2,600 =		$.462
Discontinued operations loss		
$200/2,400 =	(.083)	
$200/2,600 =		(.077)
Net income		
$1,000/2,400 =	$.417	
$1,000/2,600 =		$.385

The EPS amounts above would be reported as shown. However, the result for the discontinued operations is antidilutive because the DEPS result (negative .077) is larger (less negative) than for BEPS (negative .083). Because the result is dilutive for income from continuing operations (the control number), all EPS amounts use the same denominator.

Conversely, if income from continuing operations is negative and including the denominator effect of a PCS in the calculation of DEPS for that income figure causes it to be less negative (larger), then no PCS is assumed converted for any income amount. BEPS = DEPS in this case, for all amounts to be shown on a per-share basis.

V. **Treasury Stock Method**—Incorporating stock options and warrants into DEPS

A. To enter stock options and warrants (which are PCS) into DEPS, a three-step process is used called the *treasury stock method*.

Example
Assume a firm's BEPS = $1,200/700 = $1.71. The firm has 2,000 stock options outstanding the entire year. The exercise price is $30. The average market price of common stock for the period is $40.

1. Assume exercise of the options. Shares issued on exercise = 2,000.

2. Purchase treasury shares with the proceeds from exercise: 2,000($30)/$40 = number of treasury shares purchased = (1,500).

3. Incremental shares = denominator effect = 500.

Divide the total proceeds from exercise [$60,000 = 2,000($30)] by the average price per stock the firm would be required to pay for its own shares ($40). The result is that the firm would buy back 1,500 of its own shares. The net number of new shares outstanding as a result of the treasury stock method is 500. DEPS = $1,200/(700 + 500) = $1.00. DEPS is less than BEPS. Therefore, the options are dilutive and are entered into DEPS.

The purpose of assuming the purchase of treasury stock is to reduce the total dilution from exercise. Otherwise, the denominator effect would be 2,000, not 500. There is no numerator effect.

B. **Antidilutive Options**—Options are antidilutive when the option price exceeds the market price. In the above example, if the average market price were $25, the three steps would produce a negative number, causing DEPS to increase. The easy way to remember this is that no one would exercise such a stock option and pay more than market price.

VI. **If-Converted Method**— This method incorporates convertible securities into DEPS.

A. The convertible security is assumed converted as of the beginning of the period or date of issuance, whichever is later. The numerator and denominator effects are computed and entered into DEPS. If DEPS decreases, the PCS is dilutive and the security is included in the computation of DEPS.

Example
(Convertible bonds) BEPS for a firm is $3,000/1,000 = $3.00. The firm also has 10, 8%, $1,000 convertible bonds outstanding the entire period. Each bond is convertible into 20 shares of common stock. The tax rate is 30%. At the beginning of the period, the bonds are assumed converted under the if-converted method. The numerator effect is the interest of $560 after tax that would not have been paid (10)($1,000)(.08)(1 − .30). The denominator effect is the 200 shares of common stock that would be issued on conversion (10)(20). DEPS = ($3,000 + $560)/(1,000 + 200) = $2.97. DEPS is less than BEPS. Therefore, the bonds are dilutive and are entered into DEPS.

C. **Interest Expense**—If the bonds were sold at a discount or premium, interest expense will reflect periodic amortization. The interest expense recognized should be added back (after tax), not the cash interest paid, because earnings was reduced by the expense.

D. **Issued Midyear**—If the bonds were issued at midyear, the numerator and denominator effects each would be multiplied by one half, resulting in smaller increases to the BEPS numerator and denominator.

E. **No Tax Effect**—Convertible preferred stock is handled the same way as convertible bonds except there is no tax effect.

Example
Net income is $3,400 and WA shares are 700. The annual preferred dividend claim on convertible preferred stock is $400 and if converted, 100 common shares would be issued. In computing BEPS, convertible preferred stock is treated just like nonconvertible preferred stock.

BEPS = ($3,400 − $400)/700 = $4.29

The numerator effect is the dividends that would not be paid if the convertible preferred stock were converted. The denominator effect is the common shares issued on conversion.

DEPS = ($3,400 − $400 + $400)/(700 + 100) = $4.25

The $400 of dividends is added back (after being subtracted in calculating BEPS) in calculating DEPS. DEPS is less than BEPS. Therefore, the convertible preferred stock is dilutive and is entered into DEPS.

VII. The Dilution/Antidilution Method—This method is used when there is more than one PCS.

    A. Two or More PCSs—The previous examples have used only one PCS. What happens if there are two or more? Which one is entered into BEPS first? The solution is to incorporate the PCS into DEPS in order of most dilutive first, then the next dilutive PCS, and so forth. The PCS with the most dilutive potential is the one with the lowest ratio of numerator effect/denominator effect (N/D).

    B. Process—The process is to enter the PCS with the lowest N/D into DEPS first. Then compare the next lowest N/D with the resulting DEPS. Continue to add PCS into DEPS until a PCS is encountered with a higher N/D than the previous DEPS figure, or until all PCS are entered. Use income from continuing operations as the control number.

Example
Data for Year 5:

Income from Continuing Operations	$26,000
Discontinued Operations after tax	12,000
Net Income	$38,000

Common stock shares outstanding all period: 10,000

BEPS for income from continuing operations = $26,000/10,000 = $2.60

Potential Common Stock Outstanding All Periods:	Numerator Effect	Denominator Effect	Numerator/ Denominator (N/D)
Warrants	$0	2,000	$0
Convertible bonds issue A	3,000	1,000	3.00
Convertible bonds issue B	2,000	1,500	1.33

The warrants are considered first because the ratio of its numerator effect to denominator effect (N/D) is the lowest of the three.

Income from continuing operations is used as the control number. The warrants are entered into DEPS for income from continuing operations because its N/D of $0 is less than BEPS. The tentative DEPS = ($26,000 + $0)/(10,000 + 2,000) = $2.17.

The convertible bonds issue B is the next to consider because it has the second lowest N/D. Its ratio is $1.33 which is less than the tentative DEPS of $2.17 and thus is entered into DEPS. The new tentative DEPS = ($26,000 + $0 + $2,000)/(10,000 + 2,000 + 1,500) = $2.07.

The convertible bonds issue A is not entered into DEPS because its N/D exceeds the previous tentative DEPS of $2.07. Thus, the final DEPS for income from continuing operations is $2.07. This process thus determines the denominator for all DEPS numbers.

Complete EPS Presentation for This Firm:

	BEPS	DEPS
Income from Continuing Operations	$2.60	$2.07
Discontinued Operations		
$12,000/10,000	1.20	
$12,000/(10,000 + 2,000 + 1,500)		.89
Net Income		
$38,000/10,000	$3.80	
($38,000+ $0 + $2,000)/(10,000 + 2,000 + 1,500)		$2.96

VIII. Additional Examples—This section provides an example Income Statement and analysis of the stock options. You should verify the calculations for practice.

Example

The Complex Company is located in Knoxville, Tennessee and has an accounting year that ends on December 31. A modified income statement for the 20X7 accounting year is presented below.

Income from Continuing Operations	$1,500,000
Discontinued Operations (less Income Tax Expense of $90,000)	$210,000
Net Income	$1,710,000

The tax rate for 20X7 was 30%.

The capital structure of the Complex Company includes common stock, nonconvertible, cumulative, preferred stock, and stock options. Relevant information related to these securities is shown below.

Common Stock, Par Value of $1

Common Shares Outstanding on January 1, 20X7	270,000 Shares
Sold Common Shares on September 1, 20X7	18,000 Shares
Common Shares Outstanding on December 31, 20X7	288,000 Shares

Non-Convertible, Cumulative, 6% Preferred Stock, Par Value of $20

Preferred Shares Outstanding throughout the year	7,500 Shares

Stock Options—The options represent 6,000 shares. The option price is $20. The average market price for the 20X7 accounting year is $25. The stock options were outstanding for the entire 20X7 accounting year.

Requirement: Determine the earnings per share disclosure for the 20X7 accounting year.

Solution: Preferred Stock Dividend:

$7,500 \times \$20 \times 6\% = \$9,000$

Weighted Average of Common Shares Outstanding

Shares		Months	
270,000	$\times$	8	2,160,000
288,000	$\times$	4	1,152,000
		12	3,312,000
			3,312,000 /12 = 276,000 Shares*

*This agrees with the calculation method shown in the previous discussion: 270,000 + 18,000(4/12) = 276,000

Analysis of Stock Options—Treasury Stock Method

1. Since the average market price is greater than the option price, the stock options are dilutive.

2. To determine the impact of the stock options on the Diluted Earnings per Share Calculation, the treasury stock method is applied.

Step 1: The Stock Options are assumed exercised and 6,000 new shares are issued at $20 per share.

Step 2: The cash from the exercise of the stock options, $120,000, is used to purchase treasury stock at the average market price for the period (6,000 × $20 = $120,000). The number of treasury shares would be 4,800 shares ($120,000/25 = 4,800).

Under step 1, 6,000 new shares would be issued, and under Step 2, 4,800 shares would be acquired. The net increase in shares outstanding would be 1,200 shares, the denominator effect.

Effect of the Stock Options

Adjustment to the Numerator:	$0.00
Adjustment to the Denominator	1,200 shares
N/D Ratio $0/1,200:	$0.00

Basic Earnings per Share Calculation

Income from Continuing Operations

($1,500,000 − $9,000)/276,000 = $5.40

Discontinued Operations

$210,000/276,000 = $0.76

Net Income

($1,710,000 − $9,000)/276,000 = $6.16

Diluted Earnings per Share Calculation

Income from Continuing Operations

($1,500,000 − $9,000)/(276,000 + 1,200) = $5.38

Discontinued Operations

($210,000/276,000 + 1,200) =   0.76

Net Income

($1,710,000 − $9,000)/(276,000 + 1,200) = $6.14

 **Example**
This example has both nonconvertible preferred and convertible preferred.

Background/Requirement
The Complex Company is located in Knoxville, Tennessee and has an accounting year that ends on December 31. A modified income statement for the 20X7 accounting year is presented below.

Income from Continuing Operations	$1,500,000
Discontinued Operations (less Income Tax Expense of $90,000)	$210,000
Net Income	$1,710,000

The tax rate for 20X7 was 30%.

The capital structure of the Complex Company includes common stock, nonconvertible and convertible, cumulative, preferred stock. Relevant information related to these securities is shown below.

Common Stock, Par Value of $1

Common Shares Outstanding on January 1, 20X7	270,000 Shares
Sold Common Shares on September 1, 20X7	18,000 Shares
Common Shares Outstanding on December 31, 20X7	288,000 Shares

Nonconvertible, Cumulative, 6% Preferred Stock, Par Value of $20

Preferred Shares Outstanding throughout the year	7,500 Shares

Cumulative, Convertible 4% Preferred Stock, Par Value of $10

Preferred Shares Outstanding throughout the year	5,000 Shares

The preferred stock is convertible at the rate of 5 common shares for one preferred share.

Requirement: Determine the earnings per share disclosure for the 20X7 accounting year.

Solution: Preferred Stock Dividend on Nonconvertible Preferred Stock:

$7,500 \times \$20 \times 6\% = \$9,000$

Weighted Average of Common Shares Outstanding:

Cumulative, Convertible 4% Preferred Stock, Par Value of $10

Preferred Shares Outstanding throughout the year	5,000 Shares

Shares		Months	
270,000	×	8	2,160,000
288,000	×	4	1,152,000
		12	3,312,000
			3,312,000 /12 = 276,000 Shares*

*This agrees with the calculation method shown in the previous discussion: 270,000 + 18,000(4/12) = 276,000

214

Analysis of the Convertible Preferred Shares—If-Converted Method

To analyze the impact of the convertible preferred shares on the Diluted Earnings per Share Calculation, the If-Converted Method is applied.

Convertible Preferred Stock Dividend:	$5,000 \times \$10 \times 4\% =$	$2,000
Common Shares That Would be Issued Upon Conversion:		
	$5,000 \times 5 =$	25,000 Shares
Adjustment to the Numerator		$2,000
Adjustment to the Denominator		25,000 Shares
N/D Ratio	$2,000/25,000 Shares =	$0.08

Basic Earnings per Share Calculation:

Income from Continuing Operations	($1,500,000 − $9,000 − $2,000)/276,000 =	$5.39
Discontinued Operations	$210,000/276,000 =	.76
Net Income	($1,710,000 − $9,000 − $2,000)/276,000 =	$6.16

Diluted Earnings per Share Calculation

Note

Since the N/D ratio of the convertible preferred shares is less than the basic earnings per share for income from continuing operations, the convertible preferred shares will have a dilutive effect.

Income from Continuing Operations	($1,500,000 − $9,000)/(276,000 + 25,000) =	$4.95
Discontinued Operations	($210,000)/301,000 =	.70
Net Income	($1,710,000 − $9,000)/(276,000 + 25,000) =	$5.65

Example

This example shows the EPS disclosure for an accounting year. Example: The Complex Company is located in Knoxville, Tennessee and has an accounting year that ends on December 31. A modified income statement for the 20X7 accounting year is presented below.

Income from Continuing Operations	$1,500,000
Discontinued Operations (less Income Tax Expense of $90,000)	210,000
Net Income	$1,710,000

The tax rate for 20X7 was 30%.

The capital structure of the Complex Company includes common stock, nonconvertible, cumulative, preferred stock, and convertible bonds. Relevant information related to these securities is shown below.

Common Stock, Par Value of $1

Common Shares Outstanding on January 1, 20X7	270,000	Shares
Sold Common Shares on September 1, 20X7	18,000	Shares
Common Shares Outstanding on December 31, 20X7	288,000	Shares

Non-Convertible, Cumulative, 6% Preferred Stock, Par Value of $20

    Preferred Shares Outstanding throughout the year   7,500 Shares

6% Convertible Bonds Payable

    Total Face Value of Outstanding Bonds $1,000,000

    The bonds were outstanding throughout the year

    The bonds are convertible to common shares at the rate of 50 shares for each $1,000 bond.

Requirement: Determine the earnings per share disclosure for the 20X7 accounting year.

Solution: Preferred Stock Dividend on Non-Convertible Preferred Stock: $7,500 \times \$20 \times 6\% = \$9,000$

Weighted Average of Common Shares Outstanding

Shares		Months	
270,000	$\times$	8	2,160,000
288,000	$\times$	4	1,152,000
		12	3,312,000
			3,312,000 /12 = 276,000 Shares*

*This agrees with the calculation method shown in the previous discussion: $270,000 + 18,000(4/12) = 276,000$

Analysis of the Convertible Bonds—If-Converted Method

To analyze the impact of the convertible bonds on the Diluted Earnings per Share Calculation, the If-Converted Method is applied.

Bond Interest Expense

    $\$1,000,000 \times 6\% = \$60,000$

Bond Interest Expense, Net of Tax

    $\$60,000 (1 - .30) = \$42,000$

Common Shares That Would be Issued Upon Conversion:

    $(1,000,000/\$1,000) \times 50 \text{ Shares} = 50,000$

Adjustment to the Numerator	$42,000		
Adjustment to the Denominator	50,000	Shares	
N/D	$42,000/50,000	Shares	= $0.84

Basic Earnings Per Share Calculation:

Income from Continuing Operations	($1,500,000 − $9,000)/276,000 =	5.40
Discontinued Operations	$210,000/276,000 =	.76
Net Income	($1,710,000 − $9,000)/276,000 =	$6.16

Diluted Earnings per Share Calculation:

Note

Since the N/D ratio of the convertible bonds is less than the basic earnings per share for income from continuing operations, the convertible bonds will have a dilutive effect.

Income from Continuing Operations

	($1,500,000 − $9,000 + $42,000)/(276,000 + 50,000) =	$4.70
Discontinued Operations	$210,000/326,000 =	.64
Net Income	$1,710,000 − 9,000 + 42,000)/326,000 =	$5.35

Example

In the last three examples (Complex Company), if the firm had all three potential common stock securities at the same time (stock options, convertible preferred shares, and convertible bonds payable), the equity contracts and convertible securities would be ranked in order of N/D ratio, from lowest to highest. Based on the data from the previous examples this rank ordering is shown below.

Security	N/D
Stock Options	$0.00 = $0/1,200
Convertible Preferred Shares	$0.08 = $2,000/25,000
Convertible Bonds	$0.84 = $42,000/50,000

The calculation of DEPS for income from continuing operations is as follows (all EPS figures are for income from continuing operations):

BEPS = ($1,500,000 − $9,000 − $2,000)/276,000 = $5.39

First, enter the stock options into DEPS because the N/D ratio of $0.00 is less than $5.39. The tentative DEPS figure = ($1,500,000 − $9,000 − $2,000)/(276,000 + 1,200) = $5.37.

Second, enter the convertible preferred into DEPS because the N/D ratio of $.08 is less than $5.37. The tentative DEPS figure = ($1,500,000 − $9,000 − $2,000 + $2,000)/(276,000 + 1,200 + 25,000) = $4.93.

Last enter the convertible bonds into DEPS because the N/D ratio of $.84 is less than $4.93. The tentative DEPS figure = ($1,500,000 − $9,000 − $2,000 + $2,000 + $42,000)/(276,000 + 1,200 + 25,000 + 50,000) = $4.35.

This is the reported amount for DEPS for income from continuing operations.

Earnings per Share and IFRS

This lesson presents the significant differences in the accounting for earnings per share (EPS) under IFRS versus U.S. GAAP.

After studying this lesson, you should be able to:

1. Identify the major differences in the accounting for EPS under U.S. GAAP versus IFRS.

I. **EPS and IFRS**

A. There are a few significant differences in the accounting for EPS under U.S. GAAP than according to IFRS. The table below summarizes these differences.

U.S. GAAP	IFRS
For diluted EPS, dilution potential of ordinary shares determined cumulatively year to date	For diluted EPS, dilution potential of ordinary shares determined independently each period
Basic and diluted EPS are not allowed for alternative earnings measures.	Basic and diluted EPS can be shown on alternative earnings measures.

B. **Potentially Dilutive Securities**—The number of potentially dilutive securities is determined independently for each reporting period and not a weighted average of the dilutive potential common stock for each interim period. Therefore, the number of potentially dilutive securities in the annual or year-to-date report may not equal the potentially dilutive securities in the interim period. Under U.S. GAAP the year-to-date diluted EPS uses a year-to-date weighted average of the shares included in each quarter.

C. **Alternative Measures of Earnings**—IFRS permits presentation in the footnotes EPS information based on alternative measures of earnings. U.S. GAAP does not allow this reporting and the SEC restrict the use of non-GAAP measures.

Segment Reporting

The disclosure requirements for firms with different business segments are considered here.

After studying this lesson, you should be able to:

1. Define an operating segment.

2. Explain how a reportable segment is identified using three quantitative tests.

3. Articulate the 75% rule for reporting.

4. List the major items to be disclosed for a reportable segment.

5. Apply the quantitative tests in an actual situation.

I.   Operating Segments

A. Financial statements provide highly aggregated information. For a firm that conducts activities in several different lines of business, users would benefit from disclosures that provide more disaggregated information. To that end, GAAP requires, under certain circumstances, that information be provided by major business segment.

B. Under GAAP, business segments are identified by employing a management approach. That is, segments are identified in the same manner that management segments the company for purposes of making operating decisions. These segments are referred to as operating segments.

C. Operating segments must have three characteristics.

   1. The segment is involved in revenue producing and expense incurring activities.

   2. The operating results of the segment are reviewed by the company's chief operating decision maker on a regular basis.

   3. There is discrete financial information available for the segment.

D. Not all subunits of a corporation are operating segments. The corporate headquarters would not be an operating segment for many firms for example.

> **Note**
> *The purpose of segment reporting is to assist the financial statement users' understanding of the entity's performance. Because segment reporting provides disaggregated information, it contains predictive value and confirmatory value to the financial statement user.*

II.   Identification of Reportable Segments—Quantitative Tests—A

reportable segment is one that meets one or more of the following three quantitative tests. Not all operating segments are reportable segments. Disclosure is required only for reportable segments.

> **Note**
> *In the past, the quantitative tests have been the most frequently tested aspect of segment reporting.*

A. The operating segment's revenue from all sources (internal and external) is 10% or more of the combined (internal and external) revenues of all of the company's reported operating segments.

B. The operating segment's operating profit or loss (absolute value) is 10% or more of the greater of the following two amounts (absolute value). Operating profit is pretax.

   1. The combined operating profit of all operating segments that did not report an operating loss

   2. The combined loss of all operating segments that did report an operating loss

C. The operating segment's identifiable assets are 10% or more of the combined assets of all operating segments.

III. Aggregation of Two or More Segments

A. For the quantitative tests, two or more segments can be aggregated provided this aggregation is consistent with the objective of segment reporting, and the segments are similar in each of the following areas:

Note
Each of the three criteria uses 10% or more as the cutoff percentage. The 10% cutoff is an example of a GAAP-imposed materiality threshold.

1. The nature of products and services

2. The nature of the production processes

3. Customer type or class

4. Distribution methods for products and services

5. The nature of the regulatory environment

Example
If a firm has three major department stores in various parts of the country, each of which meets the operating segment definition, the stores can be aggregated into a single reportable segment to avoid excessive reporting.

IV. Reportable Segments—the 75% Rule—The total external revenue reported by reportable segments must be at least 75% of the company's total consolidated revenues. This is an overall materiality threshold for reporting.

A. If this test is not met initially, more reportable operating segments must be identified, even if the additional segments do not meet one of the three quantitative tests.

B. There is no stated limit on the number of reportable segments, but as a practical matter, if the number reaches ten, then the firm should assess whether adding more segments is worth the cost.

V. Reportable Segments—"All Other" Category—All nonreportable segments are grouped into an *all other* category and their results are combined for reconciliation purposes.

VI. Reportable Segments—Required Disclosures—The required disclosures for reportable segments include the following (note that operating segments that are not reportable segments are not subject to these reporting requirements). Note also that the information reported reflects the way the firm reports information internally, which may not always be in conformity with GAAP. However, this approach was considered to be more useful than a pure GAAP-based reporting model.

A. Factors used to identify operating segments

B. General information about the products and services of the operating segments

C. Internal and external sales revenue

D. A measure of profit or loss, and total assets

E. The nature of differences between the measurement of segment quantitative information such as income and assets, and the measurement of the firm's reported quantitative information.

F. Interest revenue

G. Interest expense

H. Depreciation, depletion, and amortization expense

I. Other significant noncash items

J. Unusual or infrequent items

K. Equity in net income of investees, in which the investment is accounted for under the equity method

L. Income tax expense or benefit

M. Reconciliation of the totals of segment revenues, reported profit or loss, assets, and other significant items to the total for the firm as a whole

N. Capital expenditures

VII. Other Required Disclosures—If the following information is not already provided through the required segment information, firms must separately disclose the following:

A. Revenues from external customers from each product and service or groups of similar products or services

B. Revenues from the home country of the firm and from all foreign countries in total. If the revenues from one foreign country are material, then those revenues are to be disclosed separately.

C. The same disclosure as B above is required for long-lived assets other than financial instruments, long-term customer relationships with a financial institution, mortgage and other servicing rights, and deferred tax assets.

D. Major customers: If the revenue from a single customer amounts to 10% or more of the firm's revenues, this fact must be disclosed, including the amount of revenues from each such customer, and the operating segment or segments that earn that revenue. The identity of the customer need not be disclosed.

VIII. Comprehensive Example

Example

The Smith Company has four operating segments that are identified below. Information related to the current accounting year is also shown below. The revenue column constitutes the firm's entire revenues.

Segment	Total Revenues	Operating Profit (Loss)	Identifiable Assets
Clothing	$200	$50	$100
Sports Equipment	$150	($60)	$90
Beverage	$50	($10)	$25
Furniture	$300	$150	$200
Totals	**$700**	**$130**	**$415**

Additional information: Revenues related to internal transactions totaled $20. Of this amount, $10 of revenues was recorded by the clothing segment and $10 was reported by the furniture segment.

Revenue test: 10% of $700 = $70

Reportable Segments: Clothing, Sports Equipment, and Furniture

Operating profit test: 10% of $200 = $20

Note: The combined operating profit for those segments with positive profit ($200) exceeded the absolute value of the combined operating loss for those segments with losses ($70). Therefore, $200 is used for the test.

Reportable Segments: Clothing, Sports Equipment, and Furniture.

Note that sports equipment has an operating loss but the absolute value of that loss exceeds the $20 test amount.

Identifiable asset test: 10% of $415 = $41.5

Reportable Segments: Clothing, Sports Equipment, and Furniture.

Clothing, sports equipment, and furniture all meet at least one of the tests described above and are reportable segments. Only beverages is not a reportable segment (but it is an operating segment). The results for each of the three quantitative tests are shown above for completeness but an operating segment need meet only one of the tests in order to qualify as a reporting segment.

75% Test:

75% of $680 = $510. ($680 = $700 − $20 internal revenue). Consolidated revenues are computed by removing intersegment revenues.

(The $680 amount is the firm's external revenue.)

External Revenue of Clothing Segment	$190
External Revenue of Sports Equipment Segment	$150
External Revenue of Furniture Segment	$290
Total External Revenue	**$630**

The 75% Test is met collectively by the three reportable segments because $630 equals or exceeds $510. No additional reportable segments need be identified.

IX. U.S. GAAP–IFRS Differences

A. The international standard for segment reporting conforms in most respects with the corresponding U.S. standard adopted several years before the IASB's standard. One important difference is that, for reportable segments, the international standard requires disclosure of total liabilities if that information is provided to the firm's chief operating decision maker.

B. Liabilities are also included in the reconciliations of segment information with total firm data.

Interim Financial Reporting

Interim Reporting Principles

Update Notice: In July 2015, the FASB issued ASU 2015-11 Inventory (Topic 330)—*Simplifying the Measurement of Inventory*. The ASU changes the application of lower of cost or market (LCM) in the subsequent valuation of inventory. For testing effective on or after January 1, 2017 the subsequent measurement of inventory is either lower of cost or market or lower of cost or net realizable value. Please note the content eligibility in the lesson "Subsequent Measurement of Inventory." In 2017, the subsequent measurement of inventory depends on the inventory valuation method.

The first of two lessons about interim reporting develops the basic principles and provides guidance on specific reporting topics.

After studying this lesson, you should be able to:

1. Explain the underlying approach to interim reporting.

2. List examples of applying that underlying approach.

3. Note exceptions to the underlying approach.

4. Compute income tax expense for interim periods.

5. Describe the application of the lower-of-cost-or-market procedure for interim periods.

I. **Background and General Approach to Interim Reporting**—Why interim reporting? *Timeliness* is one of our enhancing characteristics of accounting information.

  A. Interim reports are not audited although for SEC registrants the reports are reviewed—a more limited procedure relative to an audit. As such, interim reports must be analyzed with more caution, compared with annual reports. Interim reports tend to be less accurate, subject to greater estimation error due to the shorter period involved, and are less complete. However, they improve the timeliness (time period assumption) of financial reporting.

  B. The general reporting philosophy for interim reports is that interim periods are to be viewed as an integral part of the annual period, rather than as a separate or discrete period. This principle guides many of the specific accounting principles. For example, materiality is determined with reference to annual reports, not to amounts in interim reports.

  C. In general, firms must use the same accounting methods (e.g., LIFO, straight-line depreciation) for interim reporting as they do for annual reporting.

  D. **Interim Relates to Annual**—When investors read an interim report, they are interested in evaluating the interim period as it relates to the annual period.

    1. Thus, when more than one interim period is affected by an expenditure for example, the related expense is recognized in the periods benefited, rather than recognized in the period cash was paid.

    2. There are exceptions to this principle, however. Although the integral view is required by GAAP, the *discrete* view—considering each interim reporting period as a separate period—is applied in several situations. The following material first highlights items that reflect the discrete view. The later items exemplify the integral view.

  E. **Interim Period Length**—Interim periods can be of any length less than a year; they are not limited to three-month periods (quarterly periods) although for SEC registrants, the quarterly report (10-Q) is the focus of interim reporting. Revenues earned and realizable in an interim period are recognized in that interim period.

  F. The following table summarizes the general rule for recognition during interim periods.

Item	General Rule	Exceptions
Revenues	Same basis as annual reports	None
Cost of Goods Sold	Same basis as annual reports	1. Gross profit method may be used to estimate CGS and ending inventory for each interim period. 2. Liquidation of LIFO base-period inventory, if expected to be replaced by year end, should be charged to CGS at expected replacement cost. 3. Temporary declines in inventory market value not recognized, but must recognize other than temporary declines in interim period of decline 4. Planned manufacturing variances should be deferred if expected to be absorbed by year-end.
All Other Costs and Expenses	Same basis as annual reports	Expenditures which clearly benefit more than one interim period may be allocated among periods benefited, e.g., annual repairs, property taxes
Income Taxes	Estimate annual effective tax rate	None
Discontinued Operations	Recognized in interim period as incurred	None

II. **Revenue Recognition**—Revenues are recognized in each interim period, as they would be in an annual period. Revenues earned and realizable in an interim period are recognized in that interim period.

   A. A firm uses the percentage of completion method on long-term contracts. The profit recognized each quarter is based on the percentage of completion at the end of each quarter. If a loss is anticipated in quarter 3, the entire contract loss is recognized in quarter 3.

   B. Earnings Per Share (EPS) is reported under the discrete view. Each quarterly EPS amount reflects only the events of that quarter. The assumptions and computations leading to the quarterly EPS amount reflect the circumstances within each interim period separately, rather than estimations of year-end circumstances. For example, shares issued in the third quarter affect reported EPS for the third and fourth quarter only, not the first two quarters.

III. **Expense Recognition**

   A. The general rule for expense recognition is:

   1. If the cost or expense has no relationship to other quarters, recognize the entire expense in the quarter in which the cost was incurred (the discrete view).

      a. **Examples**

         i. Discontinued operations net of applicable tax (if a component qualifying for discontinued operations reporting is considered held for sale in a particular quarter, the usual discontinued operations reporting is required for that quarter with later adjustments to any gain or loss recognized in those later quarters)

         ii. Gains and losses on disposals of plant assets

      b. These items have no relationship to interim periods other than the one in which they occurred.

      c. Arbitrary allocation of these items to other quarters is not permitted.

2. If the cost or expense benefits other quarters or interim periods, allocate the cost to those other quarters and recognize the appropriate amount of expense in those quarters (the integral view).

    a. **Examples**

        i. Depreciation

        ii. Property tax expense

        iii. Rent expense if prepaid for longer than one interim period

        iv. Advertising expense if expenditures benefit more than one interim period

        v. Bad debt expense if the firm uses an annual estimation procedure

    b. These expenses are allocated to the interim periods benefited even though some may be paid in full in one interim period, because they benefit more than one interim period.

    c. Repairs and maintenance expenditures may be cyclical with significant expenditures in one quarter benefiting the entire year. If the expenditures are planned to cover an annual period (or longer), then each interim period should recognize only its portion of the total expenditure as expense.

B. **Expenses Directly Related to Revenue**—Expenses directly related to revenue (cost of goods sold, sales commissions) are recognized in the same period as the related revenue.

C. **Income Tax Expense**—Firms face a graduated annual income tax rate. The final rate(s) applicable to annual income is not known until the end of the year.

    1. The income tax expense (which is computed only for income from continuing operations) for each interim period is computed as follows:

        a. The annual rate to be applied to income from continuing operations is re-estimated each quarter (the rate does not consider the tax on discontinued operations, which would be reported in the quarter these items were incurred, at the incremental rate at the time).

        b. That rate is applied to total interim income through the end of the current quarter, yielding total estimated tax to date.

        c. The income tax reported in previous quarters is subtracted from the results in the second step to yield the income tax expense for the current quarter.

        d. This procedure is a good example of the integral view of interim reporting—the interim period is an integral part of an annual period.

Example
Income tax recognized for quarter 1 is $20,000, based on the annual rate that is expected to apply to the firm. At the end of quarter 2, the expected annual income tax rate is 30% and pretax income for the first two quarters is $130,000.

Income tax expense to be recognized for quarter 2 only is $19,000 (.30 × $130,000 − $20,000).

IV. **Declines in Inventory Application to Interim Reports**—The decline in the value of the inventory is determined by applying either the lower of cost or net realizable value (LC –NRV) or the lower of cost or market (LC-M) approach. See the Inventory lesson "Subsequent Measurement of Inventory" for further discussion on the application of these methods.

A. **Temporary declines** in inventory are those expected to reverse by year's end.

    1. These are not recognized as losses in the interim periods in which they occur. This treatment is consistent with the integral view of interim reporting.

2. No loss is expected for the year; therefore, a temporary loss should not be recognized in a specific quarter.

3. Later recoveries are not recorded because the previous loss was not recorded.

B. **Permanent declines** in inventory are those not expected to reverse in the current year are recognized as losses in the interim periods in which they occur.

1. Later recoveries are recognized as gains to the extent of previous losses only.

2. The inventory may not be marked up above cost.

C. **Related Questions**

Question
An inventory loss (decline in inventory value below cost) is incurred in quarter 2 but is expected to be recovered by year-end. However, it was not actually recovered by the end of the year. In what interim periods is the loss recognized?

Answer
The loss is recognized in quarter 4 because it was expected to be temporary as of the end of quarter 2 and no loss was recognized then.

Question
An inventory loss occurred in the first quarter and was not expected to reverse in the current year. But the loss was recovered in the second quarter with the market price increase exceeding the decline from the first quarter. How should this be treated in the interim reports for quarters 1 and 2?

Answer
Write the inventory down in quarter 1, recognize the loss, and then write it back up in quarter 2 but only to cost, recognizing a gain.

Interim Reporting—Details and IFRS

> **Update Notice:** In July 2015 the FASB issued ASU 2015-11 Inventory (Topic 330)—*Simplifying the Measurement of Inventory*. The ASU changes the application of lower of cost or market (LC-M) in the subsequent valuation of inventory. For testing effective on or after January 1, 2017 the subsequent measurement of inventory is either lower of cost or market or lower of cost or net realizable value. The new rules are tested beginning in 2017.
>
> The second lesson on interim reporting addresses additional financial reporting topics, and international standards.
>
> **After studying this lesson, you should be able to:**
>
> 1. Describe the reporting of LIFO liquidations and cost accounting variances in interim reports.
>
> 2. Explain the application of interim reporting principles to accounting changes.
>
> 3. List the minimum reporting requirements for interim reports.
>
> 4. Note the underlying approach to interim reporting for international standards.
>
> 5. List differences in interim reporting under the two sets of standards for specific reporting topics.

I. **LIFO Liquidation**—If a firm uses LIFO for annual reporting, it must also use LIFO for interim reporting. When a LIFO layer is liquidated in a particular interim period (number of units purchased is less than number of units sold in the interim period), the accounting depends on whether the liquidation is expected to be restored by the end of the annual period.

   A. **Restoration Expected**—If the liquidation is expected to be restored, then the interim period cost of goods sold should reflect the estimated cost of the replacement (this preserves the effect of LIFO for the interim period during which the liquidation took place). The firm recognizes an increase in cost of goods sold and recognizes a provision (liability) for the future purchase. This liability is extinguished in a later interim period when the inventory is replenished. As a result, overestimated earnings are avoided. Also, the ending inventory for the interim period reflects the restoration. This is another example of the integral view of interim reporting.

   B. **Restoration Not Expected**—If the liquidation is not expected to be restored, then the interim period cost of goods sold should reflect the actual cost of the layer liquidated.

II. **Cost Accounting Variances**—Purchase price variances, and volume variances expected to be absorbed by the end of the current year are deferred (not recognized in earnings) for the interim period.

   A. This is consistent with the integral view of interim reporting because there is no variance expected for the year.

   B. The reason for the deferral is that, from the point of view of the entire reporting year, there will be no volume variance.

   C. If the variances will not be absorbed (reversed) by other purchases of material or by increased production later in the year, they are recognized in the quarter of incurrence.

III. **Gross Margin Method for Inventory**—The gross margin method (also called the gross profit method) is not allowed for annual reporting purposes, but can be used for interim reporting. This method uses the gross margin percentage to estimate cost of goods sold from purchase information. The estimated cost of goods sold then is used to estimate ending inventory for the quarter without having to count inventory. Footnote disclosure of the use of this method is required.

IV. Principle Changes

A. A change in accounting principle made in an interim period is reported in the same way as for annual statements. The retained earnings balance at the beginning of that interim period is adjusted to reflect the new principle, and the balances of previous interim periods reported comparatively with the interim period of change are retrospectively adjusted.

Example
A new accounting principle is adopted in quarter 3. The beginning retained earnings balance for quarter 3 is adjusted to reflect the new method up to that point, and quarter 1 and 2 statements are retrospectively adjusted to reflect the new principle.

B. Impracticability Exception—However, the impracticability exception for annual periods does not apply to prechange interim periods in the year the change was made. When it is impracticable to apply the retrospective method to prechange interim periods of the same fiscal year, then the change is made as of the beginning of the subsequent fiscal year.

C. For interim periods after an accounting principle change, the effect of the principle change on income from continuing operations and net income, and related per share amounts are shown.

Example
If an accounting principle change is adopted in the second quarter, these disclosures are required for the last three quarters of the fiscal year.

V. Estimate Changes

A. A change in estimate is accounted for in the interim period in which the change in estimate is made. Earlier interim periods are not affected. If material, the effect of the change on net income for the interim period and subsequent periods is reported.

Example
A change in property, plant, and equipment useful lives is made in quarter 3. The new estimate is applied as of the beginning of quarter 3. The effect of the change on earnings for quarter 3 is reported in quarter 3 results. The new estimate is also applied to quarter 4 and the effect of the change on quarter 4 earnings is reported.

VI. Interim Reports and Segment Reporting—When a firm subject to the segmental disclosure requirements issues interim reports, the following interim information is required to be reported for each segment:

A. External revenues (other than from intersegment sales)

   1. Intersegment revenues.

   2. Segment profit or loss.

VII. Reporting Requirements

A. GAAP does not require interim reports. However, the SEC requires that registrants file the 10-Q report for each quarter. Also, quarterly reports are provided as supplemental information within the annual report.

B. If non-SEC registrants choose to report interim financial statements, there is no requirement that the statements be as complete as annual statements. As a result, there is considerable variation in the detail reported. The FASB encourages the reporting of an interim balance sheet and statement of cash flows. Larger firms tend to provide more complete information. When the fourth quarter interim report is not provided, the annual report should disclose significant events for that quarter, along with material adjustments at year's end including unusual or infrequent items or discontinued operations.

C. If an interim report is provided, the minimum required disclosures include information about:

1. Sales and other revenue, unusual or infrequent items, discontinued operations, net income

2. Seasonal revenues and expenses allowing users to assess the impact on both the interim period and annual period

3. Changes in estimated income tax expense

4. Contingencies

5. Fair value

6. Earnings per share

7. Changes in accounting principle and estimates

8. Significant cash flow changes

D. Cumulatives and Comparatives—At any interim period, the financial statements would present the cumulative results as well as the comparative for the prior year.

1. For example: reporting as of June/30 (Quarter 2):

   a. Income Statements (4):

      i. Income Statement for Quarter 2 (and prior year Q 2)

      ii. Cumulative Income Statement for 1/1—6/30 (and Comparatives for prior year)

   b. Balance Sheets (3):

      i. Balance Sheet as of 6/30 (and Comparatives for prior year)

      ii. Balance Sheet as of 12/31/prior year's end

   c. Statement of Cash Flows: (4)

      i. Statement of Cash Flows for Quarter II (and Comparatives for prior year)

      ii. Cumulative Statement of Cash Flows for 1/1—6/30 (and Comparatives for prior year

VIII. U.S. GAAP–IFRS Differences

A. Whereas the stated preference in U.S. reporting for interim statements is the integral view (with major exceptions), international standards have a stated preference for the discrete view, again with major exceptions. For example, assessments of materiality are made with reference to interim amounts (a lower threshold than for U.S. standards). However, neither reporting system is a pure approach.

B. One of the guiding interim reporting principles for international standards is that all recognized accounts for interim purposes must meet their IFRS definitions in the interim period. The same process for estimates, accruals, deferrals and allocations made at the end of an annual period apply to each interim period. This provision of the international standards reflects the preference for the discrete view, and is in contrast with U.S. standards.

1. **Assets**—For an expenditure in one interim period to be capitalized (and thus result in some expensing in a later interim period), the expenditure must meet the definition of an asset in the first interim period. Allocations of expenditures to more than one interim period as expense are not allowed, unless an asset exists at the end of the interim period. The balance sheet view prevails here rather than matching.

2. **Liabilities**—Accrual of planned expenses at the end of an interim period before an expenditure is made (e.g., planned maintenance to be paid for later in the same annual period) is not permitted unless the firm has a liability at the end of the interim period. Thus, international standards do not allow the allocation of accrued expenses between interim periods unless there is a liability at the end of an interim period.

> **Example**
> A year-end bonus for management is not accrued in earlier interim periods unless there is a legal or constructive obligation for the bonus, and a reliable estimate of the amount can be made.

C. Revenues are recognized when earned and realizable. As a result, interest revenue is accrued in interim periods before receipt of cash, but dividend revenue is not because dividends are not mandatory—no liability exists on the part of the issuing firm until the dividends are declared.

1. The cyclical nature of a revenue does not warrant deferral in an interim period simply because more sales revenue, for example, is recognized in one period and less is recognized in another.

D. Similar to U.S. standards, interim period income tax expense is computed on an annualized basis (integral view). For international standards, entities must estimate the average annual effective tax rate for the full fiscal year, and apply it to each quarter. Anticipated tax rate changes and the pattern of earnings must be taken into account. When the entity is subject to taxation from more than one jurisdiction, or is subject to more than one rate across categories of income, the entity is allowed to use a weighted average rate across jurisdictions and income categories provided that this process results in a reasonable approximation to the more exact calculation.

E. Specific examples of the discrete view applied in international standards:

1. The deferral of manufacturing variances that are expected to be offset in a later interim period within the same annual period is not allowed.

2. The deferral of a temporary market decline in inventory expected to be recovered in a later interim period within the same annual period is not allowed.

3. Volume rebates and other anticipated changes in the costs of inventory to be purchased for the year can be anticipated (allocated over the year) only if the cost adjustments are contractual.

F. **International Reporting Requirements**—Neither U.S. nor international standards require interim financial statements. Depending on the country, securities regulators, governments or stock markets may require interim reports, however. In the U.S., quarterly reports are required for publicly traded firms. In other countries, semi-annual reporting is more common.

1. If the entity (a) provides full interim statements as required by a securities regulator or other entity, or (b) voluntarily provides such statements described as complying with international standards, the statements must comply with IFRS.

2. If full statements are not provided, the headings and subtotals should include those presented in the most recent annual statements. Basic and diluted EPS must be reported if the entity is subject to EPS requirements for its annual statements (publicly traded firms).

3. International standards encourage publicly traded firms to provide semi-annual reports at a minimum. Firms are required to use the same accounting policies for interim reporting as they do for annual reports if they provide interim reports.

4. If a report is provided, the minimum reporting requirements include the following condensed financial statements: statement of comprehensive income, balance sheet, statement of cash flows, and statement of changes in equity.

5. The footnotes should include information about the following, if material:

   a. Statement of accounting policies

   b. Cyclical revenues and expenses

   c. Unusual items

   d. Changes in estimates

   e. Changes in debt and equity securities

   f. Dividends paid

   g. Segment information

   h. Subsequent events

   i. Contingencies

   j. Changes in composition of consolidated enterprises

| Major Differences ||
U.S. GAAP	IFRS
Based on integral view.	Based on discrete view.
Allocation of costs over each Q.	Must meet definition of asset in order to allocate.

| Major Differences ||
U.S. GAAP	IFRS
Can defer cost variances if recovery expected.	Cannot defer cost variances.
Can defer decline in inventory value if recovery expected.	Cannot defer decline in inventory value.

Special Purpose Frameworks

Cash, Modified Cash, Income Tax

In addition to the GAAP-based general-purpose financial statements described in prior lessons, there are other comprehensive bases of accounting that may be used by nonpublic business entities, specialized entities, and individuals to prepare financial statements. This lesson covers the major non-GAAP comprehensive basis of accounting used by nonpublic business entities. These bases of accounting are referred to as Other Comprehensive Basis of Accounting (OCBOA) or Special Purpose Frameworks.

This lesson covers accounting for the major non-GAAP comprehensive basis of accounting used by nonpublic business entities. A separate lesson covers the auditing of financial statements prepared using a "comprehensive basis other than GAAP" as set forth in SAS 800, *Special Considerations—Audits of Financial Statements Prepared in Accordance with Special Purpose Frameworks.* It should be noted that the cash, tax, and regulatory bases of accounting are commonly referred to as other comprehensive bases of accounting (OCBOA). The term OCBOA was replaced with the term *Special Purpose Framework* for auditors under SAS 800. OCBOA is no longer used in Generally Accepted Auditing Standards (GAAS). However, OCBOA is still commonly used in practice. A separate lesson is presented by Professor Don Tidrick, author of the Auditing and Attestation section of CPAexcel®.

After studying this lesson, you should be able to:

1. Identify each separate basis of accounting:

   Cash Basis

   Modified Cash Basis

   Income Tax Basis

   Other

2. Describe the characteristics of each separate accounting basis.

3. Know how each separate accounting basis differs from GAAP.

I. **Special Purpose Framework or Other Comprehensive Bases of Accounting**—General-purpose financial statements, as described in prior lessons, are based on generally accepted accounting principles (GAAP) for public business enterprises. There are circumstances, however, when financial statements not based on GAAP are used by nonpublic business entities to avoid the time-consuming and costly application of GAAP. For example, another comprehensive basis of accounting (other than GAAP) may be used by sole proprietorships, partnerships or small, closely held corporations when the entity does not have loan covenants or other requirements that mandate the preparation of GAAP-based financial statements. There are over 2.8 million partnerships and over 20 million sole proprietorships in the United States. Many of these nonpublic businesses use another comprehensive basis of accounting. The primary acceptable other comprehensive bases of accounting widely used by nonpublic businesses entities, including cash basis, modified cash basis, and income tax basis, are covered in the following subsections. There are several categories of Special Purpose Framework or OCBOA financial statements:

> Cash Basis
>
> Modified Cash Basis
>
> Income Tax Basis
>
> Regulatory Basis
>
> Other Basis with Substantial Support

A. Cash Basis Financial Statements

1. Cash basis financial statements are based solely on cash receipts and cash disbursements. In a pure cash basis of accounting, revenues are recognized only when cash is received and expenses are recognized only when cash is disbursed. The principles of accrual accounting are ignored. In cash basis accounting, there is no attempt to recognize revenues when they are earned and no attempt to recognize expenses when they are incurred, nor is there a matching of related expenses to revenues or to the time period in which they would be recognized in accrual basis accounting.

2. Because, in a pure cash basis of accounting, cash received is recognized as revenue (DR. Cash/CR. Revenue) and cash paid is recognized as expense (DR. Expense/CR. Cash), a balance-sheet-like statement would show only the asset Cash and Equity; there would be no other assets or liabilities shown. For example, a payment for capital assets (e.g., property, plant, or equipment) would be recognized as an expense, not as a long-term asset. Similarly, a collection of cash would be recognized as revenue, whether or not the good or service had been provided.

3. Example Journal Entries for Equipment Purchase of $10,000:

Cash Basis		Accrual Basis	
Equipment Expense	10,000	Equipment (asset)	10,000
Cash	10,000	Cash	10,000

4. A pure cash basis accounting and resulting financial statements may be appropriate for small, very closely held businesses (e.g., sole proprietorships, small partnerships, etc.) where the owners/managers whose primary interest and even survival depends on cash flows.

B. Modified Cash Basis Financial Statements

1. Modified cash basis financial statements result from using a combination of elements of cash basis accounting and accrual basis accounting. Conceptually, modified cash basis accounting would be any point on a continuum between pure cash basis at one end and full accrual basis at the other; the greater the number of accrual basis elements adopted, the greater the modification of the cash basis.

2. A modified cash basis of accounting is acceptable as another comprehensive basis of accounting if the modification(s) has substantial support in practice. Substantial support likely would be established if:

    a. The modification is equivalent to an element of accrual basis accounting, and

    b. The modification is logical and consistent with GAAP.

3. The most common and acceptable modifications to cash basis accounting include:

    a. Recognizing the acquisition of property, plant, equipment and inventory as assets (rather than as expenses), and depreciating, amortizing, or otherwise writing-off the assets in a regular manner, or

    b. Recognizing accounts receivable when revenues are earned and accounts payable when obligations are incurred, rather than deferring recognition until collections are received or payments are made, or

    c. Recognizing income taxes (and, perhaps, other significant taxes) when they become payable, rather than when paid.

4. When modifications to cash basis accounting are made, all related accounts must be reported using the same basis of accounting. For example, if long-term assets are recognized, then the related depreciation expense and accumulated depreciation must be recognized. Similarly, if debt is recognized, then the related interest expense (accrued and paid) must be recognized.

C. Income Tax Basis Financial Statements

1. Income tax basis financial statements result from using the federal income tax rules and regulations that a firm uses, or expects to use, in filing its income tax return. In income-tax basis accounting, the effects of events on a business are recognized when taxable income or deductible expense would be recognized on the tax return. Income is recognized on the financial statements in the period it is taxable and expenses are recognized on the financial statements in the period they are deductible. The specific requirements of federal income tax accounting specify different income and expense recognition rules depending on the nature of the item and the type of taxpayer. Therefore, financial statements based on the income tax basis of accounting will include items based on various recognition principles, from pure cash to full accrual accounting, depending on that tax codes treatment of these items.

2. Some items of economic and accounting consequence to an entity are never recognized for tax purposes. These are commonly called permanent differences. For example, proceeds from life insurance on officers or portions of intercompany dividends are not taxable income to an entity but provide cash to the entity. Similarly, the premium on life insurance on officers and certain fines are not deductible for income tax purposes but require the payment of cash. Under the income tax basis of accounting, nontaxable receipts (revenue) and nondeductible payments (expenses) related to these permanent differences generally would be recognized in a statement of revenues and expenses. That recognition may be made in one of three ways:

   a. As separate line items in the revenue and/or expense sections of the statement of revenues and expenses (the most common treatment)

   b. As separate line items shown as additions to or deductions from the net revenues and expenses

   c. The nature and amounts disclosed in the notes to the financial statements

3. Because items and amounts reported for tax purposes are subject to adjustment by the Internal Revenue Service (IRS), the corresponding amounts reported in tax-based financial statements are subject to change as the tax code is changed by U.S. Congress. Therefore, the notes to the financial statements should clearly indicate not only the basis on which the statements were prepared, but also that they are subject to change as a result of IRS determinations. When such adjustments do occur, the treatment in the financial statements will depend on the nature of the item adjusted.

   a. If the adjustment relates to an error in the tax return of a prior year, then a prior period adjustment is appropriate.

   b. If the adjustment relates to an item that is not an error and is not balance sheet related, then the adjustment would be treated as a current-period expense (or income).

   c. If the adjustment relates to an item that is not an error and is balance-sheet related, then the adjustment would be treated as a prior period adjustment.

D. Other Acceptable Non-GAAP Basis of Accounting—In addition to the cash basis, the modified cash basis, and the income tax basis of accounting, two additional categories of other comprehensive basis of accounting exist. These additional categories of OCBOA are:

1. A basis of accounting used to comply with a regulatory agency that has jurisdiction over the reporting entity. Regulatory financial statements do fall under the category of a Special Purpose Framework for audit purposes.

   a. Examples would include financial statements filed with state insurance or public utility regulatory agencies.

b. Regulatory-based financial statements should be restricted to use by the entity and the regulatory agency.

2. There also may be financial statements that we have not covered. These financial statements are prepared using a basis with a definite set of accounting and reporting criteria that has substantial support and which is applied to all material financial statement items. One example of these might be financial statements that had price level or inflation adjusted financial statements.

Private Company Council

The purpose of this lesson is to provide a description of the Private Company Council (PCC), its purpose, and the process for setting standards applicable to private companies. This lesson presents the definition of a Public Business Entity and the significant Accounting Standard Updates (ASUs) that relate to private companies.

After studying this lesson, you should be able to:

1. Describe the purpose of the PCC and its role in the standard-setting process.

2. Describe the definition of a public business entity.

3. Identify and describe the significant accounting differences for private companies.

I. **PCC Purpose**—In May 2012, the Financial Accounting Foundation (FAF) approved the establishment of the Private Company Council (PCC), an organization that will assist in setting accounting standards for private companies. The PCC has two principal responsibilities:

    A. To work with the Financial Accounting Standards Board (FASB) to identify places within existing Generally Accepted Accounting Principles (GAAP) where there are opportunities for alternative accounting for private companies.

    B. To serve in an advisory capacity to the FASB on the appropriate treatment of items under consideration for new GAAP and how those items may impact private companies.

II. **What Is a Public Business Entity?**

    A. The PCC provides a definition for a public business entity because any entity that is not public is a private entity. It may seem kind of backward to not give a definition of a private entity but to give a definition of a public entity, but it is easier to define the characteristics of a public entity and therefore identify what entities cannot apply the standards set by the PCC.

    B. The definition excludes not-for-profit companies and employee benefit plans. A public entity is one that (ASC 2013-12, para. 2):

        1. Is required by the SEC to file or furnish financial statements;

        2. Is required by the Securities Act of 1934 to file or furnish financial statements with a regulatory agency other than the SEC (for example debt securities);

        3. Is required to file or furnish financial statements with foreign or domestic regulatory agencies in order to sell or issue securities;

        4. Has issued securities that are traded, listed, or quoted on an exchange or over-the-counter market; *or*

        5. Has securities that are not subject to contractual restrictions and is required by law, contract, or regulation to prepare U.S. GAAP financial statements and make them publicly available on a periodic basis.

    C. The stand-alone financial statements of a subsidiary consolidated with a public company are not considered public business entities for purposes of its stand-alone financial statements. However, the subsidiary is considered a public business for purposes of the financial statements that are included in an SEC filing.

III. **PCC Process**

    A. PCC reviews existing U.S. GAAP and identifies standards that require reconsideration. Any proposed alternative GAAP requires a two-thirds vote of all PCC members.

    B. Proposed modifications to U.S. GAAP approved by the PCC are submitted to the FASB for endorsement. If endorsed by a simple majority of FASB members, the proposed modifications will be exposed for public comment. Following receipt of public comment, the PCC will determine if any changes are warranted and take a final vote. If approved, the final decision then will be submitted to the FASB for final approval.

C. If the FASB does not endorse the initial proposal or final modification, the FASB will provide to the PCC documentation describing the reason(s) for the non-endorsement and possible changes for the PCC to consider.

IV. The PCC Framework

A. The PCC Framework is used to determine whether, and in what circumstances, private companies should have guidance for alternative recognition, measurement, disclosure, display, effective date, and transition reporting under U.S. GAAP. The differences between private companies and public companies are a driving force in determining whether alternative GAAP is warranted.

B. The Framework provides direction to evaluate the trade-off between user-relevance and cost-benefit for private companies. To help identify information needs of users of public company financial statements versus users of private company financial statements, the Framework outlines five factors that differentiate the needs of the financial statement users. These factors can help identify opportunities to reduce the complexity and costs of preparing financial statements for private companies.

1. Number of primary users and their access to management

2. Investment strategies of the primary users

3. Ownership and capital structure

4. Accounting resources available to generate reporting and disclosure information

5. Resources available for learning about new financial reporting guidance on a timely basis

C. The Framework discusses the areas in which financial accounting and reporting guidance might differ for private companies and public companies:

1. The main areas of guidance for private company accounting are with respect to (a) recognition and measurement, (b) disclosures, and (c) presentation.

V. Adoption and Transition to PCC Standards

A. In 2016, the FASB revised the adoption and transition guidance for the adoption of the private company standards.

1. In essence, private companies can elect to adopt any of the PCC alternatives at the beginning of any annual period with no retrospective application. No retroactive application upon adoption significantly simplifies the adoption of a PCC accounting alternative and makes the PCC accounting much more accessible to private companies.

2. In addition, the adoption of the PCC alternative can be done without assessing the preferability of the PCC alternative. Eliminating the need to assess preferability provides private companies with greater flexibility when deciding whether or not to adopt PCC accounting.

VI. Accounting for Goodwill (ASU 2014-02)

A. This ASU allows a private entity to amortize goodwill on a straight-line basis over 10 years, or less than 10 years if it is more appropriate. This means that the entity does not have to complete annual impairment testing. At the time of adoption of this standard, the entity must make an election to test goodwill impairment at the entity level or the reporting unit level.

B. The private entity must complete impairment testing when a triggering event occurs. When that event occurs, the private entity must apply the impairment test following the guidance for a public entity. That is, the private entity has the option to apply the prestep qualitative assessment prior to the quantitative assessment. The measurements under the quantitative two steps are applied in the same manner as required under ASC 350.

VII. Simplified Accounting for Interest Rate Swaps (ASU 2014-03)

    A. This simplified hedge accounting applies only to interest rate swaps for variable rate debt to fixed rate debt (cash flow hedge). Many private companies have difficulty obtaining fixed rate debt at a competitive interest rate. Therefore these companies frequently enter into an interest rate swap to convert the variable rate debt to fixed rates.

    B. When certain criteria are met, the private entity can assume the swap is 100% effective. This assumption significantly reduces the testing needed for assessing and measuring ineffectiveness. The criteria are (815-20-25-131D):

        1. Both the variable rate on the swap and the borrowing are based on the same index and reset period.

        2. The terms of the swap are typical (a "plain-vanilla" swap), and there is no floor or cap on the variable interest rate of the swap unless the borrowing has a comparable floor or cap.

        3. The repricing and settlement dates for the swap and the borrowing match or differ by no more than a few days.

        4. The swap's fair value at inception (i.e., at the time the derivative was executed to hedge the interest rate risk of the borrowing) is at or near zero.

        5. The notional amount of the swap matches the principal amount of the borrowing. In complying with this condition, the amount of the borrowing being hedged may be less than the total principal amount of the borrowing.

        6. All interest payments occurring on the borrowing during the term of the swap are designated as hedged whether in total or in proportion to the principal amount of the borrowing being hedged.

    C. When these criteria are met, the private entity can use the practical expedient of settlement value to measure the value of the swap versus measuring the swap at fair value. Settlement value excludes the adjustment for performance risk and is generally viewed to be a simpler valuation.

    D. The private entity must complete documentation requirements related to cash flow hedge accounting and must comply with the disclosure requirements for hedge accounting (Topic 815) and fair value (Topic 820).

    E. This standard can be applied to existing swaps if the swap had a fair value at or near zero at the time the swap was initiated. The swap does not need to have a fair value at or near zero at the date the standard is elected. After the initial election, the entity cannot apply this standard to other swaps that existed at the date of election. In other words, once this standard is adopted, the entity must identify those existing swaps to which it wants to apply the standard. After application, the entity cannot go back and apply to other existing swaps—the application should happen all at once rather than piecemeal.

VIII. Applying Variable Interest Entity (VIE) Criteria to Common Control Leasing Arrangements (ASU 2014-07)

    A. Private companies are not required to apply the criteria for determining whether there is a variable interest in certain leasing arrangements. This exemption applies when:

        1. The private company lessee and lessor are under common control;

        2. The private company lessee has a leasing arrangement with the lessor;

        3. Substantially all of the activity between the private company lessee and the lessor is related to the leasing activities; and

        4. The private company lessee explicitly guarantees any obligation of the lessor related to the leased asset.

B. If this exemption is elected it should be applied to all the leasing arrangements that meet the above conditions.

C. The private company does not need to provide the disclosures associated with a VIE, but rather would disclose the information related to the lease arrangement. The disclosure should include a description of the lease arrangements that exposes the private company lessee to provide financial support to the lessor.

IX. Simplified Accounting for Intangible Assets Acquired in a Business Combination (ASU 2014-18)

A. Private companies have the option to not recognize certain intangible assets associated with a business combination. Specifically, private companies can elect to not recognize customer-related intangibles that cannot be sold or licensed independent of the business (customer contracts and relationships) and noncompete agreements separately from goodwill. These intangible assets are costly and complex to value.

B. In general, the acquirer in a business combination must recognize all intangible assets that are (1) separable or (2) arise from contractual or other legal rights.

C. Private companies will be excluded from this requirement with respect to customer contracts, customer relationships, and noncompete agreements. Customer contracts that are nontransferable would not need to be separately valued and recognized. Customer relationships are often nontransferable because the relationship is unique with the private company. Noncompete agreements are also often nontransferable because the agreement is with an employee (or former employee) and the private entity. A noncompete agreement is a legal arrangement to prohibit another party from competing with the entity in a certain market for a certain period of time.

D. Private companies must recognize other identifiable intangibles such as copyrights, trademarks, and patents, separately from goodwill. In addition, customer-related intangibles that can be sold or licensed independent of other assets of the businesses must be recognized. For example, customer lists and other customer information that can be sold or licensed independently of the business would meet the separability criterion and would be valued and recognized as part of the business combination.

E. If the private company elects the PCC guidance on intangibles, it must also adopt the goodwill accounting alternative described above (ASU 2014-02), which requires goodwill to be amortized over a period of up to 10 years. The tandem requirement ensures that the customer-related and noncompete-related intangible assets embedded in goodwill are essentially amortized. The opposite is not required—if the private company elects to amortize goodwill, it does not have to elect this guidance on the intangible assets.

Select Financial
Statement Accounts

Cash and Cash Equivalents

Cash

This lesson presents a summary of the accounting for cash.

After studying this lesson, you should be able to:

1. Define cash and cash equivalents.

2. Define compensating balances.

3. List the two main internal controls over cash.

4. Identify the main difference in reporting cash under IFRS.

I. Articulation

    A. The balance sheet and the statement of cash flows:

        1. If a business enterprise uses the term **cash** on the statement of cash flows, the term used on the balance sheet will likewise be **cash**.

        2. If a business enterprise uses the term **cash and cash equivalents** on the statement of cash Flows, the term on the balance sheet will be **cash and cash equivalents**.

    B. A cash equivalent is a security with a fixed maturity amount and an original maturity to the purchaser of three months or less.

II. Accounting for Cash—The main reporting issue for cash is what to include in this category of assets. Several items are included in the cash account for balance sheet reporting purposes, and there are others that at first appear to be cash but are excluded.

    A. **Cash**—The current asset, represents unrestricted cash. This is cash that is available to meet current operating expenses and obligations as they arise.

        1. **Included in cash**—The components of cash include coin and currency, petty cash, cash in bank, and negotiable instruments such as ordinary checks, cashier's checks, certified checks, and money orders.

        2. **Current liability**—An overdraft of a bank account occurs when checks honored by the bank exceed the balance in the account. An overdraft may be offset against other cash accounts with the same bank, but not against cash accounts with other banks. In the latter case, the overdraft is listed as a current liability.

        3. **Excluded from cash**—Cash does not include certificates of deposit, legally restricted compensating balances, or restricted cash funds (such as a bond sinking fund). These amounts are either:

            a. Not available for the immediate payment of debts; or

            b. Management's intent is to use these resources for specific purposes. In addition, cash excludes postdated checks received from customers (include these in accounts receivable), advances to employees (a receivable), and postage stamps (a prepaid expense).

    B. **Cash Equivalents** —Although not cash, cash equivalents are so near cash that they are often combined with cash for financial statement reporting.

Example
Cash equivalents include: U.S. Treasury obligations (bills, notes, and bonds), commercial paper (very short-term corporate notes), and money market funds.

C. **Compensating Balance**—This is a minimum balance that must be maintained by the firm in relation to a borrowing. Such a balance increases the effective rate of interest on the borrowing and reduces the risk to the lender.

   1. With respect to compensating balances, if the balance is related to a short-term liability, the compensating balance is shown as a current asset (as in the example below), but is not considered a part of the unrestricted cash balance. If the compensating balance is related to a long-term liability, the compensating balance is a non-current asset.

> **Example**
>
> A firm borrows $10,000 for one year at 6% but must maintain a $700 compensating balance in an account with the lender financial institution. The $700 is not included in the cash account but is rather reported in restricted cash, a current asset. The annual effective interest rate is 6.45% [($10,000 x .06)/$9,300]. The net loan is only $9,300 ($10,000 – $700).

D. **Cash is a Monetary Asset**—A monetary asset is an asset with fixed nominal (stated) value. The nominal value of a monetary asset does not change with inflation. Cash is the most "monetary" of all assets. There is no uncertainty as to the stated or nominal value of cash at present or in the future. A $100 bill is always worth exactly $100. However, the purchasing power of cash declines with inflation. The amount of real goods and services a fixed amount of cash can buy decreases as the general price level increases. The effect is the opposite during times of deflation.

III. **Cash—The Importance of Internal Control Measures**

A. Because cash is easily concealed and has universal value, companies go to great lengths to safeguard their cash. A variety of internal control measures are used to safeguard cash.

B. The auditing section of this course considers these measures in detail. For cash, the most popular ones are:

   1. Separation of duties

   2. Bank reconciliations

C. **Separation of Duties**—Separation of duties makes it more difficult for employees to perpetrate fraud and gain access to the firm's cash.

   1. Separation of Duties, in effect, forces employees to collude if they attempt to fraudulently remove any of the company's cash resources. At a minimum, the duties related to cash that should be separated are:

      a. Custody of cash

      b. Recording of cash

      c. Reconciliation of bank accounts

   2. The reason for this minimum separation is to prevent an employee from pilfering cash and concealing the action by altering the records.

D. **Bank Reconciliations**—Bank reconciliations provide a check mechanism for both the company and the financial institution. In most cases, any errors detected in a bank reconciliation are the result of **honest** mistakes on the part of the company's employees or on the part of the bank's employees.

   1. Bank reconciliations are necessary because cash transactions that occur near the end of a month or an accounting year may be recorded by the company but have not been recorded by the financial institution. Likewise, there may be some cash transactions that have been recorded by the financial institution but have not been recorded by the company.

IV. **U.S. GAAP–IFRS Differences**—The main difference between U.S. GAAP and IFRS is that bank overdrafts can be subtracted from cash, rather than classified as liabilities.

Bank Reconciliations

The purpose of this lesson is to provide guidance on bank reconciliations.

After studying this lesson, you should be able to:

1. Identify the reconciling items in a book-to-bank and bank-to-book bank reconciliation.

2. Complete a simple bank reconciliation to the true cash balance.

I. Benefits—Bank reconciliations provide the following benefits:

  A. Enable a periodic comparison of the bank account balance and cash balance

  B. Help identify errors in the firm's records or bank records

  C. Establish the correct ending cash balance

  D. Provide information for adjusting entries

  E. Help reduce cash theft by employees if the reconciler does not have access to cash records or does not have access to cash (authorization to make disbursements, or cash custody)

II. Simple Bank Reconciliation—This type of reconciliation explains the difference between the balance per books and the balance per bank at the end of the month. For example, the November 20X7 bank reconciliation would reconcile the balance per books on November 30, 20X7 with the balance per bank on November 30, 20X7.

  A. There are three formats for the simple bank reconciliation:

  1. Bank to book—The starting point is the balance per bank. All adjustments are made to this balance to arrive at the balance per book.

  2. Book to bank—The starting point is the balance per book. All adjustments are made to this balance to arrive at the balance per bank.

> **Note**
> *The third format is the format that is typically emphasized on the CPA Exam and will be the focus of our coverage.*

  3. Bank and book to true balance—In this format, the bank balance and the book balance are separately reconciled to the **true** cash balance, which is reported in the balance sheet. The adjustments to the two starting points (bank balance and book balance) are those changes in cash that have not been recorded in the bank or the books at the end of the period.

Example

Balance Per Bank, November 30, 20X7   XX

+ Deposits in Transit	+ X
+ Cash on Hand	+ X
− Outstanding Checks	− X
± Errors made by Bank	± X
True Cash	XX

Balance Per Book, November 30, 20X7   XX

+ Interest Earned	+ X
+ Note Collected	+ X
− Service Charges	− X
− NSF Check	− X
± Errors in **Firm's** Records	± X
True Cash	XX

4. **Explanations of adjustments to the bank balance**

   a. **Deposit in transit**—These deposits have been made by the company but have not cleared the bank as of November 30, 20X7. This situation is typically related to a bank policy. For example, some banks have a policy that all deposits made after 2 p.m. of a given day will be reflected by the bank on the next business day.

   b. **Cash on hand**—This amount reflects petty cash and undeposited cash receipts. You might think of cash on hand as being one step removed from being a deposit in transit. For example purposes, let's say a company makes a deposit at 3 p.m. on November 30, 20X7. Per bank policy, this deposit will be reflected by the bank on the next business day. This 3 p.m. deposit will be a deposit in transit. During the last two business hours of November 30, 20X7, the company collected additional cash of $200. This $200 of undeposited cash receipts will be considered cash on hand. This amount could not have been known by the bank as of November 30, 20X7.

   c. **Outstanding checks**—This amount represents checks written and mailed by the company which have not cleared the bank by November 30, 20X7.

   d. **Errors made by the bank**—This amount represents errors made by the bank. For CPA Exam purposes, it might be presented as a situation in which checks written by the ABC Company are subtracted from the balance of the ABZ Company. Alternatively, a deposit made by the ABZ Company may be added to the balance of the ABC Company. There are many types of errors that can be tested. The key is to determine which balance (book or bank) is in error, and by how much. The amount of the error is the adjustment to appear in the reconciliation.

5. **Adjustments to the book balance**

   a. **Interest earned**—This amount represents interest earned on the checking account. This amount was added to the company's checking balance by the bank on November 30, 20X7. The company will record this amount upon receipt of the November bank statement.

   b. **Note collected**—This amount represents principle and interest added to the company's checking balance by the bank upon collection of a note receivable. To fully understand the transaction, it must be remembered that the company secured the services of the bank to collect a note receivable. When the bank collected the note, the amount was added to the company's checking balance by the bank. The company will record the transaction when it receives the November bank statement or receives separate correspondence related to the note collection.

   c. **Service charges**—This amount represents service charges that the bank deducted from the company's checking balance on November 30, 20X7. The company will record the transaction upon receipt of the November 30, 20X7 bank statement.

   d. **NSF checks**—This represents *nonsufficient funds* checks received from customers. For example, a customer wrote a $500 check to the company, but the customer's checking balance was not large enough to cover the check payment. Upon determining the NSF check, the bank will reduce the company's checking balance. The company will record the NSF check upon receipt of the November 30, 20X7 bank statement or upon receipt of separate correspondence related to the NSF check.

   e. **Errors in firm's records**—This represents errors made in the company's records. For CPA Exam purposes, this situation might include some discussion of incorrect recording of cash receipts and disbursements. For example, a payment of $96 might have been recorded as a payment of $69. Alternatively, a cash receipt of $11,000 might have been recorded as a cash receipt of $1,100.

 **Example**

The firm received a $320 check on account (correctly written by the customer) in November but recorded the amount as $230. The check cleared the bank in November. The firm's cash account is understated. The adjustment in the reconciliation would increase the cash account by $90 ($320 – $230).

Adjusting journal entries: Upon completion of the bank reconciliation, the company will prepare adjusting entries for each of the adjustments to the balance per books. Entries are required only for the adjustments to the book balance. These entries are illustrated below.

Interest earned on checking account:

Cash	XX	
Interest Revenue		XX

Note receivable collected by the bank:

Cash	XX	
Note Receivable		XX
Interest Revenue		XX

Service charges:

Service Charge Expense	XX	
Cash		XX

NSF check received from customer:

Accounts Receivable	XX	
Cash		XX

Note: The entry for the example error above, which understated the cash account by $90 is:

Cash	90	
Accounts Receivable		90

III. U.S. GAAP–IFRS Differences—There are no differences between U.S. GAAP and IFRS in the preparation of bank reconciliations.

Receivables

Accounts Receivable—Accounting and Reporting

The purpose of this lesson is to understand the recording and valuation of accounts receivable.

After studying this lesson, you should be able to:

1. Complete the journal entries for recording AR using the gross method and the net method for discounts and allowances.

2. Identify the U.S. GAAP and IFRS differences in valuing AR.

I. **Receivables**—This subsection provides an explanation of four different types of receivables.

   A. **Accounts Receivable**—Typically related to customer transactions. That is, an account receivable is usually related to the sale of goods to customers or the provision of services to customers. The length of time related to this claim is very short, 30 to 90 days for most business enterprises. Due to this short time frame, an account receivable typically does not have an interest element.

   B. **Notes Receivable**—Often related to noncustomer transactions although many larger consumer items and transactions between businesses require a promissory note. Examples of transactions that relate to a note receivable include the sale of noncash assets, lending transactions, and the conversion of other receivables. A note receivable is usually related to a longer time frame than an account receivable, and due to that fact, all notes have an interest element. Notes provide increased security for the seller firm, are often negotiable, and usually can be converted to cash with a third party more easily than accounts receivable.

   C. **Trade Receivable**—Another name for customer accounts receivable.

   D. **Nontrade Receivables**—Those receivables created in noncustomer transactions.

II. **Balance Sheet Valuation of Receivable**

   A. Receivables are valued on the balance sheet at net realizable value, the amount of cash that the entity expects to collect at due date or at maturity. Depending on the type of receivable, there are several factors that cause the valuation of a receivable to be less than its face or nominal value.

   B. **Factors Affecting Receivable Valuation**— Several items affect the net valuation of receivables (and net sales). Accounts receivable typically reflects more adjustments than notes receivable. Accounts receivable is shown at its net collectible amount. The adjustments to accounts receivable include:

      1. Trade (quantity) discounts

      2. Cash (sales) discounts

      3. Sales returns and allowances

      4. Noncollectible accounts

   C. **Recording Methods**

      1. In addition, two different methods of accounting for receivables may be used:

         a. The *gross method,* which records receivables at gross invoice price (before cash discount)

         b. The *net method,* which records receivables at net invoice price (after cash discount)

      2. **Using gross and net**—The following example illustrates the journal entries for the first three mentioned previously above using both the gross and net methods. Noncollectible accounts are described in the next section.

Example
Trade discount and initial recording

Assume we sell $2,000 (list price) of goods, terms 3/10, n30. The sale is subject to a 5% trade discount.

	Gross	Net
Accounts Receivable	1,900	1,843
Sales	1,900*	1,843#

*{.95($2,000)}
#{$1,900(.97)}

The 3/10, n30 terminology indicates that a cash discount of 3% is available to the buyer if payment is remitted within 10 days after the sale. Otherwise, the gross price net of any returns and allowances is due 30 days after the sale. The **gross** invoice price is $1,900, the amount after the trade discount but before the cash discount. The net method records the sale at the gross amount less the 3% cash discount, or 97% of the gross invoice price.

3. **Cash discount**

Example
Payment is received within the 10-day discount period.

	Gross	Net
Cash	1,843	1,843
Sales Discounts	57	
Accounts Receivable	1,900	1,843

The Sales Discount account is a contra account to sales. It reduces gross sales to sales at its net amount. The net method records sales net of cash discount and does not require an adjustment for cash discounts taken by customers. The gross method separately records cash discounts taken by customers. Payment is received after the 10-day discount period.

	Gross	Net
Cash	1,900	1,900
Sales Discounts Forfeited		57
Accounts Receivable	1,900	1,843

The Sales Discounts Forfeited account is a miscellaneous revenue account. The net method separately records cash discounts not taken by customers.

4. **Returns and allowances**

Example

A $200 allowance is made for a defect in the merchandise on the fifth day after sale

	Gross	Net
Sales Returns and Allowances	200	194*
Accounts Receivable	200	194

*{($200).97}

Sales Returns and Allowances is a contra account to sales. "Returns" are for merchandise returned from the customer and the "allowance" is for price reductions of the merchandise. A $200 return would be accounted for in the same manner.

D. **Adjusting Entries**—At the end of the year, material probable and estimable cash discounts (under the gross method) and sales returns and allowances must be recorded in the year of sale for correct reporting of net sales and accounts receivable.

Example

At the end of 20X8, a firm estimates that $30,000 of cash discounts will be taken by customers in 20X9, on 20X8 sales. The following adjusting entry is made at the end of 20X8:

| Sales Discounts | 30,000 | |
| Allowance for Sales Discounts | | 30,000 |

Allowance for Sales Discounts is contra to accounts receivable. The entry thus reduces both net sales and net accounts receivable. In 20X9, assuming $25,000 of discounts are actually taken on 20X8 sales, the allowance for sales discounts account is debited rather than sales discounts (which were recognized in the previous entry). The remaining $5,000 is treated as an estimate change, reducing the amount of estimated sales discounts to be recognized in the 20X9 year-end adjusting entry.

A similar journal entry is required for estimated sales returns and allowances.

III. **U.S. GAAP–IFRS Differences**

A. The main difference in the recognition criteria between U.S. GAAP and IFRS is that IFRS defines revenue from a balance sheet point of view and is based on the inflow of economic benefits during the ordinary course of business. This means that accounts receivable (and revenue) can be recognized if there is a firm sales commitment and the recognition criteria have been met. The revenue and asset are recognized when:

1. There are probably future economic benefits.

2. Revenue can be measured reliably.

3. Costs can be measured reliably.

4. Significant risk and rewards of ownership are transferred.

5. Managerial involvement is not retained as to ownership or control.

6. Therefore, a firm sales commitment may meet the IFRS criteria for recognition, but in the U.S. the revenue and asset from a firm sales commitment would not be recognized.

B. The measurement criteria for reporting receivables is very similar; the future economic benefit of the accounts receivable is analogous to the net realizable value. Therefore, the valuation of AR is similar.

Uncollectible—Direct Write-Off and Allowance

This lesson presents the accounting and reporting of uncollectible accounts receivable.

After studying this lesson, you should be able to:

1. Complete the entries for the direct write-off method for uncollectibles.

2. Complete the entries for the allowance method for uncollectibles.

I. **Introduction**

   A. The fourth factor affecting accounts receivable valuation is uncollectible accounts (the first three were trade discounts, cash discounts, and sales returns and allowances). This is the major issue affecting receivable valuation and income determination in the area of receivables. Bad debt expense (also called uncollectible accounts expense on the CPA Exam) is the account that records the effect of uncollectible accounts. Bad debt expense is on the income statement. The allowance for uncollectible accounts is a balance sheet account contra to accounts receivable. Bad debt expense traditionally has been considered a cost of doing business rather than a sales adjustment.

   B. Most companies will use one of two methods to account for bad debt expense. The direct write-off method is the first method presented, followed by the allowance method.

II. **Direct Write-Off Method**—This method records bad debt expense only when a specific account receivable is considered uncollectible and is written off. It can be used only when the firm is unable to estimate uncollectible accounts receivable reliably. Most large firms do not use this method.

   A. **Negative Aspects of the Direct Write-Off Method**—First, if the direct write-off method is employed, accounts receivable are overvalued on the balance sheet. Second, for companies employing the direct write-off method, the company usually recognizes the revenue from a credit sale in one year and typically recognizes the bad debt expense in a subsequent year. So, due to poor balance-sheet valuation and poor matching of revenues and expenses, the direct write-off method is **not** considered in accordance with GAAP unless there is no basis for estimating bad debts.

   B. **Positive Aspects of the Direct Write-Off Method**—Companies that use the direct write-off method justify its use for two reasons. First, the use of the direct write-off method may not be materially different in its effect on the company's financial statements relative to the allowance method. Second, the direct write-off method is simple and practical to use.

   C. **Typical Entries**—Bad Debt Expense and Bad Debts Recovered are both income statement accounts. The first is an expense account, while the second account is a miscellaneous revenue account.

An account is deemed uncollectible:

| Bad Debt Expense | XX | |
| Accounts Receivable | | XX |

An account previously written off is collected:

| Cash | XX | |
| Bad Debts Recovered | | XX |

III. **The Allowance Method**—The allowance method is the method of choice for most large firms and is required under GAAP if uncollectible accounts are probable and estimable. This method records an estimate of bad debt expense at the end of each year in an adjusting entry. An allowance (contra accounts receivable) is created at that time and reduces net accounts receivable. Thus, both income and net accounts receivable are reduced in the year of sale by the estimate of uncollectible accounts on the year's sales.

A. **Benefits of this Method**—The positive aspects of the Allowance Method are twofold. First, the allowance method allows companies to value accounts receivables at net realizable value on the balance sheet. Second, the use of the allowance method allows companies to recognize the revenues and expenses from credit sales in the same accounting year. So, due to appropriate balance sheet valuation of receivables and much better matching of revenues and expenses, the allowance method is in accordance with GAAP when uncollectible accounts are estimable.

B. **Typical Entries**

    1. **End-of-period adjusting entry**—This is the important entry. The allowance for doubtful accounts is recorded at year-end because the identity of the specific accounts that will be uncollectible and written off in a later period is unknown. The account is contra to accounts receivable.

Bad Debt Expense	XX	
Allowance for Doubtful Accounts		XX

C. **Write-Off of Uncollectible Accounts**—This entry has no effect on income or net assets or even net accounts receivable because the income effect of uncollectibles has already been recognized in the previous adjusting entry. The debit to the allowance decreases the allowance and thus increases net accounts receivable. The credit to accounts receivable decreases net accounts receivable.

Allowance for Doubtful Accounts	XX	
Accounts Receivable		XX

D. **Recovery of Accounts Previously Written Off**—These two entries reinstate the allowance account and record cash received.

Accounts Receivable	XX	
Allowance for Doubtful Accounts		XX
Cash	XX	
Accounts Receivable		XX

Allowance—Income Statement and Balance Sheet Approach

This lesson presents the income statement and balance sheet approach for determining the allowance for doubtful accounts.

After studying this lesson, you should be able to:

1. Calculate the allowance and bad debt expense under the income statement approach and complete the necessary adjusting entry.

2. Calculate the allowance and bad debt expense under the balance sheet approach and complete the necessary adjusting entry.

I. **Estimating Bad Debt Expense**—This section takes a closer look at the estimation of bad debt expense. The amount of bad debt expense in the first entry above, the year-end adjusting entry, may be estimated using two different approaches: the income statement approach or the balance sheet approach. As per a later discussion, it is possible to combine the two approaches. Regardless of the chosen approach, a business entity generally will choose one approach and apply it consistently from year to year.

A. **Income Statement Approach**

1. Based on observations of prior years, under this approach a company may estimate bad debt expense as a percentage of credit sales.

2. If the income statement approach is chosen, the bad debt expense is equal to a percentage of the credit sales during a given accounting period. That is, if this approach is chosen, no consideration is given to the existing balance in the allowance account.

> **Note**
> *Remember that if you use the income statement approach, you are calculating an income statement number (bad debt expense).*

3. If the income statement approach is chosen, the matching objective related to the allowance method is the objective that is receiving the primary emphasis.

 **Example**
Credit sales for 20X7: $500,000

In the past five years, approximately 5% of credit sales have been uncollectible. The bad debt expense for 20X7 is $25,000 (.05 × $500,000). Please note the bad debt expense is $25,000 regardless of the balance in the allowance account prior to the adjusting entry.

B. **Balance Sheet Approach**

1. Based on observations of prior years, under this approach, the company estimates bad debt expense by analyzing the ending accounts receivable. This analysis may result in the application of a percentage to the ending accounts receivable. Alternatively, the company may analyze the ending accounts receivable by **aging** the ending accounts receivable. This aging process involves grouping receivables by the amount of time they have been outstanding. Once the aging schedule is completed, the company then applies the various estimates of inconvertibility to each group of receivables.

Note
Remember that if you use the balance sheet approach, you are calculating a balance sheet number (allowance for doubtful accounts).

2. The analysis of ending accounts receivable has one simple objective: the determination of the **needed** or desired balance in the allowance account. By **needed** balance, we mean the balance needed to properly value accounts receivable on the balance sheet. The desired allowance balance equals the expected amount of write-offs to occur in the future based on the receivables at the balance sheet date.

3. Once the **needed** balance in the allowance account has been determined, the **needed** balance is compared to the existing balance in the allowance account. The difference in these two balances is the amount of bad debt expense to be recorded for the accounting period.

4. If a company elects to use the balance sheet approach, the company is more concerned with the balance sheet valuation objective related to the allowance method.

Example
Balance Sheet Approach

Accounts receivable on December 31, 20X7—$200,000

Based on past experience, the company estimates that 6% of ending receivables will be uncollectible.

Prior to the end-of-period adjustment, the allowance for doubtful accounts had an existing $3,000 debit balance due to greater than expected write-offs.

Desired balance in the allowance account:

$200,000 × 6% = $12,000

As the existing balance in the allowance account is a $3,000 debit balance, the amount recorded in the end-of-period adjusting entry is $15,000.

C. **Combination of the Income Statement and Balance Sheet Approaches**—Some business entities prefer to combine the income statement and balance sheet approaches. For example, the entity might elect to use the income statement approach for the monthly adjusting entries for each month January through November. For the December entry, the balance sheet approach might be employed. The following example illustrates both approaches.

Example
The Allowance Method and the Two Estimation Methods

The beginning balances of the current year pertaining to accounts receivable are taken from the current asset section of the balance sheet:

January 1 Balances:

Accounts Receivable	$250,000
Less Allowance for Doubtful Accounts	(6,000)
Equals Net Accounts Receivable	$244,000

The $6,000 remaining in the allowance account at the beginning of the year represents previous years' expected uncollectible accounts that have yet to be written off.

Events for the current year:

Write off a $4,000 account:

Allowance for Doubtful Accounts	4,000	
Accounts Receivable		4,000

Collect a $1,000 account written off last year:

Accounts Receivable	1,000	
Allowance for Doubtful Accounts		1,000
Cash	1,000	
Accounts Receivable		1,000

Credit sales for the year amount to $400,000; cash of $290,000 is collected on account:

Accounts Receivable	400,000	
Sales		400,000
Cash	290,000	
Accounts Receivable		290,000

Ending balances before adjustment:

Accounts Receivable	$356,000*
Allowance for Doubtful Accounts	3,000**

* $250,000 − $4,000 + $400,000 − $290,000

** $6,000 − $4,000 + $1,000

The next two parts are independent (the firm would use only one of the two).

1. December 31 adjusting entry for bad debt estimate: assume the income statement approach and bad debts are estimated to be 3% of credit sales.

Bad Debt Expense .03($400,000)	12,000	
Allowance for Doubtful Accounts		12,000

Note that the $3,000 pre-adjustment allowance balance is not considered when recognizing bad debt expense. However, actual experience is used periodically to re-estimate the bad debt percentage of sales.

Resulting December 31 balance sheet disclosure:

Accounts Receivable	$356,000
Less Allowance for Doubtful Accounts	**(15,000)**
Equals Net Accounts Receivable	$341,000

* $3,000 + $12,000

2. Now assume the firm uses the balance sheet approach rather than the income statement approach at year end; in particular, it uses the aging approach to estimating bad debt expense. Total accounts receivable is partitioned into age categories. The older the category, the greater the probability of uncollectible accounts. The uncollectible percentage is based on past experience.

Age Category	Amount of Receivables	Uncollectible Percentage	Expected Uncollectibles
Current	$200,000	.01	$2,000
31–60 days	100,000	.05	5,000
Over 60 days	56,000	.10	5,600
	$356,000		$12,600

Total expected uncollectible accounts—the desired ending allowance balance of $12,600—is the sum of uncollectible accounts across the age categories.

The sum of the total amounts in the age categories equals total gross accounts receivable.

December 31 adjusting entry:

Bad Debt Expense ($12,600 − $3,000)	9,600	
Allowance for Doubtful Accounts		9,600

The desired or needed ending allowance balance is $12,600. With $3,000 already in the allowance account, only $9,600 is required to be reported as bad debt expense. This approach automatically updates for changes in estimates.

Resulting December 31 balance sheet disclosure:

Accounts Receivable	$356,000
Less Allowance for Doubtful Accounts	(12,600)
Equals Net Accounts Receivable	$343,400

Note

If given a problem similar to this example, the candidate may be required to compute the right-most column above. These amounts are the product of the amount of receivables in the age category and the uncollectible percentage.

II. **U.S. GAAP–IFRS Differences**—There are no differences between U.S. GAAP and IFRS for estimating the allowance for uncollectible receivables.

Notes Receivable

This lesson presents the accounting for notes receivable.

After studying this lesson, you should be able to:

1. Calculate the interest component of an interest-bearing note receivable.

2. Complete the journal entries for an interest-bearing note receivable.

3. Calculate the implicit interest on a non-interest-bearing note receivable.

4. Complete the journal entries for a non-interest-bearing note receivable.

I. Introduction

   A. A note is a more formal financial instrument than an accounts receivable. The key reporting issues are valuation of the note (at present value).

   B. The maker of a note is the buyer or borrower (the debtor firm or individual). This party is making an unconditional promise to pay principal and interest over the note term. The holder of the note (seller or lender) is the creditor and is the firm recording the note receivable on its books.

   C. All notes have an interest element. In an interest-bearing note, the interest element is explicitly stated, while in a non-interest-bearing note, the interest element is not explicitly stated but rather is included in the face value of the note.

   D. Notes typically result from the sale of property, conversion of accounts receivable, and lending transactions.

II. Types of Notes

   A. Interest-Bearing Notes Receivable—The interest element is explicitly stated. For example, the note might be identified as a three-year, 9% note receivable. The amount of cash to be collected from an interest-bearing note is the face amount of the note (principal) plus interest.

   B. Non-Interest Bearing Notes Receivable—The interest element is not explicitly stated. For example, the note might be identified as a two-year, $13,000 non-interest-bearing note. The amount of cash to be collected from a non-interest-bearing note is the face amount of the note. That is, the face amount of the note includes principal and interest that will be collected at maturity date.

III. Recording a Note Receivable

   A. Present Value—In accordance with U.S. GAAP, all notes are recorded at the present value of future cash flows (notes of less than one-year term need not be recorded at present value). The discount rate used in this calculation is the market rate of interest on the date of note creation (this rate may be different from the note's stated rate—the rate that appears on the note). Furthermore, any discounts related to notes will be amortized by applying the effective interest method.

   B. Market Value—If the stated interest rate is equal to the market rate of interest, the present value of future cash flows will be equal to the face amount of the note. In this situation, no discounts will exist.

   C. Interest/Market Rate—If the stated interest rate is not equal to the market rate of interest, the present value of future cash flows will not be equal to the face amount of the note. In this situation, a discount related to the note will exist.

   D. For a **non-interest-bearing note**, the present value of future cash flows will not be equal to the face amount of the note. In this situation, a discount related to the note will exist.

IV. Determination of Present Value of Future Cash Flows

A. **Cash Transaction**—If the transaction is a cash transaction, such as a lending transaction, the present value of future cash flows will equal the amount of cash that exchanged hands on the date of note creation.

B. **Noncash Transaction**—If the transaction is a noncash transaction, such as the sale of a noncash asset and the receipt of a note receivable, the transaction will be recorded at the fair value of the noncash asset or the fair value of the note receivable (present value of future cash flows), whichever one can be more clearly determined.

Example
Simple Interest Note, Stated Rate Equals Market Rate

A calendar-year fiscal-year firm receives a three-year, 6%, $10,000 note on March 1 of the current year from a sale. The note pays interest each September 1 and March 1. The first four entries are shown:

<u>March 1</u>

Note Receivable	10,000	
Sales		10,000

<u>September 1</u>

Cash (.06(1/2)$10,000)	300	
Interest Revenue		300

<u>December 31</u>

Interest Receivable (.06(4/12)$10,000)	200	
Interest Revenue		200

<u>March 1 (following year)</u>

Cash	300	
Interest Receivable		200
Interest Revenue (.06(2/12)$10,000)		100

Example
Simple Interest Note, Principal and Interest are Due in Annual Installments

A calendar-year fiscal-year firm receives a 12%, $300,000 note on May 1, 20X7. Beginning in 20X8, the note calls for $100,000 of principal, along with interest on the outstanding note balance at the beginning of the period, to be paid each April 30.

Interest revenue recognized:

In 20X7: $300,000(.12)(8/12) =		$24,000
In 20X8: $300,000(.12)(4/12) +	$200,000(.12)(8/12) =	28,000
In 20X9: $200,000(.12)(4/12) +	$100,000(.12)(8/12) =	16,000
In 20X0: $100,000(.12)(4/12) =		4,000

Example
Each Note Payment Includes Principal and Interest

A firm receives a 7%, two-year, $20,000 note from a sale, on January 1, 20X7. The note calls for two equal annual payments to be made beginning December 31, 20X7. The present value of an annuity of $1 for two periods at 7% is 1.80802. Let P = annual payment.

$20,000 = P(1.80802)

P = $11,062

January 1, 20X7	Note Receivable	20,000	
	Sales		20,000
December 31, 20X7	Cash	11,062	
	Interest Revenue		1,400*
	Note Receivable		9,662

*$20,000(.07) = $1,400

This is the interest portion of the first payment.

The $9,662 is return of principal.

December 31, 20X8	Cash	11,062	
	Interest Revenue		724**
	Note Receivable		10,338

**($20,000 − $9,662)(.07) = $724

This entry closes the note receivable account ($20,000 − $9,662 − $10,338 = $0).

Example
Simple interest note, stated rate, and market rates are unequal

A firm, which is not an equipment dealer, sells used equipment (cost, $40,000; accumulated depreciation, $16,000) and receives a two-year, 4%, $25,000 note on January 1, 20X8. The note calls for annual interest to be paid each December 31 beginning 20X8 with the principal due December 31, 20X9. The equipment has no known market value but the prevailing (market) interest rate at the date of sale is 8%.

Relevant present values of $1 at 8% for two years: single payment, .85734; annuity, 1.78326.

The note is recorded at present value: $25,000(.85734) + .04($25,000)(1.78326) = $23,217. Thus, the note is recorded at a discount of $1,783 ($25,000 − $23,217). The true value of the note on receipt is $23,217 because this amount reflects the current market interest rate. This amount is also used as the fair value of the equipment in computing the gain or loss on disposal.

January 1, 20X8	Note Receivable	23,217	
	Accumulated Depreciation	16,000	
	Loss on Disposal	783	
	Equipment		40,000

(This entry records the note using the net method. The gross method would record the note at $25,000 and credit Discount on Notes for $1,783. Either approach is acceptable and both report the net notes receivable balance at present value.)

December 31, 20X8	Cash .04($25,000)	1,000	
	Note Receivable	857	
	Interest Revenue		1,857*

* .08($23,217)

The $857 amount is the increase in the value of the note for 20X8 because the cash interest was less than the growth in the note's present value over time. Had the gross method been used, the discount account would have been debited for $857 rather than the note receivable account. Under either reporting approach, the net note balance is now $24,074 ($23,217 + $857). This amount is the present value of the remaining payments at December 31, 20X8, which can also be computed as ($25,000 + $1,000)/1.08.

December 31, 20X9	Cash .04($25,000)	1,000	
	Note Receivable	926	
	Interest Revenue		1,926*
	Cash	25,000	
	Note Receivable		25,000

* .08($23,217 + $857)

Example
Non-Interest-Bearing Note

A non-interest-bearing note has a zero stated rate. The term *non-interest-bearing* is a misnomer, however, because the interest is included in the note's face value. Assume the same information as in the previous example except that there is no stated rate. Now the present value of the note is $21,434 [$25,000(.85734)]. The note is recorded at this amount. The entries are similar except that no cash interest is received. The first interest entry is shown:

| December 31, 20X8 | Note Receivable | 1,715 | |
| | Interest Revenue | | 1,715* |

* .08($21,434)

Criteria for Sale of Receivables

This lesson presents the criteria for when the transfer of receivables is a sale versus security for a loan.

After studying this lesson, you should be able to:

1. List the three criteria for the transfer of AR to qualify as a sale.

2. Complete the journal entries when the transfer of AR is a sale.

3. Define what is meant by selling AR with recourse and without recourse.

4. Identify the major differences between U.S. GAAP and IFRS accounting for transfer of AR.

I. Using Accounts Receivable and Notes Receivable as Sources of Cash—Frequently, business entities use receivables as immediate sources of cash. The firm uses the receivables as collateral for a loan or sells the receivables to a third party rather than wait for the maker of the note to make all the required payments on the note. The reasons for the transactions that will be described are varied. In some cases, a company may elect to forgo the establishment of a collection department. That is, the company could decide that the establishment of a collection department is not economically feasible. In other cases, companies may need the cash related to a note receivable or accounts receivable to meet current operating expenses or to take advantage of a unique opportunity.

II. The Parties Involved in a Transfer of Receivables are

 A. The **maker**, which is the debtor that has borrowed funds or purchased an asset and provided a note to the original creditor.

 B. The **original creditor** (transferor), which is the firm that has loaned funds or sold an asset to the maker.

 C. The **third-party financial institution** (transferee), which provides the funds to the original creditor.

III. Type of Transaction—When a company transfers receivables to a third party or uses the receivables as collateral for a loan, a determination must be made as to the substance of the transaction: Is it a sale or is it a loan? Codification 860-40 identifies the key characteristics of a sales transaction.

IV. Criteria for Sale—Criteria for determining if the transfer of receivables is a sale:

 A. The transaction is a sale of the receivable if three conditions are met. If the three conditions are met, then control has effectively passed to the third party (transferee) and a sale is implied. The three conditions are:

   1. The transferred assets have been isolated from the transferor, even in bankruptcy.

   2. The transferee is free to pledge or exchange the assets.

   3. The transferor does not maintain effective control over the transferred assets either through an agreement that allows and requires the transferor to repurchase the assets or one that requires the transferor to return specific assets.

 B. **Conditions Are Met**—If the above-listed conditions are met, the transaction is accounted for as a sale. The receivable is removed from the books of the transferor and a gain or loss on the sale of the receivable will be recorded.

 C. **Conditions Are not Met**—If the listed conditions are **not** met, the transaction is actually a situation in which the transferor is borrowing funds and using the receivables as collateral for a loan. In this case, the receivable remains on the books of the transferor, and the transferor records a liability related to the borrowing transaction. In this case, the transferor will not record any gain or loss on sale of the receivable. Rather, the transferor will record interest expense related to the borrowing transaction.

V. Terms of Transaction

A. With Recourse or Without Recourse

1. The transaction can be completed with recourse or without recourse. If the transaction is completed with recourse, the transferor is responsible for nonpayment on the part of the original maker of the receivable. This means that if the maker (original debtor) defaults, the original creditor must assume all the payments on the receivable.

Example

Grotex Inc. sells merchandise to Swemby on account. Grotex is the original creditor. Grotex then transfers the receivable to a financial institution and receives 94% of the value of the receivable. Grotex is the transferor and the financial institution is the transferee. If the transfer is with recourse and Swemby fails to pay the receivable, then Grotex must pay the financial institution the full amount of the receivable. During the term of the receivable, Grotex has a contingent liability that can be noted in a footnote, or a contra asset account can be recorded, such as note receivable discounted, or the liability may need to be accrued in the accounts, depending on the probability that Grotex will be required to pay.

2. If the transaction is completed **without recourse**, the transferor is not responsible for nonpayment on the part of the maker of the receivable. Typically, nonrecourse transfers are accounted for as sales because control has passed to the transferee (financial institution).

B. Notification or Non-Notification Basis—The transaction can be completed on a notification basis or on a non-notification basis. If the transaction is completed on a notification basis, the maker of the receivable is informed of the transaction and typically is instructed to make payments to the third party. If the transaction is completed on a non-notification basis, the maker of the receivable is not informed of the transaction and continues to make payments to the original creditor.

Example

The discounting of a note receivable is a common transaction involving the transfer of a receivable. The original creditor (transferor) discounts the note to a financial institution that charges a fee on the maturity value of the note. The maturity value is the face value plus interest, at the note's original rate, over the entire term of the note. The transferor receives proceeds equal to the maturity value less the fee. The Tiger Company has a $4,000, 90-day, 8% note receivable, which was received from a customer in settlement of an account receivable. The Tiger Company held the note for 30 days and decided to discount the note at Auburn National Bank. Auburn National Bank charges a 10% discount fee on the maturity value of the note (which includes the interest for the complete term of the note) for the two months it will hold the note. The proceeds to Tiger equal the maturity value less the fee.

Accrued interest for the 30 days the note was held by Tiger: $4,000(.08)(1/12) = $26.67

Cash Proceeds from the Discounting Transaction: Maturity Value of the Note:	
$4,000 + ($4,000)(.08)(3/12) =	$4,080
Less Discount Fee: $4,080(.10)(2/12) =	(68)
Equals Cash Proceeds	$4,012

Interest expense (if transaction is a borrowing) or loss (if transaction is a sale):

Carrying Value of Note at Date of Discounting: $4,000 + $26.67	$4,026.67
Less Cash Proceeds	($4,012.00)
Equals Interest Expense or Loss	$14.67

If the transaction is a sale (i.e., if all three criteria of ASC 860 are met), a loss of $14.67 will be recorded. If the transaction is a borrowing transaction, interest expense of $14.67 will be recorded.

Entries assuming a borrowing (all three criteria are not met):

Interest Receivable	26.67	
Interest Revenue		26.67
Cash	4,012.00	
Interest Expense	14.67	
Liability on Note		4,000.00
Interest Receivable		26.67

Entries assuming a sale (all three criteria are met)

Interest Receivable	26.67	
Interest Revenue		26.67
Cash	4,012.00	
Loss on Sale	14.67	
Note Receivable		4,000.00
Interest Receivable		26.67

For the sale transaction, if the note is discounted with recourse, Tiger has a contingent liability for the remaining two months of the note term. If the maker does not pay the note, then Tiger must. Tiger may report the liability in its footnotes or credit Notes Receivable Discounted rather than Notes Receivable in the journal entry immediately above, for $4,000. The Notes Receivable Discounted account is contra to Notes Receivable. This approach more prominently discloses the contingent liability.

VI. Transfers of Receivables Under IFRS

A. Both U.S. GAAP and IFRS seek to determine if the arrangement is a sale of the receivables or a secured borrowing. U.S. GAAP focuses on whether control has shifted from the transferor to the transferee. IFRS focuses on whether the transferor has transferred the rights to receive the cash flows from the receivable and whether substantially all the risk and rewards of ownership were transferred. Application of these criteria are quite complex. However, it is often noted that under IFRS criteria the transfer is less likely to be treated as a sale.

B. Criteria for Transfer under IFRS 39

1. If the entity transfers substantially all the risks and rewards of ownership, the transfer is treated as a sale.

2. If the entity retains substantially all the risks and rewards of ownership, the transfer is treated as a secured borrowing.

3. If neither conditions 1 or 2 hold, the entity accounts for the transaction as a sale if it has transferred control and as a secured borrowing if it has retained control.

Factoring, Assignment, and Pledging

This lesson presents the accounting for factoring receivables and describes the assignment and pledging of AR.

After studying this lesson, you should be able to:

1. Describe the difference between factoring with and without recourse.

2. Describe the difference between assigning and pledging AR.

3. Complete the journal entries when AR is factored with and without recourse.

I. **Other Types of Transactions Involving Transfers of Receivables**

  A. **Factoring**

  1. **Transferor to factor**—In a factoring, the transferor (original creditor) transfers the receivables to a factor (transferee, a financial institution) immediately as a normal part of business. The transferor prefers to pay the factor a fee in return for the factor's administration of the receivables. The factor often performs credit checks and collects the payments.

  2. **Factoring without recourse**—This type of factoring is usually accounted for as a sale because the factor has no recourse against the transferor if there is a default on the receivables. The factor (transferee) bears the cost of uncollectible accounts, but the seller (transferor) bears the cost of sales adjustments such as sales discounts and returns and allowances because they are considered preconditions.

 **Example**
A firm factors $20,000 of accounts receivable without recourse. The factor charges 5% and holds back an additional 3% for sales returns. Assume that actual sales returns equal the estimated amount. The transferor records the following entries:

Cash $20,000(1.00 − .05 − .03)	18,400	
Receivable from Factor $20,000(.03)	600	
Loss on Sale of Receivables $20,000(.05)	1,000	
Accounts Receivable		20,000
Sales Returns and Allowances	600	
Receivable from Factor		600

If the actual and estimated returns are not equal, the factoring agreement will specify which party receives the savings or bears the cost.

Note
In the example above, the transfer qualified as a sale; therefore, the cost of the factoring is a loss on the sale of receivables.

  3. **Factoring with recourse**—When receivables are factored with recourse, the three criteria of Codification 860-40 must be used to determine if the transaction is accounted for as a sale or a loan. The seller (transferor) bears the cost of bad debts as well as the cost of sales adjustments.

a. If accounted for as a sale, the entries are similar to factoring without recourse except that the transferor must estimate and record a recourse liability.

Example

A firm factors $20,000 of accounts receivable with recourse. The factor charges 2%. The firm estimates that its liability for bad debts (the recourse liability) is $1,000. The three criteria of Codification 860-40 are met. The holdback for sales adjustments is not illustrated in this example but is handled the same way as for factoring without recourse. The transferor records the following entries:

Cash $20,000(1.00 − .02)	19,600	
Loss on Sale of Receivables $20,000(.02) + $1,000	1,400	
Accounts Receivable		20,000
Recourse Liability		1,000

When accounts are deemed uncollectible, the transferor remits the necessary cash to the factor:

Recourse Liability	1,000	
Cash		1,000

Note: In the example above, the transfer qualified as a sale; therefore ,the cost of the factoring is a loss on the sale of receivables.

b. If accounted for as a loan, the transferor maintains the receivables on its books, and records a loan and interest expense over the term of the agreement.

Example

A firm factors $20,000 of accounts receivable with recourse. The factor charges 2%. The firm estimates that its liability for bad debts (the recourse liability) is $1,000. The three criteria of Codification 860-40 are not met. The transferor records the following entries:

Cash $20,000(1.00 − .02)	19,600	
Discount on Factor Liability $20,000(.02)	400	
Factor Liability		20,000
Allowance for Doubtful Accounts	1,000	
Accounts Receivable		1,000

As payments on the receivables are made to the factor, the factor liability is extinguished and interest expense is recognized. The summary entry is:

Factor Liability	20,000	
Accounts Receivable		19,000
Cash (to pay for uncollectible accounts)		1,000
Interest Expense	400	
Discount on Factor Liability		400

Interest expense is recognized in proportion to collections on the receivables. If 75% of the receivables were collected by year-end, then $300 of interest would be recognized as of the balance sheet date.

Note
In the example above, the transfer DID NOT qualify as a sale; therefore, the cost of the factoring is INTEREST EXPENSE, and the accounts receivable are not removed from the books of the transferor until the receivables are collected.

II. **Assignment of Accounts Receivable**—When accounts receivable are assigned, the borrower assigns rights to specific accounts receivable as collateral for a loan. The lender has the right to seek payment from these receivables should the borrower (original creditor for the accounts receivable) default on the loan. The borrower reclassifies the receivables as accounts receivable assigned, a subcategory of total accounts receivable. The borrower maintains the receivable records, and as cash is received, it is remitted to the lender in payment of the loan. The loan and the receivables are not offset on the borrower's balance sheet. When the loan is repaid, any remaining accounts receivable assigned are returned to ordinary accounts receivable status.

III. **Pledging of Accounts Receivable**—Pledging of accounts receivable is less formal than assignment. Rights to specific receivables are not noted as collateral, and accounts receivable are not reclassified. Neither the accounting for the receivables nor the loan is affected by the pledge. Receivables in bulk are transferred to a trustee and can be used for payment of the loan in the event of default by the borrower (original creditor for the accounts receivable). The cash flows from the receivables are used to pay the loan. Footnote disclosure of the pledge is required.

Notes Receivable—Impairment

This lesson presents the definition of when a loan is impaired and presents the entries for impairment.

After studying this lesson, you should be able to:

1. Define when a note receivable is impaired.

2. Complete the journal entries for the note impairment.

I. Impaired Loans Receivables are Written Down to

A. The present value of the future cash flows expected to be collected using the original effective interest rate for the loan, or

B. Market value if this value is more determinable.

II. The Write-Down (Loss)—This is accomplished with a debit to bad debt expense and a credit to a contra-receivable account. After the write-down, interest revenue is recognized under any of several methods found in practice, including the interest method and cost-recovery methods (Codifications 310-10-35).

Example

A firm holds a 7%, $10,000 note due December 31, 20X6. Annual interest is due each December 31. The note originated on January 1 several years ago. The 20X5 interest payment was not received and the firm believes, as of December 31, 20X5, that no more interest will be received. In addition, only $7,000 of the principal is expected to be received, and that amount will be delayed one year, to December 31, 20X7.

The carrying value of the note on December 31, 20X5, is $10,700, which includes the $700 annual interest that was not paid by the debtor firm. The interest receivable is closed to note receivable. The resulting $10,700 note receivable balance remains on the books. A valuation account is used to write the note down to present value and the loss (bad debt expense) is recognized on this date. The present value of a single payment of $1 at 7% for two years is .87344. Two years is the remaining term of the note.

December 31, 20X5

Bad Debt Expense	4,586*	
Allowance for Decline in Note Value		4,586
*Carrying Value:		$10,700.00
Less Present Value: $7,000(.87344)		(6,114)
Equals Impairment Loss		$ 4,586

The allowance for decline in note value account is contra to notes receivable. The above entry reduces the net carrying value of the note to $6,114, the present value of remaining cash flows. For the remaining two years of the note term, the firm may choose from a variety of methods to recognize interest revenue. Two are illustrated here:

	Interest Method	Cost-Recovery Method
December 31, 20X6		
Allowance for Decline in Note Value	428	No entry as the new carrying value has not been recovered
Interest Revenue .07($6,114)	428	
December 31, 20X7		
Allowance for Decline in Note Value	458	No entry as the new carrying value has not been recovered
Interest Revenue .07($6,114 + $428)	458	
Cash	7,000	7,000
Allowance for Decline in Note Value	3,700	4,586
Note Receivable	10,700	10,700
Interest Revenue		886

The interest method is applied as it is in any other note or bond situation. Interest revenue for a period is based on the net note balance at the beginning of the period. The cost-recovery method delays recognition of interest revenue until the entire new carrying value ($6,114) is received. The only cash inflow in this situation occurred at the end of 20X7. Thus all the interest revenue is recognized in that year. The total interest revenue over the two years is the same for both methods.

III. Loan Impairment and IFRS

A. Impairments under IFRS have some general guidelines that will apply to loan impairment and other impairments we will discuss throughout the specific financial accounts. IAS 36 governs impairment of assets and in general the purpose of the standard is to make sure that assets are not carried at more than the recoverable amount. If the assets carrying value is greater than the amount that could be recovered through the assets use or by selling the asset, then it is impaired.

B. IFRS is more flexible in allowing reversal of impairment losses than U.S. GAAP. In each topical area where impairment is discussed, CPAexcel® will let you know when the impairment can be reversed. The following discusses some terminology:

    1. Recoverable amount: the higher of the fair value less cost to sell or value in use:

        a. Fair value less cost to sell is the amount obtainable from the sale in an arms-length transaction between knowledgeable, willing, and able parties.

        b. Value in use is the discounted present value of the futures cash flows expected from the asset.

    2. Cash-generating unit (CGU) is the smallest group of assets that can be identified that generates cash flows independently of the cash flows from other assets. Impairment tests are all applied to the individual asset level. If the cash flows for the individual asset are not identifiable, then you measure the cash flows from the cash-generating unit.

C. If there is any indication that the loan value has declined, an impairment loss would be taken as the difference between the carrying value and the recoverable amount. If the loan value subsequently increases, IFRS permits recovery of the impairment loss.

Inventory

Introduction to Inventory

This lesson presents the basics for accounting for inventory including: components of inventory, FOB shipping point, FOB destination, consigned goods, and costs capitalized to inventory.

After studying this lesson, you should be able to:

1. List the three basic components of manufacturing inventory.

2. Define FOB shipping point and FOB destination.

3. Identify what is included in year-end inventory costs (goods in transit, consigned goods and capitalized costs).

I. **Inventory Definition and Description**

   A. This section address (1) the items, and (2) costs that should be included in the inventory account.

   Definition
   Inventory: For a typical business entity inventory includes property held for resale, property in the process of production, and property consumed in the process of production.

   B. A manufacturing company has all three types of inventory items. That is, a manufacturing company has:

      1. Finished goods inventory

      2. Work-in-process inventory

      3. Raw materials inventory

   C. A merchandising company typically holds the inventory item that is best described as property held for resale. That is, a merchandising company has a single type of inventory item, usually referred to as merchandise inventory.

   D. Inventories also include land (if the firm is a real-estate development company), and partially completed buildings and bridges (if the firm is a construction company). Inventories are always current assets to the seller even though they may be noncurrent assets to the buyer.

II. **Ending Inventory**

   A. **What Items are Included in Ending Inventory?**

      1. To address this question, you simply apply the ownership criteria. If the merchandise is owned by a business enterprise on the last day of the accounting year, regardless of location, the merchandise should be included in ending inventory.

      2. Most of the merchandise owned by a business enterprise on the last day of the accounting year is typically located on the premises/property of that business enterprise. However, goods awaiting shipment to customers are not included in the firm's inventory if the customer has paid for the goods.

      3. **Merchandise owned and located off-site**

         a. **Goods in transit**

            i. Ownership of goods in transit is determined by the test of title: FOB (free-on-board). FOB destination means that title to the goods transfers to the buyer when the goods reach the destination. Therefore, shipping terms of FOB destination Chicago means that the buyer owns the goods when they reach Chicago. FOB shipping point means title passes at the shipping point (the selling company's warehouse), therefore the goods belong to the purchaser as soon as it is loaded on a common carrier. In general, FOB shipping point means title passes at the shipping point and FOB destination means title passes at the destination. The test of title is important for the year-end cut-off because goods in transit can be included in only one firm's inventory: the buyer or seller.

Examples

1. A business entity is located in Auburn, Alabama and has a major supplier located in Seattle, Washington. On December 31, 20X7, some merchandise was placed on a train or a truck and was en route to Auburn, Alabama on that date.

If the goods were shipped FOB shipping point, the purchased goods in transit should be included in the Auburn company's ending inventory.

If the goods were shipped FOB destination, the purchased goods in transit should not be included in the Auburn company's ending inventory.

2. Goods in transit to a customer—A business entity is located in Auburn, Alabama and has a major customer located in Chicago, Illinois. On December 31, 20X7, some merchandise was placed on a train or truck and was en route to Chicago on that date.

If the goods were shipped FOB destination, the sold goods in transit should be included in the Auburn company's ending inventory.

If the goods were shipped FOB shipping point, the sold goods in transit should not be included in the Auburn company's ending inventory.

b. **Goods on consignment**

   i. A business entity is located in Austin, Texas, and has signed an agreement with a manufacturer to be the sole retailer of the manufacturer's merchandise in the state of Texas. The Austin-based entity sells the merchandise in its Austin-area stores and reaches a consignment agreement with retail establishments in Houston, Dallas, San Antonio, Lubbock, and El Paso. The agreement is the typical consignment agreement. The retail stores outside of Austin will receive the merchandise and attempt to market the merchandise in their selected markets. If the merchandise is sold, the retailer will retain a sales commission and remit the remainder to the Austin-based business entity. If the merchandise is not sold, the retailer will return the merchandise to the Austin-based business entity. In this example, the Austin-based entity is the consignor, and the business establishments located in Houston, Dallas, San Antonio, Lubbock, and El Paso are all consignees.

   ii. In consignment arrangements, the merchandise is owned by the consignor. The merchandise is always included in the consignor's ending inventory even though the inventory typically is never on the consignor's premises.

Example
Trend Inc. has $40,000 worth of its inventory held by a consignee at year-end. Trend also serves as a consignee and holds $30,000 of inventory on consignment for another firm. Only the $40,000 of inventory is included in Trend's ending inventory.

III. **Valuation of Inventory**—The acquisition cost of inventory includes all costs incurred in getting the merchandise to the seller's premises and ready for sale. A good general rule is:

A. **Capitalize in Inventory All Costs Necessary to Bring the Item of Inventory to Salable Condition.**

   1. These costs include freight and insurance in transit paid to the seller firm, any taxes paid on acquisition of inventory, material handling costs, and packaging costs. Interest on the purchase or construction of inventory is never included in inventory. Purchases discounts, and returns and allowances reduce the total cost allocated to inventory. Promotional costs such as advertising are not included in inventory because these costs do not help prepare the inventory for sale.

   2. Also not included are interest costs.

Example
A firm incurred the following costs related to the acquisition and sale of inventory:

Direct Purchase Cost	$50,000
Purchases Returns	4,000
Freight-In	9,000
Freight-Out	2,000
Interest on Purchase	1,000
Sales and Other Taxes on Acquisition	3,000
Packaging Costs (for sale)	4,000
Insurance in Transit from Supplier	500
Promotional Expenses	2,500

The inventory should be recorded at the following amount:

Direct Purchase Cost	$50,000
Purchases Returns	(4,000)
Freight-In	9,000
Sales and Other Taxes on Acquisition	3,000
Packaging Costs (for sale)	4,000
Insurance in Transit from Supplier	500
Total Inventory Cost	$62,500

The excluded costs are period expenses.

B. **Inventory Costs**

   1. Intermediate accounting considers the general issue of costing inventory but limits its consideration to merchandise inventory—that is, inventory purchased for resale. The Management Accounting section of CPAexcel® addresses a related issue: how to determine the cost of manufactured inventories. Manufactured inventory ultimately should reflect the actual cost of manufacturing.

2. **Fixed overhead is one of the four manufacturing input costs**—The others are direct material, direct labor, and variable overhead. Fixed overhead does not vary with small changes in production volume and, therefore, is often allocated to production based on a predetermined overhead rate. For example, if direct labor hours is used for allocation purposes, and the fixed overhead allocation rate is $4 per direct labor hour, then a production run using 1,000 direct labor hours would receive an allocation of $4,000 of fixed overhead cost. The $4 rate is the ratio: (budgeted fixed overhead)/(budgeted direct labor hours).

3. **Fixed overhead rates**—These are subject to estimation errors and are affected by the choice of denominator measure and the budgeting horizon reflected in the denominator. Assuming no numerator (fixed overhead cost) variation, if actual production is less than the production budgeted for the denominator, less fixed overhead will be applied to product than is actually incurred. Underapplied fixed overhead resulting from low production volume must be expensed rather than allocated back to product. Low production volume does not imply that the inventory produced should carry a higher cost or is in any way more valuable.

4. To ensure that unallocated fixed overheads are expensed, Codification 330-10-30 requires for external financial reporting purposes, that **normal** activity be used for the denominator level. Normal activity is a measure of the average production volume (as measured in units, direct labor cost or hours, machine hours, or other predicted amount) expected for a budget horizon typically extending beyond one year and takes into account lost production due to planned maintenance. The range in production volume over more than one period establishes the normal capacity amount. Shorter-range budgeted volumes should not be used as the denominator. During periods of abnormally low production, the use of actual production volume would result in higher overhead rates, causing more overhead to be allocated to product. By requiring normal capacity, higher amounts of fixed overhead will not be allocated to the product during low production periods. Fixed overhead that has not benefited production is not an asset and should be expensed as incurred.

5. The standard also requires that costs **including idle facility expense**, excessive spoilage, double freight, wasted materials, and rehandling costs be treated as current-period costs rather than allocated to inventory and carried over to future periods. This is an example of invoking the conceptual framework definition of an asset rather than the matching principle.

6. The FASB also reaffirmed the concept that selling, general, and administrative expenditures not be treated as manufacturing costs but rather as period costs. Selling costs are not production costs.

Periodic Inventory System and Cost-Flow Assumption

This lesson presents the accounting for inventory under a periodic inventory system.

After studying this lesson, you should be able to:

1. Describe the determination and presentation of the net worth element of such a statement.

2. Calculate cost of goods sold.

3. Calculate ending inventory under a periodic system using specific identification, weighted average, FIFO, and LIFO cost-flow assumptions.

I.   Introduction

A. In accounting for inventories, business entities may elect to employ a periodic inventory system. If so, the beginning inventory balance is reflected in the merchandise inventory account throughout the year. That is, the merchandise inventory account will have an unchanging balance throughout the accounting year. The firm uses other means to obtain current inventory information for internal purposes. The periodic system is much less expensive to administer than is the perpetual system.

B. **Recording Acquisitions**—For companies employing the periodic inventory system, acquisitions of merchandise during the year will be recorded in the *purchases and related accounts*. The purchases account is used rather than the inventory account because a continuous record of the cost of inventory on hand at any time is not maintained under the periodic system.

C. **Typical Entries**

   1. **Beginning inventory**

Merchandise inventory: January 1, 20X7
Purchase of merchandise on account:

Purchases	XX	
Accounts Payable		XX

   a. Purchases is a holding account for inventory charges and credits and is closed to ending inventory and cost of goods sold at the end of the period. The inventory account is not used to record purchases in a periodic system.

Paid delivery charges on purchased merchandise		
Transportation In	XX	
Cash		XX
Returned damaged or defective merchandise		
Accounts Payable	XX	
Purchase Returns and Allowances		XX
Paid for merchandise and received cash discount		
Accounts Payable	XX	
Purchase Discounts		XX
Cash		XX
Sold merchandise on account		
Accounts Receivable	XX	
Sales		XX

2. **Ending inventory**

   a. **End of the period**—Under the periodic inventory system, a physical count of ending inventory is required. Once the number of units in ending inventory has been counted, a value is assigned to the ending inventory, and the following year-end adjusting entry is prepared.

Merchandise Inventory (Ending)	XX	
Purchase Returns and Allowances	XX	
Purchase Discounts	XX	
Cost of Goods Sold	XX	
Merchandise Inventory (Beginning)		XX
Purchases		XX
Transportation In		XX

Note: The entry shown above allows a business entity to achieve multiple objectives. First, the ending balance of inventory is formally entered into the accounting system. Second, the beginning balance of inventory is closed. Also, the purchases and related accounts are closed. Finally, the cost of goods sold for the year is formally entered into the accounting system. Before this entry, cost of goods sold did not exist in the accounting records. Cost of goods sold is not directly observable in a periodic system. Rather, the value recorded for cost of goods sold is derived from the other amounts in the above entry. Another common way of computing cost of goods sold is by the basic inventory equations:

Net purchases = Gross Purchases + Transportation In (Freight In)

– Purchases Returns and Allowances

– Purchases Discounts

Beginning Inventory + Net Purchases = Ending Inventory + Cost of Goods Sold

3. Cost of goods sold is the last amount computed. In other words, it is a derived amount based on the other three values in the above equation. Also, Cost of Goods Available for Sale equals the value of either side of the above equation, although in published reports, cost of goods available for sale is shown as the subtotal of beginning inventory and net purchases.

4. The challenge is to determine the allocation of the left side total to the two components of the right side of the equation. Cost of goods sold, a major expense, is not recognized until goods are sold. Costs remain in inventory until sale.

Note
Transportation out (also called delivery expense and freight-out) is not included in inventory. Transportation out is a distribution or selling expense and is not an inventoriable cost.

Example
Data for a firm's inventory and related transactions follows:

Beginning Inventory	$20,000	Ending Inventory	$32,000
Purchases	100,000	Purchases Returns	4,000
Purchases Discounts	8,000	Transportation In	9,000
Transportation Out	6,000		

The firm's cost of goods sold is determined as follows:

Net Purchases = $100,000 + $9,000 – $8,000 – $4,000

= $97,000

Cost of Goods Sold = Beginning Inventory + Net Purchases – Ending Inventory

= $20,000 + $97,000 – $32,000

= $85,000

II. Cost-Flow Assumption

A. Beginning inventory + net purchases = ending inventory + cost of goods sold

B. To assign a value to ending inventory and cost of goods sold, we apply one of four cost-flow assumptions. These cost-flow assumptions are identified below. Although the merits of each flow assumption are discussed below, remember that firms are free to decide which assumption to choose.

C. Specific Identification

1. If the business entity has somewhat large, distinguishable products, it might be appropriate to use specific identification. For example, an automobile dealer might find this cost flow assumption appropriate. To continue the example, the dealer counted a total of 49 automobiles in inventory at year-end. The dealer can identify each automobile by vehicle number and match the invoice cost by vehicle number as well. To value its ending inventory, the dealership is able to *specifically identify* the cost of each of the inventory items and then total the individual cost of all the inventory items. Likewise, the dealership can specifically identify the cost of each item sold and total these amounts to determine cost of goods sold for the period.

2. The specific identification assumption is not cost effective for most firms and allows firms to manipulate earnings.

Example

If a firm has many identical items in inventory and desires to maximize net income, it can sell the least expensive items rather than the more expensive items. This example assumes a gradual increase in the specific price level of the inventory. The resulting lower cost of goods sold may erroneously imply to users of the financial statements that the firm can continue the reported level of gross margin (sales less cost of goods sold). However, the firm must eventually begin selling the more expensive items.

D. Weighted Average Cost-Flow Assumption

1. The term *weighted average* always implies the periodic inventory system. If the business entity selects this cost flow assumption, the weighted average cost per unit must be calculated. This calculation is shown below.

Weighted Average Cost per Unit = Cost of Goods Available for Sale / Number of Units Available for Sale

2. The ending inventory valuation is equal to the number of units in ending inventory multiplied by the weighted average cost per unit. Likewise, the cost of goods sold for the period is equal to the number of units sold multiplied by the weighted average cost per unit.

3. The weighted average method treats each unit available for sale (beginning inventory and purchases) as if it were costed at the average cost during the period. It produces cost of goods sold and ending inventory results between those of FIFO and LIFO when prices change during the period.

E. FIFO

1. This cost-flow assumption is based on a *first-in, first-out* philosophy. At the end of the accounting period, it is assumed the ending inventory is composed of units of inventory most recently acquired. Conversely, the cost of goods sold is made up of the *oldest* merchandise. The FIFO cost-flow assumption reflects the way most firms actually move their inventory. *However, GAAP does not require that firms choose the inventory cost-flow assumption that reflects the actual movement of goods.*

2. During periods of rising specific inventory prices, FIFO produces the highest net income because cost of goods sold is costed with the lowest-cost (earliest) purchases in the period. Ending inventory reflects the highest (latest) costs. Sometimes FIFO ending inventory is used as an approximation to the current cost of ending inventory.

F. LIFO

    1. This cost-flow assumption is based on a *last-in, first-out* philosophy. At the end of the accounting period, it is assumed the ending inventory is composed of the *oldest* inventory layers, while the cost of goods sold is composed of the units of inventory most recently acquired.

    2. During periods of rising specific inventory prices, LIFO produces the lowest net income because cost of goods sold is costed with the highest-cost (latest) purchases in the period. This feature of LIFO is considered an advantage because reported gross margin reflects the latest purchase costs and therefore is more indicative of future gross margin.

    3. However, the ending inventory reflects the lowest (earliest) costs. Whenever the firm purchases (or produces) more units than it sells, a layer is added. This layer is costed with the earliest costs of the period in which the layer is added, under the periodic system. After several years of adding layers, ending inventory may reflect very old costs. Ending inventory under LIFO is a less reliable amount compared with FIFO ending inventory.

III. Calculating Cost of Goods Sold in a Periodic System

    A. Counting the items in inventory at the end of the year and applying the appropriate costs, depending on the cost-flow assumption, to the items on hand, typically find the ending inventory cost. Cost of goods sold is computed last.

    B. To calculate cost of goods sold for a company employing the periodic inventory system, the calculation shown below is used. This approach is the equation approach illustrated previously, placed into a schedule format.

Cost-of-Goods-Sold Calculation:

	Beginning Inventory
+	Net Cost of Purchases
=	Goods Available for Sale
−	Ending Inventory
=	Cost of Goods Sold

Example
The four cost-flow assumptions in a periodic system are illustrated in this example. The purchases and sales of the firm's one product are given in chronological order for the period. Assume the firm always actually sells the oldest units on hand first.

Beginning Inventory: 400 Units @ $10 per Unit

Purchase 1:   100 Units @ $11 per Unit

Sale 1:   200 Units

(Note: No unit cost is given. The cost assigned to each sale depends on the cost-flow assumption chosen.)

Purchase 2:   200 Units @ $12 per Unit

Sale 2:   400 Units

Purchase 3:   200 Units @ $13 per Unit

The basic equation in units helps to identify the right hand side of the equation for costing purposes:

Beginning Inventory   + Purchases   = Ending Inventory   + Sales

400 Units   + 500 Units   = 300 Units   + 600 Units

Cost of Goods Available for Sale

= Cost in Beginning Inventory + Total Purchases Cost

= 400($10) + 100($11) + 200($12) + 200($13) = $10,100

The sum of ending inventory and cost of goods sold for all four methods must sum to $10,100. This amount is the cost of goods available for sale. During the period, there were 900 units available for sale.

C. Specific Identification and FIFO

1. These two assumptions yield the same results in this case (although they need not in a given situation), because the firm always sells its oldest goods first.

Cost of Goods Sold	= the Cost of the 600 Oldest Units Available During the Period	
	= 400($10) + 100($11) + 100($12)	= $ 6,300
Ending Inventory	= the Cost of the 300 Most Recently Added Units	
	= 100($12) + 200($13)	= <u>3,800</u>
Sum of Ending Inventory and Cost of Goods Sold		$10,100

D. Weighted Average

1. The average cost per unit for the period = $10,100/900 = $11.22

2. Both cost of goods sold and ending inventory reflect the average cost during the period.

Cost of Goods Sold	$= \$11.22(600)$	$= \$6,732$
Ending Inventory	$= \$11.22(300)$	$= \underline{3,366}$
Sum of Ending Inventory and Cost of Goods Sold		$\$10,098^{*}$

(*off by $2 due to rounding of the average cost per unit)

E. LIFO

Cost of Goods Sold	$=$ the Cost of the 600 Most Recently Acquired Units Available During the Period	
	$= 200(\$13) + 200(\$12) + 100(\$11) + 100(\$10)$	$= \$7,100$
Ending Inventory	$=$ the Cost of the 300 Oldest Available Units	
	$= 300(\$10)$	$= \underline{3,000}$
Sum of Ending Inventory and Cost of Goods Sold		$\$10,100$

F. Comparison

1. The cost of the inventory item sold by this firm steadily increased during the period. The ranking, highest to lowest in terms of dollar amount, of cost of goods sold and ending inventory:

Cost of Goods Sold		Ending Inventory	
LIFO	$7,100	FIFO	$3,800
W. Ave.	6,732	W.Ave.	3,366
FIFO	6,300	LIFO	3,000

NOTE: *Calculation of cost of goods sold:* This example calculated cost of goods sold directly. Although this may be possible for firms with low unit volume, for most firms using a periodic system, the ending inventory cost is measured first through an inventory count and application of unit costs, and then cost of goods sold is computed by subtracting the ending inventory cost from cost of goods available for sale.

NOTE: *Goods to be considered in the calculation of cost of goods sold:* A periodic system assumes all goods purchased anytime during the year are available for sale. The time period assumption of accounting supports this view. In this example, the last purchase occurred *after* the last sale. Thus, the last purchase could not possibly have been sold. However, LIFO included the last purchase as the very first purchase assumed sold, and the weighted average method also included the purchase in the computation of cost per unit. Given the time period assumption of accounting, the inclusion of the last purchase in the computations is appropriate.

Perpetual Inventory System and Cost-Flow Assumption

This lesson presents the accounting for inventory under a perpetual inventory system.

After studying this lesson, you should be able to:

1. Complete the entries to record inventory under the perpetual system.

2. Calculate ending inventory under the perpetual inventory system using specific identification, weighted average, FIFO and LIFO cost flow assumptions.

I. Typical Entries

A. In illustrating the typical entries for the perpetual inventory system, assume the merchandise inventory account balance on January 1, 20X7 is $100,000.

Purchases of inventory on account

Merchandise Inventory	XX	
Accounts Payable		XX

Paid delivery charges on purchased merchandise

Merchandise Inventory	XX	
Cash		XX

Returned damaged or defective merchandise

Accounts Payable	XX	
Merchandise Inventory		XX

Paid for merchandise and received a cash discount

Accounts Payable	XX	
Merchandise Inventory		XX
Cash		XX

Sold merchandise on account

Accounts Receivable	XX	
Sales		XX
Cost of Goods Sold	XX	
Merchandise Inventory		XX

B. The main differences between these entries and those for the periodic system are:

1. the use of the inventory account rather than purchases for the acquisition of inventory and adjustments such as returns and discounts; and

2. the recording of cost of goods sold at sale, rather than at the end of the period.

C. **End of the Period**—A physical count of ending inventory should be completed to confirm inventory records. If inventory shrinkage has occurred (loss, theft, breakage), or if recording errors have been made, an appropriate adjusting entry would be prepared to reduce inventory to the amount per the physical count. The entry would reduce the inventory account and record a shrinkage loss.

D. **Cost-Flow Assumption**—A perpetual system considers only goods on hand when computing cost of goods sold for a specific sale. As opposed to the periodic system, which considers all goods on hand during the period when computing cost of goods sold, a perpetual system computes cost of goods sold only for the goods that have actually been purchased through the date of sale.

E. **Specific Identification**—The results (values placed on cost of goods sold and ending inventory) for this cost-flow assumption are the same for both the periodic and perpetual systems. The specific cost of each item sold is used to compute the cost of goods sold.

F. **Moving Average**—The term *moving average* always implies the perpetual inventory system. Rather than having a single weighted average cost per unit for the accounting period, the company computes a new weighted average cost per unit after each purchase of inventory. That moving average is used for costing all subsequent sales until another purchase takes place, at which time the moving average is modified by the new purchase. When merchandise is sold, the current weighted average cost per unit is multiplied by the number of units sold to determine the amount of the cost-of-goods-sold entry.

   1. In a period of steadily rising prices, the moving average method (perpetual) results in lower cost of goods sold than the weighted average method (periodic). The moving average method applies earlier (and, therefore, lower) costs to sales during the year relative to the overall higher weighted average cost for the entire period.

G. **FIFO**—The results (values placed on cost of goods sold and ending inventory) for this cost flow assumption are the same for both the periodic and perpetual systems. The cost of the beginning inventory and earliest units purchased are assigned to cost of goods sold leaving the most recent purchase costs to be assigned to ending inventory.

H. **LIFO**—The results for LIFO-perpetual differ from those of LIFO-periodic. In the perpetual system, each sale is costed with the most recent purchase available preceding that sale. The periodic system uses the latest purchases for the entire period. Thus in a year of steadily rising prices, perpetual LIFO yields a lower cost-of-goods-sold figure because it uses earlier purchases. Periodic LIFO would assume the sale of the very latest purchases in the period irrespective of the sequencing of sales and purchases.

Example
The data for the previous example of the four cost-flow assumptions is now applied in a perpetual system in this example. The purchases and sales of the firm's one product are given in chronological order for the period. The firm sells the oldest units on hand first.

Beginning inventory:	400 Units @ $10 per Unit
Purchase 1:	100 Units @ $11 per Unit
Sale 1:	200 Units
Purchase 2:	200 Units @ $12 per Unit
Sale 2:	400 Units
Purchase 3:	200 Units @ $13 per Unit

Beginning Inventory	+ Purchases =	Ending Inventory	+ Sales
400 Units	+ 500 Units =	300 Units	+ 600 Units

Cost of Goods Available for Sale = Cost in Beginning Inventory

+ Purchases Cost

$$= 400(\$10) + 100(\$11) + 200(\$12) + 200(\$13) = \$10,100$$

The sum of ending inventory and cost of goods sold for all four methods must sum to $10,100. This amount is the cost of goods available for sale. During the period, there were 900 units available for sale.

I. Specific Identification and FIFO —The results for both of these assumptions are the same for both the periodic and perpetual systems and are not repeated here.

A **moving average** is not needed until there is a sale to cost. The first sale occurs after the first purchase. The average unit cost of beginning inventory and the first purchase = ($4,000 + $1,100)/ 500 = $10.20. The following table illustrates the application of the moving averages.

Event	Units	Cost	Moving Average	Computation
Beginning inventory	400	$4,000		
+ Purchase 1	100	1,100		
=	500	5,100	$10.20	= $5,100/500
– Sale 1	(200)	(2,040)		= $10.20(200)
=	300	3,060		
+ Purchase 2	200	2,400		
=	500	5,460	$10.92	= $5,460/500
– Sale 2	(400)	(4,368)		= $10.92(400)
=	100	1,092		
+ Purchase 3	200	2,600		
=	300	3,692	$12.31	= $3,692/300

For example, Sale 1 is costed at $10.20, the moving average of goods on hand just before the sale. Removing those units leaves 300 units in inventory and $3,060 in cost. Purchase 2, at $12 per unit, is added into both the units and cost columns. $12 exceeds the previous moving average; therefore the moving average after Purchase 2 increases. That average is applied to Sale 2 and so forth. The final moving average of $12.31 reflects the higher purchase cost of Purchase 3 and will be used to cost sales the next period until the first purchase in that period is made.

Ending Inventory =	$3,692
Cost of Goods Sold = $2,040 + $4,368	6,408
Total = Cost of Goods Available for Sale	$10,100

J. **LIFO**—To cost sales, the latest purchases available at time of sale are used.

Cost of Goods Sold:

    Sale 1 (200 units):100($11) (Purchase 1) + 100($10)(Beg. Inv.) = $2,100

    Sale 2 (400 units):200($12) (Purchase 2) + 200($10)(Beg. Inv.) =   <u>4,400</u>

    Total Cost of Goods Sold $6,500

Ending Inventory:

    From Purchase 3 (all remaining): 200($13) = $2,600

    From Beginning Inventory (100 Units Remaining): 100($10) =   <u>1,000</u>

    Total Ending Inventory $3,600

Check:

    Cost of Goods Sold $6,500

    + Ending Inventory   <u>3,600</u>

    = Cost of Goods Available $10,100

Evaluation of FIFO and LIFO

This lesson emphasizes the differences in FIFO and LIFO cost-flow assumptions.

After studying this lesson, you should be able to:

1. Describe the income statement and balance sheet effect of using FIFO or LIFO valuation.

2. Describe what is meant by *LIFO liquidation* and the effect on the income statement.

I. **Evaluation of FIFO and LIFO**

A. Regardless of price changes, the following effects hold and form the basis for comparing the two methods:

	Ending Inventory	Cost of Goods Sold
FIFO	Reflects latest costs	Reflects earliest costs
LIFO	Reflects earliest costs	Reflects latest costs

B. Thus, if inventory costs have been rising, LIFO shows lower ending inventory, higher cost of goods sold, and lower income. The opposite is true if costs have been declining.

C. **FIFO**

1. In assessing the relative attributes of FIFO, it is important to remember three important points of emphasis.

   a. If FIFO is employed by a business entity, the flow of costs is the same as the physical flow of goods for most firms.

   b. If FIFO is employed by a business entity, the balance sheet valuation of inventory is an approximation to current cost, which is considered more relevant than historical cost.

   c. If FIFO is employed by a business entity, however, the matching of revenues and expenses on the income statement is not considered ideal. Frequently, a company will be matching the revenues of the current year with the cost of merchandise acquired in a prior accounting period.

2. Thus, if FIFO is chosen, the inventory value in the balance sheet is a current and relevant amount, but cost of goods sold (and, therefore, gross margin and income) are considered to be less current or relevant. FIFO favors the balance sheet. These effects hold regardless of the direction of price level changes (increase or decrease) during the period.

D. **LIFO**

1. In assessing the relative attributes of LIFO, it is important to remember three important points of emphasis.

   a. If LIFO is employed by a business entity, the matching of revenues and expenses on the income statement is significantly improved over FIFO. That is, the income statement involves the matching of revenues of the current year with the cost of merchandise acquired in the current year.

   b. If LIFO is employed by a business entity, there are usually income tax advantages associated with that choice. In periods of rising prices, LIFO will result in a higher cost of goods sold and a lower tax burden for the business enterprise. However, due to the LIFO conformity rule, if LIFO is chosen for tax purposes, the firm must also use it for the books. Thus, the firm cannot reduce its taxes with LIFO and at the same time use FIFO for financial reporting purposes in the quest to maximize reported income.

   c. If LIFO is employed by a business entity, the balance sheet presentation of inventory is less than ideal. For the company employing LIFO, inventory on the balance sheet typically reflects the cost of the "oldest" merchandise included in the company's inventory records. This means the balance sheet does not reflect the current cost of inventory and often times, means the inventory is undervalued on the balance sheet.

2. Thus, if LIFO is chosen, the inventory value in the balance sheet can be a very noncurrent and irrelevant amount, but cost of goods sold (and, therefore, gross margin and income) are considered to be much more current or relevant. LIFO favors the income statement. These effects hold regardless of the direction of price level changes (increase or decrease) during the period.

3. In addition, LIFO tends to minimize *inventory* profits (also called *phantom* or *illusory* profits).

> **Example**
> Inventory costs have been rising. Sales for the year are $100,000 and cost of goods sold is $70,000 under LIFO and $60,000 under FIFO. The $70,000 of cost of goods sold under LIFO is an approximation to the cost of replacing the inventory sold during the period because it represents later purchases in the year. If the firm chooses FIFO, it reports $10,000 more in pretax earnings but that amount really is not disposable income because it must be used to replace higher cost inventory in the next accounting period. The $10,000 is thus illusory income.

E. Cost-Flow Assumptions

1. In choosing the appropriate cost-flow assumption, a business entity should select the cost-flow assumption that allows the company to do the best job of determining periodic net income.

2. However, firms often choose FIFO to maximize their reported income. This in turn improves certain financial ratios and may be helpful in meeting requirements placed on the firm by its creditors. In addition, management compensation, if tied to income, will be maximized.

3. On the other hand, the main reason for choosing LIFO is to minimize income tax. The main advantage of choosing LIFO is tax minimization. The reporting benefit of providing the most current cost of goods sold figure is an unintended consequence for most LIFO firms. A negative consequence to LIFO that sometimes occurs is the tax effect of a LIFO liquidation.

II. LIFO Liquidation

A. What happens when the number of units purchased or produced is less than the number of units sold? Under LIFO, the computation of cost of goods sold for the current period first uses all the purchases for the period. Then it works backward in time and liquidates layers that were added in previous periods (latest layer added first), until the total number of units sold for the period is costed. A LIFO liquidation is that part of current-period cost of goods sold represented by the cost of goods acquired in prior years.

B. LIFO liquidations occur either from (1) poor planning, or (2) lack of supply.

Example

Assume the following for the current year for a LIFO firm. The beginning inventory is composed of a single layer added in a previous year.

	Units	Unit Cost
Beginning Inventory	100,000	$35.00
Purchases	500,000	$55.00

Merchandise Sold During the Year: 505,000 Units

Cost of goods sold for the year under LIFO = $27,675,000 = 500,000($55) + 5,000($35). Under LIFO, the current year purchases are used first, and only then are the earlier layers used. (Note: the older inventory items are not actually present; rather, only the cost of those items is included in inventory. Remember that LIFO is a cost-flow assumption, not a description of the actual movement of goods.)

The amount of the LIFO liquidation, thus, is $175,000 ($35 × 5,000). 5,000 more goods were sold than acquired in the year. The $175,000 amount is that part of cost of goods sold represented by the cost of goods acquired in earlier years.

C. LIFO Liquidations are to be Avoided for Two Reasons

1. The main purpose for using LIFO is tax minimization. In the above example, assuming the firm will replenish the 5,000 units liquidated anyway, the firm increases its taxable income by $20 per unit unnecessarily. The $20 amount is the difference between the current-period cost of $55 and the $35 cost in the older layer. Thus, taxable income will increase by $100,000 ($20 x 5,000). If the firm had been able to purchase 505,000 units in the period, this extra tax liability would have been avoided because the entire cost of goods sold would be based on the $55 unit cost.

2. For financial statement reporting, the main advantage of LIFO is in matching current-period costs with current revenues. The liquidation distorts the relationship between current sales and current cost of goods sold. The larger the liquidation, the worse the distortion.

Dollar-Value LIFO

This lesson presents the calculation to determine ending inventory value using dollar-value LIFO.

After studying this lesson, you should be able to:

1. Explain why a company would want to use dollar value LIFO.

2. Calculate ending inventory using dollar-value LIFO. This calculation includes: a) converting ending inventory to base year costs; b) determine the increase in inventory at base year cost; c) convert the current year layer to current-year costs; d) add current layer to beginning-of-year dollar-value LIFO to derive end-of-year dollar-value LIFO.

I. Introduction

A. Remember that in this entire discussion, for external purposes the firm is using LIFO, applied through the DV LIFO method. The firm may use another cost flow assumption (typically FIFO) internally.

B. Reduces the Effect of the Liquidation Problem—The dollar-value LIFO conversion technique takes a company's ending inventory in FIFO dollars (usually) and converts them to LIFO dollars. In doing so, the impact of the liquidation problem is reduced.

C. Allows Companies to Use FIFO Internally—Most companies prefer to use FIFO for internal management reports and internal operating decisions. dollar-value LIFO allows companies an opportunity to do so.

> **Note**
> *For CPA Exam candidates, a discussion question is frequently included in dollar-value LIFO problems. That discussion question involves a discussion of the advantages of dollar-value LIFO over the quantity of goods LIFO approach (shown previously). These advantages are listed below.*

D. Reduces Clerical Costs—As mentioned earlier, most LIFO companies prefer LIFO for external reporting purposes and prefer FIFO for internal purposes. Through the use of Dollar-Value LIFO, a company can maintain a FIFO system for internal purposes, and then convert those results to LIFO for external purposes. Please note that through the use of dollar-value LIFO, a company must maintain only a single inventory system (FIFO) during the accounting period, thus reducing clerical costs.

II. Steps in Implementing Dollar-Value LIFO

A. The establishment of inventory pools simply means the company needs to group similar products into inventory groups. For example, a department store might have one inventory pool that includes appliances.

B. The conversion index can be calculated internally or obtained from an external source. Regardless of the method of acquisition, the conversion index represents the calculation shown below.

Conversion Index = Ending Inventory in Current-Year Dollars / Ending Inventory in Base-Year Dollars

C. *Base-year* dollars refers to the specific price level for the pool in effect at the beginning of the year in which the firm adopted LIFO. When this index is multiplied by the increase in inventory for the year as measured in base-year dollars, the result is the increase in inventory in current costs—the layer added to DV LIFO ending inventory.

Examples

1. A firm using FIFO for many years decides to change to LIFO and use DV LIFO as the specific method of applying LIFO. The beginning inventory in that year is $40,000.

That value, if not reduced to market via the LC-M valuation process, is the beginning inventory in base year dollars for DV LIFO. If it represents market, then the value must be increased back to cost before applying LIFO.

2. If an external index is unavailable, the conversion index at the end of a year for a pool equals:

(current cost of ending inventory) / (base-year cost of ending inventory)

When FIFO is used internally, the ending inventory under FIFO is used as the current cost.

D. Conversion of the FIFO Ending Inventory to LIFO Ending Inventory for Financial Statement Reporting Purposes—This is the objective of the DV LIFO method.

Example

A numerical example illustrates the steps. A firm adopts LIFO (DV LIFO) at the beginning of the current year (Year 1). The beginning inventory under FIFO is $2,000 at cost. That amount is the beginning inventory in base-year dollars (base-year cost). The base-year price index is defined as 1.00. All price changes are measured in relation to the base-year index of 1.00 for simplicity.

The FIFO ending inventory for the current year (Year 1) is $3,200. The ending inventory in base-year dollars is determined to be $2,909. Prices of this type of inventory have increased 10% for the year. An external price index at year-end is 1.10 for this type of inventory. (Note: this agrees with the internal price index, computed as $3,200/$2,909, which also equals 1.10).

1. Convert FIFO ending inventory to ending inventory at base-year cost

Ending inventory = FIFO ending inventory(1.00/1.10)

In base-year dollars : $2,909 = $3,200(1.00/1.10)

2. Compute the change in inventory in base-year cost.

Change in inventory in base-year cost	=	Ending inventory in base-year dollars	−	Beginning inventory in base-year dollars
$909	=	$2,909	−	$2,000

This result is important because it shows that there has been a *physical* increase in inventory for the year. With the measurement of the dollar fixed at the base year, the increase could not have been caused by increases in the price level. The $909 amount is the layer added in the current year at base-year cost. But LIFO must measure layers at current cost. The next step accomplishes this objective.

3. Compute the current-year layer at current-year costs.

Current-year layer at current-year cost	=	Current-year layer at base-year cost	×	Conversion index
$1,000	=	$909		(1.10/1.00)

4. Compute ending inventory under DV LIFO (reported in the balance sheet).

Ending DV LIFO inventory	=	Beginning DV LIFO inventory	+	Current-year layer at current-year cost
$3,000	=	$2,000	+	$1,000

1. This process illustrates that DV LIFO uses price-level indices to measure the inventory increase first in base-year cost, and then expresses each year's layer at current cost through the conversion index. The result is a DV LIFO ending inventory that is the sum of layers measured in current dollars for the period the layers were added. This method is called the *double-extension* method because the ending inventory is extended at both base-year cost and ending current-year cost.

2. The balance sheet for Year 1 reports $3,000 of inventory. This amount consists of two layers: beginning inventory of $2,000 and the Year 1 layer of $1,000. The two layers reflect different price-level indices (1.00 and 1.10 respectively).

3. Cost of goods sold is computed as in any periodic inventory context. Ending inventory as computed for DV LIFO is subtracted from cost of goods available for sale. The result is cost of goods sold.

Example

This example extends the previous DV LIFO example two more years to show how layers are accumulated, and how to handle a LIFO liquidation in DV LIFO.

Current (FIFO)	FIFO Cost of Ending Inventory	Ending Price Level Index
Year 2	$4,025	1.15
Year 3	4,100	1.20

Beginning DV LIFO inventory (from Year 1) $3,000

Ending inventory at base-year cost = $4,025(1.00/1.15) = $3,500

Increase in inventory at base-year cost = $3,500 - $2,909* = $591

Increase in inventory at Year 2 prices = $591(1.15/1.00)   680

Ending inventory, DV LIFO $3,680

*This amount is from step 1 of Year 1, the ending inventory at base-year cost for Year 1.

The $3,680 amount is really the sum of three layers reflecting different prices. This schedule helps to understand the result of DV LIFO:

Layer	In Base-Year Cost	Conversion Index	DV LIFO
Base	$2,000	1.00	$2,000
Year 1	909	1.10	1,000
Year 2	591	1.15	680
Ending Year 2 DV LIFO inventory			$3,680

Beginning DV LIFO inventory (from Year 2) $3,680

Ending inventory at base-year cost = $4,100(1.00/1.20) = $3,417

Decrease in inventory at base-year cost = $3,500* − $3,417 = $83

Decrease Year 2 layer by $83 at base-year cost

Decrease in Year 2 layer at DV LIFO cost = $83(1.15/1.00) =   (95)

Ending DV LIFO $3,585

*From Year 2 base-year cost.

At current cost, inventory for Year 3 appeared to increase. However, after converting to base-year dollars (removing the effect of the price level increase), the inventory decrease, in physical quantity, was apparent. No layer was added in Year 3. The most recent layer added is reduced under LIFO.

Again, the breakdown of layers at the end of Year 3:

Layer	In Base-Year Cost	Conversion Index	DV LIFO
Base	$2,000	1.00	$2,000
Year 1	909	1.10	1,000
Year 2	508[*]	1.15	<u>584</u>
Ending Year 3 DV LIFO inventory			$3,584[#]

[*]$591 – $83 decrease in base-year dollars
[#]$1 difference due to rounding

Subsequent Measurement of Inventory

In July 2015, the FASB issued ASU 2015-11 Inventory (Topic 330), *Simplifying the Measurement of Inventory*. The ASU changes the application of lower of cost or market (LC-M) in the subsequent valuation of inventory. The effective date is for fiscal years beginning after December 15, 2016 (2017 for calendar-year companies) and early adoption is permitted. **The new rules are subject to testing on the CPA Exam beginning in January 2017.**

This material presents the calculation for lower of cost or market (LC-M) or net realizable value (LC-NRV) for subsequent inventory valuation.

After studying this lesson, you should be able to:

1. Identify and apply the appropriate method for subsequent measurement of inventory: lower of cost or market (LC-M) or net realizable value (LC-NRV).

    a. Inventory measured using FIFO or average cost utilizes subsequent measurement that is LC-NRV.

    b. Inventory measured using LIFO or retail method utilizes subsequent measurement that is LC-M.

2. Define cost, market, the floor, and the ceiling used in the LC-M calculations.

3. Complete a calculation for subsequent measurement of inventory, and determine what value should be shown on the balance sheet.

I. Loss on Inventory

A. In addition to the normal valuation of inventory at cost and choice of inventory cost-flow assumption (FIFO, LIFO), GAAP requires that firms recognize an end-of-period loss on inventory if its utility has declined. If market is below cost, then inventory must be written down to market. The loss cannot be postponed until the period of sale.

   1. If cost < market, there is no loss recognition and the inventory is reported at cost.

   2. If cost > market, a loss is recognized and the inventory is written down to market.

II. Subsequent Measurement of Inventory

A. Effective January 1, 2017, if the entity uses FIFO or weighted average inventory valuation method, then the subsequent measurement is cost (as determined by FIFO or weighted average) or net realizable value (LC-NRV).

> **Note**
> LC-NRV applies to all inventory valuation methods that are **not** LIFO or Retail Inventory Method. In essence, this means that LC-NRV is applied to inventories carried at FIFO or weighted average.

B. If the inventory is measured using LIFO or the Retail Inventory Method (RIM), then the subsequent measurement is cost (as determined by LIFO or RIM) or market (L-CM) with market defined below and limited to a ceiling and a floor.

C. The general concept is that an entity must recognize a loss on inventory if the utility of the inventory has declined. If subsequent value of the inventory is below cost, then inventory must be written down and a loss recognized. The loss resulting from a decline in value cannot be postponed until the period of sale.

   1. If cost < market or NRV, there is no loss recognition and the inventory is reported at cost.

   2. If cost > market or NRV, a loss is recognized and the inventory is written down as described below.

D. The result is that inventory is reported at the lower of cost or market (LC-M) or lower of cost or net realizable value (LC-NRV). The total expense or loss is limited to the historical cost of the inventory.

But the subsequent valuation requirement shifts a portion of the cost as a loss or expense to the period in which the inventory has declined in value.

III. Inventories NOT Carried at LIFO or RIM (i.e., Carried at FIFO or Weighted Average) use LC-NRV

A. Subsequent valuation of inventories carried at FIFO or weighted average are measured at the lower of the cost basis or net realizable value. Net realizable value is defined in the Master Glossary in the FASB's Accounting Standards Codification as the "estimated selling prices in the ordinary course of business, less reasonably predictable cost of completion, disposal, and transportation."

Example

An item of inventory had cost using FIFO of $100.

Selling price = $99

Replacement cost = $88

Cost of completion, disposal, and transportation = $9

The entity compares the FIFO cost ($100) to NRV (selling price less cost to sell $99 − $9 = $90). Since the NRV is less than cost, the inventory is written down to its NRV of $90.

IV. Inventories Carried at LIFO or RIM Use LC-M.

A. Lower of cost or market is applied when the cost is assigned using LIFO or retain inventory method.

B. Determine Market Value

1. Market is generally *replacement cost*, subject to a range of values defined by an established *ceiling value* and an established *floor value*.

2. The ceiling value is net realizable value. That is, the ceiling value is calculated by reducing the sales price by the estimated cost to complete and sell the inventory.

3. The floor value is net realizable value reduced by the normal profit margin.

C. Calculate Market Value

1. If the replacement cost value is within the range established by the ceiling value and the floor value, market is equal to replacement cost.

2. If the replacement cost value is greater than the ceiling value, market is equal to the ceiling value.

3. If the replacement cost value is less than the floor value, market is equal to the floor value.

4. Market is also simply the middle amount (in dollar terms) of the three amounts: replacement cost, net realizable value, and net realizable value less normal profit margin. Market cannot exceed the ceiling or be less than the floor.

Example

At year-end, the following values pertain to an item of inventory:

Cost—determined using LIFO	$100
Replacement cost	80
Selling price	120
Estimated cost of completion and selling	30
Normal profit margin	20

The three values to determine market value:

Replacement cost	80
Net realizable value = $120 − $30	= 90 (ceiling)
Net realizable value less normal profit margin =	$90 − $20
	= 70 (floor)

Market value = $80, which is replacement cost because it is between the ceiling and floor amounts. It is also the middle of the three figures in dollar terms. The final LC-M valuation thus is $80 because market is lower than original cost ($100). The inventory would be reported at $80 and a holding loss of $20 would be recorded (cost of $100 less market of $80). If market had exceeded cost, then the inventory would be reported at cost.

1. If replacement cost were instead $95, then market value would be $90, the middle of the three figures determining market value.

2. If replacement cost were instead $65, then market value would be $70, the middle of the three figures determining market value.

Note
Market value cannot exceed the ceiling or be less than the floor.

D. **Summary**—The LC-M valuation process has two steps:

1. Compute market value (the middle of the three amounts).

2. Value inventory at the lower of original cost or market value (LC-M).

Note
Candidates often become so involved with the first step that they forget to apply the second. Once you have found market, don't forget to compare it to cost (Step 2) for the final valuation under LC-M.

V. **Lower of Cost or Market Comparison**

A. GAAP allows flexibility in application of LC-M, but the lower of cost or market comparison must be completed on a consistent basis from year to year. In making the comparison, a company can employ one of three approaches.

1. **Individual item basis**—If a company has 1,000 inventory items and chooses the individual item approach, a total of 1,000 comparisons will be made to determine the lower of cost or market for ending inventory.

2. **Category basis**—If a company has 1,000 inventory items grouped into 10 categories, a total of 10 comparisons will be made to determine the lower of cost or market for ending inventory.

3. **Total basis**—If a company wishes, it can make a single comparison to determine the lower of cost or market for ending inventory.

B. The individual item basis yields the most conservative (lowest) inventory value (and largest holding loss) because for each item the lower of cost or market is chosen. There is no chance for items with market exceeding cost to cancel against items with cost exceeding market, as there is with the other two approaches.

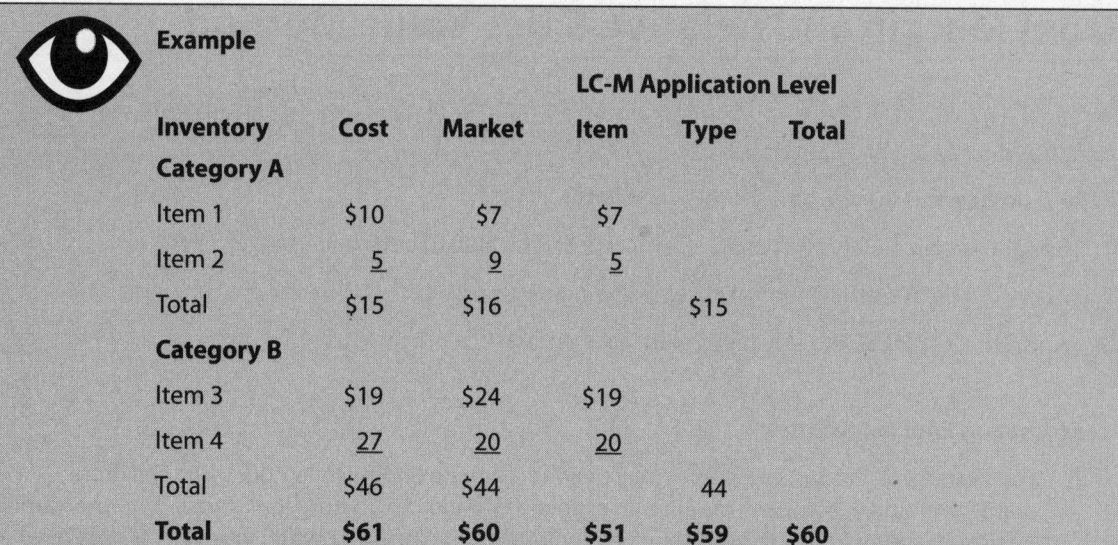

Example

LC-M Application Level

Inventory	Cost	Market	Item	Type	Total
Category A					
Item 1	$10	$7	$7		
Item 2	<u>5</u>	<u>9</u>	<u>5</u>		
Total	$15	$16		$15	
Category B					
Item 3	$19	$24	$19		
Item 4	<u>27</u>	<u>20</u>	<u>20</u>		
Total	$46	$44		44	
Total	**$61**	**$60**	**$51**	**$59**	**$60**

The firm may choose from among $51, $59, and $60 as its LC-M valuation for inventory. All three are lower than cost of $61. The higher the level of applying the LC-M valuation procedure, the higher the resulting valuation.

VI. Lower of Cost or Market—Journal Entry—Once the lower of cost or market comparison is completed and the ending valuation is found (using either LC-M or LC-NRV), the formal entry of this information can be achieved by employing the *direct method* or the *allowance method*. Under the direct method, any holding loss (difference between a higher cost and a lower market value) related to inventory is simply included in cost of goods sold. It is *directly* included in cost of goods sold. Under the allowance method, any holding loss related to inventory is separately identified in a contra inventory account with separate disclosure of the holding loss. Cost of goods sold does not include the holding loss under this method.

Example
A firm uses the category level comparison to determine market value. Total cost of inventory is $30,000, and the total market value is $27,000 at the end of the year.
To record the holding loss of $3,000, either of the two approaches can be used. The adjusting entry to record the loss under these approaches is:

Direct method:

Cost of goods sold	3,000	
Inventory		3,000

Allowance method:

Holding loss	3,000	
Allowance to reduce inventory to LC-M		3,000

The allowance method reports $3,000 less of cost of goods sold in the income statement but compensates by reporting a separate holding loss of $3,000. The allowance account, a contra inventory account, reduces net inventory in the balance sheet to $27,000. Both methods yield the same net inventory valuation and income. However, the components of income are different under the two methods.

Gross Margin and Relative Sales Value Method

This lesson presents the gross margin method for estimating ending inventory and allocation of inventory cost based on relative sales values.

After studying this lesson, you should be able to:

1. Explain margin on sales versus margin on cost and be able to determine cost to sales.

2. Apply the gross margin method to value ending inventory.

3. Apply the relative sales value method to value ending inventory.

I. **Estimating Ending Inventory**

A. For a variety of reasons, companies may need to estimate ending inventory using the gross margin method. A company may use an estimate of ending inventory for internal purposes during interim periods when a physical count is prohibitively expensive or when inventory is destroyed as the result of a casualty. The gross margin method can be used **only** for estimation purposes. It may not be used for financial reporting of inventory.

II. **Gross Margin Method**

A. The gross margin method estimates cost of goods sold from sales using a percentage based on historical data. Then, ending inventory can be inferred from beginning inventory, purchases, and cost of goods sold.

B. To use the gross margin method, a company must have a consistent gross margin percentage (margin as a percentage of sales or margin based on cost). If inventory is heterogeneous, the method should be applied to pools of inventory with relatively homogeneous gross margin percentages.

III. **Margin on Sales, Margin on Cost**

A. **Formulas:**

1. The margin on sales is gross margin divided by sales, or sales less cost of goods sold divided by sales.

> Gross Margin Percentage = Margin on Sales = (Sales − Cost of Goods Sold)/Sales

2. The margin on cost is sales less cost of goods sold divided by cost of goods sold.

> Margin on Cost = (Sales − Cost of Goods Sold) / Cost of Goods Sold

B. The use of the gross margin method depends on how the margin on sales is expressed.

C. Margin on cost is always greater than margin on sales because sales exceed cost. The two ways of expressing the margin are related. The following two examples show how each may be converted to the other.

D. The goal is to use one of the two formulas to determine cost/sales. It is the cost/sales ratio that is used to determine cost of goods sold.

Example

1. Assume gross margin (also referred to as margin on sales) is 40%. Set sales to 1.00, and margin to .40. This implies that cost is .60 times sales:

Sales	1.00
− Cost	.60
= Margin	.40

Therefore, margin / cost = .40 / .60 = .67. Thus, a gross margin percentage of 40% is equivalent to a margin on cost of 67%.

2. Assume margin on cost is 45%. Set cost to 1.00, and margin to .45. This implies that sales are 1.45 times cost.

Sales	1.40
− Cost	1.00
= Margin	.45

Therefore, margin on sales = .45 / 1.45 = .31. Thus, a gross margin percentage of 31% is equivalent to a margin on cost of 45%.

Formulas can also be used to convert one margin expression to the other:

(Margin on sales) / (1 − Margin on sales) = Margin on cost

(Margin on cost) / (1 + Margin on cost) = Margin on sales

IV. Using the Gross Margin Method

A. The purpose of the previous short section was to describe how each of the two different expressions of margin can be converted into the other. If you are comfortable with this method, the use of the gross margin method is straightforward.

> Beg. Inventory + Net Purchases = End. Inventory + Cost of Goods Sold
>
> Beg. Inventory + Net Purchases = End. Inventory + Sales (Cost/Sales)

B. The second equation shows that cost of goods sold is estimated by sales multiplied by the cost-to-sales ratio. This ratio equals 1 − gross margin %, which can easily be computed using the conversion methods shown above. The unknown in the equation is ending inventory. The gross margin method allows an estimate of ending inventory.

Example
A firm's inventory is destroyed by fire on April 4. Beginning inventory is $20,000, net purchases through April 4 are $250,000, and sales through April 4 amount to $320,000.

First, assume the gross margin is 40%. Then the cost/sales ratio is 60%.

Beg. inventory	+ Net purchases	=	End. inventory +	Sales(cost/sales)
$20,000	+ $250,000	=	? +	$320,000(.60)
			Ending inventory =	$78,000

This is an estimate of the cost of inventory destroyed (i.e., the ending inventory at April 4).

Now assume the margin on cost is 45%. From the above examples of converting margins, the gross margin percentage is 31%, and therefore the cost/sales ratio is 69%.

Beg. inventory	+ Net purchases	=	End. inventory +	Sales(cost/sales)
$20,000	+ $250,000	=	? +	$320,000(.69)
			Ending inventory =	$49,200

In this example, the firm could not have counted the inventory destroyed but is able to estimate its cost for insurance purposes by applying the gross margin method. The method is also useful for budgetary and other internal reporting purposes when an exact calculation is not needed.

V. Relative Sales Value Method

A. Firms may be able to obtain significant discounts by purchasing different types of inventory from the same supplier. This may occur, for example, in a liquidation or distress sale. U.S. GAAP requires that the total price be allocated based on the market values or selling prices of the individual inventory items.

Example
Three items of inventory were purchased for $45. The unit selling prices (for the buyer upon resale) are given below.

Inventory item	Unit sales price
A	$20
B	25
C	40
Total	$85

The cost of the inventory ($45) would be allocated to each item based on the relative sales value as demonstrated in the following calculation.

Item A is recorded at $10.59 = (($20 / $85) $45).

Item B is recorded at $13.23 = (($25 / $85) $45).

Item C is recorded at $21.18 = (($40 / $85) $45).

Retail Inventory Method

This lesson presents the retail inventory method for estimating ending inventory.

After studying this lesson, you should be able to:

1. Calculate the cost to retail percentage for the retail inventory method.

2. Calculate ending inventory using the retail inventory method.

I. **The Retail Inventory Method**—This method is used by retailers to estimate ending inventory at cost. Most retailers know the markup on the inventory items and are able to count ending inventory at retail prices (ever see the store employees counting items on a shelf?). This method is used both for internal decision purposes and for financial reporting of cost of goods sold and ending inventory.

II. **The Basic Method**

A. The retail inventory method, which is really a family of related methods, is based on three basic calculations.

B. *First*, ending inventory at retail is calculated or counted at year-end. *Second*, the cost-to-retail ratio is calculated. *Third*, the ending inventory at retail is multiplied by the cost-to-retail ratio to arrive at estimated inventory at cost.

C. Cost of goods sold is an implied amount, rather than a directly calculated amount under this method.

D. The method can be shown in equation form: $EI(cost) = EI(retail) \times C/R$, where EI is ending inventory and C/R is the cost-to-retail ratio for the period. The retail inventory method can be used with FIFO, LIFO, and average cost-flow assumptions. Cost of goods sold is found by subtracting ending inventory at cost from cost of goods available for sale.

> **Note**
> No matter which retail inventory method is used (FIFO, LIFO, or average), the entity would apply LC-M (not LC-NRV) when determining if there had been a decline in the value of the inventory that would warrant an inventory write-down.

E. **Basic Structure of the Retail Inventory Method:**

	Cost	Retail
Beginning Inventory	$200	$300
Purchases	2,000	3,000
Goods Available for Sale	2,200	3,300
Sales		(2,600)
Ending Inventory at Retail		700

Cost to Retail Ratio:
2,200/3,300 = 66 2/3%

Ending Inventory at Retail × Cost Ratio = Ending Inventory at Cost
$700 × 66 2/3% = $467

Cost of goods sold, then, is reported at the implied amount of $1,733 = $200 beginning inventory at cost + $2,000 purchases less $467 ending inventory.

F. This illustrates the "average" retail inventory method. It is one of five variations of the retail inventory method.

III. Terminology and Guidance in Applying the Retail Inventory Method

A. Original Selling Price—Cost plus initial markup.

B. Net Additional Markups—A net increase in the original selling price. This amount is the net sum of additional markups above the original selling price less additional markup cancellations. This amount is added only in the retail column and before computing the cost-to-retail ratio.

C. Net Markdowns—A net decrease in the original selling price. This amount is the net difference between markdowns, which are reductions in the original selling price, and markdown cancellations. This amount is subtracted only from the retail column and before computing the cost-to-retail ratio.

Examples

1. Cost: $20

Initial markup + 10

Additional markup $4

Additional markup cancellation (1)

Net additional markup + 3

Final selling price $33

2. Cost: $20

Initial markup + 10

Markdown ($4)

Markdown cancellation 1

Net markdown (3)

Final selling price $27

D. Transportation In—Added in the cost column only, before computing the cost-to-retail ratio.

E. Purchase Discounts—Subtracted in the cost column only, before computing the cost-to-retail ratio.

F. Purchase Returns and Allowances—The amount of merchandise available for sale has declined. This amount is subtracted in both the cost and retail columns before computing the cost-to-retail ratio.

G. Employee Discounts—The difference between the normal retail value of merchandise sold to employees and the amount actually paid by employees. This amount is subtracted along with sales from Goods Available for Sale at Retail to arrive at Ending Inventory at Retail, after computing the cost-to-retail ratio.

H. Normal Spoilage—Shown at retail value, subtracted along with sales from Goods Available for Sale at Retail to arrive at Ending Inventory at Retail, after computing the cost-to-retail ratio.

I. Abnormal Casualty Losses—Shown at both cost and retail, the amount of merchandise available for sale has declined. Reduce the cost and retail value of goods available for sale before computing the cost-to-retail ratio. This loss is usually recoverable through insurance.

IV. Variations—The variations of the retail inventory method are directly related to the calculation of the cost ratio. There are five variations, four of which are summarized below. The fifth is covered in the "Dollar-Value LIFO Retail" lesson.

    A. FIFO—The C/R excludes the cost of beginning inventory from the numerator and the retail value of beginning inventory from the denominator. Thus, C/R measures the cost-to-retail ratio only for the current-period purchases on the assumption that all beginning inventory will be sold (first-in, first-out). If ending inventory consists entirely of current-period purchases, the C/R should not include beginning inventory.

    B. FIFO, LC-M—The cost ratio excludes the cost of beginning inventory from the numerator and the retail value of beginning inventory from the denominator. Then, in an effort to arrive at a more conservative cost ratio, the calculation also excludes net markdowns from the cost ratio. This causes the denominator of C/R to be larger, because net markdowns are not subtracted, and thus the ratio itself is smaller. When C/R is multiplied by EI (retail), the resulting EI (cost) is smaller, approximating the effect of LC-M.

    C. Average—The cost ratio includes beginning inventory, along with current-period purchases in both the numerator and the denominator of C/R.

    D. Average, LC-M—The cost ratio includes beginning inventory, along with current-period purchases, in both the numerator and the denominator, but excludes net markdowns from the cost ratio calculation.

Note

On the CPA Exam, average LC-M is frequently referred to as the conventional retail inventory method. This method is the one most emphasized on the exam. The variations are presented here for completeness; however, the probability of questions on these variations is relatively low.

Example
Four variations of the retail inventory method.

	Cost	Retail
Beginning inventory	$ 100	$ 145
Net purchases	600	900
Net additional markups		70
Net markdowns		− 30
Goods available for sale	$ 700	$ 1,085
Less sales		− 800
Equals ending inventory at retail		$ 285

EI(cost) is not computed above because computing that amount is the objective of the retail method and the amount depends on the variation chosen by the firm. Also, if the *count* of ending inventory at retail is less than $285, a shrinkage loss is indicated. The actual count of ending inventory is the value to use for computing EI(cost) in that case. The $285 amount is the ending inventory *that should be present*, at retail.

FIFO: C/R = $600/($900 + $70 - $30) = .6383

EI(cost) = .6383($285) = $181.92

(Beginning inventory is excluded from the ratio.)

FIFO, LC-M: C/R = $600/($900 + $70) = .6186

EI(cost) = .6186($285) = $176.30

(Beginning inventory is excluded from the ratio and net markdowns are not subtracted in the denominator.)

Average: C/R = $700/$1,085 = .6452

EI(cost) = .6452($285) = $183.88

(Beginning inventory is included in the ratio.)

Average, LC-M : C/R = $700/($1,085 + $30) = .6278

EI(cost) = .6278($285) = $178.92

(Beginning inventory is included in the ratio and net markdowns are not subtracted in the denominator.)

Dollar-Value LIFO Retail

This lesson presents the dollar-value LIFO retail method for estimating ending inventory.

After studying this lesson, you should be able to:

1. Recognize that retail companies that use LIFO cost-flow assumption must use DV LIFO.

2. Identify the order of the DV LIFO retail calculation.

I. Introduction

A. The **dollar-value LIFO retail method (DV LIFO)** is used by companies that use the LIFO cost-flow assumption when they apply the retail inventory method. The companies must use the dollar-value approach in order to determine the LIFO layers. There are two independent steps:

1. DV LIFO is first applied to inventory at retail only—and in the same way it was illustrated before. This results in the measurement of the current-period layer measured in current retail dollars. So, DV LIFO is restricted to retail dollar application.

2. Then, the FIFO retail method (not LC-M; i.e., subtracting markdowns when computing C/R) cost-to-retail ratio is applied to this retail layer yielding the increase in cost at current prices. Finally, this cost layer is added to beginning inventory at DV LIFO cost to yield ending inventory at DV LIFO cost.

> **Note**
> Since DV LIFO is a form of LIFO, the subsequent measurement and testing for declines in inventory value would be LC-M as described in the lesson Subsequent Measurement of Inventory.

II. How to Remember which Step Comes First

A. Because inventory is counted at retail and the method is called DV LIFO retail, apply DV LIFO first, then apply the retail method that deflates the amounts back to cost.

Example

Assume the same information that was presented in the for the current year as in the previous example in the "Retail Inventory Method" lesson :

	Cost	Retail
Beginning inventory	$ 100	$ 145
Net purchases	600	900
Net additional markups		70
Net markdowns		– 30
Goods available for sale	$ 700	$ 1,085
Less sales		– 800
Equals ending inventory at retail		**$ 285**

Assume the firm adopted DV LIFO at the beginning of the current year. Therefore, the beginning inventory at retail in terms of base year dollars is $145. The price index is set at 1.00 at the beginning of the year and has climbed to 1.08 by the end of the year. The DV LIFO retail method is applied to the current year:

BI DV LIFO		$ 100.00
EI(retail, FIFO) =	$285.00	
EI(retail, base-year dollars) = $285(1.00/1.08) =	$263.89	
Increase in EI(retail, base-year dollars) = $263.89 – $145 =	$118.89	
Increase in EI(retail, FIFO) = $118.89(1.08/1.00) =	$128.40	
Increase in EI(cost, FIFO) = $128.40(.6383)*		81.96
EI DV LIFO		**$181.96**

*Cost ratio for FIFO (not LC-M) from previous example.

Later years are treated the same way. The DV LIFO method is applied as before, to subsequent year's retail dollars. Then, the FIFO cost-to-retail ratio for that year is applied to the retail layer measured in current retail dollars.

Inventory Errors

This lesson addresses how to correct for inventory errors.

After studying this lesson, you should be able to:

1. Determine the impact of an inventory error on any component of the balance sheet or income statement.

2. Complete the journal entry necessary to correct an inventory error.

I. **Introduction**

   A. Inventory effects are analyzed with the basic inventory equation:

   > Beginning Inventory + Net Purchases = Ending Inventory + Cost of Goods Sold

   B. If beginning inventory is understated, then cost of goods sold is also understated, everything else being the same, because the equation must balance. If ending inventory is understated, cost of goods sold must be overstated, again because the equation must balance.

   C. The journal entry and reporting for error corrections depend on both the error and the period of discovery.

Example

The ending inventory for Year 1 is understated $4,000 because the items in one wing of the warehouse were not counted. The effects of this error, ignoring tax effects, are:

	Year 1	Year 2
Beginning inventory:	not affected	understated $4,000
Ending inventory:	understated $4,000	not affected
Cost of goods sold:	overstated $4,000	understated $4,000
Net income:	understated $4,000	overstated $4,000
Retained earnings:	understated $4,000	is now correct*

*This is what is meant by a counterbalancing error. If it is never discovered, retained earnings automatically corrects itself, and with the new count of inventory at the end of the second year, the error disappears. However, the errors in the two years' financial statements do not automatically correct and would be present in the comparative statements.

If the error is discovered in Year 2, the following entry is made to correct the beginning balance of retained earnings:

Inventory	4,000	
Prior period adjustment (to retained earnings)		4,000

A prior-period adjustment is to the account in which the correction of an error in prior year earnings is recorded. The income statement impact of the prior-period error is closed to retained earnings. The prior-period adjustment increases the year 2 beginning balance of retained earnings to its correct amount as if year 1 income were correct. In the comparative statements for years 1 and 2, income for year 1 would be increased to its correct amount. All other affected accounts for year 1 also would be corrected.

If discovery occurs in Year 3, no entry is needed because counterbalancing has taken place. All year 2 ending account balances are correct. However, both year 1 and year 2 statements should be corrected if shown comparatively with year 3. All accounts for those years affected by the error would be restated to their correct amounts.

II. Error in Recording Purchases—What if a purchase at year-end was not recorded in the year of purchase (Year 1), but rather was recorded in the next year (Year 2), the year of payment? Assume the goods were counted in EI in year of purchase.

A. If the Error is Never Discovered

1. 1st year: purchases are understated, CGS understated, net income overstated, ending retained earnings overstated

2. 2nd year: purchases are overstated, CGS overstated, net income understated, ending retained earnings is correct (error has counterbalanced)

3. But the errors remain in both years' statements shown comparatively with later statements.

B. If the Error is Discovered in Year 2

Prior period adjustment (to retained earnings)	XX	
Purchases		XX

1. Retained earnings at the beginning of Year 2 are corrected by this entry, and year 1's income (and any other accounts affected) would be corrected in the Year 1 statement reported comparatively with Year 2.

C. If the Error is Discovered in Year 3

1. No entry is needed because retained earnings are correct—the error has counterbalanced. The statements for Years 1 and 2 would be corrected if shown comparatively with Year 3.

Losses on Purchase Commitments

This lesson addresses what to do with losses on purchase commitments.

After studying this lesson, you should be able to:

1. Explain what to do with losses when the commitment contract can be modified.

2. Explain what to do with losses when the commitment contract cannot be modified.

I. **Introduction**—Companies often commit (in a contract) to the purchase of materials to lock in the unit price of an item needed for production or resale in order to aid in cash flow budgeting and to protect against price increases. Sometime the market price of the item declines below the contract price. The accounting for this price decline depends on whether the contract can be revised in light of the changing market conditions.

II. **The Contract Can be Modified**—In this case, the loss is required to be footnoted as a contingent liability, but is not accrued in the accounts because the loss is not probable given that the contract can be revised.

III. **The Contract Cannot be Modified**—In this case, the loss must be accrued because the loss is probable and estimable. The inventory, when acquired, is recorded at market value and a loss is recognized for the difference between the market value and the contract price. If the contract has not been executed as of the balance sheet date, the following adjusting entry is made:

Loss on purchase commitment	xx	
Liability on purchase commitment		xx

The amount equals the difference between the unit contract price and market price at year-end, multiplied by the number of units required to be purchased.

A. If the market price drops further in the second year, an additional loss is recognized when the contract is executed. Recoveries result in a gain but only to the extent of the previously recognized loss.

Example
In December, a firm contracted to purchase 200 units of prefabricated housing walls at $4,000 per wall. The contract is neither cancelable nor subject to revision. By December 31, the market price per wall had dropped to $3,900.

The adjusting entry at December 31 is:

Loss on purchase commitment	20,000	
Liability on purchase commitment		20,000*

*200($4,000 − $3,900)

In January, at payment date, if the market price had decreased to $3,850, the following entry would be made:

Liability on purchase commitment	20,000	
Loss on purchase commitment	10,000*	
Inventory $3,850(200)	770,000	
Cash $4,000(200)		$800,000

*($3,900 − $3,850)200

If the market price had been $3,950 at payment date, a gain of $10,000 would be recorded and the inventory would be recorded at $3,950 per unit. If the market price exceeded $4,000 at payment date, a gain of $20,000 would be recorded and the inventory would be recorded at $800,000, the original contract price. The contract price is the ceiling for recording the inventory. There is no floor.

Inventory and IFRS

Update Notice

In July 2015, the FASB issued ASU 2015-11 Inventory (Topic 330), *Simplifying the Measurement of Inventory*. The ASU changes the subsequent valuation of inventory. The effective date is for fiscal years beginning after December 15, 2016 (2017 for calendar-year companies), and early adoption is permitted. The new rules are subject to testing on the CPA Exam beginning on January 1, 2017.

This lesson presents the significant differences in the accounting for inventory under IFRS versus U.S. GAAP.

After studying this lesson, you should be able to:

1. Identify the major differences in the accounting for inventory under IFRS versus U.S. GAAP.

I. Inventory and IFRS

    A. There are a few significant differences between the accounting for inventory under IAS 2 and under U.S. GAAP. The next table summarizes these differences.

U.S. GAAP	IFRS
Lower of cost or market (LC-M) or LC-NRV	Lower of cost or net realizable value (LC-NRV) only
May use more than one cost formula for similar inventories with similar use	Same cost formulas must be used for inventory with a similar nature and use
Reversal of the write down is prohibited.	Reversal of write down to net realizable value permitted
LIFO permitted	LIFO prohibited
Cost flow assumption does not mirror physical flow.	Cost flow assumption mirrors physical flow.

    B. Under IFRS, inventory is reported at the lower of cost or net realizable value (LC-NRV). Net realizable value is defined by IAS 2 the same as in U.S. GAAP as "the estimated selling price in the ordinary course of business less the estimated costs of completion and the estimate costs necessary to make the sale." This definition is consistent with the IASB philosophy that an asset should not be reported on the balance sheet at more than the net cash that is expected from the sale or use of that asset. Under U.S. GAAP inventory is reported at lower of cost or net realizable value (LC-NRV) for all inventory methods that are not LIFO or Retail Method and at lower of cost or market (LC-M) for all methods that are LIFO or Retail. In the LC-M application, market is defined as replacement cost with a ceiling and a floor. Although U.S. GAAP defines NRV the same as IFRS, U.S. GAAP uses NRV to determine a floor and ceiling when determining LC-M.

        1. The adjustment to net realizable value is applied on an item-by-item basis; however, inventory with similar characteristics can be grouped together. The process of applying lower of cost or NRV, and the entry made for the write-down, is similar to the process and entry used under U.S. GAAP. Under U.S. GAAP, when inventory is reported and lower of cost or market (LC-M), market is defined as replacement cost with a ceiling (NRV) and a floor (NRV less normal profit margin).

        2. The same cost formulas (e.g., valuation method FIFO) must be applied to inventory that is similar in nature and use. In the U.S., there is no restriction and different cost formulas can be applied to inventory that is similar or with similar use.

3. Inventory is reassessed at each financial reporting date, and if there are further reductions the inventory is written down again. However, if the NRV of the inventory has increased, the previous write-down can be reversed (only to the extent of the previous write-down).

C. IFRS specifically prohibits the use of LIFO as a cost-flow assumption. In the U.S. approximately 30% of publicly traded companies use LIFO. The main motivation for LIFO in the U.S. is that it lowers net income and therefore lowers taxes. This difference in accounting is viewed as a significant barrier to convergence, as U.S. companies would be forced to recognize significant gains if they had to abandon LIFO.

D. The three methods of assigning value to inventory under IFRS are: FIFO, specific identification, and weighted average. IAS 2 presumes that the inventory valuation method will follow the physical flow of goods to the extent possible.

Property, Plant, and Equipment

Categories and Presentation

This lesson presents the categories and presentation of plant asset account.

After studying this lesson, you should be able to:

1. Distinguish what is included in each category of plant assets.

2. Demonstrate ability to complete the presentation and disclosures for plant assets.

I. **Requirements for Inclusion in Plant Assets**

   A. To be included in plant assets, an asset must:

      1. Be currently used in operations;

      2. Have a useful life extending more than one year beyond the balance sheet date; *and*

      3. Have physical substance. Intangible assets are different from plant assets in that they have no physical substance.

   B. If land is held for investment purposes or for future development, it is excluded from plant assets because it currently is not a productive asset.

II. **Categories Within Plant Assets**

   A. **Plant and Equipment**—This category of fixed assets is composed of buildings, machinery, and equipment. These assets have a finite useful life and can also be referred to as depreciable assets.

   B. **Land Improvements**—This asset differs from land in that it has a finite useful life and is depreciated. Examples of land improvements include parking lots, fencing, external lighting, and some landscaping.

   C. **Land**—This category includes the site of a manufacturing facility, the site of administrative offices, and the site of any storage warehouses. Any plot of land in which a company has constructed facilities specifically related to primary business operations is included in this category. This category does not include real estate held for investment purposes. Land has an indefinite life and is, therefore, not depreciated. *It is the only asset in the plant asset category that is not depreciated or amortized.*

   D. **Natural Resources** —Include such items as a gravel pit, a coal mine, a tract of timber land, and an oil well. This category of assets will produce income until all the natural resources are extracted and sold. These assets are frequently referred to as depletable assets.

Capitalized Costs

This lesson presents what is included in the plant asset account.

After studying this lesson, you should be able to:

1. Distinguish what costs should be capitalized (versus expensed) upon acquisition of a plant assets.

2. Distinguish what costs should be capitalized (versus expensed) during the life of a plant asset.

Definition

Capitalization: The costs are added to an asset account (balance sheet) rather than to an expense account (income statement). Capitalized amounts are subsequently allocated to expense (depreciated) over time (more on this later).

I. **Costs that Are Capitalized Upon Acquisition of Plant Assets**

  A. The acquisition cost of property, plant, and equipment includes two components, the cash equivalent price or negotiated acquisition cost and the so-called **get-ready costs**.

  B. The **get-ready costs** include all costs incurred to get the asset on the company's premises and ready for use. For example, the setting up and testing of new machinery is a **get-ready cost**.

  C. The general rule for capitalizing expenditures related to the acquisition of plant assets is similar to the rule for capitalizing costs to inventory.

  D. Capitalize all expenditures necessary to bring the plant asset to its intended condition and location.

II. **Cost Capitalized During the Life of the Plant Asset**

  A. If the estimated time of benefit is related to the current accounting period only, the expenditure is recorded as an expense. Such expenditures are called "revenue expenditures" or "period costs."

  B. If the estimated time of benefit is related to the current and future accounting periods, the expenditure is capitalized. The term "capitalized" means included in an asset account.

  C. If the expenditure is immaterial, the company will account for the expenditure in the most expedient way possible. This usually means the expenditure is recorded as an expense in the period of acquisition.

  D. If the expenditure is material in amount, the accounting treatment of the expenditure will be determined by examining the estimated time of benefit related to the expenditure. To be capitalized and then depreciated, an expenditure must make the asset "bigger, better, or last longer." In other words, the asset must have increased or improved functionality, make better products, or have a longer life. Three examples of this concept follow:

  1. The estimated useful life of the asset is extended beyond the original estimation (i.e., expenditures for a major overhaul of a bread oven in a commercial bread bakery that might extend the life of the oven beyond the original estimate).

  2. The asset becomes more efficient or productive, meaning it can produce higher quantities or operate at a lower cost (i.e., a new laser product sorter might be added to a machine, replacing human efforts to sort out defective products and speeding up the process).

  3. Quality of the asset's output is improved (i.e., upgrades to equipment for a textile entity, which enable it to produce a sheet with a higher thread count).

E. If an expenditure merely maintains the asset at its anticipated level of productivity and length of life, the following occurs:

    1. The cost is *not* capitalized on the balance sheet.

    2. Instead, it is recorded as a maintenance expense on the current year income statement.

F. Be familiar with the following terms for capitalizable expenditures:

    1. An *addition* is a new major component of an asset, such as an additional room in or on a building, that did not exist before.

    2. An *improvement* is the replacement of a major component of an asset, such as an air conditioning system for a building.

    3. A *rearrangement* is a restructuring of an asset that does **not** extend its life but creates a new type of benefit. Relocation of an entity to another city is an example.

Example
The following list of expenditures shows a variety of costs related to plant assets and how to account for them.

Expenditure	Accounting treatment
Sales tax on equipment purchase	Capitalize to equipment
Cost of delivery, to set up and test equipment	Capitalize to equipment
Cost to train employees to use equipment	Expense
Title fee on land purchase	Capitalize to land
Attorney fee for land purchase	Capitalize to land
Cost to raze an old building on land purchased	Capitalize to land
Proceeds on salvage material from razing	Reduce recorded land cost
Cost of landscaping	Capitalize to land improvements
Cost to excavate foundation for a building	Capitalize to building
Interest on purchase of plant assets	Expense
Interest during construction of building	Capitalize to building
Back property taxes on land just purchased	Capitalize to land
Annual property taxes on land	Expense
Cost of permits for construction	Capitalize to building

Note
Applying the general rule helps in classifying expenditures. For example, the cost to train employees to use equipment benefits the employees, not the equipment. Razing an old building on land just purchased is part of the process of preparing the land for use. However, the cost to raze a building already owned by the firm increases the loss on disposal of the building.

Valuation

This lesson presents the valuation of plant assets when the exchange involves something other than cash.

After studying this lesson, you should be able to:

1. Calculate the value plant assets in situations where the exchange involved something other than cash (i.e., credit purchase, securities, donation, group purchase, or self-constructed asset).

Note

In general, plant assets should be valued at the market value of consideration given in exchange, or at the market value (cash equivalent price) of the asset acquired, whichever is more readily determinable and reliable.

I. **Cash Equivalent Price or Negotiated Acquisition Cost**

   A. **Methods of Acquiring Plant Assets**

   1. **Cash purchase**—The cash equivalent price is simply the amount of cash paid for the asset on acquisition date.

   2. **Deferred payment plan (credit purchase)**—The cash equivalent price for an asset acquired through a deferred payment plan is the present value of future cash payments using the market rate of interest for similar debt instruments.

Example

The list price of a plant asset is $30,000. The purchaser makes a $10,000 down payment and issues a 2-year non-interest-bearing note for the remainder. The note calls for a single lump-sum payment of $20,000 to be made at the maturity of the note. The market rate of interest on such notes is 10%. The present value of a single payment of $1 received two years in the future at 10% is .82645. The entry to record the plant asset is:

DR: Plant asset	26,529	
CR: Cash		10,000
CR: Note payable $20,000(.82645)		16,529

The note is recorded at present value. The list price of plant assets should not be used for valuation of assets. The list price is mainly a starting point for negotiations between the buyer and seller. Subsequent to acquisition, interest expense is recognized as the note approaches maturity. The interest is expensed. It is not added to the building account.

---

   3. **Issuance of securities** —The acquisition cost of an asset acquired through the issuance of stocks or bonds is the fair value of the security or the fair value of the asset acquired, whichever can be most clearly determined. When a significant number of shares is issued, care must be taken to ensure that the issuance did not affect the share price.

   4. **Donated assets**—Assets received in donation are recorded at their fair value. A revenue or gain is also recorded.

5. **Group purchases**—If a group of fixed assets is acquired in a single transaction, the total negotiated price is allocated to the individual assets acquired. This allocation is based on the respective fair values of the individual assets acquired.

Example

For a lump-sum price, a firm acquired three plant assets at a bargain price of $50,000. The individual market values of each asset are:

Market or appraised value

Building	$10,000
Land	30,000
Equipment	15,000
Total	$55,000

The recorded cost of each asset is based on its relative market value. The entry to record the purchase:

DR: Building	($10,000/$55,000)$50,000	9,091
DR: Land	($30,000/$55,000)$50,000	27,273
DR: Equipment	($15,000/$55,000)$50,000	13,636
CR: Cash		50,000

II. Self-Constructed Assets

A. **Components of Capitalized Cost**—The capitalized cost of a self-constructed asset includes four components:

1. **Labor**—The direct labor charges related to the construction of the asset will be capitalized. Usually, labor charges are expensed in the period incurred, but in this instance, the labor charges are capitalized. This component of the cost of the asset includes any fringe benefits related to the basic labor cost.

2. **Material**—The direct materials related to the construction of the asset will be capitalized.

3. **Overhead**—The overhead charges related to the construction of the asset will be capitalized. Usually, the capitalization of overhead charges is accomplished by one of two approaches.

   a. **Incremental overhead approach**—One approach is to capitalize *only* the incremental overhead. For example, if a company typically has $5,000,000 of overhead, but during the period of construction, overhead increased to $5,500,000, the incremental overhead related to the project is $500,000.

   b. **Pro rata overhead allocation approach**—Another approach is to capitalize the overhead on a pro rata basis. For example, if the project represents 15% of the total direct labor hours for the period, 15% of the total overhead will be allocated to the project.

4. **Interest cost incurred during the construction period**—(This topic is separately discussed in detail in a later lesson.) Capitalization of interest is allowed only when assets are constructed. When assets are purchased outright, any interest on debt incurred to purchase the asset cannot be capitalized.

B. Limitation on Recorded Value—Market value at completion

1. In general, GAAP prohibits the recording of assets in excess of their market values. Recording a constructed asset at an amount exceeding its market value carries forward losses due to inefficient construction to later periods, which violates conservatism. Also, the future benefit of the asset is measured at its market value.

2. If the total cost of construction exceeds market value, a loss is recognized for the difference and the asset is recorded at market value.

Example
The costs incurred to self-construct equipment are:

Labor	$20,000
Material	30,000
Incremental overhead	10,000
Applied overhead	5,000
Capitalized interest	8,000
Total	$73,000

During the construction phase, costs are accumulated in Equipment under Construction. The $73,000 amount is the final recorded amount if the market value equals or exceeds $73,000. If the market value were $80,000, the recorded value remains at $73,000 because gains cannot be recognized until realized through lower production costs. The Equipment under Construction account would be closed to Equipment.

Assume, however, that the market value is only $60,000:

Equipment	60,000	
Loss on Construction	13,000	
Equipment under Construction		73,000

Interest Capitalization Basics

This lesson is the first on interest capitalization during construction. This lesson presents when it is appropriate to capitalize interest, calculation of average accumulated expenditures and calculation of interest eligible for capitalization.

After studying this lesson, you should be able to:

1. Identify when interest capitalization is allowed.

2. Calculate the average accumulated expenditures during construction.

3. Calculate the weighted average or specific interest rate.

4. Calculate the amount of interest to be capitalized during the period.

5. Complete the journal entry for interest capitalization.

I. Introduction—Capitalization of Interest

   A. Interest cost is typically expensed in the period incurred. However, when a company constructs a fixed asset, the interest cost incurred during the construction period is considered a **get-ready cost** and is, therefore, capitalized. Interest capitalization increases both plant assets and income. Assuming that all interest is first recorded in interest expense, the following adjusting entry capitalizes some or all of that interest:

> DR: Plant Asset Under Construction   xx
>
>   CR: Interest Expense   xx

   B. Interest cost is capitalized only during the construction period. Prior to the construction period, interest cost was expensed. Any interest cost incurred subsequent to the construction period will likewise be expensed.

   C. The *justification* for interest capitalization is that had the construction not taken place, the funds used in construction could have been used to reduce interest-bearing debt. This **avoidable** interest is the amount of interest that would have been avoided had the construction not taken place. In a sense, the construction then **caused** that amount of interest, which, therefore, should be included in the cost of the asset constructed.

> **Note**
> *The definition of an asset is not the underlying justification for interest capitalization. Interest does not increase the probable future value of an asset. Capitalization of interest exemplifies the matching principle as the benefit of the constructed asset will be over its useful life.*

   D. Matching Principle—Interest capitalization exemplifies the matching principle. Until the asset is in service, it cannot produce revenue. The asset is also not yet in its intended condition and location. Thus, expensing of the interest is deferred until the asset can provide revenues against which to match the interest expense.

   E. Capitalization of interest applies only to the construction of qualifying assets, such as assets constructed for an enterprise's own use or assets intended for sale or lease that are constructed as discrete projects (ships, real estate developments, etc.).

   F. Qualifying assets require a significant time period for construction and are not routinely produced. Rather, the assets must be discrete projects individually constructed. Interest is not capitalized on the construction or manufacture of inventory items, even if the inventory requires significant time for completion (e.g., interest on the production of wine and tobacco products is not capitalized).

II. Interest Is Capitalized During Periods in Which All Three of the Following Conditions Are Met

A. Qualifying expenditures have been made. Cash payments, transfers of other assets, or the incurrence of interest-bearing debt all qualify. The incurrence of short-term non-interest-bearing debt (e.g., accounts payable) does not qualify because the firm has no opportunity cost on such debt.

> **Note**
> *If any of the three conditions is not met, interest capitalization ceases. The capitalization period concludes when the asset is substantially complete and ready for its intended use.*

B. Activities that are necessary to get the asset ready for its intended use are in progress. (Construction is proceeding.)

C. Interest cost is being incurred. Only actual interest cost is capitalized. Imputed interest is not capitalized. The total amount of interest to be capitalized for a period is limited to actual interest incurred in the period.

III. A Two-Step Process Is Involved in Computing Capitalized Interest—The two steps are: (1) compute average accumulated expenditures, and (2) apply the appropriate interest rate(s).

A. **Compute Average Accumulated Expenditures**—A key concept in determining the amount of interest to be capitalized is avoidable interest. This is the interest on debt that could have been retired had the construction not taken place. To quantify that amount of debt, average accumulated expenditures (AAE) must be computed. AAE is the measure of the amount of debt, on an annual basis, that could have been avoided.

B. AAE = average cash (or other qualifying expenditures) investment in the project during the period. This is the amount of debt that could have been retired during the period.

Examples

1. A firm begins construction on January 1 by making a $40,000 construction payment to a contractor. On July 1, another $40,000 payment is made. AAE = $40,000 + $40,000(6/12) = $60,000. The July 1 payment was invested in the project only half of a year. The $60,000 represents the amount of debt, outstanding the entire year, which could have been retired.

2. The previous example involved a small number of discrete cash payments. This example assumes that cash payments are made continuously throughout the period. The firm starts construction on January 1. By December 31 it has spent $120,000 in qualifying expenditures on the projects. Payments were made evenly throughout the year. AAE = $120,000/2 = ($0 + $120,000)/2 = $60,000. Although $120,000 was expended during the year, on average the firm had $60,000 invested in the project during the year. (This is the same logic as with a bank account; if you deposited equal amounts into your account each day for a year and ended with a $120,000 balance, your average balance would be $60,000 for the year, assuming interest is paid at year's end.)

IV. Apply the Appropriate Interest Rate—If AAE is the amount of debt that could have been retired for the year, then an interest rate multiplied by AAE is the amount of interest that could have been avoided. This is the amount of interest to be capitalized, subject to the limitation that capitalized interest cannot exceed actual interest cost for the period.

Example
Using the previous examples of AAE ($60,000), if the interest rate were 10%, then $6,000 of interest would be capitalized ($60,000 × .10) assuming at least that much interest cost was actually incurred. If total interest expense for the period before capitalizing interest amounted to $11,000, then $6,000 of interest would be debited to the asset under construction, and only $5,000 of interest expense would be reported in the income statement.

V. But What Interest Rate Should Be Used? U.S. GAAP does not limit capitalized interest to specific construction loan interest. Rather, the more general concept of **avoidable** interest is used. Two ways of computing total interest to be capitalized are allowed:

A. Weighted Average Method—Capitalizes interest using the weighted average rate on all interest bearing debt.

B. Specific Method—Capitalizes the interest on specific construction loans first. Then, if needed, capitalize interest on all other debt based on the average interest rate for that debt.

Example

A firm began construction in January and spent $100,000 in qualifying expenditures by year's end. Expenditures were made evenly throughout the period. Debt outstanding the entire year:

	Principal	Annual interest
10% construction loan	$30,000	$3,000
Other debt (average interest rate, 8%)	60,000	4,800
Total	$90,000	$7,800

AAE = $100,000/2 = $50,000

VI. Computation of Capitalized Interest

A. Weighted Average Method

Weighted average interest rate = ($7,800)/$90,000 = 8.67%

Capitalized interest = 8.67%($50,000) = $4,335. This amount is less than total interest of $7,800 for the period. Therefore the capitalized interest is $4,335 and the interest expense is $3,465 ($7,800 − $4,335).

B. Specific Method

Capitalized Interest = .10($30,000) + .08($50,000 − $30,000) = $4,600

1. This amount is less than total interest of $7,800 for the period. Therefore the capitalized interest is $4,600 and the interest expense is $3,200 ($7,800 − $4,600).

2. The specific method first uses the construction loan. The principal amount of that loan is only $30,000. But $50,000 (AAE) of debt could have been retired. The additional $20,000 of debt (to sum to the $50,000 AAE) is the portion of the nonspecific debt that could have been retired.

Note

Interest capitalized compounds over several periods. The interest capitalized in Year 1 is included in AAE for Year 2, thus increasing the amount of interest capitalized in Year 2. Interest is, therefore, compounded and included in the asset account.

Note

AAE is used only to compute capitalized interest. The ending balance in construction in progress is typically much larger than AAE for the period. Using the specific method in the above example, the ending balance in construction in progress after capitalizing interest is $104,600 ($100,000 construction payments + $4,600 interest capitalized).

Interest Capitalization Limits

This is the second lesson on interest capitalization. This lesson presents a more detailed discussion of the limits on how much interest can be capitalized. It also offers more detailed examples of the interest eligible for capitalization.

After studying this lesson, you should be able to:

1. Determine the limit on interest that is eligible for capitalization.

2. Calculate the weighted average or specific interest rate.

3. Calculate the amount of interest to be capitalized during the period.

4. Complete the journal entry for interest capitalization.

I. **Limit on Interest Capitalization**

   A. Capitalized interest is limited to actual interest incurred because avoidable debt is the lower of (1) AAE (average accumulated expenditures) and (2) total interest-bearing debt. The actual amount of interest incurred sets the ceiling on interest to be capitalized.

      1. When AAE < total interest-bearing debt, reported interest expense for the period is the difference between total interest cost and the amount of interest capitalized. In this case, because AAE is less than total debt, not all debt could have been avoided.

      2. When AAE > total interest-bearing debt, all interest cost is capitalized and there is no reported interest expense for the period. In this case, all debt could have been avoided had construction activities not taken place.

   B. These points are illustrated in the next example.

      1. **Example with more than one nonspecific construction loan**—This example shows how to compute two different weighted averages. Construction on a project began January 1, 20X6 with a construction payment of $100,000 to the contractor. One additional payment of $120,000 was made July 1, 20X6.

      2. Debt outstanding during 20X6 (entire year):

> 5%, $120,000 construction loan
>
> 6%, 20,000 note payable unrelated to construction
>
> 4%, 30,000 note payable unrelated to construction
>
> AAE = $100,000(12/12) + $120,000(6/12) = $160,000

      3. **Specific method**

> Average interest rate on nonconstruction loans =
>
> $((.06)\$20,000 + (.04)\$30,000) / (\$20,000 + \$30,000) = .048$
>
> Interest capitalized = $.05(\$120,000) + .048(\$160,000 - \$120,000) = \$7,920$

a. **Interest on the specific loan** for the construction is used first, and then interest at the average rate for all other debt is applied to the excess of AAE over the construction loan. Interest is capitalized only up to avoidable debt on the AAE.

b. **If AAE had been less** than the amount of the construction loan (e.g., $100,000), then only the construction loan interest would be capitalized (interest capitalized in that case would be .05 × $100,000 = $5,000).

c. If AAE had been $200,000 (**more than total debt**), then all the interest for the period would be capitalized because total debt is less than $200,000. All the debt could have been avoided. Interest capitalized = .05($120,000) + .048($50,000) = $8,400

4. Average Method

Average interest rate on all loans =

(.05($120,000) + (.06)$20,000 + (.04)$30,000) / ($120,000 + $20,000 + $30,000) = .0494

Interest capitalized = .0494($160,000) = $7,904

Again, if AAE had been $200,000, then all the interest for the period would be capitalized because total debt is less than $200,000. Interest capitalized = .05($120,000) + (.06)$20,000 + (.04)$30,000 = $8,400

5. Compounding of Capitalized Interest and Construction Balance

a. Interest capitalized in one period becomes part of AAE for the next period. Using the example above (average method), the balance in the construction-in-process account at the end of the first period is $227,904 ($100,000 construction payment + $120,000 construction payment + $7,904 capitalized interest).

b. The next year, the calculation of AAE will begin with $227,904(12/12), with the payments during the second year receiving the appropriate rate for the period of time in the project. Thus, the $7,904 of interest capitalized the previous period will be part of the base on which interest is capitalized the next period—interest is compounded.

Note
Interest may be capitalized on a quarterly or annual basis.

CAPITALIZATION OF INTEREST DURING CONSTRUCTION

Qualifying Assets:

Capitalize means to include an expenditure in an asset's cost.

Interest costs, when material, incurred in acquiring the following types of assets, shall be capitalized

1. Assets constructed or produced for a firm's own use

    a. Including construction by outside contractors requiring progress payments

2. Assets intended for lease or sale that are produced as discrete projects

    a. For example, ships and real estate developments

3. But **not** on

    a. Routinely produced inventories (e.g., widgets)
    b. Assets ready for their intended use when acquired
    c. Assets not being used nor being readied for use (e.g., idle equipment)
    d. Land, unless it is being developed (e.g., as a plant site, real estate development, etc.). Then capitalized interest resulting from land expenditure (cash outlay) is added to building.

When to Capitalize Interest (all three must be met):

1. Expenditures for asset have been made
2. Activities intended to get asset ready are in process
3. Interest cost is being incurred

Applicable Interest (net of discounts, premiums, and issue costs):

1. Interest obligations having explicit rates
2. Imputed interest on certain payables/receivables
3. Interest related to capital leases

How Much Interest Cost Is Capitalized?

$$\left(\begin{array}{l} \text{Accumulated expenditures beg. of period (C-I-P* bal.) +} \\ \text{Accumulated expenditures and of period (C-I-P bal.)} \end{array} \right) \div 2 \times \text{Portion of year} = \begin{array}{l}\text{Weighted-average} \\ \text{accumulated} \\ \text{expenditures}\end{array}$$

Weighted-average accumulated expenditures + (Interest rate**) = Amount capitalized (cannot exceed total interest incurred)

*C-I-P—Construction-in-Progress

**AICPA questions have given the specific borrowing rate on debt incurred to finance a project and indicated that expenditures were incurred evenly throughout the year. ASC: Topic 835 (SFAS 34) requires that the firm's weighted-average borrowing rate be used after the amount of a specific borrowing is exhausted. Alternatively, only the firm's weighted-average borrowing rate may be used on all expenditures.

Qualifications

1. Amount of interest to be capitalized cannot exceed total interest costs incurred during the entire reporting period

2. Interest earned on temporarily invested borrowings may not be offset against interest to be capitalized

II. Construction Payables—Unpaid construction input costs are not included in AAE until paid in cash. Until cash is paid, debt can be considered avoidable. Payables include wages payable, accounts payable for material, and utilities payable.

Example

If the firm incorporated $20,000 of materials into a project as of the end of the period, but paid only $15,000 for them ($5,000 in accounts payable), qualifying expenditures include only $15,000 for purposes of computing AAE.

III. Land and Capitalized Interest —The effect on interest capitalization of expenditures made for land depends on the purpose for acquiring the land.

    A. For land used as a building site, the cost of the land is included in AAE for the building, and interest is capitalized to the building; (the land is not being constructed.)

    B. For land developed for sale, interest is capitalized to the land;

    C. For land held for speculation, no interest is capitalized because the land is in its condition of intended use, and there is no asset under construction.

IV. Interest on Borrowed Funds—In some cases, the proceeds from a specific construction loan are not fully used for financing the construction until well into the construction phase. Part of the proceeds may be invested in a bank account or a debt security may be purchased. Interest revenue on unused proceeds temporarily invested is not offset against interest to be capitalized. The interest revenue is reported separately and has no effect on interest capitalized.

    A. Exception—If the funds are externally restricted tax-exempt borrowings, then a right of offset exists because the funds are restricted to use in construction.

V. Partial Year Computations—Construction projects may begin or end during a reporting period. Also, new debt may be incurred and other liabilities may be retired during a reporting period.

    A. Guidelines

        1. Interest rate—Adjust the interest rate for the fraction of the year the debt is outstanding. If new interest-bearing debt is incurred during an interest capitalization period, the interest rate reflects the period the debt was outstanding. Assume a firm capitalizes interest quarterly. If $100,000 of 12% debt is incurred May 1, then for quarter 2, $2,000 of interest is included in the numerator of the rate (2 months' interest), and $100,000 is included in the denominator.

        2. Expenditures—Weight by the percentage of the period invested in the project. An expenditure occurring at the beginning of the second month of a quarter receives a weight of 2/3.

Example

Interest Capitalization

    Assume the company is constructing an asset which qualifies for interest capitalization. By the beginning of July $3,000,000 had been spent on the asset, and an additional $800,000 was spent during July. The following debt was outstanding for the entire month.

1. A loan of $2,000,000, interest of 1% per month, specifically related to the asset.

2. A not payable of $1,500,000, interest of 1.5% per month.

3. Bonds payable of $1,000,000, interest of 1% per month.

The amount of interest to be capitalized is computed below.

Average accumulated expenditures (for the month of July) = ($3,000,000 + $3,800,000) ÷ 2 = $3,400,000

Avoidable interest			**Actual interest**		
$2,000,000 × 1%	=	$20,000	$2,000,000 × 1%	=	$20,000
1,400,000 × 1.3%*	=	18,200	1,500,000 × 1.5%	=	22,500
			1,000,000 × 1%		1,000,000
$3,400,000		$38,200	$4,500,000		$52,500

$38,200 < $52,500\\$38,200 is capitalized

Amount of interest to be capitalized is $38,200

Asset	38,200
Interest expense	38,200

*The average rate on other borrowings is ($22,500 + $10,000) ÷ ($1,500,000 + $1,000,000) = 1.3%. Notice that a specific rate is used to the extent possible and the average rate is used only on any excess. Alternatively, the rate on all debt may be used.

VI. Disclosure—The amount of interest capitalized and expensed must be disclosed during a period in which interest is capitalized. Note that the amount of interest paid for the period to be disclosed as part of the Statement of Cash Flows—either as part of the statement, as a supplemental schedule, or in a footnote.

Post-Acquisition Expenditures

This lesson presents a discussion how to treat post-acquisition expenditures.

After studying this lesson, you should be able to:

1. Distinguish when an expenditure should be capitalized or expensed.

2. Complete the entries for the capitalization of a post-acquisition expenditure.

I. **Introduction**

   A. A post-acquisition cost is capitalized if, as a result of the expenditure, the asset is:

   1. More productive (provides more benefits); *or*

   2. Has a longer useful life.

   B. Otherwise, the expenditure is expensed. Although an argument can be made that ordinary maintenance and repairs prolongs the useful life of an asset, the estimated useful life of an asset assumes a minimum level of periodic service.

   C. Repairs keep the asset in an ordinarily efficient operating condition. Repairs do not typically extend the life of the asset or increase its value. Repairs are typically expensed in the period incurred.

II. **Accounting Treatment for Capitalized Expenditures**

   A. **Additions**—Extensions or enlargements of existing assets.

   1. If an integral part of the larger asset, depreciate the addition over the shorter of its useful life or the remaining useful life of the larger asset.

   2. If not, depreciate the addition over its useful life.

   B. **Modifications**—Improvements (betterments), replacements, and extraordinary repairs all involve a modification of an existing component or part of the larger asset.

   C. **Accounting Approaches**

   1. **Substitution**—Remove the accumulated depreciation and original cost of the old component, recognize the loss, and capitalize the post-acquisition expenditure to the larger asset. This alternative is available only if the accounting system maintained records of the old component cost and accumulated depreciation.

   2. **Increase the larger asset account by the post-acquisition cost.** This approach is used when the productivity rather than the useful life of the larger asset is enhanced, and when the accounting system does not maintain records of the old component cost and accumulated depreciation.

   3. **Debit accumulated depreciation.** This approach is used when the expenditure increases the useful life of the larger asset. The debit to accumulated depreciation **turns back the clock** on the life of the larger asset. This approach is suited especially to extraordinary repairs.

   D. For each of these three approaches, the post-acquisition cost is depreciated over the shorter of its useful life or remaining useful life of the larger asset.

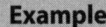

Example

The boiler of a large office building is replaced with a more efficient boiler at a cost of $65,000. The useful life of the building is unaffected but the new boiler will reduce energy costs significantly. The cost of the old boiler was $40,000, and its accumulated depreciation subsidiary ledger account reflects a balance of $35,000. To record the replacement:

DR: Accumulated Depreciation	35,000	
DR: Loss on Replacement	5,000	
CR: Boiler		40,000
DR: Boiler	65,000	
CR: Cash		65,000

Non-Accelerated Depreciation Methods

This is the first of two lessons on depreciation. This lesson presents the concepts for depreciation and certain depreciation methods.

After studying this lesson, you should be able to:

1. Explain the concepts for depreciation.

2. Calculate depreciation under the following methods: straight-line, service hours and units of production.

I. Nature of Depreciation

A. Depreciation is a *systematic and rational* allocation of capitalized plant asset cost to time periods. The term *systematic* implies that the allocation is not random but rather is made on an orderly basis. The term *rational* means that by appealing to how the asset is used, the process can be supported. The process of depreciation matches the cost of the plant asset to periods in which the asset is used to generate revenue.

B. Depreciation is *not* a process of valuation. The amount of depreciation recognized in a period is not necessarily the decline in the market value of the asset, nor is it a measure of the amount of the asset **used up**. If depreciation expense is $10,000, this does not mean that $10,000 of the cost of the asset was used in generating revenue. The $10,000 amount is simply the amount allocated to the period based on the method chosen by the firm. The book value of a depreciable plant asset (original cost less accumulated depreciation to date), is the amount of original cost yet to be depreciated. Only coincidentally does book value equal market value.

C. Justifications—There are two *justifications* for depreciation:

1. Assets wear out over time.

2. Assets become obsolete.

Example
Land is not depreciated because it does not wear out and does not become obsolete.

D. The acquisition cost of plant assets is a cost of doing business. Because plant assets have a useful life exceeding one year, their cost is allocated to the periods they benefit. Although the amount of asset decline is not observable, depreciation expense provides at least some measure of the cost of the asset to be included in total expenses on an annual basis.

E. Depreciation is not a source of funds. Although it provides a tax deduction, the same can be said for any deductible expense. Note that most firms use straightline (SL) depreciation for financial reporting, and MACRS (modified accelerated cost recovery system) for income tax reporting. MACRS is the same as the double-declining balance (DDB) method with a half-year convention applied.

F. Definitions

Definitions

Book Value: Original cost less accumulated depreciation to date.

Depreciable Cost: Total depreciation to be recognized over the life of the asset. This amount equals original cost less salvage value.

Minimum Book Value: Salvage value. In no case is salvage value depreciated. Thus, book value always includes salvage value. An asset cannot be depreciated such that its book value is less than salvage value.

1. There are three kinds of **noncurrent assets** subject to depreciation or similar process. Different terms are used for each, but all involve a systematic and rational allocation of historical cost to time periods of use:

   a. Plant assets are *depreciated;*

   b. Natural resources are *depleted;*

   c. Intangible assets are *amortized.*

Definitions

Adjusting Journal Entry: The adjusting journal entry for depreciation on nonmanufacturing assets is: DR: Depreciation expense; CR: Accumulated depreciation

Contra Account: Many firms include depreciation expense in Selling, General, and Administrative Expense and report the components in a footnote. Accumulated depreciation is a contra-plant asset account. The use of a contra account preserves the original cost information in the plant asset account.

Manufacturing Assets: For manufacturing assets, depreciation is included in overhead and allocated to production based on machine hours or direct labors. The result is that Work in Process is debited for depreciation cost. When the products are sold, Cost of Goods Sold includes depreciation. A separate expense for depreciation is not recorded for manufacturing assets.

II. Factors in Calculating

A. The amount of depreciation recognized each period is affected by the following four factors. Only the first factor, capitalized cost, is a definite amount. Two estimates are used, and the firm has a free choice among the available methods.

   1. Capitalized cost

   2. Estimated useful life

   3. Estimated salvage value (the cost of the asset not subject to depreciation—that is,the portion of initial cost expected to be returned at the end of the useful life)

   4. Method chosen

B. Several methods of depreciation are acceptable under GAAP. They can be categorized into two basic types: (1) straight-line methods and (2) accelerated methods.

   1. **Straight-line methods (a constant rate of depreciation)**

      a. **Straight-line method**—Annual depreciation is calculated by the formula shown below

---

Cost − Salvage Value / Useful Life = Annual Depreciation

---

   i. Annual depreciation is the same each year.

   ii. **Justification**—The asset will provide essentially the same benefits per year. Buildings are appropriately depreciated on an SL basis.

Example
An asset costing $22,000 with a salvage value of $2,000 and a useful life of 5 years is depreciated $4,000 each year using the SL method ($22,000 − $2,000)/5.

b. Service hours method

    i. The life of the asset is defined in terms of service hours, and the depreciation rate per service hour is calculated by using the formula shown below. The number of total service hours the asset will provide must be estimated and used as the denominator.

Depreciation Rate = (Cost − Salvage Value) / (Useful Life in Service Hours)

    ii. Depreciation for any given year is calculated by multiplying the service hours for the year by this constant depreciation rate per service hour. Annual depreciation varies with the number of service hours provided in the year. There is no expectation that depreciation will be the same amount each year.

    iii. Justification—The asset will provide essentially the same benefits per service hour. A delivery vehicle is an example of an asset appropriately depreciated on the service-hours method.

Example
An asset costing $22,000 with a salvage value of $2,000 and a useful life of 5 years is depreciated on the service-hours method. The asset is expected to provide 10,000 hours of service. In a given year, 2,500 hours of service are provided. The constant rate is $2 per service hour ($22,000 − $2,000)/10,000. Depreciation for the given year is $5,000 (2,500 × $2).

c. Units of output method

    i. The life of the asset is defined in terms of units of output, and the depreciation rate per unit of output is calculated using the formula shown below. The number of total units the asset will produce must be estimated and used as the denominator.

Depreciation Rate = (Cost − Salvage Value) / (Useful Life in Units of Production)

    ii. Depreciation for any given year is calculated by multiplying the units of output for the year by this constant depreciation rate per unit of output. Annual depreciation varies depending on the number of units produced in the year. There is no expectation that depreciation will be the same amount each year.

    iii. Justification—The asset will provide essentially the same benefits per unit produced. Oil drilling equipment is an example of an asset appropriately depreciated on the units of production method.

Example
An asset costing $22,000 with a salvage value of $2,000 and a useful life of 5 years is depreciated on the units of production method. The asset is expected to produce 1,000 units. In a given year, 300 units are produced. The constant rate is $20 per unit ($22,000 − $2,000)/1,000. Depreciation for the given year is $6,000 (300 × $20).

Accelerated Depreciation Methods

This is the second of two lessons on depreciation. This lesson presents accelerated depreciation methods.

After studying this lesson, you should be able to:

1. Calculate depreciation under the following methods: sum-of-years digits and double-declining balance.

I. **Accelerated Methods**—Accelerated methods of depreciation recognize depreciation at a faster rate early in the life of the asset. Later in the life of the asset, the amount of depreciation per period declines. This pattern of depreciation holds regardless of how the asset is used in any given period.

   A. **Justification**

   1. The theoretical justification for using an accelerated method is related to the matching principle. It is assumed the asset will be more productive in the earlier years. Therefore, more depreciation expense is recorded during those earlier, more productive years. More expense is matched against revenue in the periods of greater benefit; less expense is matched when the asset provides less benefit.

   2. Another justification is obsolescence. Assets subject to obsolescence (high-tech equipment for example) will provide most of their benefits early in their life. Therefore, more depreciation is recognized in those years.

   B. **Effect**—One effect of using accelerated methods is a stable annual total amount of expense related to plant assets. Early in the asset's life, more depreciation is recognized and less maintenance is required. Later in the asset's life just the opposite occurs. But the total annual expense is fairly stable.

   C. **Methods**

   1. **Sum-of-the-years' digits method**

   a. First, the sum of the years' digits must be calculated by using the formula shown below.

   > N = useful life in years.
   >
   > $SYD = (N(N+1))/2 = 1 + 2 + ... + N$
   >
   > SYD is the denominator of the fraction used each year to compute depreciation. The numerator is the number of years remaining at the beginning of the year.
   >
   > | | |
   > |---|---|
   > | Year 1 Depreciation: | $(N/SYD)(Cost - Salvage\ Value)$ |
   > | Year 2 Depreciation: | $((N-1)/SYD)(Cost - Salvage\ Value))$ |
   > | Year N Depreciation: | $(1/(SYD))(Cost - Salvage\ Value))$ |

   b. This method is accelerated because the highest annual amount of depreciation is recognized in year 1, the next highest in year 2, and so forth.

Example

An asset costing $22,000 with a salvage value of $2,000 and a useful life of 5 years is depreciated on the sum-of-the-years' digits method.

SYD = 1 + 2 + 3 + 4 + 5 = 15 = 5(5 + 1)/2

Depreciation, year 1 = (5/15)($22,000 − $2,000) = $6,667

Depreciation, year 2 = (4/15)($22,000 − $2,000) = $5,333

.

.

Depreciation, year 5 = (1/15)($22,000 − $2,000) = $1,333

2. **Declining-balance method**

   a. This method differs from those discussed previously in three ways:

      i. Salvage value is not used in the computation of depreciation.

      ii. Annual depreciation is based on the beginning book value of the asset. This book value declines over time, hence the name of this group of methods. This also is why salvage value is not subtracted. Book value always includes salvage value because salvage value is never depreciated.

      iii. Each year, accumulated depreciation must be checked to ensure that book value does not fall below salvage value.

   b. The method allows rates between 100% and 200% of the straight-line rate.

Double declining balance method

Depreciation in year 1	= Cost(2/N)
Depreciation in year 2	= (Cost − depreciation in year 1)(2/N)
	= (book value at beginning of year 2)(2/N)
Depreciation in year 3	= (Cost − depreciation in years 1 and 2)(2/N)

The rate (2/N) is twice the straight-line rate. N = useful life in years.

150% of declining-balance method

The calculations are the same as for double-declining balance except that (1.5/N) is the rate used.

Example

An asset costing $22,000 with a salvage value of $2,000 and a useful life of 5 years is depreciated on the double-declining-balance method.

Depreciation, year 1   = $22,000(2/5) = $8,800 Depreciation,

year 2   = ($22,000 − $8,800)(2/5) = $5,280

In some cases, strict use of the declining-balance method results in recognizing more depreciation than depreciable cost. In the year that total depreciation exceeds depreciable cost, firms will change to the straight-line method and depreciate the remaining depreciable cost over the remaining useful life beginning in that year.

3. **Partial or fractional year depreciation**

   a. Assets not purchased at the beginning of a fiscal year must be depreciated on a fractional year basis. Firms often use a simplifying convention such as: depreciate all assets a full year in the year of acquisition, and recognize no depreciation in the year of disposal. Over large groups of assets, these conventions are acceptable if applied consistently.

   b. However, a more exact approach is required on the CPA Exam.

Example

A calendar or fiscal year firm purchased an asset costing $22,000 with a salvage value of $2,000 and a useful life of 5 years on April 1, 20X7. Let:

W1 = the first whole year of depreciation (April 1, 20X7 to March 31, 20X8),

W2 = the second whole year of depreciation (April 1, 20X8 to March 31, 20X9),

and so forth.

Regardless of the depreciation method used, depreciation for reporting years is found as:

20X7 depreciation	= (9/12)W1	(asset held 9 months in 20X7)
20X8 depreciation	= (3/12)W1 + (9/12)W2	(20X8 contains the last 3 months
		of the asset's first year,
		and the first 9 months
		of the asset's second year)

The remaining years are treated the same way.

If the method chosen is double-declining balance (DDB) , then from the previous example:

W1 = $22,000(2/5) = $8,800

W2 = ($22,000 – $8,800)(2/5) = $5,280

20X7 depreciation	= (9/12)W1 = (9/12)($8,800)	= $6,600
20X8 depreciation	= (3/12)W1 + (9/12)W2	
	= (3/12)($8,800) + (9/12)($5,280)	= $6,160

For DDB, a shortcut approach is available:

20X8 depreciation = (2/5)($22,000 – $6,600) = $6,160

4. **Appraisal methods**—These methods are used when it is impractical to depreciate assets on an individual basis. Accumulated depreciation records are not maintained on individual assets, and no gain or loss is recorded on disposal.

   a. **Inventory (appraisal) method**—This method is applied to groups of smaller homogenous assets. At the end of each year, the assets are appraised and recorded at market value. The appraisal is for the entire group, which saves accounting costs. The decline in market value from the previous year is depreciation expense for the year. If assets were sold during the year, the proceeds from sale reduce depreciation expense.

Example

January 1 appraisal value of group:	$20,000
Proceeds from disposal of some assets in the group:	$3,000
December 31 appraisal value of group:	$12,000

Depreciation expense for the year

= ($20,000 – $12,000) – $3,000 = $5,000

b. Group/composite methods

    i. This system applies the straight-line method to groups of assets rather than to assets individually. Accumulated depreciation records are not maintained by asset; rather, only a control account is used to accumulate depreciation. Gains and losses are not recorded. The entry to dispose of an asset plugs the accumulated depreciation account.

> The composite depreciation rate = (Annual group SL depreciation) / (Total original cost of group)

    ii. Depreciation for a year is the product of the rate and the original cost of assets remaining at the beginning of the year. Asset additions increase the total original cost on which depreciation is computed; asset disposals reduce the total original cost.

Example
A firm purchased the following group of assets:

Asset	Number	Original unit cost	Salvage value	Useful life
A	10	$500	$100	4 years
B	5	600	300	3 years

The composite rate of depreciation = (10($500 − $100)/4 + 5($600 − $300)/3) / (10($500) + 5($600)) = .1875

The .1875 rate means that $.1875 of depreciation is recognized each year for each $1 of acquisition cost in the group. After a few years in which assets have been added and removed, if the original cost of the group of assets remaining on January 1 is $5,000, depreciation for that year is $937.50 ($5,000 × .1875).

Natural Resources

This lesson provides information on the accounting for natural resources.

After studying this lesson, you should be able to:

1. Identify acquisition, exploration and development costs.

2. Determine the costs that are capitalized as part of the natural resource asset.

3. Calculate depletion of the natural resource asset.

I. Natural Resources

> **Definition**
> *Natural Resource*: A noncurrent asset that contains the cost of acquiring, exploring, and developing a natural resource deposit (e.g., timber, oil and minerals). It does not include the cost of extracting the resource.

  A. The amount capitalized as natural resources is the sum of three different types of costs:

   1. **Acquisition costs**—The amount paid to acquire the rights to explore for undiscovered natural resources or to extract proven natural resources.

   2. **Exploration costs**—The amount paid to drill or excavate or any other costs of searching for natural resources.

   3. **Development costs**—The amount paid after the resource has been discovered but before production begins.

  B. **Methods of Accounting for Exploration Costs**

   1. **Successful-efforts method**—Only the cost of successful exploration efforts is capitalized to the natural resources account; unsuccessful efforts are expensed.

   2. **Full-costing method**—All costs of exploring for the resource are capitalized to the natural resources account. (The total amount capitalized cannot exceed the expected value of resources to be removed.)

   3. The choice between the successful-efforts and full-costing methods is among the most important a firm has to make. The choice can have a large effect on net income and total assets. The successful-efforts method best reflects the definition of an asset because only those efforts that located the resource are capitalized to the natural resource account. The full-costing method reflects the matching principle—and capitalizes all costs until the natural resource deposit produces revenue through sale of the inventory. Another justification for full costing is that all exploration efforts contributed to finding the resource.

  C. After resources are discovered on the property, the cost to develop the property to enable extraction of the resource is capitalized to the natural resources account. Development costs pertain to facilities that will not be removed when the project is finished.

  D. Removable assets such as drilling equipment, vehicles, and the like are recorded in their own separate accounts as plant assets.

II. Depletion

  A. After all costs are capitalized to the natural resources account, the resource begins to be removed and depletion is recorded. Depletion is the term used to refer to the allocation of the cost of the natural resource to inventory. Depletion is taken on the natural resource asset (sum of the three costs above less the residual value).

B. Depletion is not an expense but an allocation of the natural resource from noncurrent assets to inventory. When units of the natural resource are depleted, inventory is debited and the natural resource account is credited. Because the useful life is directly associated with the amount of resources extracted, the activity or units of production base method is widely used.

Depletion for a Period = (Depletion Rate) × (Number of Units Removed in Period)

Depletion Rate = (Natural Resources Account Balance × Residual Value) / (Total Estimated Units)

C. The successful-efforts method results in a lower depletion rate but a higher exploration expense in periods of significant exploration.

III. Other Costs Involved in Natural Resource Extraction

Definitions

Extraction Costs: Depreciation on removable assets, wages, and material costs pertaining to the extraction effort; these costs are debited to the inventory of resource, not to the natural resources account.

Production Costs: Additional processing costs after extraction; this cost also is debited to the inventory of resource, not to the natural resources account.

A. When the inventory of resource is sold, the costs that have been debited to it (depletion, extraction, production) are recognized as expense through cost of goods sold.

    1. Depreciation on Assets Used in Extraction—Depreciation on equipment used in the extraction effort is a component of total extraction costs. It does not contribute to depletion. The entry for extraction costs generally includes a debit to extraction costs and a credit to accumulated depreciation for depreciation on the cost of assets used in extraction. How the equipment is depreciated depends on whether it can be moved from one site to another.

        a. Equipment that can be used at more than one natural resource site—depreciate as usual over its useful life.

        b. Equipment dedicated to one site (often not movable or removable)—depreciate over the shorter of useful life or life of natural resource site. The most efficient method in this case is to use the units-of-production method with the same denominator as the depletion base.

IV. Financial Statement Presentation of Natural Resources

A. The natural resource account is presented as a noncurrent asset. The property associated with the natural resource is not classified as land because the land is not held as a building site, but, rather, to utilize the natural resource on the land.

B. Some firms classify the natural resource as an intangible asset because they have purchased the rights to utilize the land and do not own the land itself. These mineral rights are an intangible asset.

C. Once extracted, the natural resource noncurrent asset is transferred to resource inventory, a current asset.

Example
This example illustrates the flow of the various cost types, the calculation of depletion, and recognition of cost of goods sold.

Acquisition cost of mine	$400,000
Exploration costs, year 1	
Successful	$50,000
Unsuccessful	$150,000
Development costs	$500,000
Extraction and production costs	$200,000
Total estimated tons of ore	100,000
Estimated residual value	$ 20,000
Tons removed in year 1	40,000
Tons sold in year 1	30,000

Entries:

	Successful Efforts	Full costing
DR: Natural resources	950,000*	1,100,000**
DR: Exploration expense	150,000	
CR: Cash	1,100,000	1,100,000

*$400,000 + $50,000 + $500,000

**$400,000 + $50,000 + $500,000 + $150,000

Note: Full costing capitalizes all exploration costs whereas the successful-efforts method capitalizes only the successful efforts and expenses the rest.

	Successful Efforts	Full costing
DR: Inventory of ore	372,000*	432,000**
CR: Accumulated depletion	372,000	432,000

*(($950,000 − $20,000)/100,000 total tons)(40,000 tons removed)

**(($1,100,000 − $20,000)/100,000 total tons)(40,000 tons removed)

Accumulated depletion is contra to the natural resources account. The amounts in this entry for the two methods are the reductions in the book value of the natural resources account allocated to the inventory account. The depletion base is depleted, with the resources flowing to the inventory account. There is no change in net assets or income at this point.

	Successful Efforts	Full costing
DR: Inventory of ore	200,000	200,000
CR: Cash, materials, wages payable	200,000	200,000

The extraction and production costs also increase the inventory account. There is no income effect at this point because no inventory has been sold. Inventory cost has three components: depletion, extraction, and production.

DR: Cost of goods sold	429,000[*]	474,000[**]
CR: Inventory of ore	429,000	474,000

[*]($372,000 + $200,000)(30,000/40,000)

[**]($432,000 + $200,000)(30,000/40,000)

Of the 40,000 tons removed in the period, 30,000 were sold. Therefore, three-fourths of the inventory cost is expensed. One-fourth of the inventory cost will appear in the ending balance sheet of the firm. The entry to record the sale is not shown. It would be the same for both methods: DR Accounts receivable, CR Sales.

Impairment—Assets for Use and Held-for-Sale

This lesson presents the accounting and reporting for impairment of long-lived assets.

After studying this lesson, you should be able to:

1. Calculate the two steps in the test for impairment of assets held in use.

2. Complete the impairment test for assets held for disposal.

I. **Introduction—Asset Categories**—ASC 360 governs the subsequent measurement and accounting for impaired assets or assets held for disposal.

   A. Assets subject to impairment fall into one of three categories:

      1. Assets in use

      2. Assets held for disposal (sale)

      3. Assets to be disposed of other than by sale (by spin-off to shareholders, by exchange for other assets, or by abandonment)

   B. **Indicators of Impairment**—Impairment testing must be completed when any of the following conditions occur.

      1. Significant decrease in the fair value of the asset

      2. Significant change in the way asset is used or physical change in asset

      3. An unfavorable change in laws, regulations, or the business climate that would adversely affect the use of the asset

      4. Significantly higher than expected costs involved with the construction or acquisition of an asset

      5. There have been or projected to be negative operating or cash flow (losses) from the asset.

      6. The entity decides to sell the asset before the end of its expected life.

   C. Next is a diagram that presents an overview of the decisions that need to be made with respect to asset impairment.

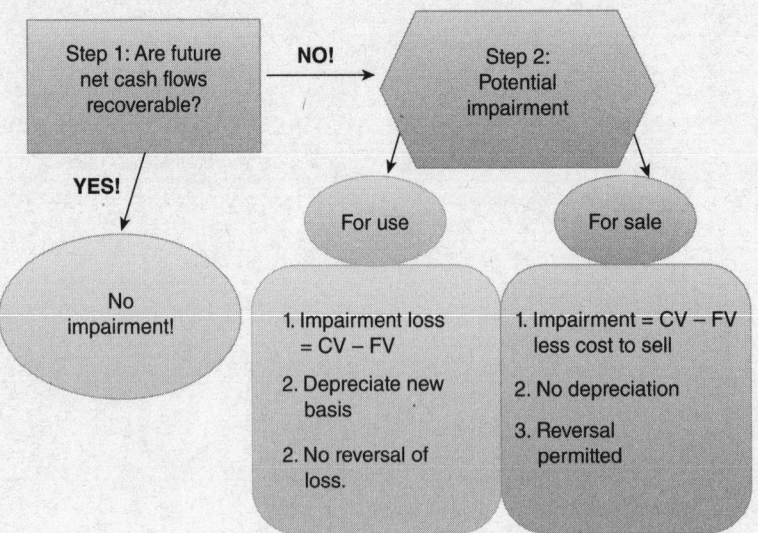

CV = carrying value; the same as net book value (BV or NBV)
FV = fair value

II. **Assets in Use**

   A. **Assets in Use**—Assets in use are written down to fair value if their recoverable cost is less than book value. The amount of the impairment loss recognized is the difference between book value and fair value. Note that the determination of impairment is a step separate from the measurement of the loss; both use different values.

1. **Fair value (FV)**—The price that would be acceptable to the firm and another party for the transfer of the asset. **Present value** is used when no active market exists for the asset.

2. **Recoverable cost (RC)**—RC is the sum of expected future net cash inflows from use and ultimate disposal. Costs of maintaining the asset are included in the computation of RC, reducing it. RC is a nominal sum, not a present value. RC is based on how the firm currently uses the asset; the expected remaining useful life is used in computing RC. RC is the net increase in cash expected from using and disposing of the asset over its remaining life. RC always exceeds FV because RC is not a discounted amount.

B. Test for Impairment

1. If book value (BV) > RC, then the asset is impaired because book value will not be recovered. If BV is $100 and RC is $70, then there is no accounting justification for reporting the asset at $100.

2. If BV ≤ RC, then the asset is not impaired and no impairment loss is recognized. In this case, the book value is recoverable.

3. Assets should be evaluated for impairment when certain indications are present, rather than on a regular basis. Significant declines in FV, changes in legal climate or physical nature of the asset are examples of signals that suggest an impairment may have occurred.

C. Measurement of Impairment Loss

1. An impaired asset is written down to FV. The loss equals BV less FV

2. Note that the *test* for impairment uses BV and RC while the *measurement* of the loss uses BV and FV.

D. Examples

Examples

1. An asset with a book value of $100 has a recoverable cost of $120 and a fair value of $75.

Test for Impairment: BV of $100 < RC of $120. The asset is not impaired because the book value is recoverable. There is no loss computation; there is no impairment loss.

2. An asset with a book value of $100 has a recoverable cost of $90 and a fair value of $75.

Test for Impairment: BV of $100 > RC of $90. The asset is impaired because the book value is not fully recoverable.

Loss Measurement: Loss = BV of $100 – FV of $75 = $25. The asset is written down to $75. The loss is a component of income from continuing operations.

The entry to record the loss of $25:

DR: Impairment loss   25

    CR: Asset or Accumulated depreciation   25

Accounting after recognizing the $25 loss

a. The new BV of the asset is the FV of 75 and is used as the cost for future depreciation. The new depreciable cost is $75 less any residual value.

b. An impairment loss on an asset in use cannot be recovered; there is no upward revaluation or gains recognized if FV increases.

c. Additional impairments are possible.

E. Asset Groups—Many, if not most, assets do not function independently but are rather part of a working group. For purposes of the **test for impairment**, assets are grouped at the *lowest* possible organizational level at which cash flows can be identified. The three amounts (BV, FV, RC) are measured at this level. One intended effect of this rule on grouping at the LOWEST level rather than a higher one is to decrease the incidence of merging assets with impairment losses with those for which FV > BV in which case there would be fewer or no impairment losses recognized.

III. Assets Held-for-Sale (Disposal)—Recoverable cost is not used for assets held for disposal. Rather, the test for impairment and the loss computation both use the same values (BV and FV less cost to sell).

A. Decision to Dispose

1. If the decision to dispose of an asset and the ultimate disposal occur in the **same period**, the actual gain or loss on disposal is recognized in income from continuing operations. The disposal loss or gain equals the difference between FV and BV (if BV > FV, then a loss occurs; if BV < FV, then a gain occurs). Depreciation should be recognized to the date of the disposal unless the firm uses a convention for fractional year depreciation. The accumulated depreciation account is removed along with the asset's original cost.

2. If the decision to dispose **precedes** the period of disposal, an estimated loss is recorded if it is probable and estimable. Estimated gains are not recognized.

B. Held for Sale Criteria

1. There are six criteria for determining when an asset is considered held for sale. All six must be met for the accounting provisions to apply. Otherwise, the asset is considered in use.

   a. Management commits to a plan to sell the asset or group of assets.

   b. The asset must be available for immediate sale in its present condition subject only to terms that are usual and customary for such sales. This criterion does not preclude a firm from using the asset while it is held for sale nor does it require a binding agreement for future sale.

   c. An active program to locate a buyer has been initiated.

   d. The sale is expected to take place within one year. In limited cases, the one-year rule is waived for circumstances beyond the firm's control (e.g., due to a new regulation or law, environmental remediation, or deteriorating market).

   e. The asset is being actively marketed for sale at a price that is reasonable in relation to its current value.

   f. Sale of the asset must be probable.

2. If the six criteria are not met at the balance sheet date but are met before issuance, treat the asset as held for use in those statements. If an asset held for sale fails to meet all six criteria at a later date, it is reclassified as held for use.

3. An asset held for sale is impaired if its BV exceeds its fair value less cost to sell at the end of the reporting period.

C. Held for Sale Accounting

1. The asset is written down to (FV less cost to sell)—here the test for impairment and the measurement of the loss are the same. The term "recoverable cost" is not used for assets for sale. If sale is expected beyond one year, the cost to sell is discounted.

2. Only direct incremental costs are used in the computation of cost to sell.

3. The impairment loss recorded equals the difference between the asset's BV and its (FV less cost to sell). The estimated cost to sell increases the loss.

4. The asset is removed from plant assets because it is no longer in use.

5. Depreciation is no longer recognized on the asset.

6. The results of operating the asset during the holding period are recognized in period of occurrence—that is, estimated future operating losses or gains are not recognized until they actually occur. Note that although these assets are held for disposal, they may require maintenance and other cash expenditures. These are expensed as incurred.

7. The asset can be written up or down if held for another period; gains are limited to the amount of the initial impairment loss. (BV cannot exceed the amount immediately before recording the initial impairment loss.)

Example

Assume that a plant asset (cost $100,000; accumulated depreciation $40,000) has a current fair value of $30,000 at the end of Year 4. Management has decided to sell the asset as soon as possible during the next reporting period. The estimated direct cost to sell is $5,000. The six criteria for determining the asset is held for sale are met.

<u>End of Year 4</u>

Plant asset	$100,000	Fair Value	$30,000
Accumulated depreciation	40,000	Cost to sell	(5,000)
Net Book Value	$ 60,000	Asset held for disposal	$25,000
		(Year 4 new net book value)	

$60,000 (old net book value) − $25,000 (Year 4 new net book value) = Year 4 loss on asset held for disposal 35,000

Assume at the end of Year 5, the asset remains unsold. The fair value is now $20,000 and the estimated cost to sell is $12,000.

<u>End of Year 5</u>

Fair Value	$ 20,000
Cost to sell	(12,000)
Asset held for disposal	$ 8,000
(Year 5 new net book value)	

$25,000 (Year 4 net book value) − $8,000 (Year 5 net book value) = Year 5 loss on asset held for disposal 17,000

Limit on gains: Assume instead that at the end of Year 5, the fair value had risen to $70,000 and estimated cost to sell remained at $5,000. The difference between fair value and estimated cost to sell has increased from $25,000 to $65,000, an increase of $40,000. This amount exceeds the previous loss of $35,000. The maximum gain allowed is $35,000, the amount of the previous loss. Therefore, the asset would be written back up to $60,000 (the book value immediately before the initial impairment), and a gain of $35,000 would be recognized.

IV. Assets to Be Disposed of Other Than by Sale

A. This category includes disposal by abandonment, by exchange for a similar asset, and by distribution to shareholders as a spin-off. Note that dissimilar asset exchange is not included in this category because that transaction is considered a sale—the culmination of an earnings process.

B. **Accounting**—Continue to classify the asset as held for use until disposal occurs, and continue to depreciate the asset. Apply the impairment standards for assets in use. Compute recoverable cost as for assets in use. These assets are treated as such because even though the plan is to dispose of the asset, the firm will derive the remaining utility of the asset (if any) from operations rather than via disposal. For exchanges and spin-offs, an additional impairment is recorded at disposal if BV > FV.

Impairment and IFRS

This lesson presents the significant differences in the accounting for impairment under IFRS versus U.S. GAAP.

After studying this lesson, you should be able to:

1. Identify the major differences in the accounting for impairment of long-lived assets under U.S. GAAP versus IFRS.

I. **Impairment and IFRS**

    A. Under IFRS, a long-lived asset is impaired when its carrying value exceeds the recoverable amount. The recoverable amount is the higher of:

        1. The asset's fair value less cost of disposal (the price that one would receive to sell an asset in an orderly transaction with a market participant); *or*

        2. The asset's value in use (which represents the entity-specific pretax cash flows discounted to present value).

    B. Impairment applies to those assets carried at cost or amortized cost. Assets carried at fair value with the unrealized gains and losses recording in income do not create an impairment loss because the impairment is already captured in the fair value.

    C. An entity must complete a review of its long-lived assets when triggering events occur and at each balance sheet date to determine if there is evidence that impairment may exist.

    D. If there is objective evidence that impairment may exist, the entity should measure and record the impairment loss.

    E. Previously recognized impairment loss is subject to reversal if the annual impairment test determines a recovery of a previously recognized impairment loss. The recovery cannot exceed the initial loss.

> **Note**
> The impairment loss exists when the recoverable amount is less than the carrying amount.

Major Differences Between U.S. GAAP and IFRS	
U.S. GAAP	**IFRS**
Two-step process	One-step process
Undiscounted cash flows from use establish recoverability (Step 1). Fair value is used for the impairment calculation (Step 2).	Recoverable amount is the higher of – Fair value less cost to sell or – Value in use
No discounting of cash flows in Step 1	Discounting required in evaluation stage
No reversals permitted	Impairment losses can be reversed if circumstances change (except for goodwill).

Examples

1. Shelby Company is assessing Asset A for impairment and has determined the following:

Carrying amount:	$42,000
Future undiscounted cash flows:	$45,000
Discounted cash flows:	$40,000
Fair value:	$37,000
Fair value less cost to sell:	$35,000

U.S. GAAP (ASC 360)

Future cash flows $45,000 > Carrying amount $42,000 therefore NO impairment

IFRS (IAS 36)

Recoverable amount the great of FV less cost to sell or value in use. $35,000 or **$40,000**.

Recoverable amount $40,000 < Carrying amount $42,000. There IS impairment.

Impairment loss: Write down to the recoverable amount: $42,000 − $40,000 = $2,000

2. Shelby Company is assessing Asset A for impairment and has determined the following:

Carrying amount:	$50,000
Future undiscounted cash flows:	$45,000
Discounted cash flows:	$40,000
Fair value:	$37,000
Fair value less cost to sell:	$35,000

U.S. GAAP (ASC 360)

Future cash flows $45,000 < Carrying amount $50,000. There IS impairment.

Impairment loss = Write down to fair value: $50,000 − $37,000 = $13,000.

IFRS (IAS 36)

Recoverable amount the great of FV less cost to sell or value in use. $35,000 or **$40,000**.

Recoverable amount $40,000 < Carrying amount $50,000. There IS impairment.

Impairment loss = Write down to the recoverable amount: $50,000 − $40,000 = $10,000.

PPE and IFRS

This lesson presents the significant differences in the accounting for property, plant, and equipment (PPE) under IFRS versus U.S. GAAP.

After studying this lesson, you should be able to:

1. Identify the major differences in the accounting for property, plant, and equipment under IFRS versus U.S. GAAP.

I. **PPE and IFRS**

A. There are a few significant differences in the accounting for PPE under IFRS than according to U.S. GAAP. The table below summarizes these differences.

U.S. GAAP	IFRS
Estimated useful life and depreciation method reviewed when events or circumstances change	Estimated useful life and depreciation method reviewed annually
No requirement for component depreciation	Component depreciation required in some cases
Revaluation to fair value is not permitted.	PPE can be revalued to fair value.
Interest earned on construction funds are not allowed to offset the interest costs.	Interest earned on construction funds can offset the interest costs.

B. **Estimated Useful Life and Depreciation Method**—Under IFRS, the company must review the remaining useful life, residual value, and depreciation method on an annual basis. Any changes in the estimated useful life, residual value, or depreciation method are accounted for prospectively.

C. **Component Depreciation**—When an item of PPE comprises individual components for which different depreciation methods or rates are appropriate, each component is depreciated separately. For example, a building can be broken down into components: roofing, electrical system, plumbing system, structural, etc. Component depreciation is based on the premise that each component of the asset has its own useful life and fair value.

D. **Fair Value Remeasurement**—Under IFRS, PPE can be remeasured to fair value if fair value can be reliably measured. If remeasurement is used, it must be applied to the entire class or components of PPE, such as land, buildings, or equipment. Increases in an assets fair value above original cost are recorded in a revaluation surplus account. Any decreases in an assets fair value below the original cost are recorded as losses to the income statement. When revaluation results in an increase in the asset, a debit is made to increase the assets value and a credit is made to an equity account (part of OCI) called revaluation surplus. If the asset is subsequently decreased during revaluation, then the previously established revaluation surplus is reduced to zero and a loss is recognized for any excess. If the fair value of the asset declines below its original cost a loss is recognized. If the fair value subsequently increases, a gain can be recognized to the extent of the loss and any additional gain is recognized in revaluation surplus.

Example
Assume Taylor Company revalued its building to fair value. The building had a net book value of $100,000 and a fair value of $120,000. The entry would be:

DR: Building   20,000

    CR: Revaluation surplus, building   20,000

Subsequent decreases in the building's fair value will first decrease the Revaluation surplus account and the excess recognized as a loss. Assume two years later the fair value of the building is $90,000:

DR: Revaluation surplus, building   20,000

DR: Revaluation loss, building   10,000

    CR: Building   30,000

E. The example is simplified by ignoring accumulated depreciation. Two methods are used to adjust accumulated depreciation: the proportional method and the reset method.

    1. In the **proportional method**, accumulated depreciation is restate proportionately so the asset's carrying value after revaluation equals the revalued amount.

Example
Assume the cost of Taylor's building is $125,000 and the accumulated depreciation is $25,000 resulting in a net book value of $100,000. Both the building and accumulated depreciation are reset using the proportionate ratio of net book value to original cost (($125,000 / $100,000) = 1.20%). The 120% ratio will increase the asset and the accumulated depreciation proportionately as displayed in the following entry.

DR: Building   25,000*

    CR: Accumulated depreciation, building   5,000#

    CR: Revaluation surplus, building   20,000

*$((125,000 \times 1.2) = 150,000 - 125,000 = 25,000)$
#$((25,000 \times 1.2) = 30,000 - 25,000 = 5,000)$

After this entry, the balances will be as follows:
New cost = $150,000 (125,000 × 1.2)
New accumulated depreciation = 30,000 (25,000 × 1.2)
New book value = 120,000 (150,000 − 30,000)

    2. In the **reset method**, accumulated depreciation is "reset" to zero by closing it to the building account, and then the building is adjusted for the revaluation.

Example
In the next entries, Taylor resets the accumulated depreciation to zero and records the revaluation surplus.

DR: Accumulated depreciation, Building   25,000

    CR: Building   25,000

DR: Building   20,000

    CR: Revaluation surplus   20,000

F. Depreciation will be computed on the newly revalued building carrying value. The balance in revaluation surplus is also depreciated over the remaining life of the asset. The depreciation on the revaluation surplus is taken directly to retained earnings.

G. The revaluation surplus is reported in equity until the property is sold. When the revalued property is sold the balance in revaluation surplus is closed directly to retained earnings.

H. **Capitalized Interest**—Under IFRS, the interest earned on the funds received for a construction loan can reduce interest cost. U.S. GAAP does not allow reduction of interest cost for the interest earned on the construction loans.

Nonmonetary Exchange

Commercial Substance

This lesson presents the accounting for nonmonetary exchanges that have commercial substance.

After studying this lesson, you should be able to:

1. Define a nonmonetary asset.

2. Define commercial substance.

3. Calculate the fair value of the asset received and the gain or loss in a nonmonetary exchange.

I. Nonmonetary Assets

Definition
Nonmonetary Asset: Such an asset does not have a fixed nominal or stated value, as is the case with cash, accounts receivable, and other monetary assets.

A. Plant assets, inventories, and many investments are nonmonetary because their value changes with the market. The determination of the fair value and recorded value of nonmonetary assets presents a challenge when they are acquired in an exchange for other nonmonetary assets.

Exam Note
This topic is frequently tested on the exam.

1. What value should be used when recording the acquired asset?

2. Should gains or losses be recorded?

3. ASC 845 governs the accounting for this area.

B. When fair value is the appropriate valuation of the acquired asset, the preferred amount is the fair value of the assets given in exchange. However, if the fair value of the asset acquired is more objectively determinable, then that amount should be used for its valuation.

C. Cash is frequently paid or received on exchange. When recording the journal entry for the exchange, the following common-sense relationships may help:

1. If cash is paid on the exchange (more common):

Fair Value of Acquired Asset = Fair Value of Asset Exchanged + Cash Paid

2. If cash is received on the exchange (less common):

Fair Value of Acquired Asset = Fair Value of Asset Exchanged − Cash Received

Example
The fair value of a plant asset exchanged for another plant asset is $40,000. Cash of $6,000 is received on the exchange. The implied fair value of the asset acquired is $34,000 ($40,000 fair value of asset exchanged − $6,000 cash received).

D. However, fair value is not always the appropriate valuation for the acquired nonmonetary asset.

E. **Gain or Loss**—The amount of the gain or loss on exchange is based solely on values pertaining to the asset exchanged. The book value of a plant asset is, for example, the difference between its cost and accumulated depreciation to date. The amount of gain or loss recorded, if any, is:

> Gain = Fair Value of Asset Exchanged − Book Value of Asset Exchanged
>
> Loss = Book Value of Asset Exchanged − Fair Value of Asset Exchanged

F. The asset exchanged should be tested for impairment before recording the exchange.

II. **Caution on List Price**—The list price of the acquired asset should not be used for fair value-list prices are notoriously inflated. Any associated trade-in allowance is used only to determine the amount of cash to be paid: List price − Trade-in allowance = Cash paid on exchange. The trade-in allowance is not equal to the fair value of the asset exchanged.

Example
The list price of a new machine is $32,000. An old machine is traded in for the new machine, and the seller gives the buyer a trade-in allowance of $18,000 for the old machine. The fair value of the old machine is $12,000.

Cash to be Paid on the Exchange	=	List Price	−	Trade-in Allowance	
	=	$32,000	−	$18,000	= $14,000

The fair value of the acquired asset equals:

Fair Value of Asset Exchanged	+	Cash Paid	
$12,000.00	+	$14,000.00	= $26,000.00

III. **ASC 845**

A. ASC 845 requires that fair value be used to record a nonmonetary asset acquired in an exchange with another nonmonetary asset, with full recognition of gains and losses, unless any of the following apply:

1. The fair value of neither asset can be determined.

2. The exchange is made solely to facilitate sales to customers (e.g., inventory is exchanged for other inventory in the same line of business to enable one of the firms to make a sale to an outside party).

3. The exchange **lacks commercial substance**—the cash flows of the firm are not expected to change significantly as a result of the exchange, which means:

a. The cash flows from the acquired asset will not be significantly different from those of the asset exchanged in terms of amount, timing, or risk; *or*

b. The use value of the acquired asset is not significantly different from that of the asset exchanged, in relation to the fair value of the assets exchanged.

B. Receipt or payment of cash to even the exchange does not necessarily imply that gains and losses should be recognized. For example, in situation 2 above, one firm may pay the other a certain amount of cash to even the exchange of inventory made to facilitate sales to customers. The cash flow does not cause the inventory to be valued at fair value.

C. If any of the above three criteria apply, then the accounting is simpler and based on book value, not fair value. No gain or loss is recorded (there are exceptions—see below), and the acquired asset is recorded at the book value of the asset exchanged plus cash paid on the exchange (or minus cash received on the exchange).

Examples

1. *Commercial Substance*

A plant asset (cost $40,000; accumulated depreciation $13,000) is exchanged for another plant asset with a fair value of $30,000. Cash of $2,000 is also paid to even the exchange. The exchange is determined to have commercial substance.

The implied fair value of the asset exchanged is $28,000 ($30,000 fair value of acquired asset less $2,000 cash paid).

Journal entry for the exchange:

Plant asset	30,000	
Accumulated depreciation	13,000	
Plant asset		40,000
Cash		2,000
Gain on exchange		1,000

The acquired plant asset is valued at the sum of the $28,000 fair value of the asset exchanged and $2,000 cash paid. The $1,000 gain equals the difference between the exchanged asset's fair value of $28,000 and its book value of $27,000 ($40,000 – $13,000). A loss would have occurred if the book value had exceeded its fair value. Both losses and gains are recognized when there is commercial substance to the exchange.

2. *Lack of Commercial Substance*

A plant asset (cost $40,000; accumulated depreciation $13,000) is exchanged for another plant asset with a fair value of $30,000. Cash of $2,000 is also paid to even the exchange. The exchange is determined to lack commercial substance. (Same data as previous example.)

Journal entry for the exchange:

Plant asset	29,000	
Accumulated depreciation	13,000	
Plant asset		40,000
Cash		2,000

The acquired asset is recorded at the sum of the $27,000 book value of the asset exchanged and $2,000 cash paid. No gain or loss is recognized. Another way to determine the debit to the new asset is to add subtract the unrecognized gain of $1,000 from the $30,000 fair value of the acquired asset.

IV. Rationale for the Exception to Fair Value Recording

A. If fair value is not available, the firm is forced into using book to record the acquired asset. If the exchange is made simply to facilitate the sale of goods to a customer, or if the exchange lacks commercial substance, then the firm is in essentially the same economic position after the exchange as before. Only the "identity" of the asset has changed. For example, exchanging an office building for a slightly different one leaves the firm in the same position. There is enough uncertainty inherent in fair values that it is considered more prudent to continue the accounting with the historically more reliable amounts (book value). Computationally, the exception also leaves future depreciation calculations unchanged.

B. Judgment is required for determining whether an exchange has commercial substance. The following characteristics of an exchange may indicate commercial substance:

1. The amount of cash paid or received on exchange is significant in relation to the fair value of the assets exchanged;

2. The functions of the assets exchanged are different. For example, exchanging land for equipment would imply at the very least a different timing and duration of cash flows.

No Commercial Substance

This lesson presents the accounting for nonmonetary exchanges that do not have commercial substance.

After studying this lesson, you should be able to:

1. Calculate the fair value of the asset received and the gain or loss in a nonmonetary exchange with no commercial substance and cash is paid or received.

I. **Accounting for an Exchange When There Is No Commercial Substance**

    A. An exchange lacks commercial substance whenever the cash flows to the firm are not expected to change significantly as a result of the exchange:

        1. The cash flows from the acquired asset will not be significantly different from those of the asset exchanged in terms of amount, timing, or risk; or

        2. The use value of the acquired asset is not significantly different from that of the asset exchanged, in relation to the fair value of the assets exchanged.

        3. When there is no commercial substance, the value of the asset acquired is the book value of the asset given.

    B. There are two exceptions to book value reporting when there is no commercial substance:

        1. When a loss is evident, it is recognized in full, and the acquired asset is recorded at market value. Cash can be paid or received on the exchange for this exception. Thus, losses are always recognized in full—an example of conservatism.

        2. When a gain is evident and cash is received (only), the gain is recognized in proportion to the amount of cash received, and the acquired asset is recorded at market value less the portion of the gain unrecognized. If the proportion represented by cash is 25% or more, then the entire gain is recognized, and the acquired asset is recorded at market value.

 **Examples**
1. *No Commercial Substance, Loss, Cash Paid*

Cost of old asset, $40,000
Accumulated depreciation, $12,000
Fair value of new asset $30,000
Cash of $6,000 is paid to even the exchange

The implied fair value of the old asset is $24,000 ($30,000 fair value of new asset − $6,000 cash paid). A $4,000 loss is evident: $28,000 book value of old asset—$24,000 fair value of old asset. Losses are recognized in full and the new asset is recorded at fair value.

Plant asset	30,000	
Accumulated depreciation	12,000	
Loss	4,000	
Plant asset		40,000
Cash		6,000

---

2. *No Commercial Substance, Loss, Cash Received*

Cost of old asset, $40,000

Accumulated depreciation, $12,000

Fair value of new asset $20,000

Cash of $3,000 is received to even the exchange

The implied fair value of the old asset is $23,000 ($20,000 fair value of new asset + $3,000 cash received). A $5,000 loss is evident: $28,000 book value of old asset − $23,000 fair value of old asset. Losses are recognized in full and the new asset is recorded at fair value.

Plant asset	20,000	
Accumulated depreciation	12,000	
Cash	3,000	
Loss	5,000	
Plant asset		40,000

3. *No Commercial Substance, Gain, Cash Received*

Cost of old asset, $40,000

Accumulated depreciation, $30,000

Fair value of new asset $20,000

Cash of $3,000 is received to even the exchange

The implied fair value of the old asset is $23,000 ($20,000 fair value of new asset + $3,000 cash received). A $13,000 gain is evident: $23,000 fair value of old asset − $10,000 book value of old asset. Cash represents ($3,000/($3,000 + $20,000)) or 13% of the value of the transaction. 13% of the old asset has been "sold" for cash allowing 13% of the gain to be recognized: 13%(13,000) = $1,690. The unrecognized gain is $13,000 − $1,690 = $11,310. The new asset is recorded at fair value less the unrecorded gain = $20,000 − $11,310 = $8,690.

Plant asset	8,690	
Accumulated depreciation	30,000	
Cash	3,000	
Plant asset		40,000
Gain		1,690

4. *No Commercial Substance, Gain, Cash Received, Proportion Represented by Cash > 25%*

Cost of old asset, $40,000

Accumulated depreciation, $30,000

Fair value of new asset $20,000

Cash of $10,000 is received to even the exchange

The implied fair value of the old asset is $30,000 ($20,000 fair value of new asset + $10,000 cash received). A $20,000 gain is evident: $30,000 fair value of old asset – $10,000 book value of old asset = $20,000. Cash represents ($10,000/($10,000 + $20,000)) of the value of the transaction or 33%, which is more than 25%. This firm has "sold" so much of its asset that the entire transaction is considered a monetary transaction. The entire gain is recognized and the new asset is recorded at fair value.

Plant asset	20,000	
Accumulated depreciation	30,000	
Cash	10,000	
Plant asset		40,000
Gain		20,000

II. Summary of All Cases for Nonmonetary Asset Exchanges

   A. Fair value not determinable: recognize no loss or gain, and record the acquired asset at book value of old asset + cash paid or – cash received.

   B. Losses (loss = book value of asset exchanged – fair value):

      1. Recognize loss in full, and record the acquired asset at fair value regardless of whether there is commercial substance. (Losses are always recognized in full.)

   C. Gains (gain = fair value of asset exchanged – book value):

      1. If there is commercial substance, recognize gain in full, and record the acquired asset at fair value.

      2. If there is no commercial substance and cash is not received on the exchange, recognize no gain, and record the acquired asset at book value of asset exchanged + cash paid.

      3. If there is no commercial substance and cash is received on the exchange, recognize the gain in proportion to the cash received and record the asset acquired at fair value less the unrecognized portion of the gain.

         a. Exception—if the proportion of cash received is 25% or more, account for the exchange as if there were commercial substance (recognize gain in full and record acquired asset at fair value).

Nonmonetary Exchanges and IFRS

This lesson presents the significant differences in the accounting for nonmonetary exchanges under IFRS versus U.S. GAAP.

After studying this lesson, you should be able to:

1. Identify the major differences in the accounting for nonmonetary exchanges under IFRS versus U.S. GAAP.

I. **Nonmonetary Exchange and IFRS**

   A. There are a few significant differences in the accounting for nonmonetary exchange under IFRS than according to U.S. GAAP. The table below summarizes these differences.

U.S. GAAP	IFRS
Advertising revenue (gain) is based on the services received or given, whichever can be most reliably measured.	Advertising revenue (gain) is recognized in barter transactions is determined by reference to a nonbarter transaction.
U.S. GAAP does not address the accounting for government grants.	Assets transferred to the entity by the government are recognized as a government grant.
Donated assets are recognized as an expense at fair value and the gain or loss is recognized on the donated asset.	There is no guidance when assets or resources are donated.

   B. **Advertising Revenue Determined by Reference to Nonbarter Transaction**—Under IFRS, advertising revenue is determined by reference to a nonbarter (another transaction in which cash is paid) transaction. U.S. GAAP permits measurement of the revenue by using the fair value of the advertising services given or received. IFRS assumes the value of these services is determinable only by referencing paid for services.

   C. **Government Grant Transfers**—IFRS specifically addresses the accounting for assets transferred to the entity from a government. These transfers in general recognize an asset and income. U.S. GAAP does not specifically address this type of transaction.

   D. **Donated Assets**—IFRS does not specifically address the accounting when an asset or other resource is donated. U.S. GAAP requires that the fair value of the donated asset or service be recognized as an expense and a gain (or loss) is recognized on the revaluation of the donated item.

Investments

Introduction—Equity and Debt Investments

When one entity acquires the debt or equity securities issued by another entity, it has made an investment in the securities of the issuing entity. How the acquiring entity accounts for and reports its investment depends on the nature, extent, and purpose of the investment, and, in some cases, whether or not the investing entity elects the fair value option. This lesson provides a frame of reference for the details of accounting for investments when the investor does not elect the fair value option. The details of accounting when the investing entity does not elect the fair value option are covered in the following lessons. The use of the fair value option is covered in a subsequent lesson.

After studying this lesson, you should be able to:

1. Define certain investment terminology.

2. Identify the major classifications of investments for accounting purposes.

3. Provide a model that shows the accounting treatment for each classification.

4. Identify the levels of influence for accounting purposes derived from investments in debt and equity securities.

5. Describe the criteria for classifying investments in debt or equity securities into the correct level of influence.

6. Define and give examples of debt and equity securities.

I. **Investments Held by Companies**

    A. **Terminology**

> **Definition**
> *Equity Securities:* Securities representing ownership interest or right to acquire or dispose of ownership interest.

        1. Includes common stock, preferred stock (except redeemable), stock warrants, call options/rights, put options

        2. Excludes debt securities (even convertible debt), redeemable preferred stock, and treasury stock

> **Definition**
> *Debt Securities:* Securities representing the right of buyer/holder (Creditor) to receive from the issuer (Debtor) a principal amount at a specified future date and (generally) to receive interest as payment for providing use of funds.

        3. Includes bonds, notes, convertible bonds/notes, redeemable preferred stock

        4. Excludes common/preferred stock, stock warrants/options/rights, futures/forward contracts

II. **Concepts**

    A. **Recognized versus Realized**

        1. A recognized gain/loss occurs when a gain or loss related to an investment (or other item) is recorded (recognized) in the financial statements, regardless of whether the investment has been sold. For example, a gain or loss would be recognized if the change in

> **Note**
> Recognition *is an accounting concept—it means that we have recognized the item on the financial statements.*

market value of investment securities is reported in the financial statements before the securities are sold.

2. A realized gain/loss occurs when an investment (or other item) is sold (or otherwise disposed of). The difference between the cash or other consideration received and the carrying value of the investment is a realized gain or loss.

> **Note**
> Realization *is an economic concept; it means that there is a culmination of the earnings process and cash or other consideration is given or received.*

III. Investment in Equity Securities

A. The accounting and reporting of an investment in equity securities depends on:

1. How much is owned

2. How long it is held

3. Whether the equity security is private or public

B. The following table depicts the accounting and reporting of equity securities. Since equity ownership provides voting rights, the level of economic influence is determined by the level of stock ownership. This level of influence is a guideline because there may be other factors that contribute to the investor's ability to exercise significant influence or control. Subsequent lessons will discuss these other factors in more detail. The purpose of this lesson is to provide an overview of the investment categories and valuation basis.

Percentage Equity Ownership	0–20%	21–50%	> 51%
Level of Economic Influence (influence over operating, investing and financing activities)	Nominal	Significant	Control
Valuation Basis	Cost or fair value	Equity method or fair value	Equity method or cost method
Reporting Classification	Trading or available for sale	Equity investment	Subsidiary
Balance Sheet Presentation	Investment—current or noncurrent	Investment—noncurrent	Consolidated financial statements

C. If the investor has < **20% ownership**, there is **nominal influence** over the operating, investing and financing activities of the investee.

1. If the investee is publicly traded, where there is a readily determinable market value for the investee, then the investment is classified as **trading or available for sale**. (These investments are discussed in the lesson "No Significant Influence.")

2. If the investee is not publicly traded, and there is not a readily determinable market value, then the investment is classified as a **cost method** investment. (The accounting for this type of investment is included in the "Equity Method" and "IFRS—Equity Method" lessons.)

3. The balance sheet presentation of **current or noncurrent** depends on management's intent for holding the security for the short term (typically the trading securities) or long term. AFS securities could be short or long-term.

D. If the investor has between **20% and 50% ownership**, then the investor can **significantly influence** the operating, investing and financing activities of the investee. Therefore, the investment is accounted for using the equity method of accounting.

1. The default accounting for an investment with significant influences is the **equity method**. A detailed discussion of equity method accounting is presented in subsequent lessons.

2. If the investee is publicly traded and there is a readily determinable market value, then the investor has the option to value this investment at **fair value**. If this option is chosen then the investment is marked-to-market value with the unrealized gains and losses recorded in earnings. Once the investor chooses the fair value option it is irrevocable and the investment continues to be recorded at fair value.

3. Investments with significant influence are usually reported as a **noncurrent** asset because buying and selling equity shares of this magnitude is relatively difficult to do. For example, if you owned 40% of a publicly traded company, it would be very difficult for you to sell that much stock in one block without severely diluting the selling price.

E. If the investor has >50% ownership of an investment, then the investor controls the investee. An investment of this magnitude creates a Parent / Subsidiary relationship.

1. The default accounting for an investment with >50% ownership is equity method. The Parent company will record its equity investment in the Subsidiary on the Parent company's books. Equity method accounting is discussed more fully in the "Equity Method" and "IFRS—Equity Method" lessons.

2. In some instances, the Parent company can choose to use the cost method to account for its subsidiary. Cost method accounting is discussed more fully in the "Equity Method" lesson. The cost method can be used by the Parent company because the Parent's stand-alone financial statements are (typically) not issued on a stand-alone basis. The Parent must consolidate and, therefore, eliminate the investment in the Subsidiary.

3. For financial statement presentation, the Parent must consolidate the Subsidiary and report consolidated financial statements of Parent + Subsidiary. Whether the Parent uses the equity method or the cost method to account for its subsidiary, the consolidated financial statements will be the same. The only difference is what is reported on the Parent's stand-alone statements. Not that the Parent's stand-alone statements are not in compliance with GAAP. GAAP requires that the Parent present consolidated statements. Consolidation is discussed more fully in the series of consolidation lessons in the "Conceptual Framework and Financial Reporting" section.

IV. Investment in Debt Securities

A. The accounting and reporting of an investment in debt securities depends on:

1. How long it is held;

2. Whether the debt security is private or public.

B. The following table depicts the accounting and reporting of debt securities. Debt ownership does not provide any voting rights; therefore, there is no economic influence from debt ownership. The critical criteria for accounting for debt investments are whether the company has the positive ability and intent to hold the debt security to maturity.

Debt Ownership	Publicly Traded		Private issue	
Positive ability and intent to hold to maturity	Held-to-maturity		Held-to-maturity	
No ability and/or intent to hold to maturity		Trading or available-for-sale		Trading or available-for-sale
Valuation Basis	Amortized cost	Fair value	Amortized cost	Fair value
Balance Sheet Presentation	Investment—noncurrent	Investment—current or noncurrent	Investment—noncurrent	Investment—current or noncurrent

C. The first criterion for a debt security to be classified as held to maturity (HTM) is that the investor must have the **positive ability and intent** to hold the security to maturity. By definition, only debt securities can be classified as HTM because equity securities do not mature.

    1. The **ability to hold** debt to maturity may be evident in prior investments in debt securities and the investor has demonstrated that he/she holds the security for its entire life.

    2. The **intent to hold** the debt to maturity may be evident by demonstrating that the investor does not need the cash associated with this investment. In other words, the investor has sufficient operating cash flows so there is no need to liquidate the investment in order to have enough cash flow for operating activities.

D. If the debt security is **publicly traded**, the investor has the option to account for the debt security at amortized cost or fair value.

    1. If the investor intends to hold the debt security to maturity and wants to classify the security as held to maturity, the debt security must be valued at amortized cost.

    2. If the debt is classified as HTM, it will be classified as a noncurrent investment until the year the security matures. At that time, the investment will be classified as current.

    3. If the investor selects the fair value option and records the security at fair value, the security will be classified as trading or available for sale and presented as current or noncurrent, depending on how long management intends to hold the debt.

E. If the debt security is **privately issued**, the investor will usually account for the debt security at amortized cost.

    1. If the investor intends to hold the debt security to maturity and wants to classify the security as held to maturity, the debt security must be valued at amortized cost.

    2. If the debt is classified as HTM, it will be classified as a noncurrent investment until the year the security matures. At that time, the investment will be classified as current.

    3. If the investor classifies the debt investment as trading or available for sale, the debt should be valued at fair value. This classification will be unlikely because it will be difficult to get a quoted price representing the fair value of private debt (Level 1 valuation). However, it is possible to use this classification; the investor would have to value the private debt using a valuation model and, depending on the extent that the inputs are observable, the debt valuation would be Level 2 or 3.

F. Below are examples for the accounting for investment in bonds. The accounting for a bond investment that is purchased and carried as an asset is the mirror image of the accounting for a bond that is issued and carried as a liability. Recall that a bond is a contract to repay borrowing at specified maturity date; interest is to be paid at specified intervals until maturity. When the entity invests in a bond, the interest received is interest income. The stated rate on the bond is the nominal rate and the effective rate of the bond is the market rate or yield.

    1. When the bond is purchased for less than face value, effective rate is greater than stated rate and the bond is purchased at a discount.

    2. When the bond is purchased for more than face value, effective rate is less than stated rate and the bond is purchased at a premium.

    3. The discount or premium is amortized to interest income over the life of the bond.

        a. Discounts or premiums should be amortized using the effective interest method. The straight-line amortization method can be used if it yields a similar result.

G. Bond investment is classified as held to maturity when there is positive ability and intent to hold the bond until maturity. Below are examples of the accounting for a bond classified as held to maturity:

 **Examples**

1. *Bond Purchased at Par*

Assume the entity purchases a 2-year, $100 bond, with 10% stated rate, pays semi-annually is purchased at 10%.

Purchase price:	PV of principle ($100, 4 periods, 5%) = .82270 =	$82.27
	PV of interest ($5, 4 periods, 5%) = 3.546 =	17.73
		$100.00

Entries at purchase date:

Bonds Investment   100

    Cash   100

Interest income—recorded every six months:

Cash   5.00

    Interest Income   5.00

2. *Bond Purchased at a Discount*

Assume a 2-year, $100 bond, with 10% stated rate, pays semi-annually is purchased at 12%.

Purchase price:	PV of principle ($100, 4 periods, 6%) = .79209 =	$79.21
	PV of interest ($5, 4 periods, 6%) = 3.46511 =	17.33
		$96.54

Beg PV	Discount	Interest Income	Cash Received	Amortization	Carrying Amount of Bond Investment
96.54	3.46	5.79	5.00	.79	97.33
97.33	2.68	5.84	5.00	.84	98.17
98.16	1.84	5.89	5.00	.89	99.06
99.05	0.95	5.94	5.00	.94	100.00
Totals		23.46	20.00	3.46	

Entries at purchase date:

Bond Investment   96.54

Cash   96.54

Interest income (effective interest method) for first 6-month period:

Cash	5.00	
Bond Investment	.79	
Interest Income		5.79

3. Bond Purchased at a Premium

Assume a 2-year, $100 bond, with 10% stated rate, pays semi-annually is purchased at 8%.

Purchase price:	PV of principal ($100, 4 periods, 4%) = .8548 =	$ 85.48
	PV of interest ($5, 4 periods, 4%) = 3.6299 =	18.15
		$103.63

Beg PV	Premium	Interest Income	Cash Received	Amortization	Carrying Value of Bond Investment
103.63	3.63	4.15	5.00	.85	102.78
102.78	2.78	4.11	5.00	.89	101.89
101.89	1.89	4.07	5.00	.93	100.96
100.96	0.96	4.04	5.00	.96	100.00
Totals	16.37		20.00	3.63	

Entries at purchase date:

Bond Investment	103.63	
Cash		103.63

Interest income (effective interest method) for first 6-month period:

Cash	5.00	
Bond Investment		.85
Interest Income		4.15

H. If there is no evidence of positive ability and intent to hold the bond investment to maturity, the bond investment must be classified as available for sale (AFS) or trading. These classifications require the bond investment to be carried at fair value.

1. A bond investment classified as AFS is reported at fair value with the unrealized gains and losses associated with the changes in fair value recorded as an unrealized holding gain or loss in comprehensive income. The interest income on the bond investment would still be accounted for as described above, but there would be an additional entry to adjust the bond investment to fair value.

2. Using the example above where the bond was purchased at a discount for $96.54, assume that at the end of the first 6-month period the fair value of the bond is $96.00. The interest income entry would be exactly the same as described above, but there would also be an entry to mark the bond investment to fair value using a valuation account for $1.33 ($97.33 – 96.00). The fair value adjustment account is used as a contra or adjunct account to adjust the unamortized value of the bond to fair value.

Fair value adjustment:

Unrealized holding gain or loss—Equity	1.33	
Fair value adjustment (AFS bond investment)		1.33

3. If the entity intends to sell the bond in the short term, the bond investment would be classified as trading. A bond investment classified as trading is reported at fair value with the unrealized gains and losses associated with the changes in fair value recorded in earnings. The fair value adjustment would be:

Fair value adjustment:

Unrealized holding gain or loss—Income	1.33	
Fair value adjustment (AFS bond investment)		1.33

No Significant Influence

No Significant Influence

This lesson covers investments where the investor does not hold significant influence over the investee. How the investor accounts for such an investment depends on the investor's intent with respect to the investment. For accounting purposes, three categories of investments are: (1) held to maturity, (2) trading, and (3) available for sale.

After studying this lesson, you should be able to:

1. Describe the criteria, accounting, and reporting for investments in debt securities classified as held to maturity.

2. Describe the accounting for the disposal of held-to-maturity investments at maturity or before maturity.

3. Describe the criteria, accounting, and reporting for investments in securities classified as trading.

4. Describe the accounting for the disposal of a trading investment.

5. Describe the criteria, accounting, and reporting for investments in securities classified as available for sale.

6. Describe the accounting for the disposal of an available-for-sale investment.

I. Overview

A. The following table presents an overview of the definition, accounting, balance sheet reporting, and treatment of realized and unrealized gains and losses. This lesson discussions the first three investments listed on the table: trading, available for sale, and held to maturity. Subsequent lessons go into detail on the accounting and reporting of the equity and cost methods.

Category	Definition	How Is Security Reported on the Balance Sheet	How Unrealized Holding Gains and Losses Are Recorded	How Realized Gains and Losses Are Reported on the Income Statement
Trading [Mark-to-Market]	**Debt and Equity** securities bought and held principally for the purpose of selling them in the near term	Reported at **fair value**, usually a current assets on the balance sheet	Unrealized gains and losses are included in **earnings** in the period they occur	Unrealized holding gains or losses will **already have been recognized**, and should not be reversed. **Dividends are income.**
Available for Sale [**Mark to Market**]	**Debt and Equity** securities not classified as trading or held to maturity	Reported at **fair value**, and may be classified as current or noncurrent	Unrealized gains and losses are **excluded from earnings**—reported as OCI—unless the decline is considered to be *other than temporary* then—recognized in earnings	Realized gains and losses are recognized (gain or loss will be difference between selling price and carrying value less any permanent decline in value recognized). **Dividends are income.**
Held to Maturity [**No market revaluation**]	**Debt securities** that the organization has the **positive intent and ability** to hold to the maturity date	Reported at **amortized cost** and grouped with noncurrent assets on the balance sheet	Unrealized gains and losses are **excluded from earnings**—unless the decline is considered to be *other-than-temporary* or the Fair Value Option is selected	Realized gains and losses are **recognized** in accordance with amortized cost method. **No dividends on debt.**
Securities—Accounted for under the Equity Method	An Equity investment whereby the investor has **significant influence** over investee—generally >20% voting shares.	Reported in accordance with the **Equity Method** - if control >50% must consolidate	These securities are **not adjusted** for changes in market value unless the decline is considered to be *other-than-temporary* or the Fair Value Option is selected	Realized gains and losses from transactions are recognized for the difference between selling price and the equity basis of the stock. **Dividends are NOT income.**
Securities—Accounted for under the Cost Method	An **Equity** investment where there is no **significant influence** and it is a security with no readily determinable market value (privately held)	**At cost.** Cost basis is reduced if there is a liquidating dividend where the dividends declared exceed the investee's profits. Dividends and profits are measured from the date the investee was purchased.	There are no unrealized gains and losses because the cost method is not marked to market.	Realized gains and losses are **recognized** (gain or loss will be difference between selling price and carrying value less any permanent decline in value recognized). **Dividends are income. WATCH for liquidating dividends!**

II. Held-to-Maturity Investments—This classification includes only investments in debt securities that the investor intends to hold until the investment matures and has the ability to do so. This lesson presents the criteria necessary to be classified as held to maturity and the accounting and financial statement reporting for such investments. Coverage includes recognition of a premium or discount at the time of investment, the amortization of a premium or discount, financial statement presentation, and disposition of held-to-maturity investments.

A. Criteria for this classification

1. Applies only to investments in **debt** securities because only debt has a maturity.

2. Applies when investor has:

   a. **Positive** intent to hold the securities to maturity; and

   b. **Ability** to hold the securities to maturity.

3. Held-to-maturity classification is not appropriate if investor may sell due to need for cash or better investment opportunities, or if the debt can be settled (e.g., prepaid) and the investor would not recover all of the recorded investment.

4. Sale of debt securities before maturity, that meet the following conditions, can be considered **held to maturity**.

   a. Sale is near enough to maturity date so that interest rate risk is substantially eliminated as a factor in pricing;

   b. Sale occurs after investor has collected (through periodic payments or prepayment) a substantial portion (at least 85%) of the principal outstanding at acquisition date.

B. Accounting and reporting for this held-to-maturity classification

1. Record investment at cost:

   a. Cost includes:

      i. Purchase price (e.g., per security cost);

      ii. Directly related costs incurred—brokerage fee, transfer fee, etc.

2. Carry and report held-to-maturity investments at amortized cost:

   a. Recognize periodic interest income

   DR: Cash

       CR: Interest Income

           Interest Receivable (accrued interest collected on first interest date, if any)

   b. Fair value option: Normally, temporary changes in the fair value of investments held-to-maturity should not be recognized; however, GAAP permits an investor to elect the fair value option for most financial assets, including debt investments, which the investor intends to hold to maturity.

   c. Report held-to-maturity investment in financial statements:

      i. Interest income or revenue (including increase/decrease from amortization of discount or premium)

      ii. Investment held to maturity (probably net of premium or discount) in Balance Sheet as:

         1. Current—if maturity is within one year (or operating cycle) of maturity;

         2. Noncurrent—if maturity is **not** within one year (or operating cycle) of maturity.

      iii. **Investment Held to Maturity in Statement of Cash Flows is an Investing Activity.**

III. Trading Investments—Overview—This classification includes both debt and equity securities. All investments in this classification must be adjusted to fair value at the balance sheet date. The process for making that adjustment, as well as the required financial statement presentation and accounting for disposal (sale) of held-for-trading investments, are also presented.

A. Criteria for this classification

1. Applies to investments in both debt and equity securities;

2. Investor buys and holds for the purpose of selling in the *near term*, generally with the objective of generating profits on short-term price changes.

B. Accounting and reporting for this held-for-trading classification

1. Record investment at cost.

    a. Cost includes:

        i. Purchase price (e.g., per security cost);

        ii. Directly related costs incurred—brokerage fee, transfer fee, etc.

2. Carry and report trading securities at fair value

    a. For debt securities:

        i. Recognize periodic interest income.

    b. For equity securities:

        i. Recognize dividends received as income.

    c. For both debt and equity securities, adjust to fair value at balance sheet date.

Example

Determine the appropriate Carrying and Reporting Values for the following data:

Trading Investment	12/31/201X/Value Carrying	Fair	Lower of Carrying or Fair
Co. A	$100,000	$ 80,000	$ 80,000
Co. B	200,000	160,000	160,000
Co. C	50,000	75,000	50,000
Totals	$350,000	$315,000	$290,000

At what net amount should the trading investments be shown on 12/31/1X? $_____

Answer: $315,000 fair value of the aggregate trading investments classification.

What is the net amount of the adjustment necessary to reflect the correct amount at which the trading investments should be shown? $_____

Answer: $35,000

          Carrying Value $350,000

          Fair Value   315,000

          Write-down $ 35,000

C. Disposition (Sale) of Trading Investments:

    1. If debt security, first recognize interest income and amortization of premium/discount to date of sale;

    2. Determining carrying value of investments to be sold:

        a. For Debt and Equity Securities = Fair Value

    3. Recognize (realized) gain or loss at date of sale, if any, as difference between sales price and carrying value of investments sold.

IV. Available-for-Sale Investments—Overview—This classification includes all investments in debt and equity securities that are not classified as held to maturity or trading, such as, for example, an equity security that the investor intends to hold indefinitely. This section presents the criteria necessary to be classified as available for sale and the accounting and financial statement reporting for such investments. Like the prior trading classification, this classification includes both debt and equity securities. Therefore, the details related to both types of securities are not repeated here. The major difference between this lesson and the prior trading section is that an unrealized holding gain or loss on an investment available for sale does not go on the income statement, but enters in the determination of Other Comprehensive Income, and subsequently shows up as (part of) accumulated other comprehensive income in Shareholders' Equity on the Balance Sheet.

A. Criteria for this classification

    1. Applies to investments in both debt and equity securities.

    2. Includes all investments in debt and (qualified) Equity securities not classified as held-to-maturity or trading investments.

B. Accounting and Reporting for this Available-for-Sale Classification

    1. Record investment at cost

        a. Cost includes:

            i. Purchase price (e.g., per security cost);

            ii. Directly related costs incurred—brokerage fee, transfer fee, etc.

    2. Carry and report securities available for sale at fair value:

        a. For debt securities:

            i. Recognize periodic interest income.

            ii. Recognize periodic amortization of premium or discount.

        b. For equity securities

            i. Recognize dividends received as dividend income.

        c. For **both Debt and Equity Securities** adjust to fair value at balance sheet date:

            i. Determine fair value of available-for-sale investments (of this classification) at balance sheet date (only).

            ii. Determine carrying value of available-for-sale investments (of this classification) at balance sheet date.

            iii. Adjusting available-for-sale investments to fair value

                1. If fair value > carrying value:

                    (a) Recognize (unrealized) holding gain.

                    (b) Gain is recorded in Other Comprehensive Income.

                2. If fair value < carrying value:

                    (a) Recognize (unrealized) holding Loss.

                    (b) Loss is recognized in Other Comprehensive Income.

d. Assess available-for-sale investments for impairment.

    i. The individual securities classified as available for sale are assessed for impairment to determine if a decline in fair value below the amortized cost basis (debt) or cost (equity) is other than temporary using a two-step process:

        1. Determine if the fair value of an investment is less than its (amortized) cost; if so, the investment is impaired.

        2. Determine if the impairment is other than temporary.

    ii. If the investment is impaired and the impairment is other than temporary, an impairment loss equal to the difference between the investment's (amortized) cost and its fair value is recognized in current income as a realized loss.

        1. The fair value becomes the new (amortized) cost basis of the investment.

        2. Subsequent recoveries in fair value would not be recognized.

e. Financial statement presentation:

    i. Unrealized holding gain/loss:

        1. Report as an item of Comprehensive Income, which is

        2. Included in Accumulated Other Comprehensive Income in Shareholders' Equity section of Balance Sheet, net of tax effects.

    ii. Available-for-sale allowance to Balance Sheet as adjustment to carrying value of Investment:

Available-for-Sale Investments	$200,000
Plus: Allowance to Increase to Fair Value	20,000
Available-for-Sale Investments at Fair Value	$220,000

    iii. Available-for-Sale Investments in Balance Sheet as current and/or noncurrent Asset. Available-for-sale investments generally will be classified as noncurrent assets, but those investments within one year (or operating cycle) of disposal will be classified as current assets.

    iv. Available-for-Sale Investments in Statement of Cash Flows as investing activity.

3. Disposition (sale) of Available-for-Sale Investments:

    a. If debt security, first recognize interest income and amortization of premium/discount to date of sale.

    b. Determine carrying value of investment to be sold:

        i. For Debt and Equity Securities = Fair Value

    c. Recognize (realized) gain or loss at date of sale, if any, as difference between sales price and carrying value of investments sold.

    d. Any related unrealized (holding) gain or loss on securities sold that is in Accumulated Other Comprehensive Income at the date of sale is recognized in income.

Cost Method and Transfers Between Classifications

When an investment security is in a privately held company for which there is no market value, the investor may use cost method accounting for this investment. A cost method investment does not change in value unless there is a liquidating dividend. In addition, while holding investments, an investor's original intent or ability to exercise that intent may change and, therefore the classification of the investment, may change. This lesson discusses those issues.

After studying this lesson, you should be able to:

1. Describe the accounting for a cost method investment.

2. Calculate the liquidating dividend for a cost method investment.

3. Identify the reasons an investor's intent with respect to his/her investments may change.

4. Describe the accounting treatment when reclassification changes occur.

I.   Cost-Method Investments

   A. The cost method of accounting for an equity investment is permitted if the investor cannot exert significant influence over the investee and there is no readily determinable fair value of the investment. In most cases, the cost method would be used because the investee is a privately held company.

   B. The cost method requires that the initial investment be recorded at historical cost and is not subsequently adjusted unless there is a liquidating dividend or a permanent decline in value.

   1. The original cost of the investment, (historical cost) is the amount paid for the investment.

   2. Dividends are recorded like normal dividends and dividend income is recognized in earnings.

   3. Once investment is recorded, no further adjustments or changes are required, unless

   a. The fair value of the investment has a permanent decline in value (such as the investee goes into bankruptcy). A permanent decline in value means that it is unlikely there would ever be a recovery of value. Under such a circumstance, a permanent write-down (or write-off) of the investment is required.

   b. There is a liquidating dividend. A liquidating dividend occurs when the dividends declared by the investee are in excess of the earnings of the investee since the acquisition by the investor. In other words, the investee is returning the capital rather than a dividend. This is an example of a return of capital rather than a return on capital.

Example

Liquidating Dividend

Company ABC purchased 15% of the equity of Company XYZ for $500,000 on January 1, 20X1. During 20X1 XYZ Company had $200,000 of earnings and declared and paid $300,000 of dividends. Company XYZ paid more dividends than earnings and there is a $100,000 liquidating dividend ($200,000 – $300,000). Therefore when Company XYZ paid $45,000 ($300,000 x 15%) dividend to ABC, XYZ was distributing the earnings in the form of dividends plus return some of the capital back to ABC. This is a liquidating dividend.

The entry would be as follows:

Cash	45,000 (300,000 × 15%)	
Dividend Income		30,000 (200,000 × 15%)
Investment in XYZ		15,000 (100,000 × 15%)

After the liquidating dividend the Investment in XYZ would have a balance of $485,000 ($500,000 – $15,000).

II. **Transfers Between Categories—Overview**—The classification of an investment that gives the investor no significant influence over the investee may change as a result of a change in investor intent or the financial status of the investor. A change in classification requires that the security value be removed from the old classification and the appropriate value be assigned to the new classification. Because the old and new classifications may require different valuations, a gain or a loss may result from the transfer. This lesson presents the requirements necessary to transfer an investment from one classification to another and the appropriate treatment of a resulting gain or loss.

III. **Transfers Between Classifications**

A. **Transfers Result From**

1. **Changes in investor intent**—For example, an investment that was initially classified as held for trading may be changed to available for sale because the investor now intends to hold the security indefinitely.

2. **Change in investor ability to hold to maturity**—For example, an investment that was initially classified as held to maturity may be changed to held for trading because the investor now intends to sell the security in the near future to raise needed cash.

B. The general rule is that transfers between classifications are accounted for at fair value (FV) at the date of transfer. That is, the value of the investment in the new category will be at fair value on the date of the transfer. The treatment of any unrealized gains or losses (G/L) is accounted for in accordance with the new classification.

C. See the following illustration.

Transfer from → Transfer to ↓	Held to maturity	Available for sale	Trading
Held to maturity	NA	Establish HTM account at FV. Unrealized G/L in AOCI is amortized over remaining life of the debt.	Establish HTM account at FV. Unrealized G/L is recorded in income. *Very rare*
Available for sale	Establish AFS account at FV. Unrealized G/L is recorded in AOCI.	NA	Establish AFS account at FV. Unrealized G/L is recorded in income. *Very rare*
Trading	Establish Trading account at FV. Unrealized G/L in is recorded in income.	Establish Trading account at FV. Unrealized G/L in AOCI is recorded in income.	NA

IFRS—Investments

This lesson summarizes the accounting for investments under IFRS No. 9 as it applies to investments, a major form of financial asset. The broader topic of accounting for financial instruments under IFRS, including financial liabilities, is covered in a later lesson in the subsection on Financial Instruments.

After studying this lesson, you should be able to:

1. Describe how investments in each of the new categories are measured and reported.

2. Describe when transfers between categories are permitted and how they are treated.

3. Describe the categories of investments under IFRS No. 9.

4. Describe the conditions that determine whether an investment should be derecognized.

I. The following table shows a high-level summary of the differences between U.S. GAAP and IFRS.

	U.S. GAAP	IFRS
Classifications	Three classifications: 1. Held to Maturity 2. Available for Sale 3. Trading	Two classifications: 1. Held to Maturity—debt measured at amortized cost 2. Fair Value through profit or loss—debt at FV and all equity at FV
HTM valuation	Effective interest rate based on contractual cash flows and contractual life	Effective interest rate based on estimated cash flow and estimated life
Impairment of debt investment	An impairment loss on debt investment cannot be reversed.	An impairment loss on debt investment can be reversed if there is objective evidence.
Requirement for classification as HTM	Positive ability and intent to hold to maturity	Business model test—holding the instrument is to collect contractual cash flows. Cash flow characteristic test—contractual terms of instrument provide cash flows on specific dates.
OCI option	Gains/losses recorded in OCI only for available-for-sale securities. These gains or losses are recycled through profit or loss when the security is sold.	Entity may elect to record gains/losses to OCI at initial recognition of investment. This election is irrevocable and gains or losses are not recycled through profit or loss when sold.
Reclassification of debt instruments	Transfers from HTM when no longer have positive ability and intent	Transfers from HTM only when the business model objective changes
Transfers	Permits transfers into or out of trading classification	Does not permit transfers into/out of trading classification (FV through profit or loss)

II. Categories and Measurement Under IFRS No. 9

    A. Categories of Investments

        1. IFRS No. 9 establishes two categories of investments (as financial assets) for accounting purposes:

            a. Debt instruments (to be measured) at amortized cost;

    b. All other investments, including debt instruments not measured at amortized cost and all equity instruments and derivative instruments.

2. In order to be classified as a debt instrument at amortized cost, the instrument must not be a derivative debt instrument and meet the following two conditions:

    a. **Business model test**—The objective of the entity (its business model) is to hold the investment to collect the contractual cash flows; its business model is not to sell the instrument prior to its contractual maturity to realize changes in fair value.

    b. **Cash flow characteristic test**—The contractual terms of the investment give rise on specified dates to cash flows that are solely payments of principal and interest on the principal outstanding, where interest is only consideration for the time value of money and credit risk.

3. Investments (and other financial assets) that meet the foregoing conditions (i.e., business model test and cash flow characteristic test) are classified as debt instruments at amortized cost (except as noted in B.1., below); all other investments constitute the other classification.

4. Financial assets that have an embedded derivative instrument (i.e., that includes a derivative within the host instrument) are not separated (bifurcated) into different instruments for accounting purposes. If the host instrument is a financial liability, or a nonfinancial item, the bifurcation requirements are still required.

5. Classification is made at the time an investment is initially recognized.

B. Measurement of Investments

1. **An investment that meets the conditions of debt instrument at amortized cost** will be measured and reported at amortized cost **unless** conditions warrant the investor electing to measure the investment at fair value with changes in fair value recognized through profit or loss (net income).

    a. The fair value option would be available when its use would eliminate or significantly reduce a measurement or recognition inconsistency that would otherwise result from measuring assets or liabilities, or recognizing the gains or losses on them, on different basis.

    b. These measurement or recognition inconsistencies are sometimes referred to as *accounting mismatches*.

2. If a debt instrument measured at amortized cost is sold or disposed of prior to maturity, the gain or loss on disposition must be separately present in the statement of comprehensive income with disclosure of the reasons for the disposal.

3. **All other investments in debt** (i.e., those not measured at amortized cost) must be measured at fair value, with changes in fair value reported through profit or loss (net income).

4. **All investments in equity** are measured and reported at fair value, with changes in fair value reported through profit or loss (net income)(FV-NI), except equity investments that the entity elects to report through other comprehensive income.

    a. Even investments in equity securities with no ready market must be reported at fair value; there is no cost method alternative as there is under U.S. GAAP. Cost, however, can be the best estimate of fair value.

    b. If the investor does not hold an equity investment for trading purposes, it may elect to report changes in fair value through other comprehensive income (FV-OCI).

        i. The election must be made when the investment is first recognized and is irrevocable.

        ii. Amounts recognized although other comprehensive income will never be reclassified to profit or loss (net income), even on disposal or impairment, but will remain in equity (e.g., transferred to retained earnings).

        iii. Dividends from these investments would be recognized in net income.

        iv. This category is analogous to the U.S. GAAP category *Available for Sale*.

C. Transfers Between Classifications Under IFRS No. 9

   1. Because there are only two categories of investments under IFRS No. 9, the only possible transfers are for debt instruments (there is no *amortized cost* for equity instruments); they are:

      a. From debt at amortized cost to fair value with changes recognized through profit/loss, or

      b. From fair value with changes recognized through profit/loss to debt at amortized cost.

   2. The transfer between categories for investments in debt can be made only when the investor's business model objective for debt investments changes so that the (previous) category no longer applies.

      a. Such transfers, if appropriate, are treated prospectively in financial statements effective the first day of the first reporting period following the change in business model.

      b. Restatement of previously recognized gains/losses or interest income is not permitted.

      c. Transfers between classifications (reclassification) is not permitted based on changes in the characteristics of the instrument (e.g., the conversion option on an investment in convertible bonds lapses/expires).

   3. A transfer between categories is not possible for investments in equity because equity investments have no amortized cost to enable that classification.

III. Derecognition of Investments

  A. Derecognition of an investment (or other financial asset) is concerned with determining whether the investment or an element thereof (e.g., cash flows from an investment) should be written off.

  B. Basically, an investment (or element thereof) should be written off when:

   1. The investment asset (or an element thereof) has been transferred, and

   2. Substantially all the risks and rewards of ownership have been transferred.

  C. An investment is considered transferred if either:

   1. The entity has transferred the contractual rights to receive the cash flows associated with the investment, or

   2. The entity has retained the contractual rights to receive the cash flows associated with the investment, but has concurrently assumed a contractual obligation to transfer those cash flows to another party under an arrangement that meets the following three conditions:

      a. The entity has no obligation to pay amounts to the eventual recipient unless it collects equivalent amounts on the original asset (investment), and

      b. The entity is prohibited from selling or pledging the original asset (other than as security to the eventual recipient), and

      c. The entity has an obligation to remit those cash flows without material delay.

  D. Whether a transferred investment should be written off, depends on whether the transferring entity has relinquished substantially all the risks and rewards of ownership.

   1. If substantially all the risks and rewards of ownership have been transferred, the transferred investment should be written off.

2. If substantially all the risks and rewards of ownership have been retained, the transferred investment should not be written off.

3. If substantially all the risks and rewards of ownership have been neither transferred nor retained, treatment depends on whether control of the investment has been relinquished.

   a. If the entity no longer controls the investment, it should be written off.

   b. If the entity has retained control of the investment, it should not be written off.

IV. **Disclosures Under IFRS No. 9**—Basic disclosures required for investments (as financial assets) are set forth in a separate IFRS (No. 7), *Financial Instruments: Disclosures.* Those requirements, which apply to all financial instruments, are not covered here. The most significant changes to those disclosure requirements (i.e., of IFRS No. 7) that are contained in IFRS No. 9 are presented here.

A. **Equity Investments at Fair Value Reported through Other Comprehensive Income (OCI)**—When equity investments are measured at fair value and reported through other comprehensive income (OCI), the entity must disclose:

   1. Identification of the investments that have been designated to be measured at fair value with changes in fair value reported through OCI and the reasons for choosing the OCI alternative for those investments

   2. The fair value of each such investment at period end

   3. Dividends recognized during the period on those equity investments, showing separately the amounts for investments held at the period end and those that were disposed of during the period

   4. Transfers during the period from accumulated OCI to retained earnings and the reasons for those transfers

   5. For equity investments reported through OCI that are disposed of (derecognized) during the period:

      a. The reasons for disposal

      b. The fair value at the date of disposal

      c. The gain or loss on disposal

B. **Reclassifications Due To Changes in Business Model**—When an entity reclassifies investments between categories due to changes in its business model, it must disclose:

   1. The date and amount of each reclassification by category;

   2. A detailed explanation of the underlying change in business model and a qualitative description of the effects on the financial statements;

   3. If the reclassification is from fair value measurement to amortized cost measurement, it must disclose:

      a. For the period of reclassification, the fair value of the reclassified investments as of the end of the period and the gain or loss that would have been recognized during the period if reclassification had not occurred;

      b. For the remaining life of the investment, the effective interest rate at the date of reclassification and interest income recognized during each period.

C. **Gains or Losses on Sale of Investments Measured at Amortized Cost**—If debt instruments measured at amortized cost are sold or disposed of prior to maturity, any gain or loss must be recognized separately on the face of the financial statements.

D. Additional disclosures are required when IFRS No. 9 is applied for the first time.

Significant Influence—Equity Method

Equity Method

When an investment in equity securities gives the investor significant influence (but not control) over the investee, the investor must carry and report that investment using the full equity method of accounting. The only exception is if the investor elects the fair value option and chooses to report the investment at fair value. This lesson describes the application of the equity method of accounting.

After studying this lesson, you should be able to:

1. Describe and illustrate the entries made by an investor using the equity method, including the impact on the investment account and the income recognized from the investee.

2. Describe the accounting when all or part of an equity method investment is disposed of.

3. Describe special disclosures required when the equity method is used.

I. **Equity Method—Overview**—The common accounting applied to an investment with >20% equity ownership (significant influence or control) is the equity method of accounting. The equity method requires the investor to periodically adjust the carrying value of the investment to (1) reflect changes in the investee's shareholders' equity (e.g., net income/loss dividends, etc.) and (2) recognize the effects of any difference between the cost of the investment assignable to the fair value of investee's amortizable assets and the book value of those assets (i.e., FV does not equal BV).

> **Note**
> *The investor can elect to record an equity ownership in an investee >20% but <50% at fair value and in some circumstances at cost. This lesson focuses on equity method accounting.*

II. **Investments Requiring the Equity Method**—The kinds of investments requiring the use of the equity method are:

A. Investments in voting equity securities; not nonvoting equity or debt securities

B. With sufficient ownership to give significant influence or control over the operating and financial policies of the investee

> **Exam Tip**
> This is a very popular topic on the CPA Exam. Study time dedicated to this area will pay off!

1. Significant influence is presumed if there is 20%–50% ownership of voting stock. Control is presumed when there is >50% ownership of voting stock. Although the Parent company will use equity method to account for the investment in its subsidiary, the Parent will consolidate the subsidiary for financial reporting purposes.

   a. Indicators of significant influence when ownership is <20%.

      i. Has representation on board of directors

      ii. Participates in investee policy making

      iii. Has material intercompany transaction

      iv. Is technologically interdependent with investee

      v. No other single investor has a material voting ownership of investee.

   2. Special indicators that the investor will **not** have significant influence and will use **fair value:**

   a. Investee opposes investment.

   b. Standstill agreement between investor and investee; this mean that the investor cannot acquire more stock or other attempts to exert significant influence.

   c. Significant influence or control is exercised by others; for example:

      i. Investor A owns 35% of the voting stock, but Investor B owns the other 65% (has control) and does not cooperate with Investor A.

      ii. Investee is in bankruptcy or legal reorganization and under the control of the courts

        iii. Investee is a foreign entity that operates under foreign government restrictions that preclude exercise of significant influence.

    d. Investor lacks information for use of equity method (very rare).

    e. Investor cannot obtain representation on investee Board of Directors.

C. If prior ownership with no significant influence is followed by additional purchase of equity shares resulting in significant influence, then:

    1. **IF you are testing prior to January 1, 2017, this paragraph applies**: A change to equity method accounting will occur when the entity switches from fair value to equity method or acquires additional shares and obtains significant influence (i.e., 10% ownership and acquires addition 15% and now at 25% ownership). A change to the equity method accounting is accounted for **retroactively**.

    2. **IF you are testing on or after January 1, 2017, this paragraph applies:** A change to equity method accounting will occur when the entity switches from fair value to equity method or acquires additional shares and obtains significant influence (i.e., 10% ownership and acquires addition 15% and now at 25% ownership). A change to the equity method accounting is accounted for **prospectively**.

II. **Recording Initial Investment**—The initial investment in securities to be accounted for using the equity method will be recorded at cost.

    A. Cost includes:

        1. Purchase price of the equity securities (e.g., price per share)

        2. Other directly related costs incurred in the acquisition (e.g., brokerage commission, transfer fee, etc.)

    B. Entry:

> DR: Equity Investment—Co. A
>> CR: Cash (or other consideration)

    C. At the time of the initial investment, the investor must also:

        1. Determine book value (BV) of assets/liabilities of investee at date of investment.

        2. Determine fair value (FV) of assets/liabilities of investee at date of investment.

        3. Allocate any difference between cost of investment and book value of net assets of the investee to:

            a. FV of identifiable assets/liabilities, then any excess balance to

            b. Goodwill (or to gain if Cost < FV)

    D. Subsequent to recording an investment that gives the investor significant influence over the investee, the investor must carry the investment on its books and report the investment in financial statements using either the equity method or, at its option, using fair value (as provided by ASC 825).

    E. **Acquiring Significant Equity Interest Decomposing The Purchase Price**

        1. It is assumed that the acquisition is considered an arms-length transaction negotiated by two independent parties. All **direct costs** related to the purchase are expensed because they are not considered an attribute of the acquiree. Direct costs are finder's fees, audit fees, legal fees related to the acquisition. Direct costs are NOT costs to finance the acquisition, such as cost of borrowing or the fees to register the acquiring company's stock.

            a. Combine **income statements** from the **date** of combination.

            b. **Assets and liabilities** of the company acquired (the acquiree) are valued at **fair value**.

c. The fair value of the consideration transferred less the net fair market value of the identifiable assets acquired and liabilities assumed is **goodwill**. Complete a decomposition of the consideration transferred as shown below.

**Fair value of the business as a whole (Bus FV)–
typically equals consideration transferred (Purchase
Price (PP))**

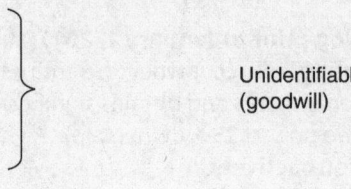

Unidentifiable intangible asset
(goodwill)

**Net fair value of assets acquired and liabilities
assumed (FV of net assets)**

Identifiable asset revalued to FV
(tangible and intangible)

Net book value of assets acquired and liabilities

IV. Summary of Equity Method—The effects of the equity method on an investor's investment (asset) and investment revenue are summarized in the following two T-accounts:

A. Investment Account

(Equity) Investment in Investee X (on Balance Sheet)	
Original cost of investment	
Pro rata share of investee's income since acquisition	Pro rata share of investee's losses since acquisition
Amortization of book value in excess of cost (i.e., on amounts allocated to write down nonfinancial assets)	Amortization of cost in excess of book value (i.e., on amounts allocated to identifiable assets, but not goodwill)
Retroactive adjustment due to change from fair value to equity method (DR or CR)	Pro rata share of investee's dividends declared
	Impairment losses
	Disposal of investee stock (write off)

B. Equity Revenue Account

Investment (Equity) Income, Investee X (on Income Statement)	
Pro rata share of investee's losses since acquisition	Pro rata share of investee's income since acquisition
Amortization of cost in excess of book value (i.e., on amounts to identifiable assets, but not goodwill)	Amortization of book value in excess of cost (i.e., on amounts allocated to write down nonfinancial assets)

Note
Dividends are NOT income.

V. Equity-Method Accounting

A. This section identifies and illustrates the basic steps in applying the equity method of accounting, including how the investor entity (1) recognizes its share of investee's net income or loss, (2) recognizes its share of investee's dividends, and (3) determines and accounts for any difference between the cost of its investment in the investee and the book value of the investee's net assets it acquired. The application of these steps (the equity method) affects both the investor's investment account (in the investee) and the revenue recognized from the investee by the investor. A chart is provided that summarizes the effects of the equity method on each of these accounts (investment and equity revenue).

VI. Equity-Method Entries—Under the equity method, the investor will recognize on its books and report in its financial statements changes in the investment (from original cost) to reflect the changing value of the investee's equity accounts. These changes include:

A. Investee results of operation (income/loss)—to be recognized by the investor when reported by the investee:

1. Investor recognizes (picks up on its books) its proportionate share of investee's reported income/loss, excluding its share of any intercompany profits/losses in assets (e.g., in inventory, etc.).

    a. Entry (assuming investee has net income):

> DR: Investment in Investee X
>
>   CR: Investment (equity) Income

    b. Entry (assuming investee has net loss):

> DR: Investment (equity) Loss
>
>   CR: Investment in Investee X

2. If investee has outstanding cumulative preferred stock, any accrued dividends on that stock must be deducted (whether paid or not) before computing the common equity investor's share of reported net income/loss.

3. If investee reports prior period adjustment, investor picks up its proportionate share as such (i.e., in investor's Retained Earnings).

4. If investee losses reduce the investment to zero, investor should discontinue applying the equity method unless investee's imminent return to profitability is assured.

5. If Investor elects to use the fair value method to measure and report an investment that otherwise would be accounted for using the equity method, the investors does NOT recognize its share of the investee's results of operation (or the effects of differences between the cost of the investment and its fair value at acquisition; see D, below). The investee's results of operation are assumed to be reflected in the change in fair value of the investment (which is recognized in net income).

B. **Investee Items of Other Comprehensive Income (OCI)**—If the investee reports changes to equity resulting from items of other comprehensive income, the investor recognizes (picks up) its proportionate share of those items when reported by the investee.

1. Items of other comprehensive income that might change equity would include:

    a. Unrealized gains/losses on available-for-sale securities

    b. Foreign currency items

    c. Pension and postretirement benefit items not recognized in period cost

2. Entry (assuming OCI items increased equity):

> DR: Investment in Investee X
>
> CR: Other Comprehensive Income (to Accumulated OCI in equity)

C. Investee Dividends

1. Investor recognizes (picks up) its proportionate share of investee dividends as a reduction in its investment in the investee.

2. For example, if the investee paid a cash dividend the investor entry would be:

> DR: Dividends Receivable/Cash
>
> CR: Investment in Investee X

3. If Investor elects to use the fair value method to measure and report an investment that otherwise would be accounted for using the equity method, the investors DOES recognize its share of the investee's cash dividends paid. Those cash dividends are considered income for the period to the investor.

> **Note**
> *Dividends under the equity method are "automatically" treated as liquidating (i.e., liquidating part of the investment).*

D. Investee Book Value (BV) Does Not Equal Investment Cost/Fair Value—If the cost of investment to the investor and the fair value of the investee's assets/liabilities is different from the investee's book value at the date of investment, the investor will recognize periodic adjustment(s) to its investment account (and to the investment revenue account).

1. Differences between the cost of the investment and the book value of the net assets to which the investment gives the investor a claim may be due to:

    a. Identifiable assets/liabilities carrying values on the books of the investee being different than the fair value of those assets/liabilities at the date of the investment

    b. Goodwill being paid for by the investor

2. Investor adjustment—assuming the cost of investment exceeds the book value of the investment at the date of investment. (Note: See 5. below for when the book value > cost of investment.)

3. Cost of investment > BV of net assets acquired (i.e., book value of investor's share of investee net assets)

4. Investor makes entry for *depreciation* or *amortization* on its share of fair value in excess of book value as it relates to identifiable depreciable or amortizable assets; but **no** amortization of Goodwill.

    a. Entry: (assuming FV of depreciable assets > BV of those assets)

> DR: Investment (Equity) Income
>
> CR: Investment in Investee X

    b. Investor does not DR: Expense, but reduces the amount of income picked up from the investee, and reduces the carrying amount of the investment.

5. **Investor adjustment**—assuming the cost of investment is less than the book value of the investment at the date of investment (i.e., a bargain purchase).

    a. Allocate **any** difference to **FV of identifiable assets/liabilities** (e.g., reduce overvalued identifiable assets and/or increase undervalued liabilities), with any balance recognized as a gain in **earnings** in the period of investment.

    b. *Negative goodwill* is **not** recognized (as a deferred charge) and amortized.

6. If Investor elects to use the fair value method to measure and report an investment that otherwise would be accounted for using the equity method, the investors do NOT recognize the effects of any differences between the cost of the investment and its fair value at acquisition (or its share of operating results). Any difference between the cost of the investment and its fair value at acquisition is assumed to be reflected in the change in fair value of the investment (which is recognized in net income).

VII. Equity Method Revenue Recognized from Investment

A. The Amount is Recognized as

1. Investment (equity) Income/Loss (one amount).

VIII. Sale of Equity-Method Investment—Upon sale of all or part of an investment accounted for using the equity method, the following would apply:

A. Update investment and investment revenue accounts to date of sale by recording:

1. Share of investee income/loss to date of sale

2. Depreciation/amortization on cost > BV (or BV > cost) to date of sale

B. Gain/loss on sale is the difference between selling price (SP) and book (carrying) value (BV) of the investment sold.

1. If SP > BV = Realize gain.

2. If SP < BV = Realize loss.

C. If sale is not for entire investment and results in the investor losing significant influence over the investee (e.g., < 20% ownership), the remaining investment should be accounted for at fair value with any difference between the carrying amount of remaining investment and its fair value recognized as a gain or loss in current income.

IX. Equity-Method Disclosures—When the equity method is used to report investments in common stock, the following disclosures are appropriate:

A. The name of each equity-method investee and the percentage of ownership

B. The name of any investee in which the investor own 20% or more (but not more than 50%) of the voting stock that is not accounted for using the equity method and the reason for that treatment

C. The name of any investee in which the investor owns less than 20% of the voting stock that is accounted for using the equity method and the reason for that treatment

D. Any difference between the carrying amount of the investment and the investor's share of the underlying claim to net assets and how that difference is treated

E. When a bargain purchase gain is recognized, the amount of the gain recognized, the line item where the gain is recognized and a description of the transaction that resulted in the gain

F. When there is a quoted market price for the common stock, the market value of each investment

G. When the equity method is used for investments in corporate joint ventures that are material to the investor, summary information about the assets, liabilities, and results of operation of those joint venture investees

H. Possible effects of conversion or exercise of outstanding securities (e.g., options, convertible securities, etc.) on the investor's ownership claim

IFRS—Equity Method

This lesson describes the U.S. GAAP/IFRS differences in the application of the equity method of accounting.

After studying this lesson, you should be able to:

1. Identify certain differences between the use of the equity method under U.S. GAAP and under IFRS.

I. Summary of Differences—Below is a summary of the differences in U.S. GAAP and IFRS with respect to equity method accounting. Each of these differences are discussed more fully in this lesson.

U.S. GAAP	IFRS
No special term for investee	Investees are referred to as "associates."
Can apply fair value option to equity investee	Only certain investors (venture capitalists, mutual funds, or unit trusts) can apply fair value option.
No requirement for accounting policies to conform	Uniform accounting policies must be applied.
It is encouraged to have reporting dates for investor and investee to be within three months.	Reporting dates for investor and associate cannot be more than three months.
Not required to adjust for significant transactions in the three-month window	Required to adjust for significant transactions in the three-month window
Can recognize investee losses if imminent return to profit is assured	Do not recognize losses
Impairment loss is measured as the carrying value less the fair value.	Impairment loss is measured as the carrying value less the recoverable amount.
Apply equity method until investment is sold.	If investment is to be sold, adjust to lower of fair value or carrying amount and reclassify as held-for-sale.

II. U.S. GAAP–IFRS Differences

A. Fair Value Option—Both U.S. GAAP and IFRS permit the use of the fair value option to measure investments, which give the investor significant influence over an investee; however, the entities that may elect the fair value option are more limited under IFRS.

1. Under U.S. GAAP, any investor that has significant influence over an investee and would otherwise use the equity method of accounting may elect to carry and report the investment at fair value.

2. Under IFRS only certain types of investors that have significant influence over an investee and would otherwise use the equity method may elect to carry and report the investment at fair value.

   a. Under IFRS, an entity over which an investor has significant influence is called an *associate*; thus, the account would be "Investment in Associate."

   b. Only the following types of investors may elect to carry and report investments in associates using fair value:

   i. Venture capital organizations—Private equity investment firms

   ii. Mutual funds—An investment company offering a managed open-end portfolio of securities

   iii. Unit trusts—An investment company offering a fixed (unmanaged) portfolio of securities with a fixed life

B. Accounting Policies—Under U.S. GAAP, the accounting policies used by an investee accounted for using the equity method do not have to conform to the accounting policies of the investor, as long as the investee accounting policies comply with U.S. GAAP. Under IFRS, in using the equity method the investor must apply uniform accounting policies to the investor and investee accounting for similar transactions and events

C. Like U.S. GAAP, IFRS presumes an investor that holds between 20% and 50% of the voting stock of an investee can exercise significant influence, unless there is evidence otherwise, and requires the use of the equity method for those investments.

    1. IFRS uses the term *associates* to refer to investees over whom the investor has significant influence.

    2. The effects on the investment account and on the equity revenue account generally would be the same under IFRS as under U.S. GAAP, with these significant exceptions:

        a. Under IFRS, entities may have *reserve* accounts, which don't exist under U.S. GAAP.

        b. Under IFRS, changes in reserve accounts of the associate (investee) are recognized by the investor under the equity method.

D. Under IFRS, the reporting dates (period ends) of the investor and its associates cannot be different by more than three months. Further, any significant transactions that occur during the up-to-three-month period must be adjusted to the accounts in recognizing the equity method effects. Under U.S. GAAP, the difference between reporting dates of the investor and investee should not be more than three months, but adjustments for significant transactions that occur during the intervening period do not have to be made to the investee accounts in applying the equity method. The entity may make adjustments for such a transaction, but it is only required to disclose such effects.

E. Under U.S. GAAP, when investee losses exceed the investor's investment, but imminent return to profitable operations by the investee appears assured, the investor may continue to recognize its share of investee losses (even if it has not guaranteed obligations of the investee or committed to provide further financial support). Under IFRS, when investee losses exceed the investor's investment, the investor should discontinue recognizing its share of investee losses even if the associate's (investee's) future profitability appears imminent and assured. However, if the investor has obligations or commitments to make payments on behalf of the associate, it may continue to recognize its share of losses to the extent of those obligations.

F. Under U.S. GAAP, if an investor determines that a decrease in the fair value of an equity investment is other than temporary, an impairment loss is measured as the excess of the carrying amount of the investment **over the fair value**. Under IFRS, if an investor determines that an equity investment is impaired, the impairment loss is measured as the excess of the carrying amount of the investment **over the recoverable amount**.

G. Under IFRS, if an equity method investment is to be sold, the investment is reported at the lower of (1) its fair value less cost to sell, or (2) the carrying amount as of the date the investment is classified as held-for-sale. Under U.S. GAAP, an investor continues to account for an equity-method investment that is to be sold using the equity method of accounting until it loses significant influence over the investee.

Investor Stock Dividends, Splits, and Rights

As a result of holding an investment in equity securities, an investor may receive a stock dividend, a stock split, or a stock right.

After studying this lesson, you should be able to:

1. Describe each of these issues.

2. Summarize the appropriate accounting treatment for each.

I. **Introduction**—An investor who has an equity investment in another entity may receive a dividend on that stock, have the stock split, or hold a right to acquire other securities. This lesson describes each of these possibilities and summarizes the accounting treatment from the perspective of the investor— the recipient of the dividend, split, or right.

II. **Stock Dividends Received by Investor**

   A. Investor receives additional shares of investee stock as dividend.

   B. Investor adjusts only **per share** (not total) cost (carrying value) of investment.

 **Example**

> Investment Carrying Value (Under Cost or Equity method) $100,000
>
> Original number of shares = 1,000
>
> Per share cost (carrying value) = $100,000/1,000 = $100
>
> Stock Dividend of 10% received = 100 shares received
>
> New Per Share Cost (Carrying Value) = $100,000/1,100 shares = $90.90 per share

   C. Upon subsequent sale (in part or total) write off shares at new per share cost (carrying value).

III. **Stock Split Received by Investor**

   A. Investor receives additional shares of investee stock in conjunction with investee decrease in par or stated value per share. In a reverse stock split the investor exchanges shares held for few shares of the investee in conjunction with investee increasing par or stated value per share.

   B. In either a stock split or a reverse stock split, the investor adjusts only per share (not total) cost (carrying value) of investment.

   C. Calculation/treatment is the same as for stock dividend.

IV. **Stock Rights Received by Investor**

   A. Investor receives privilege (right) to purchase additional shares of investee at specific (option) price within a specific time; usually evidenced by a certificate called a stock warrant.

   1. If option price < market price, the stock right has a value.

   2. The value of the right is determined by allocating cost (carrying value) of investment between the shares of stock and stock rights based on relative fair value.

   3. Two alternative possibilities exist for determining the amount of the investment to be allocated to the stock rights:

    a. The per share market value of the rights is known/given (illustrated in B., below).

    b. The per share market value of the rights is not known/given; the theoretical per share market value of the rights must be computed (illustrated in C., below).

B. **Market Value of Rights Known/Given**—Determine cost (carrying value) of stock rights (per right) assuming per share market value (MV) is given as follows:

$$\frac{\text{MV One Right}}{(\text{MV of Stock without Right} + \text{MV of One Right})} \times [\text{Cost (Carrying Value of Investment)}] = \frac{\text{Total "Cost"}}{\text{of Rights}}$$

$$\frac{(\text{Total "Cost" of Rights})}{(\text{Number of Rights Received})} = \text{Per Share "Cost" of Rights}$$

C. **Market Value of Rights not Known/Given**—Determine theoretical market value of stock rights (per right) as follows:

    1. Market Value (MV) of stock quoted **without value of right** (ex-right):

> (MV one Share of Stock w/o Right – Options Price w/Right) / Number of Rights to Buy One Share = Theoretical MV per right

    2. Market Value (MV) of stock quoted **with right** (rights on):

> (MV one Share of Stock w/Right – Option Price w/Right) / (Number of Rights to Buy One Share + 1) = Theoretical MV per right

D. **Transfer Share of Investment Carrying Value between Stock and (Now) Rights**—(Assuming investment classified as Available for Sale)

> DR: X Securities Stock Rights—Available for Sale
>
>   CR: Available-for-Sale Investment—X Securities

E. **Stock Rights are Equity Securities**—Therefore, they must be classified as Trading or Available for Sale and accounted for/reported as such.

F. **Disposition of Stock Rights**

    1. **If sold**—Write off stock rights and recognize gain/loss.

    2. Entry (assume gain):

> DR: Cash
>
>   CR: X Securities Stock Rights Available for Sale
>
>   CR: Gain on Sale of Stock Rights

    3. **If exercised**—Write off stock rights as (part of) cost of investment in securities purchased with the rights.

4. Entry:

> DR: Available-for-Sale Investment – X Securities
>
> > CR: X Securities Stock Rights Available for Sale
> >
> > CR: Cash

5. If allowed to lapse—Write off stock rights and recognize loss.

6. Entry:

> DR: Loss on Expiration of Stock Rights
>
> > CR: X Securities Stock Rights Available for Sale

V. U.S. GAAP–IFRS Differences—There are no significant differences between U.S. GAAP and IFRS in the treatment of stock dividends, stock splits, and stock rights by the investor.

Impairment of Debt and Equity Securities

This lesson presents the criteria for potential impairment of an investment in a debt or equity security. In general, an investment is potentially impaired if the fair value is less than the cost basis. There are different factors to consider if the investment is an equity security versus a debt security. However, both require an assessment of whether the impairment is other than temporary. This lesson presents how those impairment losses are recorded if the impairment is other than temporary. Once an impairment loss is recognized in earnings, the impairment loss cannot be recovered.

After studying this lesson, you should be able to:

1. Identify when losses associated with debt securities are recognized in earnings versus recognized in OCI.

2. Describe what is meant by other-than-temporary impairment (OTTI).

3. Calculate how impairment losses are measured for both debt and equity securities.

I. All investments, including debt and equity securities should be tested for impairment annually or when factors indicate. In general, an investment is potentially impaired if the fair value is less than the cost basis. Application of impairment testing and the accounting for the decline in value is different for debt and equity investments. The first section discusses impairment for equity securities and the second section discusses impairment for debt securities.

II. **Equity Securities**

    A. **Trading Securities**—Trading securities are carried at fair value with changes in fair value recording in earnings. Therefore, any impairment in value is already recognized and no impairment testing is necessary.

    B. **Available-for-Sale Securities (AFS)**—AFS securities are carried at fair value with the changes in fair value recorded in other comprehensive income. If the decline in the fair value of the AFS security is considered other-than-temporary, then the unrealized gains and losses in accumulated other comprehensive income (AOCI) should be transferred out of AOCI and recognized in earnings. Listed below are the two key factors to consider in the determination of whether the decline in value associated with the security is a loss other-than-temporary-impairment (OTTI):

        1. Whether the security will recover in value. Taking into consideration:

            a. Length of time and extent to which the fair value has been less than cost

            b. The financial condition of the issuer and the near term prospects of recovery

        2. Whether the investor has positive ability and intent to hold the security until recovery could occur

    C. If neither of the above factors indicates a recovery of the losses associated with the AFS security, then the losses in AOCI are reclassified to earnings and the AFS security is written down the fair value and that fair value becomes its new cost basis. All future considerations of impairment are based on the new cost basis. Recovery of the impairment loss is not allowed.

    D. What is meant by "other-than-temporary impairment (OTTI)?" The FASB purposefully uses the term OTTI and not the term "permanent." A decline in value need not be permanent—it would be very difficult to determine if a decline is permanent. The decline in value needs to meet the threshold of "not temporary," which means there is no recovery anticipated in the foreseeable future and the entity has the ability to hold the security until there is a recovery in value.

    E. **Cost-Method Investments**—Cost-method investments do not have a readily determinable fair value. Therefore annual impairment testing is not required. However, if fair value is determined for a cost-method investment for other purposes, then the entity must complete an impairment test. If a fair value measurement is not made for other purposes the entity must still complete an impairment test when factors indicate that there may be impairment. If the impairment is OTTI, the cost method investment is written down and a loss is recognized in earnings.

III. Debt Securities

A. If the fair value of the debt security is below the cost, you must evaluate whether the impairment is other than temporary. The decline in value is considered other than temporary if any of the following exist:

1. The holder has the intent to sell the impaired debt security.

   a. Recognize the OTTI in earnings. The impairment loss is the difference between the amortized cost and the fair value of the debt security.

2. It is more likely than not that the holder will be required to sell the impaired debt security before they can recover the amortized cost basis (i.e., the holder's need for cash for operations or other investment purposes will likely require that they sell the impaired debt security).

   a. Recognize the OTTI in earnings. The impairment loss is the difference between the amortized cost and the fair value of the debt security.

3. The holder does not expect the present value of the estimated cash flows to recover the entire amortized cost basis of the debt security, regardless of whether they intend to sell the security. The entity must evaluate whether any of the loss is due to credit loss.

   a. Recognize in earnings the portion of the OTTI that is associated with credit losses.

   b. Recognize in OCI the portion of the OTTI that is associated with other factors.

B. The table below summarizes the factors that impact the measurement and recognition of an impairment loss associated with a debt security.

Factor	Measurement of impairment loss	Recognition of impairment loss
The holder has the intent to sell the impaired debt security.	Amortized cost less fair value	Earnings
It is more likely than not that the holder will be required to sell the impaired debt security before it can recover the amortized cost basis.	Amortized cost less fair value	Earnings
The holder does not expect to recover the entire amortized cost basis of the debt security, regardless of whether it intends to sell the security.	PV of Cash flows > amortized cost	No OTTI
	PV of Cash flows < amortized cost	Earnings: Portion of OTTI associated with credit loss OCI: Portion of OTTI associated with other factors

B. Recovery of impairment losses is prohibited.

IV. Disclosure Requirements—There are significant disclosure requirements associated with impairment losses. The following items are required to be disclosed.

A. For each major security disclose the methodology and significant inputs to determine fair value and the measurement of credit losses.

B. Present the amounts recognized in earnings and in OCI.

Intangible Assets—Goodwill and Other

Introduction to Intangible Assets

This lesson provides information on the accounting for intangible assets.

After studying this lesson, you should be able to:

1. Define an intangible asset.

2. Identify the difference between a definite life and indefinite life intangible asset.

3. Describe how to test for impairment of definite life and indefinite life intangible assets.

I. Introduction

> **Definition**
> *Intangible Assets:* Long-term operational assets that lack physical substance or presence, but are currently used in the operation of a business and have a useful life extending more than one year from the balance sheet date.

A. Intangibles are similar to plant assets except that they lack physical substance. Many intangibles are legal rights. ASC 350 governs the accounting for intangibles by (1) dividing intangibles into definite or indefinite life intangibles, and (2) requiring that all intangibles be evaluated for impairment.

B. Sources of Intangibles—Intangibles are either acquired from other parties or **internally developed**.

   1. An acquired intangible is separately recognized in the accounts if either (1) the benefit of the asset is obtained through contractual or other legal rights (as in a patent), or (2) if the intangible is otherwise separable, i.e., can be sold, transferred, licensed, rented, or exchanged regardless of the acquirer's intent to do so.

   2. Internally developed intangibles (such as organization costs) are expensed immediately if they are not specifically identifiable, have indeterminate values, or are inherent in a continuing business and related to the entity as a whole. Firms routinely expense the amount of internal expenditures devoted to the development of intangibles, most notably for patents, research and development (R&D), and goodwill. The only costs related to internally developed intangibles that are capitalized are registration fees and legal costs paid to outsiders.

C. Classification

   1. Intangibles are classified as:

      a. Definite life intangibles (all of these are identifiable); or

      b. Indefinite life intangibles (further subdivided into identifiable intangibles and goodwill).

   2. An intangible has a **definite** life either if the asset has a finite legal life or if the firm believes the useful life is finite. The useful life for amortization is set by economic factors (market and obsolescence) as well as by its legal life.

   3. An intangible has an **indefinite** life if no legal, regulatory, contractual, competitive, or other factor limits the life. Indefinite means there is no foreseeable limit on the period of time over which the intangible is expected to provide cash flows. A renewable and very recognizable trademark is an example.

   4. *Only definite life intangibles are amortized.* For example, some licenses and franchises that are renewable or even perpetual are not amortized because their benefits are indefinite in duration and no means exists to determine the useful life.

Example
A city providing a perpetual license to run a ferry across a body of water. The same logic holds for land; this asset also has an indefinite life and is not depreciated, so this is not a new concept. Only now that concept is being applied to intangibles.

5. However, if an intangible has an indefinite legal life (e.g., trademark) but management believes that the asset has a finite life, then the asset is treated as a definite life intangible.

6. All intangibles are subject to impairment.

D. **Summary Table**

1. **FV** = fair value or market value;

2. **BV** = book value;

3. **R** = recoverable cost (sum of expected future net cash inflows from use and ultimate disposal; it is a nominal sum, not a present value).

Definite Life Intangibles

Capitalize	Amortization	Impairment
External costs*	Over useful life	Same as assets in use
	Usually no residual value	Impairment if BV > R
	Usually SL method	Impairment Loss = BV − FV

*see below

Indefinite Life Intangibles Other than Goodwill

Capitalize	Amortization	Impairment
External costs*	Do not amortize	Same as assets held for sale
		Impairment if BV > FV
		Impairment loss = BV − FV

Goodwill (also has indefinite life)

Capitalize	Amortization	Impairment
Price of firm acquired less fair value of net assets of firm acquired	Do not amortize	2 steps—see text

* External costs in this summary table include amounts paid for registration, legal and accounting fees, outside design costs, consulting fees, successful legal defense costs, and also the cost of direct purchases of intangibles from others.
Costs of internally developed intangibles including salaries of employees working on patents, materials used, and overhead are expensed as incurred.

E. **Amortization**

1. Amortization of definite life intangibles is recorded just like depreciation expense. The debit is to an expense account such as amortization expense or selling, general and administrative expense (SG&A) for intangibles devoted to nonmanufacturing activities, and the debit is to work in process (and ultimately cost of goods sold) for manufacturing intangibles. The credit is usually made directly to the intangible rather than to a contra account.

Example

DR: Amortization of copyright (SG&A)   xx

    CR: Copyright   xx

   2. The straight-line method is typically used to compute amortization.

F. Residual Value—For amortized intangibles, residual value is assumed to be zero unless:

   1. The useful life to the firm is less than legal or economic life;

   2. Another entity could obtain some benefit from the asset after the first firm was finished with it; *and*

   3. There is reliable evidence as to its amount (which would consist of a market for the asset at that time or a commitment from another firm to purchase the asset at end of its useful life).

G. Useful Life—For amortized intangibles, if an asset is valuable only when it is used with other assets, the useful life of the other assets in the group can be a factor in setting useful life. For example, if a number of patents are used for one combined purpose, and the patents do not have any usefulness apart from the group, then the shortest useful life of the assets in the group sets the useful life for them all.

H. Changes in Classification—If an amortized (definite life) intangible is later deemed to have an indefinite life, then amortization ceases. An impairment might result because fair value would now be used to test for impairment rather than recoverable cost.

I. Separate Recognition—Many intangibles must be separately identified: trademarks and trade names, noncompetition agreements, customer lists, order or production backlogs, copyrights and patents, secret formulas and processes, licensing agreements, and supply contracts. A major reason for identifying these is that intangibles with definite life are amortized. To include them in goodwill in an acquisition would mean they would not be amortized.

J. Types of Intangibles

   1. Marketing-related—Trademarks, Internet domain names, noncompetition agreements.

      a. Some of these items are indefinite life intangibles. Indefinite life intangibles include trademarks because they are renewable every 10 years indefinitely.

   2. Customer-related—Customer lists, contractual relationships with customers.

      a. These are definite life intangibles because they could not have benefit periods of indefinite or unlimited life.

   3. Artistic-related—Copyrights (these are not renewable).

      a. Definite life

   4. Contract-related—Franchises, licensing agreements, broadcast rights, service/supply contracts

      a. Some of these are definite life intangibles, and some are indefinite life intangibles (as in the case of a perpetual franchise or one that is renewable indefinitely).

   5. Technology-related—Patents (both product and process type) that have a 20-year life and give the holder the exclusive right to use, manufacture, or sell a product or process. Capitalize successful legal defense costs.

      a. These are definite life intangibles and, although small modifications can lead to a new patent that effectively extends the life of the old (the BV of the old is added to the new), the new patent is still considered to have a definite life.

6. **Goodwill**—Arises only from a business combination in which the fair value of the entity purchased exceeds the fair value of the entity's identifiable net assets (assets—liabilities). (More on goodwill in the next lesson!)

   a. Indefinite life and tested for impairment annually

K. **Revaluation of Book Value** —From time to time, the rights associated with an intangible asset must be legally defended. For example, a company might have a patent on a unique product. If a competitor infringes on the rights represented by the patent and manufactures a similar product, the company holding the patent might elect to defend those rights through legal action. Accounting for the legal costs of this action is dependent on the outcome of the legal action.

L. **Successful Legal Defense**—If the rights associated with the intangible asset are successfully defended, the economic benefits associated with the intangible asset have been enhanced. Therefore, the related legal costs are recorded as an increase in the capitalized value of the intangible asset.

> **Example**
> A firm owns a patent with a total capitalized cost of $45,000. At the beginning of the current year, the patent has been amortized four years of a total estimated nine-year useful life. During the current year, the firm won a patent infringement suit concerning its patent. Legal costs amounted to $15,000. The legal costs are added to the book value of the patent. The book value at the beginning of the current year plus the $15,000 legal costs are amortized over the remaining five years of the patent's life.
>
> Book value of patent at beginning of current year = $45,000 − $45,000(4/9) = $25,000

M. **Unsuccessful Legal Defense**—If the rights associated with the intangible asset are unsuccessfully defended, the economic benefits associated with the intangible asset have likely been decreased to zero. Therefore, the related legal costs are recorded as legal expenses of the period incurred. In addition, the intangible is written off as a loss.

N. **Impairment Test of Definite Life Intangibles**—The test for impairment is a two-step process and it is the same as for plant assets in use.

   1. The book value (BV) of the definite life intangible is compared to the recoverable cost (R) of the intangible asset. Recoverable cost is the sum of net cash inflows attributable to using the asset and from the ultimate disposal. If the BV is greater than the recoverable costs, then the asset is impaired.

   2. The second step is to compare the BV to the fair value (FV). If the BV is greater than the FV, the asset is written down to FV. The impairment loss equals BV − FV. Subsequent amortization proceeds based on the new BV.

O. **Impairment Test of Indefinite Life Intangibles other than Goodwill**—

   1. If the intangible asset is an indefinite life and not subject to amortization, then it must be tested for impairment at least on an annual basis, or when circumstances indicate there may be impairment. The procedure to test for impairment is the same as for plant assets held for sale. The FV is used to test for impairment AND measure the loss. An asset is impaired if BV exceeds FV.

> **Note**
> Recoverable cost is not used to test for impairment for indefinite life intangibles because it could be argued that an indefinite life intangible could have unlimited recoverable costs given the potential for indefinite life. That is, how do you determine the future cash flow streams for a life that is indefinite? You can't!

   2. Impairment losses cannot be reversed for either definite life or indefinite life intangibles. This is the same as for impairment of assets in use—impairment losses are not recoverable.

> **Note**
> Recall that for plant assets held for sale previous impairment losses can be recovered.

II. Deferred Charges

A. Deferred charges are accounts that are difficult to classify. A variety of practice exists for these accounts. They should not be included in intangibles but are often listed close to intangibles in the balance sheet and are sometimes confused with intangibles.

B. Examples of deferred charges are listed below.

1. Long-term prepaid insurance

2. Long-term prepaid rent

3. Machinery rearrangement costs—Related to an assembly line for a manufacturing concern, the costs of an efficiency study. These costs are typically amortized over five to ten years.

4. Deferred income taxes—When transactions in the current or past periods give rise to future deductible temporary differences (which reduce future taxable income relative to future pretax accounting income), a deferred tax asset is created. Coverage of this topic is significantly expanded in a subsequent lesson.

5. Deferred bond issue costs—The costs of issuing bonds is recorded in a deferred charge and amortized over the term of the bonds.

III. Cash Surrender Value of Life Insurance

A. Firms that carry whole life insurance policies on key employees enjoy an annual increase in the investment portion of the policy. Cash surrender value is appropriately classified as an investment account but may be reported by some firms in Other Assets in the balance sheet.

> **Example**
> The annual premium on a life insurance policy for a corporate executive is $800. In the third year, cash surrender value begins accumulation, at $200.
>
> Entry for third-year premium:
>
> | | | |
> |---|---|---|
> | Insurance Expense | 600 | |
> | Cash Surrender Value of Life Insurance | 200 | |
> | Cash | | 800 |
>
> In subsequent years, the cash surrender value portion of the premium increases. The fourth year might be $300, for example. At the end of the fourth year, the balance in cash surrender value then would be $500.

Goodwill

This lesson provides information on the accounting for goodwill.

After studying this lesson, you should be able to:

1. Describe how goodwill is created and initially measured.

2. Complete the steps to test for and measure goodwill impairment.

I. Introduction

Definition

Goodwill: The result of a business combination that is measured as the difference between the fair value of the acquired company as a whole (the acquiree) and the fair value of the identifiable net assets (assets—liabilities). The fair value of the acquiree as a whole is often greater than the fair value of the identifiable net assets. Goodwill is the excess of the fair value of the entity as a whole over the fair value of its identifiable assets.

A. Goodwill is the only intangible asset that is not identifiable. Goodwill is attributable to many different factors such as reputation, management skills, location, customer loyalty, etc. Goodwill is the value of the acquiree that cannot be attributable to specific identifiable tangible or intangible assets, or liabilities. Goodwill has an indefinite life because the going-concern concept assumes that, in the absence of evidence to the contrary, the combined entity (acquirer and acquiree) will continue indefinitely.

B. Goodwill is recognized only when a buyer firm (the acquirer) obtains control of another enterprise. If a firm has never acquired another enterprise, then that firm would not have goodwill listed in its balance sheet.

C. In recording the acquisition of another business enterprise, the fair value of the acquiree is compared to the fair value of net identifiable asset of the acquiree. Any **excess** of entity fair value over fair value of identifiable assets is goodwill.

Examples

1. *100% ownership of Acquiree*

Assume ABC Company acquired 100% of XYZ Company for $200,000, which is the FV of XYZ as a whole. At the time of the acquisition, XYZ's net assets had a book value of $100,000.

The fair value of the net identifiable assets of XYZ is $160,000, which means that XYZ has net assets with a fair value greater than their book value.

In the acquisition of the XYZ Company, the ABC Company paid $40,000 for goodwill ($200,000 – $160,000), as illustrated in the model below.

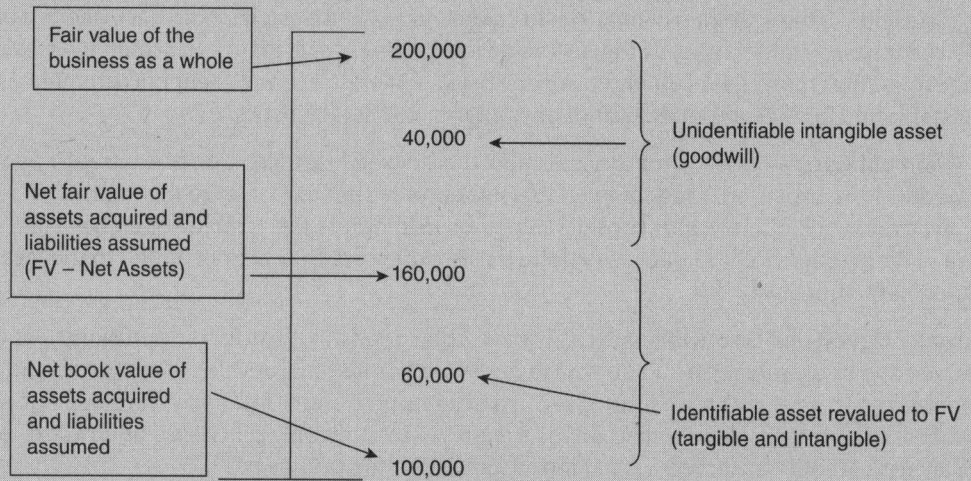

2. Now assume that ABC Company acquired 75% of XYZ Company for $150,000 and that the total value of the remaining 25% is $50,000. The diagram below depicts that the total goodwill is still $40,000, but goodwill is allocated between the controlling interest (acquirer ABC) and the noncontrolling interest (NCI). ABC Company, the controlling interest, is allocated $30,000 and the NCI is allocated the remaining 25%, or $10,000.

	Total value of XYZ 100%	ABC's share 75%	NCI's share 25%	
Total	200,000	150,000	50,000	
FV	40,000	30,000	10,000	Goodwill
	160,000	120,000	40,000	
	60,000	45,000	15,000	Fair market revaluation of identifiable net assets
BV	100,000	75,000	25,000	

D. With reference to determining the **fair value of net identifiable assets**, there are two notable points:

1. The use of the term **net** implies that all liabilities assumed in the acquisition have been subtracted from all assets acquired in the acquisition.

2. The use of the term **identifiable assets** implies that all identifiable assets are included, both tangible (such as property, plant, and equipment) and intangible (such as patents), including those that have a definite life and those that have an indefinite life.

E. Recorded goodwill remains on the books of the acquirer unless the acquiree is sold or the goodwill becomes impaired (as described in IV. below).

F. **Goodwill** represents an expectation on the part of the acquiring business enterprise that, because of synergies, there will be above normal earnings in the years immediately following the acquisition. If the acquiring company had created a new business, it would have had to develop a client base, reputation, and other favorable intangible characteristics. In acquiring an existing business enterprise, the acquiring company pays for the established client or customer base, the established business reputation, and other intangible characteristics.

G. **Goodwill Costs**—Subsequent to acquisition, the costs to maintain, enhance, or repair purchased goodwill are expensed. The acquirer understandably wishes to maximize the return on its investment and often spends considerable sums to integrate the acquiree operations into its (acquirer's) operations. All such expenditures are expensed. They are not added to the recorded purchased goodwill.

II. Internally Developed Goodwill—Internally developed goodwill exists for most business entities. However, due to conservatism and objectivity/verifiability, internally developed goodwill is not recognized as an asset in the accounting records of a business entity. Internally developed goodwill cannot easily be measured or verified. This is a major reason that only purchased goodwill, resulting from an arm's length transaction, is recognized for accounting purposes.

III. Bargain Purchases—Occasionally a firm acquires another enterprise for a price less than the fair value of the acquiree's net assets. This situation is referred to as a bargain purchase. The amount by which the fair value of the acquiree's net assets exceeds the price paid is recognized by the acquirer in the period of the acquisition as ordinary income.

> **Note**
> A full description of the determination of goodwill and a bargain purchase amount resulting from a business combination is covered in the later lesson "Recognizing/Measuring Goodwill or Bargain Purchase Amount" as part of the "Select Transactions" section.

IV. Goodwill Impairment

A. **Goodwill**, like all indefinite life intangibles, **must be tested for impairment at least annually** or when certain circumstances indicate that its carrying value may be greater than its fair value (**called an impairment**).

1. When goodwill is recognized, it must be allocated to a reporting unit. A reporting unit is a component of an operating segment for which discrete financial information is available and regularly used by management for decision-making purposes.

2. Goodwill impairment testing must be done at the reporting unit level or one level below the reporting unit.

3. An entity may elect to use a qualitative assessment of whether impairment is likely to have occurred as a basis for determining if the quantitative two-step assessment is required. This qualitative assessment is often referred to as a *prestep*.

> **Note**
> *The CPA Exam typically does not ask the candidate to identify reporting units, but to know that goodwill is tested at the reporting unit level.*

a. The ability to use a qualitative assessment about the likelihood of goodwill impairment is intended to reduce the complexity and costs associated with assessing goodwill for impairment.

b. **Only if the qualitative assessment determines that is it more likely than not that an impairment has occurred, then the subsequent complex and costly two-step assessment is required.**

c. The qualitative assessment (before the quantitative assessment) is optional; however, if the qualitative assessment indicates that the fair value of the reporting unit is more likely than not below the carrying value of the reporting unit, then the quantitative assessment is required. If the qualitative prestep is not completed, the entity must complete the quantitative two-step assessment.

B. Qualitative Assessment (Prestep)

1. An entity is permitted, and may elect, to begin its determination of whether goodwill is impaired by performing a qualitative assessment.

2. The purpose of the qualitative assessment is to determine if it is more likely than not (i.e., a likelihood of more than 50%) that the fair value of the reporting unit with which the goodwill is associated has declined below the carrying value of that reporting unit, including its goodwill.

3. In evaluating whether it is more likely than not that the fair value of a reporting unit is less than its carrying value, an entity should consider all relevant events and circumstances, including:

   a. Microeconomic conditions such as deterioration in general economic conditions, limited access to capital, fluctuation in exchange rates, or other adverse events in equity and credit markets

   b. Industry and market conditions such as deterioration in the industry environment, increased competition, decline in market-dependent multiples, change in the market for the entity's products or services, or a regulatory or political development

   c. Cost factors such as increases in raw materials, labor, or other costs that have a negative effect on earnings and cash flows

   d. Overall financial performance such as negative cash flows or actual or projected declines in revenues, earnings, or cash flows

   e. Entity-specific events such as changes in management, key personnel, strategy, or customers; contemplation of bankruptcy or litigation

   f. Factors affecting a reporting unit such as changes in composition or carrying amount of its net assets, anticipation of selling or disposing all or a portion of a reporting unit, or recognition of goodwill impairment loss by a subsidiary that is a component of a reporting unit

   g. If the reporting unit is publicly traded, a sustained decrease in share price (considered both in absolute terms and relative to the peer group)

4. **Qualitative Assessment Outcomes**

   a. After assessing the totality of the above kinds of events and circumstances, an entity determines that it **is not** more likely than not that the fair value of the reporting unit is less than its carrying value, then the quantitative steps of the goodwill impairment test **are unnecessary**.

   b. After assessing the totality of the above kinds of events and circumstances, an entity determines that it **is** more likely than not that the fair value of the reporting unit is less than its carrying value, then the first step of the two-step quantitative assessment **must be performed**.

C. Quantitative Assessment—Step 1: Testing for Potential Impairment

1. If the qualitative assessment determines that it is more likely than not that the fair value of the reporting unit is less than its carrying value, then a quantitative assessment must be performed.

2. The first quantitative step used to identify potential goodwill impairment compares the fair value of a reporting unit with its carrying amount, including any deferred income taxes and previously recognized goodwill.

3. If the carrying amount of the reporting unit is greater than zero and its fair value exceeds that carrying amount, goodwill of the reporting unit is considered not impaired and the second quantitative step of the impairment test is not required.

4. If the carrying amount of the reporting units is greater than its fair value, the second quantitative step of the impairment test is required to measure the amount of the goodwill impairment loss.

Examples

Facts: Assume Firm A acquires firm B for $400 million when B's net identifiable assets have a fair value of $300 million. Subsequent to the acquisition, Firm B is considered a reporting unit. As a consequence of the acquisition, Firm A will recognize $100 million in goodwill, determined as cost of investment (fair value of B) $400 million – fair value of identifiable assets $300 million = $100 million goodwill.

One year later, as a result of its qualitative assessment, Firm A cannot rule out the possibility that the goodwill recognized when it acquired Firm B is impaired.

1. No Potential Impairment

In carrying out Step 1 of its quantitative assessment, Firm A determines that the fair value of Firm B, as a unit, is $420 million and that the carrying value of its investment in Firm B is $410 million. Since the fair value ($420 million) is greater than the carrying value ($410), there is no potential impairment and Step 2 of the quantitative assessment is not required.

2. Potential Impairment

Assume in carrying out Step 1 of its quantitative assessment, Firm A determines that the fair value of Firm B, as a unit, is $340 million and that the carrying value of its investment in Firm B is $380 million. Since the fair value ($340 million) is less than the carrying value ($380), goodwill is potentially impaired and Step 2 of the quantitative assessment is required to measure the impairment loss, if any.

D. Quantitative Assessment—Step 2: Measuring Impairment

1. When the first step of the quantitative assessment indicates the potential that goodwill is impaired, then this second quantitative step is required to measure the goodwill impairment.

2. Goodwill impairment is measured by comparing the (current) implied fair value of a reporting unit's goodwill with the carrying amount of that goodwill.

a. The implied fair value of the goodwill is determined by assigning fair value to all the assets and liabilities of a reporting unit, including any intangible assets, and comparing that net fair value with the fair value of the reporting unit as a whole.

b. The excess of the fair value of a reporting unit over the fair value amounts assigned to its net assets is the implied goodwill of the reporting unit.

c. The assignment of fair values to assets and liabilities, including any previously unrecognized intangible assets, is used only for the purpose of measuring goodwill impairment; those assigned values are not used to change the recorded values of recognized assets or liabilities, or to recognize any previously unrecognized assets or liabilities, including intangible assets.

3. If the carrying amount of goodwill exceeds the implied fair value of that goodwill, an impairment loss is recognized for the amount of the excess.

   a. The amount of loss recognized cannot exceed the carrying amount of the goodwill.

   b. After the impairment loss is recognized, the adjusted carrying amount is the new accounting basis for goodwill.

   c. Subsequent reversal of a goodwill impairment loss is not permitted.

Example

Assume the facts in Example 2 above, specifically:

Firm A acquires firm B for $400 million when B's net identifiable assets have a fair value of $300 million. Subsequent to the acquisition, Firm B is considered a reporting unit. As a consequence of the acquisition, Firm A will recognize $100 million in goodwill, determined as cost of investment (fair value of B) $400 million – Fair value of identifiable assets $300 million = $100 million goodwill.

One year later, as a result of its qualitative assessment, Firm A cannot rule out the possibility that the goodwill recognized when it acquired Firm B is impaired. Therefore, it carries out a quantitative assessment.

In carrying out Step 1 of its quantitative assessment, Firm A determines that the fair value of Firm B as a unit is $340 million and that the carrying value of its investment in Firm B is $380 million. Since the fair value ($340 million) is less than the carrying value ($380), goodwill is potentially impaired and Step 2 of the quantitative assessment is required to measure the impairment loss, if any.

Step 2: The fair value of Firm B's identifiable net assets is determined to be $280 million.

Implied goodwill = Fair value of Firm B as a unit, $340,000 million – Fair value of Firm B's identifiable net assets, $280,000 million = $60 million implied goodwill.

Impairment loss = Carrying amount of goodwill $100 million – Implied value of current goodwill $60 million = $40 million impairment loss

Impairment Entry:

DR: Impairment Loss—Goodwill $40 million

   CR: Goodwill $40 million

E. Reporting Unit Book Value = Zero or Negative

1. If the carrying amount of a reporting unit is zero or negative, the second quantitative step must be performed to measure the amount of impairment loss, if any, when it is more likely than not that a goodwill impairment exists.

2. In evaluating whether it is more likely than not that the goodwill of a reporting unit with zero or negative book value is impaired, an entity should take into account:

   a. The events and circumstances described previously (IV. B.)

   b. Whether there are significant differences between the carrying amount and the estimated fair values of its assets and liabilities

   c. The possible existence of significant unrecognized intangible assets

V. Goodwill Impairment Test Flowchart—The following flowchart summarizes the required steps in carrying out the testing of goodwill for impairment.

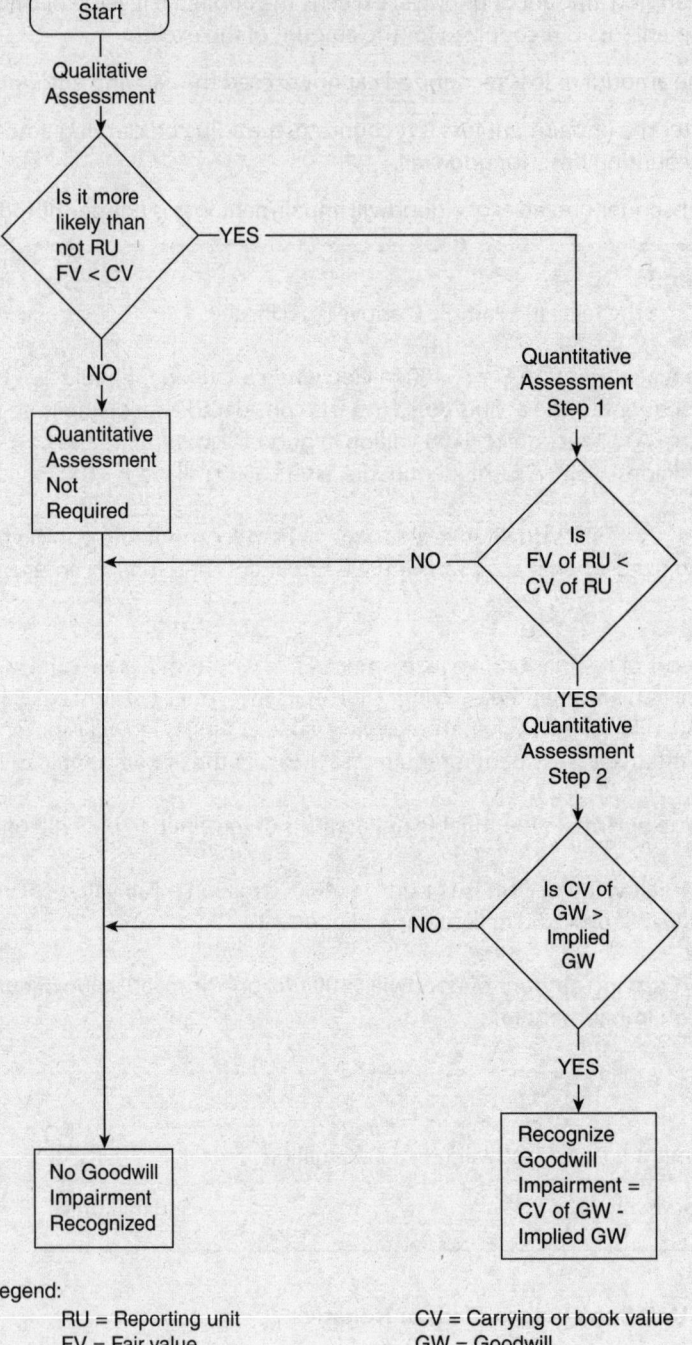

Legend:

RU = Reporting unit   CV = Carrying or book value
FV = Fair value   GW = Goodwill

Research and Development Costs

This lesson presents the accounting and reporting for research and development costs (R&D).

After studying this lesson, you should be able to:

1. Identify what costs are considered research and what costs are considered development.

2. Identify the major difference in IFRS and U.S . GAAP with respect to R&D

I. Details

A. Definitions

> **Definitions**
>
> *Research:* The attempt to discover new knowledge aimed at the development of new products, services, processes, or techniques, or the significant improvement in an existing product.
>
> *Development:* The translation of research findings or knowledge into a plan or design of a new product or significant improvement in an existing product or process whether intended for sale or use. Development includes formulation, design and testing of product alternatives, construction of prototypes, and operations of pilot plants.

1. Development does not include routine or periodic alterations to existing products, processes, or other ongoing operations. It also does not include market research.

Exam Tip
The CPA Exam frequently tests detailed knowledge of the definition and items included in R&D, and also what is not included in R&D.

B. Included in R&D Are:

1. Laboratory research

2. Conceptual formulation and design of possible products or process alternatives

3. Modification of the formulation or design of a product or process

4. Design, construction, and testing of preproduction prototypes and models

5. Design of tools, jigs, molds, and dies involving new technology

6. Design of a pilot plant

C. Excluded from R&D Are:

1. Engineering follow-through

2. Quality control and routine testing

3. Troubleshooting

4. Adaptation of an existing capability to a particular customer's needs

5. Routine design of tools, jigs, molds, and dies

6. Legal work in connection with patent applications

7. Software development costs

II. Accounting for R&D

A. General Rule—ASC 730 requires that research and development costs are expensed in the period incurred. Research and development costs include labor costs, materials costs, and overhead costs.

B. Fixed Assets—In relation to the use of fixed assets in research and development activities, three specific situations need to be addressed.

1. **Fixed Assets Used in Several Research and Development Projects**—These assets are capitalized and annual depreciation is included in the annual research and development costs. The debit is to R&D expense rather than to depreciation expense; the credit is to accumulated depreciation.

2. **Fixed Assets Used Temporarily in a Research and Development Project**—The depreciation related to the time frame of the project is included in the annual research and development costs.

3. **Fixed Assets Used in a Single Research and Development Project, the Asset has no Alternative Uses**—Even though the fixed asset has a useful life exceeding one year and the single R&D project will be in process for more than one year, the entire cost of the fixed asset is expensed as R&D immediately.

C. Patent Costs—The internal costs of developing a patent are considered R&D and therefore are expensed. The result is that the only costs capitalized for internally developed patents are registration and legal costs. This contrasts with the cost of purchasing a patent from an outside party. The entire cost of such a patent is capitalized. The treatment appears somewhat inconsistent but stems from the reasoning that it is better to err on the side of conservatism when the benefits of R&D are so uncertain.

D. Purchased Services—R&D services purchased from other firms are included in R&D. But if a firm performs R&D services for another firm, the costs are accumulated in an inventory account and expensed as cost of goods sold or cost of services provided at the conclusion of the contract.

E. R&D Examples

> **Exam Tip**
> This issue has appeared in CPA Exam questions in the past. To some candidates, the treatment in the third situation below appears unusual because the fixed asset has a useful life of more than one year. ASC 730 views the purchase of such an asset as an irrevocable commitment of resources. Since the intent is to use the equipment only in the one R&D effort, and since it has no future value, conservatism and consistency with other R&D expenses would imply immediate expensing.

Examples

1. Maple Inc. does not have the expertise in a specific research area and contracted with Oak Co. to perform research on a new product design to be used by Maple. Maple will expense all of the payments made to Oak as R&D expense. However, Oak Co. will debit inventory for the cost of its research performed for Maple until the contract is completed, at which time contract revenue and expense is recognized. This is not R&D expense to Oak.

2. The following costs were incurred by a firm in the current year:

Materials, labor, and overhead cost incurred for:

Laboratory research	$40,000
Modification of the design of a product or process	10,000
Adaptation of an existing capability to a particular customer's needs	20,000

Purchase cost of fixed assets at beginning of year:

Equipment used the full year for lab research, annual depreciation $30,000; equipment has alternative non R&D uses	$300,000 cost
Equipment used the full year for lab research, annual depreciation $15,000; equipment has alternative R&D uses	$150,000 cost
Equipment used the full year for lab research, annual depreciation $25,000; equipment has no alternative use other than in one specific R&D effort	$250,000 cost

Total R&D expense for the year equals:

$345,000 = $40,000 + $10,000 + $30,000 + $15,000 + $250,000.

The $20,000 (adaptation of existing capability) is not R&D. The full cost of the third item of equipment is included in R&D for the current year because it has no alternative use (in other R&D or non-R&D uses).

III. Research and Development and IFRS

A. IFRS distinguishes between research and development, like U.S. GAAP. However, IFRS allows companies to capitalize development costs.

Software Costs

This lesson presents the accounting and reporting for internally developed software costs and the fees associated with cloud computing.

After studying this lesson, you should be able to:

1. Describe the accounting for software costs prior to and after technological feasibility.
2. Calculate the amortization of capitalized software costs.
3. Identify the major difference in IFRS and U.S. GAAP with respect to software costs.
4. Describe when the cloud computing fees are related to a software license or a service agreement.

Internally Developed Software Costs

I. **Background**

    A. Many companies develop software internally for their specific use or to sell to others. The accounting question is: When does the research and development activity cease and when is there sufficient probability that a product will be marketed?

    B. The costs incurred during research and development (R&D) of the software will be expensed, while the costs incurred subsequent to research and development activities will be capitalized.

    C. As per ASC 985, research and development activities continue until the technological feasibility of the software has been established. The difference between R&D and Software is the latter establishes a point after which development costs are capitalized to an intangible asset and subsequently amortized. In contrast, all R&D is expensed as incurred.

II. **Technological Feasibility**

    A. The critical point for software cost accounting is technological feasibility. The establishment of the technological feasibility of the software typically occurs when the program model or working model of the software is complete. The product is not yet ready to market, but the commitment is made at this point to continue with the product. There is sufficient reason, at this point, to allocate additional resources to the effort.

    B. The costs incurred subsequent to the establishment of the technological feasibility will be capitalized and amortized over the estimated economic life of the software.

III. **Breakdown of Software Costs and Their Accounting**—This listing of costs appears in the chronological order of incurrence with respect to a particular software product.

    A. **Research and Development**—Costs incurred to establish technological feasibility (costs incurred before technological feasibility is established) *expense as incurred, as R&D expense.*

        1. The quest for technological feasibility is the activity in software development most similar to general R&D. During this period, the firm has not reached a decision on the feasibility of its product. Costs during this period include planning, designing, coding, and testing of programs.

    B. **Costs Subsequent to Establishing Technological Feasibility**—Through the completion of product masters: *capitalize as computer software costs (intangible asset) and amortize.*

        1. This second category of costs includes additional costs of coding, testing, debugging, and preparation of final product master and final documentation manual. It does not include duplication of product masters and manuals. This category ends when a product master is ready for duplication.

        2. This is the only category of software costs that is capitalized as an intangible asset and subsequently amortized.

C. Software Production Costs—(Duplication of software and manuals). Capitalize in inventory and expense through cost of goods sold as sales take place.

D. Customer Support and Maintenance—Expense as incurred.

E. Summary of Accounting Treatment of Software Costs

1. Software development (coding and testing) before technological feasibility: DR. R&D expense

2. Software development (coding and testing) after technological feasibility to production of product masters: DR. Capitalized Software Development Costs

3. Duplication of product, packaging, etc.: DR. Inventory of product

4. Sell product: DR. Cost of Goods Sold

5. Customer service: DR. Expense

IV. Amortization of Capitalized Computer Software Costs—These are amortized using one of the two following methods, whichever results in a larger amortization amount. Each year the computation for both methods must be made to ensure the larger amount is recognized. The same method need not produce the larger amount each year. The amortization is an operating expense.

A. Revenue Method

Amortization for current year $= B \times R$

Where: $B =$ book value of capitalized software costs at beginning of year

$R = $ (current year revenue) / (current year revenue + estimated future revenue)

B. Straight-Line Method

Amortization for current year $= B/N$

Where: $B =$ book value of capitalized software costs at beginning of year

$N =$ number of years remaining in product sales life at beginning of year

C. Cautions

1. Remember to choose the higher of the two amounts each period. Also, the inputs to both methods change each year. The beginning book value changes, as does the estimate of future revenue and remaining years in the product life.

2. After amortizing the capitalized costs for a particular year, the ending book value is compared with the net realizable value of the software (future estimated gross revenues less operating costs). If the ending book value exceeds the net realizable value, the book value is written down to net realizable value, with a loss recognized. The net realizable value becomes the beginning book value for the next period, for purposes of amortization. Write-ups are not allowed.

Example

The software costs incurred for a product developed for sale are:

Costs incurred to establish technological feasibility	$100,000
Costs incurred after establishment of technological feasibility and through the completion of product masters	200,000

Entries:

R&D expense	100,000	
Cash, other accounts		100,000
Computer software costs (intangible asset)	200,000	
Cash, other accounts		200,000

(The product is marketed at the beginning of year 2 and is expected to have a three-year sales life)

Revenue from software sales in year 2	$1,000,000
Estimate of revenue for years 3 and 4 (total)	3,000,000
Total current-year and future estimated revenue	4,000,000

Amortization of computer software costs:

Revenue method amortization = $200,000($1,000,000/$4,000,000) = $50,000

Straight-line method amortization = $200,000/3 = $66,667

(higher of the two amounts)

Entry:

Amortization of computer software costs	66,667	
Computer software costs		66,667

Book value of computer software costs at beginning of year $200,000 − $66,667 = $133,333

Revenue from software sales in year 3	$1,750,000
Estimate of revenue for year 4	500,000
Total current year and future estimated revenue	$2,250,000

Amortization of computer software costs:

Revenue method amortization = $133,333($1,750,000/$2,250,000) = $103,703

Straight-line method amortization = $133,333/2 = $66,667

Entry (at year-end):

Amortization of computer software costs	103,703	
Computer software costs		103,703

The ending year 3 book value of computer software costs, reported in the balance sheet, is $29,630 ($133,333 − $103,703). This example shows that the same amortization method need not be used each year.

V. Software Costs and IFRS

    A. IFRS does not specifically address internal software costs; therefore, the rules of research and development are applied. Under IFRS, software costs for research are expensed and those for development are capitalized. U.S. GAAP specifically addresses software costs and identifies the threshold of technological feasibility for capitalization.

VI. Cloud Computing—ASU 2015-05 was issued in April 2015 and provides guidance on the accounting for fees paid in a cloud computing arrangement.

    A. First the company must determine if the cloud computing arrangement includes a software license. The arrangement contains a software license if both one and two are true:

        1. The customer has the contractual right to take possession of the software at any time during the hosting period without significant penalty.

            a. Significant penalty means that the customer can take delivery without incurring significant costs and can use the software separately without a significant reduction in utility or value.

        2. It is feasible for the customer to either run the software on its own hardware or contract with another party unrelated to the vendor to host the software.

    B. If the cloud computing arrangement contains a software license then the license is accounted for like other acquired intangible license agreements. Generally this means that the license is capitalized as an intangible asset and amortized over the life of the license (if definite lived) or tested annually for impairment (if indefinite life).

Intangibles and IFRS

This lesson presents the significant differences in the accounting for intangibles assets under IFRS and U.S. GAAP.

After studying this lesson, you should be able to:

1. Identify the major differences in the accounting for intangibles assets under IFRS and U.S. GAAP.

I. **Intangibles and IFRS**

   A. IFRS defines an intangible asset as "an identifiable nonmonetary asset without physical substance." This definition has three key characteristics. (The definition and characteristics are very similar to U.S. GAAP.) The asset:

      1. Is controlled by the entity and the entity expects to derive future economic benefits

      2. Lacks physical substance

      3. Is identifiable to be distinguished from goodwill

   B. IFRS allows intangible assets to be revalued to fair value if there is an active market for the intangible assets. If an intangible asset is valued at fair value, the entire class of intangible assets must be valued this way, not just select individual intangible assets. U.S. GAAP does not allow revaluation to fair value.

   C. IFRS allows reversal of impairment losses on intangible assets to the carrying value that would have been recognized had the impairment not occurred. GAAP does not allow for reversals of impairment losses.

   D. The method and amortization method of the intangible asset should be reviewed each annual reporting period. U.S. GAAP requires a review when the events or circumstances change.

Major Differences Between U.S. GAAP and IFRS	
U.S. GAAP	**IFRS**
Revaluation to fair value is not permitted.	Intangibles can be revalued to fair value if there is an active market.
Reversal of impairment loss is not allowed.	Reversal of impairment loss is permitted.
Estimated useful life and amortization method reviewed when events or circumstances change	Estimated useful life and amortization method reviewed annually

II. Goodwill and IFRS

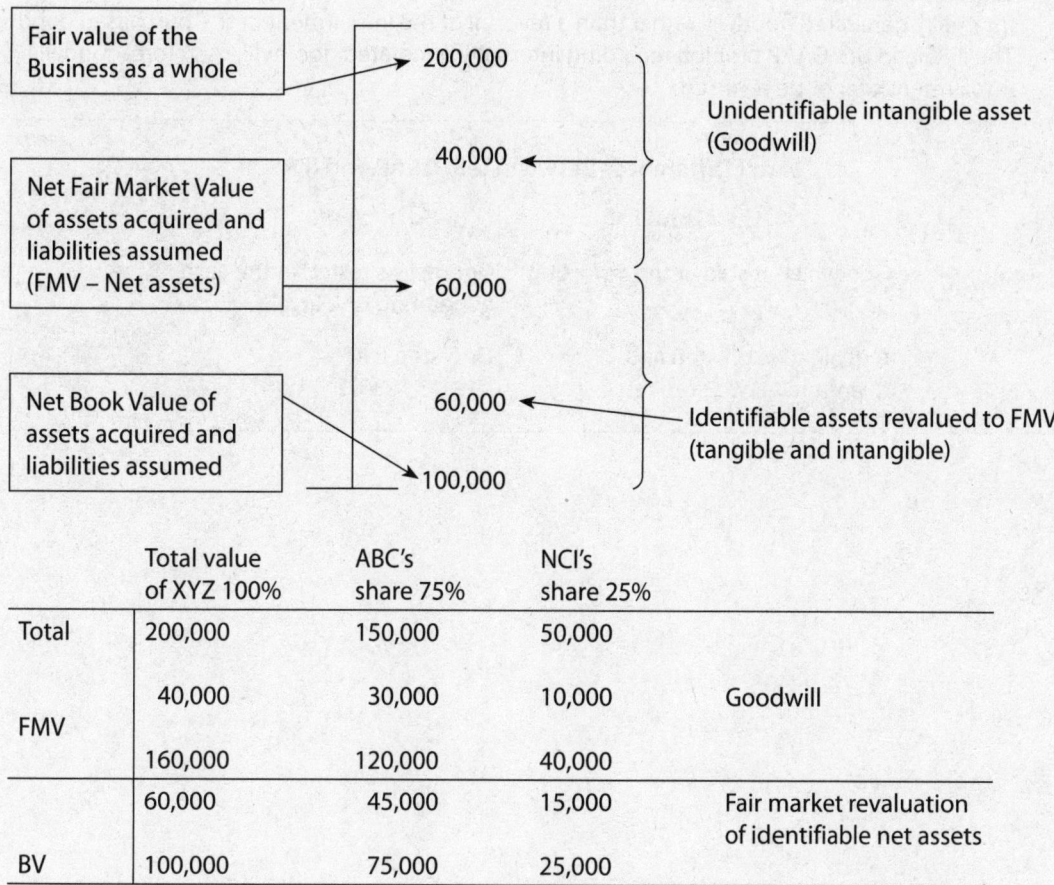

	Total value of XYZ 100%	ABC's share 75%	NCI's share 25%	
Total	200,000	150,000	50,000	
FMV	40,000	30,000	10,000	Goodwill
	160,000	120,000	40,000	
	60,000	45,000	15,000	Fair market revaluation of identifiable net assets
BV	100,000	75,000	25,000	

A. IFRS IAS 36 requires goodwill impairment testing to use a single-step quantitative test that is performed at the cash-generating unit (or group of cash-generating units). A company is likely to have more cash-generating units than reporting units. Therefore, more "buckets" of goodwill will be tested under IFRS than under U.S. GAAP within a given entity.

B. The test must be performed at least annually or whenever there is evidence that an impairment may have occurred. IFRS requires a one-step impairment test. The carrying value of the cash-generating unit is compared to its recoverable amount. The impairment loss is the excess of the carrying amount of the cash-generating unit over the recoverable amount. The calculated value of the impairment loss reduces goodwill to zero. If there is additional value associated with the impairment loss, it is allocated to the other assets of the unit pro rata based on the carrying amount of each asset in the group. The unit is not reduced below the highest amount of its fair value less cost to sell, its value in use, or zero.

C. IFRS for small and medium-sized companies require goodwill to be amortized over the estimated useful life. If an estimate useful life is not reliably determinable, the goodwill should be assigned a life of 10 years.

D. Although other types of impairment loss are reversible under IFRS, goodwill impairment loss cannot be reversed. The IFRS believes that any subsequent increase in goodwill is more likely to be internally generated goodwill rather than a reversal of the impairment of the purchased goodwill. The IFRS and U.S. GAAP prohibit recording internally generated goodwill; therefore, goodwill impairment cannot be reversed.

Major Differences Between U.S. GAAP and IFRS

U.S. GAAP	IFRS
Goodwill is tested at the reporting unit level	Goodwill is tested at the cash generating unit level
A qualitative prestep and quantitative two-step test	One-step test

Payables and Accrued Liabilities

Current Liabilities

This lesson is the first of several concerning recognition and reporting of current liabilities. The general nature and definition of liability are discussed, along with classification and valuation of liabilities.

After studying this lesson, you should be able to:

1. Define liability, current liability, and noncurrent liability.

2. Categorize liabilities two different ways.

3. Determine the valuation of current and noncurrent liabilities.

4. Distinguish current from noncurrent liabilities.

Definition
Liabilities: Represent outsider claims to a firm's assets or are enforceable claims for services to be rendered by the firm.

I. **Liabilities in General**

  A. **Definition of Liabilities**

  1. Liabilities have three key elements, which are shown below. This definition is taken from the FASB's conceptual framework.

    a. Liabilities represent probable future sacrifices of economic benefits.

    b. Liabilities are obligations to transfer assets or provide services in the future.

    c. Liabilities are the result of past transactions or events.

  2. It is important to note that, for a liability to be recognized in the accounts, it is not necessary to know the identity of the creditor, the exact amount that will be paid, or even the due date. Contingent liabilities, discussed later, are a category of liability for which one or more of these information items are not known as of the balance sheet date. However, the three elements from the conceptual framework above must be met by all liabilities if one is to be recognized in the accounts.

Examples

1. A firm signed a contract to perform services the following year. At the current balance sheet date, the firm has no liability because no resources have been exchanged. Only a contract has been signed. There is no past transaction that substantiates the liability as of the balance sheet date. There is no future obligation to provide services because neither party has executed the contract. None of the elements of the liability is met.

2. Do airline frequent flyer programs create liabilities for airline companies?
The answer is yes, because all three parts of the definition of a liability are met. The airline has (1) an obligation to provide service (2) in the future (3) as a result of a past transaction (customers achieving the requisite miles or credit card purchases for a free flight). Airline companies accrue this liability. Again, none of the following is known at the time of the accrual: the identity of the creditor, amount to be paid, or due date.

B. Classification of Liabilities—Liabilities are classified in two ways: (1) current liabilities (CL) or noncurrent liabilities (NCL), and (2) definite or contingent.

1. Most current liabilities (CL) are due within one year of the balance sheet. All other debt is noncurrent. Liabilities are presented on the balance sheet in increasing order of maturity. That is, current liabilities are presented first, and then, noncurrent liabilities are presented. CL include accounts payable, wages payable, income taxes payable, utilities payable, accrued payables, some notes payable, and many others. Noncurrent liabilities (NCL) include bonds payable, some notes payable, lease liabilities and pension liabilities.

2. Definite liabilities actually exist at the balance sheet. Contingent liabilities have some uncertainty at the balance sheet date. Their existence is contingent on an event that may or may not occur after the balance sheet. A contingent liability may be accrued as a definite liability, is disclosed as a contingency, or is not considered a liability at all. Most liabilities are definite. Examples of contingent liabilities include lawsuits, warranties, and guarantees. Contingent liabilities are covered in a subsequent lesson.

C. Distinction between Current and Noncurrent Liabilities

1. **Current liabilities**—Are those that meet two criteria:

   a. Due in the coming year or the operating cycle of the business, whichever is longer;

   b. An obligation to be met by the transfer of a current asset or the *creation of another current liability*.

   i. The operating cycle is the period from acquiring inventory and other resources, to sale, to receipt of cash from the receivable. Most firms have operating cycles much shorter than a year. One measure of the operating cycle is 365/inventory turnover + 365/AR turnover = number of days required to sell the inventory on hand + number of days required to collect receivables.

2. **Noncurrent liabilities**—Are defined by exclusion. That is, noncurrent liabilities are those that do not meet the criteria necessary for classification as a current liability.

Examples

1. A bond payable liability is due four years from the balance sheet. This liability is classified as noncurrent.

2. If the bond liability matures serially, and a portion of the principal balance is due at the end of each year, then the amount due the following year is classified as a current liability in the balance sheet for the current year and is labeled: current maturities of long-term debt.

3. **Valuation of Liabilities**

   a. CLs are reported valued at the amount due, or nominal amount. Liabilities for services are measured at the amount received. For example, the unearned revenue (liability) for an amount received by an airline before a flight is provided is measured at the amount received for the ticket.

   b. NCLs are reported at the present value of all future payments (principal and interest), discounted at the prevailing rate of interest for similar debt on the date of issuance. Present value is the current sacrifice to retire the debt. Interest is the difference between the total future payments and present value. Interest is not recognized until time passes.

Caution: A CL and NCL reported in the balance sheet at equal values (e.g., both $100,000) may require greatly different cash payment totals over their terms due to interest on the NCL principal.

c. Although in theory all debt should be reported at present value, for practical reasons CL are not discounted because the difference between present and nominal (future) value is typically not material.

II. A Closer Look at Current Liabilities (CL)

A. The essence of a CL is that it is expected to reduce the firm's liquidity within one year of the balance sheet date or operating cycle whichever is longer. A CL payable with a current asset clearly will reduce the firm's liquidity. But what about the second part of the definition *creation of another CL?*

B. CLs that are continuously refinanced (rolled over) by replacing them with other CLs due later (but within one year of the balance sheet date) must still be classified as CL, even though no current asset will be used to extinguish them in the year after the balance sheet date.

Examples

1. A note payable due 3/1/X2 is expected to be refinanced continuously on a four-month basis, each time substituting a new four-month note for the old. That is the intent of the debtor firm. The note due 3/1/X2 is classified as a CL in the 12/31/X1 balance sheet because it meets the second part of the CL definition.

Although the expectation is that no current asset will be used to retire the debt, there is no certainty that the debtor firm will be able to continue this practice. For example, the debtor firm cannot control the creditor who may decide not to refinance. Interest rates may increase substantially changing the strategy of the debtor firm.

Caution: Most liabilities due within one year of the balance sheet are CLs. But there are exceptions—some are classified as NCL.

2. A note is due five months from the balance sheet date but payable in the common stock of the debtor. The debtor does not reduce current assets in payment of this debt. A later lesson discusses another example—the refinancing of short-term debt on a long-term basis.

3. A bond liability due next year for which the firm has created a sinking fund investment (noncurrent asset) for bond retirement is classified as an NCL because payment will reduce noncurrent assets not current assets.

Caution: Most liabilities due later than one year after the balance sheet date are NCLs but there are exceptions; some are classified as CLs.

4. Long-term obligations callable on demand by the creditor are classified as current. Because the creditor can call in the debt, the debtor must report it as current. A creditor may require this provision in the debt contract to reduce the risk of losing principal. Such provisions also may be added in case the debtor violates a debt restriction. For example, a debt contract requires the debtor to maintain a current ratio (CA/CL) of 3.0 or more. If the ratio falls below 3.0, the debt is due on demand by the creditor, unless the debtor "cures" the violation within the next reporting period.

III. Definite Liabilities

Definite Liabilities—Definite liabilities are not dependent on any future event. The existence of these liabilities is determined by a current event or a past transaction or event. Definite liabilities include liabilities payable in definite amounts (e.g., accounts payable), those that can only be estimated (e.g., estimated income tax payable), and accrued liabilities that are recorded for expenses recognized before payment is made (e.g., utilities payable). Not all definite liabilities can be measured with certainty. Some are estimated and reported at an approximate amount.

A. Accounts Payable

1. These payables are also called trade payables. They represent the amount a business enterprise owes to suppliers and other entities that provide goods or services to the company.

2. These payables are typically for a short duration, usually 30 days. In some instances, the time period can be 45 or 60 days.

3. Accounts payable are recognized at the time of purchase or at the time that services are received by the business entity. In relation to purchased merchandise, the payable should be recognized at the point in which the merchandise is included in the company's inventory. The module on inventory discusses this issue in further detail (F.O.B. title test and goods on consignment). Several additional accounts such as purchases, purchases returns and allowances and others are created to accommodate the specifics of inventory purchasing.

B. Subsequent lessons provide additional examples of definite liabilities. For example, corporations often provide an estimate of fourth-quarter income taxes at year-end:

DR: Income tax expense	xxx
CR: Income tax payable	xxx

1. The amount recorded in this adjusting journal entry is an estimate of the amount due for the year; the exact amount often is subject to dispute because the process of preparing a corporation's income tax return is affected by ambiguities in the tax law and other issues. The first three quarterly payments also are estimates. Subsequent lessons consider income tax reporting in greater depth.

Specific Current Liabilities

This lesson considers several specific definite current liabilities. Recall that definite liabilities exist at the balance sheet. Additional examples appear in the context of other lessons.

After studying this lesson, you should be able to:

1. Record sales taxes payable from data about sales and the applicable tax rate.

2. Distinguish employer and employee payroll costs and which results in an employer expense.

3. Record payroll including employer payroll tax expenses, and payroll liabilities from both employer and employee sources.

4. Compute bonus liabilities with income tax effects.

I. **Sales Taxes**—Firms collect sales taxes from their customers and periodically submit them to the state or local government. Between collection and submission of the tax, the firm has a liability to the government.

Examples

The sales tax rate is 10% and the total amount collected from customers for the month is $77,000. The summary entry to record sales and the sales tax is:

Cash	77,000	
Sales		70,000*
Sales Taxes Payable		7,000

* $77,000/1.10 = $70,000 The cash collected includes the sales tax.

The sales taxes payable account is debited when paid to the state, county, or city. Note that the firm reports only $70,000 of sales.

II. **Payroll Liabilities**

A. In their role as employers, firms incur definite current payroll-related liabilities from two different sources:

1. Employer costs including gross salary, employer share of fringe benefits, employer share of FICA and Medicare, and federal and state unemployment tax (FUTA and SUTA). The employer recognizes an expense for these costs.

2. Employee costs withheld from paychecks including income tax withholding, employee share of FICA, Medicare and fringe benefits, and also personal expenses such as parking, union dues and others. The employer does not recognize an expense for these costs but acts as a collection point resulting in an employer liability.

    a. Payroll tax liabilities are paid by the employer at specific dates set by law.

    b. Social security legislation levies the OASDI (Federal Old Age, Survivor, and Disability Insurance) tax, also called FICA (Federal Insurance Contribution Act) tax, on annual salaries and wages up to a certain annual salary limit per employee. In addition, the Medicare tax is levied on all salaries and wages without limit. Both employer and employee pay the same amount for both taxes.

    c. Employers pay federal and state unemployment taxes. Both (1) Federal Unemployment Tax Act (FUTA) and (2) State Unemployment Taxes (SUTA) are levied on each employee's salary up to a certain limit per year. Only employers pay this tax.

Note

Because payroll tax rates and salary limits change, the CPA Exam will provide approximate values. However, we recommend that you be aware of the general magnitude of such costs. Approximate rates and limits: FICA, 6.5% on the first $110,000 of salary per year; Medicare, 1.5% with no limit; FUTA, 6% on the first $7,000 reduced by up to 5.5% for contributions to SUTA; SUTA, 5.5% on first $7,000.

Caution

FICA, FUTA, and SUTA all have salary limits beyond which no more tax is levied either for employer or employee (there is no limit for Medicare) for a particular year. Look for these limits in payroll problems and take care not to exceed them when computing these expenses for the employer and for FICA withholdings for the employee.

Example

Gross payroll is $60,000 for a month late in the year (gross pay limits for some employees have been exceeded). Use the approximate tax rates provided.

FICA tax, 7%, only $40,000 of gross pay subject to tax

Medicare tax, 1.5% of gross pay

State income tax withholding, $2,000 (based on withholding tables)

Federal income tax withholding, $18,000 (based on withholding tables)

State unemployment tax, 5%, only $20,000 of gross pay subject to tax

Federal unemployment tax, 1%, only $20,000 of gross pay subject to tax

Union dues withheld, $1,000

Health insurance premiums, $3,000 (1/3 paid by employees)

Retirement, $4,000 (1/4 paid by employees)

Salary or wage expense	65,000*	
State inc tax withholding payable		2,000
Federal income tax withholding payable		18,000
FICA tax payable (.07 × $40,000)		2,800
Medicare tax payable (.015 × $60,000)		900
Health insurance payable		3,000
Retirement payable		4,000
Union dues payable		1,000
Cash (net pay)		33,300

*$65,000 = $60,000 gross + 2/3($3,000 health) + 3/4($4,000 retirement).

Net pay = $60,000 – employee withholdings (excludes employer share of fringes) = $60,000 – $20,000 income tax – $2,800 FICA – $900 Medicare – $1,000 health – $1,000 retirement – $1,000 union = 33,300

The $65,000 expense includes only the employer's costs. The employees' net pay is reduced by their costs. Rather than increasing the expense debit, the net pay credit is reduced.

Remaining is to record the employer share of FICA and Medicare, and the employer's taxes for FUTA and SUTA. The next journal entry records these expenses. The two journal entries could be combined.

Payroll tax expense	4,900	
FICA tax payable (.07 × $40,000)		2,800
Medicare tax payable (.015 × $60,000)		900
FUTA tax payable (.01 × $20,000)		200
SUTA tax payable (.05 × $20,000)		1,000

The total employer expense for this payroll is $69,900 ($65,000 + $4,900).

III. Bonus Compensation Liabilities—A bonus is an additional amount of compensation in excess of a base salary. Frequently, liabilities related to bonus compensation are dependent on operating results for the accounting period. The bonus may be based on income before or after the bonus, and before or after income tax effects. We recommend converting the problem statement directly into an equation. These types of problems require solving for up to two unknowns.

Examples

1. An employee's bonus is based on operating income after income taxes but before deducting the bonus. Operating Income before bonus and taxes is $90,000, the bonus rate is 10%, and the tax rate is 40%. Let B = bonus, T = tax.

$$B = .10\,(\$90{,}000 - T)$$
$$T = .40\,(\$90{,}000 - B)$$
$$B = .10\,(\$90{,}000 - .40\,(\$90{,}000 - B))$$
$$B = \$5{,}625$$

2. An employee's bonus is based on operating income after income taxes and bonus. Operating income before bonus and tax is $90,000, the bonus rate is 10%, and the tax rate is 40%. Let B = bonus, T = tax.

$$B = .10\,(90{,}000 - T - B)$$
$$T = .40\,(90{,}000 - B)$$
$$B = .10(90{,}000 - .40\,(90{,}000 - B) - B)$$
$$B = \$5{,}094$$

Costs and Expenses

Costs and Expenses

This lesson considers the general principles for recognizing expenses and losses before and after expenditures are made. Many of the FAR lessons consider specific costs and expenses. Advertising costs and property taxes are illustrated here.

After studying this lesson, you should be able to:

1. Recognize that cost is a general term encompassing other specific accounting terms.

2. Distinguish assets, expenses and losses.

3. Describe how conceptual framework concepts affect the recognition of assets, expenses and losses.

4. Determine when advertising costs are expensed, and when they are capitalized.

5. Prepare the journal entries relevant to property taxes assessed for an annual period.

I. **General Concepts**

    A. **Cost**—Costs are the economic sacrifices incurred by firms for goods and services used in their business. Costs are measured at the cash equivalent or fair value of consideration transferred, or liability assumed, for the good or service. The conceptual framework description of cost is ". . . the value of cash or other resources given up (or the present value of an obligation incurred) in exchange for a resource measures the cost of the resource acquired."

        1. For accounting purposes, a cost can cause the recognition of an asset, expense, loss, or liability. Many costs, as evidenced by expenditures, are first recognized as assets, and then later expensed or written off as a loss. Only the expense and loss dispositions enter into the determination of income. Expenses and losses are the portions of costs that no longer have future value.

    B. **Expense versus Loss**

        1. Both expenses and losses are debited when they are recognized and both reduce net income.

        2. Only expenses provide a benefit to the firm. Expenses are outflows of resources that are incurred in production or other activities central to the ongoing primary operations of the entity. Examples include salary expense, rent expense, and many others. In each case, the firm obtains a benefit.

        3. Losses provide no benefit to the primary operations of the entity. Losses are **incidental** to the primary operations. Losses are recognized when it becomes evident that a previously recognized future benefit (an asset) has been reduced. When assets are "written off" as worthless, a loss is recognized. Losses also occur from casualties. The loss represents the amount of asset reduction for which there is no benefit. Losses also arise from the sale of assets for less than book value or the retirement of liabilities for more than book value.

II. **Timing of Cash Payment**—The incurrence of cost can occur before, at the same time, or after expense or loss recognition. Over the life of the resource obtained, total cost and total expenses (plus losses) will be of equal amount. But for any reporting period, the amounts are often different.

    A. When cash payments precede expense recognition, an asset typically is recorded because payment of the good or service occurs before its use in the business. Over the period of the asset's benefit, an expense is recognized. Examples include plant assets (depreciation) and prepaids (rent expense, insurance expense). These items are called deferrals. (Payment before expense.)

    B. When expenses precede cash payments, a liability typically is recorded. The liability is paid at a later date. The service or good is received and used before payment. These items are called accruals. (Payment after expense.)

III. Matching

A. The matching principle is frequently used to determine the amount of expense to be recognized for a given period. This is an income statement emphasis and is a major underlying concept used for determining the timing of expense recognition. The principle states that expenses are to be recognized in the same period as the related revenues. The revenues drive the recognition of expense. The wording of the principle presumes a causal relationship but depending on the expense, the strength of the relationship between expenses and revenues varies. The following is a list of expense categories from strong to weak relationship with revenue.

1. **Expenses with a direct causal link to revenues**—Cost of goods sold, and sales commissions based on sales revenue are examples. The link between revenues and expenses is the strongest for this category. For example, when inventory is sold, cost of goods sold is recognized for the cost of the item sold. Before sale, the inventory is reported as an asset.

2. **Expenses associated with revenues in a specific time period**—Salaries, property taxes, and other similar costs are examples. These costs are only indirectly related to revenues produced in the same period because they serve many different efforts. The presumption is that they contributed to the overall effort of generating revenues in that period.

3. **Expenses associated with benefits over more than one period**—This category includes depreciation and amortization expenses that are allocated on a systematic and rational basis to time periods or units of production (if the asset is involved in manufacturing). Long-term prepaids are included in this category. As they expire, they give rise to operating expenses including rent and insurance.

4. **Expenses recognized in the period incurred**—Examples are advertising and research and development (R&D) expense. The relationship between these costs and revenues is not determinable. There is no way to determine whether these expenditures have future benefit (with some exceptions).

IV. Asset and Liability Definitions versus Matching

A. Relative to matching, the recent emphasis has been on determining whether an asset or liability is to be recognized. The conceptual framework definitions are followed in this regard. This is a balance sheet emphasis and is a concept competing with matching as a major underlying concept used for determining the timing of expense recognition. An expense is a derived concept, based on the decrease in an asset or increase in a liability.

B. Interperiod tax allocation is an example of the balance sheet emphasis. The firm directly determines its income tax liability and the change in deferred tax accounts for the period. Income tax expense is the net change in these assets and liabilities. The firm is not attempting to match income tax expense with the benefits of operating in the United States.

1. Accounting for R&D is another example. Because future benefit is not probable for most R&D efforts, there is insufficient justification for recording an asset, which is a probable future benefit controlled by the firm as a result of a past transaction. Here the focus is on whether there is an asset. The definition is not met; therefore, an expense is recognized. The firm is not attempting to match R&D expense with the future revenues of inventions developed from current R&D efforts.

2. Another example is the use of the successful efforts method of accounting for natural resource exploration costs. This method capitalizes (debits an asset) only the costs of successful explorations (finding the resource). Unsuccessful efforts are expensed.

C. Matching, however, continues to be the justification for other practices including accounting for bond issue costs, the full costing method of accounting for natural resource exploration costs, and capitalization of interest. In these cases, assets are not enhanced. However, an asset is recorded in each case so that its cost can be matched against the related future revenues.

D. In many other situations, both concepts (matching, and the definitions of asset and liability) lead to the same accounting. For example, the recognition of estimated warranty expense in the year of sale both matches the expense in the year of sale, and records the probable obligation of the firm to transfer resources in the future as a result of a past transaction.

V. Advertising Costs

A. Advertising costs include the costs of content production and communicating that content.

B. The general principle is that advertising costs are either (1) expensed as incurred or (2) when the advertising first occurs. This is a policy choice and must be consistently applied. Although the advertising may be for an extended period of time, both alternatives reflect the lack of probable future benefit and are consistent with accounting for R&D.

    1. The second alternative assumes that the cost of advertising has been incurred and the advertising service will take place in the future. Examples are the first television commercial to be aired, and the first appearance of an advertisement in a newspaper.

C. Tangible assets such as catalogues and billboards are recognized as prepaids and amortized to advertising expense until they are no longer owned or expected to be used.

D. Accounting for certain direct response advertising programs is different. Direct response advertising is a promotional method designed to encourage prospective customers to respond directly to the advertiser. Methods include the use of coupons, toll-free telephone numbers and Internet links.

    1. Direct response advertising costs are capitalized if the main purpose is to produce sales from customers who respond directly to the advertising, and if it is probable that future benefits will result and extend beyond the current period.

    2. Capitalized costs are amortized as advertising expense over the expected period of benefit. Expiration of an offer is an example of the end of an amortization period.

    3. The firm must be able to support the contention that there are future benefits from this form of advertising through past experience.

    4. The types of costs that are capitalized include:

        a. Incremental direct costs such as the costs of logos, advertisements on the Internet, and others

        b. Salary costs of employees directly involved in the advertising activities including developing the concepts, artwork, advertising copy etc.

        c. Assets used as prizes directly related to direct response advertising programs

    5. Not capitalized are indirect costs such as facility costs and depreciation.

VI. Property Taxes

A. Property taxes are levied by state and local governments based on the assessed valuation of property as of a given date. The tax becomes a lien against the property on the date specified by law and thus legally the liability comes into existence on that date. From the perspective of the taxing authority, property taxes do not "accrue" over time. The fiscal periods of the taxing authority and the firm paying the tax (the property owner) often do not coincide.

B. The issues then are (1) what is the period over which to recognize the tax, and (2) what is the amount of any liability or prepayment for balance sheet reporting.

C. Accounting Principles

    1. The tax-paying firm accrues the property tax monthly as expense over the fiscal year of the taxing authority because the expense should be recognized in the same period the firm benefits from the services provided by the governmental unit (taxing authority).

> **Exam note**
> *This is the most important point to remember.*

    2. Until the amount of the tax bill for the year is known, the firm estimates the annual amount for purposes of recording the monthly property tax expense.

    3. When the amount of the tax bill for the year becomes known, the difference between the estimated annual amount and the actual annual amount is treated as an increase or decrease to the monthly property tax expense amount based on the annual estimate.

4. Until the tax is paid, the firm records a liability for the recognized expense to date. When the tax is paid, the liability is extinguished and a prepayment of tax is recognized for the remaining months of the taxing authority's fiscal year. That prepayment is reduced as the expense for the remaining months is recognized.

Example
The county in which a calendar-fiscal year firm is located has a June 30 fiscal year-end. The firm will accrue property taxes monthly and estimates the tax for the current tax fiscal year (July 1, 20X4—June 30, 20X5) to be $12,000 based on the previous year's bill. In December the actual tax bill is received showing $12,700 as the actual amount. The firm pays the tax bill on December 26, 20X4 before the December 31, 20X4 due date. The county's billing practice thus requires property owners to pay first half of the annual year tax in arrears (last six months in 20X4) and to prepay the last half (first six months of 20X5).

End-of month journal entries for July—November 20X4 (5 monthly entries)

Property tax expense	1,000	
Property tax payable		1,000

(Estimated property tax $12,000/12 months)

December 26, 20X4 entry

Property tax payable	5,000	
Prepaid property tax	7,700	
Cash		12,700

(To record payment, remove payable (5 months × $1,000) and recognize prepayment)

December 31, 20X4 entry

Property tax expense	1,100	
Prepaid property tax		1,100

(To record December property tax expense ($12,700 − $5,000)/7 months)

Starting with December, the remaining portion of the total actual property tax expense amount is allocated evenly over the remaining seven months of the county's fiscal year. This is a change in estimate and is handled prospectively. The previous five months' estimated expense amounts are not retrospectively adjusted.

In the 20X4 balance sheet, the firm reports $6,600 of prepaid property tax as a current asset ($7,700 − $1,100 or 6 × $1,100). The property tax expense is accrued by the firm over the county's fiscal period. The firm will recognize $6,600 of property tax expense for the first six months of 20X5 ($1,100 monthly).

VII. Costs and Expense under IFRS

A. In general, the recognition of costs and expenses under IFRS is similar to US GAAP. One main difference related to the topics covered in this lesson relate to advertising and promotional expenses. U.S. GAAP permits capitalization of certain direct-response advertising costs. IFRS does not allow capitalization of these costs; all must be expensed as incurred.

Costs and Expenses	
U.S. GAAP	**IFRS**
Certain direct-response advertising cost can be capitalized	All advertising and promotional costs are expensed as incurred

Compensated Absences

Accounting by the employer for vacation and holiday pay programs is the focus of this lesson.

After studying this lesson, you should be able to:

1. Explain the relevance of the four criteria for recognizing compensated absence expense and obligation.

2. Record the journal entry for recognizing the annual expense.

3. Note the exception for sick leave benefits.

4. Prepare the journal entry for payment, including situations for which the rate of pay has changed.

I. **Compensated Absences**

   A. Compensated absences include vacation, holiday, and sick-leave periods for which the employee is compensated. GAAP requires that accrual accounting be applied if certain criteria are met. The expense of these benefits is accrued during the period employees earn these benefits if all of the following four criteria are met:

      1. The obligation is attributable to services rendered as of the balance sheet date.

      2. The rights vest (benefits are no longer contingent on continued employment) or accumulate (carry over to future periods).

      3. Payment of the obligation is probable.

      4. The amount of the obligation is estimable.

   B. Some benefits do not require accrual. For example, some holiday-pay benefits, military leave, and maternity leave benefits do not accumulate if the employee does not use these benefits. Therefore, no accrual is required. In general, if the probable and estimable criteria are not met, there is no accrual. Such expenses are recognized when paid (pay-as-you-go).

   C. Vesting is more valuable to the employee than accumulation because the employee can leave the firm and be paid the benefits if they are vested. However, if benefits accumulate, the employee does not lose the benefits if the holiday or vacation is not taken by the balance sheet date. Limits on accumulation (e.g., at most 10 weeks of vacation pay can be accumulated for some firms) place a cap on the amount of liability accrued.

II. **Measurement of the Accrual**—The measurement of the accrual can be based on current or future wage rates although typically current rates are used. Current rates result in a lower expense accrual and do not telegraph future pay raises.

   A. If current rates are used for the accrual, and a pay raise is enacted between the accrual of the expense and its payment, the effect of the raise is treated as a change in estimate and is recognized currently and prospectively, retroactive application does not apply.

   B. The liability is not discounted but rather is reported at nominal (future) value.

Example
At year's end, employees had earned a total of $35,000 worth of vacation and holiday pay. Of that amount, $12,000 of vacation and holiday pay was paid during the year.

Adjusting entry at year's end:

Salary Expense	23,000	
Liability for Compensated Absences		23,000

Next year, there is an across the board 4% pay rate increase. The remaining holiday and vacation pay is paid.

Liability for Compensated Absences	23,000	
Salary Expense .04($23,000)	920	
Cash		23,920

III. **Sick Pay Benefits**—Accumulated sick pay benefits need not be accrued (but may be) because the event causing payment (illness) cannot be predicted. However, if unused sick pay benefits are routinely paid to employees (e.g., upon leaving the firm), then accrual is required because in this case the benefits vest.

IV. **Benefits not Accrued**—In practice, not all earned compensated absence benefits are accrued because not all earned benefits are taken by employees. For example, not all vacation pay benefits are taken because some employees let a portion of their benefits lapse.

Example
The beginning balance of the liability for compensated absences for the year is $50,000. During the current year, $25,000 of additional benefits are earned. The firm estimates that 15% of benefits earned each year will not be paid. Benefits paid for the year totaled $35,000.

Journal entries:

Liability for compensated absences	35,000	
Cash		35,000
Salary expense	21,250	
Liability for compensated absences		21,250

$21,250 = .85($25,000). The expense recognized reflects the amount earned in the period that will probably be paid.

The ending liability balance is $36,250 (= $50,000 − $35,000 + $21,250) and represents the expected future payment for compensated absence benefits earned through the end of the current year.

Contingencies, Commitments, and Guarantees (Provisions)

Contingent Liability Principles

This lesson introduces an important type of liability and the underlying principles for recognition.

After studying this lesson, you should be able to:

1. Define *contingent* liability.

2. Explain when they are recognized in the accounts, and when they are footnoted only.

3. Record the journal entries for a regular warranty, a common type of contingent liability.

4. Determine the amount to recognize for a contingent liability when only a range of values can be estimated.

I.   **Introduction**

> **Definition**
> *Contingency:* An existing condition (at the balance sheet date) involving uncertainty as to a possible gain or loss that will be resolved when a future event occurs or fails to occur. Resolution of the uncertainty may confirm an increase in assets (or reduction in a liability), or the incurrence of a liability or an asset impairment.

A.   Remember that all liabilities must be the result of a past event. The same holds for a contingent liability. As of the balance sheet date, there must have been a transaction or event implying that a liability may have been incurred (or asset impaired). However, a future event also plays an important role in the recognition of a contingent liability. A contingent liability is not definite as of the balance sheet date.

1.   For example, a firm is a defendant in a lawsuit. The suit is not resolved as of the balance sheet date. The firm does have a definite liability at year-end, but is contingently liable. The outcome of the suit in the following year will result in either a definite liability or no liability at all. Contingent liabilities are generally disclosed and possibly recognized, as discussed below.

2.   General risks and contingencies such as the possibility of a strike or casualty are not recognized or disclosed because no event or transaction has occurred as of the balance sheet date to substantiate that a liability has been incurred. A firm cannot accrue future casualty losses for example.

B.   The accounting for contingencies is dependent on the probability of the future event occurring, and whether the amount of the gain or loss is estimable. This lesson considers only contingent liabilities. Other contingencies such as uncollectible accounts receivable and asset impairments are discussed elsewhere.

II.   **Probability of Future Event**

A.   In accounting for contingencies, a determination must be made related to the probability of occurrence of the future event (which will resolve the contingency) and the possibility of estimation.

B.   In assessing the probability of occurrence, professional judgment is employed to classify the probability into one of three categories. These categories are described below.

1.   **Probable**—Based on professional judgment, the probability of occurrence is considered very high or a near certainty.

2. **Reasonably possible**—Based on professional judgment, the probability of occurrence is neither very high nor remote. In other words, when probability of occurrence is considered along a spectrum of possibilities, the probability of occurrence is not at either end of the spectrum, but is in the large middle section of the spectrum.

3. **Remote**—Based on professional judgment, the probability of occurrence is considered to be very low, or as the title implies, remote.

C. **Reasonable Estimate of Amount**—Based on professional judgment and experience, a determination is made about the possibility of estimating the amount of the contingency. Either the amount of resulting gain or loss is reasonably estimable or it is not. In addition, firms may be able to estimate a possible range of amounts for the gain or loss, but be unable to assign any amount in the range a higher probability of occurring than any other amount.

D. **The Loss Contingency is Probable and Can be Reasonably Estimated at the Balance Sheet Date**—GAAP requires that if a contingent loss is both *probable* and *estimable*, then an estimated loss and estimated liability will be recognized—actually recorded in the accounts in the amount estimated. The guiding theoretical considerations here are conservatism and the definition of a liability. Because the loss (asset decrease or liability increase) will most likely occur in the future and because the firm can estimate the amount, there is no reason to postpone the loss and liability recognition until it actually occurs. The general definition of a liability is essentially met when the contingent liability is probable and estimable.

Example
Recognized Contingent Liability

A large retailer offers warranties on its products. The firm estimates that total warranty costs will amount to 2% of sales for the year. Warranty claims are expected to occur on an even basis over the two years following sale. Sales were $1,000,000 for the year. There is no beginning warranty liability account balance for the year and there have been warranty claims totaling $6,000 during the year. This is a probable and estimable contingent liability. The actual loss or expense is contingent on a future event: customers making warranty claims. But a past transaction has occurred indicating it is probable that services will have to be provided in the future and the amount is estimable. Therefore, the loss or expense, and liability are recognized in the year of sale with the following adjusting entry.

Warranty Expense	20,000	
Warranty Liability		20,000

The fact that the warranty liability is a contingent liability does not change the fact that it must be recorded in the accounts. Note the entire estimated amount is recorded in the year of sale. The pattern of claims is not a factor in the recognition of the expense. When claims are actually made, the warranty liability is reduced and cash, inventory, and other assets are reduced:

Warranty Liability	6,000	
Cash, Parts Inventory, etc.		6,000

Firms must disclose the accounting policy with respect to warranty accounting, and disclose a schedule of the changes in the warranty liability for the period (increases due to expense, decreases due to claim service).

If the estimate of claims significantly overstates the actual claims cost, then the adjusting entry at the end of the year uses a smaller percentage to compensate. The opposite is true as well. There is no retroactive adjustment; rather the estimate is changed for the current and future periods to reflect the actual level of claims.

If the firm is able to estimate a range of possible losses, with no amount in the range having a higher probability of occurring than any other amount, the amount recognized in the accounts is the **lowest** amount in the range. Use of the lowest amount is the least conservative alternative. The footnotes should describe the entire range, however. In all other cases (other than probable and estimable), no accrual of the loss is required. Footnote disclosure is required unless the probability of occurrence is remote.

Exam Tip

The **range** of possible values issue appears on the CPA Exam from time to time. The candidate must remember that conservatism plays an important role in recognizing contingent liabilities, but when only a range of possible values is known, an exception is made: The lowest rather than the highest amount is used for reporting purposes. If a range of values is given but one value in the range has a higher probability assigned to it than any other, the value with the higher probability is used for reporting.

E. **The Loss Contingency is Probable and Cannot be Reasonably Estimated**—In this situation, the loss contingency should be disclosed in the footnotes to the financial statements.

F. **The Loss Contingency is Reasonably Possible**—In this situation, regardless of whether the loss can be reasonably estimated, the loss contingency is disclosed in the footnotes to the financial statements.

G. **The Loss Contingency is Remote**—In this situation, whether the loss can be reasonably estimated or not, the loss contingency can be disclosed in the footnotes to the financial statements. Please note that footnote disclosure is permitted but not required.

Examples of Contingent Liabilities and Additional Aspects

This lesson provides additional examples of recognized contingent liabilities, and addresses unasserted claims, gain contingencies and guarantees.

After studying this lesson, you should be able to:

1. Determine when an unasserted claim is recognized in the accounts.

2. State the appropriate reporting of gain contingencies.

3. Explain the reporting of guarantees.

4. Record a variety of recognized contingent liabilities.

I. Examples of Contingent Liabilities

Examples

1. *Recognized Contingent Litigation Liability*

The Lion Company was sued during the last quarter of 20X7 because of an accident involving a vehicle owned and operated by the company. After discussing the case with the company's legal representatives, it was decided that the company would probably lose the case, and the amount of damages could be reasonably estimated at $50,000.

Entry:

Estimated Loss from Pending Lawsuit	$50,000	
Estimated Liability from Pending Lawsuit		$50,000

Had the firm believed that the loss was only reasonably possible, the above entry would not be made. The lawsuit and possible loss would be discussed in the footnotes. Only a small percentage of contingent lawsuit losses are recognized.

2. *Recognized Contingent Premium Liability*

The Wolf Company offered to its customers a premium—a special coffee cup free of charge (cost per cup: $ .75) with the return of 20 coupons. One coupon is placed in each can of coffee when packed. The company estimated, on the basis of past experience that only 70% of the coupons will be redeemed. The following additional data is available for two years.

	Year 1	Year 2
Number of Coffee Cups Purchased	6,000	4,000
Number of Cans of Coffee Sold	100,000	200,000
Number of Coupons Redeemed	40,000	120,000

Entries:
Record the Purchase of Cups:

Year 1:	Premium Inventory	$4,500	
	Cash ($.75 × 6,000)		$4,500
Year 2:	Premium Inventory	$3,000	
	Cash		$3,000

Record the Estimated Premium Expense and Liability:

Year 1:	Estimated Premium Expense	$2,625	
	Estimated Premium Liability		$2,625
	$2,625 = (100,000/20) \times \$.75 \times .70$		
Year 2:	Estimated Premium Expense	$5,250	
	Estimated Premium Liability		$5,250
	$5,250 = (200,000/20) \times \$.75 \times .70$		

This is another example of a recognized contingent liability. Because it is probable and estimable, it is recorded like any other recognized liability.

Record the Redemption of the Coupons:

Year 1:	Estimated Premium Liability	$1,500	
	Premium Inventory		$1,500
	$1,500 = (40,000/20) \times \$.75 = 1,500$		
Year 2:	Estimated Premium Liability	$4,500	
	Premium Inventory		$4,500
	$4,500 = (120,000/20) \times \$.75 = 4,500$		

II. Unasserted Claims and Assessments

A. Entities may be subject to future claims and assessments not yet filed as of the balance sheet date. Examples include possible IRS actions against the entity for violations of the tax law, EPA claims against the entity for environmental violations, and other events that have occurred as of the balance sheet date.

B. If, at the balance sheet date, it is not probable that a claim or assessment will occur or if the outcome is not expected to be unfavorable to the entity, then no recognition or disclosure is required.

C. If it is probable that a claim or assessment will occur, and there is at least a reasonable probability that the outcome will be unfavorable to the entity, then the claim or assessment is treated as a contingency, even though no claim or assessment has been filed. The event before the balance sheet that would trigger the claim or assessment (such as a previous year's tax return filing or environmental violation) must have occurred, before the entity recognizes or discloses the contingency.

    1. If the amount is estimable, the contingent liability is recognized.

    2. Otherwise, it is footnoted only.

III. Contingencies Acquired in Business Combinations

A. In mergers and acquisitions, the acquiring firm may acquire contingencies of the acquired firm. The amounts ascribed to contingencies, as is the case for any other identifiable asset or liability, affect the valuation of recorded goodwill on the acquisition. The amount recognized for this type of contingent liability is somewhat different than that discussed above.

B. If the contingency is contractual (e.g., a regular warranty) at acquisition, then contingent liability is recognized by the acquirer at fair value.

C. At acquisition, if the contingency is not contractual and has more than a 50% probability of becoming a definite liability when a future event occurs or does not occur, then the liability is recognized at fair value. Otherwise, there is no recognition.

D. After acquisition, as new information is obtained, the contingency is reported at the greater of acquisition date fair value, and the amount that would be recognized under normal contingency rules. Any changes in the reported liability are recognized as gains or losses.

IV. Gain Contingencies

A. The Gain Contingency is Probable—In this situation, whether the gain can be reasonably estimated or not, the gain contingency is disclosed in the footnotes to the financial statements. Probable and estimable gain contingencies, in contrast with loss contingencies, are not recognized in the accounts. Conservatism dictates that the future event must first occur before recognizing the gain and asset increase (or liability decrease).

B. The Gain Contingency is Reasonably Possible—In this situation, regardless of whether the gain can be reasonably estimated, the gain contingency is disclosed in the footnotes to the financial statements.

C. The Gain Contingency is Remote—In this situation, regardless of whether the gain can be reasonably estimated, footnote disclosure of the gain contingency is not recommended.

V. Guarantees

A. Entities may guarantee a future payment based on a future event. An example is the guarantee of the debt of an affiliate to help the affiliate obtain a loan. Others include the guarantee of a line of credit and guarantees to repurchase receivables that have been sold or assigned.

B. There are two parts to the guarantee:

1. The first part is the obligation of the guarantor to be ready to comply with the guarantee if the triggering event occurs (e.g., default by the debtor whose debt is guaranteed by the guarantor). The guarantor recognizes this liability at fair value initially even if there is no expectation of payment. The debit depends on the nature of the guarantee.

Example

If the guarantee is for the debt of a customer incurred to buy the products of the entity guaranteeing the customer's debt, the debit is a reduction in the profit on the sale. In a stand-alone guarantee to an unrelated party without consideration, the debit is to an expense. For a lessee guarantee of residual value in an operating lease, the debit is to prepaid rent.

2. The second part is the uncertain contingent obligation—the contingent liability. This part is subject to the usual principles regarding contingent liabilities. When a contingent liability is recognized, the amount recorded is the greater of the initial fair value for part 1 above, and the amount to be recognized as a contingency. Subsequent measurement is not addressed by GAAP although recognition of the change in value is presumed with a corresponding change in earnings.

C. The guarantor is required to disclose the following:

1. The nature of the guarantee, the term of the guarantee, how the guarantee came into existence, and the triggering event

2. The maximum future amount payable under the guarantee

3. The carrying amount of the liability

4. A description of recourse provisions or available collateral enabling the guarantor to recover the amounts paid under the guarantee, if any

IFRS—Contingencies

The last lesson on contingent liabilities addresses international accounting standards.

After studying this lesson, you should be able to:

1. Define *provisions* and *contingent liability* under international accounting standards

2. Determine when provisions are recognized under international accounting standards.

3. Describe the similarities and differences in reporting between U.S. and international accounting standards.

4. Define *more likely than not* under international accounting standards

I. Contingencies

A. There are a few differences in IFRS and U.S. GAAP for the recognition and measurement of contingencies. The main difference is in terminology. The term *contingent liability* under U.S. GAAP refers to both recognized and unrecognized uncertain obligations. Under IFRS a recognized contingent obligation is referred to as a *provision* and an unrecognized contingent obligation is referred to as a *contingent liability*.

B. Another terminology difference is *probable* versus *more likely than not*. In U.S. GAAP the term *probable* is interpreted to mean "likely to occur." This distinction is usually a legal opinion made by attorneys. In IFRS, *more likely than not* is interpreted to mean more than 50%. U.S. GAAP is a higher threshold for accrual because likely to occur would mean more than 70% or so probability of occurrence—where *more likely than not* is a threshold of more than 50% likelihood of occurrence.

C. The table below summarizes the main terminology differences.

	U.S. GAAP	IFRS
Accrued contingent obligation reported on the balance sheet	Contingent liability	Provision
Contingent obligation disclosed in the footnotes	Contingent liability	Contingent liability
Threshold for accrual of the contingent obligation	Probable	More likely than not < 50%

II. Liability—Definition under IFRS—The IFRS definition for liabilities: "present obligations arising from past events, the settlement of which is expected to result in an outflow from the entity of resources embodying economic benefits."

A. There are two general sources of present obligations or liabilities:

1. Legal obligations that derive from a contract, legislation, or other legal process

2. Constructive obligations deriving from the entity's established practices, published policies or other statements that create a valid expectation on the part of other parties that the entity will discharge those responsibilities

B. Among all the possible types of liabilities, the focus in this section is on estimated liabilities. These include accruals and *provisions*. Accruals are much less uncertain than provisions. Examples of accruals include utilities payable and wages payable. Examples of provisions include income taxes payable, property taxes payable and compensated absences liabilities. Under IFRS, accruals and provisions are reported separately.

III. Provisions—A provision is a liability that is uncertain in terms of timing and amount but is not of uncertain existence. A provision is recognized if the entity has a present obligation (either legal or constructive) as a result of an obligating event that will result in an outflow that is more likely than not. In order to recognize the provision, you must be able to reliably estimate the amount.

    A. Note that except for the 50% threshold, an item meeting the above requirements would qualify as a recognized contingent liability under US standards. However, for U.S. contingent liabilities, there also must be a probable outflow of benefits, where *probable* means much higher than the 50% threshold for international standards. As a result, international standards recognize many more liabilities (as provisions) compared with recognized contingent liabilities under U.S. standards.

    B. If the outflow of benefits is not *more likely than not* but reasonably possible, then the entity discloses the possible obligation and refers to it as a contingent liability.

    C. If the outflow of benefits is *more likely than not* but not estimable, then the entity discloses the possible obligation and refers to it as a contingent liability.

    D. If the outflow of benefits is only remotely possible, there is no recognition or disclosure.

    E. In comparing the two sets of standards in this area, examples of provisions under international standards include (1) income taxes payable, property taxes payable and compensated absences liability; and also (2) warranty liability and premium liability. The first group refers to estimated liabilities under U.S. standards and the second group refers to recognized contingent liabilities under U.S. standards. Thus, provisions include but are not limited to U.S. recognized contingent liabilities.

IV. Measuring Provisions

    A. Provisions are measured at the best estimate of the amount required to settle the obligation at the balance sheet date.

    B. Discounting is required if there is a material difference between the expected amount paid, and its present value. This is contrary to U.S. standards, which, in most cases, do not apply discounting. Changes in the present value over periods are recognized as a borrowing cost.

        1. Present value measurement can be applied using either of the following techniques:

            a. The traditional present value technique applies the risk adjusted rate directly to estimates of cash flows. If the cash flows are contractual, this technique may be appropriate.

            b. The expected present value technique applies the risk-free rate to multiple cash flow projections each with an associated probability of outcome. If the cash flows are considerably uncertain and there is a wide range of possible amounts, this technique may be appropriate.

> **Note**
> *If a range of equally likely amounts is possible for a provision, international standards require recognition of the midpoint of the range (U.S. standards use the lowest amount in the range).*

V. Disclosures for Contingent Liabilities under International Standards Include—(1) an estimate of the financial effect, (2) information about the uncertainties relating to the amount and timing of the outflow of benefits, and (3) the possibility of any reimbursement or recourse for the entity.

VI. Gain Contingencies—Assets

    A. A disclosable contingent asset under international standards is one that is possible or probable (> 50%) but less than "virtually certain," arising from past events and whose existence will be confirmed by the occurrence or nonoccurence of a future uncertain event not wholly in the control of the entity. Contingent assets arise from unplanned or unexpected events that give rise to the possibility of an inflow of economic benefits to the entity.

        1. An example is a claim against an insurance company that an entity is pursuing legally. If, later, the receipt of benefits from the insurance company becomes virtually certain (much higher than probable), then it is recognized; it is no longer contingent at that point. **This is in contrast with U.S. standards, which require realization before recognition.**

    B. If the probability of receipt of benefits is remote, no disclosure is warranted.

Long-Term Debt (Financial Liabilities)

Notes Payable

This lesson is about notes payable accounting. The general principles applying to all notes payable are covered here.

After studying this lesson, you should be able to:

1. Distinguish simple interest notes, non-interest bearing notes, and installment notes.

2. Understand how two interest rates are used in accounting for notes.

3. Determine whether a note is issued at a premium or discount.

4. Compute the total interest expense over the term of the note.

5. Compute interest expense for a period on a noncurrent note.

6. Apply the gross method and the net method.

7. Apply the effective interest and straight-line methods.

8. Record the initial issuance of notes payable at present value.

9. Compute and record interest expense on notes payable for multiple periods.

10. Record the relevant journal entries for notes issued in exchange for rights or other privileges.

I. **Notes Payable Features and Reporting**

   A. Notes payable are more formal than accounts payable and involve interest. A formal document called a "promissory note" details the rights and duties of both parties to the note. Notes can be classified as current or noncurrent.

   B. Current notes payable are reported at the amount due when they mature. Noncurrent notes are reported at the present value of future payments, discounted at the prevailing interest rate at time of issuance.

   C. Simple interest notes have a face value that is also the maturity amount, the amount due at the end of the note term. The stated interest rate and face value determine the annual interest to be paid. A 5%, $10,000 (face value) note pays $500 interest per year, with the $10,000 maturity amount due at the end of the note term.

   D. **Installment Notes**—Each payment includes principal and interest—have no maturity value because the last payment reduces the note payable balance to zero. These notes are often used to purchase plant assets and may be secured by those assets. A mortgage note is an example.

   E. There are two rates of interest relevant to notes payable:

      1. Stated rate is the contractual rate listed in the note; this rate determines the cash interest payments.

      2. Yield or market rate is the rate on notes of similar risk and term (the prevailing rate).

         If the two rates are equal, the note is issued at face value.

   F. When the yield rate is greater than the stated rate, the note is issued at a discount (less than face). When the yield rate is less than the stated rate, the note is issued at a premium (more than face). The issue price or proceeds is the present value, also called principal.

G. The total interest expense over the note term equals the difference between the total payments required under the note and the principal amount. Total interest expense also equals total cash interest over the term plus the discount or minus the premium at issuance.

H. Notes issued for nonmonetary consideration (goods and services) are measured at the more reliable of (a) fair value of the consideration, or (b) present value of future cash payments discounted at the prevailing rate.

I. Periodic interest expense is computed as the product of the yield rate at the date of issuance, and the beginning net note liability (present value). This approach is called the effective interest method and is required by GAAP. The difference between cash interest paid and interest expense recognized at each payment date is the amortization of discount or premium.

J. At subsequent balance sheet dates, notes are reported at the present value of remaining payments, using the yield rate at the date of issuance. Present value also equals face value plus unamortized premium or less unamortized discount.

K. An alternative to the effective interest method is the straight-line method, which is allowed only if it results in interest expense amounts not materially different from the effective interest method. An equal amount of discount or premium amortization is recognized each period.

L. The gross or net method of recording the note and interest expense are both acceptable. The gross method separates the face value (note payable) and discount or premium in different accounts. The net method uses one combined net account (note payable), which is the present value and net note liability under the effective interest method.

M. The fair value of notes must be disclosed—that is, the estimate of the amount required to pay off the note at the balance sheet date. Also disclosed are the details of noncurrent notes such as interest rates, assets pledged, call and conversion provisions and restrictions, and the aggregate maturity amounts for each of the five years following the balance sheet date.

N. Direct loan origination fees and points are recognized over the loan term.

II. Examples

A. Noncurrent Interest-Bearing Note Payable—An interest-bearing note payable is one in which the interest element is explicitly stated. These notes are recorded at the present value of future cash flows, using the market rate of interest as the discount rate. If the stated interest rate and the market rate of interest are not equal, the present value of the future cash flows is not equal to the face amount of the note, and a discount or premium is recorded.

Example
Interest-Bearing Long-Term Notes Payable where Stated and Market Rates Unequal

The Montana Company paid for legal services received by giving the law firm a $10,000 three-year, 6% note payable (interest payable at the end of the year) on January 1 of Year 1. The market rate of interest for a note of this type is 10%. The value of the legal services is not specified. Therefore, the present value of the note is used as the amount to record both sides of the transaction. In some cases, the stated rate is intentionally lowered to ease the cash flow requirements of the debtor firm during the note term.

Present Value of Future Cash Flows

$10,000 × .75131 (PV of $1, N = 3, I = 10%)	=	$7,513
$600 × 2.48685 (PV of an Annuity, N = 3, I = 10%)	=	1,492
Total Present Value of Future Cash Flows		$9,005

Debt Amortization Schedule

Date	Cash Interest	Interest Expense	Discount Amortized	Unamortized Discount	Carrying Value
1/1/Y1				$995	$9,005
12/31/Y1	$600	$900	$300	$695	$9,305
12/31/Y2	$600	$931	$331	$364	$9,636
12/31/Y3	$600	$964	$364	$0	$10,000
Totals	$1,800	$2,795	$995		

Entries:

Year 1:	Legal Expenses	$9,005	
1/1/1	Discount on Note Payable	$995	
	Note Payable		$10,000

This discount account is contra to Note Payable.
The net note payable balance is $9,005.

12/31/1	Interest Expense	$900	
	Discount on Note Payable		$300
	Cash		$600

Year 2:	Interest Expense	$931	
12/31/2	Discount on Note Payable		$331
	Cash		$600

Year 3:	Interest Expense	$964	
12/31/3	Discount on Note Payable		$364
	Cash		$600
	Note Payable	$10,000	
	Cash		$10,000

In this example, we illustrate the gross method. The note payable is listed at face value, with separate recording of the discount. The net method is also acceptable and would record the note payable initially at $9,005 with no discount recorded. Interest expense for Year 1 is .10 × $9,005 (the net note balance at beginning of Year 1).

The legal expenses are recorded at the present value of the future payments at the market or prevailing interest rate. The stated rate of 6% is used only to compute the interest payments. Interest expense is based on the market rate of 10%.

The total interest expense over the note term ($2,795) is the difference between the principal of $9,005 and the sum of the future payments of $11,800 (3 x $600 + $10,000). It also equals the sum of the $1,800 cash interest over the term (3 × $600) and the $995 discount. The discount represents additional interest because the firm received only $9,005 worth of services but must pay $10,000 at the note's maturity.

If the straight-line (SL) method of amortization had been chosen, the journal entry for the three interest payments would be the same, as follows:

Interest expense	932	
Discount on note payable	332	(995/3)
Cash	600	

B. **Non-Interest-Bearing Notes Payable**—A non-interest-bearing note payable is one in which the interest element is not explicitly stated but rather is included in the face amount of the note. These notes are recorded at the present value of future cash flows, using the market rate of interest as the discount rate.

Example
A firm purchases a used plant asset by issuing a one-year, $10,165 face value note. The note pays no cash interest. The purchase occurred on July 1, Year 1 for this calendar-year firm. The plant asset has a market value of $9,500. The implied market rate of interest is 7% as shown below. A non-interest-bearing note is another example for which the stated rate (0% here) is less than the yield rate.

$10,165(PV of $1, I = ?, N = 1)   = $9,500

(PV of $1, I = ?, N = 1) = $9,500/$10,165 = .93458

This present value factor corresponds to I = 7%.

The purchaser included the 7% interest in the face value of the note. (Net method is shown.)

July 1, Year 1	Equipment	9,500	
	Note Payable		9,500
December 31, Year 1	Interest Expense $9,500(.07/2)	332.50	
	Note Payable		332.50

Interest expense is based on the beginning net liability balance

June 30, Year 2	Interest Expense	332.50	
	Note Payable		332.50
	Note Payable	10,165	
	Cash		10,165

Total interest on the note = $665 = $332.50(2) = $10,165 − $9,500. This solution illustrates the net method. There is no separate accounting for the discount. The gross method could also have been used. The straight-line method is inappropriate in this example, given the magnitude of the difference between the stated and yield rates.

C. **Installment Note**

Example
On 1/1/X5, a firm purchased a building by paying $100,000 down and signing a $400,000, 6%, 10-year secured mortgage note. The note calls for annual payments beginning 12/31/X5. The prevailing interest rate for a note of this type is 10%. Each payment includes principal and interest, and the note is fully paid with the last payment. The gross or net method can be used as always but the straight-line method is not appropriate because each payment reduces principal.

The annual payment (pmt) is computed using the stated rate and total note amount as indicated in the note:

400,000 = pmt(PV annuity, i = .06, n = 10) = pmt(7.36009)
400,000/7.36009 = pmt = $54,347

The amount borrowed is the present value of all payments required on the note using the prevailing or yield rate of 10%. The situation is silent on the fair value of the building. Therefore, the present value of the note (at the yield rate) is used for recording both the note and building.

Amount borrowed = $54,347(PV annuity, i = .10, n = 10) = $54,347(6.14457) =$333,939

Journal entries (net method):

1/1/X5	Building	433,939	
	Cash		100,000
	Mortgage note payable		333,939
12/31/X5	Interest expense	33,394	333,939(.10)
	Mortgage note payable	20,953	
	Cash		54,347
12/31/X6	Interest expense	31,299	(333,939 − 20,953)(.10)
	Mortgage note payable	23,048	
	Cash		54,347

The ending 20X5 balance of the note payable is $312,986 = $333,939 − $20,953, the principal portion of the first payment. The total balance is reported as follows: (1) $23,048 current liability (CL), and $289,938 noncurrent (NCL) = $312,986 − $23,048. The portion of the liability to be paid in 20X6 is the amount classified as current for 20X5 ($23,048).

The ending 20X6 balance of the note payable is $289,938 = $333,939 − $20,953 − $23,048. This balance also can be computed as $54,347(PV annuity, i = .10, n = 8) because there are eight payments remaining at this point.

Total interest over the 10 year note term equals the difference between the total payments on the note less the amount borrowed = (10 × $54,347) − $333,939 = $209,531.

Note that each payment affects both interest expense (income statement) and the balance in the net mortgage note payable (balance sheet). In analyzing the effect of the payment on the firm's financial statements, it is important to distinguish the expense from the reduction in principal. Interest is always computed first.

Erroneous reporting of the entire amount of the payment as a reduction in principal overstates the debtor's net income and understates liabilities.

D. **Note in Exchange for Rights or Other Privileges**—A firm may borrow from a customer and ask for an interest rate less than the prevailing rate in exchange for a reduced price on goods or services to be sold to the customer. Part of the consideration received on the borrowing is a prepayment by the customer for the reduced price. The note is recorded as always using the prevailing rate. The difference between the amount borrowed and the present value of the note is unearned revenue.

 **Example**
At the beginning of 20X4, Duke Inc. borrowed $40,000 by issuing a three-year non-interest-bearing note with face value of $40,000. The prevailing rate on similar notes is 10%. In exchange, Duke agrees to provide the creditor (customer of Duke) with goods at a reduced price over four years.

The present value of the note is $40,000(PV1, i = .10, n = 3) = $40,000(.75131) = $30,052.

Journal entries (gross method):

1/1/X4	Cash	40,000		
	Discount on note	9,948		40,000 – 30,052
	Note payable		40,000	
	Unearned revenue		9,948	

Duke receives an interest-free loan in exchange for reducing the prices on its goods to the creditor firm, (Duke's customer). The loan is in substance only for $30,052 and is the basis for interest expense recognition. The remaining $9,948 received by Duke is a prepayment by the customer for reduced prices on the goods it will buy from Duke.

12/31/X4	Interest expense	3,005		.10(30,052)
	Unearned revenue	2,487		9,948/4
	Discount on note		3,005	
	Sales revenue		2,487	

The remaining journal entries for interest proceed as illustrated in other examples. The ending net balance of the note immediately before payment will be $40,000 because the discount will be fully amortized. The recognition of sales revenue proceeds as above over four years assuming the customer purchases equivalent amounts of goods each year.

III. Joint and Several Liability Arrangements—Joint and several obligations arise when more than one entity agrees to be liable for the entire amount of an obligation. If one of the entities is unable to make payment when the liability is due, each of the other entities is fully liable for the debt. Such arrangements may arise through a borrowing that involves a note payable.

    A. A firm in such an arrangement for which the total amount of the debt is fixed at the reporting date, reports the obligation at the sum of:

        1. The amount the firm agreed to pay (the required amount according to the arrangement); plus

        2. Any additional amount the firm expects to pay on behalf of the others in the arrangement.

    B. If there is an amount within the range for the second part (2.) that is a better estimate than any other in the range, then that amount is used for (2.). If not, the minimum amount in the range is used.

    C. There is no corresponding international standard although joint and several liabilities are treated as contingencies under IFRS.

Bonds Payable

Bond Accounting Principles

In this lesson, the basic principles of recording bonds and recognizing interest are illustrated. Being able to apply present value is a prerequisite.

After studying this lesson, you should be able to:

1. Identify the seven items of information required to account for a bond issue.

2. Compute the selling price of a bond issue.

3. Determine whether a bond will sell at a premium or discount, without computing the bond price.

4. Apply the effective interest method of amortizing bond discount and premium.

5. Decide when the straight-line method of amortizing bond discount and premium is appropriate.

6. Apply the straight-line method of amortizing bond discount and premium.

Exam note: This is a major topic on the CPA Exam. A bond is a long-term debt instrument issued to many different creditor/investors. A bond contrasts with a note that represents the debt for a borrowing from a single creditor.

I. Bond Basics

Definition
Bond: A **bond** is a financial debt instrument that typically calls for the payment of periodic interest with the face value being due at some time in the future. The bondholder (creditor or investor) pays the issuing firm an amount based on the stated and market rates of interest and receives interest and the face amount in return, over the bond term. Bonds and notes are the major sources of general debt funding for corporations.

A. There are seven items of information that must be known to account for a bond:

1. **Face (maturity) value**—The amount paid to the bondholder at maturity. This amount is often $1,000.

2. **Stated (coupon) interest rate**—The rate at which the bond pays cash interest. The rate is stated on the bond. If the rate is 6% and the bond's face value is $1,000, then one bond pays $60 interest each year.

3. **Interest payment dates**—The dates the bond pays the cash interest. Semi-annual interest payments are the norm.

4. **Market (yield, effective) interest rate**—The rate equating the sum of the present values of the cash interest annuity and the face value single payment, with the bond price. If a 6%, $1,000 bond was issued for $900, the market rate of interest equates the $900 amount with the present value of the annuity of $60 (or $30 twice a year), and the $1,000 face value to be paid in the future. The market rate is the true compounded rate of return on the bond. This rate is determined by the market and does not appear on the bond.

5. **Bond date**—The planned issuance date. This date is listed on the bond.

6. **Issuance date**—The date the bonds are actually issued. This date cannot be earlier than the bond date but may be later. This information is not on the bond.

7. **Maturity date**—The date the maturity value is paid, the end of the bond term.

B. **Other Terminology**

1. **Bond term**—The period from issuance date to maturity date

2. **Bond issue costs**—The cost of printing, registering, and marketing the bonds

3. **Accrued interest on bond sale**—The amount of interest, based on the coupon interest rate for the period, between the issuance date and the immediately preceding interest payment date

4. **Bond price**—The current market price of a bond exclusive of accrued interest

5. **Bond proceeds**—The sum of the bond price and any accrued interest

C. **Types of bonds**—There are several classifications of bond issues. The most important for the exam are:

1. **Secured versus unsecured (debentures)**—A secured bond issue has a claim to specific assets. Otherwise, the bondholders are unsecured creditors and are grouped with other unsecured creditors. An unsecured bond is backed only by the credit of the issuing firm and is called a debenture.

2. **Serial versus single maturity term**—A serial bond matures serially, that is at regular or staggered intervals. The total face value of this issue is paid gradually rather than all at once, as is the case with a single maturity or term bond.

3. **Callable versus redeemable**—An issuer can retire callable bonds before maturity at a specified price. The bondholder can require a redeemable bond to be retired early.

4. **Convertible versus nonconvertible**—A convertible bond can be converted into capital stock by the bondholder; a nonconvertible bond cannot.

D. **Determination of Selling Price of the Bond (Initial Book Value)**—The selling price of a bond is equal to the present value of future cash flows face value and cash interest. The discount rate used for this calculation is the market rate of interest on the date the bonds are issued.

1. **Stated rate > market rate**—If the stated interest rate is greater than the market rate of interest, the bonds will sell at a premium.

   a. **The premium**—The amount received above face value and is recorded in Premium on Bonds Payable, an adjunct account to Bonds Payable. If a $1,000 bond sells for $1,100, then the premium is $100. The bond price increases (and yield rate decreases) to the point at which the yield rate equals the market rate for similar bonds.

2. **Stated rate < market rate**—If the stated interest rate is less than the market rate of interest, the bonds will sell at a discount.

   a. **The discount**—The amount below face value and is recorded in Discount on Bonds Payable, a contra account to Bonds Payable. If a $1,000 bond sells for $950, then the discount is $50. The price decreases (and yield rate increases) to the point at which the yield rate equals the market rate for similar bonds.

3. **Stated rate equals market rate**—If the stated rate and market rate are equal, the bond sells at face value and no premium or discount is recorded. (Sell at face value: stated rate = market rate)

Example
A bond issued at a discount:

A 6%, $1,000 bond dated 1/1/x7 is issued on that date to yield 8%. The bond pays interest each June 30 and December 31 and matures four years from issuance. The bond price equals:

$1,000(PV of $1, i = 4%, n = 8)
+ .03($1,000)(PV of $1 annuity, i = 4%, n = 8)
= $1,000(.73069) + $30(6.73274)
= $933

The price (present value) is computed using the market rate of interest. 4% is used rather than 8% because the bonds pay interest semiannually. The 3% interest rate is used only to compute the semiannual interest payment. The bond sells at a discount because investors can earn 8% on competing bonds.

Bond prices are expressed in percentage of face value. This bond was issued at 93.3, or 93.3% of face value. Bond prices are always quoted exclusive of any accrued interest. This example uses only one bond for simplicity. A bond issue of 1,000 bonds would provide $933,000 of debt capital. The amounts in the journal entries and financial statement sections below would be multiplied by 1,000.

The entry to record the issuance of the bond is:

Cash	933	
Discount on Bonds Payable	67	
Bonds Payable		1,000

The noncurrent liability section of the balance sheet immediately after issuance would disclose:

Bonds Payable	$ 1,000
Less Discount on Bonds Payable	(67)
Net Bonds Payable	$ 933

The $933 amount is the net bond liability or book value of the bond issue. The bonds payable account is always measured at face value. The discount and premium are contra or adjunct accounts that reduce or increase the net liability to present value. With interest rate changes after issuance, the fair value of the bond most likely is not $933. In the last year of the bond term, the net liability is reported as a current liability, often called *current maturities of long-term debt*.

E. Amortization of Premium/Discounts

1. The discount or premium on a bond issue is amortized over the bond term. The book value of the bond issue must equal face value on the maturity date because that is the amount paid to retire the bonds.

2. The amortization of premiums and discounts is accomplished through the use of the *effective interest method*. Due to materiality, many companies employ the *straight-line amortization method*. The straight-line method is acceptable only if the results do not depart materially from the effective interest method.

Exam note
Both methods of amortization are tested on the exam. Questions with more involved requirements often use the straight-line method because the amounts are easier to compute.

3. **Effective interest method**—This method first computes interest expense based on the beginning book value of the bond and the market rate at issuance. The difference between

interest expense and the cash interest paid is the amortization of the discount or the premium. The market rate at issuance is always used to compute interest expense. The rate is not changed after issuance because it represents the true interest rate over the bond term. The amortization of discount or premium is a "plug" figure.

Example

Using the previous example of computing the bond price, the June 30 entry in year of issuance under the effective interest method is:

Interest Expense $933(.04)	37	
Discount on Bonds Payable		7
Cash $1,000(.03)		30

The net book value of the bonds is now $940 ($933 + $7). That is the amount on which interest expense at December 31 is computed. The book value changes with each interest entry and will equal $1,000 at maturity. Therefore, each entry recognizes a different amount of interest expense. But the ratio of interest expense to beginning book value is constant and equals the effective interest rate. The resulting book value is the present value of remaining cash payments using the yield rate at issuance.

The initial discount of $67 represents additional interest because only $933 was received from the bondholders, but $1,000 must be paid at maturity. Therefore, total interest expense over the bond issue equals cash interest plus the discount = 8($30) + $67 = $307.

The $67 of additional interest expense (initial discount) is gradually recognized over the term of the bonds; that is why in the entry above, interest expense is $7 more than cash interest paid.

The effect of a premium is opposite that of a discount. It represents a reduction in total interest expense over the bond term because the premium is not paid at maturity. Semiannual interest expense is less than cash interest paid, by the amount of the premium amortization. The book value of the bond issue gradually decreases to face value over the bond term.

4. **Straight-line (SL) method**—This method recognizes a constant amount of amortization each month of the bond term. The straight-line method should not be used when (a) the term to maturity is quite long and there is more than a minor difference between the market and stated rates, or (b) when there is a very significant difference between the market and stated rates regardless of the length of the term. An example of (b) is a zero coupon bond. Such bonds pay no interest (stated rate = 0). However, they yield competitive rates. The effective interest method must be used for these bonds.

Example

Using the previous example of computing the bond price, the June 30 entry in year of issuance under the straight-line method is:
(Note : The interest expense amount is a "plug" figure.)

Interest Expense	38	
Discount on Bonds Payable		8 ($67/48 months)(6 months)
Cash $1,000(.03)		30

The bond term is four years long or 48 months. Six months have elapsed since the issuance of the bonds. The entry at each interest date is the same as the one above for the straight-line method. The interest expense is the same amount for each entry.

Bond Complications

This lesson incorporates additional aspects into accounting for bonds.

After studying this lesson, you should be able to:

1. Record the issuance of a zero coupon bond and subsequent interest expense.

2. Compute and record accrued interest for bonds issued between interest dates.

3. Account for bond issue costs at the issuance of the bonds and throughout the bond term.

4. Analyze the effect of accrued interest and debt issue costs on the firm's financial statements.

I. **Zero Coupon Bonds**—These bonds pay no interest (coupon rate is zero), but the accounting procedure remains the same except that no cash interest is paid during the term. The entire amount of interest is included in the face value, just like a non-interest-bearing note. Zero coupon bonds, and also "deep-discount" bonds with very low coupon rates, are issued at a large discount.

 **Example**

$400,000 (face value) of zero coupon bonds are issued to yield 5% on January 1, Year 1. The bonds mature in 20 years.

Issue price = $400,000(PV $1, i = 5%, n = 20) = $400,000(0.37689) = $150,756

Journal entries:

1/1/year 1	Cash	150,756	
	Discount on bonds	249,244	
	Bonds payable		400,000
12/31/year 1	Interest Expense	7,538	$150,756(.05)
	Discount on bonds		7,538

The SL method is not appropriate for this type of bond.

II. **Bonds Issued between Interest Dates**—When bonds are issued between interest dates, the total cash received by the company issuing the bonds equals to the selling price of the bonds plus interest (at the stated rate) accrued since the last interest date. This sum is called the "proceeds." By requiring the investor to pay the interest accrued since the last interest date, the issuing company can pay the usual amount of interest at the next interest date.

Example
A bond issue dated January 1 and paying interest each June 30 and December 31 is issued on April 30. The issuing firm collects 4 months of interest from January 1—April 30. Then, on June 30, the firm pays 6 months of interest. If the original bondholder holds the bonds on June 30, the bondholder receives 6 months of interest because the bond automatically pays 6 months of interest on that date. The bondholder nets 2 months of interest for the period the bonds were held:

> 6 months of interest received on June 30
> − 4 months paid at purchase
> = 2 months earned interest

In the entry for bond issuance, accrued interest payable is credited for the interest collected from the bondholders and cash is increased by this amount. There is no interest expense recognized at this point because the bond term has just begun. Accrued interest has no effect on the amount of premium or discount.

Example
Bender Inc. issued $8,000 of 8% bonds at 105 on March 1. The bonds pay interest each December 31 and June 30 and are dated January 1, Year 1. The bonds mature five years after the bond date. The first three entries under the straight-line method (SL) are:

March 1, Year 1

Cash $8,000(1.05) + .08(2/12)($8,000)	8,507	
Premium on Bonds Payable ($8,000).05		400
Accrued Interest Payable .08(2/12)($8,000)		107
Bonds Payable		8,000

June 30, Year 1

Interest Expense	185	
Premium on Bonds Payable ($400/58 months)(4 months)	28	
Accrued Interest Payable	107	
Cash .08(6/12)($8,000)		320

(There are 58 months in the bond term, or four years and ten months, and four months have elapsed since the bond issuance, requiring four months of amortization.) The accrued interest is a separate resource. It is not included in the price and has no effect on the discount or premium.

December 31, Year 1

Interest Expense	279	
Premium on Bonds Payable ($400/58 months)(6 months)	41	
Cash .08(6/12)($8,000)		320

The remaining entries in the bond term are identical to the December 31 entry.

III. Debt Issue Costs

These costs include legal fees, printing costs, and promotion costs related to the issuance of a debt instrument such as a bond or note. Debt issuance costs are the incremental costs of issuing debt (third-party costs), excluding those paid to the lender.

   A. Accounting and reporting:

1. Debt issue costs are reported in the balance sheet as a direct deduction from the liability's carrying amount. This is the same treatment afforded stock issue costs. Debt issue costs are not capitalized as an asset.

2. Debt issue costs are amortized to interest expense over the term of the related debt instrument.

B. IFRS accounting is the same.

Example
On January 1, Year 1, 5%, $1,000 bonds are issued at 100. The bonds mature in 10 years and pay interest each June 30 and December 31. $1,200 of debt issue costs incurred.

Calculation of the effective interest rate m:

$20,000 − $1,200 = $20,000(PV $1, m, n = 20) + (.05/2)($20,000)(PV $1 annuity, m, n = 20)

$18,800 = $20,000(PV $1, m, n = 20) + $500(PV $1 annuity, m, n = 20)

Using a spreadsheet program or business calculator, m is computed to be 5.8%.

Journal entry for bond issue:

1/1/Year 1	Cash	18,800	
	Bonds payable		18,800

Debt issue costs reduce the proceeds of borrowing and increase the effective interest rate on the bond issue. They also reduce the carrying value of the debt.

Balance sheet presentation:

January 1, Year 1
Noncurrent debt:

Bonds payable	$20,000
Unamortized bond issue costs	(1,200)
Net bond liability	$18,800

The above recording implies the *net* approach. Alternatively, the issue costs may be recorded in a valuation account (*bond issue costs* similar to bond discount) with the bonds payable account recorded at face value.

Journal entry for interest and amortization of bond issue costs:

6/30/Year 1	Interest expense	545	18,800(.058/2)	
	Bonds payable	45		
	Cash		500	20,000(.05/2)

Interest expense includes amortization of debt issue costs. Had there been a discount on the bond issue, the amortization of the discount would be included in interest expense as well.

The straight-line (SL) method is an acceptable alternative to the effective interest approach shown above, if its results are not materially different.

If the SL approach is used, the amortization of bond issue costs would be $60 each 6-month period ($1,200/20 periods).

Analysis
The effect of bond issue costs on the issuing firm's financial statements is to (1) reduce the initial net bond liability and (2) increase interest expense in the future.

If instead, the bond issue costs were erroneously recognized as expense, the firm's net income is understated and liabilities are overstated in the year of issuance.

Bond Fair Value Option, International

This lesson addresses the use of the fair value option for bond accounting, and international accounting aspects of bonds.

After studying this lesson, you should be able to:

1. Prepare a bond amortization schedule.

2. Apply the fair value option to determine the periodic unrealized gain or loss.

3. Report the unrealized gain or loss in the correct financial statement.

4. Identify differences between U.S. and international principles as they apply to bond accounting.

I. **Amortization Tables**—A bond amortization table shows the amounts for all journal entries and ending net bond liability for the entire bond term. The following is an example of an amortization table showing the use of the effective interest method. One line of an amortization conveys the same information as the journal entry for that year.

Example

On January 1, year 1, the Idaho Company issued bonds with a face value of $100,000 and a stated interest rate of 7%. The bonds will mature on December 31, year 5. Interest on the bonds is paid each December 31. The market rate of interest on January 1, year 1, was 8%.

Selling Price of the Bonds

$100,000 × .68058 (Present Value of $1, n = 5, i = 8%)	$68,058
$7,000 × 3.99271 (Present Value of Annuity, n = 5, i = 8%)	27,949
Total Price	$96,007

Partial Amortization Schedule

Date	Cash Interest	Effective Interest	Discount Amortized	Unamortized Discount	Carrying Value of Bonds
1/1/year 1				$3,993	$96,007
12/31/year 1	$7,000	$7,681	$681	$3,312	$96,688
12/31/year 2	$7,000	$7,735	$735	$2,577	$97,423
12/31/year 3	$7,000	$7,794	$794	$1,784	$98,216
12/31/year 4	$7,000	$7,857	$857	$926	$99,074
12/31/year 5	$7,000	$7,926	$926	$0	$100,000

Under the effective interest method, the carrying value of the bonds at the beginning of the year is used to compute interest expense. The year 1 interest expense of $7,681 equals ($96,007 × .08). The year 2 interest expense of $7,735 equals ($96,688 × .08).

A. When interest payment dates and fiscal year-end do not coincide, the portion of the interest period that falls within a reporting period is used to compute interest expense. The effective interest method "straight lines" the interest calculation during an interest period.

Example

If the Idaho bonds above were dated and issued on March 1, year 1, the amount of interest recognized and discount amortized would be 10/12 of the amounts in the 12/31/year 1 row of the amortization table above. Also, interest payable is credited at 12/31/year 1 for 10/12 of $7,000, rather than cash.

II. Fair Value Option (FVO)

A. The FVO allows certain financial assets and liabilities to be reported at fair value, with unrealized gains and losses reported in earnings in the year they occur. This option reduces the accounting mismatch inherent in using fair value for assets and a different measurement basis for liabilities and reduces earnings volatility because the effect of interest rate changes on investments in debt securities is opposite that on liabilities such as bonds payable.

B. The firm makes an irrevocable decision to choose the FVO on the date of issuance. The choice is by debt instrument. The option can be applied to all or a subset of debt instruments, even within the same type.

    1. If the option is not chosen, then the accounting proceeds as discussed previously.

    2. If the option is chosen, then the accounting also proceeds as discussed above but in addition, the firm increases or decreases the resulting book liability to fair value using a fair value adjustment account (FVA: adjunct or contra account).

        a. Fair value is the quoted market price of the security. If that is not available, the current market rate of interest on similar debt instruments is used to estimate fair value.

        b. The required change in the FVA for the period is recognized as an unrealized gain or loss.

            i. If the required fair value adjustment has increased, the firm recognizes an unrealized loss. The amount required to pay off the liability relative to the book value under the effective interest method at the balance sheet date has increased.

            ii. If the required fair value adjustment has decreased, the firm recognizes an unrealized gain.

            iii. Classification of the unrealized gain or loss:

                (a) The portion of the total unrealized gain or loss attributable to credit risk (risk of default or delay in payment of interest or principal) is recognized in other comprehensive income.

                (b) The portion attributable to the change in interest rates is recognized in net income.

Example

Fair value option applied. Assume the entire unrealized gain or loss is attributable to interest rate changes.

Amortization Schedule

Date	Cash Interest	Interest Expense	Premium Amortization	Unamortized Premium	Net Liability
1/1/X1				4213	10,4213
12/31/X1	7000	6253	747	3466	103,466
12/31/X2	7000	6208	792	2674	102,674
12/31/X3	7000	6160	840	1834	101,834
12/31/X4	7000	6110	890	944	100,944
12/31/X5	7000	6056	944	0	100,000

12/31/X1	Interest expense	6,253	
	Premium	747	
	Cash		7,000

The resulting 12/31/X1 book value before applying FVO is $103,466 (see amortization schedule).

Now assume that the fair value of the bond issue at 12/31/X1 is $102,200. (Interest rates have increased.)

Required fair value adjustment (FVA) = $103,466 − $102,200 = $1,266 DR

12/31/X1	FVA	1,266	
	Unrealized gain		1,266

Financial Statement Effects

Income Statement		Balance Sheet	
Interest expense	$6,253	Bonds payable	$100,000
Unrealized gain	1,266	Premium	3,466
		FVA	(1,266)
		Net liability (fair value)	$102,200

12/31/X2

The fair value of the bond issue at 12/31/X2 is $103,136. (Interest rates have decreased.) From the amortization schedule, the book value, had the FVO not been chosen is $102,674 (see amortization schedule).

Required FVA = $103,136 − $102,674 =	$462 CR
FVA before adjustment	1,266 DR
Adjustment to FVA	$ 1,728 CR

Unrealized loss	1,728	
FVA		1,728

The loss of $1,728 also equals the sum of (1) increase in fair value for the period ($103,136 − $102,200), plus (2) $792 amortization of the premium for the period. Both factors cause the difference between fair value and the net liability per the amortization schedule) to increase.

III. U.S. GAAP–IFRS Differences

A. Most aspects of bond accounting are the same for international accounting standards and U.S. standards.

B. IFRS requires the effective interest method in all cases, and the amortization period is the expected term of the bond, as opposed to the contractual period as per U.S. standards.

C. **Fair Value Option**—This option also is available under international standards but is less of a free choice compared with U.S. standards. The option works the same way. The choice is irrevocable and unrealized gains and losses are recognized in income.

   1. However, the option is limited to financial assets and liabilities that are managed and evaluated as a group on a fair value basis as part of a risk management or investment strategy. The entity cannot arbitrarily choose which liabilities will receive the optional accounting treatment. As such, the application of the FVO is more faithful to the underlying purpose of reducing the effect of different accounting measurements on financial assets and liabilities.

Modification and Debt Retirement

Refinancing Short-Term Obligations

Current liabilities can be reclassified as noncurrent under the accounting principles covered in this lesson.

After studying this lesson, you should be able to:

1. Understand the three ways a firm can reclassify current liabilities to noncurrent status under GAAP.

2. Highlight the critical difference between U.S. and international standards with regard to this type of reclassification.

I. **Introduction**

   A. **Definition**—Recall that the definition of a current liability includes *the incurrence of other current liabilities*. This means that if a firm refinances a current liability with another current liability, the liability remains classified as current. Even though no current asset may be required for extinguishment in the coming year, the debtor firm cannot guarantee it will be able to continue to refinance on a short-term basis indefinitely.

   If the debtor firm enters into a revolving credit agreement whereby one current liability is continually replaced with another current liability, even though no current assets may actually be used for a significant time period, the agreement does not allow reclassification of the liabilities to noncurrent status. This arrangement falls within the definition of a current liability.

   B. **Refinancing ST Obligations**—Many firms have a preference for classifying liabilities as noncurrent rather than current to improve their reported liquidity position and reduce the perceived immediate riskiness of the firm. Refinancing on a current basis is of no help here, but if a current liability is refinanced on a long-term basis, the classification of a current liability can be successfully changed to noncurrent without extinguishing the original liability.

II. **Criteria for Reclassifying Current Liabilities as Noncurrent Liabilities**—Reclassification of a current liability to noncurrent status is possible provided two conditions are met.

   A. **Intent**—The intent to refinance the short-term obligation as a long-term obligation must be proven. This proof might be in the form of board of directors' meeting minutes or through written correspondence with the financial institution.

   B. **Ability**

      1. The firm must also be able to refinance the obligation and demonstrate that ability before the issuance of the financial statements. There are three ways to meet this requirement. Each must occur in the period between the balance sheet date and the date the financial statements are issued or are available to be issued.

         a. Actually refinance the liability on a long-term basis. In this case, the firm replaces the current liability with a noncurrent liability.

         b. Enter into a noncancellable refinancing agreement supported by a viable lender. The agreement must extend more than one year beyond the balance sheet date. The purpose of the agreement is to refinance the liability on a noncurrent basis.

         c. Issue equity securities replacing the debt.

      2. The details of the refinancing arrangement must be disclosed in the footnotes.

Example

On December 31, 20X7, the Bulldog Company reports a current note payable that matures on April 1, 20X8. The note is payable to an equipment dealer. The 20X7 financial statements are issued March 4, 20X8. If any of the following three transactions or events occur, then the original note is classified as noncurrent in the 20X7 balance sheet:

1. On February 22, 20X8, Bulldog issues another note payable maturing in 20X9 to replace the existing note.

2. On March 1, 20X8, Bulldog signs a noncancellable refinancing agreement with a lender capable of honoring the agreement. The agreement requires the lender to pay the original note in return for a note from Bulldog due after December 31, 20X8. The refinancing need not occur before the issuance of the financial statements. Only the agreement must be set in place by that time.

3. In February, Bulldog issues shares of its common stock to the equipment dealer in full payment of the note. (If this occurs before the balance sheet date, then Bulldog has no liability to reclassify.)

However, if the firm extinguishes the original note in February by paying cash, and then replenishes the cash with the issuance of a long-term note, the original note remains a current liability in the 20X7 balance sheet because current assets were used for extinguishment.

Also, if a refinancing agreement is cancelable by either party, then there is no reclassification of the note because then there is no guarantee that current assets will not be used in 20X8 to pay the note.

Note

The amount of current debt that can be classified as noncurrent cannot exceed the amount available under the agreement (or the amount refinanced or extinguished through issuing stock). The maximum amount may also be limited to the value of collateral put up by the debtor. For example, the amount of a $60,000 note to be refinanced with another lender might be limited to $40,000, the amount of collateral put up by the debtor. In this case, only $40,000 could be classified as noncurrent.

III. U.S. GAAP–IFRS Differences

A. International standards require that the debtor firm must exhibit its ability to refinance the current liability by taking action or having an agreement in-place **before** the balance sheet date. If the action is delayed until after the balance sheet date but before the financial statements are issued or available to be issued, the current liability is not reclassified. This is in contrast with U.S. standards. The options available under international standards for refinancing a current liability to noncurrent status then are:

1. The refinancing of the current liability on a long-term basis must occur before the balance sheet date.

2. If a refinancing agreement is the chosen method, the refinancing agreement must be in place before the balance sheet date and the intent of the firm must be to refinance the obligation on a long-term basis within one year of the balance sheet date. An existing loan facility and intent of the firm to rollover the debt suffices as well.

3. Issuing equity securities to extinguish the liability before the balance sheet is not an option because the firm would have no current liability to report at the balance sheet date. Rather than reclassify the current liability, the liability would be retired.

Debt Retirement

This topic is usually tested in the context of bond retirements and reinforces the previous discussions on bond accounting

After studying this lesson, you should be able to:

1. Apply both the effective interest and straight-line methods when recording a bond retirement.

2. Record a bond retirement by removing the relevant bond account balances and recognizing a gain or loss

I. Accounting Principles

Exam note
This topic, in the context of bonds payable, is frequently tested on the CPA Exam.

A. When debt is retired at maturity, any discount or premium, and debt issue costs, are fully amortized. The final payment extinguishes the liability at its maturity value, which is also the net liability amount at maturity. No gain or loss is recognized.

B. Firms may retire their debt at any time (before maturity) unless the debt agreement prohibits it. The amount paid to retire bonds early reflects the current yield rate and may be different from the book value of the bonds on the retirement date. The result is that a gain or loss is recorded. The gain or loss is included in income from continuing operations.

C. Debt is considered extinguished when one of two conditions is met.

1. The debtor pays the creditor and is relieved of any obligation related to the debt.

2. The debtor is legally released from being the primary obligor of the liability, and it is probable that the debtor will make no further payments. This legal release may be done by the creditor or by the courts. (An example is the release from a mortgage note upon sale of the related property.)

D. If the debtor firm places assets into an irrevocable trust for the purpose of retiring debt (in-substance defeasance), the liability nonetheless remains on the balance sheet, along with the assets, separately reported. The liability is not extinguished, nor is a gain or loss recorded.

II. Accounting for Debt Extinguishment

A. Extinguishment of debt can be accomplished in a variety of ways. The company can simply pay off the debt. Also, debt may be replaced by a new debt issue (a refinancing, also called a "refunding"). For a refunding, the present value of the new debt issue is used as the price of retiring the old issue. Alternatively, the company may purchase a bond issue on the open market and retire the bonds payable. Finally, the company may retire callable bonds by exercising the *call* feature of the bonds if the bonds are callable, and pay the call price.

B. Regardless of the method, however, the accounting is the same:

1. Record interest and amortization of discount or premium, and amortization of debt issue costs, to the date of extinguishment. Accrued interest from the most recent interest payment date will be included in the amount paid to retire the bonds.

2. Remove the related debt accounts at their remaining amounts (face value, unamortized discount or premium, and any unamortized debt issue costs)

3. Record the gain or loss, which is the difference between the current bond price and the net bond liability. The net bond liability is the face value of the bond plus or minus unamortized premium or discount, and less unamortized bond issue costs. If the current bond price exceeds the net bond liability, a loss is recognized, and vice versa.

Example
The Washington Company exercised its **call** privilege related to an outstanding bond payable. The book value of the bond payable was $105,000, including unamortized premium on bond payable of $5,000. The call price was $104,000. The entry to record the transaction is shown below.

Bonds Payable	$100,000	
Premium on B/P	$ 5,000	
Cash		$104,000
Gain		$ 1,000

III. More Involved Example of Bond Retirement

Example
$10,000 of bonds were issued 5/1/Year 1 at 91. The bonds mature 12/31/Year 6. Bond issue costs of $680 were incurred on issue and the straight-line method is used to amortize both the discount and bond issue costs. The bonds pay interest each December 31. On 1/1/Year 4, 60% of the issue was retired at 97.

The bond term is 5 years and 8 months, or 68 months. The bonds are retired when 3 years or 36 months remain in the bond term. The original discount was $900 (.09 x $10,000).

Entry for retirement:

Bonds Payable .60($10,000)	6,000	
Loss	322	
Bond Discount .60($900)(36/68)		286
Bond Issue Costs .60($680)(36/68)		216
Cash .97(.60)($10,000)		5,820

IV. U.S. GAAP–IFRS Differences

A. The accounting for debt retirement is essentially the same for both sets of standards.

B. International standards use the term *derecognition* of the liability as well as *extinguishment* of debt when a liability is retired. A liability is extinguished or derecognized only when the obligation is discharged, canceled or expired. The terminology for what constitutes an extinguishment is somewhat different between U.S. and international standards, but the meaning and effect is essentially the same. The focus of both is on the economic substance of the transaction.

C. Gains and losses on debt extinguishment are reported in Other Income, the same category as interest expense, on international income statements.

D. In-substance defeasance is treated the same way as for U.S. standards. It is not accounted for as an extinguishment of debt or derecognition of the assets used for that purpose.

E. Some modifications of terms restructuring are treated as debt extinguishments for international accounting. This topic is discussed in the lessons on troubled-debt restructurings.

Troubled Debt

When a creditor makes a concession to a debtor that is unable to meet the terms of a debt agreement, the restructuring is considered "troubled." This lesson addresses the accounting for such restructures

After studying this lesson, you should be able to:

1. Identify when a debt restructure is troubled.

2. Categorize a troubled-debt restructure into one of three types.

3. Record a settlement troubled-debt restructure for both debtor and creditor.

4. Account for a modification of terms troubled-debt restructure when the restructured flows are less than the book value of the liability being restructured.

5. Determine the new interest rate to be applied by the debtor firm in a troubled-debt restructure for which the sum of restructured cash flows exceeds the original debt amount.

6. Record interest expense during the restructured debt term.

7. Identify the similarities and differences in accounting for troubled-debt restructures under U.S. and international standards.

8. Account for two types of loan modifications under international standards.

I. Introduction

A. Restructuring of debt is commonplace. Extension of terms, changes in interest rates, and other aspects of the debt agreement are examples. In a troubled debt restructure (TDR), however, the creditor grants a concession by agreeing to terms less favorable than under the original debt agreement. For a restructuring to be considered a TDR, the *both* of the following must hold:

1. The creditor granted a concession in the expectation that more ultimately will be received from the debtor compared with other strategies, such as forcing the debtor into bankruptcy.

2. The debtor is in financial difficulty, which means that without the concession, it is likely that the debtor will default.

B. The accounting for the restructure depends on whether the debt is settled (a settlement) or whether it continues (a modification of terms).

C. In all TDR cases, the present value of the consideration paid under the restructured agreement is less than the carrying value of the debt (including any unpaid interest) at date of restructure.

1. If the debt is settled, the fair value of consideration transferred is less than the carrying value of the debt at date of restructure (creditor grants a concession).

2. If the debt is modified, the present value of the restructured cash flows (computed using the original interest rate) is less than the carrying value of the debt at date of restructure (creditor grants a concession).

II. Debtor and Creditor Recording and Reporting of Settlement Troubled-Debt Restructures

A. **Debtor**—In settlement restructures, the debtor:

1. Records a gain for the difference between the book value of the debt, including any unpaid accrued interest, and the fair value of consideration transferred in full settlement of the debt (debtor always records a gain of this type and never a loss)

2. Records a gain or loss, if any, on the disposal of nonmonetary assets transferred in full settlement of the debt (if the debtor pays cash only to settle the debt, there is no gain or loss of this type recorded)

3. Removes the debt accounts from the books

4. Records any stock issued in settlement at the fair value

B. **Creditor**—In settlement restructures, the creditor:

1. Records a loss for the difference between the book value of the receivable and the fair value of assets or stock of the debtor received

2. Removes the receivable accounts from the books

3. Records assets received at fair value

Example

On January 1, a debtor owed a creditor a $10,000 note due on this date. In addition, $1,000 of unpaid interest from the previous year was also due. (A 10% original interest rate is implied.) The debtor could not pay the entire amount and the two parties agreed on a restructure in which the debtor would transfer land (cost, $4,000; fair value, $2,000) and issue stock (fair value and total par value, $5,000) in full settlement of the debt.

Debtor			Creditor		
Note Payable	10,000		Investment in Stock	5,000	
Interest Payable	1,000		Loss on Debt Restructure	4,000	
Loss on Land Disposal	2,000		Land	2,000	
Gain on Debt Restructure		4,000	Note Receivable		10,000
Capital Stock		5,000	Interest Receivable		1,000
Land		4,000			

The debtor's gain is the difference between the book value of the debt settled ($11,000, which includes interest) less the market value of items transferred ($2,000 land + $5,000 stock). This equals the creditor's loss on restructure (and equals the concession) because the two parties reported the same book value for the debt and receivable plus interest. The debtor's loss on disposal is the loss that would be recorded had the land been sold for cash.

III. Debtor Reporting of Modification of Terms for Troubled-Debt Restructure

A. For debtor accounting purposes, there are two very different cases for modification of terms for TDRs. The cases are distinguished by the relationship between the prerestructure book value of the debt, and the nominal sum of restructured future cash flows. The book value of the original debt always includes unpaid accrued interest. The creditor's accounting for modification terms TDRs is not parallel to the debtor's accounting and is covered in the lesson on loan impairment.

Note

Sometimes a restructuring is a combination settlement and modification of terms, In these cases, the settlement portion is recorded first with the liability reduced by the fair value of consideration paid (no gain is recorded). The remainder of the debt restructure is treated as a modification of terms, detailed below.

---

1. **Modification type 1**—In modification of terms, restructures in which the nominal sum of the restructured flows is *less than or equal* to the book value of the debt plus accrued interest, the debtor:

a. Reduces the carrying value of the debt to the nominal sum of restructured cash flows

b. Records a gain for the difference between the book value and the nominal sum of restructured cash flows

c. Records no further interest; all future cash payments are returns of principal

2. **Modification type 2**—In modification of terms restructures in which the nominal sum of the restructured flows is *greater* than the book value of the debt plus accrued interest, the debtor:

   a. Records no gain or loss and does not change the carrying value of the debt

   b. Computes the new rate of interest equating the present value of restructured cash flows and the book value of the debt

   c. Records interest expense based on the new rate for the remainder of the loan term

IV. Examples of Modification of Terms for TDRs

Example
Modification Type 1
On January 1, Year 1, a debtor owed a creditor a $10,000 note due on this date. In addition, $1,000 of unpaid interest from the previous year was also due. The debtor could not pay the entire amount and the two parties agreed on a restructure in which the debtor would make the following payments:

		Restructured cash flows
December 31, Year 1	Interest	400
	Principal	3,000
December 31, Year 2	Interest	400
	Principal	3,000
Total restructured cash flows		6,800

The *interest* cash flows are not really interest because all flows are returns of principal in this case. However, restructuring agreements may refer to such smaller flows as interest. The nominal sum of $6,800 is less than the $11,000 book value of debt.

Entries for Debtor:

January 1, Year 1	Interest Payable	1,000	
	Note Payable	10,000	
	Gain		4,200
	Note Payable		6,800

This entry reduces the carrying value of the debt to $6,800. The gain is the difference between the book value of the old debt plus interest ($11,000) and the nominal sum of restructured flows. The old debt accounts are closed and a new note payable is recorded. An alternative is to simply reduce the old note account $3,200 and close the interest payable account.

December 31, Year 1	Note Payable	3,400	
	Cash		3,400
December 31, Year 2	Note Payable	3,400	
	Cash		3,400

Analysis

The accounting for this case (sum of new flows < book value) is a significant departure from the normal procedure for noncurrent debt accounting, which would report the new note payable at present value, rather than nominal value as in this situation.

Compared with the normal procedure (recording at present value), there are three effects of the above accounting for modification type 1 TDRs on the debtor's financial statements:

1. Liabilities are larger (nominal sum is larger than the present value).

2. Income is smaller in year of restructure (the gain is smaller than if the note payable were recorded at present value).

3. Future interest expense is smaller (there is no interest recognized).

B. Example of Modification Type 2

Example

On January 1, Year 1, a debtor owed a creditor a $10,000 note due on this date. In addition, $1,000 of unpaid interest from the previous year was also due. The debtor was unable to pay the total amount and the parties agreed to a restructure in which the debtor would make a single lump sum payment of $11,440 on December 31, Year 1. In this case, the nominal sum of restructured cash flows ($11,440) exceeds the book value of $11,000. Thus, there will be interest paid at the end of Year 1. The new interest rate is found as:

(PV of $1, i = ?, n = 1)($11,440) = $11,000

(PV of $1, i = ?, n = 1)($11,440) = $11,000/($11,440) = .96154

This present value factor corresponds to 4%, indicating the concession made by the creditor. Rather than earning 10%, the creditor will earn only 4%. Another way to consider the concession is to compute the present value of the restructured flows using the original interest rate:

$11,440(PV of $1, i = .10, n = 1) = $11,440(.90909) = $10,400

This amount is less than the $11,000 book value of the debt, again reflecting the debtor's concession. Entries for Debtor:

January 1, Year 1	No entry needed (or the old debt accounts can be closed and a new note payable of $11,000 can be created)		
December 31, Year 1	Interest Expense .04($11,000)	440	
	Note Payable	10,000	
	Interest Payable	1,000	
	Cash		11,440

C. This illustrates a restructure agreement requiring only a single payment. Other examples might require only an annuity of payments. Either way, only one present value factor is used, and the calculation of the new interest rate is straightforward.

D. However, many restructurings include both single payments and annuities as restructured flows. In these cases, there are two unknowns in terms of present value factors. The candidate may be called upon to set up the solution for such a situation, and explain how to solve for the new effective rate. It is even possible that a simulation may enable the actual calculation. The following example is an illustration.

E. Example of Modification Type 2

Example

On 1/1/X1 a debtor owed a creditor a $6,573 (face) non-interest-bearing note due on this date. The interest rate implied on this note is 8%. The debtor was unable to pay the total amount and the parties agreed to a restructure in which the debtor would make the following restructured payments: (1) restructured face value of $5,000 due 12/31/X6, (2) annual interest payments at 10% of the new face value, beginning 12/31/X1.

In this example, the sum of restructured cash flows is $8,000 [$5,000 + (6 x $500)], which exceeds the debt book value ($6,573). It is important to be sure that the restructure is a TDR before proceeding.

There are two ways to find out.

(1) Use the original interest rate of 8% to determine the present value of new flows. If that present value is less than $6,573, then the creditor is making a concession.

PV of new flows = $5,000(pv of $1, i = .08, n = 6) + $500(pv $1 annuity, i = .08, n = 6)

PV = $5,000(.63017) + $500(4.62288) = $5,462 < $6,573 therefore, the restructuring is a troubled-debt restructure.

(2) Compute the new effective rate (m) implied by the new flows. If that rate is less than 8%, then the creditor is making a concession.

$5,000(pv of $1, m, n = 6) + $500(pv $1 annuity, m, 6) = $6,573

The solution for m can be computed using the internal rate of return (IRR) function within standard spreadsheet programs. See below. m = 4%, which is less than 8%. Therefore, the restructuring is a troubled-debt restructure.

Spreadsheet solution for m. The original liability balance is placed into cell A1 as a negative amount (the investment). Each succeeding cell is a separate cash flow in which each new cell indicates a new period. The next five cells are the annual interest payments of $500. The cash flow for 20X6 (cell A7) includes both principal ($5,000) and interest because they occur simultaneously. In cell B7 the IRR function is inserted and the spreadsheet formula returns 4% for m in that cell.

	A	B
1	− 6,573	
2	500	
3	500	
4	500	
5	500	
6	500	
7	5,500	=IRR(A1:A7)

The first two required journal entries are:

12/31/X1	Interest expense	263		(6,573)(.04)
	Note payable	237		
	Cash		500	
12/31/X2	Interest expense	253		($6,573 − $237).04
	Note payable	247		
	Cash		500	

At 12/31/X6, the note balance is $5,000 and is retired with the final payment of that amount.

V. U.S. GAAP–IFRS Differences

A. International accounting standards treat **settlements** of debt the same way as do U.S. standards, although the term *troubled* is not used. The transaction is an extinguishment of debt with a gain recognized by the debtor in profit or loss if the settlement is troubled.

B. International accounting standards do not identify **modifications** of loans as troubled. Rather, there are two cases based on whether the modification is (1) significant, (2) not significant. These do not correspond to the two modification-of-terms cases under U.S. standards.

1. **Significant modification**—When the modification of the original loan is considered significant, the transaction is treated as an extinguishment of the old debt and recognition of the new debt. The new debt is recorded at fair value. Any gain or loss is fully recognized and any costs or fees reduce the gain or increase the loss on retirement. This is consistent with the normal application of noncurrent liability accounting.

   a. A modification is significant if the difference between the present values of the two debts (computed with the original rate of interest) is 10% or more of the present value of remaining cash flows on the old debt. The original rate is used only for purposes of determining the 10% threshold. The rate used to record the new debt and recognize subsequent interest is the effective rate of interest on similar debt.

Example
Significant Modification

On January, 1, 20X2, DCo. owes a $6%, $50,000 note due four years from this date, along with one year of unpaid interest for 20X1 ($3,000 = .06 x $50,000). DCo. is experiencing significant financial difficulty and appeals to the creditor to restructure the loan. The creditor agrees in order to help DCo. avoid bankruptcy. The term is left unchanged but the interest rate is reduced to 4%, with interest payments due annually each December 31, and the principal is reduced to $30,000. The one year of unpaid interest is not forgiven but rather is required to be paid immediately. The creditor charges $1,900 to restructure the loan payable in cash.

The present value (pv) of the new loan arrangement using the original 6% rate is as follows:

pv = 30,000(pv of $1, i = 6%, n = 4) + .04(30,000)(pv $1 annuity, i = 6%, n = 4) + 3,000

pv = 30,000(.79209) + 1,200(3.46511) + $3,000 = 30,921

The present value of the new loan arrangement at 6% is $30,921, or approximately 58.3% of the $53,000 present value of the original loan. The 10% threshold is exceeded and thus the transaction is treated as an extinguishment of the original loan. The new loan is to be recognized at fair value. The comparison of present values computed under the original loan's interest rate is solely for the purpose of determining whether the modification is substantial (exceeds the 10% threshold).

Assume that the market rate of interest on the new loan is 13% given DCo.'s financial condition. The new loan is reported at its fair value, the present value of future cash flows at 13%.

   New loan initial book value =
   = 30,000(pv of $1, i = 13%, n = 4) + .04(30,000)(pv $1 annuity, i = 13%, n = 4)
   = 30,000(.61332) + 1,200(2.97447) = 21,969

Note payable	50,000	
Interest payable	3,000	
Note payable		21,969
Cash		4,900 ($3,000 interest + $1,900 costs)
Gain		26,131

The above journal entry illustrates the net method. If the gross method were used, the new note payable would be recorded at $30,000 with a discount of $8,031 debited. Either way, interest expense on the restructured note is based on the net note balance at the beginning of each period, calculated at 13%.

---

2. **Not a significant modification.** If the 10% threshold is not met, then the difference in present values is deferred and amortized over the new debt term. The new debt is not measured at fair value but rather takes on the original loan book value plus or minus the loss or gain. Any costs or fees adjust the carrying value of the debt and are thus amortized over the new debt term. A deferred gain is a liability and its amortization is reported in other income.

Example
Not a Significant Modification

A firm in financial difficulty includes in its liabilities a 4%, $80,000 loan due six years from the current balance sheet date, December 31, 20X4. The interest due on that date is paid. On the next day (1/1/x5) the firm restructures the loan with the creditor. The term is shortened to four years, principal reduced to $75,000, and the interest rate is reduced to 3% with interest payments due annually each December 31 beginning one year from the restructuring date.

The present value of the new loan using the original 4% rate is as follows:

pv = 75,000(pv of $1, i = 4%, n = 4) + .03(75,000)(pv $1 annuity, i = 4%, n = 4)

pv = 75,000(.85480) + 2,250(3.62990) = 72,277

There is less than a 10% difference between the two present values ($72,277/$80,000 = 90.3%).

Note payable	80,000	
Note payable		72,277
Deferred gain		7,723

The original interest rate of 4% continues to be applied to the new debt balance for purposes of computing interest expense.

Debt Covenant Compliance

Several aspects of debt covenants are discussed in this lesson.

After studying this lesson, you should be able to:

1. Describe the basic content of a debt covenant.

2. Articulate the reasons for debt covenants.

3. List several attributes that serve as the restriction included in debt covenants.

4. Note different ways in which compliance with a debt covenant can be demonstrated.

5. Be aware of the possible responses by the creditor in the event of noncompliance with a debt covenant.

6. Understand how reclassification of debt is involved with debt covenant compliance.

I. Background—Debt Covenants

A. A debt covenant is a part of the larger contract underlying the debt instrument. A bond indenture (contract) details the rights and duties of the issuing firm (debtor, borrower) and the bondholder (creditor, lender), for example. A covenant, also called a "restriction," is a section of the contract that describes the responses available to the creditor if certain events or conditions occur, such as the debtor's current ratio declining below a certain level. The covenant may allow the creditor to call the debt (demand immediate payment). Covenants also protect the debtor from such actions should the conditions not occur (debtor maintains compliance with the covenant).

B. Covenants can be established either unilaterally by the creditor, or through negotiation between creditor and debtor. Firms emerging from corporate reorganization or bankruptcy may be subject to more stringent covenants. A description of the covenant is disclosed in the notes to the debtor's financial statements.

C. Covenants are one form of protection for the creditor. Others include requiring the issuing firm to redeem bonds according to a prespecified schedule (sinking fund debentures), requiring the issuing firm to accumulate a sinking fund for the eventual retirement of bonds, and structuring the bonds as serial bonds.

D. The debtor must periodically demonstrate compliance with the covenants. The frequency may be quarterly, semiannually, or annually and is set at the time of borrowing. Information in the audited annual financial statements reflects a higher degree of verifiability compared with quarterly statements. The frequency may reflect the perceived riskiness of the borrower. For example, for a troubled line of credit, demonstration of compliance might be required monthly.

E. Covenants are periodically revisited and modified as debtor financial health and macroeconomic conditions change. At a minimum, adjustments should be considered annually. In a line of credit, a review also occurs upon renewal of the credit line.

II. Specific Attributes Used in Covenants

A. A wide variety of measures is used in debt covenants. Typically, a minimum or maximum value for the measure is the condition beyond which the debtor is in violation. The following list provides examples.

1. **Current ratio** (current assets/current liabilities)—A measure of liquidity. If the debtor's current ratio falls below 2.0 for example (a minimum level), the debtor has violated the covenant. The creditor then has the right to respond in specific ways defined in the contract. This aspect is discussed below.

2. **Working capital** (current assets – current liabilities)—A minimum level is specified in the covenant.

3. **Income measures,** such as net income before tax, net income, income from continuing operations, and EBITDA (earnings before interest, taxes, depreciation, and amortization). The covenant specifies a minimum absolute level, or possibly one based on a percentage of the previous year's amount.

4. **Interest coverage ratio** (EBITDA/interest expense)—A minimum level is specified.

5. **Retained earnings balance, or total owners' equity balance**—A minimum level is specified.

6. **Debt to equity ratio**—A maximum level is specified.

7. **Total debt**—A maximum level is specified.

8. **Interest expense**—A maximum level is specified.

9. **Total assets or net assets**—A minimum level is specified.

B. Covenants also may describe a restriction on the debtor's transactions during the debt term for the protection of the creditor. Otherwise, the debtor is in violation of the covenant.

   1. Limit dividends or treasury share purchases to a specific amount, or prohibit them.

   2. Limit additional borrowings. A "leverage" covenant may limit total debt to some multiple of an earnings variable, such as EBITDA. Alternatively, the firm may be required to maintain a minimum specified interest coverage ratio if additional debt capital is acquired.

   3. Require that the borrower not voluntarily cause a reduction in net assets (weakening of the balance sheet) or not take any action that might impede the ability to service the debt.

   4. Prohibit risky investments or expansion projects.

C. A covenant also may require that the firm's debt rating not fall below a minimum level. Two rating agencies are Standard & Poor's Corporation and Moody's Investor Services. S&P ratings are: Highest, AAA; High, AA; Medium, A; Minimum investment grade, BBB. Moody's corresponding ratings are: Aaa, Aa, A, Baa. A debtor, for example, may be required to maintain at least an A S&P rating for compliance with the covenant.

D. "Covenant-lite" loans are drawn with fewer or less stringent covenants. Such loans provide less protection for the creditor. One reason for less onerous covenants is that loans can be sold on a secondary market, effectively passing the risk on to investors. The ability to refinance the loans is another factor.

III. The Compliance Process

A. Ensuring compliance with covenants is an ongoing task for many debtor firms. Both management and audit committees continuously monitor the financial condition of the firm so that adjustments can be made in time to avoid situations that would cause the firm to be out of compliance. A forward-looking process facilitates risk assessment and risk management.

B. The debtor develops a system that signals conditions which may lead to a violation well before it actually happens. All relevant personnel within the organization must participate, to avoid the potentially devastating effects of a violation.

C. Periodic internal self-evaluation precedes the formal compliance review that involves the creditor. All administrative requirements pertaining to the covenant within the debt agreement including progress reports are fulfilled on a timely basis.

D. Capital budgeting and other planning processes within the firm consider the potential effect on debt covenant compliance.

E. A periodic sensitivity analysis determines the leeway available on key factors used in the covenant, within current operations. How much room does the firm have to alter its tactics and strategies and continue to comply with its covenants?

IV. Specific Compliance Strategies

A. **Operating Strategies**—Relevant strategies available to the debtor are implied by the covenant. If the covenant requires a limitation or elimination of dividends, for example, then that strategy must be followed to avoid a violation. In this example, shareholders should be informed about the reduction and the reason for it.

   1. Improving products and services, enhancing marketing, encouraging innovation, seeking the best management talent, and avoiding risk are ways to improve operating results and help

maintain compliance. Leverage should be used sparingly, and only if the expectations for increased profitability are sufficiently strong to warrant increased debt, if allowed under the covenant.

2. Increasing liquidity is another aspect that helps compliance for several types of covenants. Covenants involving the current ratio and working capital are examples. Refinancing short-term debt to noncurrent classification is a specific strategy that would assist the debtor in complying with this type of covenant. In general, specific transactions may enable compliance with covenant ratios.

Example

Beta Co. has a loan covenant requiring it to maintain a current ratio of 1.5 or better as of year-end. As Beta approaches year-end, current assets are $20 million ($1 million in cash, $9 million in accounts receivable, and $10 million in inventory), and current liabilities are $13.5 million. Therefore, its current ratio is 1.48 (20/13.5), which is below the minimum.

Several actions below are being considered to maintain compliance with the debt covenant by year-end:

A. Sell $1 million in inventory and deposit the proceeds in the entity's checking account.

B. Borrow $1 million short term and deposit the funds in the entity's checking account.

C. Sell $1 million in inventory and pay off some of its short-term creditors.

D. Do nothing at all.

Which choice will allow Beta to meet its loan covenant?

Only Action C will increase the current ratio to 1.5 or more. Current assets decrease by $1 million from paying current liabilities, which also decrease $1 million. The current ratio after Action C would be 1.52: (20 − 1)/(13.5 − 1) = 19/12.5 = 1.52.

Action A leaves current assets and current liabilities unchanged, along with the current ratio, leaving Beta in noncompliance.

Action B increases both current assets and current liabilities by $1 million, resulting in a 1.45 current ratio: (20 + 1)/(13.5 + 1) = 21/14.5 = 1.45. The noncompliance is worse after Action B.

Action D is the status quo, leaving the current ratio below the minimum.

---

3. Refinancing debt when interest rates decline can improve both earnings and liquidity.

B. **Accounting Choices**—Where GAAP allows a choice or allows leeway in estimation of certain variables, the debtor firm may consider choosing the methods which contribute to maintaining compliance with the debt covenant.

1. Although net income is not a formal variable in all covenants, higher earnings will contribute to a greater probability of compliance with many covenants. Choices such as FIFO, straight-line depreciation, longer useful lives for plant assets, higher recoverable costs for plant assets, the specific method of capitalizing interest, full-costing method of accounting for natural resource exploration costs, and others can help in this regard.

   a. However, the effect of choices on the quality of earnings must also be considered. Firms with low quality of earnings may suffer in the equity capital markets.

   b. Also, some covenants require consistent application of accounting policies and compute compliance based on the policies in effect at the time of the borrowing. An improvement in an accounting-related measure used in a debt covenant caused by a change in accounting policy therefore may not be "counted" toward improved debt covenant compliance.

2. Off-balance sheet activities, such as structuring leases as operating leases, will reduce reported debt, a variable used in several measures incorporated into covenants.

V. Creditor Response to a Covenant Violation

A. The debt contract describes the actions that may be taken by the creditor in the event of a covenant violation by the debtor. Typically these are options rather than requirements.

1. The financial position of the creditor, and the general relationship between the firms, may affect how the creditor responds to a violation.

B. If the covenant states that the debt can be called in the event of noncompliance (e.g., if the debtor's working capital falls below the minimum $20 million as specified in the covenant), then the creditor has the option to demand immediate payment.

C. Other actions include increasing the interest rate, requiring the borrower to specify assets as collateral, accelerating the payment terms (other than immediate payment), reducing the amount available in a line of credit, and repossessing collateral.

D. Additional restrictions may be placed on the debtor. If a covenant is violated because of reduced earnings, for example, then the debtor may be prohibited from paying dividends or taking on more debt until the violation is cured.

E. The creditor may agree to renegotiate or restructure the debt.

F. Legal action may be taken against the debtor, including the initiation of a breach of contract lawsuit.

VI. Debtor Strategies after a Covenant Violation

A. The debtor may have few options after a covenant violation, depending on the response by the creditor. Therefore, the debtor firm seeks to avoid a violation and the potential negative impact on its operations.

1. If a violation leads to a debt default, operations can be disrupted, access to the capital markets is hindered, higher borrowing costs and penalties may be incurred, employee morale may decline, administrative time is wasted, suppliers and customers may end their relationship with the debtor, and the debtor's going concern may be placed in doubt.

2. Likewise, creditors do not want debtors to default. Covenant violations place the creditor in an uncertain position and at a minimum cause additional work for its managers. Defaults also may attract scrutiny from bank examiners, which in turn may require an increase in a reserve against the possible loan loss. A default also raises the possibility that a loss is imminent.

B. Many debtors are not in a position to pay the debt immediately and often request a renegotiation of the debt terms enabling lower or deferred payments.

C. A debtor may also ask for a waiver granting time to cure the violation or to void the violation. These requests are more likely when the reasons for the violation are beyond the immediate control of the debtor. General economic downturns and inflation with their respective effects on the debtor's earnings and liquidity are factors. For example, goodwill impairments due to declining stock prices can cause parent firm earnings to decline with no change in the parent's core operations.

D. The debtor may request relief from the covenant. This involves a request to either eliminate or weaken the covenant by amending the debt contract. For example, if the violated leverage covenant is 5 times EBITDA, the debtor may request to increase the multiple to 6.5. Such a change to the covenant may occur when the compliance review or general review of the contract occurs or earlier, depending on the severity of the violation.

VII. Classification of Debt When a Covenant Is Violated

A. If a liability is callable on demand without qualification, then the liability is classified as a current liability, even if not due within one year from the balance sheet date. This category includes liabilities that are not callable as of the balance sheet date but will become due on demand within one year of the balance sheet date.

B. If a liability is callable on demand if a debt covenant is violated, and there is violation, the liability is classified as a current liability if there are no other relevant circumstances.

C. If a liability is callable on demand if a debt covenant is violated, and there is violation, but that violation is waived by the creditor, then the liability is classified as a noncurrent liability.

D. If a liability callable on demand if a debt covenant is violated, and there is a violation, if the creditor grants a grace period and it is probable that the debtor will rectify that violation within the grace period, then the liability is classified as a noncurrent liability. Otherwise, the liability is classified as a current liability.

E. The violations assumed above are called "objective acceleration clauses" because the potential covenant violations are listed as specific events, such as failure to make an interest payment or the current ratio has decreased below the minimum specified in the covenant.

    1. Other clauses are less objective and are called "subjective acceleration clauses." They enable the creditor to call the debt for reasons not objectively specified, such as a decline in the earnings of the debtor or deterioration of the debtor's balance sheet. If circumstances suggest the possible calling of the debt, then the liability is classified as current. However, if the likelihood of acceleration of the due date is considered remote (including similar past situations in which the creditor did not call the debt), then the classification remains noncurrent.

VIII. U.S. GAAP–IFRS Differences

A. If the debtor firm breaches a debt covenant causing the debt to be payable on demand, it is classified as current, unless the creditor agrees, by the balance sheet date, to allow a "grace" period ending at least one year after the balance sheet, during which the creditor can cure the breach and during which the debtor cannot demand payment.

B. For subjective acceleration clauses, U.S. standards require current classification when relevant conditions are present because the callable on demand feature cannot be controlled by the debtor. International standards have no such requirement.

Distinguishing Liabilities from Equity

This lesson considers the theoretical question of whether a transaction yields a liability, equity, or both.

After studying this lesson, you should be able to:

1. Discuss the basic issue.

2. Explain how mandatorily redeemable shares are classified.

3. Account for obligations to issue shares of a fixed dollar amount.

4. Record the journal entries for an obligation to issue a fixed number of shares.

5. Account for written put options.

6. Identify the main differences in this area between U.S. and international accounting standards.

I. **Background**—Although the definitions of *liability* and *equity* have been established for a long time, new transactions have developed that put these definitions to the test. The expectation is that new definitions will be forthcoming, along with affected specific accounting principles. Until then, the determination of whether an item is a liability or equity proceeds on a somewhat piecemeal basis. This lesson considers (1) transactions involving the firm's stock, and (2) compound financial instruments. Additional discussion of financial instruments as they affect liabilities and equity is found in lessons on derivatives.

II. **Adopted Standards**—The FASB has adopted accounting standards that require certain items related to equity are to be reported as liabilities. These items obligate the firm to deliver assets of a fixed monetary value, either cash or equity shares, in the future, and they include:

    A. Mandatorily redeemable shares

    B. Certain stock appreciation rights (discussed in a previous lesson)

    C. Financial instruments obligating the issuing firm to issue stock worth a fixed value

    D. Written put options and other financial instruments obligating the issuing firm to repurchase its own shares

III. **Mandatorily Redeemable Shares**—Mandatorily redeemable financial instruments are classified as liabilities if both of the following criteria are met. (1) They are obligations to repurchase the firm's equity shares or are indexed to such an obligation, and (2) They require or may require the issuer to settle the obligation by transferring assets. However, if the redemption is required only upon liquidation of the entity, then the classification is equity. An example of an instrument that is classified as debt is a written put option on the issuer's shares that is to be settled in cash. Mandatorily redeemable financial instruments are initially measured at fair value.

IV. **Obligations to Issue Shares of a Fixed Dollar Value**

    A. Firms may pay for services or goods by issuing stock after the goods or services are received. Recall that when shares are issued immediately upon receipt of goods or services, the expense or asset, and the stock issued, are measured at the more reliable of the fair values (good/service, or stock). When there is a period of time between receipt of consideration and the issuance of stock, the stock price can change. The issue then arises at the receipt of consideration: Does the firm have a liability, or equity? The answer depends on whether the agreement specifies shares worth a fixed dollar amount, or a fixed number of shares.

    B. **Shares Worth a Fixed Dollar Amount (Variable Number of Shares)**—When a firm agrees to issue shares in the future worth a fixed dollar amount, a liability rather than equity is recognized. The vendor is not at risk for fluctuations in the price of the stock to be received because shares worth the fixed amount will be received, regardless of the stock price.

> **Example**
> A firm and a vendor agree that the firm will pay for service provided April 1, 20X2 with shares of the firm's $1 par common stock two months after that date. The value of shares to be issued is $10,000; the parties agree that this is the fair valuation of the services.
>
> | 4/1/X2 | Service expense | 10,000 | | |
> |---|---|---|---|---|
> | | Liability for stock issuance (liability account) | | 10,000 | |
>
> On May 31, 20X2, the share price of the firm's stock is $40. The number of shares to be issued therefore is 250 ($10,000/$40).
>
> | 5/31/X2 | Liability for stock issuance | 10,000 | | |
> |---|---|---|---|---|
> | | Common stock | | 250 | 250($1) |
> | | Contributed capital in excess of par-common | | 9,750 | 250($40 − $1) |

C. Fixed Number of Shares—By comparison, when the number of shares is fixed rather than the dollar amount, the issuing firm records an owner's equity account upon receipt of consideration. During the period between providing the goods or service, and receipt of stock, the vendor is at risk in the same way any other shareholder is at risk. If the stock price declines during this time, the value received by the vendor will also decline.

> **Example**
> Using the information in the previous example, assume the two parties agree that the firm will issue 200 shares of $1 common stock two months after the service is provided. The market price of the stock on April 1, 20X2 is $50.
>
> | 4/1/X2 | Service expense | 10,000 | | |
> |---|---|---|---|---|
> | | Stock issuance obligation (OE account) | | 10,000 | |
> | 5/31/X2 | Stock issuance obligation | 10,000 | | |
> | | Common stock | | 200 | 200($1) |
> | | Contributed capital in excess of par-common | | 9,800 | 200($50 − $1) |
>
> The fair value of the services was $10,000 on April 1. That amount determines the increase in contributed capital. The share price at the time of issuance is not relevant.

V. Written Put Options

A. As part of a share repurchase plan, firms may write an option allowing other entities to sell the firm's stock to the firm at a fixed price (option price) on a specific date or during a specified period. The purchaser (option holder) pays a fee for the option. The fee typically approximates the fair value of the option using an option-pricing model (the same type of model used to value employee stock options discussed in a previous lesson).

B. The purchaser of the option is betting that the firm's stock will decline in price. The firm is betting the price will stay above the option price.

C. The fair value of the option is reported as a liability. Changes in the option's fair value are recognized at each year-end before the exercise. An increase in the fair value represents a potential decrease in the share price because the option is more valuable. The option will be exercised if the share price during the exercise period is less than fixed option price. At exercise, the firm extinguishes the liability and pays the option price. If the option is not exercised (because the share price exceeds the option price during the exercise period), the liability is extinguished and a gain is recorded.

Example

On January 1, 20X1, a firm wrote put options for 100 shares of its common stock. Holders of the option will be able to sell the firm's stock back to the firm for $50 per share on December 31, 20X2. The estimated fair value of one option is $10. Journal entries for the firm follow:

1/1/X1	Cash	1,000	100($10)
	Put option liability	1,000	

On December 31, 20X1, the fair value of an option is re-estimated to be $12.50. The increase in fair value reflects an increased likelihood that the price of the firm's stock will be less than $50 on the exercise date.

12/31/X1	Loss on put option	250	100($12.50 − $10)
	Put option liability	250	

On December 31, 20X2, the price of the firm's stock is $45 per share. The option is exercised because the purchaser (option holder) will receive $50 per option when the shares are worth only $45. The purchaser can purchase a share of the stock for $45 on the market and sell it back to the firm for $50—a gain of $5 per share. However, the purchaser has incurred a net loss of $500: $1,000 fee less the $500 gain on exercise [100($50 − $45)].

12/31/X2	Put option liability	1,250	
	Treasury stock	4,500	100($45) (fair value)
	Cash		5,000 100($50)
	Gain on put option		750

The treasury stock is recorded at fair value. The $500 net gain to the firm over the two years is computed two ways:

1. $500 = $750 gain for 20X2 − $250 loss for 20X1 = $500

2. $500 = $1,000 fee − $500 (excess of $5,000 paid for stock − $4,500 fair value)

D. When the option is not exercised (stock price did not fall below the option price), the put option liability is closed and a gain is recognized. The overall gain to the firm is the fee. In this example, if the stock price were $55 on December 31, 20X2, the option would not be exercised and the firm would record the following journal entry:

12/31/X2	Put option liability	1,250	
	Gain on put option		1,250

The firm's overall gain is $1,000 ($1,250 gain for 20X2 − $250 loss for 20X1).

VI. Compound Financial Instruments

A. At present, GAAP addresses this issue on an individual standard basis. The expectation is that this area will be revised based on a more general standard. Previous lessons addressed the following two items, for example.

    1. Convertible bonds are treated the same as nonconvertible bonds at issuance and throughout the term—as debt. There is no separation of the debt and equity components. Only at conversion does the equity component surface. There is an exception—when convertible bonds can be settled in cash. This exception is consistent with the notion of a liability—that is, the obligation to transfer assets in the future as a result of a past transaction.

    2. Bonds with detachable warrants separate the debt and equity components at issuance. This treatment is just the opposite as that for most convertible bonds.

VII. U.S. GAAP–IFRS Differences

A. Whereas, at present, U.S. standards address financial instruments on an individual basis, international standards apply more general concepts.

B. Under international standards, a financial instrument is classified as liability or equity, based on the substance of the transaction.

    1. If a financial instrument is an obligation to transfer cash or other financial assets, it is classified as a liability, regardless of form. It may be necessary to separate the liability and equity components as is the case with convertible bonds under international standards. The classification is made at issuance and continues until it is derecognized. When there is uncertainty about measurement, the liability component is directly measured with the equity component treated as a residual.

C. More specifically, under international standards, an item is a liability if the firm has a contractual obligation to deliver cash or other financial asset to the holder, or to exchange another financial instrument with the holder under conditions that are potentially unfavorable to the issuer.

    1. Liability classification is required under these circumstances regardless of the consideration transferred to settle the obligation, and regardless of whether the issuer has restrictions on the ability to settle the obligation or regardless of the way the obligation is settled.

    2. For example, the instrument could be settled by issuing shares and yet be classified as a liability (the obligation to issue shares of a fixed dollar amount is an example). If the circumstances are not met, then the instrument is classified as equity, which implies that the instrument evidences a residual interest in the assets of an entity after deducting its liabilities.

Equity

Owners' Equity Basics

This lesson begins the discussion of accounting for owners' equity (OE) by a corporation.

After studying this lesson, you should be able to:

1. Distinguish the two major types of OE.

2. Identify OE accounts from a list that includes other types of accounts.

3. List several different accounts that fall under *additional paid-in capital*.

4. Compare the corporate form of business organization to other forms of business organization.

5. List and distinguish the rights of common and preferred shareholders.

6. Compute the number of shares in the authorized, issued, outstanding, and treasury states or categories.

7. Apply stock dividends and splits to the computation of the number of shares in each category.

8. Identify terminology differences for OE between U.S. and international reporting.

Definition
Owners' Equity: The owners' equity (OE) accounts represent the residual interest in the net assets of an entity that remain after deducting its liabilities.

I. **Two Main OE Categories**

  A. The two main categories of OE are listed below.

    1. Earned

    2. Contributed

  B. **Earned Capital**—There is no one measurement basis for earned capital (retained earnings) because all of the measurement bases that are reflected in net income are also reflected in retained earnings.

  C. **Contributed Capital**—The primary measurement basis for contributed capital is the historical value of direct investments made in the firm by investors, in return for shares of capital stock.

  D. **Equation**

Total Owners' Equity = Total Assets − Total Liabilities

    1. This balance sheet equation can be used to show the equality of changes in the three types of balance sheet accounts during a period.

Example

The following changes in a firm's aggregate account balances occurred during the year:

	Increase
Assets	$8,900
Liabilities	2,700
Capital stock	6,000
Additional paid-in capital	600

Assume a $300 dividend declaration and that the year's earnings were the only changes in retained earnings for the year. Net income for the year can be found as follows:

Increase in Assets	=	Increase in Liabilities + Increase in OE
$8,900	=	$1,700 + $6,000 + $600 + net income − $300
Net income	=	$900

II. Presentation of Equity Accounts

A. **Major Account Types**—For a corporation, the major account types in OE are:

1. **Preferred stock,** the total par value of issued preferred stock;

2. **Common stock,** the total par value of issued common stock unless the stock is no-par stock and a stated value is not used;

3. **Additional paid-in capital, preferred**—This account reports the amount received for preferred stock issuances in excess of the par value;

   a. *Additional paid-in capital* is also referred to as *contributed capital in excess of par* and paid-in capital in excess of par.

4. **Additional paid-in capital, common**—This account reports the amount received for common stock issuances in excess of the par value;

   a. In general, additional paid-in capital is a category of OE used for several different sources such as paid-in capital from treasury stock transactions, stock award plans, and others.

5. **Retained earnings,** the net of the firm's earnings to date less dividends to date, plus or minus other items including prior period adjustments and certain accounting changes.

6. **Accumulated other comprehensive income,** the running total of all other comprehensive income items through the balance sheet date. See the lesson on the "Statement of Comprehensive Income." This category can be considered part of the "earned" component of OE, although the transactions causing changes in this category are not run through earnings and therefore are not included in retained earnings.

7. **Treasury stock,** which is the cost or par value of the common stock of a firm purchased by that firm, depending on the method used by the firm. Treasury stock of Coca-Cola Company, for example, is stock of Coca-Cola purchased by Coca-Cola. This account is a negative or contra OE account.

B. **Types of Ownership**

1. The types of ownership, and, therefore, the types of accounts recorded in OE, include

   a. A sole proprietorship

   b. The partnership form of business

   c. The corporate form of business

> **Exam note**
> *This lesson stresses the corporate form of ownership because that form is emphasized on the CPA Exam.*

2. **Sole Proprietorship**

   a. With a proprietorship, the ownership of the business enterprise consists of a single individual or party.

3. **Partnership**

   a. With a partnership, the ownership of the business enterprise consists of two or more participants.

4. **Corporation**

   a. With the corporate form of business, the stock may be closely held by a small number of investors or, in the case of a publicly traded company, the stock may be held by a large number of investors with the stock traded on an organized exchange.

   b. The stockholders' section of the corporate balance sheet includes the contributed capital accounts, such as common stock and contributed capital in excess of par, the retained earnings account and others referred to above.

   c. Capital stock (preferred or common) is the means by which ownership is conveyed. If there is only one class of stock, it is common stock.

5. **Advantages and disadvantages of the corporate form of business**

   a. Shareholders have limited liability; the corporation is a separate legal entity. Shareholders are not liable for the actions of the corporation and can lose only their investment. Partners and sole proprietors have unlimited liability. If the business cannot satisfy its debts, the creditors can seek relief from the owners of those types of businesses.

   b. A firm "goes public"—i.e., becomes a corporation—because it is easier to raise significant amounts of capital. Any investor in the world can purchase shares of a publicly traded corporation. Current shareholders can likewise sell their shares easily. In contrast, each time the ownership composition of a partnership changes, the partnership agreement is redrawn.

   c. Lack of mutual agency for a corporation. The actions of one shareholder (unless that shareholder is an officer of the corporation) do not bind the corporation or other shareholders. In contrast, each partner's actions bind the partnership.

   d. Double taxation of corporate profits. A corporation must pay income taxes and file an annual tax return. Dividends to shareholders are taxed on their personal returns. This double taxation is mitigated to some extent through the dividends received deduction if a shareholder of one corporation is another corporation (discussed in the taxation section of this review course). In contrast, partnerships and sole proprietorships file only an information return. The owners pay income tax on their portion of the income from the business.

   e. Corporations are subject to a great deal more regulation, including SEC reporting requirements for publicly held corporations.

6. **Hybrid organizations**—These organizations have some of the characteristics of both corporations and partnerships or sole proprietorships.

   a. S corporation. This is a classification for tax purposes. If the relevant tax rules are followed, limited liability is retained but the income is taxed only once, at the owner level.

   b. Limited liability companies allow all owners to be involved in the management of the business with each being liable only to the extent of their investment. Double taxation is avoided.

   c. Limited liability partnerships are less generous with respect to the limited liability feature.

III. Legal Capital—*Par* value is the minimum legal issue price for capital stock in most states and appears on the stock certificate.

    A. No Par Value Alternatives—If the stock has no par value, two alternatives exist:

        1. The firm may designate a stated value, which serves the same function as par value except that it does not appear on the certificate.

        2. The firm may not use a par value or stated value at all, in which case the stock is referred to as no par stock.

    B. Measured at Par or Stated

        1. The preferred stock and common stock accounts are always measured at par or stated value.

        2. Any excess of issuance price over the par value is credited to additional paid-in capital (preferred or common).

    C. No Par Stock Credited—If the stock is no-par stock, then the entire issuance proceeds is credited to the capital stock account and there is no additional paid-in capital account (contributed capital in excess of par).

    D. Legal Capital—The legal capital or minimum capital of a corporation is usually the par value of the stock or the stated value of the stock issued.

        1. Establishes Minimum Investment—This legal requirement establishes the minimum investment necessary to become a part of the ownership group of a corporation.

        2. Protection for Creditors—Legal capital provides a measure of protection for the creditors of the corporation.

            a. Dividends may not be paid from legal capital.

            b. If there were no such protection, management could liquidate the corporation by paying back the shareholders their investment, leaving the creditors with assets that might not be worth their book value.

            c. In many states, firms may not pay dividends to common stock in an amount that would cause total assets to be less than total liabilities plus the liquidation preference of preferred stock. The liquidation preference of preferred stock is the amount payable on liquidation of the company.

    E. Stock Not Discounted—In most states, stock cannot be sold at a discount.

        1. If stock is sold at a discount, a contingent liability equal to the difference between the par or stated value and the acquisition cost of the stock is borne by the original shareholder.

        2. This requirement is an attempt to provide some legal protection for creditors.

    F. Treasury Stock Transactions—Another attempt to provide some protection for creditors is a limit on the amount of treasury stock transactions.

        1. In many states, treasury stock may not be purchased in excess of the amount of unrestricted or unappropriated retained earnings.

        2. The corollary of this constraint is that the cost of treasury stock is a restriction on retained earnings.

Example
A firm has $100,000 of assets, but only $30,000 is liquid current assets.

Total debt equals $70,000.

The firm has no retained earnings.

The legal capital of the firm is $30,000.

Although the firm has sufficient recorded assets to cover the creditor and shareholder interests, if the $30,000 of liquid assets was paid to the shareholders, buying out their interests, the $70,000 book value of remaining assets may not be sufficient to cover the creditors' claims because the assets may have a market value significantly less than $70,000.

The creditors would incur a loss.

This would be in direct violation of the order of rights upon liquidation of a corporation: Stockholders receive assets after all the creditors are satisfied.

IV. Rights of Shareholders, States of Stock

    A. Common Stock Rights—In return for purchasing a share of common stock, the common shareholder receives the following rights:

        1. Voting rights

            a. Common shareholders have the right to participate in the decision-making process of a corporation by voting for the board of directors, the external auditors, and other major issues.

            b. That is, the shareholders have a right to participate in major operating and financing decisions through the exercise of voting rights.

            c. They do not, however, have the right to participate in day-to-day management functions.

        2. Dividend rights

            a. Common shareholders have rights related to the receipt of dividends.

            b. The dividend rights of common shareholders are subordinate rights in that preferred shareholders receive their dividend allocation prior to any allocation to the common shareholders.

            c. Dividends are not mandatory.

            d. The Board of Directors must declare dividends before the firm is liable to the shareholders for dividends.

        3. Preemptive rights

            a. The preemptive rights of common shareholders allow current shareholders to maintain their existing percentage of the firm in the event of a new stock issuance by the firm.

            b. Preemptive rights are not always present, depending on state law and the corporate charter.

            c. The preemptive right is important to shareholders owning an appreciable percentage of the firm.

            d. Without the preemptive right, management could issue shares in an effort to reduce the percentage ownership (and influence) of a shareholder who disagrees with the current management over major issues affecting the direction of the firm.

Example
A firm plans to issue 100,000 shares of common stock.

A shareholder currently owns 2% of the outstanding common stock.

The shareholder must be allowed to purchase 2,000 of the new shares if the preemptive right is present.

The shareholder cannot be compelled to make the purchase, however.

4. **Rights Related to Liquidation**—In the event of liquidation, common shareholders are again in a subordinate role.

   a. The creditors are satisfied first.

   b. Then, the preferred shareholders are eligible to receive the liquidation values for the preferred shares.

   c. Finally, the remaining assets are distributed to the common shareholders. The common shareholders are the very last to receive assets on liquidation. They have the residual interest in the firm.

   d. Positive total owners' equity does not necessarily imply that any shareholders will receive assets upon liquidation. If the fair value of assets is less than total liabilities at liquidation, no shareholder would receive any assets.

B. **Preferred Stock Rights**—Preferred stock is called *preferred* because these shares typically are paid dividends before common stock. Preferred shareholders, however, usually give up their right to vote in return for the dividend preference.

   1. **The rights of preferred shareholders are**

      a. **Nonvoting**—Typically, preferred shareholders do not have voting rights. That is, preferred shareholders are not participants in the major operating and financing decisions made by the company.

      b. **Dividend Preferences**—In relation to dividends, preferred shareholders receive their dividend allocation first. Then, the remainder of the dividend is allocated to common shareholders.

      c. **Additional Features**—Additional features, such as withcumulativepreferred stock and participating preferred stock, can enhance this dividend preference for preferred shareholders. The process of allocating dividends to the two types of stock is illustrated in a later lesson.

      d. **Dividends in Arrears**

         i. If preferred stock is cumulative and dividends for a year are not paid, then the dividends are said to be in arrears.

         ii. No dividends may be paid to any other class of stock, including the current preferred stock dividend requirement, until the dividends in arrears are paid.

         iii. This is how the dividend preference for preferred stock is preserved. However, there is no liability for dividends in arrears until the dividends are declared.

         iv. Undeclared dividends in arrears are disclosed in the footnotes until the dividends are paid.

      e. **Liquidation Preferences**

         i. In the event of liquidation, the creditors are paid first.

    ii. Second, the preferred shareholders receive their specified liquidation values per share. This amount may be different from par value, or the value paid for the shares. The liquidation preference per share of preferred stock must be disclosed in the equity section of the balance sheet when the preference exceeds par value. There is no preemptive right for preferred shareholders because preferred stock does not vote in the affairs of the corporation.

    iii. Finally, any remainder is allocated to the common shareholders.

C. Number of Common Shares Issued, Outstanding, and in the Treasury

    1. Common Stock—When a corporation is formed, the total number of shares that may be issued is called the *authorized shares*. This amount can be increased only by vote of the shareholders. For common stock, this total can be broken down into:

        a. Number issued: The number of shares ever issued by the firm but not retired

        b. Number outstanding: The number of shares currently held by stockholders

        c. Number in the treasury: The number of shares purchased by the issuing firm and not yet reissued. Treasury shares are included in the number of issued shares:

> \# Issued Shares = \# Outstanding Shares + \# Treasury Shares

> **Note**
> The number of issued shares is always greater than or equal to the number of outstanding shares.

    2. Treasury Not Outstanding—Cash and property dividends are not paid on treasury stock because treasury shares are not outstanding.

    3. Shares Outstanding—Earnings per share and most other per-share calculations are made on shares outstanding because these shares represent the *active* shares—those in the hands of the investors. These are the shares that vote and receive dividends.

    4. Dividends and Splits—Stock dividends and splits not substantive transactions. They do not cause a change in the firm's assets or relative ownership in the firm. For calculation purposes, they are retroactively applied to all issuances of stock preceding the stock dividend or split.

Examples
1. *Shares Outstanding Computation*

A corporation had 70,000 shares of common stock authorized and 30,000 shares outstanding at the beginning of the year. During the year, the following events occurred:

January	Declared 10% stock dividend
June	Purchased 10,000 shares for the treasury
August	Reissued 5,000 shares
November	Declared 2-for-l stock split

At the end of the year, the number of outstanding shares of common stock are:

$(30{,}000(1.10) - 10{,}000 + 5{,}000)2 = 56{,}000$

Stock dividends and splits are applied retroactively to all shares outstanding and are applied to all substantive changes in shares outstanding that occur before the stock dividend or split.

2. ***Number of Shares Issued and Outstanding Calculation***

Of the 12,500 shares of common stock issued by a firm, 2,500 shares were in the treasury at the beginning of the year. During the year, the following transactions occurred in chronological order:

a. 1,300 treasury shares were reissued under a stock compensation plan.

b. A 3-for-1 stock split took effect.

c. 500 shares of treasury stock were purchased.

Issued shares include outstanding shares and treasury shares. Treasury shares are issued but not outstanding. Stock splits are applied to all outstanding shares because a split reduces the par value of each share of issued stock. Treasury shares must be adjusted for splits because treasury shares typically are reissued.

Number of shares issued at year end: 12,500(3) = 37,500

Number of shares outstanding at year end: (10,000 + 1,300)3 − 500 = 33,400

3. ***Number of Shares Issued and Outstanding Computation***

A firm issued 10,000 shares of common stock. Of these, 500 were held as treasury stock at December 31, 20X3. During 20X4, transactions involving the firm's common stock were as follows:

May—100 shares of treasury stock were sold.

August—1,000 shares of previously unissued stock were sold.

November—A 2-for-1 stock split took effect.

Laws in the firm's state of incorporation protect treasury stock from dilution. At December 31, 20X4, the number of common stock issued and outstanding:

Issued = (10,000 + 1,000)2 = 22,000

Outstanding = (9,500 + 100 + 1,000)2 = 21,200

The treasury shares are already issued. Therefore, in the calculation of issued shares, no separate adjustment for treasury shares is needed.

D. Disclosures

1. Footnote disclosures for equity can be extensive if the entity has several classes of stock. The following are required disclosures.

   a. Rights and preferences of each class of stock including liquidation preferences and voting rights

   b. Number of shares authorized, issued, and outstanding for each class of stock

   c. Par value for each class of stock

   d. Treasury shares

   e. Restrictions regarding dividends and dividends in arrears

   f. Call and conversion information

E. U.S. GAAP—IFRS Differences

1. International and U.S. accounting for stockholders' equity are very similar. Some areas are not addressed by international standards and the U.S. treatment is typically prescribed in these situations. In terms of presentation on the balance sheet, OE is often presented before liabilities in international statements. Owners' equity in international statements has three main categories: issued share capital, retained earnings, and other equity including reserves. The term *reserve* is not commonly used in U.S. financial reporting.

2. **Terminology differences**

   a. Common stock and its account in the ledger are referred to as "ordinary shares" for international accounting.

   b. Preferred stock is referred to as *preference shares*.

   c. Paid-in capital in excess of par (or additional paid-in capital) is referred to as *share premium*.

   d. The term *reserve* is commonly used.

3. **Reserves**

   a. In some international jurisdictions, reserves are similar to retained earnings appropriations under U.S. GAAP in that they restrict dividends. Paid-in capital, for example, is typically off-limits for dividends as well as amounts paid for treasury stock (capital redemption reserve). Firms may set up a reserve account for that purpose (a credit to an OE account). Likewise, the revaluation surplus or reserve from upward revaluation of plant assets is not available for dividends.

   b. The items reported in other comprehensive income are referred to as "reserves" for international accounting. For example, the net unrealized gain or loss on available-for-sale securities under the fair value method is referred to as *investment revaluation reserve*. Another is the revaluation reserve from upward revaluation of plant assets.

   c. Depending on the jurisdiction, a firm may be required to establish a reserve, called a statutory or legal reserve, based on the requirements of the law. These reserves may be required for protection of creditors. The reserve is created in an account similar to an appropriation under U.S. standards.

4. **Disclosures**

   a. In addition to the usual disclosures involving equity as per U.S. statements, international disclosures also include amounts of capital not yet paid in, restrictions on the repayment of capital, and changes in reserve accounts.

   b. The amount of treasury stock can be disclosed either in the OE section of the balance sheet or in the notes.

   c. If a firm reserves shares for future issuance under stock options or subscription contracts, the number of shares, terms, and amounts are disclosed. A firm must have sufficient shares to satisfy these commitments. The reserved shares are not available for other transactions.

Stock Issuance

The different ways that stock is issued are addressed in this lesson.

After studying this lesson, you should be able to:

1. Prepare the journal entry for the issuance of par stock, no-par stock with stated value, and true no-par stock, for cash.

2. Record a stock subscription and defaults by subscribers.

3. Classify the stock subscriptions receivable account.

4. Record the journal entry for stock issued in exchange for a nonmonetary asset or service.

5. Allocate the total issuance proceeds to several securities in a basket sale.

6. Account for stock issuance costs.

I. **There Are Several Types of Stock Issuance Transactions**

   A. **Cash Transaction**—In recording a cash sale of common stock, the corporation will credit the stock account for the par or stated value of the stock sold. Any remainder is recorded in an account such as contributed capital in excess of par value or in excess of stated value.

   Example
   A firm issues 2,000 shares of $4 par common stock for $10 each.

Cash	20,000	
Common Stock		8,000 OE account, only par value
Paid-in capital in excess of par		12,000 OE account, all the rest

   B. **Preferred Stock**—Is handled the same way; the issuance of preferred stock credits the Preferred stock account and contributed capital in excess of par (preferred).

   C. **True No Par Stock**—When the stock is true no-par stock (without stated value),

      1. The entire proceeds from issuance of stock are credited to the common stock account.

      2. No contributed capital account is recorded.

   D. **Stock Sold on a Subscription Basis**

      1. Sale of stock on a subscription basis requires a contract specifying

         a. Share price

         b. Number of shares

         c. And the payment dates

      2. **When stock is sold** on a subscription basis, the implication is that the selling price of the stock will be received in a series of payments from the shareholder. Once the full amount is received, the stock will be issued.

      3. **At the signing of the contract**—Subscribers may make their first payment.

> **Note**
> *If the stock has no par value but a stated value is specified, the contributed capital account is titled: Paid-in capital in excess of stated value (common).*

4. **Initial payment**

Cash	amount of payment
Stock subscriptions receivable	sum of remaining payments
Common stock subscribed	(par) × (# of shares subscribed)
Contributed capital in excess of par	(contract price − par) × (# shares)

5. **Subsequent payments**

Cash	amount of payment
Stock subscriptions receivable	amount of payment

6. **Issuance of shares after final payment**

Common stock subscribed	(par) × (# of shares subscribed)
Common stock	(par) × (# of shares subscribed)

7. **Account classifications**—Stock subscriptions receivable: contra-common stock subscribed (contra OE)

8. **Common stock subscribed**—Owners' equity

9. **Recorded at signing**—Note that the contributed capital in excess of par is recorded when the contract is signed indicating that, in all probability, the shares will be issued.

10. **Credited upon final payment**—Common stock is not credited until the final payment is made because the shares are not issued at that time.

11. **Default by subscriber**—If the subscriber fails to make all the payments and defaults, the journal entry to record the default depends on the contract and applicable state law.

12. Possibilities include:

   a. Return all payments to subscriber.

   b. Issue shares in proportion to payments made.

   c. The subscriber receives no refund or shares.

Example
An individual subscribes to 200 shares of $10 par common stock at a subscription price of $15. After making payments totaling $1,200, the subscriber defaults.

Summary entry before default:

Cash	1,200	
Stock subscriptions receivable	1,800	
Common stock subscribed		2,000
Contributed capital in excess of par		1,000

Analysis

It is important to remember that the receivable (a confusing account name) is not an asset but rather a contra-equity account. There is no increase in OE for the unpaid portion. The increase in the firm's assets and OE from the above transaction is $1,200, not $3,000.

Default assumption (1), return all payments to subscriber:

The above entry is reversed.

Default assumption (2), issue shares in proportion to payments made:

$1,200/$15 = 80 shares fully paid. Required ending balances:

Common stock: 80($10)		= $800
Contributed capital in excess of par: 80($15-$10)		= $400

Common stock subscribed	2,000	
Contributed capital in excess of par	600	
Subscriptions receivable		1,800
Common stock		800

OE increases $1,200 as a result of this entry.

Default assumption (3), no refund or shares to subscriber:

Common stock subscribed	2,000	
Contributed capital in excess of par	1,000	
Subscriptions receivable		1,800
Contributed capital from default		1,200*

*Equals amount paid in by subscriber

E. **Stock Issued in Exchange for Nonmonetary Consideration**

1. **Value most clearly determined**—When stock is sold and a nonmonetary asset is received, the recording of the transaction will be based on the fair value of the stock sold or the fair value of the asset received (or services received), whichever can be most clearly determined.

2. **Small number of shares**—When the stock is actively traded, and the number of shares issued is small in relation to the number of shares already outstanding, generally the market price of the issued shares is the more reliable of the two measures.

3. **Significant number of shares**—If the number of shares issued is significant, then the market value of the consideration received may be a better measure because the issuance of a large number of shares could affect the market price of the stock.

Example

1. A firm issued 300 shares of $5 par common stock for used equipment.

2. The market value of the equipment is not easily determinable.

3. The firm's stock was quoted at $30 a share on a national stock exchange.

4. The firm has hundreds of thousands of shares outstanding.

Equipment 300($30)	9,000	
Common stock 300($5)		1,500
Contributed capital in excess of par - common		7,500

If services are received in exchange for stock issuance, the debit is to an expense.

II. Basket Sale

A. A basket sale occurs when two or more securities are bundled together and sold in a single transaction.

B. The total amount received must be allocated to the individual securities sold.

C. **Allocating Methods**—For example, common stock and preferred stock might be bundled together and sold in a single transaction. In allocating the proceeds to the common stock sold and the preferred stock sold, the company will use the proportional method or the incremental method.

    1. **Proportional method**—When both securities have established market values, the allocation will be based on their respective fair values.

    2. **Incremental method**—When only one security has an established fair value, that security is assigned proceeds equal to the known fair value. Any incremental proceeds are allocated to the remaining security sold.

Examples
100 shares of a firm's $10 par common stock, along with 50 shares of the firm's $12 par preferred stock are issued as a unit for a total consideration of $4,200.

1. The market prices of the shares are: common, $35; preferred, $20.

	Total market values		Allocation of proceeds	
Common	$35(100)	$3,500	($3,500/$4,500)$4,200	$3,267
Preferred	$20(50)	1,000	($1,000/$4,500)$4,200	933
Total		$4,500		$4,200

Entry to record issuance:

Cash	4,200	
Preferred stock 50 × $12		600
Contributed capital in excess of par-preferred ($933 – $600)		333
Common stock 100 × $10		1,000
Contributed capital in excess of par-common ($3,267 – $1,000)		2,267

2. The market price for the common stock is $35. The preferred stock does not sell actively and no current quote is available.

Total allocation to common = $35(100) = $3,500

Remaining amount of proceeds to preferred: $4,200 – $3,500= $700

Entry to record issuance:

Cash	4,200	
Preferred stock 50 × $12		600
Contributed capital in excess of par-preferred ($700 – $600)		100
Common stock 100 × $10		1,000
Contributed capital in excess of par-common ($3,500 – 1,000)		2,500

III. Stock Issue Costs Are Treated as a Reduction in the Proceeds of the Stock Issuance—This reduces the contributed capital in excess of par account.

    A. Rationale—There is no future benefit of the issue costs—that is, the costs have served their purpose as soon as the stock is issued. No future periods benefit. This view emphasizes the balance sheet. The accounting is the same as for debt issue costs.

Note

The annual costs of maintaining the stockholder records and processing dividends are expensed as incurred.

Example

A firm issued 100 shares of $5 par common stock for $26 per share and incurred $75 of stock issue costs.

Cash (100 × $26) − $75	2,525	
Common stock		500
Contributed capital in excess of par, common		2,025

There is no further accounting for the issue costs.

Preferred Stock

This lesson considers the accounting treatment for the issuance, redemption, retirement, and conversion of preferred stock.

After studying this lesson, you should be able to:

1. Prepare the journal entries for the issuance and retirement of preferred stock.

2. Record the conversion of convertible preferred stock.

3. Identify the type of preferred stock that is classified as debt.

I. **Issuance**

A. Preferred stock often has a larger par value than common stock, and has a dividend stated in dollar terms or as a percentage of face value. An issue of 6%, $100 par preferred stock is equivalent to an issue of $6, $100 par preferred stock for example. Upon issuance, any excess of proceeds over total par value of shares issued is credited to contributed capital in excess of par. The credit to the preferred stock account is relatively much larger than the credit to contributed capital excess compared with common stock, which usually carries a small par value.

B. Convertible preferred stock allows the preferred shareholder to convert the preferred shares to common shares. The journal entry for issuance of convertible preferred stock does not allocate any of the proceeds to the conversion feature. As with convertible bonds, the securities are recorded at issuance in the same way nonconvertible securities would be.

C. **Preferred Stock with Warrants**—Preferred stock, like bonds, may be issued with warrants for the purchase of common stock entitling the holder to purchase common stock at a fixed price. The issue price of the preferred stock is allocated to (1) the preferred stock accounts, and (2) another OE account for the common stock warrants. The allocation is based on fair value. When the warrants are exercised, cash is debited, the warrant account is closed, common shares are issued, and the common stock accounts are established.

II. **Calling and Redeeming Preferred Stock**—When preferred stock is called (by the issuer) or redeemed (by the stockholder) or is acquired and retired, all related OE accounts are removed. The issuer can call in callable preferred stock at a specified price during a specified period. No gain or loss is recognized for any of these events because the transactions are between the firm and its owners.

A. Any **debit difference** is recorded in retained earnings.

B. Any **credit difference** is recorded in a contributed capital account.

C. Any **dividends in arrears** must be paid when the shares are acquired (retained earnings is debited).

D. **The General Journal Entry:**

Preferred stock	Par value of stock called or redeemed	
Contributed capital in excess of par	Amount recorded on original issuance*	
Retained earnings	If difference is a debit	
Cash		Amount paid to the shareholders
Contributed capital from retirement of Preferred stock		If difference is a credit

*This amount is limited to the original recorded amount on the shares now acquired back by the issuing firm.

Example
100 shares of 6%, $50 par callable cumulative preferred stock with two years of dividends in arrears are called at $53. The shares were issued for $51 a share.

Journal entries:

Retained earnings 2(.06)($50)(100)	600	
Cash (for dividends in arrears)		600
Preferred stock ($50)(100)	5,000	
Contributed capital in excess of par, preferred ($51 − $50)100	100	
Retained earnings ($53 − $51)100	200	
Cash $53(100)		5,300

III. Conversion of Preferred Stock—When convertible preferred stock is converted into common stock, the preferred stock accounts are transferred to the common stock accounts. Again, there is no gain or loss.

   A. Retained Earnings Debited—If the total recorded value of the preferred stock is less than the par value of the common stock issued on conversion, retained earnings is debited for the difference.

   B. The General Journal Entry:

Preferred stock	Par value of stock converted	
Contributed capital in excess of par	Amount recorded on original issuance*	
Retained earnings	If needed	
Common stock		Par value of common stock issued
Contributed capital in excess of par, common		If difference is a credit

* This amount is limited to the original recorded amount on the shares now being converted to common.

Example
100 shares of 6%, $50 par convertible preferred stock are converted into $10 par common stock at a rate of two shares of common per share of preferred. The preferred stock was for $51 a share.

Journal entry:

Preferred stock ($50)(100)	5,000	
Contributed capital in excess of par, preferred ($51 − $50)100	100	
Common stock 100(2)($10)		2,000
Contributed capital in excess of par, common		3,100

If each share of preferred stock was convertible into six shares of common stock, the conversion entry would be:

Preferred stock ($50)(100)	5,000	
Contributed capital in excess of par, preferred ($51 − $50)100	100	
Retained earnings	900	
Common stock 100(6)($10)		6,000

IV. Redeemable Preferred Stock

A. Redeemable preferred stock may require the issuing firm to (1) redeem the stock (purchase the stock from the shareholder) at a specified future date at a specified price, or (2) redeem the stock at the option of the shareholder.

    1. A preferred stock or other financial instrument issued in the form of shares is mandatorily redeemable if the issuer is unconditionally required to redeem the instrument by transferring its assets at a specified or determinable date(s) or when an event certain to occur takes place. If the obligation to redeem is dependent on a future uncertain event, the instrument is considered to be **mandatorily redeemable** when that event occurs, or when the event becomes certain to occur.

B. **Balance Sheet Classification**—Mandatorily redeemable financial instruments (such as redeemable preferred stock) must be classified as debt (rather than owners' equity) unless the redemption is required to occur only if the issuing firm goes out of business.

    1. At the end of each year the liability is reported at the present value of the amount to be paid at maturity. The implicit rate at date of issuance is used for the discounting. Interest expense is recorded for the amount of cash dividends paid, as adjusted for the change in present value for the maturity amount.

    2. If either the maturity date or maturity value (redemption price) is not known, the fair value is used for balance sheet reporting and the change in fair value is used for interest expense measurement.

V. U.S. GAAP–IFRS Differences

A. Under international standards, when (1) preferred stock provides for mandatory redemption for a fixed or determinable amount at a fixed or determinable date, or (2) gives the holder the right to require the issuer to redeem the stock at or after a particular date for a fixed or determinable amount, then it is classified as a liability. As such, more preferred stock is reported as debt for international reporting.

    1. Under international standards, the feature that makes an item debt is that the issuer is currently, or can be required to, deliver cash or other financial instrument to the holder of the instrument with terms that are potentially unfavorable to the issuer.

B. If a preferred stock issue does not explicitly meet either of the two criteria above but is expected to meet one later during its term, then again it is treated as a liability.

    1. An example is preferred stock with a dividend that increases over time such that the issuer will be required to redeem the preferred stock. Another is if the holder has the option to require redemption if a future event occurs, and that event is probable, then the instrument is classified as debt.

Treasury Stock

This lesson covers the cost and par methods of accounting for treasury stock. Share retirement also is covered.

After studying this lesson, you should be able to:

1. Describe the accounting for share retirement.

2. Identify the differences between the cost and par methods.

3. Record the purchase and reissuance of treasury stock under the cost and par methods.

4. Identify the main accounting aspects of all treasury stock transactions.

Exam Tip
CPA Exams in the past have listed a firm's treasury stock in the investment section of the balance sheet in questions calling for the candidate to identify errors. This requires the candidate to recognize that treasury stock is not an asset of the firm. It is reported as a contra-owner's equity account. These questions are solved by reducing the investment account by the amount recorded as treasury stock and reinstating the treasury stock account as a reduction from total OE.

I. **Accounting Generalizations About Treasury Stock**—The following statements hold regardless of the method used to account for treasury stock, which are shares of a firm's common stock purchased (bought back) by that firm.

   A. No one owns treasury stock—there is no shareholder for this stock. A firm cannot own itself.

   B. Treasury stock is not an asset.

   C. A firm cannot record any income account in a treasury stock transaction.

   D. A firm cannot profit from treasury stock transactions.

   E. The treasury stock account is debited upon purchase of treasury stock. The account is a contra OE account. The common stock account is not affected by treasury stock transactions because treasury stock is considered issued stock.

   F. Treasury stock reduces the number of shares outstanding but not the number of shares issued, because treasury stock is issued stock.

   G. When treasury stock is purchased, earnings per share increases because the denominator of EPS is reduced with no effect on the numerator.

   H. The net assets and owners' equity of the firm decrease by the cost of treasury shares purchased.

   I. Retained earnings can be decreased in some cases, but never increased by treasury stock transactions.

II. **Accounting for Treasury Stock**

   A. There are two methods to account for treasury stock:

      1. **Cost Method**—Records the treasury stock account at the cost of shares reacquired;

      2. **Par Value Method**—Records the treasury stock account at the par value of shares reacquired.

   B. Owners' equity is reduced by the same amount, regardless of which method is used, but the balances of certain OE accounts are different under the two methods.

III. **Cost Method**

   A. **Description of the Cost Method**—At purchase, treasury stock is debited for the cost of the shares purchased. The contributed capital in excess of par account that was credited when the stock was issued is not affected. Reissuances credit the treasury stock account at cost, and the difference

483

between the purchase price and reissue price is recorded in contributed capital from treasury stock.

B. **Journal Entry Example:** (The par of common stock is $5, original issuance price was $20, a total of 700 shares have been issued, and retained earnings is $4,000.)

Purchase 200 shares of treasury stock for $25 a share:

Treasury stock (cost) 200 × $25	5,000	
Cash		5,000

Reissue 50 shares of treasury stock for $30 a share (greater than cost):

Cash 50 × $30	1,500	
Contributed capital from treasury stock ($30 – $25)50		250*
Treasury stock 50 × $25		1,250**

* Excess of reissue price over cost of treasury stock
** FIFO, average or specific identification can be used to measure the cost of treasury stock sold when there is more than one cost represented in the treasury stock account.

Reissue 50 shares of treasury stock for $18 a share (less than cost):

Cash 50 × $18	900	
Contributed capital from treasury stock	250*	
Retained earnings	100**	
Treasury stock 50 × $25		1,250

* Reduces the balance to zero.
** The total excess of cost over reissue price is 50($25 – $18) = $350. The contributed capital from treasury stock account accounts for $250 of that amount. The remainder is taken from retained earnings.

Analysis

Treasury stock purchases reduce the firm's total assets, net assets, and total OE. Erroneously recording treasury stock as an asset (e.g., an investment) would have no effect on these amounts and thus would serve to overstate the firm's assets and OE.

When a firm purchases its own stock, it literally contracts in size. Firms buy back their own stock for a variety of reasons, such as to increase EPS, return cash to the shareholders, and to thwart hostile takeovers.

IV. **Balance Sheet Presentation**—Treasury stock is subtracted at the very bottom of the OE section of the balance sheet. The balance is $2,500 (100 treasury shares remaining × $25 cost). The common stock and original contributed capital in excess of par accounts are unaffected.

OE section:	
Common stock 700($5)	$ 3,500
Contributed capital in excess of par 700($20 – $5)	10,500
Contributed capital from treasury stock	0
Retained earnings $4,000 – $100	3,900
Less treasury stock at cost	($2,500)
Total OE	$15,400

V. Par Value Method

A. This is the second of two methods allowed for treasury stock accounting. The first is the cost method, covered in the previous lesson.

B. **Description of the Par Value Method**—At purchase, the treasury stock account is debited for par value, and the contributed capital in excess of par account that was credited when the stock was issued is debited for the original amount recorded. Reissuances are treated as a regular issuance of stock except that treasury stock is credited, rather than common stock.

C. **Journal Entry Example**—The initial data for the cost method (previous example) is used (par of common stock is $5, original issuance price was $20, a total of 700 shares have been issued, and retained earnings is $4,000) but, the transactions in this example are not the same as for the cost method so that the main aspects of the par method can be shown.

Purchase 100 shares of treasury stock for $15 a share (less than original price):

Treasury stock (par) 100 × $5	500	
Contributed capital in excess of par, common ($20 − $5)100	1,500	
Contributed capital from treasury stock ($20 − $15)100		500
Cash		1,500

This entry reduces the original contributed capital in excess of par as if the stock were going to be retired.

Purchase 100 shares of treasury stock for $22 a share (greater than original price):

Treasury stock 100 × $5	500	
Contributed capital in excess of par, common ($20 − $5)100	1,500	
Contributed capital from treasury stock ($22 − $20)100	200	
Cash 100 × $22		2,200

It is important to remember that the contributed capital in excess of par account is always reduced by the original amount received when the stock was issued ($1,500).

The excess of the cost ($22) over original issue price ($20) is first taken from any previous contributed capital from treasury stock transactions. In this case, $500 is available from the previous treasury stock purchase.

If this amount were insufficient to complete the debit side of the entry, retained earnings would be reduced by the remaining amount. (If the purchase price had been $28, then retained earnings would be reduced by $300.)

Reissue 150 shares of treasury stock for $18 a share:

Cash 150 × $18	2,700	
Contributed capital in excess of par ($18 − $5)150		1,950
Treasury stock 150 × $5		750

This entry is essentially the same as for the issuance of unissued stock. The only difference is that treasury stock, rather than common stock, is credited.

D. **Balance Sheet Presentation**—Treasury stock is reported as a subtraction from the common stock account in the balance sheet. The balance is (50 treasury shares remaining × $5 par) = $250. The common stock and original contributed capital in excess of par accounts are unaffected. Assume that 700 shares of common stock have been issued. The balance sheet would show:

OE section:

Common stock 700 ($5)	$ 3,500
Less treasury stock at cost (50 × $5)	(250)
Common stock outstanding	3,250
Contributed capital in excess of par	
700($20-$5) − $1,500 − $1,500 + $1,950	9,450
Contributed capital from treasury stock	
$500 − $200	300
Retained earnings	4,000
Total OE	$17,000

(The total OE for the cost and par value method examples are not equal because the transactions were different. If the transactions were the same, the total OE would be the same although the component balances other than the common stock account could be different.)

VI. Comparison of Cost and Par Value Methods

A. When treasury shares are purchased at a cost greater than par but less than original issue price, what is the relative impact of the cost and the par value methods on additional paid-in capital and retained earnings?

1. **Cost Method**—Under the cost method, when treasury stock is purchased for an amount less than original price, the treasury stock account is debited. This is a contra OE account. Additional paid-in capital and retained earnings are unaffected.

2. **Par Value Method**—Under the par value method, the treasury stock account is debited for par value, and additional paid-in capital is debited for the amount in proportion to the original issue price. Because less was paid for the treasury stock than was received on original issuance, retained earnings is unaffected. Rather, additional paid-in capital from treasury stock is credited for the difference, but not by as much as the debit to the original issuance additional paid-in capital account.

3. Therefore, additional paid-in capital decreases under the par value method relative to the cost method, but there is no difference in the effect on retained earnings under the conditions imposed.

B. Use of the contributed capital from treasury stock account when treasury shares are reissued or purchased:

	Cost Method	Par Value Method
Increase in Contributed Capital from Treasury Stock	Reissue at a price exceeding cost	Purchase at a price less than original issue price
Decrease in Contributed Capital from Treasury Stock	Reissue at a price less than cost	Purchase at a price exceeding original issue price

VII. Share Retirement

A. Sometimes firms retire their shares after purchasing them on the market, rather than treating them as treasury shares. Retired shares are placed back into the authorized but unissued category.

Accounting for the purchase and retirement of shares is the same as the purchase of treasury shares under the par value method, except that common stock account is used instead of the treasury stock account.

1. If the purchase price is less than the original issue price, then contributed capital from stock retirement is credited.

2. If the purchase price is greater than the original issue price, then contributed capital from stock retirement is debited until exhausted, and retained earnings is debited for the remainder, if any.

B. Subsequent issuance of the retired shares is recorded as a normal stock issuance, because the retired shares were treated as unissued.

Dividends

This lesson considers cash and other property dividends, which are distributions of the firm's earnings (reduction in retained earnings).

After studying this lesson, you should be able to:

1. Identify the important dates for recording dividends.

2. State the accounting treatment of dividends in arrears.

3. Record a property dividend using the correct amount.

4. Prepare the journal entries for declaration and payment of a scrip dividend.

5. Note the main difference between liquidating dividends and other cash and property dividends.

I. **Cash and Other Property Dividends**

A. Cash, and other property dividends reduce the distributing firm's assets and retained earnings. A liability is recognized for these liabilities on the date of declaration. Stock dividends also reduce retained earnings but do not involve a distribution of assets. No liability is recognized for stock dividends.

1. **Relevant dates**—In relation to dividends, there are three important dates (listed in chronological order).

a. The **declarative date** is the date the board of directors formally declares the dividend. This is the most important date in terms of the effect on the firm's resources and therefore its balance sheet. At this date, the firm recognizes a liability and a reduction in retained earnings. The firm's net assets are reduced.

b. The **date of record** is simply a cut-off date. The shareholders of record on this date will be the recipients of the dividend payments. This date is used because it requires a certain amount of time to compile the list of shareholders as of a particular date.

c. The **payment date** is the date the dividends are actually distributed to the shareholders. Firms typically pay dividends quarterly. The time lag between declaration and payment can be a few weeks. The fourth-quarter dividend is declared near the end of the fiscal year, but payment often occurs early the next year. Therefore, the amount of dividends declared in a year often is not the same as the amount of dividends paid in that year. Payment does not reduce the firm's retained earnings and net assets; rather, it is the *declaration* that reduces retained earnings and net assets.

B. **Cash Dividends**

1. The distribution of earnings will take the form of a cash distribution. The related liability will be recognized on the date of declaration. The typical entries related to a cash dividend are shown below. Dividends are not recognized as an expense for the firm paying the dividends.

Date of Declaration:	Retained Earnings*	xx	
	Dividends Payable		xx

* Some firms debit the temporary account Dividends Declared rather than debit retained earnings directly. At year-end, the Dividends Declared account is closed to retained earnings.

2. Date of Record:	No Entry		

3. Date of Payment:	Dividends Payable	xx	
	Cash		xx

C. **Dividends in Arrears**—Unpaid dividends for a particular year on cumulative preferred stock. Dividends are not required to be paid but are said to accumulate if unpaid. However, no liability is recognized for dividends in arrears until there has been a dividend declaration. The cumulative feature of preferred stock simply means in the event of a dividend declaration, preferred shareholders are entitled to be paid the dividends in arrears before any distribution related to the current period occurs. Dividends in arrears are disclosed in the footnotes.

D. **Other Property Dividends**

1. In this type of dividend, the distribution of earnings will take the form of a noncash distribution. The related liability and the gain or loss on disposal of the asset is recognized on the date of declaration. The dividend is recorded at the asset's fair value *at declaration date*. The typical entries related to a property dividend are shown below.

Date of Declaration:	Retained Earnings	xx	
	Dividends Payable		xx

2. The above entry is recorded at the fair value of the asset to be distributed. Retained earnings are reduced by the true economic sacrifice of declaring the dividend at the time of making the commitment to distribute the asset. The liability is also measured at fair value. In addition to the above entry, one of the following two entries is made to adjust the asset to fair value at declaration date. The amount recorded is the difference between book value and fair value.

Asset	xx	
Gain on Disposal		xx
or		
Loss on Disposal	xx	
Asset		xx

3. Remaining entries:

Date of Record:	No Entry		
Date of Payment:	Dividends Payable	xx	
	Asset		xx

The credit to the asset is for the adjusted book value, which equals the fair value on the declaration date. Ignoring income tax effects, the net reduction in retained earnings resulting from a property dividend is the book value of the asset to be distributed. Retained earnings is reduced by the fair value of the asset distributed, but the gain or loss decreases or increases that effect to a net amount equaling the book value of the asset distributed.

 **Example**
A firm declares and pays a property dividend. The book value of the asset distributed is $4,000, and the fair value is $6,000.

Retained Earnings	6,000	
Dividends Payable		6,000
Asset	2,000	
Gain on Asset Distribution		2,000
Dividends Payable	6,000	
Asset		6,000

Retained earnings is decreased a net of $4,000 ($6,000 from recording the dividend – $2,000 gain on asset), an amount equaling the book value of the asset.

II. **Scrip Dividends**—A scrip dividend is first distributed in note payable (scrip) form because the firm does not have the cash at the date of declaration to pay the dividend but wants to assure the shareholders that the dividend is forthcoming.

   A. **Interest Paid**—Interest is paid on the note until cash is paid.

   B. **General Entries**

At declaration:	
Retained Earnings	Amount of dividend declared
Scrip Dividend Payable	A liability account
At payment:	
Scrip Dividend Payable	Amount of dividend declared
Interest Expense xx	
Cash	Dividend plus interest

   C. **Interest expense** is computed from the date of declaration to the date of payment using the interest rate in the note. The principal amount is the amount of dividend declared.

   D. **Partial Payment**—If a partial payment is made after declaration (to shareholders of record), then the interest expense is computed from the date of that partial payment to the date the final payment is made. The principal amount on which interest is computed is the amount of the final payment.

   E. **Returns on Capital**—Cash, property, and scrip dividends are returns on capital. They are distributions of earnings, not contributed capital.

III. **Liquidating Dividends**—A liquidating dividend is a return of capital, rather than a return on capital. It is a return of contributed capital—an amount invested by the shareholder.

   A. **Reduces Contributed Capital Account**—The liquidating portion of a dividend reduces a contributed capital account, rather than retained earnings, and must be disclosed as a liquidating dividend.

   B. **Capital Account Debited**—Rather than debiting retained earnings for the liquidating portion, a contributed capital account is debited.

   C. **Liquidating Dividend Occurrence**—One situation in which a liquidating dividend occurs is the payment of a dividend in excess of earnings by a firm in the extractive industries.

1. In this case, because the depletable resource will not be replaced (as would be the case for depreciable assets), a dividend equal to net income plus depletion can be distributed without harming the ability of the firm to maintain capital.

Examples

1. A firm has net income of $10,000 which reflects $2,000 of depletion. A dividend of $12,000 can be paid because the depletable resource will not be replaced. If $12,000 of dividends is declared, the entry is:

Retained Earnings	10,000	
Contributed Capital	2,000	
Dividends Payable		12,000

The liquidating portion is $2,000.

2. A firm in the extractive industries declared a cash dividend of $40,000. The dividend is legal in this state. The following data pertain to the firm just prior to the dividend:

Accumulated Depletion	$10,000
Capital Stock	50,000
Additional Paid-In Capital	15,000
Retained Earnings	30,000

Retained earnings is used first as a source of capital for the dividend ($30,000 of the $40,000 total dividend).

The remaining $10,000 reduces additional paid-in capital and is a liquidating dividend.

The accumulated depletion justifies the liquidating portion because it is a recognized reduction in net income that represents the allocated cost of an investment that will not be replaced. Dividends in excess of income are allowed to the extent of accumulated depletion less any prior liquidating dividends.

IV. U.S. GAAP–IFRS Differences

A. There is no recognition of dividends declared after the balance sheet date but before the financial statements are authorized for issue. No liability or reduction in retained earnings is recorded. This is the case for both international and U.S. reporting.

B. However, for international reporting, the amount of dividends proposed (but not formally approved) or declared before the financial statements were authorized for issue must be disclosed. This disclosure can be made within the OE section of the balance sheet or in the notes. There is no recognition until declaration.

Stock Dividends and Splits

Stock dividends reduce retained earnings but cause no reduction in the firm's assets.

After studying this lesson, you should be able to:

1. Identify the differences between cash dividends, stock dividends, and stock splits.

2. List the effects of stock dividends on shares outstanding, and on the accounts.

3. Record large and small stock dividends.

4. Note the effects of stock splits on the accounts.

I. **Stock Dividends**—A stock dividend is a distribution by a firm of its stock to its shareholders in proportion to their existing holdings. The shareholder does not pay for these shares. Stock dividends do not involve a future transfer of assets or a future provision of services. Therefore, in relation to stock dividends, no liability is recorded. Each investor simply holds more shares, but each share is worth proportionately less than before the dividend. Each investor maintains the previous ownership percentage.

Example
If a firm has 10,000 shares of common stock outstanding and issues a 5% stock dividend, then 500 shares are distributed to the current shareholders at no cost to them.

If a specific shareholder owned 2,000 shares before the dividend (20% ownership), he or she would receive 100 shares (2,000 × .05). After the dividend, the shareholder owns 2,100/10,500 or 20% of the firm (no change in percentage ownership).

A. **Effect of Dividend**—The effect of a stock dividend is to increase the number of shares issued and outstanding.

B. **EPS Decreased**—Earnings per share is decreased by a stock dividend.

C. **Stock Dividend Purpose**—Stock dividends are distributed to reduce the market price of the firm's stock (often because the stock price has become too high for potential investors) and also to reduce demand by shareholders for cash dividends.

D. **Permanent Capitalization**—A stock dividend is a permanent capitalization (reduction) of retained earnings (or possibly paid-in capital for large stock dividends) into contributed capital. The firm's net assets are unaffected. Only OE accounts are affected.

E. **Accounting for Dividends**—Accounting for stock dividends depends on the size of the stock dividend (small or large).

   1. **Small stock dividend** —(% of dividend is less than 20–25%) Capitalize at market price.

Example
Assume a firm has 20,000 shares of $5 par common stock outstanding and declares a 5% stock dividend when the market price (fair value) is $20 per share.

This is a small stock dividend because 5% is less than 20%–25%.

Entry:

Retained earnings 20,000(.05)($20)	20,000	
Common stock 20,000(.05)($5)		5,000
Contributed capital in excess of par, common		15,000

If there is a significant period of time between declaration and distribution of shares, or if the two events occur in different fiscal periods, the account Stock Dividend Distributable

492

is credited instead of Common Stock in the above entry. At distribution, Stock Dividend Distributable is debited and Common Stock is credited.

2. **Market price measure**—The market price of the stock at the **declaration date** is used to measure the stock dividend because that is the date on which the commitment to distribute the dividend is made.

   a. **Market to pay dividend**—Market price is used on the assumption that the market price of the stock will not change given the small size of the dividend, and the shareholder then can sell the shares received while maintaining the predividend market value of the investment. In effect, the firm is using the market to pay the dividend.

   b. **Debit to retained earnings**—Under the above assumption, the debit to retained earnings is the value of the stock distributed and therefore represents the amount of retained earnings to be permanently capitalized to contributed capital. This amount of retained earnings will never be available for cash dividends.

3. **Large stock dividend**—(% of dividend is greater than 20%–25%) Capitalize at par value.

Example
Assume a firm has 20,000 shares of $5 par common stock outstanding and declares a 40% stock dividend when the market price (fair value) is $20 per share.

This is a large stock dividend because 40% is greater than 20%–25%.

Entry:

Retained earnings 20,000(.40)($5)	40,000	
Common stock		40,000

In this case, the assumption cannot be made that the market price of the stock will remain unchanged because of the large dilution in the number of shares outstanding.

Thus, only the par value of shares issued is permanently capitalized. Subsequent changes in market price do not affect the accounting.

   a. Large stock dividends also can be accounted for as a stock split effected in the form of a stock dividend. The debit would be to contributed capital in excess of par, rather than retained earnings in the above example. As such, retained earnings is not capitalized to permanent capital if this alternative is chosen.

   b. We have distinguished small and large stock dividends by referring to "less than 20%–25%," which is sufficient in most cases. However, for SEC registrants, less than 25% is considered small. For other firms, if the dividend percentage is between 20% and 25%, the firm may choose to record the dividend at fair value or at par value of the shares. If less than 20%, par value is used; if more than 25%, fair value is used. The expectation is that the CPA Exam would not use a percentage of 20–25% in order to avoid this confusion.

4. **Change in total OE**—Neither type of stock dividend causes a change in total OE, but retained earnings is reduced and contributed capital is increased (except for a large stock dividend accounted for as a stock split).

   a. **No liability recorded**—It is important to remember that no liability is recorded for a stock dividend because it does not involve the distribution of goods or services, and therefore, does not meet the definition of a liability.

II. **Stock Splits**—A stock split is not a dividend. Rather it is an adjustment to par value and number of issued shares.

   A. **A 2-for-1 split** halves the par value and doubles the number of shares. The reason firms split their shares is to reduce the market price and make the shares available to a larger number of shareholders.

B. No accounting entry is needed although firms may make a memo entry to record the split.

   1. **No change in OE**—There is no change in any account balance within owner's equity.

C. Dividend/Split Similarity—Although both a 100% stock dividend and 2-for-1 stock split double the number of shares outstanding, there are few other similarities.

   1. **Comparison of dividend/split**—Comparison of a 100% stock dividend and 2-for-1 stock split.

	100% stock dividend	2-for-1 stock split
Effect on total OE	None	None
Effect on retained earnings	Decrease	None
Effect on par value	None	Cut in half
Effect on shares outstanding	Double	Double
Effect on contributed capital	Increase	None
Effect on common stock account	Increase	None

III. Additional Aspects

A. Treasury shares usually do not receive stock dividends. However, if the treasury shares were intended to be used to meet a commitment under a stock option plan for example, then the treasury shares would be adjusted for the stock dividend.

B. Real estate trusts and other firms may declare dividends that may be paid in cash or shares at the election of the shareholders with a potential limitation on the total amount of cash that all shareholders can elect to receive in the aggregate. For this type of distribution, the stock portion of the distribution is treated as a stock issuance, not a stock dividend.

Dividend Allocation

The lesson considers the order and allocation of dividends between preferred and common stock.

After studying this lesson, you should be able to:

1. Allocate dividends when there are dividends in arrears.

2. Determine the dividends to common when the firm has partially participating preferred stock.

3. Calculate the dividends to both classes of stock when the firm has fully participating preferred stock.

I. **Introduction**

   A. Nonparticipating preferred stock is entitled only to the annual dividend percentage noted in the stock certificate—the annual dividend requirement.

   B. When the full amount of preferred stock dividend is not paid on cumulative preferred stock for any given year, the unpaid dividends are in arrears and must be paid before any other dividend, including the current-year dividends on preferred stock.

   C. If the preferred stock is noncumulative and any part of the current-year dividends are not paid, then they are never paid.

   D. When preferred stock does not participate beyond its annual percentage or amount, the order of dividend payments is:

      1. Preferred: Any dividends in arrears (only if preferred stock is cumulative)

      2. Preferred: Current-period dividend

      3. Common: Remainder

Example

a. A firm has 200 shares of 5%, $100 par cumulative nonparticipating preferred stock.

b. The annual dividend requirement on the stock is $1,000 (.05 × 200 × $100).

c. This preferred stock might also be referred to as $5 preferred stock (rather than 5%) indicating the annual dividend per share.

d. The firm also has 4,000 shares of $10 par common stock outstanding.

e. Two years of dividends are in arrears as of the beginning of the current year and $7,000 of dividends are declared for the current year.

f. The dividend allocation is (P = preferred; C = common):

		P	C
i. Preferred:	arrears	$2,000	
ii. Preferred:	current	1,000	
iii. Common:	remainder		$4,000
Total		$3,000	$4,000

II. **Preferred Stock Is Participating**—When preferred stock is participating, the stock may receive dividends in addition to the annual current dividend requirement. When preferred participates, common receives a matching amount. Preferred stock may be fully or partially participating.

A. Fully Participating

1. After any dividends in arrears are allocated, the remaining dividends are allocated based on the total par value of the preferred and common stock outstanding.

2. If total dividends are not sufficient to provide common with a matching amount equal to the preferred percentage times total par value of common, then there is no participation and common receives all the dividends after the current year preferred dividend requirement and any dividends in arrears are allocated.

B. Partially Participating

1. The preferred stock receives dividends up to an additional percentage.

   a. Common stock receives a matching amount equal to the preferred percentage times total par of common stock outstanding before the preferred stock receives its additional allocation.

   b. Common stock receives any dividends in excess of the additional amount allocated to common.

2. If the total dividends declared are not sufficient to provide the maximum additional participating percentage to both preferred and common (after common receives its share based on the preferred percentage), then each class of stock receives a share of the remainder in proportion to total par.

3. The steps in the allocation are:

   a. Preferred: Any dividends in arrears

   b. Preferred: Current-period dividend

   c. Common: Matching amount: preferred percentage x total par of common outstanding

   d. Preferred: Additional percentage

   e. Common: Remainder

III. **Examples**—Common information: A firm has 200 shares of 5%, $100 par cumulative participating preferred stock. The annual dividend requirement on the stock is $1,000 (.05 × 200 × $100). The firm also has 4,000 shares of $10 par common stock outstanding.

		Percentage
Total par value of preferred stock outstanding:	$20,000	1/3
Total par value of common stock outstanding:	40,000	2/3
Total par value	$60,000	

Examples

1. *Fully participating*

The preferred stock is fully participating. Two years of dividends are in arrears and total dividends declared are $11,000.

	P	C
a. Preferred: Arrears	$2,000	
b. Preferred: Current	1,000	
c. Common: Matching amount .05($40,000)		$2,000
Dividend remaining =		
$6,000 ($11,000 − $5,000 allocated above)		
d. Preferred: Participation (1/3)($6,000)	2,000	
e. Common: Participation (2/3)($6,000)		4,000
Total	$5,000	$6,000

If total dividends were less than $5,000 but more than $3,000, then common would receive the entire amount above $3,000. There would be no dividends available for participation to either class of stock because common did not receive its matching amount.

2. *Partially participating*

The preferred stock is participating to a maximum additional percentage of 4% (for a total of 9%). Two years of dividends are in arrears, and total dividends declared are $14,000.

	P	C
a. Preferred: Arrears	$2,000	
b. Preferred: Current	1,000	
c. Common: Matching amount .05($40,000)		$2,000
Dividend remaining =		
$9,000 ($14,000 - $5,000 allocated above)		
This amount is less than 4% of total par of both classes of stock: ($2,400 = .04 × $60,000)		
d. Preferred: Participation (.04)($20,000)	800	
e. Common: Remainder ($9,000 − $800)		8,200
Total	$3,800	$10,200

If the remaining dividends after Step 3 were less than $2,400, then the remaining dividends are allocated in proportion to total par value. Using the same information except that total dividends declared are $6,800:

	P	C
a. Preferred: Arrears	$2,000	
b. Preferred: Current	1,000	
c. Common: Matching amount .05($40,000)		$2,000
Dividend remaining		
$1,800 ($6,800 − $5,000 allocated above)		
This amount exceeds 4% of total par of both classes of stock: ($2,400 = .04 × $60,000)		
Therefore the remaining dividend is allocated in proportion to total par value.		
d. Preferred: (1/3)($1,800)	600	
e. Common: (2/3)($1,800)		1,200
Total	$3,600	$3,200

Stock Rights, Retained Earnings

Accounting for stock rights and the retained earnings statement are the focus of this lesson.

After studying this lesson, you should be able to:

1. Account for stock rights issued to existing shareholders, and for rights issued to outside parties.

2. Articulate the reasons for retained earnings appropriations and restrictions.

3. Record retained earnings appropriations.

4. Prepare a statement of retained earnings.

5. Describe each item found in the statement of retained earnings.

I. **Stock Rights**—This section covers the issuance of stock rights to existing shareholders and to outside parties for services. A later lesson covers stock option plans for employees. The main question is whether the issuance of the rights is an event to be recognized in the accounts.

Definition

Stock Right: Gives the holder the option to purchase a certain number of shares of the issuing firm at a specified price during a specified time period.

  A. Stock rights are often used to convey preemptive rights.

  B. The existing shareholders are given rights (via a stock warrant) to purchase their pro rata number of shares to keep their current percentage in the firm.

  C. The rights have an expiration date and must be exercised by this date.

Entries for rights to existing shareholders

At issuance of rights:	No journal entry is made. No resources have been transferred.
At exercise of rights:	The usual entry to record the issuance of stock is made. The issue price is the exercise price as specified in the stock warrant, not the market price on the date of exercise.
If rights lapse:	No entry is made if the shareholder does not exercise the rights.

  D. **Stock Rights Issued to Outside Parties for Services**

At issuance of rights:	Record an expense and owners' equity account equal to the difference between the market price and exercise price, times the number of shares under option.
At exercise of rights:	Record the stock issuance at the exercise price and remove the OE account credited at issuance of the rights.

Example
A firm issues 300 rights to an attorney for services rendered to the firm. Three rights entitle the holder to purchase one share of the firm's $5 common stock for $20. The market value of the stock on the day the rights were issued was $30.

Entries:

At issuance:

Legal expenses ($30 – $20)(300/3)	1,000	
Stock rights outstanding (OE)		1,000

The $1,000 recorded amount represents the opportunity cost to the firm of committing to an issuance of 100 shares of stock for $20 when the market price is currently $30. Subsequent changes in market price do not enter into the accounting.

At exercise:

Cash (300/3)($20)	2,000	
Stock rights outstanding	1,000	
Common stock (300/3)($5)		500
Contributed capital in excess of par, common		2,500

II. Appropriations of Retained Earnings

A. Unappropriated Retained Earnings

1. **Available for declaration**—This portion of retained earnings is available for dividend declaration. In other words, the future use of this amount of retained earnings has not been determined.

2. **No specific purpose**—Unappropriated retained earnings have not been earmarked for a specific purpose.

3. **Not all are paid**—Not all unappropriated retained earnings must be paid in dividends, however.

B. Appropriated Retained Earnings

1. **Declared off-limits**—This amount of retained earnings has been declared off-limits for dividends so that funds may be conserved for a specific purpose or objective.

   a. **Financial planning**—The purpose might be related to financial planning, such as debt retirement or plant expansion.

   b. **Legal requirement**—The purpose or objective might be related to some legal requirement, such as the appropriation of retained earnings related to treasury stock transactions.

   c. **Contractual obligation**—Finally, the purpose of the appropriation might be related to a contractual obligation, such as a clause in a loan agreement requiring the appropriation.

2. **End result**—When retained earnings are appropriated, the amount of unappropriated retained earnings declines, and the amount of possible dividend declarations declines as well.

C. Formal communication—A retained earnings appropriation is management's formal communication that a portion of retained earnings has been declared off-limits for dividends.

D. Appropriation Entry—The entry for an appropriation is:

Retained earnings	amount appropriated
Retained earnings, appropriated for X purpose	amount appropriated

1. **No reduction**—This entry does not reduce total retained earnings nor does it necessarily reduce dividends.

2. **When purpose fulfilled**—When the purpose for which an appropriation is made has been fulfilled, the above entry is reversed, reinstating the amount to unappropriated retained earnings.

    a. **No effect**—The entry to reverse the appropriation also has no effect on total retained earnings.

E. Partition retained earnings—Retained earnings appropriations have no effect on assets. They do not "reserve" assets. They simply partition retained earnings into two parts.

III. Restrictions on Retained Earnings

Definition
Restriction on Retained Earnings: A constraint placed on a certain portion of retained earnings by an external party.

A. Effect Like Appropriation—It has the same effect as an appropriation and may be accompanied by an appropriation.

Examples
States Restrict—States may restrict retained earnings in the amount of the cost of treasury stock held by the firm. This is a protection for the creditors. It forces the firm to maintain its legal capital.

Bondholders Restrict—Bondholders may restrict retained earnings through the debt agreement or bond covenant. This is also a protection for the creditors but this time is protection for a specific group of creditors—the bondholders themselves who want the firm to conserve cash so that their claims can be met.

B. Disclosure—Both restrictions and appropriations are disclosed in the notes to the financial statements.

Note
Both restrictions and appropriations may cause the amount of dividends to be reduced. However, a firm need not appropriate retained earnings or be subject to a constraint on retained earnings in order to lower the amount of dividends paid. The firm simply needs to reduce the amount of dividends declared. However, an appropriation supports this decision and may make such a decision more acceptable to shareholders.

Example
If total retained earnings is $400,000, and a $100,000 appropriation is recorded, and the firm was planning to declare only $150,000 in dividends, the appropriation does not reduce dividends although it may still accomplish its communication objective.

IV. Statement of Retained Earnings

A. Purpose—The purpose of the **Statement of Retained Earnings** is to provide the reader of the financial report with a detailed account of increases and decreases in retained earnings that were recorded in a given accounting period. The retained earnings statement may be shown separately, or more frequently, as part of the statement of changes in equity. If part of the Statement of Changes in Equity, the Statement of Retained Earnings occupies one column.

    1. A typical Statement of Retained Earnings is shown below.

The Tiger Company
Statement of Retained Earnings
For the Year Ended December 31, 20X7

Retained Earnings, January 1, 20X7	XX
Prior Period Adjustment	(±) XX
Change in Accounting Principle (Catch-Up Adjustment)	(±) XX
Restated Balance, January 1, 20X7	XX
(±)Net Income	(±)XX
(–) Cash and Property Dividends Declared	(–)XX
(–)Stock dividends	(–) XX
(=)Retained Earnings, December 31, 20X7	XX

Footnote: The retained earnings balance on December 31, 20X7, is $XX. Of that amount, $YY has been appropriated for . . .

Note
All amounts in the statement can be negative, but cash, property, and stock dividends are always negative amounts. Also, where relevant, amounts are always after-tax amounts.

B. Adjusted for Prior Adjustments

    1. As you can see, the beginning retained earnings balance is adjusted initially for any prior period adjustment (corrections of errors in prior year net income) recorded during the year and for the catch-up adjustment related to changes in accounting principle.

    2. Restated balance—The restated balance is increased by reported income and decreased by any dividend declarations that occurred during the year.

Book Value per Share

This lesson covers the book value per share ratio and accounting for quasi-reorganizations.

After studying this lesson, you should be able to:

1. Compute book value per share.

2. Analyze the effect of transactions on book value per share.

3. Identify the reasons and effects of a quasi-reorganization.

4. Record the journal entries for a quasi-reorganization.

5. Prepare the postreorganization Balance Sheet.

I. **Book Value per Share (of Common Stock)**—Among the ratios tested on the CPA Exam, book value per share has appeared with relative frequency. Its calculation tests a number of details concerning owners' equity.

   A. **Definition**

Definition

Book Value per Share Ratio Equals: Common stockholders' equity per share of outstanding common stock, at the end of the period.

---

   1. **Common Stockholders' Equity**—Common stockholders' equity is total OE after preferred dividend claims are removed.

   2. **Statistic Represents**—The statistic represents the historical value of the firm per common share and may be used as a benchmark for comparisons with market value per share.

      a. However, it is very unlikely that book value per share would ever equal market value per share for most firms.

   B. **Equations**

Book Value per Share Outstanding =

Common Stockholders' Equity/Ending Common Shares of Common Stock Outstanding

Common Stockholder's Equity =

Total OE – Liquidation Preference of Preferred Stock – Preferred Stock Dividends in Arrears

---

   C. **Amount Payable**—The liquidation preference of preferred stock is the amount payable on liquidation of the company. It must be paid before the common stock receives any assets.

 **Examples**

1. *Book Value per Share*

The stockholders' equity section for a firm's balance sheet shows:

6% noncumulative preferred stock, $100 par (liquidation value $105 per share)	$10,000
Common stock	33,000
Retained earnings	12,500
Treasury stock	(6,000)
Total OE	$49,500

At the end of the period, the firm has 100 shares of preferred stock outstanding, 3,300 shares of common stock issued, and 300 common treasury shares.

Book value per share is $13.00 = ($49,500 − 100($105)) / 3,000. Only 3,000 shares of common are outstanding.

If the preferred stock was cumulative and there were dividends in arrears, they also would be subtracted from total owners' equity in the numerator.

The par value of preferred stock is not used in the calculation if it is different from the liquidation preference, as is the case here.

2. *Book Value per Share—Effect of Treasury Stock Purchase*

A firm purchased treasury shares at a cost exceeding the original issuance but less than book value per share. This transaction reduces total stockholders' equity but increases book value.

Explanation:

The purchase of treasury stock at any price decreases total owners' equity.

When the purchase price per share is less than book value per share, then the denominator of book value per share decreases by a greater percentage than does the numerator, and book value per share increases.

Assume that the total owners' equity and number of shares before the treasury stock purchase is $4,000 and 400 respectively. Book value per share is $10. The firm purchases 20 shares of treasury stock for $8 (less than book value). The new book value per share is: ($4,000 − $160)/(380) = $10.11. Book value per share has increased.

Note

The CPA Exam often asks candidates to analyze the effect of prospective transactions on book value per share.

II. **Quasi-Reorganization**—An alternative to bankruptcy in some cases, quasi-reorganization allows a firm a fresh start and new, more conservative asset values.

A. **Conditions**—Operating losses have created a deficit in retained earnings (negative balance) and certain asset values are overstated.

1. **Positive prospects**—However, the firm has positive prospects for the future but will be unable to pay dividends until the deficit is absorbed by future income.

2. **Updated balance sheet**—Rather than continue with unrealistic asset values and negative retained earnings (the inability to pay dividends will hurt the firm's ability to raise capital), a quasi-reorganization will provide an updated balance sheet with no retained earnings deficit.

B. **Requirements for a Quasi-Reorganization**

1. **Approval**—Shareholder and creditor approval.

2. **Balance becomes zero**—The retained earnings balance must be zero immediately after the quasi-reorganization.

3. **No negative balance after**—No contributed capital account can have a negative balance after the quasi-reorganization.

4. **Assets down to market**—Assets must be written down to market value (asset write-ups are possible but would be rare).

5. **Dated years after**—Retained earnings must be dated for a period of 3 to 10 years after the quasi-reorganization to indicate that the balance reflects income earned after the quasi-reorganization.

C. **Accounting Steps**

1. **Write assets down to market value**, further reducing retained earnings (increasing the deficit).

2. **Reduce contributed capital** to absorb the retained earnings deficit.

3. **Change value/number of shares**—If needed, change par value or the number of shares of common stock to absorb the remaining deficit.

Example

A firm has the following balance sheet (abbreviated):

Assets	$10,000	Liabilities	$4,000
		Common stock ($1 par)	3,000
		Contributed capital in excess of par	5,000
		Retained earnings	(2,000)

Certain plant assets with a book value of $5,000 are worth only $1,000. The firm elects to reduce par value to accomplish the quasi-reorganization.

Entries:

Retained earnings	4,000	
Plant assets		4,000

The retained earnings deficit is now $6,000.

Contributed capital in excess of par	5,000	
Retained earnings		5,000

The retained earnings deficit is now $1,000.
The common stock is reduced to $2,000 to absorb the remaining deficit.
This means that par value must be reduced to $.67

$2,000	= (3,000 shares)(new par value)
$2,000/3,000	= $.67 = new par value

Common stock	1,000	
Retained earnings		1,000

The balance sheet immediately following the quasi-reorganization is:

Assets	6,000	Liabilities	4,000
		Common stock ($.67 par)	2,000
		Contributed capital in excess of par	0
		Retained earnings	0

Select Transactions

Revenue Recognition

Point of Sale and Installment Method

This lesson on revenue reviews the definition and recognition criteria for revenue, and highlights the major recognition methods. The installment method is covered in detail.

After studying this lesson, you should be able to:

1. Define *revenue*.

2. State the general revenue recognition criteria.

3. Explain when major revenue recognition methods are applied.

4. Record deferred and recognized gross profit under the installment method.

5. Account for repossessions under the installment method.

6. Point to general differences in revenue recognition between U.S. and international standards.

Definition
Revenue: Inflows or other enhancements of assets of an entity or settlements of its liabilities (or a combination of the two) from delivering or producing goods, rendering services, or other activities that constitute the entity's ongoing major or central operations.

I. **Criteria for Revenue Recognition**

A. Revenues are recognized in the accounting year in which the following three criteria are met, regardless of when the cash is collected.

   1. The goods and services have been provided to the customer or client (the revenue is earned).

   2. The company is reasonably assured of collecting receivables (the revenue is realizable).

   3. The company can determine the expenses incurred in providing the goods and services. This criterion is not a constraint on recognition in most situations. *Earned* and *realizable* are the primary criteria.

B. **Criteria Not Met**—When one or more of the three criteria above are not met, revenue is deferred. If cash is collected before providing the good or service, deferred revenue (unearned revenue), a liability, is recorded.

C. **Certain Methods Accepted**—Certain established methods of revenue recognition have achieved acceptance in the business community that allow for some latitude in applying these three criteria. The major revenue recognition methods are listed below, along with the criterion that causes revenue to be postponed until it is met.

Method	Last Criterion to Be Met
Point of sale method (ordinary sale)	Seller performance (providing the good)—*earned*
Installment method	Receipt of cash—*realizable*
Cost-recovery method	Receipt of cash—*realizable*
Percentage of completion method	Seller performance (work is progressing)—*earned*
Completed contract method	Seller performance (completion)—*earned*
Sales with right of return	Expiration of return right or ability to estimate returns—*earned*

II. Installment Method of Revenue Recognition

A. Installment Sales Basis

1. The installment basis is a version of the cash basis of accounting. Profit recognition is dependent on cash being received. The method is typically employed in one of two situations.

   a. **Collectibility questionable**—The collectibility of receivables is questionable.

   b. **Extended time period**—If receivables will be collected over an extended time period, the installment sales basis might be appropriate.

2. **Gross profit formula**

   a. In applying the installment method, the gross profit percentage is calculated for merchandise sold.

   b. This percentage is: (sales − cost of goods sold) / sales.

   c. When cash is collected, the amount received is divided between recovery of cost and gross profit received. If no cash is received, no profit is recognized.

   d. The amount of recognized gross profit = (cash received in period) × (gross profit percentage). The remaining portion of the cash received is considered a return of cost.

Note
Caution: Not all installment sales are required to be accounted for under the installment method of revenue recognition. Rather, some method that bases revenue recognition on cash received should be used, such as the installment method or cost recovery method, only if the collectibility is uncertain or if the term is very long.

Example
Installment Method of Revenue Recognition
A firm sells goods with a total sales value of $80,000. The cost of the items sold is $60,000. During the year, the firm collects $25,000. The firm is uncertain about collecting the remaining sales price and elects to use the installment method of revenue recognition. The entries and balance sheet disclosure for the seller are shown below for this method. The gross profit percentage is 25%: ($80,000 − $60,000)/$80,000.

During the year:

Installment accounts receivable	80,000	
Installment sales		80,000
Cost of goods sold	60,000	
Inventory		60,000
Cash	25,000	
Installment accounts receivable		25,000

End of year adjusting entries:

The income statement accounts are closed, gross profit is deferred, and a portion of the gross profit is recognized.

Installment sales	80,000	
Deferred gross profit (contra receivable)		20,000
Cost of goods sold		60,000
Deferred gross profit(.25 × $25,000 cash)	6,250	
Recognized gross profit (to income statement)		6,250

Explanation: The firm is able to recognize gross profit, at the 25% rate, only on cash collected from the customer. Each $1 of cash collected is $.75 return of cost and $.25 gross profit. Cash collected includes any down payment or other cash paid by the customer.

The recognized gross profit account is an income statement account. Income increased only $6,250 this year because of the sale. The remaining $13,750 ($20,000 – $6,250) is deferred to the next period. When more cash is collected, more gross profit is recognized and the amount deferred is decreased.

Gross profit is not net income. The expenses below gross margin must also be taken into account when computing net income. Some firms prefer to disaggregate recognized gross profit into sales and cost of goods sold for reporting. In the example above, the firm would report $25,000 of sales and $18,750 of cost of goods sold ($25,000 × .75). Under this alternative reporting, gross margin is increased $6,250.

Balance sheet presentation of the receivable:	
Accounts receivable $80,000 – $25,000	$55,000
Less deferred gross profit	(13,750)
Equals net accounts receivable	$41,250

The net accounts receivable of $41,250 equals the cost of the inventory yet to be recovered: $41,250 = (1 – .25)($55,000). The receivable must be shown at cost.

To report the receivable at sales value ($55,000) would imply that the remaining $13,750 of gross profit had been recognized.

Note

The CPA Exam frequently asks for the amount of deferred gross profit on the installment sales method. In the above example, that amount is $13,750. Also, the gross profit percentage often changes each year. When sales from more than one period are given, be sure to apply the gross margin method that applies to each year's sales.

Example

Data for a firm using the installment method of revenue recognition follow:

Year	Sales	Cost of goods sold	Cash collected	
1	$3,000	$2,000	Year 1 sales $	500
2	$4,500	$2,250	Year 1 sales	1,500
			Year 2 sales	2,000

What is the amount of deferred gross profit to be reported at the end of year 2?

Solution

The gross profit percentages are:

Year 1: ($3,000 − $2,000)/$3,000 = 1/3

Year 2: ($4,500 − $2,250)/$4,500 = 1/2

Deferred gross profit at 12/31/Year 2 = ($3,000 − $500 − $1,500)(1/3) + ($4,500 − $2,000)(1/2)= $1,583

This amount would be subtracted from gross accounts receivable at year-end ($3,500) in deriving the net accounts receivable balance ($1,917).

B. **Repossession**—Occasionally, an item sold is repossessed due to nonpayment by the customer. Under the installment method of revenue recognition, the remaining receivable and deferred gross profit balances are closed, the repossessed inventory is recorded at fair value, and a gain or loss is recorded.

Example

Goods costing $8,000 were sold for $20,000 in a previous year. The installment method was used to recognize revenue because cash receipts were uncertain. As of the beginning of the current year, cash collections from previous years on the sale totaled $14,000. The gross margin percentage is $12,000/$20,000 or 60%. The goods are repossessed and have a fair value of $1,000 at the time of repossession.

Account balances at the beginning of the current year:

Installment accounts receivable	$6,000	($20,000 − $14,000)
Deferred gross profit	(3,600)	($6,000 x .60)

Journal entry for repossession:

Inventory	1,000	
Deferred gross profit	3,600	
Loss on repossession	1,400	
Installment accounts receivable		6,000

The loss equals the difference between the fair value of the inventory ($1,000) and the net installment receivable ($2,400).

III. U.S. GAAP–IFRS Differences

   A. The definition of revenue for international standards is substantively the same as for U.S. standards although the wording is somewhat different.

      1. International definition—Revenue is the gross inflow of economic benefits during the period arising in the course of ordinary activities when those inflows result in increases in equity, other than increases relating to contributions from equity participants.

      2. U.S. GAAP distinguishes revenue and gains; IFRS revenues include gains.

   B. International standards specifically define the sources of revenue (listed below). In contrast, U.S. standards do not.

      1. Sale of goods

      2. Rendering of services

      3. Use by others of the entity's assets yielding interest, royalty, and dividend revenue (equity method dividends are not revenue as per U.S. standards)

   C. International standards are much less specific with respect to recognition of revenue in special industry situations. There are fewer exceptions; international practice relies more on general principles.

   D. Revenue is recognized under international standards when the following criteria are met:

      1. The amount of revenue and costs associated with the transaction can be measured reliably.

      2. It is probable that the economic benefits associated with the transaction will flow to the seller.

      3. For the sale of goods, the seller must have transferred to the buyer the risks and rewards of ownership, and does not effectively manage or control the goods (a significant right of return is an example).

      4. For the rendering of services, the stage of completion can be measured reliably.

   E. In comparison, the U.S. principle focuses on when the earnings process is complete and whether cash will be collected, whereas the international definition is focused on when the transfer of risks and rewards of ownership take place. However, the two definitions usually lead to the same result.

   F. **Biological and Agricultural Assets**—When the future economic benefits are probable and can be reliably estimated for these assets, gains and losses from increases and decreases in the fair value (less estimated selling costs and taxes) are recognized as they occur, before the sale takes place.

Cost Recovery and Franchise Fees

This lesson illustrates the cost-recovery method, revenue recognition under a right of return, and revenue recognition in other specific business contexts.

After studying this lesson, you should be able to:

1. Identify when the cost-recovery method may be used.

2. Apply the cost-recovery method.

3. Determine when revenue is to be recognized under a right of return.

4. Apply the milestone method of revenue recognition.

5. Recognize the appropriate amount of revenue for an initial franchise fee.

I. Cost-Recovery Method

A. The cost-recovery method is more conservative than the installment method. No gross profit is recognized on cash collections until the cost of the item sold is fully recovered. After that point, all collections constitute gross profit.

1. **Justification for use**—Justification for the use of the cost recovery basis is identical to the reasons used to justify the installment sales basis—uncertainty about cash collection (realizable criterion).

2. **Similar to installment**—The journal entries are essentially the same although gross profit is recognized more slowly under the cost-recovery method.

Example
Merchandise with a cost of $60,000 is sold for $90,000 in Year 1. Cash collections will have to exceed $60,000 before any gross profit is realized. All gross profit is deferred until $60,000 cash is collected.

Cash collected in Year 1 is $40,000. Therefore, gross profit recognized is zero and deferred gross profit is $30,000.

Cash collected in Year 2 is $30,000. Therefore, gross profit recognized is $10,000 because total cash collected is $70,000 to this point. From here on, all cash collected is gross profit.

Cash collected in Year 3 is $20,000. Therefore, gross profit recognized is $20,000.

Note
The installment method would have recognized some profit in Year 1. The entries for the cost-recovery method are similar to the installment method and use the same accounts. The adjusting journal entry deferring the total gross profit for the year of sale is the same. But adjusting entries for gross profit recognition (and closing of deferred gross profit) are recorded only when total cash receipts exceed cost. Thus, only the timing of recognizing gross profit differs.

II. Revenue Recognized at the Completion of Production

    A. Certainly for most products, revenue is not recognized at the completion of production. However, for products such as precious metals and certain agriculture products, if three conditions are met, the revenue should be recognized at the completion of production. These three conditions are listed below.

        1. There is a relatively stable market for the products.

        2. Any related marketing costs are nominal.

        3. The units produced must be homogeneous.

    B. **Limited Applicability**—At completion of production, the usual uncertainties as to sale (and collection of cash) are absent, allowing revenue recognition to take place before sale. This method has very limited applicability.

III. Sales with a Right of Return

    A. Sellers often provide a right of return. The amount of net sales recognized for a period depends on whether six criteria (listed in B., below) are met.

        1. Sales are recognized at the point of sale if the six criteria (listed below) are met; **or**

        2. After the point of sale, when the return privilege expires, if the six criteria are not met. In this case, the sale may not be recognized as revenue until the period following the physical sale.

    B. **Six Criteria**—Revenue is recognized at the point of sale if all of the following six criteria are met:

        1. The seller's price to the buyer is substantially fixed or determinable at the date of sale.

        2. The buyer has paid the seller, or the buyer is obligated to pay the seller, and the obligation is not contingent on the resale of the product.

        3. The buyer's obligation to the seller would not be changed in the event of theft, physical destruction, or damage to the product.

        4. The buyer acquiring the product for resale has economic substance apart from that provided by the seller.

        5. The seller does not have significant obligations for future performance to directly bring about resale of the product by the buyer.

        6. The amount of future returns can be reasonably estimated.

> **Note**
> The last criterion is the most important for you to remember. If returns are not estimable as of the balance sheet date, then no sales with a right of return still effective can be recognized. (The same holds for the other five criteria as well.) The six criteria are expansions of the general earned and realizable criteria for revenue.

    C. **Recognition When All Six Criteria Are Met**

        1. Reported net sales for the year equals total sales less actual returns on those sales during the year less estimated returns at year's end.

        2. Accounts receivable is reported net of deferred gross profit on the estimated returns at year's end. The journal entries are similar to those for the installment method.

    D. **Recognition When All Six Criteria Are Not Met**

        1. If all six criteria are not met, revenue recognition is postponed until the return privilege has substantially expired, or the six criteria have been met. Reported net sales equals total sales less actual returns on those sales during the year less sales with a return privilege that is still effective.

        2. Accounts receivable is reported net of deferred gross profit on sales with a return privilege still effective.

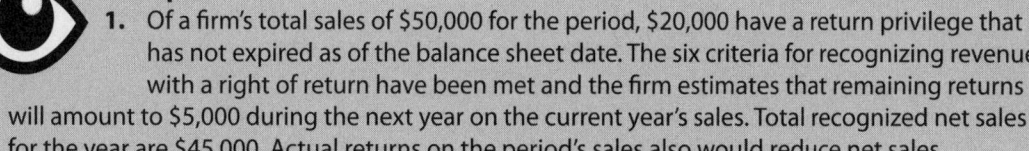

Examples

1. Of a firm's total sales of $50,000 for the period, $20,000 have a return privilege that has not expired as of the balance sheet date. The six criteria for recognizing revenue with a right of return have been met and the firm estimates that remaining returns will amount to $5,000 during the next year on the current year's sales. Total recognized net sales for the year are $45,000. Actual returns on the period's sales also would reduce net sales.

2. Of a firm's total sales of $50,000 for the period, $20,000 have a return privilege that has not expired as of the balance sheet date. The six criteria for recognizing revenue with a right of return have **not** been met. Total recognized net sales for the current year are only $30,000. Even though it is most likely that some of the remaining $20,000 of sales will not be returned, GAAP requires the most conservative possible accounting if the six criteria are met: No sales are recognized. Next year, when the return privilege expires, any unreturned sales will be recognized as sales in that year.

IV. Goods on Consignment

A. In a consignment arrangement, the consignor (owner of goods) uses the consignee's premises to sell its goods. For example, the magazines in a supermarket (consignee) often are owned by the publisher (consignor). The focus here is on the recognition of revenue for the consignor.

No revenue is recognized by consignor when it ships goods to the consignee, because no sale has yet taken place. The consignor includes unsold goods in its inventory even though they are on the consignee's premises. The consignor makes no journal entry to record the cost of goods shipped to consignee because the consignor still owns the goods.

When a retail customer purchases consigned goods on the consignee's premises, only then does the consignor recognize a sale. The consignee typically retains a percentage of each sale (its fee, a revenue) and remits the remainder to the consignor. The amount of revenue recognized by the consignor is the total sales amount. The consignee's fee is treated as an expense by the consignor.

The amount of any reimbursable expenses (e.g., handling and advertising) incurred by the consignee also is withheld and recognized as an expense by the consignor.

Example

Ron Inc. is the consignor, and Ed Co. is consignee.

Ron incurs $30 of freight cost to ship goods to Ed (recorded on Ron's books):

Inventory	30	
Cash or accounts payable		30

Ed incurs $70 of reimbursable expenses related to the goods on consignment (recorded on Ed's books):

Receivable from Ron	70	
Cash or accounts payable		70

Ed sells $500 of merchandise of Ron's goods it holds on consignment and retains a 5% commission (recorded on Ed's books):

Cash or accounts receivable	500	
Payable to Ron		475
Commission revenue		25

Ron is notified of above sale (recorded on Ron's books):

Accounts receivable	475	
Commission expense	25	
Sales		500

Ed remits payment to Ron (recorded on Ed's books):

Payable to Ron	475	
Receivable from Ron		70
Cash		405

Ron receives payment (recorded on Ron's books):

Cash	405	
Expenses	70	
Accounts receivable		475

V. Initial Franchise Fee

A. Recognized as Revenue—When the franchisor (e.g., McDonald's Corporation) sells a franchise to a franchisee, the latter can sell the franchisor's products under the franchise agreement. The franchisor charges an initial fee and continuing fees. The initial franchise fee is recognized by the franchisor as revenue when all material services or conditions have been substantially performed or satisfied by the franchiser. These services include training of the franchisee and constructing the facilities, for example. The fee is recorded as unearned revenue until it is recognized as revenue.

B. Commencement of Operations—The commencement of operations by the franchisee is generally presumed to be the earliest point at which performance has been completed.

C. Questions About Collectibility—If there are questions about the collectibility of the initial franchise fee or if the amount will be collected over an extended time period and no estimate of uncollectibility can be made, it is appropriate to employ the installment sales basis or the cost recovery basis to recognize the revenues related to the initial franchise fee.

D. Extended Time Period—If the goods and services related to the initial franchise fee are to be provided over an extended time period, it is appropriate to employ the percentage of completion method or the completed contract method to recognize the revenues related to the initial franchise fee.

E. Accrual Basis—The revenues and expenses related to continuing franchise fees should be accounted for under the accrual basis of accounting. The franchisor typically recognizes the revenue as it provides goods and services (including advertising) to the franchisee. The related costs are matched against this revenue in the same period the revenue is earned.

VI. Milestone Method for R & D Arrangements

A. Payments to a firm (vendor) conducting research for other entities may be contingent on achieving milestone events such as successful completion of the testing phase of a new product. The recognition of these payments as revenue in their entirety in the period the milestone is achieved is called the milestone method. There often are several milestones in an arrangement.

B. Revenue is recognized at milestones only if the milestone meets the following criteria to be considered substantive (complete). The consideration earned by achieving the milestone must:

    1. Be commensurate with either (a) the vendor's performance in achieving the milestone, or (b) the enhancement of the value of the item delivered as a result of achieving the milestone. In other words, the consideration must in-line with the value provided by the vendor;

    2. Relate only to work already performed;

    3. Be reasonable relative to all deliverables and payment terms in the arrangement.

C. Each milestone is evaluated separately and must be substantive in its entirety. As a result, milestones and resulting revenue recognition can occur at different times for an arrangement.

D. Choosing the milestone method is an accounting policy choice. Other appropriate methods may be applied provided that they do not recognize the consideration as revenue in its entirety. However, the firm must be consistent in its application of chosen method for similar arrangements.

Contract Accounting

This lesson about contract accounting covers the rationale for the applicable methods and the journal entries for the typical case. It also addresses the accounting for losses on a contract.

After studying this lesson, you should be able to:

1. Determine when to use the percentage of completion method and the completed contract method.

2. Record the three summary journals each year for a contract under both methods.

3. Record annual gross profit under the percentage of completion method.

4. Close the contract accounts under both methods.

5. Prepare the financial statement presentation of the accounts.

6. Distinguish the two types of losses on contract.

7. Account for a single-period loss on a profitable contract.

8. Record the loss when a contract turns unprofitable under both methods of accounting.

9. Apply the cost-recovery method to a long-term contract under international accounting standards

I. **Methods of Revenue Recognition for Long-Term Contracts**—Long-term contracts pose a unique revenue recognition problem. The seller/contractor performs its obligation over a long period of time. Cash collection generally is not an issue because projects generally are financed by third parties. Should the contractor recognize revenue as work progresses, or wait until the entire project is complete? Because of the long-term nature of construction contracts, the answer to this question has a significant impact on the contractor's income during the contract period. Two methods are used for revenue recognition in this context:

   A. **Completed Contract Method**—No gross profit or revenue is recognized until the contract is complete. This method is required if estimates of the degree of completion at interim points cannot be made.

   B. **Percentage of Completion**—Recognize gross profit in proportion to the degree of completion. This method is required if estimates of the degree of completion at interim points can be made **and** reasonable estimates of total project cost (and therefore profitability) can be made, **and** when the buyer and seller can be expected to perform under the contract. The percentage of completion equals cost incurred to date divided by the total estimated project cost.

II. **Basic Illustration**—The following example provides an illustration of both methods.

A contractor begins construction of a building for a client. The contract price is $10,000. Data for two years follows. The estimated remaining cost is updated at the end of each year. The project is incomplete at the end of Year 2 because costs remain for completion after Year 2. Each year for each contract, three summary journal entries are recorded under each method. A fourth journal entry under the percentage of completion method recognizes revenue and gross profit.

	Year 1	Year 2
Cost incurred in year	$2,000	$4,000
Estimated remaining cost to complete at end of year	6,000	1,500
Progress billings in year	1,000	3,500
Collections on billings in year	800	3,000

III. Year 1

A. The first three summary journal entries for Year 1 are the same for both methods:

Construction in progress (inventory)	2,000	
Materials, cash etc.		2,000
Accounts receivable	1,000	
Billings		1,000
Cash	800	
Accounts receivable		800

B. Construction in progress is an inventory account and a current asset. Although the contract may run for several years, the operating cycle of a construction firm is the length of its contracts. Thus, the inventory account is classified as a current asset. Construction in progress is debited only when costs are incorporated into the project. Purchases of materials for the project are recorded in the materials account.

C. Billings is contra to construction in progress. In the balance sheet, if the balance in construction in progress exceeds cumulative billings to date, the net difference is a current asset: Excess of construction in progress over billings on contracts. If cumulative billings exceed the construction in progress balance, the difference is disclosed in the current liability section. By subtracting billings from construction in progress, the seller is transferring its equity in the project from the physical asset to the financial asset (to accounts receivable and then ultimately to cash).

D. The completed contract method recognizes no gross profit in Year 1 (or even in Year 2). The percentage of completion recognizes gross profit each year. Completed contract records no further entries for the first two years.

E. The fourth entry (below) is recorded for percentage of completion only, and is an adjusting entry. This entry records the gross profit on the project for the year based on the percentage of completion, which is 25% at the end of Year 1. 25% = ($2,000/($2,000 + $6,000)). The expected total cost of the project is $8,000 at the end of Year 1 and $2,000 of cost has been incurred.

F. Adjusting entry for percentage of completion only (the fourth journal entry):

Construction in progress	500	
Construction expenses	2,000	
Construction revenue		2,500

G. $2,500 revenue = 25%($10,000). The project is 25% complete allowing 25% of the total revenue to be recognized. The $2,000 of construction expense is the cost incurred in the period. The $500 gross profit can be directly computed as the percentage of completion times the total estimated gross profit: .25($10,000 − $8,000) = $500. The $500 gross profit is recorded in the inventory account because it represents the increase in the value of the inventory. When $500 of gross profit is recognized, the net assets of the seller must also increase.

H. Caution—The total estimated cost of the project at the end of any year equals cost incurred to date + estimated remaining costs to complete at year-end. This amount generally must be computed by the candidate. This amount is the denominator of the percentage of completion and also is used to compute gross profit to date. For example, the $8,000 figure would not be provided for the candidate. This amount changes each year of the project.

I. The balance sheet and income effects for both methods at the end of Year 1:

	Completed contract	Percentage of completion
Income statement		
Recognized gross profit	$ 0	$ 500*

*The $2,500 revenue less $2,000 expense also can be reported.

Balance sheet (current assets)		
Accounts receivable	200	200
Construction in progress	$2,000	$2,500
Less billings	(1,000)	(1,000)
Excess of construction in progress over billings	1,000	1,500

If no losses are expected, the balance in construction in progress at any balance sheet date is:

Completed contract:	Total cost to date
Percentage of completion:	Total cost to date
	+ Total recognized gross profit to date

The construction in progress and billings accounts are separate accounts. Billings is subtracted from construction in progress only for reporting in the balance sheet.

Analysis

What is the impact of the four journal entries (under percentage of completion) on the Year 1 financial statements for the contractor?

Although the effects may appear involved, their entire effect is summarized in the fourth entry: an increase in net assets and pretax net income of $500. The first three journal entries cause various account balance changes but net to a zero effect on net assets and net income.

IV. Year 2

A. The first three journal entries are the same as the first year's except for the amounts. Both methods record these entries. These entries are not shown; the amounts are: $4,000, $3,500, and $3,000.

B. The fourth entry (for percentage of completion below) shows how the gross profit for the second year is computed as the total gross profit to date less the gross profit recognized in earlier years. After the first year, there is no direct way to compute gross profit for the year because total gross profit through the end of each year uses the estimated remaining cost amount and percentage of completion through the end of the year, both of which change each year.

C. The percentage of completion at the end of Year 2 = Cost to date/Total estimated cost = ($2,000 + $4,000)/($2,000 + $4,000 + $1,500) = $6,000/$7,500 = 80%.

D. Note that the estimated remaining cost to complete ($1,500) is the only difference between the numerator and denominator. When working a problem in this area, simply repeat the numerator amounts in the denominator and then add the estimated remaining cost to complete to the denominator.

Gross profit recognized in Year 2 = Total estimated gross profit through Year 2
                                − Gross profit recognized in previous periods
                                = .80($10,000 − $7,500) − $500
                                = $1,500

Adjusting entry for percentage of completion only:

Construction in progress	1,500	
Construction expenses	4,000	
Construction revenue		5,500

$5,500 = .80($10,000) − $2,500 revenue in Year 1

V. End of Contract—Year 3

A. Assume that total cost incurred by the contractor for the project was $7,500 with completion occurring in Year 3. Under percentage of completion, the final adjusting entry (fourth entry in year) would record gross profit for that year and update the construction-in-progress account. That entry is:

Construction in progress		500
Construction expenses	$7,500 − $6,000	1,500
Construction revenue	$10,000 − $8,000	2,000

B. The entries to complete the contract and close the accounts are:

Completed contract:			Percentage of completion:		
Billings	10,000		Billings	10,000	
Construction expenses	7,500		Construction in progress		10,000
Construction in progress		7,500			
Construction revenue		10,000			

C. Only in the final year of the contract is gross profit recognized under the completed contract method. At completion, $2,500 of gross profit is recognized (revenue less expenses). Under the percentage of completion method, the construction in progress account balance is total cost plus total gross profit, or $7,500 + $2,500 = total contract price of $10,000. The billings account reflects the full contract price under both methods.

VI. Contract Accounting, Losses

A. Losses on Contracts

1. For accounting purposes, there are two kinds of losses on long-term contracts: (1) single-period losses and (2) overall lossess.

2. They require very different accounting. In particular, a single-period loss is treated exactly the same way as gross profit during the year, for both percentage of completion and completed contract methods. Overall losses require very different reporting.

B. Single-Period Loss—When the total gross profit through the end of a given year is less than the gross profit recognized in previous years, a loss has occurred in the given year although the contract still may be profitable.

In the current example under percentage of completion, the firm has recognized $2,000 of gross profit through the first two years. If the normal computation of gross profit resulted in total gross profit through Year 3 of $1,700, then a single-period loss of $300 has occurred. The entries are the same as before. The adjusting entry for gross profit is computed as usual. The only difference is that construction in progress is credited (reduced) for $300 rather than debited.

1. The completed contract method is unaffected by single-period losses.

C. Overall Losses—GAAP requires, for both methods (percentage of completion and completed contract), that when an overall loss on a contract is anticipated, the loss must be recognized in full. An overall loss occurs when the total estimated costs of the project exceed the contract price.

Example
Year 3 is added to the data for the basic illustration in the previous example. The information for Years 1 and 2 are the same as before. Through Year 2, a total of $2,000 gross profit was recognized.

	Year 1	Year 2	Year 3
Cost incurred in year	$2,000	$4,000	$2,400
Estimated remaining cost to complete at end of year	6,000	1,500	1,800

At the end of Year 3 the overall anticipated loss is $200:

= total estimated project cost − contract price

= $2,000 + $4,000 + $2,400 + $1,800 − $10,000 = $200

The loss is recognized in full for both methods. Any previous gross profit under percentage of completion also is removed from the construction in process account. In the first two years under percentage of completion, recognized revenue was $8,000 and recognized gross profit was $2,000 from the previous example. The adjusting entries to record the loss are:

Adjusting entry for percentage of completion:

Construction expenses	2,435#	
Construction in progress		2,200*
Construction revenue		235^

The loss recorded by this entry is $2,200, the difference between the revenue and expense.

A plug figure. When an overall loss is anticipated, the amount recorded as construction expense is no longer the year's incurred cost

* $2,000 profit in Years 1 and 2 plus the overall loss of $200

^ The percentage of completion is now ($2,000 + $4,000 + $2,400)/($2,000 + $4,000 + $2,400 + $1,800)= .8235. .8235($10,000) − $8,000 previous revenue = $235

The construction in progress account balance is now total cost to date less the overall loss. The same holds for completed contract. No previous profit must be removed however, and the entry under the completed contract method is:

| Loss on construction contract | 200 | |
| Construction in progress | | 200 |

D. U.S. GAAP–IFRS Differences

1. International standards require the percentage of completion method when the contractor can reliably estimate total costs although international standards are less specific regarding how to measure the stage of completion. Both sets of standards require full recognition of an estimated overall loss in the year that determination is made.

2. In contrast with U.S. standards however, when the percentage of completion method is not appropriate, the completed contract method cannot be used. Rather, the cost-recovery method (also called the zero-profit method) is applied. This approach is also applied to long-term service contracts when the total estimated cost of providing the service cannot be estimated reliably.

   a. In this context, the cost-recovery method requires that the contractor recognize construction expense equal to the revenue recognized, thus generating no gross profit. The amount of revenue recognized is computed as per the percentage of completion method. This is the same journal entry for recognition of gross profit under the percentage of completion method except there is no debit to construction in progress.

Example

The basic illustration for U.S. standards in the previous lesson (no losses) is used to illustrate the cost-recovery method (assuming the percentage of completion method is not appropriate). Before the contract is completed, only the fourth journal entry each year is different compared with the percentage of completion method. Only the fourth journal entry is shown here for both methods.

Contract data: contract price, $10,000.

Year 1 cost incurred, $2,000. Year 2 cost incurred, $4,000.

Fourth journal entry under percentage of completion (from previous lesson):

Year 1			Year 2		
Construction in progress	500		Construction in progress	1,500	
Construction expenses	2,000		Construction expenses	4,000	
Construction revenue		2,500	Construction revenue		5,500

Fourth journal entry under cost-recovery method (international standards):

Year 1			Year 2		
Construction expenses	2,000		Construction expenses	4,000	
Construction revenue		2,000	Construction revenue		4,000

Under the cost-recovery method, there is no debit to construction in progress. This approach yields the same gross profit (zero) as the completed contract method but the latter records no revenue or expense until the project is complete.

---

3. When the project is completed, the total gross profit on the contract is recognized as a debit to construction in progress and the remaining cost incurred and revenue are recognized.

Example

Again, using the basic illustration for U.S. standards above (no losses), Year 3, the cost-recovery journal entry before closing the contract is as follows. The total contract price was $10,000 and the cost incurred in Year 3 was $1,500. Total contract cost is $7,500. The entry for international standards is:

Construction in progress	2,500		$10,000 − $7,500
Construction expenses	1,500		
Construction revenue		4,000	10,000 − $2,000 − $4,000

The $4,000 construction revenue is the difference between total contract price and the revenue recognized in the first two years. The entire gross profit for the project is recognized in the final year (Year 3) of the contract.

4. The cost-recovery (zero-profit) method is invoked when total project cost cannot be estimated, and also for any other reason causing completion of the contract to be uncertain.

   a. Other causes include (1) a finding that the contract is not enforceable, (2) if completion is dependent on pending litigation, and (3) if the contractor cannot complete the contract due to internal problems such as pending bankruptcy.

5. International standards distinguish fixed fee contracts (use the percentage of completion method) and cost-plus contracts for which the percentage of completion method is not used. In a cost-plus contract, the total cost of the project is variable with the customer taking the risk for cost increases. The amount of revenue recognized by the contractor in any period is the cost incurred plus the agreed-upon percentage markup above cost.

Deferred Revenue

Deferred Revenue Principles

This is the first of two lessons about deferred or unearned revenues. This lesson provides the basic concepts that apply to all such accounts.

After studying this lesson, you should be able to:

1. Identify deferred revenues and be able to record them correctly.

2. Determine the amount of revenue to be recognized, from given data about deferred revenues.

3. Compute the cash payments amount, from given data about deferred revenues.

I.   Deferred Revenues

> **Definition**
> *Deferred Revenue:* A liability recognized when cash is received before the service is provided or before the goods are shipped to customers.

- **A.** Deferred revenues are liabilities representing cash received for goods not yet delivered or services to be performed. Recognition of revenue occurs when the firm provides the good or service at which point the deferred revenue (liability) is reduced. These liabilities often are reduced in adjusting entries. For example, a company may prepare an adjusting entry to recognize rent revenue and reduce unearned rent revenue.

- **B.** Cash representing revenue that will be earned in the future is credited to one of the following accounts, which are simply different names for the same account:

    1. Deferred revenue

    2. Unearned revenue

    3. Revenue received in advance

- **C.** Each of the above accounts is a liability. CPA Exam questions in this area ask the candidate to determine the ending balances of two accounts:

    1. Revenue to be recognized in income for the period; and

    2. The amount of unearned revenue to be reported in the balance sheet.

- **D.** Under the revenue recognition principle, revenue is not recognized unless it is (1) earned, and (2) realizable. In the case of deferred revenue, the cash collection occurs before the earnings process is complete. Such revenue is common for firms that require partial or full payment before providing service. Examples include real estate management companies (unearned rent), publishing companies (magazine subscriptions) and airline companies (flight liability).

- **E.** A liability is recognized upon receipt of cash. As the service or good is provided, the liability is extinguished because the revenue is earned. In many cases, the contract need not be fully executed before some revenue is recognized. In these cases, the revenue is recognized based on the percentage of the total contract that has been provided.

II. Examples—Several examples are provided to illustrate the variations in problems that may be encountered on the CPA Exam.

Example
Duration Magazine Inc. collects subscriptions in advance from customers and records deferred revenue. As magazines are distributed over the subscription period, revenue is recognized. The beginning balance of deferred subscription revenue is $24,000. During the year, $87,000 of cash is collected. At the end of the year, the firm calculates from subscription data that the subscription value of magazines yet to be distributed is $37,000. The adjusting entry to record revenue for the period is:

Deferred Subscription Revenue	74,000	
Subscription Revenue		74,000*

* $24,000 + $87,000 − $37,000 = $74,000

Example
Journal Entries
A tenant pays a building management firm $24,000 for two years' rent on August 1, 20X3 ($1,000 per month). The rental period begins on that date and the building management firm has a calendar fiscal year. Provide the journal entries for 20X3.
Solution:

Aug 1, 20X3

Cash	24,000	
Unearned Rent		24,000

Dec 31, 20X3 (adjusting journal entry)

Unearned rent	5,000	
Rent revenue		5,000

$5,000 = $1,000 per month × 5 months August–December.

The 20X3 income statement will reflect $5,000 of rent revenue. The ending balance in unearned rent for 12/31/X3 is $19,000 ($24,000 − $5,000) of which $12,000 is a current liability (the portion relating to 20X4), and $7,000 is a noncurrent liability (the portion relating to 20X5).

Example
Account Balances Given
The beginning and ending balances of unearned revenue for an airline company appear below. These amounts represent cash collected from customers for flights to be provided in the future.

	Beginning	Ending
Unearned Revenue	$300,000	$410,000

During the year, the firm collected $760,000 from customers for flights. How much revenue was recognized during the year?

Solution: Any operating account such as unearned revenue can be analyzed using a T account or an equation. The equation approach is illustrated below:

Beginning Balance of Unearned Revenue + Increase − Decrease = Ending Balance of Unearned Revenue

Unearned Revenue

Revenue Recognized   Beginning Balance – Cash Received
Ending Balance

The increase for this account is the amount of cash received during the period; the decrease is the amount of revenue recognized.

Beginning Balance	+	Cash Received	–	Revenue Earned	=	Ending Balance
$300,000	+	$760,000	–	?	=	$410,000

Solving for revenue earned yields $650,000. This amount is reported in the income statement.

Summary entries can be reconstructed:

Cash	760,000	
Unearned Revenue		760,000
Unearned Revenue	650,000	
Revenue		650,000

Example
Reporting Cash as Revenue on Receipt
In some cases, firms record all cash received as revenue and then make an adjusting entry (1) to recognize the amount of unrecognized revenue to report in the balance sheet, and (2) to adjust revenue.

At the beginning of the year, the balance in rent collected in advance (liability) was $56,000. During the year, the firm collected $520,000 in rent from tenants representing rentals of $2,000 per month. At year-end, 10 tenants had an average of eight months rent (at $2,000 per month) remaining on their contracts. The summary journal entries assuming that cash collected is recognized immediately as rent revenue are as follows:

Cash	520,000	
Rent Revenue		520,000
Rent Revenue	104,000	
Rent Collected in Advance		104,000

The ending liability balance (rent collected in advance) = 10 tenants × 8 months remaining on average × $2,000 per month = $160,000

Beginning Balance	+	Cash Received	–	Rent Revenue Earned	=	Ending Balance
$56,000	+	$520,000	–	?	=	$160,000

Solving for rent revenue earned for the year yields $416,000. Because the firm has already recorded $520,000 in revenue upon cash collection, the adjustment is $104,000: $520,000 rent recognized previously less the actual revenue earned of $416,000. In this case, the liability balance is directly computed; the amount of revenue recognized is computed as one of the components of the change in the liability account.

III. Total Revenue to Be Recognized—You may encounter situations in which firms require cash to be paid in advance for some services, while for other services the firm bills the customer after the service is provided. In this case, both unearned revenue and accounts receivable must be analyzed to uncover the total revenue to be recognized for the period.

Example

The following amounts were taken from the comparative financial statements of a large local firm:

	12/31/X4	12/31/X3
Accounts receivable	$20,000	$12,000
Unearned revenue	34,000	28,000

The accounts receivable represents billings after service was provided to customers. Unearned revenue represents cash collected before service was provided. Total cash received from customers during 20X4: $126,000.

What amount of service revenue was recognized during the period?

Solution: Accounts receivable is recognized when revenue is earned. The customer is billed after the service is provided. Unearned revenue is recognized when customers pay in advance, before service is provided. Cash received increases the unearned revenue account while reducing accounts receivable. Recognizing earned revenue has the opposite effect: It reduces unearned revenue while increasing the accounts receivable account.

Again, a T account or equation analysis helps. Although the amount of cash received on accounts receivable and the amount of cash received in advance from customers cannot be determined from the information provided, the total cash received from both sources is provided. The solution strategy is to set up the analysis of the two balance sheet accounts and place the revenue amounts on the same side of the respective equations:

Accounts receivable:

Beg. Bal + Revenue Earned − Cash Received = End. Bal

Revenue Earned = End. Bal + Cash Received − Beg. Bal

Unearned revenue:

Beg. Bal + Cash Received − Revenue Earned = End. Bal

Revenue Earned = Beg. Bal + Cash Received − end. Bal

Repeat the last equation for each account, insert the known amounts, recall that total cash received amounted to $126,000, and add the equations together.

AR:	Revenue Earned	=	End. Bal + Cash Received	−	Beg. Bal
		=	$20,000		$12,000
Unearned Rev:	Revenue Earned	=	Beg. Bal + Cash Received	−	End. Bal
		=	$28,000		$34,000
Sum:	Revenue Earned	=	$48,000 + $126,000	−	$46,000
		=	$128,000		

Therefore, total revenue to be recognized for 20X4 equals $128,000. However, from the information provided, the revenue cannot be broken down by source (customers paying in advance versus customers paying after service is provided).

Shortcut approach: An alternative approach is to simply assume that one-half the total cash received relates to each of the two accounts (accounts receivable and unearned revenue). Again, an equation or T account may be used for the analysis; this time the account analysis can proceed separately for each account. Assume one-half of the cash (1/2 × $126,000 = $63,000) is applied to each account.

Accounts receivable:

Beg. Bal	+	Revenue Earned	−	Cash Received	=	End. Bal
$12,000	+	?		− $63,000	=	$20,000

Unearned revenue:

Beg. Bal	+	Cash Received	−	Revenue Earned	=	End. Bal
$28,000	+	$63,000	−	?	=	$34,000

Total revenue earned = $71,000 + $57,000 = $128,000. Note however that the individual amounts of revenue, $71,000 and $57,000, are most likely not the actual revenue amounts by sources. Only the total is correct.

Specific Deferred Revenues

In this, the second of two lessons about deferred revenues, the focus is on specific examples of deferred revenue.

After studying this lesson, you should be able to:

1. Record the appropriate journal entries for gift card programs.

2. Account for container deposits.

3. Determine the amount of revenue to be recognized for extended warranties.

4. Allocate the total revenue for an arrangement with more than one deliverable.

I. Gift Certificates/Cards

A. When a retailer sells a gift certificate or gift card, it records an unearned revenue account (a liability). The transaction is a cash receipt for a possible future sale. When the customer uses the card for a purchase, the liability is reduced, and sales (and cost of goods sold) are recognized.

B. In the case of forfeiture by a customer, the retailer still recognizes revenue, subject to certain legal constraints, if present. Some cards have definite expiration dates that allow for accurate determinations of forfeited cards. Other cards have no expiration dates. For these arrangements, after a certain amount of time and based on past experience, the retailer can assume that a certain percentage of cards will not be redeemed. To the extent that state law requires the firm to remit any or all of the forfeited gift revenue to the state, that portion of the gift card liability is not recognized as revenue.

 **Example**
The beginning balance of a retailer's gift card liability (unearned revenue) for the current year is $4,600,000. During the year, $32,000,000 of gift cards were sold and $28,000,000 of cards were used by customers to purchase goods at a 60% average gross margin percentage. From past experience, the firm estimates that 20% of the beginning gift card liability balance has been forfeited by customers.

Journal entries for the year:

Receipt of cash:	Cash	32,000,000	
	Gift card liability		32,000,000
Customer redemption:	Gift card liability	28,000,000	
	Sales		28,000,000
	Cost of goods sold	11,200,000	
	Inventory		11,200,000
	$11,200,000 = $28,000,000(.40)		
Forfeiture:	Gift card liability	920,000	
	Forfeited card revenue*		920,000
	$920,000 = $4,600,000(.20)		

* This account is typically merged with sales in practice; no cost of goods sold is recognized.

The ending liability balance of $7,680,000 represents the remaining sales that could be recognized in the future on card redemptions. If forfeiture experience changes, the rate applied in the adjusting journal entry at year-end uses the new rate (change in estimate). Eventually, all cash received from customers for gift cards is recognized as revenue, unless state law requires that the firm remit all or a portion of forfeited card receipts to the state.

II. Container Deposits

A. In some industries, and for certain retail products, the seller requires a container deposit, which is paid by the customer and reimbursed when the container is returned. Accounting for container deposits is similar to that for gift cards. The amount received from the customer is a liability until the container is returned. However, this liability is much less an unearned revenue account because containers are not meant to be sold. However, some containers are never returned and the deposit is forfeited; a nonsales revenue is recognized at this point. An expense is recognized for the cost of containers not returned by customers.

B. **Sample journal entries**

Receipt of deposit:	Cash
	Container deposit liability
Return of container:	Container deposit liability
	Cash
Forfeiture:	Container deposit liability
	Miscellaneous revenue
	Miscellaneous expense
	Inventory of containers

C. If there is a specified return period (e.g., one year), then the forfeiture entries are recorded after that period has elapsed. If not, and the firm honors returns indefinitely, an estimate of forfeitures is used for the forfeiture entries.

D. Are gift card and container deposit liabilities definite liabilities?

1. The answer is yes. The firm has a liability at the point of receiving cash from the customer. The liability is not contingent on a future event. The firm has an obligation for the amount received. The liability will be extinguished regardless of action or inaction by the customer. These liabilities are not contingent on a future event.

III. Extended Warranties

A. Regular warranties are offered by many companies at no charge to the customer. They create contingent liabilities and are covered in another lesson. Extended warranties are offered for additional consideration and provide coverage beyond the regular warranty. When the customer pays for the extended warranty, another unearned revenue account (liability) is recorded. The reporting issue involves the timing of revenue recognition.

B. **Accounting for Extended Warranties**

1. The unearned revenue is recognized as revenue over the life of the contract.

2. Warranty expense (cost to service claims) is recognized as incurred.

3. If the total cost of servicing claims over the contract life is estimable, then the revenue is recognized in proportion to costs incurred. Otherwise the straight-line method is used.

4. Costs directly related to individual contracts (e.g., commissions) are capitalized and amortized over the life of the contract in the same proportion as revenue is recognized.

5. Advertising and other indirect costs are expensed as incurred.

Example
A firm's sales totaled $3,000,000 for the year. This figure includes $150,000 for two-year extended warranty contracts covering the goods sold. The firm expects to incur a total of $120,000 cost in servicing warranty claims on these contracts. During year 1, $20,000 of warranty costs were incurred.

Journal entries for year 1:

Cash or Accounts receivable	3,000,000	
Sales		2,850,000
Unearned warranty revenue		150,000
Warranty expense	20,000	
Cash, inventory, other		20,000
Unearned warranty revenue	25,000	
Warranty revenue		25,000

$25,000 = ($20,000/$120,000)$150,000. One-sixth of expected total claims service has been performed. Therefore, one-sixth of $150,000 is recognized as revenue. If the firm could not estimate the $120,000 total warranty cost, then $75,000 of revenue would be recognized ($150,000/2) using the straight-line approach.

The remaining $125,000 of warranty revenue ($150,000 – $25,000) is recognized in the second year of the contract, regardless of the actual cost incurred in the second year because the benefits cease at the end of the second year. At that point all the revenue is earned.

IV. Revenue Arrangements with Multiple Deliverables

A. Vendors often provide more than one product or service as part of a single arrangement. Not all items in the arrangement are necessarily delivered at the same time. The revenue for delivered items is separately recognized if the following two criteria are met:

1. The delivered item has value to the customer on a stand-alone basis; and

2. If the arrangement includes a general right of return relative to the delivered item, delivery of the undelivered item is considered probable and substantially in the control of the vendor.

B. If the criteria are not met for a delivered item, then the arrangement is treated as one unit and revenue recognition is deferred for the delivered item until all items are delivered.

Example
A firm sells a machine and installation services to another firm. The machine is delivered. If the two criteria are met, then revenue is recognized for the machine and later for the installation when that is complete. (Note: If there is no right of return, then the second criterion does not apply.) If the two criteria are not met, the revenue for both items is recognized when the installation is complete.

C. Allocating the Total Arrangement Price—The total arrangement price is allocated to the individual items based their stand-alone selling prices (relative-selling price method). To determine the selling prices, the following hierarchy is used. Note that selling prices as set in an individual contract may not be representative of the stand-alone selling price to be used in the computation.

1. Vendor-specific objective evidence of selling price (VSOE) about the price of the item if sold separately by the vendor. If this information is not available, then use…

2. Third-party evidence of selling price (TPE) about similar or interchangeable items when sold separately by a third party on a stand-alone basis. If this information is not available, then use…

3. Best estimate of selling price (e.g., cost plus a reasonable profit margin).

D. The allocation of revenue to the individual items is not subject to change given new information; changes in estimate are not allowed.

> **Example**
> Continuing with the previous example, assume that the selling price for the combined arrangement is $40,000. The machine, if sold separately, sells for $36,000. But the vendor does not sell installation services separately and thus has no separate selling price. Nor is there any TPE of price for the installation. The vendor therefore applies its normal profit margin to the cost of the installation and determines an estimate of the installation service selling price to be $8,000. The allocation of the $40,000 arrangement price is as follows:
>
> To machine: $40,000[$36,000/($36,000 + $8,000)] = $32,727
> To installation: $40,000[$8,000/($36,000 + $8,000)] = 7,273
> Total revenue: $40,000

E. Multiple Software Deliverables—For software, the total arrangement fee is allocated to the various items based on vendor-specific objective evidence of fair value, rather than selling price, regardless of contractually stated selling prices. Vendor-specific objective evidence of fair value is limited to the price charged when the same item is sold separately. If an item is not sold separately, the price is established by management.

1. **Residual method**—For multiple deliverable software items, when the vendor is able to determine the selling price for undelivered items but is unable to determine the price of the delivered items, the residual method is applied.

2. The allocation of the total arrangement price to the delivered items is the residual after subtracting the total selling price of the undelivered items. This results in the entire discount, if any, allocated to the delivered items. The amount allocated to the delivered items is recognized upon delivery. The amount allocated to the undelivered items is deferred until delivery.

3. For the residual method to be applicable, all other applicable revenue recognition criteria must be met, and the fair value of the undelivered items must be less than the total fee.

F. Exception—If software within a multiple deliverable arrangement is an integral part of a bundle of products including nonsoftware products, then the previously discussed general guidance for revenue recognition for multiple deliverables is applied (using selling prices rather than fair value), rather than the residual method. The firm must use the relative-selling price method illustrated above.

1. The relative-selling price method is applied for all multiple deliverable situations in which software functions together with a tangible product to deliver the latter's essential functionality.

Deferred Compensation Arrangements

Pension Principles, Reporting

This lesson describes the basic principles underlying accounting for defined benefit pension plans.

After studying this lesson, you should be able to:

1. Distinguish defined contribution and defined benefit pension plans.

2. Account for defined contribution plans.

3. Describe the inputs to a pension benefit formula and the relevance of the formula to accounting for defined benefit pension plans.

4. List the main attributes of accounting for defined benefit pension plans.

5. Define projected benefit obligation.

6. Explain the two separate sides of the pension plan.

7. Calculate reported pension liability.

8. Note the components of pension expense.

I. **Types of Pension Plans**—(1) defined contribution plans, and (2) defined benefit plans.

    A. **Defined Contribution Plans**

> **Definition**
> *Defined contribution plans:* The amount of the employer contribution is defined by contract. For example, the employer contributes 5% of gross salary to the plan each month.

        1. In a defined contribution plan, the benefits paid during retirement are dependent on the return on the pension fund assets and, therefore, are not defined. The employee bears the risk of fund performance in this type of plan. The sponsoring firm has no obligation to the employee beyond the total annual contribution. A 401K plan is an example of a defined contribution plan.

        2. Accounting for defined contribution plans is straightforward: The amount of annual pension expense recognized is the required contribution. This accounting reflects the accrual basis rather than cash basis. Any shortfall represents a liability until the employer covers it. If the payment is not expected to be within one year of the balance sheet date, the liability is discounted to present value. Amendments to the plan that change benefits earned previously are immediately expensed.

 **Example**
A defined contribution plan requires the employer (sponsor) to contribute 4% of all covered employees' annual gross salary to the plan each year. Gross salary for covered employees for the current year is $1,000,000. The firm contributed $35,000 for the year and will make up the shortfall early the following year.

Summary journal entry:

Pension expense	40,000	.04($1,000,000)
Pension liability	5,000	
Cash	35,000	

3. The sponsor must disclose a description of the plan, the covered employee groups, information about how contribution amounts are determined, and any factors affecting comparability between periods.

4. Both defined contribution and benefit plans can be **contributory** or **noncontributory**.

    1. In a contributory plan, the employer and the employees make contributions to the pension plan. In noncontributory plans, only the employer makes contributions to the pension plan.

5. Note: If a firm has both a defined contribution plan and a defined benefit plan, the pension expense amounts and pension liability amounts are not combined across plans.

B. **Defined Benefit Plans**

> **Definition**
> *Defined benefit plans:* The benefits paid during retirement are based on a formula and therefore are defined.

1. In a defined benefit plan, the contribution to the pension fund is not defined. The employer bears the risk in this type of plan because the benefit is defined.

C. **Defined benefit plans** are the focus of the lessons pertaining to Pension accounting. Because the benefit during retirement is defined, the determination of annual pension expense and the ending pension obligation for a given year is complicated by the need to estimate many factors including turnover, final salary, life expectancy, and others.

D. **Accounting for Defined benefit plans** is based on accrual accounting: Pension expense is recognized as benefits are earned and the pension obligation is recognized for unpaid benefits. One of the costs of generating current-period revenue is the provision, by the employer, of employee pension benefits. That cost is matched as pension expense against the revenues it helped generate.

> **Exam note**
> *Essentially all pension questions on the CPA Exam pertain to defined benefit plans.*

E. **Trustee**—Many firms sponsoring defined benefit plans use a trustee to disburse retirement checks and perform other administrative tasks concerning the pension plan. The sponsoring firm makes periodic funding contributions to the trust company. Those contributions and the earnings on them comprise the pension plan assets available for payment of retirement benefits. The periodic trustee report provides detailed information about the funding of the pension plan and benefit payments made by the plan. Information from the trustee is the basis for the asset "side" of pension accounting. Information on the fund balance and actual return on plan assets for a period is provided by the trustee report.

F. **Benefit Formula**—The pension benefits that an employee is entitled to at retirement are explicitly stated in the pension plan. The estimated future benefits are the primary input into the determination of the pension obligation. The benefit level is based on the benefit formula, which includes such variables as:

1. Years of service

2. Age at retirement

3. Highest salary attained

>
> **Example**
> The annual benefit payment for a defined benefit plan is:
>
> (Years of service/40)(Final or highest annual salary)(Age at retirement/65).
>
> The annual benefit may not exceed final salary.
>
> An employee retiring at age 60 after 25 years of service with a final salary of $80,000 will receive an annual pension benefit of $46,154 = (25/40)(80,000)(60/65).

G. Actuary—The *actuarial* present value of those pension checks at the reporting date (well before employees have retired) is the foundation for pension accounting. Present value calculations are performed by actuaries who typically work for insurance companies and are highly trained in the mathematics relevant to employee benefits. The management of the sponsoring firm works with the actuary providing the employee information required to make estimates of life expectancy, turnover, final salary, the discount rate used for computing present values, and other amounts. Actuarial information is the basis for the liability and expense "side" of pension accounting. This information is conveyed to the firm by the report of the actuary. Without the actuary, accounting for defined benefit pension plans would not be possible.

II. Accounting for Defined-Benefit Pension Plans—This is characterized by the following special attributes:

> **Delayed recognition of certain items in pension expense**—Gradual recognition through amortization rather than immediate recognition.
>
> **Net cost reporting of pension expense**—This expense (or component of inventory cost for manufacturing personnel) is the net sum of five components, one or more of which can be negative (decrease in pension expense).
>
> **Offsetting in the balance sheet**—The pension obligation and pension-plan assets are not recognized separately in the balance sheet; rather, they are offset yielding one much smaller reported net asset or liability.

The two main accounting reporting issues are:

A. The determination and reporting of annual pension expense;

B. The determination and reporting of the ending pension obligation for the period.

    1. For the **each fiscal year**, the firm must report:

        a. Pension expense—The cost to the firm of providing the pension benefits earned during the year. This amount is reported in the income statement and has five independently computed components.

        b. PBO (projected benefit obligation)—The present value of unpaid pension benefits promised for work done through the balance sheet date, as measured by the benefit formula. PBO reflects future salaries if they are used in the formula, but PBO reflects service credits earned only through the balance sheet date. This major liability is reported only in the footnotes, not in the balance sheet. PBO is an actuarial present value that takes into account such variables as life expectancy, estimated final salary, years of service, turnover, interest rates, etc. An actuarial firm provides this information.

        c. Pension assets at market value—The current ending plan assets (with the trustee). This is the fund available for retirement benefits. Like PBO, plan assets are reported only in the footnotes, not the balance sheet (off-balance sheet). The ending plan asset balance equals: contributions made by the sponsoring firm to date + investment return to date (interest, dividends, stock appreciation, recognized gains and losses) – benefits paid to date.

        d. Pension liability—The difference between ending PBO and plan assets at the balance sheet date, reported in the balance sheet. Pension liability (PBO—assets) is the amount underfunded. If the plan is overfunded (assets exceed PBO), then pension asset is reported (assets—PBO). The pension liability (or asset) amount is also called "funded status" and represents the critical reporting value for pensions. If PBO is $40 million and plan assets at market value are $30 million, the pension fund is underfunded by $10 million. The pension liability of $10 million is the only amount reported in the balance sheet. Both PBO and assets are measured as of the balance sheet date.

    i. **Classification of liability or asset**

        1. The portion of pension liability classified as current is the excess of benefits payable for the coming year over the fair value of plan assets—this is the amount of payments that cannot be paid out of existing plan assets. The remainder is a noncurrent liability.

        2. If PBO is less than plan assets, the reported pension asset is classified as noncurrent because it is restricted and not available for other purposes.

    ii. When a firm has more than one defined benefit pension plan, the pension assets for those plans with plan assets at fair value greater than PBO are aggregated into one asset for reporting, and vice versa for plans with pension liabilities. Offsetting is not permitted because one plan's assets cannot be used to pay another plan's benefit payments.

> **Note**
>
> Two additional liability measures are reported in the footnotes:
>
> **ABO (accumulated benefit obligation)**—The present value of unpaid pension benefits through the balance sheet using current salaries. This calculation is the same as for PBO except that the latter uses future salaries.
>
> **VBO (vested benefit obligation)**—The present value of vested benefits.
>
> In most situations, the following relationship holds: PBO > ABO > VBO.

C. **Two Important Estimates**—In pension accounting are:

    1. **Discount rate**—The rate used for all actuarial present-value pension calculations. It is the rate at which the pension obligation could be settled and is pegged at the market rate of interest.

    2. **Expected rate of return**—The rate used to compute expected return on plan assets, one of the components of pension expense.

D. The two rates are independent although generally similar in magnitude.

E. **Pension Expense for a Period**—(Assume a calendar fiscal year) Is the sum of five components:

    1. **Service cost (SC)**—The actuarial present value of pension benefits earned during the current period. This amount is the increase in pension expense due to service provided during the year. For example, covered employees have increased their service credits by one year. The increase in the present value of future benefits attributable to this increase is SC. Service cost is an immediate increase in PBO.

    2. **Interest cost**—Equals growth in PBO for the period due to the passage of time = (discount rate) x (PBO at Jan. 1). This component is based on benefits earned through the end of the previous year. PBO is a present value. Because PBO is not paid until retirement benefits are paid, it grows by the interest rate as would any unpaid liability. That liability increase must be paid by the firm; therefore, the increase in PBO is part of annual pension expense.

    3. **Expected return on plan assets**—**Expected return on plan assets** equals (expected rate of return)x(plan assets at January. 1 at market value). This component **reduces** pension expense. The return on plan assets is the amount of the pension fund that is not paid by the sponsoring firm. Rather, investment returns on the assets provide a significant portion of the amounts paid to retirees. Expected return is used for component 3 rather than actual return to smooth the volatility in pension expense. Expected and actual returns on plan assets for the period are generally not the same.

    4. **Amortization of prior service cost**—(PSC—discussed later). This component causes pension expense to be increased gradually by the effect of amendments to the plan, which grant an increase in the value of pension benefits for service already provided by the employees.

5. **Amortization of net gain or loss**—(discussed later). This component causes pension expense to be gradually increased or decreased by (a) changes in PBO caused by estimate changes or experience changes, and (b) differences between expected and actual return on plan assets.

F. Each of the five components is **computed independently**.

1. Components 1 and 2 always increase pension expense.

2. Component 3 always reduces pension expense.

3. Component 4 almost always increases pension expense because benefits are usually increased by plan amendments. In rare cases, a pension plan modification may reduce pension benefits in which case component 4 would reduce pension expense.

> **Note**
> *Components 1–5 are not generally known by their numbers. Be able to recognize each component by name.*

4. Component 5 decreases pension expense for gains (PBO decreases and when actual return exceeds expected return), or increases pension expense for losses (PBO increases and when actual return falls short of expected return).

G. **Practical Expedient.** When the fiscal year end (FYE) of the sponsor (employer) does not coincide with a calendar month end, the employer may elect to measure plan assets and benefit obligations using the month end that is closest to the employer's fiscal year end. This is an option, not a requirement.

 **Example**
If the FYE is 12/20, the sponsor can choose to use 12/31 as the measurement date for plan assets and pension obligations.

An employer making the election must apply it consistently each year, and to all of its benefit plans.

Also, the sponsor must adjust the fair value of the plan assets and obligations for any contribution or other significant event caused by the employer (as opposed to events caused by market factors) that occurs between the measurement date and the employer's FYE.

The measurement date can be before or after the FYE.

Example: A firm's FYE is 12/28 and measures its assets and obligation as of 12/31. A significant contribution made on 12/30 is subtracted from plan assets. Alternatively, if the FYE is 1/5 and measurement date is 12/31, a contribution made 1/3 is added to plan assets.

Pension Expense Basics

This lesson highlights the first three components of pension expense to illustrate the model for accounting for defined benefit pension plans. It also shows the interaction of pension expense, PBO, plan assets, and pension liability.

After studying this lesson, you should be able to:

1. Calculate the first three components of pension expense.

2. Record pension expense and funding contribution.

3. Provide the financial reporting for the sponsor after recording the journal entries.

I. **Accounting for Pension Expense—Components 1–3**

   A. The first three components of pension expense occur each year. This example illustrates the first three components, resulting journal entries, and financial statement reporting. The last two components are independent of these and are discussed later. Recall that the first three components are (1) service cost, (2) interest cost, (3) expected return on plan assets.

   B. **20x1**

      1. **Component 1, service cost**—20x1 is the first year of a defined benefit plan. Service cost (SC) for 20x1, as computed by the actuary, is $3,000 (the present value of benefits earned in 20x1 taking into account estimated final salary, years of service, age at retirement, life expectancy, and other factors). Actuaries provide SC each year so you will not have to compute this amount.

      2. Discount rate is 5%, expected rate of return on plan assets is 6%.

      3. Funding contribution to trustee is $2,000 (assume year-end).

      4. **Component 2, interest cost**—There is no PBO at January 1, 20x1, because the plan was not in existence before that date. Therefore, there is no interest cost (component 2) for 20x1.

      5. **Component 3, expected return**—There was no pension fund at January 1, 20x1, so there is no expected return (component 3). SC is the only component for the first year. PBO at year-end is $3,000, the present value increase in PBO due to service credits earned in 20x1.

         a. **Journal entries**—When only components 1–3 are present, the sponsoring firm makes only two journal entries each year (the first is an adjusting entry):

Pension expense	3,000	
Pension liability		3,000
Pension liability	2,000	
Cash		2,000

         b. **Analysis**—These two entries cause:

            i. Income from continuing operations before tax to decrease $3,000.

            ii. Cash to decrease $2,000. (The cash is no longer available to the sponsoring firm because it has been placed into the pension fund, usually with the trustee.)

            iii. Reported pension liability to increase $1,000 ($3,000 − $2,000), the amount by which the plan is underfunded.

c. There is no journal entry on the sponsoring firm's books when retirement benefits are paid; these amounts are paid and recorded by the trustee. However, both PBO and plan assets are reduced by benefits paid. Because both plan assets and PBO are reduced by benefit payments, there is no effect on pension liability.

d. In the first entry above, pension expense causes pension liability (PBO − assets) to increase because SC is a direct increase to PBO. The funding contribution causes pension liability (PBO − assets) to decrease because assets reduce the pension liability.

PBO at 12/31/x1 is $3,000, the present value of benefits earned to date. The $3,000 amount is also SC because this is the first year of the plan.

Assets at 12/31/x1 = $2,000 (from funding in 20x1)

Pension liability = $1,000 = $3,000 (PBO) − $2,000 (assets)

= $1,000 = $3,000 (credit in entry for pension expense) − $2,000 (debit in entry for funding)

---

e. The pension plan is underfunded $1,000, the amount of the reported pension liability. PBO of $3,000 and assets of $2,000 are reported in the footnotes. Pension expense of $3,000 is reported in the income statement.

f. The Employee Retirement Income Security Act of 1974, as amended, requires that employee pension benefits vest within a certain period (five or seven years is typical). **Benefits are vested** if they are not contingent on continued employment. The Act also requires that firms provide minimum funding of pension plans. In addition, amounts funded by the employer are tax deductible, but only up to a maximum amount. Cash flow considerations also constrain the amounts funded.

C. 20x2

1. SC = $3,300 = the present value of benefits earned in 20x2. (This amount is larger than for 20x1; the increase may be due to an increase in the number of employees covered by the plan, higher future salaries, 20x2 is one year closer to the payment of retirement benefits, and other factors.). Again, this amount is provided by actuary.

2. Expected return = .06(fund balance at 1/1/x2) = .06($2,000) = $120. Assume expected return and actual return are the same in this example (otherwise, component 5 will come into play).

3. Funding in 20x2 is $3,000 (year-end).

Pension expense (end of 20x2):

1. SC	$3,300
2. Interest cost = (.05)($3,000 PBO at 1/1/x2)	150
3. Expected return on plan assets (.06)($2,000 assets at 1/1/x2)	(120)
Pension expense	$3,330

Journal entries:

Pension expense	3,330	
Pension liability		3,330
Pension liability	3,000	
Cash		3,000

a. Pension expense increases the pension liability (PBO – assets) by $3,330 because:

   i. SC and interest cost directly increased PBO by $3,450 ($3,300 + $150);

   ii. Expected return increased assets by $120 which reduces pension liability;

b. The net effect on pension liability therefore is $3,330.

c. To this point of coverage, ending PBO is the sum of service cost to date and interest cost to date, less benefits paid to date.

> PBO 12/31/x2 = $3,000 SC(20x1) + $3,300 SC(20x2) + $150 interest cost (20x2) = $6,450.
>
> PBO is the actuarial present value of benefits earned for the first 2 years, based on the benefit formula. If the firm invested $6,450 at end of 20x2 at the discount rate of 5%, then there would be just enough to cover all benefits earned through 20x2. (Benefits will be paid much later, during the retirement period.)

d. Assets at 12/31/x2 = $2,000 beginning balance + $120 (20x2 actual return) + $3,000 20x2 funding = $5,120.

   i. Plan assets always reflect actual return. Pension expense uses expected return. These amounts are the same in this example but will be different for the coverage of component 5 (discussed later).

> Pension liability at 12/31/x2 = $6,450 (PBO) – 5,120 (assets) = $1,330. This computation uses the ending amounts for the two components of pension liability.
>
> Also,
>
> Pension liability at 12/31/x2 = $1,000 (1/1/x2 balance) + 3,330 (pension expense entry) – 3,000 (funding entry)= $1,330. This is the ending ledger account balance after posting the two journal entries for 20x2.

e. The pension plan is underfunded $1,330, the amount of the reported pension liability. PBO, and assets are reported in the footnotes. Pension expense of $3,330 is reported in the income statement.

Exam note
Time permitting, verify the ending pension liability balance by computing both ways as shown above. These two ways of computing the ending pension liability are (1) the component approach using ending PBO and asset amounts and (2) the ledger account approach using the beginning balance and changes during the current year. If the amounts are different, you know an error has been made.

Pension Expense, Delayed Recognition

This lesson completes the discussion of pension expense by covering the last two components, which are subject to delayed recognition in earnings. The last two components are the amortization of prior service cost, and pension gains and losses.

After studying this lesson, you should be able to:

1. Describe the effects of delayed recognition on the accounting and reporting by the employer (sponsor).

2. Explain how prior service cost arises and interpret the initial recognized amount.

3. Record prior service cost.

4. Apply two methods of amortizing prior service cost and record the resulting journal entry.

5. Describe the composition of the pension gain or loss amount that is subject to amortization.

6. Record the net pension gain or loss for a year.

7. Apply two methods for amortizing pension gain or loss for the year.

I. **Delayed Recognition—Components 4 and 5**

    A. Components 1–3 of pension expense are recognized immediately, but components 4 and 5 are subject to delayed recognition in pension expense. The items causing these last two components are recognized immediately in pension liability and other comprehensive income (OCI), however.

    B. Defined benefit pension plans are subject to **two significant changes**:

        1. **Prior service cost (PSC)**—This is an immediate increase in PBO from the retroactive application of an increase in benefits for service already rendered (from plan amendments or from retroactive application to employee service before the plan's adoption). This is the source for component 4 of pension expense.

        It is called "prior" service cost because the service cost of previous years has been increased. For example, a defined benefit pension plan provides benefits equal to 2% of final salary for each year of service. The plan is later amended to increase the rate 2.10%, and the amendment is retroactive. The present value of the increased benefits (.10%) earned prior to the amendment is PSC. Employees have already rendered the service for a PSC grant. In rare cases, a retroactive grant may decrease the benefits for service already rendered.

        2. **Pension gains and losses**—There are two sources of pension gains and losses: (a) changes in PBO due to estimate changes and experience changes, and (b) the difference between expected and actual return. This is the source for component 5 of pension expense.

        For example, if employee turnover decreases or life expectancy increases, then future benefits will exceed the previous estimates used to compute PBO. The increase in PBO is called an actuarial loss or PBO loss. Also, recall that component 3 of pension expense is expected return. If actual return exceeds expected return, the difference is a gain, and vice versa. The gains and losses from both sources are netted into one amount at the beginning of each year.

    C. **PSC, and PBO Gains and Losses**—These are immediate changes to PBO and therefore to pension liability (PBO – assets). Asset gains or losses also affect the pension liability because component 3 is expected return. The impact on pension liability is recognized immediately along with an equal effect on Other Comprehensive Income (OCI), but due to the long-run nature of pension costs and the desire to decrease the volatility of reported pension expense, these two pension plan changes are not immediately recognized in pension expense.

Rather, they are recognized on a delayed basis by gradually amortizing them as components 4 and 5. Also, for gains and losses, delayed recognition allows for the canceling out of opposite items without bringing significant amounts into pension expense. A gain of $10 combines with a $7 loss to yield a $3 net gain, for example.

D. Recall that comprehensive income (CI) is the sum of net income (NI) and other comprehensive income (OCI) for a period:

> CI = NI + OCI

E. CI is a "global" measure of income. Its purpose is to report most changes in owners' equity other than transactions with owners. OCI items are similar to items currently recognized in net income but that are not so reported. Rather, they bypass the income statement and are recorded directly into an owners' equity account. They cause OCI, and therefore CI, to change, but not NI.

Example

The present value of a PSC amendment is $40,000. PBO therefore is increased by $40,000 immediately. In the same year, the actuary recomputes PBO because of new information on turnover, which has increased. The result is a decrease in PBO of $10,000 (with higher turnover, pension benefits will decrease because employees will remain with the firm a shorter time than previously expected).

The net result is that PBO is increased $30,000 ($40,000 − $10,000) and OCI is decreased $30,000 for the year. CI is also decreased $30,000 for the year. If it were not for delayed recognition, the entire $30,000 would have increased pension expense thus reducing net income. Instead, OCI is reduced immediately by the full change in PBO.

II. Component 4 of Pension Expense—Amortization of Prior Service Cost (PSC)

The amortization of the initial present value amount for PSC is component 4 of pension expense. In most cases, component 4 increases pension expense although retroactive amendments have decreased pension benefits.

A. Amortization is computed using one of two methods (a free choice but the firm must be consistent):

1. **Straight-line method** (amortize PSC over the average remaining service period of employees covered by the amendment); *or*

2. **Service method** (amortize an equal amount of PSC per service year, more amortization is recognized when more employees are working).

Example

Prior service cost is $15,000 as determined on January 1, 20x0. There are three employees with the following remaining service periods affected by the amendment:

Employee	Service years remaining
A	9
B	2
C	4
Total	15

The average remaining service period is 5 years: 15/(3 employees).

B. Straight-Line Method

1. Amortization each year is $3,000 ($15,000/5). Pension expense is increased $3,000 for the years 20x0–20x4. After that, unless another prior service grant is awarded, pension expense will no longer reflect this component. Only the initial PSC amount is amortized—as component 2 (interest cost) automatically includes interest on the growth in PSC because the $15,000 is included in PBO.

C. Service Method

1. A constant amount of amortization is recognized for each service year: $1,000 = $15,000/15. For the first two years (20x0 and 20x1), all three employees are working (three service years). Therefore, 3($1,000) or $3,000 of PSC is amortized (included in pension expense). The amortization (component 4) for each year is shown below.

Year	Service Years	Calculation	Amortization
20x0	3	3($1,000)	$3,000
20x1	3	3($1,000)	$3,000
20x2	2 (B is retired)	2($1,000)	$2,000
20x3	2	2($1,000)	$2,000
20x4	1 (C is retired)	1($1,000)	$1,000
20x5	1	1($1,000)	$1,000
20x6	1	1($1,000)	$1,000
20x7	1	1($1,000)	$1,000
20x8	1	1($1,000)	$1,000
			$15,000

2. The rationale for delayed recognition of PSC is that the firm will receive a benefit from the retroactive increase in pension benefits (higher morale, lower demands for future pay increases, etc.). The cost of the amendment should be matched against the benefits to be received in the future. The service method is preferable in this regard because more cost is included in pension expense when more employees are working.

Note
The two methods always yield the same amortization amount for the first year (in this example, $3,000).

3. The two methods always yield the same amortization amount for the first year (in this example, $3,000).

> The formula for PBO now includes PSC. There are two different ways to express ending PBO for a year, with the second being more useful in solving problems:
>
> PBO ending amount = SC to date + Interest cost to date − Benefits paid to date + PSC
>
> PBO ending amount = PBO beginning balance + SC for year + Interest cost for year − Benefits paid in year + PSC if granted in year

III. Journal Entries for Recognition of PSC and Its Amortization

1. Recognition of PSC (amount from above example). This is recorded only once, in the year of granting the retroactive benefits. This amount is a present value:

PSC-OCI	15,000	
Pension liability		15,000

2. Pension liability (PBO − assets) is increased immediately because PBO is increased immediately. The account PSC-OCI represents a specific OCI item (the "OCI" in the account title simply indicates that PSC is included in OCI). OCI is immediately reduced by $15,000 because the cost of the pension plan has increased that amount. All OCI items are merged into one net change in owners' equity called "Accumulated Other Comprehensive Income (AOCI)".

3. Amortization of PSC for 20x0 (same amount for each method in first year). This entry is in addition to the entry to record the components 1–3 and may be merged with that entry:

Pension expense	3,000	
PSC-OCI		3,000

4. Analysis: The above entry reclassifies a part of PSC-OCI to pension expense —this is delayed recognition. Pension expense is increased $3,000 by this entry. The $3,000 amount is called a reclassification adjustment because a portion of the $15,000 reduction in OCI has now been transferred to net income. This journal entry has no effect on CI for the year because net income has been reduced and OCI has been increased (credited).

   Amortization is recorded each year until the $15,000 PSC amount is fully amortized. The amount recorded after the first year depends on the method of amortization chosen (discussed above).

Formal versus Informal Record

A. **Formal Record**—The pension information maintained in the accounts is called the formal record. These accounts include pension expense, pension liability, PSC-OCI, pension gain/loss-OCI.

B. **Informal Record**—Any pension information not formally recorded in the accounts. These amounts include PBO and assets at market value.

IV. Component 5 of Pension Expense—Amortization of Net Gain or Loss

A. This component may cause pension expense to decrease (for a net gain) or to increase (for a net loss). Each fiscal period begins with a net gain or loss (but not both) because all gains and losses are merged into one amount. Gains and losses cancel each other dollar for dollar.

B. Component 5 is the amortization of the net gain or loss at the *beginning* of the year.

C. The net gain or loss at the beginning of a year is the net sum of all previous gains and losses less previous amortization. The following table illustrates the two sources of gains and losses.

	PBO Change	Asset Return
Gain	Decrease in PBO from increase in expected or actual turnover, decrease in life expectancy, etc.	Actual return > expected return
Loss	Increase in PBO from decrease in discount rate, decrease in turnover, etc.	Actual return < expected return

1. PBO gains and losses stem from both (1) experience not equal to a prior estimate, and (2) change in estimate of future events. No distinction is made between these two types for purposes of component 5.

Example
The current year began with no net gain or loss. There is no component 5 for the current year because there is no net gain or loss to amortize as of the beginning of the year.

At the end of the current year, the actuary informs the sponsoring firm that PBO has increased $14,000 due to a decrease in expected turnover, and actual return exceeded expected return by $4,000. The net loss is $10,000 for the current year ($14,000 PBO loss – $4,000 asset gain).

The **net loss** of $10,000 is the source of amortization (component 5) for the next year.

D. There are **two computations** for component 5 each year:

1. Determining the amortization of the net gain or loss at the beginning of the current year to include in pension expense for the year. There are two methods of amortization allowed: (1) minimum (corridor) amortization and (2) SL amortization. Both use average remaining service period of employees as the denominator. The firm must be consistent in its application. If corridor amortization is not chosen, any consistently applied method resulting in an amortization amount is acceptable. SL is the most popular choice for the second alternative.

2. Determining the net gain or loss at the end of the current year for amortization the following year. The ending net gain or loss = beginning net gain or loss – amortization of beginning net gain or loss ± PBO gain or loss for the current year ± asset gain or loss for the current year.

E. Journal Entries—These mirror the entries for PSC above.

a. Recognition of the gain or loss for the year (assume a net gain of $2,000, which is the net of the PBO gain or loss for the year, and the asset gain or loss for the year):

Pension liability	2,000	
Pension gain/loss – OCI		2,000

b. Amortization of beginning net gain or loss (assume year started with $40,000 net gain):

Pension gain/loss – OCI	4,000	(assumed amount, see example below)
Pension expense		4,000

As with PSC, for pension gains and losses there are two journal entries beyond the basic two always present for components 1–3.

The first is recorded each year and recognizes the net pension gain or loss for the year ($2,000 net gain here).

The second is the amortization of the beginning net gain or loss that stems from previous years ($4,000 amortization here). In this example, pension expense is reduced by the $4,000 amortization because the beginning amount is a net gain—a reduction in the cost of the pension plan not yet brought into pension expense. The determination of the amount amortized is illustrated in detail below.

> **Note:** The final (complete) formula for PBO at a balance sheet date is: PBO = SC to date + interest cost to date – benefits paid to date + PSC + net PBO gain or loss to date.
>
> Also:
>
> PBO = PBO beginning balance + SC for year + interest cost for year – benefits paid in year + PSC if granted in year + PBO gain or loss for year
>
> Asset gains and losses are not part of the PBO calculation above, but they are a part of the determination of net gain or loss for component 5.

V. **Full Example**—This example illustrates all of the computational aspects for component 5 of pension expense and also provides an overall review of defined benefit pension accounting in a comprehensive context.

A. **Assumed Data at 12/3/x4**

1. PBO, $50,000

2. Assets, $30,000

3. There is no net gain or loss at the end of 20x4;

4. Average remaining service period of employees covered by the plan is 10 years. Assume this value remains constant over the next several years as employees retire and new employees are hired;

5. Discount rate, 5%

6. Expected long-term rate of return, 6%

B. **20x5 (End of Year)**—There is no component 5 (amortization) for 20x5 because there is no net gain or loss at 1/1/x5.

C. **Assumed Data at 12/31/x5**

1. Ending PBO after including SC, interest cost, and subtracting benefits paid for 20x5, but before PBO loss, $90,000

2. PBO loss from change in estimated turnover, $15,000

3. PBO after including PBO loss, $105,000 ($90,000 + $15,000)

4. Ending assets at market value, $75,000

5. Ending pension liability = $105,000 PBO – $75,000 assets = $30,000

6. Actual return on assets, $2,000

D. Computation of Net Loss at 12/31/x5

Asset gain = actual return $2,000 − expected return ($30,000 × .06 = $1,800) =	($200)
PBO loss	15,000
Net loss	$14,800

1. The net loss of $14,800 is the amount subject to amortization for 20x6 because there was no net gain or loss at the beginning of 20x5. The entry to record the net loss (alternatively, the gain and loss can be recorded separately):

Pension gain/loss-OCI	14,800	
Pension liability		14,800

2. This entry, like the one recording PSC-OCI, recognizes the net loss as a component of OCI and increases the pension liability. "Pension gain/loss-OCI" is so named to indicate the account can be a gain or loss. The PBO loss immediately increased the pension liability (PBO − assets). The journal entry to record pension expense (first three components) used expected return thus reducing pension expense by $1,800. As a result, pension liability was not reduced by actual return, which was $200 more. Therefore, the pension liability must be reduced an additional $200. That amount is netted against the PBO loss resulting in the $14,800 increase in the pension liability.

E. 20x6 (End of Year)

1. The $14,800 net loss from 20x5 is the amount subject to amortization yielding component 5 of pension expense for 20x6. The results of applying the two allowable methods are as follows.

   a. **SL method**—amortization = $14,800/10 years = $1,480. If this method is chosen, component 5 of pension expense is a $1,480 increase (because this portion of the loss is being recognized in pension expense—a loss represents an increase in the firm's pension cost).

   b. **Corridor (minimum) method**—The amount of the $14,800 subject to amortization is the amount outside a "corridor." The corridor is plus or minus 10% of the larger of PBO and assets, both at the beginning of the year. This method results in lower amortization relative to the SL method, allowing for more cancellation of gains and losses over time. This method results in amortization only if the amount of net gain or loss is significant, as defined by the corridor.

Amortization =

($14,800 − .10(larger of $105,000 PBO at Jan. 1, or $75,000 assets at Jan. 1)) / 10 years =

($14,800 − .10($105,000)) / 10 = $430.

If this method is chosen, component 5 of pension expense is a $430 increase.

F. Assume the Following Data for 20x6

1. SC is $8,000 for 20x6

2. The firm chooses corridor amortization of net gain or loss.

3. Benefits paid to retirees during the year, $12,000

4. Funding contribution, $15,000

5. Actual return on assets, $400

6. PBO gain from reduction in rate of compensation increase (reduces estimated final salaries), $22,000 (year-end)

7. Amounts to be determined by firm (or candidate for CPA Exam):

   a. Interest cost for 20x6 = .05($105,000) = $5,250

   b. Expected return on plan assets = .06($75,000) = $4,500

   c. Asset loss for 20x6 = $4,500 expected return − $400 actual return = $4,100

   d. Pension expense for 20x6 = $8,000 SC + $5,250 interest cost − $4,500 expected return + $430 amortization of net loss = $9,180. If there were unamortized PSC, the amortization of PSC would be added to this total.

   e. Ending PBO = $105,000 beginning PBO + $8,000 SC + $5,250 interest cost − $22,000 PBO gain − $12,000 benefits paid = $84,250

   f. Ending assets at market value = $75,000 beginning assets + $400 actual return + $15,000 funding − $12,000 benefits paid = $78,400

G. Journal Entry to Record the 20x6 PBO Gain and Asset Loss ($22,000 − $4,100 = $17,900)

Pension liability	17,900	
Pension gain/loss-OCI		17,900

H. Journal Entry to Record Pension Expense —

Pension expense	9,180	
Pension liability		8,750
Pension gain/loss-OCI		430

1. $8,750 = $8,000 SC + $5,250 interest cost − $4,500 expected return. This amount is the net sum of the first three components. The $430 amortization of the net loss from the previous period increases pension expense with no additional effect on the pension liability. The recording of the loss increased pension liability that year.

I. Journal Entry to Record Funding

Pension liability	15,000	
Cash		15,000

Computation of net gain at 12/31/x6

Net loss, 1/1/x6	$14,800
Amortization	(430)
Asset loss	4,100
PBO gain	(22,000)
Net gain	(3,530)

J. This example illustrates how a net loss can turn into a net gain in one period. The ability of gains and losses to cancel each other supports corridor amortization.

K. Verification of Ending Pension Liability (Via Components and Journal Entry Effects)

1. Ending PBO – ending assets: $84,250 – $78,400 = $5,850

2. Ledger account: $30,000 beginning 20x6 balance – $17,900 recording net gain for 20x6 + $8,750 pension expense entry – $15,000 funding entry = $5,850

L. 20x7 (End of Year)

1. To complete the example, only the calculation of component 5 is illustrated:

    a. **SL method**—amortization = $3,530/10 years = $353, decreases pension expense. This amount is shown for illustration. The firm chose corridor amortization for 20x6 which also should be chosen for 20x7 for consistency.

    b. **Corridor (minimum) method**—the corridor amount = .10(larger of $84,250 PBO at January 1, or $78,400 assets at January 1) = $8,425. Because the $3,530 net gain is not outside (larger than) the corridor amount, there is no amortization required under this method. Because the firm chose this method, there is no component 5 for 20x7.

2. If there were no PBO gain or loss for 20x7, and actual return equals expected return, the net gain of $3,530 is carried over to 20x8. The corridor amount will most likely change because the ending balance of both PBO and assets typically changes each year.

Pension Plan Reporting, International

The lesson addresses the main differences between U.S. and international standards regarding pension accounting and reporting by the pension plan.

After studying this lesson, you should be able to:

1. Note terminology differences between U.S. and international standards.

2. Describe the international approach to accounting for prior service cost.

3. Distinguish accounting for pension gains and losses between the two sets of standards.

4. Understand the basics of reporting by the pension plan.

I. U.S. GAAP–IFRS Differences

A. In many significant ways, international and U.S. pension accounting standards are the same. For example, pension expense has the same five components, and the plan obligation and plan assets are not reported on the balance sheet. However, because the governments of many countries provide significant contributions, pensions may have less of a material impact on sponsors' financial statements in these countries. Accounting differences are discussed below.

B. Terminology and Presentation

1. PBO for U.S. standards is called defined benefit obligation (DBO) for international standards.

2. Pension liability or asset reported in the balance sheet (for the United States) is called defined benefit liability or asset (international).

3. PSC is prior service cost for United States, but is called past-service cost for international accounting.

4. Under international standards, pension expense is reported in separate components rather than as a single amount on the income statement. These components are: service cost (including past service cost), and net interest cost (interest cost netted against expected return).

5. Pension gains/losses for U.S. standards are called "remeasurement gains/losses" for international standards.

C. A multiemployer plan has two or more unrelated firms contributing assets to the same plan for the payment of pension benefits of the employees of the participating firms. Under U.S. standards, each participant firm accounts for the plan as a defined contribution plan. Pension expense is simply the required contribution for the period, and any unpaid amount at year-end is reported as a liability. International standards allow such plans to be accounted for as defined benefit plans if there is sufficient information.

D. Under IFRS, the discount rate used to compute interest cost must also be used to compute expected return on plan assets. Therefore, net interest cost is the difference between interest cost and expected return on plan assets.

In contrast, under U.S. standards, expected return is based on any reasonable rate of return chosen by management. As a result, the asset gain or loss for IFRS will not be the same amount as per U.S. standards.

E. Accounting for pension gains and losses. Under IFRS, gains and losses from both sources (liability, assets) are recognized immediately in DBO and OCI. This is the treatment under U.S. standards. However, under IFRS, gains and losses are not subsequently amortized into pension expense. Net income is never affected. Rather, pension gains and losses are treated as permanent owners' equity items.

Example

An actuarial loss of $1,000,000 million is recorded as follows for international standards:

Remeasurement gain/loss—OCI   1,000,000

    Defined benefit liability   1,000,000

(There is no subsequent amortization of the remeasurement loss to pension expense.)

F.   Accounting for past-service cost (PSC). Under international standards, PSC (called past-service cost for IFRS) is expensed immediately in pension expense as part of service cost.

II. Disclosures by Sponsor

A. Disclosures for Defined Contribution Plans

1. Pension expense should be presented separately from defined benefit plan pension expense.

2. Description of the plan

3. Description of the nature and effect of significant changes during the period affecting comparability (e.g., a divestiture, business combination, or a change in the rate of contributions)

4. Reconciliation of beginning and ending pension liability balance

B. Disclosures for Defined Benefit Plans

1. Pension expense and its components

2. Funded status (pension liability)

3. Reconciliation of beginning and ending balances for PBO including SC, interest cost, gains and losses, amendments and other changes; and for plan assets including contributions, benefits, and other changes

4. Accumulated benefit obligation (ABO) and vested benefit obligation (VBO)

5. Any settlements or curtailments. A settlement occurs when a transaction relieves the employer of primary responsibility for a pension or postretirement benefit obligation and eliminates significant associated risks. A curtailment is an event that significantly reduces the expected years of future service of an active plan participant or eliminates the accrual of a defined benefit for a significant number of active plan participants.

6. Estimates and assumptions including benefits expected to be paid in each of the next five years, employer contributions expected to be paid in the next 12 months, discount rates, rate of compensation increase, and expected long-term rate of return on plan assets

7. Amounts recognized in OCI and reclassification adjustments, and OCI amounts not yet recognized in pension expense

III. Reporting by the Pension Plan

A. The entity that administers pension plans is required to separately provide accrual-based financial statements for the plans they administer. This section discusses the requirements pertaining to those financial statements. Previous lessons referred to accounting and reporting by the sponsor of the plan.

Typically an insurance company or trust company administers the plans, but the reporting requirements also apply to firms that administer their own plans.

B. Requirements for the Annual Accrual Basis Financial Statements for Defined Contribution Plans

1. A statement of net assets available for benefits as of the end of the plan year

2. A statement of changes in net assets available for benefits for the year then ended

3. A statement of cash flows is not required but encouraged

4. A general description of the plan agreement including vesting, allocation provisions, the disposition of forfeitures, and a description of significant plan amendments adopted during the period

C. Requirements for the Annual Accrual Basis Financial Statements for Defined Benefit Plans

1. A statement reporting net plan assets at fair value available to pay pension benefits at the beginning or end of the year (end of year preferable)

2. A financial statement reporting the changes for the year in net plan assets at fair value available to pay pension benefits

3. A statement of the actuarial present value of accumulated plan benefits as of the beginning or end of the year (using the same date as plan assets in 1)

4. Additional information about factors affecting the change in actuarial present value of accumulated plan benefits from the previous year

5. The term *"accumulated plan benefits"* is used because this reporting requirement applies to other types of employee benefits, in addition to pension plans.

6. A statement of cash flows is not required but encouraged.

7. A general description of the plan including vesting and benefit provisions, plan amendments adopted in the current year, funding policy, and a description of the priority order of participant's claims upon plan termination

Postretirement Benefits

This lesson covers the accounting for retirement benefits other than pensions. The most significant benefit in this category is postretirement healthcare. The accounting is similar to the accounting for defined benefit pension plans.

After studying this lesson, you should be able to:

1. Explain EPBO and its relevance to the reported obligation.

2. Describe how APBO is computed and what it represents.

3. Express how to measure the reported liability and expense.

4. Determine an employee's full eligibility date and explain how it affects the measurement of the plan obligation and reported liability.

I. **Potential Benefits**

    A. In addition to pensions, many firms provide other postretirement benefits to retirees based on the service they provided during their years as employees. Such benefits are often referred to as **OPEB** or other postemployment benefits. These benefits may include one or more of the following:

        1. Healthcare or medical care benefits

        2. Dental care benefits

        3. Eye care benefits

        4. Life insurance benefits

        5. Benefits related to legal services

        6. Benefits related to tax services

        7. Benefits related to tuition assistance

        8. Benefits related to day care

        9. Benefits related to housing assistance

    B. By far, the largest in magnitude in terms of cost is postretirement healthcare coverage. The recipients of these benefits may include retirees, their spouses, and their other dependents and beneficiaries. This is in contrast to pensions in which only the employee receives the benefit.

II. **Accounting for Postretirement Benefit Plans**

    A. **Liability Reporting**—As with pensions, the primary measure of the postretirement benefit obligation is netted against plan assets. The difference, postretirement benefit liability, is reported in the balance sheet.

    B. The primary measure of postretirement benefit obligation is **Accumulated Postretirement Benefit Obligation (APBO)**. It is used and reported the same way as PBO in pension accounting, but is computed differently.

        1. **Expected Postretirement Benefit Obligation (EPBO)** is computed first. This is the present value of benefits expected to be paid based on the level of coverage the employees are expected to attain. Postretirement healthcare plans provide services based on years of service, retirement age, and other variables. An employee may receive 50%, 75%, or 100% coverage during retirement, for example, depending on age at retirement and years of service. The benefit levels thus increase in steps rather than gradually with each year of service, as is the case with pensions. EPBO is estimated each year based on the coverage expected to be attained by each employee and based on estimates of healthcare costs during the employee's retirement.

    a. EPBO is the present value of benefits to be paid by the firm, after deducting the contributions of the employee and any Medicare or other government-sponsored plan payments. In contrast to pension accounting, there is no benefit formula. Rather, EPBO reflects the level of service expected to be attained by the employee.

  2. APBO is then computed as the fraction of EPBO earned by the employee as of the balance sheet date. For example, Pat is expected to attain a coverage level of 75% of full coverage based on her expected service period. If Pat must work for 20 years to obtain that level, and Pat has worked 12 years as of the balance sheet date, APBO for Pat is $(12/20) \times$ EPBO. Remember that EPBO is the present value of the total cost expected to be paid by the firm and includes service projected all the way to retirement. The measurement of APBO stops at the balance sheet date. EPBO is used only to compute APBO.

C. Postretirement benefit liability as reported in the balance sheet = APBO − plan assets at market value. APBO and plan assets are reported in the footnotes only, not in the balance sheet.

D. **Postretirement Benefit Expense**—As with pensions, postretirement benefit expense has five components, and one additional component (which is also present in some pension plans but has essentially disappeared from pension accounting). Except for a few differences, postretirement benefit expense is computed the same way as pension expense. Delayed recognition applies to components 4–6.

  1. **Service cost (SC)**—The increase in APBO attributable to service provided in the period. SC is recognized only during the attribution period—the period to full eligibility (see below). This often occurs before retirement, in contrast with pension accounting.

  2. **Interest cost**—The increase in APBO due to the passage of time = (discount rate) × (APBO at January 1).

  3. **Expected return on assets**—(expected rate of return) × (assets at January 1).

  4. **Amortization of prior service cost (PSC)**—The same two amortization methods allowed in pensions are allowed for PSC in postretirement benefit plans.

    a. Initial full recognition of PSC is recorded in PSC-OCI and postretirement benefit liability, as is the procedure for pensions.

  5. **Amortization of net gain or loss at January 1**—The same two amortization methods allowed in pensions are allowed for postretirement benefit expense. Changes in APBO and the difference between actual and expected return on plan assets are the two sources for gains and losses, as with pensions. However, firms may recognize postretirement benefit gains or losses immediately, with some limitations.

    a. Initial full recognition of postretirement benefit gains and losses is recorded in postretirement benefit gain/loss-OCI and postretirement benefit liability, as is the procedure for pensions.

  6. **Amortization of transition obligation**—Before accrual accounting was mandated for postretirement benefits, most firms used cash basis accounting for postretirement benefits. As a result, most if not all, of APBO at the date of transition to accrual accounting was not recognized. Many firms elected to recognize immediately that entire amount as an accounting change, decreasing income in the year of transition. For these firms, there is no component 6. Those that did not recognize the transition obligation (APBO at transition) immediately in income, chose the other available option at the time which was to amortize the initial APBO amount over average remaining service period (if less than 20 years, the firm may use 20 years) on a straight-line basis (similar to amortization of PSC if SL is used). The result is component 6 of pension expense. Under either option, the entire transition obligation was recognized in postretirement benefit liability.

> **Note**
> As with pension accounting, the actuary provides all of the information on the liability side of the plan including SC, EPBO, APBO, PSC, and gains/losses. The candidate should be able to compute the other amounts.

III. Full Eligibility

A. In contrast with pensions, employees often reach full eligibility before retirement. In these cases, no additional benefits are earned beyond the full eligibility date. (With pensions, each year of service typically increases the retirement benefit.) An employee is fully eligible for the benefits expected to be received when the employee renders the necessary years of service and meets any other requirements necessary to receive those benefits. Full eligibility does not mean that the employee will receive full benefits. Rather, it means that the employee has reached the service level required to receive the benefits that will most likely be granted to the employee during retirement.

> **Example**
> A postretirement healthcare plan provides 50% of full postretirement healthcare coverage for 20 years of service rendered after age 40, 70% coverage for 25 years of service after age 40, and 100% coverage for 30 years of service after age 40. If an employee hired at age 35 is expected to retire at age 62, then the employee is expected to work 22 years after age 40. This employee therefore is expected to be eligible to receive 50% of full healthcare coverage during retirement. Note that, depending on the plan, the attribution period may not begin with the date of employment.
>
> The employee's full eligibility date is age 60, at which time the requisite 20 years of service after age 40 has been rendered. Service cost, the first component of postretirement benefit expense, for this employee, is attributed to service from age 40 to age 60. After that point, SC no longer is computed for the employee, but interest cost continues. The period during which the employee earns benefits toward full eligibility is 20 years.
>
> APBO is a fraction of EPBO. The fraction is the number of years of the full eligibility period actually served by the employee as of the balance sheet date. When our employee above, who is expected to receive 50% of full coverage, reaches the age of 45, the employee will have rendered 5 years of the total period to full eligibility. On this date, APBO = (5/20)EPBO. The next year APBO = (6/20)(EPBO).
>
> Note, however, that EPBO increases each year with the passage of time, as does APBO. When the employee reaches full eligibility at age 60, no more service cost is computed. At that point, APBO = EPBO, and both grow with interest cost until the employee retires at age 62.

Example

Assume the following data for the current year(assumes one covered employee for simplicity):

EPBO at Jan. 1 of the current year, $4,000

Plan assets at Jan. 1, $1,000;

Discount rate, 6%;

Expected rate of return on assets, 7%;

Actual return on plan assets, $70;

Funding (year-end), $900;

Years required to full eligibility, 20 years;

Years worked as of Jan. 1, 9 years;

APBO, Jan. 1 = $4,000(9/20) = $1,800;

Postretirement benefit liability reported in the balance sheet, Jan. 1 = $1,800 APBO − $1,000 assets = $800;

EPBO, Dec. 31 = $4,000(1.06) = 4,240 (6% growth due to interest;)

APBO, Dec. 31 = $4,240(10/20) = $2,120 (one more year of service provided);

Assets, Dec. 31 = $1,000 beginning assets + $70 actual return + $900 funding = $1,970. Any benefits paid would be subtracted from assets.

Postretirement benefit expense:

1. SC = $4,240(1/20) (the portion of ending EPBO attributable to service in the current year) =	$212
2. Interest cost = $1,800(.06) (growth in APBO for the year) =	108
Expected return on plan assets = $1,000(.07) =	(70)
Total	$250

Postretirement benefit expense	250	
Postretirement benefit liability		250

Postretirement benefit liability	900	
Cash		900

Ending balance of postretirement benefit liability ($150) computed two ways:

$2,120 ending APBO − $1,970 ending assets = $150

$800 beginning balance + $250 increase from pension expense entry − $900 decrease from current year funding = $150

IV. Example—Ending Postretirement Benefit Liability:

Example

The previous example illustrated the relationship between APBO and EPBO for a single employee. In practice, the actuary provides the underlying amounts relevant to the reported obligation and for computing postretirement benefit expense across the entire employee group. The following example uses data at the firm level and also illustrates PSC and gains/losses.

Data for the postretirement healthcare plan for a firm is as follows, for the current year (in millions):

Service cost	$100
Accumulated postretirement benefit obligation, Jan. 1	800
Plan assets at fair value, Jan. 1	200
Prior service cost ($100 initial amount, $10 amortization per year)	80
Net loss at Jan. 1 (current year amortization, $4)	56
APBO gain (actuarial gain), Dec. 31	40
Retiree benefits paid	120
Funding contribution (year-end)	240
Return on plan assets, actual	19
Discount rate	5%
Expected return on plan assets	6%

Required: (1) Record postretirement benefit expense and any other required journal entries; (2) determine ending postretirement benefit liability using two different calculations; and (3) determine the amount of net gain or loss to carry over to the next year.

Solution

(1) Postretirement benefit expense:

1. SC	$100
2. Interest cost (.05)($800)	40
3. Expected return (.06)(200)	(12)
4. Amortization of PSC	10
5. Amortization of net loss	4
Total	$142

Postretirement benefit expense	142	
Postretirement benefit liability		128
PSC-OCI		10
Postretirement benefit gain/loss-OCI		4
Postretirement benefit liability	240	
Cash		240

Asset gain for the year = $19 actual return − $12 expected return = $7

APBO gain =   <u>40</u>

Total gain for period $47

Postretirement benefit liability   47

    Postretirement benefit gain/loss-OCI   47

(2) Beginning postretirement benefit liability = $800 beginning APBO − $200 beginning assets = $600

Ending APBO = $800 beginning APBO + $100 SC + $40 Interest cost − $120 benefits paid − $40 APBO gain = $780

Ending assets = $200 beginning assets + $240 funding + $19 actual return − $120 benefits paid = $339

(3) Ending postretirement benefit liability
$780 ending APBO − $339 ending assets = $441

$600 beginning balance + $128 (pension expense entry) − $240 (funding entry) − $47 current year gain entry = $441

V. Disclosures

A. The disclosures required for postretirement benefit plans are essentially the same as covered for defined benefit pension plans. Where PBO (projected benefit obligation) for pension plans is disclosed for example, APBO and EPBO are disclosed for postretirement plans. As with pension plans, the components of postretirement benefit expense are disclosed. And where the rate of compensation increase is disclosed for pensions, the expected rate of increase in future medical and dental benefit costs is disclosed for postretirement benefit plans.

B. Many firms are combining these disclosures. Review the listing of disclosures in the section on defined pension benefit plans.

VI. U.S. GAAP–IFRS Differences

A. The international accounting standard applicable to defined benefit pension accounting also applies to postretirement benefits. The lessons on pension accounting provide details about the differences between international and U.S. standards. These differences apply as well to postretirement benefits.

B. Firms use appropriate account titles to distinguish pension expense and postretirement benefit expense, and DBO for pensions and the analogous obligation measure for retirement benefits.

C. In many countries, funding is on a pay-as-you-go basis which reduces or eliminates component 3 of postretirement benefit expense, expected return on plan assets. The fund (the basis for expected return) is nonexistent or very small.

Stock Compensation (Share-Based Payments)

Stock Options

This lesson addresses stock purchase plans open to the rank and file and stock option plans, which typically are available only to top management. Both are examples of share-based payment plans concerning.

After studying this lesson, you should be able to:

1. Account for plans available to most or all employees of the firm.

2. Understand how the variables used as inputs to the calculation of the fair value of an option affect their value.

3. Compute and record compensation expense for a stock option plan.

4. Prepare the entry for the exercise and expiration of options.

5. Include forfeitures in the accounting.

I. **Stock Purchase Plans Open to All Employees**

   A. Before discussing stock option plans, plans for the rank and file are presented as a background to this significant reporting area. In this type of plan, employees purchase stock directly from firms, they may receive a small discount, and the employer may match a portion of the purchase.

   1. **Criteria for recognizing compensation expense**

      a. Such plans are considered **noncompensatory** (no significant compensation is provided) if all apply:

         i. Essentially all employees can participate.

         ii. Employee must decide within one month of the firm setting the price for the stock whether to enroll in the plan.

         iii. Discount does not exceed the employer cost savings inherent in issuing directly to employees ($\leq$ 5% market price meets this criterion).

         iv. Purchase price must be based solely on the market price of the stock.

         v. Employees can cancel their enrollment before purchase date and obtain a full refund.

   2. **Noncompensatory plan**—If noncompensatory, the shares are recorded as any other stock issuance. The only expense is the portion "paid for" by the firm (the matching portion), if any. The employer does not actually pay any cash; rather, it bears the matching portion as its cost.

Example
The par value of common stock is $1 and market price is $100. Employees of the firm can purchase their firm's stock for $98 (2% discount)—and the other criteria are met.

This plan is noncompensatory (2% < 5%).

The firm pays 50% of the employee's cost, and an employee buys 20 shares.

Compensation expense	980		employer cost .50($98)(20)
Cash	980		employee payment 20($1 par)
Common stock		20	
Paid-in capital in excess of par, common		1,940	20($98 – $1)

If the firm did not match any of the cost, the employee would pay $1,960 (= 20 × $98), and no compensation expense would be recognized. The $100 market price is not used because the discount is considered small.

3. **Compensatory plan**—If not all five criteria are met, then the plan is compensatory. For example, if the discount is substantial, then that total discount amount is recorded as expense.

Example
Assume the same facts as for the above noncompensatory example except that the employee can purchase the stock for $90 (10% discount). This is a compensatory plan because the discount exceeds 5% of the market price.

Compensation expense	1,100*		
Cash	900		.50($90)20 employee payment
Common stock		20	20($1 par)
Paid-in capital in excess of par, common		1,980	20($100 – $1)

* .50($90)(20) matching portion + ($100 – $90)20 the discount portion (the total discount)

In the first example (noncompensatory), total contributed capital is based on the discounted price (< 5%). Compensation expense reflects only the portion not paid by the employee.

In the second example (compensatory), total contributed capital is based on the current share price, and compensation expense reflects the larger discount and the portion paid by the employer.

B. The remaining parts of this lesson pertain to incentive plans for selected employees—typically upper management. The terms of these plans provide an incentive for the employee to provide significant value and be well-compensated.

II. Stock Option Plans

Definition
Stock Option Plan: Provides an employee with the option to purchase shares of employer firm stock at a fixed price in the future, after a reasonable service period. The options expire beyond a certain point.

A. The value of such a grant stems from the potential for the stock price to increase. The ability of employees to influence the stock price provides the incentive.

B. Basic Example—On 1/1/x1, selected executives of Flowers Inc. are granted the option to purchase 10,000 shares of the firm's $1 par common stock for $5 per share during the two-year period beginning 1/1/x5 and ending 12/31/x6 (exercise period). The market price of the stock on the grant date also is $5. To maintain their eligibility for the option plan, the employees must continue to be employed by the firm for the four years after the grant date.

1. **Features of the plan**

   a. The $5 fixed price of the stock is called the option price or exercise price.

   b. The four-year period before the option can be exercised is called the service period, vesting period and amortization period.

   c. During the service period, compensation expense is recognized.

   d. To fully exercise the option, the employees must pay $50,000 for the 10,000 shares.

   e. The options vest at the end of the service period. (The ability to exercise the option is no longer contingent on continued employment with the firm at this point.)

   f. This type of plan is called a *fixed* plan because the relevant terms are set at the grant date.

   g. This plan illustrates *cliff* vesting because all options vest at the same time.

C. Measuring Compensation Expense

1. GAAP requires that the fair value of the options granted be estimated using an option-pricing model as of the grant date. Various option-pricing models are available that use the following six variables at grant date to determine the value of the option (including Black-Scholes, lattice, and others):

   a. Exercise price (option price)—*Higher fair value with lower option price (less must be paid to obtain the shares)*

   b. Expected average life of the option (service period + exercise period)—*Higher fair value with longer option period (there is a greater chance the stock price will increase and the time value of money is greater)*

   c. Current stock price—*Higher fair value with higher price (the fair value of the option is in part a function of current stock price)*

   d. Expected volatility of the stock—*Higher fair value with greater volatility (there is a greater chance of price increase – decreases don't hurt the holder)*

   e. Risk-free rate of interest—*Higher fair value with higher interest rate (the option holder can invest the exercise price and earn interest during service period)*

   f. Dividend yield at the grant date—*Higher fair value with lower dividend yield (higher stock price with lower dividends)*

2. **Fair Value Method**—Assume that Flowers's choice of option-pricing model at grant date establishes the fair value of one option to be $2.20. Note that the market price of the stock at grant date is not used for measuring the cost of the option plan to the firm.

   a. Total compensation expense for the four-year service period is $22,000 (10,000 × $2.20). This amount is allocated on a straight-line basis. The following journal entries illustrate the accounting.

12/31/x1, x2, x3, x4			
Compensation expense	5,500		$22,000/4
PIC-stock options		5,500	

    b. If stock options vest immediately at grant, then the entire compensation expense as measured by the option's fair value is recognized immediately.

    c. When the firm issues a stock dividend or splits its stock, unexercised options are adjusted. The number of shares under option, fair value and exercise price are proportionately adjusted. For example, a two-for-one split doubles the number of shares under option, and halves the fair value and exercise price. The total fair value and compensation expense to be recognized remain unchanged.

    d. Compensation expense is reported as a component of income from continuing operations. For manufacturing firms, a portion may be allocated first to an inventory account and then to cost of goods sold. PIC-stock options (paid-in capital from stock options) is an owners' equity account which will be closed to another contributed capital account upon exercise.

D. At Exercise

At exercise			
Cash	50,000		10,000($5)
PIC-stock options	22,000		5,500 (4)
Common stock		10,000	10,000($1)
PIC-CS		62,000	

1. **Analysis**—What is the net effect of the accounting through exercise?

    a. Earnings is reduced $5,500 for each year in the service period.

    b. Retained earnings is reduced $22,000 from compensation expense.

    c. Contributed capital increases $72,000 = the fair value of the options at grant date ($22,000) + cash paid in by employee ($50,000).

    d. Net effect on total OE = $72,000 − $22,000 = $50,000 = cash increase.

2. Essentially, retained earnings is converted into permanent capital for the amount of the fair value of the option, but its placement on the income statement is the key idea. The firm increases its permanent value by the value of the manager's services. The stock price at exercise date is not used in the accounting.

E. Expiration of Options—When the market price fails to increase above the option price (here $5), the options expire. There is no retroactive adjustment and the compensation expense remains (because there was value at grant date), and the PIC-stock options account is simply renamed.

1. Assume all 10,000 options expire—entry at end of exercise period:

PIC-stock options	22,000	
PIC-expired stock options		22,000

2. Net effect of all the journal entries is to reduce retained earnings by $22,000 (through compensation expense), and increase permanent capital by the value of the grant ($22,000).

F. **Forfeitures**—Employees may leave the firm before completing the service requirement under the grant. This results in a forfeiture of their shares, requiring an adjustment to total compensation expense. Firms must make an entity-wide accounting policy election concerning accounting for forfeitures. This election affects all share-based payment plans where forfeitures relate to employee turnover; the policy must be disclosed. This election does not affect performance plans. Firms must choose one of the following:

1. Recognize forfeitures as they occur (when employees leave). If this alternative is chosen, the initial total compensation expense amount is based on all covered employees until some employees forfeit their grants.

2. Estimate forfeitures and adjust the estimate as new information is forthcoming. Forfeitures are estimated when it is no longer probable that an employee will continue with the firm and therefore the employee will not meet the service requirement of the grant.

Example
Assume Flowers chooses to estimate forfeitures:

If, as of the grant date, 10% of the 10,000 options were expected to be forfeited, then only 90% of the $22,000 total fair value is used for the accounting (.9 × $22,000 = $19,800). The entries would be the same except use $19,800 in place of $22,000, and 9,000 options in place of 10,000.

If there is a change in estimated forfeitures, the amount of compensation expense in the year the change is determined is increased or decreased by the effect of the change on all previous years and current year (but no retroactive application). The year of the change receives the entire "catch up" adjustment.

The result is that the amount of compensation expense recognized through the end of that year reflects the amount of expense that would have been recognized using the new estimate all along. In effect, the new estimate is applied to periods before it was known. This procedure is contrary to the usual approach to estimate changes that would allocate the remaining expense over the remaining service period.

Example
Assume in the Flowers example that initially there were no forfeitures expected, but in 20X3 new information implies that a total of 10% of the options will be forfeited. The entries for the first two years are as above. Relevant amounts at the end of 20X2:

PIC-stock options balance, $11,000 (5,500 × 2)

Compensation expense recognized to date, $11,000

New estimate of total compensation expense, $19,800 (.9 × $22,000)

12/31/x3

    Compensation expense   3,850 $19,800(3/4) − $11,000
      PIC-stock options   3,850

By the end of 20X3, three-quarters of the total compensation expense is recognized. The entire impact of the estimate change on three years is recognized in the year of the change (20x3) rather than spread over the remaining years in the service period.

12/31/x4

    Compensation expense   4,950 $19,800(1/4) (SL)
      PIC-stock options   4,950

Total compensation expense recognized over the 4 years = $11,000 + $3,850 + $4,950 = $19,800.

Constant percentage of estimated forfeiture: A quick calculation of total compensation cost is possible if the firm anticipates a constant percentage of estimated forfeitures each year during the service period. For example, a plan grants 100,000 options on 1/1/x1. The fair value of each option is $2.45, service period is four years, and the anticipated forfeiture rate is 4% per year during the service period.

Total compensation expense = $100,000($2.45)(1 - .04)^4 = $208,090$

G. **Use of Actual Forfeitures Rather than Estimated Forfeitures**—If the firm instead chose to recognize forfeitures as they occur rather than estimate, the same procedure illustrated above is used except actual forfeitures are used rather than estimated forfeitures. Total compensation expense is adjusted when actual forfeitures occur, and a catch-up adjustment to compensation expense is made in that year.

Example

Assume the Flowers data with no forfeitures the first year (20x1). Then in 20x2, employees holding 2,000 options leave the firm. As of 1/1/x2, PIC-stock options balance, $5,500, compensation expense recognized to date, $5,500.

New total compensation expense, $17,600 (8,000 options × $2.20).

12/31/x2

Compensation expense	3,300*	
PIC-stock options		3,300

* $3,300 = $17,600(2/4) - $5,500$

Compensation expense recognized in each of the last two years is $17,600/4 or $4,400.

III. **Deferred Tax Asset (DTA)**

1. The lessons on accounting for income tax provide in-depth coverage of deferred income tax assets. In order to explain the effect of share-based compensation plans on the DTA, a quick review is in order.

   Whenever a current temporary difference between books and tax yields a future deductible difference causing future taxable income to be less than future pretax account income, a DTA is recorded for the tax effect of that difference.

   In the case of compensation expense recognized for share-based plans, pretax accounting income is reduced currently for the amount of compensation expense recognized. The tax deduction typically will not be received by the firm until the shares vest or are exercised (in the future). Therefore, in the future, the firm will reduce its taxable income due to a transaction that has already occurred. As a result, a DTA is created during the years compensation expense is recorded and is eliminated in the future years when the deduction is received.

   The increase in the DTA each year during the service period equals the future tax rate multiplied by compensation expense for that year.

   In some cases—for example, when the market price of the stock equals the option (exercise) price at grant date (there are other tax requirements as well)—there is no tax deduction, in which case there are no tax consequences and no effect on the deferred tax asset (DTA).

2. For plans providing a tax deduction to the firm, the recognized compensation expense per GAAP may be different from the tax deduction ultimately received by the firm. The difference between the actual tax benefit and the recognized DTA through vesting is recognized in income tax expense.

Example

a. The total compensation expense for a stock option plan computed at grant date is $3,000,000. The plan has a three-year service period. Assume a 30% tax rate.

b. Each year during the service period, $1,000,000 of compensation expense is recognized and the required ending DTA is increased $300,000 ($1,000,000 × .30). Income tax expense is reduced $300,000 each year without a tax deduction; therefore, the DTA is increased. By the end of the three-year service period, the DTA has an ending balance of $900,000.

c. The actual amount of the future tax deduction is not known until exercise. Until then, total compensation expense is used as the estimate of the future deduction.

d. When the options are exercised, the firm's tax deduction becomes known. Any difference between the tax benefit already recognized (the DTA) and the tax benefit of the actual deduction is recognized as an increase or decrease in income tax expense in the year of exercise.

Assume the allowed deduction is $3,300,000, which is the number of shares exercised multiplied by the difference between the market price at exercise and the option price. This amount exceeds total compensation expense of $3,000,000 recognized over the three years.

The tax benefit of the $3,300,000 deduction is $990,000 (.30 × $3,300,000) which exceeds the DTA by $90,000 ($990,000 − $900,000). The $90,000 difference is recognized as a decrease in current income tax expense. If the deduction were less than $3,000,000, the tax effect of the difference is recognized as an increase in income tax expense

IV. U.S. GAAP–IFRS Differences

A. International and U.S. standards are similar for stock-based compensation plans. However, they have a larger effect on the financial statements of U.S. firms because share-based compensation is less common outside the United States.

B. Deferred Tax Asset

1. The increase in the deferred tax asset for a stock award or stock option plan under U.S. standards is based on the cumulative compensation expense to date. That amount is used as the estimate of the future tax deduction and is the basis for increasing the deferred tax asset.

2. Under international standards, the deferred tax asset is increased only when the option has intrinsic value (market price > option price) during the service period. Under this approach, if there is no intrinsic value, there is no estimated tax deduction and no increase in deferred tax asset is recognized.

C. Graded Vesting Options—"Graded vesting" refers to groups of options within one award that vest at different dates. For example, one-third of the options in an award may vest one year from grant date, with the rest vesting two years after the grant date.

Under U.S. standards, the entire award may be accounted for as a single award using the fair value of the "average" option in the award.

Alternatively, each group may be accounted for separately (with separate fair values). In addition, if this approach is chosen, firms may choose a simplified straight-line method whereby the total compensation expense for all groups is allocated over the longest vesting period. Either way, the minimum annual expense is the amount applicable to vested options.

For international standards, the straight-line method is not allowed nor is the minimum amount of expense required to be recognized.

Stock Awards

This lesson discusses stock awards and restricted stock units, which are incentive stock-based compensation plans. The calculation of total compensation expense is more direct under stock awards, relative to stock options. Also summarized is the reporting for employee stock ownership plans (ESOPs).

After studying this lesson, you should be able to:

1. Compute total compensation expense for stock awards.

2. Record periodic compensation expense using the gross or net methods.

3. Prepare the journal entry for vesting.

4. Modify the recording of compensation expense for forfeitures.

5. Understand how RSUs are similar to stock award plans.

6. Understand the basics for ESOPs.

I. **Stock Award Plans (Restricted Stock)**

   A. Under stock award plans, stock is awarded for continuing employment but the employee cannot sell the stock (the main restriction) until the award is vested—and the employee may not receive the shares until vested. Employees acquire the normal rights of shareholders at grant.

   B. For such plans, total compensation expense is the number of shares awarded multiplied by the market price of the stock at grant date (the fair value at that date). This amount is recognized as expense over the period the employee provides the service for which the grant was awarded. When the award vests, there is no additional incentive and expensing is complete. Changes in stock price after the grant have no effect on the accounting. If the award vests immediately at grant, then the entire compensation expense is recognized immediately.

Example

January 1, 20x1, 500 shares of restricted stock are granted to each of two employees (1,000 shares in total). The stock is $1 par common stock and the market price is $6 on the grant date. The employees must work 3 years at which time the award is vested. This example shows the *gross* method whereas the previous illustrations of accounting for stock options used the *net* method. Both are acceptable and yield the same financial reporting.

Total compensation expense = $6,000 (1,000 × $6)

1/1/x1 (Grant date)

Deferred comp expense	6,000	
Common stock		1,000
PIC-CS		5,000

Deferred compensation expense is a contra OE account. The effect of the above entry on total OE is zero.

12/31/x1, x2, x3

Compensation expense	2,000	
Deferred comp expense		2,000

Under the "net" method, the firm makes no entry on 1/1/x1. At each 12/31, compensation expense is debited for $2,000 and a PIC account is credited. (PIC-stock award)

12/31/x3 (Vesting)

No entry is needed under the "gross" method because the full amount of compensation expense is recorded, deferred compensation expense is closed, and the stock was recorded at grant date. Under the "net" method, the vesting entry replaces the PIC account created during the service period and the permanent OE accounts are credited:

PIC-stock award	6,000	
Common stock		1,000
PIC-CS		5,000

The net effect of the accounting:

- An expense equal to the value of the stock at grant date is recognized.

- Contributed capital increases by that amount.

- Retained earnings is reduced by the same amount permanently.

- There is no net effect on OE. (The firm did not pay or receive anything that can be objectively measured.)

C. Forfeitures: As with stock options, firms must decide whether to estimate forfeitures or to wait and recognize them as they occur. If employees do not continue employment through the vesting date then the expense recognized on those awards is reversed. The effect is to reduce compensation expense in the current year by the amount of compensation expense recognized in previous years' on the forfeited stock. Reversal is recorded because the stock is taken back—ultimately the firm did not give anything to the employee in this case. The forfeiture is treated as an estimate change; retrospective application is not permitted.

Example

Assume the firm recognizes forfeitures when they occur. One of the two employees in the example above leaves the firm at the end of 20x2. The deferred compensation expense balance under the gross method is $4,000 ($2,000 for the employee leaving) before recognizing compensation expense.

12/31/x2

Common stock	500	
PIC-CS	2,500	
Deferred comp expense		2,000
Compensation expense		1,000

The above gross method entry "takes back" the $1,000 of compensation expense recognized on this employee in 20X1, and removes the contributed capital accounts for the employee. The entries continue for the remaining employee. Under the net method, PIC-stock award is debited $1,000 and compensation expense credited $1,000.

12/31/x2, x3 (gross method)

Compensation expense	1,000	
Deferred comp expense		1,000

Under the net method, the 12/31/x2, x3 entries are:

Compensation expense	1,000	
PIC-stock award		1,000

Either way, the $1,000 compensation expense for remaining two years before removing the prior expense recognized on forfeited shares = (500 remaining shares)($6)/(3 year service period) = $1,000. Another way to calculate this amount is: ($6,000 original total compensation expense − $2,000 expense for x1 − $2,000 expense for x2 and x3 on forfeited shares)/2.

For 20x2, there is no net compensation expense ($1,000 decrease and $1,000 increase), and in 20x3, $1,000 of compensation expense is recognized. With the $2,000 recognized in 20x1, a total of $3,000 of compensation expense is recognized for one employee for which the award vested. At this point, the deferred compensation expense balance is zero and there are no further entries.

If the firm chooses to estimate forfeitures, the procedure followed for stock options is applied to stock awards as well. The initial total compensation expense amount is reduced by estimated forfeitures before allocating to the service periods. There is no need to reverse previous compensation expense amounts in this case unless actual and estimated forfeitures are different.

II. Restricted Stock Units (RSUs)

An RSU is the right to receive a specified number of shares. When vested, the shares are issued. Such awards are very similar to stock awards. The benefits are the same. The difference is that the shares are not issued until vested and thus the holders typically do not receive the normal rights of shareholders until the RSU vests.

The accounting is the same as for restricted stock awards. Total compensation expense is determined at grant date using the share price on that date. That total expense is allocated over the vesting period. The same JEs are recorded (gross or net method). Forfeitures are treated the same way as under stock awards.

III. Employee Stock Ownership Plans (ESOPs)

A. An employee stock ownership plan (ESOP) is a qualified stock bonus plan whereby the firm invests primarily in qualifying employer securities, including stock and other marketable obligations for the benefit of the employees. The shares are distributed to the employees as part of their compensation, and often are held by the firm until the employee retires. This discussion focuses on accounting by the employer.

B. Income Statement Effects

1. The employer recognizes compensation expense for the amount the employer contributed, or committed to contributing to an ESOP in the year. This includes cash, and its stock measured at fair value.

C. Balance Sheet Effects

1. In some instances, the ESOP will borrow funds from a bank or other lender in order to acquire shares of the employer's stock. If such an obligation of the ESOP is guaranteed by the employer (assumption by the employer of the ESOP's debt), it should be recorded as a liability in the employer's financial statements. The offsetting debit to the liability should be accounted for as a reduction of shareholders' equity.

2. Shareholders' equity will increase symmetrically with the reduction of the liability as the ESOP makes payments on the debt.

3. Assets held by an ESOP are not to be included in the employer's financial statements, because such assets are owned by the employees, not the employer.

Example
On January 1, Year 1, Fay Corporation established an employee stock ownership plan (ESOP). Selected transactions relating to the ESOP during year 1 were as follows:

- On April 1, Year 1, Fay contributed $30,000 cash and 3,000 shares of its $10 par common stock to the ESOP. On this date, the market price of the stock was $18 a share.

- On October 1, Year 1, the ESOP borrowed $100,000 from Union National Bank and acquired 5,000 shares of Fay's common stock in the open market at $17 a share. The note is for one year, bears interest at 10%, and is guaranteed by Fay.

- On December 15, Year 1, the ESOP distributed 6,000 shares of Fay common stock to employees of Fay in accordance with the plan formula.

In its Year 1 income statement, Fay reports $84,000 of compensation expense relating to the ESOP. his is the amount contributed or committed to be contributed to the ESOP in Year 1: the contribution of $30,000 cash plus the common stock with a fair value of $54,000 (3,000 × $18).

In its December 31, Year 1 balance sheet, Fay will report $100,000 in liabilities for its ESOP obligation because the obligation is covered by either a guarantee by Fay or a commitment by Fay to make future contributions to the ESOP sufficient to meet the debt service requirements.

The offsetting $100,000 debit is reported as a reduction of Fay's stockholders' equity.

Stock Appreciation Rights

The lesson addresses the accounting for a share-based payment plan that bases total compensation on the increase in the firm's stock price over a period of years. A liability is recorded under certain circumstances.

After studying this lesson, you should be able to:

1. Explain when a liability is recorded for an SAR.

2. Compute and record periodic compensation expense.

3. Modify the calculation of periodic compensation expense for forfeitures.

4. Identify the period over which compensation expense is computed.

I. **Stock Appreciation Rights (SARs)**

A. These plans are different from stock option plans: (1) employee receives the difference between the stock price at grant date, and the stock price at exercise date, (2) pays nothing, (3) the SAR specifies payment of the benefit in either cash or stock (employee may have a choice). The accounting issue is whether the arrangement involves debt or equity.

B. If the SAR plan allows the employer to issue stock, then the SAR is accounted for as a stock option plan. The fair value of the SAR is estimated at grant date and the total fair value is allocated to compensation expense over the service period.

C. If the SAR plan specifies that payment is in cash or allows the employee to choose cash payment:

1. The firm records a liability rather than paid-in-capital when compensation expense is recognized.

2. For each year in the service period, the fair value of each right is reestimated in light of new information using an option pricing model.

3. Compensation expense is recorded each year based on the fair value at the end of the period (fair value is reestimated each year through exercise), for the portion of the service period elapsed using the catch up procedure for stock options. Expense recognition continues through the exercise date.

4. Estimated forfeitures are built into the calculation of total compensation expense as illustrated previously for stock options; or the firm may choose to recognize forfeitures as they occur.

5. At exercise date, the fair value of the SAR equals the difference between price at grant date and the price paid for the stock.

Example

On 1/1/x1, several executives are granted SARS on a total of 10,000 shares, which, at exercise, pay cash equal to the difference between the $5 per share market price at grant date and the market price at exercise. The market price of the stock on the grant date is $5. To continue owning the SARs, the employees must work for four years at which time the SARs are exercisable, for the two years following that date.

Fair value per SAR:

12/31/x1 $3

12/31/x2 4.50

12/31/x3 2.80

12/31/x4 3.50

12/31/x5 3.90

1/1/x1

no entry

12/3/x1

Compensation expense 10,000($3)/4	7,500	
Liability under SAR plan		7,500

12/3/x2

Compensation expense 10,000($4.50)(2/4) – $7,500	15,000	
Liability under SAR plan		15,000

12/3/x3

Liability under SAR plan 10,000($2.80)(3/4)—$22,500	1,500	
Compensation expense		1,500

(Through this date, $21,000 of compensation expense has been recognized: $21,000 = 10,000($2.80)(3/4) = $7,500 + $15,000 − $1,500) Note that both the liability and compensation expense are reduced this year.

12/3/x4

Compensation expense 10,000($3.50)(4/4)—$21,000	14,000	
Liability under SAR plan		14,000

The SARs have vested, but the liability and expense continue to be adjusted until exercise or lapsing because the firm must report the liability at the amount of probable payment.

12/3/x5

Compensation expense 10,000($3.90) – $35,000	4,000	
Liability under SAR plan		4,000

During 20x6, the SARs are exercised. The market price at exercise date is $8.40 (fair value of SAR is $3.40, the difference between $8.40 and $5 price at grant).

Liability under SAR plan 10,000(3.40) – $39,000	5,000	
Compensation expense		5,000
Liability under SAR plan	34,000	
Cash 10,000($8.40 – $5)		34,000

Total compensation expense recognized over the entire period is $34,000. If the SAR had no value at the end of exercise period (because the market price was not greater than $5), the entire liability is extinguished and compensation expense is reduced by the same amount as the liability balance at that time.

Income Taxes

Income Tax Basics

This lesson provides an overview of accounting for income taxes. Terminology is emphasized so that later tax lessons can be understood within the context of the larger issues.

After studying this lesson, you should be able to:

1. Note that the emphasis of interperiod tax allocation measurement is on the appropriate recognition of assets and liabilities.

2. Explain how income tax expense is computed in general.

3. Identify the major categories of differences between tax accounting and financial reporting.

4. Define taxable income, income tax liability, current and deferred income tax provision, and other terms.

I. **Overview**

   A. The reporting principles for GAAP and for tax law are not the same. The amount of taxes due for a period is set by tax law, not by GAAP. The question then is: how to measure income tax expense? In determining the income tax cost and the related ending balances of tax assets and liabilities for the period, GAAP applies the accrual basis of accounting. Income tax expense as reported for the books is generally not the same as the amount of tax due for the period.

   B. Income tax expense is recognized when it is incurred, regardless of when the payment is actually made to the Internal Revenue Service. The process of recognizing income tax expense and associated deferred tax accounts is called "interperiod tax allocation." Interperiod tax allocation is the application of accrual accounting to the measurement of income tax effects on the financial statements.

   C. GAAP adopted the asset/liability approach for measurement of income tax effects.

      1. The emphasis is on the correct measurement of the income tax assets and liabilities.

      2. Deferred tax assets and liabilities are measured directly, along with the income tax liability.

      3. Income tax expense is a derived amount—a derived figure.

   D. **Summary**—The main effects of applying the asset/liability approach for interperiod tax allocation are:

      1. Income tax expense for the period reflects the amount that will ultimately be payable on the year's transactions, even though the timing of payment and expense recognition will not coincide.

      2. The income tax payable account, deferred tax asset account, and deferred tax liability account report the tax receivables and obligations from transactions that have already occurred as of the balance sheet date but that have not yet been received or paid.

II. **Terminology and Definitions**—Several terms and definitions are provided early in the discussion to help you with the concepts and procedure.

   A. **Taxable Items**—Amounts that cause income tax to increase. This is an Internal Revenue Code term and typically refers to revenues that cause taxable income to increase.

   B. **Deductible Items**—Amounts that cause income tax to decrease. This is an Internal Revenue Code term and typically refers to expenses that cause taxable income to decrease.

C. **Pretax Accounting Income**—Income before income tax for financial accounting purposes as determined by GAAP.

D. **Taxable Income**—Income before income tax for tax purposes. This is the analog of pretax accounting income. Taxable income is the amount to which the tax rates are applied in determining the income tax liability for the year.

E. **Income Tax Liability**—The amount of income tax the firm must pay on taxable income for a year. Firms pay this liability in estimated quarterly installments with the last installment due early in the year following the tax year.

F. **Income Tax Expense**—The account reported in the income statement that measures the income tax cost for the year's transactions. Income tax expense equals the income tax liability plus or minus the net change in the deferred tax accounts for the period.

G. **Current Income Tax Provision**—Also called current portion of income tax expense and current provision for income tax. This term is used in the income statement to refer to the amount of income taxes due for the year. This amount is the same as the income tax liability for the year.

H. **Deferred Income Tax Provision**—The amount of income tax expense for the year that is not currently due. This amount equals the net sum of the changes in the deferred tax accounts.

Example

Assume the following year-end income tax accrual entry. For simplicity, we assume that the entire year's tax liability is paid early the following year. The $40,000 income tax expense amount is derived from the other amounts. It is not directly computed.

Income Tax Expense	40,000	
Deferred Tax Asset	6,000	
Deferred Tax Liability		9,000
Income Tax Payable		37,000

Current income tax provision:	$37,000 (income tax liability)
Plus deferred income tax provision	3,000*
Equals total income tax expense	$40,000

*$9,000 increase in deferred tax liability less $6,000 increase in deferred tax asset

---

I. **Permanent Difference**—An amount that appears in the tax return or income statement but never both. These include items of revenue or expense that are never taxable or deductible; also taxable and deductible items that never appear in the income statement. This type of difference is also called a nontemporary difference.

Example

A fine or penalty that is never deductible but is treated as an expense or loss for income statement purposes is a permanent difference. These types of differences do not enter into the process of interperiod tax allocation. They have no deferred tax consequences.

J. **Temporary Difference**—An item of revenue or expense that, over the total life of the item, will affect pretax accounting income and taxable income in the same total amount, but will be recognized in different amounts in any given year for financial reporting and tax purposes.

Example
Depreciation can be different in any given year for income reporting and tax purposes, but total depreciation is the same over the life of the asset under the two reporting systems.

K. Net Operating Loss—Negative taxable income (strictly a tax term). A net operating loss can be carried back 2 years to reduce taxable income in those years for a refund of taxes, and carried forward 20 years to reduce taxable income and therefore the tax liability in future years.

L. Deferred Tax Asset—The recognized tax effect of future deductible temporary differences. These differences, caused by transactions that have occurred as of the balance sheet date, will cause future taxable income to **decrease** relative to pretax accounting income.

M. Deferred Tax Liability—The recognized tax effect of future taxable temporary differences. These differences, caused by transactions that have occurred as of the balance sheet date, will cause future taxable income to **increase** relative to pretax accounting income.

N. Interperiod Tax Allocation—The process of measuring and recognizing the total income tax consequences of transactions in the year. Only temporary differences and net operating loss carryforwards enter into this process. Interperiod tax allocation gives rise to deferred tax accounts because the total tax consequence of the period's transactions is not equal to the current income tax liability. The current tax liability (measured at the current tax rate) measures a part of that total, but there will be additional tax consequences in the future because of transactions that have occurred as of the balance sheet date. Hence the need for the deferred tax accounts. Deferred tax accounts are measured at the **future enacted** tax rate.

III. Three Types of Differences—Between GAAP and Income Tax Law

A. The three types of differences between the two reporting systems in terms of their effect on accounting for income taxes are:

1. Permanent differences

2. Temporary differences

3. Net operating losses

B. For interperiod tax allocation, temporary differences are the most important. Most firms have both temporary and permanent differences, but net operating losses are less common. Thus, the two main differences to be aware of in accounting for income taxes are temporary and permanent differences.

Permanent Differences

The specifics concerning permanent differences between tax accounting and financial reporting are discussed here. This type of difference does not cause a deferral of tax and is treated in a more straightforward way relative to temporary differences.

After studying this lesson, you should be able to:

1. Describe the general effect of permanent differences on the measurement of income tax expense.

2. List important specific permanent differences.

3. Note how each specific difference affects the tax accrual entry.

I. Nature of Permanent Differences

A. The permanent differences are those, due to the existing tax laws, that will not reverse themselves over an extended period of time. The treatment of permanent differences under the two reporting systems is **permanently** different. Some of the more common permanent differences follow. Permanent (nontemporary) differences are not used in computing the change in deferred tax accounts.

B. For purposes of the CPA Exam, our recommendation is to be familiar with the most common specific permanent differences. There are far fewer of these relative to temporary differences. Also, be able to identify a new difference as permanent, if given sufficient information about how the item is treated for financial reporting and for tax.

II. Specific Permanent Differences

A. **Tax-Free Interest Income**—An example of this difference is the interest income earned on an investment in state or municipal bonds. The interest income is included in pretax accounting income, but not in taxable income.

B. **Life Insurance Expense**—The insurance premiums on a life insurance policy for a key employee where the firm is the beneficiary are not deductible from taxable income, but are an expense for financial reporting.

C. **Proceeds on Life Insurance**—In the event of the death of the key employee, the proceeds from the insurance policy are not taxable but are included as a gain for financial reporting purposes.

D. **Dividends Received Deduction**—The dividends received deduction is a deduction for tax purposes equal to 80% (amount subject to change) of qualified dividends received. It is an amount of dividends received that is not subject to tax. However, the entire amount of dividends received is included in pretax accounting income. There is no similar deduction for financial reporting purposes. The difference between the total dividend (included in book income) and the amount taxable (e.g., 20%) is the permanent difference (80% of the dividend).

E. **Fines and Penalties**—Many fines, penalties, and expenses resulting from a violation of law are not deductible for tax purposes, but are recognized as an expense or loss for financial reporting purposes.

F. **Depletion**—GAAP depletion (cost depletion) is based on the cost of a natural resource used up. Tax depletion is based on revenues of resource sold. The difference in any year is a permanent difference.

III. General Rule for Accounting for Permanent Differences

For each of the differences listed above, an amount is recognized in one system of reporting but not in the other. The difference never reverses as it does with temporary differences. But the income tax law is what ultimately determines whether an item is considered for tax purposes. Hence the rule for permanent differences: **The effect of a permanent difference on income tax expense is the same as its effect on the income tax liability for the period.**

Example

Pretax accounting income is $20,000 and taxable income is $22,000. The only difference is a $2,000 fine that is recognized for accounting purposes but is not deductible for tax purposes. If the tax rate is 30%, the income tax accrual entry is:

Income Tax Expense*	6,600	
Income Tax Payable		6,600

*($22,000 × .30)

The fine will never be deductible for tax purposes. Therefore, financial reporting treats the item giving rise to the permanent difference (through income tax expense) in the same way the tax code treats the item—it is not deductible. Permanent differences are not considered when computing the balances of deferred tax accounts. Permanent differences are not allocated; they do not affect the process of interperiod tax allocation.

Note that income tax payable is directly computed as taxable income multiplied by the current tax rate. Because there are no changes in deferred tax accounts, income tax expense equals income tax payable because income tax expense is a derived amount. It is the amount that completes the entry in terms of equality of debits and credits. Income tax expense is not directly computed.

Temporary Differences

This lesson discusses the basics of accounting for the more involved type of difference between tax accounting and financial reporting—temporary differences.

After studying this lesson, you should be able to:

1. Explain the basic nature of an item causing a temporary difference.

2. Identify specific temporary differences.

3. Note that both revenues and expenses can be recognized for financial reporting before or after they are recognized for tax reporting.

4. Define originating and reversing temporary differences.

5. Categorize temporary differences into taxable and deductible differences.

6. Calculate taxable income from pretax accounting income and additional information.

I. **Nature of Temporary Differences**

   A. In contrast with permanent differences, which never reverse over time, temporary differences do reverse. These are the differences involved with the process of interperiod tax allocation—the recognition of deferred tax accounts.

   Example
   A firm provides services for a client for a fee of $4,000. The service is provided near the end of the year. The client is expected to remit the fee early the following year. For financial accounting purposes, the $4,000 of revenue is recognized in the year the service is provided but for tax purposes is taxable in the year the fee is received. Over the two years, both systems recognize the same amount of revenue. The temporary difference of $4,000 originated in the first year, and reversed in the second. At the end of the first year, the firm has a future difference of $4,000. That is the basis for the recorded deferred tax account at the end of the first year.

   1. The only difference between the two reporting systems (GAAP and tax) is one of timing of recognition.

   2. The concept of future temporary differences is one way to refer to the underlying differences leading to the deferred tax accounts. Another is in reference to an item's tax basis compared with its amount for financial reporting purposes. For example, the cost of a plant asset is $100,000 and for financial reporting the asset has been depreciated $15,000 through the current balance sheet date (book value $85,000). The asset has been depreciated $25,000 for tax purposes through the balance sheet date. For tax purposes, this asset is said to have a tax basis of $75,000. The difference between the book value and tax basis is $10,000, which also is the future taxable difference. The $10,000 future difference is the amount that enters into the computation of the deferred tax liability at the end of the current year.

II. **Some Temporary Differences**—Some of the more frequently observed temporary differences are listed and described below. In many cases, a balance sheet account reflects the amount of the difference to reverse in the future.

   A. **Taxable After Recognized for the Books**—Revenues or gains that are taxable after they are recognized in financial income.

Examples

1. An example of this type of difference involves the use of the installment sales basis of accounting for income tax purposes. The accrual basis of accounting is used by the entity for financial reporting purposes, while a version of the cash basis, the installment sales basis, is used for income tax purposes. The net installment accounts receivable at year-end reflects the future temporary difference. Only the amount of cash received in a year is taxable in that year; but the entire sale is recognized as revenue for the books in the year of sale.

2. The use of the equity method to recognize income from investments in equity securities is another example. The equity method is used for financial reporting purposes, and the amount of income reported on the income statement corresponds to the percentage of stock owned in the investee multiplied by the reported earnings of the investee. Investment income recognized for tax purposes will be equal to the dividends received in a given year (after the dividends received deduction, if applicable).

B. **Deductible After Recognized for the Books** — Expenses or losses that are deductible after they are recognized in financial income

Example

An example of this type of difference involves the recognition of warranty expense. For financial reporting purposes, warranty expense is usually estimated and recognized in the year the related merchandise is sold. For tax purposes, warranty expense is recognized in the year customers request warranty service, often after the year of sale. The warranty liability reflects the future temporary difference.

C. **Taxable Before Recognized for the Books**—Revenues or gains that are taxable before they are recognized in financial income

Examples

1. An example of this type of difference involves the recognition of rent revenue or subscription revenue. For financial reporting purposes, the rent revenue or subscription revenue is recognized in the year that it is earned. For tax purposes, the rent revenue or subscription revenue is recognized in the year that the related cash payment is received. The unearned subscription revenue account reflects the future temporary difference.

2. On September 1, 20X7, the Dolphin Company rented a vacant warehouse to the Raider Company. The lease term was one year, from September 1, 20X7 through August 31, 20X8. The warehouse annual rental fee was $24,000, which was paid in full on September 1, 20X7. For financial reporting purposes, $8,000 rental revenue will be reported in 20X7, and $16,000 rental revenue will be reported in 20X8. For tax purposes, the entire $24,000 will be reported on the 20X7 tax return. The total rent revenue is the same under the two systems of reporting but the timing of recognition is different in each year affected. At the end of 20X7, the $16,000 balance in unearned rent (a liability) equals the future temporary difference to reverse in 20X8.

D. **Deductible Before Recognized for the Books**—Expenses or losses that are deductible before they are recognized in financial income

Example

An example of this type of difference is depreciation recorded for income tax purposes. For financial reporting purposes, depreciation is recorded over the estimated useful life of an asset. For tax purposes, depreciation is recorded over shorter time frames called recovery periods. In addition, for tax purposes, an accelerated depreciation method is typically employed.

III. Categorizing Temporary Differences

A. Originating/Reversing

1. When an item causing a temporary difference first occurs, the difference is called an originating difference.

2. In later years, the difference attributable to the item is called the reversing difference.

B. Future Differences—The classification of temporary differences is based on the future reversal rather than the originating amount because deferred tax asset and liability balances reflect the future tax consequences of transactions that have already occurred.

C. Two Categories—For purposes of interperiod tax allocation and recording the annual income tax accrual entry, temporary differences are classified into two categories.

1. The first category, called **Taxable Temporary Differences**, involves differences that initially cause a postponement in the payment of taxes.

   a. In the year of origination, the item causes taxable income to decline relative to pretax accounting income.

   b. When the item reverses, the item causes future taxable income to exceed pretax accounting income. This is why these differences are called taxable differences. They increase taxable income relative to pretax accounting income in the *future*.

   c. Future taxable differences give rise to deferred tax liabilities.

2. The second category, called **Deductible Temporary Differences**, involves differences that initially cause a prepayment of taxes.

   a. In the year of origination, the item causes taxable income to increase relative to pretax accounting income.

   b. When the item reverses, the item causes future taxable income to be less than pretax accounting income. This is why these differences are called deductible differences. They reduce taxable income relative to pretax accounting income in the *future*.

   c. Future deductible differences give rise to deferred tax assets.

D. Examples of Taxable Temporary Differences—Future taxable income > future pretax accounting income:

1. **Depreciation**

Example
For financial reporting and tax purposes, depreciation on a plant asset purchased Year 1 will be:

Year	Book Depreciation	Tax Depreciation
1	$10,000	$16,000
2	10,000	9,000
3	10,000	5,000
Totals	$30,000	$30,000

At the end of Year 1, the future taxable difference is $6,000, because in the future, after Year 1, $20,000 of depreciation expense will be recognized for book purposes ($10,000 + $10,000), but only $14,000 of depreciation will be deducted for tax purposes ($9,000 + $5,000). After Year 1, the future difference of $6,000 will cause taxable income to exceed pretax book income by $6,000 because less depreciation will be deducted than expensed for book purposes. At the end of Year 1, if the future tax rate is 30%, this difference contributes $1,800 to the firm's ending deferred tax liability balance ($6,000 × .30).

At the end of Year 2, the difference in Year 2 has reversed, reducing the future taxable difference to $5,000 ($10,000 book depreciation – $5,000 tax depreciation) which contributes $1,500 to the firm's ending deferred tax liability balance ($5,000 × .30). If there were no other differences, the deferred tax liability would be reduced $300 at the end of Year 2 ($1,800 – $1,500)

At the end of Year 3, there are no future differences, and the deferred tax liability is closed (assuming no other differences).

2. Installment Sales

Example

During Year 1, a firm sells $6,000 worth of goods on the installment basis. For financial reporting purposes, the firm uses the point-of-sales method to record revenue and recognizes the entire $6,000 in Year 1. For tax purposes, the firm uses the installment method, which postpones revenue recognition until cash is received. No cash is received in Year 1 on the sale and the firm has no tax liability for this amount.

At the end of Year 1, the firm has a future taxable difference of $6,000. In a later year, when cash is received, the firm's taxable income will exceed pretax accounting income by $6,000 because of transactions that have occurred through the end of Year 1.

The future temporary difference is found on the balance sheet in the Installment Receivable account, which has a balance of $6,000, the amount not yet collected.

E. Examples of Deductible Temporary Differences—(future taxable income < future pretax accounting income)

1. Warranty expense

Examples—Warranty expense

On sales for Year 1, the firm recognizes $8,000 of estimated warranty expense. For the books, the entire estimated expense is recognized in the year of sale. Also during Year 1, $1,000 was spent servicing warranty claims. The firm can deduct only the $1,000 on its Year 1 tax return because tax law limits the deduction to the actual cost of claims service. At the end of Year 1, the firm has a $7,000 future deductible difference because the firm expects to spend $7,000 in the future servicing warranty claims at which time that amount will be deductible. Next year, when the remaining claims are serviced, the firm's taxable income will fall by $7,000 relative to pretax accounting income.

The future temporary difference is found in the warranty liability, which has a balance of $7,000, the amount of future claims expected.

2. Revenue received in advance

Examples
Revenue Received in Advance

During Year 1, the firm collected $22,000 in advance of providing its services to customers. By the end of the year, the firm had performed $10,000 worth of service. The full $22,000 is taxable in Year 1 but only $10,000 of revenue is recognized in the income statement. At the end of Year 1, the firm has a $12,000 deductible difference. Next year, when the remaining service is provided, the firm's pretax accounting income will increase $12,000 with no effect on taxable income. Future taxable income will be less than pretax accounting income.

The future temporary difference is found in the unearned revenue account, which has a balance of $12,000, the amount of paid services yet to be provided.

IV. Relationship Between Pretax Accounting Income and Taxable Income

A. Frequently, examination problems provide only one of the two before-tax income measures: (pretax accounting income or taxable income). If taxable income is not provided, it must be computed from pretax accounting income and the differences between the two reporting systems. To prepare the year-end tax accrual entry, which involves the deferred tax account changes, and income tax expense, the candidate must be able to determine taxable income. The income tax liability equals the tax rate multiplied by taxable income and is recorded in the journal entry.

Only current-year differences (both temporary and permanent) are involved in determining taxable income from pretax accounting income. This is in contrast with deferred tax account balances, which use only future temporary differences.

B. When taxable income is not provided, start with pretax accounting income and adjust for differences between pretax accounting income and taxable income. Both temporary and permanent differences are involved. Ask yourself how each difference affects both pretax accounting income and taxable income. The difference in these effects leads to the amount of the adjustment and also the decision about whether to add or subtract from pretax accounting income.

Examples
1. *Short Example*

Pretax accounting income is given and is $40,000. But you need to determine taxable income. Prepaid rent of $5,000 from the beginning of the year was expensed during the year (a reversing temporary difference). $7,000 of insurance was prepaid at year-end (an originating temporary difference). $3,000 of tax-free interest was received from municipal bonds (a permanent difference). To prepare the tax accrual entry, you need taxable income.

Pretax accounting income	$40,000
Rent expense	5,000
Prepaid insurance	(7,000)
Tax-free interest	(3,000)
Taxable income	$35,000

The logic: Pretax accounting income was reduced by $5,000 of rent expense not paid for this year. This amount was deducted in a previous year when paid. There is no deduction this year so taxable income is not reduced this year; add back to pretax accounting income.

Pretax accounting income was not reduced by the insurance expenditure because no expense was recognized. But it is deductible in the year paid (this year); subtract from pretax accounting income.

Pretax accounting income includes the tax-free interest because it is a revenue, but taxable income excludes it due to its nontaxable nature; subtract from pretax accounting income.

2. Longer Example

The four temporary differences from previous examples are repeated below, along with additional information for Year 1. Pretax income is given; you must determine taxable income.

Year 1 Information

Pretax accounting income	$100,000
Fines and penalties	9,000
Municipal bond interest received	14,000
Depreciation deduction	16,000
Depreciation expense recognized for books	10,000
Taxable installment sales	0
Installment sales revenue recognized for books	6,000
Warranty deduction	1,000
Warranty expense recognized for books	8,000
Taxable service revenue	22,000
Service revenue recognized for books	10,000

Computation of taxable income:		Balance sheet account:
Pretax accounting income	$100,000	
Plus nondeductible fines and penalties	9,000	
Less nontaxable municipal bond interest received	(14,000)	
Excess of tax over book depreciation	(6,000)	Equipment book value
Excess of book over tax sales revenue	(6,000)	Installment receivable
Excess of book over tax warranty expense	7,000	Warranty liability
Excess of tax over book service revenue	12,000	Unearned revenue
Taxable income	$102,000	

The first two adjustments—fines and penalties, and municipal bond interest—are permanent differences. Pretax accounting income was reduced by fines and penalties but they are not deductible for tax purposes and therefore must be added back in computing taxable income. The opposite is true for municipal bond interest. It is included in pretax accounting income but is not taxable and therefore is subtracted in computing taxable income.

The remaining adjustments are temporary differences. $16,000 of depreciation is deducted for tax purposes, but pretax accounting income reflects only $10,000 of depreciation. Thus, an additional $6,000 must be subtracted in computing taxable income.

Pretax accounting income reflects $8,000 of warranty expense, but only $1,000 of deduction was allowed (cost to service claims). To adjust pretax accounting income that was reduced $8,000 to taxable income that is reduced only $1,000, the difference of $7,000 must be added to pretax accounting income.

Pretax accounting income reflects $10,000 of service revenue, but taxable income includes all $22,000 received from customers. Therefore, add $12,000 to pretax accounting income. Taxable income then reflects all $22,000 collected in the year.

Tax Accrual Entry

This lesson integrates previous lessons on accounting for income tax by illustrating the tax accrual entry. This entry recognizes the firm's tax liability, changes in deferred tax accounts, and income tax expense.

After studying this lesson, you should be able to:

1. Identify the types of differences causing deferred tax assets and liabilities.

2. Record the tax accrual entry when there are no beginning balances in deferred tax accounts.

3. Compute income tax expense as a derived amount.

4. Note that it is the future temporary differences which are involved in computing deferred tax account balances.

I. General Tax Accrual Entry

A. The previous definitions and categorization of future differences as permanent and temporary are used in this lesson to develop the year-end tax accrual entry.

B. The following entry is a generalization of the year-end tax accrual entry assuming that the year's full tax liability is paid early the following year. Both the deferred tax asset and liability show an increase, but both can be decreases as well, depending on the situation.

Income Tax Expense	a "plug" figure
Deferred Tax Asset	see below*
Deferred Tax Liability	see below**
Income Tax Payable	taxable income x current tax rate

* The amount to increase the deferred tax asset to its required ending balance, which is the total future deductible temporary difference multiplied by the future enacted tax rate. Estimated tax rates are not used, only enacted tax rates. If the required change were a decrease, the asset would be credited.

** The amount to increase the deferred tax liability to its required ending balance which is the total future taxable temporary difference multiplied by the future enacted tax rate. If the required change were a decrease, the liability would be debited. Future tax rates are used to measure the deferred tax accounts because the future tax consequences will be settled or recovered at the future tax rate.

Note
The future and current tax rates are the same if Congress has not enacted a new rate for future years by the end of the current year.

II. Illustrative Example (No Beginning Deferred Tax Balances)

A. A firm in its first year has $100,000 of operating income composed of items that are recognized in the same amounts for both financial reporting and tax purposes. **In addition**, the firm has:

1. $10,000 of municipal bond interest

2. Rent expense of $20,000 for book purposes

3. Rent expense of $25,000 for tax purposes

B. The $5,000 difference in rent expense is the ending prepaid rent. This amount is deductible in Year 1 but is not recognized as rent expense until Year 2. The tax rate for year 1 is 30% but the Year 2 rate, enacted at the close of Year 1, was increased to 35%.

C. Tax accrual entry for Year 1:

Income Tax Expense	24,250	
Deferred Tax Liability ($5,000 × .35)		1,750
Income Tax Payable ($75,000 × .30)		22,500*

*Taxable income = $100,000 − $25,000 = $75,000. The municipal bond interest is not taxable. It is not included in the $100,000 amount common to the two reporting systems. Taxable income applies the current (Year 1) tax rate, while the computation of the deferred tax liability uses the future enacted tax rate.

D. The future temporary difference of $5,000 is a taxable temporary difference because taxable income in Year 2 will increase relative to pretax accounting income by this amount when the prepaid rent is recognized as expense for book purposes only. The resulting deferred tax liability is measured using the future enacted tax rate at which the tax will be paid.

E. Income tax expense is the sum of the increase in the deferred tax liability and income taxes payable. This is the only way to compute income tax expense. It is not the product of the current tax rate and pretax accounting income. The $24,250 income tax expense is the total amount of tax expected to be paid on transactions occurring in Year 1. This total amount is allocated via interperiod tax allocation to the current provision of $22,500 (the income tax liability for Year 1) and $1,750 (the amount deferred to Year 2). The $1,750 is the amount of tax payable in the future based on transactions that occurred by the end of Year 1.

Abbreviated income statement for Year 1

Operating Income Before Rent Expense	$100,000
Rent Expense	(20,000)
Municipal Bond Interest	10,000
Pretax Accounting Income	90,000
Income Tax Expense (from tax accrual entry)	(24,250)
Net income	$ 65,750

F. The **total income tax expense** is classified into two parts, which must be reported either on the face of the income statement or in the footnotes:

Current Provision of Income Tax	$22,500
Plus Deferred Provision of Income Tax	1,750
Total Income Tax Expense	$24,250

G. **Notice** that the income tax expense recognized is not equal to the current tax rate times pretax accounting income (.30 × $90,000 = $27,000). In other words, the current tax rate of 30% is not the effective tax rate for this firm. The effective tax rate is the ratio of income tax expense to pretax accounting income. For this firm, that rate is 26.95% ($24,250/$90,000).

H. Two factors explain the difference: (1) the municipal bond interest is included in pretax accounting income but is not taxed (this lowers the effective tax rate), and (2) the higher rate of 35% is applied to the future temporary difference and is reflected in income tax expense (this raises the effective rate). Because of these types of differences, a tax reconciliation footnote is a required disclosure. That footnote would show:

Statutory Tax Rate:	.3000	
Effect of Nontaxable Municipal Bond Interest	(.0333)	$10,000(.3)/$90,000
Effect of Future Rate Increase on Future Temporary Differences	.0028	$5,000(.35 − 30)/$90,000
Effective Tax Rate	.2695	$24,250/$90,000

III. Analysis: Practice Example (Permanent and Temporary Difference)—Gem has no beginning deferred tax balances and uses the equity method to account for its 25% investment in Gold. During 20X2, Gem received dividends of $30,000 from Gold and recorded $180,000 as its equity in the earnings of Gold. Additional information follows:

A. All the undistributed earnings of Gold will be distributed as dividends in future periods.

B. The dividends received from Gold are eligible for the 80% dividends received deduction.

C. There are no other temporary differences.

D. Enacted income tax rates are 30% for 20X2 and thereafter.

E. Required: In its December 31, 20X2 balance sheet, what amount should Gem report for deferred income tax liability?

F. Solution: With no beginning deferred tax balances, the ending balance in the deferred tax liability equals the change in the deferred tax liability for the period. The change in the deferred tax liability is the future tax effect of the amount of income from the investment that is expected to be taxable in the future, using enacted tax rates. That amount is $9,000 = .30(.20)($180,000 − $30,000). The ($180,000 − $30,000) factor is the total future earnings difference between tax and book accounting. The .20 is the amount taxable after considering the dividends received deduction. The tax rate is 30%. The final result, $9,000, is the anticipated future tax liability, based on current transactions.

G. This problem has both permanent and temporary differences. The permanent difference is the 80% dividends received deduction. Of the $180,000 earnings, 80% or $144,000 will never be taxed. Therefore, 20% or $36,000 will be taxed. By 20X2 year's end, .20($30,000 dividends received) or $6,000 has been taxed, leaving $30,000 as the future temporary difference. The $30,000 is the amount recognized in 20X2 earnings but will not be taxed until later years. The tax effect of this difference, $9,000 (.30 × $30,000) is the ending deferred tax liability.

IV. Differences Originating and Reversing Over More than One Period

A. Depreciable plant assets often require more than one year for the full temporary difference to originate. In early years, future temporary differences appear to be deductible but should not be treated as such. The entire net future temporary difference for a depreciable asset is treated as a taxable temporary difference.

Example

A plant asset is purchased at the beginning of Year 1 and will be depreciated as indicated:

Year	Tax Depreciation	Book Depreciation
1	$400	$200
2	300	200
3	200	200
4	100	200
5	0	200
Totals	$1,000	$1,000

At the end of Year 1, the total future temporary difference is $200, the difference between Years 2–5 depreciation for the two systems ($200 + $200 + $200 + $200) − ($300 + $200 + $100). More depreciation ($200 more) in the future (after Year 1) will be recognized for book purposes than for tax purposes. Thus, future taxable income will exceed pretax accounting in the future in total causing the difference to be classified as taxable at the end of Year 1.

Although the difference for Year 2 (only) appears to be a deductible difference (because Year 2 taxable income will be less than pretax accounting income by $100), that difference is an originating difference, not a reversing difference. Thus, the correct approach is to treat the entire future difference at the end of Year 1 as a taxable difference.

B. Other examples include prepaids and warranties covering more than one year. In each case, the full future difference at the end of each year is treated the same—either as a future taxable difference (prepaid) or deductible difference (warranty).

Tax Allocation Process

This lesson provides a summary of the interperiod tax allocation process by including beginning balances of deferred tax accounts, temporary differences reversing in the current period, and new temporary differences originating in the current period.

After studying this lesson, you should be able to:

1. List the steps leading to the tax accrual entry in the most general case.

2. Compute the ending balance in the deferred tax asset and liability accounts.

3. Determine the change in the deferred tax asset and liability accounts.

4. Complete the tax accrual entry.

5. Identify the treatment of temporary differences that do not originate in only one period.

6. Modify the tax accrual entry for changes in tax rate and tax law.

I. **General Steps for Interperiod Tax Allocation: Adjusting the Deferred Tax Accounts**

   A. In the previous examples, only one temporary difference was used, and there were no beginning deferred tax account balances. This section completes the discussion by including more than one temporary difference and beginning deferred tax account balances. A general process leading to the tax accrual entry is used.

   B. Steps leading to the tax accrual entry at year-end. The amounts appearing in the journal entry are those on the right side of the next table.

1. Compute taxable income and multiply by current tax rate.	
Result = income tax payable ——————— to tax accrual entry ——————————>	XX
2. Analyze all future individual temporary differences, separating them into taxable and deductible categories.	
3. Apply the future enacted rate(s) to the taxable differences and aggregate.	
Result = required ending deferred tax liability balance =	XX
Subtract beginning deferred tax liability balance	(XX)
Equals required increase or decrease in deferred tax liability ——————————>	XX
4. Apply the future enacted rate(s) to the deductible differences and aggregate.	
Result = required ending deferred tax asset balance =	XX
Subtract beginning deferred tax asset balance	(XX)
Equals required increase or decrease in deferred tax asset ——————————>	XX
5. Net sum equals income tax expense	XX

   C. **Caution**—Occasionally the CPA Exam has asked questions requiring the candidate to determine the income tax payable ending balance after the payment of estimated tax payments. Assume the current tax liability is $50,000 (taxable income × current tax rate). If the firm has made a total of $35,000 of estimated tax payments, then the income tax liability to be reported in the balance sheet is $15,000 ($50,000 – $35,000). This aspect has little effect on the main issue at hand: completing the tax accrual entry.

II. Example—Beginning Deferred Tax Account Balances, Multiple Differences

> **Example**
>
> **Year 1 Pretax accounting income**: $60,000
>
> Ending prepaid insurance balance (coverage for Year 2)   10,000
>
> Recognized lawsuit contingent liability (recognized loss) (to be resolved in Year 2)   15,000
>
> Tax rates: current (30%), enacted for Year 2 and later (35%)

Steps:		To tax accrual entry
1. Taxable income = $60,000 − $10,000 + $15,000 = $65,000		
The prepaid insurance is subtracted because it is an amount paid in Year 1, but not recognized as expense for the books. The contingent loss is added because it is a recognized loss for the books but is not deductible for taxes until paid. Income tax payable = $65,000(.30)	=	$19,500
2. Future taxable difference: $10,000 prepaid insurance. (Future pretax accounting income will decrease relative to taxable income when the insurance expense is recognized for the books.) Future deductible difference: $15,000 contingent liability. (Future taxable income will recognize the loss as a deduction when paid reducing taxable income relative to pretax accounting income.)		
3. Required ending deferred tax liability = $10,000(.35) = $3,500		
Beginning deferred tax liability	(0)	
Increase in deferred tax liability		3,500
4. Required ending deferred tax asset = $15,000(.35) = $5,250		
Beginning deferred tax asset	(0)	
Increase in deferred tax asset		(5,250)
5. Income Tax Expense		$17,750

Year 1 Tax Accrual Entry:

Income Tax Expense	17,750	
Deferred Tax Asset	5,250	
Deferred Tax Liability		3,500
Income Tax Payable		19,500

Current Provision of Income Tax Expense	$ 19,500
Less Deferred Provision ($5,250 − $3,500)	(1,750)
Equals Total Income Tax Expense	$17,750

Example (continued)
Year 2 Pretax Accounting Income $80,000
Depreciation for financial reporting and tax purposes on a plant asset purchased Year 2 will be:

Year	Book Depreciation	Tax Depreciation
2	$10,000	$16,000
3	10,000	9,000
4	10,000	5,000
Totals	$30,000	$30,000

$5,000 of municipal bond interest was received.
$8,000 worth of goods was sold on the installment basis. The entire amount is recognized in revenue for book purposes. No cash is collected in Year 2.
$11,000 of estimated warranty expense is recognized; $4,000 was spent to service claims.
Tax rates have not changed. Current and future years are taxed at 35%.

Steps:

	To tax accrual entry
1. Taxable Income:	
Pretax Accounting Income	$80,000
Municipal Bond Interest	(5,000)
Expiration of Prepaid Insurance from Year 1	10,000
Lawsuit Loss from Year 1, Paid in Year 2	(15,000)
Excess of Tax Depreciation over Book Depreciation	(6,000)
Installment Sales Revenue Recognized for Books	(8,000)
Excess of Warranty Expense over Warranty Deduction	7,000
Taxable Income	$63,000

Income Tax Payable = $63,000 × (.35) = $22,050

The expiration of the prepaid insurance from Year 1 reduced pretax accounting income but does not reduce taxable income in Year 2 because the entire prepayment was deducted in Year 1. The lawsuit loss was not recognized in pretax accounting income because it was recognized in Year 1. It is paid in Year 2 and therefore deducted in Year 2.

	To tax accrual entry
2. Future taxable differences:	
Excess of book depreciation over tax depreciation	$ 6,000
Installment sales revenue to be recognized for tax	8,000
Total future taxable differences	$14,000
Future deductible difference:	
Excess of warranty expense over warranty deduction	$7,000

(Note that the temporary differences from Year 1 have reversed and no longer are *future* differences with respect to the end of Year 2.)

	To tax accrual entry	
3. Required Ending Deferred Tax Liability = $14,000(.35) =	$4,900	
Beginning Deferred Tax Liability	(3,500)	
Increase in Deferred Tax Liability		1,400
4. Required Ending Deferred Tax Asset = $7,000(.35) =	$2,450	
Beginning Deferred Tax Asset	(5,250)	
Decrease in Deferred Tax Asset		2,800
5. Income Tax Expense		$26,250

Year 2 Tax Accrual Entry

Income Tax Expense	26,250	
Deferred Tax Asset		2,800
Deferred Tax Liability		1,400
Income Tax Payable		22,050

Current provision of income tax expense	$22,050
Plus deferred provision ($1,400 + $2,800)	4,200
Equals total income tax expense	$26,250

III. Tax Rate Considerations

A. As already discussed, the future enacted tax rate is used to measure the change in the deferred tax accounts for the year-end tax accrual entry. The tax effect of a change in the future tax rate is recognized in the current period because the change in deferred tax accounts directly affects income tax expense (a derived amount).

B. When the tax rate is changed **during** the year, the new rate is applied as of the beginning of the year (estimate change) to recompute the deferred tax balances. This results in an immediate change to income tax expense. For annual reporting, the normal year-end tax accrual entry automatically accomplishes this effect.

C. Corporations are taxed at an increasing rate as taxable income increases. The average tax rate is used for computing the changes in the deferred tax accounts.

D. When a future temporary difference is expected to reverse at a different rate than the regular tax rate (e.g., a capital gains rate), then the specific rate applying to the difference is used when measuring that portion of the change in the deferred tax account.

IV. Classification of Deferred Tax Accounts

A. Deferred tax assets (DTA) (and associated valuation allowances) and deferred tax liabilities (DTL) are classified noncurrent.

B. For balance sheet reporting, the *net* of the noncurrent DTA and DTL is reported as one net noncurrent asset or liability.

Example

The ending internal deferred tax account balances are as follows (both noncurrent):

DTA: $200,000

DTL: 900,000

The firm will report a $700,000 noncurrent deferred tax liability in its balance sheet.

C. As discussed in a later section, there may be a valuation allowance (contra DTA). In the above example, if there were a valuation allowance of $50,000 for the DTA, then the firm reports a $750,000 noncurrent deferred tax liability in its balance sheet.

$$\$750,000 = \$900,000 - (\$200,000 - \$50,000)$$

D. Netting occurs only within each tax jurisdiction. A separate net noncurrent item is reported for each tax jurisdiction.

Valuation Allowance for Deferred Tax Assets

This lesson discusses the valuation allowance for deferred tax assets leading to the reported net deferred tax asset.

After studying this lesson, you should be able to:

1. Determine when a valuation allowance is required for a deferred tax asset.

2. Describe the evidence used to determine whether a valuation allowance is required.

3. Explain the sources of support for the realization of a deferred tax asset.

4. Record the appropriate amount of a valuation allowance from given information.

I. Limitation on Deferred Tax Assets

A. A deferred tax asset, like any other asset, is an asset only if it has future benefit. A deferred tax asset will reduce income tax payments in the future, if there is taxable income in the future to reduce. (A few other sources of benefit exist as well but future taxable income is the main one).

B. When there is not a sufficient probability of realizing the deferred tax asset, a valuation allowance (contra account) is recorded to reduce the deferred tax asset to the amount expected to be realized.

II. Net Amount of Deferred Tax Asset Reported

A. **Definition—Realization** of a deferred tax asset means that the asset will provide its expected benefits.

B. When there is **at least a 50% chance of realizing** the deferred tax asset, it is reported free of any valuation account.

C. When there is less than a 50% chance of the deferred tax asset being fully realized, it is reported but also is reduced by a valuation allowance (contra to deferred tax asset) to the amount that has at least a 50% chance of being realized.

D. Another way to say this is: If, based on available evidence, it is more likely than not that some portion of the deferred tax asset will not be realized, the deferred tax asset is reduced by a valuation allowance to the amount more likely than not to be realized.

E. The valuation allowance account, if needed, is treated as a negative deferred tax asset account. The ending balance is the amount required at the end of a period, and the change in the valuation account is the increase or decrease from the previous period. Thus, the same process for updating deferred tax accounts applies to the valuation allowance account.

III. Assessing Whether a Valuation Allowance Valuation Account Is Needed

A. A valuation account is suggested if any of the following are present:

1. A history of unused net operating losses;

2. A history of operating losses;

3. Losses expected in future years; *or*

4. Very unfavorable contingencies.

5. A very brief carryback or carryforward period should raise serious doubts about the realization of the deferred tax asset. For example, a significant deductible temporary difference may be expected to reverse in a single year. Alternatively, the enterprise might operate in a traditionally cyclical business that would limit the length of the carryback or carryforward time period.

B. Evidence suggesting that a valuation account is not needed must also be considered, as exemplified by the following:

    1. Existing contracts or sales backlog will produce more than enough taxable income to realize the deferred tax asset.

    2. An excess of appreciated asset value over the tax basis of the entity's net assets will produce more than enough taxable income to realize the deferred tax asset.

    3. A strong earnings history suggests that taxable income in the future will be enough to realize the deferred tax asset.

C. Both positive and negative evidence is used when making the decision about whether to recognize a valuation allowance.

IV. Sources for Realizing the Deferred Tax Asset

A. If any one of the following sources is present in sufficient amount (to achieve the 50% threshold), then no valuation allowance is required. More than one source can be used to support a deferred tax asset.

    1. Expectation of future taxable income;

    2. Taxable income in prior years within the two-year carryback period for net operating losses;

    3. Future taxable differences; *or*

    4. Tax planning strategies.

B. **First Source**—The *first* source is the one most frequently used. If sufficient future taxable income is expected, then the deferred tax asset most likely will be realized. The deferred tax asset is credited upon realization, rather than crediting income taxes payable. No valuation account is necessary.

C. **Second Source**—The *second* source involves carrybacks of net operating losses. If a future deductible amount (giving rise to the deferred tax asset) were the only item to appear in the future tax return, a net operating loss would occur. A net operating loss may be carried back two years for a refund of taxes paid earlier. Thus, if a firm has a deferred tax asset at 12/31/X7 and the associated future deductible difference is scheduled to reverse in 20X8, that deductible difference could be carried back first to 20X6 and reduce taxable income in that year causing a refund of taxes.

    1. If large enough, the remainder then could be carried back to 20X7 for additional refund. Thus, prior year taxable income within the carryback period is a source of realizing the deferred tax asset, and, if present, alleviates the need for a valuation allowance.

    2. **Example of source 2 and journal entry**—A firm has a $20,000 future deductible difference at the end of 20X8. The difference is expected to reverse in 20X9. The future tax rate is 30%. Thus, a $6,000 deferred tax asset is recorded. However, the firm has little prospect for future taxable income, has no available tax strategies, and has no future taxable temporary differences (i.e. no other sources of realization). But assume the firm earned $6,000 taxable income in both 20X7 and 20X8.

        a. Therefore, $12,000 of prior years' taxable income can be used to support the deferred tax asset. If the only item on the tax return in 20X9 is the reversing deductible difference, then 20X9 will report a net operating loss of $20,000, which can be carried back to the previous two years to obtain a refund of the tax paid on the $12,000 of taxable income. The tax accrual entry for 20X8 assuming no beginning deferred tax balances for 20X8:

Deferred Tax Asset ($20,000 × .3)	6,000	
Valuation Allowance ($8,000 × .3)		2,400
Income Tax Payable ($6,000 × .30)		1,800
Income Tax Benefit		1,800

    b. Of the $20,000 deductible difference, $12,000 is supported by prior taxable income within the carryback period. The remaining $8,000 is unsupported. The valuation allowance reduces the net reported deferred tax asset to $3,600 ($12,000 × .30). The income tax expense is negative in this year and is labeled Income Tax Benefit. This amount increases net income for 20X8.

  D. **Third Source**—The *third* source involves the ability of future taxable differences and the future deductible differences (giving rise to the deferred tax asset) to cancel within the carryback or carryforward period. Assume a firm has a future $4,000 deductible temporary difference (giving rise to a $1,200 deferred tax asset assuming a 30% tax rate), and it also has a $6,000 future taxable difference. The deductible difference can be carried back two years or forward 20 years. If the taxable difference is within that total carryback or carryforward period, then the deductible difference will cancel $4,000 of the taxable difference, which realizes the deferred tax asset, and no valuation allowance is needed.

  E. **Fourth Source**—The *fourth* source, tax planning strategies, are actions that (1) must result in the realization of deferred tax assets, (2) might not be taken otherwise, and (3) are prudent and feasible. An example of such a strategy is to accelerate the timing of a future deductible difference so that it falls within the carryback period to enable a tax refund of prior year taxes. Another is the ability to sell a building at a taxable gain (and leasing it back to avoid the disruption of moving the business) to avoid the expiration of a deductible difference in the current year. The resulting increase in taxable income will help to cancel (use) the deductible difference before it expires.

V. **Reporting the Deferred Tax Asset and Valuation Allowance**

  A. The full-deferred tax asset and valuation allowance are reported in the balance sheet. Alternatively, the deferred tax asset is reported net in the balance sheet with the footnotes reporting the full asset and the valuation allowance.

  B. The valuation allowance is classified as is the deferred tax asset—noncurrent.

  C. The tax rate used to measure the deferred tax asset is based on the source of realization. For example, if the only source of realization of the deferred tax asset is the carryback of the relevant deductible difference, the tax rate in the years available for carryback is used to measure the deferred tax asset.

Uncertain Tax Positions

This lesson considers the accounting for beneficial tax positions that are uncertain.

After studying this lesson, you should be able to:

1. Determine the appropriate reporting when the chance of the position being sustained is less than or equal to 50%.

2. Record the resolution of the uncertainty for a tax position with less than or equal to a 50% chance of being sustained.

3. Prepare the journal entry when it is more likely than not that the position will be sustained.

4. Record the resolution of the uncertainty for a tax position with more than a 50% chance of being sustained.

I. Uncertainty in Income Tax—The Issue

A. The preparation of a firm's tax return is affected by many estimates and uncertainties. Uncertain tax positions are those that may not be sustainable on audit by the IRS. Examples include uncertain deductions, tax credits, and revenue exemptions. The firm includes the uncertain position in its tax return thus reducing its income tax liability, but there remains uncertainty about the actual benefit of that deduction. If there is at least a one-third probability that the tax position will be sustained, there is no legal or professional censure for taking that position.

B. This lesson explains how the financial benefit of such uncertain tax positions is reported. Income tax expense is reduced (benefit recognized) for an uncertain tax position only if it is "more likely than not" (> 50%) that the position will be sustained upon audit by the IRS.

C. A two-step approach is applied: (1) Is the uncertain position more likely than not to be sustained?; (2) If yes, then a probabilistic approach is applied to determine the amount of benefit recognized in the current year.

II. Probability Less than or Equal to 50%

A. If it is **not** "more likely than not" that the position will be sustained upon audit by the IRS, then income tax expense is not reduced and an additional tax liability is recognized. No benefit is recognized in the current year.

Example
Taxable income is $20,000 and the tax rate is 30%. Taxable income reflects an uncertain deduction of $2,000. The firm believes there is less than a 50% chance of the $2,000 deduction being allowed.

Income tax expense	6,600	
Income tax payable ($20,000 × .30)		6,000
Liability for unrecognized tax benefit ($2,000 × .30)		600

Income tax expense is not reduced by the uncertain deduction—the deduction is not recognized in the financial statements. Upon resolution however, future income tax expense is reduced if the deduction is upheld.

The liability for unrecognized tax benefits should not be netted against deferred tax accounts. The reason for this second liability is that the firm is proceeding with the uncertain benefit on its tax return; thus the income tax payable reflects the uncertain deduction. The firm will pay only the smaller amount in the current year with resolution of the unrecognized benefit later. The above entry reflects the expectation that the firm will have to pay the additional $600 at a later date.

B. Resolution of the Uncertainty

    1. If the deduction is disallowed, the journal entry in the year of resolution is:

Liability for unrecognized tax benefit	600	
Cash		600

Additional amounts may be due for interest and penalties. These amounts are recognized as an expense in the year of payment.

    2. If all or a portion of the deduction is allowed, income tax expense is reduced in the year of payment (change in estimate) for the tax benefit received. Assume that $667 of the deduction was allowed (one-third of the $2,000 deduction taken) yielding a $200 reduction in the amount of tax due, and income tax expense ($667 × .30 = $200).

Liability for unrecognized tax benefit	600	
Cash		400
Income tax expense		200

III. Probability > 50%

A. If it **is** "more likely than not" that the position will be sustained upon audit by the IRS, then the firm must estimate specific outcomes of the audit and probabilities associated with each. The amount of benefit recognized is the largest amount for which the cumulative probability of realization exceeds 50%.

Example
Taxable income is $20,000 and the tax rate is 30%. Taxable income reflects an uncertain deduction of $2,000. The firm believes there is more than a 50% chance of a deduction in some amount being allowed. Estimated amounts of allowable deductions along with their probabilities appear below:

Amount Allowed	Probability	Cumulative Probability
$2,000	.15	.15
1,600	.20	.35
1,400	.30	.65
400	.20	.85
200	.15	1.00

The tax benefit recognized is based on the $1,400 amount, which is the largest amount for which the cumulative probability exceeds 50%. No reduction in income tax expense is recognized for the remaining portion of the deduction ($600).

Income tax expense	6,180	
Income tax payable ($20,000 × .30)		6,000
Liability for unrecognized tax benefit ($600 × .30)		180

Income tax expense is reduced by $420 as a result of the recognition of the current tax benefit associated with the $1,400 amount ($1,400 × .30 = $420).

B. The process of identifying outcomes and estimating probabilities must assume that the taxing authority will have full knowledge of the tax situation.

C. The classification of the liability for unrecognized tax benefit is based on the period of expected settlement. Tax cases often require more than one year for resolution. Therefore, the liability is classified as noncurrent unless there is reason to believe resolution will occur within one year of the balance sheet, in which case the liability is classified as current.

IV. Resolution of the Uncertainty

A. *In a later year, if the expected $1,400 deduction is allowed:*

Liability for unrecognized tax benefit	180	
Cash ($2,000 − $1,400).30		180

B. When the benefit recognized in income tax expense in a prior year is not the same amount as the final actual benefit determined upon resolution, the difference is recognized in income tax expense in the year of resolution (change in estimate).

1. *If no deduction is allowed:*

Income tax expense	420	
Liability for unrecognized tax benefit	180	
Cash ($2,000 × .30)		600

2. *If a $1,600 deduction is allowed:*

Liability for unrecognized tax benefit	180	
Income tax expense ($1,600 − $1,400) × .30		60
Cash ($2,000 − $1,600).30		120

3. If the entire $2,000 deduction is allowed:

Liability for unrecognized tax benefit	180	
Income tax expense ($2,000 − $1,400).30		180

V. The Same Approach Is Applied to Future Temporary Differences—For example, if there is uncertainty about the deductibility of a future deductible difference giving rise to a deferred tax asset, the same two-step approach is applied. The result is a reduced deferred tax asset, increased deferred tax liability, or both.

Net Operating Losses

This lesson considers accounting for tax loss carrybacks and carryforwards. Journal entries are illustrated for both options available under the tax law. Other aspects including disclosures for taxes and international standards are discussed.

After studying this lesson, you should be able to:

1. Highlight the important differences in accounting for income tax between U.S. and international standards.

2. Note the important footnote disclosures for income tax.

3. Record the journal entry for the carryback of a net operating loss.

4. Record the journal entry for the carryforward of a net operating loss under both options available

I. **Net Operating Losses**

 A. A net operating loss (NOL) is negative taxable income for a year—a loss for income tax purposes. An NOL occurs when taxable deductions exceed taxable revenues. This provision is solely within the tax code.

 B. The tax law allows an NOL to be carried back two years for a refund of taxes paid in those years and forward 20 years to reduce taxes in those years.

 C. Recognition of the carryback produces a refund receivable; recognition of the carryforward produces a deferred tax asset (DTA). Now there are two sources of DTAs: future deductible differences and tax loss carryforwards.

II. **Two Options**—When a firm has an NOL, it can choose from two options. The choice is irrevocable for a given NOL year.

 A. **Carryback, Carryforward Option**—Under this option, the NOL is first carried back to the two years before the year of the NOL. The NOL absorbs prior years' taxable income for a refund of taxes paid in those prior years. The refund is limited to the amount of taxes actually paid. The earlier of the two years is used first.

 1. If the NOL exceeds taxable income for the two preceding years, the remainder then is carried forward for at most 20 years to absorb future taxable income. Earliest years are used first. No taxes are paid on taxable income absorbed by the NOL in those future years.

 B. **Carryforward Only Option**—In this option the firm chooses only to carryforward the NOL rather than carry it back first for a refund.

III. **Choosing Among the Two Options**

 A. The carryforward aspect is present in both options. The only difference between the options is the carryback feature. The main reason for the carryforward-only option is to take advantage of significantly higher tax rates in the future. The difference must be large enough to offset the present value benefits of the immediate refund available from the carryback, for option B to make sense.

 1. Some tax credits also have the carryback/carryforward feature and may expire more quickly than the NOL. Tax credits reduce income tax by the amount of the credit and are thus more valuable dollar for dollar. Thus, it may be advantageous to use prior year taxable income for these credits.

IV. **Cautions in Applying the Options**

 A. An NOL absorbs taxable income through the carryback and carryforward features, NOT income tax. A $10,000 NOL is worth only $3,000 to the firm if the tax rate is 30%.

 B. The taxable income of the earliest year of the two years before the NOL is absorbed first in a carryback (FIFO)

 C. The taxable income of the earliest future year is absorbed first, in a carryforward. (FIFO)

D. NOLs themselves are used on a FIFO basis. An NOL must be completely utilized before a later NOL can be carried back or forward.

E. The positive taxable income of any year can be absorbed only once in the realization of the tax benefit of an NOL carryback or carryforward.

V. Example: Two Options

This example illustrates how the two options operate. A firm's history of taxable income follows:

Year	Taxable Income	Tax Rate
A	$1,000	20%
B	2,000	25%
C	3,500	30%
D	4,000	35%
E	(11,000)	38%
F	1,500	40%
G	6,000	40%

A. Carryback, Carryforward Option

1. **Year E**—The firm pays no income tax because taxable income is negative $11,000. $3,500 of the $11,000 NOL is carried back to year C first and then $4,000 is carried back to year D. The resulting refund generated in year E is $2,450.

$3,500(.30) + $4,000(.35) = $2,450.

Of the original $11,000 NOL, $3,500 of NOL remains to carryforward ($11,000 − $3,500 − $4,000).

    a. **Caution for candidates:** Remember to go back only 2 years. Often the data includes more than two previous years of taxable income (as in this example), and there is a tendency to use the earliest taxable income provided. Years A and B are unavailable for carryback in this example.

2. **Year F**—The firm pays no income tax because the taxable income of $1,500 is completely absorbed by the carryforward of $1,500 of the $3,500 NOL remaining. Now only $2,000 of NOL remains to carryforward to year G.

3. **Year G**—The remaining $2,000 of NOL absorbs a like amount of taxable income, leaving only $4,000 ($6,000 taxable income less the $2,000 NOL carryforward) subject to tax. Therefore, the firm pays $1,600 in income tax ($4,000 × .40).

    a. If the sum of the taxable income of years C and D equaled or exceeded $11,000, there would be no NOL to carry forward.

B. Carryforward-Only Option

1. The NOL is carried forward to years F and G completely absorbing the taxable income in those years. No tax is paid in those years. The combined taxable income for the two years is $7,500. Thus, $3,500 of the NOL remains to be carried forward to future years (18 years remain in the carryforward period after year G). The value to the firm of the remaining NOL at the end of year G is $1,400 ($3,500 × .40) assuming a future tax rate of 40%.

2. If the combined taxable income for years F and G had exceeded $11,000, there would be no remaining carryforward of NOL, and the firm would pay taxes on the amount of taxable income exceeding $11,000.

VI. Accounting for NOLs

A. Carryback

1. A *carryback* generates an immediate refund of tax. The carryback is recorded as follows (in the NOL year):

Refund Receivable	amount of refund
Income Tax Benefit	amount of refund

2. The amount of the refund is limited to the taxes paid in the previous two years. The receivable is a current asset and the income tax benefit is a gain account (or negative income tax expense), reducing the loss for the year.

B. Carryforward

1. The carryforward feature is present in both options. A *carryforward* generates a deferred tax asset. This is the same account that is produced by future deductible differences. Both a carryforward of an NOL and a future deductible difference reduce future taxable income relative to pretax accounting income. The tax benefit of a carryforward is recognized in income in the period of the loss. The carryforward is recorded as follows (in the NOL year):

Deferred Tax Asset	(future enacted rate)(remaining NOL)
Income Tax Benefit	(future enacted rate)(remaining NOL)

2. The "remaining NOL" amount in the above entry depends on the option chosen.

   a. If the carryback/carryforward option is chosen, the remaining NOL amount is the portion of the total NOL remaining after carrying it back to the previous two years to absorb taxable income in those years.

   b. If the carryforward only option is chosen, the remaining NOL amount is the full NOL.

3. The required amount of deferred tax asset from a carryforward contributes to the total required ending deferred tax asset balance, along with the future deductible differences. The deferred tax asset stemming from an NOL is subject to the valuation allowance requirements.

VII. Example—Accounting for Both Options

VII. Example—Accounting for Both Options—The data from the previous example on the two options is repeated below. Assume no temporary or permanent differences (pretax income equals taxable income). The tax rates are enacted in the year before they are effective. For example, the tax rate listed for year F (40%) applies to year F but was enacted in year E. Assume sufficient estimated future taxable income to support a deferred tax asset. (No valuation allowance is required.)

Year	Taxable Income	Tax Rate
A	$1,000	20%
B	2,000	25%
C	3,500	30%
D	4,000	35%
E	(11,000)	38%
F	1,500	40%
G	6,000	40%

1. **Carryback, Carryforward Option**

Year E Accounting:

Refund Receivable	2,450	
Income Tax Benefit		2,450

$3,500(.30) + $4,000(.35) = $2,450

Of the original $11,000 NOL, $3,500 remains to carry forward ($11,000 − $3,500 − $4,000).

Deferred tax asset	1,400	
Income Tax Benefit		1,400

$3,500(.40) = $1,400

The total benefit recorded is $3,850 ($2,450 + $1,400). The 40% tax rate is used because it was enacted in year E. The tax benefit of the remaining $3,500 NOL is $1,400 because in years after year E, the $3,500 NOL will reduce taxable income that would have been taxed at 40%.

Reported net income for year E is negative $7,150 (− $11,000 + $2,450 + $1,400). The bottom of the income statement appears as follows:

Pretax accounting income	($11,000)
Income tax benefit	3,850
Net income	($7,150)

Year F Accounting:

The taxable income of $1,500 is completely absorbed by the carryforward of $1,500 of the $3,500 NOL remaining. Now only $2,000 of NOL remains to carry forward to year G. The calculation of the change in deferred tax asset (DTA) is as follows.

Required ending DTA balance:	$800	$2,000 remaining NOL × .40
Beginning DTA balance	1,400	
Decrease in DTA	$600	

Journal Entry:

Income tax expense	600	
Deferred tax asset		600

At the end of year F, the firm can carry forward $2,000 of NOL. The value of that carryforward at a 40% tax rate is $800. The tax journal entry adjusts the DTA to the correct ending balance.

The firm pays no income tax in year F.

Year G Accounting:

Income tax expense	2,400	
Deferred tax asset		800
Income tax payable		1,600

$1,600 = .40($6,000 − $2,000 NOL remaining). The NOL carryforward reduces the amount on which tax is levied by $2,000. There is no remaining NOL to carry forward; therefore, the DTA balance is closed. The income tax expense amount is a derived amount, as always.

2. Carryforward Only Option

Year E Accounting:

Deferred tax asset	4,400	
Income tax benefit		4,400

$4,400 = $11,000(.40). The total income tax benefit of $4,400 exceeds the amount in the carryback, carryforward option ($3,850) for year E because the tax rates in years C and D were lower than in years after year E. This is an example of a situation for which the firm might choose the carryforward-only option.

Reported net income in year E is negative $6,600 (− $11,000 + $4,400).

Year F Accounting:

$1,500 of the $11,000 NOL is used to absorb taxable income in year F, leaving $9,500 to carry forward.

Required ending DTA balance:	$3,800	$9,500 remaining NOL × .40
Beginning DTA balance	4,400	
Decrease in DTA	$ 600	

Journal entry:

Income tax expense	600	
Deferred tax asset		600

The firm pays no tax in year F.

Year G Accounting:

$6,000 of the remaining $9,500 NOL is used to absorb taxable income in year G leaving $3,500 to carry forward.

Required ending DTA balance:	$1,400	$3,500 remaining NOL × .40
Beginning DTA balance	3,800	
Decrease in DTA	$2,400	

Journal entry:

Income tax expense	2,400	
Deferred tax asset		2,400

The firm pays no tax in year G.

Caution: One of the most important aspects of NOL accounting illustrated by this example is to remember to first compute the ending DTA from the remaining NOL. Computing the amount of NOL "used up" by the current year's taxable income using the current year rate will not always yield the correct answer because the tax rate may have changed, as illustrated in this example.

VIII. NOLs and Temporary Differences; International Standards

A. **Temporary Differences and Carryforwards**—Both (1) future deductible temporary differences and (2) NOL carryforwards (which occur in both NOL options) give rise to the required ending deferred tax asset balance. Treat the remaining NOL carryforward amount just like you would a future deductible difference. Always compute the required ending deferred tax asset balance first. Then compare that amount to the beginning balance to determine the change—the amount to enter into the journal entry. The required ending deferred tax asset will reflect the remaining NOL.

> **Note**
> *The NOL carryforward and the future deductible difference are treated the same way for purposes of computing the deferred tax asset balance.*

 **Example**
A firm has the following beginning deferred tax account balances for the current year (year 3):

Deferred tax liability	$4,000
Deferred tax asset	6,000

The tax rate for year 3 is 40%, and the enacted tax rate for future years is 30%. At the end of year 3, the firm anticipates the following future temporary differences:

Taxable	$5,600
Deductible	3,000

The firm's tax return shows an NOL of $30,000 in year 3 (negative taxable income). The carryforward-only option is chosen. Note that the computation of the ending deferred tax liability and asset balances are independent. They do not interact.

Required ending deferred tax liability: $5,600(.30) =	$1,680
Beginning deferred tax liability	4,000
Decrease in deferred tax liability	$2,320
Required ending deferred tax asset = ($3,000 + $30,000)(.30) =	$9,900
Beginning deferred asset	6,000
Increase in deferred tax asset	3,900

Entry for year 3:

Deferred tax asset	3,900	
Deferred tax liability	2,320	
Income tax benefit		6,220

B. **Disclosures for Income Taxes**

1. Current and deferred portions of income tax expense

2. Any investment tax credits and other credits taken

3. Benefits of operating tax loss carryforwards, remaining amounts, and expiration dates

4. Government grants to the extent they are used to reduce income tax

5. Adjustments to deferred tax accounts (and valuation allowance) as a result of a change in enacted tax rates or tax status of the firm

6. Total of all deferred tax liabilities

7. Total of all deferred tax assets

8. Total valuation allowance recognized for deferred tax assets

9. Net change in the valuation allowance

10. Approximate tax effect of each type of temporary difference (and carryforward)

11. Reconciliation of reported income tax expense on income from continuing operations, with the tax that would have resulted from applying the statutory tax rate to income from continuing operations

I2. Any change in the tax status of the firm

C. U.S. GAAP–IFRS Differences

1. Although the basic procedures and logic of interperiod tax allocation are similar for international and US standards, many of the differences between the two sets of standards unrelated to taxation cause differences in the outcome of applying interperiod tax allocation.

   a. For example, the international–US differences concerning the recognition of contingent liabilities cause differences in when and how much is recorded in the resulting deferred tax asset for the two systems.

   b. In addition, countries have different systems of taxation.

2. To measure the change in deferred tax accounts, international standards apply the tax rates that have been enacted or "substantively enacted" by the end of the period. This is an example of substance over form because the time lag between the announcement of the change and enactment may require a few months. For US purposes, the rates must be enacted.

3. International accounting standards allow for an upward revaluation of plant assets and other assets to fair value. The difference between the book value of the revalued asset and its taxable basis is a temporary difference causing a change in the relevant deferred tax account. These changes are reported in equity, rather than income tax expense.

4. **Deferred tax asset**

   a. For international reporting, a deferred tax asset is recognized only when it is probable that it will be realized (the same sources are available as for US standards). Valuation allowance accounts are not used; the deferred tax asset is either recognized or not. Although *probable* is not defined, it is generally understood to be significantly higher than the 50% threshold used in US standards. As a result, all other factors being the same, it is less likely for a deferred tax asset to be reported under international standards, and if they are reported, the amounts may be less, relative to US standards.

   b. For both international and US standards, it is possible for a deferred tax asset not to be recognized in one period (international: not probable; U.S: 50% or less chance of realization), but for the same future deductible difference, the deferred tax asset could be recognized in a later period, as circumstances change. The opposite is also possible. Both systems, however, use different thresholds and recording procedures as mentioned above

5. International standards do not specifically address uncertain tax positions. Currently, they are treated as contingencies.

Accounting Changes and Error Corrections

Types of Changes and Accounting Approaches

This is the first of several lessons addressing accounting changes. This lesson provides a description of the types of changes, and of the accounting approaches that apply to them.

After studying this lesson, you should be able to:

1. Identify the types of accounting changes allowed by GAAP.

2. Note the available accounting approaches.

3. Choose the appropriate accounting approach for a given accounting change.

4. List items that do not qualify as accounting principle changes.

5. Contrast the basic aspects of the two available accounting approaches.

6. Distinguish direct and indirect effects of accounting principle changes.

I. **Background and Summary**

    A. **Accounting Changes and Error Corrections**—GAAP specifies how to account for changes in accounting. The four items addressed:

        1. Accounting principle changes (example: change from FIFO to weighted-average method)

        2. Accounting estimate changes (example: change the useful life of a plant asset)

        3. Changes in reporting entity (example: change in the composition of the subsidiary group in a consolidated enterprise)

        4. Corrections of errors in prior financial statements (example: discover that an item expensed in a prior year should have been capitalized and amortized)

    B. Error corrections are not considered an accounting change but the procedures for recording are the same as for accounting principle changes and thus are covered in this set of lessons.

II. **Accounting Approaches are Specified for Accounting Changes and Errors**

    A. **Retrospective**—Application of a principle to prior periods as if that principle had always been used. The procedure records the effect of the change on prior years as an adjustment to the beginning balance in retained earnings for the year of change rather than in income; prior year financial statements reported comparatively with the current year statements are adjusted to reflect the new method. The result is that the financial statements of all periods presented reflect the same (new) accounting principle. Retrospective application enhances comparability (a quality from the conceptual framework) across the financial statements of different years reported comparatively. Therefore the term *retrospective application* implies that the company applied the new standard it adopted to all periods shown unless it was impracticable to determine the cumulative effect or the period-specific change. When there is retrospective application the entity must disclose the effects on income and income taxes.

    B. **Prospective**—Apply the change to current and future periods only; prior year statements are unaffected.

    C. Restatement is the term reserved specifically for error changes. Restatement requires correcting the comparative financial information presented along with correcting the opening retained earnings balance. The entity must disclose the nature of the error and the effect on current and prior periods.

III. **Summary of Accounting**—The following summarizes the types of items found in the accounting changes area, and the associated accounting approach.

Accounting Change or Item	Accounting Approach
Accounting principle change	Retrospective
Accounting principle change—determining prior year effects impracticable	Prospective
Accounting estimate change*	Prospective
Change in reporting entity	Retrospective
Correction of accounting error	Restatement**

*Includes changes in depreciation, amortization and depletion methods, which are treated as a change in estimate effected by a change in accounting principle.

**This is the same accounting procedure as retrospective but the difference in terminology highlights the distinction between a voluntary accounting principle change and the correction of an error, called a *prior period adjustment*.

IV. **Accounting for Principle Changes—Retrospective Application**

Definition
Change in Accounting Principle: A change from one generally accepted accounting principle to another when there are at least two acceptable principles, or when the current principle used is no longer generally accepted. A change in the method of **applying** a principle is also considered a change in accounting principle.

Example
Changing inventory cost flow assumption (LIFO to FIFO); changing the accounting for long-term construction contracts (completed contract to percentage of completion), change in method of applying LC-M / LC-NRV to inventory (individual, group, aggregate).

A. Changes in depreciation method, amortization method, and depletion method are treated as **estimate changes**.

B. The following are **not accounting principle changes:**

1. Initial adoption of a new principle to new events for the first time or for events that were immaterial in their effect in the past

Example
Capitalizing interest for the first time because in the past the firm was not involved in construction activities to a significant extent. This is not an accounting principle change.

2. Adoption or modification of a principle for transactions that are clearly different in substance from those in the past

3. A change in method that is a planned procedure as part of the normal application of a method (example: the change to the straight-line method late in the life of an asset depreciated on the double-declining balance method)

4. The change from a principle that is not generally accepted to one that is accepted (treat as an error correction)

C. **Retrospective Application**—The following steps are performed to implement retrospective application of an accounting principle change.

1. The cumulative effect of the change on periods before those presented is reflected in the carrying amounts of affected assets and liabilities as of the beginning of the earliest period presented, along with an offsetting adjustment to the opening balance of retained earnings for that period.

2. The financial statements for prior periods presented comparatively are recast to reflect the period-specific effects of applying the new principle. Each account affected by the change is adjusted as if the new method had been used in those periods.

3. Through a journal entry, the beginning balance of retained earnings in the year of the change is adjusted to reflect the use of the new principle through that date. The amount of this cumulative effect is generally not the same amount as that for Step 1 above because different periods are covered in each.

Example

In 20X5, a firm changes from the weighted-average (WA) method of accounting for inventory to FIFO. The 20X3 and 20X4 reports reissued comparatively with 20X5 will now reflect the FIFO method even though in those prior years the WA had been used. The journal entry to record the change will adjust beginning 20X5 inventory and retained earnings to the amounts that would have been in those accounts at that date had FIFO always been used (this is the cumulative effect recorded in the entry, through 1/1/X5). In the retained earnings statement, the beginning balance in retained earnings for 20X3 will be adjusted for the effects of the change on income for all years before 20X3 (this is the cumulative effect reported in the retained earnings statement, through 1/1/X3). The two cumulative effect amounts cover different numbers of years.

D. **Justification for Principle Change**—An accounting principle change can be made only if the change is required by a new pronouncement, or if the entity can justify the use of an allowable new principle on the basis that it is preferable in terms of financial reporting. The allowable new principle must improve financial reporting given the environment of the firm. Common justifications include changing business conditions, and better matching of revenues and expenses.

1. **Caution:** When new accounting standards are adopted, retrospective application may not be required, even though the standard may require that a new accounting principle or method be applied. In such cases, the transitional guidance of the new standard is to be followed.

E. **Direct and Indirect Effects**—Retrospective application of a change in accounting principle is limited to the direct effects of the change and related tax effects. *Direct effects* are those recognized changes in assets or liabilities necessary to effect the change (e.g., the change to inventory due to change in cost flow assumption). Related effects on deferred tax accounts, or an impairment adjustment resulting from applying LC-M valuation to the new inventory balance are also examples of direct effects.

1. *Indirect effects* are changes in current or future cash flows resulting from making a change in accounting principle applied retrospectively. Such changes are recognized in the period of change. Prior period financial statements are not adjusted although a description of the effects, amounts and per share amounts are disclosed in the footnotes.

Example
A change in nondiscretionary profit-sharing plan resulting from a principle change affecting earnings causes the firm to increase profit-sharing payments in the current period as a result of restating prior period income. The payments are recognized in the current year, not retrospectively.

2. Litigation settlements from lawsuits initiated in previous years but paid or received in the current year are also not treated retrospectively. They are considered an event of the period of settlement and included in that period's earnings.

F. **Disclosures for Principle Changes**—Disclosures in the year of change and also the interim period of change include the following. Subsequent financial statements need not repeat these disclosures.

1. Nature and reason for the change including why the new change is preferable (a change caused by the adoption of a new standard is sufficient justification)

2. Method of applying the change

3. For current and prior periods retrospectively adjusted, the effect of the change on income from continuing operations and net income, and all other affected line items (for income statement, balance sheet, and statement of cash flows), and any affected per-share amounts. A firm may provide only the line item information, or may disclose the entire statements as adjusted, in the notes

4. The cumulative effect on retained earnings (or other relevant equity accounts) as of the beginning of the earliest period presented

5. If it was not practicable to apply the retrospective method to all periods, the reasons why and a description of the alternative method used report the change

6. Summaries of financial results (such as major financial statement subtotals for the previous ten years) as reported in the notes are also retrospectively adjusted for the change

Retrospective Application

This lesson provides detailed guidance on how to account for accounting principle changes.

After studying this lesson, you should be able to:

1. Record the journal entry for an accounting principle change.

2. Discuss how prior year financial statements are recast for reporting in the year of change.

3. Prepare the comparative retained earnings statements for an accounting principle change.

4. Explain the modifications to the procedures when it is impracticable to determine prior year effects.

I. **Accounting Principle Change—Retrospective Application**

A. A firm changed its method of inventory valuation from WA (weighted-average) to FIFO in 20X8 and reports the previous two years' financial statements comparatively with 20X8. The change was made for financial reporting purposes only. Management believes that the FIFO method more accurately portrays the movement of goods and provides a better matching of revenues and expenses. The income tax rate is 40%. Net income for 20X8 as computed under WA would have been $12,000. The retained earnings balance at the beginning of 20X6 was $42,000. The firm has not declared dividends during the last four years.

	Ending inventory balances		Income recomputed under
	WA	**FIFO**	**FIFO**
20X8	$56,000	$68,000	$14,400
20X7	42,000	50,000	12,800
20X6	30,000	34,000	10,200
20X5	25,000	27,000	

B. Journal entry to record the principle change:

1/1/X8		
Inventory ($50,000 – $42,000)	8,000	
Cumulative effect of accounting change (.60 × $8,000)		4,800
Deferred income tax liability		3,200

C. **The Cumulative Effect**—Is closed to retained earnings. It does not appear in the income statement. The $8,000 amount is the difference in total pretax income for the firm from its beginning to 12/31/x7 between WA and FIFO. If the firm had been on FIFO for those years, then cost of goods sold for those years would have been $8,000 less because FIFO ends that period with $8,000 more inventory.

1. The accounting change increases income for financial reporting in years before 20X8. Therefore, income tax expense has increased for those years causing the deferred tax liability to increase as well through the beginning of 20X8.

D. The 20X8 journal involving inventory and cost of goods sold will reflect the FIFO method.

E. Comparative Statements

1. The income statements and balance sheets for 20X7 and 20X6 will now report cost of sales, income, inventory, and any other related account based on the FIFO method.

2. 20X8 statements reflect the application of the FIFO method.

3. The retained earnings statement reports the effect of the change on income for all years before 20X6. The income amounts reported in the statement reflect the FIFO method.

F. Retained Earnings Statements

	20X8	20X7	20X6
Retained earnings, January 1			$42,000
			1,200*
	$66,200	$53,400	$43,200
Net income	14,400	12,800	10,200
Retained earnings, December 31	$80,600	$66,200	$53,400

*Post-tax difference in beginning 20X6 inventory amounts ($27,000 – $25,000) x .6 = $1,200. Note that the $1,200 amount is the *reported* cumulative effect and is different from the $4,800 amount *recorded.* The income amounts shown for 20X6 and 20X7 are the updated amounts reflecting FIFO and thus update the retained earnings balances subsequent to the 1/1/X6 retained earnings balance. Ultimately, by 1/1/X8, a $4,800 increase is reflected in the retained earnings balances reported.

II. Inability to Determine Prior Year Effects—It is not always possible to apply a method retrospectively because required information is not available. In such cases, the usual procedures are not applied.

Example
The change to LIFO requires the firm to apply LIFO all the way back to the beginning of the firm (or a point at which there was no inventory). The procedure requires the identification of cost layers for any prior year for which inventory increased in physical amount. This information may be difficult or impossible to obtain. Purchase price information may no longer be available. Even more challenging would be to apply LIFO retrospectively in a manufacturing context where possibly hundreds of different items are integrated into many different products.

A. Impracticability Exception—The retrospective approach is not to be applied if any of the following applies:

1. After making a reasonable effort to apply the principle to prior periods, the entity is unable to do so.

2. Assumptions about management's intent in prior periods are required and such assumptions cannot be independently substantiated.

3. Retrospective application requires estimates of amounts based on information that was unavailable in the prior periods or on circumstances that did not exist in the prior periods.

B. Two Impracticability Cases

1. When it is impracticable to determine the period-specific effects of the change for one or more prior periods presented, the change is applied as of the beginning of the earliest period for which retrospective application is practicable (which may be the current period).

2. When the cumulative effect as of the beginning of the current period cannot be determined, then the change is made prospectively as of the earliest date possible.

 **Example**
A firm changes from FIFO to LIFO in 20X4, but the cumulative effect for prior years cannot be determined. However, records enable the firm to apply LIFO beginning in 20X1. The FIFO ending inventory balance for 20X0 is used as the beginning LIFO balance for 20X1. LIFO is applied from that point. No cumulative effect is recorded.

III. Change in Reporting Entity—Retrospective Application

A. **Change in Reporting Entity**—A change in reporting entity results in financial statements of a different reporting entity. A change in reporting entity is limited mainly to:

    1. Presenting consolidated or combined financial statements in place of financial statements of individual entities

    2. Changing the set of subsidiaries that make up a consolidated group

    3. Changing the entities included in combined financial statements

B. A business combination accounted for by the purchase method, or the consolidation of a variable interest entity is not a change in reporting entity.

C. **Retrospective Method**—The retrospective method is applied (not considered a restatement of prior financial statements). Prior financial statements are recast as if the new entity existed in those prior periods.

D. **Disclosures Required for Current Period**—(Subsidiary sequent financial statements need not repeat these disclosures).

    1. Nature of the change and reason for it

    2. Effect of the change on income from continuing operations, net income, other comprehensive income, and related per-share amounts

Prospective Application

This lesson takes a closer look at accounting for estimate changes, including changes in depreciation, amortization, and depletion methods.

After studying this lesson, you should be able to:

1. Identify accounting estimate changes.

2. Prepare the appropriate reporting for estimate changes.

3. Account for changes in depreciation, amortization and depletion methods.

I. Accounting for Estimate Changes—Prospective Application

Definition

Change in Accounting Estimate: Is derived from new information and is a change that causes the carrying amount of an asset or liability to change, or that changes the subsequent accounting for an asset or liability. Estimate changes are the most frequent type of accounting change.

Example
Most areas within financial accounting are subject to estimation. Bad debts, warranties, depreciation, pension accounting, lower of cost or market, asset impairment, and many others are examples.

A. Recall that this category of accounting change—**estimate changes**—now also includes changing a method of depreciation, amortization, or depletion. Such a principle change cannot be distinguished from a change in estimate, because the method change reflects a change in the expected pattern of benefits to be received from the asset in the future. Therefore, a change in depreciation method is considered to be a change in estimate affected by a change in accounting principle.

   1. In general, when a change in principle cannot be distinguished from a change in estimate, the change is treated as a change in estimate (prospectively). For example, a cost that has been capitalized and amortized in the past is now expensed immediately because future benefits are no longer probable. The change to immediate expensing is treated as a change in estimate (no future periods are expected to benefit).

B. **Prospective Application**—Changes in accounting estimate are accounted for in the current and future periods (if affected). Prior period statements are not affected in anyway nor are there disclosures with respect to prior statements. The new information prompting the change was not known until the current year and is not relevant to prior periods.

   1. There is no *cumulative effect* account for estimate changes.

   2. For estimate changes affecting only the current period, the new estimate is used and the usual accounting procedure applies.

   3. For changes affecting current and future periods, the book value of the relevant account at the beginning of the current year is used as the basis for applying the new estimate.

   4. For changes in method of depreciation, amortization, or depletion, the book value at the beginning of the current period is used as the basis for expense recognition over the asset's remaining useful life, along with new estimates of salvage value and useful life if necessary. The new method is applied as of the beginning of the period of change.

C. **Disclosures for Estimate Changes**—For the current period, the following are required:

1. Effect of the change on income from continuing operations, net income, and related per-share amounts for the period of change for estimate changes affecting current and future periods

2. For estimate changes affecting only the period of change, the above disclosures are required only if material.

D. **Numerical Example—Change in Estimate of Useful Life**—In 20X8, a firm using the sum-of-years-digits (SYD) method of depreciation changed the total useful life of a plant asset (cost $19,000; residual value $4,000) from ten years to five years. The revised estimate of residual value is $1,000. The asset was purchased 1/1/X5.

 **Example**

Original SYD = $1 + 2 + ... + 9 + 10 = 55$

Revised SYD = $1 + 2 = 3$ (only two years remain in revised useful life at 1/1/X8)

Book value at 1/1/X8 = $19,000 − ($19,000 − $4,000)[(10+9+8)/55] = $11,636

Depreciation for 20X8 = ($11,636 - $1,000)*[(2/3)] = $7,091

Journal entry for depreciation, 12/31/X8

Depreciation expense	7,091	
Accumulated depreciation		7,091

If the estimates were not changed, depreciation in 20X8 would have been: ($19,000 − $4,000)(7/55) = $1,909. The increase in depreciation is $7,091 − $1,909 = $5,182. Assume a 30% tax rate. The decrease in income for the current year due to the estimate change is .70($5,182) = $3,627.

Footnote: During the current year, the useful life and salvage values of equipment were reduced resulting in a decrease in current year income of $3,627.

E. **Numerical Example—Change in Depreciation Method**—In 20X6, management changes from the double-declining balance method (DDB) to the straight-line method (SL) to reflect new information suggesting that the asset will provide more uniform benefits and for a longer period of time than originally expected. The affected asset was purchased at the beginning of 20X5 for $22,000. Original estimates were: 5-year total useful life; $2,000 residual value. As of the beginning of 20X6, the revised estimates are: 9-year total useful life; $200 residual value.

Example

Book value at 1/1/X6 = $22,000 − $22,000(2/5) = $13,200

Depreciation for 20X6 = ($13,200 − $200)/(9 − 1) = $1,625

(at the beginning of 20X6, eight years remain in the asset's useful life)

Journal entry for depreciation, 12/31/X6

Depreciation expense	1,625	
Accumulated depreciation		1,625

The same entry would be recorded for the remaining seven years of the asset's life after 20X6 unless additional estimate or method changes were made.

Accounting Errors—Restatement

The last lesson on accounting changes considers errors affecting income of prior periods.

After studying this lesson, you should be able to:

1. Identify when an error has occurred, and if it affects income of prior periods.

2. Record a prior period adjustment from given information.

3. Describe how statements of prior periods are restated for an error correction.

4. Determine when a prior period adjustment is recorded in a journal entry, and when it is reported in the retained earnings statement.

I. **Correction of Error in Prior Financial Statements—Restatement**

A. **Error in Prior-Period Financial Statements**—An error in a prior-period financial statement is caused when information existed at the time the statements were prepared enabling correct reporting, but a misstatement was made causing erroneous recognition, measurement, or disclosure. The presumption is that the correct reporting could have been accomplished in the past. Errors made in the current year but discovered before the closing process are corrected without special procedures.

   1. Recall that the change from an inappropriate accounting principle to one that is generally accepted is considered an error correction.

   2. Changes in estimates that reflect negligence or those that were made in bad faith are also considered error corrections.

B. **Restatement of Prior Financial Statements**—Although not an accounting change, an error correction uses the same accounting procedures as accounting principle changes and is addressed by the same accounting standard. However, the term *restatement* is used rather than *retrospective application* to distinguish voluntary principle changes from restatements due to errors and to reduce potential confusion between the two.

C. The procedure for **error corrections** is the same as for retrospective application except for the use of the term *restatement*.

   1. The effect of the error correction on periods before those presented is reflected in the affected real accounts as of the beginning of the earliest period presented, including an adjustment to the opening balance of retained earnings (prior period adjustment) for that period, for the effect of the change on all periods before that date.

   2. The financial statements for prior periods presented comparatively are recast to reflect the effect of the error correction.

   3. Through a journal entry, the beginning balance of retained earnings in the year of the correction is adjusted to reflect the correct accounting through that date (prior period adjustment).

D. **Numerical Example**—In 20X8, a firm discovered that in 20X5, a cash advance of $600,000 received from a client as a prepayment for advertising services was credited to revenue. The contract called for the firm to provide services evenly over the five years ending 12/31/X9. Net income for 20X7 was $300,000 and for 20X8 was $400,000 before the error correction. The retained earnings (RE) balance 1/1/X7 was $800,000. 20X8 and 20X7 are shown comparatively in 20X8 annual report. No dividends were paid in either year. Ignore income tax effects.

 **Example**

1. **Journal entry to record the error correction:**

   1/1/X8:

Prior period adjustment	240,000	
Unearned revenue		240,000

The prior period adjustment is closed to retained earnings.

2. **Analysis of error:**

   (annual revenue = $120,000 = ($600,000/5))

Amount of revenue recorded through 1/1/X8:	$600,000
Correct amount of revenue earned through 1/1/X8:	
$120,000(3 years)	360,000
Overstatement of RE at 1/1/X8	$240,000
(this is the prior period adjustment through 1/1/X8)	
Amount of revenue recorded through 1/1/X7:	$600,000
Correct amount of revenue earned through 1/1/X7:	
$120,000(2 years)	240,000
Overstatement of RE at 1/1/X7	$360,000
(this is the prior period adjustment through 1/1/X7)	

3. **Corrected net income amounts:**

   20X8: $400,000 + $120,000 = $520,000 (correct)

   20X7: $300,000 + $120,000 = $420,000 (correct)

4. **Journal entry 12/31/X8:**

Unearned revenue	120,000	
Revenue		120,000

5. **Comparative statements:** The 20X7 statements will be recast to show the corrected amounts of unearned revenue, revenue, and other affected accounts.

6. **Retained Earnings Statements**

	20X8	20X7
Retained earnings, January 1		$800,000
Prior period adjustment, error correction		(360,000)
Retained earnings, January 1, as corrected	$ 860,000	440,000
Net income	520,000	420,000
E 12/31	$1,380,000	$860,000

   Footnote: The firm discovered an error in recognizing revenue recorded in 20X5 and has restated the financials for 20X7 and 20X8. The error understated income for 20X7 previously reported by $120,000.

7. The amount of the prior period adjustment to the beginning balance of retained earnings for each year shown is to be reported. For consistency with accounting principle changes, this example reports the adjustment only for the earliest year reported in the retained earnings statement. Firms may report the other amounts in the footnotes.

E. **Disclosures for Error Corrections**—Disclosures in the period of correction include the following. Subsequent financial statements need not repeat these disclosures.

    1. A statement that previous financial statements were restated, and the nature of the error

    2. Effect of the correction on each financial statement line item and related per share amounts for each prior period presented

    3. The total cumulative effect of the change on retained earnings as of the beginning of the first period presented

    4. Pre- and post-tax effects of the correction on net income for each prior period presented

II. **Counter-Balancing Errors**—Many accounting errors counterbalance or *self-correct* after a certain period of time if they are not corrected. These errors require no entry to correct retained earnings or other current account balance after the error counterbalances. However, prior year financial statements remain in error.

Examples

1. In counting its ending inventory for the 20X3 accounting year, one row of merchandise in the warehouse was counted twice. The result of this error is that ending inventory for 20X3 was overstated by $5,000. The error was detected on December 28, 20X7. Ignore income tax considerations.

20X3 effects:

*ending inventory is overstated $5,000

*cost of goods sold is understated $5,000

*net income is overstated $5,000

*ending retained earnings is overstated $5,000

20X4 effects:

*beginning inventory is overstated $5,000

*cost of goods sold is overstated $5,000

*net income is understated $5,000

*ending retained earnings is now correct because the income effects for 20X3 and 20X4 cancel each other

The error was detected on December 28, 20X7. At that time, the balance in retained earnings was correct, and no correcting entry is needed. Most likely, neither the 20X3 nor 20X4 statements will be reissued comparatively with those of 20X7—no prior year financial statements require restatement.

2. However, now assume the same error was discovered in 20X4 instead. Beginning retained earnings is overstated $5,000, and beginning inventory for 20X4 is overstated. The following entry is required and illustrates a prior period adjustment:

As of 1/1/X4:

Prior period adjustment   5,000

    Inventory   5,000

Although this is a counterbalancing error, if it is discovered before it has a chance to counterbalance, an error-correcting entry is needed.

III. U.S. GAAP–IFRS Differences

A. One of the early convergence efforts between the IASB and FASB occurred in the area of accounting changes. However, minor differences continue. The terminology between the two standards is somewhat different. For example, the term *accounting policies* is used for international standards; the term *accounting principles* or *accounting methods* is used in the United States. Also, the disclosure requirements are more detailed for U.S. reporting.

Major Differences

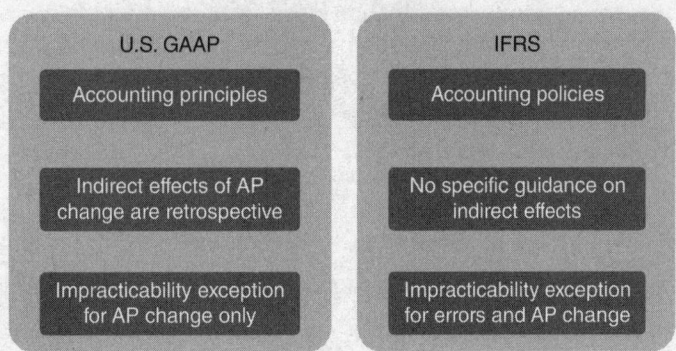

B. International standards do not address the accounting for the indirect effects of an accounting principle change.

1. Indirect effects of a change in accounting principle is any changes to current or future cash flows of an entity that result from making a change in accounting principle that is applied retrospectively. An example of an indirect effect is a change in a nondiscretionary profit sharing or royalty payment that is based on a reported amount such as revenue or net income. (ASC 250-10-55-6)

C. The change to or from LIFO is not an issue for international reporting because LIFO is not permitted.

D. International standards allow for the impracticability exception for errors as well as for accounting principle changes. U.S. GAAP standards allow this exception only for accounting principle changes.

1. For international reporting, the error is corrected by restating the financial statements for the earliest period practicable, which may result in the reporting of the correction in a year other than the year in which the error occurred. For U.S. reporting, the presumption is that if an error is discovered, it can be corrected as of the date it occurred.

E. Occasionally, a new international standard is adopted with a delayed effective date. If the firm does not elect early adoption, the following must be disclosed:

1. Nature of the future change

2. Date by which the standard is required to be adopted

3. Planned date of adoption

4. Estimate of the effect the new standard will have on the firm's financial position or a statement explaining why such an estimate cannot be made

Business Combinations

Introduction to Business Combinations

This lesson addresses accounting requirements when control is acquired and, therefore, a business combination has occurred. This lesson also discusses that one of the elements in determining the correct accounting to use for a business combination is the legal form that the combination takes. When a business combination occurs, the operating results of two or more entities are combined. This lesson considers the determination of combined operating results of entities included in a business combination as of the date of the business combination and at the end of subsequent periods.

After studying this lesson, you should be able to:

1. Define *business combination*.

2. Provide a frame of reference for understanding the accounting for business combinations.

3. Present a model that depicts the issues relevant to accounting for business combinations.

4. Describe the accounting elements (accounts) and entries determined by the legal form of combination.

5. Account for stock issuance costs.

6. Understand what constitutes the consolidated income of affiliated entities: (a) as of the date of the business combination, (b) as of the end of the period of the combination, and (c) for periods subsequent to the period of the combination.

I. Definition—*A business combination* is a **transaction or an event** in which an acquirer obtains **control** of a **business**:

   A. A **transaction** means that there was an exchange of consideration between two parties. Sometimes an **event** occurs where one party may gain control over another party without an exchange transaction or outright purchase.

   1. For example, in the diagram below, Co A is a 40% owner with veto rights and Co B is a 60% owner of Co C. The veto rights require that Co A be in agreement with any major decisions made by Co B. Since Co A has veto rights Co B does not control Co C. However, if Co A's veto rights expire, then Co B now controls Co C.

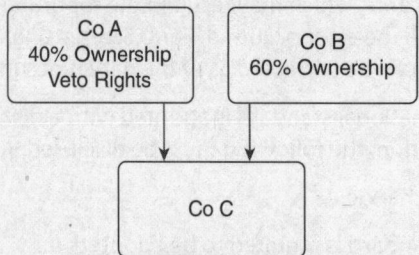

   B. **Control** is currently defined as voting control and is essentially greater than 50% voting interest.

   C. A **business** is defined as "an integrated set of activities and assets that is capable of being conducted and managed for the purpose of providing a return . . ." This definition means that the set of activities and assets does not need to be profitable to be considered a business. A startup company that has yet to generate profits would be considered a business.

II. Considerations

   A. The accounting for recording a business combination depends on the legal (or statutory) form that the combination takes and the application of the acquisition method of accounting. The alternative legal forms of a business combination are: (1) merger, (2) consolidation, and (3) acquisition; each is described and illustrated below.

   B. The acquisition method of accounting must be used to record all business combinations for which the acquisition date is on or after the first annual reporting period beginning on or after

December 15, 2008. (Prior to that date, a business combination would be accounted for using either the purchase method or the pooling of interests method. The pooling of interests method was allowed for combinations initiated before June 30, 2001.)

C. The following lessons cover accounting for a business combination under the alternative legal forms and the requirements of the acquisition method of accounting. In addition, lessons identify the circumstance under which a business combination will result in the need to prepare consolidated financial statements and the alternative methods that an investor might use to carry an investment on its books prior to consolidation.

D. Since a primary means of accomplishing a business combination is the acquisition by one entity (investor/parent) of the common stock of another entity (investee) so as to gain control of the investee/subsidiary, the current topic of "Business Combinations" is an extension of the prior topic dealing with investments in equity securities and also the next topic dealing with consolidated financial statements. Those relationships can be illustrated as:

1. **Investments in equity securities** may result in

2. **Business combinations**, which will likely require preparation of

3. **Consolidated financial statements** for the "combined" businesses.

E. The lessons in this section deal with the second of those related issues, accounting for business combinations.

III. Business Combination Overview

A. The diagram below summarizes the alternative issues and treatments in accounting for business combinations. Specifically, this diagram, is used to show (1) the relationships between the legal forms of business combinations, (2) the use of the acquisition method of accounting to record those combinations, (3) whether consolidated financial statements will be required, and (4) the accounting methods the parent may use to carry its investment in the subsidiary on its (parent's) books prior to preparing consolidated financial statements.

B. The lessons in this section ("Business Combinations") describe and illustrate the accounting treatments for the alternatives depicted in this model. One of the fundamental differences in treatments derives from differences in the legal form of a business combination, as shown in the second column (from the left) in the model. The next lesson describes the different legal forms of business combinations and the accounting consequences of those different forms.

C. This overview should be used as a frame of reference as you study the lessons in this Business Combinations section.

INVESTMENT MADE CONTROLLING INTEREST IS ACQUIRED	LEGAL FORM OF COMBINATION	ACCOUNTING TREATMENT	ELIGIBILITY FOR CONSOLIDATION	CARRY ON BOOKS AT	REPORT AT
	MERGER OR CONSOLIDATION	ACQUISITION (Purchase)	N/A	N/A	SINGLE ENTITY
>50% VOTING STOCK Or GROUP OF ASSETS that constitute a Business	ACQUISITION	ACQUISITION (Purchase)	YES	COST / EQUITY	CONSOLIDATED STATEMENTS
			NO (Lack Control)	COST OR EQUITY	COST OR EQUITY

IV. Introduction to Legal Forms of Business Combinations—The legal form of a business combination is concerned with the legal (or statutory) means by which businesses are combined or come under common control. Although the legal form of a combination is distinct from the accounting treatment of the combination, the legal form will determine certain aspects of accounting for a combination.

    A. Legal Forms of Business Combinations—The three legal forms of business combinations are merger, consolidation, and acquisition.

        1. Merger—One preexisting entity acquires either a group of assets that constitute a business or controlling equity interest of another preexisting entity and "collapses" the acquired assets or entity into the acquiring entity.

            a. Graphic illustration

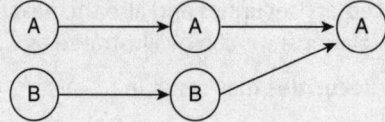

            b. Note, that only one entity (A) survives. (B) (a group of assets or another entity) ceases to exist separate from (A).

        2. Consolidation—A new entity consolidates the net assets or the equity interests of two (or more) preexisting entities.

            a. Graphic illustration

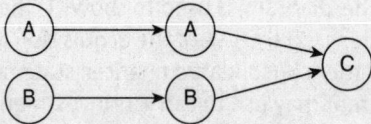

            b. Note: Only one entity (new C) exists; it consolidated the net assets or equity interests of (A) and (B) into it. (A) and (B) cease to exist as legal entities.

        3. Acquisition—One preexisting entity acquires controlling equity interest of another preexisting entity, but both continue to exist and operate as separate legal entities.

            a. Graphic illustration

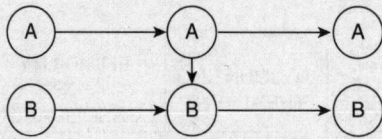

            b. Note that both entities survive, with (A) owning controlling interest in (B). Both (A) and (B) continue to exist and operate as separate legal entities.

    B. For Accounting Purposes—Because both a merger and a consolidation result in only one entity surviving, they can be treated alike.

    C. Merger/Consolidation—In a merger or consolidation, one entity (the acquirer) buys either a group of assets that constitute a business or controlling interest (typically > 50% of the common stock) of one or more target companies (the acquiree) and the group of assets or the assets and liabilities of the acquired entity become a part of the acquiring entity.

        1. The acquirer records (picks up) the group of assets or the assets and liabilities of the acquiree(s) onto its books. (The acquired entity/entities will no longer exist.)

> **Example Entry:**
>
> DR: Assets   \$_____(per Acquisition Method)
>
>   CR: Liabilities (assumed)   \$_____(per Acquisition Method)
>
>   CR: Consideration given   \$_____(at date of acquisition)

2. The legal form—merger or combination—determines the kinds of accounts (i.e., various assets and liabilities) used to record the combination.

3. The acquisition method of accounting determines the values to be used in the combination entry. (Determination of those values is covered in detail in later lessons.)

4. After this type of combination, only one entity exists, therefore there is no need to prepare Consolidated Financial Statements.

D. Acquisition—In an acquisition, one entity (the acquirer) buys controlling interest (> 50%) of the voting stock of a target entity (the acquiree) and both entities (acquiring and acquired entities) continue as separate legal and accounting entities.

    1. The acquirer records its ownership of the stock of the acquiree as a Long-Term Investment.

       a. The acquirer does **not** record (pick up) on its books the assets and liabilities of the acquiree.

       b. The assets and liabilities of the acquiree stay on that entity's (separate) books.

> **Example Entry:**
>
> DR: Investment in subsidiary   \$_____(Per Acquisition Method)
>
>   CR: Consideration given   \$_____(at date of Acquisition)

       c. The legal form—acquisition—determines the kind of asset (Investment!) used to record the combination.

       d. The acquisition method of accounting determines the values to be used in the combination entry. (Determination of those values is covered in detail in later lessons.)

       e. Since, after an acquisition, two entities exist, one controlled by the other, an acquisition usually **does** require preparation of Consolidated Financial Statements, those of the acquirer together with those of the acquiree(s).

E. Income Determination at Date of Combination

    1. Only the acquirer's (acquiring firm's) operating results (income/loss) up to the date of combination enter into determination of consolidated net income **as of the date of the combination**.

    2. The acquiree's (acquired firm's) operating results (income/loss) up to the date of combination are part of what the acquirer purchases when it acquires the acquiree (i.e., makes its investment in the acquiree), and are not part of consolidated net income as of the date of combination.

       a. The acquiree's operating results up to the date of the combination will be closed (or treated as closed) to its retained earnings.

       b. The acquiree's retained earnings as of the date of the combination is part of the equity "paid for" by the acquirer when it makes its investment.

    c. The acquiree's retained earnings as of the date of the combination will be part of the acquiree's equity eliminated against the acquirer's investment account in the consolidating process. (The consolidating process is covered as the next major topic.)

V. Income Determination at the End of the Year of Combination and Subsequent Years

    A. Income at the End of the Period (e.g., year) of Combination: The acquirer's operating results (income/loss) for the entire year **plus** the acquiree's operating results (income/loss) **after the date of the combination** enter into the determination of consolidated income for the year of combination.

    B. Income for periods (e.g., years) subsequent to combination: In periods subsequent to the period in which the combination occurs, both the acquirer's and the acquiree's operating results (income/loss) for the entire reporting period enter into the determination of consolidated net income or loss.

VI. Summary of Determining Income/Loss Associated with a Business Combination—The following timeline graphic summarizes what operating results are included or excluded in determining consolidated income or loss following a business combination. The timeline should be read from left to right.

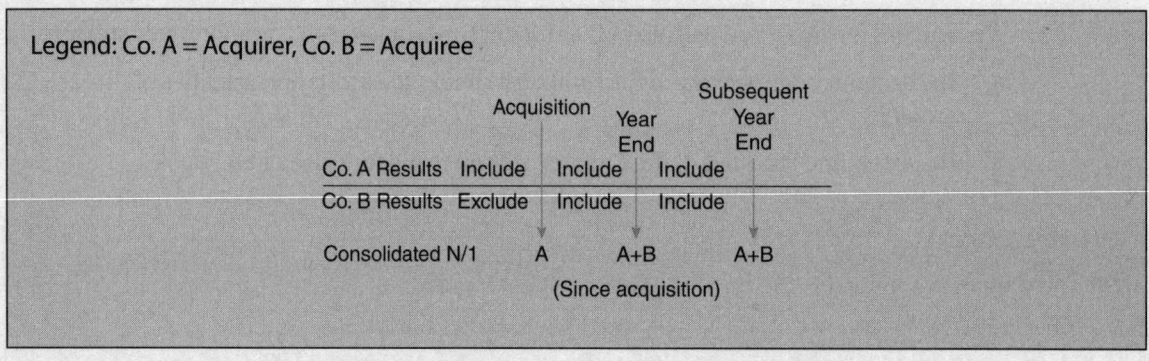

Legend: Co. A = Acquirer, Co. B = Acquiree

	Acquisition	Year End	Subsequent Year End
Co. A Results	Include	Include	Include
Co. B Results	Exclude	Include	Include
Consolidated N/1	A	A+B	A+B

(Since acquisition)

Acquisition Method of Accounting

Introduction to Acquisition Method of Accounting

Application of the acquisition method of accounting to a business combination involves several requirements: (1) identifying the acquirer, (2) determining the acquisition date and measurement period, (3) determining the cost of the acquisition, (4) recognizing and measuring the assets acquired, liabilities assumed, and noncontrolling interest in the acquiree, and (5) recognizing and measuring any goodwill or bargain purchase amount. This lesson covers the first and second of those requirements. Subsequent lessons cover the remaining acquisition requirements and related issues.

After studying this lesson, you should be able to:

1. Identify the requirements (steps) for applying the acquisition method of accounting to a business combination.

2. Identify the nature of the acquirer.

3. Provide guidelines for determining the acquiring entity (acquirer) in a business combination.

4. Define and determine the acquisition date and the measurement period.

5. Describe the effects of changes made to accounts and amounts during the measurement period.

I. **Historical Perspective**

A. Prior to 2001, Accounting Principles Board Opinion No. 16, *Business Combinations*, permitted the use of two different methods to account for business combinations: (1) the purchase method and (2) the pooling-of-interests method. The method used in a particular case depended on the facts and circumstances of the combination. FASB No. 141, *Business Combinations*, which became effective in 2001, eliminated the pooling-of-interests method as an acceptable method of accounting for business combinations. Between 2001 and 2009 only the purchase method was used to account for new business combinations.

B. In 2002, as part of their ongoing convergence project, the FASB and the International Accounting Standards Board (IASB) agreed to work together to reconsider standards for applying the purchase method of accounting for business combinations. The objective of that joint undertaking was to develop "a common and comprehensive standard for accounting for business combinations that could be used for both domestic and international financial reporting." That joint effort resulted in ACS 805 issued in December 2007, and IFRS 3 issued in January 2008. Although the requirements of those pronouncements resulted in a high degree of convergence between U.S. GAAP and the international standard for business combinations, some differences still remain. Those differences are in the areas of scope (especially as relates to not-for-profit organizations); the definition of control; how fair value, contingencies, employee benefit obligations, noncontrolling interest (FASB requires the use of fair value; IASB permits either fair value or proportionate share of acquiree's net assets) and goodwill are measured; and certain disclosure requirements.

II. **Current Standard**

A. The topic of business combinations is part of ASC 805 in the codification of accounting standards. ASC 805 requires the use of the acquisition method of accounting for business combinations, which is a variation of the purchase method of accounting, and applies to all transactions or events in which an entity obtains control of one or more businesses (including a group of assets that constitute a business) except the following:

1. The formation of a joint venture

2. The acquisition of an asset or group of assets that does not constitute a business

3. A combination between entities under common control

  4. A combination between not-for-profit organizations

  5. The acquisition of a for-profit entity by a not-for-profit organization

 B. ASC 805 specifies how the acquiring entity (acquirer) in a business combination should:

  1. Recognize and measure the identifiable assets acquired, the liabilities assumed, and any noncontrolling interest in the acquired business

  2. Recognize and measure goodwill or a bargain purchase amount

  3. Disclose information about a business combination to enable financial statement users to evaluate the business combination

III. Applying the Acquisition Method

 A. Recording a business combination using the acquisition method of accounting involves the following steps:

  1. Identifying the acquiring entity (the acquirer)

  2. Determining the acquisition date and measurement period

  3. Determining the cost of the acquisition

  4. Recognizing and measuring the identifiable assets acquired, the liabilities assumed and any noncontrolling interest in the acquired business (the acquiree)

  5. Recognizing and measuring goodwill or a gain from a bargain purchase, if any

IV. The First Step in Applying the Acquisition Method—Identifying the Acquiring Entity.

 A. **Use of the Acquisition Method**—Use of the acquisition method requires identifying the acquiring entity (i.e., the acquirer).

  1. The acquirer is the entity that obtains control of a business.

  2. A business (as defined by the FASB) is an integrated set of activities and assets that is capable of being conducted and managed through the use of inputs and processes for the purpose of providing economic benefits to owners, members, or participants.

  3. A business may be a group of assets/net assets (which constitute a business as defined in B, above) or a separate legal entity.

 B. **Determining the Acquirer**—The acquirer should be determined based on the facts and the circumstances of the combination.

  1. In a combination affected primarily through the distribution of cash or other assets or by incurring liabilities (or a combination thereof) to obtain control of a group of assets or a separate entity, the entity that distributes assets or incurs liabilities is generally the acquiring entity.

  2. As a general rule, ownership by one entity (investor), directly or indirectly, of more than 50% of the outstanding voting shares of another entity (investee) establishes the investor as the acquiring entity.

  3. In a combination effected through an exchange of equity interest (e.g., common stock for common stock), the entity that issues (new) equity interest is generally the acquiring entity; however, all pertinent facts and circumstances should be considered, including:

   a. The relative voting rights in the combined entity after the combination—If all else is equal, the acquiring entity is the combining entity whose owners as a group have the larger portion of the voting rights in the combined entity.

   b. The existence of a large minority voting interest when no other owner(s) have a significant voting interest—If all else is equal, the acquiring entity is the combining entity whose owner(s) hold the largest minority voting interest in the combined entity.

    c. The composition of the governing body of the combined entity—If all else is equal, the acquiring entity is the combining entity whose owner(s) have the ability to select or remove a voting majority of the governing body of the combined entity.

    d. The composition of the senior management of the combined entity—If all else is equal, the acquiring entity is the combining entity whose former management dominates that of the combined entity.

    e. The terms of the equity exchange—If all else is equal, the acquiring entity is the combining entity that pays a premium over the precombination fair value of the equity interest of the other combining entity(ies).

4. The acquirer usually is the combining entity whose relative size (e.g., measured in assets, revenues or earnings) is significantly larger than that of the other combining entity(ies).

5. A new entity formed to effect a business combination is not necessarily the acquirer.

    a. If the new entity transfers cash or other assets or incurs liabilities to effect a business combination, the new entity is likely the acquirer.

    b. If a new entity is formed to issue equity interest to effect a business combination, one of the preexisting combining entities must be determined to be the acquiring entity based on available evidence, including taking into account the guidance in C and D, above.

6. If more than two entities are in the combination, in addition to the guidance in C and D, above, consideration should be given to which combining entity initiated the combination and the relative assets, revenues and earnings of the combining entities.

7. The acquirer of a variable interest entity is the primary beneficiary of the variable interest entity.

    a. Simply put, a variable interest entity is one in which contractual, ownership or other pecuniary interests in the entity change with changes in the fair value of the entity's net assets, excluding the variable interest.

    b. An entity will consolidate a variable interest entity when it has an investment or other interest that will absorb a majority of the investee entity's expected losses, receive a majority of the entity's expected residual returns, or both.

    c. The entity that consolidates a variable interest entity is the primary beneficiary of that entity.

V. The Second Step in Applying the Acquisition Method—Determining the Acquisition Date and Measurement Period.

  A. The Acquisition Date—The acquisition date is the date on which the acquirer obtains control of the acquiree (i.e., the business).

    1. It is normally the date on which the acquirer legally transfers consideration for, acquires the assets of, and assumes the liabilities of the acquiree.

    2. It is also called the *closing date* for the combination.

    3. The acquisition date can be before or after the closing date, if by agreement or otherwise the acquirer gains control of the acquiree at an earlier or later date.

    4. An acquirer should consider all pertinent facts and circumstances in determining the acquisition date.

  B. Measurement Period—If the initial accounting for a business combination is not complete by the end of the reporting period in which the combination occurs, the acquirer will report provisional amounts in its financial statements for items for which the accounting is incomplete and adjust those amounts during the measurement period.

    1. The **measurement period** is the period after the acquisition date during which the acquirer may adjust any provisional amounts.

2. The measurement period provides the acquirer reasonable time (usually one year) to obtain information needed to identify and measure, **as of the acquisition date**, the following:

   a. Identifiable assets, liabilities, and noncontrolling interest in the acquiree

   b. Consideration transferred to obtain the acquiree

   c. Any precombination interest held in the acquiree

   d. Any goodwill or bargain purchase gain

3. During the measurement period, new information about facts **that existed at the acquisition date** that would have affected the recognition of assets or liabilities, or that would have affected the measurement of amounts recognized, will be used to adjust the provisional amounts in the reporting period in which the adjustment amounts are determined.

   a. The recognition of additional identifiable assets or asset amounts will result in a decrease in the amount of (provisional) goodwill, if any.

   b. The recognition of additional identifiable liabilities or liability amounts will result in an increase in the amount of (provisional) goodwill, if any.

   c. Adjustments to provisional accounts and/or amounts must be reflected in current period earnings for changes in depreciation, amortization, or other income effects. Effective with ASU 2015–2016, retroactive application to prior period financial statements is **not** required.

   d. The effect of the changes in provisional amounts must also be disclosed in the footnotes of the financial statements.

4. The measurement period ends when the acquirer obtains information it was seeking about facts **that existed at the acquisition date** or learn that no additional information is available.

   a. In no case should the measurement period exceed one year from the acquisition date.

   b. After the measurement period, accounting for the business combination should be changed only to correct an error (following the provisions of ASC 250, *Accounting Changes and Error Corrections*).

Determining the Cost of the Business Acquired

Application of the acquisition method of accounting to a business combination involves the following requirements: (1) identifying the acquirer; (2) determining the acquisition date and measurement period, (3) determining the cost of the acquired business; (4) recognizing and measuring the assets acquired, liabilities assumed, and noncontrolling interest in the acquiree; and (5) recognizing and measuring any goodwill or bargain purchase amount. This lesson covers the third of these requirements, determining the cost of the acquired business. Subsequent lessons cover the remaining requirements and related issues.

After studying this lesson, you should be able to:

1. Identify the ways that an acquirer may gain control of a business.

2. Identify and measure the elements of consideration that may be used to carry out a combination.

3. Describe the appropriate treatment when control is obtained without transferring consideration.

4. Describe how costs of carrying out a business combination should be treated.

I. **The Third Step in Applying the Acquisition Method**—Determining the cost of an acquired business.

II. **An Acquirer May Obtain Control of a Business in Two Ways**

   A. By transferring consideration to either another entity or its owner(s):

   1. To obtain a group of assets that constitute a business, *or*

   2. To gain control of another entity.

   B. Without transferring consideration—For example, by contract or through the lapse of the minority veto rights of others.

III. **Obtaining Control by Transferring Consideration**

   A. The consideration used by the acquirer may take a number of forms, including:

   1. Transferring cash, cash equivalents, or other assets

   2. Incurring liabilities

   3. Issuing equity interests, including common and preferred stock, options and warrants

   4. A combination of transferring assets, incurring liabilities or issuing equity

   B. The consideration used to effect a business combination generally must be measured at fair value (see exception in D, below).

   C. If any assets or liabilities transferred by the acquirer (except as noted in D, below) have a carrying value before transfer that is different than fair value at acquisition, the assets or liabilities must be adjusted (remeasured) to fair value at the date of the combination and the related gains or losses recognized in current income by the acquirer.

Example
P, Inc. acquires a group of assets that constitute a business from S, Inc. As payment for the group of assets, P transfers cash and land to S. The land was acquired by P 12 years ago for $126,000. It had a fair value of $150,000 at the time of the business acquisition. Prior to transferring the land to S, P should make an entry to revalue the land to fair value and recognize a gain.

DR: Land	$24,000	
CR: Gain on Land Revaluation		$24,000

(Fair value $150,000 – Carrying value $126,000 = $24,000 gain.)

The land, with a new carrying value of $150,000, would then be transferred to Sill as part of the consideration for the acquired business.

D. An exception to the requirement that assets and liabilities to be transferred as consideration in a business combination be remeasured to fair value applies when the transferred assets or liabilities remain under the control of the acquirer.

    1. In that case, the assets or liabilities are not adjusted to fair value, but are transferred at carrying value and no gain or loss is recognized.

Example
P, Inc. gained control of S, Inc. by acquiring more than 50% of S's voting common stock. As a part of its acquisition of S's stock, P transferred land with a carrying value of $126,000 and a fair value of $150,000 to S for 10,000 shares of S's common stock. Because it has controlling interest in S, P also retains control of the land transferred to S. Therefore, the land should be transferred at the carrying value, $126,000, not fair value, and no gain (or loss) will be recognized.

E. Contingent Consideration as Cost Elements

    1. The consideration transferred by the acquirer to acquire a business may include a contingent element.

    2. Contingent consideration is either:

        a. An obligation of the acquirer to transfer additional assets or equity interest to the former owner(s) of the acquired business as part of the consideration if future events occur or conditions are met, or

        b. A right of the acquirer to a return of previously transferred consideration if specific conditions are met.

    3. Contingent consideration should be recognized on the acquisition date at fair value as part of the consideration transferred in exchange for the acquired business.

        a. An obligation to pay contingent consideration should be recognized as either a liability or as equity (according to the provisions of ASC 480, *Distinguishing Liabilities from Equity*).

        b. A right to the return of previously transferred consideration should be recognized as an asset.

    4. Changes in the fair value of contingent consideration after the acquisition date that result from new information about facts and circumstances **that existed at the acquisition date** should be accounted for as measurement period adjustments (and, therefore, as adjustments to the cost of the acquired business).

    5. Changes in the fair value of contingent consideration **resulting from occurrences after the acquisition date**—including meeting earning targets, reaching a specified share market price, or reaching research and development milestones—are not measurement period adjustments and do not enter into the cost of the business combination.

    a. Changes resulting from occurrences after the acquisition date related to contingent consideration classified as equity are not remeasured; subsequent settlement should be accounted for as an equity adjustment.

    b. Changes resulting from occurrences after the acquisition date related to contingent consideration classified as assets or liabilities are remeasured to fair value at each balance sheet date until the contingency is resolved, with changes recognized in current income.

F. Acquirer's Share-Based Payment Awards as Cost Elements

  1. An acquirer may exchange its share-based payment awards for awards held by the acquiree's employees as part of a business combination.

    a. For example, in a merger the acquirer may exchange its stock options (options to acquire its stock) for the stock options in the acquiree held by the acquiree's employees at the date of the merger.

    b. Such an exchange would be a modification of share-based payment awards under ASC 718, *Stock Compensation*, and would be treated as the exchange of the original award for a new award.

  2. The treatment of the exchange of share-based awards in a business combination depends on whether the acquirer is obligated to make the exchange or does so at its own discretion.

  3. An acquirer may be obligated to exchange share-based awards because of:

    a. The terms of the acquisition agreement

    b. The terms of the acquiree's awards

    c. Applicable laws or regulations

  4. If the acquirer is obligated to exchange awards:

    a. The portion (all or part) of the replacement awards (measured in accord with the provisions of ASC 718) that relates to precombination services based on conditions of the acquiree's awards will be part of the consideration transferred in the business combination.

    b. The portion (all or part) of the replacement awards (measured in accord with the provisions of ASC 718) that relates to postcombination services (the amount not allocated to precombination services) will be treated as compensation expense in post-combination financial statements.

  5. If the acquirer elects to replace acquiree share-based awards, even though it is not obligated to do so, all the value of the awards (measured in accord with the provisions of ASC 718) will be treated as compensation expense in postcombination financial statements.

IV. Obtaining Control Without Transferring Consideration

  A. An entity (acquirer) may acquire control of another entity (acquiree) without transferring any consideration. Examples include:

  1. An entity (acquiree) reacquires a sufficient number of its own outstanding shares from selected investors so that another investor (acquirer) obtains control with its existing ownership.

  2. Minority veto rights lapse that previously kept a majority owner (acquirer) from controlling the investee (acquiree).

  3. Two entities agree to combine by contract alone; neither entity owns controlling equity interest in the other entity.

B. When a business combination occurs as a result of a contract between entities:

    1. One of the combining entities must be identified as the acquirer and, therefore, the other entity is the acquiree.

    2. The equity interests in the acquiree held by parties other than the acquirer are noncontrolling interest in the postcombination financial statements of the acquirer, even if all (100%) of the equity interest in the acquiree is attributable to the noncontrolling interest (i.e., the entity designated as the acquirer has no equity interest in the acquiree).

V. Treatment of Acquisition-Related Costs

A. Acquisition-related costs are costs the acquirer incurs to carry out the acquisition (of a group of assets that constitute a business or an entity).

B. Acquisition costs include:

    1. Finder's fees

    2. Advising, legal, accounting, valuation (appraisal) and other professional and consulting fees

    3. General administrative costs, including the cost of an internal acquisitions department

    4. Cost of registering and issuing debt and equity securities in connection with an acquisition

C. Acquisition-related costs (except as noted in D, below) should be expensed in the period in which the costs are incurred and the services are received; these costs are not included as part of the cost of an acquired business.

D. The cost of issuing debt and equity securities for the purposes of a business combination are not treated as cost of the acquired business, but should be accounted for as provided for by other applicable GAAP. Although current GAAP is not uniform with respect to treatment of issuance costs, generally, the following would apply:

    1. Debt issuance costs (legal, printing, etc.) may be either recognized as a deferred asset and amortized over the life of the debt, or expensed when incurred.

    2. Equity issuance costs (legal, printing, registering, etc.) reduce the proceeds from the securities issued and, in effect, reduce Additional Paid-in Capital.

VI. Summary—In summary, the cost of an acquired business is the sum of:

A. Fair value of assets transferred by the acquirer

B. Fair value of liabilities incurred by the acquirer

C. Fair value of equity interest issued by the acquirer

D. Fair value of contingent consideration (net) obligations of the acquirer

E. Fair value of share-based payment awards for precombination services that the acquirer is obligated to provide

Recognizing/Measuring Assets, Liabilities, and Noncontrolling Interest

Application of the acquisition method of accounting to a business combination involves the following requirements: (1) identifying the acquirer, (2) determining the acquisition date and measurement period, (3) Determining the cost of the acquisition, (4) recognizing and measuring the assets acquired, liabilities assumed, and noncontrolling interest in the acquiree, and (5) recognizing and measuring any goodwill or bargain purchase amount. This lesson covers the fourth of these requirements, recognizing and measuring the assets acquired, liabilities assumed, and noncontrolling interest in the acquiree. Subsequent lessons cover the remaining requirement and related issues.

After studying this lesson, you should be able to:

1. Identify the items that should be recognized as assets or liabilities in a business combination.

2. Identify items that are exceptions to the general recognition and measurement guidelines.

3. Describe the requirements when a business is acquired in stages.

4. Describe how noncontrolling interest in an acquiree is recognized and measured.

5. Identify the differences between U.S. GAAP and IFRS that relate to this lesson.

I. **The Fourth Step in Applying the Acquisition Method**—In the fourth step, you would recognize and measure the assets acquired, liabilities assumed, and any noncontrolling interest in an acquiree.

II. **Recognition**—At the acquisition date, the acquirer must recognize (distinct from goodwill, if any) the identifiable assets acquired, liabilities assumed and any noncontrolling interest in the acquiree.

    A. Identifiable assets and liabilities must meet the definition of assets and liabilities in FASB Conceptual Framework, *Elements of Financial Statements*.

        1. Rights or obligations that do not exist at the date of acquisition, even if expected to exist in the future, are not recognized as assets or liabilities acquired.

        2. Benefits received or obligations that occur but do not exist at the date of acquisition are recognized as post-combination items, as called for by the provisions of other appropriate GAAP. They are not part of the business acquisition. For example:

            a. Costs expected to be incurred to exit an acquired activity

            b. Costs expected to be incurred in terminating or relocating employees of the acquiree

    B. To qualify for recognition as part of the business combination, the assets and liabilities must be part of what the acquirer and acquiree exchanged in the business combination, not the subject matter of any separate transaction.

        1. A pre-combination transaction or arrangement that primarily benefits the acquirer or the subsequent combined entity, rather than the acquiree or the former owner(s), is likely to be a separate transaction.

        2. The following would be separate transactions, not a part of the combination transaction:

            a. A transaction that settles a preexisting relationship between the acquirer and the acquiree

            b. A transaction that compensates employees or former owner(s) of the acquiree for future services

            c. A transaction that reimburses the acquiree or its former owner(s) for paying the acquirer's acquisition-related costs

C. The acquirer can recognize assets and/or liabilities not previously recognized by the acquiree. For example, an internally developed brand name, patent or other asset for which costs were expensed by the acquiree would be recognized as identifiable assets by the acquirer.

    1. This would include in-process research and development (IPRD) costs incurred by the acquiree. That is, the acquirer can capitalize IPRD purchased from the acquiree as part of a business combination. This will result in the acquirer recording an intangible asset for this IPRD.

D. An intangible asset (separate from goodwill) is identifiable and would be recognized by the acquirer if it either:

    1. Is capable of being separated from the acquiree and sold, transferred, leased, rented, or exchanged (e.g., customer lists); *or*

    2. Arises from contractual or other legal rights.

E. Goodwill on the books of the acquired entity prior to a business combination would not be recognized by the acquirer in recording the combination. Any goodwill attributable to the acquiree would be separately determined by the acquirer. (See the "Recognizing/Measuring Goodwill or Bargain Purchase Amount" lesson.)

III. Classification and Designation—At the acquisition date, the acquirer must classify or designate the identifiable assets acquired and liabilities assumed so as to subsequently apply GAAP requirements.

A. Classification or designation will be made on the basis of related contractual terms, economic conditions, operating and accounting policies, and other relevant conditions that exist at the acquisition date.

B. Example of items that need classification or designation include:

    1. Investments in debt and equity securities as being held to maturity, trading, or available for sale

    2. Derivatives to determine whether they are hedging instruments, and if so, the particulars

    3. Embedded derivatives to determine whether they will be treated as separate from the host instrument

    4. Long-term assets to determine whether they will be used or held for sale

C. Leases (lease contracts) and insurance/reinsurance contracts should continue to be classified as established at inception of the contract (unless subsequent modifications of the contract have warranted reclassification).

IV. Measuring (Recording) at Fair Value—At the acquisition date, identifiable assets, liabilities and any noncontrolling interest in the acquiree should be measured (recorded) at fair value at that date.

A. Fair value for identifiable assets and liabilities acquired should be determined using the guidelines and techniques established in ASC No. 820, *Fair Value Measurement*.

B. Fair value for each identifiable asset and liability, or group of related assets or related liabilities, should be determined based on its specific attributes, including condition, location, highest and best use, and so on.

C. Subject to the requirements of ASC 820, the following may be a basis for determining fair value of certain assets acquired and liabilities assumed:

    1. Marketable securities—Quoted prices in active markets

    2. Receivables—Present value of amounts to be received

    3. Inventories (finished goods and merchandise)—(Estimated selling price less the cost of disposal and a reasonable profit

4. **Inventories** (work-in-process)—Estimated selling price less costs to complete, cost of disposal, and a reasonable profit

5. **Inventories** (raw materials)—Current replacement cost

6. **Plant and equipment held for use**—Current replacement cost

7. **Plant and equipment held for disposal**—Fair value (based on market or cost valuation) less cost of disposal

8. **Intangible assets**—Estimated fair value (based on market, income, or cost valuation)

9. **Land and natural resources**—Fair value (based on market, income or cost valuation)

10. **Accounts and notes payable, long-term debt, and other liabilities**—Present values of amounts to be paid determined using appropriate current interest rates

V. **Exceptions**—Certain exceptions to the general recognition and/or measurement principles apply to specific identifiable assets and liabilities; those exceptions include:

A. **Contingencies**—Recognition principle exception—to ASC 450

1. A contingency is an existing condition involving uncertainty as to possible gain or loss that will be resolved when one or more future events occur or fail to occur.

2. Contingencies related to existing contracts (*contractual contingencies*—e.g., warranty obligations) should be recognized and measured at fair value.

3. Contingencies not related to existing contracts (*noncontractual contingencies*—e.g., lawsuits) should be recognized and measured at fair value only if it is more likely than not as of the acquisition date that the contingency will give rise to an asset or a liability.

B. **Income Tax Issues**—(Recognition and measurement principles exceptions):

1. The acquirer will recognize and measure a deferred tax asset or liability related to assets acquired and liabilities assumed in a business combination as provided by the provisions of ASC 740.

2. The acquirer will account for the potential tax effects of temporary differences, carry forwards and income tax uncertainties of an acquiree at the acquisition date, or that will result from the acquisition, as provided for by the provisions of ASC 740, *Tax Provisions*.

C. **Employee Benefits**—(Recognition and measurement principles exceptions). The acquirer will recognize and measure a liability (or asset, if any) related to the acquiree's employee benefit arrangements in accord with applicable GAAP.

D. **Indemnification Provisions**—(Recognition and measurement principles exceptions):

1. An indemnification provision in a business combination would establish a seller's guarantee that limits the acquirer's liability for the outcome of an uncertainty related to an identifiable asset or liability.

2. The acquirer normally should recognize the indemnification benefit as an asset (indemnification asset) at the time and using the same measurement basis as the indemnified asset or liability.

E. Reacquisition Rights—(Measurement principle exception):

  1. Prior to a business combination, the acquirer may have granted the acquiree the right to use an asset of the acquirer; for example, the right to use the acquirer's trade name as part of a franchise agreement.

  2. If, as part of the business combination, the acquirer reacquires that right, it should be recognized by the acquirer as an intangible asset and measured on the basis of the remaining contractual term of the contract that granted the right.

  3. Subsequent to the business combination, the intangible asset "reacquired right" should be amortized over the remaining period of the contract that granted the right.

F. Share-Based Payment Awards—(Measurement principle exception):

  1. An acquirer may grant its share-based payment awards (e.g., employee stock options) for awards held by the acquiree's employees.

  2. The liability or equity recognized as a result of such awards should be measured in accord with the provisions of ASC 718.

G. Assets Held for Sale—(Measurement principle exception):

  1. Long-term assets acquired by the acquirer, which it classifies as held for sale at the acquisition date should be measured in accord with the provisions of ASC 360.

  2. Basically, ASC 360 requires that assets held for sale must be measured at fair value less cost to dispose.

VI. Fair Value of Previously Held Equity—Fair value of acquirer's previously held equity interest in acquiree, if any.

  A. At the acquisition date, the acquirer must measure (determine) the fair value of its previously held equity interest in the acquiree, if any.

    1. An acquirer would have an equity interest in the acquiree prior to the acquisition date if the business combination were achieved in stages (also called a step acquisition).

Example

On January 2, 2007, Investco, Inc. acquired 35% of the voting stock of Lowco, Inc. That level of equity ownership likely gives Investco significant influence over Lowco, but does not give it control. Therefore, Investco would account for its investment in Lowco using the equity method of accounting. On January 2, 2009, Investco acquires in the market an additional 40% of Lowco's voting equity. Thus, as of January 2, 2009, Investco owns 75% of Lowco's voting equity, which gives it control of Lowco, and a business combination has occurred as of January 2, 2009.

In this example, Investco would need to determine the fair value of its 35% ownership of Lowco as of January 2, 2009, the date of the business combination.

  B. Any difference between the fair value of the acquirer's precombination equity interest in the acquiree and the carrying value of that interest on the acquirer's books would be recognized by the acquirer as a gain or loss in income of the period of the combination.

    1. If the acquirer had accounted for its precombination equity ownership using the equity method of accounting (as in the preceding example), the carrying amount of the investment using that method would be used in determining any gain or loss related to the previously held equity interest.

Example

On January 2, 2007, Investco, Inc. acquired 35% of the voting stock of Lowco, Inc. for $150,000. Because its investment gave Investco significant influence over Lowco, it used the equity method to account for its investment. On January 2, 2009, Investco acquired in the market an additional 40% of Lowco's voting stock, which resulted in a business combination. At that time, Investco's investment in the 35% of Lowco acquired in January, 2007, had a carrying value of $185,000 and a market value of $200,000. As a part of its acquisition accounting for the business combination, Investco must revalue its 35% precombination investment in Lowco to fair value at the date of the business combination and recognize a gain.

Entry

DR: Investment in Lowco, Inc.	$15,000	
CR: Gain on Investment Revaluation		$15,000

(Fair value =$200,000 – Carrying value $185,000 =$15,000 gain)

The fair value of Investco's precombination investment in Lowco ($200,000) would be included as a part of the cost of Investco's acquisition of Lowco.

If the acquirer had accounted for its precombination equity ownership as an available-for-sale investment, any amount recognized in prior periods in other comprehensive income would be removed from accumulated other comprehensive income and included in calculating the gain or loss as of the date of the combination.

C. The fair value of the equity owned prior to the acquisition date (i.e., the business combination) would become part of the "cost" of the investment in the acquiree.

VII. Fair Value of Noncontrolling Interest

A. At the acquisition date, the acquirer must measure (determine) the fair value of the noncontrolling interest in the acquiree.

   1. A noncontrolling interest in an acquiree occurs when the acquirer obtains less than 100% of the equity interest of the acquiree.

   2. The percentage of equity interest not owned either directly or indirectly by the acquirer is the noncontrolling interest (formerly called "minority interest") and must be measured at fair value at the acquisition date.

B. The value assigned to the noncontrolling interest should not be based simply on the noncontrolling interest's proportional interest in the identifiable assets acquired, liabilities assumed and share of goodwill, but rather on the separately determined fair value of the noncontrolling interest in the acquiree.

   1. If an active market price for the equity shares of the acquiree is available, the acquisition date fair value of the noncontrolling interest would be based on the market value of the equity shares not held by the acquirer.

   2. If an active market price for the equity shares of the acquiree is not available, the acquirer would use some other valuation technique to value the equity shares not held by the acquirer.

C. The fair value of the acquirer's interest on a per-share basis may be different than the fair value of the noncontrolling interest on a per-share basis, due mainly to a *control premium* associated with the acquirer's ownership.

Recognizing/Measuring Goodwill or Bargain Purchase Amount

Application of the acquisition method of accounting to a business combination involves the following requirements: (1) identifying the acquirer, (2) determining the acquisition date and measurement period, (3) determining the cost of the acquisition, (4) recognizing and measuring the assets acquired, liabilities assumed, and noncontrolling interest in the acquiree, and (5) recognizing and measuring any goodwill or bargain purchase amount. This lesson covers the last of these requirements, recognizing and measuring goodwill or a bargain purchase amount in a business combination. Subsequent lessons cover post-combination issues.

After studying this lesson, you should be able to:

1. Describe how to determine whether or not goodwill or a bargain purchase amount exists.

2. Determine the amount of any goodwill or bargain purchase amount.

3. Understand certain special circumstances that may be relevant to determining goodwill or a bargain purchase amount.

4. Identify the differences between U.S. GAAP and IFRS related to this lesson.

I. **The Fifth and Final Step in Applying the Acquisition Method**—Recognizing and measuring goodwill or a gain from a bargain purchase, if any.

II. **At the Acquisition Date**—The acquirer must recognize and measure any goodwill or gain from a bargain purchase that resulted from the business combination.

III. **Amount of Gain**—The amount of that goodwill or bargain purchase gain, if any is determined using

   A. The *investment value* of the acquired business, *and*

   B. The fair value of the net of identifiable assets acquired and liabilities assumed in the business combination.

IV. **Investment Value**—The *investment value* is the sum of the following elements (The term *investment value* is not used in the FASB, but has been adopted here to include the sum of A. and B., as follows):

   A. The consideration transferred (cost) to affect the business combination (as detailed in the earlier lesson "Determining the Cost of the Business Acquired"), including the fair value of the following:

   1. Assets transferred

   2. Liabilities incurred

   3. Equity interest issued

   4. Contingent consideration (at acquisition date)

   5. Required share-based payment awards to employees for precombination services

   6. Precombination equity of the acquiree held by the acquirer (if the combination was achieved in stages or steps)

   B. The fair value of the noncontrolling interest in the acquiree, if any (as detailed in the prior lesson "Recognizing/Measuring Assets, Liabilities, and Noncontrolling Interest.")

   Investment Value = Costs (in A., above) + FV of NCI

V. **Measured at Fair Value**—The identifiable assets acquired, the liabilities assumed and any noncontrolling interest in the acquiree as of the acquisition date generally would be measured at fair value (with certain exceptions as noted in the prior lesson "Recognizing/Measuring Assets, Liabilities and Noncontrolling Interest").

VI. **Goodwill**—Goodwill results when the investment value (see IV., above) is **greater** than the net fair value of assets assumed and liabilities incurred at the date of the business combination (see IV., above).

    A. Simply put, goodwill (if it exists) is the excess of the fair value of the investment in the acquiree (including the fair value of the claim of the noncontrolling interest) over the fair value (or other required measure) of the identifiable net assets of the acquired business.

Example

1. On January 2, 2009, Investco, Inc. acquired all of the outstanding common stock of Lowco, Inc. in the market for $1,000,000 cash and merged the assets acquired and liabilities assumed into Investco. At that date the fair values of Lowco's identifiable assets and liabilities were:

Accounts Receivable	$ 200,000
Inventories	400,000
Property, Plant and Equipment	800,000
Other Identifiable Assets	200,000
TOTAL ASSETS	$1,600,000
Accounts Payable	300,000
Other Current Liabilities	200,000
Long-term Liabilities	200,000
TOTAL LIABILITIES	$ 700,000
FAIR VALUE OF NET ASSETS	$ 900,000

2. Goodwill calculation:

Investment value = $1,000,000 – Fair value of net assets = $900,000 = $100,000 Goodwill.

    B. Postcombination treatment of goodwill provides that:

        1. Goodwill is not amortized.

        2. Goodwill is assessed at least annually for impairment, as provided by ASC 350.

VII. **Bargain Purchase**—A bargain purchase results when the investment value (see IV., above) is **less** than the net fair value of assets assumed and liabilities incurred as of the date of the business combination (see V, above).

    A. Simply put, a bargain purchase (if it exists) is the excess of the fair value (or other required measure) of the net assets of the acquired business over the fair value of the investment in the acquiree (including the fair value of the claim of noncontrolling interest).

    B. A bargain purchase may result from the following reasons, among others:

        1. The business combination occurs when the owner(s) of the acquired entity are under compulsion to carry out the sale (i.e., a "forced" sale), resulting in a bargain purchase by the acquirer.

        2. The valuation of assets acquired and/or liabilities assumed is constrained by the exceptions to the use of fair value, as detailed in the prior lesson "Recognizing/Measuring Assets, Liabilities and Noncontrolling Interest."

C. If the acquirer determines that the fair value (or other required measure) of the net assets of the acquiree is greater than the investment in the acquiree (an apparent bargain purchase), before recognizing a gain from a bargain purchase the acquirer must fully reassess whether all assets acquired and liabilities assumed have been identified and properly measured according to the provisions of ASC 805, including the measurement of:

1. Identifiable assets acquired and liabilities assumed

2. Acquirer's precombination equity interest in the acquiree

3. Noncontrolling interest in the acquiree

4. Consideration transferred

D. If, after reassessment, the acquirer still concludes that a bargain purchase exists, the amount of that bargain purchase shall be recognized as a gain in earnings as of the date of the business combination.

Example

1. On January 2, 20X9, Investco, Inc. acquired all the outstanding common stock of Lowco, Inc. in the market for $850,000 cash and merged the assets acquired and liabilities assumed into Investco. At that date, the fair values of Lowco's identifiable assets and liabilities were:

Accounts Receivable	$ 200,000
Inventories	400,000
Property, Plant and Equipment	800,000
Other Identifiable Assets	200,000
TOTAL ASSETS	$1,600,000
Accounts Payable	300,000
Other Current Liabilities	200,000
Long-term Liabilities	200,000
TOTAL LIABILITIES	$ 700,000
FAIR VALUE OF NET ASSETS	$ 900,000

2. Bargain purchase calculation:

Fair value of net assets = $900,000 - Investment value = $850,000 = $50,000 Bargain purchase amount. This amount would be recognized as a gain in the period of the business combination.

(Note: See the entry for this example in the subsequent lesson, "Recording Business Combinations.")

3. The gain is attributable only to the acquirer.

VIII. Special Circumstances—Special circumstances may affect the determination and measurement of goodwill or a bargain purchase amount. These include the following:

A. If the business combination is carried out solely through the exchange of equity (e.g., acquirer's common stock for acquiree's common stock), the fair value of the acquiree's equity interest at the acquisition date may be a more reliable measure of fair value than the acquirer's equity interest and, if so, the amount of goodwill or bargain purchase should be based on the acquiree's equity interest instead of the equity interest transferred by the acquirer.

B. If no consideration is transferred in carrying out the business combination, goodwill or a bargain purchase amount should be determined using a valuation technique, instead of the value of the consideration transferred.

Post-Acquisition Issues

Prior lessons presented the steps required in the application of the acquisition method of accounting to a business combination. Following the combination, most items recognized in a combination will be measured and accounted for following the requirements of GAAP for those specific items. However, some items recognized in a combination have specific postcombination requirements. This lesson is concerned with those items.

After studying this lesson, you should be able to:

1. Know the items recognized in a business combination that require specific postcombination treatment.

2. Understand how to measure and account for items that require specific postcombination treatment.

3. Understand and know how to recognize post-acquisition measurement period adjustments for assets acquired.

4. Understand pushdown accounting and how it impacts the financial statements of the acquiree.

I. **Conventional Treatment**—Once the business combination has been recorded using the acquisition method of accounting, the acquirer generally will measure and account for assets acquired, liabilities assumed or incurred, and equity issued in the combination in accord with the provisions of established GAAP for those items.

II. **Specific Treatment**—However, certain items acquired or issued in carrying out a combination require specific treatment as provided by ASC 805; those items are:

   A. **Assets and Liabilities Arising from Contingencies**

   1. An asset or liability arising from a contingency recognized at the time of a business combination should be accounted for based on subsequent information about the contingency.

   2. Until new information about the possible outcome of a contingency is received, the acquirer will continue to report the contingency at its fair value at the date of the combination.

   3. When new information about the possible outcome of a contingency is received, the acquirer will measure and report the item according to the following rule:

      a. If the contingency is a liability, it will be measured and reported at the higher of:

         i. Its acquisition-date fair value, *or*

         ii. The amount that would be recognized if the requirements of ASC 450 were followed.

      b. If the contingency is an asset, it will be measured and reported at the lower of:

         i. Its acquisition-date fair value, *or*

         ii. The best estimate of its future settlement amount.

   4. A contingency recognized in a business combination will be derecognized only when the contingency is settled or expires.

   B. **Indemnification Assets**

   1. An indemnification asset recognized in a business combination should be measured and reported on the same basis as the liability or asset that is indemnified, subject to any contractual limitations.

   2. An indemnification assets recognized in a business combination will be derecognized only when it is settled or expires.

C. Contingent Consideration

1. Contingent consideration recognized in a business combination should be measured and reported at fair value.

2. Changes in information about the fair value of contingent consideration as it existed at the date of the business combination are measurement period adjustments and change the cost of the investment.

3. Changes in the fair value of contingent consideration that results from events after the business combination (including reaching a specific share price, meeting an earnings target, etc.) are not measurement period adjustments and do not change the cost of the investment; these changes should be accounted for as follows:

   a. Contingent consideration classified as equity is not remeasured and its subsequent settlement is accounted for within (by adjusting) equity;

   b. Contingent consideration classified as an asset or liability is remeasured at each reporting date and recognized in earnings (unless the contingent consideration is a hedging arrangement, in which case the changes in value are recognized in other comprehensive income).

III. Post-Acquisition Measurement Period Adjustment

There is much complexity associated with determining acquisition-date fair value of the assets acquired and liabilities assumed. Added to this complexity is the timing of the acquisition in relation to the issuance of the financial statements, where the acquisition could occur on December 15 and the financial statements are issued on December 31. Therefore, it is likely that the initial values of the assets acquired and liabilities assumed are measured at a provisional value based on best estimates available as of the reporting date.

A. The measurement period for the provisional values is one year post-acquisition for information that existed as of the acquisition date and, if known, would have impacted the valuation of the assets and liabilities as of that date.

B. During the measurement period, the acquirer recognizes increases (or decreases) in the value of the provisional amounts with the respective adjustments to depreciation, amortization, and goodwill. The impact on the income statement is reported in the period in which the adjustments to the provisional amounts are determined.

Example
The Appendix to ASU 2015-16 provides the following example of how the measurement period adjustment would be reflected in the current financial statements.

Assume the Acquirer purchases the Target on September 20, 20X7, and obtained a tentative fair value estimate for plant equipment of $30,000 and estimated the remaining life to be 5 years. In the December 31, 20X7, financial statements, the Acquirer reported the plant equipment at $30,000 and accumulated depreciation and depreciation of $1,500 ($30,000/5 years × 3/12).

At the end of March, the appraisal of the equipment is completed and the acquisition-date fair value is determined to be $40,000. In the March 31, 20X8, interim financial statements, the acquirer would report the effect of the measurement period adjustment as follows:

1. The carrying amount of the plant equipment would be increased by $9,000. The $10,000 increase in fair value less the $1,000 difference in additional depreciation that would have been taken [$40,000 / 5 years × 6/12] − ($30,000 / 5 years × 6/12) = $1,000].

2. The carrying value of goodwill would be increased by $10,000.

3. Depreciation expense for the period ended March 31, 20X8, would be increased by $1,000 to reflect the impact on earnings for the change in the provisional amount of the plant equipment.

IV. Pushdown Accounting

A. In November 2014, the FASB issued ASU 2014-17 to address pushdown accounting to provide guidance on when and how a new accounting and reporting basis (pushdown accounting) should be used. ASU 2014-17 applies to both public and nonpublic companies and increases the consistency of the application of pushdown accounting in practice. The ASU allows an acquiree the option to apply pushdown accounting anytime there is a change in control as defined in ASC 805 and 810. If the acquiree elects to apply pushdown accounting, it would revalue all of the assets and liabilities to acquisition date fair value as determined by the acquirer in its application of ASC 805. The acquiree may elect to apply pushdown accounting each time there is a change in control. If the acquiree elects to apply pushdown accounting in a reporting period subsequent to the change in control, then the election is a change in accounting principle and should be accounted for in accordance with ASC 250.

B. Pushdown accounting allows the acquiree to recognize a new basis for all assets and liabilities and any goodwill that results from the application of acquisition method accounting. If there was a bargain purchase the acquiree would recognize an adjustment to additional paid-in capital, not a gain on the income statement. All subsequent accounting for the new basis of the assets and liabilities of the acquired company would be in accordance with the applicable U.S. GAAP. If the acquirer was not required to apply ASC 805 (e.g., the acquirer was an investment company), the acquiree can still elect pushdown accounting and would recognize the new basis for assets and liabilities had ASC 805 been applied by the acquirer.

> **Note**
> *Acquisition accounting at the parent level is the same, regardless of whether it is pushed down to the acquired subsidiary.*

Example

Assume that Passing Corporation (P) acquired Score Company (S) for $400,000 on July 1, 2015, and on that date S had the following summarized balance sheet with the book values and fair values shown:

	Book Value	Fair Value
Accounts Receivable (net)	$40,000	$40,000
Inventories	80,000	80,000
Plant and Equipment (net)	160,000	200,000
Land	120,000	160,000
TOTAL ASSETS	$400,000	$480,000
Accounts Payable	$20,000	$20,000
Short-term Note	30,000	30,000
Bonds Payable	70,000	90,000
TOTAL LIABILITIES	$120,000	$140,000

If S elects to use pushdown accounting, the incremental fair values of the assets and liabilities would be recorded by S. In addition, S would record the goodwill that results from the business combination. Below is the entry that would be recorded by S on July 1, 2015:

Plant and Equipment (200,000 – 160,000)	40,000	
Land (160,000 – 120,000)	40,000	
Goodwill (400,000 – (480,000 – 140,000))	60,000	
Bonds Payable (90,000 – 70,000)		20,000
Revaluation Capital		120,000

C. If the acquiree applies pushdown accounting, it should disclose the effects of the pushdown accounting on its separate financial statements so that the financial statement user can evaluate the effects of pushdown accounting. If the acquiree does not elect to apply pushdown accounting, the entity should disclose that it has undergone a change in control event and that it elects to prepare its separate financial statements using its historical basis.

D. The standard is effective for any change in control events that occur after November 18, 2014. If this guidance is applied retrospectively to the most recent change in control event, it is treated as a change in accounting principle.

Disclosure Requirements—Acquisition Method

When a business combination has been carried out, considerable disclosure is required of the acquirer. Disclosures are required not only for the period in which the combination occurs, but also in subsequent period during the measurement period. This lesson identifies the most significant disclosures when a business combination occurs

After studying this lesson, you should be able to:

1. Know the required disclosures that enable financial statement users to evaluate: a) the nature and financial effects of a business combination; b) the financial effects of adjustments related to business combinations.

I. **Business Combination Disclosure Requirements**—The acquirer in a business combination is required to disclose considerable information related both directly to the combination and to certain post-combination effects. The following summarizes those disclosure requirements.

   A. Required information that enables users of the acquirer's financial statements to evaluate the nature and financial effects of a business combination that occurs either: (1) during the current reporting period, or (2) after the reporting period, but before the financial statements for that period are released, including the following:

      1. The name and a description of the acquiree, the acquisition date, and the percentage voting equity interest acquired (if any)

      2. The primary reasons for the business combination and a description of how the acquirer obtained control of the acquiree

      3. A quantitative description of the factors that make up the goodwill recognized (if any), such as expected synergies from combining operations, intangible assets that do not qualify for separate recognition (e.g., an assembled workforce), and other factors

      4. The acquisition-date fair value of the total consideration transferred and the acquisition-date fair value of **each major class** of consideration transferred

      5. For contingent consideration and indemnification assets the following:

        a. The amount recognized as of the acquisition date

        b. A description of the arrangement and the basis for determining the amount of payment

        c. An estimate of the (undiscounted) range of outcomes or, if a range cannot be estimated, that fact and the reasons why a range cannot be estimated

        d. If the maximum amount of payment is unlimited, disclosure of that fact

      6. For most receivables, disclosure for **each major class** of receivable the fair value, the gross contractual amounts receivable, and the best estimate as of the acquisition date of the contractual cash flows not expected to be collected

      7. The amount recognized at the acquisition date for **each major class** of assets acquired and liabilities assumed

      8. For assets and liabilities arising from contingencies, the amount recognized or why no amount was recognized, the nature of recognized and unrecognized contingencies, and an estimate of the (undiscounted) range of outcomes or, if a range cannot be estimated, that fact and the reasons why a range cannot be estimated

      9. The total amount of goodwill that is expected to be deductible for tax purposes

      10. The amount of goodwill assigned to each reportable segment (if segment information is required)

      11. For any transactions between the acquirer and acquiree (or its former owners) that are recognized separately from the acquisition of assets and assumption of liabilities in the business combination the following:

        a. A description of each transaction

    b. How the acquirer accounted for each transaction

    c. The amounts recognized for each transaction and the line item(s) in the financial statements where each amount is recognized, including those amounts recognized as expenses and, separately, issuance costs not recognized as expenses

12. For a bargain purchase, the amount of gain recognized, the line item in the income statement where the gain is recognized, and a description of why the transaction resulted in a gain

13. For business combinations in which the acquirer owns less than 100% of the equity interest of the acquiree at the acquisition date, the fair value of the noncontrolling interest at the acquisition date and the valuation techniques and inputs used to measure that fair value

14. For a business combination achieved in stages, the fair value of the equity interest held by the acquirer immediately prior to the combination, the amount of any gain or loss resulting from remeasuring the interest to fair value at the date of the combination, and the line item in the income statement where the gain or loss is recognized

15. For public business enterprises (basically, publicly traded entities), the following:

    a. The amount of revenue and earnings of the acquiree occurring since the acquisition date that is included in consolidated statements for the period

    b. The revenue and earnings of the combined entity for the current reporting period as though the acquisition date for all business combinations that occurred during the period had been at the beginning of the annual reporting period (this would be *supplemental pro forma information*)

    c. For comparative statements, the revenue and earnings of the combined entity for the comparable prior reporting period(s) as though the acquisition date for all business combinations that occurred during the current year had occurred as of the beginning of the comparable prior annual reporting period(s) (this would be *supplemental pro forma information*)

    d. For any of the above information that is impracticable to provide, disclosure of that fact and the reasons why the disclosure is impracticable

B. Required information that enables users of the acquirer's financial statements to evaluate the financial effects of adjustments recognized in the current reporting period that relate to business combinations that occurred in the current or prior reporting periods, including the following:

1. If the initial accounting for a business combination is incomplete for particular assets, liabilities, noncontrolling interests, or items of consideration, and only provisional amounts have been recognized, the following information:

    a. The reasons that the initial accounting is incomplete

    b. The assets, liabilities, equity interests, or items of consideration for which the initial accounting is incomplete

    c. The nature and amount of any measurement period adjustments recognized during the reporting period

2. For contingent consideration assets or liabilities that remain unsettled, the following should be provided in each reporting period:

    a. Any changes in the recognized amounts, including any differences arising as a result of settlement

    b. Any changes in the (undiscounted) range of outcomes and the reasons for those changes

    c. The disclosures required by ASC 820, *Fair Value Measurement*, which deal with how fair value was determined

3. Reconciliation of the carrying amount of goodwill at the beginning and end of the reporting period.

C. Any additional information necessary to meet the objectives set forth in A and B, above.

Recording Business Combinations

Previous lessons have identified and illustrated the legal forms of business—merger, consolidation, and acquisition, Those lessons have described the requirements of the acquisition method of accounting for a business combination. This lesson is concerned with the entries that will be made in recording a business combination under the alternative legal forms.

After studying this lesson, you should be able to:

1. Recall the nature of the various legal forms of business and understand the effects of the alternative legal forms on the accounting entry.

2. Make the entry to record a merger/consolidation under the following circumstances:

   - When there is goodwill and the acquirer has no precombination ownership of the acquiree.

   - When there is goodwill and the acquirer has precombination ownership of the acquiree.

   - When there is a bargain purchase and the acquirer has no precombination ownership of the acquiree.

   - When there is a bargain purchase and the acquirer has precombination ownership of the acquiree.

3. Make the entry to record an acquisition, both when the acquirer has no precombination ownership of the acquiree and when the acquirer has precombination ownership of the acquiree.

I. **Legal Form and Acquisition Accounting**—The legal form of a business combination determines the accounts that the acquirer will use in recording a business combination; the acquisition method of accounting determines the amounts at which those accounts will be recorded and is required, regardless of the legal form.

II. **Recording a Legal Merger or Legal Consolidation**

   A. Recall the characteristics of a legal merger and legal consolidation:

   1. **Legal merger**—One preexisting entity (acquirer) acquires either a group of assets that constitutes a business or controlling interest in the stock of another preexisting entity (acquiree) and merges the acquired assets or other entity (assets and liabilities) into the acquirer entity.

   2. **Legal consolidation**—A new entity is created to consolidate two or more preexisting entities.

      a. The preexisting entities cease to exist as legal entities.

      b. Under the acquisition method of accounting, if only equity interest is issued by the new entity, one of the preexisting entities must be determined to be the acquirer, not the new legal entity.

   3. **In either legal form**—Only one entity remains after the business combination.

   B. The basic entry by the acquirer to record a legal merger (or group of assets that constitute a business) or a legal consolidation using the acquisition method of accounting is:

   1. Entry:

   DR: Assets acquired (at FV)
      CR: Liabilities assumed (at FV) $\left.\right\}$ = A − L = Net Assets
      CR: Consideration Paid (at FV)

2. Assets acquired and recognized may be:

    a. Tangible (e.g., equipment) or intangible (e.g., patent)

    b. Severable—separately "sellable" (e.g., investments) or nonseverable (e.g., trademark)

3. Assets recognized would *not* include preexisting goodwill of the acquiree.

4. Assets acquired and liabilities assumed by the acquirer would be measured at fair value, with the following exceptions:

    a. Acquired income tax-related items, including deferred tax asset or deferred tax liability related to assets acquired or liabilities assumed, and tax effects of temporary differences, carry forwards, and tax uncertainties, would be measured under the provisions of FASB No. 109 and FASB Interpretation No. 48

    b. Employee benefit liabilities (or assets), using the provisions of other applicable FASBs

    c. Indemnification asset, using the same measurement basis as the indemnified asset or liability

    d. Reacquisition rights, using the remaining contractual term of the contract that granted the right

    e. Share-based employee payment awards, using the provisions of ASC 718

    f. Assets held for sale, using the provisions of ASC 360

5. Consideration used by the acquirer could include the following and would be measured at fair value (except when transferred assets (or liabilities) remain under the control of the acquirer; then, they would be measured at carrying value to the acquirer):

    a. Cash and cash equivalents transferred

    b. Other assets transferred

    c. Liabilities incurred

    d. Equity interest issued, including common and preferred stock, options, and warrants

    e. Any combination of the above forms of consideration

C. **Goodwill**—Would be recognized if the investment value in the acquiree is greater than the fair value of the net assets of the acquiree at the acquisition date.

1. Investment value in the acquiree is the sum of the fair value of consideration transferred to effect the combination + the fair value of any precombination equity owned by the acquirer + the fair value of the noncontrolling interest in the acquiree, if any.

2. The fair value of the acquiree's net assets is the difference between the acquiree's total assets at fair value and total liabilities at fair value:

> Total Assets (@ FV) − Total Liabilities (@ FV) = FV of Net Assets

3. If investment value > fair value of net assets, goodwill is recognized.

Example
No Precombination Ownership of the Acquiree by the Acquirer

a. Facts: On January 2, 20X9, Investco, Inc. acquired all of the outstanding common stock of Lowco, Inc. in the market for $1,000,000 cash and merged the assets acquired and liabilities assumed into Investco. At that date the fair values of Lowco's identifiable assets and liabilities were:

Accounts receivable	$ 200,000
Inventories	400,000
Property, plant, and equipment	800,000
Other identifiable assets	200,000
TOTAL ASSETS	$1,600,000
Accounts payable	300,000
Other current liabilities	200,000
Long-term liabilities	200,000
TOTAL LIABILITIES	$ 700,000
FAIR VALUE OF NET ASSETS	$ 900,000

b. Goodwill calculation:

Investment value = $1,000,000 − Fair value of net assets = $900,000 = $100,000 Goodwill.

c. Entry:

DR: Accounts receivable	$ 200,000	
Inventories	400,000	
Property, plant, and equipment	800,000	
Other identifiable assets	200,000	
Goodwill	100,000	
CR: Accounts payable		$ 300,000
Other current liabilities		200,000
Long-term liabilities		200,000
Cash		1,000,000

Example
With Precombination Ownership of the Acquiree by the Acquirer

a. Facts: (The following accounts and amounts are taken from a disclosure illustration in ASC 805; the other facts are assumed.)

On January 2, 20X8, Topco, Inc. acquired 15% of the voting equity of Noco, Inc. for $1,200 and subsequently treated the investment as available for sale. On June 30, 20X9, Topco, Inc. acquired the remaining 85% of Noco, using the following consideration:

Cash	$ 8,300
Common stock (1,000 shares × $4)	4,000
Contingent consideration obligation	1,000
Total consideration at combination	$13,300

At that date, the fair value of Topco's original 15% was $2,000. Topco incurred $1,250 of acquisition-related costs. Topco's common stock is $1.00 par, with a market value of $4.00 per share at the acquisition date

The fair values and other appropriate values assigned to Noco's identifiable assets and liabilities were:

Financial assets	$ 3,500
Inventory	1,000
Property, plant, and equipment	10,000
Identifiable intangible assets	3,300
Total Assets	$17,800

Financial liabilities	$ 4,000
Liability arising from a contingency	1,000
Total Liabilities	$ 5,000

b. Goodwill calculation:

Investment value:

Acquirer's consideration at combination	$13,300
Acquirer's precombination equity @ FV	2,000
Total Investment Value	$15,300

Fair Value of Net Assets ($17,800 − $5,000)	$12,800
Goodwill = Investment Value > FV of NA	$ 2.500

c. Entry:

DR:	Financial assets*	$ 3,500	
	Inventory*	1,000	
	Property, plant, and equipment*	10,000	
	Identifiable intangible assets*	3,300	
	Goodwill****	2,500	
	CR: Financial liabilities*		4,000
	Liability arising from contingency*		1,000
	Contingent consideration obligation**		1,000
	Cash**		8,300
	Investment—available for sale***		2,000
	Common stock ($1 par)**		1,000
	Additional paid-in capital**		3,000

*Identifiable assets and liabilities acquired.

**Consideration transferred at combination.

***Precombination Investment in Noco at fair value—now part of the cost of the assets and liabilities acquired.

****Computed goodwill

d. Comments on Entry:

[1]The acquirer would have to classify or designate the assets acquired and liabilities assumed to subsequently apply the appropriate GAAP. For example, if any financial assets are investments, the acquirer would need to classify as held to maturity, held for trading, or available for sale.

[2]Since the precombination investment in Noco was classified as available for sale, the difference between the cost ($1,200) and the fair value at the date of combination ($2,000), or $800, would be removed from Accumulated Other Comprehensive Income and recognized by Noco as a realized gain.

[3] Goodwill recognized by Topco will not be amortized, but will be assessed at least annually for impairment.

[4]The $1,250 cost incurred to carry out the combination is not part of the consideration used to acquire Noco, but would be expensed by Topco when incurred.

D. A Bargain Purchase—Would be recognized if the fair value of the net assets of the acquiree at the acquisition date is greater than the investment value in the acquiree.

1. Investment value in the acquiree is the sum of the fair value of consideration transferred to effect the combination + the fair value of any precombination equity owned by the acquirer + the fair value of the noncontrolling interest in the acquiree, if any.

2. The fair value of the acquiree's net assets is the difference between the acquiree's total assets at fair value and total liabilities at fair value:

Total Assets (@ FV) − Total Liabilities (@ FV) = FV of Net Assets

3. If fair value of net assets > investment value, a bargain purchase gain is recognized.

Example

No precombination ownership of the acquiree by the acquirer

a. Facts: On January 2, 20X9, Investco, Inc. acquired all of the outstanding common stock of Lowco, Inc. in the market for $850,000 cash and merged the assets acquired and liabilities assumed into Investco. At that date the fair values of Lowco's identifiable assets and liabilities were:

Accounts receivable	$ 200,000
Inventories	400,000
Property, plant, and equipment	800,000
Other identifiable assets	200,000
TOTAL ASSETS	$1,600,000
Accounts payable	300,000
Other current liabilities	200,000
Long-term liabilities	200,000
TOTAL LIABILITIES	$ 700,000
FAIR VALUE OF NET ASSETS	$ 900,000

b. Bargain purchase calculation: Fair value of net assets = $900,000 − investment value = $850,000 = $50,000 bargain purchase amount. This amount would be recognized as a gain in the period of the business combination.

c. Entry:

DR: Accounts receivable	$ 200,000	
Inventories	400,000	
Property, plant, and equipment	800,000	
Other identifiable assets	200,000	
CR: Accounts payable		$300,000
Other current liabilities		200,000
Long-term liabilities		200,000
Cash		850,000
Bargain Purchase Gain		50,000

Example

With precombination ownership of the acquiree by the acquirer

a. Facts: (The following accounts and amounts are taken from a disclosure illustration in ASC 805; the other facts are assumed.)

On January 2, 20X8, Topco, Inc. acquired 15% of the voting equity of Noco, Inc. for $1,200 and subsequently treated the investment as available for sale. On June 30, 20X9, Topco, Inc. acquired the remaining 85% of Noco, using the following consideration:

Cash	$ 5,000
Common stock (1,000 shares × $4)	4,000
Contingent consideration obligation	1,000
Total consideration at combination	$10,000

At that date, the fair value of Topco's original 15% was $2,000. Topco incurred $1,250 of acquisition-related costs. Topco's common stock is $1.00 par, with a market value of $4.00 per share at the acquisition date.

The fair values and other appropriate values assigned to Noco's identifiable assets and liabilities were:

Financial assets	$ 3,500
Inventory	1,000
Property, plant, and equipment	10,000
Identifiable intangible assets	3,300
Total Assets	$ 17,800

Financial liabilities	$ 4,000
Liability arising from a contingency	1,000
Total Liabilities	$ 5,000

b. Bargain purchase calculation:

Investment value:	
Acquirer's consideration at combination	$10,000
Acquirer's precombination equity @ FV	2,000
Total Investment Value	$12,000
Fair Value of Net Assets ($17,800 – $5,000)	$12,800
Bargain Purchase Gain:	
FV of NA > Investment Value	$ 800

c. Entry:

DR:	Financial assets*	$ 3,500
	Inventory*	1,000
	Property, plant, and equipment*	10,000
	Identifiable intangible assets*	3,300
	CR: Financial liabilities*	4,000
	Liability arising from contingency*	1,000
	Contingent consideration obligation**	1,000
	Cash**	5,000
	Investment—available for Sale***	2,000
	Common stock ($1 par)**	1,000
	Additional paid-in capital**	3,000
	Bargain purchase gain****	800

> *Identifiable assets and liabilities acquired.
>
> **Consideration transferred at combination.
>
> ***Precombination investment in Noco at fair value—now part of the cost of the assets and liabilities acquired.
>
> ****Computed bargain purchase gain

d. Comments on Entry:

[1] The acquirer would have to classify or designate the assets acquired and liabilities assumed to subsequently apply the appropriate GAAP. For example, if any financial assets are investments, the acquirer would need to classify as held to maturity, held for trading, or available for sale.

[2] Since the precombination investment in Noco was classified as available for sale, the difference between the cost ($1,200) and the fair value at the date of combination ($2,000), or $800, would be removed from Accumulated Other Comprehensive Income and recognized by Noco as a realized gain.

[3] The bargain purchase gain will be recognized by Topco in its earnings for the period of the business combination.

[4] The $1,250 cost incurred to carry out the combination is not part of the consideration used to acquire Noco, but would be expensed by Topco when incurred.

III. Recording a Legal Acquisition.

A. Recall the characteristics of a legal acquisition:

1. One preexisting entity (acquirer) acquires controlling interest in the voting stock of another preexisting entity (acquiree) and both entities continue to exist and operate as separate legal entities.

2. Example: Company P acquires more than 50% of the voting stock of Company S and Company P does not merge Company S into Company P; rather, Company S continues to exist as a separate corporation with Company P holding the majority of its voting stock.

3. In this legal form, both entities continue to exist, operate, and maintain separate accounting records, but one entity has controlling interest in the other entity.

4. Since the controlling entity may not have 100% ownership of the acquired entity's voting stock, there can be other shareholders with an interest in the acquired entity; those shareholders are the noncontrolling interest (formerly called *minority interest*).

B. The basic entry by the acquirer to record a legal acquisition using the acquisition method of accounting is:

1. Entry:

> DR: Investment in Subsidiary X (at FV of Consideration Paid)
> CR: Consideration Paid (at FV)

2. Consideration used by the acquirer could include the following and would be measured at fair value (except when transferred assets (or liabilities) remain under the control of the acquirer—then, they would be measured at carrying value to the acquirer):

a. Cash and cash equivalents transferred

b. Other assets transferred

c. Liabilities incurred

d. Equity interest issued, including common and preferred stock, options and warrants

e. Any combination of the above forms of consideration

3. As a result of the acquisition and related entry:

a. A parent-subsidiary relationship is established.

b. The firms operate and maintain accounting books and records as separate entities.

c. The parent carries Investment in Subsidiary on its books using the cost, equity, or other method.

4. The subsidiary will be reported in the consolidated statements of the parent, unless the parent lacks effective control of the subsidiary. (The consolidating process, including when a parent lacks effective control over a subsidiary, is covered in later lessons.)

Example
No precombination ownership of the acquiree by the acquirer and no noncontrolling ownership.

1. Facts: On January 2, 20X9, Investco, Inc. acquired all of the outstanding common stock of Lowco, Inc. in the market for $1,000,000 cash in a legal acquisition.

2. Entry:

> DR: Investment in Lowco, Inc. (Subsidiary) $1,000,000
> CR: Cash $1,000,000

3. At that date, Investco also would have to determine the following information:

a. The book values of Lowco's assets and liabilities

b. The fair value of Lowco's assets and liabilities

c. Any goodwill or bargain purchase amount implicit in the relationship between its investment and the fair value of Lowco's net assets

4. The information determined and "captured" in 3, above, will be the basis for the preparation of consolidated financial statements; the preparation of those statements will include, among other things:

a. Revaluing Lowco's assets and liabilities to fair value as of the date of the business combination

b. Recognizing any goodwill or bargain purchase amount implicit in the business combination

Example
With precombination ownership of the acquiree by the acquirer and a noncontrolling interest.

1. Facts: (The following accounts and amounts are taken from a disclosure illustration in ASC 805; the other facts are assumed.)

   On January 2, 20X8, Topco, Inc. acquired 15% of the voting equity of Noco, Inc. for $1,200 and subsequently treated the investment as available for sale. On June 30, 20X9, Topco, Inc. acquired an additional 65% of Noco, using the following consideration:

Cash	$ 5,000
Common stock (1,000 shares × $4)	4,000
Contingent consideration obligation	1,000
Total consideration at combination	$10,000

   At that date, the fair value of Topco's original 15% was $2,000. Topco incurred $1,250 cost of acquisition-related costs. The remaining 20% ownership in Noco is the noncontrolling interest. Topco's common stock is $1.00 par, with a market value of $4.00 per share at the acquisition date.

2. Entry:

DR: Investment in Noco, Inc. (Subsidiary)	$12,000	
CR: Contingent consideration obligation		1,000
Cash		5,000
Investment—available for sale		2,000
Common stock ($1 par)		1,000
Additional paid-in capital		3,000

3. Comments on Entry:

   a. Since the precombination investment in Noco was classified as available for sale, the difference between the cost ($1,200) and the fair value at the date of combination ($2,000), or $800, would be removed from Accumulated Other Comprehensive Income and recognized by Noco as a realized gain.

   b. The $1,250 cost incurred to carry out the combination is not part of the consideration used to acquire Noco, but would be expensed by Topco when incurred.

4. At that date, Topco would also have to determine the following information:

   a. The book values of Noco's assets and liabilities.

   b. The fair value of Noco's assets and liabilities.

   c. The fair value of the 20% noncontrolling interest.

   d. Any goodwill or bargain purchase amount implicit in the relationship between the investment value in Noco (Topco's consideration transferred—$10,000, plus its precombination investment at fair value—$2,000, plus the fair value of the noncontrolling interest) and the fair value of Noco's net assets.

5. The information determined and "captured" in 4, above, will be the basis for the preparation of consolidated financial statements; the preparation of those statements will include, among other things:

   a. Revaluing Noco's assets and liabilities to fair value as of the date of the business combination

   b. Recognizing the fair value of the noncontrolling interest in Noco as an equity item

   c. Recognizing any goodwill or bargain purchase amount implicit in the business combination

6. On Topco's books, it will carry its investment in its subsidiary Noco as an asset using the cost method, the equity method, or some other method; that investment will be eliminated in the consolidating process and consolidated financial statements will be issued for Topco and Noco.

IFRS—Business Combinations

The accounting standard on Business Combinations was a joint project of the FASB and IFRS. Therefore, there are very few differences between U.S. GAAP and IFRS. The major differences arise from the implementation of acquisition method accounting.

After studying this lesson, you should be able to:

1. Identify the major differences in the application of acquisition method accounting under IFRS versus U.S. GAAP.

I. IFRS Business Combinations

A. The most significant differences in the application of the acquisition method of accounting between U.S. GAAP and IFRS are related to the differences in the accounting for the acquired item. Below is a table of the major differences. Each difference is discussed further in the study text.

U.S. GAAP	IFRS
Contingent assets and liabilities can be recognized if criterion are met.	Contingent assets are not recognized.
Goodwill allocation is to the reporting units.	Goodwill is allocated to the cash generating units.
Goodwill impairment testing has a qualitative *prestep* and then, if needed, a two-step approach.	Goodwill impairment testing is a one-step test.
Must disclose pro forma information for current and prior periods presented	Must disclose pro forma information only for current period
Not required to disclose assumptions related to acquired contingencies	Required to disclose assumptions related to acquired contingencies

B. Contingency Recognition and Measurement

1. There are significant differences between U.S. GAAP and IFRS in accounting for contingencies acquired in a business combination.

   a. Under U.S. GAAP, both contingent assets and contingent liabilities are recognized. A distinction is made between contingencies that are contractual (e.g., a warranty obligation) and those that are not contractual (e.g., an unsettled law suit). Contractual contingencies are recognized at fair value if that value can be determined during the measurement period. Noncontractual contingencies are recognized only if it is more likely than not that they qualify as an asset or liability.

   b. Under IFRS, contingent assets are not recognized. Contingent liabilities are recognized if they:

      i. Are a present obligation that arises from a past event, *and*

      ii. Fair value can be measured reliably.

2. Subsequent to recognition, the treatments between U.S. GAAP and IFRS differ, as follows:

   a. Under U.S. GAAP, recognized contingent assets and liabilities will continue to be reported at their acquisition-date fair value until new information about the outcome of the contingency becomes known. When new information about the outcome becomes known, the contingency will be remeasured using criteria based on whether the contingency is an asset or liability (as described in IIB, above).

b. Under IFRS, recognized contingent liabilities subsequently are remeasured at the higher of the amount initially recognized or the best estimate of the amount required to settle the contingent liability. Since contingent assets are not recognized under IFRS, no subsequent treatment applies.

C. Goodwill Allocation—Both U.S. GAAP and IFRS require that recognized goodwill be allocated to component units of the entity, but there is a difference in the specification of those component units.

1. Under U.S. GAAP, goodwill must be allocated to the **reporting units** of the entity. A reporting unit is an operating segment of the entity that:

   a. Constitutes a business;

   b. Has discrete financial information available; *and*

   c. Has operating results regularly reviewed by management.

2. The difference between U.S. GAAP and IFRS in the allocation of goodwill is likely to result in the allocation of goodwill to more units under IFRS than under GAAP, which may result in more frequent goodwill impairment.

3. Under both U.S. GAAP and IFRS goodwill must be tested for impairment at the unit level (reporting unit under U.S. GAAP; cash-generating unit under IFRS).

4. Goodwill Impairment—Both U.S. GAAP and IFRS require that recognized goodwill be tested for impairment at least annually, but there are differences in the testing methodology that can create differences in loss recognition.

   a. Under U.S. GAAP, goodwill may be tested for impairment using one of two general approaches:

   i. The first general approach begins by conducting a qualitative assessment to determine if it is more likely than not (i.e., a likelihood of greater than 50%) that the fair value of the reporting unit has declined below its carrying value. If it is determined to be more likely than not that fair value is less than carrying value, then the first of a two-step process must be followed to make a quantitative determination of whether or not an impairment has occurred and, if so, measure the amount of the related loss. If it is determined in the qualitative assessment that it is NOT more likely than not that the fair value of the reporting unit is less than its carrying value, then no further assessment for impairment is required.

   ii. The second general approach, which is an alternative to the first described above, is to skip the qualitative assessment and carry out the two-step quantitative process to determine if goodwill is impaired and, if so, to measure that impairment loss.

   b. Under IFRS, goodwill is tested for impairment using a one-step approach, measured as the excess of the carrying amount (CV) of the cash-generating unit over the recoverable amount (RA) of the cash-generating unit. If CV > RA, adjust goodwill and recognize a loss in operating results.

   c. Goodwill impairment testing and measurement is covered in detail in the lesson "Goodwill" in the "Intangible Assets—Goodwill and Other" topic.

D. Disclosure Requirements—There are differences in disclosure requirements between the standards. The most significant of their disclosure differences are identified here.

1. **Pro forma disclosures**—Under U.S. GAAP, public business enterprises (basically, publicly traded entities) are required to disclose certain supplemental pro forma information, including revenue and earnings information. This pro forma information must be disclosed for the current and prior periods presented. Similar disclosures are not required for other (nonpublic) entities. Under IFRS, however, all acquirers are required to provide pro forma information, but only for the period of the combination, not for prior periods presented. The pro forma disclosures required by IFRS include:

a. The amount of revenue and profit or loss of the acquiree since the acquisition date included in the consolidated statement of comprehensive income for the reporting period;

b. The revenue and profit or loss of the combined entity for the current reporting period through the acquisition date for all business combinations that occurred during the year as if they had been as of the beginning of the annual reporting period.

2. **Acquired contingencies**—Under U.S. GAAP, when contingent assets or contingent liabilities are acquired in a business combination, the acquirer is not required to disclose the major assumptions made about the future events or the amount of any expected reimbursement used in valuing the contingencies. Under IFRS, the acquirer is required to disclose major assumptions made about future events and the amount of expected reimbursement, if any, used in valuing the contingencies.

3. **Goodwill**—Under U.S. GAAP (ASC 280), public business enterprise acquirers that recognize goodwill must disclose the amount of the goodwill allocated to each reportable segment as of the acquisition date. Under IFRS (No. 3), acquirers are not required to disclose the amount of goodwill allocated to each cash-generating unit (comparable to a reportable segment under U.S. GAAP); however, other IFRS (IAS No. 36) requires disclosure by all entities (not just public business enterprises) of goodwill for each cash-generating unit as of each balance sheet date.

Financial Instruments

Financial Instruments Introduction

This lesson begins a series of lessons that cover financial instruments, including derivatives, and the use of financial instruments for hedging and speculative purposes. This lesson introduces the material by defining financial instruments, giving common examples of financial assets and financial liabilities that are considered financial instruments.

After studying this lesson, you should be able to:

1. Define financial instruments.

2. Identify asset and liability accounts that are financial instruments.

I.   **Introduction**—The term **financial instruments** includes a diverse variety of items found in business activity. Financial instruments include cash, accounts/notes receivable, accounts/notes payable, bonds, common stock, preferred stock, stock options, foreign currency forward contracts, futures contracts, various financial swaps, and so on. Some of these items are common, well understood, and have long-established accounting treatments. Other financial instruments are not so common nor are they well understood, and often they challenge accounting principles. Those challenges are further complicated by the ongoing development of even more exotic financial instruments.

II. **Financial Instruments**

   A. **Defined**—Other contracts that are also considered financial instruments meet the following criteria as presented in ASC 825:

   1. **Cash**—Including foreign currency and demand deposits

   2. **Evidence of an ownership interest in an entity**—(Including investments in common and preferred stock, warrants and options to purchase stock, and partnership and limited liability company interest)

   3. **Contracts that result in an exchange of cash or ownership interest in an entity and that both**

      a. **Impose on one entity a contractual obligation or duty (liability)**

         i.   To deliver cash (e.g., trade accounts payable, loan obligations, bonds payable, etc.) or another financial instrument (e.g., a note payable in US Treasury bonds) to a **second entity**, *or*

         ii. To exchange financial instruments on potentially unfavorable terms with a **second entity**.

      b. **Conveys to a second entity a contractual right (asset)**

         i.   To receive cash (e.g., accounts receivable, investment in bonds, etc.) or another financial instrument from the **first entity**, *or*

         ii. To exchange financial instruments on potentially favorable terms with the **first entity**.

   4. Derivatives are a special form of financial instrument, which will be defined and described in a subsequent lesson.

B. **Common Examples**—Many of the items covered in prior lessons were financial instruments, either financial assets or financial liabilities. Those items (accounts), as well as other financial assets and financial liabilities, include:

1. **Financial assets**

   a. Cash and cash equivalents

   b. Accounts receivable

   c. Investments in debt (notes, bonds, etc.) and equity securities (common and preferred stock, etc.)

   d. Interest in partnerships, limited liability entities, and joint ventures

   e. Option contracts (w/favorable terms)

   f. Futures and forward contracts (w/favorable terms)

   g. Swap contracts (w/favorable terms)

2. **Financial Liabilities**

   a. Accounts payable

   b. Notes and bonds payable

   c. Option contracts (w/unfavorable terms)

   d. Futures and forward contracts (w/unfavorable terms)

   e. Swap contracts (w/unfavorable terms)

III. **Transaction Costs**—The treatment of cost associated with acquiring a financial asset or incurring a financial liability depends on the nature and treatment of the particular financial instrument:

A. For all financial instruments (assets or liabilities) to be measured at fair value, the transaction costs associated with acquiring or incurring the item are excluded from the cost of the financial instrument.

B. Except for certain costs associated with the purchase of (investment in) debt and lending activities, transaction costs directly attributable to the financial item are expensed when incurred.

C. Costs associated with debt issuance (incurring financial liabilities) are treated as deferred charges.

IV. **Impairment Assessment**—Financial assets must be assessed for impairment and, if it is determined that fair value is less than carrying value and the decline is other than temporary, the asset must be written down and (generally) a loss recognized in current income.

A. If the financial asset is classified as available for sale, it must be assessed for impairment because, even though it is carried at fair value, changes in fair value are not reported through income; an impairment loss must be reported through income.

B. If the financial asset is a debt security, then the treatment of the loss depends on whether or not the entity expects to dispose of the security before its carrying amount is recovered.

1. If the entity does not expect to hold the debt security until recovery of its carrying amount, the loss is recognized in current income.

2. If the entity expects to hold the debt security until recovery of its carrying amount, the loss must be separated into two components:

   a. Any portion of loss in fair value attributable to credit standing of the issuer is recognized in income; *and*

   b. Any other loss in fair value is recognized in other comprehensive income, net of tax.

V. **Preview**—The following lessons dealing with financial instruments cover:

A. The required and recommended disclosures that apply to all financial instruments, including derivatives.

B. The definition of derivatives, as a special form of financial instrument, and the measurement requirements, which apply to all derivatives.

C. The different accounting requirements, which apply depending on the specific purpose for which a derivative instrument is held. Four possible purposes are identified for accounting:

   1. To speculate;

   2. As a fair value hedge;

   3. As a cash flow hedge; *or*

   4. As a foreign currency hedge.

IFRS—Financial Instruments

Although there are many similarities between U.S. GAAP and IFRS in accounting for financial instruments, there are also notable differences. This lesson describes the most significant differences between U.S. GAAP and IFRS accounting requirements for financial instruments.

After studying this lesson, you should be able to:

1. Identify significant areas of difference between U.S. GAAP and IFRS in accounting for financial instruments.

2. Describe the measurement and recognition criteria in the accounting for financial instruments under IFRS.

I. Introduction

A. **Background**—The first version of IFRS 9, *Financial Instruments*, was issued in November 2009 with the completion of the first phase on the classification and measurement of financial assets. In years following, subsequent phases were completed addressing financial liabilities, the fair value option, and derivatives and hedging. In 2014, the final comprehensive standard was released with the completion of the single asset impairment model phase.

IFRS 9 is effective for annual periods beginning on or after January 1, 2018, with early adoption permitted. IFRS 9 replaces IAS 39, *Financial Instruments: Recognition and Measurement*; however, since early adoption of IFRS 9 is permitted but not yet mandatory, both IAS 39 and IFRS 9 are eligible for testing on the FAR exam.

> **Note**
> IFRS 9 was not a convergence standard with U.S. GAAP. Different guidance applies under U.S. GAAP for financial instruments.

B. **Financial Instrument**—A financial instrument is any contract that gives rise to a financial asset of one entity and a financial liability or equity instrument of another entity.

   1. **Financial asset**—Any asset that is

      a. Cash;

      b. An equity instrument of another entity (such as stock issuance);

      c. A contractual right to receive cash or another financial asset from another entity; *or*

      d. A contractual right to exchange financial instruments with another entity under conditions that are potentially favorable.

   2. **Financial liability**—Any liability that is a contractual obligation to

      a. Deliver cash or another financial asset to another entity; *or*

      b. Exchange financial instruments with another entity under conditions that are potentially unfavorable.

   3. **Recognition**—Financial instruments should be recognized in the statement of financial position when the entity becomes a party to the contractual provision of the instrument.

   4. **Measurement**

      a. **Initial measurement**—An entity should recognize a financial asset or a financial liability initially at its fair value. Except in the case of assets or liabilities at fair value through profit or loss, directly attributable transaction costs are added to an asset or deducted from a liability.

    b. Subsequent measurement—An entity will subsequently measure the financial instrument depending on its classification.

      i. IFRS 9 replaces classifying financial assets under one of four measurement classifications as required in IAS 39. Under IAS 39, financial assets could be classified as financial assets at fair value through profit or loss, available-for-sale financial assets, loans and receivables, or held-to-maturity investments. Under IFRS 9, financial assets are classified as one of the following: amortized cost, fair value through profit or loss, or fair value through other comprehensive income.

      ii. Financial liabilities are classified as either amortized cost or fair value through profit or loss.

II. Classification and Measurement of Financial Assets—Classification and measurement of an entity's financial assets depend on the entity's *business model objective* for managing the financial asset and the *contractual cash flow characteristics* of the financial asset. A business model refers to how an entity manages its financial assets in order to generate cash flows (collecting contractual cash flows, selling financial assets, or both). Classification is made at the time the financial instrument is initially recognized. Reclassification between the two categories is permitted if the business model objective has changed since its initial assessment.

  A. Fair Value through Profit or Loss (FVTPL)

    1. This is the default classification category for financial assets. This classification includes any financial assets held for trading and also derivatives, unless they are part of a properly designated hedging arrangement. Debt instruments will be classified as FVTPL unless they have been correctly designated to be measured at amortized cost or fair value through other comprehensive income.

    2. Changes in value are reported as gains or losses in profit or loss (net income) at each reporting date. This effectively incorporates an annual impairment review.

    3. In addition, transaction costs incurred are expensed and charged to profit or loss when incurred.

  B. Fair Value through Other Comprehensive Income (FVTOCI)

    1. For equity securities, this classification must be elected and is irrevocable.

    2. For debt instruments, this classification is used if the entity's business model objective is achieved by both collecting contractual cash flows and selling financial assets. For debt instruments, the FVTOCI classification is mandatory for certain assets unless using this classification creates an accounting mismatch, in which case the fair value option (FVTPL) may be elected.

      a. Business model test—The entity's objective is achieved by both holding financial assets to collect cash flows and by selling financial assets.

      b. Cash flow characteristic test—The requirement is that the contractual cash flows collected on specified dates are solely payment of principal and interest (SPPI) on the principal amount outstanding. If this test is not met, the asset is measured at fair value.

    3. Changes in value are reported in other comprehensive income at each reporting date; only dividend income is recognized in profit or loss.

    4. The requirements for reclassifying gains or losses recognized in other comprehensive income are different for debt instruments and equity investments.

  C. Amortized Cost—A debt instrument is reported at amortized cost, net of any write-down for impairment, if it meets the following two conditions:

    1. Business model test—The entity's objective is to hold the financial asset to contractual maturity. If this test is not met, the asset is measured at FVTPL or FVTOC.

    2. Cash flow characteristic test—The requirement is that the contractual cash flows collected on specified dates are solely payment of principal and interest (SPPI) on the principal amount outstanding. If this test is not met, the asset is measured at FVTPL.

Example
A financial instrument that fails the amortized cost classification test is a convertible bond because the entity has the choice to convert into shares or cash, which affect cash flows. (The nominal rate of interest is lower due to this conversion option as compared to a bond without this option.)

Note
If an instrument meets the above tests, an entity still may choose to report it at fair value if it significantly reduces an accounting mismatch (measurement or recognition inconsistency).

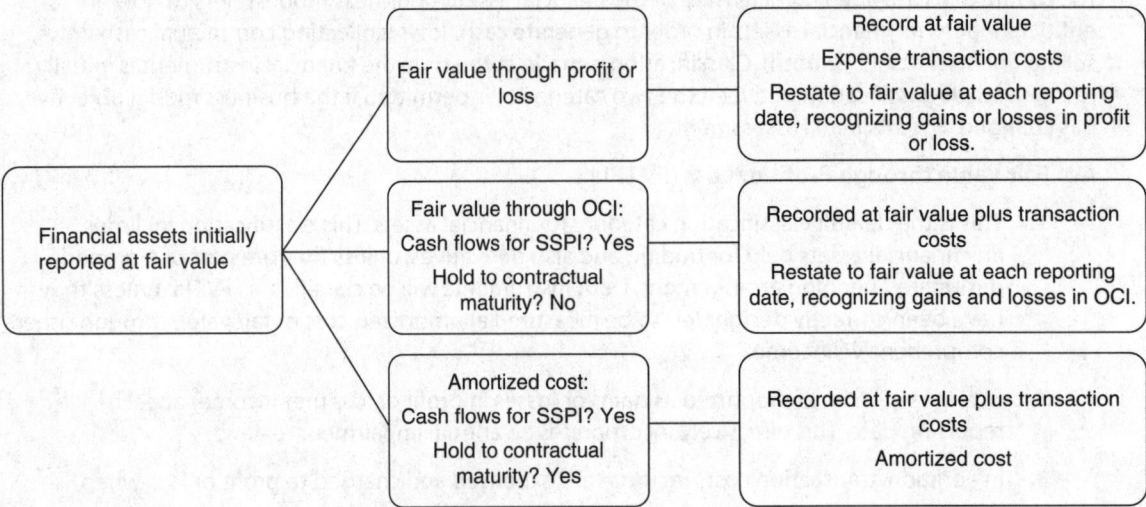

III. Impairment

A. IAS 39 not only had multiple impairment models, it also used an incurred loss model for recognizing impairments causing delays in recognition of losses, especially evident during the financial crisis of 2007–2008.

1. IFRS 9 requires that a single impairment model is applied to debt instruments measured at amortized cost or FVOCI as well as loan commitments (e.g., lease receivables, trade receivables, and commitments to lend money) and financial guarantee contracts.

2. The IFRS 9 model requires an entity to recognize expected credit losses at all times and to update the expected credit losses at each reporting date. This model is forward-looking and eliminates the threshold for recognizing expected credit losses (i.e., waiting for a trigger event to be identified first), resulting in more timely information about expected losses.

B. **General Impairment Approach**

1. With the exception of purchased or originated credit impaired financial assets, expected credit losses are required to be measured through a loss allowance at an amount equal to:

   a. The 12-month expected credit losses (EL; expected credit losses that result from those default events on the financial instrument that are possible within 12 months after the reporting date); *or*

   b. The full life-time expected credit losses (ELL; expected credit losses that result from all possible default events over the life of the financial instrument), depending on the stage of the financial asset.

C. The entity will make the following distinction about the stage of the financial instrument: performing, underperforming, or nonperforming.

1. **Performing instruments** (stage 1) have not deteriorated significantly in credit quality since initial recognition or have low credit risk.

> **Note**
> "Significantly" has not been defined under IFRS 9 for the impairment model; thus, judgment is required.

    a. The 12-month expected credit losses are recognized.

    b. Interest revenue is calculated on the gross carrying amount of the asset.

2. **Underperforming** (stage 2) financial assets have deteriorated significantly in credit quality, and their credit risk has increased significantly since initial recognition. The instrument does not have objective evidence of a credit loss event.

    a. Lifetime expected credit losses are recognized.

    b. Interest revenue is still calculated on the asset's gross carrying amount.

3. **Nonperforming** (stage 3) financial assets do have objective evidence of impairment at the reporting date.

    a. Lifetime expected credit losses are recognized.

    b. Interest revenue is calculated on the net carrying amount (reduced for expected credit losses).

D. Impairment Disclosures

1. Information must be disclosed explaining the entity's basis for its expected credit loss calculations and how it measures expected credit losses and assesses changes in credit risk.

2. Entities are required to provide a reconciliation from the opening allowance balance for 12-month loss allowance to the closing balance, separate from the lifetime loss allowance balances and provided along with a reconciliation of the related financial instrument's carrying amounts.

IV. Measurement of Financial Liabilities

A. IFRS 9 does not impose major changes from IAS 39 regarding financial liabilities. The instruments are recognized when the entity enters into the obligation of the financial liability.

B. Financial liabilities under IFRS are initially measured at fair value, taking into account transaction costs as discussed previously.

C. Subsequent measurement depends on the category to which the instrument has been assigned:

1. **Financial liabilities held for trading** are measured at fair value with changes in fair value through profit or loss (FVTPL).

2. **All other financial liabilities** are measured at amortized cost using the effective interest rate method unless the fair value option is applied. Trade payables generally are not subject to discounting unless discounting is material.

V. Derecognition of Financial Instruments

A. IAS 39 requirements for derecognition of financial assets and liabilities is carried over to IFRS 9. That is, derecognition occurs when substantially all risks and rewards of ownership have been transferred.

B. Financial liabilities are removed from the balance sheet when extinguished (obligation is discharged, expired, or canceled). If there is a substantial modification of terms on a liability, the original liability is extinguished and the new financial liability is recognized. A gain or loss on the extinguishment of the original financial liability is reported in the P&L statement.

VI. U.S. GAAP and IFRS—Major Differences

A. Under IFRS, the classification of an item that is a financial asset is based on the business model. Under U.S. GAAP, the classification is based on the nature, use, and other characteristics of the specific financial item.

B. Under IFRS, financial assets must be reviewed for impairment.

   1. When there is objective evidence that a financial asset is impaired, its recoverable amount (not its fair value, as under U.S. GAAP) must be determined.

   2. The difference between recoverable amount and carrying value is the impairment loss.

   3. Impairment losses are recognized in income.

      a. Unlike U.S. GAAP, the treatment of impairment losses on debt securities does not depend on whether the entity expects to dispose of the security before recovery of its carrying amount.

Financial Instruments Disclosures

This lesson identifies and describes the financial statement disclosures for all financial instruments, including derivatives. Required disclosures include information about fair value and concentration of credit risk. Disclosures related to market risk are recommended, but not required.

After studying this lesson, you should be able to:

1. Describe the disclosure requirements recommended (but not required) for all financial instruments.

2. Describe the disclosures that are required.

I. **Fair Value and Related Disclosure Requirements That Apply to All Financial Instruments**

   A. **The following must be disclosed for all financial instruments, whether recognized or not recognized in the balance sheet (except as noted in D, below), for which it is practicable to estimate fair value.**

      1. Fair value

      2. Related carrying amount

      3. Whether the instrument/amount is an asset or liability

   B. **Practicable to Estimate**—Means that fair value estimates can be made without incurring excessive costs; it is a cost/benefit assessment. If it is not practicable to estimate fair value, the following must be disclosed:

      1. The reasons that it is not practicable to estimate fair value, *and*

      2. Information pertinent to estimating fair value, such as carrying amount, effective interest rate, and maturity.

   C. **Fair Value Measurement**—Should be determined in accordance with the definition and requirements of ASC 820, *Fair-Value Measurement*.

      1. *Fair value* is the price that would be received to sell an asset or paid to transfer a liability in an orderly transaction between market participants at the measurement date.

      2. Quoted market prices in an active market provide the most reliable evidence of fair value.

   D. Disclosures about fair value **are not required** for the following financial items:

      1. Employer's and plan's obligations for pension benefits, postretirement benefits, postemployment benefits, employee stock option and stock purchase plans, and other forms of deferred compensation arrangements

      2. Substantially extinguished debt

      3. Insurance contracts (other than financial guarantee insurance contracts) and certain investments made by insurance entities

      4. Lease contracts

      5. Warranty obligations and rights

      6. Unconditional purchase contracts

      7. Investments accounted for under the equity method

      8. Noncontrolling interest in a consolidated subsidiary

      9. Equity instruments issued and classified in shareholders' equity

E. No fair value disclosure is required for trade accounts receivable or trade accounts payable when their carrying amounts approximate fair value.

F. **Netting**—Fair values of different financial instruments may not be netted, even if they are of the same class or otherwise related.

G. **Required Disclosures**—May be in either the body of the financial statements or in the footnotes. If in the footnotes, one note must show fair values and carrying amounts for all financial instruments.

II. Concentration of Credit Risk Disclosure Requirement That Apply to All Financial Instruments

A. **Disclosures Required**—Entities must disclose all significant concentrations of credit risks arising from all financial instruments (with limited exceptions) whether from a single party or a group of parties engaged in similar activities and that have similar economic characteristics.

B. **Credit Risk Defined**—Credit risk is the possibility of loss from the failure of another party (or parties) to perform according to the terms of a contract.

C. **Concentrations of Credit Risk Defined**—Concentration of credit risk occurs when an entity has contracts of material value with one or more parties in the same industry or region or having similar economic characteristics (e.g., receivables from a group of highly leveraged entities).

D. **The Following Must be Disclosed**—About each significant concentration of credit risk:

1. **Information about the common activity, region, or economic characteristic that identifies the concentration;**

2. **The maximum amount of loss due to the credit risk** (measured as the gross fair value of the financial instruments) that would occur if the other parties failed completely to perform according to the terms of the contract and assuming any collateral was of no value;

3. **The entity's policy of requiring collateral or other security to support financial instruments subject to credit risk**, a brief description of any collateral, and information about the entity's access to the collateral; *and*

4. **The entity's policy of entering into master netting arrangements to reduce the credit risk associated with financial instruments**, a brief description of any such arrangements, and the extent to which such arrangements would reduce the entity's maximum risk of loss.

III. Market Risk Disclosures Are Recommended

A. **Market risk disclosures for financial instruments are NOT required** but are encouraged.

B. **Market risk** is the possibility of loss from changes in market value due to changes in economic circumstances, not necessarily due to the failure of another party.

C. **Entities are encouraged to disclose quantitative information about the market risk of financial instruments**, including the following possible disclosures:

1. More details about current position and related period activity

2. Hypothetical effects on income of different changes in market prices

3. An analysis of interest rate repricing or maturity dates

4. Duration of financial instruments

5. The entity's value at risk from derivatives

IV. Other Disclosures

A. Qualitative Disclosures

1. Except for disclosures related to concentrations of credit risk, U.S. GAAP does not require substantive qualitative disclosures about financial instruments.

    2. Under SEC requirements, SEC registrants are required to provide qualitative disclosures about:

       a. Market risk

       b. Interest rate risk

       c. Foreign currency risk

       d. Commodity price risk

       e. Similar risks

    3. The SEC qualitative disclosures are provided in management's discussion and analysis and not in the financial statements or notes thereto.

B. Quantitative Disclosures

    1. Except for disclosures related to concentrations of credit risk, required quantitative disclosures about financial instruments under GAAP are nominal.

    2. Under SEC requirements, SEC registrants are required to provide quantitative disclosures only about financial instrument market risk, and those disclosures are in management's discussion and analysis, not in the financial statements or notes thereto.

C. Class Disclosures—Under SEC requirements, SEC registrants are required to provide separate presentation in the balance sheet of financial instruments by class; however, there is no comparable requirement under GAAP for entities that are not SEC registrants.

Derivatives and Hedging

Derivatives Introduction

This lesson defines derivatives and provides guidance on recognition and measurement. Specifically, it identifies the elements necessary for a financial instrument to be a derivative, gives examples of common derivatives and items that are not derivatives, and explains the concept of embedded derivatives. The general recognition and measurement requirement applicable to all derivatives is also presented.

After studying this lesson, you should be able to:

1. Define and describe a derivative financial instrument.

2. Identify common derivatives and contracts that are not derivatives for accounting purposes.

3. Identify the criteria for determining when a contract includes an embedded derivative.

4. Describe the general recognition and measurement requirement applicable to all derivatives.

I. **Definitions**

    A. A **derivative** is a financial instrument (or other contract) with all three of the following elements:

        1. **It has one or more** *underlyings* **and one or more** *notional amounts* or payment provisions (if this happens, then that will happen).

            a. An **underlying** is any financial or physical variable that has either observable changes or objectively verifiable changes. Therefore, underlyings include traditional financial measures such as commodity prices, interest rates, exchange rates, or indexes related to any of these items. More broadly, measures such as an entity's credit rating, rainfall, or temperature changes also meet the definition of an underlying.

            b. **Notional** amounts are the "number of currency or other units" specified in the financial instrument or other contract. In the case of options, this could include bushels of wheat, shares of stock, and so on.

            c. The **settlement amount** of a financial instrument or other contract is calculated using the underlying(s) and notional amount(s) in some combination.

                i. Computation of the settlement amount may be as simple as multiplying the fair value of a stock times a specified number of shares.

                ii. However, calculation of the settlement amount may require a very complex calculation, involving ratios, stepwise variables, and other leveraging techniques.

        2. **Derivatives require little or no initial net investment.** Derivatives can be purchased for an amount that is smaller than would be required for other types of similar contracts.

            a. Many derivative instruments require no net investment or simply a premium as compensation for the time value of money.

                i. Futures contracts may require the establishment of a margin account with a balance equal to a small percentage (2–3%) of the value of the contract.

                ii. A call option on a foreign currency contract would cost only a small fraction of the value of the contract.

                iii. These are typical contracts that would meet this definition and would be included in the definition of derivative instruments.

3. **Its terms require or permit a net settlement**—The instrument can be settled for cash or an asset readily convertible to cash in lieu of physical delivery of the subject matter of the contract.

    a. Require or permit net settlement, either within the contract or by a means outside the contract.

        i. Net settlement means that a contract can be settled through the payment of cash rather than the exchange of the specific assets referenced in the contract.

        ii. This type of settlement typically occurs with a currency swap or an interest rate swap.

    b. Provide for the delivery of an asset that puts the recipient in a position not substantially different from net settlement.

        i. This might include a futures contract where one party to the contract delivers an asset but a "market mechanism" exists (such as an exchange) so that the asset can be readily converted to cash. Convertibility to cash requires an active market and is a determining factor in whether a financial instrument or other contract will be treated as a derivative instrument.

> **Note:** The term *notional amount* is sometimes used interchangeably with *settlement amount*.
>
> Read carefully to determine if the context in which the term is used calls for a number of units (notional amount) or a dollar value (settlement amount).

II. **Derivative Examples**—The following contracts are examples of common derivatives.

    A. **Option Contracts**—For example, a stock option that requires the maker to deliver shares of stock at a later time in exchange for a fixed—option—price. The value of the option contract is a function of market price of the stock (compared to the option or strike price) and the number of shares.

    B. **Futures Contracts**—Made through a clearinghouse (e.g., to deliver or receive a commodity or foreign currency in the future at a price set at the present).

    C. **Forward Contracts**—Not made through a clearinghouse (e.g., like a futures contract, but made directly between contracting parties).

    D. **Swap Contracts**—For example, an agreement to exchange currencies, debt securities, or interest rates (e.g., swap fixed rate debt for variable rate debt).

    E. **Other Contracts**—Some contracts have characteristics comparable with those in the above list and should be accounted for as derivative contracts.

III. **Items Not Derivatives**—The following contracts are not derivatives for accounting purposes:

    A. Normal purchases and sales contracts (for something other than a financial instrument)

    B. Regular security trades

    C. Traditional life insurance and property and casualty insurance contracts

    D. Investments in life insurance

    E. Contracts indexed to a company's own stock

    F. Contracts issued in connection with stock-based compensation arrangements

    G. Contracts to enter into a business combination at a future date

    H. Other contracts as listed in ASC 815

IV. **Recognition and Measurement**—All derivative instruments must be recognized as either an asset (contractual right) or a liability (contractual obligation) and measured at fair value.

    A. The measurement of derivatives at fair value will result in gains and losses.

    B. The accounting treatment of the resulting gains and losses depends on whether the derivative has been designated (and qualifies) as a hedge and, if so, the purpose of the hedge.

V. Embedded Derivative Instruments

A. A host contract (debt instrument, lease, or equity instrument) may have a feature that results in a derivative *embedded* into the contract.

1. An embedded derivative exists when the host contract contains a term or component that behaves like a derivative. That is, if the feature stood alone, it would meet the definition of a derivative.

2. The instrument containing both the host contract and the embedded derivative is called a hybrid instrument.

B. Bifurcation is the process of separating an embedded derivative from its host contract. The process is necessary so that hybrid instruments can be separated into their component parts, each being accounted for by using the appropriate valuation techniques. Bifurcation occurs if the embedded feature meets all of the following requirements:

1. The economic characteristics and risks of the embedded derivative are not clearly and closely related to the characteristics and risks of the host contract (Example: Debt instrument that is convertible into a fixed number of the debtor's common stock is contingent on an event that has nothing to do with the debt element or the potential equity interest. The contingent event could be a hostile take-over that is not clearly and closely related to the host);

2. The hybrid instrument (host contact with derivative instrument) is not itself remeasured to fair value with changes reported in current income as they occur; *and*

3. As a separate instrument, the embedded instrument would meet the requirements of a derivative instrument.

C. If a single host contract contains more than one embedded derivative that meets the requirements to be accounted for as a separate derivative instrument, those embedded derivatives must be bundled together and treated as a single, compound embedded derivative, which is accounted for separately.

D. When an embedded derivative is separated from its host contract, the carrying value of the host contract (before bifurcation) is allocated between the embedded derivative and the host contract as follows:

1. The derivative is initially recorded at its fair value.

2. The difference between the carrying value of the hybrid contract and the fair value of the derivative element is the initial value of the remaining host contract.

E. The host contract, without the embedded derivative, will be accounted for based on GAAP applicable to that type of instrument.

F. A number of hybrid instruments that would normally require bifurcation are listed next.

1. A bond payable with an interest rate based on the S&P 500 index

2. An equity instrument (stock) with a call option, allowing the issuing company to buy back the stock

3. An equity instrument with a put option, requiring the issuing company to buy back the stock at the request of the holder

4. A loan agreement that permits the debtor to pay off the loan prior to its maturity with the loan payoff penalty based on the short-term T-bill rates

VI. Accounting for Derivatives Not Designated for Hedge Accounting

A. In this case, the derivative (contract) is not intended to hedge (offset) a separate risk or does not meet the accounting requirements to qualify as a hedge. For example, the derivative (e.g., a stock option contract) may have been entered into for speculative purposes (i.e., to make a profit).

B. Initial Recognition

1. An acquired contract that is a derivative instrument is initially measured and recorded at the then-current fair value.

2. Sample entry, assuming the acquisition of a derivative asset with value at the date of acquisition:

DR: Investment in Derivative

   CR: Cash (or other compensation)

C. **Subsequent Measurement and Recognition**—Changes in the fair value of these derivatives result in:

1. **Adjusting the carrying value of the derivative instrument to current fair value** (i.e., increase or decrease an asset or a liability); *and*

2. **Recognizing the related gain or loss in current income**.

D. Below is a brief description of the value components of options. Options have both intrinsic value (strike price less market price) and time value (option value less intrinsic value). Option can also be *in-the-money* or *out-of-the-money*.

1. **Options**

   a. **Call** (right to buy)—A call is in-the-money when the strike price less than the spot price.

   b. **Put** (right to sell)—A put is in-the-money when the strike price is greater than the spot.

   c. **Assume**—Stock with a $30 market value has an at-the-money option with a strike price of $30 (market = strike so the entire option value at the time of purchase is time value—this is an *at-the-money* option), and this option sells for $2 and is good for 60 days.

	Market price $35	Market price $25
Call (right to buy)	In the money	Out of the money
Put (right to sell)	Out of the money	In the money

---

   d. **Option value = intrinsic value + time value.** In the next table, assume that the option prices is quoted to be $8 per option.

   e. **Intrinsic value = in-the-money (ITM) value**

	Option value = (quoted value)	Intrinsic Value + (ITM value)	Time value (quoted value—ITM)
Call (right to buy)	8	5 (35 Market—30 Strike)	3
	8	0 (25 Market—30 Strike)	8
Put (right to sell)	8	0 (35 Market—30 Strike)	8
	8	5 (25 Market—30 Strike)	3

f. The accounting for the intrinsic value and time value can be different depending on how the derivative is used. Time value is associated with the time value of money or the anticipated passage of time—where intrinsic value is value associated with the amount of benefit that is associated with the derivative terms relative to the market price.

2. **Futures and Forwards**

   a. Time value for futures and forwards is most commonly calculated as the time value of money.

E. The following simplified example illustrates the accounting for a derivative held for speculative purposes (i.e., to make a profit).

Example

On December 1, year 1, Echo, Inc. purchased options to buy (a call option) 1,000 shares of Levy, Inc. in 60 days at a strike price of $45 per share when Levy's stock was selling for $43 per share in the market. Echo's purchase of the options was based on its intent to earn a profit on expected short-term increases in the market price of Levy's stock. On December 31, year 1, Levy stock was selling in the market for $46 per share.

Because the options have a strike price of $45 per share, Echo can purchase 1,000 shares of Levy from the option counterparty for $45 per share, even though the stock is selling in the market for $46 per share. Thus, on December 31 the options have a fair value of $1,000 (1,000 options × ($46 − $45) = $1,000).

1. Echo would make the following entry as of December 31, year 1:

   DR: Stock Options (market price > strike price) $1,000

       CR: Gain on Stock Options $1,000

2. The gain would be recognized in current income.

VII. Hedging

A. Hedging is a risk management strategy—Hedging involves using offsetting (or counter) transactions or positions so that a loss on one transaction or position would be offset (at least in part) by a gain on another transaction or position (and vice versa).

1. You would "hedge a bet" by offsetting a possible loss (from betting on one team to win) by also betting on the other team to win.

2. You would hedge against a possible loss in inventory value by entering into a contract to sell comparable inventory at a fixed price (set now) for future delivery.

B. For accounting purposes, derivative financial instruments that meet certain criteria may be used as hedges of the risks associated with certain economic undertakings and account balances.

C. For accounting purposes, nonderivative financial instruments may not be used to hedge an asset, liability, unrecognized firm commitment, or forecasted transaction, except that a nonderivative instrument denominated in a foreign currency may be used to hedge the foreign currency exposure of an unrecognized firm commitment to be settled in a foreign currency or a net investment in a foreign operation. (Certain concepts used in this item are developed in the immediate following lessons dealing with hedging.)

Hedging Introduction

This lesson makes the distinction between hedging and hedge accounting. There are three broad categories of hedge accounting. This lesson identifies those categories and the documentation required in order to get hedge accounting. In addition, this lesson describes the elements in a hedging relationship, the general kinds of risk that may be hedged, the specific risk components that may be hedged for accounting purposes, and the items and instruments that cannot be used for accounting hedges.

After studying this lesson, you should be able to:

1. Identify the possible uses of derivatives for accounting purposes.

2. Identify and describe the basic elements of a hedge relationship.

3. Identify the basic kinds of hedges for accounting purposes.

4. Identify the specific kinds of risks that can be hedged for accounting purposes.

5. Identify items and instruments that cannot be used for accounting hedges.

I. Hedging

A. Hedging means that the entity utilizes a derivative financial instrument to offset the risk related to a transaction, item, or event:

1. **Natural or economic hedges**—A derivative can be used as a natural hedge with no special hedge accounting treatment. In a natural hedge, both the underlying risk and the derivative instrument are marked-to-market value through earnings. The changes in the value of the hedged risk and derivative offset—to the extent these match, there is no impact on net income.

2. **Hedge accounting**—If certain conditions are met, a derivative may be specifically designated as a hedging instrument and special hedge accounting can be used. The gain (loss) on the derivative (the hedging instrument) is used to match the loss (gain) on the hedged item.

II. Criteria to Use Hedge Accounting

A. **Criterion #1**—Formal designation and documentation at inception of the hedge including the hedging relationship, the entity's strategy and objective for undertaking the hedge, the nature of the risk being hedged, and the methods used to assess effectiveness and measure ineffectiveness

B. **Criterion #2**—Eligibility of hedged items and transactions

C. **Criterion #3**—Eligibility of hedging instruments

D. **Criterion #4**—Hedge effectiveness; the hedge should be expected to be highly effective throughout its life

1. Effectiveness is measured by analyzing the hedging instrument's ability to generate changes in fair value or cash flows that offset the changes in value or cash flows of the hedged risk item both retrospectively and prospectively.

2. At a minimum, effectiveness will be measured quarterly and whenever earnings or financial statements are reported. The entity will determine whether the hedging relationship has been highly effective in achieving offsetting changes in fair value or cash flows through the date of assessment. An entity can base the measurement on regression or other statistical analysis.

3. The method used to assess effectiveness must be used throughout the hedge period and must be consistent with the approach used for managing risk.

III. Hedge Elements—Hedging involves two basic elements; those elements are:

    A. Hedged Item—The recognized asset, recognized liability, commitment, or planned transaction that is at risk of loss; it is the possible loss on the hedged item that is hedged.

    B. Hedging Instrument—The contract or derivative instrument that is entered into to mitigate or eliminate the risk of loss associated with the hedged item.

IV. Types of Hedge Accounting—Hedge accounting generally provides for matching the recognition of gains and losses of the hedging instrument and the hedged asset or liability. Instruments that qualify as hedging instruments will be accounted for using hedge accounting in one of the following three ways:

    A. Fair Value Hedge:

        1. A hedge of the exposure to changes in the fair value of the following, because of a particular risk:

            a. A recognized asset or liability *or*

            b. An unrecognized firm commitment

    B. Cash Flow Hedge:

        1. A hedge of the exposure to variability in the cash flows of the following, because of a particular risk:

            a. A recognized asset or liability *or*

            b. A forecasted transaction

    C. Foreign Currency Hedge:

        1. A hedge of the foreign currency exposure of any of the following:

            a. An unrecognized firm commitment

            b. An available-for-sale security

            c. A forecasted transaction

            d. A net investment in a foreign operation *or*

            e. Foreign currency—denominated assets and liabilities

V. Items Eligible for Hedge Accounting—For accounting purposes, there are risks that can be designated as the hedged item.

    A. For financial assets and financial liabilities, the following risks can be hedged:

        1. Commodity price risk

        2. Interest rate risk, where the interest rate being hedged is a benchmark rate

        3. Foreign exchange risk

        4. Credit risk (except not for investments in available-for-sale securities)

VI. Items Not Eligible for Hedge Accounting—For accounting purposes, a number of items (recognized assets/liabilities, commitments, planned transactions, etc.) are specifically excluded from being designated as a hedged item. Those include, among others, the following:

    A. An investment accounted for using the equity method of accounting

    B. A firm commitment to carry out a business combination

    C. A noncontrolling interest in a subsidiary

    D. Transactions between entities included in consolidated statements, except for foreign currency–denominated forecasted intra-entity transactions

E. Transactions with shareholders as shareholders (e.g., projected purchase of treasury stock or payment of dividends)

F. The risk of changes in fair value of held-to-maturity securities due to changes in interest rates (interest rate risk)

G. Part of the term (or life) of a hedged item (e.g., cannot hedge the first five years of a 10-year fixed rate bond investment)

VII. Summary of Hedged Item and Fair Value Versus Cash Flow Hedge Accounting

Item	Fair Value Hedge	Cash Flow Hedge
A recognized asset or liability	Hedges the risk of changes in the fair value of the hedged item	Hedges the risk related to the cash flows of the hedged item
Firm commitment	Hedges the risk related to the fair value changes of the commitment. The firm commitment is recognized as an asset or liability if hedged.	Not applicable
Forecasted transaction	Not applicable	Hedges the cash flows related to a forecasted transaction. The forecasted transaction must be specifically identifiable, probable, and with a party external to the reporting entity.
Foreign currency	1. Hedge of unrecognized firm commitment, denominated in a foreign currency.[3] 2. Hedge of available-for-sale securities, denominated in a foreign currency.	3. Hedge of a net investment in foreign operations: include changes in fair value as other comprehensive income. 4. Hedge of foreign currency denominated forecasted transactions.[4]
Gain or loss on hedged item	Included in net income[1]	Ineffective portion in net income. Effective portion in other comprehensive income[2]
Gain or loss on hedging instrument	Included in net income[1]	Ineffective portion in net income. Effective portion in other comprehensive income[2]

[1]Gains and losses on hedged asset/liability and the hedging instrument shall be recognized in current earnings. To the extent that the hedge is effective, the gains and losses will offset. To the extent the hedge is ineffective, the effect will show in current earnings as a gain or loss with no offset.

[2]The effective portion of the hedge is reported in other comprehensive income (check to make sure of linking of hedged asset/liability and hedging instrument; i.e., that value of both are valued from same index or rate). The ineffective portion is reported in earnings immediately.

[3]A foreign currency–denominated firm commitment has two risks: (1) the risk associated with the change in the price of the item associated with the firm commitment (a fixed price risk; therefore a fair value hedge) and (2) the risk associated with the change in the exchange rate for the value of the foreign currency (a floating price risk; therefore, a cash flow hedge). This distinction is discussed further in the lesson "Foreign Currency Hedges: Hedging Forecasted Transactions and Firm Commitments."

[4]The accounting for the hedge of a net investment in foreign operations is similar to cash flow hedge accounting (effective portion of gains and losses to OCI). The FASB classifies this type of hedge as a fair value hedge—with the effective gains/losses deferred in OCI.

VIII. Two Common Transactions to Which Hedge Accounting Is Applied

A. Forecasted Transaction

1. A transaction that is expected to occur for which there is no firm commitment. Because no transaction or event has yet occurred, when the transaction or event does occur, it will be at the prevailing market price (ASC 815).

2. The forecasted transaction must be:

   a. Specifically identifiable, probable to occur (ASC 450), with an external party, and does not involve future assets/liabilities that will be remeasured through earnings

3. Accounting for a forecasted transaction—unhedged:

   a. A forecasted item is recorded at the market value on the day the forecasted transaction occurs.

Example

Assume that on May 1, the company anticipates the purchase of 1,000 barrels (bbls) of fuel oil in six months (November 1). The quantity of the fuel oil is what is normally used in the course of business. The company has not selected a specific vendor or set a price. The spot price of fuel oil on May 1 is $70 bbl and the spot price on November 1 is $85 bbl. No entry would be made at the forecast date or at any time during the forecast period. An entry is made on November 1 when the fuel oil is actually purchased. The entries would be:

Date	May 1	November 1
Price	($70 bbl)	($85 bbl)
Entry	No entry	DR: Fuel Oil $85,000
		CR: Cash $85,000

4. **Risk—cash flows**—The cash flows on November 1 are uncertain and have variability and are dependent on the price on November 1.

5. **Benefits of a forecasted transaction:**

   a. Flexibility with respect to vendor, price, quantity, quality, delivery specifics

   b. Allows the company to complete due diligence on potential vendors

   c. Allows the company to "shop around" on the days prior to the purchase

   d. Increased possibility for price concessions in the days prior to the purchase (i.e., discounts and incentives)

   e. Prices may decrease and the purchase price will be lower

6. Limitations of a forecasted transaction:

   a. Prices may increase.

   b. Shortage of supply and cannot obtain the fuel oil (or must obtain substandard quality)

   c. No opportunity to build a relationship with a single vendor

B. **Firm Commitment**

   1. An agreement with an unrelated party that is binding on both parties and usually legally enforceable. The agreement usually specifies all significant terms (including quantity to be exchanged, fixed price, timing of the transaction) and includes a disincentive for nonperformance that is sufficiently large enough to make performance probable (ASC 815).

   2. Accounting for a firm commitment—unhedged:

      a. A firm commitment is also known as a purchase (or sales) commitment and is recorded at the commitment price on the date specified in the firm commitment.

Example

Assume that on May 1, the company enters into a firm commitment with a specific vendor to purchase 1,000 barrels (bbls) of fuel oil in six months. The firm commitment specifies the quantity, quality, price and delivery terms. The firm commitment price agreed to on May 1 is $70 bbl with delivery on November 1. The spot price of fuel oil on May 1 is $70 bbl and the spot price on November 1 is $85 bbl. No entry would be made on the date of the firm commitment (May 1) or at any time during the firm commitment period. An entry is made on November 1 when the fuel oil is actually purchased and the fuel oil would be recorded at the firm commitment price. The entries are as follows:

Date	May 1	November 1	
Price	($70 bbl)	($85 bbl)	
Entry	No entry	DR: Fuel Oil	$70,000
		CR: Cash	$70,000

3. **Risk—fair value**—The fair value of the $70,000 contract goes up if the price goes up to $85 (because you can get the oil cheaper than the market price). The fair value of the contract goes down if the price goes down to $65 (because you have to pay a price higher than the market price).

4. Benefits of a firm commitment:

   a. Certainty with respect to vendor, price, quantity, quality, delivery specifics

   b. Permits better budgeting

   c. Allows the company to develop a relationship with a specific vendor

   d. Increases the likelihood of obtaining the product if there is a shortage

   e. Mitigates the risk of prices increasing

5. Limitations of a firm commitment:

   a. Prices may decrease.

   b. Vendor may go bankrupt.

   c. Less opportunity to build relationships with other vendors

   d. Cannot take advantage of last minute discounts

IX. **Exclusions**—For accounting purposes, a number of instruments (contracts, options, etc.) are specifically excluded from being used as a hedging instrument. Those include, among other, the following:

A. A nonderivative instrument (e.g., U.S. Treasury note), except as permitted in certain intracompany cases for:

   1. Hedging changes in the fair value of an unrecognized firm commitment attributable to foreign currency exchange rates, *or*

   2. Hedging the foreign currency exposure of a net investment in a foreign operation.

B. Components of a compound derivative instrument used for different risks.

C. A hybrid financial instrument if:

   1. It is irrevocably elected to be measured in its entirety at fair value under the fair value option, *or*

   2. It has an embedded derivative that cannot be reliably identified and measured.

Fair Value Hedges

This lesson covers the accounting for fair value hedges. As the name implies, the purpose of this hedge is to offset changes in the fair value of the hedged item. This lesson will define fair value hedges, the requirements that must be met in order for a derivative to be treated as a fair value hedge, and the accounting treatment of derivatives and related hedged items in a fair value hedge.

After studying this lesson, you should be able to:

1. Define a fair value hedge.

2. Describe the criteria that must be met for a derivative to qualify as a fair value hedge.

3. Demonstrate the accounting for derivatives used as fair value hedges and for the related hedged item.

4. Describe the accounting when the requirements for a fair value hedge are no longer satisfied.

I. **Accounting for Fair Value Hedges**

   A. A fair value hedge is the hedge of an exposure to changes in fair value of a (recognized) asset, liability, or an unrecognized firm commitment due to a particular risk. A fair value hedge converts a fixed price to a floating price.

   1. For example, the use of a futures contract to hedge the fair value of a recognized asset or liability such as inventory.

   2. A derivative can also be used to hedge the fair value of an **unrecognized firm commitment.** A firm commitment exists when an entity enters into a contract to buy or sell (i.e., a purchase commitment).

   a. Unhedged firm commitments are not recognized because the purchase has not yet occurred. Once the firm commitment is designated as the hedged item, the changes in the fair value of the firm commitment are recognized.

   b. A firm commitment to purchase an item is at a fixed price. The changes in the market price relative to the firm commitment price will increase or decrease the fair value of the firm commitment contract.

   i. For example: Assume a company has a firm commitment to purchase fuel oil at $60 barrel. If the market price of the fuel oil rises to $65 a barrel, the fair value of the firm commitment contract has increased because the company can buy the fuel oil at a price less than the market price. If the price of the fuel oil declines to $50 a barrel, then the fair value of the firm commitment contract will decrease because the company is locked into a price that is higher than the market price.

   B. A derivative may be used to create a fair value hedge only if both the hedging instrument (the derivative) and the hedged item (asset, liability, or firm commitment) meet **certain criteria**, including:

   1. At inception of the hedge, there must be **formal documentation** of (1) the hedging relationship, (2) the objective and strategy for undertaking the hedge, (3) identification of the hedging instrument and the hedged item, (4) the nature of the risk being hedged, (5) how effectiveness of the hedge will be assessed, and (6) when a firm commitment is the hedged item, how the related asset or liability will be recognized.

   2. Both at inception of the hedge and on an ongoing basis, the hedge must be expected to be **highly effective** in offsetting changes in fair value of the hedged item, **with an assessment** of effectiveness required **when financial statements are prepared and at least every three months**.

   3. The hedged item (1) is specifically identified as a recognized asset, liability, or firm commitment (or portion thereof), (2) presents exposure to changes in fair value that could affect reported income, (3) is not accounted for at fair value with changes reported in income, (4) not an investment accounted for using the equity method, (5) not a noncontrolling interest or an equity interest in a consolidated subsidiary and (6) if a debt security classified as

held-to-maturity, the risk being hedged is the creditworthiness of the obligor (not the interest rate because the investor intends to hold to maturity).

C. Additional Qualifications

1. If the hedged item is an interest-rate risk, only a benchmark interest rate may be hedged. Only two interest rates are considered to be benchmark interest rates:

   a. Direct U.S. Treasury obligations

   b. London Interbank Offer Rate (LIBOR)

2. If the hedged item is a nonfinancial asset or liability, the risk being hedged is the risk of change in the fair value of the entire hedged asset or liability, not a portion of the asset or liability.

D. Changes—Changes in fair value of both the derivative qualifying as a fair value hedge (hedging instrument) and the asset, liability, or firm commitment being hedged (hedged item) are accounted for by:

1. **Adjusting the carrying amount of both the derivative and the hedged item to fair value**.

   a. If the hedged item is a firm commitment, a new asset or liability will have to be recognized on the balance sheet when the initial adjustment occurs.

   b. The amount of the adjustment to the hedged item becomes a part of the carrying amount of the item and is accounted for as such.

2. **Recognizing gains and losses from revaluing both the derivative and the hedged item *in current income***.

   a. If the hedged item is normally adjusted through "other comprehensive income" (i.e., an available-for-sale investment), the change in fair value, if hedged, must be recognized in current income.

   b. To the extent the gain or loss on the hedging instrument offsets the loss or gain on the hedged item, the hedge is "effective." To the extent the gain or loss on the hedging instrument is more or less than that on the hedged item, the hedge is "ineffective" and will result in a net effect (gain or loss) on current income.

E. If the criteria for fair value hedges are no longer met, the derivative may no longer be accounted for as a hedge.

1. If the hedged item was an unrecognized firm commitment, the asset or liability created to account for its change in value must be written off and a corresponding gain or loss recognized in current income.

F. Hedged assets and liabilities should continue to be assessed for impairment.

G. A Hedge of a Recognized Asset or Liability—Can be *either a cash flow hedge or a fair value hedge*.

1. To qualify as a cash flow hedge, the hedging instrument must completely offset the variability in (dollar) cash flows associated with the receivable or payable.

2. If the instrument does not qualify as a cash flow hedge, or if management so designates, the hedging instrument will be a fair value hedge.

H. Accounting Treatment—The accounting for the hedge of a recognized asset or liability would depend on the designated purpose of the hedge whether to hedge cash flow or to hedge fair value.

1. If to hedge fair value, the treatment would include:

   a. Adjusting the hedged item (receivable or payable) to fair value each balance sheet date and recognizing the change in fair value as a gain or loss in current income

   b. Adjusting the hedging instrument to fair value each balance sheet date and recognizing the change in fair value in current income

      i. To the extent the change in fair value of the hedging instrument and the change in the fair value of the hedged item are different, there will be a net effect in current income.

II. Fair Value Hedge of a Firm Commitment

Example

Assume that the company enters into a firm commitment with a supplier of cotton on January 1 to buy 1,000,000 tons of cotton on March 31 for $42/ton. The terms and conditions of the firm commitment meet all the required criteria. In order to protect against the risk of prices decreasing in the first quarter, the company enters into a futures contract on January 1 to sell cotton on March 31 for $42/ton. The futures contract is purchased "at the money" and a margin account is established with the broker. Therefore, there is no cash outlay for the purchase of the futures contract. The example below ignores the time value of money (the ineffective portion of the hedge). The table below shows the entries that would be made at the date the transaction is initiated (January 1), at an interim date (February 28 is an assumed date), and the settlement date (March 31).

	Jan 1, 20X9	Feb 28, 20X9	Mar 31, 20X9
Spot price per ton	$40	$38	$37
Futures rate per ton	$42	$41	$37

Entries with broker for futures contact	none	Futures contract 1,000,000
		   Gain/loss(I/S) 1,000,000
		($41 − $42) × 1,000,000
			Futures contract 4,000,000
			   Gain/loss(I/S) 4,000,000
			($37 − $41) × 1,000,000
			
			Cash 5,000,000
			   Futures Contract 5,000,000

Entries for firm commitment with supplier	none	Gain/loss(I/S) 1,000,000
		   Firm commitment 1,000,000
		($41 − $42) × 1,000,000
			Gain/loss(I/S) 4,000,000
			   Firm commitment 4,000,000
			($37 − $41) × 1,000,000
			
			Inventory—cotton 37,000,000
			Firm commitment 5,000,000
			   Cash at the money 42,000,000

After production and sale of the end product, the inventory is reduced and cost of goods sold is recorded. Assume that the product is sold on June 1, 20X9. The following entries would be made on June 1.

DR: Cost of goods sold   37,000,000
    CR: Inventory   37,000,000
    (to record CGS)

III. Items to Note

A. The firm commitment is recognized and marked to market using the changes in the futures rate.

B. The futures contract is marked to market using the changes in the futures rate.

C. The gains and losses perfectly offset each other. If there were any ineffectiveness, it would be a residual amount reflected in earnings.

D. The value of the inventory is reduced for the amount of deferred gains or losses in the firm commitment account.

E. The fair value hedge converted the fixed price of the firm commitment ($42/ton) to a floating price on March 31 ($42/ton paid less $5/ton received from the futures contract = $37/ton which was the March 31 spot price).

Cash-Flow Hedges

This lesson covers the accounting for a cash-flow hedge. As the name of the use implies, the purpose of this hedge is to reduce the variability related to uncertain future cash flows. This lesson defines cash-flow hedges, the requirements that must be met in order for cash-flow hedge accounting, and the accounting for the derivative and related hedged item.

After studying this lesson, you should be able to:

1. Define a *cash-flow hedge*.

2. Describe the criteria that must be met for a derivative to qualify as a cash-flow hedge.

3. Demonstrate the accounting for derivatives used as cash-flow hedges and for the related hedged item.

4. Describe the accounting when the requirements for a cash-flow hedge are no longer satisfied.

I. **Accounting for Cash Flow Hedges**

   A. A cash-flow hedge is the hedge of an exposure to variability (changes) in the cash flow associated with a (recognized) asset, liability, or a forecasted transaction due to a particular risk. A cash-flow hedge converts a floating price to a fixed price.

      1. For example, the use of an interest-rate swap to hedge the cash outflow from variable-rate debt, or the use of a futures contract to hedge the cash inflow from a forecasted sale.

      2. A **forecasted transaction** is a planned or expected transaction with a third party, but for which there is not yet a firm commitment and there are not yet any established rights or obligations associated with the planned transaction.

   B. A derivative may be accounted for as a cash-flow hedge only if both the hedging instrument (the derivative) and the hedged item (asset, liability, or forecasted transaction) meet **certain criteria**, including:

      1. At inception of the hedge, there must be **formal documentation** of (1) the hedging relationship, (2) the objective and strategy for undertaking the hedge, (3) identification of the hedging instrument and the hedged item, (4) the nature of the risk being hedged, and (5) how effectiveness of the hedge will be assessed.

      2. Both at inception of the hedge and on an ongoing basis, the hedge must be expected to **be highly effective** in offsetting change in cash flow of the hedged item, with an assessment of effectiveness required when financial statements are prepared and at least every 3 months.

      3. A forecasted transaction can be hedged only if it is (1) specifically identified as a single transaction or group of individual transactions with the same risk exposure, (2) probable of occurring, (3) with an external party (except for certain intercompany hedges), (4) capable of affecting cash flows that would affect earnings, and (5) not for the acquisition of an asset or the incurrence of a liability, which is accounted for at fair value with the change reported in current income.

   C. **Additional Qualifications**

      1. If the hedged item is the cash flow from a forecasted transaction related to an investment classified as held to maturity, the risk being hedged is the risk of changes in cash flow attributable to credit risk, foreign exchange risk, or both.

      2. If the hedged item is the cash flow from a forecasted transaction, it cannot involve:

         a. A business combination;

         b. A parent's equity interest in a subsidiary; *or*

         c. An entity's own equity instruments.

D. Changes in Fair Value of Derivatives Qualifying as Cash Flow Hedges (Hedging Instrument) are Accounted for by

1. Determining for each period the change in (1) the fair value of the derivative (hedging instrument) and (2) the present value of the cash flows associated with the asset, liability, or forecasted transaction being hedged (hedged item)

2. Determining for each period (1) the cumulative change in the fair value of the derivative and (2) the cumulative change in the present value of the cash flows associated with the hedged item

3. Recognizing the change in the fair value of the derivative for the period (write up or write down the derivative)

4. Recognizing as an item of Other Comprehensive Income an amount equal to the (cumulative) change in the present value of cash flows associated with the hedged item. This is the **effective portion** of the hedge; the extent to which the change in the value of the hedge offsets the change in value of the hedged item.

5. Recognizing as a gain or loss in current income the amount by which the (cumulative) change in the derivative is different from the (cumulative) change in the present value of the cash flows associated with the hedged item. This is the **ineffective portion** of the hedge; the extent to which the hedge is more or less than the change in value of the hedged item.

Example

The following two-period example illustrates the process for determining and recording (1) the change in the fair value of a derivative that hedges the cash flow of a hedged item (asset, liability, or forecasted transaction), (2) the effective portion of the gain or loss on the hedge, and (3) the ineffective portion of the gain or loss on the hedge.

Assume Alpha Company anticipates selling inventory (say, silver) to a third party two years in the future. To protect the cash value of that sale against future declines, Alpha enters into a futures contract to sell that inventory at a (futures) price set now. The relevant values, analysis, and entries are as follows:

End of Period	Hedging Instrument Derivative Fair Value		Hedged Item PV of Expected Cash Flows		Hedge Allocation	
	Period Change	Cumulative Change	Period Change	Cumulative Change	Effective Portion	Ineffective Portion
1	$150	$150	$(148)	$(148)	$148	$2 (Gain)
2	147	297	(151)	(299)	149	2 (Loss)

Period 1 Entry: DR: Futures Contract (Derivative) $150
                      CR: Other Comprehensive Income $148
                      CR: Gain on Cash Value Hedge   2

Period 2 Entry: DR: Futures Contract $147
                      DR: Loss on Cash Value Hedge   2
                      CR: Other Comprehensive Income $149

E. The effective portion of cash-flow hedges (deferred gains/losses) are reported as a component of **Other Comprehensive Income** in the Statement of Comprehensive Income for the period and in **Accumulated Other Comprehensive Income** in the Balance Sheet **until the period(s) in which the hedged item affects income**. For example:

1. The effective portion of a hedge of a forecasted sale (example above) would be reclassified to (and recognized in) income in the period of the sale.

2. The effective portion of a hedge of a forecasted purchase of a depreciable asset would be reclassified to (and recognized in) income over the periods depreciation expense is taken on the asset.

F. If the criteria for cash flow hedges are no longer met, the derivative may no longer be accounted for as a hedge.

   1. The deferred gain or loss remaining in accumulated other comprehensive income should continue to be reclassified to (and recognized in) income in the period(s) in which the hedged items affect income.

   2. If a hedged forecasted transactions is no longer expected to occur, the deferred gain or loss in accumulated other comprehensive income should be reclassified to (and recognized in) income immediately.

G. Assets and liabilities for which related cash flows have been hedged should continue to be assessed for impairment.

   1. If an impairment loss is recognized, any deferred gain in accumulated other comprehensive income should be reclassified (recognized) to offset the loss.

H. **A hedge of a recognized asset or liability** can be *either a cash-flow hedge or a fair value hedge*.

   1. To qualify as a cash-flow hedge, the hedging instrument must completely offset the variability in (dollar) cash flows associated with the receivable or payable.

   2. If the instrument does not qualify as a cash-flow hedge, or if management so designates, the hedging instrument will be a fair value hedge.

I. **Accounting Treatment**—The accounting for the hedge of a recognized asset or liability would depend on the designated purpose of the hedge—that is, whether to hedge cash flow or to hedge fair value.

   1. If to hedge cash flow, the treatment would include:

      a. Adjusting the hedged item (receivable or payable) to fair value each balance sheet date and recognizing the change in fair value in comprehensive income.

      b. Adjusting the hedging instrument to fair value each balance sheet date and recognizing the change in fair value as follows:

         i. An amount up to the amount equal to the gain or loss recognized on the hedged item is recognized in comprehensive income to offset the gain or loss on the hedged item.

         ii. The amount greater than the amount of gain or loss recognized on the hedged item is recognized in current income (income or expense).

Example
Cash Flow Hedge of a Forecasted Transaction

Assume at the beginning of the year the company anticipates the production needs and will need 1,000,000 tons of cotton at the end of each quarter. In order to protect against the risk of prices increasing in the first quarter, the company enters into a futures contract on January 1 to buy cotton on March 31 for $42/ton. The futures contract is purchased "at the money" and a margin account is established with the broker. Therefore, there is no cash outlay for the purchase of the futures contract. This example ignores the time value of money (the ineffective portion of the hedge).

	Jan 1, 20X9	Feb 28, 20X9	Mar 31, 20X9
Spot price per ton	$40	$46	$44
Futures rate per ton	$42	$45	$44

Entries with Broker for Futures Contract	none	Futures Contract 3,000,000
		  G/L on Futures (OCI) 3,000,000*
		  ($42 − $45) × 1,000,000
			G/L on Futures (OCI) 1,000,000*
			  Futures Contract 1,000,000
			  ($45 − $44) × 1,000,000
			
			Cash 2,000,000
			  Futures Contract 2,000,000
			  ($42 − $44) × 1,000,000

Entries for Forecasted Transaction with Supplier	none	none	Inventory—cotton 44,000,000
			  Cash 44,000,000
			  ($44 × 1,000,000)

Impact on Balance Sheet	none	Increase assets 3,000,000 Increase equity 3,000,000	Decrease assets 1,000,000 Decrease equity 1,000,000
Impact on Income Statement	none	none	none

*The unrealized gain or loss in OCI remains in that account until the inventory is sold. After production and sale of the end product, the inventory is reduced and cost of goods sold is recorded. Cost of goods sold is then adjusted for the cumulated gain or loss in OCI. Assume that the product is sold on June 1, 20X9. The following entries would be made on June 1.

DR: Cost of goods sold 44,000,000   DR: Gain/loss on futures (OCI)   2,000,000
  CR: Inventory   44,000,000   CR: Cost of goods sold   2,000,000
(to record CGS)   (to close OCI into CGS)

II. **Items to Note**

    A. The forecasted transaction is not recognized until the item is purchased.

    B. The futures contract is marked to market using the changes in the futures rate.

    C. The gains and losses on the futures contract are deferred into OCI until the item that is hedged effects earnings.

    D. The value of the cost of goods sold is reduced for the amount of deferred gains or losses once the inventory is sold.

    E. The cash-flow hedge converted the floating price of the forecasted transaction (unknown) to a fixed price on Jan 1 ($42/ ton the price of the futures contract). Total cash paid on March 31 is $42/ton (the spot price) = $44/ton (the spot price paid) less the cash received on the futures contract $2/ton.

Foreign Currency Hedges

This lesson covers the final use of derivatives for accounting purposes—as a hedge of amounts denominated (to be settled) in a foreign currency. As the name of the use implies, the purpose of these derivatives is to offset changes in the dollar value of expected transactions, commitments, transactions, and balances measured in a foreign currency. This lesson identifies and describes the alternative foreign currency hedges; lessons included in the "Foreign Currency Denominated Transactions" topic cover these hedges in detail.

After studying this lesson, you should be able to:

1. Define a foreign currency hedge.

2. Identify and describe the specific kinds of foreign currency items that may be hedged.

I. **Accounting for Derivatives That Qualify as Foreign Currency Hedges and Other Eligible Contracts Used as Foreign Currency Hedges**—(This is a summary introduction; the full details of such hedges are covered in subsequent lessons.)

> **Definition**
> *Foreign Currency Hedge:* The hedge of an exposure to changes in the dollar value of assets or liabilities (including certain investments) and planned transactions that are denominated (to be settled) in a currency other than an entity's functional currency (i.e., a foreign currency).

A. An entity may **hedge foreign currency exposure of** the following kinds:

1. **Forecasted foreign-currency-denominated transactions**—(including inter-company transactions). The risk being hedged is the risk that exchange rate changes will have on the **cash flow** from nonfirm but planned transactions to be settled in a foreign currency. For example, the dollar value of royalty revenue **forecasted to be received** in a foreign currency from a foreign entity, including a related entity.

2. **Unrecognized foreign-currency-denominated firm commitments**—The risk being hedged is the risk that exchange rate changes will have on the **fair value** or **cash flow** of firm commitments for a future sale or purchase to be settled in a foreign currency. For example, a commitment (contract) to purchase custom-built equipment from a foreign manufacturer with payment to be made in a foreign currency.

3. **Foreign-currency-denominated recognized assets**—(e.g., receivables) **or liabilities** (e.g., payables). The risk being hedged is the **fair value** or **cash flow**, measured in dollars of:

   a. An already booked asset or liability to be settled in a foreign currency (fair value or cash flow hedge), *or*

   b. A forecasted functional-currency-equivalent cash flow associated with a recognized asset or liability (cash-flow hedge), *or*

   > **Note**
   > *The dollar value of or cash flows from such assets and liabilities may change as a result of changes in the foreign exchange rate between recognition and settlement of the asset or liability.*

   c. An investment denominated in a foreign currency.

4. **Investments in available-for-sale securities**—The risk being hedged is the risk that exchange rate changes will have on the **fair value** of investments in available-for-sale securities (debt or equity) denominated in a foreign currency.

5. **Net investments in foreign operations**—The risk being hedged is the risk that exchange rate changes will have on the **fair (economic) value** of financial statements converted from a foreign currency to the functional currency. In this case, the accounting for the hedging instrument (derivative) must be treated like the accounting for the translation adjustment for the associated foreign investment.

B. The accounting treatments for these foreign currency-hedging purposes generally are consistent with the fair value and cash-flow hedge treatments described in earlier lessons and are discussed in detail in subsequent material.

Effectiveness and Disclosure

In order to qualify for hedge accounting, the company must document how it will assess hedge effectiveness and measure hedge ineffectiveness. In addition, this lesson presents the disclosure requirements associated with hedging.

After studying this lesson, you should be able to:

1. Identify and describe how effectiveness is assessed when hedging is used.

2. Describe the ways by which ineffectiveness can be measured.

3. Describe the treatment of ineffectiveness resulting from the use of hedging.

4. Describe the shortcut method of effectiveness assessment.

5. Describe the most significant disclosures required when hedging is used.

I. **Effectiveness**

A. There are two terms associated with *effectiveness*. **Assessing hedge effectiveness** is the necessary criteria in order to get hedge accounting. To qualify for hedge accounting, the hedging instrument must be highly effective, both at inception of the hedge and on an ongoing basis, in offsetting changes in the fair value or the cash flows of the hedge item. This correlation must be between 80 and 125% in order for the hedge to qualify for hedge accounting.

B. If the hedge is determined to be effective, and hedge accounting is permitted, the ineffective portion of the hedge needs to be measured—**measuring ineffectiveness**. The measurement of the ineffectiveness is important because in hedge accounting the ineffective portion of the hedge is accounted for separate from the effective portion of the hedge.

II. **Assessing Hedge Effectiveness**—Hedge effectiveness is assessed in two stages.

A. **Prospective Consideration**—A forward-looking assessment of the entity's expectations that a planned hedging relationship will be highly effective over future periods in achieving offsetting changes in fair value or cash flows.

1. The prospective assessment should consider all reasonable possible changes in fair value and/or cash flows of both the hedged item and the hedging instrument.

2. The prospective assessment can be based on:

a. Regression analysis or other statistical analysis of past changes in fair value or cash flows

b. Qualitative assessment of the extent to which the critical terms (e.g., nominal amounts, expiration date, etc.) of the hedging instrument and the hedged item match

3. Generally, the prospective assessment involves a probability-weighted analysis of the possible changes in fair value and/or cash flows.

B. **Retrospective Evaluation**—When a relationship between an instrument and an item qualifies as a hedge for accounting purposes, the relationship must continue to be assessed for effectiveness and measured for ineffectiveness whenever financial statements are reported, and at least every three months.

1. A single method of evaluating effectiveness or measuring ineffectiveness is not specified by GAAP.

2. The retrospective evaluation can be accomplished using a number of approaches, including:

   a. A dollar-offset approach—An assessment based on how well the dollar change in the hedging instrument actually has offset the dollar change in the hedged item, with the assessment performed either on a period-by-period basis or on a cumulative basis.

   b. Regression analysis or other statistical analysis.

   c. Qualitative assessment.

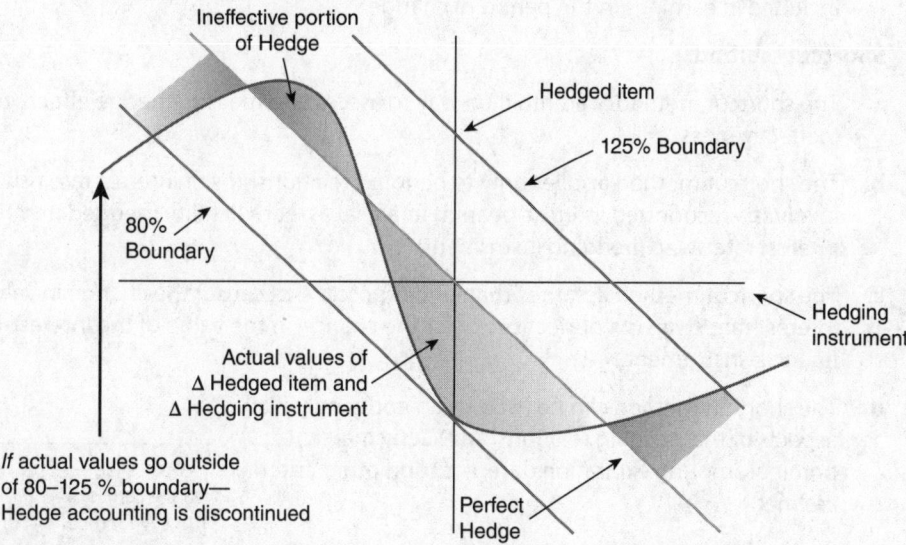

III. Effectiveness Testing

A. In order to qualify for hedge accounting, the hedge must be "highly effective." Highly effective means the correlation between the hedged item and the hedging instrument must be between 80 and 125%. In the graph above, the boundaries of 80–125% indicate that the plotted changes in the value of the hedged item and the hedging instrument need to fall within these boundaries. As long as the change in the hedged item and hedging instrument is between the boundaries of 80% and 125%, the hedge is permitted. If the change is outside of this range (shown at either end of the curve) hedge accounting is no longer permitted.

B. Effectiveness is the change in the fair value of the derivative divided by the change in the value of the hedged item.

$$\frac{\Delta FV\ derivative}{\Delta FV\ hedged\ risk} = 80\text{–}125\%$$

C. Effectiveness of the hedge must be assessed as highly effective throughout its life with a review at least every three months (i.e., that hedging instrument gain or loss covers hedged item's loss or gain).

D. **Measuring Ineffectiveness**—The straight line through the axis of the above graph represents a "perfect hedge" where changes in the value of the hedged item and hedging instrument offset each other perfectly. Since very few circumstances will result in a perfect hedge, the ineffective part of the hedge must be measured and reported on the income statement. Ineffectiveness is the distance measured on the curved line to the straight line within the 80–125% boundaries. This area is designated with grey shading to show what amount of the hedge is ineffective.

1. **Measuring ineffectiveness treatment**—Ineffectiveness, as measured by the extent to which there is not an exact offset in the hedging relationship, must be included in earnings in the period of the ineffectiveness.

2. **Time value**

   a. In establishing its effectiveness assessment policy, an entity must specify whether all or a part of the time value of the hedging instrument will be included in the assessment.

   b. Any element of time value that is excluded from effectiveness assessment must be included in earnings in the period of change.

3. **Shortcut method**

   a. The shortcut method is a simplified way to assess and measure hedge effectiveness/ineffectiveness.

   b. The shortcut method applies only to hedging relationships of interest rate risk that involves a recognized interest-bearing financial asset or liability (hedged item) and an interest rate swap (hedging instrument).

   c. The shortcut method assumes that (and is possible because) the change in value of the interest-rate swap is a perfect proxy for the change in the value of the interest-bearing financial instrument.

   d. The shortcut method can be used by an entity only if all aspects of the hedging relationship exactly match (e.g., nominal amount, expiration date, etc.) and other criteria are met.

   > **Note**
   > *It is becoming very difficult to qualify for the shortcut method and, therefore, it is becoming more and more rare in practice.*

   e. If all of the criteria are met, an entity may assume no ineffectiveness in the hedging relationship and does not have to carry out an effectiveness assessment.

IV. Disclosure Requirements

A. An entity that issues or holds derivatives (or other contracts used for hedging) must disclose (mostly in the footnotes) a considerable amount of information in both annual and interim financial statements, including:

1. **General Disclosure Requirements**

   a. Its objectives for issuing or holding the derivatives (or other contracts), the context needed to understand those objectives, and its strategies for achieving those objectives.

   b. Information must distinguish between instruments used for risk management (hedging) and those used for other purposes (e.g., profit).

   c. Information must be disclosed in the context of each instrument's underlying risk exposure, including, for example: interest rate risk, credit risk, foreign currency exchange risk, overall price risk, etc.

   d. Information must distinguish between instruments designated as fair value hedges, cash flow hedges, hedges of foreign currency exposure of net investments in foreign operations, and any other derivatives.

   e. Information that would enable users to understand the volume of its derivative activities

   f. Quantitative disclosures must be presented in tabular format.

   g. If information on derivatives is disclosed in multiple footnotes, the derivative-related footnotes must be cross-referenced.

B. Balance Sheet–Related Disclosures—The following specific balance-sheet-related disclosures are required:

1. The location (line item) and fair value amounts of derivative instruments

2. Fair value must be presented as a gross (not net) amount.

3. Fair value amounts must be shown separately as assets and liabilities, and segregated between those derivatives that are hedges and those that are not.

4. For derivatives used as hedges, the fair value amounts must be presented separately for each type of hedge contract (e.g., interest rate contract, foreign currency contract, commodity contract, etc.).

5. The amounts reclassified from Accumulated Other Comprehensive Income to current income

C. Income Statement–Related Disclosures—The following specific income-statement-related disclosures are required:

1. The location (line item) and amounts of gains/losses on derivative instruments.

2. Gains/losses must be presented separately for:

   a. Derivatives designated as fair value hedges and for the related hedged item

   b. Derivatives designated as cash-flow hedges and net-investment hedges, separating the effective and ineffective portions

   c. Derivatives not functioning as hedges

   d. Amounts reclassified from Accumulated Other Comprehensive Income to Current Income

   e. Amounts recognized from hedged firm commitments that no longer qualify for hedge treatment

D. Cash Flow–Specific Disclosures—For derivatives designated as cash flow hedges and for the related hedged item the following specific disclosures are required:

1. A description of transactions or other events that will result in the reclassification (recognition) of accumulated other comprehensive income into income and an estimate of the amount to be reclassified during the next 12 months

2. The maximum length of time over which the entity is hedging cash flows for forecasted transactions

3. The gain/loss recognized in earnings from hedged forecasted transactions that no longer qualify for hedge treatment

E. Credit-Risk-Related Contingent Features—Specific Disclosures

1. Credit-risk-related contingent features are provisions in a derivative (or other instrument) that trigger immediate settlement (or other consequences) if a specific event or condition occurs or fails to occur. For example, an interest rate swap may provide for immediate settlement if an entity's credit rating is downgraded.

2. For derivatives that contain credit-risk-related contingent features the following specific disclosures are required:

   a. The existence and nature of credit-risk-related contingent features and the circumstances in which the features could be triggered for derivatives that are liabilities

   b. The aggregate fair value amounts of derivatives that contain credit-risk-related contingent features that are liabilities

    c. The aggregate fair value of assets (1) that are already posted as collateral, (2) additional assets that would be required as collateral and/or (3) needed to settle the instrument immediately if the contingent feature is triggered

V. Note on Derivatives and Hedging Disclosures—The required disclosures related to the issuing and/or holding of derivatives and the use of derivatives (and other instruments) for hedging purposes are extensive, detailed, and continuously changing (usually resulting in more disclosures). The disclosures identified and described above are those that are most significant and, therefore, most likely to occur on the CPA Exam.

IFRS—Hedging

There are many similarities between U.S. GAAP and IFRS in the accounting for derivatives and hedging. This lesson identifies and describes the major differences between U.S. GAAP and IFRS with respect to hedge accounting.

After studying this lesson, you should be able to:

1. Identify significant areas of difference between U.S. GAAP and IFRS in accounting for derivatives.

2. Identify the significant areas of difference between U.S. GAAP and IFRS in hedge accounting.

I. Derivatives: U.S. GAAP–IFRS Differences

U.S. GAAP	IFRS
Definition of derivative includes identifying a notional amount.	Definition of a derivative does not include a notional amount.
Normal purchase/sales contracts not considered a derivative if documented	Normal purchase/sales contracts not considered a derivative and no formal documentation necessary
Embedded derivatives assessed throughout life of contract	Embedded derivatives assessed only at initiation of contract
Embedded derivatives within a single host separated and bundled as one derivative	Embedded derivatives within a single host separated as multiple derivatives

A. **Definition**—The definition of a derivative under IFRS is different from the definition under U.S. GAAP. Like U.S. GAAP, the IFRS definition establishes a derivative as a financial instrument whose value changes with changes in an underlying and one that requires a minimal or no initial net investment. Unlike U.S. GAAP, the IFRS definition does not:

1. Include reference to a *notional* concept or element; *or*

2. Specify that net settlement is required or permitted, only that the contract will be settled at a future date.

B. **Documentation**—Under both U.S. GAAP and IFRS, normal purchase and sales contracts are not considered derivatives. U.S. GAAP requires that a financial instrument that is a normal purchase or sale be formally documented to establish that it is not a derivative; IFRS does not require such formal documentation.

C. **Embedded Derivatives**

1. **Recognition**—Under IFRS an embedded derivative is separated from the host contract only if

   a. The entire (hybrid) contract is not measured at fair value with changes recognized in profit or loss, and

   b. The economic characteristics and risks of the embedded derivative are not *closely related* to those of the host contract.

> **Note**
> *Although this recognition standard is similar to that under U.S. GAAP, application of the separate standards can sometimes result in differences in the recognition of embedded derivatives as separate instruments.*

2. **Assessment**—Under U.S. GAAP, the assessment of whether there is an embedded derivative that must be separated from the host contract and accounted for as a separate derivative generally must occur throughout the life of the contract. Under IFRS, however, that assessment generally occurs only when the reporting party becomes a party to the contract.

3. **Multiple Embedded Derivatives**—Under U.S. GAAP, when a single host contract contains more than one embedded derivative that meets the requirements to be accounted for as a separate derivative instrument, those embedded derivatives must be bundled together and treated as a single, compound embedded derivative. Under IFRS, however, when a single host contract contains more than one embedded derivative with different underlying risk exposures that are readily separable and are independent of each other, the embedded derivative elements must be accounted for separately.

4. **Measurement**—There are no significant differences between U.S. GAAP and IFRS with respect to the measurement of derivative instruments; however, there are differences with respect to the use of derivatives for hedging purposes. Those differences will be covered in the appropriate lessons on hedging.

II. **Hedging: U.S. GAAP–IFRS Differences**

The next table summarizes the significant differences with respect to hedge accounting

U.S. GAAP	IFRS
Risk associated with business combination cannot be hedged.	Foreign exchange risk associated with business combination can be hedged.
Part-term hedges not permitted	Part-term hedges are permitted.
Very limited when nonderivative items can be used as hedging instruments	Nonderivative items can be used as hedging instruments.
Only benchmark rates can be hedged.	Interest rate does not need to be the benchmark rate.
The shortcut method is permitted.	The shortcut method is not permitted.

A. Under IFRS, unlike under U.S. GAAP, a forecasted (planned) business combination that is subject to foreign exchange risk can be hedged.

B. Under IFRS, hedging part of the term (or life) of a hedged item is permitted; part-term hedges are not permitted under U.S. GAAP.

C. Under IFRS, nonderivative financial instruments can be used as hedging instruments for hedging any kind of item; under U.S. GAAP, nonderivative instruments can be used only in very limited circumstances.

III. **Fair Value Hedges—U.S. GAAP–IFRS Differences**—Under IFRS, the risks associated with financial items that can be hedged are less restrictive than under U.S. GAAP.

A. Generally, any financial item can be hedged as long as effectiveness can be measured. In addition, under IFRS, hedge effectiveness is required only at each reporting date, which may not be as often as every three months.

B. Unlike U.S. GAAP, under IFRS, a hedged interest rate does not have to be a benchmark rate.

C. Unlike U.S. GAAP, IFRS permits fair value hedging of a portion of a specified risk and/or for a portion of a time period unit maturity.

IV. **Cash Flow Hedges—U.S. GAAP–IFRS Differences**

A. Under IFRS, the gain or loss on the hedge of a forecasted transaction of a nonfinancial asset or liability (e.g., inventory, equipment, etc.) may be used, at the option of the entity, to adjust the basis of the hedged item; under U.S. GAAP, that gain or loss must be deferred through other comprehensive income until the hedged item affects income.

B. Under U.S. GAAP, for consolidated purposes, foreign currency risk can be hedged with internal derivatives (between entities to be consolidated) provided comparable derivatives are entered into (by the intercompany counterparty) with an unrelated third party so that net basis hedging is accomplished. Under IFRS, for consolidated purposes, only instruments with parties external to the reporting entity can be designated as hedging instruments.

V. Foreign Currency Hedges—GAAP–IFRS Differences

A. Under IFRS, the kinds of intercompany transactions subject to hedging of foreign currency exchange risk are more limited than under U.S. GAAP. Generally, only intercompany monetary items and certain intercompany forecasted purchases and sales can be hedged under IFRS. Thus, for example, forecasted or recognized intercompany royalties cannot be hedged under IFRS.

VI. Effectiveness—GAAP–IFRS Differences

A. Under IFRS, an assessment of hedge effectiveness is required only on a reporting date; there is no requirement, as under U.S. GAAP, that an assessment be conducted at least every three months.

B. Under IFRS, qualitative assessment of effectiveness (i.e., using the extent to which critical terms of the hedging instrument and the hedged item match) can be used only in limited circumstances in carrying out prospective assessment; such assessment may not be used to assume perfect effectiveness in retrospective assessment.

C. Under IFRS, the shortcut method for assessing effectiveness is not permitted. U.S. GAAP and IFRS generally have the same disclosure requirement: Both require extensive disclosures.

Foreign Currency Denominated Transactions

Introduction and Definitions

This lesson begins a series of lessons covering foreign currency denominated transactions. The first set of lessons discusses the accounting for foreign currency denominated transactions; the second set of lessons deal with foreign currency conversion. This lesson distinguishes between foreign currency transactions and foreign currency translation and gives examples of each. In addition, currency exchange rates and the alternative ways those rates may be expressed are presented.

After studying this lesson, you should be able to:

1. Define and describe foreign currency conversion.

2. Display your understanding of changes in exchange rates.

3. Define direct quote, indirect quote, spot rates and forward rates.

4. Describe how to account for changes in currency exchange rates at the following dates:

    • When transaction is initiated; and

    • On the balance sheet date; and

    • On the settlement date.

5. Define and describe foreign currency denominated transactions.

I. Foreign Currency Denominated Transactions

Definition
Foreign Currency Transactions: Transactions of a domestic entity denominated in (to be settled in) a foreign currency, but to be recorded on the domestic entity's books in the domestic currency.

Example
A U.S company buys goods from a Japanese company and agrees to pay for the goods with yen, rather than dollars. In this case, the transaction is denominated in yen, but the amount recorded on the books of the U.S. entity is measured in U.S. dollars; therefore, the transaction amount must be converted from yen to dollars.

II. Foreign Currency Translation

Definition
Foreign Currency Translation: Financial statements denominated in (expressed in terms of) a foreign currency, but to be reported in the financial statements expressed in the domestic currency.

Example
A U.S. company has a French subsidiary that maintains its books and prepares its financial statements in euros. In this case, the financial statements are denominated in euros, but must be converted to dollars in order to be consolidated by the U.S. parent.

III. Terms and Definitions

- **A. Direct Quote**—This is a direct exchange rate and it measures how much domestic currency must be exchanged to receive one unit of a foreign currency. $1.25 = 1 €.

- **B. Indirect Quote**—This is an indirect exchange rates and it measures how many units of foreign currency may be purchased with one unit of domestic currency. $1.00 = .80 €. The indirect quote is the reciprocal of the direct quote (1 € / $1.25 = .80 €).

- **C. Spot Rate**—The number of units of a currency that would be exchanged for one unit of another currency on a given date.

- **D. Forward Rate**—The number of units of one currency that would be exchanged for units of another currency at a specified future point in time.

KEY CONCEPTS

1. A foreign currency transaction is when a transaction is denominated in a currency other than the domestic currency.

2. An unsettled foreign currency transaction creates a payable or receivable in a foreign currency.

3. This payable or receivable presents a risk because of the changes in the exchange rates before settlement.

IV. Strengthening or Weakening of Currencies

- **A.** A strengthening or weakening dollar means that the dollar buys more or less of the foreign currency. It also means we receive less or more of the foreign currency owed to us.

- **B.** If we have a payable denominated in the € and the dollar strengthens, since we have to pay a fixed amount of €s, and they are now worth fewer dollars, we have experienced a gain on the liability. The gains or losses arising from transactions denominated in a foreign currency are foreign currency transaction gains or losses.

- **C.** The following chart illustrates the relationship between fluctuations in exchange rates and exchange gains and losses.

	Accounts Receivable Denominated in Foreign Currency	Accounts Payable Denominated in Foreign Currency
Domestic Currency **Weakens**	Exchange Gain	Exchange Loss
Domestic Currency **Strengthens**	Exchange Loss	Exchange Gain

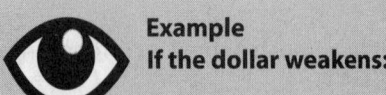

Example
If the dollar weakens:

	from	to
indirect	$1.00 = 0.80 €	$1.00 = 0.625 €
direct	$1.25 = 1 €	$1.60 = 1 €

It will take more U.S. dollars to acquire one unit of foreign currency (€ = foreign currency unit).

Imports become more expensive to the U.S.

U.S. exports become less expensive to the foreign country.

If the dollar strengthens:

	from	to
indirect	$1.00 = 0.80 €	$1.00 = 0.909 €
direct	$1.25 = 1 €	$1.10 = 1 €

It will take fewer U.S. dollars to acquire one unit of foreign currency.

Imports become less expensive to the U.S.

U.S. exports become more expensive to the foreign country.

V. General Principles/Rules

A. Transaction terms provide that the transaction will be settled (by a domestic entity) in a foreign currency.

B. The domestic entity will ultimately pay or receive a foreign currency.

VI. General Rules

A. Measure and record transaction on books in terms of the functional currency.

Example
For a U.S. entity, the transaction must be measured and recorded in dollars.

B. Convert foreign currency units (FC units) to functional currency units ($) using spot exchange rate at date of transaction.

C. Recognize the effects of exchange rate changes:

1. On accounts denominated in a foreign currency (e.g., Receivables/Payables)

2. In the period in which the exchange rate changes

3. As adjustment to account balance, and as exchange loss or gain

VII. Application at Date of Transaction

    A. Determine FC units to settle transaction.

    B. Translate (convert) FC units to reporting currency (U.S. dollars) by:

> \# FC Units × Spot Exchange Rate = Dollar Amount to Settle

    C. Record transaction at dollar amount to settle.

VIII. Application at Balance Sheet Date

    A. Determine (New) Dollar Amount to Settle Currently by

> \#FC Units × Balance Sheet Date Spot Exchange Rate = Dollar Amount at Balance Sheet Date

    B. Determine difference between recorded dollar amount to settle and new (current) dollar amount at balance sheet date.

    C. Record Difference as

        1. Adjustment to recorded receivable/payable

        2. Exchange loss or gain

    D. Report exchange loss or gain in current-period income statement as component of income from continuing operations.

IX. Application at Settlement Date

    A. Determine (New) Dollar Amount to Settle Currently by

> \#FC Units × Settlement Date Spot Exchange Rate = Dollar Amount to Settle.

    B. Determine difference between recorded dollar amount to settle and new (current) dollar amount to settle at settlement date.

    C. Record Difference as

        1. Adjustment to recorded receivable/payable

        2. Exchange loss or gain

    D. Report exchange loss or gain in current-period income statement as component of income from continuing operations.

    E. Record settlement of adjusted receivable/payable account balance.

X. Summary

    A. Below is a summary of the accounting for foreign currency denominated transactions (described above) in table form:

At Date Transaction Initiated	At Balance Sheet Date, If Before Settlement Date	At Date Transaction Is Settled
Translate transaction into dollars using current spot exchange rate:	Determine dollar amount to settle transaction at balance sheet date (settlement amount):	Determine dollar amount to settle transaction (settlement amount):
(#FC units × ER/spot = $ value)	(#FC units × ER/spot = $ value)	(#FC units × ER/spot = $ value)
Record asset, liability, revenue, expense, loss and/or gain on transaction at dollar amount.	Determine difference between recorded amount and settlement amount.	Determine difference between recorded amount and settlement amount.
	Record difference as:	Record difference as:
	—Adjustment to recorded account balance (receivable/payable), and	—Adjustment to recorded account balance (receivable/payable), and
	—Loss or gain for the period.	—Loss or gain for the period.
	Report loss or gain in current-period income statement as component of income from continuing operations.	Record settlement of adjusted account balance.
		Report loss or gain in current-period income statement as component of income from continuing operations.

Import Transactions

When a domestic entity (assume U.S. entity) imports (purchases) an item from a foreign entity and the settlement of the transaction is in the foreign currency, the transaction is denominated in the foreign currency, but reported in the U.S. dollar equivalent of that foreign currency. This lesson illustrates a foreign currency denominated import transaction at initiation of the transaction, adjustment for changes in exchange rates at the balance sheet date, and settlement of the transaction.

After studying this lesson, you should be able to:

1. Record the entries for foreign currency denominated import transactions:

- Calculate the effect of the changes in the exchange rates and related gains and losses, and

- Record the entries for the initial transaction, interim balance sheet date, and the settlement date.

I. Simple Illustration—Purchase (Import) Transaction Denominated in Foreign Currency

Assume: On October 1, 20X2 we entered into a transaction to purchase goods payable in a Foreign Currency (FC) on January 31, 20X3. The purchase was for 1 FC worth of merchandise.

The exchange rates are as follows:

Transaction date:	October 1	$2.00 = 1 FC (direct quotation)
Balance sheet date:	December 31	$1.00 = 1 FC
Settlement date:	January 31	$1.50 = 1 FC

October 1: The entry to record the purchase.

Inventory	$2	
Accounts Payable (FC)		$2

December 31: The FC is worth $1. The change in the exchange rate is recorded.

Accounts Payable (FC)	$1	
Foreign currency transaction G/L (IS)		$1

Note: Foreign currency transaction gain/loss (G/L could be a debit (loss) or credit (gain) depending on the changes in the exchange rates. Also, this account is recognized in earnings on the Income Statement (IS).

January 31: The FC is worth $1.5. Below are the following entries to: 1) record the change in the exchange rate, 2) the purchase of the FC, and 3) settle the transaction.

1. Foreign currency transaction G/L (IS)	$.50	
Accounts Payable (FC)		$.50
2. Investment in FC	$1.50	
Cash		$1.50
3. Accounts Payable (FC)	$1.50	
Investment in FC		$1.50

II. Illustration: Purchase (Import) Transaction Denominated in Foreign Currency

Assume: On November 15 a U.S. Co. purchases equipment from Foreign Co. for 500,000 units of Foreign currency (500,000 FC) with the full amount payable on January 31.

The exchange rates are as follows:

November 15	1 FC = $.75 (direct quotation)
December 31	1 FC = $.74
January 31	1 FC = $.76

November 1: The entry to record the purchase (500,000 × .75 = 375,000).

Equipment	$375,000	
Accounts Payable (FC)		$375,000

December 31: The change in the exchange rate is recorded. It will now take fewer dollars to settle the obligation in FC. (500,000 × (.75 − .74)) = 5,000

Accounts Payable (FC)	$5,000	
Foreign currency transaction G/L (IS)		$5,000

January 31: It will now take more dollars to settle the obligation in FC. Below are the following entries to: 1) record the change in the exchange rate from December 31 to January 31 (500,000 × (.74 − .76) = 10,000), 2) the purchase of the FC (500,000 × .76 = 380,000), and 3) settle the Accounts Payable in FC.

1. Foreign currency transaction G/L (IS)	$10,000	
Accounts Payable (FC)		$10,000
2. Investment in FC	$380,000	
Cash		$380,000
3. Accounts Payable (FC)	$380,000	
Investment in FC		$380,000

Complete a T-account for the Account Payable in Foreign Currency (FC) as a double check to make sure you have recorded everything properly:

Accounts Payable FC

		375,000 (500,000 × .75)	Nov 1
Dec 31 MTM	5,000		
		370,000 (500,000 × .74)	Dec 31
		10,000 MTM	Jan 1
		380,000 (500,000 × .76)	Jan 31
Jan 31 Payment	380,000		
		0 Ending Balance	

Now try to work through the above problem using indirect exchange rates. With indirect exchange rates you divide the foreign currency amount by the exchange rate. Using the rates below, you will get the exact same journal entries and T-accounts shown above.

The exchange rates are as follows:

November 15   1.333333 FC = $1 (direct quotation)

December 31   1.351351 FC = $1

January 31   1.315789 FC = $1

Export Transactions

When a domestic entity (assume U.S. entity) exports (sells) an item to a foreign entity and the settlement of the transaction is in the foreign currency, the transaction is denominated in the foreign currency but reported in the U.S. dollar equivalent of that foreign currency. This lesson illustrates a foreign-currency denominated export transaction. At initiation of the transaction, adjustment for changes in exchange rates at the balance sheet date, and settlement of the transaction.

After studying this lesson, you should be able to:

1. Record the entries for foreign currency denominated export transactions:

- Calculate the effect of the changes in the exchange rates and related gains and losses, and

- Record the entries for the initial transaction, interim balance sheet date, and the settlement date.

I. Simple Illustration—Sale (Export) Transaction Denominated in Foreign Currency

Assume: On October 1, 20X2 we agreed to sell goods with the receivable to be paid in euros on February 1, 20X3, for 1 FC worth of merchandise.

The exchange rates are as follows:

Transaction date:	October 1	$2 = 1 FC
Balance sheet date:	December 31	$1 = 1 FC
Settlement date:	February 1	$3 = 1 FC

October 1: The entry to record the sale at the current exchange rate.

Accounts Receivable (FC)	$2	
Sales		$2

December 31: The entry to record the change in the exchange rate. (We will now receive only $1 worth of FC instead of $2).

Foreign currency transaction G/L (IS)	$1	
Accounts Receivable (FC)		$1

Note: Foreign currency transaction gain/loss (G/L could be a debit (loss) or credit (gain) depending on the changes in the exchange rates. Also, this account is recognized in earnings on the Income Statement (IS).

February 1: The FC is now worth $3. Below are the following entries to: 1) record the change in the exchange rate, 2) the receipt of FCs, and 3) convert the FCs to dollars.

1. Accounts Receivable (FC)	$2	
Foreign currency transaction G/L (IS)		$2
2. Investment in FC	$3	
Accounts receivable (FC)		$3
3. Cash	$3	
Investment in FC		$3

II. Illustration: Sale (Export) Transaction Denominated in Foreign Currency

Assume: On December 15 a U.S. Co. sells goods to a Foreign Co. for 500,000 units of Foreign Currency (500,000 FC) with the full amount payable on January 15.

The exchange rates are as follows:

December 15	1 FC = $.75 (direct quotation)
December 31	1 FC = $.72
January 15	1 FC = $.74

December 15: The entry to record the sale (500,000 × .75 = 375,000).

Accounts Receivable (FC)	$375,000	
Sales		$375,000

December 31: The change in the exchange rate is recorded. When 1 FC is received, it is worth fewer dollars. (500,000 × (.75 − .72)) = 15,000

Foreign currency transaction G/L (IS)	$15,000	
Accounts Receivable (FC)		$15,000

January 31: When 1 FC is received, it is worth more dollars. Below are the following entries to: 1) record the change in the exchange rate (500,000 × (.72 − .74) = 10,000), 2) the receipt of the FC to settle the account receivable (500,000 × .74 = 370,000), and 3) convert the FC to dollars.

1. Accounts Receivable (FC)	$10,000	
Foreign currency transaction G/L (IS)		$10,000
2. Investment in FC	$370,000	
Accounts Receivable (FC)		$370,000
3. Cash	$370,000	
Investment in FC		$370,000

Complete a T-account for the Account Receivable in Foreign Currency (FC) as a double check to make sure you have recorded everything properly:

		Accounts Receivable FC			
Dec 15	(500,000 × .75)	375,000			
			15,000	MTM	Dec 31
Dec 31	(500,000 × .72)	360,000			
Jan 31	MTM	10,000			
Jan 31	(500,000 × .74)	370,000			
			370,000	Collection	Jan 31
		0			

Now try to work through the above problem using indirect exchange rates. With indirect exchange rates you divide the foreign currency amount by the exchange rate. Using the rates below, you will get the exact same journal entries and T-accounts shown above.

The exchange rates are as follows:

December 15	1.333333 FC = $1 (direct quotation)
December 31	1.388888 FC = $1
January 15	1.351351 FC = $1

Foreign Currency Hedges

Introduction to Forward and Option Contracts

The objective of this lesson is to provide an overview of the accounting for forward and option contracts to buy or sell a foreign currency. This lesson defines forward and option and gives examples of each.

After studying this lesson, you should be able to:

1. Define terms related to forward and option contracts, including:

   - Forward contracts,
   - Foreign currency forward exchange contracts, and
   - Foreign currency option contracts.

2. Describe and compute the value of a forward and option contract, including:

   - At inception of the contract,
   - At subsequent Balance Sheet dates, and
   - At settlement of the contract.

3. Record the entries to account for both forward exchange contract and forward option contracts.

I. Definitions

   A. Forward Contract

   > **Definition**
   > *Forward Contracts:* Agreements (contracts) to buy or sell (or which give the right to buy or sell) a specified commodity in the future at a price (rate) determined at the time the forward contract is executed.

   B. For Accounting Purposes—The most important types of forward contracts are:

   1. Foreign Currency Forward Exchange Contracts (FXFC)

   > **Definition**
   > *Foreign Currency Forward Exchange Contracts (FXFC):* An agreement to buy or sell a specified amount of a foreign currency at a specified future date at a specified (forward) rate.

   a. Under an FXFC contract, the obligation to buy or sell is firm; the exchange must occur.

   b. This contract is an *exchange* because the contract provides for trading (exchanging) one currency for another currency.

   Example
   A U.S. entity enters into an FXFC to pay a predetermined price in U.S. dollars for a predetermined quantity of euros.

2. Foreign Currency Option Contracts (FCO)

> **Definition**
> *Foreign Currency Option Contracts (FCO):* An agreement that gives the right (option) to buy (call option) or sell (put option) a specified amount of a foreign currency at a specified (forward) rate during or at the end of a specified time period.

    a. Under an FCO contract, the party holding the option has the right (option) to buy or sell, but does not have to exercise that option. The exchange will occur at the option of the option holder.

> **Example**
> A U.S. entity acquires an option (right) to buy euros but does not have to buy the euros.

    b. If the option is exercised, there is an exchange of currencies.

    c. FCO contracts are significantly more costly to execute than FXFC contracts because the option must be purchased by paying an option premium to the counterparty for the right to buy or sell the currency.

    d. The benefit of an FCO (over an FXFC) is that if changes in the exchange rate do not warrant it, the contract does not have to be exercised; therefore, only the option premium (cost) is incurred.

II. The Accounting Treatment

  A. Derivative Instruments—Both foreign currency forward exchange contracts and foreign currency option contracts are derivative instruments.

    1. All derivative instruments are adjusted to and reported at fair value.

    2. Changing fair value of derivatives result in gains and losses.

    3. When derivatives are used for hedging purposes, gains and losses on those derivatives serve to offset losses or gains on the hedged item.

  B. Determining Fair Value of Forward Exchange Contracts

    1. A forward exchange contract requires the parties to the contract to exchange currencies at the maturity of the contract (or to otherwise settle the contract).

    2. The fair value of a forward exchange contract is determined by **changes** in the forward (exchange) rate during the life of the contract, discounted to its present value.

    3. Changes in the forward rate can result in an increase in fair value (a gain) or a decrease in fair value (a loss).

    4. At the inception of a forward contract, it typically has no value (there has been no **change** in the forward rate); changes in value (and gains or losses) occur as the forward rate changes.

    5. Illustration

      a. Facts: On November 2, year 1, Usco, Inc. enters into a forward exchange contract to sell 10,000 euros (€) in 90 days. The relevant direct exchange rates are:

	Spot Rates	Forward Rates (to January 31, year 2)
November 2, year 1	$1.20	$1.25
December 31, year 1	1.22	1.23
January 31, year 2	1.24	1.24

b. November 2—Contract Initiated:

    i. The contract amount is 10,000€ × $1.25 = $12,500, and since that is based on the quoted rate at that date, it has no intrinsic value; anyone could obtain a 90-day forward contract at $1.25.

    ii. Entry: No entry required; no payment was made and the contract has no value.

c. December 31—Balance Sheet Date:

    i. The forward rate at December 31 is $1.23, a decrease of .02 per euro. Thus, the contract amount is now 10,000€ × $1.23 = $12,300, a change (decrease) of $200. Since Usco has a contract that enables it to sell 10,000€ for $1.25 each and 10,000€ could be sold now (December 31) for only $1.23 each, the $200 change is the nominal value of the contract—the value of Usco's right to sell 10,000€ at $1.25 each. The fair value (and amount of gain) is the present value of the $200. That would be determined by discounting the $200 for one month (31 days in January) at the appropriate discount rate (e.g., the firm's incremental borrowing rate).

    ii. If the appropriate discount rate is 12%, or 1% per month, the present value of $200 due in one month (January 1–31) would be $200 × .99 = $198, the fair value of the contract asset on December 31. The entry would be:

DR: Forward Contract	$198	
CR: Gain on Forward Contract		$198

    1. If the contract was entered into for speculative purposes (i.e., to make a profit), the gain would be recognized in current (year 1) income.

    2. If the contract was entered into as a qualifying hedge, the treatment of the gain would depend on the nature of the hedge (see subsequent lessons).

d. January 31—Settlement Date:

e. The forward rate is the spot rate, $1.24 (the forward and spot rate converge upon the maturity of the forward contract), an increase of .01 per euro since December 31. Thus, the current amount to, an increase of .01 per euro since December 31. Thus, the current amount to satisfy the contract is 10,000€ × $1.24 = $12,400, the amount that would be paid to acquire 10,000€ to satisfy the contract (and the amount that would be received if the euros were sold on the current spot market). As provided by its forward contract, however, Usco will received 10,000€ × $1.25 = $12,500, not $12,400. Thus, its entry would be:

DR: Cash (sell 10,000€ × $1.25)	$12,500	
Loss on Forward contract	98	
CR: Cash (buy 10,000€ × $1.24)		$12,400
Forward Contract (booked 12/31)		198

f. The net effect over the life of the contract is a $198 gain in year 1 and a $98 loss in year 2, for a net gain of $100, which is the difference between the dollar cost of buying 10,000€ at $1.24 = $12,400 and the dollar amount received from reselling the euros under the forward contract, 10,000€ at $1.25 = $12,500.

C. Determining Fair Value of Forward Exchange Option Contracts

1. A forward exchange option contract gives the holder of the contract the right to buy (call option) or sell (put option) a foreign currency, but does not require the holder to do so.

2. The determination of the fair value of a forward exchange option contract depends on the market in which the option is traded, if any.

3. Alternatives for determining forward exchange option fair value:

a. Exchange-traded options: Market price quoted on exchange = fair value

b. Over-the-counter options: Price quoted from option dealer = fair value

c. Not traded in active market: Option pricing model (e.g., modified Black-Scholes option price model) = fair value

4. At the inception of a forward option contract, the buyer will pay a premium (option premium) to the counter party for the right to buy from or sell to the counterparty according to the terms of the contract; the amount of the premium would be a function of the intrinsic value of the option and the "time value" factor.

a. Intrinsic value: The difference between the current spot rate for the currency and the strike price—that is, the price at which exercise of the option would result in a gain

b. Time value: The "value" assigned to the probability that the relationship between the changing spot price and the strike price will increase the value of the option during its life

5. Illustration

a. Facts: On November 2, year 1, Usco, Inc. enters into a call option contract to buy 10,000 euros (€) in 90 days with a strike price of $1.21. The exchange rates and option premiums for the option period are:

	Spot Rate	Forward Rates (to January 31, year 2)	Option Premium
November 2, year 1	$1.20	$1.25	$200
December 31, year 1	1.22	1.23	350
January 31, year 2	1.24	1.24	300

b. November 2—Contract Initiated:

    i. Usco paid a premium of $200 for the contract; that is its fair value at that date.

Entry:

DR:	Foreign Currency Option	$200	
	CR: Cash		$200

c. December 31—Balance Sheet Date:

    i. The option premium, as quoted by option sellers for a contract with comparable terms, has increased from $200 to $350, an increase (gain) of $150.

Entry:

DR:	Foreign Currency Option	$150	
	CR: Foreign Currency Option Gain		$150

If the contract was entered into for speculative purposes (i.e., to make a profit), the gain would be recognized in current (year 1) income.

If the contract was entered into as a qualified hedge, the treatment of the gain would depend on the nature of the hedge (see subsequent lessons).

d. January 31—Settlement Date:

    i. The option premium is $300, the intrinsic value of the option at that date, computed as 10,000€ × ($1.24 − $1.21) = 10,000€ × .03 = $300. At the settlement date, there is no time value associated with the contract; it has only intrinsic value.

Entry:

DR:	Foreign Currency (Euros)	$12,400	
	Loss on Foreign Currency Option	50	
	CR: Cash (10,000€ × $1.21)		$12,100
	Foreign Currency Option		350

e. The net effect over the life of the contract is a $150 gain in year 1 and a $50 loss in year 2, or a net gain of $100. Thus, the difference between the cost of euros if purchased January 31 of $12,400 (10,000€ × $1.24) and the cost of the euros purchased under the option contract of $12,100 (10,000€ × $1.21) of $300 is reflected in the $200 cost of the option and a net gain of $100.

D. Both foreign currency forward exchange contracts and foreign currency option contracts are referred to as *forward contracts* in these lessons.

Natural (Economic) Hedge

This lesson illustrates a natural or economic hedge that is not accounted for using hedge accounting. This lesson illustrates the hedge of a purchase and sale denominated in a foreign currency.

After studying this lesson, you should be able to:

1. Define *hedging.*

2. Describe how a forward exchange contract can be used to hedge a receivable denominated in a foreign currency.

3. Record entries associated with a foreign currency receivable, the hedging of that receivable, and the settlement of both the receivable and the hedging instrument.

I. Hedging Definition

Definition

Hedging: A risk management strategy, which generally involves offsetting or counter transactions so that a loss on one transaction would be offset (at least in part) by a gain on the other transaction.

A. You would "hedge a bet" by offsetting a possible loss from betting on one team (to win) by betting on the other team to win.

B. You would hedge against a possible loss in the dollar value of a foreign currency to be received in the future by selling that foreign currency now at a specified rate for delivery when you receive it in the future (a forward contract).

II. Simple Illustration

	November 2	December 31	January 31
Spot rates	$2.00 = 1€	$3.00 = 1€	$2.80 = 1€
Forward rates	$2.10 = 1€	$3.20 = 1€	$2.80 = 1€

Entries with the Broker
 	
At forward rates
	AR—Broker (€) $2.10
	   AP—Broker ($) $2.10
	
	Record the forward contract with the broker. We will pay the broker $2.10 on 1/31 and he will give us 1€.
		AR—Broker (€) $1.10
		   G/L on FX (IS) $1.10
		
		($2.10 – $3.20)
		
		Record the gain on the forward contract with the Broker. The € due from the Broker is now worth more dollars.
			G/L on FX (IS) $ .40
			   AR—Broker (€) $ .40
			
			($3.20 – $2.80)
			
			AP—Broker ($) $2.10
			   Cash $2.10
			
			Investment in € $2.80
			   AR—Broker (€)
			        $2.80
			
			Record the settlement with the Broker.

Entries with the Spain Comany
 	
At spot rates
	Inventory $2.00
	   AP—Spain Co (€) $2.00
	
	Record the commitment to pay 1€ to Spain Co. which will cost us $2.
		Gain/Loss on FX (IS) $1.00
		   AP—Spain Co (€) $1.00
		
		($2.00 – $3.00)
		
		Record the loss from the weakening dollar.
			AP—Spain Co (€) $ .20
			   G/L on FX (IS) $ .20
			
			($3.00 – $2.80)
			
			AP—Spain Co (€) $2.80
			   Investment in € $2.80
			
			Record the settlement of our AP with the Spain Company.

A. Purchase Denominated in Foreign Currency with Natural Hedge

1. Pumped Up Company purchased equipment from Switzerland for 140,000 francs on December 16, 20X7, with payment due on February 14, 20X8. On December 16, 20X7, Pumped Up also acquired a 60-day forward contract to purchase francs at a forward rate of SFr 1 = $.67. On December 31, 20X7, the forward rate for an exchange on February 14, 20X8, is SFr 1 = $.695. The spot rates were:

December 16, 20X7	1 SFr = $.68	
December 31, 20X7	1 SFr = .70	
February 14, 20X8	1 SFr = .69	

	December 16	December 31	February 14
Spot rate	$.68	$.70	$.69
Forward rate	$.67	$.695	$.69

Entries with Company
 	
Hedged item
 	
Changes in the spot
	Equip 95,200
	   AP (SFr) 95,200
	   (140,000 SFr × .68)
		Fx G/L (IS) 2,800
		   AP (SFr) 2,800
		   (140,000 × (.68 − .70))
			AP (SFr) 1,400
			   Fx G/L (IS) 1,400
			   (140,000 × (.70 − .69))
			
			AP (SFr) 96,600
			   Invest in (SFr) 96,600
			   (Pay Swiss Co.)
			   (.69 × 140,000)

Entries with Broker
 	
Hedging instrument
 	
Changes in the forward
	AR (SFr) 93,800
	   AP ($) 93,800
	   (140,000 SFr × .67)
		AP (SFr) 3,500
		   Fx G/L (IS) 3,500
		   (140,000 × (.67 − .695))
			Fx G/L (IS) 700
			   AP (SFr) 700
			   (140,000 × (.695 − .69))
			
			AP ($) 93,800
			   Cash 93,800
			   (Pay Broker)
			   (.67 × 140,000)
			
			Invest in (SFr) 96,600
			   AR (SFr) 96,600
			   Receive SFr (.69 × 140,000)

Accounts Receivable Sfr		Accounts Payable Sfr	
(140,000 x .67) 93,800			95,200 (140,000 x .68)
3,500			2,800
(140,000 x .695) 97,300	700	1,400	98,000 (140,000 x .70)
(140,000 x .69) 96,600			96,600 (140,000 x .69)

III. Sale Denominated in Foreign Currency with Natural Hedge

A. Alman Company sold pharmaceuticals to a Swedish company for 200,000 kronor (SKr) on April 20, with settlement to be in 60 days. On the same date, Alman entered into a 60-day forward contract to sell 200,000 SKr at a forward rate of 1 SKr = $.167 in order to manage its exposed foreign currency receivable. The forward rate on May 31 was 1 SKr = $.168. The forward contract is not designated as a hedge. The spot rates were:

April 20	SKr 1 = $.170
May 31	SKr 1 = .172
June 19	SKr 1 = .165

Select Transactions

	April 20	May 31	June 19
Spot rate SKr	.170	.172	.165
Forward Rate	.167	.168	–

Entries with Company
 	
Hedged item
 	
Changes in the spot
	AR (SKr) 34,000
	     Sales 34,000
	
	(200,000 × .17)
		AR (SKr) 400
		   FX G/L (IS) 400
		
		((.170 − .172) × 200,000)
			Fx G/L(IS) 1,400
			   AR (SKr) 1,400
			
			((.172 − .165) × 200,000)
			
			Invest in SKr 33,000
			   AR (SKr) 33,000
			
			(Receive SKr)
			(.165 × 200,000)

Entries with Broker
 	
Hedging instrument
 	
Changes in the forward
	AR $ 33,400
	   AP (SKr) 33,400
	
	(200,000 × .167)
		Fx (G/L) (IS) 200
		   AP (SKr) 200
		
		((.167 − .168) × 200,000)
			AP(SKr) 600
			   Fx G/L (IS) 600
			
			((.168 − .165) × 200,000)
			
			AP (SKr) 33,000
			   Invest in SKr 33,000
			   (Pay Broker)
			
			Cash 33,400
			   AR 33,400
			   (Receive $)

Accounts Receivable SKr		Accounts Payable SKr	
(200,000 x .17) 34,000			33,400 (200,000 x .167)
400			200
(200,000 x .172) 34,400	1400	600	33,600 (200,000 x .168)
(200,000 x .165) 33,000			33,000 (200,000 x .165)

IV. **Hedging Costs**

A. **Hedging Minimizes or Prevents Losses**—From exchange rate changes (per se), but usually involves some costs of doing so, including:

1. Fees or other charges imposed by the other party to the forward contract

2. Differences between spot rates and forward rates at the date the forward contract is initiated

Hedging Forecasted Transactions and Firm Commitment

When forward currency forward exchange contracts are used for hedging, GAAP defines the kinds of risks that may be hedged for accounting purposes. This lesson identifies those types of risks and provides discussion of the hedge of a foreign-currency denominated forecasted transaction and firm commitment.

After studying this lesson, you should be able to:

1. Describe the criteria and accounting treatment for the hedge of a foreign currency denominated transaction.

2. Describe the criteria and accounting treatment for the hedge of a foreign currency denominated transaction.

3. Identify and describe the items that can be hedged for accounting purposes.

I. **Purpose of Hedging**—GAAP identifies the following types/purposes of using forward contracts for hedging purposes when the item hedged is denominated in a foreign currency:

   A. **Forecasted Transaction**—Hedge a forecasted transaction denominated in a foreign currency; to offset the risk of exchange rate changes on nonfirm but budgeted (planned) transactions to be denominated in a foreign currency

   B. **Unrecognized, Firm Commitment**—Hedge an unrecognized, but firm commitment denominated in a foreign currency; to offset the risk of exchange rate changes on firm commitments for a future purchase or sale to be denominated in a foreign currency

   C. **Recognized Assets or Liabilities**—Hedge recognized (exposed) assets (e.g., receivables) or liabilities (e.g., payables); to offset the risk of exchange rate changes on already booked assets and liabilities denominated in a foreign currency

   D. **Available-for-Sale Investment**—Hedge an investment in available-for-sale securities; to offset the risk of exchange rate changes on this class of investments denominated in a foreign currency

   E. **Net Investment in Foreign Operation**—Hedge a net investment in a foreign operation (e.g., subsidiary); to offset the risk of exchange rate changes on an investment in a foreign operation (e.g., translated value of financial statements expressed in a foreign currency)

II. **Relationships**

   A. The first three types of hedges listed above can occur as a sequence of events (hedges). In sequence of occurrences, these hedges are of:

      1. A forecasted transaction, which may become

      2. An identifiable foreign-currency commitment, which results in a recorded transaction that creates

      3. A recognized asset (receivable) or liability (payable).

Example

A U.S. entity may include in its annual budget the purchase of a major piece of equipment from a foreign entity to be paid in the foreign currency (a forecasted transaction).

During the budget period, the U.S. entity enters into a contract with a foreign entity to construct the equipment (an identifiable firm commitment).

Upon receiving the equipment, the U.S. entity records the asset and the payable to the foreign entity (a recognized liability).

    B. The **purpose**, **criteria**, and **accounting treatment** for each of the five types of hedges and for speculation are presented in the following lessons.

III. Hedging Forecasted Transactions

    A. Purpose—To offset the risk of exchange rate changes on non-firm, but budgeted (planned) foreign currency transactions (e.g., purchase or sale) between the time the transaction is planned and when it becomes firm or is executed.

Examples

    1. Hedge import or export transactions (denominated in a foreign currency), which are included in a firm's annual budget (i.e., planned).

2. Hedge dividends from a foreign subsidiary that are budgeted for the coming year.

    B. Designation

        1. Criteria for Designation—Use of a forward contract, either an exchange contract or an option contract, to hedge a forecasted transaction requires that (these requirements generally apply to all hedges):

            a. The forecasted transaction must be identified, probable of occurring, and present an exposure to foreign-currency price changes.

            b. Use of a forward contract to hedge must be consistent with company risk management policy, designated and documented in advance as intended as a hedge, and be highly effective as a hedge.

        2. Nature of Designation—A hedge of a forecasted transaction is a cash-flow hedge; the hedge is to offset changes in cash flow associated with the forecasted transaction.

        3. Accounting Treatment

            a. The **change in the fair value** of the forward exchange contract, measured as the change in the forward exchange rate, should be recognized as an increase or decrease in the contract carrying value with a corresponding loss or gain recognized.

            b. To the extent the change in the value of the forward contract (the hedge) is effective in offsetting a decrease (loss) or an increase (gain) in the expected cash flow of the forecasted transaction, the gain or the loss should be deferred and reported as a component of *other comprehensive income*.

            c. To the extent the change in the value of the forward contract (the hedge) is ineffective in offsetting the change in the expected cash flow of the forecasted transaction (i.e., to the extent the changes in the forward contract and the expected cash flow are different), that amount of loss or gain should be reported in current income.

d. Illustration—Assume for a period the following changes occurred in the present value (PV) of a forecasted cash flow and the fair value (FV) of a forward contract designated as a hedge of the forecasted cash flow:

Decrease in PV of expected cash flow of forecasted transaction	$48,000
Increase in FV of forward contract	$50,000
Increase in FV > Decrease in PV	$ 2,000

Related Entry (at B/S date):		
DR: Forward Contract	$50,000	
CR: Other Comprehensive Income		$48,000
Gain on Cash Flow Hedge		$2,000

e. Amounts (losses and gains) deferred in *other comprehensive income* should be recognized in net income in the period(s) in which the related forecasted transaction(s) affect net income.

IV. Hedging Firm Commitments

A. Purpose—To offset the risk of exchange rate changes on a firm commitment for a future purchase or sale denominated in a foreign currency; a contract has been entered into, but the related transaction has not been recorded under GAAP. The risk of an exchange rate change on the contract is the same as if the purchase or sale were recorded.

Example
Hedge the obligation incurred when a purchase order is placed with a foreign entity to manufacture and deliver equipment with payment to be made in a specified amount of foreign currency. The buying party has a contractual obligation to "take and pay" on delivery of the equipment, but under GAAP will not record the obligation until the equipment is delivered.

B. Risk of Exchange Rate Changes—Since the contract is to pay a specified amount of foreign currency, the party is at risk of exchange rate changes between the date of the contract (purchase order) and the date the purchase and obligation to pay (accounts payable) are recorded.

C. Designation

1. Criteria for Designation—Use of a forward contract, either an exchange contract or an option contract, to hedge a firm commitment requires that:

a. The commitment being hedged **must be firm**, be identified, and present exposure to foreign currency prices changes.

b. The forward contract must be designated and effective as a hedge of a commitment and be in an amount that does not exceed the amount of the commitment. (To the extent the amount of the forward contract exceeds the amount of the commitment, the forward contract is treated as speculation, not a hedge.)

2. Nature of Designation—A hedge of a firm commitment can be either a *fair value hedge* (the hedge is to offset changes in (dollar) fair value of the firm commitment); or a *cash flow* *hedge* (the hedge is to offset changes in expected cash flow associated with settling the firm commitment).

3. **Accounting Treatment (Assuming a Fair Value Hedge)**

   a. The change in fair value of the forward contract (the hedging instrument), measured as the change in the forward exchange rate, should be recognized as an increase or decrease in the carrying value of the forward contract with a corresponding gain or loss recognized in net income.

   b. The change in fair value of the firm commitment (the hedged item), measured as the change in the forward exchange rate, should be recognized as in increase or decrease in the carrying value of the firm commitment with a corresponding gain or loss recognized in net income. (Note: This treatment requires recognizing an asset or liability for the firm commitment that otherwise would not be recognized under GAAP.)

   c. To the extent the gain or loss on the forward contract does not exactly offset the loss or gain on the firm commitment (i.e., the de facto ineffectiveness of the hedge), there will be a net gain or loss reported in current net income.

4. **Accounting Treatment (Assuming a Cash-Flow Hedge)**

   a. The change in the fair value of the forward exchange contract, measured as the change in the forward exchange rate, should be recognized as an increase or decrease in the contract carrying value with a corresponding loss or gain recognized.

   b. To the extent the change in the value of the forward contract (the hedging instrument) is effective in offsetting a decrease (loss) or an increase (gain) in the expected cash flow of the firm commitment, the gain or the loss should be deferred and reported as a component of *other comprehensive income*.

   c. To the extent the change in the value of the forward contract (the hedging instrument) is ineffective in offsetting the change in the expected cash flow of the firm commitment (i.e., to the extent the changes in the forward contract and the expected cash flow are different), that amount of loss or gain should be reported in current income.

5. These treatments as fair value hedge or cash flow hedge are the same as described and illustrated for fair value and cash flow hedges in the financial instruments topic.

Hedging Asset/Liability, Available for Sale, and Foreign Operations

This lesson covers the hedge accounting for a foreign currency denominated asset or liability, an available-for-sale security, and an investment in foreign operations.

After studying this lesson, you should be able to:

1. Describe the hedge accounting of a hedge of a foreign currency denominated asset or liability.

2. Describe the hedge accounting of a hedge of a foreign currency denominated available-for-sale security.

3. Describe the hedge accounting of a hedge of an investment in foreign operations.

I. **Hedging Foreign Currency Denominated Asset or Liability**—To offset the risk of exchange rate changes on an existing (already booked) asset or liability.

> **Example**
> Hedge the risk of exchange rate changes reducing the dollar value of a receivable denominated (to be received) in a foreign currency, or the risk of exchange rate changes increasing the dollars required to settle a payable denominated (to be paid) in a foreign currency. For example, a receivable denominated in a foreign currency will result in collection of a fixed number of foreign currency units, but the dollar value of those units will vary with changes in the exchange rate between that foreign currency and the dollar. A U.S. company could enter into a forward contract now to sell those foreign currency units when received in the future and thus hedge the receivable.

A. **Criteria for Designation**—Use of a forward contract, either an exchange contract or an option contract, to hedge a recognized asset or liability requires that:

1. The asset or liability is denominated in a foreign currency and has already been booked (recognized).

2. The gain or loss on the hedged asset or liability must be recognized in earnings.

B. **Nature of Designation**—A hedge of a recognized asset or liability can be either a cash-flow hedge or a fair value hedge.

1. To qualify as a cash-flow hedge, the hedging instrument must completely offset the variability in (dollar) cash flows associated with the receivable or payable.

2. If the instrument does not qualify as a cash-flow hedge or if management so designates, the hedging instrument will be a fair value hedge.

C. **Accounting Treatment**—The accounting for the hedge of a recognized asset or liability would depend on the designated purpose of the hedge—whether to hedge cash flow or to hedge fair value.

1. If to hedge cash flow, the treatment would include:

   a. Adjusting the hedged item (receivable or payable) to fair value each balance sheet date using the spot exchange rate and recognizing the change in fair value as a gain or loss in comprehensive income.

b. Adjusting the hedging instrument to fair value each balance sheet date using the forward exchange rate and recognizing the change in fair value as follows:

    i. An amount up to the amount equal to the gain or loss recognized on the hedged item is recognized as a loss or gain in comprehensive income to offset the gain or loss on the hedged item.

    ii. The amount greater than the gain or loss on the hedged item is recognized in current income (income or expense). Typically this excess is the current-period amortization of any premium or discount on the hedging instrument.

2. If to hedge fair value, the treatment would include:

    a. Adjusting the hedged item (receivable or payable) to fair value each balance sheet date using the spot exchange rate and recognizing the change in fair value as a gain or loss in current income

    b. Adjusting the hedging instrument to fair value each balance sheet date using the forward exchange rate and recognizing the change in fair value as a gain or loss in current income

    c. To the extent the change in fair value of the hedging instrument and the change in the fair value of the hedged item are different there will be a net effect in current income.

D. Alternate Accounting Treatment—A firm can mitigate the risk of exchange rate changes on recognized accounts receivable and accounts payable denominated in a foreign currency without using hedge accounting. See the lesson "Natural (Economic) Hedge" for an illustration of this type of hedge.

II. Hedging Foreign Currency Denominated Available-for-Sale Security—To offset the risk of exchange rate changes on an investment in securities (debt or equity) that are held available for sale.

Example
Hedge the risk of exchange rate changes on the (dollar) fair value of an investment in debt or equity securities held available for sale that will be settled in (sold for) a foreign currency.

A. Criteria for Designation—Use of a forward contract, either an exchange contract or an option contract, to hedge an available-for-sale investment requires that:

1. The securities being hedged must be identified and must not be traded in the investor's currency.

2. The forward contract must be designated and highly effective as a hedge of the investment, and in an amount that does not exceed the amount of the investment being hedged. (To the extent the amount of the forward contract exceeds the investment, the forward contract is treated as speculation, not a hedge.)

B. Nature of Designation—A hedge of an investment available for sale Is a fair value hedge; the hedge is to offset changes in (dollar) fair value of an investment.

1. Accounting treatment

    a. The change in fair value of the forward contract (the hedge), measured as the change in the forward exchange rate, should be recognized as an increase or decrease in the carrying value of the forward contract with a corresponding gain or loss in net income.

    b. The change in fair value of the investment (the hedged item), measured as the change in market value, should be recognized as an increase or decrease in the carrying value of the investment with a corresponding gain or loss in net income.

> **Note**
> *This treatment requires recognizing changes in the fair value of available-for-sale investments in net income, not in other comprehensive income as otherwise would be required under GAAP.*

      c. To the extent the gain or loss on the forward contract does not exactly offset the loss or gain on the investment (i.e., the de facto ineffectiveness of the hedge), there will be a net gain or loss reported in current net income.

III. Hedging Foreign Investment in Foreign Operations—To offset the risk of exchange rate changes on the translation (conversion) of the financial statements of a foreign operation, (branch, investee or subsidiary) from the foreign currency to dollars.

Example

Hedge the risk that the dollar value of an investment in a foreign subsidiary will fluctuate as a result of exchange rate changes. Translation (conversion from foreign currency units to dollars) of accounts on the financial statements of the foreign subsidiary requires use of changing exchange rates, which subject the investment carried by the parent to fluctuate solely as a result of exchange rate changes.

The U.S. parent could (1) borrow in the foreign currency of the subsidiary (a liability) to offset (hedge) the effects of changes in the exchange rate on conversion of the financial statements (a net asset), (2) acquire a foreign currency call option to offset (hedge) the effects of changes in exchange rate on the conversion of the financial statements (a net asset).

A. Criteria for Designation—Use of a hedge instrument (e.g., borrowing or derivative contract) to hedge a net investment in a foreign operation requires that the contract be designated as a hedge of the net investment and be highly effective. The FASB classified this type of hedge as a **fair value hedge** because the **changes in the value** of the foreign investment (foreign investment using the equity method or foreign subsidiary to be consolidated). It is not classified as a cash flow hedge because it is highly unlikely that the investor will be liquidating its foreign investment to create a cash-flow risk. That is, if the investor holds significant ownership (>20% for equity method) or control (>50%), the investor is not likely to frequently sell that foreign investment; therefore, the **risk is the changes in value,** not the cash flows from liquidating the investment. The unrealized gains and losses are classified in OCI to offset the translation adjustment associated with the conversion of the foreign investment.

B. Nature of Designation—A hedge of a net investment in a foreign operation is accounted for like a cash flow hedge with the effective portion recorded in Other Comprehensive Income.

C. Accounting Treatment

    1. The change in fair value (in dollars) of both the hedging instrument (e.g., a borrowing) and the change in the translated value of the balance sheet of the foreign entity (hedged item) should be determined.

    2. To the extent the change in fair value (in dollars) of the hedging instrument is equal to, or less than, the change in the translated balance sheet, both changes enter into the cumulative translation adjustment (an item of other comprehensive income) as offsets to each other.

    3. To the extent the change in fair value (in dollars) of the hedging instrument is greater than the change in the translated balance sheet, the excess (of change in the hedging instrument) is recognized as a gain and reported in current net income.

Speculation and Summary

Forward contracts can be used for speculative purposes. In this case, there is no existing obligation (to pay or receive a foreign currency) being hedged, rather the forward contract is entered into to make money. This lesson also presents a summary of the use of forward contracts and the accounting treatment for such contracts .

After studying this lesson, you should be able to:

1. Describe the accounting treatment of a forward contract used for speculation.

I. Purpose

A. To make a gain as a result of exchange rate changes either by buying foreign currency for future delivery at a price lower than its value when delivered or by selling foreign currency for future delivery at a price higher than it can be bought at the delivery date. In this case, there is no existing obligation or other conversion being hedged; rather, the forward contract is entered into to make a profit (i.e., for speculative purposes).

> **Example**
> A U.S. entity enters into a forward contract to purchase euros in 180 days at a rate (forward rate) existing now in the belief that the existing forward rate is less than the spot rate will be in 180 days. To the extent the forward contract rate is less than the spot rate on the date the contract expires, the entity would make a gain. (Of course, if the spot rate at expiration is less than the forward contract rate, the entity would incur a loss.)

B. Any derivative that does not meet the requirements to qualify as a hedging instrument would be treated as held for speculative purposes.

II. Criteria for, and Nature of, Designation—When a forward contract is used for speculation, there is no separate risk being hedged. The forward contract and the resulting loss or gain stand alone. They are not intended to offset any existing exposure.

III. Accounting Treatment

A. The forward exchange contract is measured (valued) and recorded at the forward exchange rate (quoted now) for exchanges that will occur at the maturity date of the contract.

B. If a balance sheet date occurs between initiation of the contract and maturity (settlement) of the contract, the contract must be revalued (at the balance sheet date) by using the forward exchange rate quoted at that time for the maturity date of the contract. Any change between the balance sheet date value of the contract and the already recorded value of the contract, will be recognized as a gain or loss in net income for the period.

C. At the settlement date (maturity date of the contract), the contract must be revalued by using the spot (current) exchange rate for the maturity date of the contract. Any change between the settlement date value of the contract and the already recorded value of the contract, will be recognized as a gain or loss in net income for the current period.

D. In summary, all gains and losses on derivative instruments held for speculative purposes or treated as for speculative purposes are recognized in current income.

IV. Summary of Foreign Currency Hedges

A. Summary of Accounting for Forward Exchange Contracts by Purpose of Contracts

HEDGE OF:	Type of Hedge	Basic Approach	Treat Gain/Loss	Comments
Forecasted Transaction: To offset risk of exchange rate changes on planned (forecasted) transaction	Cash Flow	Adjust Forward Contract to Fair Value	Effective portion deferred in Other Comprehensive Income. Ineffective portion recognize in Current Income	Only derivative instruments qualify. Deferred gain/loss recognized when forecasted transaction affects income.
Unrecognized Firm Commitment: To offset risk of exchange rate changes on a firm commitment	Cash Flow OR Fair Value	Adjust carrying value to Fair Value for both Forward Contract and Firm Commitment (recognize asset or liability)	Cash Flow: Effective Portion deferred in Other Comprehensive Income, Ineffective portion in Current Income. Fair Value: Recognize in current income for both Forward Contract and Firm Commitment; any difference will affect net income	Either derivative instruments or non-derivative financial instruments may be used.
Recognized Asset or Liability: To offset risk of exchange rate changes on booked assets or liabilities	Cash Flow OR Fair Value	Adjust carrying value to Fair Value for both Forward Contract and Recognized Asset or Liability	Cash Flow: Effective portion in Other Comprehensive Income; Ineffective portion in Current Income. Fair Value: Recognize in current income for both Forward Contract and Recognized Asset or Liability; any difference will affect net income.	Gain/Loss on Hedged Item must be recognized in earnings.
Investment in Available-for-Sale Securities: To offset risk of exchange rate changes on investment	Fair Value	Adjust carrying value to Fair Value for Forward Contract and Investment	Recognize both Forward Contract and Investment change in FV in Current Income; any difference will affect Current Net Income	Only derivative instruments qualify. Gain/loss is not recognized in Other Comprehensive Income.
Net Investment in Foreign Operation: To offset risk of exchange rate changes on conversion of financial statements	ASC 815-35 does not classify this hedge—the accounting is similar to CF hedge because effective portion of gains/loss are reported in OCI	Adjust carrying value of Forward Contract to Fair Value	Recognize as adjustment to Translation Adjustment; Gain in excess of Translation Adjustment to Net Income of current period	Either derivative instruments or non-derivative financial instruments may be used. Adjustment offsets gain/loss on translation of foreign financial statements.
SPECULATION: Entered into for profit; not hedging an exposure to currency risk	(None)	Adjust carrying value of Forward Contract to Fair Value	Recognize in Current Net Income	Not offsetting any obligation or other translation.

Conversion of Foreign Financial Statements

Introduction to Conversion of Foreign Financial Statements

This lesson begins a series of lessons covering foreign currency conversion. Conversion is the process expressing of financial statements expressed in one (foreign) currency to a (domestic) currency. There are two methods of conversion: translation and remeasurement. The key criteria for determining the method of conversion is to determine the entities function currency. This lesson describes the nature of foreign currency conversion and how to determine the functional currency.

After studying this lesson, you should be able to:

1. Identify and define currency concept relevant to foreign currency conversion, including: a) recording currency; b) reporting currency; and c) functional currency.

2. Determine which currency is the functional currency of an entity.

I. Conversion—The Conversion of Financial Statements from One Currency to Another Currency Involves Two Major Steps:

    A. Determining the functional currency of the entity that prepared the original financial statements, and

    B. Applying the correct conversion process based on the functional currency of the entity that prepared the original financial statements.

    C. Foreign-currency conversion occurs when a domestic (U.S.) entity must convert financial statements denominated (expressed) in a foreign currency into their domestic (dollar) equivalents.

II. Sources of Financial Statements—The financial statements denominated in the foreign currency could be those of a branch, joint venture, partnership, equity investee or subsidiary of the domestic entity.

III. Conversion Needed—The conversion could be needed in order to:

    A. Apply equity method by U.S. investor

    B. Combine with other entities

    C. Consolidate with U.S. parent (and other subsidiaries)

IV. Conversion Objectives—The objectives of foreign-currency conversion are:

    A. To provide information that is generally compatible with the expected economic effects of rate changes on an enterprise's cash flows and equity, *and*

    B. To reflect in consolidated statements the financial results and relationships of the individual consolidated entities as measured in their functional primary currencies in conformity with U.S. GAAP.

V. Currency Concepts—The following currency concepts are relevant to foreign currency translation:

    A. Recording Currency—The currency in which the foreign entity's books of account are maintained

    B. Reporting Currency—The currency in which the final (e.g., consolidated) financial statements are expressed

    C. Functional Currency—The currency of the primary economic environment in which an entity operates and generates net cash flows

VI. Conversion Methodology—The specific translation methodology to use to convert financial statements expressed in a foreign currency into domestic (dollar) equivalents depends on the functional currency of the foreign entity. The functional currency of the foreign entity can be:

A. The Recording Currency—The foreign entity's local foreign currency

B. The Reporting Currency—The currency of the final reporting entity (the dollar for a U.S. entity)

C. Another Foreign Currency—A foreign currency other than the recording currency

VII. Determining Functional Currency—Generally, the functional currency of the foreign entity will be determined according to the following guidelines:

A. Functional Currency = (Local, Foreign) Recording Currency—If operations of the foreign entity are relatively self-contained and integrated within the country in which it is located.

    1. EXCEPTION—If the local economy is highly inflationary (i.e., cumulative inflation of 100% or more over a three-year period) the functional currency = reporting currency (the $ if a U.S. subsidiary).

B. Functional Currency = U.S. Reporting Currency

    1. If operations are a direct and integral component or extension of a U.S. entity's (e.g., Parent's) operations, or

    2. When the foreign entity is located in a country with a highly inflationary economy, defined as cumulative inflation of 100% or more over a three-year period.

C. Functional Currency = Another Foreign Currency—(Other than local foreign recording currency or the reporting currency) If the foreign entity generates most of its cash flows in the currency of another foreign country or if required by law or contract.

VIII. Role of Functional Currency—The functional currency of the entity issuing financial statements to be converted to another currency will determine the method to be used to convert the financial statements. Two methods are possible:

A. Translation

B. Remeasurement

Conversion Using Translation

This lesson identifies the exchange rates to use when the translation method of conversion is used and how to treat the resulting translation adjustment.

After studying this lesson, you should be able to:

1. Describe the sequence of requirements when financial statements are converted using translation.

2. Identify the exchange rates to use for converting different financial statement accounts using translation.

3. Describe how the translation adjustment amount is treated when financial statements are converted using translation.

4. Apply the translation method in converting financial statements from one currency to another currency.

5. Describe and apply the reporting of the translation adjustment in a set of converted financial statements.

I. **Translation Process—Local Recording Currency = Functional Currency**—Use translation to convert from foreign currency to reporting currency (the $):

   A. Convert accounts from foreign-currency units (FCU) to dollars using a current exchange rate (CR)—also called spot rate.

      1. **Example**—Conversion: FCU × CR = $

   B. **Current Exchange Rates (CR) to use**

      1. **Revenues, expenses, gains, and losses**—Use exchange rate at dates on which earned or incurred; however, a weighted average rate for the period can be used.

      2. **Assets and liabilities**—Use spot rate at Balance Sheet date (except paid-in-capital and retained earnings, see below).

      3. **Paid-in capital**—Use historic rate in existence when paid-in capital arose (but not earlier than investment in foreign entity).

      4. **Retained earnings**—Calculated as beginning R/E (end of prior period) + translated N/I – dividends declared converted at spot rate at date of declaration = ending R/E ($).

II. **Translation Adjustment**—The amount needed to make the Balance Sheet (expressed in dollars) balance is the amount of the translation adjustment.

   A. Under **Translation** (method of converting) the Translation Adjustment does NOT enter into determination of Net Income, but is treated as Other Comprehensive Income for reporting purposes.

   B. Accumulated Other Comprehensive Income (including the accumulated translation adjustment) is reported as an item in Shareholders' Equity in the translated ($) Balance Sheet.

III. Illustration (simple) of translation (local foreign currency is the functional currency):

Example

Assume a U.S. entity has a Mexican subsidiary, which maintains its accounting records and prepares its financial statements in the local currency, the Mexican peso (MP).

Relevant exchange rates are:

Historic rate when subsidiary was established:

1MP = $.0950

Average rate for the current-period 20X8:

1 MP = $.1000

Spot rate at date of dividend declaration:

1 MP = $.1010

Spot rate at end of current-period 12/31/X8:

1 MP = $.1020

IV. Translation—Of the (simple) financial statements from MP to U.S. dollars would occur as follows:

Foreign Subsidiary Statements			
For the Year Ended 12/31/X8		**Translation Process**	
Statement of Net Income and Comprehensive Income (20X8)	**MP**	**Rate for Translation**	**US$**
Sales	100,000	$.1000	$10,000
COGS	(50,000)	.1000	(5,000)
Depreciation	(10,000)	.1000	(1,000)
Other Expenses	(5,000)	.1000	(500)
Net Income	35,000		$ 3,500
Net Income	=====		
Other (Items of) Comprehensive Income: (from B/S below) Translation Adjustment			680
Comprehensive Income			4,180
Retained Earnings (20X8)			
Beginning R/E	60,000	(End 20X7)	$ 5,700
Add: N/I (20X8)	35,000	(Above)	3,500
Deduct: Dividends 20X8	(20,000)	.1010	(2,020)
Ending R/E	75,000		$ 7,180
	=====		=====

Balance Sheet (12/31/X8)

Cash and Accounts Receivable	20,000	.1020	$ 2,040
Inventory	80,000	.1020	8,160
Fixed Assets	25,000	.1020	2,250
Total Assets	125,000		12,750
Liabilities	20,000	.1020	2,040
Common Stock	30,000	.0950	2,850
Retained Earnings	75,000	(Above)	7,180
Subsidary Totals	125,000		12,070
Accumulated Other Comprehensive Income		(To Balance)	680
Total Liability + Equity	125,000		$12,750

A. Items to note in above illustration:

1. All revenue (sales) and expense items were assumed to have occurred evenly throughout the year.

2. Beginning Retained Earnings is the dollar value at the end of the prior year.

3. Dividends are translated at the exchange rate in effect on the date of declaration.

4. Common stock is translated at the exchange rate in effect the day the stock was issued (since parent created the sub).

5. The translated Balance Sheet does not balance (Assets = $12,750; Liabilities + Equity = $12,070) until the translation adjustment is included. The amount of the translation adjustment is the amount needed to make the Balance Sheet balance ($680). The $680 is "plugged."

6. The Translation Adjustment is reported in the Shareholders' Equity Section of the Balance Sheet and as an item of Other Comprehensive Income in reporting Comprehensive Income.

Conversion Using Remeasurement

If the final reporting currency is the functional currency, rather than the local foreign currency, the foreign financial statements will be converted using remeasurement, instead of translation. Similarly, if another foreign currency (other than the recording currency) is the functional currency, the foreign financial statements will have to be remeasured to the functional currency, and then translated to the reporting currency. This lesson identifies the exchange rates to be used when the remeasurement method of conversion is used and how to treat any resulting remeasurement adjustment.

After studying this lesson, you should be able to:

1. Describe the sequence of requirements when converting financial statements using remeasurement.

2. Identify the exchange rates to use for converting different financial statement accounts using remeasurement.

3. Describe how the translation adjustment amount is treated when financial statements are converted using remeasurement.

4. Apply the remeasurement method in converting financial statements from one currency to another currency.

5. Describe and apply the reporting of the remeasurement translation adjustment in a set of converted financial statements.

I. **Remeasurement Process—U.S. Dollar** = **Functional Currency**—Use remeasurement to convert from foreign currency to reporting currency (the $):

   A. Convert accounts from foreign currency units (FCU) to dollars using temporal method:

      1. For monetary items—current exchange rate (CR).

      2. For nonmonetary items—historical exchange rate (HR), that is, exchange rate in existence when account item arose. Monetary items are those where value is fixed by contract (examples: cash, accounts receivable, accounts payable, bonds and notes, etc.)

      3. Examples

FCU of Monetary × CR = $

FCU of Non-Monetary × HR = $

   B. **Historic Exchange Rate**—Basically, use historic exchange rate for nonmonetary items:

      1. **Past Price Valuation**—Assets and liabilities valued at past prices (not for assets and liabilities measured at amounts promised).

         a. **Examples**

            i. Securities carried at cost, if any

            ii. Inventories carried at cost

            iii. Prepaid costs

            iv. Fixed assets/accumulated depreciation

            v. Intangibles (goodwill, etc.)

            vi. Deferred revenue

            vii. Paid-in capital

2. **Historic Rate Conversion**—Revenue and expenses related to assets and liabilities converted at Historic Rate (only).

   a. **Examples**

      i. COGS (when Inventory at cost)

      ii. Depreciation

      iii. Amortization of Intangibles (not GW!)

II. Use Current Exchange Rates for

A. All other (monetary) Assets and Liabilities

B. All other Revenue, Expense, Gain, and Loss Items

III. Remeasurement Adjustment—Amount needed to make the trial balance debit and credits (expressed in dollars) balance is amount of remeasurement adjustment:

A. The remeasurement adjustment is reported as a gain or loss in the income from continuing operations section of the income statement (expressed in dollars).

B. The remeasurement adjustment "flows through" the Income Statement to Retained Earnings.

IV. Illustration (Simple) of Remeasurement (Reporting Currency Is the Functional Currency)

Example

Assume a U.S. entity has a Mexican subsidiary, which maintains its accounting records and prepares its financial statements in the local currency, the Mexican peso (MP). Because the Mexican subsidiary is a sales unit that purchases its inventory for its U.S. parent, it is basically an extension of its parent, not independent of it. Therefore, its functional currency is the U.S. dollar.

Relevant exchange rates are:

Historic rate when subsidiary was established:

1 MP = $.0950

Historic rate when subsidiary Fixed Assets were acquired:

1 MP = $.0975

Average rate for the current-period 20X8:

1 MP = $.1000

Spot rate at date dividend declared:

1 MP = $.1010

Spot rate at end of current-period 12/31/X8:

1 MP = $.1020

V. Remeasurement Illustration

Remeasurement Illustration

For the Year Ended 12/31/X8 Income Statement (20X8)	MP	Translation Process Rate for Translation	US$
Sales	$100,000	.1000	$10,000
COGS	(50,000)	.1000	(5,000)
Depreciation Expense	(10,000)	.0975	(975)
Other Expenses	(5,000)	.1000	(500)
Preliminary Net Income	35,000		$ 3,525
Translation Adjustment			
Gain			383
Net Income			3,908
Retained Earnings (20X8)			
Beginning R/E	$60,000	(End 20X7)	$ 5,700
Add: Preliminary N/I (20X8)	35,000	(Above)	3,525
Deduct: Dividends 20X8	(20,000)	.1010	(2,020)
Preliminary End R/E	75,000		$ 7,205
Add: Adjustment to NI			
(Translation Gain)			383
Ending R/E (Final)			$ 7,588
Balance Sheet (12/31/X8)			
Cash and Accounts Receivable	$20,000	.1020	$ 2,040
Inventory (at cost)	80,000	.1000	8,000
Fixed Assets	25,000	.0975	2,438
Total Assets	125,000		12,478
Liabilities	$20,000	.1020	$2,040
Common Stock	30,000	.0950	2,850
Preliminary R/E	75,000	(Above)	7,205
Preliminary subsidiary totals	$125,000		$12,095
Deduct: Preliminary R/E			$7,205
Add: Final R/E			7,588
Total Liability + Equity			$12,478

Calculation of Cumulative Translation Adjustment (to be carried to Preliminary Net Income)		
Total Assets	$12,478	
subsidiarytotal L + C	12,095	
Adjustment to NI	$ 383	("Flows through" to Retained Earnings)

A. Items to note in previous illustration:

1. Revenues (sales) are assumed to have occurred evenly throughout the year.

2. All inventory sold during the year and remaining on hand at year-end is assumed to have been acquired from the parent evenly throughout the year.

3. Fixed assets and depreciation expense are translated at the exchange rate in effect when the fixed assets were acquired.

4. Dividends are translated at the exchange rate in effect on the date of declaration.

5. Common stock is translated at the exchange rate in effect the day the stock was issued (since the parent created the subsidiary).

6. The preliminary translated Balance Sheet does not balance (assets = $12,478; Preliminary Liabilities + Equity = $12,095). The difference ($383) is not reported as a Translation Adjustment in Shareholders' Equity.

7. The amount needed to balance the Balance Sheet ($383) is recognized as a Translation Adjustment Gain in the Income from Continuing Operations section of the Income Statement, which increases Net Income, which, in turn, increases Ending Retained Earnings resulting in balancing the Balance Sheet.

8. Since the translation adjustment is recognized in net income, it is not shown as an item of Other Comprehensive Income.

Remeasurement, Translation, and IFRS

Under special circumstances, both the remeasurement and the translation methods of converting foreign currency financial statements will be required. This lesson identifies when that would be necessary and the accounting treatment, including the handling of the remeasurement and translation adjustments.

After studying this lesson, you should be able to:

1. Describe when both the remeasurement and translation forms of conversion of financial statements will be required.

2. Describe the application of the remeasurement and translation processes in combination when they are both required.

I. **Remeasurement, then Translation**—A foreign currency other than the recording currency = functional currency.

    A. In this case, both remeasurement and translation will be required:

        1. **Remeasure**—(As previously described) from recording currency to functional currency (which is another foreign currency), then

        2. **Translate**—(As previously described) from functional currency to U.S. $ reporting currency.

II. **The Translation Adjustments**—Resulting from each of the conversion processes will be reported as follows:

    A. **Remeasurement (Translation) Adjustment**—In Income Statement.

    B. **Translation (Translation) Adjustment**—In Other Comprehensive Income for reporting purposes and, subsequently, in Accumulated Other Comprehensive Income in the Shareholders' Equity section of the Balance Sheet.

Example
A subsidiary of a company in the United States is in England. The subsidiary functions in the euro. The local currency is the British pound, the functional currency is the euro, and the reporting currency is the U.S. dollar.

The financial statements would be *remeasured* from British pound to euro and then *translated* from euro to the U.S. dollar.

III. **IFRS**

    A. There are many similarities between U.S. GAAP and IFRS with respect to the accounting for foreign currency translation. There are some slightly different criteria for determining the functional currency, but the result is essentially the same (the currency of the entity's primary business activities). Both require foreign currency—denominated financial statements to be remeasured to the functional currency of the entity. The results from the exchange rates are reported in income. The method to translate from the functional currency to the reporting currency is also the same (except for financial statements hyperinflationary countries).

U.S. GAAP	IFRS
Functional currency is the currency of the primary economic activities.	Functional currency is the currency of the primary economic activities. Determination based on primary and secondary indicators.
Equity is translated at historical rates.	No specific guidance on what rate to use. Once management has chosen to use either the historical rate or the closing rate, the policy should be applied consistently.
Financial statements in hyperinflationary economies are remeasured as if the functional currency were the reporting currency (U.S. dollar).	Financial statements in functional currencies in hyperinflationary economies are indexed using the general price index and then translated to the reporting currency. The indexing results in restatements in terms of the measuring unit at the balance sheet date with the resulting gain or loss in income.

Leases

Background, Operating Leases

This is the first of several lessons addressing the accounting for leases. This lesson provides an overview of accounting for leases and specific guidance on accounting for operating leases.

After studying this lesson, you should be able to:

1. Distinguish between operating and capital leases and describe the general accounting for both types of lease on the lessor and lessee.

2. Articulate the general rationale for capitalizing a lease.

3. Compute annual rent expense and revenue for an operating lease with uneven periodic rentals.

4. Account for leasehold improvements in an operating lease.

I. Definitions

Definitions

Lease: A lease is a contract conveying the right to use property, plant, and equipment for a stated period of time.

Operating Lease: A lease that does not transfer the risks and rewards of ownership to the lessee. The lessee (renter) records rent expense; the lessor (owner) records rent revenue. The asset remains on the lessor's books.

Capital Lease: A lease that transfers the risks and rewards of ownership to the lessee. The lessee recognizes a leased asset and a lease liability on its books and recognizes interest expense and depreciation over the lease term. The lessee "capitalizes" the leased asset. The lessor removes the asset from its books, replaces it with a financial asset, and recognizes interest revenue over the lease term.

    A. When a lease is capitalized by the lessee, the present value of the future lease payments is debited to the leased asset and credited to the lease liability accounts. For the lessor, the present value of lease payments is debited to the net financial asset (a receivable) created at inception (beginning of the lease).

    B. A lease is capitalized when it meets the lease capitalization criteria (discussed later).

II. Accounting for Operating Leases

    1. A lease is accounted for as an operating lease when the capitalization criteria are not met. An operating lease is a lease that is not a capital lease.

    2. Rental contracts often specify that the lessee must pay the first period's rent at the inception. In addition, a bonus or special payment may be required to secure the lease and the last period's rent may also be required to be paid at inception. Also, rent payments may not be of equal amount each year per the rental contract.

3. GAAP requires that the straight-line method of recognizing rent expense and revenue be applied unless another method more accurately reflects the pattern of use. The straight-line method allocates the total rentals, regardless of their timing, on an equal basis to each period. Thus, without regard to the rental schedule, the amount of rent revenue (lessor) and rent expense (lessee) to be recognized each year is:

> Annual Rent Expense or Revenue = Total Rentals over the Lease Term/Number of Years in Lease Term

4. The total rentals include any amounts that will be retained by the lessor as rent. They do not include damage or cleaning deposits. Free rental periods are automatically included in the computation. For example, if the first year of a 10-year operating lease is rent-free, the numerator of the equation above reflects only nine years of rent while the denominator includes 10 years. Each of the 10 years would recognize the same rent expense or revenue.

5. The rationale for the application of the straight-line method is the assumption that the asset will provide equal benefits to the lessee each year. This is the usual assumption. Unless explicit information to the contrary is provided, assume the straight-line method.

6. In some cases, the annual (or monthly) rental begins at a relatively low amount and progressively increases. In the early years of the rental, the amount paid is less than the constant amount expensed per period. As a result, a liability is recorded for the difference. In later years, when the payment amounts exceed the constant expense amount, the liability is gradually extinguished.

7. Leasehold improvements are improvements made to a rental property that revert to the owner at the end of the lease term. These are typically structural changes that cannot be removed at the end of the rental period without damaging the rented property. The cost of leasehold improvements is capitalized by the lessee to a plant asset or an intangible asset and depreciated or amortized to expense over the shorter of (a) remaining term of the rental, and (b) useful life of the improvements. Typically, the remaining term is used for amortization, which is an expense separate from rent expense.

8. The lessor reclassifies the leased asset from plant assets to another category such as *other assets* or *investment in leased assets* during the lease term. However, depreciation continues during the lease term because the asset is being used by the lessee.

III. Examples

> ### Examples
>
> **1.** Ace Co. signed a contract to rent office space from Deuce Co. for three years beginning January 1, Year 1. The rental contract called for annual rentals of $2,000 due at the beginning of each year. However, at inception Ace was required to pay a $600 bonus to obtain the space. Ace was also required to pay the third year's rent at inception. Both parties account for the lease as an operating lease.
>
> Rent expense for Ace (revenue for Deuce) to be recognized each year is $2,200: = (3($2,000) + $600) / 3.
>
> | Entries: | Ace | | Deuce | |
> |---|---|---|---|---|
> | January 1, Year 1 | | | | |
> | Prepaid Rent | 4,600 | | Cash | 4,600 |
> | Cash | | 4,600 | Unearned Rent | 4,600* |
>
> *Unearned rent is a liability; $4,600 = 2($2,000) + $600
>
> | | Ace | | Deuce | |
> |---|---|---|---|---|
> | December 31, Year 1 | | | | |
> | Rent Expense | 2,200 | | Unearned Rent | 2,200 |
> | Prepaid Rent | | 2,200 | Rent Revenue | 2,200 |
> | January 1, Year 2 | | | | |
> | Prepaid Rent | 2,000 | | Cash | 2,000 |
> | Cash | | 2,000 | Unearned Rent | 2,000 |
> | December 31, Year 2 | | | | |
> | Rent Expense | 2,200 | | Unearned Rent | 2,200 |
> | Prepaid Rent | | 2,200 | Rent Revenue | 2,200 |
> | December 31, Year 3 | | | | |
> | Rent Expense | 2,200 | | Unearned Rent | 2,200 |
> | Prepaid Rent | | 2,200 | Rent Revenue | 2,200 |

2. A firm rents office space beginning January 1, Year 1 for five years. The first year rental rate is $1,200 per year, and the rate for the last four years is $1,800 per year.
As an added inducement, the first six-months of the first year are rent-free (a rent abatement). A refundable damage deposit of $800 is collected at inception. The firm accounts for the lease as an operating lease.

The annual rent expense to be recognized for each of the five years of the lease term is $1,560 = [(1/2)($1,200) + 4($1,800)]/5. Only one-half year's rent is required to be paid for the first year. The damage deposit is not included in the rentals because it is to be refunded to the lessee. The lessee records a receivable for the deposit; the lessor records a payable.

Capital Lease Basics

This lesson establishes the terminology and conceptual underpinnings for capital lease accounting.

After studying this lesson, you should be able to:

1. Define the important terms relevant to capital lease accounting including lease term, bargain purchase option, unguaranteed residual value, minimum lease payments, and others.

2. List the items included in minimum lease payments for both parties to the lease.

3. Determine the applicable interest rate for both parties.

4. List and understand the four criteria for capitalizing a lease.

5. Note the additional two criteria for lessors.

I. Capital Lease Terminology

A. The **lease term** is the period during which the lessee can reasonably be expected to continue leasing the asset. The inception of the lease is the first day of the lease term. The lease term is the fixed noncancellable term of the lease plus periods covered by bargain renewal options plus all periods covered by renewal options during which there is a loan outstanding from the lessor to the lessee. The lease term cannot extend beyond the exercise date of a bargain purchase option, even if the lease specifies payments after the date of the bargain purchase option (those later payments would not be paid because the asset will be purchased before those payments).

B. The **bargain purchase option (BPO)** is an option whereby the lessee will have an opportunity in the future to purchase the asset at an amount that is significantly less than the asset's fair value on that future date. The price is sufficiently low to reasonably assure exercise of the option by the lessee. If the lessee accepts the terms of the lease contract, the accounting for both parties assumes the purchase option will be exercised, in which case title transfers to the lessee. The exercise ends the lease term.

   1. The option is not really a bargain, however. The lessor expects the option to be taken and structures all of the payments, including the BPO, to provide the required rate of return. The BPO amount is really just another lease payment.

C. The **guaranteed residual value** clause often is present in lease agreements in which there is no bargain purchase option or transfer of title. (The asset reverts to lessor at the end of the lease term.) The guaranteed residual value refers to the condition of the property at the time that it reverts back to the lessor. If the lessee guarantees the residual value, the lessee is responsible for the condition of the asset at the conclusion of the lease term. Third parties may also guarantee residual values.

   1. If the lessee guarantees a residual value, the lessee will pay the lessor any shortfall between the amount guaranteed and the actual fair value of the asset at the end of the lease term.

   2. An unguaranteed residual value is the expected salvage value of the leased asset at the end of the term that has not been guaranteed.

> **Example**
> The estimated value of a leased asset at the end of the lease term is $3,000. With or without a guarantee, the value is expected to be $3,000. This is the same residual or salvage value discussed in the lessons on depreciation of plant assets, except that it is measured at the end of the lease term, which may be well before the end of the asset's economic life.

D. The **executory costs** involved in a capital lease include casualty insurance, maintenance, and property taxes. These costs are not capitalized by any party, but rather represent annual expenses associated with owning and maintaining the asset. They are not considered when determining whether the lease is a capital or operating lease, and they are not capitalized in a capital lease.

E. **Lessee Minimum Lease Payments**—The minimum lease payments for the lessee are all the payments the lessee is expected to make under the lease, excluding executory costs. The components of the lessee's minimum lease payments are listed below.

1. The annual lease payments

2. Bargain purchase option

3. A residual value guaranteed by the lessee at the expiration of the lease term

4. Any penalty payments the lessee is required to make for not renewing the lease term

5. Excluded are payments required by the lessee for damage, extraordinary wear and tear, or excessive usage because they cannot be estimated. Rather, they are treated as expenses or losses in the period incurred.

F. **Lessor Minimum Lease Payments**—The minimum lease payments from the lessor's perspective are the same as those identified for the lessee with one additional element. The minimum lease payments also include any residual value guaranteed by a third party unrelated to either the lessee or the lessor. An unguaranteed residual is not included in the minimum lease payments of the lessor or lessee because it is a cash flow outside the lease arrangement.

G. The **implicit interest rate** is sometimes described as the lessor's required rate of interest. Mathematically, the implicit interest rate is the rate that equates the fair value of the leased asset with the sum of the present value of the minimum lease payments (lessor's perspective) plus the present value of any unguaranteed residual value. This is the rate used by the lessor for all present value calculations in a capital lease, and for computing interest revenue.

1. This rate is the annual compounded rate of return to the lessor over the lease term. The unguaranteed residual value is included in the calculation because it is part of the value of the asset (as is the case with the salvage value for any plant asset).

Example

A lease requires 10 equal annual lease payments of $4,000 to be paid each January 1. The inception of the lease is January 1, Year 1. The fair value of the asset leased is $27,807. The unguaranteed residual value at the end of the lease term is $2,000. The lessor's implicit rate in the lease is 10%. The discounted cash flows, including the unguaranteed residual value, are related to the fair value as shown in the equation:

$27,807 = market value of asset = present value of the lease payments +

present value of unguaranteed residual value

$27,807 = $4,000(PV ann. due, I = 10%, N = 10) + $2,000(PV $1, I = 10%, N = 10)

= $4,000(6.75902) + $2,000(.38554)

If the cash flows are received as expected, the lessor will earn 10% on a compounded basis annually from its investment in the leased asset. All residual values at the end of the lease term are treated the same way in the above equation. It makes no difference in terms of the lessor's equation if the residual is guaranteed or not.

H. The **lessee's incremental borrowing rate** is the rate, at lease inception date, the lessee would have incurred to borrow the funds necessary to purchase the leased asset rather than lease it.

II. Capital Lease Criteria

A. The four criteria used to determine whether a lease is a capital lease follow. Both parties use these criteria. If one or more of the criteria is met, the lease is a capital lease for the lessee. The lessor also must meet two additional criteria, listed later, for the lease to be capitalized. If none of the first four is met, the lease is an operating lease for both parties.

Study Tip
Caution: To facilitate the discussion, the lease capitalization criteria are referred to by number, but for the CPA Exam, candidates should know the criteria by their descriptions as provided below.

B. In all cases, the lease must be noncancellable for it to be a capital lease. This is generally assumed, if not mentioned, in a problem.

1. **Criterion 1**—The lease agreement transfers ownership of the leased asset to the lessee at the conclusion of the lease term (title transfer).

2. **Criterion 2**—The lease contains a bargain purchase option (BPO).

3. **Criterion 3**—The lease term is at least 75% of the remaining estimated economic life of the leased asset at inception (term is 75% or more of useful life).

Example
A lessor leases an asset with an original useful life when new of 20 years. After two years, the asset is leased for 12 years. The third criterion is not met because 12/18 = .67 which is less than .75. The remaining useful life at inception is 18 years. The lease term is less than 75% of the 18 years of remaining useful life. If none of the other three criteria is met, the lease is an operating lease.

4. **Criterion 4**—The present value of minimum lease payments at the inception of the lease is at least 90% of the fair value of the leased asset at that time (PV is 90% or more of fair value). Review the definition of minimum lease payments. Criterion 4 is the reason that minimum lease payments were defined.

C. For criterion 4, the lessor uses the rate implicit in the lease to measure the present value. The lessee uses the lower of implicit interest rate, if the lessee knows the rate or can determine it, and the lessee's borrowing rate. The lower rate will cause the present value to be higher resulting in a better chance of the lessee fulfilling the fourth criterion and thus having a capital lease. The parties use these interest rates not only in measuring the present value for criterion 4, but also for capitalizing the minimum lease payments for recording purposes and for computing interest.

Example
A lessor leases an asset with a fair value of $100,000 for 10 years. Annual end-of-year lease payments are $15,000. The lessor's implicit rate and lessee's borrowing rate are 10%. The lease calls for no other payments by the lessee and the asset reverts to the lessor at the end of the lease term.

PV of minimum lease payments   = $15,000(PV ord. ann., I = 10%, N = 10)

           = $15,000 × 6.14457

           = $92,169 > .90($100,000)

The fourth criterion is met for both parties because the present value of minimum lease payments for both lessor and lessee ($92,169) exceeds 90% of the fair value of the asset. Thus, the lease is a capital lease.

Caution 1: The present value of minimum lease payments may be different for the lessor and lessee because:

1. Different cash flows may be included in their minimum lease payments (e.g., third-party guarantee of residual); *and*

2. Their interest rates may be different.

Caution 2: When the lease term begins within the last 25% of the total useful life of the asset, critera 3 and 4 no longer can be used to determine whether a lease is capitalized. In this case, title must transfer or a bargain purchase option must be present for a lease to be capitalized.

Example
An asset's original useful life is 20 years. After 15 years of using the asset, a firm leases it to another firm for 4 years. Normally, this lease would qualify as a capital lease because the lease term is 80% of the remaining useful life at inception (4/5). But at inception, only 25% of the total useful life of the asset remains (5/20). Therefore, criterion 3 and criterion 4 can no longer be used for lease capitalization. Most of the asset's useful life is over. If this lease does not transfer title or include a bargain purchase option, then it is an operating lease.

III. Rationale for Lease Capitalization

A. The fundamental rationale for lease capitalization is that if most of the benefits and responsibilities of asset ownership are passed to the lessee, the lessee should record an asset and a lease liability equal to the present value of the minimum lease payments. The four criteria operationalize this concept.

B. If **either of criterion 1 or criterion 2** is met, the lease is essentially an installment purchase of the asset. There is little question that the lessee will obtain most of the benefits of the asset under such an agreement because in both cases, the lessee retains the asset at the end of the lease term.

C. If **criterion 3** is met, the lessee obtains at least 75% of the useful life of the asset. For many assets, this means the lessee will receive considerably more than 75% of the benefits of the asset because many assets are more productive earlier in their useful lives.

D. If **criterion 4** is met, the lessee is making payments with a present value of at least 90% of the fair value of the asset. The lessee is essentially purchasing most of the asset's value. The lessee would not commit to such a stream of payments unless most of the asset's benefits were being purchased through the lease.

IV. Two Additional Criteria for the Lessor—For the lease to be accounted for as a capital lease, the lessor must meet at least one of the first four criteria and both of the next two, which apply only to the lessor:

A. **Criterion 5**—There are no material cost uncertainties that would require unreimbursable costs to be incurred by the lessor.

1. This means that there are no uncertainties that would call into question the capitalization of the lease payments by the lessor. For example, if the lessor guaranteed the asset against obsolescence (not usual in a capital lease), there would be significant uncertainty concerning the net amount of cash inflow per period to the lessor. If that were the case, the uncertain cash flows should not be capitalized, and the lease is accounted for as an operating lease by the lessor.

B. **Criterion 6**—Collectibility of the minimum lease payments is reasonably assured.

1. If collectibility of the lease payments is uncertain, there is no justification for capitalizing them into an asset account. Again, this means the lease is an operating lease for the lessor although it could be a capital lease for the lessee.

V. Summary—Lease Capitalization Criteria

A. To capitalize a lease:

   1. The lessee must meet one of criteria 1–4 (otherwise, the lease is an operating lease).

   2. The lessor must meet one of criteria 1–4, and both 5 and 6 (otherwise, the lease is an operating lease).

B. With the lessor using more criteria than the lessee, it is possible for a lease to be a capital lease for the lessee and an operating lease for the lessor. All that would be required is for the lessor to fail to meet either criteria 5 or 6.

C. Another possibility occurs with criterion 4. The lessor's implicit rate might be considerably lower than the lessee's borrowing rate and the lessee is unable to determine the lessor's rate. The present value of the minimum lease payments might then exceed 90% of the fair value of the property for the lessor, but not for the lessee. Also, the lessor may include payments such as the third party guarantee of residual value in minimum lease payments, whereas the lessee does not.

Note

When examining a lease agreement for the possible failure to meet criteria 5 and 6, the potential problem usually rests with criterion 6. For example, the prime interest rate at the inception of the lease is 7%, but the lessee's incremental borrowing rate is 13%. From that information, you should conclude the lessee is a poor credit risk and conclude the collectibility of lease payments is not assured.

For CPA Exam purposes, assume criteria 1–4 are not met unless there is positive information indicating that one or more of the criteria is met. But for criteria 5 and 6, assume they are met unless there is negative information, as exemplified immediately above.

VI. Classification of Leases

A. A capital lease from the lessor's perspective will be further classified as a direct financing capital lease or a sales-type capital lease. No such classification exists for the lessee. Lessee capital lease accounting is unaffected by whether the lessor has a direct financing lease or a sales-type lease. The following is the breakdown of leases for both parties.

B. Lessee

   1. Operating

   2. Capital

C. Lessor

   1. Operating

   2. Capital

      a. Direct financing (defined later)

      b. Sales type (defined later)

Direct Financing Leases

This lease accounting lesson covers the specifics for recording a direct financing lease for both parties.

After studying this lesson, you should be able to:

1. Identify a direct financing lease from given information.

2. Record the inception journal entry for both parties.

3. Prepare the journal entries for interest recognition for both parties over more than one period.

I. **Direct Financing Capital Lease (DFL) Basics**

    A. A DFL is one of two types of capital leases for the lessor. The other is a STL (Sales Type Lease). This distinction does not affect the lessee. A capital lease is a DFL if the book value of the lessor's asset equals its fair value.

    B. The only revenue a lessor derives from a DFL is interest revenue.

    C. The general entries for a DFL for both parties appear below. The numerical examples illustrate the procedures. The entries are affected by whether the lease payment stream is an annuity due or an ordinary annuity.

    D. **Lessor**

At inception (assumes a new asset)	
Lease Receivable	sum of minimum lease payments + any unguaranteed residual
Unearned Interest revenue	total interest over term
Asset	fair value = cost value

    1. The lessor typically uses the gross method, which records the lease receivable at nominal amounts rather than present value. The present value of the nominal amounts is the net lease receivable balance, which also is the difference between the Lease Receivable and Unearned Interest Revenue accounts.

    2. The present value is computed using the lessor's implicit interest rate. The financial asset replaces the physical asset. The receivable is a noncurrent asset. Unearned Interest Revenue is contra to Lease Receivable.

    3. For a new asset, cost and book value are the same. If the asset is no longer new at inception, then the accumulated depreciation account is closed (debited). In this case, fair value equals book value or carrying value.

    E. **Recognition of Periodic Interest Revenue**

Cash	lease payment amount
Unearned Interest Revenue	equals interest revenue amount
Lease Receivable	lease payment amount
Interest Revenue	beginning net lease receivable × lessor's implicit interest rate

F. The lease payment amount includes principal and interest. The reduction in principal is the difference between the lease payment and the interest revenue amounts. The last lease payment closes the remaining balances in the lease receivable and unearned interest accounts.

Study Tip:
The lessor computes interest revenue based on the net lease receivable, even though the gross method is used for recording.

G. Lessee

At inception	
Leased Asset	present value of minimum lease payments
Lease Liability	present value of minimum lease payments

1. The lessee is capitalizing an asset it does not own and is recording a significant liability based on a contract. The lessee typically uses the net method. (Liability is recorded at present value.) The leased asset is included in plant assets. The lease liability has both current and noncurrent components. The present value is computed using the lower of implicit interest rate if the lessee knows the rate or can determine it, and the lessee's implicit rate. This is the same rate used by the lessee for criterion 4 for lease capitalization.

2. The amount recorded for the asset and liability cannot exceed the asset's fair value. If the present value, as computed, exceeds the fair value, the lease is recorded at the fair value. A new (higher) interest rate, equating the present value of the lease payments and the fair value, is used for computing interest. This provision applies to both lessee and lessor.

H. Recognition of Periodic Interest Expense

Interest Expense	beginning liability balance × interest rate
Lease Liability	amount of liability reduction
Cash	lease payment amount

I. Recognition of Periodic Depreciation

Depreciation expense	amount discussed later
Accumulated depreciation	

1. In a later lesson, the computation of depreciation is discussed. The amount depends on whether title is transferred to the lessee at the end of the lease. Accumulated depreciation is contra to the leased asset.

II. Example—Direct Financing Lease

A. On January 1, Year 1 lessor leases equipment to lessee. Data on the lease:

1. Equipment fair value and Lessor's book value, $25,771 (asset is new);

2. Lessor's implicit rate and Lessee's implicit borrowing rate, 8%;

3. Lease payments due each December 31 through Year 3 (three-year lease term);

4. Useful life of equipment, three years (no residual value).

B. The annual lease payment (L) is computed as:

$25,771 = L(PV ord.ann, I = 8\%, N = 3)$

$25,771 = L(2.57710)$

$L = 10,000$

C. This example illustrates an ordinary annuity payment stream. Later examples illustrate an annuity due.

D. This is a capital lease for both parties because criterion 3 is met (lease term of three years = 100% of useful life at inception). Criterion 4 is also met (present value of minimum lease payments of $25,771 = 100% of fair value at inception). There is no information about criterion 1 or criterion 2 (title transfer, BPO), and we cannot assume those are met.

E. The entries for the first two years are shown for both parties.

F. Lessor, Inception

1/1/Year 1	Lease Receivable 3($10,000)	30,000	
	Unearned Interest ($30,000 –$25,771)		4,229
	Equipment		25,771

The net lease receivable equals $25,771 ($30,000 − $4,229). If the net method were used in the entry above, the lease receivable would be recorded at $25,771 and no contra account (unearned revenue) would be used.

G. Recognition of Interest Revenue, Year 1

12/31/Year 1	Cash	10,000	
	Unearned Interest	2,062	
	Lease Receivable		10,000
	Interest Revenue ($25,771 × .08)		2,062

H. The net lease receivable is now $17,833 [$25,771 − ($10,000 − $2,062)]. The reduction in principal is the lease payment less the interest revenue included in the lease payment.

If the net method were used in the entry above, the lease receivable would be reduced by $7,938 ($10,000 − $2,062), and there would be no unearned interest account in the entry. Whether the gross or net method is used, interest revenue is always computed on the net lease receivable amount.

I.   Recognition of Interest, Year 2

12/31/Year 2	Cash	10,000	
	Unearned Interest	1,427	
	Lease Receivable		10,000
	Interest Revenue ($17,833 × .08)		1,427

J.   The Year 3 entry reduces the net lease receivable to zero.

K.   Lessee Inception, and Year 1 Interest and Depreciation

1/1/Year 1	Leased Asset	25,771	
	Lease Liability		25,771
12/31/Year 1	Lease Liability	7,938	
	Interest Expense ($25,771 × .08)	2,062	
	Cash		10,000
	Depreciation Expense $25,771/3	8,590	
	Accumulated Depreciation		8,590

1.   The lessee records the leased asset and lease liability at present value (net method). One year later, interest expense is based on the lease liability one year before. Assuming the straight-line method, depreciation expense is computed using no residual value per the given information. The lease term and service life are equal. $8,590 of depreciation expense is recognized in each of the three years. The net book value of the asset and net lease liability are the same only at inception. At 12/31/year 1: Book value of leased asset = $25,771 − $8,590 = $17,181. Net lease liability = $25,771 − $7,938 = $17,833. This is the amount on which interest expense for Year 2 is based.

L.   Interest and depreciation recognition, Year 2

12/31/Year 2	Leased Liability	8,573	
	Interest Expense ($25,771 − $7,938)(.08)	1,427	
	Cash		10,000
	Depreciation Expense $25,771/3	8,590	
	Accumulated Depreciation		8,590

M.   The Year 3 entries reduce both the lease liability and net asset book value to zero.

Sales-Type Leases, International

This lesson addresses the specifics for sales-type leases, and the main differences between U.S. and international standards regarding lease accounting.

After studying this lesson, you should be able to:

1. Identify and define a sales-type lease from given information.

2. Prepare the inception journal entry for both parties.

3. Be aware of differences in accounting for leases between U.S. and international accounting standards.

I.   Sales-Type Capital Lease (STL) Basics

A. An STL is one of two types of capital leases for the lessor (the other being DFL). This distinction does not affect the lessee. The lessor derives two types of income from a sales-type capital lease: interest revenue recognized over the lease term, and gross profit recognized at the inception of the lease agreement.

B. In an STL, the book value of the lessor's asset is not equal to (usually less than) its fair value. There is gross profit (or loss) on the lease that is recorded at inception. The lessor need not be a manufacturer or dealer for a capital lease to be a STL for the lessor.

C. The general inception entries for an STL for the lessor appear below. The numerical examples add additional aspects to the entries.

D. Lessor—At inception (although two entries are shown, they can be combined into one):

Lease Receivable	sum of minimum lease payments + any unguaranteed residual
Unearned Interest Revenue	total interest over term
Sales	fair value = selling price
Cost of Goods Sold	cost of asset
Asset	cost of asset

1. The above entry recognizes gross profit immediately. In comparison, a DFL does not. A sale is recorded, as is the cost of goods sold. The gross profit equals sales (recorded at selling price) less cost of goods sold. The net lease receivable (lease receivable less unearned interest revenue) equals the fair value of the asset, which also equals sales. The above entry assumes a new asset. If the asset were used, accumulated depreciation would be debited (closed) and cost of goods sold would reflect the book value of the asset.

2. The generalized entry above shows the unguaranteed residual value included in the receivable for completeness. If there is no unguaranteed residual, then the sales and cost of goods sold are recorded as shown. But if there is an unguaranteed residual, both sales and cost of goods sold are reduced by the present value of the residual because that portion of the asset is not considered sold. The gross margin is unaffected. This aspect is shown in an example in a later lesson.

E. The lease payments are based on the fair value, as they are in a DFL. Interest is also computed on the fair value of the asset. The lessor is financing the lessee's purchase at the selling price, as would be the case in any sale arrangement for which the seller is also acting as the financing source.

F. The remaining entries for the lessor are the same as for a DFL.

II. Example—Sales-Type Capital Lease

   A. Sales-Type Lease (uses the same data as the DFL example in a previous lesson except: cost and fair value are not equal and the payments occur on the first of the year—annuity due). On January 1, Year 1, Lessor leases equipment to Lessee. Data on the lease:

     1. Equipment fair value, $25,771 (asset is new)

     2. Lessor's book value (same as cost because asset is new), $20,000

     3. Lessor's implicit rate and Lessee's implicit borrowing rate, 8%

     4. Lease payments due each January 1 through Year 3 (three-year lease term)

     5. Useful life of equipment, three years (no residual value)

   B. The annual lease payment (L) is computed as:

$25,771 = L (PV ann. due, I = 8%, N = 3)

$25,771 = L (2.78326)

L = $9,259 (smaller than in the previous ordinary annuity example because the payments are made one year earlier, reducing the total interest over the lease term)

   C. This is a capital lease for both parties because criterion 3 is met (lease term of 3 years = 100% of useful life at inception). Criterion 4 is also met (present value of minimum lease payments of $25,771 = 100% of fair value at inception).

   D. The entries for the first two years are shown for both parties.

   E. Lessor Inception

1/1/year 1	Lease Receivable 3($9,259)	27,777	
	Unearned Interest ($27,777 − $25,771)		2,006
	Sales		25,771
	Cost of Goods Sold	20,000	
	Equipment		20,000
	Cash	9,259	
	Lease Receivable		9,259

     1. Analysis: Gross profit of $5,771 ($25,771 − $20,000) is recognized at inception. Economically, the lease is an installment sale. There is no interest component to the first payment because it takes place at inception. The net lease receivable now equals $16,512 ($27,777 − $2,006 − $9,259).

     The above entries increase the lessor's net assets and pretax earnings by the gross profit of $5,771.

F.   Interest Recognition, Year 1

12/31/year 1	Unearned Interest ($16,512 × .08)	1,321	
	Interest Revenue		1,321

G. A year has passed and although no payment is due until the next day, the interest revenue for Year 1 must be accrued as recorded above. The lessor has "loaned" its asset to the lessee for a year. Under accrual accounting, the interest is recognized when earned.

The net lease receivable at 12/31/year 1 = $27,777 − $2,006 − $9,259 + $1,321 = $17,833. The reduction (debit) in unearned interest in the above entry causes the net lease receivable to increase by the amount of recognized interest that has not yet been received. If the lessor used the net method, the lease receivable would be debited for the unpaid interest. Either way, the financial reporting is the same.

The entry for receipt of payment the next day is:

1/1/year 2	Cash	9,259	
	Lease Receivable		9,259

H. The net lease receivable is now $8,574 ($17,833 − $9,259). This is the amount on which interest revenue is computed at the end of year 2.

I.   Interest Recognition, Year 2

12/31/year 2	Unearned Interest ($8,574 × .08)	686	
	Interest Revenue		686

J.   Lessee Inception— Although the accounting by the lessee is unaffected by whether the lessor has a DFL or STL, the lessee's entries are shown here to provide an example of an annuity due (first payment due at inception).

1/1/year 1	Leased Asset	25,771	
	Lease Liability		25,771
1/1/year 1	Lease Liability	9,259	
	Cash		9,259

1. The lease liability is now $16,512 ($25,771 − $9,259).

K. Interest and Depreciation Recognition, Year 1, and Payment at 1/1/Year 2

12/31/year 1	Interest Expense ($16,512 × .08)	1,321	
	Lease Liability		1,321

This entry records accrued but unpaid interest and is easy to forget when taking the CPA Exam because no payment is due on this date. Note that the lease liability is increased rather than interest payable, because interest is not separately paid but rather is a component of the lease payment.

	Depreciation Expense $25,771/3	8,590	
	Accumulated Depreciation		8,590
1/1/Year 2	Lease Liability	9,529	
	Cash		9,529

L. The lease liability is now $8,574 ($16,512 + $1,321 − $9,259).

M. Interest and Depreciation Recognition, Year 2

12/31/year 2	Interest Expense ($8,574 × .08)	686	
	Lease Liability		686
	Depreciation Expense $25,771/3	8,590	
	Accumulated Depreciation		8,590

III. U.S. GAAP–IFRS Differences

A. Overall, international and U.S. accounting standards are similar in the leasing area but there are some significant differences in the details. International standards refer to capital leases as *finance leases*; to direct financing leases (DFLs) as regular finance leases; and to sales-type leases (STLs) as *manufacturer or dealer finance leases*.

B. The classification of leases as capital leases is similar to U.S. standards although the details are somewhat different. A capital lease (finance lease for international standards) is one that transfers substantially all the risks and rewards of ownership to the lessee. Otherwise, it is an operating lease. The international standard does not define *substantially all* as compared with US standards, which use quantitative thresholds (75% and 90%).

C. The determination of whether a lease is a capital lease is based on two sets of conditions. Except for the first two below, judgment is required. If any one of the first five is met (with judgment required for 3–5), then the lease is a finance lease. Conditions 6–8 *could* point to a finance lease—the implication is that the evidence must be stronger for these last three criteria.

1. Title transfer (same as United States)

2. Bargain purchase option (same as United States)

3. The term is for a major portion of the remaining life of the asset (United States uses 75% or more).

4. The present value of minimum lease payments is substantially all of the fair value of the asset (United States uses 90% or more).

5. The asset under lease is specialized or unique such that only the specific lessee can use it without major modification.

6. If the lease is canceled, the lessee bears any loss of the lessor associated with cancellation.

7. Gains and losses from changes in the fair value of the asset accrue to the lessee (e.g., by reductions or increases in the lease payments).

8. There is a bargain renewal option allowing the lessee to continue leasing the asset after the term for substantially less than fair rental at that time.

D. More than one indicator may be required for lease capitalization. The international standard stresses economic substance over legal form, which requires professional judgment to be applied in many cases.

E. The lessee for international standards uses the lessor's implicit interest rate in all cases, unless the lessee is unable to determine that rate. In that case, the lessee's incremental borrowing rate is used. Recall that for U.S. standards, the lessee uses the lower of the two rates.

F. International standards do not formally use criteria 5 and 6 for lessors for lease capitalization. However, the standard does discuss the possibility that the two parties may account for the same lease differently, thus opening up the possibility that a lessor entity might use uncollectibility of payments or cost uncertainties as a reason for not capitalizing a lease.

Additional Aspects of Capital Leases

Several miscellaneous issues affecting lease accounting are covered here. These issues affect the journal entries and financial statement presentation of leases.

After studying this lesson, you should be able to:

1. Determine the capitalizable amount for a lease when executory costs are given.

2. Describe residuals in a capital lease and how they may affect whether a lease is capitalized.

3. Modify the accounting for leases when the asset under lease involves land.

4. Account for initial direct costs depending on the classification of the lease.

5. Describe the accounting for contingent rentals.

I. Executory Costs

A. These costs are flow-through costs and do not affect lease capitalization. They include property taxes, casualty insurance, and maintenance. They are not capitalized because they do not contribute to the asset's value beyond one year. However, if executory costs are included in the annual lease payment, they must be subtracted before computing the present value for determining the present value of the minimum lease payments and for determining the amounts to capitalize in the accounts.

Example

If the total annual lease payment is $12,000 of which $2,000 is executory costs, only the $10,000 amount is used in the present value calculations and capitalization of the lease. The $2,000 amount is treated as an expense by the lessee. If the lessor pays all or a part of these costs (e.g., because the property tax is paid by the legal owner), the lessee reimburses the lessor.

II. Unguaranteed Residual Value (End of Lease Term)

A. The **unguaranteed residual value** is an amount that is outside the lease agreement. It is not an expected payment to be made by the lessee, nor is it a payment the lessor expects to receive under the lease. Therefore, it is excluded from the minimum lease payments and not considered for criterion 4. However, it is part of the value of the asset. The lessor includes it (at present value) in the net lease receivable. The Lease Receivable account will equal the amount of the unguaranteed residual (at nominal value) at the end of the lease term.

B. The unguaranteed residual is the only item included in the lessor's accounts but excluded from minimum lease payments. Therefore the unguaranteed residual does not help a lease meet criterion 4, but if the lease is capitalized, it is included in the lessor's lease receivable.

III. Third-Party Guarantee of Residual Value (End of Lease Term)

A. A **third party** (financial institution) may be enlisted to guarantee the residual value of a leased asset (for a fee). The lessee is not involved and, therefore, does not include the guarantee in its minimum lease payments or lease liability. The lessor does include the guarantee because it is a payment expected to be received under the lease.

B. This is another instance in which the lessee and lessor may classify the lease differently. If the third party guarantee is large enough, the lessor can reduce the annual lease payments to the point where the present value of the lessee's minimum lease payments is less than 90% of the market value of the property. The lessor will continue to earn its implicit rate because of the guarantee. If the lessee meets no other lease capitalization criterion, the lessee will account for the lease as an operating lease with the lessor treating the lease as a capital lease. One of the main reasons third-party guarantees are used is to achieve this very result. The lessee keeps the lease off its balance sheet.

IV. Leases Involving Land

   A. When land is the only asset under capital lease, criteria 3 and 4 do not apply. Only criterion 1 and criterion 2 are applicable for determining whether the lease is a capital lease, and depreciation expense is not recognized by the lessee if the lease is capitalized. If neither criterion 1 or 2 is met, then the lease is an operating lease.

   B. Land and Building Leases

   1. When the assets under lease are land and a building, the lessee records the two leases separately if criterion 1 or 2 is met, because land is not depreciated. For recording purposes, the total present value is allocated to the assets on the basis of fair value. The lessor combines the assets into one lease receivable.

   2. If neither criterion 1 or 2 is met, and the fair value of the land is less than 25% of the combined fair value, the assets are treated as one single asset for purposes of accounting for the capital lease by both parties. The single asset is depreciated even though land is a component of that single asset, if the lease is capitalized i.e. meets criteria 3 or 4.

   3. If neither criterion 1 or 2 is met, and the fair value of the land is 25% or more of the combined value, the land lease is treated as an operating lease (because title will not transfer to the lessee) and the building lease as is an operating or capital lease, depending on whether the building lease meets the lease capitalization criteria.

V. U.S. GAAP–IFRS Differences—For leases involving land, the land and building elements are treated separately unless the land is an immaterial part (United States uses a 25% threshold for materiality for the land portion). This is another example of U.S. standards using a quantitative or rule-based threshold, whereas international standards use a principles-based determination.

VI. Initial Direct Costs

   A. Initial direct costs often are incurred by a lessor in negotiating and completing lease arrangements. Legal fees, costs of credit investigations, employee compensation related to initiating the lease, and any clerical costs are included. Initial direct costs are identified after a specific party is considered a potential lessee. They exclude advertising and solicitation costs and the costs of servicing leases.

   B. Lessee accounting is unaffected by these costs.

   C. Lessor accounting: The accounting treatment of initial direct costs is consistent with the type of lease to which they pertain.

   1. Operating leases

   a. Capitalize the initial direct costs and amortize to expense over the term of the lease in proportion to revenue recognized (usually the straight-line basis).

   2. Sales-type leases

   a. Recognize the initial direct costs immediately as a selling expense. The costs are, therefore, matched against the sale recognized on the lease arrangement at inception.

   3. Direct financing leases

   a. The initial direct costs are included in the lessor's gross receivable (investment in the lease). Cash and other assets are decreased (credited) as a result of the costs. The initial direct costs, therefore, are included in the base on which the annual payments are computed. The resulting interest rate is reduced causing total interest revenue over the lease term to be reduced by the amount of the initial direct costs, gradually over the lease term. There is no separate accounting for the initial direct costs in this case; their recognition is automatic by virtue of their inclusion in the receivable.

Depreciation, BPO, and Residuals

This lesson provides specific guidance for recording capital leases with bargain purchase options and residuals.

After studying this lesson, you should be able to:

1. Compute the lease payment for a lease in different situations.

2. Explain the inception journal entry when there is a bargain purchase option, or one of three different types of residuals.

3. Describe how annual depreciation on a capital lease is affected when the lease meets different capitalization criteria.

I. Clustering of Capitalization Criteria

A. The lease capitalization criterion or criteria met in a particular lease has a significant effect on the accounting. This lesson discusses these effects and later lessons provide examples.

B. If criterion 1 or 2 is met (title transfer and BPO), then the lessee retains the asset at the end of the lease term. There is no residual to the lessor at the end of the lease term; it is not used in the accounting. However, there may be a residual value at the end of the asset's service life. In that case, it is used by the lessee in determining depreciation if the lessee retains the asset at the end of the lease term.

C. If only one or both of criterion 3 or criterion 4 are met (75% of term, 90% of fair value), but not criterion 1 or criterion 2, then the asset reverts to the lessor. The lessor obtains the residual at the end of the term, which becomes important to the accounting. This residual can be (a) unguaranteed, (b) guaranteed by the lessee, or (c) guaranteed by a third party.

II. Lessor's Equation

A. The lessor's equation describes the relevant cash flows and residuals in the lease, and incorporates the interest rate implicit in the lease—that is, the annual compounded rate of return to the lessor.

B. The equation is:

Fair Value of the Asset under Lease at Inception	=	Present Value of Annual Lease Payments	+	Z (Present Value of a Single Payment)

C. In calculating the present values, the lessor's implicit rate is used. The first present value can be either an ordinary annuity, or an annuity due. The second present value is always a single payment.

D. The amount Z in the equation can be the BPO or one of the three residuals noted above. A BPO and a residual would not occur in the same situation.

1. If criterion 2 is met, then Z is the amount of the BPO—the amount the lessee would pay to purchase the asset at the end of the lease term.

2. If only one or both of criterion 3 or criterion 4 are met, but not criterion 1 or criterion 2, then Z is one of the three residuals at the end of the term: (a) unguaranteed, (b) guaranteed by the lessee, or (c) guaranteed by a third party.

E. Problems may require you to compute the amount of the annual lease payment, which you need for the journal entries. You will be given the fair value of the asset under lease, the book value or cost, and any amount Z. Insert the relevant values (do not use book value or cost; always use fair value), and solve for the ordinary lease payment, as in the example that follows. Remember that the lease payment is always based on fair value, not cost (in a DFL cost and fair value are equal).

Example

An asset with a fair value of $60,000 and cost of $50,000 is leased for four years on 1/1/x1. The lease calls for equal annual lease payments each December 31 during the term. The useful life at inception is six years. The asset reverts to the lessor at the end of the term at which time it is expected to be worth $5,857. This is an unguaranteed residual. If there is no statement about a guarantee, the residual is unguaranteed. The lessor's implicit rate is 10%. The lessor's equation below shows how the annual lease payment (L) is determined.

$$60,000 = L(pva, .10, 4) \quad + 5,857(pv1, .10, 4)$$

$$60,000 = L(3.16987) \quad + 5,857(.68301)$$

$$60,000 = L(3.16987) \quad + 4,000$$

$$56,000 = L(3.16987)$$

$$56,000/(3.16987) = L = 17,666$$

Although the unguaranteed residual is not included in the minimum lease payments of either party, it is part of the return to the lessor. The larger the residual, the smaller the annual lease payment.

III. Depreciation of the Leased Asset by the Lessee

A. Knowing the criterion met by the lease is required for the correct lessee depreciation calculation in a capital lease. The lessee does not depreciate the lease in an operating lease. The lessor does not depreciate the asset in a capital lease.

B. Any acceptable depreciation method (straight-line, accelerated) can be used by the lessee.

C. The annual journal entry was shown previously and is:

Depreciation expense*

   Accumulated depreciation

*The amount recognized for depreciation, assuming straight-line depreciation, equals (leased asset balance at inception—residual value)/number of years

D. The values to use for the residual value and number of years in the above expression depend on the capitalization criteria met by the lease:

Criteria Met by Lease	Residual Value	Number of Years
1 or 2 (title transfer, BPO)	residual value at end of asset's useful life	useful life at inception
3 or 4 only (not 1 or 2)		
Unguaranteed residual	0	lease term
Lessee guarantee	lessee guarantee	lease term
Third-party guarantee	0	lease term

1. For example, if the lease contains a BPO, the lessee is expected to use the asset for its entire economic life, beginning with the date of inception. If there is any residual at the end of that period, it is used in the depreciation calculations for that entire period.

2. If the lessee guarantees the residual value at the end of the lease term, that is the amount of the asset not used by the lessee and is the appropriate residual value to use for the lessee's annual depreciation. The asset reverts to the lessor at the end of term thus defining the period of use by the lessee.

IV. Amounts to Include in Minimum Lease Payments and Accounts

A. In a capital lease, the amounts to include in minimum lease payments for the lessor and lessee, and to include in the reported amounts, also depend on which criterion is met by the lease. Criterion 4 is often the critical one for capital leases, hence the importance of minimum lease payments.

B. The following summary table shows the inclusions for a BPO, the three residuals discussed above, and for executory costs and the annual lease payment. "No" means the item is not included in the attribute listed. "Yes" means it is included. The net account balance columns show whether to include the item in the accounts at present value (a net account is measured at present value). The related gross amount follows the same guide for the lessor. The table provides a roadmap for solving almost any capital lease journal entry problem you might encounter. Any amount included in the lessee's lease liability is also included in the leased asset account.

Include in	Minimum Lease Payments		Net Account Balance	
Item	Lessee	Lessor	Lease Liability	Lease Receivable
Executory costs	No	No	No	No
Annual lease payment	Yes	Yes	Yes	Yes
Bargain purchase				
Option	Yes	Yes	Yes	Yes
Unguaranteed				
Residual	No	No	No	Yes
Lessee guarantee of				
Residual	Yes	Yes	Yes	Yes
Third-party guarantee of				
Residual	No	Yes	No	Yes

1. For example, a lease includes an unguaranteed residual. Neither party includes this amount in minimum lease payments because it is outside the lease. The unguaranteed residual thus does not contribute to capitalizing the lease. The lessee does not receive the residual, and the lease payments do not reflect it. Therefore, the lessee does not include it in the lease liability (or asset). But the unguaranteed residual is part of the asset's value. When the lessor removes the physical asset from its books at inception, it replaces it with a receivable. Part of that receivable is the residual value—that is, the value the asset will be worth at the end of the term. The net lease receivable includes the unguaranteed residual at present value. The unguaranteed residual is the only example of an item excluded from minimum lease payments but included in the account balances, for a particular party.

2. The third-party guarantee of residual does not involve the lessee; therefore, it is excluded from the lessee's minimum lease payments and accounts. It is included in the lessor's minimum lease payments and accounts.

3. Executory costs are ignored for lease capitalization purposes, except remember to subtract them if they are included in the lease payment before discounting the lease payments, determining whether criterion 4 is met, and recording the journal entries.

C. A later lesson provides several examples of using this roadmap and provides practice with more complex capital lease situations.

Capital Lease Examples

This lesson illustrates detailed accounting for several capital lease situations.

After studying this lesson, you should be able to:

1. Record all the journal entries for both parties to a capital lease with a bargain purchase option, guarantee of residual, and unguaranteed residual

2. Modify your entries depending on whether the lease is a direct financing lease or sales-type lease.

I. Direct Financing Lease with a BPO

A. On January 1, 20xA, Lessor and Lessee signed a three-year lease that qualifies as a direct financing lease to the Lessor and a capital lease to the Lessee. The leased asset cost the lessor $100,000, and the negotiated lease price is also $100,000 (fair value), making the lease a DFL. The estimated economic life of the asset is four years, and the estimated residual value of the asset at the end of four years is zero.

B. The lessee has an option to purchase the asset for $10,000 on December 31, 20xC. At that date, the estimated residual value is $15,000. The option is a BPO because the purchase option is for an amount significantly less than the estimated value.

C. The lease requires three annual rentals of $33,809, payable each January 1. Lessor has an implicit interest rate of 10% on the cost of the asset. The calculation of the periodic rentals (L) is shown below. The BPO amount is included in the lessor's equation because it is an amount expected to be received. It should be considered just another lease payment.

$$100,000 = L(\text{PV ann.due}, N = 3, I = 10\%) + 10,000(\text{PV } \$1, N = 3, I = 10\%)$$

$$100,000 = L(2.73554) + 10,000(.75131)$$

$$92,487 = L(2.73554)$$

$$L = 33,809$$

D. The lease is a capital lease for both parties because criterion 2 is met (BPO), criterion 3 is met (term = 75% of useful life at inception), and criterion 4 is met (PV of minimum lease payments is 100% of the market value of the asset). When no information is given concerning the lessee's interest rate, you can assume it is the same as the lessor's.

E. Selected Entries—You should verify the calculations for practice. Not all entries are shown. The unearned revenue account is the same account as unearned interest used previously. There is variation in the account names used in practice.

Lessor			Lessee		
January 1, 20xA:					
Lease Receivable	111,427		Leased Property	100,000	
Asset		100,000	Lease Liability		100,000
Unearned Revenue		11,427			

$111,427 = 3(\$33,809) + \$10,000$

Cash	33,809		Lease Liability	33,809	
Lease Receivable		33,809	Cash		33,809

December 31, 20xA:

Unearned Revenue	6,619		Interest Expense	6,619	
Interest Revenue		6,619	Lease Liability		6,619

$\$6,619 = (\$111,427 - \$11,427 - \$33,809).10$

			Depreciation Expense	25,000	
			Acc.Depreciation		25,000

(100,000/4)(Useful life is four years).

If there was an estimated residual value at the end of the useful life, it would be subtracted in the numerator.

January 1, 20xB:

Cash	33,809		Lease Liability	33,809	
Lease Receivable		33,809	Cash		33,809

December 31, 20xC:

Cash	10,000		Lease Liability	10,000	
Lease Receivable		10,000	Cash		10,000

1. The net lease receivable and lease liability balances equal the $10,000 BPO at the end of the lease term because the BPO was included in both at present value. By the end of the term, that amount had grown to its full nominal value. The net book value of the asset on the lessee's balance sheet is $25,000 after three years of depreciation. The lessee keeps the asset for its remaining year of useful life because of the BPO. The following amortization schedule provides information leading to the entries for the entire lease term.

F. Amortization Schedule

Date	Annual Lease Payments	10% Annual Interest	Decrease (Increase) in Net Receivable or Liability	Net Lease Receivable or Liability Balance
1/1/20xA				100,000
1/1/20xA	33,809		33,809	66,191
12/31/20xA		6,619	(6,619)	72,810
1/1/20xB	33,809		33,809	39,001
12/31/20xB		3,900	(3,900)	42,901
1/1/20xC	33,809		33,809	9,092
12/31/20xC		908	(908)	10,000
12/31/20xC	10,000	___	10,000	0
Totals	111,427	11,427	100,000	

II. Sales-Type Lease with a BPO

A. On January 1, 20xA, Lessor and Lessee signed a three-year lease that qualifies as a sales-type lease to the Lessor and a capital lease to the Lessee. The leased asset cost the lessor $100,000 and the negotiated lease price is $120,000 (fair value). The estimated economic life of the asset is four years and the estimated residual value of the asset at the end of four years is zero.

B. The lessee has an option to purchase the asset for $10,000 on December 31, 20xC. At that date, the estimated residual value is $15,000.

C. The lease requires three annual rentals of $41,121, payable each January 1. Lessor has an implicit interest rate of 10% on the cost of the asset. The calculation of the periodic rentals (L) is shown below.

$$120,000 = L(\text{PV ann.due}, N = 3, I = 10\%) + 10,000(\text{PV } \$1, N = 3, I = 10\%)$$

$$120,000 = L(2.73554) + 10,000(.75131)$$

$$112,487 = L(2.73554)$$

$$L = 41,121$$

D. The lease is a capital lease for both parties because criterion 2 is met (BPO), criterion 3 is met (term = 75% of useful life at inception), and criterion 4 is met (PV of minimum lease payments is 100% of the fair value of the asset).

E. Selected Entries—You should verify the calculations for practice; not all entries are shown.

Lessor			**Lessee**		
January 1, 20xA:					
Lease Receivable	133,363				
Cost of Goods Sold	100,000		Leased Property	120,000	
Sales Revenue		120,000	Lease Liability		120,000
Unearned Revenue		13,363			
Asset		100,000			

$$\$133,363 = 3(41,121) + 10,000$$

Cash	41,121		Lease Liability	41,121	
Lease Receivable		41,121	Cash		41,121

December 31, 20xA:					
Unearned Revenue	7,888		Interest Expense	7,888	
Interest Revenue		7,888	Lease Liability		7,888

$$\$7,888 = .10(\$133,363 - \$13,363 - \$41,121)$$

			Depreciation Expense	30,000	
			Acc.Depreciation		30,000
			($120,000/4 years)		

January 1, 20xB:					
Cash	41,121		Lease Liability	41,121	
Lease Receivable		41,121	Cash		41,121

December 31, 20xC:					
Cash	10,000		Lease Liability	10,000	
Lease Receivable		10,000	Cash		10,000

F. Amortization Schedule

Date	Annual Lease Payments	10% Annual Interest	Decrease (Increase) in Net Receivable or Liability	Net Lease Receivable or Liability Balance
1/1/20xA				120,000
1/1/20xA	41,121		41,121	78,879
12/31/20xA		7,888	(7,888)	86,767
1/1/20xB	41,121		41,121	45,646
12/31/20xB		4,565	(4,565)	50,211
1/1/20xC	41,121		41,121	9,090
12/31/20xC		910	(910)	10,000
12/31/20xC	10,000		10,000	0
Totals	133,363	13,363	120,000	

G. Classification of the total lease liability at the end of any year into current (CL) and noncurrent (NCL) portions is handled in one of two acceptable ways: (1) the CL is the present value of the next year's payment, or (2) the CL is the reduction of the total lease liability in the succeeding year. In either case, the NCL portion is the total lease liability less the CL portion.

Example
In the above amortization schedule, the 12/31/20xA total lease liability is $86,767.

1. Under the first approach, the CL portion is $41,121, which is the present value of the payment occurring one day after the 20A balance sheet date. The NCL portion is the rest, or $45,646 ($86,767 − $41,121). If the 20xB lease payment were due 12/31/20xB instead, the present value of $41,121 for one year would be the CL portion.

2. Under the second approach, the CL portion is the decrease in the total lease liability in 20B, or $36,556 ($86,767 − $50,211). The NCL portion is the rest, or $50,211 ($86,767 − $36,556). Note that the two approaches yield somewhat different results.

III. Direct Financing Lease, Lessee Guarantee, Third-Party Guarantee

A. On January 1, 20xA, Lessor and Lessee signed a three-year lease that qualifies as a direct financing lease to the Lessor and a capital lease to the Lessee. The leased asset cost the lessor $100,000, and the negotiated lease price is also $100,000 (fair value). The estimated economic life of the asset is four years, and the estimated residual value of the asset at the end of four years is zero.

B. Lessor retains ownership of the leased asset at the termination of the lease. On January 1, 20xA, lessor and lessee estimated a residual value of $10,000 at the end of the three-year lease term. The terms of the lease agreement specify that the lessee will guarantee a minimum residual value of $10,000. If the actual residual value determined at the end of the lease term is less than $10,000, the lessee must pay the difference in cash.

C. The lease requires three annual rentals of $33,809, payable each January 1. Lessor has an implicit interest rate of 10% on the cost of the asset. The calculation of the periodic rentals (L) is shown below. Note that this calculation is the same as for the DFL-BPO example. Both the BPO and guaranteed residual value provide the lessor with $10,000 at the end of the lease term. Thus, the lease payments should be the same for both situations. The amortization schedule is the same as well.

$$100,000 = L(\text{PV ann.due}, N = 3, I = 10\%) + 10,000(\text{PV } \$1, N = 3, I = 10\%)$$

$$100,000 = L(2.73554) + 10,000(.75131)$$

$$92,487 = L(2.73554)$$

$$L = 33,809$$

D. The lessee includes the present value of the guarantee in the leased asset and liability because it is part of the cost of the asset. The lease is a capital lease for both parties because criterion 3 is met (term = 75% of useful life at inception) and criterion 4 is met (PV of minimum lease payments is 100% of the fair value of the asset). The actual residual value at December 31, 20xC is $9,000. (Lessee must pay the $1,000 difference between fair value and guarantee amount.)

E. **Selected Entries**—You should verify the calculations for practice; not all entries are shown.

Lessor			Lessee		
January 1, 20xA:					
Lease Receivable	111,427		Leased Property	100,000	
Asset		100,000	Lease Liability		100,000
Unearned Revenue		11,427			
Cash	33,809		Lease Liability	33,809	
Lease Receivable		33,809	Cash		33,809
December 31, 20xA:					
Unearned Revenue	6,619		Interest Expense	6,619	
Interest Revenue		6,619	Lease Liability		6,619
			Depreciation Expense	30,000	
			Acc.Depreciation		30,000
			(($100,000 − $10,000)/3)		

1. The lessee guarantees the residual value. This is the portion of the value of the asset that will not be used by the lessee and thus is treated as a salvage value. The lessee will use the asset only three years.

January 1, 20xB:

Cash	33,809	Lease Liability	33,809	
Lease Receivable		33,809	Cash		33,809

December 31, 20xC:

Asset	9,000	Acc.Depreciation	90,000	
Cash	1,000	Lease Liability	10,000	
Lease Receivable		10,000	Leased Property		100,000
		Loss on Contract	1,000	
		Cash		1,000

2. The balance of the net lease receivable and the lease liability are $10,000 at the end of the lease term because both included the guaranteed residual at present value at inception. By the end of the lease term, that value has grown to its full nominal value. The asset is transferred to the lessor at fair value. The lessee sustains a loss of $1,000 because the fair value was less than the guaranteed amount.

F. Amortization Schedule

Date	Annual Lease Payments	10% Annual Interest	Decrease (Increase) in Net Receivable or Liability	Net Lease Receivable or Liability Balance
1/1/20xA				100,000
1/1/20xA	33,809		33,809	66,191
12/31/20xA		6,619	(6,619)	72,810
1/1/20xB	33,809		33,809	39,001
12/31/20xB		3,900	(3,900)	42,901
1/1/20xC	33,809		33,809	9,092
12/31/20xC		908	(908)	10,000
12/31/20xC	10,000	___	10,000	0
Totals	111,427	11,427	100,000	

G. Now assume that, instead of the lessee guaranteeing the residual, a third party provides the guarantee. There is no change in the lease payment or the accounting by the lessor because either way, the lessor will receive $10,000 at the end of the lease. But the lessee no longer includes the guarantee in its minimum lease payments and its account balances.

H. The lessee's present value of minimum lease payments = $92,487 = $33,809 (PV ann. due, N = 3, I = 10%) = $33,809(2.73554). This amount exceeds 90% of the fair value of the property ($100,000) so the lease continues to be a capital lease. Also, criterion 3 continues to be met. The lessee would record the leased asset and lease liability at $92,487 rather than $100,000. The payments are the same, but interest expense is somewhat smaller because of the smaller beginning lease liability. Finally, depreciation expense would be computed as $92,487/3 = $30,829. There is no residual value to deduct in this case.

IV. Sales-Type Lease, Unguaranteed Residual

A. On January 1, 20xA, lessor and lessee signed a three-year lease that qualifies as a sales-type lease to the lessor and a capital lease to the Lessee. The leased asset cost the lessor $100,000 and the negotiated lease price is $120,000 (fair value). The estimated economic life of the asset is four years and the estimated residual value of the asset at the end of four years is zero.

B. The lessor retains ownership of the leased asset at the termination of the lease. On January 1, 20xA, lessor and lessee estimated a residual of $10,000, which is not guaranteed by the lessee or any other party.

C. The lease requires three annual rentals of $41,121, payable each January 1. Lessor has an implicit interest rate of 10% on the cost of the asset. The calculation of the periodic rentals (L) is shown below.

120,000	= L(PV ann.due, N = 3, I = 10%) + 10,000(PV $1, N = 3, I = 10%)
120,000	= L(2.73554) + 10,000(.75131)
112,487	= L(2.73554)
L	= 41,121

D. The present value of minimum lease payments is $112,487 ($41,121 × 2.73554), the amount excluding the unguaranteed residual value. The latter amount is not included in either party's minimum lease payments. However, it is included in the lessor's lease receivable.

E. The lease is a capital lease for both parties because criterion 3 is met (term = 75% of useful life at inception) and criterion 4 is met (PV of minimum lease payments is 94% of the fair value of the asset—$112,487/$120,000).

F. The actual residual value on December 31, 20xC is $10,000.

G. **Selected Entries**—You should verify the calculations for practice; not all entries are shown.

Lessor			Lessee		
January 1, 20xA:					
Lease Receivable	133,363				
Cost of Goods Sold	92,487		Leased Property	112,487	
Sales Revenue		112,487	Lease Liability		112,487
Unearned Revenue		13,363			
Asset		100,000			

1. The present value of the unguaranteed residual is $7,513 ($10,000 × 0.75131). This amount must be subtracted from both cost of goods sold and sales. Cost of Goods Sold = $100,000 − $7,513, and Sales = $120,000 − $7,513. The lessee capitalizes only the lease payments.

Cash	41,121		Lease Liability	41,121	
Lease Receivable		41,121	Cash		41,121

December 31, 20xA:

Unearned Revenue	7,888		Interest Expense	7,137	
Interest Revenue		7,888	Lease Liability		7,137
			Depreciation Expense	37,496	
			Acc.Depreciation		37,496
			($112,487/3 years)		

2. The lessee will have the asset for three years. There is no residual value for the lessee.

January 1, 20xB:

Cash	41,121		Lease Liability	41,121	
Lease Receivable		41,121	Cash		41,121

December 31, 20xC:

Asset	10,000		Acc.Depreciation	112,487	
Lease Receivable		10,000	Leased Property		112,487

H. Lessor's Amortization Schedule:

Date	Annual Lease Payments	10% Annual Interest	Decrease (Increase) in Net Receivable	Net Lease Receivable Balance
1/1/20xA				120,000
1/1/20xA	41,121		41,121	78,879
12/31/20xA		7,888	(7,888)	86,767
1/1/20xB	41,121		41,121	45,646
12/31/20xB		4,565	(4,565)	50,211
1/1/20xC	41,121		41,121	9,090
12/31/20xC		910	(910)	10,000
12/31/20xC	10,000	____	10,000	0
Totals	133,363	13,363	120,000	

I. Lessee's Amortization Schedule—In this case, the lessee's amortization is based on a different starting value because the lessor included the unguaranteed residual in its net receivable, but the lessee does not include it in the leased asset and liability.

Date	Annual Lease Payments	10% Annual Interest	Decrease (Increase) in Liability	Lease Liability Balance
1/1/20xA				112,487
1/1/20xA	41,121		41,121	71,366
12/31/20xA		7,137	(7,137)	78,503
1/1/20xB	41,121		41,121	37,382
12/31/20xB		3,739	(3,739)	41,121
1/1/20xC	41,121		41,121	0
Totals	123,363	10,876	112,487	

J. Purchase of asset during lease term. In some capital leases that do not meet criteria 1 or 2, the lessee may have the option to purchase the asset during the lease term. The price may be a negotiated price, or the prices may be preset at inception, with the price decreasing over the term.

1. At the purchase date, the lessee records interest expense and the increase in the lease liability from the last payment date through the purchase date, and also records depreciation since the most recent fiscal year-end. The lease liability, accumulated depreciation and leased asset accounts are closed, and cash is credited for the price. A new asset account is established and recorded at the updated book value of the leased asset at the time of purchase plus the excess of the purchase price over the updated book value of the lease liability. In other words, the lessee has paid more than the amount owed on the leased asset to purchase it; the excess is treated as an increase in the purchase cost. No loss is recognized. If the book value of the lease liability exceeds the purchase price, the difference is subtracted from the book value of the leased asset. No gain is recognized. The asset under lease is now being purchased; therefore no gain or loss is recognized. The lessee is in the same economic position with respect to the asset.

2. The lessor's accounting is somewhat different; a gain or loss is recognized immediately for the difference between the net receivable balance and the selling price of the asset. Interest revenue is first recognized to the point of sale to update the receivable balance. The entry for the sale closes the receivable and unearned interest revenue accounts.

3. **Analysis**—Assume now that the lease in the current example (STL—unguaranteed residual)allows the lessee to purchase the asset during the lease term. At 12/31/20xA the lessee purchases the asset for $80,000, a negotiated price. Both parties first record the usual journal entries at that date. The net receivable balance at that date is $86,767 per the above amortization schedules (gross receivable balance is $92,242 = $133,363 − $41,121; unearned revenue balance is $5,475 =$92,242 − $86,767). The net lease liability is $78,503 per the above amortization schedule. The accumulated depreciation balance is $37,496. The book value of the asset is $74,991 ($112,487 − $37,496). The excess of the purchase price over the liability balance is $1,497 ($80,000 − $78,503).

Lessee entry:

Equipment	76,488	$74,991 + $1,497
Accumulated depreciation	37,496	
Lease liability	78,503	
Leased property		112,487
Cash		80,000

Lessor entry:

Cash	80,000	
Unearned revenue	5,475	
Loss on sale	6,767	$86,767 − $80,000
Lease receivable		92,242

Sale Leasebacks and Disclosures

Lessee accounting for the sale of an asset and immediate leaseback is addressed in this lesson.

After studying this lesson, you should be able to:

1. Explain why a firm would enter into a sales-leaseback transaction.

2. Compute the related gain or loss.

3. Account for three different levels of leaseback: major, minor, and in-between.

4. Modify your accounting depending on whether the lease is a capital or operating lease.

5. Identify when a loss is real or artificial.

6. Note the general footnote disclosures for leases for both parties.

I. Nature of the Transaction and Accounting Issues

A. A sale-leaseback transaction is actually two related transactions. The owner of property sells its asset and immediately leases it back. The asset is not physically moved. It is entirely a financial transaction. The seller-lessee is simply refinancing the asset but is no longer the owner. For the seller-lessee, leasing may be more attractive than financing the asset with other types of debt. The sale provides immediate cash, and the asset continues to be used as before.

B. The accounting issue for the seller-lessee is how to account for the gain or loss on the sale because often the sales price and payments under the leaseback are not independent. The seller-lessee lease is treated as a capital or operating lease depending on whether at least one of the usual four criteria are met. The accounting for the lessor-owner is not affected by sales-leasebacks—the usual procedures for lease accounting apply. Our coverage of sales-leasebacks therefore applies only to the seller-lessee. The following generalizations apply:

1. The recorded gain on the sale part of the transaction = selling price − book value.

2. The recorded loss on the sale part of the transaction = book value − selling price.

3. The recorded gain or loss is not always recognized in earnings immediately; in some cases it is deferred.

II. Accounting Situations

A. The accounting for a gain depends on the proportion of the asset value leased back. The accounting for a loss depends on whether the loss is real or artificial. The following situations are relevant. Remember that in each case only the sale entry is affected and any subsequent recognition of gain or loss. Accounting for the leaseback proceeds as previously discussed.

1. Gain: major leaseback

2. Gain: minor leaseback

3. Gain: less than major, but more than minor leaseback

4. Losses: real and artificial

B. Gain—Major Leaseback—The gain is computed as always: the difference between the selling price and book value of the asset. However, the selling price may not be the same as fair value. The lessor pays the seller-lessee the selling price. If the price is greater than fair value, the difference will be returned to the lessor in the form of higher rentals. If the price is less than fair value, the rentals will be reduced. (In this case, acceptance of a lower selling price is in effect a prepayment of rent by the lessee.)

1. **Accounting**—If the present value of the minimum lease payments is ≥ 90% of the asset's fair value (major leaseback), then the gain is deferred (not immediately recognized in earnings) and amortized. In this case, the sale is not the dominant aspect of the transaction because the lessee retains most or all of the use of the asset. Because the lessee will continue to use the same asset, the gain should be recognized over the period the asset will be used. The seller has simply refinanced the asset and is in the same economic position as before the sale. In addition, an inflated selling price may be part of the cause of the gain.

2. **Capital lease**—If the lease is a capital lease, the gain is recorded in a contra-leased asset account and amortized as a reduction in depreciation expense in the same proportion as depreciation expense is recognized. The gain is thus recognized gradually over the lease term.

   a. If asset is retained by lessee at the end of the lease term, depreciation and amortization of the deferred gain continues to the end of the asset's life. If the asset reverts to the lessor, the lease term is used for the amortization period. If the asset is land, the amortization of the deferred gain is recognized as revenue because land is not depreciated.

3. **Operating lease**—If the lease is an operating lease, the gain is recorded in a liability account and amortized as a reduction in rent expense (there is no leased asset to depreciate). Again, the gain is recognized gradually over the lease term.

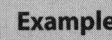

Example

On 1/1/X1 QWEL Inc. sells an asset for its fair value of $25,771 (cost $40,000; accumulated depreciation $20,000) and leases it back under a three-year noncancellable lease. The lease payments are based on the asset's fair value. The implicit rate of interest is 8%, remaining useful life of the asset is three at lease inception, and the annual lease payments are due each December 31 beginning 20X1. Assume the seller-lessee uses SL depreciation.

The annual lease payment (LP) for this ordinary annuity is computed as:

$25,771 = LP(pva, 8\%, 3)$

$25,771 = LP(2.57710); LP = \$10,000$

This is a major leaseback because the present value of the minimum lease payments is 100% (≥ 90%) of fair value.

Journal entries for QWEL (seller-lessee):

1/1/x1

Cash	25,771	
Accumulated depreciation	20,000	
Asset		40,000
Deferred gain		5,771
Leased asset	25,771	
Lease liability		25,771

A balance sheet at this point reports a net leased asset of $20,000 ($25,771 − $5,771 deferred gain) − the same value just before the sale-leaseback ($40,000 − $20,000).

12/31/X1

Interest expense (.08)25,771	2,062	
Lease liability	7,938	
Cash		10,000
Depreciation expense $25,771/3	8,590	
Accumulated depreciation		8,590
Deferred gain 5,771/3	1,924	
Depreciation expense		1,924

The reduction in depreciation expense has the same effect on earnings as recognizing an equivalent part of the gain each year during the term.

Had the lease instead been classified as an operating lease (e.g., if at inception the asset is within its last 25% of original useful life and criterion 1—title transfer, and criterion 2— bargain purchase option, are not met, then criterion 3 and 4 do not apply), the same entry above would be recorded for the sale, but the deferred gain account is classified as a liability. Each year, after recording rent expense, the following entry would be made:

Deferred gain	(total gain)/lease term
Rent expense	

C. Gain—Minor Leaseback—In this situation, the two transactions (sale and leaseback) are considered separate because the lessee is not retaining most of the usefulness of the asset.

1. **Accounting**—If the present value of the minimum lease payments is ≤ 10% of the asset's fair value (minor leaseback), then the sale and leaseback are considered unrelated. The gain is recognized immediately in the entry for sale, and the lease proceeds as usual.

 **Example**

Fair value and selling price	$800,000
Carrying value of asset	600,000
Present value of lease payments	72,000

$72,000/$800,000 < 10% of $800,000

Gain of $200,000 implied ($800,000 − $600,000)

The journal entry for sale recognizes the gain of $200,000 in earnings. The lease is recorded as an operating lease.

D. Gain—Less than Major but More than Minor Leaseback

1. This case has attributes of both the previous two and occurs when the present value of minimum lease payments is between 90% and 10% of fair value:

   a. (90% of fair value) > (present value of minimum lease payments) > (10% of fair value).

   b. **Accounting**—The lessee immediately recognizes the gain to the extent that it exceeds the present value of minimum lease payments. The amount of the gain up to the present value of minimum lease payments is deferred and amortized.

 **Example**

Sales price and fair value of asset	$900,000
Carrying value of asset	300,000
Present value of lease payments	450,000

The present value of minimum lease payments is 50% of fair value (less than major but more than minor leaseback).

Gain of $600,000 is implied ($900,000 − $300,000)

Deferred gain, amortized over term or life, $450,000

Immediately recognized gain, $150,000

E. Losses—Real and Artificial—The selling price of an asset in a sale-leaseback is not necessarily equal to fair value. For example, the lessee may accept a selling price below fair value in return for lower rentals during the lease term.

1. The recorded loss on sale is always the difference between selling price and book value (same for a gain). But the selling price may be set low to achieve a particular economic or reporting goal, even though the fair value exceeds book value. In this case, the loss is artificial.

2. In an outright sale of an asset, the selling price and fair value are equal. A real loss occurs when fair value is less than book value. If fair value exceeds book value, there is no real loss. Any recorded loss in this case (occurring because selling price is less than book value) is deferred and amortized.

3. In a sale-leaseback, the lessee immediately recognizes the loss to the extent that the fair value is less than book value (the real loss). Any loss in excess of that amount is deferred and amortized as in the case of gains, discussed above. However, when a loss is amortized the opposite effect occurs: depreciation expense (capital lease) is increased, or rent expense (operating lease) is increased.

Examples

1. The selling price of an asset in a sale-leaseback is $10,000. Its fair value is $13,000, and its carrying value is $12,000. The recorded loss on sale is $2,000 ($12,000 carrying value − $10,000 selling price). But the firm really does not have a loss because fair value exceeds carrying value. This is an "artificial" loss. The loss will be made up through lower rentals on the leaseback side of the transaction. In this case, the entire loss is deferred and amortized as an increase in depreciation expense for a capital lease or rent expense for an operating lease.

2. Selling price $10,000; fair value $10,000; book value $12,000. Recorded loss is $2,000 (selling price less book value). Fair value is less than book value by that amount. Therefore, the entire loss is recognized immediately. The leaseback side of the transaction continues based on fair value, as usual.

3. Selling price $10,000; fair value $10,500; book value $12,000. Recorded loss is $2,000 (selling price less book value). Fair value is less than book value by $1,500. That amount of loss is recognized immediately. The remaining $500 is deferred and amortized.

III. U.S. GAAP–IFRS Differences

A. For operating leases in a sales leaseback arrangement, under international standards, if the selling price equals fair value, any gain or loss on the sale is recognized immediately rather than deferred and amortized as under U.S. standards.

1. If the selling price is less than fair value without lower than fair value rentals, the loss is also recognized immediately. But if the rentals are lower than fair value to compensate for the lower sales price, the loss is deferred and amortized in proportion to the payments.

2. If the selling price exceeds fair value, the excess is also deferred and amortized.

3. If the fair value is less than book value (which implies an impairment), the resulting loss is recognized immediately.

B. For finance (capital) leases, the gain is deferred and recognized over the lease term in all cases, even if the asset is acquired by the lessee at the end of the term (title transfer or BPO). U.S. standards, by contrast, distinguish among major, in-between, and minor leasebacks. In some cases, gains are immediately recognized.

IV. Lease Disclosures

A. Lessees are required to disclose:

1. The gross amount of assets recorded under capital leases

2. Future minimum lease payments in the aggregate and for each of the five succeeding years (capital leases)

3. Future minimum rentals in the aggregate and for each of the five succeeding years (operating leases)

4. General description of the lease arrangement, executory costs, contingent rentals, residual values, and other features

5. Rent expense for operating leases

B. Lessors are required to disclose:

1. The components of the net lease receivable (net investment in capital leases) including future minimum lease payments to be received, unguaranteed residual values, and unearned interest revenue

2. Minimum future rentals on noncancelable operating leases in the aggregate and for each of the five succeeding fiscal years

3. General description of the lease arrangement, executory costs, contingent rentals, residual values, and other features

4. The cost and carrying amount of assets leased by others

State and Local Governments

Not-for-Profit Accounting and Reporting

Introduction to Types of Not-for-Profit Entities and Standard Setting

This lesson presents a brief overview of the types of not-for-profit entities and the organizations that set accounting standards for these entities.

After studying this lesson, you should be able to:

1. Recall the purpose and characteristics in the conceptual framework for no business entities.

2. List the four main categories of not-for-profit organizations.

I. **Background**—Not-for-profit (NFP) organizations comprise a wide variety of institutions, including some governmentally affiliated entities such as state universities and city and county hospitals. For many years, these organizations received little attention and guidance regarding their recording and reporting rules. As a result, standards were developed piecemeal by national industry associations (e.g., National Association of College & University Business Officers) and "industry" audit guides produced by the AICPA. When FASB was created in 1973, NFP organizations were included under its purview, but it was not until the release of Statements #116 (FASB Codification ASC 958-205 through ASC 958-230) and #117 (ASC 958-658) nearly twenty years later that accounting and reporting issues for NFP organizations were addressed in a meaningful, comprehensive manner.

II. **Categories of Not-for-Profit Organizations**

A. Historically, NFPOs have been grouped into the following four categories. Although accounting and reporting differences among the categories have been dramatically reduced, each category retains a few unique characteristics. The four categories of NFP organizations that follow FASB accounting and financial reporting are:

1. **Hospitals and other healthcare entities**—Includes private hospitals (which includes both *for-profit* and *not-for-profit*), as well as nursing homes, home health agencies, continuing care retirement communities, health maintenance organizations, and others:

    a. **Exception:** Public (i.e., government-run) healthcare entities follow accounting and financial reporting standards established by GASB.

2. **Colleges, universities and other educational organizations**—Includes private (e.g., NFP) four-year colleges and universities and other types of schools.

    a. **Exception**—Two-year institutions with taxing authority (i.e., most community colleges) are excluded from this category, as are public (i.e., government-run) educational institutions, such as state-run universities. These types of educational organizations follow the financial reporting model established by GASB.

3. **Voluntary health and welfare organizations (VHWOs)**—These organizations promote research and education in a wide variety of social and health-related areas; they frequently offer free or low cost services to the general public or to special groups; they receive the majority of their funding from voluntary contributions from the general public and from grants; many of these organizations have local branches that are associated with national organizations with the same objectives.

Example
Arthritis Foundation, United Way, American Cancer Society, Boy Scouts, Girl Scouts, and so on. Almost all these organizations are classified as *private* not-for-profit organizations.

4. **Other nonprofit organizations (ONPOs)**—These encompass a diverse group of organizations including social clubs, political parties, museums, fraternities, unions, athletic clubs, environmental action organizations, etc.; while the vast majority of these organizations are classified as private, governmentally affiliated organizations are occasionally found within this category (public museums, historical sites, etc.).

III. **Jurisdiction over Not-for-Profit Organizations**

A. **FASB**—Regulates the accounting and reporting practices for all private not-for-profit-organizations; GASB governs governmentally affiliated organizations.

Note
Colleges and universities and healthcare organizations can be organized as not-for-profit, governmental, or for-profit commercial entities. If organized as a governmental entity, GASB standards apply. When organized as a not-for-profit or for-profit entity, FASB standards apply.

B. **Private NFPs**—Most not-for-profit organizations fall under this category; FAS 116 (ASC 958-685) prescribes the rules for recognition of contributions and FAS 117 (ASC 958-205 through 230) prescribes the external reporting requirements for all private NFP organizations.

1. Traditional reporting practices (fund model) are still expected to be used for internal reporting and still may appear on the CPA Exam; however, funds are not used for external reporting.

C. **Public (Governmentally Affiliated) NFPs**—These organizations are predominantly publicly funded hospitals and universities, although museums, parks, and landmarks can fall into this category as well.

1. They use fund reporting in their independent statements, and for reporting purposes are usually combined with the primary government entity and accounting and financial reporting is determined by the GASB.

D. **Basis of Accounting for Private NFP**—Generally accepted accounting principles established by FASB requires NFP organizations to use full accrual basis accounting. The main objective of financial reporting is to disclose the sources of an NFP's resources and how they were expended rather than the determination of net income.

Financial Reporting

This lesson presents a summary of the primary financial statements for not-for-profit entities.

After studying this lesson, you should be able to:

1. Describe the form and content of the Statement of Financial Position.

2. Describe the form and content of the Statement of Activities.

3. Describe the form and content of the Statement of Cash Flows.

4. Describe the form and content of the Statement of Functional Expenses and know which type of not-for-profit should prepare this statement.

5. Describe the three categories of net assets.

I. **Statement #117 (ASC 958-205 through 958-230)—Financial Statement Presentation**—This statement identifies a single set of statements that is to be prepared for all private NFP organizations. In these statements, **fund information is no longer presented**; assets and liabilities from all funds are combined, and the Fund Balances are **translated to one of three classifications of net assets: unrestricted net assets, temporarily restricted net assets, or permanently restricted net assets.**

   A. Three statements are required for all organizations:

      1. **Statement of Financial Position**

      2. **Statement of Activity**

      3. **Statement of Cash Flows**

   B. An additional statement, the **Statement of Functional Expenses**, is required for voluntary health and welfare organizations only (e.g., American Red Cross, Volunteers of America).

II. **Statement of Financial Position**

   A. The Statement of Financial Position is **required** for all NFP organizations.

      1. It does not include any fund information but instead is presented **"for the organization as a whole."**

      2. Net assets (the residual of assets over liabilities) are broken down into three categories based on the nature of any **donor-imposed restrictions**:

         a. Unrestricted

            i. Unrestricted net assets represent net assets that are free of donor restrictions on usage and the NFP can use these net assets for any purpose.

         b. Temporarily restricted

            i. A donor may place restrictions on a donation that temporarily restrict its use in one of two ways. When the temporary restriction is met, the amount of the restriction met is reclassified from temporarily-restricted net assets to unrestricted net assets. The two types of restrictions are:

               1. **Purpose-type restriction**, occurs when the donor stipulates that the resources from the donation must be spent on something specific (e.g., drug-free youth education programs at the YMCA).

               2. **Time restriction**, occurs when the donor stipulates that the resources must be spent in a certain time period (e.g., a $50,000 donation to be spent $10,000 yearly for five years). NFPs can also elect to have a policy of implied time restriction on donated fixed assets, which reclassifies an amount equal to annual depreciation from temporarily-restricted net assets to unrestricted net assets.

    c. Permanently restricted

        i. A donor may make a contribution with restrictions that it never be spent, such as an endowment fund that is to remain intact but the income from the endowment can be used by the NFP in accordance with the donor's stipulations, if any.

B. Statement of Financial Position

Not-for-Profit Organization

Statements of Financial Position

June 30, 20X1 and 20X0

(in thousands)

	20X1	**20X0**
Assets:		
Cash and Cash Equivalents	$ 75	$ 460
Accounts and Interest Receivable	2,250	1,670
Inventories and Prepaid Expenses	610	1,000
Contributions Receivable	3,025	2,700
Short-term Investments	1,400	1,000
Assets Restricted to Investment in Land, Buildings, and Equipment	5,210	4,560
Land, Buildings, and Equipment (Note A)	61,700	63,590
Long-Term Investments	217,950	203,500
Total Assets	$292,220	$278,480
Liabilities and Net Assets:		
Accounts Payable	$ 2,570	$ 1,050
Refundable Advance		650
Grants Payable	875	1,300
Notes Payable		1,140
Annuity Obligations	1,685	1,700
Long-Term Debt	5,500	6,500
Total Liabilities	$ 10,630	$ 12,340
Net Assets:		
Unrestricted (Note E)	$ 90,838	$ 78,940
Temporarily Restricted (Note B)	48,732	50,200
Permanently Restricted (Note C)	142,020	137,000
Total Net Assets	281,590	266,140
Total Liabilities and Net Assets	$292,220	$278,480

III. Statement of Activity

    A. The Statement of Activity is required for all organizations. The principal requirement of the statement is to provide the change in net assets for each of the three classifications of net assets (unrestricted, temporarily restricted, and permanently restricted) and for the organization as a whole. This means that all revenue amounts must be reported as belonging to one of these three classifications. Expense amounts are reported only in the **unrestricted net asset** classification.

Note

FASB guidance includes a couple of alternative presentation formats for the Statement of Activity; the format shown in this lesson is the one you will usually see on the CPA Exam.

B. The Statement of Activity has four principal sections:

1. Revenues and Gains

2. Net Assets Released from Restrictions

3. Expenses and Losses

4. Change in Net Assets (including reconciliation of beginning and ending Net Assets)

Note

The reporting of revenues and expenses on the Statement of Activities is heavily tested on the CPA Exam. Be sure to memorize the format of this statement and understand how it is used. The areas of emphasis are classification of revenues, classification of expenses, timing of release of assets from restrictions, and evaluation of the effect on temporarily restricted net assets and restricted net assets when donor restricted monies are spent for their intended purpose.

C. **Statement of Activity Format A**

Format A
Not-for-Profit Organization
Statement of Activities
Year Ended June 30, 20X1
(in thousands)

Changes in unrestricted assets:

Revenues and gains:

Contributions	$ 8,500
Fees	5,400
Investment Income on Endowment	3,600
Other Investment Income	2,850
Net Unrealized and Realized Gains on Endowment	4,428
Net Unrealized and Realized Gains on other Investments	3,800
Other	150
Total Unrestricted Revenues and Gains	28,728
Net Assets Released from Restrictions (Note D)	15,220
Total Unrestricted Revenues, Gains, and Other Support	43,948

Expenses and losses:	
Program A	13,100
Program B	8,540
Program C	5,760
Management and General	2,420
Fund Raising	2,150
Total Expenses (Note G)	31,970
Fire Loss	80
Total Expenses and Losses	32,050
Increase in Unrestricted Net Assets	11,898
Changes in Temporarily Restricted Net Assets:	
Contributions	8,250
Investment Income on Annuity Agreements	180
Investment Income on Endowment	2,400
Net Unrealized and Realized Gains on Endowment	2,952
Actuarial Loss on Annuity Obligations	(30)
Net Assets Released from Restrictions (Note D)	(15,220)
Decrease in Temporarily Restricted Net Assets	(1,468)
Changes in permanently Restricted Net Assets:	
Contributions	280
Investment Income on Endowment	120
Net Unrealized and Realized Gains on Endowment (Note F)	4,620
Increase in Permanently Restricted Net Assets	5,020
Increase in Net Assets	15,450
Net Assets at beginning of year	266,140
Net Assets at end of year	$281,590

IV. Revenues and Gains Section

A. Note the following items in this section:

1. Contribution revenue can be reported in all three classifications of net assets; this is also true of investment income and realized and unrealized gains on securities.

2. Exchange revenues (fees, dues, charges for services, etc.) can only be reported under unrestricted net assets.

V. Expenses and Losses Section

A. Note the following items in this section:

1. *All expenses are incurred from unrestricted net assets.*

2. Expenses must be reported using **functional classifications.** There are two primary ways to classifying the expenses.

3. **Programming services**—Expenditures made to further the main mission of the organization. The line items listed under this category vary substantially from organization to organization but frequently include items such as education, outreach, research, clinical care, etc.

4. **Supporting services**—Expenditures made to provide the organizational infrastructure and to raise resources. Supporting services are always reported on two line items:

   a. **Management and general**—Administrative and support expenses such as the director's salary, office supplies, computer services;

   b. **Fund raising**—Monies used to encourage contributions to the organization including advertisements, promotional literature and mailings, and "special events" such as galas, telethons, auctions, and other fund drives.

Note

The separation of expenses into Program Services and Supporting Services classifications is extremely important as the percentage of revenues spent on Supporting Services is frequently used to measure the efficiency of a NFP organization. The examiners often include questions in which an expenditure is partially for a program service and partially for a supporting service (management and general or fund raising). In these instances, it is important to split the expenditure into the correct functional classifications.

Losses are shown as line items after expenses and can occur in any classification of Net Assets.

VI. Net Assets Released from the Restrictions Section

A. Although contributions, which have restrictions on their use, are reported under temporarily restricted net assets, when the monies are expended for the intended purpose, the expense is reported under unrestricted net assets, we need a mechanism to **reduce the amount of temporarily restricted net assets** and to **increase the amount of unrestricted net assets** to cover the expenditure. This is the function of the section titled **net assets released from restrictions.** Whenever the temporary restrictions placed on resources have been "satisfied," we transfer assets from temporarily restricted net assets into unrestricted net assets.

B. We can move these resources in three instances, which correspond with the three types of restrictions placed on the resources:

   1. **Satisfaction of program restrictions**—The resources have been spent for the intended operating purpose, which always results in the recognition of an expense.

   2. **Satisfaction of asset acquisition restrictions**—The resources have been spent for the intended capital purpose, which always results in the increase of an asset account.

   3. **Satisfaction of time restrictions**—The time or event specified in the restriction on the resources has occurred; note that it is not necessary that the resources be spent.

C. **Note the Following on the Statement of Activities:**

   1. There is always an increase in unrestricted net assets.

   2. There is always a decrease in temporarily restricted net assets.

   3. There is never an entry under permanently restricted net assets.

> **Exam Tip**
> *Most questions in this area will ask for the "effect on net assets when monies restricted to a certain type of expenditure are actually expended for that purpose." Two separate transactions must be considered: the expense itself, which will reduce unrestricted net assets, and the transfer of resources in the net assets released from restrictions section, which increases unrestricted net assets and decreases temporarily restricted net assets.*

VII. Change in Net Assets

A. The "bottom line" of the Statement of Activity is entitled **Change in Net Assets,** *not* Net Income. The Change in Net Assets line item is always followed by the reconciliation of the ending balance in each of the three categories of Net Assets. That is:

+ Change in Net Assets
± Beginning Net Assets
= Ending Net Assets

B. Ending net assets totals on the Statement of Activity should reconcile to the Net Asset totals on the Statement of Financial Position.

VIII. Statement of Cash Flows

A. The Statement of Cash Flows is required for all organizations. Its format is identical to the Statement of Cash Flows required by for-profit organizations and consequently it is not heavily tested. The principal difference lies in the treatment of contributions that are restricted for long-term purposes—that is, resources that are subject to capital restrictions—which are reported in the Financing Activities section. Unrestricted contributions and contributions subject to Program or Time Restrictions are reported in the Operating Activities section.

B. The three classifications of cash flows and some examples of the items found in each section are shown below:

1. **Cash flows from operating activities**—Includes **unrestricted contributions, unrestricted investment earnings, revenue restricted for operating purposes (program restrictions)**, revenue from exchange transactions, and **operating expenditures** (salaries, supplies, interest expense), including grants to other organizations;

2. **Cash flows from investing activities**—Includes inflows from the sale of capital assets, marketable securities, etc., and outflows for the purchase of capital assets, etc.;

3. **Cash flows from financing activities**—Has two subsections (i) include contributions and investment revenues restricted for long-term purposes (e.g., restrictions for acquisition of capital assets, endowments) and (ii) other financing activities for debt proceeds, debt repayment, lease payments, etc.

C. Statement of Cash Flows

Indirect Method
Not-for-Profit Organizations
Statement of Cash Flows
Year Ended June 30, 20X1
(in thousands)

Cash Flows from Operating Activities:	
Change in Net Assets	$ 15,450
Adjustments to Reconcile Change in Net Assets to Net Cash Used by Operating Activities:	
Depreciation	3,200
Fire Loss	80
Actuarial Loss on Annuity Obligations	30
Increase in Accounts and Interest Receivable	(460)
Decrease in Inventories and Prepaid Expenses	390
Increase in Contributions Receivable	(325)
Increase in Accounts Payable	1,520
Decrease in Refundable Advance	(650)
Decrease in Grants Payable	(425)
Contributions Restricted for Long-Term Investment	(2,740)
Interest and Dividends Restricted for Long-Term Investment	(300)
Net Unrealized and Realized Gains on Long-Term Investments	(15,800)
Net Cash Used by Operating Activities	(30)

Cash Flows from Investing Activities:	
Insurance Proceeds from Fire Loss on Building	250
Purchase of Equipment	(1,500)
Proceeds from Sale of Investments	76,100
Purchase of Investments	(74,900)
Net Cash Used by Investing Activities	(50)
Cash Flows from Financing Activities	
Proceeds from Contributions Restricted for:	
Investment in Endowment	200
Investment in Term Endowment	70
Investment in Plant	1,200
Investment Subject to Annuity Agreements	200
	1,680
Other Financing Activities:	
Interest and Dividends Restricted for Reinvestment	300
Payments of Annuity Obligations	(145)
Payments on Notes Payable	(1,140)
Payments on Long-Term Debt	(1,000)
	(1,985)
Net Cash used by Financing Activities	(305)
Net Decrease in Cash and Cash Equivalents	(385)
Cash and Cash Equivalents at Beginning of Year	460
Cash and Cash Equivalents at End of Year	$ 75

IX. Statement of Functional Expenses

A. The Statement of Functional Expenses is **required *only for voluntary health and welfare organizations but is recommended* for all NFP organizations**. (This is the most frequently asked question about this statement!) The purpose of the Statement of Functional Expenses is to take the functional expense categories shown in the Statement of Activities (Program Services and Supporting Services) and break them down into "natural expense" categories (i.e. rent, utilities, salaries, depreciation, etc.).

B. Statement of Functional Expenses

Statement of Functional Expenses
Illustrative VHWO/ONPO

Statement of Functional Expenses

For the Year Ended December 31, 20X1

	Program Services			Supporting Services			
	Research	Education	Total	Management and General	Fund Raising	Total	Total Expenses
Salaries	$16,000	$27,000	$43,000	$30,000	$15,000	$45,000	$88,000
Employee Health and Retirement Benefits	1,289	3,340	4,629	4,648	1,284	5,932	10,561
Payroll Taxes, etc.	644	1,670	2,314	2,324	642	2,966	5,280
Total Salaries and Related Expenses	17,933	32,010	49,943	36,972	16,926	53,898	103,841
Professional Fees and Contract Service Payments	34,996	90,710	125,706	13,428	2,283	15,711	141,417
Supplies	4,852		4,852	9,296	6,000	15,296	20,148
Telephone and Telegraph	1,245	1,670	2,915	7,747	5,965	13,712	16,627
Postage and Shipping	1,192	1,670	2,862	6,714	8,015	14,729	17,391
Occupancy	10,000		10,000	15,494	7,707	23,201	33,201
Rental of Equipment	322	835	1,157	1,549	4,567	6,116	7,273
Local Transportation	966	2,305	3,471	11,879	8,563	20,442	23,913
Conferences, Conventions, Meetings	2,577	6,680	9,257	19,626	3,711	23,337	32,594
Printing and Publications	1,289	3,340	4,629	7,231	18,268	25,499	30,128
Awards and Grants	16,106	41,747	57,853				57,853
Interest				20,000		20,000	20,000
Meals					20,000	20,000	20,000
Gratuities					5,000	5,000	5,000
Miscellaneous	322	833	1,155	8,264	5,995	14,259	15,414
Total Expenses before Depreciation	91,800	182,000	273,800	113,000	271,200	246,200	545,000
Depreciation of Buildings, Improvements, and Equipment	12,000	2,000	14,000	13,000	3,000	16,000	30,000
Total Expenses	103,800	184,000	287,800	171,200	116,000	287,200	575,000
Less: Expenses Deducted Directly from Revenues					(25,000)	(25,000)	(25,000)
Total Expenses Reported by Function	$103,800	$184,000	$287,800	$171,200	$91,000	$262,200	$550,000

Donations, Pledges, Contributions, and Net Assets

This lesson describes contribution revenue recognition for not-for-profit entities.

After studying this lesson, you should be able to:

1. Describe the three categories of net assets.

2. Describe the difference between purpose restrictions and time restrictions.

3. Recall the criteria for recognizing a promise to contribute ("pledge") as contribution revenue.

4. Determine revenue to be recognized for donated services, donated fixed assets, and donated collections.

5. Identify transfers to a nongovernmental, not-for-profit entity acting as an agent or intermediary that are not recognized as contributions in the statement of activities.

I. **Nonexchange Transactions**—*Contributions* are unconditional, nonreciprocal receipts of assets or services. They are not *exchange* transactions, in which each party in the transaction gives up something of value. They are asymmetrical transactions in which one party relinquishes something of value to another party, but the other party provides nothing in return. The item of value may be cash, marketable securities, inventory, property, or even services (subject to limitations noted later). Statement #116, *Accounting for Contributions Received and Contributions Made*, provides guidance on revenue recognition for non-exchange transactions.

II. **Contribution Recognition**

   A. *All unconditional contributions are recognized as contribution revenue in the period in which the contribution is made, regardless of whether it is received in cash.* Donations other than cash are recorded at **fair value as of the date of the gift**.

   B. **Conditional** contributions depend on the occurrence of some future, uncertain event. In this case, revenue recognition occurs when the condition is met or the chance of not meeting the condition becomes remote. The not-for-profit should account for conditional contributions received (e.g., cash is deposited) as a refundable advance (liability) until the condition is met.

III. **Revenue Classifications**

   A. All revenue must be reported in one of three categories based on the type of restrictions, if any, *placed by the donor* on its use. The three categories are:

Unrestricted	Resources are available for expenditure *in the current period for any purpose.*
Temporarily Restricted	Resources are available for expenditure in the current period but only for **specified (operating) purposes**; these restrictions are known as **program restrictions.**
	or
Temporarily Restricted	Resources are available for expenditure in the current period only for **capital purposes**; these restrictions are known as **asset acquisition** or **capital restrictions.**
	or
Temporarily Restricted	Resources are available only after a specified time has elapsed or event has taken place: these restrictions are known as **time restrictions.**
Permanently Restricted	Resources are not available for expenditure at any time, although the earnings on the resources *may* be expended; permanently restricted assets are known as **endowments.**

Note
Only revenue from nonexchange transactions (e.g., contributions) can be classified as Temporarily Restricted or Permanently Restricted because the restriction must be made by an external party (the donor); **revenue subject to internal restrictions**, such as might be made by the Board of Directors, **and revenue from exchange transactions** (i.e., dues, sales of goods, charges for services, etc.) are **always classified as Unrestricted.**

Example
Animal Action recently received $100,000 in contributions. $30,000 of this amount was restricted by donors to covering the costs of a spay/neuter clinic. The director set aside an additional $50,000 of this amount to be used to build an addition to the animal shelter. Animal Action reports $30,000 of the Contribution Revenue as Temporarily Restricted and reports $70,000 as Unrestricted. The $50,000 set aside by the director should be reported as designated resources within the Unrestricted category; it does not qualify for inclusion in the Temporarily Restricted category.

IV. Pledges (ASC 958-605-25-7-15)

A. Promises to contribute (pledges) may also be recognized as contributions as long as they are unconditional. Conditional promises to give are promises that depend on a specific event occurring in the future. They cannot be recognized as contributions until the uncertain future event has occurred. Conditional promises to give are recognized when the conditions are substantially met or when the likelihood that the conditions will **not** be met is remote. An allowance for uncollectible pledges should be recorded in a manner similar to a for-profit organization's accounting for accounts receivable.

Study Tip
The timing of the receipt of cash related to pledges is a frequent distracter in CPA Exam questions. The examiners will give information about the pledge and about when the pledge was paid. The cash payment information should almost always be ignored. **Revenue recognition is not tied to the receipt of cash;** a pledge to contribute in the current period is recognized as revenue when the pledge is made, **not** when the cash is received (but see special rules for multiyear pledges below).

Examples

1. Simmons promises to give $1,000,000 to World Crisis Services to purchase food supplies for a drought-ridden country. Simmons also promises to give an additional $500,000 if the drought is not broken in six months. The $1,000,000 should be recognized as a Contribution since it is an unconditional promise. The $500,000 cannot be recognized as a Contribution since it is conditioned upon an uncertain future event.

2. Jesse Morgan pledges $10,000 to the McMillan School, a private not-for-profit elementary school that maintains a culturally diverse student body, as long as the average standardized test scores for the student body are above 75% of the national average. The average standardized tests scores for the McMillan School student body have always been above 85% in its 25-year history. Since the likelihood that the test average would fall below 75% for this year is remote, McMillan would recognize the promise to give immediately.

3. QuickCure Hospital receives pledges of $80,000 in November of the current year. It receives $50,000 cash related to the pledges in December and the remaining $30,000 in January. QuickCure's fiscal year runs from January 1 to December 31. QuickCure recognizes revenue of $80,000 in the current year.

B. Unconditional Pledges—Are recognized as contribution revenue *net* **of the estimated uncollectible pledges (allowance for uncollectible pledges)**.

Example

Little City Public Television recently held a fund drive and received $300,000 in pledges. Historically, the station has been unable to collect 30% of its pledges. Little City Public Television should recognize the contribution revenue of $210,000 ($300,000 − ($300,000 × 30%)).

The accounting entry for pledges is sometimes tested on the exam:

DR: Pledges Receivable	$300,000	
CR: Estimated Uncollectible Pledges		$ 90,000
CR: Contribution Revenue		$210,000

V. Pledges Made Over Multiple Fiscal Periods—When revenue is to be received over multiple fiscal periods, as happens when contributions are pledged over several years (e.g., a pledge $10,000 per year for four years), special recognition rules apply:

A. Recognize revenue at the *net present value* of the contribution.

B. The portion of the pledge that is to be received in subsequent fiscal periods is considered **Temporarily Restricted** (time restricted—see below); the portion that is to be received in the current period is recognized as **Unrestricted**, assuming that no other restrictions, such as a purpose restriction, are specified.

C. The net present value of the pledge is recalculated at the end of the period (or whenever the financial statements are prepared) and increases in net present value are booked as *contribution revenue*, **not interest**.

D. When the future payments are received, the assets are reclassified to unrestricted net assets, assuming that there are no other restrictions on how the money may be spent, but **revenue is not recognized**. (It was recognized when the pledge was made and as the interest element was realized.)

Example

On January 1, Fly Free, a raptor preservation organization, received an unrestricted pledge of $10,000 per year for three years (the current year and the next two years).

Assuming an interest rate of 10% and that the first payment is made immediately, the present value of the pledge is $27,355. Fly Free recognizes $10,000 Contribution Revenue in the Unrestricted category (the current year's payment) and $17,355 Contribution Revenue in the Temporarily Restricted category (the present value of the two remaining payments).

Cash	10,000	
Contributions Receivable	20,000	
Contributions—Unrestricted		10,000
Contributions—Temporarily Restricted		17,355
Discount on Contributions Receivable		2,645

At year-end, Fly Free recalculates the present value of the remaining pledge as $19,091. The difference of $1,736 ($19,091 − $17,355) is recognized as Contribution Revenue in the Temporarily Restricted category. Note: Interest revenue is not recognized.

Discount on Contributions Receivable	1,736	
Contribution—Temporarily Restricted		1,736

When the second year's payment of $10,000 is received, no additional revenue is recognized (cash increases and pledges decrease). The $10,000 will, however, be reclassified from Temporarily Restricted to Unrestricted since the *time restriction* has now been met. (See ASC 958-605-30-4 through 7 for an explanation of how assets are *released from restriction*.)

Cash	10,000	
Contributions Receivable		10,000
Net Assets Released—Temporarily Restricted	10,000	
Net Assets Released—Unrestricted		10,000

At the end of the second year, Fly Free recalculates the present value of the remaining pledge as $10,000. The difference of $909 ($10,000 − $9,091) is recognized as Contribution Revenue in the Temporarily Restricted category.

Discount on Contributions Receivable	909	
Contribution—Temporarily Restricted		909

When the final payment of $10,000 is received, it will again be reclassified from Temporarily Restricted to Unrestricted. The total amount of Contribution Revenue recognized over the life of the pledge is $30,000 ($27,355 + $1,736 + $909).

Cash	10,000	
Contributions Receivable		10,000
Net Assets Released—Temporarily Restricted	10,000	
Net Assets Released—Unrestricted		10,000

VI. Donated Services (ASC 958-605-25-16-17)

A. FASB allows NPF organizations to recognize the value of services that are donated to the organization, but only if certain conditions are met. Donated services are recognized if *either:*

  1. Nonfinancial assets are enhanced **or**

  2. Services requiring a) *special skills* are provided b) *by persons possessing those skills* and the services would c) *normally have been purchased* by the organization (e.g., CPA who donates audit services).

B. The entry to record the donated service recognizes the fair value of the service as a *credit to Contribution Revenue* and as a *debit to either an asset* (if nonfinancial assets are enhanced) *or as an expense* (if services are provided) account.

Examples

1. Nonfinancial Assets Are Enhanced—Prairie View Prep School is building an auditorium for their fine arts department. The parent of an eighth grade student is an architect and donates his services to design the auditorium. He normally charges $150,000 for this work, though the going market rate in the area for similar work is $100,000.

Since architectural fees are normally capitalized as part of the building cost, a nonfinancial asset has been enhanced. Prairie View can recognize the donated services at the fair value of $100,000 with the following entry:

```
DR: Building                          100,000
    CR: Contribution Revenue                      100,000
```

2. Service Requiring Special Skills—Jennifer Rhodes, a professional deep-sea diver, has been hired by Sea Mammals R Us, an international sea mammal conservation group, to help record the activities of migrating whales. The original contract is for five days at $600 per day. However, the process requires an additional two days to complete, and the contract is extended.

Rather than bill for the additional time, Jennifer contributes her time to the organization. Because Sea Mammals R Us would normally have had to purchase these services and because they are skilled services, they can recognize the value of the services with the following entry:

```
DR: Research Expenses (Diving Expense)   1,200
    CR: Contribution Revenue                      1,200
```

3. Donated Services Not Recognized—Students at Central University have recently been accosted and robbed and/or threatened when crossing campus late at night. To combat this problem, student groups have banded together to offer escort services to students free of charge. The students estimate that a fair charge for such a service is approximately $10 per trip or $4,500 per month. The university has increased its campus police force in response to the problem and has decided against providing escort services to students.

Central is *not* able to recognize the value of these services because, even though this might arguably be classified as a "skilled" service, there is no indication that the students possess these skills and this is not a service that the university would normally provide.

Note: This is a consistently tested area on the exam. Most of the time the value of the services is recognized. Frequently, there are differences between rates charged and *standard* or *fair value* rates: Always record at fair value.

VII. Donated Fixed Assets and Donated Collections

A. Donated fixed assets are **recorded at FMV** at date of donation. These assets are generally subject to depreciation.

B. **Classification of revenue from the donation**—Fixed assets are normally considered to be unrestricted so contribution revenue related to the donation is usually recognized as Unrestricted. If, however, there are restrictions on how the asset must be used or on how proceeds from the sale of the asset may be expended, it should be classified as Temporarily Restricted or even Permanently Restricted.

C. Not-for-profit organizations have the option of not recognizing donated works or art, historical artifacts, rare books, and other similar donated collections as revenues or gains and assets if all of the following conditions are met (ASC 958-360-20):

1. Held for public exhibition, education, or research in furtherance of public sector rather than financial gain

2. Protected, kept unencumbered, care for, and preserved

3. Subject to an organizational policy that requires the proceeds from sales of collection items to be used to acquire other items for collections

---

Examples

1. *Unrestricted Fixed Asset*—Newberry Cars donated a demonstration car to the McGrary Foundation, a not-for-profit organization. The car cost Newberry $15,000 and had a retail sales value of $22,000 when new. The car's current market value is $16,000. McGrary records the donation and reports Contribution Revenue of $16,000 under Unrestricted Net Assets.

2. *Permanently Restricted Fixed Asset*—Mary Cochoran donates land to the Newport Home, a not-for-profit organization that provides temporary living accommodations for foster children, with the stipulation that the land be maintained by Newport Home in perpetuity and is used to provide recreational opportunities to the foster children. The land has a basis of $50,000 to Ms. Cochoran and a fair value of $80,000. Newport Home records the donation and reports Contribution Revenue of $80,000 under Permanently Restricted Net Assets.

3. *Donated Work of Art Not Recognized*—Pedro Picasso donates a work of art having a fair value of $50,000 to become part of the permanent collection at the Modern Art Museum. The museum has a policy of not recognizing donations to its collection as revenue or assets. The museum does not recognize the contrition as revenue or record an asset—it should report the donation in the notes to the financial statements.

4. *Donated Work of Art Recognized*—Pedro Picasso donates a work of art having a fair value $5,000 with the understanding that the Modern Art Museum will sell it at an auction and use the funds for its general operating activities. The museum will report $5,000 Contribution Revenue under Unrestricted Net Assets.

VIII. Contributions Raised or Held for Others

A. NFP organizations sometimes receive resources that are restricted by the donor to specific recipients. Depending on the degree of the restriction, these monies may represent Contribution Revenue to the NFP organization or they may actually be liabilities of the NFP organization. FASB ASC 958-605 *(Statement 136), Transfers of Assets to a Not-For-Profit Organization That Raises or Holds Contributions for Others,* **addresses these recognition issues.**

B. **What transactions are covered**—ASC 958-605 applies to transactions in which three entities are identified:

1. A **donor** who has sent resources to a NFP;

2. A **recipient** who is responsible for disbursing the money to a NFP;

3. A **specified beneficiary**, who will ultimately be able to use the funds.

C. FASB requires that when an NFP organization is an intermediary or an agent for the transfer of assets to another NFP organization (beneficiary), that intermediary or agent would not recognize contribution revenue, unless it is granted *variance power* to redirect the resources (i.e., change the beneficiary) or it is financially interrelated to the beneficiary.

1. **Variance power**—The unilateral power to redirect the transferred assets to another beneficiary. Unilateral power means that the recipient entity can override the donor's instructions without seeking approval.

2. **Donor**—The contributor of cash or other assets. The donor decides who the intended beneficiary is. However, if the donor decides to grant variance power, the agent is ultimately responsible for who eventually receives the donation.

3. **Intermediary, agent, or trustee**—The conduit or go-between that holds the contribution. If variance power is granted, the agent acts more as a donee or recipient organization until the contribution is redistributed.

4. **Specified beneficiary**—The ultimate intended recipient of the contribution.

> **Example**
>
> Consider the NFP organization United Way and its work collecting contributions and redirecting the funds to feeder organizations. To the extent that United Way is able to control which feeder organization receives the contribution, it would have variance power.
>
> If a donation is made to a disaster relief NFP organization (e.g., the Red Cross) specifically for the Katrina hurricane relief victims, the NFP is not able to redirect the funds to build a new administrative facility in the state of New York because variance power is not granted.

D. Recognition

1. *Without variance power*, the intermediary will record the receipt of resources (debit) at fair value with an offsetting recognition of a liability (credit) to the ultimate recipient (i.e., specified beneficiary). Likewise, the specified beneficiary is required to recognize a receivable (debit) and contribution revenue (credit).

2. *If variance power is granted*, the NFP recipient organization (i.e., intermediary) would recognize the receipt of resources (debit) and corresponding contribution revenue (credit) instead of a liability because the NFP now has control over the ultimate distribution of the contribution. When the asset is transferred to the beneficiary, an expense is recognized by the NFP (intermediary). A beneficiary would make no entry until contribution is actually received.

3. When the intermediary or agent and the beneficiary are financially interrelated, the intermediary or agent would recognize the receipt of the asset and the associated contribution revenue; the beneficiary would recognize its interest in the net assets of the intermediary or agent. The intermediary would adjust its net assets for the beneficiary's share of the change.

Special Issues—Recent Developments

This lesson describes some special issues pertaining to financial reporting for not-for-profit entities.

After studying this lesson, you should be able to:

1. Describe the accounting and reporting of inexhaustible fixed assets (e.g., collections).

2. List three types of endowments that do not meet the requirements of a regular, "pure" endowment.

3. Describe the reporting for earnings on endowments.

4. Describe the financial reporting for investments.

5. Describe the funds that are used for internal reporting purposes.

I. **Inexhaustible Fixed Assets (ASC 958-605-25-19)**

   A. Inexhaustible fixed assets include works of art, cultural treasures, historical documents and property, and so on, and are subject to special rules. In particular:

   1. Inexhaustible fixed assets donated to the organization need *not be capitalized*. This means that, when such an asset is donated to the organization, we do not need to make an accounting entry to record the transaction and the value of the contribution and asset will not appear on the face of the financial statements. Further, if such an item is sold and the proceeds are used to purchase another inexhaustible fixed asset, those transactions also need not be recorded or reported on the face of the financial statements. Note that, although these transactions do not appear on the face of the financial statements, *they are disclosed in the notes*.

   2. Depreciation on these inexhaustible fixed assets *need not* be recorded.

   B. In order to use these procedures, the assets must fit the requirements of assets known as *collectibles* or *collections*: Three conditions of the assets must be met. The assets must be:

   1. Held for public exhibition, education, or research rather than financial gain;

   2. Protected, kept unencumbered, cared for, and preserved; *and*

   3. Subject to a policy that requires proceeds from sales of collection items to be used to acquire other items for collections.

   Example
   A local collector donates a Picasso painting to the Henderson Museum of Modern Art. Since Henderson already has several Picassos, it sells the painting and uses the proceeds to purchase a Calder mobile. The mobile will be displayed in Henderson's public galleries and will be well protected. Because the art works meet the definition of a *collectible*, Henderson need not record the donation of the Picasso or the subsequent sale and purchase of the Calder. Instead, these transactions are disclosed in the notes.

II. **Investments**

   A. NFP organizations frequently hold significant amounts of investments. ASC 954-320-35 (Statement #124), *Accounting for Certain Investments Held by Not-for-Profit Organizations*, addresses the accounting issues associated with these investments by NFP organizations. For the most part, accounting for these investments is handled in the same manner as it is for for-profit organizations. That is, NFP organizations must report (all) their marketable securities at fair value. Changes in market value are recognized on the Statement of Activities as unrealized gains and losses during the period of the change.

B. However, unlike for-profit organizations, NFP organizations do not break debt securities out into Trading, Available-for-Sale, and Held-to-Maturity categories. Because the Held-to-Maturity category is the only one that allows for valuation at other than market value, for NFP organizations, *debt securities* **are** *always* **valued at fair value**.

III. Endowments

A. **Permanent endowments** are contributions to the organization from third parties for which the principal (corpus) must *remain intact in perpetuity*. Earnings on the endowment may be **expendable-restricted** (expendable but only for specified purposes), **expendable-unrestricted** (expendable at any time, for any purpose) or **nonexpendable**, depending on the stipulations of the donor. Endowments that have these characteristics are called *regular* endowments or *pure* endowments and are recorded as Permanently Restricted assets. Fund accounting is typically used for endowments for internal purposes but is not used for external reporting for private not-for-profit organizations. Funds are reported for governmental not-for-profit organizations (e.g., county hospital).

B. **Split-interest agreements** are arrangements whereby both a donor (or beneficiary) and a not-for-profit organization receive benefits, often at different times in a multiyear arrangement. A typical split-interest agreement has two components: a lead interest and a remainder interest. A lead interest provides disbursements throughout the term of the agreement. A final disbursement at the termination of the agreement is a remainder interest.

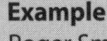

Example

Roger Smith established a charitable lead trust for a donation to the Salvation Army. Roger put $1,000,000 in the trust to be invested for 10 years. The Salvation Army receives the trust income for the 10-year period (a lead interest). At the end of the 10-year period, the principal of the trust goes to Roger's children (the remainder interest).

C. Other types of contributions are similar to regular endowments but fail to meet one of the regular endowment criteria.

1. **Quasi-endowments**—Amounts set aside by the governing board of the organization, rather than outside sources, of which the principal must be retained and invested. Although these resources act like an endowment, they cannot be considered regular endowments as the restrictions on endowment resources must come from an external party. This type of endowment is known as **quasi-endowment**. Quasi-endowments are not included in Permanently Restricted Net Assets but are **included with Unrestricted Net Assets**.

> **Study Tip**
>
> The examiners frequently try to confuse board designated funds with quasi-endowments. Candidates should pay particular attention to indications of how the principal is to be treated: *If the principal can be spent, it is a board-designated fund; If only the earnings can be spent, it is a quasi-endowment.*

2. **Term endowments**—Gifts and bequests from third parties that are to be retained and invested for a period of time or until a specific event occurs. However, after the criterion has been met, the full amount can be spent. The earnings on the invested amount are paid to a separate beneficiary (usually a spouse or a child) until the criterion is met. These contributions are known as **term endowments.** Because they can ultimately be spent, they are **classified as Temporarily Restricted Net Assets.**

3. **Board designated funds**—Amounts set aside by the governing board of the organization to be spent for specific purposes; these funds are not endowments because the principal can be spent. Board-designated funds frequently are set apart from other unrestricted assets by establishing an account similar to a reservation of Retained Earnings by for profit entities. The account is normally titled Unrestricted Net Assets Designated for _____ and is deducted from the total Unrestricted Net Assets.

Example
Mantega Hospital received a $50,000 gift of securities that are to be retained and invested. The earnings may be used as Mantega wishes. Mantega's governing board designated, for special uses, $30,000 that had originated from unrestricted gifts. It set aside $80,000, the earnings from which are to be used to help fund charity care.

Mantega reports $50,000 as a regular endowment (Permanently Restricted Net Assets); $30,000 is classified as a board designated fund (included in Unrestricted Net Assets); the remaining $80,000 is classified as a quasi-endowment (included in Unrestricted Net Assets).

IV. Earnings on Endowments

A. Earnings on endowments are reported as Endowment Income or Investment Income on the accrual basis. The income may be reported in any of the three classes of net assets depending on the restrictions on the use of the income:

1. If there are no restrictions on use, then report income under Unrestricted Net Assets.

2. If the income must be spent for specified purposes, or may not be spent until a specified time or event, report under Temporarily Restricted Net Assets.

3. If the income may not be spent but must be used to increase or maintain the corpus, report under Permanently Restricted Net Assets.

Example
Erica Gardner gives $100,000 to Borgans Children's Hospital to be used as a loan fund for families traveling to be with their children at the hospital. Interest charged on the loans (endowment earnings) is put back into the fund to increase the amount available to lend. The interest is reported under Permanently Restricted Net Assets.

V. Types of Funds Used by Not-for-Profit Organizations

Types of Funds Used by Not-for-Profit Organizations—Not-for-profit organizations may use fund accounting for internal purposes. If so, the following seven types of funds are used by not-for-profit organizations:

A. **Unrestricted Current Funds**—Account for resources over which the governing board has discretionary control and fund balance is **Unrestricted Net Assets**

B. **Restricted Current Funds**—Account for resources whose use is restricted by external parties for a specific purpose, in which case fund balance is **Temporarily Restricted**

C. **Plant Funds**—Account for investments in plant and resources available for capital asset acquisition and net assets are typically separated into Unrestricted, Temporarily Restricted, or Permanently Restricted. Plant funds frequently take on other names such as Land, Building, and Equipment Funds, or Plant Expansion Fund; colleges and universities frequently use four subfunds: (1) Unexpended Plant Funds, (2) Funds for Renewal and Replacement, (3) Funds for Retirement of Indebtedness, and (4) Net Investment in Plant.

D. **Loan Funds**—Commonly used by colleges and universities to account for loans made to students

E. **Endowment Funds**—Permanent, term, or quasi (board designated)

F. **Annuity (Life Income) Funds**—Account for *split-interest funds* in which the not-for-profit organization shares a beneficial interest with another external party

G. **Agency Funds**—Account for resources held by the not-for-profit organization as an agent for a third party

State and Local Government Concepts

Introduction to Governmental Organizations

> **After studying this lesson, you should be able to:**
>
> 1. Describe the characteristics that governments operate in that influence their accounting and financial reporting.
>
> 2. Describe the how fund accounting is used by governmental entities.
>
> 3. Describe the hierarchy of GAAP for state and local governments as established by GASB Statement No. 76.

I. **Exam Coverage**—The AICPA content specifications for accounting for governmental and not-for-profit organizations, including the approximate weighting of the questions, is shown below.

II. **Accounting and Reporting for Governmental Entities (5–15%)**

   A. **Governmental Accounting Concepts**

      1. Measurement focus and basis of accounting

      2. Fund accounting concepts and application

      3. Budgetary process

   B. **Format and Content of Governmental Financial Statements**

      1. Government-wide financial statements

      2. Governmental funds financial statements

      3. Conversion from fund to government-wide financial statements

      4. Proprietary fund financial statements

      5. Fiduciary fund financial statements

      6. Notes to financial statements

      7. Required supplementary information, including management's discussion and analysis

      8. Comprehensive annual financial report (CAFR)

   C. **Financial Reporting Entity Including Blended and Discrete Component Units**

   D. **Typical Items and Specific Types of Transactions and Events**—Recognition, measurement, valuation and presentation in governmental entity financial statements in conformity with GAAP

      1. Net position and its three categories:

         a. Net investment in capital assets

         b. Restricted

         c. Unrestricted

      2. Capital assets and infrastructure

      3. Transfers

      4. Other financing sources and uses

    5. Fund balance and its five types:

        a. Nonspendable

        b. Restricted

        c. Committed

        d. Assigned

        e. Unassigned

    6. Nonexchange revenues

    7. Expenditures

    8. Special items

    9. Encumbrances

    10. Deferred outflows of resources and deferred inflows of resources

  E. **Accounting and Financial Reporting for Governmental Not-for-Profit Organizations**

III. **Characteristics and Types of Governmental Organizations**—Accounting and financial reporting for government organizations is greatly influenced by the following unique characteristics of these organizations:

  A. Lack of a clear profit motive

  B. Ownership is collective and nontransferable (i.e., cannot be sold or traded).

  C. Nonexchange transaction—financial resources contributed to the organization are often not in exchange for a direct or proportionate share of services. (e.g., property taxes are paid to finance public schools regardless of the number of children the taxpayer has in school).

  D. Policy decisions are made by a vote of elected or appointed governing bodies.

  E. Policymaking is often open to the public and news media.

  F. The budget is an expression of the policies of the organization and success is frequently determined by the ability or inability to meet the budget.

  G. All the foregoing characteristics lead to an elaborate accounting and financial reporting structure.

IV. **Types of State and Local Governments (SLGs)**—*General-purpose governments* (cities, states, and counties), *limited or special-purpose governments* (school districts, transit authorities, and municipal utility districts) and various *agencies and commissions* (e.g., employment commission, economic development commission, etc.).

> **Note**
> Although the federal government is a form of government, it is not included in the state and local government category and, in general, it is not tested on the CPA Exam. The Financial Accounting Standards Advisory Board (FASAB) considers and recommends accounting principles for the federal government.

V. **Who Makes the Rules?**

  A. The governmental GAAP hierarchy is established by GASB Statement No. 76 for fiscal years beginning after June 15, 2015. Statement No. 76 superseded GASB Statement No. 55.

    1. **State and local governments**—The Governmental Accounting Standards Board (GASB) is the primary authority. **GASB Statement No.** 76 lists the sources of accounting principles in two categories in descending order of authority as follows:

        a. Category A: Officially established accounting principles; that is, GASB Statements and Interpretations.

b. Category B: GASB Technical Bulletins, GASB Implementation Guides, and literature of the AICPA cleared by the GASB.

[Statement No. 55, which was superseded by Statement No. 76, contained four (4) categories:

i. GASB Statements and Interpretations

ii. GASB Technical Bulletins and AICPA Industry Guides and Statements of Position cleared by GASB

iii. AICPA Practice Bulletins cleared by GASB and consensus opinions of a group of accountants organized by GASB

iv. Implementation guides published by GASB staff and widely recognized practices prevalent in the state and local government.]

c. If the accounting treatment for a transaction or event is not specified by a pronouncement in Category A, then the governmental entity should consider whether the accounting treatment is specified by a source in Category B.

d. If the accounting treatment for a transaction or event is not specified by sources in Categories A and B, then the government entity should first consider accounting principles for similar transactions or events within a source in Category A and B and then may consider nonauthoritative accounting literature from other sources—provided it does not contradict authoritative GAAP—such as GASB Concepts Statements, pronouncements and other literature of the FASB, Federal Accounting Standards Advisory Board (FASAB), International Public Sector Accounting Standards Board, and the International Accounting Standards Board, AICPA literature not cleared by GASB, practices that are widely recognized and prevalent in state and local governments, literature of other professional associations and regulatory agencies, and accounting textbooks, handbooks, and articles. Nonauthoritative accounting literature should be evaluated for consistency with GASB Concepts Statements.

2. **Hybrid organizations (governmentally affiliated hospitals, universities, and museums)**—GASB is the ultimate authority for governmentally affiliated hospitals, universities, and other not-for-profits (e.g., museums). Remember that nongovernmental, not-for-profit hospitals, universities, and other types of not-for-profit organizations follow FASB standards.

GASB Concepts Statements

This lesson describes GASB's conceptual framework by covering GASB Concepts Statements

After studying this lesson, you should be able to:

1. Understand the unique characteristics of the governmental environment and the two main purposes of financial reporting by governments.

2. List the seven elements of financial statements and describe some examples of deferred items.

3. List the hierarchy of communication methods to convey information to users of the general-purpose external financial reports.

4. Understand the types of measures that can be used to report on service efforts and accomplishments.

5. List the six characteristics of information in financial reporting by governments.

I. **GASB Concepts Statements**—GASB Concepts Statements do not provide authoritative guidance on accounting and reporting; rather, these statements provide the conceptual framework the GASB uses in developing new standards and revising existing standards. Consequently, it is important to understand the main concepts found in the GASB Concepts Statements.

II. **Concepts Statement No. 1,** *Objectives of Financial Reporting.* (issued May 1987)

A. **Scope**

1. It establishes the objectives of general-purpose external financial reporting by state and local governmental entities.

2. It applies to both governmental-type and business-type activities.

3. The concepts statement **does not establish financial reporting standards—it establishes the conceptual framework to be used by GASB in evaluating existing standards and establishing future standards.**

4. General-purpose external financial reporting includes general-purpose financial statements, notes to the financial statements, required supplemental information, and other supplementary information.

5. This statement may not meet the needs of users of specific purpose financial reporting:

   a. Characteristics

      i. Used to meet the needs of specific users

      ii. Presents financial information on a basis of accounting that differs from GAAP

      iii. Presents financial information in a prescribed format

      iv. Reports on specified elements, accounts, or items taken from the general-purpose financial statements

   b. Examples

      i. Offering statements

      ii. Budgets

      iii. Reports to grantor agencies

B. Governmental Environment

1. **Primary characteristics**

   a. Representative form of government and separation of powers.

   b. Federal system of government and the prevalence of intergovernmental revenues—intergovernmental revenues require state and local governments to be accountable to the governmental entity that provided the resources and to citizenry.

   c. The relationship of taxpayers to services received—governments impose taxes and provide services that may not have a direct relationship between the fees paid the services received:

      i. Taxpayers are involuntary resource providers—They cannot choose whether or not to pay taxes.

      ii. The amount of taxes paid by an individual seldom bears a proportional relationship to the cost or value of services received by the individual.

      iii. There is no "exchange" relationship between resources provided and services received.

      iv. Governments often have a monopoly on the services they provide.

2. **Control aspects**

   a. The budget is an expression of public policy and financial intent and as a method of providing control—The budget is:

      i. An expression of public policy

      ii. A financial plan

      iii. A form of control having the force of law

      iv. It provides a basis for evaluating performance

   b. The use of fund accounting for control purposes

3. **Other characteristics**

   a. The dissimilarities between similarly designated governments

   b. Significant investment in nonrevenue producing capital assets

   c. The nature of the political process—Balance the conflicting demands of different groups within the citizenry with the resources made available by the citizenry

C. Users of Financial Reports

1. **The citizenry**—Those to whom government is primarily accountable (e.g., taxpayers, voters, service recipients, the media, advocate groups, public finance researchers)

2. **Legislative and oversight bodies**—Those who directly represent the citizens (e.g., state legislatures, county commissions, city councils, board of trustees, school boards)

3. **Investors and creditors**—Those who lend or participate in the lending process (e.g., institutional investors, underwriters, bond rating agencies, bond insurers, financial institutions)

D. Uses of Financial Reports

1. Comparing actual financial reports with the legally adopted budget

2. Assessing financial condition and results of operations

3. Assisting in determining compliance with finance-related laws, rules, and regulators

4. Assisting in evaluating efficiency and effectiveness

E. **Purpose of Financial Reporting**

1. **Accountability**—This is based on the belief that the taxpayer has a "right to know" is accomplished by providing information to assist users in determining whether the government was operated within the legal constraints imposed by the citizenry.

2. **Interperiod equity**—This is a significant part of accountability by showing whether current-year revenues are sufficient to pay for current-year services or whether future taxpayers will be required to assume burdens for services previously provided.

> **Note**
> *The concepts of* accountability *and* interperiod equity *are extremely important in establishing authoritative guidance by GASB and are consistently asked on the CPA Exam.*

F. **Characteristics of Information in Financial Reporting** (TRUCCR ["TRUCKER"])

1. **T**imeliness

2. **R**elevance

3. **U**nderstandability

4. **C**omparability

5. **C**onsistency

6. **R**eliability

III. **Concepts Statement No. 2,** *Service Efforts and Accomplishments (SEA) Reporting* (issued April 1994), and **Concepts Statement No. 5**, *Service Efforts and Accomplishments Reporting—An amendment of GASB Concepts Statement No. 2* (issued November 2008)

A. GASB believes that service effort and accomplishment (SEA) information assists users in assessing accountability and making better informed decisions. However, SEA is voluntary. In June 2010, GASB issue suggested guidelines for voluntary reporting of SEA performance information.

B. **Elements of SEA Performance**

1. Measures of **service efforts** (inputs)—the amount of financial (e.g., cost of road maintenance) and nonfinancial resources (e.g., number of employee hours used in road maintenance) that are applied to a service.

2. Measures of **service accomplishments** (outputs and outcomes)—report what was provided or achieved with the resources used. There are two types of measures of accomplishments:

   a. **Output measures**—Quantity of service provided (e.g., miles of road repaired) or that meets a certain quality requirement (e.g., percentage of buses that meet a prescribed on-time standard).

   b. **Outcome measures**—Indicate the results that occur because of services provided including accomplishments as a result of the services provided (e.g., the clearance rate of serious crimes) and measures of public perception (e.g., residents' rating of their neighborhood's safety).

3. Measures that relate service efforts to service accomplishments (efficiency) measure the resources used to achieve the level of output (e.g., the cost per lane-mile to resurface roads) or measure the resources used to achieve a particular outcome (e.g., cost per lane-mile of road maintained in good condition).

4. GASB states that SEA performance information should focus on measures of service accomplishments (outputs and outcomes) and measures that relate service efforts and service accomplishments (efficiency).

C. **Characteristics of SEA Performance Information**—Should meet the same six characteristics for general-purpose external financial reporting (i.e., GASB Concepts Statement No. 1)—timeliness, relevance, understandability, comparability, consistency, reliability (TRUCCR).

D. **Providing Context for SEA Performance Information**

1. **Comparisons**

   a. With previous years

   b. Entity established targets

   c. Progress toward achievement of goals or objectives

   d. With accepted norms and standards

   e. With other parts of the entity

   f. With other comparable jurisdictions

2. **Unintended effects**—Significant positive or negative indirect consequences

3. **Demand for services**—Competing demand for resources

4. **Factors that influence results**—External (e.g., extreme weather conditions) and internal (e.g., staff shortages)

5. Narrative information

IV. **Concepts Statement No. 3,** *Communication Methods in General Purpose External Financial Reports that Contain Basic Financial Statements* (issued April 2005).

A. **Hierarchy of Communication Methods**

1. Recognition in basic financial statements

2. Disclosure in notes to basic financial statements

3. Presentation as required supplementary information (RSI) is *essential* for placing basic financial statements and notes to basic financial statements in an appropriate context. **RSI is required**

4. Presentation as other supplementary information (SI) is *useful* for placing basic financial statements and notes to basic financial statements in an appropriate context. **SI is *not* required**, but applicable GASB guidance should be followed when SI is presented.

V. **Concepts Statement No. 4,** *Elements of Financial Statements* (issued June 2007)

A. **Five Elements of the Statement of Financial Position**

1. **Assets**—Resource with present service capacity that the government presently controls

2. **Liabilities**—Present obligations to sacrifice resources that the government has little or no discretion to avoid

3. **Deferred outflow of resources**—A consumption of net assets by the government that is applicable to a future reporting period

4. **Deferred inflow of resources**—An acquisition of net assets by the government that is applicable to a future reporting period

5. **Net position**—The residual of all other elements presented in the statement of financial position

---

Note

GASB issued Statement No. 63, *Financial Reporting of Deferred Outflows of Resources, Deferred Inflows of Resources, and Net Position*, to provide financial reporting guidance for deferred outflows of resources, deferred inflows of resources, and the renaming of net assets as net position. Only items identified by GASB as deferred outflows or deferred inflows can be reported as such. For example, GASB Statement No. 53, on derivatives, and GASB Statement No. 60, on service concessions, identify certain items as deferred outflows of resources or deferred inflows of resources.

B. Two Elements of Resource Flow Statements

1. **Outflow of resources**—Consumption of net assets by the government that is applicable to the reporting period; for example, a decrease in fair value of a hedging derivative is a deferred outflow

2. **Inflow of resources**—Acquisition of net assets by the government that is applicable to the reporting period; for example, an increase in fair value of a hedging derivative is a deferred inflow

---

Definition

Resource: An item that can be drawn on to provide services to the citizenry.

C. Recognition of deferred inflows or resources and deferred outflows of resources is limited to those instances identified and required by GASB in authoritative pronouncements.

Example

GASB Statement No. 53, *Accounting and Financial Reporting for Derivative Instruments*, requires that changes in fair values of hedging derivative instruments be reported as either deferred inflows or deferred outflows of resources.

GASB Statement No. 60, *Accounting and Financial Reporting for Service Concession Arrangements*, requires that certain up-front payments that a government receives from an entity it has contracted with to operate a major capital asset, such as a toll road, be recognized as a deferred inflow of resources. Revenue should be recognized as the deferred inflow of resources is reduced.

GASB Statement No. 65, *Items Previously Reported as Assets and Liabilities*, revises a number of items previously reported as either assets or liabilities.

- **Refunding of debt:** The difference between the reacquisition price and the net carrying amount of the old debt should be reported as a deferred outflow of resources, if a loss occurred, or as a deferred inflow of resources, if a gain occurred.

- **Imposed nonexchange revenue transactions:** Deferred inflows of resources should be reported when resources are received or reported as a receivable before the period in which the levy occurs (e.g., before the property tax levy).

- **Government-mandated nonexchange transactions and voluntary exchange transactions:** In multiyear transactions, such as a grant, time restrictions may exist. The provider should report all resources received before the time requirements are met but all other eligibility requirements are met as a deferred outflow of resources, and the recipient should report them as deferred inflow of resources. The provider should report all resources transmitted before the eligibility requirements are met and without a time requirement as assets, and the recipient should report them as liabilities.

- **Sales of future revenues and intra-entity transfers of future revenues:** The sale or interentity transfer of future revenues should report the amount received as deferred inflows of resources.

- **Leases:** The gain or loss on the sale of property that is accompanied by a leaseback provision should be recorded as a deferred inflow of resources or as a deferred outflow of resources.

- **Loan origination fees and costs:** Points received by a lender in relation to loan origination should be reported as a deferred inflow of resources when received.

- **Rate regulators:** The portion of current rates intended to recover costs that are expected to be incurred in the future (e.g., for utility expansion) should be reported as a deferred inflow of resources when there is an understanding that unused amounts will be returned to the users by a reduction in rate or refund.

- **Revenue recognition in governmental funds:** When an asset is recorded in governmental fund financial statements before the revenue should be recognized, the government should report a deferred inflow of resources until such time as the revenue can be recognized.

GASB Statement No. 68, *Accounting and Financial Reporting for Pensions*, requires that the effects on the total pension liability of (a) changes in assumptions and (b) differences in assumptions and actual experience are to be recognized initially as deferred outflows of resources or deferred inflows of resources and then systematically allocated to expense over the average remaining years of employment of employees. Similarly, the differences between the expected earnings on plan investments and actual experience are to be recognized as deferred outflows of resources or deferred inflows of resources and allocated to expense over a five-year period.

VI. **Concepts Statement No. 6, *Measurement of Elements of Financial Statements***

  A. **Two Approaches to Measuring Assets and Liabilities**

    1. **Initial amount**—Determined at the time the assets is acquired or a liability is incurred.

    2. **Remeasured amounts**—Determined as of the date of the financial statements.

  B. **Four measurement attributes**

    1. **Historical cost**—Price paid to acquire an asset or the amount received as a result of incurring a liability in an actual exchange transaction. This is an **entry value**.

    2. **Fair value**—Price paid that would be received to sell an asset or paid to transfer a liability in an orderly transaction between market participants at the measurement date. This is an **exit value**.

    3. **Replacement cost**—Price that would be paid to acquire an asset with equivalent service potential in an orderly market transaction at the measurement date. This is an **entry value**. A measurement of an asset at the initial transaction date using the replacement cost measurement attribute is referred to as **acquisition value**; such as assets acquired as part of a group of items and donated assets.

    4. **Settlement amount**—The amount at which an asset could be realized or a liability could be liquidated with the counterparty, other than in an active market. A measurement of a liability at the initial transaction date using the settlement amount measurement attribute is referred to as **acquisition value**.

Fund Accounting

This lesson describes fund accounting.

After studying this lesson, you should be able to:

1. List the 11 types of funds used by governmental entities.

2. Describe the measurement focus basis of accounting for each type of fund.

3. Describe the primary purpose of each type of fund.

I. **Governmental Accounting Concepts**

   A. **Governmental entities use several unique accounting methods to provide organizational control**

      1. **Funds**—Segregate resources according to restrictions on use. In the absence of a profit motive, **budgetary accounts** provide control over expenditures. Modification of revenue and expenditure recognition rules changes the flow of transactions through the accounting records to reflect better the nature of the nonexchange transactions that provide most of the resources for governmental expenditures.

   B. **Fund Accounting**—Many resources received by government entities are restricted to use for specified purposes. Further, they are often required by law to be "separately accounted for." Governmental entities **use funds to segregate resources** by type of restriction.

> **Definition**
> *Fund:* A separate **fiscal** and **accounting** entity with a self-balancing set of accounts (i.e., assets, liabilities, and residual balances).

   1. The accounting equation for a fund is:

> Assets + Deferred Outflows of Resources = Liabilities + Deferred Inflows of Resources + Fund Balance (for governmental fund types or net position for proprietary fund types and government-wide financial statements)

   2. **Purpose of a fund**—Funds exist:

      a. To improve management accountability and control; *and*

      b. To meet legal requirements.

   3. **Types of funds**—Governmental entities engage in nonexchange, exchange, and fiduciary transactions. These transactions are segregated into three fund categories:

      a. **Governmental funds**—Nonexchange revenues such as taxes, intergovernmental revenues, and grants provide resources for the majority of general government expenditures (i.e., expenditures for public health and safety, government infrastructure assets such as roads and bridges, government administration, etc.) These transactions are recorded in a group of funds collectively referred to as governmental funds.

      b. **Proprietary funds**—Governmental entities sometimes engage in activities in which they operate much like for-profit organizations. Public utilities, convention centers, motor pools, and airports are common examples of these activities. These activities result in exchange transactions, that is, charges to users for the goods and services that they receive. Most exchange transactions are recorded in a group of funds called proprietary funds.

    c. Fiduciary funds—Governmental entities frequently manage and/or process resources on behalf of other entities or individuals. Since these resources do not truly belong to the governmental entity, they are recorded separately in a group of funds called fiduciary funds.

C. Budgetary Accounting

1. Because governmental entities do not try to earn a profit, they cannot rely on the profit motive—that is, the need to have a positive net income—to control their spending. Instead, **several types of budgetary accounts are incorporated into the accounting records** to control revenues and expenditures and they are **subject to legal spending limits**. In budgetary accounting:

    a. Formal DR/CR accounting entries—Are made at the beginning of the period to record estimated revenues and authorized expenditures (appropriations).

    b. These entries serve as a basis of comparison for actual revenues and expenditures.

    c. Unless there are changes in the budget, the budgetary accounts remain unaltered during the fiscal year.

    d. Since appropriations are usually valid for only one fiscal period, budgetary accounts are closed at the end of the period.

2. **Purpose of budgetary accounting**—Budgetary accounting permits organizations to **demonstrate compliance with legislatively prescribed spending limits and purposes**.

D. Encumbrance Accounting—To ensure that the entity does not order more goods than it has the authority to purchase, an estimate of expenditures is recorded at the time an order is placed rather than waiting until the goods are received. This is known as encumbrance accounting.

E. Financial Reporting—Governmental entities produce two distinct sets of financial statements: the **fund statements** and the **government-wide** (or entity-wide) **statements**.

1. **Fund statements**—The Fund statements include three separate sets of financial statements—one for each of the three fund categories (Governmental, Proprietary, and Fiduciary). Each of these sets of statements is prepared using the "native" basis of accounting for the fund:

    a. Governmental funds—Modified accrual basis

    b. Proprietary funds—Full accrual basis

    c. Fiduciary funds—Full accrual basis

2. **Government-wide statements**—The government-wide (or entity-wide) statements are presented for the *organization as a whole* and, therefore, include information from both the governmental and proprietary funds. (Note that fiduciary funds are not included as these resources are managed only on behalf of others and do not actually belong to the governmental entity.) In order to combine information from these two fund categories, they must both use the same basis of accounting. For these statements, the governmental fund transactions are converted from modified accrual basis to full accrual basis so that the **government-wide statements can be presented on a full accrual basis.**

F. Objective of Governmental Accounting

1. The objective of a governmental entity is the provision of services to its constituents. The objectives of governmental accounting are to:

    a. Assess the availability of current-period resources to finance current-period expenditures (interperiod equity);

    b. Assess the service efforts and accomplishments of the governmental entity; *and*

    c. Demonstrate compliance with the legal authorization to expend.

2. Interperiod equity measures the extent to which current resources are sufficient to finance current expenditures (i.e., we have a balanced budget). Interperiod equity is fundamental to public administration and is a component of accountability.

II. Fund Structure

A. Fund Categories

> **Tip**
>
> Remember the acronym **DRIP-CEG-PIPPA**—**DRIP**: **D**ebt service funds, special **R**evenue funds, **I**nternal service funds, **P**ermanent funds; (**CEG**): **C**apital projects funds, **E**nterprise funds, **G**eneral fund; **PIPPA**: **P**ension trust funds, **I**nvestment trust funds, **P**rivate **P**urpose trust funds, **A**gency funds—a mnemonic for remembering the 11 types of funds. Governmental funds are the consonants; D, R, P, C, and G, in DRIP-CEG.

1. Governmental entities are organized into **three fund categories**. The fund category determines the basis of accounting that is used for funds within that category, whether budgetary transactions are recorded in the funds, and whether the funds can report capital assets and/or long-term debt and the financial statements that will be prepared for the funds. A fund category may use either modified accrual basis accounting or full accrual basis accounting depending on the fund's activities.

   a. Governmental fund category (modified accrual basis)

   b. Proprietary fund category (full accrual basis)

   c. Fiduciary fund category (full accrual basis)

2. **Fund types**—Within the **three fund categories** are 11 **fund types**.

   a. **Governmental funds (consonants in DRIP CEG)**

      i. **G**eneral fund

      ii. Special **R**evenue funds

      iii. **D**ebt service funds

      iv. **C**apital project funds

      v. **P**ermanent funds

   b. **Proprietary funds (vowels in DRIP CEG)**

      i. **E**nterprise funds

      ii. **I**nternal service funds

   c. **Fiduciary funds (PIPPA)**

      i. **P**ension trust funds

      ii. **I**nvestment trust funds

      iii. **P**rivate **P**urpose trust funds

      iv. **A**gency trust funds

3. There is only one general fund. All other fund types may be comprised of many individual funds.

4. **Number of funds principle**—The number of funds principle states that an organization should **use the minimum number of funds possible, consistent with**:

   a. **Laws and contracts**, *and*

   b. **Sound financial management**.

B. Governmental Fund Category

1. The five fund types in this category finance most *general government* activities (law enforcement, public safety, schools, capital projects, etc.) All governmental funds are current funds (i.e., they have only current asset and current liability accounts—no long-term items).

   a. They are **expendable funds**—they are not concerned with preserving capital. All resources that are recognized in these funds should be expended, not retained.

b. All governmental funds use **modified accrual basis accounting**.

c. All governmental funds can use **budgetary accounting** and **encumbrance accounting** (However, at least on the CPA Exam, not all governmental funds use both.)

d. **Capital assets** and **long-term debt** related to these funds are **recorded separately in off-books records**. They are not reported in the fund statements, although they **are** included in the government-wide statements.

Accounting Equation
Current Assets + Deferred Outflows of Resources − *Current* Liabilities − Deferred Inflows of Resources = *Fund Balance*

---

2. Governmental fund types (consonants in DRIP CEG)

a. General fund—The general fund accounts for ordinary operations of the government.

   i. Revenues typically come from taxes, licenses, fines, fees, etc.

   ii. Most **unrestricted resources** are accounted for in this fund.

   iii. Expenditures can be made for **any general government services** not specifically accounted for in another fund.

   iv. This is the **only required fund** of a governmental unit.

   v. There is **only one general fund**.

3. Special revenue funds—Account for the proceeds of specific revenues from taxes, grants, entitlements, or other earmarked sources that are restricted or committed to expenditures for specified purposes other than debt service or major capital projects (e.g., a gasoline tax that must be spent on road maintenance, private foundation grants that must be used to provide training opportunities for disadvantaged workers).

> **Exam Tip**
> *Special revenue funds never account for capital asset acquisition, capital asset construction, or debt service transactions on the CPA Exam. CPA Exam questions always assume that these transactions are recorded in the capital projects or debt service funds, respectively.*

4. Capital projects funds—Account for **monies designated for acquisition or construction of significant capital items** (land, buildings, and equipment). Capital project funds are **short-lived**, existing only long enough to accumulate resources to acquire or construct an asset and to account for the expenditures related to the asset. After acquisition or construction, the fund is closed. Any **monies remaining** in the fund are usually **transferred to a debt service fund** or, if no debt was issued to finance the project, to the general fund.

5. Debt service funds—Account for **monies set aside to pay interest and principal** on the governmental unit's **long-term general obligation debt**. Note that the debt service fund **does not account for the liability** itself, only for the monies that are set aside to pay the principal and interest. Its function resembles that of a bond sinking fund in financial accounting.

6. Permanent funds—Account for resources received by the governmental entity with the stipulation that the principal amount remain "intact" but that earnings must be spent, for purposes that benefit the governmental entity (i.e., purchase of library books, park improvements, and cemetery maintenance). These types of funds are more generally known as **endowments**.

a. Although the permanent fund receives the endowment earnings, any **expendable earnings are transferred to an appropriate governmental fund** (usually a special revenue fund) to make the actual expenditure.

C. Proprietary Fund Category

1. The two fund types in this category account for governmental unit activities that charge fees in exchange for goods or services. The activities accounted for in these funds are similar to those of for-profit businesses.

   a. Activities that are *self-supporting*—that is, in which **50% or more of costs are covered by fees**—*must* **be accounted for as proprietary funds**. Additionally, activities where there is *intent* to cover 50% or more of costs through fees *or* activities that would **benefit from the additional control measures provided by full accrual basis accounting** *may* be accounted for as proprietary funds. These activities:

      i. Record and report their own capital assets and long-term debt

      ii. Use full accrual basis accounting

Accounting Equation
(Current Assets + Capital Assets + Deferred Outflows of Resources) –
(Current Liabilities + Long-Term Liabilities + Deferred Inflows of Resources) = Net Position

---

2. **Proprietary fund types (vowels in DRIP CEG)**

   a. **Enterprise funds**—Account for activities that provide goods and services to the **general public** as well as to the governmental entity itself (i.e., utilities, transit services, golf courses, etc.). A **service fee commensurate with the benefits received** is generally charged.

   b. **Internal service funds**—Account for activities that provide goods and services **only to other government agencies and departments** (i.e. motor pools, printing services, data processing services, central supplies, etc.). Fees for these services are generally paid through inter-departmental charges.

D. Fiduciary Fund Category (PIPPA)—These funds account for monies and other resources held by the governmental unit in a trustee or agent capacity. In general, fiduciary funds use full accrual accounting to record transactions.

1. **Pension trust funds**—Pension trust funds account for **contributions made by or on behalf of government employees to provide them with retirement income and postretirement benefits** and for the **actual expenditures made to retirees** and terminated employees. Related transactions such as pension investment earnings and investment management expenses are recorded here as well.

2. **Agency funds**—Account for monies for which the governmental unit serves as merely an agent in the process of distributing/delivering the monies to their rightful recipient; that is, when the governmental unit acts as a clearing house, collecting monies for other units and then remitting them as appropriate, usually for a small fee. These funds have only current assets and current liabilities—they do not recognize revenues or expenses.

3. **Private purpose trust funds**—Account for trust arrangements for which **other entities** (i.e., external organizations or individuals and other governmental entities) **are the beneficiaries rather than the governmental unit itself**. Private purpose trust funds differ from agency funds in that they **often hold assets for long periods of time** (These funds are often in the form of endowments.), whereas agency funds hold monies only briefly before they are distributed to the proper recipient.

4. **Investment trust funds**—Account for **monies received from other governmental agencies to be included in the governmental entity's investment pool** (Note: larger, general-purpose governments frequently provide this service to smaller agencies that lie within their jurisdiction). Earnings on the monies invested are also recorded in the investment trust fund. Note that **resources belonging to the governmental entity itself** that are included in the Investment Pool are not reported in the investment trust fund: **only resources from external entities are reported here**. Resources belonging to the governmental entity itself are reported in the funds that made the Investment Pool contributions.

E. Treatment of Fixed Assets and Long-Term Liabilities—Prior to GASB Statement No. 34, account groups were used to track long-term items (fixed assets and long-term debt) associated with governmental funds. These amounts were also included in the financial statements on the Combined Balance Sheet. The account groups are not part of the GASB Statement No. 34 model and are not included in the fund statements. They are, however, reported in government-wide statements.

1. In practice, many organizations may still use the two account groups to track long-term items associated with the Government funds. These systems are well established and the information they provide is still needed, so there is little reason to abandon them.

2. With this in mind, the following information is of interest:

   a. **General Fixed Asset Account Group (GFAAG)**—Used to record fixed (long-term) assets purchased by any of the governmental funds (principally the general fund, special revenue fund, and the capital projects fund), as well as items donated to the governmental unit. Assets were recorded at historical cost or at FMV at the date of donation.

   b. **General Long-Term Debt Account Group (GLTDAG)**—Used to record general obligation long-term debt of the governmental unit, including bonds, notes, and capital leases. As the debt matures (becomes current) the liability is removed from the GLTDAG and placed in a debt service fund for repayment.

> **Study Tip**
> Even though the Account Groups are not part of the GASB Statement No. 34 reporting model, it is possible that the terms may still appear as possible answers to questions and even that the examiners might ask how transactions that used to be reported in the Account Groups are now reported. Because of this, it is probably a good idea to become familiar with how these account groups were used.

> **Note**
> Risk Financing Activities—GASB Statement No. 10 required that if a single fund is used to accounting for an entity's risk financing activities, that fund should be either the general fund or an internal service fund. GASB Statement No. 66 modifies GASB Statement No. 10 when monies are set aside for risk management by statute. GASB Statement No. 66 states that dedicated revenue restricted by statute for risk financing (e.g., tax levy for tort liabilities) should be accounted for in a special revenue fund.

Measurement Focus Basis of Accounting

After studying this lesson, you should be able to:

1. Describe how the 60-day rule is used.

2. Identify revenues that are subject-to-accrual under the modified accrual basis of accounting.

3. Describe the two criteria that determine revenue recognition under the modified accrual basis of accounting.

4. Describe how capital expenditures are classified under the modified accrual basis of accounting.

I. **Basis of Accounting**—The basis of accounting defines the way in which inflows and outflows of resources are measured and recognized. In governmental accounting, the basis of accounting that is used varies depending on (1) the fund that is used to record the transaction and (2) the report that displays the transaction results. Two bases of accounting are used: **modified accrual basis and full accrual basis.**

   A. **Governmental Fund Transactions**—The governmental funds depend on nonexchange revenues to provide the bulk of their resources. Full accrual accounting, which relies on the matching principal to determine the timing of revenue and expense recognition, is not appropriate for these types of transactions. Governmental entities modify the full accrual basis revenue and expenditure recognition rules so that their governmental funds better match the characteristics of these transactions. The resulting basis is known as the modified accrual basis, which is used to record transactions in governmental funds.

      1. A major concern for governmental entities is that they have received sufficient *financial resources* to cover their *financial expenses* (*financial resources* can be roughly translated to mean cash and near-cash equivalents). Therefore, the measurement focus for changes in resources during the period (i.e. revenues and expenditures) under modified accrual basis accounting is on *the flow of financial resources*: that is, on *cash* inflows and outflows.

      2. Governmental entities also need to know where they stand financially. That is, they need to know the total amount of assets available and liabilities payable at any given point in time. Thus, at the end of the period (e.g., for the balance sheet), the focus of modified accrual basis accounting is on the *financial position* of the organization.

   B. **Proprietary Fund Transactions**—Proprietary funds, like for-profit businesses, incur expenses in order to generate revenues sufficient to cover the expenses and maintain the capital invested in the organization. Moreover, like for-profit businesses, most transactions of proprietary funds are exchange transactions. **Full accrual accounting** is, therefore, an appropriate basis of accounting for proprietary funds.

      1. A major concern of proprietary entities is that, over the long run, they earn a sufficient return to cover the full cost of providing goods and/or services (i.e., direct expense items such as salaries and cost of goods, as well as the cost of the capital assets used by the entity). The measurement focus of full-accrual basis accounting for changes during the period (revenues and expenses) is, therefore, on *the flow of economic resources, income determination,* or *capital maintenance. Economic resources* are broader in scope than *financial resources* as they encompass financial resources that are not immediately available (e.g., long-term investments, property, plant and equipment).

      2. Proprietary entities also need to know where they stand financially. That is, they need to know the total amount of assets available and liabilities payable at any given point in time. Thus, at the end of the period (e.g., for the balance sheet), the focus of **full accrual basis accounting** is on the *financial position* of the organization.

Exam Tip

Questions asking you to relate the basis of accounting to its "measurement focus" appear on almost every CPA Exam. You should memorize the following relationships:

	Measurement Focus	
Basis of Accounting	**During the Period**	**At the End of the Period**
Modified accrual	*flow of* **financial** *resources*	*net current financial position*
Full accrual	*flow of* **economic** *resources*	*financial position*

II. Modified Accrual Basis Accounting

A. **A primary objective of for-profit organizations** is to generate a positive **net income**, which ensures that the capital invested in the organization is maintained and that there is a return to the investors. Full accrual basis accounting is designed to measure a for-profit organization's success in achieving this objective. It focuses on the matching of revenues with related expenses to determine net income.

1. Since governments neither have investors who provide capital to fund the organization nor do they raise revenues through the expending of resources (i.e., exchange transactions), the matching of revenues and expenses is not relevant or even possible, for governmental entities. Instead, the emphasis in **governmental entities** is on the **provision of services** and the **availability of resources** to provide those services.

2. Because of the differences in the objectives, full accrual basis accounting is not appropriate for governmental entities. A modification of the full accrual basis revenue and expenditure recognition rules is necessary to create a basis of accounting that is more closely aligned with their objectives. This basis of accounting is called ***modified accrual basis***.

B. **Characteristics of Modified Accrual Basis Accounting**

1. **Measurement focus**—The measurement focus of modified accrual basis accounting is on the *flow of financial resources,* that is, the inflows and outflows of *expendable resources* (i.e., cash and near cash assets such as marketable securities, receivables, etc.), not on the *flow of economic resources, income determination*, and *capital maintenance* as would be the case in the full accrual basis.

> **Study Tip**
> *Full accrual basis revenues are recognized when measurable and earned. The examiners frequently try to confuse candidates by including* earned *as a factor in modified accrual basis revenue recognition.* **Earned** *revenue always denotes full accrual basis accounting.*

2. **Revenue recognition**—Revenues are recognized in the period in which they become ***measurable and available*** (not when they are *earned*).

a. The terms *measurable* and *available* have very specific meanings:

   i. **Measurable**—The amount is known or can be reasonably estimated.

   ii. **Available**—The amount is both:

      1. Legally due

      2. Received in cash either:

         1. By the end of the fiscal period *or*

         2. *In time to pay for obligations of the current fiscal period* (known as the 60-day rule).

b. **60-day rule**—A governmental entity may recognize monies received during the first 60 days of a new fiscal period as revenue of the old fiscal period.

   i. **Rationale**—Because many expenditures for the old fiscal period are not known and/ or not due until the new fiscal period (e.g., utility bills), monies received within the first 60 days of the new fiscal period are usually considered received *in time to pay for obligations of the current fiscal period.*

Example
In Fiscal Year X, Bishop County levied property taxes totaling $5,000,000. The County received payments of $4,000,000 by the end of Fiscal Year X, received $300,000 during the first 60 days of the Fiscal Year Y, received an additional $500,000 by the end of Fiscal Year Y, and received the remaining $200,000 during the first 60 days of Fiscal Year Z.

Bishop County recognizes $4,300,000 (4,000,000 + 300,000) of property tax revenue in Fiscal Year X and $700,000 (500,000 + 200,000) of property tax revenue in Fiscal Year Y.

Note
This means that most governmental revenues are recognized when received in cash, as long as they are legally due. Income taxes, sales taxes, licenses, fines, etc. are usually recognized in this manner.

Study Tip
Although governmental entities frequently recognize revenue only when cash is received, this is **not** cash basis accounting. **Cash basis accounting is *never* GAAP** for governmental entities.

---

c. **Revenues subject to accrual**—Revenues that are measurable and legally due prior to the receipt of cash are **normally recognized on the accrual basis**. These revenues typically result from charges that are billed to the customer/constituent by the governmental entity. Revenues that are subject to accrual include:

   i.   **Property taxes**

   ii. **Interest and penalties on delinquent taxes**

   iii. **Investment revenue**

   iv. **Regularly billed charges for services**

   v.   **Taxes collected by other government units but not yet remitted**

Note
Even though revenue is recognized "up front" for these items (e.g., when the receivable is recognized), an adjusting entry is made at the end of the period to defer revenue recognition for any amounts that have not been received in cash within 60 days after the end of the fiscal period.

---

d. Therefore, even though we credit revenue when the bill is sent out, the amount of revenue actually reported on the financial statements is consistent with the modified accrual basis revenue recognition rules.

Example
Fayette County Sheriff's Department billed residents $1,200,000 for special security services provided during the year. Of these receivables, $800,000 was paid within the fiscal period and an additional $200,000 was paid during the first 60 days of the next period.

How much revenue should Fayette County recognize when the bills for these services are sent out?

When the bills are sent out, Fayette County recognizes revenue in the full amount of the billing:

DR: Receivables	$1,200,000	
CR: Revenue		$1,200,000

How much revenue is reported for these services on the financial statements?

The revenue reported on the financial statements equals the amount received in cash during the fiscal period or within the first 60 days of the next fiscal period: $1,000,000 ($800,0000 + $200,000)

How should any amounts not recognized as revenue be reported?

The remaining amount should be reported as Deferred Inflows of Resources. The following adjusting entry is made to recognize the deferral:

DR: Revenue	$200,000	
CR: Deferred Inflows of Resources		$200,000

3. **Expenditure recognition**—Expenditures, in general, are recognized on the **accrual basis**, that is, when the liability is measurable and has been incurred, **except for the following four items:**

   a. **Interest on general long-term debt** is not recorded until it is actually due. *Due* in this instance means **on the due date.**

      i. **General long-term debt**—Refers to long-term debt incurred by governmental funds, which are the funds that provide general government services.

      ii. **Specific long-term debt**—Refers to long-term debt incurred by the proprietary funds. Specific debt is reported in the proprietary funds. Interest on specific long-term debt *is accrued.*

Note
Only interest on general long-term debt is treated in this manner. Interest on short-term debt (e.g., accounts payable) and interest on specific long-term debt **are** accrued. The examiners will frequently try to trick you into treating these items as if they were general long-term debt.

Example
The City of Middleton uses a calendar fiscal year. On January 8, $3,000,000 of interest on its general obligation bonds will be due and payable to the bondholders. How much accrued interest on these bonds should be reported on its financial statements dated December 31?

No interest ($0.00) on this debt should be reported on the December 31 financial statements as interest on general, long-term debt is not reported until it is due.

   b. **No distinction is made between capital expenditures** (land, buildings, and equipment) **and period expenditures** (wages, rent, utilities, etc.). **All are simply reported as expenditures**.

Example
The City of Bighorn uses general fund resources to purchase a new copier costing $3,000 for the mayor's office as well as $400 of paper, toner, and other supplies to support the copier. Bighorn's Duplicating Service, an internal service fund, purchases a copier costing $10,000 and $600 of supplies, all of which were consumed during the period.

The general fund uses modified accrual basis accounting and the Internal Service Fund uses full accrual basis accounting. Bighorn reports general fund expenditures of $3,400.

The Internal Service Fund reports $600 of expenses and reports an additional asset of $10,000.

c. **Inventoriable materials and supplies**—These may be recognized as **expenditures either when purchased** (purchases method) *or* **when used** (consumption method).

>
> **Example**
> Marriot County purchases $80,000 of inventoriable supplies during the year. Marriot had $40,000 of supplies on hand at the beginning of the year and $30,000 of supplies on hand at the end of the year. If Marriot uses the purchases method, it reports supplies expenditures of $80,000. If Marriot uses the consumption method, it reports supplies expenditures of $90,000 (40,000 + 80,000 – 30,000).

d. **Prepaid items**—These may be recognized as **expenditures either when purchased** (purchases method) *or* **when used** (consumption method). Unlike inventoriable materials, however, prepaid items are almost always expenditures in full when paid (purchases method).

>
> **Example**
> At the beginning of the year, the City of Whittenville leased space in a strip mall to use for a neighborhood outreach center. Whittenville used general fund resources to pay $36,000 in advance for the three-year lease. If Whittenville uses the purchases method, it reports lease expenditures of $36,000. If Whittenville uses the consumption method, it reports lease expenditures of $12,000 (36,000/3), the value of the lease benefits that expired during the year.

4. **Increases and decreases in fund balance other than revenues and expenditures**—Funds using the modified accrual basis of accounting have a number of transactions that create increases or decreases in fund balance that cannot be classified as revenues or expenditures.

a. **Other financing sources (OFS)**—Increases in the fund balance of a fund that do not result in an increase in the net position of the organization as a whole.

> **Example**
> Receipt of the **proceeds of long-term debt** and **transfers of assets from another fund** are the most common examples of OFS. Other financing sources are either reported with Revenues or netted against other financing uses. In either event, they are **part of the net change in fund balance during the period.**

b. **Other financing uses (OFU)**—Decreases in the fund balance of a fund that do not result in a decrease in the net position of the organization as a whole.

> **Example**
> The transfer of assets to another fund is the most common example of an OFU. Other financing uses are either reported with expenditures or netted against other financing sources. In either event, they are **part of the net change in fund balance during the period.**

> **Note**
> The ability to distinguish OFS and OFU from revenues and expenditures is a consistent area of emphasis on the CPA Exam.

Budgetary Accounting

This lesson describes typical accounting entries related to the government's budget.

After studying this lesson, you should be able to:

1. List the accounts used to record the budget.

2. Prepare journal entries to record the budget.

I. **Budgetary Accounting Requirements**

   A. Budgetary accounting requires the creation of special budgetary accounts, recording of budgetary entries, and preparation of reports that compare budget amounts to actual amounts.

   B. In general, only funds that use modified accrual basis of accounting use budgetary accounting. Even then, not all modified accrual basis funds use budgetary accounts. The general fund and special revenue funds are usually budgeted, debt service funds are sometimes are budgeted, but capital projects funds are not usually budgeted.

II. **Budgetary Accounts**—Budgetary accounts are used to record budget entries. The budgetary accounts parallel the *actual* nominal accounts found in governmental funds. The actual accounts and their normal balances are shown below:

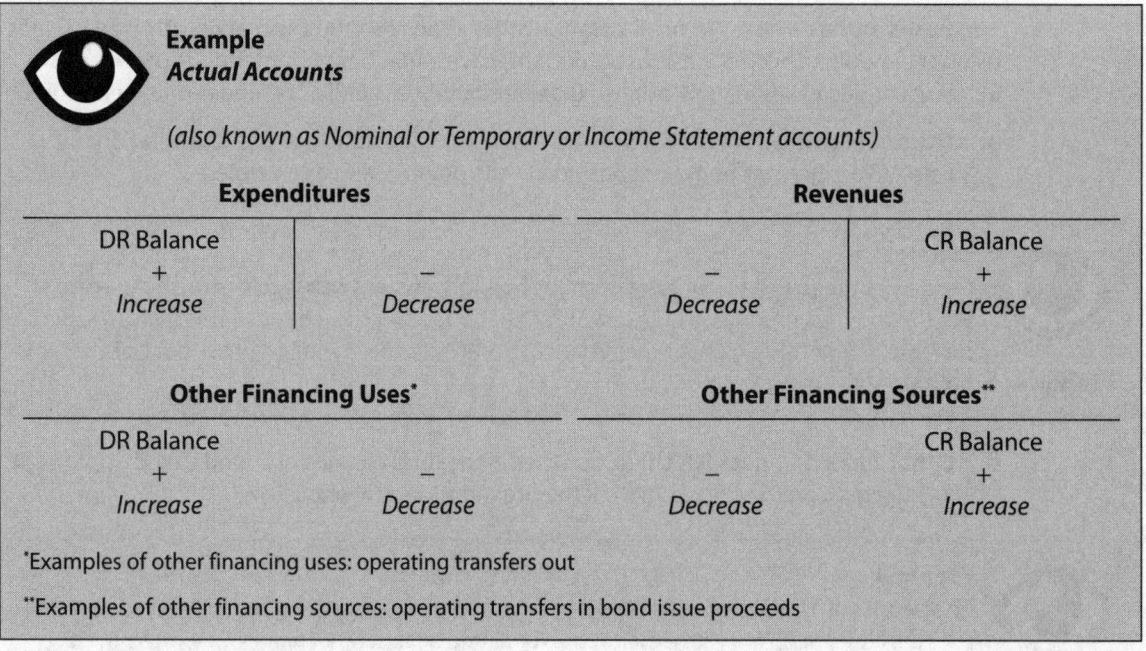

Example
Actual Accounts

(also known as Nominal or Temporary or Income Statement accounts)

Expenditures			Revenues
DR Balance			CR Balance
+	–	–	+
Increase	*Decrease*	*Decrease*	*Increase*

Other Financing Uses*			Other Financing Sources**
DR Balance			CR Balance
+	–	–	+
Increase	*Decrease*	*Decrease*	*Increase*

*Examples of other financing uses: operating transfers out

**Examples of other financing sources: operating transfers in bond issue proceeds

A. **A parallel budgetary account** is established for each of the actual revenue, expenditure, other financing source, and other financing-use accounts. The budgetary accounts and their normal balances are shown below.

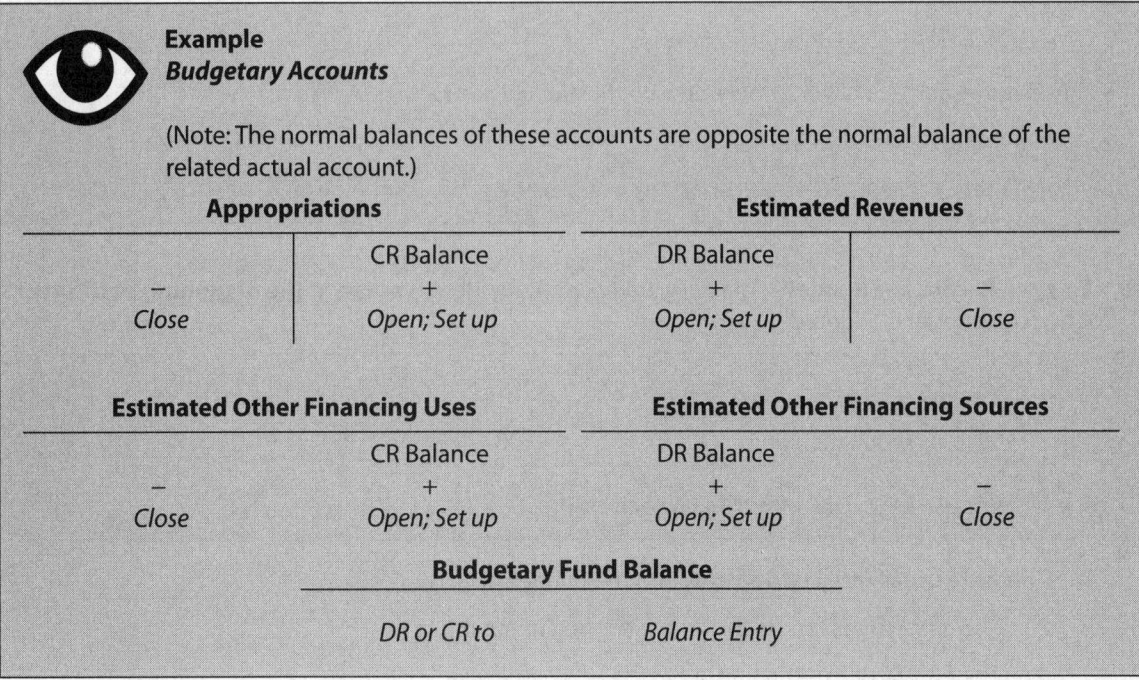

Example
Budgetary Accounts

(Note: The normal balances of these accounts are opposite the normal balance of the related actual account.)

Appropriations			Estimated Revenues		
	CR Balance		DR Balance		
−	+		+		−
Close	*Open; Set up*		*Open; Set up*		*Close*

Estimated Other Financing Uses			Estimated Other Financing Sources		
	CR Balance		DR Balance		
−	+		+		−
Close	*Open; Set up*		*Open; Set up*		*Close*

Budgetary Fund Balance

DR or CR to   *Balance Entry*

B. First, and most important, note that budgetary accounts have **normal balances** *opposite* those of their actual account counterparts. This is the most commonly tested characteristic of the budgetary accounts. You must know whether a DR or a CR is used to "set up" (increase) the budget at the beginning of the year or "close" (decrease) the budget at the end of the year for each of the four budgetary accounts.

1. **Estimated revenues**—Normal balance is a **DR**; the budget office established estimates for this account.

2. **Appropriations**—Normal balance is a **CR**; the legislative body sets these **legally authorized spending limits**.

> **Note**
> There is not an account titled estimated expenditures. The correct title is appropriations.

3. **Estimated other financing sources**—Normal balance is a **DR**; this account estimates the inflow of funds that are not properly categorized as revenues (operating transfers from other funds, proceeds of bond issues, etc.)

4. **Estimated other financing uses**—Normal balance is a **CR**; this account estimates the outflow of funds that are not properly categorized as expenditures (operating transfers to other funds, etc.).

5. **Budgetary fund balance**—This is an **offset account** used to balance the budgetary entry; as such, it **does not have a normal balance** but is **debited or credited as necessary** to make debits equal credits within the budgetary entry.

> **Note**
> **The budgetary fund balance** is the technically correct title for this account and is consistently used on the CPA Exam. Some textbooks, however, use **fund balance** as the offset account but this is not what you will see on the CPA Exam. Moreover, for financial reporting GASB Statement No. 54 prohibits reporting reserved and unreserved categories within fund balance and provides five new categories within fund balance to be reported in fund-level financial statements. The five categories are as follows: Nonspendable, Restricted, Committed, Assigned, and Unassigned. Please refer to the "Net Position and Fund Balance" lesson for a more detailed explanation of this change.

Study Tip

Budgetary accounting is always tested on the CPA Exam. The questions are usually quite simple as long as the candidate remembers:

- The names of the budgetary accounts

- Budgetary account balances are opposite their actual account counterparts.

- When budgetary entries are made

- All of these concepts are tested on nearly every exam.

III. Entry to Record the Budget—The entry to record the budget is **made at the beginning of the year** when the budget is adopted:

Estimated Revenues	XXX	
Appropriations		XXX

DR or CR Budgetary Fund Balance to balance the entry.

    A. There are usually only **two entries** into the budgetary accounts:

        1. The entry to **set up the budget** at the beginning of the year

        2. The entry to **close the budget** at the end of the year

    B. Midyear entries occur only when the legislative body convenes and authorizes additional appropriations or when actual revenues are significantly different from predictions. Note that the offset account used to balance the entry is Budgetary Fund Balance.

 **Example**

In midyear, the Lawrence City Council authorized $150,000 in additional expenditures to repair damages from spring flooding. The entry to record the additional appropriation is:

Budgetary Fund Balance	XXX	
Appropriations		XXX

IV. Entry to Close the Budget—If there have been no changes to the budget during the year, the entry to close the budgetary accounts at the end of the fiscal period simply reverses the original entry.

Appropriations	XXX	
Estimated Revenues		XXX

DR or CR Budgetary Fund Balance to balance the entry.

    A. If there have been changes to the original budget, remember that the purpose of the entry is to close (zero out) the balances in the budgetary accounts, whatever those balances may be. Always DR or CR the Budgetary Fund Balance account to balance the entry.

Encumbrance Accounting

After studying this lesson, you should be able to:

1. Describe the difference between an encumbrance and an expenditure.

2. Calculate the available balance of an appropriation.

3. Describe how outstanding encumbrances at fiscal year-end are classified in the financial statements.

4. Prepare journal entries related to encumbrances.

I. Encumbrances Represent the Estimated Dollar Value of Purchase Orders Outstanding

    A. Using Encumbrances to Control Expenditures—Appropriations represent legal spending limits prescribed by the entity's governing body. Appropriations are usually established for departmental units and/or for various types of expenditures (salaries, equipment, supplies, etc.). The *unexpended, unencumbered appropriation* is the remaining authorization to spend after taking into account goods still on order (encumbrances) and goods received to date (expenditures). Synonymous terms include: uncommitted appropriations, available balance, unencumbered balance, and free balance. It is calculated as:

>   + Appropriations
>   − Encumbrances
>   <u>− Expenditures</u>
>   = Unencumbered, Unexpended Appropriation

Example

Niles County has an appropriation of $10,000 for computer supplies. So far this year, Niles has received and paid for $4,500 of computer supplies. An additional $2,000 of computer supplies have just been ordered. What is Niles' unencumbered, unexpended balance?

	P/O Let
+ Appropriation	+10,000
− Encumbrances	−2,000
− Expenditures	<u>−4,500</u>
= Unencumbered, Unexpended Appropriation	**3,500**

The unexpended, unencumbered balance is immediately reduced by the $2,000 order to $3,500. When the goods arrive, the encumbrance entry is liquidated (reversed) and the actual cost is recognized as an expenditure, as shown below.

>   + Appropriations
>   − Encumbrances
>   <u>− Expenditures</u>
>   = Unencumbered, Unexpended Appropriation

Example
Niles County has an appropriation of $10,000 for computer supplies. So far this year, Niles has received and paid for $4,500 of computer supplies. An additional $2,000 of computer supplies have just been ordered. What is Niles' unencumbered, unexpended balance?

	P/O Let	Goods Received
+ Appropriation	+10,000	10,000
− Encumbrances	−2,000	0
− Expenditures	−4,500	6,500
= Unencumbered, Unexpended Appropriation	**3,500**	**3,500**

1. Note that when the goods are actually received, there is no change in the unencumbered, unexpended appropriation amount: The effect of the transaction has been moved forward to the point of order rather than waiting until the goods arrive.

B. **Encumbrance Accounts**—Two additional budgetary accounts are created to record encumbrances:

Encumbrances		Budgetary Fund Balance Assigned (or Committed) for Encumbrances	
DR Balance		−	CR Balance
+	−	−	+
PO Issued	Goods Rec'd	Goods Rec'd	PO Issued

C. **Encumbrances**, like expenditures, is **a debit balance account**. It is increased (debited) when a purchase order is issued. The **fund balance assigned (or committed) for encumbrances** is simply an **offset account** for encumbrances. The balances in the encumbrances and the budgetary fund balance accounts **are always equal, but are opposite each other**. Whether *assigned* or *committed* is used depends on the level of authority required to make the expenditure (i.e., to encumber the amount). If the expenditure is authorized by a formal act of the government's highest decision-maker (i.e., the city council) then *committed* should be used. On the other hand, if the expenditure is authorized by a group (i.e., finance committee) or an official (i.e., business manager) then *assigned* should be used.

II. **Encumbrance Entries** (Note: In this example we assume the expenditures are authorized by a group or an official of the government and, therefore, *Fund Balance—Assigned* is the appropriate category.)

A. **When a Purchase Order is Prepared (or *Let*)**—The estimated amount of the purchase is recorded as an encumbrance. The entry to record the processing of a purchase order is:

Encumbrances	XXX	
Budgetary Fund Balance—Assigned		XXX

B. When Goods/Services are Received—A two-part entry is required.

    1. The **encumbrance amount is reversed** (liquidated)

    2. The **actual expenditure is recognized:**

Budgetary Fund Balance—Assigned	XXX	
Encumbrances		XXX
Expenditures	XXX	
Vouchers Payable/Cash		XXX

III. Differences Between Estimated and Actual Expenditures—When encumbered goods are received at an actual, invoiced price that differs from the estimated (encumbered) amount, the encumbrance is liquidated at the original, estimated amount and the expenditure is recorded at the actual, invoiced amount. As a result of this entry, a corresponding change in the unencumbered, unexpended appropriation balance occurs.

Example

Previously encumbered goods are received at an invoiced cost of $5,500. The estimated cost of the goods was $6,000. The entry to record the receipt of goods is as follows:

Budgetary Fund Balance	$6,000	
Encumbrances		$6,000
Expenditures	$5,500	
Vouchers Payable		$5,500

As a result of this transaction, the balance of the unencumbered, unexpended appropriation increases by $500.

A. At Year-End—Encumbered orders not received at fiscal year-end are generally closed out, sometimes as part of the budgetary closing entry. In addition, a portion of the fund balance is set aside to cover the estimated amount of orders outstanding at year-end. Depending on the level of authority by which the encumbrances were established, either Fund Balance—Committed or Fund Balance—Assigned (both are actual Balance Sheet accounts), is used to account for these monies.

Budgetary Fund Balance	XXX	
Encumbrances		XXX
Unassigned Fund Balance	XXX	
Fund Balance—Assigned (or Committed)		XXX

Exam Tip

In the past, the CPA Exam often used these account titles interchangeably: Fund Balance; Unreserved Fund Balance; Unreserved, Undesignated Fund Balance. GASB Statement No. 54 replaced these categories of fund balance with the following five categories: Nonspendable, Restricted, Committed, Assigned, or Unassigned.

Example

After closing all nominal accounts except encumbrances, Morgan City had the following account balances at the end of the year:

Assets	$10,000,000
Liabilities	$7,000,000

There were $2,000,000 of purchase orders outstanding at the end of the year. There were no nonspendable, restricted, committed, or assigned amounts in the fund balance.

Currently, Morgan City's general fund has an unassigned, undesignated fund balance of $3,000,000 ($10,000,000 assets less $7,000,000 liabilities). Since there are no nonspendable, restrictions, commitments, or assigned amounts within the fund balance, this entire amount is available for appropriation (e.g., the legislative body can decide to spend the money).

However, is that money truly available? Consider the outstanding purchase orders. They are not included in liabilities, but they are legal obligations to purchase goods. Should the amount available for appropriation really be $1,000,000 ($3,000,000 less $2,000,000 outstanding purchase orders)?

The closing entry for the encumbrances takes note of this legal obligation:

Budgetary Fund Balance	$2,000,000	
Encumbrances		$2,000,000
Unassigned Fund Balance	$2,000,000	
Fund Balance—Assigned for Encumbrances		$2,000,000

As a result of these entries, the unassigned fund balance is now $1,000,000 ($10,000,000 assets less $7,000,000 liabilities less $2,000,000 outstanding purchase orders/encumbrances). The obligation for the outstanding purchase orders is seen in the Fund Balance—Assigned account balance of $2,000,000.

1. Note that after all closing entries have been made, the balance in the fund balance—assigned (or committed) account includes the amount outstanding encumbrances at year-end. According to GASB Statement No. 54, the fund-level financial statements are not separately displayed in the financial statements, but they should be disclosed in the notes to the financial statements.

IV. **Reversing Entries**—At the beginning of the next fiscal year: The closing entry for encumbrances is usually at least partially reversed. Because of this entry, the prior year encumbrances are then treated like any other encumbrance when the order is received.

Encumbrances—Prior Year	2,000,000	
Budgetary Fund Balance		2,000,000
Fund Balance—Assigned for Encumbrances	2,000,000	
Unassigned Fund Balance		2,000,000

A. Since the fund balance and reservations of fund balance accounts are used only for financial reporting and, therefore, do not affect transaction processing during the year, the reversing entries may not occur. Instead, the balance in the assigned account stays in place throughout the year, and it is simply adjusted to equal the total outstanding encumbrances at the end of the year.

Example

At the beginning of the fiscal year, Bremerton County reported $15,000,000 in its unassigned fund balance and $4,000,000 in its fund balance assigned (for outstanding encumbrances). The outstanding purchase orders were recognized as encumbrances of prior year at the beginning of the year but the fund balance assigned for encumbrances account was not adjusted.

At the end of the fiscal year, all the orders from the prior year had been received but there were $5,000,000 of purchase orders outstanding from the current year. What entry is necessary to close the encumbrance accounts and recognize the outstanding purchase orders on the financial statements?

Budgetary Fund Balance	$5,000,000	
Encumbrances		$5,000,000
Unassigned Fund Balance	$1,000,000*	
Fund Balance—Assigned for encumbrances		$1,000,000*

* Calculation of entry for Fund Balance—Assigned for Encumbrances:

$5,000,000 CR desired ending balance

$4,000,000 CR beginning balance

$1,000,000 CR is required to achieve the ending balance

Deferred Outflows and Deferred Inflows of Resources

After studying this lesson, you should be able to:

1. Describe examples of deferred outflows and deferred inflows of resources.

2. Describe how deferred outflows and deferred inflows of resources are determined.

I. **Overview**—GASB Statement No. 63 provides guidance on deferred outflows and deferred inflows of resources. Unlike revenues and expenses, which are inflows and outflows of resources related to the period in which they occur, deferred outflows and deferred inflows of resources are related to future periods. Recognition of deferred inflows or revenues and expenses is deferred until the future period to which the inflows and outflows are related. Consequently, segregating deferred outflows from expenses and deferred inflows from revenues in any given period provides users with information to assess a government's interperiod equity.

II. **Financial Statement Presentation**

   A. **Governmental-Wide Statement of Net Position**

   (Assets + Deferred Outflows of Resources) − (Liabilities + Deferred Inflows of Resources) = Net Position

   B. **Fund-Level Financial Statements**

   1. **Governmental Fund Balance Sheet**

   (Current Assets + Deferred Outflows of Resources) − (Current Liabilities + Deferred Inflows of Resources) = Fund Balance

   2. **Proprietary Fund Statement of Net Position**

   (Assets + Deferred Outflows of Resources) − (Liabilities + Deferred Inflows of Resources) = Net Position

   3. **Fiduciary Fund Statement of Net Position**

   (Assets + Deferred Outflows of Resources) − (Liabilities + Deferred Inflows of Resources) = Net Position

   C. **Types of Deferred Outflows and Deferred Inflows of Resources**—GASB Concepts Statement No. 4 (para. 38) stipulates that recognition of deferred outflows and deferred inflows are limited to those items identified by GASB. The following items have been identified by GASB:

   1. **Derivatives (GASB Statements No. 53 and 64)**—Derivative instruments are reported at fair value. Changes in the fair value of derivatives used for hedging activities are reported as either a deferred outflow (loss in fair value) or a deferred inflow (gain in fair value). On the other hand, changes in the fair value of derivative instruments used for investment purposes are reported as part of current-period earnings. The table below describes how changes in the fair value of derivative instruments are reported:

	Purpose of Derivative Instrument	
	Investment	Hedging
Reporting of change in the fair value of the derivative instrument	Investment Revenue—Loss	Deferred Outflow or Deferred Inflow of Resources
Reported in:	Statement of Activities	Statement of Net Position—Balance Sheet

GASBS Statement No. 53 limits the use of the deferred recognition approach to those it describes as effective hedges. In essence, a hedge is considered effective when a change in the fair value of the hedging derivative is offset by the change in the fair value of the underlying hedged item. The standard provides three methods to evaluate the effectiveness of a hedge (this material taken from the lesson "Special Items—Recent Developments"):

a. **Consistent critical terms method**—If the critical terms of the hedgeable item and the derivative instrument are the same, or very similar, the changes in cash flows or fair values of the derivative instrument will substantially offset the changes in the cash flows or fair values of the hedgeable item.

b. **Quantitative methods**

   i. **Dollar-offset method**—This method evaluates effectiveness by comparing the expected cash flows or fair values of the derivative instrument with the changes in the expected cash flows or fair values of the hedgeable item. If the changes of either the hedgeable item or the derivative instrument divided by the other falls in the range of 80% to 125%, these changes substantially offset and the derivative instrument is considered to be an effective hedge. For example, if the actual results are such that the change in fair value of the derivative instrument is a decrease of $100 and the fair value of the hedgeable item increased by 110, the dollar-offset percentage is 110/100, which is 110%, or 100/110, which is 91%. In either case, the hedging derivative instrument is determined to be effective.

   ii. **Regression analysis method**—This method evaluates effectiveness by considering the statistical relationship between the cash flows or fair values of the derivative instrument and the hedgeable item. The changes in cash flows or fair values of the derivative instrument substantially offset the changes in the cash flows or fair value of the hedgeable item, if all of the following criteria are met:

      (a) The R-squared of the regression analysis is at least 0.80.

      (b) The F-statistic calculated for the regression model demonstrates that the model is significant using a 95% confidence level.

      (c) The regression coefficient for the slope is between −1.25 and −0.80.

c. **Synthetic instrument method**—Sometimes a government will combine an interest-bearing hedgeable item with a derivative instrument to create a third synthetic instrument. This method is limited to cash flow hedges in which the hedgeable items are interest bearing and carry a variable rate. Under this method, the derivative instrument is effective if the actual synthetic rate is substantially fixed. The hedge is considered substantially fixed if the actual synthetic rate is within 90% to 111% of the fixed rate. For example, if an interest-rate swap's fixed payment rate is 7.00%, an actual synthetic instrument rate that falls within a range between 6.30% (90% of 7.00%) and 7.77% (111% of 7.00%) is considered to be substantially fixed and, therefore, the derivative instrument is considered effective.

d. Changes in the fair value of derivative instruments, that do not qualify as effective using one of the methods described above, are reported in the Statement of Activities.

2. **Service concession arrangements (GASB Statement No. 60)**—Service concession arrangements are usually public-private partnerships in which a government receives payments from an operator in return for the right to build, operate, and/or collect user fees on public infrastructure and other public assets during the term of the agreement. Examples include construction and operation of toll roads, operation of convention centers, construction and operation of rest areas, operation of correctional facilities, operation of public golf courses, and so on.

Example
Suppose Blake City contracts with Kameron Golf for a five-year period to operate its municipal golf course in Year 1. In return for an up-front fee of $250,000 Blake City will allow Kameron Golf to retain 50% of profits. Blake City records the up-front fee in Year 1:

Cash	250,000	
Deferred Inflow of Resources		250,000

Blake City systematically recognizes the revenues in each of the five years:

Deferred Inflow of Resources	50,000	
Revenues		50,000

3. **Items previously reported as assets and liabilities (GASB Statement No. 65)**—Prior to GASB Statement No. 63, deferred outflows of resources had been reported among assets and deferred inflows of resources were reported among liabilities. For example, **imposed nonexchange revenue transaction**, such as property taxes, received in the year before they were due were reported as deferred revenue even though the government has no liability. GASB Statement No. 65 was issued to correct this problem.

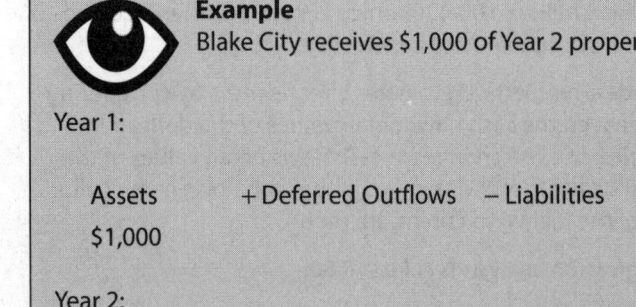

Example
Blake City receives $1,000 of Year 2 property taxes in Year 1.

Year 1:

Assets	+ Deferred Outflows	– Liabilities	– Deferred Inflows	= Net Position
$1,000			$1,000	No change

Year 2:

Assets	+ Deferred Outflows	– Liabilities	– Deferred Inflows	= Net Position
			$(1,000)	$1,000

a. **Refunding of debt**—The difference between the reacquisition price and the net carrying amount of the old debt is reported as a deferred outflow of resources (loss) or deferred inflow of resources (gain) and recognized as a component of interest expense in a systematic manner over the shorter of the remaining life of the old or new debt.

b. **Nonexchange transactions**

i. **Imposed nonexchange revenue transactions**—Deferred inflows of resources should be reported for resources associated with imposed nonexchange revenue transactions that are received or reported as receivable before the taxes are levied or before the period that the resources are required to be used according to enabling legislation that includes time requirements.

ii. Government-mandated and voluntary nonexchange transactions—Amounts provided by a grant or a government mandated program (e.g., environmental clean-up) in which all eligibility requirements are met other than a time requirement should be reported as a deferred outflow of resources by the provider and as a deferred inflow of resources by the recipient.

Example
Blake City receives a $50,000 cash grant and has not yet met all eligibility requirements including a time requirement:

Eligibility requirements not met, including time requirement

Assets	+ Deferred Outflows	– Liabilities	– Deferred Inflows	= Net Position
$50,000		$50,000		No change

Blake City recognized a liability because it will have to return the monies if it never meets the eligibility requirements.

Example
Kameron City requires a $40,000 cash grant and all eligibility requirements have been met except for a time requirement:

Assets	+ Deferred Outflows	– Liabilities	– Deferred Inflows	= Net Position
$40,000			$40,000	No change

Kameron City recognizes the grant as a deferred inflow of resources because it will have to wait for the time requirement to be met, the inflow is related to a future period and therefore recognition is deferred until the future period.

---

c. Sales and intra-entity transfers of future revenues—Sales of future revenues or intra-entity transfers of future revenues (e.g., sale of future tobacco settlement revenues by a county government to its county tobacco settlement authority are recognized as deferred inflows of resources by the county.

d. Debt issuance costs—These costs are expensed when incurred; that is, they are not deferred outflows.

e. Leases—Gain or loss on a sale and leaseback transaction are recorded as a deferred outflow (loss) or deferred inflow (gain). Points received by the lender in relation to loan origination are reported as deferred inflow of resources. Loan origination fees, other than points, are reported as revenue.

f. Regulatory operations—A regulator may set a rate that includes a component to cover expected future costs with the understanding that the rate will be reduced by a corresponding amount if those costs are not incurred. Those amounts should be reported as a deferred inflow of resources and recognized as revenue when associated costs are incurred.

g. Pension (GASB Statement No. 68)—Employer accounting and reporting for pensions was dramatically changed by GASB Statement No. 68. GASB Statement No. 68 changed pension accounting from a funding-based approach to an accounting-based approach, which changed from focus from an actuarially required contribution to a net pension liability. The impacts of benefit changes are immediately recognized. Differences between projected earnings and actual earnings on plan investments are recognized as deferred outflows or deferred inflows and amortized into pension expense over a five-year period. Changes in actuarial assumptions are recognized as deferred outflows or deferred inflows and amortized into pension expense over the average remaining service period of all employees. In general, beginning balances of deferred outflows of resources and deferred inflows of resources related to pensions should be reported at transition only when it is practical to determine all such amounts (**GASB Statement No. 68, para. 137**). However, at transition a government should recognize a beginning deferred outflow of resources for its pension contributions, if any, made subsequent to the measurement date of the beginning net pension liability and the end of the government's reporting period (**GASB Statement No. 71, para. 3**).

    h.   **Government acquisitions**—A government may pay and/or assume liabilities of former owner to acquire another entity (e.g., acquire a hospital, private school, or golf course). The acquiring government measures the acquired financial elements at their acquisition value as of the acquisition date. If the payment made by the government exceeds the net position acquired, the difference is reported as a deferred outflow of resources. For example, Blake City acquired King's Crossing Golf Course for $2 million but the net position was $1.7 million. Blake City will report a deferred outflow of resources of $300,000. If Blake City had paid $1.5 million, $200,000 less than the net position acquired, noncurrent asset values will usually be decreased by a corresponding amount.

D.   **Use of the "Term Deferred"**—This term is limited to items reported as deferred outflows of resources and deferred inflows of resources (GASB Statement No. 65, para. 31).

E.   **Major Fund Criteria**—Combine: (1) assets and deferred outflows of resources and (2) liabilities and deferred inflows of resources in applying the 10% and 5% threshold criteria to determine major funds (GASB Statement No. 65, para. 33).

Net Position and Fund Balance

This lesson describes the equity section of each fund type.

After studying this lesson, you should be able to:

1. List the three categories of net position.

2. List the five categories of fund balance.

3. Describe when each category of fund balance should be used.

I. **GASB Statement No. 54,** *Fund Balance Reporting and Governmental Fund Type Definitions*

   A. **Fund Balance and Governmental Fund Types**—In February 2009, GASB issued Statement No. 54, entitled *Fund Balance Reporting and Governmental Fund Type Definitions*. The Statement replaces the former *reserved* and *unreserved* fund balance classifications with new classifications and it provides guidance for the types of activities that are accounted for in special revenue, capital projects, and debt service funds. The Statement year-end pertains to fund balance amounts reported in fund-level financial statements for governmental fund types. You should expect questions on the fund balance categories established by GASBS Statement No. 54 on the CPA Exam.

   1. **GASB Statement No. 54,** *Fund Balance Classifications*

      a. **Nonspendable**—This classification is for amounts that cannot be spent because they are either not in spendable form (e.g., inventory, long-term receivables, or property held for resale) or the government is legally or contractually bound to maintain the amount (e.g., endowments in a permanent fund). However, if the proceeds from the collection of long-term receivables or from the sale of properties are restricted, committed, or assigned, then these amounts should be included in the appropriate spendable fund balance category (i.e., restricted, committed, or assigned). Note also that for government-wide financial statements, amounts held in perpetuity are classified as nonexpendable in the restricted net position category. For fund-level financial statements, however, those amounts should be classified as nonspendable.

      b. **Spendable**—There are four classifications for amounts that are in spendable form (e.g., fund balance amounts associated with cash, investments, receivables).

         i. **Restricted fund balance**—Amounts that are restricted to a specific purpose when constraints are placed on the use of resources that are either (1) externally imposed by creditors, grantors, contributors, or laws or regulations of other governments or (2) imposed by law through constitutional provisions or enabling legislation. Enabling legislation refers to legislation that authorizes the government to assess, levy, charge, or mandate the payment of resources and includes a legally enforceable requirement that those resources be used only for the specific purposes stipulated in the legislation. Moreover, the government can be compelled by external parties (e.g., citizens, public interest groups, or the judiciary) to use the resources created by the enabling legislation only for the purposes specified by it.

         ii. **Committed fund balance**—Amounts that are committed for a specific purpose by formal action of the government's highest level of decision-making (e.g., by city council resolution). In contrast to fund balance restricted by enabling legislation, amounts in the committed fund balance category may be redeployed for other purposes by taking the same kind of formal action (e.g., resolution, ordinance, or legislation) it employed to previously commit the amounts. Moreover, constraints imposed by the governing body are not considered legally enforceable.

         iii. **Assigned fund balance**—Amounts that are intended by the government to be used for specific purposes that are not classified as restricted or committed. Intent is usually expressed by the governing body, a committee or group (e.g., finance committee), or an official to which the governing body has delegated the authority to assign amounts for specific purposes. In contrast to committed fund balance classification, the authority for making an assignment is not required to be the government's highest decision-making authority. Moreover, constraints imposed on the use of assigned amounts are more easily removed or modified than amounts that are committed. (Note: This is the residual catchall classification for spendable amounts not restricted or committed in a special revenue, capital projects, or debt service fund.) Governments should not report an assignment in the general fund for a specific purpose if the assignment would result in a deficit in unassigned fund balance in the general fund.

    iv. **Unassigned fund balance**—The residual classification for the general fund for amounts not classified as restricted, committed, or assigned. (Note: Typically, this classification is only used by the general fund with one exception: negative fund balance amounts in other governmental fund types are reported as unassigned.)

2. **Comparing Old and New Rules on Fund Balance**

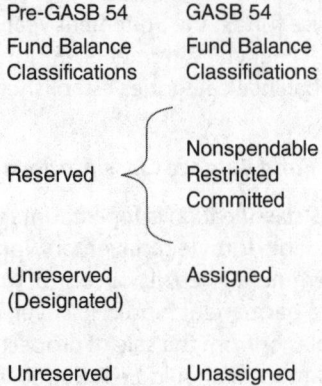

Pre-GASB 54 Fund Balance Classifications	GASB 54 Fund Balance Classifications
Reserved	Nonspendable Restricted Committed
Unreserved (Designated)	Assigned
Unreserved	Unassigned

    a. **Stabilization "rainy day" funds**—Many state and local governments formally and systematically set aside amounts for use in emergency situations. Stabilization amounts should be reported as a restricted or committed fund balance if they meet the criteria for being either restricted or committed. Otherwise, the amount should be reported as unassigned fund balance in the general fund.

    b. **Encumbrances**—Prior to GASB Statement No. 54, encumbrances outstanding at the end of the year were shown as a reserve in the fund balance section ("Fund balance reserved for encumbrances"). Since GASB Statement No. 54 removes the *reserved* classification, encumbrances should not be shown in the financial statements. If the encumbered amount has not previously been restricted, committed, or assigned, it should be included within the committed or assigned fund balance depending on the level of authority used to encumber the amount. GASB states that amounts related to encumbrances should be disclosed in the notes to the financial statements.

    c. **Government-wide financial statements**—The term "fund balance" is not used in government-wide financial statements. A summary reconciliation of conversion of total governmental fund balances to net position of governmental activities in the government-wide statement of net position must be prepared.

3. The Statement provides guidance on the types of activities accounted for in the following governmental fund types:

    a. **Special revenue funds**—Used to account for and report the proceeds of specific revenue sources that are restricted or committed to expenditure for specified purposes other than debt service or major capital projects. The "specific revenue sources" should be the foundation of the special revenue fund. Special revenue funds should not be used to account for resources held in trust for individuals, private organizations, or other governments. Restricted or committed fund balance amounts should comprise a significant portion of total fund balance. Effect: This is a *revenues-based* approach. Governments that use an *activity-based* approach (e.g., street maintenance expenditures) will need to examine whether the resources in the fund are restricted or committed amounts.

b. **Capital projects funds**—Used to account for and report financial resources that are restricted, committed, or assigned to expenditure for the acquisition or construction of major capital facilities of the general government. Effect: These must be capital, rather than operating expenditures, in addition to nonroutine such as buildings, major building improvements, and infrastructure assets. Nonproject, routine expenditures such as buses, fire trucks, and computers should not be accounted for in a capital project fund.

c. **Debt service funds**—Used to account for and report financial resources that are restricted, committed, or assigned to expenditure for principal and interest payments.

II. **Net Position (GASBS Statement No. 63)**

A. **Net position** represents the difference between assets and liabilities in government-wide financial statements (GASB Statement No. 34) and in fund-level financial statements for proprietary fund types and fiduciary fund types. Basically, there are three categories of net position:

1. **Net investment in capital assets**—This category indicates the fund's net investment in capital assets and is calculated as the fund's gross capital assets less accumulated depreciation and less the outstanding balance of any capital asset related debt (e.g., mortgages, bonds, and other borrowings). However, the unexpended portion of capital-asset-related debt is not included in this net asset category.

2. **Restricted net position**—At the fund level, this category indicates the amount of restrictions in excess of noncapital related debt and liabilities directly associated with those restricted assets. To be considered a restriction at the fund level, the constraint on the asset use must be narrower than the general limits of the activity. For example, a Water Utility enterprise fund does not report revenues restricted to use by the water utility as restricted net position. According to GASB Statement No. 46, restrictions may be imposed:

   a. Externally by creditors (e.g., debt covenants), grantors, contributors, or laws and regulations of other governments;

   b. By constitutional provisions; *or*

   c. By enabling legislation of the government that authorizes it to assess, levy, charge, or otherwise mandate payment of resources externally and places a legally enforceable purpose restriction on those net resources.

3. **Unrestricted**—This category represents the remainder of the fund's net position that does not meet the definition of the other two categories.

B. **At the Government-Wide Level**—Restricted net position for proprietary fund types (i.e., business-type activities) in the government-wide financial statements may be larger than (and unrestricted net position corresponding less than) the sum of the restricted net position used in the individual proprietary funds because the restriction on asset use is more limited in scope at the fund level than at the government-wide level. For example, assets that are restricted for water utility purposes but can be used for any legitimate purpose by the Water Utility Enterprise Fund increase unrestricted net position in the fund level financial statements. However, the same amount is an increase in restricted net position in the government-wide financial statements because the amounts can only be used by the water utility; they cannot be used by the parks department, street and repair maintenance, and so on.

C. Other Points

1. Restricted net position can never be a negative amount.

2. Although it is rare, if some assets are required to be retained in perpetuity (e.g., a permanent endowment), then two subcomponents are used—expendable and nonexpendable restricted net position.

3. The net position of a fiduciary fund is held in trust or in an agent capacity for specific individuals (e.g., employees and retirees), private organizations, or other governments rather than for other funds or component units of the government itself. Therefore, the net position in a fiduciary fund is a restricted net position that is typically labeled as "Net Position Held in Trust."

> **Note**
> *Designations of unrestricted net position by management indicate that the government does not intend to use those resources for the general operations of the fund. GASB* **prohibits** *reporting designations of net position on the face of fund or government-wide financial statements.*

> **Note**
> GASBS Statement No. 63, *Financial Reporting of Deferred Outflows of Resources, Deferred Inflows of Resources, and Net Position*, replaces *Net Assets* with *Net Position*. GASBS Statement No. 63 was issued because GASB Concepts Statement No. 4 includes net position as one of five elements that make up the government-wide Statement of Financial Position. The need for the change was necessary because GASBS Statement No. 53, on derivatives, and GASBS Statement No. 60, on service concession agreements, provide for the possible reporting of deferred outflows of resources and deferred inflows of resources, which triggers the use of the term "net position" rather than net assets. Under GASBS Statement No. 63, the statement of net position can take the following form:
>
> Assets
> + Deferred Outflows of Resources
> – Liabilities
> – Deferred Inflows of Resources
> = Net Position
> Net position has three categories: (1) net investment in capital assets, (2) restricted, and (3) unrestricted.

Governmental Funds

This lesson provides examples of typical accounting entries made in each type of governmental fund.

After studying this lesson, you should be able to:

1. List the five types of government funds and describe the purpose of each.

2. Prepare typical entries for each type of fund.

3. Describe how the modified accrual basis of accounting affects the accounting and reporting for major revenue sources such as property taxes and the acquisition of fixed assets within the fund-level financial statements.

Study Tip

Remember the acronym **DRIP-CEG-PIPPA**—**DRIP**: **D**ebt service funds, special **R**evenue funds, **I**nternal service funds, **P**ermanent funds; **CEG**: **C**apital projects funds, **E**nterprise funds, **G**eneral fund; **PIPPA**: **P**ension trust funds, **I**nvestment trust funds, **P**rivate **P**urpose trust funds, **A**gency funds—a mnemonic for remembering the 11 types of funds. Governmental funds are the consonants; D, R, P, C, and G, in **DRIP-CEG**.

I. General Fund

    A. General Fund—The principal operating fund for all governmental entities. Most "general" revenues (property taxes, fines, penalties, licenses, etc.) and "general" expenditures (police, fire, city administration, etc.) are accounted for in the general fund.

    B. General Fund Characteristics—The general fund is the only fund that is absolutely required in governmental accounting. There is only one general fund. Like all government funds, the general fund:

        1. Uses modified accrual basis accounting

        2. Uses budgetary and encumbrance accounting

        3. Accounts for current items only

            a. Purchases of fixed assets are recorded in the general fund as expenditures.

            b. Proceeds from the issuance of long-term debt are recorded in the general fund as Other Financial Sources.

Note

Although the fixed assets and the long-term debt are not recorded in the general fund, they *are* recorded "off-books" and are included in the government-wide financial statements. These statements are discussed later in the "Deriving Government-Wide Financial Statements and Reconciliation Requirements" lesson.

    C. General Fund Functions—In addition to funding most of the current operating costs of the governmental entity, the general fund frequently finances many other funds, such as debt service, capital projects, enterprise, and internal service funds, just to name a few—by transferring monies to these funds. These transfers can take one of several forms:

        1. **Loans**—Monies that are transferred to another fund and are expected to be repaid are recorded either as **short-term inter-fund receivables** (*Due from xxxxx fund*) or **long-term inter-fund receivables** (*Advances to xxxxx fund*).

 **Example**
The general fund transferred $80,000 to a newly created capital projects fund to pay for project start-up expenses. The general fund expects the capital projects fund to repay the money in six months when its revenues arrive.

General Fund

    DR: Due from Capital Projects Fund $80,000

          CR: Cash $80,000

Capital Projects Fund

    DR: Cash $80,000

          CR: Due to General Fund $80,000

If the debt were not to be repaid for several years, the entry would be:

General Fund

    DR: Advances to Capital Projects Fund $80,000

          CR: Cash $80,000

Capital Projects Fund

    DR: Cash $80,000

          CR: Advances from General Fund $80,000

2. **Transfers**—Monies that are transferred to another fund and are **not** expected to be repaid are recorded as Transfers. Although the general fund occasionally receives monies transferred in from other funds, transfers out from the general fund to another fund are much more common. Transfers are usually made to finance another fund's ongoing operations, to provide investment capital to a fund (purchase fixed assets, increase working capital, etc.) or to remove a deficit position. These transfers are recorded by the fund providing the resources as Other Financing Uses—Transfers Out and by the fund receiving the resources as Other Financing Sources—Transfers In.

Exam Tip:
Questions on the CPA Exam may refer to transfer accounts by their full title:
Other Financing Sources—Transfers In and
Other Financing Uses—Transfers Out
or by either part of the account title:
Transfers In and *Transfers Out* or
Other Financing Sources or *Other Financing Uses.*
Any of the three forms is equally likely to appear in a question.

D. Common General Fund Entries

1. **Property Taxes**—Property taxes are one of the few governmental revenues that are *susceptible to accrual*. This means that the revenues are recorded when the property taxes are levied (i.e., when bills are sent out), rather than waiting until payment is received. The standard entry to record property taxes is:

Property Taxes Receivable—Current	XXX
Est. Uncollectible Taxes—Current	XXX
Revenues (or Property Tax Revenue)	XXX

    a. Notice that property tax revenue is recognized net of the estimated uncollectible taxes. That is, there is **no** *Bad Debt Expense*. Note also that both the property tax levy and the related uncollectible are designated *Current*.

Exam Tip

Examiners sometimes test candidates' algebraic skills along with their accounting knowledge by asking them how to calculate the amount of the property tax levy based on a specified dollar amount of revenues and given percentage of estimated uncollectible taxes.

 **Examples**

1. Property taxes are levied in December, Year X. The taxes are not due until Year Y and are intended to finance activities in Year Y. The entry to record the tax levy is:

DR: Property Taxes Receivable—Current	XXXX
CR: Est. Uncollectible Taxes—Current	XXXX
CR: Deferred Inflow of Resources	XXXX

2. Hillborough County levies property taxes sufficient to produce revenue of $475,000. If Hillborough anticipates uncollectible taxes to equal 5% of the total levy, what is the amount of the levy?

$$\text{Levy} - (.05 \times \text{Levy}) = \text{Revenue}$$
$$.95 \times \text{Levy} = \text{Revenue}$$
$$.95 \times \text{Levy} = 475,000$$
$$\text{Levy} = 475,000/.95$$
$$\text{Levy} = 500,000$$

E. Accounting for Delinquent Taxes—When taxes are not received within a specified period of time, both the receivables and the related uncollectible taxes are reclassified as delinquent.

Property Taxes Receivable—Delinquent	XXX	
Est. Uncollectible Taxes—Current	XXX	
Property Taxes Receivable—Current		XXX
Est. Uncollectible Taxes—Delinquent		XXX

1. **Changes in estimate of uncollectible taxes**—At the end of the period, the Estimated Uncollectible Taxes are reevaluated and the allowance account is adjusted appropriately. Note that the offsetting entry is to Revenue. Since property tax revenues are reported net of the allowance for uncollectible taxes, a change in the estimated uncollectible dictates that the revenue recognized from those transactions is also changed.

2. **Original estimate was too high**—Lower the revenue amount.

DR: Revenues (or Property Tax Revenue)	XXX	
CR: Est. Uncollectible Taxes		XXX

---

3. **Original estimate was too low**—Increase the revenue amount.

```
DR:  Est. Uncollectible Taxes              XXX
     CR:  Revenues (or Property Tax Revenue)      XXX
```

4. **End-of-period revenue deferral**—Although property tax revenue is recognized when the property tax bills are sent out (e.g., the property taxes are levied), if the taxes are not paid during the fiscal year or in the first 60 days of the subsequent fiscal year, then revenue cannot be recognized. At the end of the period, any revenues not received within the allowable period must be backed out and revenue recognition deferred.

Example

Belmont City levies property taxes totaling $5,000,000 during the current fiscal year. Uncollectible taxes are estimated to be $50,000. When the bills are sent out, Belmont recognizes $4,950,000 in property tax revenue. During the year and in the first 60 days of the subsequent year, Belmont collects property taxes from this levy totaling $4,500,000. Belmont may only recognize the $4,500,000 as revenue during the current fiscal year. Recognition of the remaining $450,000 is deferred by the following entry until the monies are actually collected:

```
Revenues (or Property Tax Revenues)     450,000
    Deferred Inflow of Resources                450,000
```

F. **Fines and Penalties on Delinquent Taxes**—Fines and penalties assessed by the governmental unit on unpaid taxes are handled exactly as the taxes themselves. That is, they are considered to be "susceptible to accrual" and thus revenue net of estimated uncollectible taxes and penalties is recorded when the fines are levied.

```
Fines and Penalties Receivable—Current       XXX
    Est. Uncollectible Fines and Penalties—Current    XXX
    Revenues                                          XXX
```

G. **Revenues that are not Susceptible to Accrual**—Unlike property taxes, most general fund revenues (i.e., fees for licenses and permits, charges for services, parking fines, etc.) are *not susceptible to accrual*. These revenues are recorded when they are received in cash, as long as they are legally due.

```
Cash               XXX
    Revenues Control        XXX
```

1. If they are not yet legally due yet are received by the government, Deferred Inflows of Resources are recognized.

 **Example—The Use of Deferred Inflow of Resources as Required by GASB Statement No. 65**
Note: This is a likely exam question.

Rintner County received an $8,000 property tax payment that was not due until the subsequent fiscal year. Rintner recognizes the receipt as Deferred Inflow of Resources, which is neither revenue nor a liability account, until the taxes are due. (The account title is usually Taxes Received in Advance.)

Cash	8,000	
Deferred Inflow of Resources		8,000

In the subsequent year:

Deferred Inflow of Resources	8,000	
Property Tax Revenues		8,000

Note

GASB Statement No. 65 limits the use of the term "deferred" to deferred outflows of resources and deferred inflows of resources

H. **Long-Term Debt Proceeds**—Proceeds received from bonds or other long-term debt issues are not classified as revenues but as Other Financing Sources.

Cash	XXX	
Other Financing Sources—Bond Proceeds		XXX

I. **Direct Expenditures**—Not all expenditures are encumbered. Bills for services rendered, monthly billings in irregular amounts (e.g., utilities), and items purchased in a retail environment are not usually encumbered. These types of payments are often called **direct expenditures.** They are recorded as expenditures immediately without going through the encumbrance process.

Expenditures	XXX	
Cash/Vouchers Payable		XXX

J. **Capital Expenditures**—There is no difference in the entry to record payment for a fixed asset such as a computer and a period expenditure such as rent. Both represent *outflows of financial resources* and both are recorded as expenditures. The entry to record purchase of a new fixed asset is:

Expenditures	XXX	
Cash/Vouchers Payable		XXX

II. Special Revenue Funds

Definition
Special Revenue Funds: Funds used to account for monies restricted or "earmarked" for specific types of general government expenditures

A. **Examples of Resources Usually Accounted For**—Special revenue funds include entitlement monies, which must be used to improve public safety, grants to provide housing assistance to low-income constituents, and taxes, which must be used for specified purposes.

1. All restricted resources can be accounted for in special revenue funds except:

   a. Monies restricted to debt service (these are accounted for in a debt service fund)

   b. Monies restricted for capital projects (these are accounted for in a capital projects fund)

   c. Monies that are permanently restricted (e.g., endowments—these are accounted for in a permanent fund)

B. **Special Revenue Fund Characteristics**—The special revenue fund functions like the general fund except that it accounts only for *restricted resources*. That is, it:

   1. Uses modified accrual basis accounting

   2. Uses budgetary and encumbrance accounting

   3. Accounts for current items only

C. **Special Revenue Fund Entries**—Special revenue funds receive most of their resources from:

   1. Monies transferred to them from the general fund

   2. Intergovernmental transfers

   3. Voluntary grants

D. **Transfers from the General Fund**—These receipts are *always* recorded as Other Financing Sources, *never* as Revenues.

DR: Cash	50,000	
CR: Other Financing Sources—Transfers In		50,000

E. **Intergovernmental Transfers**—Intergovernmental transfers include items such as **grants, entitlements and shared revenues,** which are usually distributed from larger government entities (i.e., the federal government) to smaller government entities (i.e., states, counties, cities).

   1. **Grants, entitlements, and shared revenues**—These are always subject to a **purpose restriction** and may also be subject to **eligibility requirements** and/or **time restrictions**. Recognition of these resources is governed by GASB Statement No. 33. (However, see the note below the examples.)

      a. **Eligibility requirements**—Revenue can be recognized only when all eligibility requirements have been met. *Most* eligibility requirements for entitlements and shared revenues are generic (e.g., they "must provide for the safety of its citizens") and can *usually* be assumed to be met. When there are specific requirements that are **not** met (e.g., they "must have provided training in CPR to all public safety officers"), a liability is recognized until the eligibility requirements are met.

Example
A $50,000 state grant for assistance to single parents of children under the age of three is received. The monies cannot be expended until matching local monies have been appropriated and transferred to the fund (an eligibility requirement).

When the monies are received:

DR: Cash	50,000	
CR: Grant Received in Advance		50,000

After matching monies are transferred to the fund:

DR: Grant Received in Advance	50,000	
CR: Revenues		50,000

b. **Time requirements**—When resources cannot be used before a specified time or event has taken place, revenue recognition must be deferred.

Example
On February 1, the McClain School District received $500,000 in federal education entitlement monies. $200,000 of the money can be spent in the current period; the remaining $300,000 cannot be spent until September 1 of the following year.

When the monies are received:

DR: Cash	50,000	
CR: Revenues		200,000
CR: Deferred Inflow of Resources		300,000

On September 1 of the subsequent year:

DR: Deferred Inflow of Resources	300,000	
CR: Revenues		300,000

c. **Purpose restrictions**—The existence of a purpose restriction alone does not delay revenue recognition. This is particularly true when the specified type of expenditure is of an ongoing nature, such as public safety, road maintenance and repair, emergency services, and the like. As long as all other eligibility requirements are met, revenue is recognized immediately.

Example
Lakeland County receives 30% of the tax collected on gasoline sales made inside the county limits. On April 10, Lakeland received $1.5M as its share of taxes collected during the first quarter. By law, these monies must be used to maintain existing roads and bridges.

The requirement to use the money to maintain existing roads and bridges is a purpose restriction, **not** an eligibility requirement. Therefore, revenue related to the transaction can be recognized immediately.

DR: Cash	1.5M	
CR: Revenue		1.5M

F. **Voluntary Grants**—While intergovernmental revenues are usually transferred directly to the recipient government for expenditure, most voluntary grants and contracts require that, after a grant is awarded, the recipient government makes the expenditure first and then bills the granting entity for reimbursement. These types of grants are known as expenditure-driven or reimbursement grants.

1. From a revenue recognition viewpoint, the requirement that the governmental entity must first expend resources for the purpose specified in the grant contract can be viewed as an eligibility requirement. Thus, no revenue is recognized when the grant is awarded. When an expenditure is made for the specified purpose, the government entity prepares a reimbursement request. Assuming all other eligibility requirements have been met, the government entity can recognize a receivable and revenue when the reimbursement request is submitted.

Note
Recall that GASB Statement No. 33, which governs revenue recognition for nonexchange transactions such as grants, entitlements, and shared revenues, is a full accrual basis standard. It defines how these revenues will be reported in the government-wide statements (which are prepared on a full accrual basis). However, since special revenue funds use modified accrual basis accounting, GASB Statement No. 33 is not sufficient to determine whether revenue will be recorded in the special revenue funds and reported in the fund statements. The rules governing revenue recognition under the modified accrual basis must be considered on top of the GASB Statement No. 33 rules to make this determination.

Examples

1. A school board makes $20,000 of expenditures in accordance with the specifications of a federal education assistance grant. Documentation of the expenditure and a request for reimbursement is sent to the granting agency.

Expenditure is made:

DR: Expenditures	20,000	
CR: Cash		20,000

Reimbursement is requested:

DR: Grants Receivable	20,000	
CR: Revenue		20,000

2. On November 15, the Town of Live Oak was awarded an expenditure-driven grant of $50,000 by the State Parks Board. This award is appropriately accounted for in a Special Revenue Fund. In December, The town spent $30,000 in accordance with the grant guidelines and properly billed the State Parks Board for the expenditure. Since the State Parks Board normally requires 90 days to process a reimbursement billing request, the Town does not expect to receive the $30,000 reimbursement until late in March. The Town of Live Oak uses a calendar fiscal year.

According to GASB Statement No. 33, the Town should recognize revenue of $30,000 when the billing is sent to the State Parks Board. However, since the Town will not receive the reimbursement within the current fiscal period or the first 60 days of the subsequent period, modified accrual basis accounting does not permit the revenue to be recognized. Instead, revenue recognition is postponed until the subsequent period. Therefore, the $30,000 is not available under revenue recognition in the modified accrual basis of accounting used by the special revenue fund. GASB Statement No. 65 (para. 30) required use of a Deferred Inflow of Resources in this situation. The entry to record the billing to the State Parks Board then becomes:

DR: Grants Receivable	30,000	
CR: Deferred Inflow of Resources		30,000

However, the government-wide statements will report revenue of $30,000 during the current year since full accrual basis accounting does not require cash to be received in order to recognize revenue.

III. Debt Service Funds

Definition
Debt Service Funds: Funds used to make interest and principal payments on general long-term debt.

A. **General Debt**—Debt that has been incurred by the governmental fund types. Bonds are the most common form of general obligation long-term debt but other types of long-term debt (i.e., capital leases, long-term notes payable and long-term claims and judgments against the governmental entity, etc.) are also included in this category.

B. **Debt Service Funds**—Do not make payments on *short-term* liabilities or *specific debt* (revenue bonds and other long-term debt attributable to proprietary funds).

Note
Debt service funds do not record or report the long-term debt. They only *service* the debt by making the required interest payments and principal re-payments. The long-term debt is recorded in off-books schedules until it matures (e.g., becomes due). Once the debt has matured, the debt service funds record the currently due portions of the debt. When used in reference to general long-term debt, the terms "current", "due," and "currently due" mean *matured* debt, that is, debt that is on or past the *due date*.

Example
The City of Mayfield uses a calendar fiscal year. On December 31, it has $100,000,000 of general obligation bonds outstanding. Of this amount, $15,000,000 will mature during the next 12 months; $5,000,000 of this amount matures on January 4.

On its fund financial statements dated December 31, Mayfield's debt service funds will not report any of this general obligation debt because none of it is currently due (i.e., *matured*).

On January 4, the due date of the debt, the debt service fund will record the $5,000,000 of debt that matures on that day. The entry to recognize the liability is:

DR: Expenditures—Principal $5,000,000

CR: Bonds Payable $5,000,000

Typically, this liability will remain on the books for less than 24 hours, because the repayment checks to the bondholders are usually written on the maturity date.

DR: Bonds Payable $5,000,000

CR: Cash $5,000,000

C. **Debt Service Fund Characteristics**—Debt service funds use **modified accrual basis accounting** and may use budgetary accounting. Because they use modified accrual basis accounting, **interest expense** on the outstanding debt is **not** accrued, but recorded only when it is actually **due** (i.e., *on the due date*).

1. **Debt Service Fund Entries**

   a. Debt service funds include entries that:

      i. Record receipt of resources to be used to pay interest and repay principal on general obligation long-term debt

      ii. Record investment of those resources and recognition of investment earnings

      iii. Record liabilities related to matured interest and principal on general obligation long-term debt

      iv. Record payment of matured interest and principal

D. **Receipt of Resources**—The majority of resources received by the debt service funds are transferred from the general fund. These transfers are never recorded as revenue; they are always recorded as Other Financing Sources.

Cash	XXX	
Other Financing Sources—Transfers In		XXX

1. **Investment related entries**—are resources accumulated to repay the principal of bonds are usually **invested until they are needed.**

Investments	XXX	
Cash		XXX

    a.   **Investment earnings**—Earnings recognized as **revenues.**

Cash/Interest receivable	XXX	
Interest revenue		XXX

Note

Interest revenue on the debt service fund investments, *unlike interest expense on the long-term liabilities*, **is accrued** as long as the earnings will be received in time to meet modified accrual revenue recognition criteria (e.g., within 60 days of year-end, which is *usually the case.*

    b.   **Investment management fees**—Recognized as **expenditures** in the debt service fund.

Expenditures—Management fees	XXX	
Cash		XXX

2. **Recognition of matured liabilities—Interest payable** on general long-term debt is recognized on the day that it becomes due. It is *not* accrued.

Expenditures—Interest	XXX	
Interest Payable		XXX

3. The liability for repayment of matured portions of general long-term debt is recognized on the day that the debt matures.

Expenditures—Principal	XXX	
Bonds Payable		XXX

Note

Under modified accrual basis accounting, both the repayment of principal and payment of interest are recognized as **expenditures** (both require an outflow of financial resources). GASB requires separate reporting of each type of expenditure: **Expenditures—Interest** and **Expenditures—Principal**.

E. **Payments to Bondholders**—If the payable has been accrued, the following entry is used to record payment to the bondholders:

Interest Payable	XXX	
Bonds Payable	XXX	
Cash		XXX

1. Often, however, the expenditure is *not* accrued but is recognized when the payment is made:

Expenditures—Interest	XXX	
Expenditures—Principal	XXX	
Cash		XXX

IV. Capital Projects Funds

Definition
Capital Projects Funds: Funds that are used to facilitate resource accumulation and manage expenditures for major capital projects.

A. **Capital Projects Funds**—Do not have to be used for all capital asset acquisition or construction. The general fund frequently finances purchases of smaller capital assets, such as computers, furniture, and vehicles. Capital projects funds are most useful for large purchases or projects in which funding from multiple sources is involved.

B. **Capital Projects Fund Characteristics**—Capital projects funds use modified accrual basis accounting and recognized encumbrances. They may also use budgetary accounting (although they almost never do on the CPA Exam).

1. Capital projects funds are *limited life funds:* They exist for the life of the project and are then closed.

2. Surplus monies in the fund at closing are transferred either to a debt service fund or to the general fund. Assets acquired or constructed through capital projects funds are reported in the Government-wide financial statements.

Note
Although the **expenditures** made to construct or acquire capital assets are recognized in the capital projects funds, the **capital asset** itself is **not** recognized in the capital projects fund. Like all governmental funds, capital asset funds cannot recognize fixed assets. This includes *construction in progress*, which represents the cost of an incomplete fixed asset. Assets constructed and construction in progress are reported on the government-wide statements at the actual amount expended to acquire them.

C. **Capital Projects Fund Entries**—Entries in capital projects funds record:

1. **Receipt of the resources** used to finance the project;

2. **Expenditures** to construct or acquire the capital asset;

3. **Transfers of excess resources** are made when the project is complete (something that rarely happens in practice but is frequently tested on the CPA Exam).

D. **Receipt of Resources**—Capital projects are usually funded through a combination of bond proceeds, grants, and contributions from the general fund.

1. **Debt funding**—If **bonds** provide funding, recognize Another Financing Source:

Cash	XXX	
Other Financing Sources—Bond Proceeds		XXX

Note

If bonds are sold at a **premium**, the premium amount is not available for expenditure in to the capital projects fund but is transferred to a debt service fund where it can be used to repay bondholders.

Example

Daley City issued $4 M par value bonds to finance construction of a new police headquarters. The bonds were sold for $4.1 M and the proceeds were accounted for in a capital projects fund. The premium amount is in excess of the amount authorized by voters for expenditure on the project and cannot be expended in the capital projects fund. The bond covenant usually specifies that proceeds received in excess of par value must be used to repay the bond liability. Consequently, premiums are usually transferred to a **debt service fund**.

Record the full amount of the proceeds as an Other Financing Source in the capital projects fund.

Cash	4,100,000	
Other Financing Sources-Bond Proceeds		4,100,000

Record the transfer of the premium to the debt service fund as an Other Financing Use in the capital projects fund and as an Other Financing Source in the debt service fund.

Capital Projects Fund

Other Financing Use—Operating Transfer Out	100,000	
Cash		100,000

Debt Service Fund

Cash	100,000	
Other Financing Source—Operating Transfer In		100,000

E. **Alternative Treatment**—Capital projects funds sometimes separate the premium from the bonds upon receipt of the proceeds, showing only the par value of the bonds as an Other Financing Source and showing the premium as a **liability** (Due to Debt Service Fund). In these instances, the debt service fund may recognize the receipt of the premium as revenue rather than an Other Financing Source. However, most CPA Exam questions do **not** follow this approach.

F. **Grant Funding**

1. If grants provide funding, *Revenue* is usually recognized when the grant is received. However, depending on the terms of the grant contract, revenue recognition may be deferred until eligibility requirements are met or until the monies are actually expended. The general rules prescribed by GASB Statement No. 33 govern recognition of grant proceeds.

Cash	XXX	
Grant Revenues or Grant Received in Advance (a liability)		XXX

2. **Transfers from other funds**—If transfers from the general fund or other fund provide funding, recognize the receipt as an Other Financing Source:

Cash	XXX	
Other Financing Sources—Transfer In		XXX

G. **Expenditures**—All amounts paid for the acquisition or construction of a capital asset, whether for materials, labor, or equipment, are recorded as Expenditures. Somewhat specialized entries occur, however, when construction of the asset is contracted to a private company.

1. When the contract is signed, an encumbrance is created for the entire amount of the contract. As the contractor submits progress billings, the encumbrance is partially liquidated.

 **Examples**

1. Amestown signed a $2 M contract with Bowie Construction to build a new auditorium. Bowie submitted a progress billing for $200,000 when the building was 10% complete.

Entry to Recognize the Contract

Encumbrances	2,000,000	
Budgetary Fund Balance		2,000,000

Entry to Record the Progress Billing

Budgetary Fund Balance	200,000	
Encumbrances		200,000
Expenditures	200,000	
Contracts Payable		200,000

When the progress billing is paid, a portion of the payment is usually withheld. This amount is known as a *retained percentage*. The retained percentage is withheld until the project is satisfactorily completed. If corrections need to be made and the original contractor is unable or unwilling to make the corrections, these monies are available to fund the work. Once the project has been approved any remaining money is remitted to the original contractor.

2. Amestown's contract with Bowie Construction specified that 10% of all billings would be retained.

Entry to Record Payment of the $200,000 Progress Billing Already Recorded

Contracts Payable	200,000	
Retained Percentage		20,000
Cash		180,000

If corrections are required in order for the project to be approved and the original contractor does not elect to complete the work, the work is paid from the Retained Percentage account.

2. **Payments**— Payments for additional work made from the Retained Percentage account do **not** create any additional expenditures

Example
Upon completion of the auditorium, inspection revealed that an additional $80,000 work was needed to correct deficiencies in construction. Bowie elects to forfeit that amount from its retained percentage and let another contractor complete the job.

Entry to Pay the Other Contractor

Retained Percentage	80,000	
Cash		80,000

H. **Transfer of Excess Resources**—After construction is completed, the capital projects fund is eliminated.

   1. Any remaining monies are transferred to other funds. If bonds have been used to finance the project, the transfer is usually to the debt service fund.

Example
Patterson County recently completed a new park headquarters building. The building was financed through bond issues and the construction was accounted for in a Capital Projects Fund. After all bills were paid, $30,000 cash remained in the fund.

Entry to Record the Transfer of the Cash to the Debt Service Fund

Capital Projects Fund:

Other Financing Use—Transfer Out	30,000	
Cash		30,000

Debt Service Fund:

Cash	30,000	
Other Financing Source—Transfer In		30,000

Entry to Close the Capital Projects Fund (assuming all other accounts had been closed prior to transfer of the cash to the debt service fund)

Capital Projects Fund:

Fund Balance	30,000	
Other Financing Use—Operating Transfer Out		30,000

V. **Permanent Funds**

Definition
Permanent Funds: Funds that account for the principal and earnings of endowments that must be used for the benefit of governmental programs

A. The Endowment Principal—This is typically received as a contribution or a bequest from a private individual or organization. By accepting the endowment, the governmental entity agrees to invest and maintain the principal intact, usually in perpetuity, and to expend the net earnings on the investment for the purposes stated in the endowment agreement. In order to be accounted for in a permanent fund, the purposes must be in support of government programs or for the benefit of the constituents in general.

> **Note**
> Most CPA Exam questions about permanent funds focus on whether it is appropriate to account for a contribution or bequest in a permanent fund. If the resources contributed need **not** be held in perpetuity but may be expended for the governmental purpose, they should be not accounted for in a permanent fund but would most likely be accounted for in a **special revenue fund**. If the purpose of the expenditures is for a nongovernmental purpose or the benefit of specific individuals (e.g., to provide an annual award to recognize an outstanding business), the resources should be accounted for in a **private purpose trust fund**.

B. Characteristics of Permanent Funds—Permanent funds use modified accrual basis accounting, but they are not usually budgeted nor do they typically use encumbrances. Although they account for the nonexpendable endowment principal and the expendable earnings on the endowment, they do **not** account for the related expenditures (i.e., expenditures for the purpose(s) specified in the endowment agreement). Instead, the net expendable earnings are transferred to the fund responsible for the specified type of expenditure, which is usually a special revenue fund.

C. Permanent Fund Entries—Entries in permanent funds are usually limited to recognition of:

1. Receipt of the endowment principal

2. Receipt of investment earnings

3. Transfer of net expendable earnings

D. Receipt of Endowment Principal—GASB Statement No. 33 specifically requires that the receipt of endowment principal (a nonexchange transaction) be recognized as Revenue when received.

E. Investment Earnings—Investment earnings have two components: **periodic income** (i.e. interest and dividends) and **capital gains** (gains and losses on the sale of investments). Depending on the endowment agreement, these two components can receive very different accounting treatments.

1. **Interest and dividends**—Interest and dividends, net of any related expenses, are usually considered fully expendable. The gross revenue is recognized in the permanent fund.

2. Investment management fees and other expenditures required to maintain the endowment principal are also recognized in the permanent fund. These fees are deducted from investment earnings to determine net expendable earnings.

3. **Capital gains (and losses)**—In the absence of specific instructions to the contrary, gains (and losses) on the sale of investments are usually considered to be adjustments to the principal. That is, they are **not** expendable.

F. Transfer of Net Expendable Earnings—The permanent fund does not make Expenditures for the purpose(s) identified in the endowment agreement. Instead, the earnings are transferred to the fund responsible for the type of expenditure specified in the agreement.

G. Net Expendable Earnings—Determined by deducting management fees and other charges necessary to maintain the principal from periodic investment income (interest and dividends).

H. GASB Statement No. 52, Land and Other Real Estate Held as Investments by Endowments—Prior to this standard, permanent and term endowments, including permanent funds, reported land and other real estate held as investments at their historical cost. This statement requires that endowments report their land and other real estate investments at fair value. Changes in fair value should be reported as investment income.

Example

The City of Towson recently received an endowment consisting of $1,000,000 of cash and securities. The endowment agreement specified that the net earnings on the endowment were to be used to support after-school recreational activities in the city parks. During the year, the endowment received $45,000 of interest revenue and paid $2,000 in investment management fees. Expenditures totaling $20,000 were made for the purposes designated in the endowment agreement.

Entry to Record Receipt of Endowment Principal

Note: The permanent fund is the appropriate fund in which to record the endowment as a provision of recreational activities is a governmental function that benefits the citizenry in general.

Permanent Fund:

Cash/Securities	1,0000,000	
Revenue		1,0000,000

Entry to Record Receipt of Interest Revenue

Permanent Fund:

Cash	45,000	
Revenue—Interest		45,000

Entry to Record Payment of Investment Management Fees

Permanent funds can make expenditures necessary to maintain and manage the endowment principal.

Permanent Fund:

Expenditures—Investment Management	2,000	
Cash		2,000

Entry to Record Transfer of Net Expendable Earnings to an Expendable Fund

In this case, we assume a special revenue fund.

Permanent Fund:

Other Financing Uses—Transfer Out	43,000	
Cash		43,000

Special Revenue Fund:

Cash	43,000	
Other Financing Sources		43,000

Entry to Record Expenditure for the Purpose of the Endowment

Special Revenue Fund:

Expenditures	20,000	
Cash		20,000

Proprietary Funds

This lesson describes the financial reporting for proprietary funds.

After studying this lesson, you should be able to:

1. List the two types of proprietary funds and describe the purpose of each.

2. List the three types of financial statements for proprietary funds.

3. Explain the difference in the primary service user and fee pricing policies for internal service funds and enterprise funds.

4. List the four sections of the Statement of Cash Flows for proprietary funds.

Tip

Remember the acronym **DRIP-CEG-PIPPA**—(**DRIP**): **D**ebt service funds, special **R**evenue funds, **I**nternal service funds, **P**ermanent funds; (**CEG**): **C**apital projects funds, **E**nterprise funds, **G**eneral fund; (**PIPPA**): **P**ension trust funds, **I**nvestment trust funds, **P**rivate **P**urpose trust funds, **A**gency funds—a mnemonic for remembering the eleven types of funds. Proprietary funds are the vowels, I and E, in **DRIP-CEG**.

I. **Internal Service Funds**

   A. **Characteristics**—These funds use full accrual accounting since they are concerned with measuring profit and maintaining capital. Therefore, they:

      1. Carry their own fixed assets and long-term debt

      2. Record depreciation expense

      3. Use standard accounting terminology (i.e., expenses, not expenditures, and net position, not fund balance)

   B. **Reporting in Government-Wide Financial Statements**—Internal service funds are not reported as part of business activities in the government-wide financial statements. Since internal service funds provide services primarily to the reporting government itself, the internal service fund accounts are primarily adjusted into the governmental activities of the government-wide financial statements. Moreover, an internal service fund can never be classified as a major fund for funds-level financial reporting and internal service fund account balances (e.g., total assets) are not used in determining major funds when applying the 10% and 5% rules.

   C. **Look to the customer**—GASB states that internal service funds should be only if the reporting government is the predominant customer in the activity, otherwise an enterprise fund should be used.

   D. **Financed**—Internal service funds are financed through charges to user departments (which are usually intended to recover at least 50% of operating costs) and contributions from the general fund. Although there are exceptions, the general **pricing policy** in establishing user fees for services and goods provided by internal service funds is to achieve breakeven of user fees compared to operating expenses.

   E. **Receive Transfers**—Internal service funds most often receive transfers from the General Fund to provide capital for the initial start-up of the fund or for later expansion. These transfers are reported as Transfers (In) by the internal service fund and as Other Financing Uses—Transfers (Out) by the General Fund. At year-end, the internal service fund will close this amount to its Net Position account.

F. Subsidized—Transfers from the general fund may also subsidize the day-to-day operations of the internal service fund. These transfers are reported as Transfers (In) by the internal service fund and as Other Financing Uses-Transfers (Out) by the general fund. At year-end, the internal service fund will close this amount to its Net Position account.

> **Note**
> *Under GASB Statement No. 33, no distinctions are made between Residual Equity Transfers (start-up funds- or funds transferred out when closing a fund) and Operating Transfers.*

👁 **Example**

ABC County maintains a motor pool to provide transportation for county administrators on official business. ABC follows a practice of subsidizing 30% of the operating costs of the motor pool from General Fund resources. During the current period, ABC transferred $36,000 to subsidize current operations and transferred another $80,000 to expand the motor pool by four vehicles. How should these transfers be reported?

General Fund

Other Financing Uses—Operating Transfer-Out	116,000	
Cash		116,000

Internal Service Fund

Cash	116,000	
Operating Transfer-In		116,000

G. Transactions—When the internal service fund charges fees to other departments for goods and services, the transactions are recorded just as they would be if the transaction was with an external business. That is, the internal service fund recognizes operating revenue and the recipient fund recognizes an expenditure (or expense, as appropriate for the fund). These transactions are called Quasi-External Transactions.

1. All charges for services (i.e., revenue) that would normally result in a debit to the Accounts Receivable account, are shown as amounts "Due from (fund name)."

Due from General Fund	XXX	
Billings to Departments (an Operating Revenue)		XXX

2. Statement of Revenues, Expenses, and Changes in Fund Net Position distinguishes *operating revenues* (charges for goods and services) from *nonoperating revenues* (interest) from *operating transfers* (regular, recurring transfers from the general fund intended to subsidize operations and grants).

a. Earnings retained in an internal service fund and contributions to equity made by another fund (e.g., general fund) that are not to be repaid are closed to the equity account—Net Position—Unrestricted. Excess of Net Billings to Departments over Costs, if a gain, (or Excess of Costs over Net Billings to Departments, if a loss) is the account title typically used in closing temporary accounts at year's end (i.e., the income summary account name);

b. Monies from another fund (e.g., general fund) that are used for temporary financing needs and are expected to be repaid are accounted for by crediting "Advances from (fund name)," which is a liability account.

3. The equity section of the Balance Sheet has three principal accounts:

    a. Net Investment in Capital Assets (Note: If interfund loans and other debt exceed the internal service fund amount of capital assets net of accumulated depreciation, then there is no net investment in capital assets to report; i.e., only a positive net investment in capital assets is reported),

    b. Restricted Net Position—(Typically, internal service funds do not have assets restricted for use by external resource providers or legislative action; when that is the case restricted net position will not appear in the internal service fund Statement of Net Position),

    c. Unrestricted Net Position

    d. The general format for the Statement of Revenues, Expenses, and Changes in Fund Net Position is:

Operating Revenues (detailed)

Total Operating Revenues

Operating Expenses (detailed)

Total Operating Expenses

Operating Income (Loss)

Nonoperating Revenues, Expenses, Gains, Losses, and Transfers (detailed)

Change in Net Position

Net Position—Beginning of Period

Net Position—End of Period

---

    e. Generally, the Statement of Net Position follows the following format. (Note: Deferred outflows and deferred inflow of resources are not shown since they are unlikely for internal service funds):

Assets:

Current Assets (detailed)

Capital Assets (detailed)

Total Assets

Liabilities:

Current Liabilities (detailed)

Long-Term Liabilities

Total Liabilities

Net Position:

Net Investment in Capital Assets (a positive amount only)

Restricted (by external resource providers or legislative action)

Unrestricted

Total Net Position

---

4. The Statement of Cash Flows has four categories (as opposed to the three categories found in for-profit statements):

   a. **Operations**—From the production of goods and services only (i.e., operating income, not net income) using the **direct method**; this excludes items such as interest and operating transfers, Note: GASB requires a reconciliation of operating income to net cash provided by operating activities is required,

   b. **Noncapital financing**—from debtor activities not clearly related to capital transactions (e.g., operating grants),

   c. **Capital financing**—from the acquisition or disposal of capital assets or borrowing and repayment clearly related to capital activities, which can include advances from other funds for the purpose of financing capital acquisitions,

   d. **Investing**—from gains and losses on investments and creditor activities and interest (less likely for internal services funds than for enterprise funds).

H. Enterprise Funds

1. These funds account for entities that provide goods and services to the general public, such as urban transportation departments, swimming pools, electric and water utilities, airports, ports, government run hospitals, toll roads and bridges, parking lots, parking garages, public housing projects, state-run lotteries, and the like.

2. GASB requires activities to be reported as enterprise funds if any one of the following criteria in the context of the activity's principal revenues sources is met:

   a. The activity is financed with debt that is secured solely by a pledge of the net revenues from fees and charges of the activity (e.g., revenue bonds);

   b. Laws or regulations require that the activity's costs of providing services including capital costs be recovered with fees and changes, rather than with taxes or similar revenues; or

   c. The pricing policies of the activity establish fees and charges designed to recover the costs, including capital costs (such as depreciation or debt service).

3. **Restricted assets**—Enterprise funds, especially utilities, frequently have assets whose use is restricted by contractual or legal requirements. For example, refundable customer deposits held by a utility are classified as Cash under the Restricted Assets category in the utility's Statement of Net Position. Similarly, assets held for the retirement of revenue bonds as required by bond covenants are also classified under the Restricted Asset category. Another common restricted asset is assets set aside to fund capital acquisitions, replacements, and improvements **Liabilities payable from Restricted Assets**: liabilities Payable from Restricted Assets, such as Refundable Customer Deposits, are reported separately from Current Liabilities. The difference between Restricted Net Assets and Liabilities Payable from Restricted Net Assets is reported as **Restricted Net Position**.

   a. **Liabilities Payable from Restricted Assets**—Such as refundable customer deposits, are reported separately from Current Liabilities. The difference between Restricted Net Assets and Liabilities Payable from Restricted Net Assets is reported as **Restricted Net Position**.

4. **Utility plant and construction work in process**—It is common for utility enterprise funds to report utility plant assets and construction work in process in the Statement of Net Position. Net utility plant less related debt is reported in **Net Position as Net Investment in Capital Assets**.

5. **Customer Advances for Construction**—It is common practice for utilities to require its customers to advance a portion of the estimated cost of construction projects that occur at the request of the customers. These advances are reported as a separate item under liabilities. The amount of the advance refunded to the customer, either wholly or partially, is usually applied against billings for service (i.e., a reduction in account receivable). The balance of customer advances not refunded (retained by the utility) is reported as

Contributions from Customers in the statement of revenues, expenses, and changes in fund net position.

6. **Long-term liabilities**—Bonds secured by an enterprise fund's revenues are a common form of long-term debt. However, some bonds also are secured either in part of wholly by the government's full faith and credit. If the intent is to service the bonds from enterprise fund's revenues GASB standards require the bonds to be reported as a liability of the enterprise fund.

7. The general format of a utility enterprise fund statement of net position is:

Assets:

Current Assets

Restricted Assets

Utility Plant

Other Noncurrent Assets

Total Assets

Liabilities:

Current Liabilities

Liabilities Payable from Restricted Assets

Long-Term Liabilities

Total Liabilities

Net Position:

Net Investment in Capital Assets

Restricted

Unrestricted

Total Net Position

Note

GASB Statement No. 62, *Codification of Accounting and Financial Reporting Guidance Contain in Pre-November 30, 1989 FASB and AICPA Pronouncements*, incorporates into the GASB codification guidance that was found in FASB and AICPA pronouncements. The change was necessary because the FASB Accounting Standards Codification, which supersedes the previous FASB pronouncements, would no longer be readily available to some GASB constituents. Through the issuance of GASBS Statement No. 62, that guidance is now readily available within the GASB codification. In addition, GASBS Statement No. 62 eliminated an election for enterprise funds and business-type activities to apply post-November 30, 1989 FASB Statements and Interpretations that do not conflict with or contradict GASB pronouncements. (November 30, 1989 was the date that the Financial Accounting Foundation reaffirmed GASB as the standard-setting body for governmental entities.)

Fiduciary Funds

This lesson describes the financial reporting for fiduciary funds.

After studying this lesson, you should be able to:

1. List the four types of fiduciary funds and describe the purpose of each.

2. Describe the fund-level financial statements required for each type of fiduciary fund.

3. Understand the difference between single employer and multiple-employer pension plans.

> **Tip**
> Remember the acronym **DRIP-CEG-PIPPA—(DRIP): D**ebt service funds, special **R**evenue funds, **I**nternal service funds, **P**ermanent funds; **(CEG): C**apital projects funds, **E**nterprise funds, **G**eneral fund; **(PIPPA): P**ension trust funds, **I**nvestment trust funds, **P**rivate **P**urpose trust funds, **A**gency funds—a mnemonic for remembering the eleven types of funds. Fiduciary Funds are **PIPPA**.

I. **Agency Funds**

  A. **Overview of Agency Fund Transactions**—Governmental entities frequently act as intermediaries in the process of disbursing monies from one governmental entity to another. For example, in a federal program designed to distribute monies to cities across the country, it is common for the federal program to disburse money to the states, which are required to disburse the money to the counties within the state, which are in turn required to disburse the monies to the cities within the counties. When the intermediate entities make these disbursements according to predetermined instructions or a formula, with little or no judgment required, they are acting as agents and appropriately account for the transactions in an agency fund.

   1. Since the governmental entity has no claim on these resources, but merely acts as a cash conduit, it does not recognize revenues when it receives the monies or recognize expenses when it disburses the monies.

      a. Instead, it recognizes a liability when the monies are received and a reduction in liabilities when the monies are disbursed.

      b. Because the assets (usually cash) recorded in an agency fund are always fully offset by a related liability, agency funds do not have a net position: Assets minus liabilities always equals zero.

> **Example**
> On July 13, Markson County received $800,000 from the state that is to be distributed to the school districts within the county in proportion to the number of students in each district. On July 22, Markson distributed $250,000 to the Peabody School District, $150,000 to Jim Pierce School District, and $400,000 to Central School District. Prepare the entries to record the receipt of the monies from the state and the disbursement of the monies to school districts:
>
> **Agency Fund**
>
> DR: Cash   800,000
>
>   CR: Due to School Districts   800,000
>
> To record receipt of monies payable to the school districts
>
> DR: Due to School Districts   800,000
>
>   CR: Cash   800,000
>
> To record distribution of monies to the school districts

2. **Financial reporting for agency funds**—Agency funds, like all fiduciary funds, use full accrual basis accounting. Technically, also like all fiduciary funds, agency funds prepare a Statement of Net Position and a Statement of Changes in Net Position. However, since agency fund assets are always completely offset by liabilities, they do not report Net Position (Assets – Liabilities = 0).

   a. Because agency funds do not report any Net Position, they cannot have any changes in Net Position and consequently do not prepare a Statement of Changes in Net Position.

B. **Tax Agency Funds**—When several governmental entities have taxing authority over a single piece of property, the governmental entities typically work together to send out a single bill to the taxpayer. The taxpayer returns a single payment to one of the taxing entities (the *collecting entity*, which is typically a county or parish), which in turn disburses the appropriate amount to each of the other taxing entities. These transactions are recorded in a tax agency fund.

   1. **Five entries are commonly made in the tax agency fund**

      a. **Recognizing the tax levy**—Each taxing entity records its portion of the tax levy in its general fund (or other governmental fund, as appropriate). The gross amount of the total levy across all taxing entities is recorded in the tax agency fund by debiting a receivable account and crediting a generic liability account (e.g., Due to Other Governments).

> **Example**
> The Brower County tax agency fund has been established to account for the collection and distribution of the county's and the City of Thurman's property taxes. The tax levies for the year were $600,000 for the County and $400,000 for the City. It is expected that the uncollectible taxes will be $15,000 for the County and $10,000 for the City.
>
> **Agency Fund:**
>
> DR: Taxes Receivable for Other Governments   1,000,000
>
>   CR: Due to Other Governments   1,000,000
>
> To record levy of taxes (note that the full amount of the levy is recognized: *the estimated uncollectible is ignored*).

b. **Recording payments**—When tax payments are received, the collecting entity recognizes the receipt of cash in the tax agency fund and reduces the outstanding Taxes Receivable.

Example
The previous example is continued. The county received $540,000 of tax payments.

Agency Fund

DR: Cash	540,000	
CR: Taxes Receivable for Other Governments		540,000

To record receipt of $540,000 of tax payments

c. **Recognizing amounts payable to specific taxing entities**—When tax payments are received, the collecting entity determines the amounts due to each of the taxing entities according to tax rate schedules. The amount payable to each entity is recognized by creating a specific liability account for each entity and reduces the generic liability account.

Example
The previous example is again continued. After reviewing the relevant tax rate documents, the county determined that $300,000 of the total $540,000 of tax payments belonged to the county and the remaining $240,000 belonged to the city.

Tax Agency Fund

DR: Due to Other Governments	540,000	
CR: Due to Brower County General Fund		300,000
CR: Due to City of Thurman		240,000

To recognize amounts due to specific taxing entities

d. **Recognizing processing fees**—It is usual for the collecting entity to charge a small fee, usually a percentage of the amount collected, to the other taxing entities. The fee is recognized in the agency fund by reducing the amounts owed to the other taxing entities and increasing the amount owed to the collecting entity. Note that revenue and expenses related to this transaction are not recognized in the agency fund: The individual taxing entities will recognize revenue or expense when the monies are distributed.

Example
Suppose that, in the previous example, the county charged a 1% fee to the city to cover the administrative costs associated with collecting and disbursing the property taxes. The processing fee associated with the $240,000 of taxes due to the City of Thurman is $2,400 and is recognized by reducing the amount due to the City of Thurman and increasing the amount due to Brower County.

Agency Fund

DR: Due to City of Thurman	2,400	
CR: Due to Brower County General Fund		2,400

e. **Disbursing the cash payments**—Periodically (once a week, once a month), the collecting entity disburses the collections to the taxing entities. This is recorded in the agency fund by simply crediting cash and debiting the appropriate liability accounts.

Example
The previous example is completed. At the end of the week, the county disburses the tax payments to its general fund and to the City of Thurmond General Fund in accordance with the individual entity liability accounts.

Agency Fund

DR: Due to City of Thurman ($240,000 − $2,400)   237,600

DR: Due to Brower County General Fund   302,400
($300,000 + $2,400)

    CR: Cash   540,000

To disburse tax collections to taxing entities

2. When the taxing entity receives payment for the taxes collected on its behalf, it reduces its Property Tax Receivable account and increases its Cash account. To the extent that there is a difference between the amount of taxes actually collected and the amount disbursed to the taxing entity, the taxing entity recognizes revenues or expenditures for the difference.

Example
In the previous example, Brower County received $302,400, which represented the tax payments collected on its behalf plus a processing fee paid by the City of Thurman. The City of Thurman received $237,600, which consisted of the tax payments collected on its behalf less the processing fee paid to Brower County. Each entity records the receipt of the payment in its general fund as shown next.

Brower County General Fund

DR: Cash   302,400

    CR: Property Taxes Receivable—Current   300,000

    CR: Revenue—Processing Fee   2,400

To record receipt of tax payments and processing fee

City of Thurman General Fund

DR: Cash   237,600

DR: Expenditures—Processing Fee   2,400

    CR: Property Taxes Receivable—Current   240,000

To record receipt of tax payments and payment of processing fee

C. **Special Assessment Agency Funds**—Special assessment projects are often financed with debt issues. Though the debt is to be repaid from special assessments levied on the property owners, the governmental entity usually assumes secondary liability for the debt in the event that the property owners default on their payments. Under these circumstances, the levy of the special assessment and the payments to the bondholders are accounted for in a debt service fund and the special assessment debt is included with other general long-term debt.

1. Sometimes, however, the governmental entity does not assume secondary liability for the debt and merely acts as an agent for the bondholders by collecting the special assessment levy from the property owners and remitting payments for interest and principal to the bondholders. In these cases, the levy of the special assessment and the payments to the bondholders are accounted for in an agency fund and the special assessment debt is not reported with other general long-term debt.

   a. **Five entries are commonly made in the special assessment agency fund**

      i. **Levy of the special assessment**—After the project is completed, the special assessment is levied. The full amount of the special assessment is recorded at this time, although it is split into a current and a deferred portion. The debit for the special assessments receivable is recorded just as it would be in a debt service fund. However, instead of crediting revenues, the offsetting credit is to a liability account (usually titled Due to Bondholders).

Example

Mill City recently completed a street improvement project that was to be paid for in part by a special assessment of $800,000 levied on the property owners who benefited from the improvements. The special assessment is payable over 10 years, with $80,000 of the assessment becoming current each year. $800,000 of special assessment bonds, which were not secondarily backed by the city, were issued to cover the construction costs. Interest expense and principal repayments on the bonds are to be paid from the special assessment collections. The entry to record the levy of the special assessment is as follows (Note that the actual liability for the bonds is not recorded as the city does not assume any liability for the bonds but merely acts as an agent in remitting payments to the bondholders.)

Special Assessment Agency Fund

DR:	Special Assessments Receivable—Current	80,000	
DR:	Special Assessments Receivable—Deferred	720,000	
	CR: Due to Bondholders		800,000

To record levy of the special assessment

ii. **Receipt of payments from the property owners**—In general, the entry to record payment of the currently due portion of the special assessment is straightforward: Debit Cash and credit Special Assessments Receivable for the amount of the payment. Sometimes, however, the payment may also include interest and penalties for late payment. If the additional amounts have not been accrued (as is usually the case), these amounts are simply shown as being "due to the bondholders."

Example

Mill City received $78,000 in special assessment collections. This amount represented payment of $77,000 of currently due special assessment receivables and $1,000 in interest and penalties associated with assessments that were not paid on a timely basis. (The interest and penalties have not been recorded as receivables.)

Special Assessment Agency Fund

DR:	Cash	78,000	
	CR: Special Assessments Receivable—Current		77,000
	CR: Due to Bondholders		1,000

To payment of special assessments

iii. **Payment of interest and principal to bondholders**—The payment of interest and any currently due portions of principal to the bondholders is recorded by decreasing cash and decreasing the liability account Due to Bondholders by a corresponding amount. No expense is recognized.

Example

At the end of the year, interest of $32,000 was due to the bondholders. In addition, $40,000 of the bond principal matured at the end of the year. The entry to record this payment to the bondholders is shown next.

Special Assessment Agency Fund

DR: Due to Bondholders   72,000

    CR: Cash   72,000

To payment of interest and principal to bondholders

II. Investment Trust Funds

A. **Overview of Investment Trust Fund Transactions**—In order to maximize earnings on their investments, governmental entities frequently *pool* or commingle idle cash from many funds into a single Pooled Investment account. Some governments also permit external governmental entities to contribute monies to the investment pool, especially if the external entities lack sufficient size and/or the expertise to manage efficiently their investments themselves. When an investment pool includes external participants, GASB requires the use of an investment trust fund to record and report the interests of the external participants.

1. **Valuation of the investment pool assets**—Securities held by the investment pool are reported at fair value. The pool is revalued whenever investment income is distributed to the participants and whenever a participating entity adds to or withdraws resources from the pool.

    a. Because of this, investment income is typically distributed to participants on a monthly or quarterly basis and participants can change their investment in the pool only at these points in time.

2. **Distribution of investment income**—Interest, dividends, and realized and unrealized gains and losses on investments are distributed to participants in the pool based on their proportionate share of the investment.

    a. Income-sharing ratios are established whenever participants add to or withdraw resources from the pool. However, distribution of income does not change the income-sharing ratio since the income is distributed to all participants proportionately.

3. **Reporting participation of external entities**—The net interest of external entities participating in the investment pool is reported as Net Position of Investment Trust Fund.

    a. Each external entity has a separate Net Position account, which is typically listed as Net Position Held in Trust for XXXXX.

    b. Investment pool resources related to internal participants are shown as a liability in the Investment Trust Fund. See the following illustration.

Statement of Net Position Investment Trust Fund

Assets		Liabilities	
Cash	$ 1,000,000	Due to General Fund	$ 10,000,000
Investments	19,000,000	Due to Capital Projects Fund	5,000,000
Total Assets	$20,000,000	*Total Liabilities*	*$15,000,000*
		Net Position	
		Held in Trust for City X	$ 3,000,000
		Held in Trust for School District	2,000,000
		Total Net Position	*$5,000,000*
		Total Liabilities and Net Position	*$20,000,000*

4. **Reporting changes in investment**—Changes in a participant's investment in the investment pool arise from three principal sources:

   a. Contribution of resources to the investment pool—This may be the initial contribution of a new participant or an additional contribution from a current participant.

   b. Withdrawal of resources from the investment pool—The withdrawal may be a partial or complete withdrawal.

   c. Net investment earnings (here used in the broadest sense to include realized and unrealized gains and losses on the investment assets, interest revenue, and dividends) Net of any management fees and transaction costs.

   d. Although the investment trust fund, like the other fiduciary funds, uses full accrual basis accounting rules to recognize revenues and expenses, because these resources do not belong to the governmental entity, they are reported on the financial statements as Additions and Deductions, respectively.

     i. Common items listed under Additions include Contributions and Investment Earnings.

     ii. Common items listed under Deductions include Withdrawals and Management Fees.

   e. Only increases and decreases in the investment assets of external pool participants are reported in the investment trust fund's statements. The internal pool participants report increases and decreases in their respective funds.

Statement of Changes in Net Position Investment Trust Fund

Additions:

Investment Earnings	$ 300,000
Contributions	50,000
Total additions:	350,000

Deductions:

Withdrawals	100,000
Total withdrawals:	100,000
Change in Net Position	$ 250,000
Beginning Net Position	4,750,000
Ending Net Position	$5,000,000

Note

The following entries are provided to add depth to your understanding of the purpose and use of investment trust funds. However, the entries themselves are rarely tested on the CPA Exam.

B. **Recognition and Distribution of Investment Income**—Although most investment pools distribute income to participants periodically, investment income, such as interest revenue, dividends, and the like, accrues on a continuous basis. Therefore, as income accrues, it is first recorded in a holding account and then later distributed to the pool participants. Changes in the fair value of the pool investments are handled in a similar manner.

1. **Common entries in investment trust funds**—There are four principal entries in investment trust funds.

    a. **Entry to record investment income**—When investment income is received or accrues, the appropriate asset account is debited and a holding account titled Undistributed Earnings on Pooled Investments is credited.

Example

During the quarter, the Investment Pool for Grimes County received dividends totaling $50,000 and interest totaling $120,000. At the end of the quarter, an additional $30,000 in interest had accrued. The income is placed in the holding account to await distribution as shown next.

Investment Trust Fund

DR:	Cash	170,000	
DR:	Interest Receivable	30,000	
	CR: Undistributed Earnings on Pooled Investments		200,000

To record investment income for the quarter

b. **Entry to record sale of securities**—When securities are sold, the gain or loss on the sale is placed in a holding account until the end of the period. See the following example.

Example
During the quarter, the securities costing $500,000 were sold for $450,000, resulting in a realized loss of $50,000. The entry to record the sale is shown next.

Investment Trust Fund

DR:	Cash	450,000	
DR:	Undistributed Change in Fair Value of Pooled Investments	50,000	
	CR: Investments		500,000

To record sale of securities at a loss

c. **Entry to record revaluation of the portfolio**—Whenever income is scheduled to be distributed to the pool participants or when participants add or withdraw resources from the investment pool, the fair value of the investment pool is determined and the change in fair value is calculated. This unrealized gain or loss is combined in the holding account with the realized gains and losses on the sale of securities for distribution to the pool participants.

Example
At the end of the quarter, the fair value of the securities held in the investment pool was $19,350,000. The book value of the investments at the end of the quarter was $18,500,000, resulting in an unrealized gain of $850,000. This gain is recorded as shown next.

Investment Trust Fund

DR:	Investments	850,000	
	CR: Undistributed Change in Fair Value of Pooled Investments		850,000

To record change in fair value of the investment portfolio

d. **Entry to record distribution of investment earnings to pool participants**—Both the Undistributed Earnings on Pooled Investments and the Undistributed Change in Fair Value of Pooled Investments are periodically distributed to the pool participants in accordance with their proportionate interest in the investment pool. Since distributions to external participants increase the net position of the investment trust fund, they are recorded as revenues (additions) to the investment trust fund. Distributions to internal participants, however, simply increase the liability to the internal participants recorded in the investment trust fund: The internal participants will report the revenue in their fund statements.

> **Example**
>
> At the end of the quarter, the investment earnings and change in the fair value of the investment portfolio are distributed to the participants in proportion to their interest in the pooled investment. The internal and external participants interests are:
>
> | Internal Participants | | Proportionate Interest |
> |---|---|---|
> | General Fund | $ 10,000,000 | 50% |
> | Capital Projects Fund | 5,000,000 | 25% |
>
> | External Participants | | |
> |---|---|---|
> | City X | $ 3,000,000 | 15% |
> | School District | 2,000,000 | 10% |
> | Total Interest in Investment Pool | $20,000,000 | 100% |
>
> The balance in the Undistributed Earnings on Pooled Investments account of $200,000 and the balance in the Undistributed Change in Fair Value of Pooled Investments account of $800,000 are distributed as shown next.
>
> **Investment Trust Fund**
>
> | | | | |
> |---|---|---|---|
> | DR: | Undistributed Earnings on Pooled Investments | 200,000 | |
> | | CR: Due to General Fund (50% × $200,000) | | 100,000 |
> | | CR: Due to Capital Projects Fund (25% × $200,000) | | 50,000 |
> | | CR: Additions—Investment Income (10% + 15%) × $200,000) | | 50,000 |
>
> To distribute investment earnings to investment pool participants
>
> **Investment Trust Fund**
>
> | | | | |
> |---|---|---|---|
> | DR: | Undistributed Change in Fair Value of Pooled Investments | 800,000 | |
> | | CR: Due to General Fund (50% × $800,000) | | 400,000 |
> | | CR: Due to Capital Projects Fund (25% × $800,000) | | 200,000 |
> | | CR: Additions—Investment Income (10% + 15%) × $800,000) | | 200,000 |
>
> To distribute realized and unrealized gains and losses on investments to participants

2. **Recognition of investment earnings of internal participants**—Internal participants are notified when investment earnings are distributed to investment pool participants. Each internal participant makes an entry to recognize revenue in the appropriate fund and increases their Pooled Investment account to reflect the increase in the investment trust fund.

Example
The investment trust fund notifies the internal participants of their earnings. Each fund makes an appropriate entry in their fund accounts, as shown.

General Fund

DR: Pooled Investments ($100,000 + $400,000) 500,000

CR: Investment Revenue 500,000

To record quarterly earnings on pooled investments

Capital Projects Fund

DR: Pooled Investments ($50,000 + $200,000) 250,000

CR: Investment Revenue 250,000

To record quarterly earnings on pooled investments

III. **Pension Trust Funds and Other Postemployment Benefit Plan (OPEB) Trust Funds**

  A. **Overview of Pension Plans**—Pension plans are categorized in several different ways.

    1. **Defined contribution versus defined benefit plans**—There are two broad types of pension plans: **defined contribution** plans and **defined benefit** plans. In defined contribution plans, the employer and the employee make contributions to the plan, which are invested and earn a return. Upon retirement, the employee is entitled to the total contributions made on his or her behalf plus the accumulated earnings on those contributions, whatever they may be. Thus, while the *contributions* to these funds are defined, the *benefits* are determined by the performance of the invested assets. Because plan benefits are based on existing resources, *no actuarial calculations are necessary* to determine the plan liability or the required contribution to the plan. In **defined benefit plans**, the employer promises the retiree a defined future benefit over a future time period and the employer bears the risk associated with unknown future economic factors.

      a. Defined benefit plans specify, in relative terms, the future benefits that the plan will pay out (e.g., two-thirds of the average annual salary during the last three years of employment). Actuarial calculations are necessary to establish the present dollar value of these benefits and to determine the annual contribution necessary in order to have sufficient resources available to pay retirement benefits.

    2. **Single employer plans versus multiple employer plans**—*Single-employer* plans are exactly what they say. They are individual plans set up by an individual governmental employer to cover a specified class or classes of employees. A single-employer plan, however, does not necessarily mean single-*plan*. Many governmental entities offer several different pension plans to different classes of employees (e.g., one plan for public safety personnel and another plan for administrative personnel). A governmental entity may offer several different single-employer plans.

      a. Sometimes, in an effort to provide better-quality, lower-cost plans to their employees, smaller employers band together and jointly create a retirement plan that covers all of their employees. These plans are known as *multiple-employer plans*. States frequently provide a plan that is available to all the employees of any governmental entity within its jurisdiction. These plans are known as Public Employee Retirement Systems (PERS). There are two types of multiple-employer plans.

        i. Agent multiple-employer plans pool the administrative and investment functions for multiple employers to reduce overhead but each individual employer plan assets maintained in separate accounts to pay benefits to only its plan members.

ii. Cost-sharing multiple-employer plans pool the assets and obligations of all participating employers and use plan assets to pay benefits to any participating plan members.

B. Reporting for Pension Trust Funds—GASB Statement No. 67 establishes reporting requirements for defined benefit pension trust funds. Two financial statements are required: (1) Statement of Fiduciary Net Position and (2) Statement of Changes in Fiduciary Net Position. All of the amounts presented in the pension trust fund statements are in nominal (actual) dollar amount: *No actuarial amounts are presented*.

1. **Statement of fiduciary net position**—This statement is required for all types of pension plans. The most distinctive feature of the statement is the title of the net position section: Net Position Held in Trust for Pension Benefits.

Statement of Fiduciary Net Position

Pension Trust Fund

Assets

Cash	$ 15,000,000
Interest Receivable	500,000
Investments	54,500,000
Total Assets	*70,000,000*

Deferred Outflows of Resources

Liabilities

Accounts Payable	$ 500,000
Annuities Payable	1,500,000
Total Liabilities	*$ 2,000,000*

Deferred Inflows of Resources

Net Position Held in Trust for Pension Benefits $68,000,000

2. **Statement of changes in fiduciary net position**—This statement is also prepared for both defined contribution and defined benefit plans. Note that the statement presents *Additions* and *Deductions* rather than Revenues and Expenses. This terminology reflects the fact that these resources do not belong to the governmental entity and so cannot generate revenues and expenses for the governmental entity.

a. Additions (revenues) and Deductions (expenses) are recognized on the full accrual basis.

b. The principal Additions (revenues) recognized in the pension trust fund consist of:

i. Contributions to the plan from the employee

ii. Contributions to the plan from the employer

iii. Investment earnings

Exam Tip
Some CPA Exam questions still ask about the amount of Revenue or Expense recognized in Fiduciary Funds. Although GASB now requires Fiduciary Funds to *report* Additions and Deductions in their financial statements, it is permissible to *record* Revenues and Expenses in the fund and simply convert them to Additions and Deductions for reporting purposes. Consequently, questions that ask about Revenue or Expense recognition in the funds can be answered without undue concern about the terminology used in the question.

Statement of Changes in Fiduciary Net Position

Pension Trust Fund

Additions:

Contributions:

Employer	$ 1,200,000
Employee	800,000
Total Contributions:	2,000,000

Investment Income:

Interest and dividends	1,800,000
Net increase in fair value of investments	400,000
Total Investment Income:	2,200,000
Total additions	*4,200,000*

Deductions:

Retirement annuities	1,400,000
Disability benefits	400,000
Refunds to terminated employees	200,000
Administrative expenses	300,000
Total deductions	*2,300,000*

Net Increase 1,900,000

Net Position Held in Trust for Pension Benefits:

Beginning of year 66,100,000

End of year $68,000,000

c. The principal Deductions (expenses) recognized in the pension trust fund consist of payments to retirees, refunds to terminated employees, and investment management fees.

    i.   Required supplementary information (RSI)

        (a)   All plans:

            (i)   Plan description

            (ii)   Investment policies

            (iii)   Receivables

            (iv)   Allocated insurance contracts

            (v)   Reserves

            (vi)   Deferred Retirement Option Program (DROP)

            (vii)   10-year schedule of Actuarially Determined Contributions

        (b)   Single-employer and cost-sharing multiple employer plans:

            (i)   Components of net pension liability

            (ii)   Significant assumptions

            (iii)   Actuarial valuation date

            (iv)   10-year schedule of changes in net pension liability

            (v)   10-year schedule of Net Pension Liability

            (vi)   10-year schedule of Money-Weighted Rates of Return

C.   **Accounting for Pension Trust Funds**—The transactions accounted for in pension trust funds are straightforward. The funds follow full accrual basis accounting rules when recognizing Revenues (Additions) and Expenses (Deductions) and adjust their investments to reflect market value at the end of the period. Questions on the CPA Exam usually ask only whether a particular item can be recognized as a Revenue (Addition) or an Expense (Deduction) in the fund.

> **Note**
> GASB Statement No. 68 provides new standards for accounting and financial reporting for pensions that apply to most governments that provide their employees with pension benefits. Together with GASB Statement No. 67, GASB Statement No. 68 represents a significant shift from the ***fund-based*** approach used in the past to an ***accounting-based*** approach. GASB 68 is effective for fiscal years beginning after June 15, 2014.

D.   **Annual Pension Expense**—Annual pension expense includes the following items:

Benefits earned during the year

   + Interest on the total pension liability

+/– Changes in benefit terms

   – Projected earnings on plan investments

+/– Changes in plan net position from other than investments

Changes in plan net position from other than investments: Differences between projected and actual earnings on plan investments are initially recognized as deferred outflows or resources or deferred inflows of resources and will be amortized to pension expense over a five-year period. Differences in some assumptions used to develop the projected total future pension benefit are initially recognized as deferred outflows or resources or deferred inflows of resources and will be amortized over the average remaining service period of all employees in the plan (active and inactive). (Prior to GASB Statement No. 68 this difference was amortized in a period up to 30 years. Be on guard for a question that includes a 30-year amortization answer—this is a trick answer!) The unamortized amounts are reported in the balance sheet as either a deferred outflow of resources, if the difference is unfavorable, or as a deferred inflow of resources, if the difference is favorable.

1. **Pension liability**—For **single-employers** and **agent employers** is the net pension liability calculated as the difference between the employer's total pension liability less the amount of plan assets as indicated by the net position of the plan. For cost-sharing employers the net pension liability is its proportionate share of the cumulate net pension liability in the cost-sharing plan. Measuring total pension liability is a three-step process:

   a. **Projection of the future benefit payments**—For current and inactive employees including projected salary increases, service credits, automatic cost-of-living adjustments (COLA), and other automatic benefit changes.

   b. **Discount rate**—This is used to determine the present value of the projected future benefit payments. The rate is based on the long-term expected rate of return on plan investments to the extent that plan assets are available to meet the pension liability; thereafter, a tax-exempt, high-quality (an average rating of AA/As or higher) 20-year municipal bond index rate would be incorporated into the measurement of a blended **discount rate** (in effect the premise is that the government would issue bonds to meet the pension obligation remaining after plan assets are exhausted).

   c. **Attributing the present value to specific time periods**—After the projected benefit payments have been discounted they are allocated to past, current, and future time periods. Total pension liability represents the portion that is attributed to each employee's past and current periods of service. GASB Statement No. 68 requires employers to use the entry age actuarial cost method applied as a level percentage of payroll.

2. **Actuarial valuations**—Should be performed at least biennially. If a valuation is not prepared as of the measurement date, the total pension liability will be based on a roll forward of information from an earlier actuarial valuation to the measurement date (the earlier valuation should be no more than 24 months earlier than the pension plan's fiscal year-end).

Example

Planerville City maintains a single-employer, defined benefit pension plan for city employees and, as required by GASB, records transactions related to the plan assets in a Pension Trust Fund. The current balances in the Pension Trust Fund are as follows:

Account	DR	CR
Cash	35,000	
Interest Receivable	5,000	
Investments	530,000	
Pension Annuities Payable		10,000
Net Position Held in Trust—Pension Benefits		560,000

During the year, the following transactions occurred:

- Planerville contributed $30,000 to the pension plan on behalf of city employees. Contributions from the employees totaled $20,000.

- Interest of $18,000 and dividends of $4,000 were received in cash during the year ($5,000 of the interest had been previously accrued). Accrued interest at year's end totaled $7,000.

- Annuity payments to retirees during the year totaled $35,000, including the $10,000 that had been previously accrued. Accrued pensions payable at the end of the year totaled $15,000.

- Terminated employees requested and received refunds of their contributions totaling $5,000.
- Investment management fees of $8,000 were paid.

Pension Trust Fund

DR: Cash	50,000	
CR: Contributions—Employers		30,000
CR: Contributions—Employees		20,000

To record receipt of employer and employee contributions.

DR: Cash	22,000	
CR: Interest Receivable		5,000
CR: Additions (Revenue): Investment Income		17,000

To record receipt of investment income.

DR: Interest Receivable	7,000	
CR: Additions (Revenue): Investment Income		7,000

DR: Deductions (Expenses): Retirement Annuities	25,000	
DR: Pension Annuities Payable	10,000	
CR: Cash		35,000

To record payment of retirement annuities.

DR: Deductions (Expenses): Retirement Annuities	15,000	
CR: Pension Annuities Payable		15,000

To record accrual of retirement annuities.

DR: Deductions (Expenses): Refunds	5,000	
CR: Cash		5,000

To record payment of refunds to terminated employees.

DR: Deductions (Expenses): Management Fees	8,000	
CR: Cash		8,000

To record payment of refunds to terminated employees.

E. Supplemental Disclosures—Although the Pension Trust Fund accounts for pension assets only in nominal dollars, actuarial information must be disclosed in two required schedules by GASB Statement Nos. 67 and 68: the Schedule of Changes in Net Pension Liability (which replaced the Schedule of Funding Progress) and the Schedule of Employer Contributions (similar to what was required before GASB Statement Nos. 67 and 68). Both schedules are included in the Required Supplementary Information (RSI) section of the Comprehensive Annual Financial Report (CAFR).

1. **Schedule of Changes in Net Pension Liability**

   a. This is a 10-year schedule of changes in the net pension liability, presenting for each year; the beginning and ending balances of total pension liability, the pension plan's fiduciary net position, and net pension liability; service cost, interest on the total pension liability, changes in benefits terms, differences between expected and actual experience in measurement of the total pension liability, changes of assumptions or other inputs, contributions from the employer, contributions from nonemployer contributing entities, contributions from employees, pension plan net investment income, benefit payments, pension plan administration expense, and other changes.

   b. Two key ratios are also presented:

      (i) The **funded ratio**, which is the ratio of the plan fiduciary net position divided by total pension liability

      (ii) Net pension liability (asset) as a percentage of covered payroll.

      b. As required supplemental information (RSI) contributions to the actuarially determined contribution as a percentage of covered payroll is presented.

2. **Schedule of Employer Contributions**—This schedule presents the actuarially determined contribution, the amount actually contributed by the government, the difference between the two, and the percentage of the amount that was actually contributed to the actuarially determined contribution amount. A ratio of the amount of contribution recognized by the pension plan as a percentage of covered payroll is also presented. This schedule also presents information for a 10-year period.

Note

Prior to GASB 67 and 68, the actuarially determined contribution was termed as the "annual required contribution." With GASB Statement Nos. 67 and 68, GASB shifted the focus from a *funding-based approach* to an *accounting-based approach*. GASB stated that *funding* was a policy decision by the government. Hence, the change from annual required contribution to actuarially determined contribution reflects GASB's shift in philosophy regarding pensions.

3. **GASB Statement No. 78 Exclusion**—Excludes GASB Statement No. 68 requirements for pensions provided to employees of state or local governments through a cost-sharing multiple-employer defined benefit plan that (a) is not a state or local governmental pension plan, (b) is used to provided defined benefit pensions both to employees of state and local government employers and to employees of employers that are not state or local governments, and (c) has no predominant state or local governmental employer. In these situations, a government employer may not be able to obtain the measurements and other information needed to comply with the requirements of GASB Statement No. 68. Therefore, GASB Statement No. 78 excludes those government employers from the requirements of Statement No. 68 and prescribes recognition and measurement of pension expense, expenditures, liabilities, disclosures, and RSI for these pension plans.

   a. **Recognition and measurement in financial statements prepared using the economic resources measurement focus**—Pension expense equal to the employer's required contributions to the pension plan for the reporting period and a payable for unpaid required contributions at the end of the reporting period.

b. Recognition and measurement in financial statements prepared using the current financial resources measurement focus—Pension expenditures equal to the employer's required contributions to the pension plan for pay periods within the reporting period and a payable to the extent it is normally expected to be liquidated with expendable available resources.

c. Disclosures

    i. Description of the plan

    ii. Whether the pension plan issues a publicly available report

    iii. Description of benefits

    iv. Description of contribution requirements

    v. Information about employer's payables

d. Required supplemental information (RSI)—A 10-year schedule of the employer's required contributions.

F. Recognition of Pension Costs in the Employing Funds—The amount of pension costs actually recognized in the employing fund varies according to the basis of accounting used by the fund.

    1. Governmental funds—Governmental funds recognize pension cost on the modified accrual basis: Employers report the portion of the annual pension cost that has been or will be *funded with current resources of the governmental funds* as expenditures. This amount may be more or less than the current period's annual pension cost.

        a. Liability for any unfunded amount is not recorded in the fund but is maintained off-books by adding it to the Schedule of General Long-Term Debt.

Example

Largo County's offers a defined benefit pension plan to its employees. The annual pension cost for the fund for the current year is $100,000. However, the county was only able to contribute $50,000 to the pension plan. The county does not currently have plans to pay the additional $50,000 due to the pension plan.

DR:	Expenditures—Pension Cost	50,000	
	CR: Cash		50,000

To record pension cost.
(Note that no fund liability is accrued for the additional $50,000 that the county should have paid into the pension plan for the current year because the county has not yet committed resources to pay these costs.)

---

    2. Proprietary funds—When employees are paid using proprietary fund resources, the employer's pension contributions are recognized on the full accrual basis (i.e., whenever a fund liability is incurred. A fund liability is incurred whenever an enforceable claim is made against fund resources.

Example
The previous example is continued with the exception that the employees are paid using proprietary fund resources.

DR: Expenses—Pension Cost   100,000

    CR: Pension Liability   50,000

    CR: Cash   50,000

To record pension cost
(Note that the full actuarially calculated pension cost is recognized even though the county has not yet committed resources to pay these costs; this is because full accrual basis accounting requires recognition of the full actuarially calculated liability in the period that the employee services were rendered.)

G. **Other Postemployment Benefit Plan (OPEB) Trust Funds**—Fortunately with GASB Statement No. 74, on financial reporting by plans that administer OPEB benefits, and GASB Statement No. 75, on a government's accounting and financial reporting of OPEB benefits that it provides to its employees, GASB adopted approaches that are similar to those used for pensions under GASB Statement Nos. 67 and 68. The next table provides a summary.

	Pensions (GASB Statement Nos. 67 and 68)	**OPEB (GASB Statement Nos. 74 and 75)**
Total liability	Total pension liability	Total OPEB liability
Difference between total liability and plan fiduciary net position	Net pension liability	Net OPEB liability
Discount rate	Long-term expected rate of return on plan assets, if any, are expected to be available to make projected benefit payments and be invested using a strategy to achieve a return and a 20-year tax-exempt high quality general obligation municipal bond yield or index rate to the extent the plan assets are projected to be insufficient to cover projected benefits and administrative expenses	Same
Actuarial cost method	Entry age actuarial cost method with each period's service cost determined as a level percentage of pay	Same
Required supplementary information	Schedule of Changes in Net Pension Liability (ten years) Schedule of Employer Contributions (10 years)	Schedule of Changes in Net OPEB Liability (10 years) Schedule of Employer Contributions (10 years)

> **Note**
> Governments that fund OPEB on a "pay-as-you-go" approach will not have an OPEB Trust Fund and will report the Total OPEB Liability in their financial statements.

IV. Private Purpose Trust Funds

A. Resources Managed in Trust

> **Definition**
> *Private Purpose Trust Funds:* Funds used to account for any resources managed in trust by the governmental entity, where the beneficiaries are outside of the governmental entity itself. The beneficiaries may be individuals, private organizations or businesses, or other governmental entities.

1. Individual private purpose trusts may be either expendable or nonexpendable (e.g., endowments, where the principal must be retained and only the earnings may be expended).

2. Earnings from nonexpendable trust funds are often transferred to another fund for the actual disbursements to be made.

3. As with permanent Funds, capital gains and losses related to nonexpendable trusts are attributed to the principal unless specifically directed to attribute elsewhere.

4. Under GASBS Statement No. 52, land and other real estate held as investments are reported at fair value with the change in fair value for the period reported as investment income/loss.

Format and Content of Comprehensive Annual Financial Report (CAFR)

The Comprehensive Annual Financial Report

This lesson describes the components of the Comprehensive Annual Financial Report (CAFR) and the types of financial statements presented in it.

After studying this lesson, you should be able to:

1. List two government-wide financial statements and describe which fund types are included in the statements.

2. List the three main sections of the CAFR and the three items that make up the *basic financial statements*.

3. Describe items that require supplemental information (RSI).

I. Comprehensive Annual Financial Report (CAFR)

    A. Reporting Requirements—GASB specifies two levels of reporting for governmental entities: the General Purpose Financial Statements and the Comprehensive Annual Financial Report (CAFR).

        1. General Purpose Financial Statements (GPFS)—The General Purpose Financial Statements represent the minimum requirements for external reporting. The GPFS contain three principal components (all three components are discussed in more detail both below and in the GASBS Statement No. 34, *Basic Financial Statements-and Management's Discussion and Analysis-for State and Local Governments*, Reporting lesson):

            a. Management's discussion and analysis (MD&A)

            b. Basic financial statements

            c. Required supplementary information (RSI)

        2. Though the GPFS represent the minimum reporting requirements (sometimes phrased on the exam as the "minimum that can be separately released"), most medium to large governmental entities find it necessary to provide significantly more information in order to meet the needs of the users of the financial statements.

        3. Comprehensive Annual Financial Report (CAFR)—In order to meet the information needs of external users of the financial statements, most governmental entities produce a Comprehensive Annual Financial Report (CAFR), which is the equivalent of the annual report of a for-profit organization. GASB specifies the structure of the CAFR, which is broken up into three main sections. Each section contains several required elements:

            a. Introductory section

            b. Financial section

            c. Statistical section

> **Study Tip**
> The items included in each of the sections of the CAFR are frequently tested on the CPA Exam.

CAFR Structure

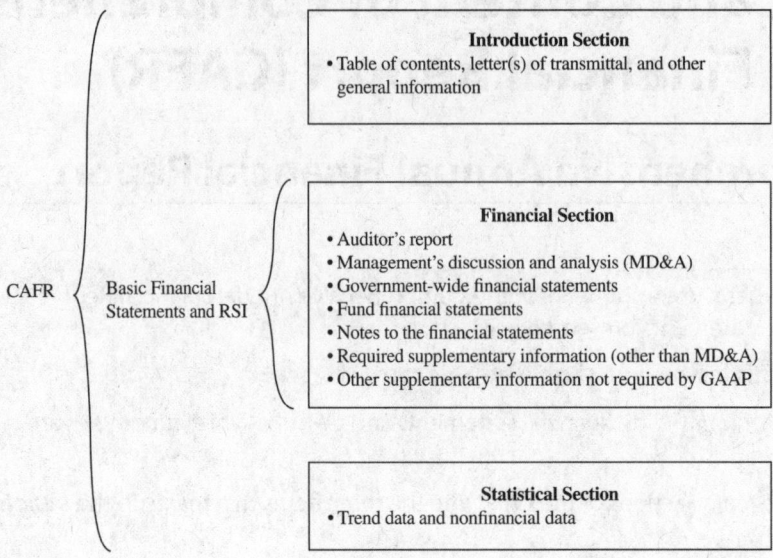

B. CAFR—Financial Section—In addition to the required financial statements, the Financial section includes explanatory text and a number of supporting schedules. The following items are included in the Financial section:

1. **Auditor's Report**—This is the first item presented in the section and, in addition to providing the auditor's opinion on the fairness of the statements, specifies the scope of the audit.

   a. The Basic Financial Statements are always covered by the auditor's opinion but the accompanying information in the management's discussion and analysis (MD&A), the required supplementary information, the combining statements, and other schedules, is **not** usually audited.

2. **Management's discussion and analysis (MD&A)**—The purpose of the MD&A is to help the user assess the overall financial condition of the governmental entity and determine whether the government's position has improved or deteriorated during the period. MD&A should compare current year results to prior year results with an emphasis on the current year.

   a. The analysis of the MD&A is based on currently known facts and conditions. In its evaluations, forecasts or subjective information are not permitted.

   b. The information presented typically includes an analysis of balances and transactions in individual funds, descriptions of capital asset and long-term debt activity during the year, and an analysis of balances and transactions of individual funds.

3. **Basic financial statements**—Basic financial statements consist of three separate items:

   a. Government-Wide Statements

   b. Fund Statements

   c. Notes to the Financial Statements

4. **Government-Wide statements**—These statements present information for the government as a whole and are presented on a full accrual basis. Two statements are required:

Note
GASB Statement No. 63 replaced *"net assets"* with the term *"net position"* for Government-Wide Financial Statements, Proprietary Fund Financial Statements, and Fiduciary Fund Financial Statements. Governmental Fund Financial Statements report fund balances rather than Net Position.

    a. Government-Wide Statement of Net Position

    b. Government-Wide Statement of Activities

    c. Government-Wide Statements include financial data from the governmental and proprietary funds only. Fiduciary fund financial data is **not** included in these statements.

5. **Fund Statements**—Information from each of the three fund categories is presented using its native accounting basis. Each fund category has a unique set of required statements.

    a. Governmental fund category—These statements are produced using modified accrual basis accounting.

        i. Balance Sheet (five categories of fund balance)

        ii. Statement of Revenues, **Expenditures**, and Changes in **Fund Balance**

    b. Proprietary fund category—These statements are produced using full accrual basis accounting.

        i. Statement of Net Position (three categories of net position)

        ii. Statement of Revenues, **Expenses**, and Changes in **Net Position**

        iii. Statement of Cash Flows (four categories of cash flows)

    c. Fiduciary fund category—These statements are produced using full accrual basis accounting.

        i. Statement of Fiduciary Net Position

        ii. Statement of Changes in Fiduciary Net Position

> **Exam Tip**
> *The examiners frequently ask candidates to identify which statements are required for a fund type or category or, conversely, what funds are included in a specified statement.*

6. **Notes to the Financial Statements**—The GASB requires numerous disclosures in the Notes. The Notes are considered an integral part of the Financial Statements. Common disclosures include:

    a. Summary of significant accounting policies, including policies for:

        i. Budgetary basis of accounting

        ii. Reporting capital assets, including estimating useful lives and depreciation expense

        iii. Description of pension plans and other postemployment benefits, annual pension cost, and net pension obligation

        iv. Schedule of debt service costs to maturity

        v. Schedule of capital assets (beginning balances, additions, deductions, ending balances)

        vi. Schedule of long-term liabilities (beginning balances, additions, deductions, ending balances)

    b. Other required supplementary information (RSI)—The RSI is presented after the Basic Financial Statements and is used to display additional information other than that included in the MD&A or the Notes. The information presented in the section varies depending on the activities of the governmental entity:

7. **Budgetary Comparison Statement**—This statement is required for **all funds subject to an annual budget.** The statement must present:

    a. Original budget (**required**)

    b. Final budget (*as amended*) (**required**)

    c. Actual revenues and expenditures (**required**)

    d. Variance (final budgeted amounts less actual amounts) (**encouraged but not required**)

    e.   The Budgetary Comparison Statement is **presented on the budgetary basis that is used by the legislative body, which may be cash basis or near cash basis** (**required when applicable**).

    f.   A reconciliation between the revenues and expenditures using the GAAP basis (usually modified accrual basis) and the budgetary basis is required when the budget basis is non-GAAP.

8. **Pension plan and other postemployment benefit (OPEB) plan disclosures**—Actuarial information about pension plan liabilities and funding is presented in two required schedules (the specific requirements of these schedules are discussed in the Fiduciary Fund study text):

    a.   For pensions: Schedule of Changes in Net Pension Liability and Related Ratios; For OPEB: Schedule of Changes in Net OPEB Liability and Related Ratios

    b.   For pensions: Schedule of Employer Contributions; For OPEB: Schedule of Employer Contributions;

    c.   The schedules show historical trends by presenting information for a 10-year period.

9. **Information related to infrastructure assets accounted for using the modified approach**—Governmental entities using the modified approach to calculation and reporting of depreciation expense related to infrastructure assets (streets, bridges, sidewalks, drainage systems, etc.) are required to disclose and justify their methods for determining depreciation in this section. The following information is usually presented:

    a.   Description of the method used to assess condition of the assets

    b.   Results of the most recent condition assessments

    c.   Estimate of costs necessary to maintain the assets at the prescribed level of condition

    d.   Comparison of actual maintenance costs to estimated costs

10. **Combining financial statements and individual fund financial statements**—Although they are not specifically required by GASB, most governmental entities provide combining statements for all aggregate columns. Individual fund statements may be presented whenever the governmental entity deems it appropriate.

    a.   Combining statements are used to show the individual entities included in the aggregated columns of the Financial Statements, for example, the "Non-Major Funds" columns found in the Fund Statements and the Component Units column in the Government-Wide Statements.

C. **CAFR—Statistical section**—The purpose of the Statistical section is to assist the user in evaluating the current and future performance of the governmental entity in the broader context of its social and economic environment. GASBS 44 defines five categories of information that should be presented in the Statistical section and recommends that data be provided for a **10-year** period in order to facilitate trend evaluation.

1. **Financial Trends Information**—Schedules in this category help the user understand how the governmental entity's financial position has changed over the past 10 years. It typically displays key fund balances and key net position category balances for this period.

2. **Revenue Capacity Information**—This information helps the user understand the ability of the governmental entity to generate its own revenues. Information included in this section typically includes:

    a.   Significant sources of revenue

    b.   Principal taxpayers

    c.   Property tax levy and collection

3. **Debt capacity information**—This section assists the user in understanding the governmental entity's obligation to service existing debt as well as its ability to finance future operations through debt. It includes information such as:

   a. Ratios of outstanding debt to personal income

   b. Schedules of direct and overlapping debt

   c. Legal debt limitations and debt margins

   d. Revenues pledged to service debt

4. **Demographics and economic information**—The economic and social environment in which the governmental organization operates is presented in this section. Trend information that is frequently provided includes:

   a. Per capita income

   b. Level of education achieved and distribution of current students across educational level

   c. Major employers and industries

   d. Employment and unemployment rates

5. **Operating information**—The purpose of this section is to provide the user with a better understanding of the government's operations and resources. At a minimum, the following schedules of operating information should be provided:

   a. Number of government employees

   b. Operating indicators—Indicators are indicators of the demand or level of service provided, such as the number of building permits issued, number of park visits, average daily school attendance, etc.

6. **Narrative explanations**—The statement requires explanatory information regarding the sources, methodologies, and assumptions used to produce each schedule and to provide narrative explanations of:

   a. The objectives of statistical section information

   b. Unfamiliar concepts

   c. Relationships between information in the statistical section and elsewhere in the financial report

   d. Atypical trends and anomalous data that users would not otherwise understand

II. **GASB Statement No. 34,** *Financial Reporting*

A. **GASB Statement No. 34 Reporting Model**—This reporting model modifies the traditional "fund-based" statements somewhat and then adds to them two highly aggregated, entity-wide statements. This set of nine statements constitutes the *Basic Financial Statements*. The Basic Financial Statements represent the minimum amount of financial information that can be taken out of the CAFR and released separately.

MD&A	Basic Financial Statements	RSI

Government-Wide Financial Statements	Fund-Level Financial Statements	Notes to the Financial Statements
• Statement of Net Position • Statement of Activities	**Governmental Funds** • Balance Sheet • Statement of Revenues, Expenditures, and Changes in Fund Balance **Proprietary Funds** • Statement of Net Position • Statement of Revenues, Expenses, and Changes in Fund Net Position • Statement of Cash Flows **Fiduciary Funds** • Statement of Net Position • Statement of Changes in Net Position	

B.   Government-Wide Financial Statements—The traditional fund-based statements are complemented by two highly aggregated/government-wide statements.

   1.   Characteristics of Government-Wide Statements

   a.   Distinguish *governmental activities* from *business-type activities* but do **not** identify funds.

   b.   The measurement focus is on *economic resources* (i.e., revenues and expenses) and thus uses full accrual based accounting.

   2.   Classification of funds

Governmental Activities	Business-Type Activities	Not Reported in Government-wide Statements
General Fund	Enterprise Fund	Pension Trust Fund
Special Revenue Fund		Investment Trust Fund
Debt Service Fund		Private Purpose Trust Fund
Capital Projects Fund		Agency Fund
Permanent Fund		

Internal service funds are not reported in the government-wide financial statements; rather, the amounts in the ISF are blended into governmental activities and business activities according to the use by each of ISF services.

   3.   The account groups are not reported in the GASB Statement No. 34 model, but the net position and long-term debt from the account groups are included under Governmental Activities.

C.   Statement of Net Position

   1.   Government-Wide Financial Statements

| | Primary Government | | | |
	Governmental Activities	Business-Type Activities	Total	Component Units
Assets				
(listed by liquidity)	XXXXX	XXXXX	XXXXX	XXXXX
Deferred Outflows of Resources	XXXXX	XXXXX	XXXXX	
Total Assets	XXXXX	XXXXX	XXXXX	XXXXX
Liabilities				
(listed by maturity)	XXXXX	XXXXX	XXXXX	XXXXX
Deferred Inflows of Resources	XXXXX	XXXXX	XXXXX	
Total Liabilities	XXXXX	XXXXX	XXXXX	XXXXX
Net Position				
Net Investment in Capital Assets	XXXXX	XXXXX	XXXXX	XXXXX
Restricted for:				
Capital Projects	XXXXX	XXXXX	XXXXX	XXXXX
Debt Service	XXXXX	XXXXX	XXXXX	XXXXX
Community Development	XXXXX	XXXXX	XXXXX	XXXXX
Other Purposes	XXXXX	XXXXX	XXXXX	XXXXX
Unrestricted	XXXXX	XXXXX	XXXXX	XXXXX
Total Net Position	XXXXX	XXXXX	XXXXX	XXXXX

2. **Assets**—These include both current and fixed assets.

   a. **Interfund payables and receivables**—Among governmental activities funds and among business-type activities funds have been eliminated.

   b. **Internal Balances**—Any remaining interfund payables and receivables between government-type and business-type funds are identified as **Internal Balances** under each activity type and are eliminated in the Total column.

   c. **Capital Assets**—include fixed assets previously reported in the General Fixed Assets account group but they must be reported net of accumulated depreciation and includes intangible assets, as provided by GASBS Statement No. 51, net of amortization.

   d. **GASBS Statement No. 51,** *Accounting and Financial Reporting for Intangible Assets.* (This content is from the lesson "Special Items—Recent Developments.") GASBS Statement No. 51 was issued to resolve inconsistencies that had developed in accounting and financial reporting for intangible assets. The types of intangible assets held by governments include the following: water rights, timber rights, patents, trademarks, computer software, and easements. Easements are mentioned in GASBS Statement No. 34 para. 19, as a type of capital asset, and it is this reference that is considered the source of the inconsistencies in accounting for intangible assets observed in practice.

      i. **Characteristics of intangible assets**—An intangible asset is an asset that possesses all of the following characteristics:

         (a) **Lack of physical substance**—The asset may be contained in, or on an item of, physical substance (e.g., software on a computer disc) or closely associated with another item that has physical substance (e.g., the underlying land in the case of a right-of-way). These modes of containment and associated items are not considered when determining whether an asset lacks physical substance.

(b) Nonfinancial nature—The asset is not in monetary form nor does it represent a claim or rights to assets in monetary form.

(c) Initial useful life extending beyond a single reporting period

ii. **Exceptions**—The provisions of GASBS Statement No. 51 do not apply to the following intangible assets:

(a) Those acquired or created for the purpose of obtaining income or profit, which should follow guidance for investments

(b) Assets resulted from capital lease transactions reported by lessees

(c) Goodwill created through combination

iii. **Recognition**—An intangible asset should be recognized in the statement of net position, if it is identifiable. One of the following two conditions must be met for intangible assets to be considered identifiable:

(a) The asset is separable. It is capable of being separated or divided from the government and sold, transferred, licensed, rented, or exchanged

(b) The asset arises from contractual or other legal rights

iv. **Internally generated intangible assets**—Internally generated intangible assets are capitalized only when all three of the following conditions are met. Outlays prior to meeting the three conditions should be expensed as incurred.

(a) The project is expected to provide an intangible asset upon completion of the project.

(b) Technical or technological feasibility for completion of the project is demonstrated so that the intangible asset will provide its expected service capability.

(c) The intention, ability, and presence of effort to complete or continue development of the intangible asset is demonstrated.

v. **Internally generated computer software**—Activities involved in developing and installing internally generated computer software can be grouped into three stages:

(a) Preliminary project stage—Activities include the conceptual formulation and evaluation of alternatives, the determination of the needed technology, and the final selection of alternatives. Treatment: Expense.

(b) Application development stage—Activities include design, software configuration and interfaces, coding, hardware installation, and testing. Treatment: Capitalize.

(c) Postimplementation/operation stage—Activities include application training and software maintenance. Treatment: Expense.

(d) Activities in the preliminary project stage and the postimplementation/operation stage should be expensed. Outlays in the application development stage should be capitalized; however, the following two criteria must be met in order to capitalize application development stage activities:

(i) The activities in the preliminary project stage are completed; *and*

(ii) There is an ongoing authorization and commitment to funding.

vi. **Modification of computer software**—Additional criteria must be met to capitalize outlays associated with an internally generated modification of computer software that is already in operation. One of the following criteria must be met:

(a) An increase in the functionality of the computer software;

(b) An increase in the efficiency of the computer software; *or*

(c) An extension of the estimated useful life of the software.

vii. Amortization—The amortization period should not exceed the period of service capacity provided in contractual or legal rights. Renewal periods related to such rights may be considered if there is evidence that the government will seek to achieve the renewal and that the outlays associated with the renewal are nominal in relation to the level of service capacity expected to be obtained by the renewal. An intangible with an indefinite useful life should not be amortized (e.g., a permanent right-of-way easement).

viii. Estimated historical cost—If the actual historical cost of an intangible asset is not known, the government should report the estimated historical cost for intangible assets acquired after June 30, 1980.

e. Infrastructure assets—Roads, sidewalks, street lights, signs, and bridges must be included as part of capital assets net of depreciation.

  i. Modified approach—The depreciation requirement for infrastructure assets can be waived under the following conditions:

   (a) The inventory of infrastructure assets is up-to-date, information on asset condition is available, and the amount necessary to maintain and preserve the infrastructure assets is estimated.

   (b) Complete condition assessments of infrastructure assets are made every three years.

f. Artwork and historical treasures—Capitalize at historical cost or fair value at date of donation. However, these items do not have to be depreciated.

g. Collections—Special rules are available, however, for collections. Items are considered part of a collection if they are:

  i. Held for public exhibition, education, or research;

  ii. Protected and preserved; *or*

  iii. Subject to a policy that requires proceeds from sales of collection items to be used to acquire other items for collections.

h. Impairments—GASBS No. 42, *Accounting and Financial Reporting for Impairment of Capital Assets and for Insurance Recoveries*. This Statement requires governmental entities to recognize impairments of capital assets using criteria that mirror the requirements in financial accounting.

  i. Recognition—A capital asset should be considered impaired if its service utility has declined significantly and unexpectedly.

   (a) The decline must be large in magnitude and the event or change in circumstance that caused the decline must be outside the normal life cycle of the capital asset. Exclusions:

    (i) Events or changes that might be expected to occur during the life of the asset

    (ii) Capital assets accounted for under the modified approach (GASB Statement No. 34)

    (iii) Impairments caused by deferred maintenance

  ii. Procedures

   (a) Indicators of impairment

    (i) Evidence of physical damage

    (ii) Change in legal or environmental factors

    (iii) Technological development or evidence of obsolescence

    (iv) Change in the manner or expected duration of usage of a capital asset

    (v) Construction stoppage

(b) Tests of impairment—factors to consider:

    (i) Magnitude of the decline in service utility

    (ii) Unexpected nature of the decline

(c) Measurement depends on whether the capital asset will continue to be used by the government.

    (i) Assets continue to be used. The amount of the impairment is a portion of the historical cost. Use one of the following methods that best reflects the value-in-use or remaining service utility of the impaired capital asset:

        (a) The restoration cost approach is typically used for impairments resulting from physical damage (e.g., fire damage to a city building). The amount of the impairment is derived from the estimated costs to restore the utility of the capital asset.

        (b) The service units approach is generally used for impairments resulting from changes in legal or environmental factors or from technological development or obsolescence (e.g., new water quality standards that a water treatment plant does not meet). The amount of impairments is determined by evaluating the maximum service units or total estimated service units throughout the life of the asset before and after the event or change in circumstances.

        (c) The deflated depreciated replacement cost approach is generally used for impairments resulting from a change in the manner or duration of use. The current cost for a capital asset to replace the current level of service is identified. This cost is depreciated to reflect the fact that the existing capital asset is not new and then is deflated to convert to historical cost dollars.

        (d) Assets are no longer used. Impaired capital assets that will not continue to be used by the government and those impaired from construction stoppage should be reported at the lower of carrying value or fair value.

iii. **Reporting**—Impaired capital assets should be reported at the lower of carrying value or fair value.

(a) Depending on the circumstances, the impairment loss, if significant, may be reported either as a special item or as an extraordinary item:

    (i) Special items are within the control of management but are either unusual in nature or infrequent in occurrence. Special items are reported separately in the statement of activities and before extraordinary items.

    (ii) Extraordinary items are unusual in nature, infrequent in occurrence, and outside the control of management.

(b) Insurance Recoveries. GASB Statement No. 42 also provides guidance on all insurance recoveries. Impairment losses are reported net of insurance recoveries. Only realized or realizable insurance recoveries should be recognized. If an insurer has admitted or acknowledged coverage, an insurance recovery is considered realizable.

iv. **Liabilities**—Include both short-term and long-term liabilities and are valued using the effective *interest rate method.* This results in long-term liabilities being shown at their *present value,* rather than at their face value, which was the case when they were reported in the General Long-Term Debt account group.

    iv. Net Position—Contains three component parts:

        (a) Net investment in capital assets—These assets are all fixed, including infrastructure assets, and net of accumulated depreciation less the total of all general obligation long-term debt.

        (b) Restricted net position—These assets are subject to third-party restrictions governing how they may be spent (primarily the fund balances from the restricted funds—special revenue fund, debt service fund, capital projects fund, and permanent fund).

        (c) Unrestricted net position—These assets may be used at any time and for any purpose. They are primarily the fund balance from the general fund.

D. The Statement of Activities—This statement is developed in a functional format that highlights Program revenues and costs. The top half of the statement measures revenues and expenses by Program and categorizes the net result as either a governmental activity or a business-type activity. Net results at the program level are typically negative as much of the cost of providing these programs is financed from other sources. These other sources—general revenues, transfers, and special items—are shown in the bottom half of the statement. The overall net effect is usually to bring overall cash flows to a positive number. All reporting is on the full-accrual basis.

Government-Wide Financial Statements

Statement of Activities

		Program Revenues		Net Revenue (Expense) and Changes Primary Government			
Functions	**Expenses**	**Charges for Services**	**Operating Grants**	**Governmental Activities**	**Business Activities**	**Total**	**Comp. Units**
Primary Government							
Governmental Activities							
Function #1	xxx	xxx	xxx	xxx		xxx	
Function #2	xxx	xxx	xxx	xxx		xxx	
Total Governmental Activities	xxx	xxx	xxx	xxx		xxx	
Business Type Activities:							
BTA #1	xxx	xxx	xxx		xxx	xxx	
BTA #2	xxx	xxx	xxx		xxx	xxx	
Total Business Type Activities	xxx	xxx	xxx		xxx	xxx	
Total Primary Government	xxx	xxx	xxx	xxx	xxx	xxx	xxx
Component Units	xxx	xxx		xxx			xxx
General Revenues—detailed				xxx	xxx	xxx	xxx
Contributions to Permanent Funds				xxx		xxx	
Special Items				xxx		xxx	
Total General Revenues, etc.				xxx	xxx	xxx	xxx
Change in Net Position				xxx	xxx	xxx	xxx
Net Position—beginning				xxx	xxx	xxx	xxx
Net Position—ending				xxx	xxx	xxx	xxx

1. The **functional format** is divided into governmental activities, business-type activities, and Component Units.

2. A function's **Net Revenue (Expense)** is calculated as: the function's program revenues less the function's expenses.

   a. **Exchange revenue** is recognized on the full-accrual basis.

   b. **Nonexchange revenue** is recognized when all conditions surrounding the receipt of the monies have been met (purpose, time, reimbursement, and other contingencies).

   c. **Derived revenue** (sales taxes, income taxes, gasoline taxes, etc.) should be recognized in the same period as the underlying transaction.

   d. **Imposed nonexchange transactions** (property taxes, fines, penalties, etc.) are recognized as soon as a legally enforceable claim exists.

3. **General revenues, special items, and transfers** are reported below the function section.

E. **Required supplementary information (RSI)**—This information presents schedules and statistical data that supplement the basic financial statements. Note that the RSI is not part of the Basic Financial Statements.

   1. **Budgetary comparison schedules**—include the budget as originally adopted, the final budget, and the actual results.

      a. The basis of accounting used for this schedule **matches the basis used to develop the budget.** Note that **many** governmental entities use the **cash basis** to develop budgets.

F. **Balance Sheet Conversion Adjustments**—Following is a summary of the adjustments required to convert from the GASB Statement No. 34 – mandated fund-based balance sheets to the government-wide statement of net position. Note that, with the exception of interfund payables and receivables to enterprise funds and the wholesale inclusion of internal service funds as part of governmental activities, all modifications are made to governmental funds.

   1. Add all internal service fund assets and liabilities to the governmental activities balance sheet. The internal service fund Net Position are added to the Fund Balance of the governmental fund.

   2. Eliminate all interfund payables/receivables except those to/from Enterprise funds.

      a. The Net payable/receivable balance to/from enterprise funds is labeled *internal balances.*

   3. Add *net* general government fixed assets.

      a. Accumulated depreciation *must* be deducted from the assets.

   4. Add *net* general government long-term debt.

      a. Report using the effective interest rate method, instead of par value.

   5. Bring accruals and deferrals up-to-date according to the economic resources measurement focus (full accrual basis).

   6. Report Net Position instead of fund balances.

   See the following illustration.

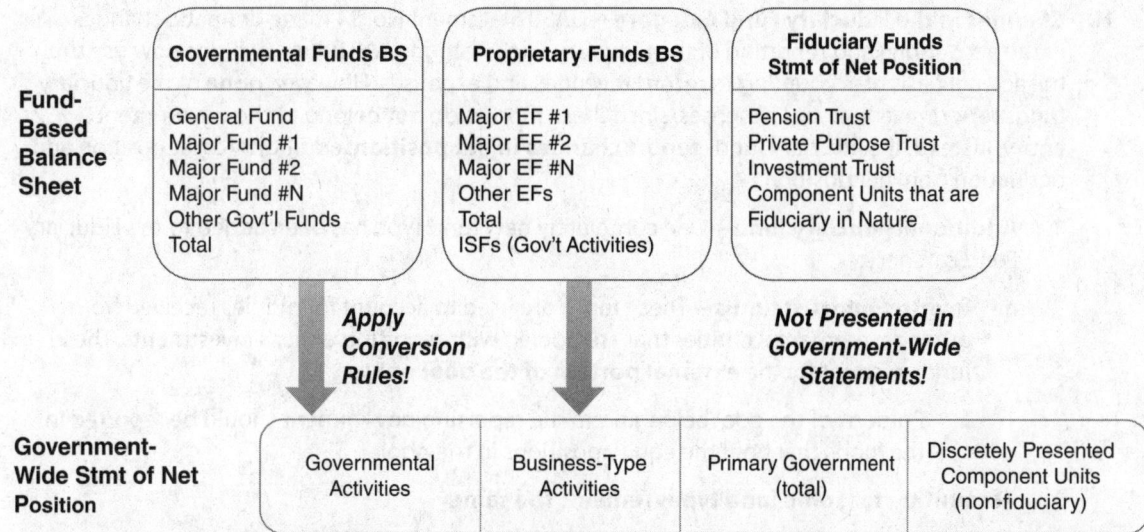

G. **Operating Statement Conversion Adjustments**—Following is a summary of the adjustments required to convert from the GASB Statement No. 34 mandated fund-based operating statements to the government-wide statement of activities. Note that, with the exception of interfund payables and receivables to Enterprise funds and the wholesale inclusion of Internal Service funds as part of governmental activities, all modifications are made to governmental funds.

1. Add all net revenue (expense) related to internal service funds:

   a. Add internal service funds' Net Position to governmental funds' total Fund Balance.

2. Eliminate capital outlay expenditures and debt principal expenditures.

   a. Increase the governmental funds' total Fund Balance for these items.

3. Eliminate proceeds from issuance of GLTD and proceeds from fixed asset sales.

   a. Decrease the governmental funds' total Fund Balance for these items.

4. Adjust governmental fund interest expenditures to interest expense under the effective interest method.

   a. Includes amortization of premiums, discounts, and bond issue costs.

   b. Depending on where you are in the amortization process, this could cause the governmental funds' total Fund Balance to increase OR decrease.

5. Record gains/losses on the sale of fixed assets.

   a. Increase or decrease the total Fund Balance of governmental funds for these items, as appropriate.

6. Record depreciation expense on GFA.

   a. Decrease the governmental funds' total Fund Balance for this item.

7. Adjust revenues from modified accrual to accrual amounts.

   a. Increase or decrease the governmental funds' total Fund Balance for these items, as appropriate.

8. Convert expenditures to expenses and adjust for differences between the modified accrual and accrual bases.

   a. Increase or decrease the governmental funds' total Fund Balance for these items, as appropriate.

H. Changes in the Fiduciary Fund Category—GASB Statement No. 34 made dramatic changes in the accounting and reporting of the Fiduciary Fund Category. All fiduciary funds now use the full accrual basis of accounting to record revenues and expenses. However, **none** of the fiduciary funds report revenues and expenses, since these monies do not belong to the government entity. Instead, the fiduciary funds **report changes in net position:** additions to net position and deduction from net position.

1. **Additional fiduciary fund**—One completely new fund type has been added to the Fiduciary Fund category:

   a. **Investment trust funds**—These funds are used to account for monies received from other governmental entities that are pooled with reporting entity's investments. These funds account for the **external portion of the pool only.**

      i. Portions of the pool belonging to the reporting government should be reported in the funds that hold the equity positions in the pool.

2. **Accounting for some fund types remains the same**

   a. **Pension trust funds**—Report the contributions to and distributions from the governmental entity's pension funds.

   b. **Agency funds**—These may include only those assets that are ultimately payable to entities outside the reporting government.

      i. For example, a property tax agency fund could only include those amounts due to other government entities.

      ii. Monies payable to the reporting government must be reported in the appropriate fund.

III. GASBS Statement No. 56, *Codification of Accounting and Financial Reporting Guidance Contained in the AICPA Statements on Auditing Standards*

A. This Statement adds accounting guidance in the AICPA auditing literature to the GASB codification in three areas:

1. **Related party transactions**—State and local governments are required to disclose related-party transactions and should recognize the substance of the transaction rather than its legal form.

2. **Subsequent events**—Two types of subsequent events are described in the Statement. Recognized events consist of events that provide additional evidence with respect to conditions that existed at the date of the statement of net position and require adjustments to the financial statements. **Nonrecognized events** consist of those events that provide evidence with respect to conditions that did not exist at the date of the statement of net position. These events should not result in adjustment of the financial statements, but they may be disclosed in the notes of the financial statements.

3. **Going concern considerations**—The Statement requires financial statement preparers to evaluate whether there is a substantial doubt about a government's ability to continue as a going concern for 12 months beyond the financial statement date (or shortly thereafter, which GASB describes as "an additional three months"). Indicators of substantial doubt include:

   a. Negative trends (e.g., recurring budget deficits)

   b. Other indicators of financial difficulties (e.g., loan default)

   c. Internal matters (e.g., work stoppages)

   d. External matters (e.g., legal proceedings)

4. If the evaluation determines that there is substantial doubt about a governmental entity's ability to continue as a going concern, then the notes to the financial statements should include the following disclosures:

   a. Pertinent conditions and events giving rise to the assessment that a substantial doubt exists about the ability of the entity to continue as a going concern

   b. The possible effects of such conditions and events

   c. Government officials' evaluation of the significance of those conditions and events

   d. Possible discontinuance of operations

   e. Government officials' plans

   f. Information about the recoverability or classification of recorded assets amounts or the amounts or classification of liabilities

Determining the Financial Reporting Entity

This lesson describes how the financial reporting entity is determined.

After studying this lesson, you should be able to:

1. Describe a primary government and a component unit.

2. Describe the difference between the blended presentation and discrete presentation of component unit information.

3. Describe the criteria for *fiscal independence* and *financially accountable*.

I. **Other Entities**—Because many governmental entities either authorize or are otherwise associated with a variety of other commissions, agencies, boards, and special districts, a question arises about which, if any, of these *other entities* should be included in the financial statements of the primary governmental unit. If the other entities are included, a further question concerns how their financial information should be presented. Most of these entities are legally separate organizations and enjoy some degree of financial and/or management independence.

II. **Terminology**

Definitions

Primary Government: A state government, a general-purpose local government (cities, counties) or a special purpose government that (1) has a separately elected governing body, (2) is legally separate, and (3) is fiscally independent of other state and local governments. The primary government is also known as the oversight unit. To be *fiscally independent*, the organization must be authorized to take all three of these specific actions without the approval of another government:

Component Units: Legally separate organizations for which the primary government officials are financially accountable or for which the relationship with the primary government is such that it would be misleading or incomplete to exclude it from the primary government's financial statements.

Financial Reporting Entity: A primary government and its component units.

III. **Deciding Whether an Entity Is a Component Unit**

A. The following circumstances set forth a primary government's financial accountability for a legally separate organization:

1. The primary government is financially accountable if it appoints a voting majority of the organization's governing body *and* either:

   a. It is able to impose its will on that organization if primary government has the ability to do any one of the following:

      i. Remove appointed members of the organization's governing board at will

      ii. Modify or approve the budget of the organization

      iii. Modify or approve rate or fee changes affecting revenues, such as utility rate increases

      iv. Veto, overrule, or modify decision of the organization's governing body

      v. Appoint, hire, reassign, or dismiss those persons responsible for the day-to-day operations of the organization

   b. **OR** there is potential for the organization to provide specific financial benefits to or impose specific financial burdens on the primary government as evidenced by any one of the following conditions where the primary government is:

      i.   Legally entitled to or can otherwise access the organization's resources

      ii.   Legally obligated or has otherwise assumed the obligation to finance the deficits of, or provide financial support to, the organization

      iii. Obligated in some manner for the debt of the organization

2. The primary government is financial accountable if an organization is **fiscally dependent** on the primary government and there is a potential for the organization to provide specific benefits to, or impose specific financial burdens on, the primary government regardless of how the organization's governing body is determined.

Recap of combinations of criteria of a potential component unit should be included in the primary government's reporting entity:

	Financial Accountability	
Appointment Authority	**Appointment Authority**	**Fiscal Dependence**
+	+	+
Financial Benefit or Burden	**Ability to Impose Will**	**Financial Benefit or Burden**

3. Include the organization as a component unit in the primary government's financial statements when it would be misleading without the inclusion of the other entity. (Component units can be other organizations for which the nature and significance of their relationship with a primary government are such that exclusion would cause the reporting entity's financial statements to be misleading.)

4. Component units can be other organizations for which the nature and significance of their relationship with a primary government are such that exclusion would cause the reporting entity's financial statements to be misleading.

Example

What are the criteria for recognizing an independent agency as a component unit of a general-purpose governmental unit (i.e., city, county, or state)?

The component unit must be fiscally dependent on the primary government or, if not fiscally dependent, then its board must be appointed by the primary government and either the primary government can impose its will on the component unit or significant financial burdens or benefits can be shifted from one to the other.

IV. GASB Satement No. 39, *Determining Whether Certain Organizations Are Component Units*—This statement broadens the definition of a component unit. It requires legally separate organizations that are not fiscally dependent on the primary government, and for which the primary government is not financially accountable, to be included in the primary government's financial statements as component units if the organization raises and holds economic resources for the direct benefit of a governmental unit.

A. Criteria—Legally separate entities that meet all of the following criteria, should be discretely presented as component units if:

1. The separate organization holds economic resources entirely, or almost entirely, for the direct benefit of the primary government, its component units, or its constituents

2. The primary government is entitled to, or has the ability to otherwise access, a majority of the economic resources received or held by the separate organization

3. The economic resources received or held by the separate organization are significant to the primary government

4. GASB Statement No. 80, issued January 2016, provides the blending method should be used for a component unit organized as a not-for-profit corporation in which the primary government is the sole corporate member, as identified in the component unit's articles of incorporation or bylaws.

B. GASB Statement No. 39 requires discrete presentation of component units included in the reporting entity due to the requirements of Statement No. 39.

Example

The Business School alumni of Big X University establish a legally separate, not-for-profit foundation to provide scholarships to students and to establish chaired faculty positions. Although neither the Business School nor the University appoint members of the governing board of the foundation or exert any control over the foundation, all of the money raised by the foundation is channeled to the Business School, which constitutes a significant resource to the Business School and the University. Because all three requirements are met, the foundation is included as a component unit of Big X University.

V. Presenting the Financial Information

A. Blending

1. If the component unit is, in substance, a part of the primary government (i.e., a building authority established to construct facilities for the primary government) then the balances for its funds should be included with similar funds in the primary government.

Example

The component unit's capital projects fund should be added to the primary government's capital projects funds; the component unit's debt service fund should be added to the primary government's debt service funds; and so on.

2. **Exception**—An exception is made for the component unit's general fund, which is considered a special revenue fund for the primary unit.

3. **A component unit is deemed to be part of the primary government *in substance* when any one of the following characteristics occur:**

   a. It has substantively the same governing body as the primary government (i.e., a voting majority of the component unit's governing body is the same as the primary government's governing body; e.g., 4 out of 7) and (1) there is a financial burden/benefit relationship or (2) the primary government's management has day-to-day operational responsibility for the component unit.

   b. The component unit provides services only or provides benefits only to the primary government.

   c. The component unit's total debt outstanding is expected to be repaid entirely, or almost entirely by the primary government.

B. Discrete Presentation

1. **For all other component units, a special column is added to the right of the primary government's data.** If there are multiple component units, their data may be aggregated into a single column and a combining statement that details the individual units prepared.

Example

How and when is a component unit's financial information presented discreetly with the primary government?

All other component units (i.e., those that provide services to other than the primary government) use discrete presentation. The component unit(s) data is displayed in a separate column to the right of the primary government's information.

VI. Reporting Entity Component Unit Disclosures

    A. The component units included in the reporting entity

    B. The rationale for including each component unit

    C. Information about how each component unit was included in the financial statements—blended or discretely presented in the government-wide financial statements or included in the fiduciary fund financial statements (recall that fiduciary funds are not included in the government-wide financial statements)

    D. The availability of separate financial statements of each component unit

Major Funds and Fund-Level Reporting

After studying this lesson, you should be able to:

1. Describe how major funds are determined.

2. List the types of financial statements required at the fund-level for fiduciary funds.

3. List the types of financial statements required at the fund-level for proprietary funds.

4. List the types of financial statements required at the fund-level for governmental funds.

5. Describe financial reporting for internal service funds.

I. Major Funds and Fund-Based Statements

A. **Reporting**—Based on *major funds*.

1. A major fund is one that comprises 10% of the total assets plus deferred outflows, or liabilities plus deferred inflows, revenues, or expenditures/expenses (excluding extraordinary items) for its fund category (governmental or enterprise funds) **and** one that comprises at least 5% of the corresponding total for all governmental and enterprise funds combined.

Note: Fiduciary funds are never major funds because the assets in fiduciary funds are not government assets and, therefore, are not used to calculate the 5% and 10% tests. The government acts as a trustee, custodian, or agent of assets held by the government for the benefit of others. Fiduciary funds are not included in the government-wide financial statements. In the Comprehensive Annual Financial Report (CAFR) fiduciary funds are reported at the fund level to provide accountability to those for whom the government is acting in a fiduciary capacity.

2. The general fund is always considered a major fund.

3. Other funds may be considered major funds because of their significance to the governmental unit and/or the users of the financial statements (based on *professional judgment*).

4. Nonmajor funds are segregated by type (governmental or *business-like*), then presented in total by type in separate columns.

B. A **reconciliation** of amounts listed on the fund-based statements to amounts listed on the government-wide statements must be presented a) on the face of the fund-based financial statements or b) on a separate schedule.

C. **Financial Statements**

1. Proprietary funds and fiduciary funds present a Statement of Net Position, rather than a Balance Sheet (governmental funds still call their statement a Balance Sheet).

2. Since fiduciary funds do not recognize revenue or expense, they produce a Statement of Changes in Net Position, rather than a Statement of Revenues and Expenses.

3. The Statement of Revenues and Expenditures Budget to Actual—essentially the budget comparison statement—appears with Other Required Supplementary Information.

II. Treatment of Fiduciary Funds—The only statements required for fiduciary funds are a Statement of Fiduciary Net Position and a Statement of Changes in Fiduciary Net Position.

A. Although we **record** revenues and expenses in the trust funds (pension trust, investment trust, and private purpose trust), we **do not report** revenues and expenses for these funds in the government-wide financial statements.

    1. Because these monies do not belong to us, we cannot recognize either revenue or expense related to them.

  B. Instead, we report Additions to Net Position and Deductions from Net Position.

  C. The agency fund does not even RECORD revenues and expenses, because these funds act simply as a cash conduit;

    1. Monies in these funds belong to someone else and simply flow through the agency fund.

    2. Hence, the agency fund records and reports only assets and liabilities.

III. **Treatment of Internal Service Funds**—Internal service funds are not aggregated with enterprise funds but are, instead, combined with the governmental funds in the government-wide financial statements.

IV. **Infrastructure Capital Assets**

  A. Capital assets include infrastructure (sidewalks, street lights, roads, etc.) and easements.

Deriving Government-Wide Financial Statements from Fund-Level Financial Statements

This lesson presents an approach to create the government-wide Statement of Net Position from fund-level financial statements.

After studying this lesson, you should be able to:

1. Describe which fund types make up governmental activities and which fund types make up business-type activities.

2. Describe how internal service fund financial information is integrated into the government-wide financial statement.

3. Prepare standard entries to adjust fund-level information in deriving governmental activities in the Statement of Net Position.

4. Describe what creates "internal balances" in the Statement of Net Position.

I. **Governmental Activities**—Recall that governmental funds (DRIP CEG) use the modified accrual basis of accounting, which has the flow of financial resources measurement focus. Consequently, a number of conversion steps are required in converting fund-level information to government-wide information. Capital assets and long-term liabilities are not included in the fund-level financial statements of governmental funds; revenues and expenditures are not measured in accordance with accrual accounting; and the five types of fund balances need to be restated in one of the three categories of net position. The conversion process can be summarized as follows (GF: General Fund; ISF: Internal Service Fund; MF: Major Fund; NMF: Nonmajor Funds):

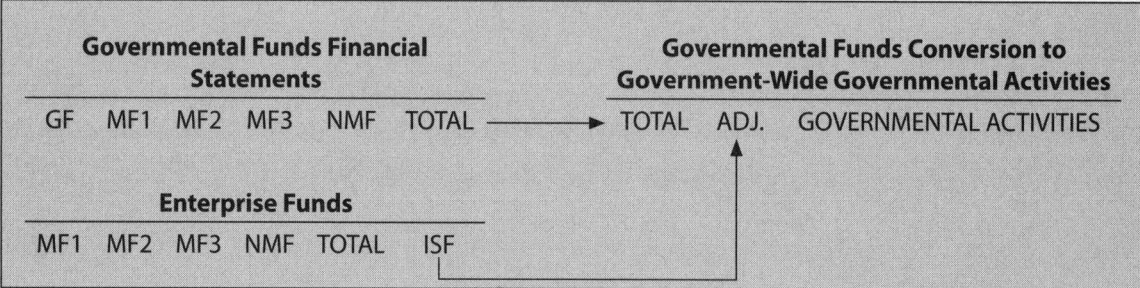

The adjustments need to convert fund level governmental fund balance sheet information into the government-wide balance sheet can be summarized by examining the accounting equation for governmental funds, the government-wide statement, and the adjustments necessary to make the conversion:

Governmental Funds Accounting Equation	Adjustments to Make the Conversion to Government Wide	Governmental Activities Accounting Equation
Current Assets		Current Assets
	General Capital Assets	**+ Capital Assets**
+ Deferred Outflows		+ Deferred Outflows
– Current Liabilities		– Current Liabilities
	General Long-term Liabilities	**– Long-term Liabilities**
– Deferred Inflows		– Deferred Inflows
	Deferred Revenues	**– Deferred Revenues**
= Fund balance	+/– Net Effect of Changes	**= Net Position**

Adjustments:

Adjustments	Government-Wide Financial Statements	
	Balance Sheet	Statement of Activities
General Capital Assets	Add capital assets and accumulated depreciation	Eliminate capital outlay expenditures, add depreciation expense, deduct carrying value of capital asset disposals
General Long-Term Liabilities	Add bonds payable and add (deduct) bond premium (discount), add accrued interest payable	Eliminate other financing sources for bonds and bond premium (or other financing use for bond discount), eliminate expenditures or other financing use for bond retirements, convert interest expenditure to interest expense
	Add other long-term liabilities such as pensions, other post-employment benefits (OPEB), claims, judgments, compensated absences, etc.	Convert expenditures to expenses
Other Adjustments	Add Internal Service Fund (ISF) assets and liabilities	Allocate ISF profit (loss) from interfund sales/services to decrease (increase) expenses
	Eliminate interfund payables to and receivables from governmental funds	Eliminate transfers to and from governmental funds
	Reclassify net interfund payables and receivables from enterprise funds as internal balances	Reclassify net amount of transfers to or from Enterprise Funds as transfers to and from business-type activities
	Reduce Deferred Revenues to eliminate amounts deferred due to resources not available	Convert revenues from modified accrual to accrual

II. **Business-Type Activities**—Enterprise funds (EFs) are reported as business-type activities in the government-wide financial statements. Since EFs are reported using the flow of economic resources measurement focus and the accrual basis of accounting, the conversion process is rather simple. The main adjustments are to eliminate various interfund transactions and balances. When an Internal Service Fund provides sales and services to EF departments, the profit (loss) experienced by the ISF overstates (understates) the amount recorded by the EF, and an adjustment is required to derive business-type activity expenses in the statement of activities. The net amount of interfund receivables and payables between EFs and governmental funds are reclassified as **internal balances** in the balance sheet (Statement of Net Position). The conversion process can be summarized as follows (GF: general fund; ISF: internal service fund; MF: major fund; NMF: nonmajor funds):

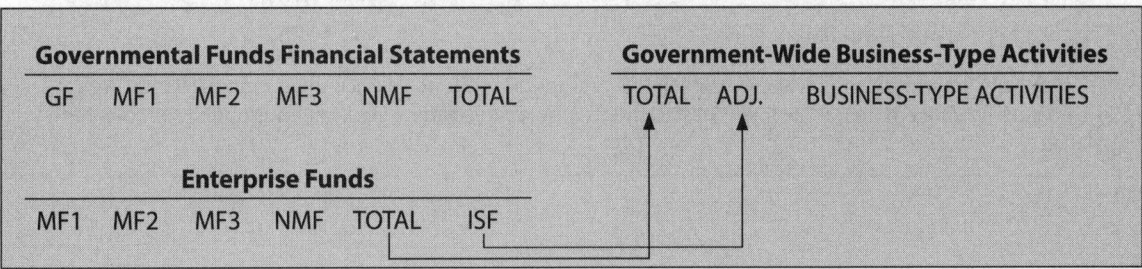

III. Internal Service Funds—Internal service fund (ISF) activities that primarily serve governmental activities are reported as governmental activities. Similarly, ISF activities that primarily serve enterprise funds are reported as business-type activities. If the ISF makes a profit or a loss then the funds the recorded expenditures or expenses from ISF services require an adjustment for the amount of overcharge or undercharge by the ISF.

IV. Fiduciary Funds—Fiduciary fund activities **(PIPPA)** are **not** included in the government-wide financial statements because the government primarily holds and manages resources in fiduciary funds for the benefit of others.

V. Conversion Worksheet—The standard worksheet used to convert governmental funds to government activities takes the following form:

	Adjustments			
Governmental Funds	General Capital Asset Balances and Changes	General Long-Term Liabilities Balances and Changes	Other Balances, Changes, and Interfund Items	Governmental Activities

Example

The City of Carrolton, Texas had the following balances in its balance sheet for governmental funds as of September 30, 2014:

Assets

Cash and cash equivalents	$122,925,945
Receivables	
Ad valorem taxes	149,350
Sales taxes	2,385,722
Franchise taxes	3,006,119
Accrued interest	191,398
Other	1,182,311
Due from other funds	1,153,976
Due from other governments	1,067,617
Prepaid items	51,584
Land held for resale	3,032,558
Total Assets	$135,146,580

Liabilities and Fund Balance

Liabilities	
Accounts payable	$11,543,454
Unearned revenue	723,293
Total Liabilities	12,266,747
Total Fund Balance*	122,879,833
Total Liabilities and Fund Balance	$135,146,850

*For simplicity, only total fund balance is used in this example. Carrolton's balance sheet reports all five categories of fund balance. Government-wide financial statements report three categories of net position rather than fund balance.

Other information related to governmental activities:

1. Capital assets:

Land	$102,700,673
Construction in progress	4,865,419
Buildings	65,622,079
Equipment	30,822,739
Intangibles	6,156,150
Improvements	43,784,292
Infrastructure	259,110,959
Accumulated Depreciation:	
Buildings	(36,944,523)
Equipment	(17,777,803)
Intangibles	(5,637,553)
Improvements	(15,442,257)
Infrastructure	(67,926,595)

2. Long-term liabilities:

Bonds payable	$168,728,244
Compensated absences	890,740
Health claims liability	1,105,000
Other post-employment benefits	411,049
Long-term risk liability	2,028,558

3. Internal service fund:

Cash and cash equivalents	$16,854,237
Receivables:	
Accrued interest	22,597
Other	65,477
Inventories	71,275
Prepaid items	176,367
Accounts payable	1,043,264
Net amount allocated to business-type activities	194,753

Other items:

4. Equity interest in North Texas Emergency Communications Center joint venture with two other cities: $583,200

5. Net pension asset: $1,352,103

6. Deferred charges on debt refunding: $2,122,111

7. Interest payable not reported under modified accrual basis of accounting: $971,993

8. Cash and investments restricted by legal and contractual obligations: $30,442,879

9. Adjustment for internal balances

Assets	Governmental Funds	(1) Capital Assets	(2) Long-Term Liabilities	(3) ISF	#	Other Items	Government-Wide
Cash and cash equivalents	$122,925,945			16,854,237	8	(30,442,879)	$109,337,303
Receivables							
Ad valorem taxes	149,350						149,350
Sales taxes	2,385,722						2,385,722
Franchise taxes	3,006,119						3,006,119
Accrued interest	191,398			22,597			213,995
Other	1,182,311			65,477			1,247,788
Due from other funds	1,153,976				9	(1,153,976)	—
Due from other governments	1,067,617						1,067,617
Internal balances				194,753	9	1,153,976	1,348,729
Inventories				71,275			71,275
Prepaid items	51,584			176,367			227,951
Equity interest in joint venture					4	583,200	583,200
Land held for resale	3,032,558						3,032,558
Restricted assets, cash					8	30,442,879	30,442,879
Net pension assets					5	1,352,103	1,352,103
Capital assets (Net)		369,333,580					369,333,580
Total Assets	$135,146,580	369,333,580		17,384,706		1,935,303	523,800,169
Deferred outflow or resources—Debt Refunding Charges					6	2,122,111	2,122,111
Liabilities and Fund Balance							
Liabilities							
Accounts payable	$11,543,454			1,043,264			12,586,718
Accrued interest payable					7	971,993	971,993
Unearned revenue	723,293						723,293
Long-Term Liabilities (Total)			185,978,505				185,978,505
Total Liabilities	12,266,747		185,978,505	1,043,264		971,993	200,260,509
Total Fund Balance*/Net Position	122,879,833	369,333,580	(185,978,505)	16,341,442		963,310	325,661,771

Conversion worksheet: To simplify the example, capital assets are added in the worksheet as a single amount net of accumulated depreciation in adjustment (1) and long-term liabilities are added in total in adjustment (3). It highlight the adjustment for internal service funds adjustment (3) is shown in a separate column. All other adjustments appear in the "Other Items" column with the appropriate reference in the "#" column.

VI. Reconciliation of the Changes in Fund Balance to Changes in Net Position—A reconciliation for the changes in fund balance in the government fund balance sheet to changes in net position in the government-wide statement of net position accompanies the government fund balance sheet.

City of Carrollton, TX

Reconciliation of Governmental Funds Fund Balances to Governmental Activities Net Position

30-Sep-X4

Reconciliation of Fund Balances to Net Assets

	in 000s
Fund Balances—Total Governmental Funds	$122,880
Capital Assets, net of accumulated depreciation, are not reported on the Balance Sheet but are reported on the Statement of Net Position	369,334
Long-term liabilities are not due and payable in the current period and therefore are not reported in the funds.	(185,979)
Unamortized balance of debt refunding costs reported when refunding occurred by the governmental refunding occurred.	2,112
Internal service fund current assets and accounts payable	16,147
Internal balances between governmental activities and business activities	195
Interest is not accrued on long-term debt on the Balance Sheet but is reported on the Statement of Net Position	(972)
Deferred Revenue reported in the funds are not on the Statement of Net Position because of differences in revenue recognition.	1,352
Equity investment in joint venture is not reported in governmental funds balance sheet	583
Net Position of Governmental Activities	$325,662

Note

The $195 amount of internal service fund net position allocated to business-type entities is the only reconciling item between total net position for enterprise funds and net position for business-type activities in the government-wide statement of net position.

Typical Items and Specific Types of Transactions and Events

Interfund Transactions, Construction Projects, and Infrastructure

This lesson describes the types of interfund transactions and special rules related to infrastructure.

After studying this lesson, you should be able to:

1. List the four types of interfund transactions.

2. Understand typical entries related to construction projects.

3. Describe when the *modified approach* for infrastructure can be used.

I. Interfund Transactions

    A. Loans

        1. One fund transfers cash (usually) to another fund with the expectation that this amount will be repaid. The general fund frequently loans or advances monies to an enterprise fund.

            a. General fund

Advances to Enterprise Fund*	XXX	
Cash		XXX

*This account title assumes that the debt is a long-term item; if it is a short-term item, the account titles are changed to Due from the enterprise fund (receivable) and Due to the general fund (payable)

            b. Enterprise fund

Cash	XXX	
Advances from General Fund*		XXX

*This account title assumes that the debt is a long-term item; if it is a short-term item, the account titles are changed to Due from the enterprise fund (receivable) and Due to the general fund (payable)

        2. When the monies are repaid, the entries are simply reversed.

    B. Quasi-External (Interfund Sales and Purchase) Transactions—These transactions occur when one fund (usually an enterprise or internal service fund) supplies goods/services to another fund. The transaction gives rise to a revenue entry in the fund supplying the services and an expenditure in the fund using the services.

        1. For instance, if the general fund receives copying services from the printing and duplication department (an internal service fund), the following entry is recorded:

            a. General fund

Expenditures	XXX	
Due to Internal Service Fund		XXX

    b. Internal service fund

Due from General Fund	XXX
Revenues	XXX

    c. When the amounts are paid in cash, the liability/receivable is eliminated in each of the funds.

C. Expenditure Reimbursements—When one fund pays an expenditure on behalf of another fund and subsequently receives repayment, the expenditure is reduced in the fund that receives the repayment and increased in the fund making the repayment.

   1. For example, if the general fund previously paid for an expenditure on behalf of a capital projects fund and the capital projects fund is now reimbursing the general fund, the entry to record the reimbursement is:

   2. General fund

Cash	XXX
Expenditures	XXX

   3. Capital projects fund

Expenditures	XXX
Cash	XXX

D. Residual Equity Transfers—These are nonrecurring, relatively infrequent, transfers of monies between funds, typically to establish or expand the activities of a Proprietary fund (i.e., for capital purposes), remove a deficit equity position in a Proprietary fund, or transfer a remaining balance out of a fund that is being closed.

> **Note**
> Transfers from the general or special revenue fund to capital projects or debt service funds are classified as operating transfers, not residual equity transfers!)

   1. Reporting for Residual Equity Transfers

    a. In the GASB Statement No. 33 model, they are titled simply Transfers and are reported in the other financing sources/(uses) section of the government fund fund-based statements and as Transfers by the proprietary fund in a separate line item after the operating income line of the proprietary fund statement of revenues, expenses, and changes in net position.

    b. The transfers of proprietary funds are closed to net position.

   2. To record the transfer of remaining funds from a terminated debt service fund to the general fund:

   3. Debt service fund

DR: OFU—Residual Equity Transfer to General Fund	XXX
CR: Cash	XXX

4. General fund

DR: Cash	XXX	
CR: OFS—Residual Equity Transfer from Debt Service Fund		XXX

E. Operating Transfers—These are regular, routine, or recurring transfers of resources between funds to subsidize current activities. They are classified as Operating Transfers. Examples are when the general fund transfers money to the stores fund (and ISF) to subsidize salary costs or when the general fund transfers monies to a debt service fund to be used for the repayment of a long term liability.

1. Since these transfers do not represent revenues or expenditures for the governmental unit, they are reported as other financing sources/uses in governmental funds and as Transfers In or Out in proprietary funds (in a line(s) after Operating Income).

2. The entry to record a routine transfer from the general fund to the debt service fund is shown below.

3. General fund

DR: OFU—Operating Transfer to Debt Service Fund	XXX	
CR: Cash		XXX

4. Debt service fund

DR: Cash	XXX	
CR: OFS—Operating Transfer from General Fund		XXX

II. Entries Relating to Major Construction Projects

A. Major Construction Projects—When a major building project is begun, a series of entries occur that affect the debt service fund and the general fund. These entries are illustrated below.

B. Introduction

1. Bonds are issued to pay for the constructions (no entry required for authorization of bond issue).

a. Capital projects fund

Cash	10,000,000	
Other Financing Sources—Bond Proceeds		10,000,000

b. Governmental activities (government-wide financial statements)

Cash	10,000,000	
Bonds Payable		10,000,000

2. Bonds payable are shown at present value calculated using the effective interest rate method on the government-wide financial statements but are not shown in the fund-level financial statements of the capital projects fund.

3. Progress proceeds on the building.

    a. Capital projects fund

Expenditures	5,000,000	
Cash (or Vouchers Payable)		5,000,000

    b. Governmental activities (Government-wide financial statements)

Construction-in-Progress	5,000,000	
Cash (or Vouchers Payable)		5,000,000

4. The general fund transfers monies to the debt service fund to cover interest that is now due on the debt and to provide for retirement of the bonds; the debt service fund pays the interest.

    a. General fund

Operating Transfer to Debt Service Fund	2,000,000	
Cash		2,000,000

    b. Debt service fund

Cash	2,000,000	
Operating Transfer from General Fund		2,000,000
Expenditures—Interest	1,000,000	
Interest Payable		1,000,000

    c. Governmental activities (Government-wide financial statements)

Interest Expense	1,000,000	
Interest Payable		1,000,000

5. The project is completed at an additional cost of $4,500,000.

    a. Capital projects fund

Expenditures	4,500,000	
Cash (or Vouchers Payable)		4,500,000

    b. Governmental activities (Government-wide financial statements)

Note
The asset is reported with Net Investment in Capital Assets in the Government-Wide Financial Statements.

Capital Asset	9,500,000	
Cash (or Vouchers Payable)		4,500,000
Construction-in-Process		5,000,000

6. The capital projects fund is closed and the remaining balance is transferred to the debt service fund to be used to repay the bond liability.

   a. Capital projects fund

Other Financing Sources	10,000,000	
Expenditures		9,500,000
Fund Balance		500,000
Residual Equity Transfer to Debt Service Fund**	500,000	
Cash		500,000
Fund Balance	500,000	
Residual Equity Transfer to Debt Service Fund**		500,000
Debt Service Fund:		
Cash	500,000	
Residual Equity Transfer from Capital Projects Fund**		500,000

** Per GASB Statement No. 33, these would be reported as transfers.

III. Infrastructure

A. Infrastructure is capital assets such as highways, bridges, streets, sidewalks, water and sewerage systems, storm drainage, seawalls, and lighting systems that are stationary in nature and can be preserved much longer than most other capital assets (e.g., buildings and equipment).

B. The financial reporting treatment of public infrastructure follows that of other capital assets.

   1. In **government-wide financial statements** infrastructure is reported as assets in the Statement of Net Position and, unless the modified approach is adopted, depreciation expense for infrastructure is reported in the government-wide Statement of Activities. Depreciation is also recognized in proprietary and fiduciary fund-level financial statements.

   2. In **governmental fund financial statements** additions to infrastructure assets are reported as expenditures.

C. Under the **modified approach** a government can elect not to depreciate certain eligible infrastructure, provided that the following two requirements are met:

   1. The government manages the eligible infrastructure assets using an asset management system that includes (a) an up-to-date inventory of eligible assets, (b) condition assessments of the assets and summary of results using a measurement scale, and (c) estimates each year of the annual amount needed to maintain and preserve the eligible assets at a condition level established and disclosed by the government, and

2. The government documents that the eligible infrastructure assets are being preserved approximately at (or above) the condition level established and disclosed in 1(c).

3. Using the modified approach, the government will expense maintenance costs in lieu of depreciation expense. Additions and improvements to infrastructure assets are still capitalized in the government-wide statement of net position and in the proprietary and fiduciary fund-level statements of net position.

Long-Term Liabilities Other Than Bonded Debt

This lesson describes the common types of long-term liabilities other than bonded debt.

After studying this lesson, you should be able to:

1. List four common types of long-term liabilities other than bonded debt.

2. Describe the *general rule* at the fund level, for recognition of expenditures and liabilities.

3. Describe the *general rule* at the government-wide level, for recognition of expenses and liabilities.

I. Recognition and Reporting of Long-Term Liabilities Other Than Debt in Governmental Funds

    A. Recognize a Liability—In the fund-based statements only when the use of current resources is required. Governmental funds are used to account for sources, uses, and balances of expendable general government financial assets. As a result, in governmental funds:

        1. Long-term assets purchased are reported as fund expenditures rather than as fixed assets.

        2. Proceeds of long-term debt are recorded as other financing sources rather than as long-term debt.

        3. Long-term portions of the liability are kept off the fund-based statements.

            a. Only those portions of the potential liability that are likely to be paid in cash are included. For example, if sick leave does not vest to the employee, then only those portions of sick leave that are reasonably expected to be paid to the employee are reported.

        4. General long-term liabilities are reported in the government-wide financial statements.

            a. All unmatured long-term debt, except for that of proprietary funds or trust funds, is reported in the government-wide Statement of Net Position. Matured general obligation debt, that has been recorded in or will be paid from a debt service fund, is excluded from general long-term liabilities.

            b. General long-term liabilities include unmatured principal of bonds, warrants, notes, capital leases, claims and judgments, certificates of participation, compensated absences, landfill closure and postclosure care, underfunded pension plan and underfunded OPEB contributions, and other forms of general government debt. Unmatured long-term special assessment debt is also included if the government is obligated in any manner on the debt and the debt is not being serviced through an enterprise fund.

    B. Liabilities in the government-wide statements—may be reported either at face value or at discounted value, depending on the circumstances.

        1. If there is a *structured settlement plan* (contractual obligations to pay money on fixed or determinable dates as a means of settling a liability), then the discounted value of the plan to discharge the liability is used;

        2. In the absence of a structured settlement plan, the liability is simply reported at face value.

Example

The City of Tima Springs was assessed damages of $1,000,000 pursuant to a liability claim from a citizen who fell into an uncovered manhole. Payment of the claim is scheduled to take place over a 10-year period, with the first payment of $115,000 due in six weeks; the PV of the remaining cash flow is $465,000.

Tima would recognize the currently due portion of the settlement as an Expenditure in its fund-based statements. The government-wide statements would report expenses of $580,000 ($465K + $115K) and report the liability at its $465,000 PV.

II. Common Types of Long-Term Debt Other Than Bonded Debt

A. Claims and Judgments—These primarily related to construction activities of a government. Litigated and adjudicated claims adverse to the government should be recorded. For claims that not yet been litigated or judgments have not been made, liabilities may be estimated on a case-by-case basis. Accounting and reporting for claims and judgments varies as follows:

1. The amount of claims and judgments recognized as expenditures and liabilities of governmental funds is limited to amount that is payable with current expendable resources available in the fund.

2. The full known or estimated liability and expense is reported in the government activities column of the government-wide statement of net position and statement of activities.

B. Compensated Absences—Such absences represent paid time off that employees earn in vacation and sick leave. The accounting and reporting for compensated absences is similar to that for claims and judgments, and varies as follows:

1. The amount of expenditure and liability recognized in the financial statements of governmental funds is only that portion of the compensated absences that employees will use in the upcoming fiscal period. That is, the amount that will be paid from current financial resources.

2. The full amount of the liability and expense is recognized in the government-wide financial statements.

Example

General Fund recognizes $50,000 in the amount that it estimates employees will use in the next year:

Expenditures—Compensated Absences	$50,000	
Liability—Compensated Absences		$50,000

The full expense and liability of $200,000 is recognized in the government-wide financial statements:

Expense—Compensated Absences	$250,000	
Liability—Compensated Absences		$250,000

C. Capital Leases—Accounting rules for capital leases are established by GASB Statement No. 62. A lease is a capital lease if it meets any one of the following classification criteria:

1. The lease transfers ownership of the property to the lessee by the end of the lease term.

2. The lease contains an option to purchase the leased property at a bargain price.

3. The lease term is equal to or greater than 75% of the estimated economic life of the leased property.

4. The present value of the rental or other minimum lease payments equals or exceeds 90% of the fair value of the leased property less any investment tax credit retained by the lessor.

D. In the government-wide financial statements and in the fund financial statements of proprietary funds, a capital lease is recognized in the same manner as a purchase of a capital asset. The leased asset is capitalized at the present value of the minimum lease payments and a liability is recognized equal to the amount of the asset less any initial cash payment made.

E. Governmental funds, conversely, will only recognize the expenditure of lease payments as they are made in its fund-level financial statements. This is consistent with the flow of current financial resource approach in the modified accrual basis of accounting.

F. Municipal Solid Waste Landfills—Landfills incur a variety of costs during the period of operation and after closure. The EPA requires postclosure maintenance and monitoring over a landfill for thirty years. GASB requires measuring and reported estimated total closure and postclosure costs. A portion of the total cost is recognized yearly using the units-of-production method. For example, a landfill in its first year of operation has an estimated capacity of 5,000,000 cubic years and $10,000,000 in currently estimated closure and postclosure costs. A total of 50,000 cubic yards were used in the first year of operation. Since 10% of the landfills capacity was used, 10% ($1,000,000) of the total closure and postclosure cost will be recognized. The journal entry is as follows:

Expense for Landfill Closure and Postclosure	$1,000,000	
Accrued Landfill Closure and Postclosure Liability		$1,000,000

1. Obviously, the liability amount will increase yearly. Actual costs for closure and postclosure are reported as a reduction of the accrued liability, not as capital assets or expenses.

2. Usually landfills are operated as a proprietary fund. IF the landfill is operated as a governmental fund; e.g., by the general fund, then only amounts actually spent on closure or postclosure activities will be recognized as an expenditure of the fund. The government-wide activities, however, will report the expense and liability in the same manner that a proprietary fund would report.

G. Pension Plans—These plans represent significant costs and liabilities for many governments. Accounting and reporting for pension plans are discussed in the lesson on Fiduciary Funds. Accounting for pensions in funds that employ government workers is similar to accounting for claims and judgments and compensated absences. Governmental fund types will recognized pension expenditures and liabilities to the extent that the amounts are payable with current available financial resources. Proprietary funds will recognize the full expense and liability.

H. Other Postemployment Plans (OPEB)—Such plans provide retirement benefits other than pensions such as medical, dental, and vision plans. Generally, accounting and reporting for OPEB is similar to that for pension plans and is discussed in the lesson on "Fiduciary Funds".

III. Accounting and Reporting for Pollution Remediation Obligations—Many state and local governments are faced with high costs in their attempts to remediate existing pollution problems. Note, that the statement does not address costs associated with control or prevention of future pollution problems.

A. Liability Recognition Triggers—The government must recognize a liability for pollution remediation if the cost can be reasonably estimated and one of the following five events occurs:

1. **Pollution poses an imminent danger** to the public or environment and a government has little or no discretion to avoid fixing the problem.

2. The government has **violated a pollution prevention-related permit or license.**

3. **The government has been identified by a regulator** (i.e., the Environmental Protection Agency (EPA) as being responsible (or potentially responsible) for cleaning up pollution, or for paying all or some of the cost of the clean-up.

4. **An outcome (or likely outcome) of a lawsuit** will compel the governmental entity to address a pollution problem.

5. **The government begins to clean up pollution** or conducts related remediation activities (or the government legally obligates itself to do so).

B. Expense or Expenditure Recognition—Recognition of the expense varies with the fund responsible for the clean-up costs.

    1. Government-wide financial statements and proprietary fund statements—Report expenses as the liability related to the pollution remediation is accrued. As the work is preformed and payments are made, the liability is reduced.

    2. Governmental fund statements—Report expenditures when the payment for the clean-up is made.

C. Capitalization of Pollution Remediation Costs—Not every pollution remediation is recognized as an expense. Pollution remediation costs can instead be capitalized when they are used for the following:

    1. Prepare property for sale in **anticipation of a sale**;

    2. Prepare property for use when the **property was acquired with known or suspected pollution that was expected to be remediated**;

    3. Perform pollution remediation that **restores a pollution-caused decline in service utility, which was previously recognized as an asset impairment**;

    4. Acquire property, plant, and equipment that have **future alternative use other than remediation efforts**.

IV. GASB Statement No. 70—Accounting and Financial Reporting of Nonexchange Financial Guarantees

A. Nonexchange Financial Guarantees—A government may extend or receive a financial guarantee without receiving or providing equal or approximately equal value in return. For example, a school district may receive a financial guarantee from the state government for its bonds used to construct a new school without providing considering to the state government. (Note: GASB 70 does not apply to guarantees related to special assessment debt, which is covered by GASB 6).

B. Recognition—A government that has extended a nonexchange financial guarantee should consider qualitative factors in assessing the likelihood that the government will **more-likely-than not** be required to make a payment in relation to the guarantee. Example qualitative factors include:

    1. Initiation of a process of entering bankruptcy or financial reorganization;

    2. Breach of debt contract, debt covenants, default on interest or principal payments;

    3. Other indicators of significant financial difficulty.

C. Measurement

    1. Proprietary funds (economic resource measurement focus). Recognize the liability and an expense at the discounted present value of the best estimate of future outflows expected to be incurred as a result of the guarantee. If a best estimate is not available then recognize the minimum value within the range of estimates.

    2. Governmental funds (current financial resources measurement focus). Recognize a fund liability and expenditure to the extent of the liability expected to be liquidated with expendable and available resources when payments are due and payable on the guaranteed obligation.

Terminology and Nonexchange Transactions

This lesson describes unique terminology and classification schemes used in governmental accounting.

After studying this lesson, you should be able to:

1. List six expenditure classification schemes.

2. Distinguish between an expense and an expenditure.

3. List four types of nonexchange transactions.

4. List seven revenue classifications.

I. **Account Terminology and Classifications**

   A. **Revenue Classifications**—Revenues of governmental funds are classified by source. The main revenue source classes are:

      1. **Taxes**—Property, sales, income, and other taxes; penalties and interest on delinquent taxes

      2. **Licenses and permits**—Motor vehicle permits, fishing permits, building permits, alcoholic beverage licenses

      3. **Intergovernmental**—Grants, shared revenues, and payments to other governments in lieu of taxes

      4. **Charges for services**—Building inspection fees, copying fees, recording fees

      5. **Fines and forfeits**—Parking fines, traffic fines

      6. **Investment earnings**—Usually on short-term investments

      7. **Miscellaneous**—Rents and royalties, escheats. (The net assets of deceased persons who die without a will and with no known relatives revert back to the state.)

   B. **Expenditure Classifications**—Most expenditures of governmental funds are authorized through appropriations. During the budgeting process, appropriations are identified not just by the type of expenditure (i.e., salaries, supplies, utilities) but also by the purpose(s) of the expenditure and its funding source. In order to show compliance with the appropriations, expenditures must also be coded to identify these characteristics.

      1. **Fund**—The fund supplying the financial resources

      2. **Program or function**—The broad purpose of the expenditure (i.e., public safety, education, health, etc.)

      3. **Activity**—A specific goal or objective under a program (i.e., child vaccination, low-income healthcare, AIDS awareness, etc.)

      4. **Organizational unit**—The department or agency within the governmental entity that is responsible for managing the expenditure (i.e., community clinic, emergency services, health department, etc.)

      5. **Character**—Identifies the period of time benefited by the expenditure:

         a. **Current expenditures**—Benefit the current period only

         b. **Capital outlay**—Benefits current and future periods

         c. **Debt service**—Benefits past periods (and, potentially, current and future periods)

         d. **Intergovernmental transfers**—Nonexchange (and frequently mandatory) transfers of resources from one governmental entity to another

6. **Object**—The "natural" expense category, the specific purpose of the expenditures (e.g., salaries, supplies, and rent).

Study Tip

Of the six classifications listed, four are most frequently seen in CPA Exam questions: *Fund*, *Program/ Function*, *Character*, and *Object*.

Study Tip

Expenditures in the fund statements for the governmental funds are reported by character. Expenditures in the government-wide statements for the governmental funds are reported by program/function.

C. **Special Terminology**—Used in Modified Accrual Basis Accounting.

   1. **Modified accrual basis**—Uses alternate titles for some common accounting terms:

      a. **Expenditures, not expenses**—Under modified accrual basis accounting, decreases in net assets are called **expenditures**, not expenses.

      b. **Fund balance, not retained earnings or owner's equity**—Under modified accrual basis accounting residual equity is called Fund Balance, not Retained Earnings or Owner's Equity.

Study Tip

The examiners frequently use these two terms to indicate which type of fund is being discussed. If the question uses the terms "expenditures" or "fund balance," then the fund or report in question must be one of the governmental funds, as these are the only funds that use modified accrual basis accounting.

If the question uses the terms "expenses" or "net position," then the fund or report in question must be one of the proprietary funds or fiduciary funds, as these are the only funds that use full accrual basis accounting.

---

      c. **Vouchers payable, not accounts payable**—The term "Accounts Payable" may be replaced by the term "Vouchers Payable" in any of a governmental entity's funds. No differences in treatment are signified by the alternate terminology.

      d. **Warrants, not checks**—The term *check* may be replaced by the term *warrant* in any of a governmental entity's funds. No differences in treatment are signified by the alternate terminology.

D. **Use of Control Accounts in Governmental Accounting**

   1. Accounts such as revenues, estimated revenues, expenditures, appropriations, and encumbrances frequently have the word *control* appended to the account title. The account titles revenues and revenues control refer to precisely the same account (as do expenditures and expenditures control, etc.).

   2. The concept of a *control* account here is the same as in financial accounting when it is used with accounts receivable control.

   3. The **control account** is a general ledger summary account that reflects the grand total balance of the subsidiary ledger accounts.

   4. For example, A/R control represents the total dollar amount of the individual customer accounts:

Cust 1		Cust 2		Cust 3		A/R Control	
	500		100		300		900

5. In government accounting, this concept is applied to the budgetary and actual revenue and expenditure accounts: the account **revenue control** represents the total of the individual revenue accounts:

Rev-Taxes	–	Rev-Fines	–	Rev-Licenses	–	Revenue Control	__
600		200		300		1100	

> **Note**
> The form of the account name does not influence the answer to the question. A question about a revenue transaction may refer to the revenue account as revenue control, revenue or zoning fee revenue; in all instances, the answer to the question would be the same.

II. GASB Statement No. 33, *Accounting and Financial Reporting for Nonexchange Transactions*

A. **GASB Statement No. 33** provides a comprehensive basis for recognizing nonexchange revenues such as property taxes, sales taxes, shared revenues, entitlements, and grants. It divides the revenues into four classes of transactions and defines separate recognition criteria for each class.

1. Because GASB Statement No. 33 is a full accrual basis standard and most nonexchange revenues are recorded in governmental funds, application of the revenue recognition rules when recording the transactions and when reporting them in the fund statements is a two-step process:

  a. Determine whether revenue can be recognized under GASB Statement No. 33 recognition rules. If revenue cannot be recognized, there is no need to go on to the second step: the transaction is recognized as deferred inflow of resources; *and*

  b. If revenue can be recognized under GASB Statement No. 33, then we must apply the modified accrual basis recognition standards to determine whether revenue can be recorded in the (governmental) funds. If revenue cannot be recognized under modified accrual basis as well as under GASB Statement No. 33, then the transaction is recognized as deferred inflow of resources.

> **Note**
> *These timing differences create an ongoing set of adjustments between revenue recognized in the funds and reported in the fund statements and revenue reported in the government-wide statements.*

2. Again, this two-step process is necessary because we use a full accrual basis standard to record and report transactions in funds that use the modified accrual basis of accounting. For reporting in the government-wide statements, which are presented on the full accrual basis, this two-step process is not necessary: Transactions are evaluated using only GASB Statement No. 33 rules.

> **Study Tip**
> The examiners sometimes ask questions about nonexchange revenue recognition in the government-wide statements and sometimes ask questions about nonexchange revenue recognition in the fund statements and about when the transactions are recorded. Timing differences from revenue recognized/not recognized in prior periods may complicate these questions. It is extremely important to read the question carefully to determine which basis of accounting is being used before attempting to answer the question.

B. **Nonexchange Revenue Classifications**—The following four transaction classifications are used to define and apply revenue recognition rules:

1. **Imposed nonexchange revenues**—Government-assessed amounts, such as property taxes, fines, and interest on delinquent property taxes, are billed and charged to individuals and businesses.

  a. Recognize revenue in the period for which the taxes are levied; *and*

b. Recognize an asset (property taxes receivable) when there is an enforceable claim or when payment is received (cash).

Example
Property Tax Example
The City of Wellston uses a calendar fiscal year. In November, Year X, the City levied property taxes totaling $25 M to be used to finance the next fiscal year, Year Y. The taxes were due by January 31, Year Y. The City posted collections as follows:

Through December 31, Year X:	$1,5 M
Through December 31, Year Y:	$20.0 M
January 1–February 28, Year Z	$2.5 M
March 1–December 31, Year Z	$1.0 M

According to GASB Statement No. 33, *all* revenue would be recognized in Year Y because the taxes were levied for use in Year Y. Note that when the taxes are levied in Year X, deferred inflow of resources is credited because the revenue cannot be recognized until the following year. Therefore, the Government-wide statements would report:

Year X	Deferred Inflow of Resources	$25 M
Year Y	Property Tax Revenue	$25 M
Year Z	No revenue—all previously recognized	$0 M

In order to record the taxes in the general fund, the requirements of modified accrual basis accounting must be considered in addition to the GASB Statement No. 33 rules (i.e., revenues must be received in cash within 60 days after the end of the fiscal year). This changes the timing of the revenue recognition. Revenue is recorded in the general fund and reported in the fund statements as follows:

Year X	*Deferred* Inflow of Resources	$25 M
Year Y	Property Tax Revenue ($1.5M + $20.0M + $2.5M)	$24 M
Year Z	Property Tax Revenue (amount rec'd after 60 days)	$1 M

2. **Derived tax revenues**—Taxes resulting from the taxable exchange transactions of individuals and businesses. Principal examples are sales taxes and income taxes. These revenues differ from imposed revenues as the government does not know what the amount will be until it receives the tax.

   a. Recognize both assets and revenue at the time the underlying exchange transaction takes place.

> **Example**
> *Sales Tax Example*
> In December, Year X, merchants collected $58M in sales taxes. The merchants filed tax forms on January 31, Year Y and remitted $50M to the state. Because of a downturn in the economy, it was expected that only $5M of the remaining $8M would be collected and that $5M would not be collected until April, Year Y.
>
> The government-wide statements report the net revenue in the period in which the underlying exchange transaction (e.g., the purchase of goods from the merchants) took place:
>
> **Year X: Sales Tax Revenue** ($58M – $3M estimated uncollectible) $55 M
>
> **Year Y:** Nothing—all revenue recognized in the prior period $0 M
>
> To record the taxes in the general fund, we must consider the timing of the cash receipts in addition to the GASB Statement No. 33 requirements. Thus, the sales taxes would be recorded in the general fund and reported in the Fund statements as follows:
>
> Year X: Sales Tax Revenue ($50M received within first 60 days of Year Y) $50 M
>
> Year Y: Sales Tax Revenue ($5 M received after first 60 days of Year Y) $5 M
>
> Notice that the total amount of revenue recognized over the two-year period is the same in the government-wide statements as in the fund statements. Only the timing of the recognition differs.

C. **Government-Mandated Nonexchange Transactions**—These are intergovernmental transfers of resources including entitlements, shared revenues, and payments in lieu of taxes. Most of these resources: 1) have restrictions on how they may be used; and 2) are only available to the recipient entity if they meet specific conditions known as **eligibility requirements.**

1. Recognize both assets and revenue when **all** eligibility requirements have been met:

   a. Eligibility requirements include achievement of specified objectives and time requirements.

   b. *Generic* eligibility requirements may be assumed to be met (i.e., in order to receive highway funds, a state must have interstate highways in need of repair; even though no specific repairs may be scheduled when the monies are received, eligibility is assumed to be met because it would be unusual not to have interstate highways in need of repair).

2. **"On-behalf of" payments**—These are, by definition, recognized as revenue and as a corresponding expenditure. (For example, state governments may make the employer portion payments for elementary and secondary schools on behalf of the school districts in order to provide equal pension benefits to teachers across the state.)

Example
Shared Revenue Example
A state is entitled to 40% of the federal gasoline tax collected on gas sales within its borders. The state receives these monies directly from the retailers and periodically remits 60% of the tax to the federal government. In order to be eligible to receive these monies, the drinking age in the state must be no less than 21 and the state must maintain all interstate highways within its borders at or above a specified level of condition for the entire year.

If the drinking age in this state is below 21, the state may not recognize revenue, even though it has the cash in its possession, because this specific eligibility requirement has not been met. This is the case both for reporting on the government-wide statements and on the fund statements and for recording in the general fund.

If the drinking age is 21, the state may recognize revenue immediately in the Government-wide statements even though it has not maintained all of the interstate highways at the specified condition level for the entire year because this is a generic eligibility requirement and the presumption is that it will be met. Revenue reporting in the fund statements and recording in the general fund is dependent upon the timing of the receipt of cash.

D. **Voluntary Nonexchange Transactions Contracts**—Entered into voluntarily by the participants, who may include individuals and/or other governmental entities; this classification includes competitively awarded grants, cash and/or property contributions or bequests, and endowments; frequently subject to use/purpose restrictions and/or eligibility requirements

1. Recognize both assets and revenue when **all eligibility requirements have been met**:

   a. The existence of purpose restrictions does **not** affect revenue recognition.

   b. For reimbursement/expenditure-driven grants, reimbursement requirements are considered to be eligibility requirements, so revenue is **not** recognized until the expenditure is made.

   c. Endowments, which could be considered to have an indefinite time restriction, are explicitly required to be recognized as revenue upon receipt.

Example
Bexar City received a $100,000 grant from the Alliance for Education to be used to provide reading programs at neighborhood recreation centers. In order to receive these monies, the city must operate programs in at least three recreation centers, each with an enrollment of at least 30 children between the ages of 5 and 7. Bexar currently operates two centers with substantially more than 30 children within the required age range enrolled in programs. It plans to open a third center in two months and anticipates an enrollment of 5–7 year olds sufficient to meet the grant requirement.

When the grant monies are received, they cannot be recognized as revenue in either the government-wide or fund statements because the specific eligibility requirements have not been met. As soon as the third center is completed and enrollments have reached the specified level (i.e., the eligibility requirements have been met), revenue can be recognized in both the government-wide and the fund statements.

E. **Other Considerations Affecting Revenue Recognition**—Resources from nonexchange transactions often have timing restrictions (restrictions on *when* the resources are to be used) and purpose restrictions (restrictions on how the resources are to be used).

1. **Time restrictions**—Resources may not be used until a specific date or event has taken place, and revenue must **not** be recognized until the time requirement has been met and a deferred inflow of resources is recognized;

2. **Purpose restrictions**—When resources must be used for specific purposes, revenue is recognized *immediately*; limitations to the availability of the resources are shown by reporting a fund balance—restricted, committed, or assigned depending on the level of authority (fund-based statements) or a restricted net asset (government-wide statements).

IV. **GASB Statement No. 72,** *Fair Value Measurement and Application*

A. **Definition of Fair Value**—Fair value is the price that would be received to sell an asset or paid to transfer a liability in an orderly transaction between market participants at the measurement date. (Note this definition is the same as that in GASB Concepts Statement No. 6, para. 38.)

B. **Valuation Approaches**

1. **Market approach**—Utilizes information resulting from market transactions for identical or similar assets or liabilities (an exit price).

2. **Cost approach**—Based on the amount necessary to replace an asset's present capacity for providing service (an entry price often referred to as current replacement cost).

3. **Income approach**—Calculated by converting future amounts to a single current discounted amount.

C. **Fair Value Hierarchy**—Three levels of inputs into the measurement of fair value pertain to the reliability of the measurement of an asset or liability's fair value.

1. Level 1 inputs are quoted prices from markets with many transactions for *identical* assets and liabilities. Level 1 inputs are derived directly from the market and need not be adjusted in any way.

2. Level 2 inputs are inputs that are observable for *similar* assets or liabilities. Level 2 inputs should not be used unless Level 1 inputs are unavailable.

3. Level 3 inputs are unobservable and based on assumptions a government develops based on information available to it. Level 3 inputs should not be used unless Level 1 and Level 2 inputs are unavailable.

D. **Application of Fair Value**

1. Investments—Securities and other assets that a government holds primarily for the purpose of income or profit and with a present capacity that is based solely on its ability to generate cash or to be sold to generate case should be measured a fair value.

2. Securitized Loans—Loans acquired or originated by a government that have been securitized should be measured at fair value.

3. Exceptions:

   a. Alternative investments—Some government entities, particularly pension funds and endowments, hold investments for which fair value is not readily determinable. In such circumstances the investment can be valued using a *net asset value per share* (or its equivalent) amount; e.g., the government's proportionate share of the net assets

   b. Acquisition value—The price paid to acquire an asset with equivalent service potential in an orderly market transaction at the acquisition date or the amount at which a liability could be liquidated with the counterparty at the acquisition date (an entry price). The following assets should be measured at acquisition value:

      i. Donated capital assets

      ii. Donated works of art, historical treasures, and similar assets

      iii. Capital assets that a government received in a service concession arrangement

    c. Equity interests in common stock—Should be accounted for using the equity method. However, the following investments in common stock are excluded from using the equity method and will use the cost method instead:

        i. External investment pools—GASB Statement No. 79, *Certain External Investment Pools and Pool Participants*, describes the criteria for qualifying external investment pools to elect to report investments at amortized cost. Statement No. 79 was issued December 2015, is effective for financial statements beginning after December 15, 2015, and is eligible for testing starting July 1, 2016.

        ii. Pension or other postemployment benefit plans

        iii. IRS Section 457 deferred compensation plans

        iv. Endowments or permanent funds

        v. Investments in entities that calculate a net asset value per share (or equivalent)

        vi. Equity interest ownership in joint ventures or component units

        vii. Investments with a maturity of one year or less at the time of purchase such as money market investments.

        viii. Investments in life insurance other than investments in life settlement contracts.

    d. Synthetic guaranteed investment contracts that are fully benefit-responsive (GASB Statement No. 53).

E. Disclosures

    1. The nature, characteristics, and risks of the assets and liabilities.

    2. The level of inputs used to measure the fair value of assets or liabilities.

    3. Whether standards specifically require separate disclosure of an asset or liability (such as derivatives per GASB Statement No. 53).

    4. The relative significance of assets and liabilities measured at fair value compared to total assets and liabilities.

    5. For each type of asset or liability measured at fair value:

        a. The fair value measurement at the end of the reporting period

        b. The value hierarchy (Level 1, Level 2, or Level 3)

        c. A description of the valuation approach used (market, cost, or income)

        d. Any changes in valuation approach and inputs that had a significant impact on the measurement of fair value and the reasons for the changes

V. GASB Statement No. 77, *Tax Abatement Disclosures*

    A. Effective Date—GASB Statement No. 77 was issued August 2015 and is effective for financial statement periods beginning after December 15, 2015. Therefore, it is eligible for testing in July 2016.

    B. Definition of Tax Abatement—A reduction in tax revenues that results from an agreement between one or more governments and an individual or entity in which (a) one or more governments promises to forgo tax revenues to which it is entitled and (b) the individual or entity promises to take a specific action after the agreement has been entered into that contributes to economic development or otherwise benefits the entity or the citizens of those entities.

    C. General Disclosure Principles

        1. Disclosures should distinguish between tax abatements resulting from agreements entered into by (a) the reporting government and (b) other governments that reduce the reporting government's tax revenues.

2. Disclosure information may be provided individually or in aggregate. (Note: A government that chooses to disclose information about individual tax abatements agreements should present only those that meet or surpass a quantitative threshold selected by the government.)

3. Disclosure information should be organized by each major tax abatement program, such as economic development program or film production incentive program.

4. Disclosure information resulting from agreements entered into by other governments should be organized by the government that entered into the abatement agreement and the specific tax being abated.

5. Disclosure should commence in the period in which a tax abatement agreement is entered into and continue until the tax abatement agreement expires. (Note: If the government made commitments other than to reduce taxes as part of a tax abatement agreement, information about those commitments should be disclosed until the government has fulfilled the commitments.)

D. Disclosure Requirements

	Tax Abatement Agreement Entered into by:	
Required Disclosures:	1. Reporting Government:	2. Other Governments
(a) Brief description information:		
(1) Names and purpose of the tax abatement program	✓	✓
(2) Specific taxes being abated	✓	✓
(3) Authority under which agreements are entered into	✓	
(4) Criteria that make a recipient eligible to receive abatement	✓	
(5) The mechanism by which taxes are abated including:	✓	
(i) how the taxes are reduced		
(ii) How the amount of the abatement is determined		
(b) Gross dollar amount, on an accrual basis, by which the government's taxes were reduced during the reporting period	✓	✓
(c) If amounts are received or receivable from other governments:		
(1) Names of the governments		
(2) Authority under which the amounts were or will be paid.	✓	✓
(3) Dollar amount received or receivable		
(d) If commitments other than to reduce taxes are made, disclose the types of commitments and the most significant individual commitments made.	✓	

(e) For individually disclosed tax abatements, describe the quantitative threshold the government used to determine which agreements to disclose.	✓	✓
(f) Describe the specific source of any legal prohibition that prohibits a government from disclosing specific required disclosures.	✓	✓

Note

Tax abatement agreements entered into by a government's discretely represented component units should report disclosures according to the requirements for agreements entered into by the reporting government. For blended component units, disclosures should be in accordance with the requirements for agreements entered into by other governments.

Special Items—Recent Developments

This lesson describes recent accounting standards affecting governmental entities.

After studying this lesson, you should be able to:

1. List five types of obligating events related to pollution remediation.

2. Describe the conditions necessary to be met in order to capitalize internally generated assets.

3. Understand expense reporting for pensions and OPEB.

4. Describe the financial statement reporting for other post-employment benefit (OPEB) plans.

I. **Statements**—The following statements have been issued and/or implemented by GASB during the past years. Though some of these topics have been addressed in other parts of the study text, they are included in this section because, historically, the Board of Examiners tends to include questions on new statements more often than they might otherwise warrant.

II. **GASB Statement No. 49, *Accounting and Reporting for Pollution Remediation Obligations*—**Many state and local governments are faced with high costs in their attempts to remediate existing pollution problems. Note, that the statement does not address costs associated with control or prevention of future pollution problems.

    A. **Liability Recognition Triggers**—The government must recognize a liability for pollution remediation if the cost can be reasonably estimated and one of the following five events occurs:

        1. Pollution poses an imminent danger to the public or environment and a government has little or no discretion to avoid fixing the problem.

        2. The government has violated a pollution prevention-related permit or license.

        3. The government has been identified by a regulator (i.e., the Environmental Protection Agency (EPA)) as being responsible (or potentially responsible) for cleaning up pollution, or for paying all or some of the cost of the clean-up.

        4. An outcome (or likely outcome) of a lawsuit will compel the governmental entity to address a pollution problem.

        5. The government begins to clean up pollution or conducts related remediation activities (or the government legally obligates itself to do so).

    B. **Expense or Expenditure Recognition**—Recognition of the expense varies with the fund responsible for the clean-up costs.

        1. **Government-wide financial statements and proprietary fund statements**—Report expenses as the liability related to the pollution remediation is accrued. As the work is preformed and payments are made, the liability is reduced.

        2. **Governmental fund statements**—Report expenditures when the payment for the clean-up is made.

    C. **Capitalization of Pollution Remediation Costs**—Not every pollution remediation is recognized as an expense. Pollution remediation costs can instead be capitalized when they are used for the following:

        1. Prepare property for sale in anticipation of a sale.

        2. Prepare property for use when the property was acquired with known or suspected pollution that was expected to be remediated.

        3. Perform pollution remediation that restores a pollution-caused decline in service utility, which was previously recognized as an asset impairment.

        4. Acquire property, plant, and equipment that has a future alternative use other than remediation efforts.

III. **GASB Statement No. 51,** *Accounting and Financial Reporting for Intangible Assets*—GASBS Statement No. 51 was issued to resolve inconsistencies that had developed in accounting and financial reporting for intangible assets. The types of intangible assets held by governments include the following: water rights, timber rights, patents, trademarks, computer software, and easements. Easements are mentioned in GASBS Statement No. 34 (para. 19) as a type of capital asset, and it is this reference that is considered the source of the inconsistencies in accounting for intangible assets observed in practice.

    A. **Characteristics of Intangible Assets**—An intangible asset is an asset that possess all of the following characteristics:

        1. **Lack of physical substance**—The asset may be contained in, or on an item of, physical substance (e.g., software on a computer disc) or closely associated with another item that has physical substance (e.g., the underlying land in the case of a right-of-way). These modes of containment and associated items are not considered when determining whether an asset lacks physical substance.

        2. **Nonfinancial nature**—The asset is not in monetary form nor does it represent a claim or rights to assets in monetary form.

        3. **Initial useful life** extending beyond a single reporting period.

    B. **Exceptions**—The provisions of GASBS Statement No. 51 do not apply to the following intangible assets:

        1. Those acquired or created for the purpose of obtaining income or profit, which should follow guidance for investments;

        2. Assets resulted from capital lease transactions reported by lessees;

        3. Goodwill created through combination.

    C. **Recognition**—An intangible asset should be recognized in the statement of net position if it is identifiable. One of the following two conditions must be met for intangible assets to be considered identifiable:

        1. The asset is separable. It is capable of being separated or divided from the government and sold, transferred, licensed, rented, or exchanged;

        2. The asset arises from contractual or other legal rights.

    D. **Internally Generated Intangible Assets**—Internally generated intangible assets are capitalized only when all three of the following conditions are met. Outlays prior to meeting the three conditions should be expensed as incurred.

        1. The project is expected to provide an intangible asset upon completion of the project.

        2. Technical or technological feasibility for completion of the project is demonstrated so that the intangible asset will provide its expected service capability.

        3. The intention, ability, and presence of effort to complete or continue development of the intangible asset is demonstrated.

    E. **Internally Generated Computer Software**—Activities involved in developing and installing internally generated computer software can be grouped into three stages:

        1. **Preliminary project stage:** Activities include the conceptual formulation and evaluation of alternatives, the determination of the needed technology, and the final selection of alternatives. Treatment: Expense.

        2. **Application development stage:** Activities include design, software configuration and interfaces, coding, hardware installation, and testing. Treatment: Capitalize.

        3. **Postimplementation/operation stage:** Activities include application training and software maintenance. Treatment: Expense.

4. Activities in the preliminary project stage and the post-implementation/operation stage should be expensed. Outlays in the application development stage should be capitalized; however, the following two criteria must be met in order to capitalize application development stage activities:

    a. The activities in the preliminary project stage are completed.

    b. There is an ongoing authorization and commitment to funding.

F. **Modification of Computer Software**—Additional criteria must be met to capitalize outlays associated with an internally generated modification of computer software that is already in operation. One of the following criteria must be met:

    1. An increase in the functionality of the computer software;

    2. An increase in the efficiency of the computer software; *or*

    3. An extension of the estimated useful life of the software.

G. **Amortization**—The amortization period should not exceed the period of service capacity provided in contractual or legal rights. Renewal periods related to such rights may be considered if there is evidence that the government will seek to achieve the renewal and that the outlays associated with the renewal are nominal in relation to the level of service capacity expected to be obtained by the renewal. An intangible with an indefinite useful life should not be amortized (e.g., a permanent right-of-way easement).

H. **Effective Date**—Financial statements for periods beginning after June 15, 2009. Applied retroactively by restating financial statements for all prior periods presented. If the actual historical cost of an intangible asset is not known, the government should report the estimated historical cost for intangible assets acquired after June 30, 1980.

IV. **GASB Statement No. 52,** *Land and Other Real Estate Held as Investments by Endowments*—Prior to this standard, permanent and term endowments reported land and other real estate held as investments at their historical cost. This statement requires that endowments report their land and other real estate investments at fair value. Changes in fair value should be reported as investment income.

V. **GASB Statement No. 53,** *Accounting and Financial Reporting for Derivative Instruments*—The key provision of this statement is that derivative instruments, with the exception of synthetic guaranteed investment contracts, are reported at fair value. The next table describes how changes in the fair value of derivative instruments are reported:

	Purpose of Derivative Instrument	
	Investment	**Hedging**
Reporting of change in the fair value of the derivative instrument	Investment Revenue—Loss	Deferred Outflow or Deferred Inflow of Resources
Reported in:	Statement of Activities	Statement of Net Position—Balance Sheet

A. GASBS Statement No. 53 limits the use of the deferred recognition approach to those it describes as effective hedges. In essence, a hedge is considered effective when a change in the fair value of the hedging derivative is offset by the change in the fair value of the underlying hedged item. The standard provides three methods to evaluate the effectiveness of a hedge:

    1. **Consistent critical terms method**—If the critical terms of the hedgeable item and the derivative instrument are the same, or very similar, the changes in cash flows or fair values of the derivative instrument will substantially offset the changes in the cash flows or fair values of the hedgeable item.

2. **Quantitative Methods**

   a. **Dollar-offset method**—This method evaluates effectiveness by comparing the expected cash flows or fair values of the derivative instrument with the changes in the expected cash flows or fair values of the hedgeable item. If the changes of either the hedgeable item or the derivative instrument divided by the other falls in the range of 80% to 125%, these changes substantially offset and the derivative instrument is considered to be an effective hedge. For example, if the actual results are such that the change in fair value of the derivative instrument is a decrease of $100 and the fair value of the hedgeable item increased by 110, the dollar-offset percentage is 110/100, which is 110%, or 100/110, which is 91%. In either case, the hedging derivative instrument is determined to be effective.

   b. **Regression analysis method**—This method evaluates effectiveness by considering the statistical relationship between the cash flows or fair values of the derivative instrument and the hedgeable item. The changes in cash flows or fair values of the derivative instrument substantially offset the changes in the cash flows or fair value of the hedgeable item, if all of the following criteria are met:

      i. The R-squared of the regression analysis is at least 0.80;

      ii. The F-statistic calculated for the regression model demonstrates that the model is significant using a 95% confidence level; *and*

      iii. The regression coefficient for the slope is between −1.25 and −0.80.

3. **Synthetic instrument method**—Sometimes, a government will combine an interest-bearing hedgeable item with a derivative instrument to create a third synthetic instrument. This method is limited to cash flow hedges in which the hedgeable items are interest bearing and carry a variable rate. Under this method, the derivative instrument is effective if the actual synthetic rate is substantially fixed. The hedge is considered substantially fixed if the actual synthetic rate is within 90% to 111% of the fixed rate. For example, if an interest-rate swap's fixed payment rate is 7.00 percent, an actual synthetic instrument rate that falls within a range between 6.30% (90% of 7.00% and 7.77% (111% of 7.00% is considered to be substantially fixed and, therefore, the derivative instrument is considered effective.

B. Changes in the fair value of derivative instruments that do not qualify as effective use of one the methods described above are reported in the statement of activities.

VI. **GASB Statement No. 72, *Fair Value Measurement and Application***

A. **Definition of Fair Value**—Fair value is the price that would be received to sell an asset or paid to transfer a liability in an orderly transaction between market participants at the measurement date. (Note this definition is the same as that in GASB Concepts Statement No. 6, para. 38.)

B. **Valuation Approaches**

   1. **Market approach**—Utilizes information resulting from market transactions for identical or similar assets or liabilities (an exit price).

   2. **Cost approach**—Based on the amount necessary to replace an asset's present capacity for providing service (an entry price often referred to as current replacement cost).

   3. **Income approach**—Calculated by converting future amounts to a single current discounted amount.

C. **Fair Value Hierarchy**—Three levels of inputs into the measurement of fair value pertain to the reliability of the measurement of an asset or liability's fair value.

   1. Level 1 inputs are quoted prices from markets with many transactions for *identical* assets and liabilities. Level 1 inputs are derived directly from the market and need not be adjusted in any way.

   2. Level 2 inputs are inputs that are observable for *similar* assets or liabilities. Level 2 inputs should not be used unless Level 1 inputs are unavailable.

3. Level 3 inputs are unobservable and based on assumptions a government develops based on information available to it. Level 3 inputs should not be used unless Level 1 and Level 2 inputs are unavailable.

D. Application of Fair Value

1. **Investments**—Securities and other assets that a government holds primarily for the purpose of income or profit and with a present capacity that is based solely on its ability to generate cash or to be sold to generate case should be measured a fair value.

2. **Securitized loans**—Loans acquired or originated by a government that have been securitized should be measured at fair value.

3. **Exceptions**

   a. **Alternative investments**—Some government entities, particularly pension funds and endowments, hold investments for which fair value is not readily determinable. In such circumstances the investment can be valued using a *net asset value per share* (or its equivalent) amount; e.g., the government's proportionate share of the net assets

   b. **Acquisition value**—The price paid to acquire an asset with equivalent service potential in an orderly market transaction at the acquisition date or the amount at which a liability could be liquidated with the counterparty at the acquisition date (an entry price). The following assets should be measured at acquisition value:

      i. Donated capital assets

      ii. Donated works of art, historical treasures, and similar assets

      iii. Capital assets that a government received in a service concession arrangement

   c. **Equity interests in common stock**—Should be accounted for using the equity method. However, the following investments in common stock are excluded from using the equity method and will use the cost method instead:

      i. External investment pools

      ii. Pension or other postemployment benefit plans

      iii. IRS Section 457 deferred compensation plans

      iv. Endowments or permanent funds

      v. Investments in entities that calculate a net asset value per share (or equivalent)

      vi. Equity interest ownership in joint ventures or component units

   d. Investments with a maturity of one year or less at the time of purchase such as money market investments

   e. Investments in life insurance other than investments in life settlement contracts

   f. Synthetic guaranteed investment contracts that are fully benefit-responsive (GASB Statement No. 53)

E. Disclosures

1. The nature, characteristics, and risks of the assets and liabilities

2. The level of inputs used to measure the fair value of assets or liabilities

3. Whether standards specifically require separate disclosure of an asset or liability (such as derivatives per GASB Statement No. 53)

4. The relative significance of assets and liabilities measured at fair value compared to total assets and liabilities

5. For each type of asset or liability measured at fair value:

   a. The fair value measurement at the end of the reporting period

   b. The value hierarchy (Level 1, Level 2, or Level 3)

   c. A description of the valuation approach used (market, cost, or income)

   d. Any changes in valuation approach and inputs that had a significant impact on the measurement of fair value and the reasons for the changes

VII. **GASB Statement No. 79,** *Certain External Investment Pools and Pool Participants*—Similar to private sector money market funds, government investment funds pool the resources of participating governments and invest in short-term, high-quality securities. In 2014, the SEC changed rule 2a7 of the Investment Company Act of 1940 that is applicable to money market funds. GASB Statement No. 31 allowed government-run external investment pools (that are "2a7-like") to measure their investments at amortized cost, as allowed under rule 2a7. GASB considered some of the major changes the SEC made to rule 2a7 to be inappropriate for governments. Therefore, it issued Statement No. 79 to replace the reference in GASB literature to rule 2a7 and to provide guidance to allow pools to continue to qualify for amortized cost accounting. Statement No. 79 was issued and is effective December 2015 and is eligible for testing beginning in July 2016.

A. **Definition of External Investment Pool**—GASB Statement No. 31 defines an external investment pool as "an arrangement that commingles (pools) the moneys of more than one legally separate entity and invests, on the participants' behalf, in an investment portfolio; one or more of the participants is not part of the sponsor's reporting entity."

B. **Amortized Cost Criteria**—An external investment pool may elect to measure investments at amortized cost if it meets all of these criteria:

   1. **Transacts with participants at a stable net asset value per share** (e.g., $1.00 net asset value per share);

   2. **Meets portfolio maturity requirements**—Should acquire a security or other investment only if the remaining maturity is 397 calendar days or less, the portfolio has a weighted average maturity of 60 days or less, the portfolio has a weighted average life of 120 days or less

   3. **Meets portfolio quality requirements**—Should acquire securities of the highest rating by a nationally recognized statistical rating organization. If an acquired security subsequently declines in rating, the pools can hold no more than 3% of total assets in the second-highest category. The pool should not hold any securities with a rating below the second-highest category.

   4. **Meets portfolio diversity requirements**—Normally the pool should hold no more than 5% of its total assets in investments of any one issue of securities. For securities with some form of a guarantee, the pool may hold no more than 10% of its total assets in that issuer's securities. A pool is limited to no more than one-half of 1% to total assets in securities of any one issuer that have the second-highest credit rating or 2.5% if there is guarantee. U.S government securities are exempt from these calculations.

   5. **Meets portfolio liquidity requirements**—10% of total assets in daily liquid assets, 30% in weekly liquid assets, and no more than 5% of illiquid assets (assets that cannot be sold with five business days).

   6. **Meets shadow pricing requirements**—The shadow price is the net asset value per share of the pool measured at fair value at the calculation date. The pool should calculate its shadow price at least once a month.

Note

In comparison, the 2014 SEC regulatory change to rule 2a7 requires daily shadow price calculations by private sector money market funds. The shadow price should not deviate by more than one-half of 1% from the net asset value calculated using the total investments at amortized cost.

VIII. GASB Statement No. 81, *Irrevocable Split-Interest Agreements*

   A. Definition of an Irrevocable Split-Interest Agreement—An irrevocable split-interest agreement is created through a trust, or other legally enforceable agreement, in which the donor irrevocably transfers resources to an intermediary (which may be the government or a third party). The intermediary administers the resources for the unconditional benefit of a government and at least one other beneficiary.

   B. Types of Interests

     1. Lead interest—Receives resources from the throughout the term of the split-interest agreement.

     2. Remainder interest—Receives resources as a final disbursement at the termination of the split-interest agreement.

   C. Term of the Agreement

     1. Period-certain term—A specified time period (e.g., 10 years)

     2. Life-contingent term—Upon the occurrence of a specified event, commonly the death of the donor or a lead interest beneficiary.

   D. Recognition when the Government Is the Intermediary

     1. Government has a remainder interest—The government should recognize the following:

       a. Assets for the resources received or receivable

       b. A liability for the lead interest assigned to other beneficiaries

       c. A deferred inflow of resource for the government's unconditional remainder interest

       d. At the termination of the agreement, the amount reported as a deferred inflow of resources should be recognized as revenue.

     2. Government has a lead interest—The government should recognize the following:

       a. Assets for the resources received or receivable

       b. A liability for the remainder interest that is assigned to other parties

       c. A deferred inflow of resources for the government's unconditional lead interest

       d. The amount of benefits the government receives in a period should be recognized as revenue and a decrease in the deferred inflow of resources.

   E. Recognition when a Third Party Is the Intermediary—The government should recognize an asset and a deferred inflow of resources when the government becomes aware of the agreement and has sufficient information to measure the beneficial interest.

   F. Asset Recognition Criteria—Assets should be recognized when *all* of the following criteria are met:

     1. The government is specified by name as a beneficiary in the legal document underlying the donation;

     2. The donation agreement is irrevocable;

     3. The donor has not granted variance power to the intermediary with respect to the donated resources;

     4. The donor does not control the intermediary, such that the actions of the intermediary are not influenced by the donor beyond the specified stipulations of the agreement; *and*

     5. The irrevocable split-interest agreement establishes a legally enforceable right for the government's benefit (an unconditional beneficial interest).

   G. Measurement—The beneficial interest asset initially should be measured at fair value and remeasured at fair value at each financial reporting date. Changes in the fair value of the beneficial interest asset also should be recognized as an increase or decrease in the related deferred inflow of resources.

Special Industries: Healthcare and Colleges

Healthcare Organizations

This lesson describes basic accounting and financial reporting for healthcare organizations.

After studying this lesson, you should be able to:

1. Recall the financial statements of a not-for-profit hospital.

2. Recall the financial statements of a governmental hospital.

3. Calculate Net Patient Service Revenue.

I. **Unique Reporting Features for Not-for-Profit Hospitals**

A. **Hospitals Modify the Overall Format of the Statement of Activities**—To include an operating section and a nonoperating section. The general outline of the statement is:

> + Operating Revenues
> – Operating Expenses
> = Operating Income
> +/– Nonoperating Gains & Losses
> = Change in Net Assets
> + Beginning Net Assets
> = Ending Net Assets

B. **Operating Section**—Several unique items of revenue are included in the operating section:

> + Net Patient Service Revenues
> – Provision for Bad Debts
> = Net Patient Service Revenues less Provision for Bad Debts
> + Other Operating Revenues
> + Premium Revenues (e.g., Capitation Fees)
> = Total Operating Revenue

II. **Patient Service Revenues**

A. **Patient Service Revenues**—These are gross charges for direct patient care. They include such things as room charges, doctors' fees, medicines, bandages, etc.; *ancillary revenues*—which are revenues for patient-related services such as radiology, pathology, laboratory work, and so on—are also part of patient services revenues.

B. **Charity Care**—When patients enter the hospital, the *charity cases* are immediately identified and eliminated from the patient service revenue calculations. The amount of revenue as "donated" to charity cases is separately tracked and disclosed in the notes.

C. As paying patients begin to receive services, the charges for those services are *recorded in gross* (e.g., for the full amount). *Patient services revenues* are reduced by *contractual allowances* (price reductions allowed to third party payers such as insurance companies, Medicare, Medicaid, etc.), policy discounts, and administrative adjustments to determine **Net Patient Service Revenues**. Net Patient Service Revenue is the first line in the Statement of Activity. Gross Patient Service Revenues and Contractual Adjustments are displayed in the notes.

+ Gross Patient Service Revenues (*including Ancillary Revenues*)

− Charitable Services

= Patient Service Revenue

− Less Contractual Adjustments

= Net Patient Service Revenue (first line in Statement Activities)

Example

Daily charges for a semiprivate room are $110. However, the hospital has an agreement with an HMO to accept $70 as full payment for the room. The hospital records Patient Service Revenue of $110, records a Contractual Allowance of $40, and reports Net Patient Service Revenues of $70 on the financial statements.

D. Note that FASB ASC 954-605-45-4 requires the financial statement presentation of the provision for bad debts associated with patient service revenue. A provision for bad debts must be presented on a separate line as a deduction from net patient service revenue; that is, as a contra–revenue account rather than as an expense. Moreover, the healthcare entity must disclose net patient revenues for each major payor source (e.g., third-party payor and self-pay). Bad debt expense related to receivables other than patient service revenue continues to be presented as an operating expense.

E. Example presentation in the statement of operations:

Patient service revenue (net of contractual allowances and discounts)	$ 90,000
Provision for bad debts	(8,000)
Net patient service revenue less provision for bad debts	81,000
Premium revenue	20,000
Other revenue	12,000
Total revenue	$113,000

III. Other Revenue and Support

A. Other operating revenues and support include revenues from items related to the main operations of the hospital, but not directly related to patient care. Other operating revenues and support include:

1. Gift shop sales

2. Parking garage receipts

3. Cafeteria sales

4. Tuition from classes offered by the hospital

5. FMV of donated materials and supplies

6. *Restricted* contributions

7. Research grants

Example

Bay City Hospital recorded the following revenues:

Delivery room charges (only $15,000 is expected to be collected due to agreements with third-party providers)	$20,000
Cafeteria sales	$3,000
Research grants	$10,000
Radiology charges	$2,000
Nursing fees	$12,000
Gift of medicines used for direct patient care	$1,000

Bay City reports: Net Patient Service Revenues of $29,000 (15,000 + 2,000 + 12,000) and Other Operating Revenues of $14,000 (3,000 + 10,000 + 1,000).

Note

Categorization of hospital revenue as Patient Service Revenue, Other Operating Revenue, or Nonoperating Gains has been a consistent area of emphasis on the exam. It is important to know how individual contributions and revenues fit into these categories. Less emphasis has been placed on the expense categories.

IV. Premium Revenues (Capitation Fee Revenues)

A. Capitation fees are payments made to healthcare providers for comprehensive client coverage provided for a fixed fee (e.g., HMOs). Capitation fee revenues should be recognized during the period covered and estimated obligations related to patient care for this period should be accrued. Capitation fees are shown as a separate line item in the operating section of the statement and may be disclosed as Premium Revenues.

V. Operating Expenses

A. Operating expenses include virtually all costs associated with running a hospital, including depreciation, bad debt expense (**except for bad debt related to patient service revenue**) and losses on disposal of fixed assets. Expenses can be reported by natural categories (salary, supplies, rent, etc.) or by functional categories (inpatient services, ancillary services, administrative, etc.). However, if the NFP healthcare entity chooses to report expenses using natural expense categories (salary, supplies, rent, etc.) in its income statement, then it must disclose functional classifications in the notes to the financial statements; accordingly, functional classifications are most commonly used in the income statement. Functional expenses are based on full cost allocation. Unlike most not-for-profit organizations, nongovernmental not-for-profit healthcare organizations may report depreciation, interest, and bad debt expense, along with functional categories. Following not-for-profit financial reporting guidelines, the NFP healthcare entity must separately disclose program services from supporting activities as the example that follows shows:

1. **Program services**—Inpatient services, outpatient procedures, home health services, research, teaching

2. **Supporting activities**—Management, administrative, fiscal

VI. Nonoperating Revenue and Gains/Losses

A. This category includes most **unrestricted** bequests and cash donations, most **donated services**, and **unrestricted** earnings on investments, including endowment income.

Example
Belpark Hospital received the following contributions:

Contributions restricted for cancer research	$50,000
Unrestricted bequest	$25,000
Record-keeping services donated by current employees (these services would have been purchased)	$10,000
Bandages and ointments contributed by a supplier	$5,000
Government grant to fund research on birth defects	$20,000

Belpark reports Other Operating Revenue of $75,000 (50,000 + 5,000 + 20,000) and Nonoperating Gains of $35,000 (25,000 + 10,000).

VII. Contributions Other than Cash—To properly report these donations, you must carefully evaluate the type and purpose of the contributions:

   A. Materials—When goods and supplies normally purchased by the organization are donated, the items are **recorded as inventory or as an expense**, as appropriate, and the contribution is reported as Other Operating Revenue.

   B. Services—Donated services may only be recorded if: (1) a nonfinancial asset is enhanced or (2) special skills are required and the service is provided by someone possessing those skills and the services would have otherwise have been purchased by the organization. If the service can be recognized, then it is necessary to look at the purpose of the service in order to report it:

      1. If the service relates to the main operating mission of the hospital (e.g., a doctor donates a surgical procedure), record it as an operating expense and as Other Operating Revenue

      2. If the service is of a support or administrative nature (e.g., a bookkeeper volunteers to enter transactions), record it as an operating expense and a Nonoperating Gain.

VIII. Statement Format—Not-for-Profit Healthcare Entity—The following format is commonly used to report hospital/healthcare entity activities. The statement of operations should include a **performance indicator**, such as operating income, revenues over expenses, and so on. Note disclosure must indicate the policies adopted by the entity to determine what is and what is not included in the performance indicator. The following must be reported separately from (underneath) that performance indicator:

   a. Equity transfers involving other entities that control the reporting entity, are controlled by the reporting entity, or are under the common control of the reporting entity

   b. Receipt of restricted contributions

   c. Contributions of (and assets released from donor restrictions related to) long-lived assets

   d. Unrealized gains and losses on investments not restricted by donors or by law, except for those investments classified as trading securities

   e. Investment returns restricted by donors or by law

Sample Not-for-Profit Hospital
Statements of Operations
Years Ended December 31, 20X7 and 20X6
(in thousands)

	20X7	20X6
Unrestricted revenues, gains and other support:		
Patient service revenue (net of contractual allowances and discounts)	$85,156	$78,942
Provision for bad debts	(1,000)	(1,300)
Net patient service revenue less provision for bad debts	$84,156	$77,642
Premium revenue	11,150	10,950
Other revenue	2,601	5,212
Net assets released from restrictions used for operations	300	
Total revenues, gains and other support	99,207	95,104
Expenses:		
Operating expenses	88,521	80,585
Depreciation and amortization	4,782	4,280
Interest	1,752	1,825
Other	2,000	1,300
Total expenses	97,055	87,990
Operating income	1,152	5,814
Other income:		
Investment income	3,900	3,025
Excess of revenues over expenses	5,052	8,839
Change in net unrealized gains and losses on other than trading securities	300	375
Net assets released from restrictions used for purchase of property and equipment	200	
Change in interest in net assets of Sample Hospital Foundation	283	536
Transfers to parent	(688)	(3,051)
Increase in unrestricted net assets, before extraordinary item	5,147	6,699
Extraordinary loss from extinguishment of debt	(500)	
Increase in unrestricted net assets	$ 4,647	$ 6,699

See accompanying notes to financial statements.

Source: AICPA Audit and Accounting Guide, *Health Care Organizations*.

Sample Not-for-Profit Hospital
Statements of Changes in Net Assets
Years Ended December 31, 20X7 and 20X6
(in thousands)

	20X7	20X6
Unrestricted net assets:		
Excess of revenues over expenses	$ 5,052	$ 8,839
Net unrealized gains on investments, other than trading securities	300	375
Change in interest in net assets of Sample Hospital Foundation	283	536
Transfers to parent	(688)	(3,051)
Net assets released from restrictions used for purchase of property and equipment	200	
Increase in unrestricted net assets before extraordinary item	5,147	6,699
Extraordinary loss from extinguishment of debt	(500)	
Increase in unrestricted net assets	4,647	6,699
Temporarily restricted net assets:		
Contributions for charity care	140	996
Net realized and unrealized gains on investments	5	8
Net assets released from restrictions	(500)	
Increase (decrease) in temporarily restricted net assets	(355)	1,004
Permanently restricted net assets:		
Contributions for endowment funds	50	411
Net realized and unrealized gains on investments	5	2
Increase in permanently restricted net assets	55	413
Increase in net assets	4,347	8,116
Net assets, beginning of year	72,202	64,086
Net assets, end of year	$76,549	$72,202

See accompanying notes to financial statements.

Source: AICPA Audit and Accounting Guide, *Health Care Organizations*.

IX. **Reporting for Governmental Hospitals**—Governmental hospitals are subject to the accounting and reporting requirements for governmental **proprietary funds** that are discussed in the earlier lessons in the "State and Local Governments" section. The financial statements of a governmental healthcare entity include:

A. Statement of Net Position (net position has three categories: (1) net investment in capital assets, (2) restricted, and (3) unrestricted)

B. Statement of Revenues, Expenses, and Changes in Net Position

C. Statement of Cash Flows (with four categories of cash flows as prescribed by the Governmental Accounting Standards Board)

Colleges and Universities

Colleges and universities, like hospitals, may be private NFP organizations, or they may be public institutions. Private institutions must follow the rules as set by the FASB and, therefore, must present the same three financial statements (Statement of Financial Position, Activities Statement, and Statement of Cash Flows) and meet the same minimum display requirements of all other nonprofit organizations. Public colleges and universities must follow the rules as set by the GASB. They have the option to use either the governmental or AICPA audit guide reporting models when conditions warrant, and those conditions should be explained in the notes to the financial statement.

GASB Statement No. 35 (SGAS 35), *Basic Financial Statements—and Management's Discussion and Analysis—for Public Colleges and Universities* permits public colleges to report as special-purpose entities engaged in governmental or business-type activities, or both. Most four-year institutions are expected to report as special-purpose entities engaged only in business-type activities. Some community colleges may choose to report as special-purpose entities engaged in governmental activities, due to the extent of state and local government tax support.

This lesson describes basic accounting and financial reporting for colleges and universities.

After studying this lesson, you should be able to:

1. Recall the financial statements for a public (i.e., governmental) college and university.

2. Recall the financial statements for a not-for-profit college and university.

3. Describe the difference between scholarship allowances and scholarships and how each is reported in the Statement of Activities.

I. Colleges and Universities

A. **Introduction**—Colleges and universities use their own unique functional classifications for revenues and expenses.

1. The following summary highlights the major sections of the statement. The following table shows a formal Statement of Activity for a private college. Boldface titles indicate areas often used for CPA Exam questions.

Revenues, gains, and other support:	Unrestricted	Temporarily Restricted	Permanently Restricted	Total
Tuition and Fees, Net	XXX			XXX
Government Grants and Contracts	XXX			XXX
Contributions and Private Gifts	XXX	XXX	XXX	XXX
Investment Income	XXX	XXX		XXX
Auxiliary Enterprises	<u>XXX</u>			XXX
Other revenues	XXX			XXX
Net assets Released from Restrictions	XXX	(XXX)		
Total Revenues:	XXX	XXX	XXX	XXX
Expenditures				
Educational and General				
Instruction	(XXX)			XXX
Research	(XXX)			XXX
Scholarships and Fellowships	(XXX)			XXX
Academic Support	(XXX)			XXX
Student Services	(XXX)			XXX

Institutional Support	(XXX)			XXX
Plant Operation	(XXX)			XXX
Total Educational and General Expenditures	(XXX)			XXX
Auxiliary Enterprises	(XXX)			XXX
Total Expenditures	XXX			XXX
Change in Net Asset	XXX	XXX	XXX	XXX
Net Assets at Beginning of Year	XXX	XXX	XXX	XXX

II. Tuition Revenues

A. Shown at net of scholarship allowances and uncollectible amounts. Scholarships, assistantships, fellowships, and tuition waivers that are given in return for services provided to the institutions are reported as expenses for the department and function where the services are provided.

Misconception: Scholarship allowances and scholarships are not the same thing. Scholarship allowances are the difference between the stated tuition rate and the amount that is actually paid by the student and/or third parties making payments on behalf of the student. Scholarships are actual amounts paid to students by the college, rather than a reduction of charges. Tuition waivers given as a result of employment by the university—such as those given to graduate assistants—are reported as expenses. Tuition refunds (i.e., money returned to students because they *did not take* classes) **are** deducted from assessed student tuition and fees to derive gross tuition revenues.

 **Examples**

1. Students at Maplewood College register for classes for which the gross tuition is $1,000,000.

The college grants student assistantships totaling $250,000 to 50 students, in return for a service requirement, scholarships without a work requirement totaling $100,000 to 10 students, and waives tuition of $30,000 for college employees who are also taking classes.

Refunds of $50,000 are given to students who drop classes before classes start.

Maplewood reports Gross Tuition Revenue of $950,000 (1,000,000 – 50,000), Tuition and Fees (net) of $850,000 (950,000 – 100,000) and reports $280,000 (250,000+30,000) as Scholarship and Fellowship Expense.

2. Assume a university provides a student a $2,000 scholarship based on grades, entering ACT or SAT, and so on. Total tuition and fees for the student is $10,000. The scholarship would be recorded as follows:

Cash	8,000	
Revenue Deduction—Student Scholarships	2,000	
Revenue—Student Tuition and Fees		10,000

3. Assume that a student receives a $2,000 assistantship for services provided to the Biology Department. The assistantship would be recorded as follows:

Cash	8,000	
Expense—Instruction (Biology Department)	2,000	
Revenue—Student Tuition and Fees		10,000

B. Tuition for **academic periods encompassing two fiscal periods** (common in summer semesters) should be recognized proportionately in the two fiscal years affected.

Example
Blondell College's 10-week summer session runs from June 1 until August 15. By the beginning of classes, Blondell had received $500,000 for tuition charges. Another $200,000 was receivable on July 15.

Blondell's fiscal year ends on June 30. The first four weeks of the summer semester occur in June.

The college should recognize $280,000 in tuition revenue (4/10ths) and $220,000 as deferred revenue in the fiscal year ended June 30. $420,000 ($220,000 deferred revenue from the first fiscal year and $200,000 collected in the second fiscal year) is subsequently recognized as Tuition Revenue for the second fiscal year.

Expenditures are handled in a similar fashion.

C. Revenues for **auxiliary enterprises** are aggregated and reported as a single line item in the Revenues section. Expenditures for auxiliary enterprises are aggregated and reported as a single line item in the Expenditures section.

Definition
Auxiliary Enterprises: Activities carried on by the educational institution but not related to the delivery of instruction. Examples include housing services, dining services, athletic programs, college stores, student unions, etc.

D. Functional Classifications

Revenues:
Tuition and Fees
Federal Appropriations
State Appropriations
Local Appropriations
Federal Grants and Contracts
State Grants and Contracts
Private Gifts
Investment Income
Auxiliary Services
Expenses:
Instruction
Research
Public Service
Academic Support
Student Services
Instructional Support
Student Aid
Auxiliary Services
Note: Program and support expenses should be disclosed in the notes to the financial statements if not shown in the financial statement.

III. Financial Statements for Not-for-Profit Colleges and Universities—Not-for-profit colleges and universities, like other not-for-profit organizations are required to prepare a Statement of Financial Position, a Statement of Activities, and a Statement of Cash Flows following **FASB standards**. Consequently, the college of universities will also report three classifications of net assets:

    A. Unrestricted

    B. Temporarily restricted

    C. Permanently restricted

IV. Financial Statements for Governmental Colleges and Universities

    A. Governmental colleges and universities, such as the University of North Carolina, are usually reported as a component unit of the primary government that is financially accountable for the college or university (e.g., the State of North Carolina). Separately issued financial statements for the governmental college and university will follow **GASB guidelines** for proprietary funds and, therefore, will include the following:

        1. Statement of Net Position

        2. Statement of Revenues, Expenses, and Changes in Net Position

        3. Statement of Cash Flows

    B. Three components of Net Position are reported:

        1. Net investment in Capital Assets

        2. Restricted

        3. Unrestricted

V. Because private colleges and universities follow FASB reporting guidelines and governmental colleges and universities follow GASB reporting guidelines, differences exist in the format and classification of some items within the financial statements. Please refer to the lesson on healthcare entities for a description of these differences.

Multiple Choice Questions

I. Conceptual Framework and Financial Reporting

Financial Accounting Standards Board (FASB) Overview of U.S. GAAP

FASB and Standard Setting

AICPA.040201FAR-SIM

1. What group currently writes the Generally Accepted Accounting Principles?

   A. Internal Revenue Service.
   B. Securities and Exchange Commission.
   C. Financial Accounting Foundation.
   D. Financial Accounting Standards Board.

AICPA.040202FAR-SIM

2. The FASB is a(n):

   A. Private sector body.
   B. Governmental unit.
   C. International organization.
   D. Group of accounting firms.

AICPA.040212FAR-SIM

3. Choose the correct statement about GAAP.

   A. GAAP are laws.
   B. Only publicly traded companies must comply with GAAP.
   C. It is a violation of SEC regulations for publicly traded companies to depart from GAAP.
   D. Firms may not restate financial statements previously issued.

AICPA.040207FAR-SIM

4. The FASB has maintained that:

   A. The interests of the reporting firms will be a primary consideration when developing new GAAP.
   B. GAAP should have little or no cost of compliance.
   C. New GAAP should be neutral and not favor any particular reporting objective.
   D. GAAP should result in the most conservative possible financial statements.

AICPA.040203FAR-SIM

5. The purpose of financial accounting is to provide information primarily for which of the following groups?

   A. Government.
   B. Internal Revenue Service.
   C. Financial Accounting Standards Board.
   D. Investors and creditors.

Accrual Accounting

AICPA.101044FAR

6. Young & Jamison's modified cash-basis financial statements indicate cash paid for operating expenses of $150,000, end-of-year prepaid expenses of $15,000, and accrued liabilities of $25,000. At the beginning of the year, Young & Jamison had prepaid expenses of $10,000, while accrued liabilities were $5,000. If cash paid for operating expenses is converted to accrual-basis operating expenses, what would be the amount of operating expenses?

   A. $125,000
   B. $135,000
   C. $165,000
   D. $175,000

AICPA.130726FAR

7. Ina Co. had the following beginning and ending balances in its prepaid expense and accrued liabilities accounts for the current year:

	Prepaid Expenses	Accrued Liabilities
Beginning balance	$5,000	$8,000
Ending balance	10,000	20,000

   Debits to operating expenses totaled $100,000. What amount did Ina pay for operating expenses during the current year?

   A. $83,000
   B. $93,000
   C. $107,000
   D. $117,000

AICPA.920538FAR-P1-FA

8. The following information pertains to Spee Co.'s 20X4 sales:

Cash Sales	
Gross	$40,000
Returns and allowances	2,000
Credit Sales	
Gross	60,000
Discounts	3,000

On January 1, 20X4, customers owed Spee $20,000. On December 31, 20X4, customers owed Spee $15,000. Spee uses the direct write-off method for bad debts. No bad debts were recorded in 20X4. Under the cash basis of accounting, what amount of revenue should Spee report for 20X4?

A. $100,000
B. $95,000
C. $85,000
D. $38,000

AICPA.920506FAR-TH-FA

9. Before 20X1, Droit Co. used the cash basis of accounting. As of December 31, 20X1, Droit changed to the accrual basis. Droit cannot determine the beginning balance of supplies inventory.

What is the effect of Droit's inability to determine beginning supplies inventory on its 20X1 accrual basis net income and December 31, 20X1, accrual basis owners' equity?

	20X1 Net Income	12/31/20X1 Owners' Equity
A.	No effect	No effect
B.	No effect	Overstated
C.	Overstated	No effect
D.	Overstated	Overstated

AICPA.110583FAR

10. A company records items on a cash basis throughout the year and converts to an accrual basis for year-end reporting. Its cash-basis net income for the year is $70,000. The company has gathered the following comparative Balance Sheet information:

	Beginning of Year	End of Year
Accounts payable	$3,000	$1,000
Unearned revenue	300	500
Wages payable	300	400
Prepaid rent	1,200	1,500
Accounts receivable	1,400	600

What amount should the company report as its accrual-based net income for the current year?

A. $68,800
B. $70,200
C. $71,200
D. $73,200

Financial Statements

AICPA.101047FAR

11. Which of the following would be reported as an investing activity in a company's statement of cash flows?

A. Collection of proceeds from a note payable.
B. Collection of a note receivable from a related party.
C. Collection of an overdue account receivable from a customer.
D. Collection of a tax refund from the government.

AICPA.101046FAR

12. In Dart Co.'s year 2 single-step Income Statement, as prepared by Dart's controller, the section titled "Revenues" consisted of the following:

Sales	$250,000
Purchase discounts	3,000
Recovery of accounts written off	10,000
Total revenues	$263,000

In its year 2 single-step Income Statement, what amount should Dart report as total revenues?

A. $250,000
B. $253,000
C. $260,000
D. $263,000

assess.AICPA.FAR.fin.state-0025

13. A partial listing of a company's accounts is presented below:

Revenues	$80,000
Operating expenses	50,000
Foreign currency translation adjustment gain, net of tax	4,000
Income tax expense	10,000

What amount should the company report as net income?

A. $20,000
B. $24,000
C. $30,000
D. $34,000

Financial Accounting Standards Codification

AICPA.130717FAR

14. Which of the following documents is typically issued as part of the due-process activities of the Financial Accounting Standards Board (FASB) for amending the FASB Accounting Standards Codification?

A. A proposed statement of position.
B. A proposed accounting standards update.
C. A proposed accounting research bulletin.
D. A proposed staff accounting bulletin.

AICPA.100884FAR-SIM

15. U.S. GAAP includes a very large set of accounting guidance. Choose the correct statement.

A. The FASB Accounting Standards Codification includes guidance about items that are not under the purview of the Generally Accepted Accounting Principles, such as the income tax basis of accounting.
B. Authoritative guidance from FASB Statements adopted before the FASB Accounting Standards Codification does not appear in the Codification.
C. There is an implied hierarchy within the FASB Accounting Standards Codification, with FASB Statements assuming the top level.
D. International accounting standards are not included in the FASB Accounting Standards Codification.

AICPA.100883FAR-SIM

16. Which of the following statements includes the most useful guidance for practicing accountants concerning the FASB Accounting Standards Codification.

A. The Codification includes only FASB Statements.
B. The Codification is the sole source of U.S. GAAP, for nongovernmental entities.
C. The Codification significantly modified the content of GAAP when it became effective.
D. An accountant can be sure that all SEC rules are included in the Codification.

Conceptual Framework of Financial Reporting by Business Enterprises

Objectives and Qualitative Characteristics

AICPA.120623FAR

17. Which of the following characteristics of accounting information primarily allows users of financial statements to generate predictions about an organization?

A. Reliability.
B. Timeliness.
C. Neutrality.
D. Relevance.

AICPA.090636FAR-I-A

18. Which of the following characteristics relates to both accounting relevance and faithful representation?

A. Free from material error.
B. Completeness.
C. Neutrality.
D. Comparability.

AICPA.901101FAR-TH-FA

19. According to the conceptual framework, the process of reporting an item in the financial statements of an entity is:

A. Recognition.
B. Realization.
C. Allocation.
D. Matching.

AICPA.951106FAR-FA

20. Conceptually, interim financial statements can be described as emphasizing:

A. Timeliness over faithful representation.
B. Faithful representation over relevance.
C. Relevance over comparability.
D. Comparability over neutrality.

AICPA.900501FAR-TH-FA

21. According to the FASB conceptual framework, predictive value is an ingredient of:

	Relevance	Faithful Representation
A.	No	No
B.	Yes	Yes
C.	No	Yes
D.	Yes	No

Assumptions and Accounting Principles

AICPA.930505FAR-TH-FA

22. When a parent-subsidiary relationship exists, consolidated financial statements are prepared in recognition of the accounting concept of:

A. Reliability.
B. Materiality.
C. Legal entity.
D. Economic entity.

AICPA.082114FAR-I.A.II

23. According to the FASB conceptual framework, certain assets are reported in financial statements at the amount of cash or its equivalent that would have to be paid if the same or equivalent assets were acquired currently. What is the name of the reporting concept?

A. Replacement cost.
B. Current market value.
C. Historical cost.
D. Net realizable value.

AICPA.930503FAR-TH-FA

24. On December 31, 20X2, Brooks Co. decided to end operations and dispose of its assets within three months. December 31, 20X2, the net realizable value of the equipment was below historical cost.

   What is the appropriate measurement basis for equipment included in Brooks' December 31, 20X2, Balance Sheet?

   A. Historical cost.
   B. Current reproduction cost.
   C. Net realizable value.
   D. Current replacement cost.

AICPA.940503FAR-FA

25. Reporting inventory at the lower of cost or market is a departure from the accounting principle of:

   A. Historical cost.
   B. Consistency.
   C. Conservatism.
   D. Full disclosure.

AICPA.061241FAR

26. Which of the following assumptions means that money is the common denominator of economic activity and provides an appropriate basis for accounting measurement and analysis?

   A. Going concern.
   B. Periodicity.
   C. Monetary unit.
   D. Economic entity.

Constraints and Present Value

AICPA.951103FAR-FA

27. What is the underlying concept governing the Generally Accepted Accounting Principles pertaining to recording gain contingencies?

   A. Conservatism.
   B. Relevance.
   C. Consistency.
   D. Faithful representation.

AICPA.951102FAR-FA

28. According to the conceptual framework, the usefulness of providing information in financial statements is subject to the constraint of:

   A. Consistency.
   B. Cost-benefit.
   C. Relevance.
   D. Representational faithfulness.

Fair Value Framework

Fair Value Framework—Introduction and Definitions

AICPA.090417FAR-SIM

29. Which of the following benefits is the fair value framework intended to accomplish with respect to fair value measurement and fair value reporting?

	Increased Consistency	Increased Comparability
A.	Yes	Yes
B.	Yes	No
C.	No	Yes
D.	No	No

AICPA.090416FAR-SIM

30. Which one of the following is not a purpose of the fair value framework as set forth in ASC 820, "Fair Value Measurement"?

   A. Provide a uniform definition of "fair value" for GAAP purposes.
   B. Provide a framework for determining fair value for GAAP purposes.
   C. Establish new measurement requirements for financial instruments.
   D. Establish expanded disclosures about fair value when it is used.

AICPA.090421FAR-SIM

31. In determining the fair value of a nonfinancial asset, assessing the highest and best use of the asset must take into account all but which one of the following?

   A. What is physically possible.
   B. What is financially feasible.
   C. How the reporting entity would use the asset.
   D. What is legally permissible.

AICPA.090419FAR-SIM

32. The determination of fair value may be for:

	A Standalone Asset or Liability	A Group of Assets or Liabilities
A.	Yes	Yes
B.	Yes	No
C.	No	Yes
D.	No	No

AICPA.090418FAR-SIM

33. For which of the following circumstances is the guidance for determining fair value as provided in the fair value framework presented in ASC 820, "Fair Value Measurement," least likely to apply?

A. Determination of the fair value to be assigned to land acquired in a business combination.
B. Determination of the fair value of a bond liability for applying the fair value option.
C. Determination of the fair value of legal services received in exchange for an entity's common stock.
D. Determination of the fair value of a production facility when assessing whether an impairment loss has occurred.

Recognition and Measurement

AICPA.090423FAR-SIM

34. Papa Company acquired land with an office building on it from its subsidiary, Sonny Company, for $110,000. Prior to the sale, Sonny's carrying value of the land was $60,000 and its net carrying value of the building was $50,000. At the time of the transaction, Papa appropriately determined that the land had a fair value of $75,000 and the building had a fair value of $35,000. At what amount should Papa record the land and building on its books at the date of the transaction?

	Land	Building
A.	$75,000	$35,000
B.	$55,000	$55,000
C.	$60,000	$50,000
D.	$50,000	$60,000

AICPA.090428FAR-SIM

35. Marco has an investment that is traded in two different markets, Front market and Side market. Marco has equal access to each market. In order to determine the fair value of its investment, Marco has obtained the following per share information for the securities as of the close of business December 31, the end of its fiscal year:

	Front Market	Side Market
Selling Price	$52/sh	$50/sh
Transaction Cost	$6/sh	$1/sh

If Front market is the principal market for the security for Marco, using the market approach, which one of the following would be the per share amount used for measuring the investment at fair value?

A. $52/sh
B. $50/sh
C. $49/sh
D. $46/sh

AICPA.120618FAR

36. Giaconda, Inc. acquires an asset for which it will measure the fair value by discounting future cash flows of the asset. Which of the following terms best describes this fair value measurement approach?

A. Market.
B. Income.
C. Cost.
D. Observable inputs.

AICPA.090425FAR-SIM

37. In which of the following circumstances, if any, would an auditor likely be especially concerned as to whether or not the price paid to acquire an asset was the fair value of the asset?

I. The asset was acquired from the acquiring firm's majority shareholder.
II. The asset was acquired in an active exchange market.

A. I only.
B. II only.
C. Both I and II.
D. Neither I nor II.

080107FAR-FVO

38. On January 15, 2008, Able Co. made a significant investment in the debt securities of Baker Co., which it intends to hold until the debt matures. Able's fiscal year-end is December 31. If Able Co. intends to measure and report its investment in Baker Co. debt securities at fair value as permitted by FASB #159, "The Fair Value Option...," on which one of the following dates must Able elect to implement the fair value option?

A. January 15, 2008
B. January 31, 2008
C. March 31, 2008
D. December 31, 2008

Inputs and Hierarchy

AICPA.090431FAR-SIM

39. Which of the following statements concerning inputs used in ascertaining fair value is/are correct?

I. Only observable inputs can be used.
II. Inputs that incorporate the entity's assumptions may be used.

A. I only.
B. II only.
C. Both I and II.
D. Neither I nor II.

AICPA.090433FAR-SIM

40. Which of the following levels of the fair value hierarchy is the highest and which is the lowest in terms of desirability for use in determining fair value?

	Highest Level	Lowest Level
A.	Level 3	Level 1
B.	Level 1	Level 4
C.	Level 1	Level 3
D.	Level 4	Level 1

AICPA.090432FAR-SIM

41. Which of the following statements concerning the fair value hierarchy used in ascertaining fair value is/are correct?

I. Quoted market prices should be adjusted for a "blockage factor" when a firm holds a sizable portion of the asset being valued.
II. Quoted market prices in markets that are not active because there are few relevant transactions cannot be used.

A. I only.
B. II only.
C. Both I and II.
D. Neither I nor II.

AICPA.130735FAR

42. Each of the following would be considered a Level 2 observable input that could be used to determine an asset or liability's fair value, **except**

A. Quoted prices for identical assets and liabilities in markets that are not active.
B. Quoted prices for similar assets and liabilities in markets that are active.
C. Internally generated cash flow projections for a related asset or liability.
D. Interest rates that are observable at commonly quoted intervals.

AICPA.110548FAR

43. Which of the following items would best enable Driver Co. to determine whether the fair value of its investment in Favre Corp. is properly stated in the balance sheet?

A. Discounted cash flow of Favre's operations.
B. Quoted market prices available from a business broker for a similar asset.
C. Quoted market prices on a stock exchange for an identical asset.
D. Historical performance and return on Driver's investment in Favre.

Disclosure Requirements

AICPA.080120FAR-FVO

44. For a firm that elects to measure certain of its financial assets and financial liabilities at fair value, required financial statement disclosures are intended to facilitate which of the following comparisons?

I. Comparisons between entities that use different measurement methods for similar assets and liabilities.
II. Comparisons between assets and liabilities of a single entity that uses different measurement methods for similar assets and liabilities.

A. Neither I nor II.
B. I only.
C. II only.
D. Both I and II.

AICPA.080131FAR-FVF

45. Which of the following statements, if any, concerning disclosures about fair value measurements in periods subsequent to initial recognition is/are correct?

I. The fair value hierarchy level within which fair value measurements fall must be disclosed.
II. Quantitative fair value measurement disclosures must be in tabular format.

A. Both I and II are correct.
B. I only.
C. II only.
D. Neither I nor II are correct.

AICPA.090434FAR-SIM

46. Under U.S. GAAP the disclosure requirements when fair value measurement is used are differentiated by which of the following classifications?

A. Between assets measured at fair value and liabilities measured at fair value.
B. Between fair value measurements that result in gains and fair value measurements that result in losses.
C. Between items measured at fair value on a recurring basis and items measured at fair value on nonrecurring a basis.
D. Between items for which fair value measurement is required and items for which fair value measurement is elected.

AICPA.090394FAR-SIM

47. When an entity uses the fair value option for eligible financial assets and liabilities, which one of the following is not an expected outcome of the disclosures required of that entity?

A. Users being able to understand management's reasons for using the fair value option.

B. Users being able to understand how changes in fair value affect net income.

C. Replace the kind and amount of information that would have been provided if the fair value option had not been used with information related to fair value.

D. Users being able to understand the difference between fair value and cash flows.

AICPA.090436FAR-SIM

48. Which one of the following is not a required disclosure in annual financial reports for an entity that uses fair value measurement?

A. The level of the fair value hierarchy within which fair value measurements fall.

B. The valuation techniques used to measure fair value.

C. Combined disclosures about fair value measurements required by all pronouncements.

D. A discussion of any change from the prior period in valuation techniques used to measure fair value.

International Financial Reporting Standards (IFRS)

IASB Accounting Standards

AICPA.101189FAR-SIM

49. The IFRS Foundation serves as the administrative umbrella for a group of bodies. Which of the following bodies are NOT included under the IFRS Foundation umbrella?

A. International Federation of Accountants (IFAC).

B. International Accounting Standards Board.

C. IFRS Interpretations Committee.

D. IFRS Advisory Council.

AICPA.101186FAR-SIM

50. Which of the following is responsible for fund raising for entire operations involving the IASB?

A. IFRS Interpretations Committee.

B. IFRS Advisory Council.

C. IFRS Foundation.

D. Standard Advisory Council.

AICPA.101188FAR-SIM

51. Which of the following is not a role of the trustees of the IFRS Foundation?

A. Appoint the members of the IASB and establish their contracts of service and performance criteria.

B. Appoint the members of the IFRS Interpretations Committee and the IFRS Advisory Council.

C. Approve the annual budget of the IFRS Foundation and determine the basis for funding.

D. Annually review the strategy of the IFRS Foundation and the IASB and its effectiveness, including the determination of the IASB's agenda.

AICPA.101190FAR-SIM

52. Which of the following is a member of the Monitoring Board?

A. Global Accounting Technical Officer of the World Bank.

B. CEO of the Financial Executives International.

C. Chair of the CFA Institute.

D. Chair of the U.S. Securities and Exchange Commission.

AICPA.101187FAR-SIM

53. Which of the following is an objective of the IFRS Foundation?

A. To enforce the use and rigorous application of those standards.

B. To take account of, as appropriate, the needs of a range of sizes and types of entities in diverse economic settings.

C. To develop, in the public interest, a single set of high-quality, understandable, enforceable, and globally accepted financial-reporting standards (IFRSs) through its member associations.

D. To require adoption of international financial reporting standards (IFRSs) globally.

IASB Framework

AICPA.101159FAR-SIM

54. Identify which of the following is an assumption(s) underlying the preparation and presentation of financial statements under the IASB Framework.

	Accrual Basis	Going Concern
A.	Yes	No
B.	Yes	Yes
C.	No	Yes
D.	No	No

AICPA.101158FAR-SIM

55. Which of the following is a fundamental (primary) qualitative characteristic of useful financial information included in IASB's Framework?

    A. Comparability.
    B. Timeliness.
    C. Relevance.
    D. Understandability.

AICPA.101157FAR-SIM

56. According to the IASB Framework, the process of reporting an item in the financial statements of an entity is:

    A. Recognition.
    B. Statement of Financial Position.
    C. Disclosure.
    D. Presentation.

AICPA.101160FAR-SIM

57. When should an item that meets the definition of an element be recognized?

    A. The item has a cost or value that can be measured reliably.
    B. It is highly unlikely that any future economic benefit associated with the item will flow to the entity.
    C. Both A and B.
    D. Neither A nor B.

IFRS for SMEs

AICPA.100903FAR-OFS-SIM

58. Which one of the following is not an other comprehensive basis of accounting (OCBOA)?

    A. Cash basis.
    B. Modified cash basis.
    C. Income tax basis.
    D. IFRS for SMEs.

AICPA.100904FAR-OFS-SIM

59. Under IFRS for SMEs, which of the following, if any, must be disclosed in financial statements?

	Earnings per Share (EPS)	Information by Segment
A.	Yes	Yes
B.	Yes	No
C.	No	Yes
D.	No	No

AICPA.100905FAR-OFS-SIM

60. Which one of the following is a characteristic of accounting under IFRS for SMEs?

    A. Interest incurred during construction must be capitalized.
    B. Earnings per share must be provided in the financial statements.

    C. Goodwill must be amortized.
    D. The LIFO cost flow assumption can be used in valuing inventories.

AICPA.100902FAR-OFS-SIM

61. Under IFRS for SMEs, which of the following methods, if any, can be used by an investor to account for an investment in another entity (an associate) over which the investor has significant influence?

	Cost Method	Equity Method
A.	Yes	Yes
B.	Yes	No
C.	No	Yes
D.	No	No

IFRS—General Purpose Financial Statements

AICPA.101212FAR-SIM

62. Which of the following items would not appear on the Income Statement prepared using IFRS?

    A. Discontinued operations.
    B. Gross Profit.
    C. Depreciation and amortization.
    D. All items would appear on the income statement when using IFRS.

AICPA.101207FAR-SIM

63. IFRS requires a classified Statement of Financial Position. What are the required classifications?

    A. Cash; trade receivables and payables; property, plant and equipment; long-term assets and liabilities; and other assets and liabilities.
    B. Cash; trade receivables and payables; property, plant and equipment; and other assets and liabilities.
    C. Current, long-term, and other assets and liabilities.
    D. Current and non-current assets and liabilities.

General-Purpose Financial Statements

Balance Sheet / Statement of Financial Position

AICPA.101198FAR-SIM

64. Reporting accounts receivable at net realizable value is a departure from the accounting principle of:

    A. Conservatism.
    B. Fair value.
    C. Market value.
    D. Historical cost.

AICPA.101204FAR-SIM

65. Which of the following accounts is a contra account?

    A. Accumulated depreciation, equipment.
    B. Depreciation expense, office equipment.
    C. Dividends.
    D. Unearned revenue.

AICPA.101201FAR-SIM

66. The following trial balance of JB Company at December 31, Year 5, has been adjusted except for income taxes. The income tax rate is 30%.

	DR	CR
Accounts receivable, net	$725,000	
Accounts payable		250,000
Accumulated depreciation		125,000
Cash	185,000	
Contributed capital		650,000
Expenses	3,750,000	
Goodwill	140,000	
Prepaid taxes	225,000	
Property, plant, and equipment	850,000	
Retained earnings, 1/1/year five		350,000
Revenues		4,500,000
	5,875,000	5,875,000

During year five, estimated tax payments of $225,000 were paid and debited to prepaid taxes. There were no differences between financial statement and taxable income for year five.

Included in accounts receivable is $400,000 due from a loyal customer. Special terms were granted to this customer to make payments of $100,000 semi-annually every March 1 and September 1.

In JB Company's December 31, year 5 Balance Sheet, what amount should be reported as current assets?

    A. 710,000
    B. 910,000
    C. 935,000
    D. 1,135,000

AICPA.101202FAR-SIM

67. The following trial balance of JB Company at December 31, year five, has been adjusted except for income taxes. The income tax rate is 30%.

	DR	CR
Accounts receivable, net	725,000	
Accounts payable		250,000
Accumulated depreciation		125,000
Cash	185,000	
Contributed capital		650,000
Expenses	3,750,000	
Goodwill	140,000	
Prepaid taxes	225,000	
Property, plant, and equipment	850,000	
Retained earnings, 1/1/ Yr. 5		350,000
Revenues		4,500,000
	5,875,000	5,875,000

During year five, estimated tax payments of $225,000 were paid and debited to prepaid taxes. There were no differences between financial statement and taxable income for year five.

Included in accounts receivable is $400,000 due from a loyal customer. Special terms were granted to this customer to make payments of $100,000 semi-annually every March 1 and September 1.

In JB Company's December 31, year 5 Balance Sheet, what amount should be reported as total retained earnings?

    A. 225,000
    B. 525,000
    C. 750,000
    D. Some other amount

Income Statement

AICPA.901140FAR-P1-FA

68. Brock Corp. reports operating expenses in two categories: (1) selling and (2) general and administrative. The adjusted trial balance at December 31, 20X5 included the following expense and loss accounts:

Accounting and legal fees	$120,000
Advertising	150,000
Freight-out	80,000
Interest	70,000
Loss on the sale of long-term investments	30,000
Officers' salaries	225,000
Rent for office space	220,000
Sales salaries and commissions	140,000

One-half of the rented premises is occupied by the sales department.

Brock's total selling expenses for 20X5 are:

A. $480,000
B. $400,000
C. $370,000
D. $360,000

AICPA.950534FAR-FA

69. Which of the following should be included in general and administrative expenses?

	Interest	Advertising
A.	Yes	Yes
B.	Yes	No
C.	No	Yes
D.	No	No

AICPA.110580FAR

70. A company's activities for year 2 included the following:

Gross sales	$3,600,000
Cost of goods sold	1,200,000
Selling and administrative expense	500,000
Adjustment for a prior-year understatement of amortization expense	59,000
Sales returns	34,000
Gain on sale of available-for-sale securities	8,000
Gain on disposal of a discontinued business segment	4,000
Unrealized gain on available-for-sale securities	2,000

The company has a 30% effective income tax rate. What is the company's net income for year 2?

A. $1,267,700
B. $1,273,300
C. $1,314,600
D. $1,316,000

AICPA.101211FAR-SIM

71. If the accountant forgets to record salary expense in the Statement of Income, what is the result?

A. Net income is too high.
B. Net income is too low.
C. Retained earnings is too low.
D. Retained earnings is correctly stated, as the omission only affects the Income Statement.

AICPA.101208FAR-SIM

72. In a multi-step income statement:

A. Total expenses are subtracted from total revenues.
B. Gross profit (margin) is shown as a separate item.
C. Cost of sales and operating expense are subtracted from total revenues.
D. Other income is added to revenue from sales.

Statement of Comprehensive Income

AICPA.110600FAR

73. Which of the following is included in other comprehensive income?

A. Unrealized holding gains and losses on trading securities.
B. Unrealized holding gains and losses that result from a debt security being transferred into the held-to-maturity category from the available-for-sale category.
C. Foreign currency translation adjustments.
D. The difference between the accumulated benefit obligation and the fair value of pension plan assets.

AICPA.130719FAR

74. Palmyra Co. has net income of $11,000, a positive $1,000 net cumulative effect of a change in accounting principle, a $3,000 unrealized loss on available-for-sale securities, a positive $2,000 foreign currency translation adjustment, and a $6,000 increase in its common stock. What amount is Palmyra's comprehensive income?

A. $4,000
B. $10,000
C. $11,000
D. $17,000

AICPA.990501FAR-FA

75. When a full set of general-purpose financial statements are presented, comprehensive income and its components should:

A. Appear below income from continuing operations in the Income Statement.
B. Reported net of related income tax effect, in total and individually.
C. Appear in a supplemental schedule in the notes to the financial statements.
D. Be presented as part of the Income Statement or as a separate financial statement following the Income Statement.

AICPA.110582FAR

76. Which of the following is a component of other comprehensive income?

A. Minimum accrual of vacation pay.
B. Cumulative currency-translation adjustments.
C. Changes in market value of inventory.
D. Unrealized gain or loss on trading securities.

AICPA.090633FAR-I-B

77. A company reports the following information as of December 31:

Sales revenue	$800,000
Cost of goods sold	600,000
Operating expenses	90,000
Unrealized holding gain on the available-for-sale securities, net of tax	30,000

What amount should the company report as comprehensive income as of December 31?

A. $30,000
B. $110,000
C. $140,000
D. $200,000

Statement of Changes in Equity

AICPA.101241FAR-SIM

78. Which of the following items would appear on the Statement of Owner's Equity?

	Notes Payable	Treasury Stock	Advertising Expense	Retained Earnings
A.	Yes	Yes	Yes	Yes
B.	No	Yes	Yes	Yes
C.	No	Yes	No	Yes
D.	No	No	No	No

AICPA.101239FAR-SIM

79. The Statement of Changes in Equity shows an increase in the common stock account of $2,000 and an increase in the additional paid-in capital account of $10,000. If the common stock has a par value of $2, and the only transactions affecting these accounts were these issues of common stock, what was the average issue price of the common stock during the year?

A. $2
B. $5
C. $10
D. $12

AICPA.101238FAR-SIM

80. The Statement of Changes in Equity:

A. Is one of the required financial statements under U.S. GAAP.
B. Includes accounts such as the retained earnings and common share accounts but not other comprehensive income items.
C. Is used only if a corporation frequently issues common shares.
D. Reconciles all of the beginning and ending balances in the equity accounts.

Statement of Cash Flows

Sources and Uses of Cash

AICPA.040213FAR-SIM

81. Which of the following sets of financial statements generally cannot be prepared directly from the adjusted trial balance?

A. Income Statement, Balance Sheet, Statement of Cash Flows.
B. Income Statement, Statement of Cash Flows.
C. Statement of Cash Flows.
D. Balance Sheet and Statement of Cash Flows.

AICPA.951148FAR-FA

82. Which of the following is not disclosed on the Statement of Cash Flows, either on the face of the statement or in a separate schedule, when prepared under the direct method?

A. The major classes of gross cash receipts and gross cash payments.
B. The amount of income taxes paid.
C. A reconciliation of net income to net cash flow from operations.
D. A reconciliation of ending retained earnings to net cash flow from operations.

AICPA.070771FAR

83. Paper Co. had net income of $70,000 during the year. The dividend payment was $10,000. The following information is available:

Mortgage repayment	$20,000
Available-for-sale securities purchased	10,000 increase
Bonds payable-issued	50,000 increase
Inventory	40,000 increase
Accounts payable	30,000 decrease

What amount should Paper report as net cash provided by operating activities in its Statement of Cash Flows for the year?

A. $0
B. $10,000
C. $20,000
D. $30,000

AICPA.950549FAR-FA

84. Which of the following information should be disclosed as supplemental information in the Statement of Cash Flows?

	Cash Flow per Share	Conversion of Debt to Equity
A.	Yes	Yes
B.	Yes	No
C.	No	Yes
D.	No	No

AICPA.940505FAR-FA

85. The primary purpose of a Statement of Cash Flows is to provide relevant information about:

A. Differences between net income and associated cash receipts and disbursements.
B. An enterprise's ability to generate future positive net cash flows.
C. The cash receipts and cash disbursements of an enterprise during a period.
D. An enterprise's ability to meet cash operating needs.

Operating, Investing, and Financing Activities

AICPA.130711FAR

86. A company is preparing its year-end cash flow statement using the indirect method. During the year, the following transactions occurred:

Dividends paid	$300
Proceeds from the issuance of common stock	$250
Borrowings under a line of credit	$200
Proceeds from the issuance of convertible bonds	$100
Proceeds from the sale of a building	$150

What is the company's increase in cash flows provided by financing activities for the year?

A. $50
B. $150
C. $250
D. $550

AICPA.110566FAR

87. Abbott Co. is preparing its Statement of Cash Flows for the year. Abbott's cash disbursements during the year included the following:

Payment of interest on bonds payable	$500,000
Payment of dividends to stockholders	300,000
Payment to acquire 1,000 shares of Marks Co. common stock	100,000

What should Abbott report as total cash outflows for financing activities in its Statement of Cash Flows?

A. $0
B. $300,000
C. $800,000
D. $900,000

AICPA.110569FAR

88. A company calculated the following data for the period:

Cash received from customers	$25,000
Cash received from sale of equipment	1,000
Interest paid to bank on note	3,000
Cash paid to employees	8,000

What amount should the company report as net cash provided by operating activities in its Statement of Cash Flows?

A. $14,000
B. $15,000
C. $18,000
D. $26,000

AICPA.061224FAR

89. Which of the following items is included in the Financing Activities section of the Statement of Cash Flows?

A. Cash effects of transactions involving making and collecting loans.
B. Cash effects of acquiring and disposing of investments and property, plant, and equipment.
C. Cash effects of transactions obtaining resources from owners and providing them with a return on their investment.
D. Cash effects of transactions that enter into the determination of net income.

AICPA.900527FAR-TH-FA

90. A company acquired a building, paying a portion of the purchase price in cash and issuing a mortgage note payable to the seller for the balance.

In a Statement of Cash Flows, what amount is included in investing activities for the above transaction?

A. Cash payment.
B. Acquisition price.
C. Zero.
D. Mortgage amount.

Operating Cash Flows—Indirect Method

AICPA.120608FAR

91. Baler Co. prepared its statement of cash flows at year-end using the direct method. The following amounts were used in the computation of cash flows from operating activities:

Beginning inventory	$ 200,000
Ending inventory	150,000
Cost of goods sold	1,200,000
Beginning accounts payable	300,000
Ending accounts payable	200,000

What amount should Baler report as cash paid to suppliers for inventory purchases?

A. $1,200,000
B. $1,250,000
C. $1,300,000
D. $1,350,000

AICPA.920547FAR-P1-FA

92. The following balances were reported by Mall Co. December 31, 20X5 and 20X4:

	12/31/x5	12/31/x4
Inventory	$260,000	$290,000
Accounts payable	75,000	50,000

Mall paid suppliers $490,000 during the year ended December 31, 20X5. What amount should Mall report for cost of goods sold in 20X5?

A. $545,000
B. $495,000
C. $485,000
D. $435,000

AICPA.08211239FAR-III

93. How should the amortization of a bond discount on long-term debt be reported in a Statement of Cash Flows prepared using the indirect method?

A. As a financing activities inflow.
B. As a financing activities outflow.
C. In operating activities as a deduction from income.
D. In operating activities as an addition to income.

AICPA.911106FAR-P1-FA

94. The differences in some of Beal Inc.'s Balance Sheet accounts December 31, 20X4 and 20X3, are presented below:

Assets	Increase (Decrease)
Cash and cash equivalents	$120,000
Investments in trading securities	300,000
Accounts receivable, net	–
Inventory	80,000
Long-term investments	(100,000)
Plant assets (gross)	700,000
Liabilities and stockholders' equity	
Accounts payable and accrued liabilities	$(5,000)
Dividends payable	160,000
Short-term bank debt	325,000
Long-term debt	110,000
Common stock, $10 par	100,000
Additional paid-in capital	120,000
Retained Earnings	290,000

The following additional information relates to 20X4: net income was $790,000; cash dividends of $500,000 were declared; building costing $600,000, with a carrying amount of $350,000, was sold for $350,000; equipment costing $110,000 was acquired through the issuance of long-term debt; and a long-term investment was sold for $135,000. There were no other transactions affecting long-term investments. 10,000 shares of common stock were issued for $22 a share. In Beal's 20X4 Statement of Cash Flows, Net cash used in investing activities was:

A. $705,000
B. $1,190,000
C. $1,005,000
D. $165,000

AICPA.910506FAR-P1-FA

95. Metro, Inc. reported net income of $150,000 for 20X5. Changes occurred in several Balance Sheet accounts during 20X5 as follows:

Investment in Videogold, Inc. stock, carried on the equity basis	$5,500 increase
Accumulated depreciation, caused by major repair to projection equipment	2,100 decrease
Premium on bonds payable	1,400 decrease
Deferred income tax liability (long-term)	1,800 increase

In Metro's 20X5 cash flow statement, the reported net cash provided by operating activities should be:

A. $150,400
B. $148,300
C. $144,900
D. $142,800

Notes to Financial Statements

Notes to Financial Statements

AICPA.900530FAR-TH-FA

96. Which of the following facts concerning fixed assets should be included in the summary of significant accounting policies?

	Depreciation Method	Composition
A.	No	Yes
B.	Yes	Yes
C.	Yes	No
D.	No	No

AICPA.910532FAR-TH-FA

97. The summary of significant accounting policies should disclose the

A. Pro forma effect of retroactive application of an accounting change.
B. Basis of profit recognition on long-term construction contracts.
C. Adequacy of pension plan assets in relation to vested benefits.
D. Future minimum lease payments in the aggregate and for each of the five succeeding fiscal years.

AICPA.930531FAR-TH-FA

98. The summary of significant accounting policies should disclose the

A. Maturity dates of noncurrent debts.
B. Terms for convertible debt to be exchanged for common stock.
C. Concentration of credit risk of all financial instruments by geographical region.
D. Criteria for determining which investments are treated as cash equivalents.

AICPA.061215FAR

99. Which of the following must be included in the notes to the financial statements in a company's summary of significant accounting policies?

A. Description of current-year equity transactions.
B. Summary of long-term debt outstanding.

C. Schedule of fixed assets.
D. Revenue recognition policies.

AICPA.061201FAR

100. Which of the following should be disclosed in a summary of significant accounting policies?

A. Basis of profit recognition on long-term construction contracts.
B. Future minimum lease payments in the aggregate and for each of the five succeeding fiscal years.
C. Depreciation expense.
D. Composition of sales by segment.

Risks and Uncertainties

AICPA.101115FAR

101. Which of the following is not one of the concentrations about which disclosures are required?

A. Concentrations in revenue
B. Concentrations in sources of supply
C. Concentrations in the market for the firm's products
D. Concentrations in investment in other firm's stock for which ownership is less than 20% in any specific investment

AICPA.101112FAR

102. Which of the following is not a source of risk and uncertainty for which disclosures are required by GAAP?

A. Nature of a firm's operations
B. Effect of changes in government regulations
C. Use of estimates in financial statements
D. Vulnerability to significant concentrations

AICPA.101114FAR

103. What information about estimates is not required to be disclosed?

A. That estimates involve assumptions about future events
B. Possible material financial statement effects of estimate changes
C. That estimates are required in preparing financial statements
D. The old and new estimate in quantitative terms

AICPA.101116FAR

104. Under what conditions is disclosure about risks and uncertainty pertaining to concentrations required?

A. If the firm has any of the concentrations for which disclosures are required by GAAP
B. If events affecting the firm negatively have already occurred, with respect to a concentration

C. If the firm is vulnerable to a severe impact in the near term because of a concentration, and it is at least reasonably possible that the impact will occur

D. If the Board of Directors has taken a direct action serving to reduce risk and uncertainty within a given concentration

AICPA.101113FAR

105. Which of the following is not an aspect of a firm's operations necessitating disclosure of risks and uncertainties?

A. Principal markets
B. Products and services
C. Pension plan
D. Geographical location

Subsequent Events

AICPA.120632FAR

106. On March 21, year 2, a company with a calendar-year-end issued its year 1 financial statements. On February 28, year 2, the company's only manufacturing plant was severely damaged by a storm and had to be shut down. Total property losses were $10 million and determined to be material. The amount of business disruption losses is unknown. How should the impact of the storm be reflected in the company's year 1 financial statements?

A. Provide NO information related to the storm losses in the financial statements until losses and expenses become fully known.
B. Accrue and disclose the property loss with NO accrual or disclosure of the business disruption loss.
C. Do NOT accrue the property loss or the business disruption loss, but disclose them in the notes to the financial statements.
D. Accrue and disclose the property loss and additional business disruption losses in the financial statements.

AICPA.040405FAR

107. Adel Inc. uses the allowance method of accounting for bad debts.

During 20X5, the financial condition of Botel Co., one of Adel's major customers, deteriorated rapidly due to accounting and other scandals. In February 20X6 it has become clear that Botel will go out of business, although the firm has not declared bankruptcy or been forced into formal bankruptcy proceedings. Adel's receivable from Botel, nine months old as of the issuance of Adel's 20X5 financial statements, is 20 times the amount of bad debt expense otherwise reported by Adel.

How should the Botel situation be reflected in Adel's 20X5 financial statements?

A. No recognition other than that implied by the bad debt expense already recorded by Adel is necessary.
B. The footnotes should describe the potential loss, but no separate loss or expense for the Botel receivable should be recognized.
C. A loss in the amount of the Botel receivable should be recognized along with appropriate footnote disclosure.
D. Increase bad debt expense by a percentage of the Botel receivable amount because bankruptcy has not been declared as of the issuance of the financial statements.

AICPA.010405FAR

108. A large manufacturing firm made two significant acquisitions around the close of 20X6 (assume a calendar fiscal year).

The first was to purchase all the outstanding voting stock of Pernod, Inc. in December 20X6. The second was to purchase 40% of the outstanding voting stock of Weynod, Inc. in January 20X7. The manufacturing firm's 20X6 financial statements were issued in February 20X7.

Choose the correct statement regarding the accounting for these acquisitions in the 20X6 financial statements of the manufacturing firm.

	Pernod	Weynod
A.	consolidated	described in the footnotes only
B.	described in the footnotes only	described in the footnotes only
C.	consolidated	apply equity method
D.	apply equity method	apply equity method

AICPA.030405FAR

109. In October 20X2, a large U.S. aircraft manufacturer signed a significant contract with the government of France to build 50 jumbo jets, with delivery scheduled for 20X5.

In February 20X3, the firm signed a second contract with the government of Germany to build 35 jumbo jets. The 20X2 financial statements were issued in early March 20X3. The firm did not begin work on either contract before the issuance of the 20X2 statements.

Which contract(s) should be recognized in the accounts for the 20X2 financial statements?

	Contract 1 (French)	Contract 2 (German)
A.	Yes	No
B.	No	Yes
C.	Yes	Yes
D.	No	No

AICPA.020405FAR

110. During the last quarter of 20X4, a firm violated U.S. securities laws, and 20X4 revenues were overestimated as a result.

Although no lawsuit was brought against the firm before the 20X4 financial statements were released, management knows that in all likelihood the firm will be sued by shareholder groups and a range of possible loss amounts is estimated.

Therefore,

A. The firm has no recognized liability for 20X4.
B. The firm should recognize the estimated loss and liability.
C. The firm should only footnote the potential loss.
D. The firm should wait until being sued before considering any kind of disclosure.

Evaluating Financial Statements

Ratios—Liquidity/Solvency and Operational

AICPA.910538FAR-TH-FA

111. On December 30, 2004, Solomon Co. had a current ratio greater than 1:1 and a quick ratio less than 1:1.

On December 31, 2004, all cash was used to reduce accounts payable. How did these cash payments affect the ratios?

	Current Ratio	Quick Ratio
A.	Decreased	Decreased
B.	Decreased	Increased
C.	Increased	Decreased
D.	Increased	Increased

AICPA.950558FAR-FA

112. Selected data pertaining to Lore Co. for the calendar year 2005 is as follows:

Net cash sales	$3,000
Cost of goods sold	18,000
Inventory at beginning of year	6,000
Purchases	24,000
Accounts receivable at the beginning of the year	20,000
Accounts receivable at the end of the year	22,000

The accounts receivable turnover for 2005 was 5.0 times. What were Lore's 2005 net credit sales?

A. $105,000
B. $107,000
C. $110,000
D. $210,000

AICPA.082119FAR-I.C

113. The following information was taken from Baxter Department Store's financial statements:

Inventory on January 1	$100,000
Inventory on December 31	300,000
Net sales	2,000,000
Net purchases	700,000

What was Baxter's inventory turnover for the year ending December 31?

A. 2.5
B. 3.5
C. 5
D. 10

AICPA.082117FAR-I.C

114. TGR Enterprises provided the following information from its statement of financial position for the year ended December 31, Year 1:

	January 1	December 31
Cash	$10,000	$50,000
Accounts receivable	120,000	100,000
Inventories	200,000	160,000
Prepaid expenses	20,000	10,000
Accounts payable	175,000	120,000
Accrued liabilities	25,000	30,000

TGR's sales and cost of sales for Year 1 were $1,400,000 and $840,000, respectively. What is the accounts receivable turnover, in days?

A. 26.1
B. 28.7
C. 31.3
D. 41.7

AICPA.082121FAR-I.C

115. A company's year-end balance sheet is shown below:

Assets		Liabilities and shareholder equity	
Cash	$300,000	Current liabilities	$700,000
Accounts receivable	350,000	Long-term liabilities	600,000
Inventory	600,000	Common stock	800,000
Property, plant, and equipment (net)	2,000,000	Retained earnings	1,150,000
	$3,250,000		$3,250,000

What is the current ratio as of December 31?

A. 1.79
B. 0.93
C. 0.67
D. 0.43

Ratios—Profitability and Equity

AICPA.082120FAR-I.C

116. The following is the stockholders' equity section of Harbor Co.'s balance sheet on December 31:

Common stock $10 par, 100,000 shares authorized, 50,000 shares issued of which 5,000 have been reacquired, and are held in treasury	$450,000
Additional paid-in capital common stock	1,100,000
Retained earnings	800,000
Subtotal	$2,350,000
Less treasury stock	(150,000)
Total stockholders' equity	$2,200,000

Harbor has insignificant amounts of convertible securities, stock warrants, and stock options. What is the book value per share of Harbor's common stock?

A. $31
B. $44
C. $46
D. $49

AICPA.951160FAR-FA

117. The following data pertain to Cowl, Inc., for the year ended December 31, 2004:

Net sales	$600,000
Net income	150,000
Total assets, January 1, 2004	2,000,000
Total assets, December 31, 2004	3,000,000

What was Cowl's rate of return on assets for 2004?

A. 5%
B. 6%
C. 20%
D. 24%

AICPA.901110FAR-TH-FA

118. Are the following ratios useful in assessing the liquidity position of a company?

	Defensive-Interval Ratio	Return on Stockholders' Equity
A.	Yes	Yes
B.	Yes	No
C.	No	Yes
D.	No	No

AICPA.070776FAR

119. Stent Co. had total assets of $760,000, capital stock of $150,000, and retained earnings of $215,000. What was Stent's debt-to-equity ratio?

A. 2.63
B. 1.08
C. 0.52
D. 0.48

Consolidated Financial Statements

Introduction to Consolidated Financial Statements

AICPA.090104FAR-SIM

120. The results of the consolidating process are recorded in the books of the:

	Parent	Subsidiary
A.	Yes	Yes
B.	Yes	No
C.	No	Yes
D.	No	No

AICPA.090107FAR-SIM

121. Which one of the following kinds of accounts is least likely to be eliminated through an eliminating entry on the consolidating worksheet?

A. Receivables.
B. Investment.
C. Goodwill.
D. Payables.

AICPA.081273FAR-SIM

122. Which one of the following methods, if any, may a parent use on its books to carry an investment in a subsidiary that it will consolidate?

	Cost Method	Equity Method
A.	Yes	Yes
B.	Yes	No
C.	No	Yes
D.	No	No

AICPA.081277FAR-SIM

123. Which one of the following levels of voting ownership is normally assumed to convey significant influence over an investee?

A. 0%–10%.
B. 20%–50%.
C. 50%–100%.
D. 100%.

AICPA.070729FAR-P1-FA

124. The preparation of consolidated statements likely will require the following information about the subsidiary's assets and liabilities at the date of acquisition:

	Book Value	Fair Value
A.	Yes	No
B.	No	Yes
C.	Yes	Yes
D.	No	No

Consolidating Process

Consolidation at Acquisition

AICPA.071011FAR

125. A subsidiary, acquired for cash in a business combination, owned inventories with a market value different from the book value as of the date of combination. A consolidated balance sheet prepared immediately after the acquisition would include this difference as part of:

A. Deferred Credits
B. Goodwill
C. Inventories
D. Retained Earnings

AICPA.930508FAR-P2-FA

126. Penn Corp. paid $300,000 for the outstanding common stock of Star Co. At that time, Star had the following condensed balance sheet:

	Carrying Amounts
Current assets	$40,000
Plant and equipment, net	380,000
Liabilities	200,000
Stockholders' equity	220,000

The fair value of the plant and equipment was $60,000 more than its recorded carrying amount. The fair values and carrying amounts were equal for all other assets and liabilities. What amount of goodwill, related to Star's acquisition, should Penn report in its consolidated balance sheet?

A. $20,000
B. $40,000
C. $60,000
D. $80,000

AICPA.901109FAR-P1-FA

127. *This question has been adapted from the original AICPA-released question.*

On April 1, 2005, Dart Co. paid $620,000 for all the issued and outstanding common stock of Wall Corp. in a transaction properly accounted for as an acquisition.

The recorded assets and liabilities of Wall Corp. on April 1, 2005 follow:

Cash	$60,000
Inventory	180,000
Property and equipment (net of accumulated depreciation of $220,000)	320,000
Goodwill (net of accumulated amortization of $50,000)	100,000
Liabilities	(120,000)
Net assets	$540,000

On April 1, 2005, Wall's inventory had a fair value of $150,000, and the property and equipment (net) had a fair value of $380,000. What is the amount of goodwill resulting from the business combination?

A. $150,000
B. $120,000
C. $50,000
D. $20,000

AICPA.911110FAR-P2-FA

128. Beni Corp. purchased 100% of Carr Corp.'s outstanding capital stock for $430,000 cash. Immediately before the purchase, the balance sheets of both corporations reported the following:

	Beni	Carr
Assets	$2,000,000	$750,000
Liabilities	$750,000	$400,000
Common stock	1,000,000	310,000
Retained earnings	250,000	40,000
Liabilities and stockholders' equity	$2,000,000	$750,000

On the date of purchase, the fair value of Carr's assets was $50,000 more than the aggregate carrying amounts. In the consolidated balance sheet prepared immediately after the purchase, the consolidated stockholders' equity should amount to:

A. $1,680,000
B. $1,650,000
C. $1,600,000
D. $1,250,000

AICPA.071010FAR

129. A subsidiary, acquired for cash in a business combination, owned equipment with a market value in excess of book value as of the date of combination. A consolidated balance sheet prepared immediately after the acquisition would treat this excess as:

 A. Goodwill
 B. Plant and Equipment
 C. Retained Earnings
 D. Deferred Credits

Consolidation Subsequent to Acquisition

AICPA.090442FAR-SIM

130. When a parent company uses the cost method on its books to carry its investment in a subsidiary, which one of the following will be recorded by the parent on its books?

 A. Parent's share of subsidiary's net income/net loss.
 B. Parent's amortization of goodwill resulting from excess investment cost over fair value of subsidiary's net assets.
 C. Parent's share of subsidiary's cash dividends declared.
 D. Parent's depreciation of excess investment cost over book values of subsidiary's net assets.

AICPA.090444FAR-SIM

131. On October 1, 2008, Potato Company acquired 100% of the voting stock of Spud Company in a legal acquisition. Potato chose to account for its investment in Spud on its books using the cost method. Spud had the following incomes and dividends for the periods shown:

	10/1 – 12/31/08	1/1 – 12/31/09
Net Income	$3,000	$15,000
Dividends Declared/Paid	1,000	3,000

In its December 31, 2009, consolidating process, which one of the following is the amount of the reciprocity entry Potato will make on the consolidating worksheet?

 A. $2,000
 B. $3,000
 C. $14,000
 D. $18,000

AICPA.071015FAR

132. On January 1, 20X1, Prim, Inc. acquired all the outstanding common shares of Scarp, Inc. for cash equal to the book value of the stock. The carrying amount of Scarp's assets and liabilities approximated their fair values, except that the carrying amount of its building was more than fair value. In preparing Prim's 20X1 consolidated income statement, which of the following adjustments would be made?

 A. Depreciation expense would be decreased, and goodwill would be recognized.
 B. Depreciation expense would be increased, and goodwill would be recognized.
 C. Depreciation expense would be decreased, and no goodwill would be recognized.
 D. Depreciation expense would be increased, and no goodwill would be recognized.

AICPA.071017FAR-SIM

133. If the parent uses the cost method to account for its investment in a subsidiary, the parent will recognize:

 A. The parent's share of the subsidiary's net income.
 B. The parent's share of the subsidiary's dividends.
 C. Amortization of parent's excess cost of investment over the book value of the subsidiary.
 D. The parent's share of the subsidiary's net loss.

Consolidation Less than 100% Ownership

AICPA.090114FAR-SIM

134. If a parent uses the equity method on its books to account for its investment in a subsidiary, which one of the following will result in an increase in the investment account on the parent's books?

	Subsidiary Reports Income	Subsidiary Declares Dividend
A.	Yes	Yes
B.	Yes	No
C.	No	Yes
D.	No	No

AICPA.090117FAR-SIM

135. Assume that in acquiring a subsidiary, the parent determined there were several depreciable assets of the subsidiary that had a fair value greater than book value. What effect will the excess fair value over book value of the subsidiary's assets have on the following accounts in the preparation of consolidated statements?

	Depreciable Assets	Depreciation Expense
A.	Increase	Increase
B.	Increase	Decrease
C.	Decrease	Increase
D.	Decrease	Decrease

AICPA.090118FAR-SIM

136. Assume that in acquiring a subsidiary, the parent determined there were several depreciable assets of the subsidiary that had a fair value less than book value. What effect will this fair value less than book value of the subsidiary's assets have on the following accounts in the preparation of consolidated statements?

	Depreciable Assets	Depreciation Expense
A.	Increase	Increase
B.	Increase	Decrease
C.	Decrease	Increase
D.	Decrease	Decrease

AICPA.090764.FAR-SIM

137. On January 1, 20X1, Ritt Corp. purchased 80% of Shaw Corp.'s $10 par common stock for $975,000. Ritt's cost reflects an appropriate fair value measure for all of Shaw's outstanding common stock. The original cost to the noncontrolling investors for the 20% of Shaw's common stock not acquired by Ritt was $200,000. At the date of Ritt's purchase, the carrying amount of Shaw's net assets was $1,000,000. The fair values of Shaw's identifiable assets and liabilities were the same as their carrying amounts except for plant assets (net), which were $100,000 in excess of the carrying amount. Which one of the following is the amount of noncontrolling interest that should be reported in a consolidated balance sheet prepared immediately following the business combination?

A. $125,000
B. $200,000
C. $220,000
D. $243,750

AICPA.090113FAR-SIM

138. If a parent uses the equity method on its books to carry its investment in a subsidiary, which one of the following current-year entries (made by the parent) must be reversed on the consolidating worksheet?

	Income from Subsidiary	Dividends from Subsidiary
A.	Yes	Yes
B.	Yes	No
C.	No	Yes
D.	No	No

Intercompany (I/C) Transactions and Balances

Intercompany (I/C) Transactions and Balances—Introduction

AICPA.911109FAR-TH-FA

139. Pride, Inc. owns 80% of Simba, Inc.'s outstanding common stock. Simba, in turn, owns 10% of Pride's outstanding common stock.

What percentage of the common stock cash dividends declared by the individual companies should be reported as dividends declared in the consolidated financial statements?

	Dividends Declared by Pride	Dividends Declared by Simba
A.	90%	0%
B.	90%	20%
C.	100%	0%
D.	100%	20%

AICPA.090446FAR-SIM

140. Which one of the following is not a characteristic associated with intercompany transactions?

A. Intercompany transactions must be eliminated in the consolidating process.
B. Gains and losses must be eliminated in the consolidating process.
C. Transactions that originate with a subsidiary must be eliminated in the consolidating process.
D. Transactions between two subsidiaries to be consolidated with the same parent do not need to be eliminated.

AICPA.920510FAR-P1-FA

141. Lion, Inc. owns 60% of Gray Corp.'s common stock. On December 31, 2005, Gray owes Lion $400,000 for a cash advance.

In preparing the consolidated balance sheet on that date, what amount of the advance should be eliminated?

A. $400,000
B. $240,000
C. $160,000
D. $0

AICPA.900511FAR-P1-FA

142. On December 31, 2005, Grey, Inc. owned 90% of Winn Corp., a consolidated subsidiary, and 20% of Carr Corp., an investee in which Grey cannot exercise significant influence. On the same date, Grey had receivables of $300,000 from Winn and $200,000 from Carr.

In its December 31, 2005, consolidated balance sheet, Grey should report accounts receivable from affiliates of:

A. $500,000
B. $340,000
C. $230,000
D. $200,000

AICPA.130713FAR

143. King, Inc. owns 70% of Simmon Co.'s outstanding common stock. King's liabilities total $450,000, and Simmon's liabilities total $200,000. Included in Simmon's financial statements is a $100,000 note payable to King. What amount of total liabilities should be reported in the consolidated financial statements?

A. $520,000
B. $550,000
C. $590,000
D. $650,000

Intercompany (I/C) Inventory Transactions

AICPA.090449FAR-SIM

144. Pine Company acquired goods for resale from its manufacturing subsidiary, Strawco, at Strawco's cost to manufacture of $12,000. Pine subsequently resold the goods to a nonaffiliate for $18,000. Which one of the following is the amount of the elimination that will be needed as a result of the intercompany inventory transaction?

A. $-0-
B. $6,000
C. $12,000
D. $18,000

AICPA.090448FAR-SIM

145. Which one of the following will occur on consolidated financial statements if an intercompany inventory transaction is not eliminated?

A. An understatement of sales.
B. An overstatement of sales.
C. An understatement of purchases.
D. An overstatement of accounts receivable.

AICPA.090452FAR-SIM

146. During 200X, Papa Company sold inventory, which cost it $18,000, to its subsidiary, Sonnyco, for $27,000. At the end of 200X, Sonnyco had $9,000 of the intercompany goods still on its books. The balance had been resold to unaffiliated customers for $24,000. Which one of the following is the amount of ending inventory

that should be eliminated for consolidated statements?

A. $3,000
B. $6,000
C. $9,000
D. $15,000

AICPA.090451FAR-SIM

147. During 200X, Papa Company sold inventory, which cost it $18,000, to its subsidiary, Sonnyco, for $27,000. At the end of 200X, Sonnyco had $9,000 of the intercompany goods still on its books. The balance had been resold to unaffiliated customers for $24,000. Which one of the following is the amount of intercompany sales that should be eliminated for 200X consolidated statements?

A. $27,000
B. $24,000
C. $18,000
D. $12,000

AICPA.090450FAR-SIM

148. Which of the following can be overstated on consolidated financial statements if intercompany inventory balances on-hand at the end of a period are not eliminated?

	Consolidated Income	Consolidated Loss
A.	Yes	Yes
B.	Yes	No
C.	No	Yes
D.	No	No

Intercompany (I/C) Fixed Asset Transactions

AICPA.071027FAR

149. Assume that on January 2, Company P recognized a $3,000 gain on the sale of a depreciable fixed asset to its subsidiary, Company S. Company S will depreciate the asset using straight-line depreciation over the remaining three-year life of the asset. What amount of intercompany gain will be eliminated from P's retained earnings at the end of the year following the year of the intercompany fixed asset transactions?

A. $- 0 -
B. $1,000
C. $2,000
D. $3,000

AICPA.090459FAR-SIM

150. Which of the following can be overstated on consolidated financial statements if

intercompany fixed asset balances on-hand at
the end of a period are not eliminated?

	Consolidated Income	Consolidated Loss
A.	No	No
B.	No	Yes
C.	Yes	No
D.	Yes	Yes

AICPA.901102FAR-TH-FA

151. Water Co. owns 80% of the outstanding
common stock of Fire Co. On December 31,
2005, Fire sold equipment to Water at a price in
excess of Fire's carrying amount but less than its
original cost. On a consolidated balance sheet
on December 31, 2005, the carrying amount of
the equipment should be reported at:

   A. Water's original cost.
   B. Fire's original cost.
   C. Water's original cost less Fire's recorded gain.
   D. Water's original cost less 80% of Fire's recorded gain.

AICPA.071026FAR

152. For consolidated purposes, what effect will the
intercompany sale of a fixed asset at a profit
or at a loss have on depreciation expense
recognized by the buying affiliate?

	At a Profit	At a Loss
A.	Overstate	Overstate
B.	Overstate	Understate
C.	Understate	Overstate
D.	Understate	Understate

AICPA.090460FAR-SIM

153. An intercompany depreciable fixed asset
transaction resulted in an intercompany gain.
Which one of the following is least likely to
be reflected in the consolidated financial
statements prepared at the end of the period in
which the intercompany transaction occurred?

   A. Consolidated income will be less than
   the sum of the incomes of the separate
   companies being combined.
   B. Consolidated assets will be less than the
   sum of the assets of the separate companies
   being combined.
   C. Consolidated depreciation expense will be
   more than the sum depreciation expense of
   the separate companies being combined.
   D. Consolidated accumulated depreciation
   will be more than the sum of accumulated
   depreciation of the separate companies
   being combined.

Intercompany (I/C) Bonds

AICPA.071029FAR

154. In which of the following ownership
arrangements would intercompany bonds
exist?

	Parent Owns Subsidiary Bonds	Subsidiary Owns Parent Bonds
A.	Yes	Yes
B.	Yes	No
C.	No	Yes
D.	No	No

AICPA.090465FAR-SIM

155. On December 31, 2008, Pico acquired $250,000
par value of the outstanding $1,000,000
bonds of its subsidiary, Sico, in the market for
$200,000. On that date, Sico had a $100,000
premium on its total bond liability.

   Which one of the following is the net amount
   of gain or loss that will be recognized by Pico in
   its December 31, 2008, consolidated financial
   statements as a result of its intercompany
   bonds?

   A. $25,000
   B. $50,000
   C. $75,000
   D. $150,000

AICPA.090464FAR-SIM

156. On December 31, 2008, Pico acquired $250,000
par value of the outstanding $1,000,000
bonds of its subsidiary, Sico, in the market for
$200,000. On that date, Sico had a $100,000
premium on its total bond liability.

   Which one of the following is the net carrying
   value of Sico's total bond liability?

   A. $900,000
   B. $1,000,000
   C. $1,050,000
   D. $1,100,000

AICPA.090463FAR-SIM

157. On December 31, 2008, Pico acquired $250,000
par value of the outstanding $1,000,000
bonds of its subsidiary, Sico, in the market for
$200,000. On that date, Sico had a $100,000
premium on its total bond liability.

   Which one of the following is the amount of
   premium or discount on Pico's investment in
   Sico's bonds?

   A. $250,000 premium
   B. $100,000 premium
   C. $50,000 premium
   D. $50,000 discount

AICPA.090462FAR-SIM

158. Which one of the following is not a characteristic of intercompany bonds?

   A. Intercompany bonds may occur on the date of a business combination or subsequent to a business combination.
   B. When bonds become intercompany, it is as though the bonds have been retired for consolidated purposes.
   C. Intercompany bonds can result in the recognition of a gain or a loss for consolidating purposes.
   D. When bonds become intercompany, they are written off of the books of the issuing affiliate and the investing affiliate.

IFRS—Consolidations

BCC-0068B

159. Under IFRS the asset goodwill may be recognized:

   A. When it is acquired by purchase.
   B. When it is internally generated or acquired by purchase.
   C. When it is clear that it exists and has value.
   D. When it has future economic benefits.

BCC-0043

160. Under IFRS, a parent may exclude a subsidiary from consolidation if all of the following conditions exist, **except**:

   A. It is wholly or partially owned and its other owners do not object to nonconsolidation.
   B. It reports only one class of stock in its balance sheet.
   C. Its parent prepares consolidated financial statements that comply with IFRS.
   D. It does not have any debt or equity instruments publicly traded.

BCC-0042

161. Which statement is **true** with respect to noncontrolling interest?

   A. U.S. GAAP records noncontrolling interest at the proportionate share of the value of identifiable net assets of the acquiree.
   B. IFRS only records noncontrolling interest at the proportionate share of the value of identifiable net assets of the acquiree.
   C. Both U.S. GAAP and IFRS record noncontrolling interest at the proportionate share of the value of identifiable net assets of the acquiree.
   D. IFRS permits recording noncontrolling interests at either fair value or the proportionate share of the value of identifiable net assets of the acquiree.

BCC-0041

162. Which statement is true with respect to push-down accounting?

   A. IFRS permits the use of push-down accounting.
   B. IFRS does not permit the use of push-down accounting.
   C. SEC accounting does not permit the use of push-down accounting.
   D. Both SEC accounting and IFRS permit the use of push-down accounting.

AICPA.100978FAR-SIM

163. Which of the following statements about the differences between U.S. GAAP and IFRS in determining whether to consolidate an entity is/are correct?

   I. IFRS guidelines for determining the eligibility of an entity to be consolidated are more principles-based than are U.S. GAAP guidelines.
   II. In assessing an investor's level of ownership of an investee, both U.S. GAAP and IFRS consider outstanding securities that are exercisable or convertible into voting shares.
   III. Under both U.S. GAAP and IFRS, there are circumstances under which a majority-owned subsidiary does not have to be consolidated.

   A. I only.
   B. I and II only.
   C. I and III only.
   D. I, II, and III.

Combined Financial Statements

AICPA.082080FAR-I.A

164. Nolan owns 100% of the capital stock of both Twill Corp. and Webb Corp. Twill purchases merchandise inventory from Webb at 140% of Webb's cost. During 2007, merchandise that cost Webb $40,000 was sold to Twill. Twill sold all of this merchandise to unrelated customers for $81,200 during 2007. In preparing combined financial statements for 2007, Nolan's bookkeeper disregarded the common ownership of Twill and Webb.

What amount should be eliminated from cost of goods sold in the combined income statement for 2007?

   A. $56,000
   B. $40,000
   C. $24,000
   D. $16,000

AICPA.082078FAR-I.A

165. Mr. Allen owns all of the common stock of Astro Company and 80% of the common stock of Bio Company. Astro owns the remaining 20% interest in Bio's common stock, for which it paid $8,000, and which it carries at cost, because there is no ready market for Bio's stock. The condensed balance sheets for Astro and Bio as of December 31, 2007, were:

	Astro	Bio
Assets	$300,000	120,000
Liabilities	$100,000	$60,000
Common Stock	50,000	40,000
Retained Earnings	150,000	20,000
Total	$300,000	120,000

What amount should be reported as total owners' equity in a combined balance sheet for Astro and Bio as of December 31, 2007?

A. $260,000
B. $252,000
C. $212,000
D. $200,000

AICPA.910519FAR-P2-FA

166. Nolan owns 100% of the capital stock of both Twill Corp. and Webb Corp.

Twill purchases merchandise inventory from Webb at 140% of Webb's cost. During 2004, merchandise that cost Webb $40,000 was sold to Twill. Twill sold all of this merchandise to unrelated customers for $81,200 during 2004. In preparing combined financial statements for 2004, Nolan's bookkeeper disregarded the common ownership of Twill and Webb.

By what amount was unadjusted revenue overstated in the combined income statement for 2004?

A. $16,000
B. $40,000
C. $56,000
D. $81,200

AICPA.082079FAR-I.A

167. In the preparation of combined financial statements, would the following issues be treated in the same way as when preparing consolidated financial statements or in a different way?

	Minority Interest	Foreign Operations	Different Fiscal Periods
A.	Different	Different	Different
B.	Different	Same	Same
C.	Same	Same	Different
D.	Same	Same	Same

AICPA.082082FAR-I.A

168. The following information pertains to shipments of merchandise from Home Office to Branch during 2007:

Home Office's cost of merchandise	$160,000
Intracompany billing	200,000
Sales by Branch	250,000
Unsold merchandise at Branch on December 31, 2007	20,000

In the combined income statement of Home Office and Branch for the year ended December 31, 2007, what amount of the above transactions should be included in sales?

A. $250,000
B. $230,000
C. $200,000
D. $180,000

Variable Interest Entities (VIEs)

AICPA.081267FAR-SIM

169. Which of the following legal forms of business combination will result in the need to prepare consolidated financial statements?

	Merger	Acquisition	Consolidation
A.	Yes	Yes	Yes
B.	Yes	Yes	No
C.	No	No	Yes
D.	No	Yes	No

AICPA.081268FAR-SIM

170. In which one of the following cases is the subsidiary most likely to be reported as an unconsolidated subsidiary?

A. The subsidiary is in an industry unrelated to the parent.
B. The subsidiary has a fiscal year-end that is one month different from the parent's year-end.
C. The subsidiary is in legal bankruptcy.
D. The subsidiary has a controlling interest in another entity.

AICPA.081269FAR-SIM

171. Parco has the following three subsidiaries: Finco, Serco, and Euroco. Finco is a 100% owned finance subsidiary. Serco is an 80% owned service company. Euroco is a 100% owned foreign subsidiary that conducts operations in Western Europe. Which one of the following is the most likely number of entities, including Parco, to be included in Parco's consolidated financial statements?

A. One.
B. Two.
C. Three.
D. Four.

Exit or Disposal Activities and Discontinued Operations

AICPA.081295FAR-SIM

172. In 20X5, a firm decided to discontinue a segment with a book value of $200 million and a fair value of $250 million. The cost to dispose of the segment in 20X6 is estimated to be $10 million. In the 20X5 income statement, what amount of disposal gain or loss will be reported in the discontinued operations section?

    A. $-0-
    B. $50 million loss.
    C. $50 million gain.
    D. $40 million gain.

AICPA.082105FAR-III.C.I

173. On April 30, 20X5, Carty Corp. approved a plan to dispose of a segment of its business. The disposal loss is $480,000, including severance pay of $55,000 and employee relocation costs of $25,000, both of which are directly associated with the decision to dispose of the segment. The firm is a calendar-fiscal-year firm, and the segment's operating loss for the entire year (20X5) through the date of disposal was $120,000.

    Before income taxes, what amount should be reported in Carty's income statement for the year ended December 31, 20X5, as the total income effect (loss) from discontinued operations?

    A. $600,000
    B. $480,000
    C. $120,000
    D. $360,000

AICPA.110578FAR

174. A company decided to sell an unprofitable division of its business. The company can sell the entire operation for $800,000, and the buyer will assume all assets and liabilities of the operations. The tax rate is 30%. The assets and liabilities of the discontinued operation are as follows:

Buildings	$5,000,000
Accumulated depreciation	3,000,000
Mortgage on buildings	1,100,000
Inventory	500,000
Accounts payable	600,000
Accounts receivable	200,000

What is the after-tax net loss on the disposal of the division?

    A. $140,000
    B. $200,000
    C. $1,540,000
    D. $2,200,000

AICPA.082106FAR-III.C.I

175. On May 15, Year 1, Munn, Inc. approved a plan to dispose of a segment of its business. It is expected that the sale will occur on February 1, Year 2, at a selling price of $500,000. The segment reported $195,000 in operating losses for year 1. The segment is expected to lose $30,000 from operations in Year 2. The carrying amount of the segment at the date of sale was expected to be $850,000. Before income taxes, what amount should Munn report as a loss from discontinued operations in its Year 1 income statement?

    A. $575,000
    B. $225,000
    C. $195,000
    D. $545,000

AICPA.110574FAR

176. Which of the following transactions qualifies as a discontinued operation?

    A. Disposal of a group of assets that are fully depreciated and have no remaining useful life.
    B. Approved sale of a segment that represents a strategic shift in the entities operations.
    C. Phasing out of a production line.
    D. Changes related to technological improvements.

Public Company Reporting Topics (SEC, EPS, Interim, and Segment)

U.S. Securities and Exchange Commission (SEC)

SEC—Role and Standard-Setting Process

AICPA.101192FAR-SIM

177. The SEC enforces the corporate registration requirements of the Securities Act of 1933 as one of its principal objectives. These requirements are intended to provide information that enables the SEC to:

    A. Evaluate the financial merits of the corporation offering the securities to the public.
    B. Ensure that investors are provided with adequate information on which to base investment decisions.
    C. Guarantee that the facts contained in the registration statement are accurate.
    D. Assure investors of the accuracy of the financial statements.

AICPA.101193FAR-SIM

178. Even though the SEC delegates the creation of accounting standards to the private sector, the SEC frequently comments on accounting and auditing issues. The main pronouncements published by the SEC are:

    A. Federal Reporting Updates (FRU).
    B. Financial Reporting Releases (FRR).
    C. Staff Auditing Bulletins (SAB).
    D. Accounting Principles Opinions (APO).

AICPA.101191FAR-SIM

179. The SEC is comprised of five commissioners, appointed by the President of the United States, and four divisions. Which of the following divisions is responsible for overseeing compliance with the securities acts?

    A. Division of Corporate Finance.
    B. Division of Enforcement.
    C. Division of Trading and Markets.
    D. Division of Investment Management.

SEC Reporting Requirements

AICPA.110562FAR-SIM

180. Which regulation governs the form and content of financial statement disclosures?

    A. Regulation S-X.
    B. Sarbanes-Oxley.
    C. Regulation S-K.
    D. Regulation S-Q.

AICPA.101179FAR

181. Which of the following is not a required component of the 10-K filing?

    A. Product market share.
    B. Description of the business.
    C. Market price of common stock.
    D. Executive compensation.

AICPA.120625FAR

182. A company that is a large accelerated filer must file its Form 10-Q with the United States Securities and Exchange Commission within how many days after the end of the period?

    A. 30 days.
    B. 40 days.
    C. 45 days.
    D. 60 days.

assess.AICPA.FAR.sec.report-0028

183. U.S. Securities and Exchange Commission (SEC) regulations for the financial statement presentation and disclosure requirements of SEC filings can be found in:

    A. Regulation S-B.
    B. Regulation S-K.
    C. Regulation S-T.
    D. Regulation S-X.

AICPA.110563FAR-SIM

184. Which of the following is required by Regulation S-K to be included in the Management's Discussion and Analysis (MD&A) that is part of the 10-K?

    A. The Balance Sheet.
    B. Discussion of risks and uncertainties.
    C. Accounting fees and services.
    D. Executive compensation.

Earnings per Share

Introduction to Earnings per Share

AICPA.070766FAR

185. Jen Co. had 200,000 shares of common stock and 20,000 shares of 10%, $100 par value cumulative preferred stock. No dividends on common stock were declared during the year. Net income was $2,000,000. What was Jen's basic earnings per share?

    A. $9.00
    B. $9.09
    C. $10.00
    D. $11.11

AICPA.120638FAR

186. Wood Co.'s dividends on noncumulative preferred stock have been declared but not paid. Wood has not declared or paid dividends on its cumulative preferred stock in the current or the prior year and has reported a net loss in the current year. For the purpose of computing basic earnings per share, how should the income available to common stockholders be calculated?

    A. The current-year dividends and the dividends in arrears on the cumulative preferred stock should be added to the net loss, but the dividends on the noncumulative preferred stock should NOT be included in the calculation.
    B. The dividends on the noncumulative preferred stock should be added to the net loss, but the current-year dividends and the dividends in arrears on the cumulative preferred stock should NOT be included in the calculation.
    C. The dividends on the noncumulative preferred stock and the current-year

dividends on the cumulative preferred stock should be added to the net loss.

D. Neither the dividends on the noncumulative preferred stock nor the current-year dividends and the dividends in arrears on cumulative preferred stock should be included in the calculation.

AICPA.051183FAR-FA

187. During the current year, Comma Co. had outstanding: 25,000 shares of common stock, 8,000 shares of $20 par, 10% cumulative preferred stock, and 3,000 bonds that are $1,000 par and 9% convertible. The bonds were originally issued at par, and each bond was convertible into 30 shares of common stock. During the year, net income was $200,000, no dividends were declared, and the tax rate was 30%.

What amount was Comma's basic earnings per share for the current year?

A. $3.38
B. $7.36
C. $7.55
D. $8.00

Basic Earnings Per Share

AICPA.930560FAR-P1-FA

188. The following information pertains to Jet Corp.'s outstanding stock for Year 1:

Common stock, $5 par value	
Shares outstanding, 1/1/04	20,000
2-for-1 stock split, 4/1/Year 1	20,000
Shares issued, 7/1/Year 1	10,000
Preferred stock, $10 par value, 5% cumulative	
Shares outstanding, 1/1/Year 1	4,000

What are the number of shares Jet should use to calculate Year 1 earnings per share?

A. 40,000
B. 45,000
C. 50,000
D. 54,000

AICPA.130728FAR

189. A company had the following outstanding shares as of January 1, year 2:

Preferred stock, $60 par, 4% cumulative	10,000 shares
Common stock, $3 par	50,000 shares

On April 1, year 2, the company sold 8,000 shares of previously unissued common stock.

No dividends were in arrears on January 1, year 2, and no dividends were declared or paid during year 2. Net income for year 2 totaled $236,000. What amount is basic earnings per share for the year ended December 31, year 2?

A. $3.66
B. $3.79
C. $4.07
D. $4.21

AICPA.120633FAR

190. Balm Co. had 100,000 shares of common stock outstanding as of January 1. The following events occurred during the year:

4/1	Issued 30,000 shares of common stock.
6/1	Issued 36,000 shares of common stock.
7/1	Declared a 5% stock dividend.
9/1	Purchased as treasury stock 35,000 shares of its common stock. Balm used the cost method to account for the treasury stock.

What is Balm's weighted average of common stock outstanding at December 31?

A. 131,000
B. 139,008
C. 150,675
D. 162,342

AICPA.110575FAR

191. Chape Co. had the following information related to common and preferred shares during the year:

Common shares outstanding,	1/1	700,000
Common shares repurchased,	3/31	20,000
Conversion of preferred shares,	6/30	40,000
Common shares repurchased,	12/1	36,000

Chape reported net income of $2,000,000 at December 31. What amount of shares should Chape use as the denominator in the computation of basic earnings per share?

A. 684,000
B. 700,000
C. 702,000
D. 740,000

AICPA.911160FAR-P1-FA

192. Strauch Co. has one class of common stock outstanding and no other securities that are potentially convertible into common stock. During Year 1, 100,000 shares of common stock were outstanding. In Year 2, two distributions of additional common shares occurred:

On April 1, 20,000 shares of treasury stock were sold, and on July 1, a 2-for-1 stock split was issued.

Net income was $410,000 in Year 2 and $350,000 in Year 1.

What amounts should Strauch report as earnings per share in its Year 2 and Year 1 comparative income statements?

	Year 2	Year 1
A.	$1.78	$3.50
B.	$1.78	$1.75
C.	$2.34	$1.75
D.	$2.34	$3.50

Diluted Earnings Per Share

AICPA.070789FAR

193. The following information pertains to Ceil Co., a company whose common stock trades in a public market:

Shares outstanding at 1/1	100,000
Stock dividend at 3/31	24,000
Stock issuance at 6/30	5,000

What is the weighted average number of shares Ceil should use to calculate its basic earnings per share for the year ended December 31?

A. 120,500
B. 123,000
C. 126,500
D. 129,000

AICPA.083700FAR-SIM

194. The treasury stock method of entering stock options into the calculation of diluted EPS:

A. Is used only for dilutive treasury stock.
B. Computes the increase in common shares outstanding from assumed exercise of options to be the number of shares under option.
C. Is called the treasury stock method because the proceeds from assumed exercise are assumed to be used to purchase treasury stock.
D. Assumes the treasury shares are purchased at year-end.

AICPA.083701FAR-SIM

195. A firm with a net income of $30,000 and weighted average actual shares outstanding of 15,000 for the year also had the following two securities outstanding the entire year: (1) 2,000 options to purchase one share of stock for $12 per share. The average share price during the year was $20, (2) cumulative convertible preferred stock with an annual dividend commitment of $4,500. Total common shares

issued on conversion are 2,900. Compute diluted EPS for this firm.

A. $1.70
B. $1.60
C. $1.55
D. $1.61

Earnings per Share and IFRS

AICPA.101225FAR-SIM

196. For which of the following income statement sections is earnings per share calculated?

A. Sales.
B. Gross profit.
C. Income before discontinued operations.
D. Dividends paid to common shareholders.

AICPA.101223FAR-SIM

197. LM Company has net income of $130,000, weighted average shares of common stock outstanding of 50,000, and preferred dividends for the period of $20,000. What is LM's earnings per share of common stock?

A. $2.60
B. $2.50
C. $2.20
D. $0.40

AICPA.101221FAR-SIM

198. If everything else is held constant, earnings per share is increased by:

A. Purchase of treasury stock.
B. Issuance of new shares of common stock.
C. Payment of a cash dividend to common stockholders.
D. Payment of a cash dividend to both preferred and common stockholders.

AICPA.101224FAR-SIM

199. Why do preferred stock dividends appear in the calculation of earnings per share (EPS)?

A. Preferred stock may be converted into common stock at the option of the shareholder.
B. Preferred stock dividends are not included in the calculation of EPS unless they have been outstanding for the entire year.
C. The denominator includes the weighted average number of shares of both preferred and common shares outstanding.
D. Preferred stock dividends are subtracted from the earnings for the period in the calculation of earnings per share.

AICPA.101222FAR-SIM

200. AB Company reported earnings per share of $10.50 on income before discontinued operations, ($2.00) on income (loss) attributed to discontinued operations, and $8.50 on net income. Which EPS figure is more relevant to a potential investor?

    A. ($2.00)
    B. $7.50
    C. $8.50
    D. $10.50

Segment Reporting

AICPA.051164FAR-ST

201. Opto Co. is a publicly traded, consolidated enterprise reporting segment information. Which of the following items is a required enterprise-wide disclosure regarding external customers?

    A. The fact that transactions with a particular external customer constitute more than 10% of the total enterprise revenues
    B. The identity of any external customer providing 10% or more of a particular operating segment's revenue
    C. The identity of any external customer considered to be "major" by management
    D. Information on major customers is not required in segment reporting.

AICPA.900556FAR-P2-FA

202. Correy Corp. and its divisions are engaged solely in manufacturing operations. The following data (consistent with prior years' data) pertain to the industries in which operations were conducted for the year ending December 31, 2005:

Industry	Total Revenue	Operating Profit	Identifiable Assets at 12/31/1989
A	$10,000,000	$1,750,000	$20,000,000
B	8,000,000	1,400,000	17,500,000
C	6,000,000	1,200,000	12,500,000
D	3,000,000	550,000	7,500,000
E	4,250,000	675,000	7,000,000
F	1,500,000	225,000	3,000,000
	$32,750,000	$5,800,000	$67,500,000

In its segment information for 2005, how many reportable segments does Correy have?

    A. Three
    B. Four
    C. Five
    D. Six

AICPA.070790FAR

203. In financial reporting of segment data, which of the following must be considered in determining if an industry segment is a reportable segment?

	Sales to Unaffiliated Customers	Intersegment Sales
A.	Yes	Yes
B.	Yes	No
C.	No	Yes
D.	No	No

AICPA.951108FAR-FA

204. Terra Co.'s total revenues from its three business segments were as follows:

Segment	Sales to Unaffiliated Customers	Intersegment Sales	Total Revenues
Lion	$70,000	$30,000	$100,000
Monk	22,000	4,000	26,000
Nevi	8,000	16,000	24,000
Combined	$100,000	$50,000	$150,000
Elimination	–	(50,000)	(50,000)
Consolidated	$100,000	$–	$100,000

Which business segment(s) is (are) deemed to be reportable segment(s)?

    A. None
    B. Lion only
    C. Lion and Monk only
    D. Lion, Monk, and Nevi

AICPA.921136FAR-TH-FA

205. Cott Co.'s four business segments have revenues and identifiable assets expressed as percentages of Cott's total revenues and total assets as follows:

	Revenues	Assets
Ebon	64%	66%
Fair	14%	18%
Gel	14%	4%
Hak	8%	12%
	100%	100%

Which of these business segments are deemed to be reportable segments?

    A. Ebon only
    B. Ebon and Fair only
    C. Ebon, Fair, and Gel only
    D. Ebon, Fair, Gel, and Hak

Interim Financial Reporting

Interim Reporting Principles

AICPA.921116FAR-TH-FA

206. An inventory loss from a market price decline occurred in the first quarter, and the decline was not expected to reverse during the fiscal year.

However, in the third quarter, the inventory's market price recovery exceeded the market decline that occurred in the first quarter.

For interim financial reporting, the dollar amount of net inventory should:

A. Decrease in the first quarter by the amount of the market price decline and increase in the third quarter by the amount of the decrease in the first quarter.
B. Decrease in the first quarter by the amount of the market price decline and increase in the third quarter by the amount of the market price recovery.
C. Decrease in the first quarter by the amount of the market price decline and not be affected in the third quarter.
D. Not be affected in either the first quarter or the third quarter.

AICPA.101128FAR

207. How are discontinued operations that occur at midyear initially reported?

A. Disclosed only in the notes to the year-end financial statements.
B. Included in net income and disclosed in the notes to the year-end financial statements.
C. Included in net income and disclosed in the notes to interim financial statements.
D. Disclosed only in the notes to interim financial statements.

AICPA.110563FAR-TI

208. In general, an enterprise preparing interim financial statements should:

A. Defer recognition of seasonal revenue.
B. Disregard permanent decreases in the market value of its inventory.
C. Allocate revenues and expenses evenly over the quarters, regardless of when they actually occurred.
D. Use the same accounting principles followed in preparing its latest annual financial statements.

AICPA.101138FAR

209. Bard Co., a calendar-year corporation, reported income before income tax expense of $10,000 and income tax expense of $1,500 in its interim income statement for the first quarter of the year. Bard had income before income tax expense of $20,000 for the second quarter and an estimated effective annual rate of 25%. What amount should Bard report as income tax expense in its interim income statement for the second quarter?

A. $3,500
B. $5,000
C. $6,000
D. $7,500

AICPA.900543FAR-P2-FA

210. An inventory loss from a permanent market decline of $360,000 occurred in May Year 1. Cox Co. appropriately recorded this loss in May Year 1 after its March 31, Year 1, quarterly report was issued.

What amount of inventory loss should be reported in Cox's quarterly income statement for the three months ended June 30, year 1?

A. $0
B. $90,000
C. $180,000
D. $360,000

Interim Reporting—Details and IFRS

AICPA.911113FAR-P2-FA

211. Kell Corp. reported $111,000 of net income for the quarter ended September 30, 20X5. Additional information for the quarter:

1 A $60,000 gain from discontinued operation, realized on April 30, 20X5, was allocated equally to the second, third, and fourth quarters of 2005.
2 A $16,000 cumulative-effect adjustment (dr.) resulting from a change in inventory valuation method was recognized on August 2, 20X5. The new method was used for the quarter ended September 30. The $111,000 earnings amount does not reflect the cumulative effect.

In addition, Kell paid $48,000 on February 1, 20X5, for 20X5 calendar-year property taxes. Of this amount, $12,000 was allocated to the third quarter of 20X5.

For the quarter ended September 30, 20X5, Kell should report net income of:

A. $91,000
B. $75,000
C. $111,000
D. $95,000

AICPA.910536FAR-TH-FA

212. A planned volume variance in the first quarter, which is expected to be absorbed by the end of the fiscal period, ordinarily should be deferred at the end of the first quarter if it is:

	Favorable	Unfavorable
A.	Yes	No
B.	No	Yes
C.	No	No
D.	Yes	Yes

Special Purpose Frameworks

Cash, Modified Cash, Income Tax

AICPA.100916FAR-OCB-SIM

213. Which of the following items would be recognized in financial statements prepared using an income tax basis of accounting relating to permanent differences?

	Nontaxable Income	Nondeductible Expenses
A.	Yes	Yes
B.	Yes	No
C.	No	Yes
D.	No	No

AICPA.100915FAR-OCB-SIM

214. Which of the following statements, if any, concerning the modified cash basis of accounting is/are correct?

I. The modified cash basis of accounting employs some elements of accrual accounting.

II. To be acceptable, modifications to the cash basis of accounting must have substantial support in practice.

A. I only.
B. II only.
C. Both I and II.
D. Neither I nor II.

AICPA.100911FAR-OCB-SIM

215. Which one of the following is not an other comprehensive basis of accounting?

A. Pure cash basis.
B. Modified cash basis.
C. Pure accrual basis.
D. Income tax basis.

AICPA.100912FAR-OCB-SIM

216. When a set of financial statements is prepared using the cash basis or the modified cash basis of accounting, which one of the following is least likely to be an appropriate financial statement title?

A. Statement of Cash Receipts and Cash Disbursements.
B. Balance Sheet.
C. Income Statement.
D. Statement of Financial Position.

AICPA.100917FAR-OCB-SIM

217. Alco, Inc., a small manufacturing company, prepares its financial statements using its income tax basis of accounting. In December, 2012, it determined that an error had been made in the amount of rent expense reported in its 2011 tax return. How should Alco account for the amount of the rental expense error in its 2012 financial statements?

A. As an adjustment to 2012 rental income.
B. As an income tax expense in 2012.
C. As a prior-period adjustment.
D. No reporting in 2012 required.

Private Company Council/Little GAAP

AICPA.140416FAR-SIM

218. Which of the following is not measured at the expected cash to be paid or received?

A. Notes payable.
B. Equipment in use.
C. Unrecorded patent.
D. Equipment held for sale.

aq.private.comp.001

219. A private company decided to adopt one of the standards issued by the Private Company Council. What are the requirements upon adoption of the PCC standard?

A. Apply the new standard on a retrospective basis.
B. Apply the new standard on a prospective basis.
C. Assess whether application of the new standard is preferable and apply on a retrospective basis.
D. Assess whether application of the new standard is preferable and apply on a prospective basis.

II.   Select Financial Statement Accounts

Cash and Cash Equivalents

Cash

AICPA.940512FAR-FA

220. The following information pertains to Grey Co. on December 31, 2003:

Checkbook balance	$12,000
Bank statement balance	16,000
Check drawn on Grey's account, payable to a vendor, dated and recorded 12/31/03 but not mailed until 1/10/04	1,800

On Grey's December 31, 2003 balance sheet, what amount should be reported as cash?

A. $12,000
B. $13,800
C. $14,200
D. $16,000

AICPA.930510FAR-P1-FA

221. Cook Co. had the following balances on December 31, 2004:

Cash in checking account	$350,000
Cash in money market account	250,000
U.S. Treasury bill, purchased 12/1/04, maturing 2/28/05	800,000
U.S. Treasury bond, purchased 3/1/04, maturing 2/28/05	500,000

Cook's policy is to treat as cash equivalents all highly liquid investments with a maturity of three months or less when purchased. What amount should Cook report as cash and cash equivalents in its December 31, 2004 balance sheet?

A. $600,000
B. $1,150,000
C. $1,400,000
D. $1,900,000

AICPA.921113FAR-TH-FA

222. On October 31, 2005 Dingo, Inc. had cash accounts at three different banks. One account balance is segregated solely for a November 15, 2005 payment into a bond sinking fund. A second account, used for branch operations, is overdrawn. The third account, used for regular corporate operations, has a positive balance.

How should these accounts be reported in Dingo's October 31, 2005, classified balance sheet?

A. The segregated account should be reported as a noncurrent asset, the regular account should be reported as a current asset, and the overdraft should be reported as a current liability.
B. The segregated and regular accounts should be reported as current assets, and the overdraft should be reported as a current liability.
C. The segregated account should be reported as a noncurrent asset, and the regular account should be reported as a current asset net of the overdraft.
D. The segregated and regular accounts should be reported as current assets net of the overdraft.

AICPA.051178FAR-FA

223. The following are held by Smite Co.:

Cash in checking account	$20,000
Cash in bond sinking fund account	30,000
Post-dated check from customer dated one month from balance sheet date	250
Petty cash	200
Commercial paper (matures in two months)	7,000
Certificate of deposit (matures in six months)	5,000

What amount should be reported as cash and cash equivalents on Smite's balance sheet?

A. $57,200
B. $32,200
C. $27,450
D. $27,200

AICPA.930501FAR-P1-FA

224. The following is Gold Corp.'s June 30, 2004 trial balance:

Cash overdraft		$10,000
Accounts receivable, net	$35,000	
Inventory	58,000	
Prepaid expenses	12,000	
Land held for resale	100,000	
Property, plant, and equipment, net	95,000	
Accounts payable and accrued expenses		32,000
Common stock		25,000
Additional paid-in capital		150,000
Retained earnings		83,000
	$300,000	$300,000

977

Additional information:

1 Checks amounting to $30,000 were written to vendors and recorded on June 29, 2004, resulting in a cash overdraft of $10,000. The checks were mailed on July 9, 2004.
2 Land held for resale was sold for cash on July 15, 2004.
3 Gold issued its financial statements on July 31, 2004.

In its June 30, 2004, balance sheet, what amount should Gold report as current assets?

A. $225,000
B. $205,000
C. $195,000
D. $125,000

Bank Reconciliations

AICPA.911103FAR-P1-FA

225. The following information pertains to Park Co. on December 31, 2005:

Bank statement balance	$10,000
Checkbook balance	14,000
Deposit in transit	5,000
Outstanding checks	1,000

In Park's December 31, 2005 balance sheet, cash should be reported as

A. $9,000
B. $10,000
C. $14,000
D. $15,000

AICPA.083703FAR-SIM

226. A bank reconciliation with the headings "Balance per Books" and "Balance per Bank" lists three adjustments under the former and four adjustments under the latter. The company makes separate adjusting entries for each item in the reconciliation that requires an adjustment. How many adjusting entries are recorded?

A. 3
B. 4
C. 7
D. 0

AICPA.110568FAR

227. Hilltop Co.'s monthly bank statement shows a balance of $54,200. Reconciliation of the

statement with company books reveals the following information:

Bank service charge	$10
Insufficient funds check	650
Checks outstanding	1,500
Deposits in transit	350
Check deposited by Hilltop and cleared by the bank for $125, but improperly recorded by Hilltop as $152	

What is the net cash balance after the reconciliation?

A. $52,363
B. $53,023
C. $53,050
D. $53,077

AICPA.901101FAR-P1-FA

228. In preparing its August 31, 1990 bank reconciliation, Apex Corp. has the following information available:

Balance per bank statement, 8/31/90	$18,050
Deposit in transit, 8/31/90	3,250
Return of customer's check for insufficient funds, 8/31/90	600
Outstanding checks, 8/31/90	2,750
Bank service charges for August	100

On August 31, 1990, Apex's correct cash balance is

A. $18,550
B. $17,950
C. $17,850
D. $17,550

AICPA.900501FAR-P1-FA

229. Poe, Inc. had the following bank reconciliation at March 31, 2005:

Balance per bank statement, 3/31/05	$46,500
Add deposit in transit	10,300
	56,800
Less outstanding checks	12,600
Balance per books, 3/31/05	$44,200
Data per bank for the month of April 2005 follow:	
Deposits	$58,400
Disbursements	49,700

All reconciling items at March 31, 2005 cleared the bank in April. Outstanding checks at April 30, 2005 totaled $7,000. There were no deposits in transit at April 30, 2005. What is the cash balance per books at April 30, 2005?

A. $48,200
B. $52,900
C. $55,200
D. $45,900

Receivables

Accounts Receivable—Accounting and Reporting

AICPA.900510FAR-P1-FA

230. On June 1, 2005, Pitt Corp. sold merchandise with a list price of $5,000 to Burr on account. Pitt allowed trade discounts of 30% and 20%.

Credit terms were 2/15, n/40 and the sale was made FOB shipping point. Pitt prepaid $200 of delivery costs for Burr as an accommodation.

On June 12, 2005, Pitt received from Burr a remittance in full payment amounting to

A. $2,744
B. $2,940
C. $2,944
D. $3,140

Uncollectable—Direct Write-Off and Allowance

AICPA.910510FAR-TH-FA

231. Gibbs Co. uses the allowance method for recognizing uncollectible accounts. Ignoring deferred taxes, the entry to record the write-off of a specific uncollectible account

A. Affects neither net income nor working capital.
B. Affects neither net income nor accounts receivable.
C. Decreases both net income and accounts receivable.
D. Decreases both net income and working capital.

AICPA.120626FAR

232. During the year, Hauser Co. wrote off a customer's account receivable. Hauser used the allowance method for uncollectible accounts. What impact would the write-off have on net income and total assets?

	Net income	Total Assets
A.	Decrease	Decrease
B.	Decrease	No effect
C.	No effect	Decrease
D.	No effect	No effect

AICPA.900543FAR-P1-FA

233. Adam Co. reported sales revenue of $2,300,000 in its income statement for the year ended December 31, 2005. Additional information was as follows:

	12/31/04	12/31/05
Accounts receivable	$500,000	$650,000
Allowance for uncollectible accounts	(30,000)	(55,000)

Uncollectible accounts totaling $10,000 were written off during 2005. Under the cash basis of accounting, Adam would have reported 2005 sales of

A. $2,140,000
B. $2,150,000
C. $2,175,000
D. $2,450,000

AICPA.910509FAR-TH-FA

234. Bee Co. uses the direct write-off method to account for uncollectible accounts receivable.

During an accounting period, Bee's cash collections from customers equal sales adjusted for the addition or deduction of the following amounts:

	Accounts Written Off	Increase in Accounts Receivable Balance
A.	Deduction	Deduction
B.	Addition	Deduction
C.	Deduction	Addition
D.	Addition	Addition

AICPA.901145FAR-P1-FA

235. Orr Co. prepared an aging of its accounts receivable at December 31, 2005 and determined that the net realizable value of the receivables was $250,000. Additional information is available as follows:

Allowance for uncollectible accounts at 1/1/05—credit balance	$28,000
Accounts written off as uncollectible during 2005	23,000
Accounts receivable at 12/31/05	270,000
Uncollectible accounts recovery during 2005	5,000

For the year ended December 31, 2005, Orr's uncollectible accounts expense would be

A. $23,000
B. $20,000
C. $15,000
D. $10,000

Allowance—Income Statement and Balance Sheet Approach

AICPA.941145FAR-FA

236. Inge Co. determined that the net value of its accounts receivable on December 31, 2005, based on an aging of the receivables, was $325,000. Additional information is as follows:

Allowance for uncollectible accounts—1/1/05	$30,000
Uncollectible accounts written off during 2005	18,000
Uncollectible accounts recovered during 2005	2,000
Accounts receivable at 12/31/05	350,000

For 2005, what would be Inge's uncollectible accounts expense?

A. $5,000
B. $11,000
C. $15,000
D. $21,000

AICPA.930547FAR-P1-FA

237. Hall Co.'s allowance for uncollectible accounts had a credit balance of $24,000 on December 31, 2003. During 2004, Hall wrote off uncollectible accounts of $96,000. The aging of accounts receivable indicated that a $100,000 allowance for doubtful accounts was required on December 31, 2004. What amount of uncollectible accounts expense should Hall report for 2004?

A. $172,000
B. $120,000
C. $100,000
D. $96,000

AICPA.930551FAR-P1-FA

238. Ward Co. estimates its uncollectible accounts expense to be 2% of credit sales. Ward's credit sales for 2004 were $1,000,000. During 2004, Ward wrote off $18,000 of uncollectible accounts. Ward's allowance for uncollectible accounts had a $15,000 balance on January 1, 2004. In its December 31, 2004 income statement, what amount should Ward report as uncollectible accounts expense?

A. $23,000
B. $20,000
C. $18,000
D. $17,000

AICPA.110576FAR

239. Marr Co. had the following sales and accounts receivable balances, prior to any adjustments at year end:

Credit sales	$10,000,000
Accounts receivable	3,000,000
Allowance for uncollectible accounts (debit balance)	50,000

Marr uses 3% of accounts receivable to determine its allowance for uncollectible accounts at year end. By what amount should Marr adjust its allowance for uncollectible accounts at year end?

A. $0
B. $40,000
C. $90,000
D. $140,000

AICPA.900509FAR-P1-FA

240. The following accounts were abstracted from Roxy Co.'s unadjusted trial balance on December 31, 2005:

	Debit	Credit
Accounts receivable	$1,000,000	
Allowance for uncollectible accounts	8,000	
Net credit sales		$3,000,000

Roxy estimates that 3% of the gross accounts receivable will become uncollectible. After adjustment at December 31, 2005, the allowance for uncollectible accounts should have a credit balance of

A. $90,000
B. $82,000
C. $38,000
D. $30,000

Notes Receivable

AICPA.920516FAR-P1-FA

241. On December 1, 2005, Tigg Mortgage Co. gave Pod Corp. a $200,000, 12% loan.

Pod received proceeds of $194,000 after the deduction of a $6,000 nonrefundable loan origination fee. Principal and interest are due in 60 monthly installments of $4,450, beginning January 1, 2006. The repayments yield an effective interest rate of 12% at a present value of $200,000 and 13.4% at a present value of $194,000.

What amount of accrued interest receivable should Tigg include in its December 31, 2005 balance sheet?

A. $4,450
B. $2,166
C. $2,000
D. $0

AICPA.931117FAR-P1-FA

242. Frame Co. has an 8% note receivable, in the original amount of $150,000, dated June 30, 2003. Payments of $50,000 in principal plus accrued interest are due annually on July 1, 2004, 2005, and 2006.

In its June 30, 2005, balance sheet, what amount should Frame report as a current asset for interest on the note receivable?

A. $0
B. $4,000
C. $8,000
D. $12,000

AICPA.911127FAR-P1-FA

243. Each of Potter Pie Co.'s 21 new franchisees contracted to pay an initial franchise fee of $30,000.

By December 31, 2005, each franchisee had paid a nonrefundable $10,000 fee and signed a note to pay $10,000 principal plus the market rate of interest on December 31, 2006 and December 31, 2007.

Experience indicates that one franchise will default on the additional payments. Services for the initial fee will be performed in 2006.

What amount of net unearned franchise fees would Potter report on December 31, 2005?

A. $400,000
B. $600,000
C. $610,000
D. $630,000

AICPA.901103FAR-P2-FA

244. On June 1, 2005, Yola Corp. loaned Dale $500,000 on a 12% note, payable in five annual installments of $100,000 beginning January 2, 2006. In connection with this loan, Dale was required to deposit $5,000 in a noninterest-bearing escrow account.

The amount held in escrow is to be returned to Dale after all principal and interest payments have been made. Interest on the note is payable on the first day of each month beginning July 1, 2005. Dale made timely payments through November 1, 2005. On January 2, 2006, Yola received payment of the first principal installment plus all interest due.

On December 31, 2005, Yola's interest receivable on the loan to Dale should be

A. $0
B. $5,000
C. $10,000
D. $15,000

AICPA.941138FAR-FA

245. Leaf Co. purchased from Oak Co. a $20,000, 8%, 5-year note that required five equal annual year-end payments of $5,009. The note was discounted to yield a 9% rate to Leaf. At the date of purchase, Leaf recorded the note at its present value of $19,485.

What should be the total interest revenue earned by Leaf over the life of this note?

A. $5,045
B. $5,560
C. $8,000
D. $9,000

Criteria for Sale of Receivables

AICPA.920541FAR-P1-FA

246. Ace Co. sold King Co. a $20,000, 8%, 5-year note that required five equal annual year-end payments. This note was discounted to yield a 9% rate to King. The present value factors of an ordinary annuity of $1 for five periods are as follows:

| 8% | 3.992 |
| 9% | 3.890 |

What should be the total interest revenue earned by King on this note?

A. $9,000
B. $8,000
C. $5,560
D. $5,050

AICPA.931115FAR-P1-FA

247. Roth, Inc. received from a customer a one-year, $500,000 note bearing annual interest of 8%. After holding the note for six months, Roth discounted the note at Regional Bank at an effective interest rate of 10%. What amount of cash did Roth receive from the bank?

A. $540,000
B. $523,810
C. $513,000
D. $495,238

AICPA.911117FAR-P1-FA

248. On July 1, 2005, Lee Co. sold goods in exchange for a $200,000, 8-month, noninterest-bearing note receivable. At the time of the sale, the note's market rate of interest was 12%.

What amount did Lee receive when it discounted the note at 10% on September 1, 2005?

A. $194,000
B. $193,800
C. $190,000
D. $188,000

AICPA.070781FAR

249. Red Co. had $3 million in accounts receivable recorded on its books. Red wanted to convert the $3 million in receivables to cash in a more timely manner than waiting the 45 days for payment as indicated on its invoices. Which of the following would alter the timing of Red's cash flows for the $3 million in receivables already recorded on its books?

A. Change the due date of the invoice.
B. Factor the receivables outstanding.
C. Discount the receivables outstanding.
D. Demand payment from customers before the due date.

AICPA.921104FAR-TH-FA

250. After being held for 40 days, a 120-day, 12% interest-bearing note receivable was discounted at a bank at 15%. The proceeds received from the bank equal

A. Maturity value less the discount at 12%.
B. Maturity value less the discount at 15%.
C. Face value less the discount at 12%.
D. Face value less the discount at 15%.

Factoring, Assignment, and Pledging

AICPA.101058FAR

251. Milton Co. pledged some of its accounts receivable to Good Neighbor Financing Corporation in return for a loan. Which of the following statements is correct?

A. Good Neighbor Financing cannot take title to the receivables if Milton does not repay the loan. Title can only be taken if the receivables are factored.
B. Good Neighbor Financing will assume the responsibility of collecting the receivables.
C. Milton will retain control of the receivables.
D. Good Neighbor Financing will take title to the receivables, and will return title to Milton after the loan is paid.

AICPA.101059FAR

252. On April 1, Aloe, Inc. factored $80,000 of its accounts receivable without recourse. The factor retained 10% of the accounts receivable as an allowance for sales returns

and charged a 5% commission on the gross amount of the factored receivables. What amount of cash did Aloe receive from the factored receivables?

A. $68,000
B. $68,400
C. $72,000
D. $76,000

AICPA.931141FAR-P1-FA

253. On November 1, 2004, Davis Co. discounted with recourse at 10%, a one-year, noninterest-bearing, $20,500 note receivable maturing on January 31, 2005.

What amount of contingent liability for this note must Davis disclose in its financial statements for the year ended December 31, 2004?

A. $0
B. $20,000
C. $20,333
D. $20,500

Notes Receivable—Impairment

AICPA.110603FAR-SIM

254. Under IFRS, a cash generating unit (CGU) is:

A. The smallest business segment.
B. Any grouping of assets that generates cash flows.
C. Any group of assets that are reported separately to management.
D. The smallest group of assets that generates independent cash flows from continuing use.

AICPA.082108FAR-II.B

255. Choose the correct accounting by the creditor for a loan impairment. Column (1): recognize a loss or expense upon recognizing the impairment. Column (2): rate of interest to use in computing the revised book value of the receivable after the impairment.

	1	2
A.	Yes	Original effective rate
B.	Yes	New implied effective rate
C.	No	Original effective rate
D.	No	New implied effective rate

AICPA.083707FAR-SIM

256. When a note receivable is determined to be impaired,

A. The note is written-off.
B. No recognition of the impairment is required until a formal troubled-debt restructuring takes place.

C. The note is written down to the nominal sum of future cash flows expected to be collected, including interest.

D. A loss or expense is recognized as equal to the difference between the note carrying value and the present value of the cash flows expected to be received.

AICPA.083708FAR-SIM

257. A creditor's note receivable has a carrying value of $60,000 at the end of Year 1. Based on information about the debtor, the creditor believes the note is impaired and establishes the new carrying value of the note to be $25,000 at the end of Year 1. During Years 2 and 3, the debtor pays $14,000 on the note each year (total payments, $28,000). For Year 3, under which method of the two indicated is interest revenue recognized?

	Interest Method	Cost Recovery Method
A.	Yes	Yes
B.	No	No
C.	Yes	No
D.	No	Yes

Inventory

Introduction to Inventory

AICPA.900514FAR-P1-FA

258. West Retailers purchased merchandise with a list price of $20,000, subject to trade discounts of 20% and 10%, with no cash discounts allowable.

West should record the cost of this merchandise as

A. $14,000
B. $14,400
C. $15,600
D. $20,000

AICPA.911112FAR-P1-FA

259. On December 28, 2005, Kerr Manufacturing Co. purchased goods costing $50,000. The terms were FOB destination. Some of the costs incurred in connection with the sale and delivery of the goods were as follows:

Packaging for shipment	$1,000
Shipping	1,500
Special handling charges	2,000

These goods were received on December 31, 2005. In Kerr's December 31, 2005 balance sheet, what amount of cost for these goods should be included in inventory?

A. $54,500
B. $53,500

C. $52,000
D. $50,000

AICPA.941113FAR-FA

260. Herc Co.'s inventory on December 31, 2005 was $1,500,000, based on a physical count priced at cost, and before any necessary adjustment for the following:

1 Merchandise costing $90,000, shipped FOB shipping point from a vendor on December 30, 2005, was received and recorded on January 5, 2006.

2 Goods in the shipping area were excluded from inventory although shipment was not made until January 4, 2006. The goods, billed to the customer FOB shipping point on December 30, 2005, had a cost of $120,000.

What amount should Herc report as inventory in its December 31, 2005, balance sheet?

A. $1,500,000
B. $1,590,000
C. $1,620,000
D. $1,710,000

AICPA.900544FAR-P1-FA

261. On October 20, 2005, Grimm Co. consigned 40 freezers to Holden Co. for sale at $1,000 each and paid $800 in transportation costs.

On December 30, 2005, Holden reported the sale of 10 freezers and remitted $8,500. The remittance was net of the agreed 15% commission.

What amount should Grimm recognize as consignment sales revenue for 2005?

A. $7,700
B. $8,500
C. $9,800
D. $10,000

AICPA.901107FAR-P1-FA

262. The following information applied to Fenn, Inc. for 2005:

Merchandise purchased for resale	$400,000
Freight-in	10,000
Freight-out	5,000
Purchase returns	2,000

Fenn's 2005 inventoriable cost was

A. $400,000
B. $403,000
C. $408,000
D. $413,000

Periodic Inventory System and Cost Flow Assumption

AICPA.900549FAR-P1-FA

263. The following information was taken from Cody Co.'s accounting records for the year ended December 31, 2005:

Decrease in raw materials inventory	$15,000
Increase in finished goods inventory	35,000
Raw materials purchased	430,000
Direct labor payroll	200,000
Factory overhead	300,000
Freight-out	45,000

There was no work-in-process inventory at the beginning or end of the year. Cody's 2005 cost of goods sold is

A. $895,000
B. $910,000
C. $950,000
D. $955,000

AICPA.930548FAR-P1-FA

264. The following information pertains to Deal Corp.'s 2004 cost of goods sold:

Inventory, 12/31/03	$90,000
2004 purchases	124,000
2004 write-off of obsolete inventory	34,000
Inventory, 12/31/04	30,000

The inventory written off became obsolete due to an unexpected and unusual technological advance by a competitor. In its 2004 income statement, what amount should Deal report as cost of goods sold?

A. $218,000
B. $184,000
C. $150,000
D. $124,000

AICPA.990511FAR-FA

265. The following information pertained to Azur Co. for the year:

Purchases	$102,800
Purchase discounts	10,280
Freight-in	15,420
Freight-out	5,140
Beginning inventory	30,840
Ending inventory	20,560

What amount should Azur report as cost of goods sold for the year?

A. $102,800
B. $118,220
C. $123,360
D. $128,500

Perpetual Inventory System and Cost Flow Assumption

AICPA051165FAR-TI

266. Which of the following statements regarding inventory accounting systems is true?

A. A disadvantage of the perpetual inventory system is that the inventory dollar amounts used for interim reporting purposes are estimated amounts.
B. A disadvantage of the periodic inventory system is that the cost of goods sold amount used for financial reporting purposes includes both the cost of inventory sold and inventory shortages.
C. An advantage of the perpetual inventory system is that the record keeping required to maintain the system is relatively simple.
D. An advantage of the periodic inventory system is that it provides a continuous record of the inventory balance.

AICPA.020507FAR-FA

267. During periods of inflation, a perpetual inventory system would result in the same dollar amount of ending inventory as a periodic inventory system under which of the following inventory valuation methods?

	FIFO	LIFO
A.	Yes	No
B.	Yes	Yes
C.	No	Yes
D.	No	No

AICPA.901108FAR-P1-FA

268. Ashe Co. recorded the following data pertaining to raw material X during January 2005:

	Units			
Date	Received	Cost	Issued	On Hand
1/1/05 Inventory		$8.00		3,200
1/11/05 Issue			1,600	1,600
1/22/05 Purchase	4,800	$9.60		6,400

The moving-average unit cost of X inventory on January 31, 2005 is

A. $8.80
B. $8.96
C. $9.20
D. $9.60

AICPA.010502FAR-FA

269.

	Units	Unit Cost	Total Cost	Units on Hand
Balance on 1/1	2,000	$1	$2,000	2,000
Purchased on 1/8	1,200	3	3,600	3,200
Sold on 1/23	1,800			1,400
Purchased on 1/28	800	5	4,000	2,200

Nest uses the LIFO method to cost inventory. What amount should Nest report as inventory on January 31 under each of the following methods of recording inventory?

	Perpetual	Periodic
A.	$2,600	$5,400
B.	$5,400	$2,600
C.	$2,600	$2,600
D.	$5,400	$5,400

A. A
B. B
C. C
D. D

Evaluation of FIFO and LIFO

AICPA.920524FAR-TH-FA

270. When the FIFO inventory method is used during periods of rising prices, a perpetual inventory system results in an ending inventory cost that is

A. The same as in a periodic inventory system.
B. Higher than in a periodic inventory system.
C. Lower than in a periodic inventory system.
D. Higher or lower than in a periodic inventory system, depending on whether physical quantities have increased or decreased.

AICPA.951109FAR-FA

271. A company decided to change its inventory valuation method from FIFO to LIFO in a period of rising prices. What was the result of the change on ending inventory and net income in the year of the change?

	Ending inventory	Net income
A.	Increase	Increase
B.	Increase	Decrease
C.	Decrease	Decrease
D.	Decrease	Increase

AICPA.0821122FAR-II.C

272. Which inventory costing method would a company that wishes to maximize profits in a period of rising prices use?

A. FIFO
B. Dollar-value LIFO.
C. Weighted average.
D. Moving average.

AICPA.911107FAR-TH-FA

273. Generally, which inventory costing method approximates most closely the current cost for each of the following?

	Cost of Goods Sold	Ending Inventory
A.	LIFO	FIFO
B.	LIFO	LIFO
C.	FIFO	FIFO
D.	FIFO	LIFO

Dollar Value LIFO

AICPA.110564FAR

274. In January, Stitch, Inc. adopted the dollar-value LIFO method of inventory valuation. At adoption, inventory was valued at $50,000. During the year, inventory increased $30,000 using base-year prices, and prices increased 10%. The designated market value of Stitch's inventory exceeded its cost at year-end. What amount of inventory should Stitch report in its year-end balance sheet?

A. $80,000
B. $83,000
C. $85,000
D. $88,000

AICPA.931120FAR-P1-FA

275. Brock Co. adopted the dollar-value LIFO inventory method as of January 1, 2003. A single inventory pool and an internally computed price index are used to compute Brock's LIFO inventory layers.

Information about Brock's dollar-value inventory follows:

Date	Inventory At Base-Year Cost	At Current-Year Cost	At Dollar-Value LIFO
1/1/03	$40,000	$40,000	$40,000
2003 layer	5,000	14,000	6,000
12/31/03	45,000	54,000	46,000
2004 layer	15,000	26,000	?
12/31/04	$60,000	$80,000	?

What was Brock's dollar-value LIFO inventory on December 31, 2004?

A. $80,000
B. $74,000
C. $66,000
D. $60,000

AICPA.911113FAR-P1-FA

276. In 2005, Cobb adopted the dollar-value LIFO inventory method.

At that time, Cobb's ending inventory had a base-year cost and an end-of-year cost of $300,000. In 2006, the ending inventory had a $400,000 base-year cost and a $440,000 end-of-year cost.

What dollar-value LIFO inventory cost would be reported in Cobb's December 31, 2006 balance sheet?

A. $440,000
B. $430,000
C. $410,000
D. $400,000

AICPA.010501FAR-FA

277. Bach Co. adopted the dollar-value LIFO inventory method as of January 1, 2006.

A single inventory pool and an internally computed price index are used to compute Bach's LIFO inventory layers. Information about Bach's dollar-value inventory follows:

Date	Inventory At Base-Year Cost	At Current-Year Cost
1/1/06	$90,000	$90,000
2006 layer	20,000	30,000
2007 layer	40,000	80,000

What was the price index used to compute Bach's 2007 dollar-value LIFO inventory layer?

A. 1.09
B. 1.25
C. 1.33
D. 2.00

Subsequent Measurement of Inventory

AICPA.930521FAR-P1-FA

278. Moss Co. has determined its December 31, 20X4 inventory to be $400,000 on a FIFO basis. Information pertaining to that inventory follows:

Estimated selling price	$408,000
Estimated cost of disposal	20,000
Normal profit margin	60,000
Current replacement cost	360,000

Moss records losses that result from applying the lower of cost or market rule. On December 31, 20X4, what should be the net carrying value of Moss' inventory?

A. $400,000
B. $388,000
C. $360,000
D. $328,000

AICPA.120627FAR

279. The original cost of an inventory item is above the replacement cost. The inventory item's replacement cost is above the net realizable value. Under the lower of cost or market method, the inventory item should be valued at

A. Original cost.
B. Replacement cost.
C. Net realizable value.
D. Net realizable value LESS normal profit margin.

AICPA.0821123FAR-II.C

280. At the end of the year, Ian Co. determined its inventory to be $258,000 on a FIFO (first in, first out) basis. The current replacement cost of this inventory was $230,000. Ian estimates that it could sell the inventory for $275,000 at a disposal cost of $14,000. If Ian's normal profit margin for its inventory was $10,000, what would be its net carrying value?

A. $244,000
B. $251,000
C. $258,000
D. $261,000

AICPA.901117FAR-TH-FA

281. The replacement cost of an inventory item is below the net realizable value and above the net realizable value less the normal profit margin. The original cost of the inventory item is below the net realizable value less the normal profit margin.

Under the lower of cost or market method, the inventory item should be valued at

A. Net realizable value.
B. Net realizable value less the normal profit margin.
C. Original cost.
D. Replacement cost.

AICPA.110573FAR

282. The replacement cost of an inventory item is below the net realizable value and above the net realizable value less a normal profit margin. The inventory item's original cost is above the net realizable value. Under the lower of cost or market method, the inventory item should be valued at

A. Original cost.
B. Replacement cost.
C. Net realizable value.
D. Net realizable value less normal profit margin.

Gross Margin and Relative Sales Value Method

AICPA.083711FAR-SIM

283. When marking up a specific line of household items for resale, a retailer computes its markup as 40% of cost. For purposes of estimating ending inventory using the gross margin method, what percentage is applied to sales when estimating cost of goods sold?

A. 40
B. 71
C. 60
D. 29

AICPA.083712FAR-SIM

284. A firm's inventory was destroyed by fire on August 14 of the current year. Fortunately, the firm had insurance to cover the loss. However, most of the inventory records were also destroyed in the fire. The average gross margin percentage is 40%, beginning inventory was $200,000, and $1,000,000 of purchases had been made through August 13. The firm had recorded sales of $1,200,000 through that date. Estimate the cost of the inventory lost in the fire.

A. $0
B. $480,000
C. $720,000
D. $280,000

AICPA.083710FAR-SIM

285. The following two inventory items were purchased as a group in a liquidation sale for $1,000.

Item	Replacement Cost	Carrying Value on Seller's Books
A	$400	$390
B	700	755

The firm purchasing the inventory records item A at what amount?

A. $341
B. $390
C. $364
D. $500

AICPA.061203FAR

286. A flash flood swept through Hat, Inc.'s warehouse on May 1. After the flood, Hat's accounting records showed the following:

Inventory, January 1	$35,000
Purchases, January 1 through May 1	200,000
Sales, January 1 through May 1	250,000
Inventory not damaged by flood	30,000
Gross profit percentage on sales	40%

What amount of inventory was lost in the flood?

A. $55,000
B. $85,000
C. $120,000
D. $150,000

Retail Inventory Method

AICPA.901116FAR-TH-FA

287. The retail inventory method includes which of the following in the calculation of both cost and retail amounts of goods available for sale?

A. Purchase returns.
B. Sales returns.
C. Net markups.
D. Freight-in.

AICPA.083714FAR-SIM

288. Data for a firm using the FIFO-LCM retail inventory method is as follows:

	Cost	Retail
Beginning inventory	$300	$467
Net purchases	1,200	2,000
Net additional markups		100
Net markdowns		(300)
Sales		$1,700

Compute cost of goods sold.

A. $1,169
B. $1,160
C. $1,177
D. $1,122

AICPA.083713FAR-SIM

289. How does the retail inventory method establish the lower-of-cost-or-market valuation for ending inventory?

    A. The procedure is applied on a cost basis at the unit level.
    B. By excluding net markups from the cost-to-retail ratio.
    C. By excluding beginning inventory from the cost-to-retail ratio.
    D. By excluding net markdowns from the cost-to-retail ratio.

AICPA.900513FAR-P1-FA

290. Union Corp. uses the first-in, first-out retail method of inventory valuation. The following information is available:

	Cost	Retail
Beginning inventory	$12,000	$30,000
Purchases	60,000	110,000
Net additional markups		10,000
Net markdowns		20,000
Sales revenue		90,000

If the lower of cost or market rule is disregarded, what would be the estimated cost of the ending inventory?

    A. $24,000
    B. $20,800
    C. $20,000
    D. $19,200

Dollar Value LIFO Retail

AICPA.082111FAR-II.C

291. A firm uses the dollar value LIFO retail method and has $2,000 in beginning inventory at retail at the beginning of the current year. The base year equivalent of this amount is $1,600. The base year index is 1.00. The beginning inventory reported in the Balance Sheet is $800. During the current year, the firm purchased $12,000 of inventory at cost and marked that up to $40,000. Sales for the year were $28,000. The relevant ending price index is 1.60. What amount does this firm report as inventory in its Balance Sheet at the end of the current year?

    A. $4,286
    B. $13,440
    C. $4,232
    D. $4,200

AICPA.083716FAR-SIM

292. Information for a firm using the dollar value (DV) LIFO retail method follows. The cost to retail (C/R) is provided along with price level indices. The data reflects the use of the method through year one.

Layer	Retail Base	Retail Index	Retail Current	DV LIFO C/R	DV LIFO Cost
Base	$200	1.00	$200	.40	$80
Year 1	80	1.10	88	.34	$30

For year two, ending inventory at retail (by count) totaled $450. The ending price-level index for the year was 1.15. The cost-to-retail ratio was .42. What is the ending inventory for financial reporting purposes for this firm?

    A. $164
    B. $54
    C. $189
    D. $177

AICPA.083715FAR-SIM

293. Choose the correct inclusions to the cost-to-retail ratio computation under the dollar-value LIFO retail method.

	Beginning Inventory	Net Markdowns
A.	Yes	Yes
B.	Yes	No
C.	No	Yes
D.	No	No

Inventory Errors

AICPA.941143FAR-FA

294. Bren Co.'s beginning inventory at January 1, 2005 was understated by $26,000, and its ending inventory was overstated by $52,000. As a result, Bren's cost of goods sold for 2005 was:

    A. Understated by $26,000.
    B. Overstated by $26,000.
    C. Understated by $78,000.
    D. Overstated by $78,000.

AICPA.083719FAR-SIM

295. When an inventory overstatement in year one counterbalances in year two, this means:

    A. There are no reporting errors, even if the overstatement is never discovered.
    B. A prior-period adjustment is recorded if the error is discovered in year three.
    C. The year one Balance Sheet does not need to be restated if the error is discovered in year three.
    D. A prior-period adjustment is recorded if the error is discovered in year two.

AICPA.083718FAR-SIM

296. If ending inventory for 20X5 is understated because certain items were missed in the count, then:

    A. Net income for 20X5 will be overstated.
    B. CGS for 20X5 will be understated.

C. Net income for 20X5 will be understated, but net income for 20X6 will be unaffected.

D. Net income for 20X5 will be understated and CGS for 20X6 will be understated.

Losses on Purchase Commitments

AICPA.083722FAR-SIM

297. In October of year one, a firm committed to a purchase of inventory at a total cost of $26,000. The contract is irrevocable and specifies a delivery date in March of year two. At the end of year one, the market value of the inventory under contract is worth $23,000 at current cost. Choose the correct reporting for the year one financial statements:

A. A liability of $3,000 is reported in the Balance Sheet.

B. An extraordinary loss of $3,000 is reported in the Income Statement.

C. The potential loss on contract is reported in the footnotes, but there is no recognition in the financial statements.

D. No reporting is required.

AICPA.083721FAR-SIM

298. Losses on purchase commitments are recorded at the end of the current year when:

A. The current cost of the inventory is less than the inventory cost in the purchase contract.

B. The purchase contract is irrevocable.

C. The contractual cost of the inventory in an irrevocable purchase contract exceeds the current cost.

D. The buyer purchased a quantity of inventory that was not sufficient to avoid a LIFO liquidation.

AICPA.083723FAR-SIM

299. At the end of 20X4, a firm recognized a loss on a contractual commitment to purchase inventory for $60,000. The value of the inventory at the end of 20X4 is $52,000. When the inventory was actually purchased in 20X5, its value had risen to $62,000. Choose the correct statement concerning reporting in 20X5.

A. A $10,000 gain is recognized.

B. The inventory is recorded at $60,000.

C. The inventory is recorded at $52,000.

D. There is no additional loss or gain recognized.

AICPA.08211246FAR-II.C

300. A corporation entered into a purchase commitment to buy inventory. At the end of the accounting period, the current market value of the inventory was less than the fixed purchase price, by a material amount. Which of the following accounting treatments is most appropriate?

A. Describe the nature of the contract in a note to the financial statements, recognize a loss in the Income Statement, and recognize a liability for the accrued loss.

B. Describe the nature of the contract and the estimated amount of the loss in a note to the financial statements, but do not recognize a loss in the Income Statement.

C. Describe the nature of the contract in a note to the financial statements, recognize a loss in the Income Statement, and recognize a reduction in inventory equal to the amount of the loss by use of a valuation account.

D. Neither describe the purchase obligation nor recognize a loss on the Income Statement or Balance Sheet.

Inventory and IFRS

assess.AICPA.FAR.invent.ifrs-0014

301. At the end of year 1, a company reduced its inventory cost from $100 to its net realizable value of $80. As of the end of year 2, the inventory was still on hand, and its net realizable value increased to $150. Under IFRS, what journal entry should the company record for year 2 to properly report the inventory value?

A. Debit inventory for $20 and credit expense for $20.

B. Debit inventory for $70 and credit expense for $70.

C. Debit inventory for $70, credit retained earnings for $50, and credit expense for $20.

D. Debit inventory for $20, debit expense for $30, and credit retained earnings for $50.

assess.AICPA.FAR.invent.ifrs-0030

302. The following information relates to a company's year-end inventory:

Inventory cost	$910
Selling price of inventory	$1,000
Normal profit margin	10% of selling price
Current replacement cost	$740
Cost of completion and disposal	$100

Under IFRS, what is the company's year-end inventory balance?

A. $740

B. $800

C. $900

D. $910

Property, Plant, and Equipment

Categories and Presentation

AICPA.130723FAR

303. A company recently moved to a new building. The old building is being actively marketed for sale, and the company expects to complete the sale in four months. Each of the following statements is correct regarding the old building, **except**:

    A. It will be reclassified as an asset held for sale.
    B. It will be classified as a current asset.
    C. It will **no** longer be depreciated.
    D. It will be valued at historical cost.

AICPA.101216FAR-SIM

304. Which of the following is not a requirement for an asset to be categorized as a plant asset?

    A. Have physical substance.
    B. Have a useful life of at least three years.
    C. Currently used in operations.
    D. Not held for investment purposes.

AICPA.101217FAR-SIM

305. Which of the following is a required footnote disclosure on property, plant, and equipment?

    A. Range of useful lives of plant assets.
    B. Depreciation methods of plant assets.
    C. Accumulated depreciation related to plant assets.
    D. All of the above.

Capitalized Costs

AICPA.931122FAR-P1-FA

306. Merry Co. purchased a machine costing $125,000 for its manufacturing operations and paid shipping costs of $20,000. Merry spent an additional $10,000 testing and preparing the machine for use.

    What amount should Merry record as the cost of the machine?

    A. $155,000
    B. $145,000
    C. $135,000
    D. $125,000

AICPA.101048FAR

307. Newt Co. sold a warehouse and used the proceeds to acquire a new warehouse. The excess of the proceeds over the carrying amount of the warehouse sold should be reported as a(an):

    A. Reduction of the cost of the new warehouse.
    B. Gain from discontinued operations, net of income taxes.
    C. Part of continuing operations.
    D. Extraordinary gain, net of taxes.

AICPA.900515FAR-P1-FA

308. On December 1, 20X5, East Co. purchased a tract of land as a factory site for $300,000. The old building on the property was razed and salvaged materials resulting from demolition were sold.

    Additional costs incurred and salvage proceeds realized during December 20X5 were as follows:

Cost to raze old building	$25,000
Legal fees for purchase contract and to record ownership	5,000
Title guarantee insurance	6,000
Proceeds from sale of salvaged materials	4,000

    In East's December 31, 20X5 Balance Sheet, what amount should be reported as land?

    A. $311,000
    B. $321,000
    C. $332,000
    D. $336,000

AICPA.910523FAR-P1-FA

309. On October 1, 20X4, Shaw Corp. purchased a machine for $126,000 that was placed in service on November 30, 20X4. Shaw incurred additional costs for this machine, as follows:

Shipping	$3,000
Installation	4,000
Testing	5,000

    In Shaw's December 31, 20X4 Balance Sheet, the machine's cost should be reported as:

    A. $126,000
    B. $129,000
    C. $133,000
    D. $138,000

AICPA.101049FAR

310. Talton Co. installed new assembly line production equipment at a cost of $185,000. Talton had to rearrange the assembly line and remove a wall to install the equipment. The rearrangement cost was $12,000 and the wall removal cost was $3,000. The rearrangement did not increase the life of the assembly line but it did make it more efficient. What amount of these costs should be capitalized by Talton?

    A. $185,000
    B. $188,000
    C. $197,000
    D. $200,000

Valuation

AICPA.083725FAR-SIM

311. Plant assets are occasionally acquired by means other than by paying cash. Choose the correct statement about such acquisitions.

    A. If equipment is acquired with 100% debt financing, the equipment is capitalized at the sum of all interest and principal payments on the debt.
    B. If a building is acquired by issuing an amount of stock that is significant in relation to the amount of stock outstanding before the exchange, the fair value of the building should be used to initially debit the building account.
    C. If land is received by a firm as a donation, no amount should be recorded for the land because there is no cost to the firm.
    D. If land is acquired as one component of a group of plant assets for a discounted aggregate price, the amount capitalized for the land is its market value.

AICPA.083724FAR-SIM

312. A plant asset under construction by a firm for its own use was completed at the end of the current year. The following costs were incurred:

Materials	$60,000
Labor	30,000
Incremental overhead	10,000
Capitalized interest	20,000

The asset has a service life of 10 years, estimated residual value of $10,000, and will be depreciated under the double-declining balance method. At completion, the asset was worth $105,000 at fair value. What amount of depreciation will be recognized on the asset in total over its service life?

    A. $105,000
    B. $120,000
    C. $95,000
    D. $90,000

AICPA.090629FAR-II-D

313. Young Corp. purchased equipment by making a down payment of $4,000 and issuing a note payable for $18,000. A payment of $6,000 is to be made at the end of each year for three years. The applicable rate of interest is 8%. The present value of an ordinary annuity factor for three years at 8% is 2.58, and the present value for the future amount of a single sum of one dollar for three years at 8% is .735. Shipping charges for the equipment were $2,000, and installation charges were $3,500. What is the capitalized cost of the equipment?

    A. $19,480
    B. $21,480
    C. $24,980
    D. $27,500

AICPA.070770FAR

314. Oak Co., a newly formed corporation, incurred the following expenditures related to land and building:

County assessment for sewer lines	$ 2,500
Title search fees	625
Cash paid for land with a building to be demolished	135,000
Excavation for construction of basement	21,000
Removal of old building $21,000 less salvage of $5,000	16,000

At what amount should Oak record the land?

    A. $138,125
    B. $153,500
    C. $154,125
    D. $175,625

AICPA.083726FAR-SIM

315. Immediately after a note payable was signed, its present value was $30,000. This note and $20,000 cash were used to acquire a used plant asset at the beginning of the current year. The interest rate implied in the note is 6%. Total interest payments due on the note over its term amount to $4,000. The term exceeds one year. No payments on the note are due during the current year. What amount of interest expense is recognized for the first year (current year) on this note, and what amount is capitalized to the plant asset account?

	Interest Expense	Capitalized Amount
A.	$1,800	$50,000
B.	$3,000	$50,000
C.	$4,000	$30,000
D.	$0	$50,000

Interest Capitalization Basics

AICPA.120629FAR

316. At the beginning of the year, Cann Co. started construction on a new $2 million addition to its plant. Total construction expenditures made during the year were $200,000 on January 2, $600,000 on May 1, and $300,000 on December 1. On January 2, the company

borrowed $500,000 for the construction at 12%. The only other outstanding debt the company had was a 10% interest rate, long-term mortgage of $800,000, which had been outstanding the entire year. What amount of interest should Cann capitalize as part of the cost of the plant addition?

A. $140,000
B. $132,000
C. $72,500
D. $60,000

AICPA.101068FAR

317. Sun Co. was constructing fixed assets that qualified for interest capitalization. Sun had the following outstanding debt issuances during the entire year of construction:

$6,000,000 face value, 8% interest

$8,000,000 face value, 9% interest

None of the borrowings were specified for the construction of the qualified fixed asset. Average expenditures for the year were $1,000,000. What interest rate should Sun use to calculate capitalized interest on the construction?

A. 8.00%
B. 8.50%
C. 8.57%
D. 9.00%

AICPA.083728FAR-SIM

318. A firm began the construction of its new manufacturing facility in January of 20X2. The following expenditures were made on construction in that year:

Jan. 1	$40,000
Mar. 1	120,000
Oct. 31	96,000

Debt outstanding the entire year:

6%, $60,000 construction loan

4%, $90,000 note payable not related to construction

6%, $90,000 note payable not related to construction

Compute interest to be capitalized using the weighted-average method.

A. $6,720
B. $12,600
C. $8,400
D. $8,190

AICPA.910523FAR-TH-FA

319. During Year 1, Bay Co. constructed machinery for its own use and for sale to customers. Bank loans financed these assets both during construction and after construction was complete.

How much of the interest incurred should be reported as interest expense in the Year 1 Income Statement?

	Interest Incurred for Machinery for Own Use	Interest Incurred for Machinery Held for Sale
A.	All interest incurred	All interest incurred
B.	All interest incurred	Interest incurred after completion
C.	Interest incurred after completion	Interest incurred after completion
D.	Interest incurred after completion	All interest incurred

AICPA.083730FAR-SIM

320. Debt is frequently incurred when plant assets are acquired. For example, debt may be incurred on the purchase of plant assets. Debt may also be incurred during the construction of plant assets. How is the interest in these two cases treated for financial reporting?

	Debt for Purchase	Debt during Construction
A.	expense	capitalize
B.	expense	expense
C.	capitalize	capitalize
D.	capitalize	expense

Interest Capitalization Limits

AICPA.083731FAR-SIM

321. Average accumulated expenditures for year five on a construction project amounted to $70,000. The total cash invested in the project by the end of year five, was $160,000. During year six, the firm spent another $240,000 (total) on the project, uniformly throughout the year. Compute average accumulated expenditures for year six.

A. $240,000
B. $400,000
C. $190,000
D. $280,000

AICPA.083733FAR-SIM

322. A firm has spent the last two years constructing a building to be used as the firm's headquarters. At the end of the first year of construction, the balance of building under construction was $400,000, which includes capitalized interest. During year 2, the firm paid $240,000 to the contractor on March 1 and $600,000 on October 1.

The building was not finished by the end of the second year. The firm had one loan outstanding all year, an 8%, $3,000,000 construction loan. Compute capitalized interest for year two.

A. $28,000
B. $240,000
C. $60,000
D. $65,600

assess.AICPA.FAR.int.cap2-0015

323. A company with a June 30 fiscal year-end entered into a $3,000,000 construction project on April 1 to be completed on September 30. The cumulative construction-in-progress balances at April 30, May 31, and June 30 were $500,000, $800,000, and $1,500,000, respectively. The interest rate on company debt used to finance the construction project was 5% from April 1 through June 30 and 6% from July 1 through September 30. Assuming that the asset is placed into service on October 1, what amount of interest should be capitalized to the project on June 30?

A. $11,666
B. $18,750
C. $75,000
D. $90,000

AICPA.083732FAR-SIM

324. A firm is constructing a warehouse for its own use and purchased the land for the site immediately before beginning construction. Interest is capitalized on which of the following?

	Warehouse	Land
A.	Yes	Yes
B.	Yes	No
C.	No	Yes
D.	No	No

Post-Acquisition Expenditures

AICPA.930526FAR-TH-FA

325. A building suffered uninsured fire damage. The damaged portion of the building was refurbished with higher-quality materials. The cost and related accumulated depreciation of the damaged portion are identifiable. To account for these events, the owner should:

A. Reduce accumulated depreciation equal to the cost of refurbishing.
B. Record a loss in the current period equal to the sum of the cost of refurbishing and the carrying amount of the damaged portion of the building.
C. Capitalize the cost of refurbishing and record a loss in the current period equal to the carrying amount of the damaged portion of the building.

D. Capitalize the cost of refurbishing by adding the cost to the carrying amount of the building.

AICPA.911115FAR-P1-FA

326. On January 1, 20X5, Dix Co. replaced its old boiler. The following information was available on that date:

Carrying amount of old boiler	$ 8,000
Fair value of old boiler	2,000
Purchase and installation price of new boiler	100,000

The old boiler was sold for $2,000. What amount should Dix capitalize as the cost of the new boiler?

A. $92,000
B. $94,000
C. $98,000
D. $100,000

AICPA.900516FAR-P1-FA

327. On June 18, 20X5, Dell Printing Co. incurred the following costs for one of its printing presses:

Purchase of collating and stapling attachment	$84,000
Installation of attachment	36,000
Replacement parts for overhaul of press	26,000
Labor and overhead in connection with overhaul	14,000

The overhaul resulted in a significant increase in production. Neither the attachment nor the overhaul increased the estimated useful life of the press. What amount of the above costs should be capitalized?

A. $0
B. $84,000
C. $120,000
D. $160,000

AICPA.901113FAR-TH-FA

328. A building suffered uninsured water and related damage. The damaged portion of the building was refurbished with upgraded materials. The cost and related accumulated depreciation of the damaged portion are identifiable.

To account for these events, the owner should:

A. Capitalize the cost of refurbishing and record a loss in the current period equal to the carrying amount of the damaged portion of the building.
B. Capitalize the cost of refurbishing by adding the cost to the carrying amount of the building.

C. Record a loss in the current period equal to the cost of refurbishing and continue to depreciate the original cost of the building.

D. Record a loss in the current period equal to the sum of the cost of refurbishing and the carrying amount of the damaged portion of the building.

AICPA.083734FAR-SIM

329. Many years after constructing a plant asset, management spent a significant sum on the asset. Which of the following types of expenditures should be capitalized in this instance?

(1) An expenditure for routine maintenance that increases the useful life compared with deferring the maintenance

(2) An expenditure that increases the useful life of the asset compared with the original estimate, assuming normal maintenance at the required intervals

(3) An expenditure that increases the utility of the asset

	(1)	(2)	(3)
A.	Yes	Yes	Yes
B.	No	Yes	Yes
C.	No	No	Yes
D.	No	Yes	No

Non-Accelerated Depreciation Methods

AICPA.920515FAR-TH-FA

330. What factor must be present to use the units of production (activity) method of depreciation?

A. Total units to be produced can be estimated.

B. Production is constant over the life of the asset.

C. Repair costs increase with use.

D. Obsolescence is expected.

AICPA.931134FAR-TH-FA

331. In which of the following situations is the units of production method of depreciation most appropriate?

A. An asset's service potential declines with use.

B. An asset's service potential declines with the passage of time.

C. An asset is subject to rapid obsolescence.

D. An asset incurs increasing repairs and maintenance with use.

AICPA.940545FAR-FA

332. On January 2, Year 1, Lem Corp. bought machinery under a contract that required a down payment of $10,000, plus 24 monthly payments of $5,000 each, for total cash payments of $130,000.

The cash-equivalent price of the machinery was $110,000. The machinery has an estimated useful life of 10 years and estimated salvage value of $5,000. Lem uses straight-line depreciation.

In its Year 1 Income Statement, what amount should Lem report as depreciation for this machinery?

A. $10,500

B. $11,000

C. $12,500

D. $13,000

AICPA.901112FAR-P2-FA

333. Zahn Corp.'s comprehensive Balance Sheet at December 31, 20X5 and 20X4 reported accumulated depreciation balances of $800,000 and $600,000, respectively. Property with a cost of $50,000 and a carrying amount of $40,000 was the only property sold in 20X5.

Depreciation charged to operations in 20X5 was:

A. $190,000

B. $200,000

C. $210,000

D. $220,000

AICPA.08211231FAR-II.D

334. In 20X2, Spirit, Inc. determined that the 12-year estimated useful life of a machine purchased for $48,000 in January 1997 should be extended by three years. The machine is being depreciated using the straight-line method and has no salvage value. What amount of depreciation expense should Spirit report in its financial statements for the year ending December 31, 20X2?

A. $2,800

B. $3,200

C. $43,200

D. $4,800

Accelerated Depreciation Methods

AICPA.901113FAR-P2-FA

335. Vore Corp. bought equipment on January 2, 20X4 for $200,000. This equipment had an estimated useful life of five years and a salvage value of $20,000. Depreciation was computed by the 150% declining balance method.

The accumulated depreciation balance at December 31, 20X5 should be:

A. $102,000
B. $98,000
C. $91,800
D. $72,000

AICPA.900517FAR-P1-FA

336.   On April 1, 20X4, Kew Co. purchased new machinery for $300,000. The machinery has an estimated useful life of five years, and depreciation is computed by the sum-of-the-years'-digits method.

The accumulated depreciation on this machinery at March 31, 20X6 should be:

A. $192,000
B. $180,000
C. $120,000
D. $100,000

AICPA.990507FAR-FA

337.   Spiro Corp. uses the sum-of-the-years' digits method to depreciate equipment purchased in January 20X3 for $20,000. The estimated salvage value of the equipment is $2,000, and the estimated useful life is four years.

What should Spiro report as the asset's carrying amount as of December 31, 20X5?

A. $1,800
B. $2,000
C. $3,800
D. $4,500

AICPA.090635FAR-II-D

338.   Carr, Inc. purchased equipment for $100,000 on January 1, 20X2. The equipment had an estimated 10-year useful life and a $15,000 salvage value. Carr uses the 200% declining-balance depreciation method. In its 20X3 Income Statement, what amount should Carr report as depreciation expense for the equipment?

A. $13,600
B. $16,000
C. $17,000
D. $20,000

AICPA.920550FAR-P1-FA

339.   South Co. purchased a machine that was installed and placed in service on January 1, 20X4 at a cost of $240,000. Salvage value was estimated at $40,000. The machine is being depreciated over 10 years by the double-declining balance method. For the year ended

December 31, 20X5, what amount should South report as depreciation expense?

A. $48,000
B. $38,400
C. $32,000
D. $21,600

Natural Resources

AICPA.083737FAR-SIM

340.   A firm began a mineral exploitation venture during the current year by spending (1) $40 million for the mineral rights; (2) $100 million exploring for the minerals, one-fourth of which were successful; and (3) $60 million to develop the site. Management estimated that 20 million tons of ore would ultimately be removed from the property. Wages and other extraction costs for the current year amounted to $10 million. In total, 2 million tons of ore were removed from the deposit in the current year. The entire production for the period was sold. Compute cost of goods sold under the successful efforts method.

A. $30 million
B. $12.5 million
C. $10 million
D. $22.5 million

AICPA.083736FAR-SIM

341.   A firm began a mineral exploitation venture during the current year by spending (1) $40 million for the mineral rights; (2) $100 million exploring for the minerals, one-fourth of which were successful; and (3) $60 million to develop the site. Management estimated that 20 million tons of ore would ultimately be removed from the property. Wages and other extraction costs for the current year amounted to $10 million. In total, 2 million tons of ore were removed from the deposit in the current year. The entire production for the period was sold. What amount of depletion is recognized during the current year under the full costing method?

A. $20 million
B. $12.5 million
C. $10 million
D. $21 million

AICPA.083735FAR-SIM

342.   Choose the best association of terms in the natural resources accounting area with the conceptual framework.

A.   Successful efforts method-matching.
B.   Full costing method-definition of asset.
C.   Depletion-fair value accounting.
D.   Successful efforts method-definition of asset.

Impairment—Assets for Use and Held-for-Sale

AICPA.900519FAR-P1-FA

343. On December 31, 20X4, a building owned by Pine Corp. was totally destroyed by fire. The building had fire insurance coverage up to $500,000.

Other pertinent information as of December 31, 20X4, follows:

Building, carrying amount	$520,000
Building, fair market value	550,000
Removal and cleanup cost	10,000

During January 20X5, before the 20X4 financial statements were issued, Pine received insurance proceeds of $500,000. On what amount should Pine base the determination of its loss on involuntary conversion?

A. $520,000
B. $530,000
C. $550,000
D. $560,000

AICPA.920545FAR-P1-FA

344. On July 1, 20X4, one of Rudd Co.'s delivery vans was destroyed in an accident. On that date, the van's carrying value was $2,500.

On July 15, 20X4, Rudd received and recorded a $700 invoice for a new engine installed in the van in May 20X4, and another $500 invoice for various repairs. In August, Rudd received $3,500 under its insurance policy on the van, which it plans to use to replace the van.

What amount should Rudd report as gain (loss) on disposal of the van in its 20X4 income statement?

A. $1,000
B. $300
C. $0
D. $(200)

AICPA.061212FAR

345. Which of the following conditions must exist in order for an impairment loss to be recognized?

I. The carrying amount of the long-lived asset is less than its fair value.
II. The carrying amount of the long-lived asset is not recoverable.

A. I only.
B. II only.
C. Both I and II.
D. Neither I nor II.

AICPA.101074FAR

346. Last year, Katt Co. reduced the carrying amount of its long-lived assets used in operations from $120,000 to $100,000 in connection with its annual impairment review. During the current year, Katt determined that the fair value of the same assets had increased to $130,000. What amount should Katt record as restoration of previously recognized impairment loss in the current year's financial statements?

A. $0
B. $10,000
C. $20,000
D. $30,000

AICPA.110579FAR

347. Four years ago on January 2, Randall Co. purchased a long-lived asset. The purchase price of the asset was $250,000, with no salvage value. The estimated useful life of the asset was 10 years. Randall used the straight-line method to calculate depreciation expense. An impairment loss on the asset of $30,000 was recognized on December 31 of the current year. The estimated useful life of the asset at December 31 of the current year did not change. What amount should Randall report as depreciation expense in its income statement for the next year?

A. $20,000
B. $22,000
C. $25,000
D. $30,000

Impairment and IFRS

AICPA.120204FAR-SIM

348. A company has a long-lived asset with a carrying value of $120,000, expected future cash flows of $130,000, present value of expected future cash flows of $100,000, and a market value of $105,000. Under IFRS what amount of impairment loss should be reported?

A. $0
B. $5,000
C. $15,000
D. $20,000

AICPA.120206FAR-SIM

349. Under IFRS the test for asset impairment is to compare the carrying value of the asset to its recoverable amount. Which of the following is the recoverable amount according to IFRS?

A. The greater of future undiscounted cash flows or future discounted cash flows.
B. The greater of future discounted cash flows or fair value.

C.   The greater of fair value less cost to sell or value in use.

D.   The greater of fair value or value in use.

AICPA.120205FAR-SIM

350.   Restoration of the carrying value of a long-lived asset is permitted under IFRS if the asset's fair value increases subsequent to recording an impairment loss for which of the following?

	Held for Use	Held for Disposal
A.	Yes	Yes
B.	Yes	No
C.	No	Yes
D.	No	No

PPE and IFRS

AICPA.101067FAR

351.   On January 1, year one, an entity acquires a new piece of machinery for $100,000 with an estimated useful life of 10 years. The machine has a drum that must be replaced every five years and costs $20,000 to replace. Also included in the cost of the machine is an inspection fee of $8,000. Continued operations of the machine requires an inspection every four years after purchase. The company uses the straight-line method of depreciation. Under IFRS what is the depreciation expense for year one?

A. $10,000

B. $10,800

C. $12,000

D. $13,200

AICPA.101065FAR

352.   Under IFRS, when an entity chooses the revaluation model as its accounting policy for measuring property, plant, and equipment, which of the following statements is correct?

A.   When an asset is revalued, the entire class of property, plant, and equipment to which that asset belongs must be revalued.

B.   When an asset is revalued, individual assets within a class of property, plant, and equipment to which that asset belongs can be revalued.

C.   Revaluations of property, plant, and equipment must be made at least every three years.

D.   Increases in an asset's carry value as a result of the first revaluation must be recognized as a component of profit and loss.

assess.AICPA.FAR.ppe.ifrs-0031

353.   A transportation company purchased a passenger bus for $100,000 on January 1, year 1. The company expects the bus to be used for

20 years if it follows a maintenance schedule of replacing the engine after 10 years and replacing the seats every 8 years. It estimates that the current cost to replace the engine is $25,000 and the current cost to replace the seats is $10,000. The company uses straight-line depreciation, and the bus has no residual value. The company considers any component equal to or greater than 10% of the overall cost to be significant. Under IFRS, how much depreciation expense should the company recognize for the bus for the year ended December 31, year 1?

A. $5,000

B. $7,000

C. $7,250

D. $8,500

AICPA.130725FAR

354.   A company has a parcel of land to be used for a future production facility. The company applies the revaluation model under IFRS to this class of assets. In year 1, the company acquired the land for $100,000. At the end of year 1, the carrying amount was reduced to $90,000, which represented the fair value at that date. At the end of year 2, the land was revalued, and the fair value increased to $105,000. How should the company account for the year 2 change in fair value?

A.   By recognizing $10,000 in other comprehensive income.

B.   By recognizing $15,000 in other comprehensive income.

C.   By recognizing $15,000 in profit or loss.

D.   By recognizing $10,000 in profit or loss and $5,000 in other comprehensive income.

Nonmonetary Exchange

Commercial Substance

AICPA.920519FAR-P1-FA

355.   On December 31, 2005, Vey Co. traded equipment with an original cost of $100,000 and accumulated depreciation of $40,000 for productive equipment with a fair value of $60,000.

In addition, Vey received $30,000 cash in connection with this exchange. There is commercial substance to the exchange.

What should be Vey's carrying amount for the equipment received at December 31, 2005?

A. $30,000

B. $40,000

C. $60,000

D. $80,000

AICPA.090644FAR-II-D

356. On January 1, Feld traded a delivery truck and paid $10,000 cash for a tow truck owned by Baker. The delivery truck had an original cost of $140,000, accumulated depreciation of $80,000, and an estimated fair value of $90,000. Feld estimated the fair value of Baker's tow truck to be $100,000. The transaction had commercial substance. What amount of gain should be recognized by Feld?

   A. $0
   B. $3,000
   C. $10,000
   D. $30,000

AICPA.090664.FAR.II.D

357. Which of the following statements describes the proper accounting for losses when nonmonetary assets are exchanged for other nonmonetary assets?

   A. A loss is recognized immediately, because assets received should not be valued at more than their cash-equivalent price.
   B. A loss is deferred so that the asset received in the exchange is properly valued.
   C. A loss, if any, that is unrelated to the determination of the amount of the asset received should be recorded.
   D. A loss can occur only when assets are sold or disposed of in a monetary transaction.

AICPA.110571FAR

358. Which of the following statements correctly describes the proper accounting for nonmonetary exchanges that are deemed to have commercial substance?

   A. It defers any gains and losses.
   B. It defers losses to the extent of any gains.
   C. It recognizes gains and losses immediately.
   D. It defers gains and recognizes losses immediately.

AICPA.130737FAR

359. A company exchanged land with an appraised value of $50,000 and an original cost of $20,000 for machinery with a fair value of $55,000. Assuming that the transaction has commercial substance, what is the gain on the exchange?

   A. $0
   B. $5,000
   C. $30,000
   D. $35,000

No Commercial Substance

AICPA.901112FAR-TH-FA

360. Solen Co. and Nolse Co. exchanged trucks with fair values in excess of carrying amounts. In addition, Solen paid Nolse to compensate for the difference in truck values.

   The exchange lacks commercial substance.

   As a consequence of the exchange, Solen recognizes

   A. A gain equal to the difference between the fair value and carrying amount of the truck given up.
   B. A gain determined by the proportion of cash paid to the total consideration.
   C. A loss determined by the proportion of cash paid to the total consideration.
   D. Neither a gain nor a loss.

AICPA.930510FAR-P2-FA

361. Amble, Inc. exchanged a truck with a carrying amount of $12,000 and a fair value of $20,000 for a truck and $5,000 cash. The fair value of the truck received was $15,000.

   At what amount should Amble record the truck received in the exchange, assuming the exchange lacks commercial substance?

   A. $7,000
   B. $9,000
   C. $12,000
   D. $15,000

AICPA.930516FAR-TH-FA

362. In an exchange of plant assets, Transit Co. received equipment with a fair value equal to the carrying amount of equipment given up. Transit also contributed cash.

   The exchange lacks commercial substance.

   As a result of the exchange, Transit recognized

   A. A loss equal to the cash given up.
   B. A loss determined by the proportion of cash paid to the total transaction value.
   C. A gain determined by the proportion of cash paid to the total transaction value.
   D. Neither gain nor loss.

AICPA.950530FAR-FA

363. Slate Co. and Talse Co. exchanged similar plots of land with fair values in excess of carrying amounts. In addition, Slate received cash from Talse to compensate for the difference in land values.

   The exchange lacks commercial substance.

As a result of the exchange, Slate should recognize:

A. A gain equal to the difference between the fair value and the carrying amount of the land given up.

B. A gain in an amount determined by the ratio of cash received to total consideration.

C. A loss in an amount determined by the ratio of cash received to total consideration.

D. Neither a gain nor a loss.

AICPA.910535FAR-TH-FA

364. May Co. and Sty Co. exchanged nonmonetary assets. The exchange did not culminate in an earning process for either May or Sty (the exchange lacked commercial substance). May paid cash to Sty in connection with the exchange.

The book value of the asset exchanged exceeded its fair value for both firms. Therefore, a loss on the exchange should be recognized by

	May	Sty
A.	Yes	Yes
B.	Yes	No
C.	No	Yes
D.	No	No

Nonmonetary Exchanges and IFRS

AICPA.101237FAR-SIM

365. In a barter transaction where advertising services provided are exchanged for advertising services received, under which of the following situations can the advertising provider recognize revenue for the services performed? Assume the accounting is under IFRS guidelines.

A. When the advertising services in the exchange are similar

B. When the fair value of the advertising services received can be reliably measured

C. When there is a nonbarter transaction for similar advertising services that can be reliably measured with the same counterparty

D. When there is a nonbarter transaction for similar advertising services that can be reliably measured with a different counterparty

Investments

Introduction—Equity and Debt Investments

AICPA.081222FAR-SIM

366. In which one of the following circumstances would an investor most likely have control of an investee?

A. The investor owns more than 50% of the voting common stock of an investee.

B. The investor owns 100% of the nonvoting preferred stock of an investee.

C. The investor owns 90% of the voting common stock of a foreign investee on which the foreign government imposes significant financial and operating restrictions.

D. The investor owns 100% of the voting common stock of a domestic investee that is in bankruptcy.

AICPA.081218FAR-SIM

367. Which one of the following is least likely to be a factor in determining how an investment in debt or equity securities is accounted for and reported in financial statements?

A. The nature of the investment

B. The method of payment used to acquire the investment

C. The extent or proportion of the investment securities acquired

D. The purpose for which the investment was made

AICPA.081224FAR-SIM

368. In which one of the following cases would an investor be presumed to have significant influence over the investee?

A. Investor acquires more than 50% of the investee's nonvoting preferred stock.

B. Investor acquires 10% of investee voting common stock.

C. Investor acquires 40% of investee voting common stock, which it intends to hold for 60 days.

D. Investor acquires 18% of investee voting common stock and is the primary buyer of the investee's output.

AICPA.081217FAR-SIM

369. On April 1, North Company issued bonds in the market. Upon issue, South Company acquired 10% of North Company's issue. On November 30, South sold the North Company bonds in the market; the bonds were acquired by East

Company. On December 31, which, if any, of the following companies is an investee?

	North	South	East
A.	Yes	Yes	No
B.	Yes	No	No
C.	No	Yes	Yes
D.	No	No	Yes

AICPA.081222FAR-SIM

370. In which one of the following circumstances would an investor most likely have control of an investee?

 A. The investor owns more than 50% of the voting common stock of an investee.
 B. The investor owns 100% of the nonvoting preferred stock of an investee.
 C. The investor owns 90% of the voting common stock of a foreign investee on which the foreign government imposes significant financial and operating restrictions.
 D. The investor owns 100% of the voting common stock of a domestic investee that is in bankruptcy.

No Significant Influence

No Significant Influence

AICPA.061273FAR-FA

371. An investor purchased a bond as a long-term investment between interest dates at a premium. At the purchase date, the cash paid to the seller is:

 A. The same as the face amount of the bond.
 B. The same as the face amount of the bond plus accrued interest.
 C. More than the face amount of the bond.
 D. Less than the face amount of the bond.

AICPA.910504FAR-TH-FA

372. An investor purchased a bond classified as a held-to-maturity investment between interest dates at a discount.

At the purchase date, the carrying amount of the bond is more than the:

	Cash Paid to Seller	Face Amount of Bond
A.	No	Yes
B.	No	No
C.	Yes	No
D.	Yes	Yes

AICPA.120636FAR

373. On January 1 of the current year, Barton Co. paid $900,000 to purchase two-year, 8%, $1,000,000 face value bonds that were issued by another publicly traded corporation. Barton plans to sell the bonds in the first quarter of the following year. The fair value of the bonds at the end of the current year was $1,020,000. At what amount should Barton report the bonds in its balance sheet at the end of the current year?

 A. $900,000
 B. $950,000
 C. $1,000,000
 D. $1,020,000

AICPA.110544FAR

374. In year 1, a company reported in other comprehensive income an unrealized holding loss on an investment in available-for-sale securities. During year 2, these securities were sold at a loss equal to the unrealized loss previously recognized. The reclassification adjustment should include which of the following?

 A. The unrealized loss should be credited to the investment account.
 B. The unrealized loss should be credited to the other comprehensive income account.
 C. The unrealized loss should be debited to the other comprehensive income account.
 D. The unrealized loss should be credited to beginning retained earnings.

AICPA.070501FAR-TH-FA

375. When the fair value of an investment in debt securities exceeds its carrying amount, how should each of the following assets be reported at the end of the year?

	Held-to-Maturity Securities	Available-for-Sale Securities
A.	Fair value	Carrying amount
B.	Carrying amount	Fair value
C.	Carrying amount	Carrying amount
D.	Fair Value	Fair Value

Cost Method and Transfers Between Classifications

AICPA.081230FAR-SIM

376. The method of accounting for investments that does not give the investor significant influence over the investee is based on the investor's intent in making the investment. When investor intent changes, the classification of and accounting for the investment changes. When investments are transferred between classifications, which one of the following

valuation basis is most likely to be used when recording the investment in the new classification?

A. Historic cost
B. Amortized cost
C. Prior carrying value
D. Fair market value

AICPA.081228FAR-SIM

377. Which, if any, of the following transfers between classifications of investments (which do not give the investor significant influence) are possible?

	Held-to-Maturity to Held-for-Trading	Held-for-Trading to Held-to-Maturity
A.	Yes	Yes
B.	Yes	No
C.	No	Yes
D.	No	No

AICPA.930504FAR-P1-FA

378. Sun Corp. had investments in marketable equity securities costing $650,000. On June 30, 20X2, Sun decided to hold the investments indefinitely and, accordingly, reclassified them from held-for-trading to available-for-sale on that date. The investments' market value was $575,000 as of December 31, 20X1, $530,000 as of June 30, 20X2, and $490,000 as of December 31, 20X2.

What amount should Sun report as net unrealized loss on noncurrent marketable equity securities in its 20X2 statement of stockholders' equity?

A. $40,000
B. $45,000
C. $85,000
D. $160,000

AICPA.920542FAR-TH-FA

379. A marketable equity security is transferred from the held-for-trading portfolio to the available-for-sale portfolio. At the transfer date, the security's cost exceeds its market value.

What amount is used at the transfer date to record the security in the available-for-sale portfolio?

A. Market value, regardless of whether the decline in market value below cost is considered permanent or temporary.
B. Market value, only if the decline in market value below cost is considered permanent.
C. Cost, if the decline in market value below cost is considered temporary.
D. Cost, regardless of whether the decline in market value below cost is considered permanent or temporary.

IFRS—Investments

AICPA.100947FAR-NSI-SIM

380. Which, if either, of the following statements concerning the transfer of investments between categories under IFRS No. 9 is/are correct?

I. Only investments in debt securities may be transferred between categories.
II. When investments are transferred between categories, financial statements of prior periods presented for comparative purposes must not be restated.

A. I only.
B. II only.
C. Both I and II.
D. Neither I nor II.

AICPA.100944FAR-NSI-SIM

381. Inco, Inc., a U.S. entity, has elected to prepare financial statements in accordance with IFRS to provide to its foreign suppliers. Inco has the following information concerning an investment in the bonds of Tryco, Inc., as of December 31, 2011:

Par value	$100,000
Original cost	108,000
Current premium	3,500
Fair value	105,000

Inco's business model is to regularly invest in debt to receive the cash flow provided by interest and the repayment of principal on maturity. The bonds are not associated with any other asset or liability. Which one of the following is the amount at which Inco should report its investment in Tryco in its December 31, 2011 IFRS-based Statement of Financial Position?

A. $100,000
B. $103,500
C. $105,000
D. $108,000

AICPA.100946FAR-NSI-SIM

382. Which, if any, of the following transfers between categories is possible under IFRS No. 9 for investments in debt securities?

	Amortized Cost to Fair Value	Fair Value to Amortized Cost
A.	Yes	Yes
B.	Yes	No
C.	No	Yes
D.	No	No

AICPA.100948FAR-NSI-SIM

383. Which of the following are possible ways that gains or losses on changes in the fair value of investments in equity securities may be reported under IFRS requirements?

	In Profit/Loss (Income Statement)	In Other Comprehensive Income
A.	Yes	Yes
B.	Yes	No
C.	No	Yes
D.	No	No

AICPA.100943FAR-NSI-SIM

384. Which, if any, of the following characteristics concerning the categories of investments under IFRS No. 9 is/are correct?

I. There is a single category for debt investments and a single category for equity investments.

II. The business model test used in evaluating debt instruments for classification purposes is concerned with the investor's intent.

A. I only.
B. II only.
C. Both I and II.
D. Neither I nor II.

Significant Influence—Equity Method

Equity Method

AICPA.070502FAR-TH-FA

385. When the equity method is used to account for investments in common stock, which one of the following affect(s) the investor's reported investment income?

	A Change in Market Value of Investee's Common Stock	Cash Dividends from Investee
A.	Yes	Yes
B.	Yes	No
C.	No	Yes
D.	No	No

AICPA.100951FAR-SI-SIM

386. In which one of the following cases is an investor most likely to use the equity method to carry and report an investment in an investee?

A. Investor owns 15% of the voting stock of the investee and has no other affiliation with the investee.

B. Investor owns 40% of the voting stock of the investee, and the investee is in bankruptcy.

C. Investor is a manufacturing firm that owns 25% of the voting stock of a consulting firm.

D. Investor owns 30% of the voting stock of the investee but is unable to obtain representation on the investee's Board of Directors or obtain significant information from the investee.

AICPA.082068FAR-II.E

387. Anchor Co. owns 40% of Main Co.'s common stock outstanding and 75% of Main's noncumulative preferred stock outstanding. Anchor exercises significant influence over Main's operations. During the current period, Main declared dividends of $200,000 on its common stock and $100,000 on its noncumulative preferred stock. What amount of dividend income should Anchor report on its Income Statement for the period related to its investment in Main?

A. $75,000
B. $80,000
C. $120,000
D. $225,000

AICPA.951126FAR-FA

388. Grant, Inc. acquired 30% of South Co.'s voting stock for $200,000 on January 2, 2004.

Grant's 30% interest in South gave Grant the ability to exercise significant influence over South's operating and financial policies. During 2004, South earned $80,000 and paid dividends of $50,000. South reported earnings of $100,000 for the six months ended June 30, 2005, and $200,000 for the year ended December 31, 2005. On July 1, 2005, Grant sold half of its stock in South for $150,000 cash. South paid dividends of $60,000 on October 1, 2005.

Before income taxes, what amount should Grant include in its 2004 Income Statement as a result of the investment?

A. $15,000
B. $24,000
C. $50,000
D. $80,000

AICPA.110547FAR

389. Larkin Co. has owned 25% of the common stock of Devon Co. for a number of years, and has the ability to exercise significant influence over Devon. The following information relates to Larkin's investment in Devon during the most recent year:

Carrying amount of Larkin's investment in Devon at the beginning of the year	$200,000
Net income of Devon for the year	600,000
Total dividends paid to Devon's stockholders during the year	400,000

What is the carrying amount of Larkin's investment in Devon at year-end?

A. $100,000
B. $200,000
C. $250,000
D. $350,000

IFRS—Equity Method

AICPA.130502FAR

390. According to IFRS guidance on equity method accounting, under what circumstances would the investor be required to recognize the associate's (investee's) losses that exceed the investor's investment?

I. The associate's return to profitability is imminent and assured.
II. The investor has guaranteed the obligations and commitments of the associate.

A. I only.
B. II only.
C. Both I and II.
D. Neither I nor II.

AICPA.130500FAR

391. Which of the following is not required under IFRS with respect to equity method accounting?

A. The accounting policies of the "associate" must conform with the accounting policies of the investor.
B. Any investor can elect to apply the fair value option to the accounting for the "associate."
C. The reporting dates for the investor and "associate" cannot be more than 3 months apart.
D. Any impairment loss on an equity investment is measured as the carrying value less the recoverable amount.

AICPA.130501FAR

392. Which of the following methods may a mutual fund investor use to measure and report an equity method investment under IFRS?

	Fair Value Method	Equity Method
A.	Yes	Yes
B.	Yes	No
C.	No	Yes
D.	No	No

Investor Stock Dividends, Splits, and Rights

AICPA.941139FAR-FA

393. Stock dividends on common stock should be recorded at their fair market value by the investor when the related investment is accounted for under which of the following methods?

	Cost	Equity
A.	Yes	Yes
B.	Yes	No
C.	No	Yes
D.	No	No

AICPA.931148FAR-P1-FA

394. Cobb Co. purchased 10,000 shares (2% ownership) of Roe Co. on February 12, 2004. Cobb received a stock dividend of 2,000 shares on March 31, 2004, when the carrying amount per share on Roe's books was $35 and the market value per share was $40. Roe paid a cash dividend of $1.50 per share on September 15, 2004.

In Cobb's Income Statement for the year ended October 31, 2004, what amount should Cobb report as dividend income?

A. $98,000
B. $88,000
C. $18,000
D. $15,000

AICPA.900547FAR-P1-FA

395. Simpson Co. received dividends from its common stock investments during the year ended December 31, 2005 as follows:

1 A cash dividend of $8,000 from Wren Corp., in which Simpson owns a 2% interest.

2 A cash dividend of $45,000 from Brill Corp., in which Simpson owns a 30% interest. This investment is appropriately accounted for using the equity method.

3 A stock dividend of 500 shares from Paul Corp. was received on December 15, 2005, when the quoted market value of Paul's shares was $10 per share. Simpson owns less than 1% of Paul's common stock.

In Simpson's 2005 Income Statement, dividend revenue should be:

A. $58,000
B. $53,000
C. $13,000
D. $8,000

AICPA.010505FAR-FA

396. Plack Co. purchased 10,000 shares (2% ownership) of Ty Corp. on February 14, 2005.

    Plack received a stock dividend of 2,000 shares on April 30, 2005, when the market value per share was $35. Ty paid a cash dividend of $2 per share on December 15, 2005.

    In its 2005 Income Statement, what amount should Plack report as dividend income?

    A. $20,000
    B. $24,000
    C. $90,000
    D. $94,000

AICPA.990508FAR-FA

397. Band Co. uses the equity method to account for its investment in Guard, Inc. common stock. How should Band record a 2% stock dividend received from Guard?

    A. As dividend revenue at Guard's carrying value of the stock.
    B. As dividend revenue at the market value of the stock.
    C. As a reduction in the total cost of Guard stock owned.
    D. As a memorandum entry, reducing the unit cost of all Guard stock owned.

Impairment of Debt and Equity Securities

AICPA.140414FAR-SIM

398. The credit losses associated with the impairment of debt securities are separated in which of the following circumstances?

    A. When the entity has the positive ability and intent to sell the impaired security.
    B. When the entity has the positive ability and intent to hold the impaired security.
    C. When the entity has positive ability and intent to hold the impaired security and expects to recover the entire cost basis of the impaired security.
    D. When the entity has positive ability and intent to hold the impaired security and does not expect to recover the entire cost basis of the impaired security.

AICPA.140412FAR-SIM

399. Which of the following is **not** a factor to take into consideration when determining if the decline in fair value of an equity security is other-than-temporary?

    A. The length of time and extent to which the market value has been less than cost.
    B. The length of time the holder has held the security.

C. The financial condition and near-term prospects of the issuer.
D. The intent and ability of the holder to retain its investment for a period of time to allow for any anticipated recovery in the market value.

AICPA.140413FAR-SIM

400. Which of the following is true with respect to impairment of available-for-sale securities?

    A. If the decline in fair value is considered to be other-than-temporary, the unrealized losses in OCI are reclassified to earnings.
    B. If the decline in fair value is considered to be other-than-temporary, the unrealized losses are recorded in OCI.
    C. If the decline in fair value is not considered to be other-than-temporary, the unrealized gains in OCI are reclassified to earnings.
    D. If the decline in fair value is not considered to be other-than-temporary, the unrealized gains are recorded in OCI.

Intangible Assets—Goodwill and Other

Introduction to Intangible Assets

AICPA.101070FAR

401. Northstar Co. acquired a registered trademark for $600,000. The trademark has a remaining legal life of five years, but can be renewed every 10 years for a nominal fee. Northstar expects to renew the trademark indefinitely. What amount of amortization expense should Northstar record for the trademark in the current year?

    A. $0
    B. $15,000
    C. $40,000
    D. $120,000

AICPA.901102FAR-P2-FA

402. On January 2, 20X5, Ral Co. leased land and a building from an unrelated lessor for a 10-year term. The lease has a renewal option for an additional 10 years, but Ral has not reached a decision with regard to the renewal option. In early January of 2005, Ral completed the following improvements to the property:

Description	Estimated Life	Cost
Sales office	10 years	$47,000
Warehouse	25 years	75,000
Parking lot	15 years	18,000

Amortization of leasehold improvements for 20X6 should be:

A. $7,000
B. $8,900
C. $12,200
D. $14,000

AICPA.110577FAR

403. Grayson Co. incurred significant costs in defending its patent rights. Which of the following is the appropriate treatment of the related litigation costs?

A. Litigation costs would be capitalized regardless of the outcome of the litigation.
B. Litigation costs would be expensed regardless of the outcome of the litigation.
C. Litigation costs would be capitalized if the patent rights are successfully defended.
D. Litigation costs would be capitalized only if the patent was purchased rather than internally developed.

AICPA.951135FAR-FA

404. Upon the death of an officer, Jung Co. received the proceeds of a life insurance policy held by Jung on the officer. The proceeds were not taxable. The policy's cash-surrender value had been recorded on Jung's books at the time of payment.

What amount of revenue should Jung report in its statements?

A. Proceeds received
B. Proceeds received less cash surrender value
C. Proceeds received plus cash surrender value
D. None

AICPA.101071FAR

405. A company recently acquired a copyright that now has a remaining legal life of 30 years. The copyright initially had a 38-year useful life assigned to it. An analysis of market trends and consumer habits indicated that the copyrighted material will generate positive cash flows for approximately 25 years. What is the remaining useful life, if any, over which the company can amortize the copyright for accounting purposes?

A. 0 years
B. 25 years
C. 30 years
D. 38 years

Goodwill

AICPA.110601FAR-SIM

406. Which of the following is **not** one of the qualitative factors considered to determine if it is more likely than not that the reporting unit is less than its carrying value?

A. Industry and market conditions, such as deterioration in the industry environment, increased competition, decline in market-dependent multiples, change in the market for the entity's products or services, or a regulatory or political development.
B. Cost factors, such as increases in raw materials, labor, or other costs that have a negative effect on earnings and cash flows.
C. Decline in the implied goodwill by using a discounted cash flow model.
D. Overall financial performance, such as negative cash flows or actual or projected declines in revenues, earnings, or cash flows.

AICPA.110606FAR-SIM

407. Large purchased all of Small's voting stock for $11 million when Small's total owners' equity was $4 million. The book value and market value of Small's liabilities equal $3 million. However, the market value of Small's total assets equals $9 million. What amount of goodwill is recorded by Large (in millions)?

A. $7
B. $2
C. $5
D. $6

AICPA.110607FAR-SIM

408. Firm A purchased Firm B for $4,000 when B's total owners' equity was $2,000. Firm A completed the qualitative test for goodwill impairment and determined that it is more likely than not that goodwill may be impaired. B had one asset worth $500 more than the book value. One year after the purchase, Firm B's total market value had dropped to $3,200 and the market value of its net identifiable assets was $2,000. What amount of goodwill impairment loss is recorded?

A. $0
B. $800
C. $400
D. $300

AICPA.110602FAR-SIM

409. A company reported $6 million of goodwill in last year's statement of financial position. How

should the company account for the reported goodwill in the current year?

A. Determine the current year's amortizable amount and report the current year's amortization expense.
B. Determine whether the fair value of the reporting unit is greater than the carrying amount and report a gain on goodwill in the income statement.
C. Perform a qualitative assessment to determine if it is more likely than not that the fair value of the reporting unit is less than its carrying value.
D. Determine whether the fair value of the reporting unit is greater than the carrying amount and report the recovery of any previous impairment in the income statement.

assess.AICPA.FAR.goodwill-0017

410. If both an asset group and goodwill in one of a company's reporting units have to be tested for impairment, which of the following statements is correct regarding impairment testing and impairment losses?

A. The other asset group should be tested for an impairment loss before goodwill is tested.
B. Impairment testing may be conducted concurrently for the other asset group and goodwill.
C. If the other asset group is impaired, the loss should **not** be recognized prior to goodwill being tested for impairment.
D. If goodwill is impaired, the loss should be recognized prior to testing the other assets for impairment.

Research and Development Costs

AICPA.120617FAR

411. Under U.S. GAAP, how should NSB, Inc. report significant research and development costs incurred?

A. Expense all costs in the year incurred.
B. Capitalize the costs and amortize over a five-year period.
C. Capitalize the costs and amortize over a 40-year period.
D. Expense all costs two years before and five years after the year incurred.

AICPA.900553FAR-P1-FA

412. During 2005, Vest Co. incurred the following costs:

Testing in search for process alternatives	$280,000
Routine design of tools, jigs, molds, and dies	250,000
Modification of the formulation of a process	410,000
Research and development services performed by Acme Corp. for Vest	325,000

In Vest's 2005 income statement, research and development expense should be

A. $410,000
B. $735,000
C. $1,015,000
D. $1,265,000

AICPA.911147FAR-P1-FA

413. In 2005, Ball Labs incurred the following costs:

Direct costs of doing contract research and development work for the government to be reimbursed by governmental unit	$400,000

Research and development costs not included above were:

Depreciation	$300,000
Salaries	700,000
Indirect costs appropriately allocated	200,000
Materials	180,000

What was Ball's total research and development expense in 2005?

A. $1,080,000
B. $1,380,000
C. $1,580,000
D. $1,780,000

AICPA.921153FAR-P1-FA

414. Heller Co. incurred the following costs in 2005:

Research and development services performed by Kay Corp. for Heller	$150,000
Testing for evaluation of new products	125,000
Laboratory research aimed at discovery of new knowledge	185,000

What amount should Heller report as research and development costs in its income statement for the year ending December 31, 2005?

A. $125,000
B. $150,000
C. $335,000
D. $460,000

AICPA.901142FAR-P1-FA

415. Cody Corp. incurred the following costs during 2006:

Design of tools, jigs, molds, and dies involving new technology	$125,000
Modification of the formulation of a process	160,000
Troubleshooting in connection with breakdowns during commercial production	100,000
Adaptation of an existing capability to a particular customer's need as part of a continuing commercial activity	110,000

In its 2006 income statement, Cody should report research and development expense of

A. $125,000
B. $160,000
C. $235,000
D. $285,000

Software Costs

AICPA.010503FAR-FA

416. On December 31, 2004, Byte Co. had capitalized software costs of $600,000 with an economic life of 4 years. Sales for 2005 were 10% of expected total sales of the software.

At December 31, 2005, the software had a net realizable value of $480,000.

In its December 31, 2005 balance sheet, what amount should Byte report as net capitalized cost of computer software?

A. $432,000
B. $450,000
C. $480,000
D. $540,000

AICPA.910521FAR-P1-FA

417. During 2004, Pitt Corp. incurred costs to develop and produce a routine, low-risk computer software product as follows:

Completion of detailed program design	$13,000
Costs incurred for coding and testing to establish technological feasibility	10,000
Other coding costs after establishment of technological feasibility	24,000
Other testing costs after establishment of technological feasibility	20,000
Costs of producing product masters for training materials	15,000
Duplication of computer software and training materials from product masters (1,000 units)	25,000
Packaging product (500 units)	9,000

In Pitt's December 31, 2004 balance sheet, what amount should be reported in inventory?

A. $25,000
B. $34,000
C. $40,000
D. $49,000

AICPA.910522FAR-P1-FA

418. During 2004, Pitt Corp. incurred costs to develop and produce a routine, low-risk computer software product as follows:

Completion of detail program design	$13,000
Costs incurred for coding and testing to establish technological feasibility	10,000
Other coding costs after establishment of technological feasibility	24,000
Other testing costs after establishment of technological feasibility	20,000
Costs of producing product masters for training materials	15,000
Duplication of computer software and training materials from product masters (1,000 units)	25,000
Packaging product (500 units)	9,000

In Pitt's December 31, 2004 balance sheet, what amount should be capitalized as software cost, subject to amortization?

A. $54,000
B. $57,000
C. $59,000
D. $69,000

AICPA.061225FAR

419. Yellow Co. spent $12,000,000 during the current year developing its new software package. Of this amount, $4,000,000 was spent before it was at the application development stage and the package was only to be used internally. The package was completed during the year and is expected to have a 4-year useful life.

Yellow has a policy of taking a full-year's amortization in the first year. After the development stage, $50,000 was spent on training employees to use the program.

What amount should Yellow report as an expense for the current year?

A. $1,600,000
B. $2,000,000
C. $6,012,500
D. $6,050,000

AICPA.061211FAR

420. Standard Co. spent $10,000,000 on its new software package that is to be used only for internal use. The amount spent is for costs after the application development stage. The economic life of the product is expected to be three years. The equipment on which the package is to be used is being depreciated over five years.

What amount of expense should Standard report on its income statement for the first full year?

A. $0
B. $2,000,000
C. $3,333,333
D. $10,000,000

Intangibles and IFRS

AICPA.130729FAR

421. A company is completing its annual impairment analysis of the goodwill included in one of its cash generating units (CGUs). The recoverable amount of the CGU is $32,000. The company noted the following related to the CGU:

	Good-will	Patents	Other Assets	Total
Historical cost	$15,000	$10,000	$35,000	$60,000
Depreciation and amortization	0	3,333	11,667	15,000
Carrying amount, December 31	$15,000	$6,667	$23,333	$45,000

Under IFRS, which of the following adjustments should be recognized in the company's consolidated financial statements?

A. Decrease goodwill by $13,000.
B. Decrease goodwill by $15,000.
C. Decrease goodwill by $3,250; patents by $2,167; and other assets by $7,583.
D. Decrease goodwill by $4,333; patents by $1,926; and other assets by $6,741.

AICPA.101079FAR

422. Under IFRS, an entity that acquires an intangible asset may use the revaluation model for subsequent measurement only if:

A. The useful life of the intangible asset can be reliably determined.
B. An active market exists for the intangible asset.
C. The cost of the intangible asset can be measured reliably.
D. The intangible asset is a monetary asset.

AICPA.120201FAR-SIM

423. Under IFRS, the test for asset impairment is to compare the carrying value of the intangible asset to its recoverable amount. Which of the following is the recoverable amount according to IFRS?

A. The greater of future undiscounted cash flows or future discounted cash flows.
B. The greater of future discounted cash flows or fair value.
C. The greater of fair value less cost to sell or value in use.
D. The greater of fair value or value in use.

AICPA.120202FAR-SIM

424. After an impairment loss is recognized, the adjusted carrying amount of the intangible asset shall be its new accounting basis. Under IFRS, which of the following statements about subsequent reversal of a previously recognized impairment loss is correct?

A. It is prohibited.
B. It is allowed when events and circumstances change.
C. It is allowed only if the intangible asset is recorded at fair value.
D. The recovery amount can exceed the carrying value at the time of the initial impairment.

AICPA.101080FAR

425. Under IFRS, which of the following is a criterion, other than goodwill, that must be met in order for an item to be recognized as an intangible asset?

A. The item's fair value can be measured reliably.
B. The item is part of the entity's activities aimed at gaining new scientific or technical knowledge.
C. The item is expected to be used in the production or supply of goods or services.
D. The item is identifiable and lacks physical substance.

Payables and Accrued Liabilities

Current Liabilities

AICPA.070792FAR

426. Bake Co.'s trial balance included the following at December 31, Year 1:

Accounts payable	$ 80,000
Bonds payable, due Year 2	300,000
Discount on bonds payable	15,000
Deferred income tax liability	25,000

The deferred income tax liability is not related to an asset for financial accounting purposes and is expected to reverse in Year 2. What amount should be included in the current liability section of Bake's December 31, Year 1 balance sheet?

A. $365,000
B. $390,000
C. $395,000
D. $420,000

AICPA.901110FAR-P1-FA

427. Black Corp.'s accounts payable at December 31, 20X4 totaled $900,000 before any necessary year-end adjustments relating to the following transactions:

1   On December 27, 20X4, Black wrote and recorded checks to creditors totaling $400,000, causing an overdraft of $100,000 in Black's bank account at December 31, 20X4. The checks were mailed out on January 10, 20X5.
2   On December 28, 20X4, Black purchased and received goods for $153,061, terms 2/10, n/30. Black records purchases and accounts payable at net amounts. The invoice was recorded and paid on January 3, 20X5.
3   Goods shipped F.O.B. destination on December 20, 20X4 from a vendor to Black were received January 2, 20X5. The invoice cost was $65,000.

At December 31, 20X4, what amount should Black report as total accounts payable?

A. $1,515,000
B. $1,450,000
C. $1,153,061
D. $1,053,061

AICPA.911101FAR-P1-FA

428. Gar, Inc.'s trial balance reflected the following liability account balances at December 31, 20X5:

Accounts payable	$19,000
Bonds payable, due 20X6	34,000
Deferred income tax payable	4,000
Discount on bonds payable	2,000
Dividends payable on 2/15/X6	5,000
Income tax payable	9,000
Notes payable, due 1/19/X7	6,000

The deferred income tax payable is based on temporary differences that will reverse in 20X7 and 20X8.

In Gar's December 31, 20X5 balance sheet, the current liabilities total was

A. $71,000
B. $69,000
C. $67,000
D. $65,000

AICPA.101131FAR

429. Acme Co.'s accounts payable balance at December 31 was $850,000 before necessary year-end adjustments, if any, related to the following information:

At December 31, Acme has a $50,000 debit balance in its accounts payable resulting from a payment to a supplier for goods to be manufactured to Acme's specifications.

Goods shipped F.O.B. destination on December 20 were received and recorded by Acme on January 2. The invoice cost was $45,000.

In its December 31 balance sheet, what amount should Acme report as accounts payable?

A. $850,000
B. $895,000
C. $900,000
D. $945,000

AICPA.130718FAR

430. As of December 1, year 2 a company obtained a $1,000,000 line of credit maturing in one year on which it has drawn $250,000, a $750,000 secured note due in five annual installments, and a $300,000 three-year balloon note. The company has no other liabilities. How should the company's debt be presented in its classified balance sheet on December 31, year 2 if **no** debt repayments were made in December?

A. Current liabilities of $1,000,000; long-term liabilities of $1,050,000.
B. Current liabilities of $500,000; long-term liabilities of $1,550,000.
C. Current liabilities of $400,000; long-term liabilities of $900,000.
D. Current liabilities of $500,000; long-term liabilities of $800,000.

Specific Current Liabilities

AICPA.930552FAR-P1-FA

431. Dana Co.'s officers' compensation expense account had a balance of $224,000 at December 31, 20X4 before any appropriate year-end adjustment relating to the following:

No salary accrual was made for December 30-31, 20X4. Salaries for the two-day period totaled $3,500.

20X4 officers' bonuses of $62,500 were paid on January 31, 20X5.

In its 20X4 income statement, what amount should Dana report as officers' compensation expense?

A. $290,000
B. $286,500
C. $227,500
D. $224,000

AICPA.940522FAR-FA

432. Under state law, Acme may pay 3% of eligible gross wages or it may reimburse the state directly for actual unemployment claims.

Acme believes that actual unemployment claims will be 2% of eligible gross wages and has chosen to reimburse the state. Eligible gross wages are defined as the first $10,000 of gross wages paid to each employee. Acme had five employees, each of whom earned $20,000 during 20X4.

In its December 31, 20X4 balance sheet, what amount should Acme report as accrued liability for unemployment claims?

A. $1,000
B. $1,500
C. $2,000
D. $3,000

AICPA.940521FAR-FA

433. Hudson Hotel collects 15% in city sales taxes on room rentals, in addition to a $2 per room, per night, occupancy tax.

Sales taxes for each month are due at the end of the following month, and occupancy taxes are due 15 days after the end of each calendar quarter. On January 3, 20X5 Hudson paid its November 20X4 sales taxes and its fourth quarter 20X4 occupancy taxes. Additional information pertaining to Hudson's operations is:

20X4	Room Rentals	Room Nights
October	$100,000	1,100
November	110,000	1,200
December	150,000	1,800

What amounts should Hudson report as sales taxes payable and occupancy taxes payable in its December 31, 20X4 balance sheet?

	Sales Taxes	Occupancy Taxes
A.	$39,000	$6,000
B.	$39,000	$8,200
C.	$54,000	$6,000
D.	$54,000	$8,200

AICPA.051158FAR-FA

434. As of December 15, Year 1, Aviator had dividends in arrears of $200,000 on its cumulative preferred stock. Dividends for Year 1 of $100,000 have not yet been declared. The Board of Directors plans to declare cash dividends on its preferred and common stock on January 16, Year 2. Aviator paid an annual bonus to its CEO based on the company's annual profits. The bonus for Year 1 was $50,000, which will be paid on February 10, Year 2. What amount should Aviator report as current liabilities on its balance sheet at December 31, Year 1?

A. $ 50,000
B. $150,000
C. $200,000
D. $350,000

AICPA.901112FAR-P1-FA

435. Bloy Corp.'s payroll for the pay period ended October 31, 2005 is summarized as follows:

	Federal Income		Amount of Wages Subject to Payroll Taxes	
Department Payroll	Total Wages	Tax With-held	F.I.C.A.	Unem-ployment
Factory	22,000	3,000	16,000	2,000
Sales	18,000	2,000	8,000	-
Office	60,000	7,000	56,000	18,000
Total	$100,000	$12,000	$80,000	$20,000

Assume the following payroll tax rates:

F.I.C.A. for employer and employee 7% each

Unemployment 3%

What amount should Bloy accrue as its share of payroll taxes in its October 31, 2005 balance sheet?

A. $18,200
B. $12,600
C. $11,800
D. $6,200

Costs and Expenses

AICPA.130716FAR

436. On October 31, year 1, a company with a calendar year-end paid $90,000 for services that will be performed evenly over a six-month period from November 1, year 1, through April 30, year 2. The company expensed the $90,000 cash payment in October, year 1, to its services expense general ledger account. The company did not record any additional

journal entries in year 1 related to the payment. What is the adjusting journal entry that the company should record to properly report the prepayment in its year 1 financial statements?

A. Debit prepaid services and credit services expense for $30,000.
B. Debit prepaid services and credit services expense for $60,000.
C. Debit services expense and credit prepaid services for $30,000.
D. Debit services expense and credit prepaid services for $60,000.

AICPA.130715FAR

437. On January 1, year 1, Alpha Co. signed an annual maintenance agreement with a software provider for $15,000 and the maintenance period begins on March 1, year 1. Alpha also incurred $5,000 of costs on January 1, year 1, related to software modification requests that will increase the functionality of the software. Alpha depreciates and amortizes its computer and software assets over five years using the straight-line method. What amount is the total expense that Alpha should recognize related to the maintenance agreement and the software modifications for the year ended December 31, year 1?

A. $5,000
B. $13,500
C. $16,000
D. $20,000

AICPA.911126FAR-P1-FA

438. On the first day of each month, Bell Mortgage Co. receives from Kent Corp. an escrow deposit of $2,500 for real estate taxes.

Bell records the $2,500 in an escrow account. Kent's 2005 real estate tax is $28,000, payable in equal installments on the first day of each calendar quarter. On December 31, 2004, the balance in the escrow account is $3,000.

On September 30, 2005, what amount should Bell show as an escrow liability to Kent?

A. $1,500
B. $4,500
C. $8,500
D. $11,500

AICPA.941119FAR-FA

439. On July 1, 2005, Ran County issued realty tax assessments for its fiscal year ended June 30, 2006.

On September 1, 2005, Day Co. purchased a warehouse in Ran County. The purchase price was reduced by a credit for accrued realty taxes.

Day did not record the entire year's real estate tax obligation, but instead records tax expenses at the end of each month by adjusting pre-paid real estate taxes or real estate taxes payable, as appropriate. On November 1, 2005, Day paid the first of two equal installments of $12,000 for realty taxes.

What amount of this payment should Day record as a debit to real estate taxes payable?

A. $4,000
B. $8,000
C. $10,000
D. $12,000

AICPA.931132FAR-P1-FA

440. Kent Co., a division of National Realty, Inc., maintains escrow accounts and pays real estate taxes for National's mortgage customers. Escrow funds are kept in interest-bearing accounts. Interest, less a 10% service fee, is credited to the mortgagee's account and used to reduce future escrow payments.

Additional information follows:

Escrow accounts liability, 1 January, 2004	$700,000
Escrow payments received during 2004	$1.58mn
Real estate taxes paid during 2004	$1.72mn
Interest on escrow funds during 2004	50,000

What amount should Kent report as escrow accounts liability in its December 31, 2004 balance sheet?

A. $510,000
B. $515,000
C. $605,000
D. $610,000

Compensated Absences

AICPA.931128FAR-TH-FA

441. If the payment of employees' compensation for future absences is probable, the amount can be reasonably estimated, and the obligation relates to rights that accumulate, the compensation should be

A. Accrued if attributable to employees' services not already rendered.
B. Accrued if attributable to employees' services already rendered.
C. Accrued if attributable to employees' services, whether already rendered or not.
D. Recognized when paid.

AICPA.920515FAR-P2-FA

442. The following information pertains to Rik Co.'s two employees:

Name	Weekly Salary	Number of Weeks Worked in 2005	Vacation Rights Vest or Accumulate
Ryan	$800	52	Yes
Todd	600	52	No

Neither Ryan nor Todd took the usual two-week vacation in 2005. In Rik's December 31, 2005, financial statements, what amount of vacation expense and liability should be reported?

A. $2,800
B. $1,600
C. $1,400
D. $0

AICPA.930530FAR-P1-FA

443. North Corp. has an employee benefit plan for compensated absences that gives employees ten paid vacation days and ten paid sick days per year.

Both vacation and sick days can be carried over indefinitely. Employees can elect to receive payment in lieu of vacation days; however, no payment is given for sick days not taken.

At December 31, 2004, North's unadjusted balance of liability for compensated absences was $21,000. North estimated that there were 150 vacation days and 75 sick days available at December 31, 2004. North's employees earn an average of $100 per day.

In its December 31, 2004 balance sheet, what amount of liability for compensated absences is North required to report?

A. $36,000
B. $22,500
C. $21,000
D. $15,000

AICPA.921125FAR-TH-FA

444. At December 31, 2004, Taos Co. estimates that its employees have earned vacation pay of $100,000. Employees will receive their vacation pay in 2005.

Should Taos accrue a liability at December 31, 2004 if the rights to this compensation accumulated over time or if the rights are vested?

	Accumulated	Vested
A.	Yes	No
B.	No	No
C.	Yes	Yes
D.	No	Yes

AICPA.900553FAR-P2-FA

445. Gavin Co. grants all employees two weeks of paid vacation for each full year of employment. Unused vacation time can be accumulated and carried forward to succeeding years and will be paid at the salaries in effect when vacations are taken or when employment is terminated.

There was no employee turnover in 2005.

Additional information relating to the year ended December 31, 2005 is as follows:

Liability for accumulated vacations at December 31, 2004	$35,000
Pre-2005 accrued vacations taken from January 1, 2005 to 30 September 2005 (the authorized period for vacations)	20,000
Vacations earned for work in 2005 (adjusted to current rates)	30,000

Gavin granted a 10% salary increase to all employees on October 1, 2005, its annual salary increase date. For the year ended December 31, 2005, Gavin should report vacation pay expense of

A. $45,000
B. $33,500
C. $31,500
D. $30,000

Contingencies, Commitments, and Guarantees (Provisions)

Contingent Liability Principles

AICPA.120631FAR

446. Hudson Corp. operates several factories that manufacture medical equipment. The factories have a historical cost of $200 million. Near the end of the company's fiscal year, a change in business climate related to a competitor's innovative products indicated to Hudson's management that the $170 million carrying amount of the assets of one of Hudson's factories may not be recoverable. Management identified cash flows from this factory and estimated that the undiscounted future cash flows over the remaining useful life of the factory would be $150 million. The fair value of the factory's assets is reliably estimated to be $135 million. The change in business climate requires investigation of possible impairment. Which of the following amounts is the impairment loss?

A. $15 million
B. $20 million
C. $35 million
D. $65 million

AICPA.920527FAR-TH-FA

447. Snelling Co. did not record an accrual for a contingent loss, but disclosed the nature of the contingency and the range of the possible loss.

How likely is the loss?

A. Remote.
B. Reasonably possible.
C. Probable.
D. Certain.

AICPA.900512FAR-TH-FA

448. Management can estimate the amount of the loss that will occur if a foreign government expropriates some company assets.

If expropriation is reasonably possible, a loss contingency should be:

A. Neither accrued as a liability nor disclosed.
B. Accrued as a liability but not disclosed.
C. Disclosed and accrued as a liability.
D. Disclosed but not accrued as a liability.

AICPA.941127FAR-FA

449. Vadis Co. sells appliances that include a three-year warranty. Service calls under the warranty are performed by an independent mechanic under a contract with Vadis. Based on experience, warranty costs are estimated at $30 for each machine sold.

When should Vadis recognize these warranty costs?

A. Evenly over the life of the warranty.
B. When the service calls are performed.
C. When payments are made to the mechanic.
D. When the machines are sold.

AICPA.930534FAR-P1-FA

450. In 2003, a personal injury lawsuit was brought against Halsey Co.

Based on counsel's estimate, Halsey reported a $50,000 liability in its December 31, 2003, balance sheet. In November 2004, Halsey received a favorable judgment, requiring the plaintiff to reimburse Halsey for expenses of $30,000. The plaintiff has appealed the decision, and Halsey's counsel is unable to predict the outcome of the appeal.

In its December 31, 2004, balance sheet, Halsey should report what amounts of asset and liability related to these legal actions?

	Asset	Liability
A.	$30,000	$50,000
B.	$30,000	$0
C.	$0	$20,000
D.	$0	$0

Examples of Contingent Liabilities and Additional Aspects

AICPA.951117FAR-FA

451. Eagle Co. has cosigned the mortgage note on the home of its president, guaranteeing the indebtedness in the event that the president should default. Eagle considers the likelihood of default to be remote.

How should the guarantee be treated in Eagle's financial statements?

A. Disclosed only.
B. Accrued only.
C. Accrued and disclosed.
D. Neither accrued nor disclosed.

AICPA.900535FAR-TH-FA

452. Grim Corporation operates a plant in a foreign country. It is probable that the plant will be expropriated. However, the foreign government has indicated that Grim will receive a definite amount of compensation for the plant.

The amount of compensation is less than the fair market value but exceeds the carrying amount of the plant.

The contingency should be reported:

A. As a valuation allowance as a part of stockholders' equity.
B. As a fixed asset valuation allowance account.
C. In the notes to the financial statements.
D. In the income statement.

AICPA.940557FAR-FA

453. During 2005, Smith Co. filed suit against West, Inc. seeking damages for patent infringement.

At December 31, 2005, Smith's legal counsel believed that it was probable that Smith would be successful against West for an estimated amount in the range of $75,000 to $150,000, with all amounts in the range considered equally likely. In March 2006, Smith was awarded $100,000 and received full payment thereof.

In its 2005 financial statements, issued in February 2006, how should this award be reported?

A. As a receivable and revenue of $100,000.
B. As a receivable and deferred revenue of $100,000.
C. As a disclosure of a contingent gain of $100,000.
D. As a disclosure of a contingent gain of an undetermined amount in the range of $75,000 to $150,000.

AICPA.921131FAR-P1-FA

454. During 2003, Manfred Corp. guaranteed a supplier's $500,000 loan from a bank.

On October 1, 2004, Manfred was notified that the supplier had defaulted on the loan and filed for bankruptcy protection. Counsel believes Manfred will probably have to pay between $250,000 and $450,000 under its guarantee.

As a result of the supplier's bankruptcy, Manfred entered into a contract in December 2004 to retool its machines so that Manfred could accept parts from other suppliers. Retooling costs are estimated to be $300,000.

What amount should Manfred report as a liability in its December 31, 2004, balance sheet?

A. $250,000
B. $450,000
C. $550,000
D. $750,000

AICPA.900559FAR-P1-FA

455. During 2005, Tedd Co. became involved in a tax dispute with the IRS. At December 31, 2005, Tedd's tax advisor believed that an unfavorable outcome was probable.

A reasonable estimate of additional taxes was $400,000 but could be as much as $600,000.

After the 2005 financial statements were issued, Tedd received and accepted an IRS settlement offer of $450,000.

What amount of accrued liability should Tedd have reported in its December 31, 2005 balance sheet?

A. $400,000
B. $450,000
C. $500,000
D. $600,000

IFRS Contingencies

AICPA.101111FAR

456. Which of the following is not a contingent liability under international accounting standards?

A. A provision with a 60% chance of requiring an outflow of benefits, amount is estimable.
B. A provision with a 40% chance of requiring an outflow of benefits, amount is estimable.
C. A provision with a 90% chance of requiring an outflow of benefits, amount not estimable.
D. A possible obligation.

AICPA.101107FAR

457. Choose the correct statement about international accounting standards as they relate to contingent liabilities and similar items.

A. A provision that has a reasonably possible chance of requiring the outflow of benefits is treated as a contingent liability.
B. Provisions are recognized only when there is greater than a 90% probability of an outflow of benefits occurring.
C. A recognized provision is a contingent liability.
D. A provision for which it is probable that an outflow of benefits will be required is recognized, even if it is not of estimable amount.

AICPA.101109FAR

458. A firm considers its regular warranty liability to be an existing liability of uncertain amount. At year-end, the firm estimates that the amount required to extinguish its warranty liability in the future is in the range of $20 to $60 million, with no amount more likely than any other. Under the two sets of standards, what amount will be recognized?

	International	U.S.
A.	40	40
B.	40	20
C.	20	20
D.	0	40

AICPA.101110FAR

459. Which of the following is a recognized liability for both international accounting standards and U.S. standards?

A. Regular warranty liability, 60% probability of occurring.
B. Obligation to provide rebates to customers, 90% probability of occurring.
C. Possible loss due to lawsuit, 60% probability of occurring.
D. Possible loss due to lawsuit, 40% probability of occurring.

Long-Term Debt (Financial Liabilities)

Notes Payable

AICPA.931131FAR-P1-FA

460. On September 1, 20X3, Brak Co. borrowed on a $1,350,000 note payable from the Federal Bank.

The note bears interest at 12% and is payable in three equal annual principal payments of $450,000. On this date, the bank's prime rate was 11%. The first annual payment for interest and principal was made on September 1, 20X4.

At December 31, 20X4, what amount should Brak report as accrued interest payable?

A. $54,000
B. $49,500
C. $36,000
D. $33,000

AICPA.900523FAR-P1-FA

461. At December 31, Year 1, a $1,200,000 note payable was included in Cobb Corp.'s liability account balances. The note is dated October 1, Year 1, bears interest at 15%, and is payable in three equal annual payments of $400,000. The first interest and principal payment was made on October 1, Year 2. In its December 31, Year 2 balance sheet, what amount should Cobb report as accrued interest payable for this note?

A. $135,000
B. $90,000
C. $45,000
D. $30,000

AICPA.101132FAR

462. On September 30, World Co. borrowed $1,000,000 on a 9% note payable. World paid the first of four quarterly payments of $264,200 when due on December 30. In its December 31 balance sheet, what amount should World report as note payable?

A. $735,800
B. $750,000
C. $758,300
D. $825,800

AICPA.911154FAR-P1-FA

463. Loeb's Corp. frequently borrows from the bank in order to maintain sufficient operating cash. The following loans were at a 12% interest rate, with interest payable at maturity. Loeb repaid each loan on its scheduled maturity date.

Date of Loan	Amount	Maturity Date	Term of Loan
11/1/X4	$5,000	10/31/X5	1 Year
2/1/X5	15,000	7/31/X5	6 Months
5/1/05	8,000	1/31/X6	9 Months

Loeb records interest expense when the loans are repaid. As a result, the interest expense of $1,500 was recorded in 2005. If no correction is made, by what amount would 2005 interest expense be understated?

A. $540
B. $620
C. $640
D. $720

AICPA.951116FAR-FA

464. On March 1, 20X4, Fine Co. borrowed $10,000 and signed a two-year note bearing interest at 12% per annum compounded annually. Interest is payable in full at maturity on February 28, 20X6.

What amount should Fine report as a liability for accrued interest at December 31, 20X5?

A. $0
B. $1,000
C. $1,200
D. $2,320

Bond Accounting Principles

Bond Accounting Principles

AICPA.061220FAR

465. On September 30, World Co. borrowed $1,000,000 on a 9% note payable. World paid the first of four quarterly payments of $264,200 when due on December 30.

In its income statement for the year, what amount should World report as interest expense?

A. $0
B. $14,200
C. $22,500
D. $30,000

AICPA.061206FAR

466. When debt is issued at a discount, interest expense over the term of debt equals the cash interest paid

A. Minus discount
B. Minus discount minus par value
C. Plus discount
D. Plus discount plus par value

AICPA.0821129FAR-II

467. On January 1, a company issued a $50,000 face value, 8% five-year bond for $46,139 that will yield 10%. Interest is payable on June 30 and December 31. What is the bond-carrying amount on December 31 of the current year?

A. $46,139
B. $46,446
C. $46,768
D. $47,106

AICPA.120602FAR

468. What type of bonds mature in installments?

A. Debenture
B. Term
C. Variable rate
D. Serial

AICPA.110561FAR

469. When the effective interest method of amortization is used for bonds issued at a premium, the amount of interest payable for an interest period is calculated by multiplying the:

A. Face value of the bonds at the beginning of the period by the contractual interest rate.
B. Face value of the bonds at the beginning of the period by the effective interest rate.
C. Carrying value of the bonds at the beginning of the period by the contractual interest rate.
D. Carrying value of the bonds at the beginning of the period by the effective interest rate.

Bond Complications

AICPA.920522FAR-TH-FA

470. A bond issued on June 1, 20X5 has interest payment dates of April 1 and October 1.

The bond interest expense for the year ended December 31, 20X5 is for a period of

A. Seven months.
B. Six months.
C. Four months.
D. Three months.

AICPA.901113FAR-P1-FA

471. On September 1, Year 1, Cobb Co. issued a note payable to the National Bank in the amount of $900,000, bearing interest at 12%, and payable in three equal annual principal payments of $300,000.

On this date, the bank's prime rate was 11%. The first payment for interest and principal was made on September 1, Year 2.

At December 31, Year 2, Cobb should record accrued interest payable of

A. $36,000
B. $33,000
C. $24,000
D. $22,000

AICPA.921123FAR-P1-FA

472. On November 1, 20X5, Mason Corp. issued $800,000 of its 10-year, 8% term bonds dated October 1, 20X5. The bonds were sold to yield 10%, with total proceeds of $700,000 plus accrued interest. Interest is paid every April 1 and October 1. What amount should Mason report for interest payable in its December 31, 20X5 balance sheet?

A. $17,500
B. $16,000
C. $11,667
D. $10,667

AICPA.921136FAR-P1-FA

473. On April 1, 20X4, Hill Corp. issued 200 of its $1,000 face value bonds at 101 plus accrued interest. The bonds were dated November 1, 20X3, and bear interest at an annual rate of 9% payable semiannually on November 1 and May 1. What amount did Hill receive from the bond issuance?

A. $194,500
B. $200,000
C. $202,000
D. $209,500

AICPA.931134FAR-P1-FA

474. On January 2, year 4, Gill Co. issued $2,000,000 of 10-year, 8% bonds at par. The bonds, dated January 1, year 4, pay interest semiannually on January 1 and July 1. Bond issue costs were $250,000.

What amount of bond issue costs are unamortized at June 30, year 5 assuming straight-line method?

A. $237,500
B. $225,000
C. $220,800
D. $212,500

Bond Fair Value Option, International

assess.AICPA.FAR.bond.fair-0047

475. A company leases trucks and properly classifies the leases as capital leases. The leases have a 10-year term, and the lease calculations were done three years ago when interest rates were lower. Which of the following is the appropriate accounting treatment, if any, for the application of the fair value option to lease transactions?

A. Leases are **not** eligible for the fair value option.
B. Recognize the change to fair value accounting with a cumulative adjustment to beginning retained earnings.
C. Recognize the change to fair value accounting with an unrealized loss in the income statement.
D. Recognize the change to fair value accounting with an unrealized loss in accumulated other comprehensive income.

AICPA.070779FAR

476. Foley Co. is preparing the electronic spreadsheet below to amortize the discount on its 10-year, 6%, $100,000 bonds payable. Bonds were issued on December 31 to yield 8%. Interest is paid annually. Foley uses the effective interest method to amortize bond discounts.

	A	B	C	D	E
1	Year	Cash paid	Interest expense	Discount amortization	Carrying amount
2	1				$86,580
3	2	$6,000			

Which formula should Foley use in cell E3 to calculate the carrying amount of the bonds at the end of Year 2?

A. E2 + D3
B. E2 − D3
C. E2 + C3
D. E2 − C3

Modification and Debt Retirement

Refinancing Short-Term Obligations

AICPA.090646FAR-II-G

477. Willem Co. reported the following liabilities at December 31, 20X1:

Accounts payable-trade	$750,000
Short-term borrowings	400,000
Mortgage payable, current portion $100,000	3,500,000
Other bank loan, matures June 30, 20X2	1,000,000

The $1,000,000 bank loan was refinanced with a 20-year loan on January 15, 20X2, with the first principal payment due January 15, 20X3. Willem's audited financial statements were issued February 28, 20X2. What amount should Willem report as current liabilities at December 31, 2001?

A. $850,000
B. $1,150,000
C. $1,250,000
D. $2,250,000

AICPA.070788FAR

478. On December 31, 20X2, Paxton Co. had a note payable due on August 1, 20X3. On January 20, 20X3, Paxton signed a financing agreement to borrow the balance of the note payable from a lending institution to refinance the note. The agreement does not expire within one year, and no violation of any provision in the financing agreement exists. On February 1, 2003, Paxton was informed by its financial advisor that the lender is not expected to be financially capable of honoring the agreement. Paxton's financial statements were issued on March 31, 20X3. How should Paxton classify the note on its balance sheet at December 31, 20X2?

A. As a current liability because the financing agreement was signed after the balance sheet date.
B. As a current liability because the lender is not expected to be financially capable of honoring the agreement.
C. As a long-term liability because the agreement does not expire within one year.
D. As a long-term liability because no violation of any provision in the financing agreement exists.

AICPA.051156FAR-ST

479. Verona Co. had $500,000 in short-term liabilities at the end of the current year. Verona issued $400,000 of common stock subsequent to the end of the year, but before the financial statements were issued. The proceeds from the stock issue were intended to be used to pay the short-term debt. What amount should Verona report as a short-term liability on its balance sheet at the end of the current year?

A. $0
B. $100,000
C. $400,000
D. $500,000

AICPA.070767FAR

480. On December 31, year 1, Taylor, Inc. signed a binding agreement with a bank for the refinancing of an existing note payable scheduled to mature in February, year 2. The terms of the refinancing included extending the maturity date of the note by three years. On January 15, year 2, the note was refinanced. How should Taylor report the note payable in its December 31, year 1 balance sheet?

A. As a current liability
B. As a long-term liability
C. As a long-term note receivable
D. As a current note receivable

AICPA.930502FAR-P1-FA

481. On December 31, 20X4, Largo, Inc. had a $750,000 note payable outstanding, due July 31, 20X5.

Largo borrowed the money to finance construction of a new plant. Largo planned to refinance the note by issuing long-term bonds.

Because Largo temporarily had excess cash, it prepaid $250,000 of the note on January 12, 20X5.

In February 20X5, Largo completed a $1,500,000 bond offering. Largo will use the bond offering proceeds to repay the note payable at its maturity and to pay construction costs during 2005.

On March 3, 20X5, Largo issued its 2004 financial statements.

What amount of the note payable should Largo include in the current liabilities section of its December 31, 20X4 balance sheet?

A. $750,000
B. $500,000
C. $250,000
D. $0

Debt Retirement

AICPA.900540FAR-P1-FA

482. On January 1, year 1, Fox Corp. issued 1,000 of its 10%, $1,000 bonds for $1,040,000. These bonds were to mature on January 1, year 11 but were callable at 101 any time after December 31, year 4. Interest was payable semiannually on July 1 and January 1.

On July 1, year 6, Fox called all of the bonds and retired them.

The bond premium was amortized on a straight-line basis. Before income taxes, Fox's gain or loss in year 6 on this early extinguishment of debt was

A. $30,000 gain.
B. $12,000 gain.
C. $10,000 loss.
D. $8,000 gain

AICPA.910526FAR-TH-FA

483. Gains or losses from the early extinguishment of debt, if material, should be

A. Recognized in income from continuing operations in the period of extinguishment.
B. Recognized as other comprehensive income in the period of extinguishment.
C. Amortized over the life of the new issue,
D. Amortized over the remaining original life of the extinguished issue.

AICPA.901127FAR-P1-FA

484. On June 30, 2005, Town Co. had outstanding 8%, $2,000,000 face amount, 15-year bonds that matured on June 30, 2015. Interest is payable on June 30 and December 31.

The unamortized balances in the bond discount and deferred bond issue costs accounts on June 30, 2005 were $70,000 and $20,000, respectively. On June 30, 2005, Town acquired all these bonds at 94 and retired them.

What net carrying amount should be used in computing gain or loss on this early extinguishment of debt?

A. $1,980,000
B. $1,930,000
C. $1,910,000
D. $1,880,000

AICPA.931140FAR-P1-FA

485. On June 2, year 1, Tory, Inc. issued $500,000 of 10%, 15-year bonds at par. Interest is payable semiannually on June 1 and December 1. Bond issue costs were $6,000. On June 2, year 6, Tory retired half of the bonds at 98.

What is the net amount that Tory should use in computing the gain or loss on the retirement of debt?

A. $249,000
B. $248,500
C. $248,000
D. $247,000

AICPA.930518FAR-TH-FA

486. Weald Co. took advantage of market conditions to refund debt. This was the fifth refunding operation carried out by Weald within the last four years.

The excess of the carrying amount of the old debt over the amount paid to extinguish it should be reported as a:

A. Deferred credit to be amortized over life of new debt.
B. Part of continuing operations.
C. Part of other comprehensive income for the year.
D. Loss.

Troubled Debt

AICPA.010509FAR-FA

487. For a troubled debt restructuring involving only a modification of terms, which of the following items specified by the new terms would be compared to the carrying amount of the debt to determine if the debtor should report a gain on restructuring?

A. The total future cash payments
B. The present value of the debt at the original interest rate

C. The present value of the debt at the modified interest rate

D. The amount of future cash payments designated as principal repayments

AICPA.101083FAR

488. On 12/31/X1, DInc. owed CInc. the full face value of a 10%, $350,000 note that requires interest payments annually on Dec. 31. DInc. paid the interest due 12/31/X1, but is experiencing financial problems and requested that the loan agreement be restructured. Three years remain in the note term as of today. The two parties agree to the following restructuring agreement:

DInc. will pay no more interest.

DInc. will pay $196,270 one year from today, and that same amount again two years from today (total of two payments of $196,270 each).

What amount of interest expense will DInc. recognize on 12/31/X2 when the firm makes the first of two payments of $196,270?

Factor for PV Ordinary Annuity for 2 periods at 8%	= 1.78326
Factor for PV Annuity Due for 2 periods at 8%	= 1.92593
Factor for Single Sum for 2 periods at 8%	= .85734

A. $0
B. $28,000
C. $35,000
D. $19,627

AICPA.101082FAR

489. A debtor and a creditor have negotiated new terms on a note. How can you determine whether the restructuring is a troubled debt restructure?

A. If the interest rate as stated in the restructuring agreement has been reduced relative to the original loan agreement

B. If the present value of the restructured flows using the original interest rate is less than the book value of the debt at the date of the restructure

C. If the interest rate that equates (1) the book value of the debt at the date of the restructure and (2) the present value of restructured cash flows exceeds the original interest rate

D. If the present value of the restructured flows using the original interest rate is less than the market value of the original debt at the date of the restructure

AICPA.931157FAR-P1-FA

490. The following information pertains to the transfer of real estate pursuant to a troubled debt restructuring by Knob Co. to Mene Corp. in full liquidation of Knob's liability to Mene:

Carrying amount of liability liquidated	$150,000
Carrying amount of real estate transferred	100,000
Fair value of real estate transferred	90,000

What amount should Knob report as a gain (loss) on restructuring of payables?

A. ($10,000)
B. $0
C. $50,000
D. $60,000

AICPA.920553FAR-P1-FA

491. Nu Corp. agreed to give Rand Co. a machine in full settlement of a note payable to Rand. The machine's original cost was $140,000. The note's face amount was $110,000. On the date of the agreement, the note's carrying amount was $105,000, and its present value was $96,000.

1 The machine's carrying amount was $109,000, and its fair value was $96,000.

2 What amount of net gain (or losses) should Nu recognize?

A. ($4,000)
B. $0
C. ($13,000)
D. $9,000

Debt Covenant Compliance

AICPA.101088FAR

492. A firm's debt-to-equity ratio (total debt to total owners' equity) cannot exceed 3.0 without allowing a major creditor to call a loan to the firm. The ratio is currently at the maximum before any of the transactions are listed. Which of the following transactions would not subject the firm to an immediate call by the creditor?

A. Recognize an increase in the current deferred income tax liability.

B. Purchase treasury stock for less than its original issue price.

C. Purchase treasury stock for more than its original issue price.

D. Retire a different loan by issuing common stock.

AICPA.101087FAR

493. A firm is required by its creditors to maintain a 2.00 (or greater) current ratio in order to maintain compliance with a debt covenant. The current ratio of the firm is currently at the minimum before any of the transactions are listed. Which of the following actions would cause the firm to fall out of compliance?

A. Sell a used plant asset at book value.
B. Pay an account payable.
C. Declare cash dividends.
D. Pay cash dividends previously declared.

AICPA.101089FAR

494. Which of the following accounting strategies (for financial reporting purposes) is the least likely for a firm that is currently only marginally fulfilling the quantitative measures (all involving earnings) of its debt covenants?

A. Using straight-line depreciation.
B. Changing to FIFO.
C. Using the weighted-average method for capitalizing interest during times of reduced interest rates, rather than the specific method.
D. Changing to the successful efforts method of accounting for natural resource exploration costs.

AICPA.101091FAR

495. Choose the correct statement concerning the classification of a liability when a firm is subject to a debt covenant.

A. All liabilities callable on demand are classified as current in all circumstances.
B. If the liability is callable on demand, the covenant is violated, and if the covenant is violated, then the liability is classified as current if the violation is waived by the creditor.
C. If the covenant includes a subjective acceleration clause and there is only a remote chance that debt will be called, then the liability is classified as noncurrent.
D. If a covenant grants a grace period during which it is possible that the violation will be cured, then the liability is classified as noncurrent.

AICPA.101090FAR

496. Which of the following actions helps a firm to maintain compliance with a debt covenant that includes a minimum current ratio and a minimum retained earnings balance: (1) refinancing current debt on a long-term basis, (2) appropriating retained earnings, (3)

purchasing treasury stock, (4) declaring cash dividends?

A. 1 and 3
B. 2 and 4
C. 1 and 2
D. 1, 2, and 3

Distinguishing Liabilities from Equity

AICPA.101120FAR

497. A firm selling put options to sell the firm's stock

A. Increases owners' equity for the fair value of the options.
B. Does not recognize any change in its financial position at sale of the options.
C. Increases a liability for the fair value of the options.
D. Records an expense equal to the fair value of the options.

AICPA.101119FAR

498. Renwood, Inc. contracted for services to be provided over a period of time in return for 2,000 shares of Renwood's $5 par common stock when the service is completed. At the time, Renwood stock was selling for $10 per share. When the service was completed, Renwood's stock price was $12 per share. Therefore, Renwood

A. Recognizes $24,000 of expense.
B. Increases the common stock account $12,000.
C. Increases contributed capital in excess of par $10,000.
D. Credits a liability for $20,000.

AICPA.101121FAR

499. Early in 20X3, Shifter, Inc. wrote put options for 1,000 shares of its common stock. Purchasers of the options can sell Shifter stock back to Shifter for $20 per share on 12/31/X3. The estimated fair value of each option is $2 at the time of sale. At 12/31/X3, the share price is $15 and the options are exercised. As a result, Shifter

A. Recognizes a $3,000 loss.
B. Recognizes a $5,000 loss.
C. Increases the treasury stock account $20,000 upon purchase.
D. Decreases contributed capital $3,000.

AICPA.101117FAR

500. Allam, Inc. contracted for services to be provided over a period of time with full payment in Allam's $2 par common stock when the service is completed. At the time of the agreement, Allam stock was trading at

$20 per share. The agreed-upon total value of the contract is $20,000. When the service was completed, Allam's stock price was $25 per share. Therefore, Allam

A. Recognizes $25,000 of expense.
B. Increases the common stock account $1,600.
C. Increases contributed capital in excess of par $23,000.
D. Debits a liability for $25,000.

AICPA.101118FAR

501. Choose the correct statement concerning transactions involving the issuance of shares in payment of obligations for goods and services.

A. When the value of shares to be issued is fixed, the number of shares to be issued is variable.
B. When the value of shares to be issued is fixed, the number of shares to be issued is fixed.
C. When the number of shares to be issued is fixed, the expense to be recorded is variable.
D. When the number of shares to be issued is fixed, the issuing firm records a liability.

Equity

Owners' Equity Basics

AICPA.911101FAR-P2-FA

502. Of the 125,000 shares of common stock issued by Vey Corp., 25,000 shares were held as treasury stock at December 31, 20X4. During 20X5, transactions involving Vey's common stock were as follows:

January 1 through October 31 – 13,000 treasury shares were distributed to officers as part of a stock compensation plan.

November 1 – A 3-for-1 stock split took effect.

December 1 – Vey purchased 5,000 of its own shares to discourage an unfriendly takeover. These shares were not retired.

At December 31, 20X5, how many shares of Vey's common stock were issued and outstanding?

	Shares Issued	Shares Outstanding
A.	375,000	334,000
B.	375,000	324,000
C.	334,000	334,000
D.	324,000	324,000

AICPA.120605FAR

503. Jones Co. had 50,000 shares of $5 par value common stock outstanding at January 1. On August 1, Jones declared a 5% stock dividend followed by a two-for-one stock split on September 1. What amount should Jones report as common shares outstanding at December 31?

A. 105,000
B. 100,000
C. 52,500
D. 50,000

AICPA.930517FAR-TH-FA

504. Which of the following errors could result in an overstatement of both current assets and stockholders' equity?

A. An understatement of accrued sales expenses.
B. Noncurrent note receivable principal is misclassified as a current asset.
C. Annual depreciation on manufacturing machinery is understated.
D. Holiday pay expense for administrative employees is misclassified as manufacturing overhead.

AICPA.911104FAR-P2-FA

505. At December 31, 20X5, Salo Corp.'s balance sheet accounts increased by the following amounts compared with those at the end of the prior year:

Assets	$178,000
Liabilities	54,000
Capital stock	120,000
Additional paid-in capital	12,000

The only charge to retained earnings during 20X5 was for a dividend payment of $26,000. Net income for 20X5 amounted to:

A. $34,000
B. $26,000
C. $18,000
D. $8,000

AICPA.930501FAR-P2-FA

506. Rudd Corp. had 700,000 shares of common stock authorized and 300,000 shares outstanding at December 31, Year 1. The following events occurred during Year 2:

January 31	Declared 10% stock dividend
June 30	Purchased 100,000 shares
August 1	Reissued 50,000 shares
November 30	Declared 2-for-1 stock split

At December 31, Year 2, how many shares of common stock did Rudd have outstanding?

A. 560,000
B. 600,000
C. 630,000
D. 660,000

Stock Issuance

AICPA.921107FAR-P1-FA

507. On September 1, 20X4, Hyde Corp., a newly formed company, had the following stock issued and outstanding:

1 Common stock, no par, $1 stated value, 5,000 shares originally issued at $15 per share.

2 Preferred stock, $10 par value, 1,500 shares originally issued for $25 per share.

Hyde's September 1, 20X4 statement of stockholders' equity should report

	Common Stock	Additional Preferred Stock	Paid-in Capital
A.	$5,000	$15,000	$92,500
B.	$5,000	$37,500	$70,000
C.	$75,000	$37,000	$0
D.	$75,000	$15,000	$22,500

AICPA.921144FAR-P2-FA

508. On July 1, 20X5, Cove Corp., a closely-held corporation, issued 6% bonds with a maturity value of $60,000, together with 1,000 shares of its $5 par value common stock, for a combined cash amount of $110,000.

The market value of Cove's stock cannot be ascertained. If the bonds were issued separately, they would have sold for $40,000 on an 8% yield to maturity basis.

What amount should Cove report for additional paid-in capital on the issuance of the stock?

A. $75,000
B. $65,000
C. $55,000
D. $45,000

AICPA.920501FAR-P2-FA

509. On March 1, 20X5, Rya Corp. issued 1,000 shares of its $20 par value common stock and 2,000 shares of its $20 par value convertible preferred stock for a total of $80,000.

At this date, Rya's common stock was selling for $36 per share, and the convertible preferred stock was selling for $27 per share.

What amount of the proceeds should be allocated to Rya's convertible preferred stock?

A. $60,000
B. $54,000
C. $48,000
D. $44,000

AICPA.083744FAR-SIM

510. An individual contracts for the purchase of 200 shares of $10 par common stock at a subscription price of $15. After making payments totaling $1,200, the subscriber defaults. Shares are issued in proportion to the amount of cash paid by the investor. The summary journal entry to record the net effect of these two transactions includes:

A. Debit share purchase contract receivable $1,800.
B. Credit common stock $2,000.
C. Credit paid in capital in excess of par on common, $400.
D. Credit share purchase contract receivable $600.

AICPA.930506FAR-P1-FA

511. On April 1, 20X4, Hyde Corp., a newly formed company, had the following stock issued and outstanding:

1 Common stock, no par, $1 stated value, 20,000 shares originally issued for $30 per share.

2 Preferred stock, $10 par value, 6,000 shares originally issued for $50 per share.

Hyde's April 1, 20X4 statement of stockholders' equity should report

	Common Stock	Preferred Stock	Additional Paid-in Capital
A.	$20,000	$60,000	$820,000
B.	$20,000	$300,000	$580,000
C.	$600,000	$300,000	$0
D.	$600,000	$60,000	$240,000

Preferred Stock

AICPA.921142FAR-P2-FA

512. Cross Corp. had outstanding 2,000 shares of 11% preferred stock, $50 par. On August 8, 1992, Cross redeemed and retired 25% of these shares for $22,500. On that date, Cross' additional paid-in capital from preferred stock totaled $30,000.

To record this transaction, Cross should debit (credit) its capital accounts as follows:

	Preferred Stock	Additional Paid-in Capital	Retained Earnings
A.	$25,000	$7,500	($10,000)
B.	$25,000	–	($2,500)
C.	$25,000	($2,500)	–
D.	$22,500	–	–

AICPA.083749FAR-SIM

513. 500 shares of 6%, $100 par callable preferred stock are called at $101. The shares were issued at $103 per share. The journal entry to record the retirement includes which of the following?

   A. Cr. paid-in capital from retirement of preferred stock, $1,000
   B. Dr. paid-in capital from retirement of preferred stock $1,500
   C. Cr. retained earnings $1,000
   D. Dr. preferred stock $51,500

AICPA.083748FAR-SIM

514. When preferred stock is called and retired, which account or aggregate category of accounts can be increased?

	Total Owners' Equity	Retained Earnings
A.	Yes	Yes
B.	No	No
C.	Yes	No
D.	No	Yes

AICPA.083750FAR-SIM

515. 500 shares of 6%, $100 par convertible preferred stock were issued at $103 per share. Each share is convertible into 20 shares of $5 par common stock. The journal entry to record conversion includes which of the following?

   A. Dr. preferred stock $51,500
   B. Dr. retained earnings $1,500
   C. Cr. paid-in capital in excess of par, common $1,500
   D. Cr. common stock $51,500

Treasury Stock

AICPA.090640FAR-II-K

516. During the current year, Onal Co. purchased 10,000 shares of its own stock at $7 per share. The stock was originally issued at $6. The firm sold 5,000 of the treasury shares for $10 per share. The firm uses the cost method to account for treasury stock. What amount should

Onal report in its income statement for these transactions?

   A. $0
   B. $5,000 gain
   C. $10,000 loss
   D. $15,000 gain

AICPA.910518FAR-TH-FA

517. On incorporation, Dee Inc. issued common stock at a price in excess of its par value. No other stock transactions occurred, except treasury stock was acquired for an amount exceeding this issue price.

If Dee uses the par value method of accounting for treasury stock appropriate for retired stock, what is the effect of the acquisition on the following?

	Net Common Stock	Additional Paid-in Capital	Retained Earnings
A.	No effect	Decrease	No effect
B.	Decrease	Decrease	Decrease
C.	Decrease	No effect	Decrease
D.	No effect	Decrease	Decrease

AICPA.921150FAR-P2-FA

518. On December 31, 20X4, Pack Corp.'s Board of Directors canceled 50,000 shares of $2.50 par value common stock held in treasury at an average cost of $13 per share. Before recording the cancellation of the treasury stock, Pack had the following balances in its stockholders' equity accounts:

Common stock	$540,000
Additional paid-in capital	750,000
Retained earnings	900,000
Treasury stock, at cost	650,000

In its balance sheet at December 31, 20X4, Pack should report common stock outstanding of

   A. $0
   B. $250,000
   C. $415,000
   D. $540,000

AICPA.901133FAR-TH-FA

519. At its date of incorporation, Glean, Inc. issued 100,000 shares of its $10 par common stock at $11 per share. During the current year, Glean acquired 30,000 shares of its common stock at a price of $16 per share and accounted for them by the cost method. Subsequently, these shares were reissued at a price of $12 per share.

There have been no other issuances or acquisitions of its own common stock.

What effect does the reissue of the stock have on the following accounts?

	Retained Earnings	Additional Paid-in Capital
A.	Decrease	Decrease
B.	No effect	Decrease
C.	Decrease	No effect
D.	No effect	No effect

AICPA.930510FAR-TH-FA

520. In 20X3, Fogg, Inc. issued $10 par value common stock for $25 per share. No other common stock transactions occurred until March 31, 20X5, when Fogg acquired some of the issued shares for $20 per share and retired them.

Which of the following statements correctly states an effect of this acquisition and retirement?

A. 20X5 net income is decreased.
B. 20X5 net income is increased.
C. Additional paid-in capital is decreased.
D. Retained earnings is increased.

Dividends

AICPA.930502FAR-TH-FA

521. A property dividend should be recorded in retained earnings at the property's

A. Market value at date of declaration.
B. Market value at date of issuance (payment).
C. Book value at date of declaration.
D. Book value at date of issuance (payment).

AICPA.941130FAR-FA

522. When a company declares a cash dividend, retained earnings is decreased by the amount of the dividend on the date of

A. Declaration.
B. Record.
C. Payment.
D. Declaration or record, whichever is earlier.

AICPA.911106FAR-P2-FA

523. Ole Corp. declared and paid a liquidating dividend of $100,000. This distribution resulted in a decrease in Ole's

	Paid-in Capital	Retained Earnings
A.	No	No
B.	Yes	Yes
C.	No	Yes
D.	Yes	No

AICPA.940508FAR-FA

524. At December 31, 20X4 and 20X5, Apex Co. had 3,000 shares of $100 par, 5% cumulative preferred stock outstanding. No dividends were in arrears as of December 31, 20X3. Apex did not declare a dividend during 20X4. During 20X5, Apex paid a cash dividend of $10,000 on its preferred stock.

Apex should report dividends in arrears in its 20X5 financial statements as a(an)

A. Accrued liability of $15,000.
B. Disclosure of $15,000.
C. Accrued liability of $20,000.
D. Disclosure of $20,000.

AICPA.920503FAR-P2-FA

525. Bal Corp. declared a $25,000 cash dividend on May 8, 20X5, to stockholders of record on May 23, 20X5, payable on June 3, 20X5. As a result of this cash dividend, working capital

A. Was not affected.
B. Decreased on June 3.
C. Decreased on May 23.
D. Decreased on May 8.

Stock Dividends and Splits

AICPA.910512FAR-P2-FA

526. The following stock dividends were declared and distributed by Sol Corp:

Percentage of Common Shares Outstanding at Declaration Date	Fair Value	Par Value
10	$15,000	$10,000
28	40,000	30,800

What aggregate amount should be debited to retained earnings for these stock dividends?

A. $40,800
B. $45,800
C. $50,000
D. $55,000

AICPA.130747FAR

527. A company whose stock is trading at $10 per share has 1,000 shares of $1 par common stock outstanding when the board of directors declares a 30% common stock dividend. Which of the following adjustments should be made when recording the stock dividend?

A. Treasury stock is debited for $300.
B. Additional paid-in capital is credited for $2,700.

C. Retained earnings is debited for $300.

D. Common stock is debited for $3,000.

AICPA.950529FAR-FA

528. Wood Co. owns 2,000 shares of Arlo, Inc.'s 20,000 shares of $100 par, 6% cumulative, non-participating preferred stock and 1,000 shares (2%) of Arlo's common stock.

During 20X5, Arlo declared and paid dividends of $240,000 on preferred stock. No dividends had been declared or paid during 20X4. In addition, Wood received a 5% common stock dividend from Arlo when the quoted market price of Arlo's common stock was $10 per share.

What amount should Wood report as dividend income in its 20X5 income statement?

A. $12,000

B. $12,500

C. $24,000

D. $24,500

AICPA.941131FAR-FA

529. Long Co. had 100,000 shares of common stock issued and outstanding at January 1, 20X6. During 20X6, Long took the following actions:

March 15—Declared a 2-for-1 stock split, when the fair value of the stock was $80 per share.

December 15—Declared a $.50 per share cash dividend.

In Long's statement of stockholders' equity for 20X6, what amount should Long report as dividends?

A. $50,000

B. $100,000

C. $850,000

D. $950,000

AICPA.921141FAR-P2-FA

530. On May 18, 20X4, Sol Corp.'s board of directors declared a 10% stock dividend.

The market price of Sol's 3,000 outstanding shares of $2 par value common stock was $9 per share on that date. The stock dividend was distributed on July 21, 20X4, when the stock's market price was $10 per share.

What amount should Sol credit to additional paid-in capital for this stock dividend?

A. $2,100

B. $2,400

C. $2,700

D. $3,000

Dividend Allocation

AICPA.083747FAR-SIM

531. The owners' equity section of a firm includes (1) $10,000 of 8%, $100 par cumulative preferred stock, and (2) $40,000 of $5 par common stock. There is additional paid-in capital on both issues. The preferred is fully participating and there are two years of dividends in arrears as of the beginning of the current year. If the firm pays $30,000 in dividends, what amount is allocated to common?

A. $23,360

B. $22,720

C. $22,080

D. $24,320

AICPA.911105FAR-P2-FA

532. Arp Corp.'s outstanding capital stock at December 15, 20X5 consisted of the following:

1. 30,000 shares of 5% cumulative preferred stock, par value $10 per share, fully participating as to dividends. No dividends were in arrears.

2. 200,000 shares of common stock, par value $1 per share.

On December 15, 20X5, Arp declared dividends of $100,000. What was the amount of dividends payable to Arp's common stockholders?

A. $10,000

B. $34,000

C. $40,000

D. $47,500

AICPA.083746FAR-SIM

533. The owners' equity section of a firm includes (1) $10,000 of 8%, $100 par cumulative preferred stock, and (2) $40,000 of $5 par common stock. There is additional paid-in capital on both issues. The preferred participates up to an additional 4% and there are two years of dividends in arrears as of the beginning of the current year. If the firm pays $7,100 in dividends, what amount is allocated to common?

A. $4,400

B. $3,200

C. $4,700

D. $6,000

AICPA.083745FAR-SIM

534. The owners' equity section of a firm includes (1) $10,000 of 8%, $100 par cumulative preferred stock, and (2) $40,000 of $5 par common stock. There is additional paid-in capital on both issues. The preferred participates up to an additional 4% and there are two years

of dividends in arrears as of the beginning of the current year. If the firm pays $30,000 in dividends, what amount is allocated to common?

A. $27,600
B. $28,800
C. $27,200
D. $24,000

Stock Rights, Retained Earnings

AICPA.920505FAR-P1-FA

535. Zinc Co.'s adjusted trial balance December 31, 20X5 includes the following account balances:

Common stock, $3 par	$600,000
Additional paid-in capital	800,000
Treasury stock, at cost	50,000
Net unrealized loss on noncurrent marketable equity securities	20,000
Retained earnings: appropriated for uninsured earthquake losses	150,000
Retained earnings: unappropriated	200,000

What amount should Zinc report as total stockholders' equity in its December 31, 20X5 balance sheet?

A. $1.68mn
B. $1.72mn
C. $1.78mn
D. $1.82mn

AICPA.951122FAR-FA

536. In September Year 1, West Corp. made a dividend distribution of one right for each of its 120,000 shares of outstanding common stock.

Each right was exercisable for the purchase of one-hundredth of a share of West's $50 variable-rate preferred stock at an exercise price of $80 per share. On March 20, Year 5, none of the rights had been exercised, and West redeemed them by paying each stockholder $0.10 per right.

As a result of this redemption, West's stockholders' equity was reduced by

A. $120
B. $2,400
C. $12,000
D. $36,000

AICPA.910519FAR-TH-FA

537. Cricket Corp. issued, without consideration, rights allowing stockholders to subscribe for additional shares at an amount greater than par value, but less than both market and book values.

When the rights are exercised, how are the following accounts affected?

	Retained Earnings	Additional Paid-in Capital
A.	Decreased	Not affected
B.	Not affected	Not affected
C.	Decreased	Increased
D.	Not affected	Increased

AICPA.920537FAR-TH-FA

538. A retained earnings appropriation can be used to

A. Absorb a fire loss when a company is self-insured.
B. Provide for a contingent loss that is probable and reasonable.
C. Smooth periodic income.
D. Restrict earnings available for dividends.

AICPA.941109FAR-FA

539. The following trial balance of Trey Co. at December 31, 20X5 has been adjusted, except for income tax expense.

	Dr.	Cr.
Cash	$550,000	
Accounts receivable, net	1,650,000	
Prepaid taxes	300,000	
Accounts payable		$120,000
Common stock		500,000
Additional paid-in capital		680,000
Retained earnings		630,000
Foreign currency translation adjustment	430,000	
Revenues		3.6mn
Expenses	2.6mn	
	$5.53mn	$5.53mn

Additional information:

1. During 20X5, estimated tax payments of $300,000 were charged to prepaid taxes. Trey has not yet recorded income tax expense. There were no differences between financial statement and income tax income, and Trey's tax rate is 30%.

2. Included in accounts receivable is $500,000 due from a customer. Special terms granted to this customer require payment in equal semiannual installments of $125,000 every April 1 and October 1.

In Trey's December 31, 20X5 balance sheet, what amount should be reported as total retained earnings?

A. $1.029mn
B. $1.2mn
C. $1.33mn
D. $1.63mn

Book Value Per Share

AICPA.911140FAR-TH-FA

540. Grid Corp. acquired some of its own common shares at a price greater than both their par value and original issue price, but less than their book value. Grid uses the cost method of accounting for treasury stock.

What is the impact of this acquisition on total stockholders' equity and the book value per common share?

	Total Stockholders' Equity	Book Value per Share
A.	Increase	Increase
B.	Increase	Decrease
C.	Decrease	Increase
D.	Decrease	Decrease

AICPA.951125FAR-FA

541. The stockholders' equity section of Brown Co.'s December 31, 20X5 balance sheet consisted of the following:

Common stock, $30 par, 10,000 shares authorized and outstanding	$300,000
Additional paid-in capital	150,000
Retained earnings (deficit)	(210,000)

On January 2, 20X6, Brown put into effect a stockholder-approved quasi-reorganization by reducing the par value of the stock to $5 and eliminating the deficit against additional paid-in capital. Immediately after the quasi-reorganization, what amount should Brown report as additional paid-in capital?

A. $(60,000)
B. $150,000
C. $190,000
D. $400,000

AICPA.921143FAR-P2-FA

542. Boe Corp.'s stockholders' equity at December 31, 20X4 was as follows:

6% noncumulative preferred stock, $100 par (liquidation value $105 per share)	$100,000
Common stock, $10 par	300,000
Retained earnings	95,000

At December 31, 20X4, Boe's book value per common share was:

A. $13.17
B. $13.00
C. $12.97
D. $12.80

AICPA.921119FAR-TH-FA

543. When a company goes through a quasi-reorganization, its balance sheet carrying amounts are stated at:

A. Original cost.
B. Original book value.
C. Replacement value.
D. Fair value.

AICPA.911103FAR-P2-FA

544. Hoyt Corp.'s current balance sheet reports the following stockholders' equity:

5% cumulative preferred stock, par value $100 per share; 2,500 shares issued and outstanding	$250,000
Common stock, par value $3.50 per share; 100,000 shares issued and outstanding	350,000
Additional paid-in capital in excess of par value of common stock	125,000
Retained earnings	300,000

Dividends in arrears on the preferred stock amount to $25,000. If Hoyt were to be liquidated, the preferred stockholders would receive par value plus a premium of $50,000. The book value of common stock is

A. $7.75
B. $7.50
C. $7.25
D. $7.00

III. Select Transactions

Revenue Recognition

Point of Sale and Installment Method

AICPA.901118FAR-P1-FA

545. Lane Co., which began operations on January 1, 20X5, appropriately uses the installment method of accounting. The following information pertains to Lane's operations for 20X5:

Installment sales	$1,000,000
Regular sales	600,000
Cost of installment sales	500,000
Cost of regular sales	300,000
General and administrative expenses	100,000
Collections on installment sales	200,000

The deferred gross profit account in Lane's December 31, 20X5 balance sheet should be

A. $150,000
B. $320,000
C. $400,000
D. $500,000

AICPA.910508FAR-TH-FA

546. Drew Co. produces expensive equipment for sale on installment contracts. When there is doubt about eventual collectibility, the income-recognition method least likely to overstate income is

A. At the time the equipment is completed.
B. The installment method.
C. The cost-recovery method.
D. At the time of delivery.

AICPA.090642FAR-II

547. When would a company use the installment sales method of revenue recognition?

A. When collectibility of installment accounts receivable is reasonably predictable.
B. When repossessions of merchandise sold on the installment plan may result in a future gain or loss.
C. When installment sales are material, and there is no reasonable basis for estimating collectibility.
D. When collection expenses and bad debts on installment accounts receivable are deemed to be immaterial.

AICPA.070773FAR

548. Entor Co. sold equipment to Pane Co. for $50,000. The equipment had a net book amount of $30,000. The collections were $20,000 in the first year, $15,000 in the next year, and $15,000 in the last year. What is the amount of gross profit for the third year if Entor used the installment-sales accounting method for the transaction?

A. $0
B. $5,000
C. $6,000
D. $15,000

AICPA.070780FAR

549. During Year 1, Fleet Co.'s trademark was licensed to Hitch Corp. for royalties of 10% of net sales of the trademarked items. Returns were estimated to be 1% of gross sales. On signing the licensing agreement, Hitch paid Fleet $75,000 as an advance against future royalty earnings. Gross sales of the trademarked items during the year were $600,000. What amount should Fleet report as royalty income for Year 1?

A. $54,000
B. $59,400
C. $60,000
D. $75,000

Cost Recovery and Franchise Fees

AICPA.061239FAR

550. North Co. entered into a franchise agreement with South Co. for an initial fee of $50,000. North received $10,000 at the agreement's signing. The remaining balance was to be paid at a rate of $10,000 per year, beginning the following year. North's services per the agreement were not complete in the current year. Operating activities will commence next year.

What amount should North report as franchise revenue in the current year?

A. $0
B. $10,000
C. $20,000
D. $50,000

AICPA.08211243FAR-II.C

551. On December 31, 20X3, Moon, Inc. authorized Luna Co. to operate as a franchisee for an initial franchise fee of $100,000. Luna paid $40,000 on signing the agreement and signed an interest-free note to pay the balance in three annual installments of $20,000, beginning December 31, 20X4. On December 31, 20X3, the present value of the note, appropriately discounted, is $48,000. Services for the initial fee will be performed in 20X4. In its December 31, 20X3, balance sheet, what amount should Moon report as unearned franchise fees?

   A. $0
   B. $48,000
   C. $88,000
   D. $100,000

AICPA.130744FAR

552. A shoe retailer allows customers to return shoes within 90 days of purchase. The company estimates that 5% of sales will be returned within the 90-day period. During the month, the company has sales of $200,000 and returns of sales made in prior months of $5,000. What amount should the company record as net sales revenue for new sales made during the month?

   A. $185,000
   B. $190,000
   C. $195,000
   D. $200,000

AICPA.051157FAR-FA

553. Baker Co. has a franchise restaurant business. On January 15 of the current year, Baker charged an investor a franchise fee of $65,000 for the right to operate as a franchisee of one of Baker's restaurants. A cash payment of $25,000 toward the fee was required to be paid to Baker during the current year.

   Four subsequent annual payments of $10,000, with a present value of $34,000 at the current market interest rate, represent the balance of the fee, which is expected to be collected in full. The initial cash payment is nonrefundable and no future services are required by Baker.

   What amount should Baker report as franchise revenue during the current year?

   A. $0
   B. $25,000
   C. $59,000
   D. $65,000

AICPA.051173FAR-FA

554. Macklin Co. entered into a franchise agreement with Heath Co. for an initial fee of $50,000. Macklin received $10,000 when the agreement was signed. The balance was to be paid at a rate of $10,000 per year, starting the next year. All services were performed by Macklin and the refund period had expired. Operations started in the current year.

   What amount should Macklin recognize as revenue in the current year?

   A. $0
   B. $10,000
   C. $20,000
   D. $50,000

Contract Accounting

AICPA.900557FAR-P2-FA

555. Mill Construction Co. uses the percentage-of-completion method of accounting. During 20X5, Mill contracts to build an apartment complex for Drew for $20mn. Mill estimates that total costs would amount to $16mn over the period of construction.

   In connection with this contract, Mill incurs $2mn of construction costs during 20X5. Mill bills and collects $3mn from Drew in 20X5.

   What amount should Mill recognize as gross profit for 20X5?

   A. $250,000
   B. $375,000
   C. $500,000
   D. $600,000

AICPA.110554FAR

556. Frame Construction Company's contract requires the construction of a bridge in three years. The expected total cost of the bridge is $2mn, and Frame will receive $2.5mn for the project. The actual costs incurred to complete the project were $500,000, $900,000, and $600,000, respectively, during each of the three years. Progress payments received by Frame were $600,000, $1.2mn, and $700,000 in each year, respectively. Assuming that the percentage-of-completion method is used, what amount of gross profit should Frame report during the last year of the project?

   A. $120,000
   B. $125,000
   C. $140,000
   D. $150,000

AICPA.051185FA

557. The calculation of the income recognized in the third year of a five-year construction contract accounted for using the percentage of completion method includes the ratio of

A. Costs incurred in year three to total billings.
B. Costs incurred in year three to total estimated costs.
C. Total costs incurred to date to total billings.
D. Total costs incurred to date to total estimated costs.

AICPA.101096FAR

558. The following information relates to a contract through its second year. The contract price is $50,000.

	Year 1	Year 2
Cost incurred through end of	$10,000	$34,000
Estimated cost remaining at end of	30,000	20,000

Under the completed contract method, by what amount will pretax income for the second year be affected?

A. Reduced $14,000
B. Reduced $4,000
C. Reduced $2,000
D. No effect

AICPA.101095FAR

559. At the end of the third year of a contract, total estimated project cost exceeds the contract price. In both of the first two years, the firm recognized gross profit on the contract under percentage of completion. What is the ending balance in the construction-in-progress account at the beginning of year four on the contract under the percentage-of-completion method (PC), and under the completed-contract method (CC), had that method been used?

	PC	CC
A.	Cost to date less overall loss	Cost to date less overall loss
B.	Cost to date less billings	Cost to date less billings
C.	Cost to date	Cost to date
D.	Cost to date	Cost to date less overall loss

Deferred Revenue Principles

AICPA.921126FAR-P1-FA

560. Barnel Corp. owns and manages 19 apartment complexes. On signing a lease, each tenant must pay the first and last month's rent and a $500 refundable security deposit.

The security deposits are rarely refunded in total, because cleaning costs of $150 per apartment are almost always deducted. About 30% of the time, the tenants are also charged for damages to the apartment, which typically cost $100 to repair.

If a one-year lease is signed on a $900 per month apartment, what amount would Barnel report as a refundable security deposit?

A. $1,400
B. $500
C. $350
D. $320

AICPA.920526FAR-TH-FA

561. On March 31, 20X5, Dallas Co. received an advance payment of 60% of the sales price for special order goods to be manufactured and delivered within five months.

At the same time, Dallas subcontracted for production of the special order goods at a price equal to 40% of the main contract price.

What liabilities should be reported in Dallas' March 31, 20X5 balance sheet?

	Deferred Revenues	Payables to Subcontractor
A.	None	None
B.	60% of main contract price	40% of main contract price
C.	60% of main contract price	None
D.	None	40% of main contract price

AICPA.120612FAR

562. A retail store sold gift certificates that are redeemable in merchandise. The gift certificates lapse one year after they are issued. How would the deferred revenue account be affected by each of the following?

	Redemption of Certificates	Lapse of Certificates
A.	Decrease	Decrease
B.	Decrease	No effect
C.	No effect	Decrease
D.	No effect	No effect

Specific Deferred Revenues

AICPA.910538FAR-P1-FA

563. Bart Co. requires nonrefundable advance payments with special orders for machinery constructed to customer specifications.

Information for 2004 is as follows:

Customer advances—balance 12/31/X3	$590,000
Advances received with orders in 20X4	920,000
Advances applied to orders shipped in 20X4	820,000
Advances applicable to orders canceled in 20X4	250,000

In Bart's December 31, 20X4 balance sheet, what amount should be reported as a current liability for customer deposits?

A. $740,000
B. $690,000
C. $440,000
D. $0

0821128FAR-II.G

564. At the beginning of the current year, Hayworth Co. sold equipment with a two-year service contract for a single payment of $20,000. The fair value of the equipment was $18,000. Hayworth recorded this transaction with a debit of $20,000 to cash and a credit of $20,000 to sales revenue. Which of the following statements is correct regarding Hayworth's current-year financial statements?

A. The financial statements are correct.
B. Net income will be overstated.
C. Total assets will be overstated.
D. Total liabilities will be overstated.

AICPA.910515FAR-TH-FA

565. An automobile dealer sells service contracts. The contracts stipulate that the dealer will perform specific repairs on covered vehicles. The contracts vary in length from 12 to 36 months.

Do the following increase when service contracts are sold?

	Deferred Revenue	Service Revenue
A.	Yes	Yes
B.	No	No
C.	No	Yes
D.	Yes	No

AICPA.910539FAR-P1-FA

566. Fell, Inc. operates a retail grocery store that is required by law to collect refundable deposits of $.05 on soda cans.

Information for 20X4 follows:

Liability for returnable deposits—12/31/X3	$150,000
Cans of soda sold in 20X4	10,000,000
Soda cans returned in 20X4	11,000,000

On February 1, 20X4, Fell subleased space and received a $25,000 deposit to be applied toward rent at the expiration of the lease in 20X8. In Fell's December 31, 20X4 balance sheet, the current and noncurrent liabilities for deposits were:

	Current	Noncurrent
A.	$125,000	$0
B.	$100,000	$25,000
C.	$100,000	$0
D.	$25,000	$100,000

Deferred Compensation

Pension Principles, Reporting

AICPA.070754FAR

567. Data for a defined benefit pension plan for the current year are as follows:

PBO, January 1, $200mn

Assets, January 1, $160mn

Pension expense, $60mn

Funding contribution, $50mn

The ending pension liability balance is

A. $40mn
B. $10mn
C. $50mn
D. $200mn

AICPA.110556FAR

568. A company has a defined benefit pension plan for its employees. On December 31, year one, the accumulated benefit obligation is $45,900, the projected benefit obligation is $68,100, and the fair value of the plan assets is $62,000. What amount, if any, related to the defined benefit plan should be recognized in the balance sheet at December 31, year one?

A. An asset of $16,100.
B. A liability of $6,100.

C. Nothing, as the fair value of the plan assets exceeds the accumulated benefit obligation.

D. An unrealized loss of $6,100.

AICPA.061232FAR

569. What is the present value of all future retirement payments attributed by the pension benefit formula to employee services rendered prior to that date only?

A. Service cost.
B. Interest cost.
C. Projected benefit obligation.
D. Accumulated benefit obligation.

AICPA.110557FAR

570. How should plan investments be reported in a defined benefit plan's financial statements?

A. At actuarial present value.
B. At cost.
C. At net realizable value.
D. At fair value.

AICPA.900537FAR-TH-FA

571. Barrett Co. maintains a defined benefit pension plan for its employees. At each balance sheet date, Barrett should report pension liability equal to the

A. Accumulated benefit obligation.
B. Projected benefit obligation.
C. Unfunded accumulated benefit obligation.
D. Unfunded projected benefit obligation.

Pension Expense Basics

AICPA.101137FAR

572. An entity sponsors a defined-benefit pension plan that is underfunded by $800,000. A $500,000 increase in the fair value of plan assets would have which of the following effects on the financial statements of the entity?

A. An increase in the assets of the entity.
B. An increase in accumulated other comprehensive income of the entity for the full amount of the increase in the value of the assets.
C. A decrease in accumulated other comprehensive income of the entity for the full amount of the increase in the value of the assets.
D. A decrease in the liabilities of the entity.

AICPA.070760FAR

573. The recognition of a $5,000 actuarial gain at year-end causes:

A. an increase in pension liability.
B. an increase in PBO.
C. a decrease in pension asset.
D. a credit to pension gain/loss-other comprehensive income.

AICPA.070761FAR

574. The recognition of the amortization of $50 of net gain causes what effect on (1) pension expense, and (2) pension liability?

	(1)	(2)
A.	decrease	decrease
B.	decrease	no effect
C.	no effect	decrease
D.	no effect	no effect

AICPA.130741FAR

575. In the financial statements of employee benefit pension plans and trusts, the plan investments are reported at

A. Fair value.
B. Historical cost.
C. Net realizable value.
D. Lower of historical cost or market.

AICPA.901116FAR-P2-FA

576. The following information pertains to Seda Co.'s pension plan:

Actuarial estimate of projected benefit obligation at January 1, 2005	$72,000
Assumed discount rate	10%
Service costs for 2005	$18,000
Pension benefits paid during 2005	$15,000

If no change in actuarial estimates occurred during 2005, Seda's projected benefit obligation at December 31, 2005 was

A. $64,200
B. $75,000
C. $79,200
D. $82,200

Pension Expense Delayed Recognition

AICPA.101099FAR

577. A firm is applying international accounting standards to its defined-benefit pension plan and has pension gains and losses. As a result,

    A. The gains and losses are gradually recognized in defined benefit obligation.
    B. The gains and losses are never recognized in defined benefit obligation.
    C. The firm's earnings will not be affected.
    D. The gains and losses will be amortized as gradually in pension expense.

AICPA.140411FAR-SIM

578. A firm is applying international accounting standards to its defined-benefit pension plan. At the end of the current year, the actuary informs the firm that the plan has experienced an actuarial gain of $2mn. The average remaining service period of plan participants is ten years. Therefore,

    A. Defined-benefit obligation does not reflect the decrease of $2mn immediately.
    B. Pension expense will be reduced by $200,000 the following year.
    C. Other comprehensive income is immediately increased.
    D. The unrecognized net gain or loss account is immediately debited.

AICPA.101097FAR

579. Choose the correct statement regarding the treatment of prior service cost (PSC) for defined benefit plans under international accounting.

    A. Firms have an option to record PSC directly into other comprehensive income or in earnings.
    B. The entire PSC amount, at present value, is recognized immediately in pension expense.
    C. The entire PSC amount, at present value, is recognized immediately in other comprehensive income, as per U.S. standards.
    D. The estimated nominal increase in benefits is recognized immediately in pension expense.

Pension Plan Reporting, International

AICPA.101102FAR

580. Accounting for nonretirement post-employment benefits is an example of :

    A. Accrual accounting.
    B. Cash-basis accounting.
    C. Fair-value accounting.
    D. Historical-cost accounting.

AICPA.101105FAR

581. A firm provides nonretirement postemployment benefits for its employees for a limited time after employment. At the beginning of the current year, the balance of the liability for unpaid benefits was $67,000. During the year, the firm accrued an additional $34,000. At year-end, the ending liability balance was $56,000 after a year-end downward adjustment of $5,000 due to a change in estimate. What amount of benefits were paid during the year?

    A. 40,000
    B. 45,000
    C. 34,000
    D. 29,000

AICPA.101104FAR

582. Which of the following is not a criterion that must be met in order for nonretirement postemployment benefits to be accrued, rather than being treated as a cash expense upon payment

    A. The benefits are attributable to services rendered.
    B. The benefits accumulate or vest.
    C. The benefits are contingent on continued employment.
    D. The benefits are estimable.

AICPA.101106FAR

583. Under certain circumstances, a firm provides severance pay and tuition assistance to employees who are laid off. The beginning balance in the associated liability for the current year is $112,000. During the year, employees earned $48,000 of additional benefits, 60% of which are expected to be used by terminated employees, based on past experience. During the year, the firm paid $38,000 to reimburse previous employees for benefits taken. Compute the ending balance of the benefit liability.

    A. $122,000
    B. $102,800
    C. $58,000
    D. $77,200

AICPA.101103FAR

584. Which of the following is not covered by the accounting standard applicable to non-retirement post-employment benefits?

    A. Severance-pay benefits.
    B. Post-retirement healthcare benefits.
    C. Salary-continuation benefits.
    D. Job-training benefits.

Postretirement Benefits

AICPA.110552FAR

585. Which of the following costs is unique to post-retirement healthcare benefits?

   A. Per capita claims.
   B. Service.
   C. Prior service.
   D. Interest.

AICPA.130746FAR

586. An overfunded single-employer defined benefit postretirement plan should be recognized in a classified statement of financial position as a

   A. Noncurrent liability.
   B. Current liability.
   C. Noncurrent asset.
   D. Current asset.

AICPA.083755FAR-SIM

587. An employee covered by a post-retirement healthcare plan just completed her 18th year of service for a firm. Each year of employment to full eligibility provides credit for post-retirement healthcare benefits for this firm. She must work an additional seven years from today to be eligible for 75% healthcare coverage during retirement. She is expected to work ten more years from today. If this employee worked 15 more years from today, the firm would pay all her healthcare costs during retirement. Choose the correct statement.

   A. The employee's full eligibility date is reached when she has worked 33 years in total.
   B. Accumulated post-retirement benefit obligation equals expected post-retirement benefit obligation for the employee, as of today.
   C. Service cost will not be computed for the employee during her last three years of service to the firm.
   D. Expected post-retirement benefit obligation reflects only 18 years of service, as of today, for the employee.

AICPA.070763FAR

588. The following information relates to a post-retirement benefit plan:

   APBO beginning, $300mn

   Plan assets beginning, $100mn

   Net post-retirement benefit gain, beginning, $20mn

   Amortization of net gain or loss is based on SL method, ten-year average remaining service period

Prior-service cost, initial amount, recognized four years ago, $50mn

Amortization of prior-service cost is based on SL method, ten-year average remaining service period

Service cost, $40mn

Discount rate, 5%

Expected rate of return, 6%

Actual return, $10mn

Change in estimated life expectancy caused a gain of $16mn, year-end

Funding contribution, $20mn

What amount will be reported in the ending balance sheet for post-retirement benefit liability?

   A. $209mn
   B. $213m
   C. $9mn
   D. $212mn

AICPA.061219FAR

589. An employer's obligation for post-retirement healthcare benefits that are expected to be fully provided to or for an employee must be fully accrued by the date the

   A. Benefits are paid.
   B. Benefits are utilized.
   C. Employee retires.
   D. Employee is fully eligible for benefits.

Share-Based Payments

Stock Options

AICPA.120634FAR

590. The stockholders of Meadow Corp. approved a stock-option plan that grants the company's top three executives options to purchase a maximum of 1,000 shares each of Meadow's $2 par common stock for $19 per share. The options were granted on January 1 when the fair value of the stock was $20 per share. Meadow determined that the fair value of the compensation is $300,000 and the vesting period is three years. What amount of compensation expense from the options should Meadow record in the year the options were granted?

   A. $20,000
   B. $60,000
   C. $100,000
   D. $300,000

AICPA.061262FAR-P1-FA

591. A stock option plan with a positive fair value at grant date caused compensation expense of $50,000 per year to be recorded over the five-year service period. During the exercise period (two years), the stock price never exceeded the option price. Therefore, none of the options was exercised.

Choose the correct statement about the accounting for these options.

A. The contributed capital increase from recording compensation expense is reversed, causing compensation expense to be reduced in the eighth year after grant.
B. The contributed capital increase from recording compensation expense is left intact.
C. The financial statements during the service period are retroactively restated by removing the compensation expense.
D. The compensation expense for later option grants is reduced by the amount recognized on the options that expired.

AICPA.101136FAR

592. On which of the following dates is a public entity required to measure the cost of employee services in exchange for an award of equity interests, based on the fair market value of the award?

A. Date of grant.
B. Date of restriction lapse.
C. Date of vesting.
D. Date of exercise.

assess.AICPA.FAR.stock.comp-0046

593. On January 1, year 1, the board of directors of a corporation granted 10,000 stock options to the CEO. Each option permits the purchase of one share of stock at $25 per share, the current market price of the stock. The options are exercisable on December 31, year 4, as long as the CEO is still employed. The options expire on December 31, year 5. The grant date fair value of each option is $5. The corporation must recognize

A. $50,000 of compensation expense when the options are exercised.
B. $50,000 of compensation expense in year 1.
C. $12,500 of compensation expense per year for four years.
D. $10,000 of compensation expense per year for five years.

AICPA.061258FAR-P1-FA

594. Under the fair-value method of accounting for stock option plans, total compensation recognized

A. Is based on the value of the option at the grant date, adjusted for forfeitures.
B. Equals the net increase in OE after all relevant journal entries are recorded.
C. Is the difference between market price and option price at the grant date.
D. Is unaffected by the option price.

Stock Awards

AICPA.130748FAR

595. On January 1, year 1, a company issued its employees 10,000 shares of restricted stock. On January 1, year 2, the company issued to its employees an additional 20,000 shares of restricted stock. Additional information about the company's stock is as follows:

Date	Fair Value of Stock (per share)
January 1, year 1	$20
December 31, year 1	22
January 1, year 2	25
December 31, year 2	30

The shares vest at the end of a four-year period. There are no forfeitures. What amount should be recorded as compensation expense for the 12-month period ended December 31, year 2?

A. $175,000
B. $205,000
C. $225,000
D. $500,000

AICPA.061264FAR-P1-FA

596. A restricted stock award was granted at the beginning of 2005 calling for 3,000 shares of stock to be awarded to executives at the beginning of 2009. The fair value of one option was $20 at grant date. During 2007, 100 shares were forfeited because an executive left the firm.

What amount of compensation expense is recognized for 2007?

A. $14,000
B. $15,000
C. $14,500
D. $13,500

Stock Appreciation Rights

AICPA.900555FAR-P1-FA

597. On January 2, 2005, Morey Corp. granted Dean, its president, 20,000 stock appreciation rights for past services. Those rights are exercisable immediately and expire on January 1, 2008.

On exercise, Dean is entitled to receive cash for the excess of the stock's market price on the exercise date over the market price on the grant date. Dean did not exercise any of the rights during 2005. The market price of Morey's stock was $30 on January 2, 2005 and $45 on December 31, 2005.

As a result of the stock appreciation rights, Morey should recognize compensation expense for 2005 of

A. $0
B. $100,000
C. $300,000
D. $600,000

AICPA.083751FAR-SIM

598. Select the correct statement about executive compensation plans involving stock.

A. The total amount of compensation expense for a restricted stock award plan is recognized when the stock is issued.
B. The total amount of compensation expense for a restricted stock award plan is determined at the grant date.
C. For stock-appreciation rights plans payable in cash, compensation expense is recognized only during the service period.
D. For stock-appreciation rights plans payable in cash, compensation expense recognized in any given reporting period cannot be negative.

Income Taxes

Income Tax Basics

AICPA.921141FAR-TH-FA

599. Rein Inc. reported deferred tax assets and deferred tax liabilities at the end of 20X3 and at the end of 20X4.

According to FASB Statements No. 109 Accounting for Income Taxes, for the year ended 20X4, Rein should report deferred income tax expense or benefit equal to the

A. Decrease in the deferred tax assets.
B. Increase in the deferred tax liabilities.

C. Amount of the current tax liability, plus the sum of the net changes in deferred tax assets and deferred tax liabilities.
D. Sum of the net changes in deferred tax assets and deferred tax liabilities.

AICPA.901128FAR-TH-FA

600. Nala Inc. reported deferred tax assets and deferred tax liabilities at the end of 20X4 and at the end of 20X5.

According to FASB 109, for the year ended 20X5, Nala should report deferred income tax expense or benefit equal to the

A. Sum of the net changes in deferred tax assets and deferred tax liabilities.
B. Decrease in the deferred tax assets.
C. Increase in the deferred tax liabilities.
D. Amount of income tax liability, plus the sum of the net changes in deferred tax assets and deferred tax liabilities.

AICPA.911103FAR-TH-FA

601. According to FASB Statement No. 109, Accounting for Income Taxes, justification for the method of determining periodic deferred tax expense is based on the concept of

A. Matching of periodic expense to periodic revenue.
B. Objectivity in the calculation of periodic expense.
C. Recognition of assets and liabilities.
D. Consistency of tax-expense measurements with actual tax-planning strategies.

Permanent Differences

AICPA.911132FAR-P1-FA

602. Lake Corp., a newly organized company, reported pretax financial income of $100,000 for Year 1.

Among the items reported in Lake's Year 1 income statement are the following:

Premium on officer's life insurance with Lake as owner and beneficiary	$15,000
Interest received on municipal bonds	20,000

The enacted tax rate for Year 1 is 30% and 25% thereafter. In its December 31, Year 1 balance sheet, Lake should report a deferred income tax liability of

A. $28,500
B. $4,500
C. $3,750
D. $0

AICPA.910541FAR-P1-FA

603. On June 31, 20X4, Ank Corp. prepaid a $19,000 premium on an annual insurance policy.

The premium payment was a tax-deductible expense in Ank's 20X4 cash-basis tax return. The accrual-basis income statement will report a $9,500 insurance expense in 20X4 and 20X5.

Ank elected early application of FASB Statement No. 109, Accounting for Income Taxes.

Ank's income tax rate is 30% in 20X4 and 25% thereafter. In Ank's December 31, 20X4 balance sheet, what amount related to the insurance should be reported as a deferred income tax liability?

A. $5,700
B. $4,750
C. $2,850
D. $2,375

Temporary Differences

AICPA.920509FAR-TH-FA

604. Orleans Co., a cash-basis taxpayer, prepares accrual-basis financial statements. Since Year 1, Orleans has applied FASB ASC 740, Income Taxes. In its Year 3 balance sheet, Orleans' deferred income tax liabilities increased compared to Year 2.

Which of the following changes would cause this increase in deferred income tax liabilities?

I. An increase in pre-paid insurance.
II. An increase in rent receivable.
III. An increase in warranty obligations.

A. I only.
B. I and II.
C. II and III.
D. III only.

AICPA.101127FAR

605. When accounting for income taxes, a temporary difference occurs in which of the following scenarios?

A. An item is included in the calculation of net income, but is neither taxable nor deductible.
B. An item is included in the calculation of net income in one year and in taxable income in a different year.
C. An item is no longer taxable, owing to a change in the tax law.
D. The accrual method of accounting is used.

AICPA.921127FAR-P1-FA

606. For the year ended December 31, 20X4, Mont Co.'s books showed income of $600,000 before provision for income tax expense. To compute taxable income for federal income tax purposes, the following items should be noted:

Income from exempt municipal bonds	$60,000
Depreciation deducted for tax purposes in excess of depreciation recorded on the books	$120,000
Proceeds received from life insurance on death of officer	$100,000
Estimated tax payments	0
Enacted corporate tax rate	30%

Ignoring the alternative minimum tax provisions, what amount should Mont report at December 31, 20X4 as its current federal income tax liability?

A. $96,000
B. $114,000
C. $150,000
D. $162,000

AICPA.911104FAR-TH-FA

607. At the end of year 1, Cody Co. reported a profit on a partially completed construction contract by applying the percentage-of-completion method.

By the end of year two, the total estimated profit on the contract at completion in year three had been drastically reduced from the amount estimated at the end of year one.

Consequently, in year two, a loss equal to one-half of the year-one profit was recognized. Cody used the completed-contract method for income tax purposes and had no other contracts.

According to FASB Statement No. 109, Accounting for Income Taxes, the year-two balance sheet should include a deferred tax

	Asset	Liability
A.	Yes	Yes
B.	No	Yes
C.	Yes	No
D.	No	No

AICPA.911125FAR-P1-FA

608. Dunn Co.'s 20X5 income statement reported $90,000 income before provision for income taxes.

To compute the provision for federal income taxes, the following 20X5 data are provided:

Rent received in advance	$16,000
Income from exempt municipal bonds	20,000
Depreciation deducted for income tax purposes in excess of depreciation reported for financial-statement purposes	10,000
Enacted corporate income tax rate	30%

If the alternative minimum tax provisions are ignored, what amount of current federal income tax liability should be reported in Dunn's December 31, 20X5 balance sheet?

A. $18,000
B. $22,800
C. $25,800
D. $28,800

Tax Accrual Entry

AICPA.950541FAR-FA

609. For the year ended December 31, 20X5, Tyre Co. reported pre-tax financial statement income of $750,000. Its taxable income was $650,000. The difference is owing to accelerated depreciation for income tax purposes. Tyre's effective income tax rate is 30%, and Tyre made estimated tax payments during 20X5 of $90,000.

What amount should Tyre report as current income tax expense for 20X5?

A. $105,000
B. $135,000
C. $195,000
D. $225,000

AICPA.951138FAR-FA

610. Zeff Co. prepared the following reconciliation of its pre-tax financial statement income to taxable income for the year ended December 31, 20X5, its first year of operations:

Pre-tax financial income	$160,000
Non-taxable interest received on municipal securities	($5,000)
Long-term loss accrual in excess of deductible amount	$10,000
Depreciation in excess of financial-statement amount	($25,000)
Taxable income	$140,000

Zeff's tax rate for 20X5 is 40%.

In its December 31, 20X5 balance sheet, what should Zeff report as deferred income tax liability?

A. $2,000
B. $4,000
C. $6,000
D. $8,000

AICPA.101126FAR

611. In year two, Ajax, Inc. reported taxable income of $400,000 and pre-tax financial-statement income of $300,000. The difference resulted from $60,000 of non-deductible premiums on Ajax's officers' life insurance and $40,000 of rental income received in advance. Rental income is taxable when received. Ajax's effective tax rate is 30%. In its year-two income statement, what amount should Ajax report as income tax expense (current portion)?

A. $90,000
B. $102,000
C. $108,000
D. $120,000

AICPA.090637FAR-III

612. Lion Co.'s income statement for its first year of operations shows pre-tax income of $6,000,000. In addition, the following differences existed between Lion's tax return and records:

	Tax Return	Accounting Records
Uncollectible accounts expense	$220,000	$250,000
Depreciation expense	860,000	570,000
Tax-exempt interest revenue	–	50,000

Lion's current year tax rate is 30% and the enacted rate for future years is 40%. What amount should Lion report as deferred tax expense in its income statement for the year?

A. $148,000
B. $124,000
C. $104,000
D. $78,000

AICPA.980510FAR-FA

613. Black Co., organized on January 2, 20X4, had pre-tax financial statement income of $500,000 and taxable income of $800,000 for the year ended December 31, 20X4.

The only temporary differences are accrued product-warranty costs, which Black expects to pay as follows:

20X5	$100,000
20X6	$50,000
20X7	$50,000
20X8	$100,000

The enacted income tax rates are 25% for 20X4, 30% for 20X5 through 20X7, and 35% for 20X8. Black believes that future years' operations will produce profits. In its December 31, 20X4 balance sheet, what amount should Black report as deferred tax asset?

A. $50,000
B. $75,000
C. $90,000
D. $95,000

Tax Allocation Process

AICPA.941149FAR-FA

614. Kent, Inc.'s reconciliation between financial statement and taxable income for 20X5 is as follows:

Pre-tax financial income	$150,000
Permanent difference	($12,000)
	$138,000
Temporary difference—depreciation	($9,000)
Taxable income	$129,000

Additional information:

	At	
	December 31, 20X4	December 31, 20X5
Cumulative temporary differences (future taxable amounts)	$11,000	$20,000

The enacted tax rate was 34% for 20X4, and 40% for 20X5 and years thereafter.

In its December 31, 20X5 balance sheet, what amount should Kent report as deferred income tax liability?

A. $3,600
B. $6,800
C. $7,340
D. $8,000

AICPA.911138FAR-P1-FA

615. Mill, which began operations on January 1, 20X3, recognizes income from long-term construction contracts under the percentage-of-completion method in its financial statements and under the completed-contract method for income tax reporting.

Income under each method follows:

Year	Completed-Contract	Percentage-of-Completion
20X3	$-	$300,000
20X4	$400,000	$600,000
20X5	$700,000	$850,000

The income tax rate was 30% for 20X3 through 20X5. For years after 20X5, the enacted tax rate is 25%. There are no other temporary differences. Mill should report in its December 31, 20X5 balance sheet a deferred income tax liability of

A. $87,500
B. $105,000
C. $162,500
D. $195,000

AICPA.920526FAR-P1-FA

616. On January 2, 20X4, Ross Co. purchases a machine for $70,000. This machine has a five-year useful life, a residual value of $10,000, and is depreciated using the straight-line method for financial-statement purposes.

For tax purposes, depreciation expense was $25,000 for 20X4 and $20,000 for 20X5. Ross elected early application of FASB Statement No. 109, Accounting for Income Taxes. Ross' 20X5 income, before income tax and depreciation expense, was $100,000 and its tax rate was 30%.

If Ross had made no estimated tax payments during 20X5, what amount of current income tax liability would Ross report in its December 31, 20X5 balance sheet?

A. $26,400
B. $25,800
C. $24,000
D. $22,500

AICPA.901107FAR-P2-FA

617. Ram Corp. prepared the following reconciliation of income per books with income per tax return for the year ended December 31, 20X5:

Book income before income taxes	$750,000
Add temporary difference construction contract revenue, which will reverse in 20X9	$100,000
Deduct temporary difference depreciation expense, which will reverse in equal amounts in each of the next four years	($400,000)
Taxable income	$450,000

Ram's effective income tax rate is 34% for 20X5. What amount should Ram report in its 20X5 income statement as the current provision for income tax?

A. $34,000
B. $153,000
C. $255,000
D. $289,000

AICPA.051155FAR-FA

618. Miro Co. began business on January 2, 20X0. Miro uses the double-declining balance method of depreciation for financial statement purposes for its building, and the straight-line method for income taxes.

On January 16, 20X2 Miro elected to switch to the straight-line method for both financial statement and tax purposes. The building cost $240,000 in 20X0, which has an estimated useful life of 15 years and no salvage value.

Data related to the building are as follows:

Year	Double-Declining Depreciation	Straight-Line Depreciation
20X0	$30,000	$16,000
20X1	$20,000	$16,000

Miro's tax rate is 40%.

A. There should be no reduction in Miro's deferred tax liabilities or deferred tax assets in 2002.
B. Miro's deferred tax liability should be reduced by $7,200 in 20X2.
C. Miro's deferred tax asset should be reduced by $7,200 in 20X2.
D. Miro's deferred tax asset should be increased by $7,200 in 20X2.

Valuation Allowance for Deferred Tax Assets

AICPA.940524FAR-FA

619. Because Jab Co. uses different methods to depreciate equipment for financial statement and income tax purposes, Jab has temporary differences that will reverse during the next year and add to taxable income.

Deferred income taxes that are based on these temporary differences should be classified in Jab's balance sheet as a

A. Contra account to current assets.
B. Contra account to non-current assets.
C. Current liability.
D. Non-current liability.

AICPA.970511FAR-FA

620. Hut Co. has temporary taxable differences that will reverse during the next year and add to taxable income. These differences relate to non-current assets. Deferred income taxes based on these temporary differences should be classified in Hut's balance sheet as a

A. Current asset.
B. Non-current asset.
C. Current liability.
D. Non-current liability.

AICPA.950517FAR-FA

621. At December 31, Year 1, Bren Co. has the following deferred income tax items:

1. A deferred income tax liability of $15,000 related to a non-current asset
2. A deferred income tax asset of $3,000 related to a non-current liability
3. A deferred income tax asset of $8,000 related to a current liability

Which of the following should Bren report in the non-current section of its December 31, Year 1 balance sheet?

A. A non-current asset of $3,000 and a non-current liability of $15,000.
B. A non-current liability of $12,000.
C. A non-current asset of $11,000 and a non-current liability of $15,000.
D. A non-current liability of $4,000.

AICPA.941106FAR-FA

622. Thorn Co. applies FASB ASC 740, Income Taxes. At the end of 20X5, the tax effects of temporary differences are as follows:

	Tax Assets (Liabilities)	Deferred Related Asset Classification
Accelerated tax depreciation	($75,000)	Non-current asset
Additional costs in inventory for tax purposes	$25,000	Current asset
	($50,000)	

A valuation allowance was not considered necessary. Thorn anticipates that $10,000 of the deferred tax liability will reverse in 20X6. In Thorn's December 31, 20X5 balance sheet, what amount should Thorn report as non-current deferred tax liability?

A. $40,000
B. $50,000
C. $65,000
D. $75,000

Uncertain Tax Positions

AICPA.951136FAR-FA

623. On its December 31, 20X5 balance sheet, Shin Co. has income tax payable of $13,000 and a current deferred tax asset of $20,000, before determining the need for a valuation account.

Shin had reported a current deferred tax asset of $15,000 at December 31, 20X4. No estimated tax payments are made during 20X5. At December 31, 20X5, Shin determines that it is more likely than not that 10% of the deferred tax asset would not be realized.

In its 20X5 income statement, what amount should Shin report as total income tax expense?

A. $8,000
B. $8,500
C. $10,000
D. $13,000

Net Operating Losses

AICPA.090876FAR

624. At the end of the current year, Swen Inc. prepares its tax return, which reflects an uncertain amount, reducing the firm's tax liability by $40,000. Swen estimates that, upon

audit by the IRS, there is a 20% chance that the full $40,000 benefit will be upheld, and a 40% chance that the benefit will be only $25,000. As a result of the required recognition and measurement principles for uncertain tax positions, current-year income tax expense is reduced by what amount?

A. $18,000
B. $25,000
C. $40,000
D. $15,000

AICPA.090877FAR

625. Two years ago, Aggre Inc. recognized the tax benefit of an uncertain tax position. income tax expense in that year was reduced by $20,000 as a result. In addition, Aggre recorded a $5,000 tax liability for unrecognized benefits for the same tax position. During the current year, the uncertainty is resolved and a benefit of $22,000 is upheld. By what amount is current-year income tax expense affected by the resolution of the prior uncertainty?

A. $2,000 decrease.
B. $22,000 decrease.
C. $5,000 decrease.
D. There is no effect.

Accounting Changes and Error Corrections

AICPA.083752FAR-SIM

626. At the end of the previous year, a firm reported a $6,000 deferred tax asset from a net-operating-loss carry-forward that can be carried forward several years into the future. The tax rate is 30%. For the current year, the firm records estimated warranty expense of $30,000 for the year and incurred $10,000 of warranty-claims costs. Taxable income for the current year is $12,000. Compute income tax expense (benefit) for the current year.

A. ($5,400)
B. ($2,400)
C. $3,600
D. Neither expense nor benefit.

AICPA.930556FAR-P1-FA

627. Venus Corp.'s worksheet for calculating current and deferred income taxes for 20X4 is as follows:

	20X4	20X5	20X6
Pre-tax income	$1,400		
Temporary differences:			
Depreciation	($800)	($1,200)	$2,000
Warranty costs	$400	($100)	($300)
Taxable income	$1,000	($1,300)	$1,700
Loss carry-back	(1,000)	$1,000	
Loss carry-forward	$300	($300)	
	$0	$0	$1,400
Enacted rate	30%	30%	25%
Deferred tax liability (asset):			
Current	($300)		
Non-current		$350	

Venus elected early adoption of FASB Statement No. 109, Accounting for Income Taxes. Venus had no prior deferred tax balances. In its 20X4 income statement, what amount should Venus report as:

A. $350
B. $300
C. $120
D. $35

AICPA.061213FAR

628. Which of the following should be disclosed in a company's financial statements related to deferred taxes?

I. The types and amounts of existing temporary differences.
II. The types and amounts of existing permanent differences.
III. The nature and amount of each type of operating loss and tax credit carry-forward.

A. I and II only.
B. I and III only.
C. II and III only.
D. I, II, and III.

AICPA.900525FAR-TH-FA

629. No deferred tax asset was recognized in the year 1 financial statements by the Chaise Company when a loss from discontinued segments was carried forward for tax purposes. Chaise had no temporary differences. The tax benefit of

the loss carried forward reduced current taxes payable on Year 2 continuing operations.

The Year 2 financial statements would include the tax benefit from the loss brought forward in

A. Income from continuing operations.
B. Gain or loss from discontinued segments.
C. Owners' equity.
D. Cumulative effect of accounting changes.

Types of Changes and Accounting Approaches

AICPA.931126FAR-TH-FA

630. The cumulative effect of a change in accounting principle should be recorded as an adjustment to retained earnings, when the change is:

A. Cash basis of accounting for vacation pay to the accrual basis.
B. Straight-line method of depreciation for previously recorded assets to the double-declining-balance method.
C. Longer useful life of equipment to shorter useful life.
D. Completed-contract method of accounting for long-term construction-type contracts to the percentage-of-completion method.

AICPA.941155FAR-FA

631. Foy Corp. failed to accrue warranty costs of $50,000 in its December 31, 2003 financial statements. In addition, a change from straight-line to accelerated-depreciation made at the beginning of 2004 resulted in a $30,000 decrease in income for the year. Both the $50,000 and the $30,000 are net of related income taxes.

What amount should Foy report as prior period adjustments in 2004?

A. $0
B. $30,000
C. $50,000
D. $80,000

AICPA.911124FAR-TH-FA

632. The effect of a change in accounting principle that is inseparable from the effect of a change in accounting estimate should be reported:

A. By restating the financial statements of all prior periods presented.
B. As a correction of an error.
C. As a component of income from continuing operations, in the period of change and future periods if the change affects both.
D. As a separate disclosure after income from continuing operations, in the period of

change and future periods if the change affects both.

AICPA.090665.FAR.III

633. How should a company report its decision to change from a cash-basis to an accrual-basis of accounting?

A. As a change in accounting principle, requiring the cumulative effect of the change (net of tax) to be reported in the income statement.
B. Prospectively, with no amounts restated and no cumulative adjustment.
C. As an extraordinary item (net of tax).
D. As a Prior period adjustment (net of tax), by adjusting the beginning balance of retained earnings.

AICPA.951143FAR-FA

634. Lore Co. changed from the cash basis to the accrual basis of accounting during 2005. The cumulative effect of this change should be reported in Lore's 2005 financial statements as a

A. Prior period adjustment resulting from the correction of an error.
B. Prior period adjustment resulting from the change in accounting principle.
C. Adjustment to retained earnings for an accounting principle change.
D. Component of income after extraordinary item.

Retrospective Application

AICPA.950545FAR-FA

635. During 2005, Orca Corp. decided to change from the FIFO method of inventory valuation to the weighted-average method. Inventory balances under each method were as follows:

	FIFO	Weighted-Average
January 1, 2005	$71,000	$77,000
December 31, 2005	$79,000	$83,000

Orca's income tax rate is 30%.

In its 2005 financial statements, what amount should Orca report as the cumulative effect of this accounting change?

A. $2,800
B. $4,000
C. $4,200
D. $6,000

AICPA.950546FAR-FA

636. During 2006, Orca Corp. decides to change from the FIFO method of inventory valuation to the weighted-average method. Inventory balances under each method were as follows:

	FIFO	Weighted-Average
January 1, 2006	$71,000	$77,000
December 31, 2006	$79,000	$83,000

Orca's income tax rate is 30%.

Orca should report the cumulative effect of this accounting change as a(n):

A. Prior period adjustment.
B. Adjustment to retained earnings.
C. Extraordinary item.
D. Component of income after discontinued operations.

AICPA.911156FAR-P1-FA

637. Goddard has used the FIFO method of inventory valuation since it began operations in 2002. Goddard decides to change to the weighted-average (WA) method for determining inventory costs at the beginning of 2005.

The following schedule shows year-end inventory balances under the FIFO and weighted-average methods:

Year	FIFO	Weighted-Average
2002	$45,000	$54,000
2003	$78,000	$71,000
2004	$83,000	$78,000

What amount, before income taxes, should be reported in the 2005 financial statements as the cumulative effect of the change in accounting principle?

A. $5,000 decrease.
B. $3,000 decrease.
C. $2,000 increase.
D. $0.

Prospective Application

AICPA.930519FAR-TH-FA

638. During 2005, Krey Co. increased the estimated quantity of copper recoverable from its mine. Krey uses the units-of-production-depletion method.

Which of the following statements correctly describes the appropriate accounting for this change?

A. Accumulated depletion is recalculated back to the date of acquiring the mine and the depletion for each period included in the annual report will reflect the new estimate.

B. The effect of the change on all prior years is treated as a catch-up adjustment in the 2005 income statement.

C. The change in estimate is applied as of the beginning of 2005 for current and future periods.

D. The retained-earnings balance at the beginning of 2005 is adjusted for the effect of the change on prior years.

AICPA.901151FAR-P1-FA

639. On January 1, 2002, Flax Co. purchased a machine for $528,000 and depreciated it by the straight-line method using an estimated useful life of eight years with no salvage value.

On January 1, 2005, Flax determines that the machine had a useful life of six years from the date of acquisition and will have a salvage value of $48,000. An accounting change is made in 2005 to reflect these additional data.

The accumulated depreciation for this machine should have a balance at December 31, 2005 of

A. $292,000
B. $308,000
C. $320,000
D. $352,000

AICPA.061216FAR

640. Mellow Co. depreciates a $12,000 asset over five years, using the straight-line method with no salvage value. At the beginning of the fifth year, it is determined that the asset will last another four years.

What amount should Mellow report as depreciation expense for year five?

A. $600
B. $900
C. $1,500
D. $2,400

AICPA.130727FAR

641. Which of the following statements is correct as it relates to changes in accounting estimates?

A. Most changes in accounting estimates are accounted for retrospectively.

B. Whenever it is impossible to determine whether a change in an estimate or a change in accounting principle occurred, the change should be considered a change in principle.

C. Whenever it is impossible to determine whether a change in accounting estimate or a change in accounting principle has

occurred, the change should be considered a change in estimate.

D. It is easier to differentiate between a change in accounting estimate and a change in accounting principle than it is to differentiate between a change in accounting estimate and a correction of an error.

AICPA.070777FAR

642. Belle Co. determined after four years that the estimated useful life of its labeling machine should be ten, rather than 12 years. The machine originally cost $46,000 and had an estimated salvage value of $1,000. Belle uses straight-line depreciation. What amount should Belle report as depreciation expense for the current year?

A. $3,200
B. $3,750
C. $4,500
D. $5,000

Accounting Errors—Restatement

AICPA.061226FAR

643. Miller Co. discovers that in the prior year, it failed to report $40,000 of depreciation related to a newly constructed building. The depreciation was computed correctly for tax purposes. The tax rate for the current year is 40%.

What was the impact of the error on Miller's financial statements for the prior year?

A. Understatement of accumulated depreciation of $24,000.

B. Understatement of accumulated depreciation of $40,000.

C. Understatement of depreciation expense of $24,000.

D. Understatement of net income of $24,000.

AICPA.101125FAR

644. The senior accountant for Carlton Co., a public company with a complex capital structure, has just finished preparing Carlton's income statement for the current fiscal year. While reviewing the income statement, Carlton's finance director noticed that the earnings-per-share data have been omitted. What changes will have to be made to Carlton's income statement as a result of the omission of the earnings-per-share data?

A. No changes will have to be made to Carlton's income statement. The income statement is complete without the earnings-per-share data.

B. Carlton's income statement will have to be revised to include the earnings-per-share data.

C. Carlton's income statement will only have to be revised to include the earnings-per-share data if Carlton's market capitalization is greater than $5mn.

D. Carlton's income statement will only have to be revised to include the earnings-per-share data if Carlton's net income for the past two years is greater than $5mn.

AICPA.911125FAR-TH-FA

645. In single-period statements, which of the following should be reflected as an adjustment to the opening balance of retained earnings?

A. Effect of a failure to provide for uncollectible accounts in the previous period.

B. Effect of a decrease in the estimated useful life of depreciable equipment.

C. Adoption of a new accounting method for transactions that in the past had an immaterial effect on the financial statements.

D. Cumulative effect of a change from an accelerated method to straight-line depreciation.

AICPA.921146FAR-P2-FA

646. On January 2, 2005, Air, Inc. agrees to pay its former president $300,000 under a deferred-compensation arrangement.

Air should have recorded this expense in 2004, but did not do so. Air's reported income tax expense would have been $70,000 lower in 2004 had it properly accrued this deferred compensation.

In its December 31, 2005 financial statements, Air should adjust the beginning balance of its retained earnings by a

A. $230,000 credit.

B. $230,000 debit.

C. $300,000 credit.

D. $370,000 debit.

AICPA.911102FAR-P2-FA

647. During 2005, Dale Corp. made the following accounting changes:

Method Used in 2004	After-Tax Method Used in 2005	Effect
Sum-of-the-years' digits depreciation	Straight-line depreciation	$30,000
Weighted-average for inventory valuation	First-in, first-out for inventory valuation	$98,000

What amounts should be classified in 2005 as prior period adjustments?

A. $0

B. $30,000

C. $98,000

D. $128,000

Business Combinations

Introduction to Business Combinations

AICPA.081243FAR-SIM

648. In which of the following legal forms of business combination does at least one preexisting entity cease to exist?

	Merger	Consolidation	Acquisition
A.	Yes	Yes	Yes
B.	Yes	Yes	No
C.	Yes	No	No
D.	No	No	Yes

AICPA.081266FAR-SIM

649. On December 1, 200X, Betaco agreed to be acquired 100% by Alphaco at a cost equal to Betaco's book value. The combination was initiated at that time, and the closing date for the acquisition was December 31, 200X. Both firms have December 31 fiscal year-ends. There were no other transactions between the firms during 200X or 200Y. Each firm had the following net incomes for the periods shown:

	Alphaco	Betaco
1/1/0X–11/30/0X	$20,000	$5,000
12/1/0X–12/31/0X	4,000	1,000
1/1/0Y–1/31/0Y	2,000	3,000

Which one of the following is the amount of consolidated net income that should be recognized for January 200Y?

A. $2,000

B. $3,000

C. $5,000

D. $10,000

AICPA.081264FAR-SIM

650. On October 1, 200X, Parco acquired 100% controlling interest of Setco in a legal acquisition. There were no other transactions between the entities during 200X. The two companies reported the following net incomes/(losses) for the periods shown:

	Parco	Setco
1/1/0X–9/30/0X	$125,000	$40,000
10/1/0X–12/31/0X	30,000	($15,000)

Which one of the following would be the amount of income recognized by Parco in its consolidated financial statements for the year ended December 31, 200X?

A. $140,000
B. $155,000
C. $180,000
D. $210,000

AICPA.081241FAR-SIM

651. In which of the following legal forms of business combination are two or more entities combined into one new entity?

	Merger	Consolidation	Acquisition
A.	Yes	Yes	Yes
B.	Yes	Yes	No
C.	No	Yes	No
D.	No	No	Yes

AICPA.081244FAR-SIM

652. In which of the following legal forms of business combination are the assets and liabilities of an acquired entity or entities recorded on the books of the acquiring entity?

	Merger	Acquisition	Consolidation
A.	Yes	Yes	Yes
B.	Yes	Yes	No
C.	Yes	No	Yes
D.	No	Yes	No

Acquisition Method of Accounting

Introduction to Acquisition Method of Accounting

AICPA.090682.FAR.III.A-SIM

653. At the closing date of a business combination, goodwill was recognized. During the subsequent measurement period, additional identifiable assets were properly recognized as part of the business combination. If no other changes occurred during the measurement period, which one of the following would be the effect, if any, of the additional assets recognized on the amount of goodwill recognized in the combination?

A. No change in the amount of goodwill recognized.
B. An increase in the amount of goodwill recognized.
C. A decrease in the amount of goodwill recognized.
D. An increase or decrease in the amount of goodwill recognized, depending on the underlying reason(s) for the goodwill.

AICPA.090675.FAR.III.A-SIM

654. Which of the following statements concerning the nature of an acquired business in a business combination is/are correct?

I. A business may be a group of assets.
II. A business may be a group of net assets.
III. A business may be a separate legal entity.

A. I only
B. I and III only.
C. III only.
D. I, II, and III.

AICPA.090671.FAR.III.A-SIM

655. Which of the following are requirements of using the acquisition method of accounting for a business combination?

I. Determining the acquiring entity.
II. Determining the acquisition date of the business combination.
III. Determining the cost of the acquisition.

A. I only.
B. I and II only.
C. I and III only.
D. I, II, and III.

AICPA.090679.FAR.III.A-SIM

656. Company Z is formed to consolidate three preexisting entities: Companies W, X, and Y. Company Z pays cash to acquire the net assets of Company W and issues debt to acquire the net assets of Company X. Company Z acquires all of the stock of Company Y in the market for cash. Which one of the companies is most likely the acquirer in the business combination?

A. Company W.
B. Company X.
C. Company Y.
D. Company Z.

AICPA.090676.FAR.III.A-SIM

657. In which one of the following cases is Company A most likely to be the acquirer of Company B in a business combination?

A. Company A owns 80% of Company B's long-term debt.
B. Company A owns 40% of Company B's voting stock and 40% of Company C's voting stock, which owns 20% of Company B's voting stock.

C. Company A owns 35% of Company B's voting stock and 60% of Company C's voting stock, which owns 20% of Company B's voting stock.

D. Company A owns 40% of Company B's outstanding bonds and 20% of Company B's voting stock.

Determining the Cost of the Business Acquired

AICPA.090694.FAR.III.A-SIM

658. Which of the following statements concerning the acquisition of a business is/are correct?

I. Most consideration transferred to effect a business combination should be measured at fair value.

II. Contingent consideration should be included in the cost of an acquired business at fair value existing on the acquisition date.

III. The cost of carrying out a business combination should be included in the cost of an acquired business.

A. I only.
B. I and II only.
C. I and III only.
D. I, II, and III.

AICPA.090697.FAR.III.A-SIM

659. Which one of the following, incurred by an acquiring entity in carrying out a business combination, would not be included in the cost of an acquired entity?

A. Cash paid as consideration in the combination.

B. Fair value of liabilities incurred in the combination.

C. Cost of legal fees to carry out the combination.

D. Fair value of contingent consideration at the acquisition date.

AICPA.130734FAR

660. Bale Co. incurred $100,000 of acquisition costs related to the purchase of the net assets of Dixon Co. The $100,000 should be

A. Allocated on a pro rata basis to the nonmonetary assets acquired.

B. Capitalized as part of goodwill and tested annually for impairment.

C. Capitalized as an other asset and amortized over five years.

D. Expensed as incurred in the current period.

AICPA.090807.FAR.III.A-SIM

661. A business combination is accounted for using the acquisition method. Which of the following should be deducted in determining the combined corporation's net income for the current period?

	Direct Costs of Acquisition	General Expenses Related to Acquisition
A.	Yes	Yes
B.	Yes	No
C.	No	Yes
D.	No	No

AICPA.090693.FAR.III.A-SIM

662. Changes in the fair value of contingent consideration transferred in a business combination resulting from occurrences after the acquisition date should be recognized as a gain or loss in the current income when the contingent consideration is classified as:

	An Asset or a Liability	An Equity Item
A.	Yes	Yes
B.	Yes	No
C.	No	Yes
D.	No	No

Recognizing/Measuring Assets, Liabilities and Noncontrolling Interest

AICPA.090709.FAR.III.A-SIM

663. Which of the following statements, if any, concerning a noncontrolling interest in an acquiree is/are correct?

I. The value assigned to a noncontrolling interest in an acquiree should be based on the proportional share of that interest in the net assets of the acquiree.

II. The fair value per share of the noncontrolling interest in an acquiree must be the same as the fair value per share of the controlling (acquirer) interest.

A. Both I and II.
B. I only.
C. II only.
D. Neither I nor II.

AICPA.090704.FAR.III.A-SIM

664. Generally, which of the following items acquired in a business combination should be measured at fair value?

	Identifiable Assets Acquired	Liabilities Assumed	Noncontrolling Interest
A.	Yes	Yes	No
B.	Yes	No	No
C.	Yes	No	Yes
D.	Yes	Yes	Yes

AICPA.090702.FAR.III.A-SIM

665. Which one of the following payments by an acquirer in a business combination is most likely to be a part of the cost in recording a business combination transaction?

A. Payment by the acquirer to settle a trade payable due to the acquired entity.

B. Payment by the acquirer to the acquiree's management personnel to remain with the firm for one year following the business combination.

C. Payment by the acquirer to the acquiree for a valid patent not previously recognized by the acquiree.

D. Payment by the acquirer to reimburse the acquiree for cost it incurred in carrying out the business combination.

AICPA.090703.FAR.III.A-SIM

666. Which one of the following items acquired in a business combination is least likely to require that the acquirer reconsider the acquiree's classification?

A. An investment classified as held-to-maturity by the acquiree.

B. An investment classified as held-for-trading by the acquiree.

C. A lease classified as a sales-type capital lease by the acquiree.

D. A derivative instrument used for speculative purposes by the acquiree.

AICPA.090705.FAR.III.A-SIM

667. Which of the following contingencies that exist on the acquisition date should be recognized by the acquirer in a business combination?

I. A contractual contingency to provide warranty services to prior customers of the acquiree.

II. An outstanding lawsuit against the acquiree for which an expert legal authority believes there is a 20% probability that the suit will be successful.

A. Neither I nor II.
B. I only.
C. II only.
D. Both I and II.

Recognizing/Measuring Goodwill or Bargain Purchase Amount

AICPA.110546FAR

668. Damon Co. purchased 100% of the outstanding common stock of Smith Co. in an acquisition by issuing 20,000 shares of its $1 par common stock that had a fair value of $10 per share and providing contingent consideration that had a fair value of $10,000 on the acquisition date. Damon also incurred $15,000 in direct acquisition costs. On the acquisition date, Smith had assets with a book value of $200,000, a fair value of $350,000, and related liabilities with a book and fair value of $70,000. What amount of gain should Damon report related to this transaction?

A. $55,000
B. $70,000
C. $80,000
D. $250,000

AICPA.090717.FAR.III.A-SIM

669. On July 1, 2009, Nexto, Inc. had the following summarized balance sheet with the book values and fair values shown:

	Book Value	Fair Value
Accounts Receivable (net)	$40,000	$40,000
Inventories	80,000	80,000
Plant and Equipment (net)	160,000	200,000
Land	120,000	160,000
TOTAL ASSETS	$400,000	$480,000
Accounts Payable	$20,000	$20,000
Short-Term Note	30,000	30,000
Bonds Payable	70,000	70,000
TOTAL LIABILITIES	$120,000	$120,000

On that date, Pesto, Inc. acquired 100% of Nexto's voting stock from its shareholders by paying the following consideration:

Cash	$200,000
10,000 newly-issued shares of Pesto's $10 par common stock	100,000 (par)

Prior to the combination, Pesto had 1,000,000 shares of voting stock outstanding trading in an active market at $15 per share. Pesto paid $25,000 for legal and accounting fees to carry out the combination.

Which one of the following is the amount of goodwill or bargain purchase gain that Pesto should recognize as a result of its acquisition of Nexto?

Goodwill	Bargain Purchase Gain
$10,000	$– 0 –
$15,000	$– 0 –
$– 0 –	$10,000
$– 0 –	$60,000

AICPA.090720.FAR.III.A-SIM

670. In a business combination accounted for as an acquisition, the fair value of the identifiable net assets acquired exceeds the fair value of the consideration paid by the acquirer and the fair value of the noncontrolling interest in the acquiree. The excess fair value of net assets over investment value should be reported as a:

A. Gain.
B. Reduction of the values assigned to current assets and a deferred credit ("Negative Goodwill") for any unallocated portion.
C. Reduction of the values assigned to non-financial assets and a gain for any unallocated portion.
D. Pro-rata reduction of the values assigned to current and noncurrent assets.

AICPA.090718.FAR.III.A-SIM

671. In which of the following circumstances will goodwill be recognized in a business combination?

A. The acquired entity had the asset "Goodwill" on its books immediately prior to the business combination.
B. The fair value of the investment by the acquiring entity and any noncontrolling interest in the acquired entity is greater than the book value of the acquired entity's net assets.
C. The fair value of the investment by the acquiring entity and any noncontrolling interest in the acquired entity is greater than the fair value of the acquired entity's net assets.
D. The fair value of the investment by the acquiring entity and any noncontrolling interest in the acquired entity is less than the fair value of the acquired entity's net assets.

AICPA.090713.FAR.III.A-SIM

672. Windco, Inc. acquired 100% of the voting common stock of Trace, Inc. by transferring the following consideration to Trace's shareholders:

Cash	$100,000
5,000 new shares of Windco's $10 par common stock (which is less than 1% of Windco's outstanding stock)	$50,000 (par)

In addition, Windco paid $12,000 direct cost of carrying out the combination.

At the date of the acquisition, Windco's common stock was selling in an active market for $18 per share. Also, at the date of the acquisition, Trace had the following assets and liabilities with the book values and fair values shown:

	Book Value	Market Value
Accounts Receivable	$20,000	$20,000
Property and Equipment	80,000	100,000
Land	60,000	80,000
Other Assets	40,000	40,000
Total Assets	$200,000	$240,000
Accounts Payable	$15,000	$15,000
Other Short-term Debt	10,000	10,000
Long-term Debt	35,000	35,000
Total Liabilities	$60,000	$60,000

Which one of the following is the amount of gain Windco will recognize in connection with its acquisition of Trace?

A. $– 0 - (no gain)
B. $10,000
C. $40,000
D. $80,000

Post-Acquisition Issues

AICPA.130733FAR

673. How should the acquirer recognize a bargain purchase in a business acquisition?

A. As negative goodwill in the statement of financial position.
B. As goodwill in the statement of financial position.
C. As a gain in earnings at the acquisition date.
D. As a deferred gain that is amortized into earnings over the estimated future periods benefited.

AICPA.090722.FAR.III.A-SIM

674. Which one of the following assets recognized in a business combination will require that the amount recognized be amortized over future periods?

    A. An asset arising from a contingency.
    B. A reacquired right asset.
    C. An indemnification asset.
    D. A contingent consideration asset.

AICPA.090724.FAR.III.A-SIM

675. Which of the following statements, if any, concerning a contingency that arises in a business combination is/are correct?

    I. After an acquisition and until it is settled, a contingency that is a liability will be measured at no less than the fair value reported on the acquisition date.
    II. After an acquisition and until it is settled, a contingency that is an asset will be measured at no less than the fair value reported on the acquisition date.

    A. Neither I nor II.
    B. I only.
    C. II only.
    D. Both I and II.

AICPA.090726.FAR.III.A-SIM

676. In recording its acquisition of Lambda, Inc., Omega, Inc. properly recognized a contingent consideration liability of $28,000 associated with a possible payment based on a target amount of post-combination cash flow from operations. Shortly after the combination, but during the measurement period, the national economy experienced a significant downturn, which made it unlikely that the target amount would be reached. As a consequence, at the end of Omega's fiscal period, the liability was properly revalued to a fair value of $9,000. Which one of the following is the amount of increase or decrease, if any, in the consideration paid to acquire Lambda that results from the change in the fair value of the contingent liability?

    A. $ - 0 - (no increase or decrease),
    B. $19,000 increase.
    C. $19,000 decrease.
    D. $9,000 decrease.

AICPA.090725.FAR.III.A-SIM

677. In recording its acquisition of Lambda, Inc., Omega, Inc. properly recognized a contingent consideration liability of $28,000 associated with a possible payment based on a target amount of post-combination cash flow from operations. Shortly after the combination, but during the

measurement period, the national economy experienced a significant downturn, which made it unlikely that the target amount would be reached. As a consequence, at the end of Omega's fiscal period, the liability was properly revalued to a fair value of $9,000. Which one of the following is the amount of gain or loss that will be recognized in income as a result of the reevaluation of the contingent liability?

    A. $ - 0 - (no gain or loss).
    B. $19,000 gain.
    C. $19,000 loss.
    D. $9,000 loss.

Disclosure Requirements—Acquisition Method

AICPA.090730.FAR.III.A-SIM

678. When goodwill is recognized in a business combination, which of the following types of information about that goodwill must be disclosed?

    I. A quantitative description of the factors that make up the goodwill.
    II. The amount of goodwill that is expected to be deductible for tax purposes.
    III. The amount of goodwill allocated to each reportable segment.

    A. I and II only.
    B. I and III only.
    C. II and III only.
    D. I, II, and III.

AICPA.090733.FAR.III.A-SIM

679. When a bargain purchase occurs in a business combination, which of the following types of information must be disclosed in the period of the combination?

    I. The amount of gain recognized.
    II. The income statement line item that includes the gain.
    III. A description of the basis for the bargain purchase amount.

    A. I only.
    B. I and II only.
    C. I and III only.
    D. I, II, and III.

AICPA.090732.FAR.III.A-SIM

680. If provisional amounts are reported for items recognized in a business combination, which of the following kinds of information must be disclosed?

    I. The reasons why the accounting is incomplete.
    II. The amount of adjustment(s) made to the provisional amounts during the period.

III. The date at which each provisional amount is expected to be resolved.

A. I and II only.
B. II only.
C. I and III only.
D. I, II, and III.

AICPA.090728.FAR.III.A-SIM

681. An entity must disclose information about a business combination it carries out if the acquisition date occurs:

	During the Reporting Period	After the Reporting Period but Before Statements Are Released
A.	Yes	Yes
B.	Yes	No
C.	No	Yes
D.	No	No

AICPA.090729.FAR.III.A-SIM

682. Which of the following general types of information about a business combination must be disclosed?

I. The primary reason for a business combination.
II. How the acquirer gained control of the business.
III. The acquisition-date fair value of consideration transferred and each major class of asset acquired and liability assumed.

A. I and II only.
B. I and III only.
C. II and III only.
D. I, II, and III.

Recording Business Combinations

AICPA.090736.FAR.III.A-SIM

683. Sayon Co. issues 200,000 shares of $5 par value common stock to acquire Trask Co. in an acquisition-business combination. The market value of Sayon's common stock is $12 per share. Legal and consulting fees incurred in relation to the acquisition are $110,000 paid in cash. Registration and issuance costs for the common stock are $35,000. What should be recorded in Sayon's additional paid-in capital account for this business combination?

A. $1,545,000
B. $1,400,000
C. $1,365,000
D. $1,255,000

AICPA.081262FAR-SIM

684. Plant Company acquired controlling interest in Seed Company in a legal acquisition. Which one of the following could not be part of the entry to record the acquisition?

A. Debit: Investment in Seed Company
B. Debit: Goodwill
C. Credit: Cash
D. Credit: Common stock

AICPA.910513FAR-P2-FA

685. On August 31, 2005, Wood Corp. issued 100,000 shares of its $20 par value common stock for the net assets of Pine, Inc. in a business combination accounted for by the acquisition method. The market value of Wood's common stock on August 31 was $36 per share. Wood paid a fee of $160,000 to the consultant who arranged this acquisition. Costs of registering and issuing the equity securities amounted to $80,000. No goodwill was involved in the purchase.

What should Wood capitalize as the cost of acquiring Pine's net assets?

A. $3,600,000
B. $3,680,000
C. $3,760,000
D. $3,840,000

AICPA.081259FAR-SIM

686. Seashell Corp. was organized to consolidate Sea Company and Shell Company in a business combination. Seashell issued 25,000 shares of its newly authorized $10 par value common stock in exchange for all of the outstanding common stock of Sea and Shell. At the time of the consolidation, the fair market value of Sea's and Shell's assets and liabilities are equal to their book values. The shareholders' equity accounts of Sea and Shell on the date of the consolidation were:

	Sea	Shell	Total
Common stock, at par	$100,000	$200,000	$300,000
Additional paid-in capital	50,000	75,000	125,000
Retained Earnings	22,500	47,500	70,000
Totals	$172,500	$322,500	$495,000

Which one of the following is the amount of goodwill Seashell would recognize upon issuing its common stock to effect the consolidation?

A. $-0-
B. $50,000
C. $195,000
D. $245,000

AICPA.081258FAR-SIM

687. Under which one of the following circumstances will goodwill be recognized in a business combination carried out as a legal merger?

   A. Book value of net assets acquired > Cost of investment.
   B. Fair value of net assets acquired > Book value of net assets acquired.
   C. Fair value of net assets acquired > Cost of investment.
   D. Fair value of net assets acquired < Cost of investment.

IFRS—Business Combinations

AICPA.121101FAR-SIM

688. Under IFRS which of the following would not be recognized as part of a business combination?

   A. Contingent asset.
   B. Contingent liability.
   C. Goodwill.
   D. Fair value of the consideration transferred.

Financial Instruments

Financial Instruments Introduction

AICPA.090150FAR-SIM

689. Which one of the following is not a characteristic of financial instruments?

   A. Financial instruments include derivative instruments.
   B. Certain disclosure requirements apply to all financial instruments.
   C. Financial instruments can be used for hedging purposes.
   D. All financial instruments have the same accounting requirements.

AICPA.090152FAR-SIM

690. For financial accounting purposes, which one of the following is not a type of hedge carried out using derivatives?

   A. Fair value.
   B. Cash flow.
   C. Speculative.
   D. Foreign currency.

AICPA.090151FAR-SIM

691. Which one of the following is not a characteristic of derivative instruments?

   A. Derivative instruments are a form of financial instrument.
   B. All derivative instruments have the same accounting requirements.

   C. Derivative instruments can be used for hedging purposes.
   D. Derivative instruments can be used to hedge foreign currency risk.

AICPA.070730FAR.SIM

692. Which of the following accounts would reflect the existence of a financial instrument(s)?

	Investments in Debt Securities	Investments in Equity Securities	Bonds Payable
A.	Yes	Yes	Yes
B.	Yes	Yes	No
C.	Yes	No	Yes
D.	No	No	No

IFRS—Financial Instruments

AICPA.101233FAR-SIM

693. Which of the following describes an "accounting mismatch" as that expression is used in IFRS?

   A. Debts don't equal credits.
   B. Liabilities exceed assets.
   C. Related assets and liabilities are valued using different measures.
   D. The value of a hedging instrument does not equal the value of the hedged item.

AICPA.101234FAR-SIM

694. Which of the following is the correct accounting measurement and treatment under IFRS for assets classified as "Loans and Receivables"?

   A. Amortized cost, with interest and amortization recognized in current income.
   B. Amortized cost, with interest and amortization recognized in other comprehensive income.
   C. Fair value, with changes in fair value recognized in current income.
   D. Fair value, with changes in fair value recognized in other comprehensive income.

AICPA.101231FAR-SIM

695. Under IFRS, which one of the following instruments is most likely to be treated in its entirety as a financial liability?

   A. Convertible debt.
   B. Convertible preferred stock.
   C. Redeemable preferred stock.
   D. Common stock with a preemptive right.

Financial Instruments Disclosures

AICPA.070731FAR

696. If it is not practicable for an entity to estimate the fair value of a financial instrument, which of the following should be disclosed?

   I. Information pertinent to estimating the fair value of the instrument.
   II. The reasons it is not practicable to estimate fair value.

   A. I only.
   B. II only.
   C. Both I and II.
   D. Neither I nor II.

AICPA.090319FAR-SIM

697. Disclosure of information about significant concentrations of credit risk is required for:

   A. All financial instruments.
   B. Financial instruments with off-balance-sheet credit risk only.
   C. Financial instruments with off-balance-sheet market risk only.
   D. Financial instruments with off-balance-sheet risk of accounting loss only.

AICPA.070733FAR

698. Fair value disclosure of financial instruments may be made in the:

	Body of Financial Statements	Footnotes to Financial Statements
A.	Yes	Yes
B.	Yes	No
C.	No	Yes
D.	No	No

AICPA.090318FAR-SIM

699. When a concentration of credit risk must be disclosed and the exact amount is uncertain, which one of the following amounts must be disclosed?

   A. Minimum amount at risk.
   B. Current period average amount at risk.
   C. Historic average amount at risk.
   D. Maximum amount at risk.

Derivatives and Hedging

Derivatives Introduction

AICPA.130736FAR

700. Smythe Co. invested $200 in a call option for 100 shares of Gin Co. $.50 par common stock, when the market price was $10 per share. The option expired in three months and had an exercise price of $9 per share. What was the intrinsic value of the call option at the time of initial investment?

   A. $50
   B. $100
   C. $200
   D. $900

AICPA.090320FAR-SIM

701. Which one of the following is not a characteristic of a derivative?

   A. A derivative is a financial instrument or similar contract.
   B. A derivative requires contractual satisfaction by delivery of the subject matter of the contract.
   C. A derivative identifies a specific price, rate, or other monetary measure.
   D. A derivative identifies a specific quantity or other quantitative unit of measure.

AICPA.082071FAR-III.A

702. Which of the following is the characteristic of a perfect hedge?

   A. No possibility of future gain or loss.
   B. No possibility of future gain only.
   C. No possibility of future loss only.
   D. The possibility of future gain and no future loss.

AICPA.090322FAR-SIM

703. Assume Instco acquires an option to buy (a call option) 100 shares of Opco for $50 per share when the market price of Opco is $45 per share and that Instco paid a premium of $1.00 per share to acquire the options. Which one of the following is the underlying related to Instco's options?

   A. 100 shares.
   B. $1.00 per option.
   C. $45.00 per option.
   D. $50.00 per option.

AICPA.101197FAR

704. A derivative financial instrument is best described as:

   A. Evidence of an ownership interest in an entity such as shares of common stock.
   B. A contract that has its settlement value tied to an underlying notional amount.
   C. A contract that conveys to a second entity a right to receive cash from a first entity.
   D. A contract that conveys to a second entity a right to future collections on accounts receivable from a first entity.

Hedging Introduction

AICPA.101229FAR-SIM

705. Which one of the following is an item for which risk associated with the item cannot be hedged for accounting purposes?

   A. Foreign currency risk of a net investment in a foreign operation.
   B. Fair value of an investment accounted for using the equity method of accounting.
   C. Credit risk of investments classified as held for trading.
   D. Overall change in the fair value of a non-financial asset.

AICPA.101228FAR-SIM

706. Hedges of foreign currency risks can be the hedge of:

	Fair Value	Cash Flows
A.	Yes	Yes
B.	Yes	No
C.	No	Yes
D.	No	No

AICPA.101226FAR-SIM

707. Which of the following statements, if either, concerning accounting for derivative financial instruments is/are correct?

   I. Derivative instruments can be used only for hedging purposes.
   II. Derivative instruments can be used only to hedge fair value.

   A. I only.
   B. II only.
   C. Both I and II.
   D. Neither I nor II.

AICPA.101227FAR-SIM

708. Which of the following are basic kinds of risks that can be hedged for accounting purposes?

	Fair Value	Cash Flows
A.	Yes	Yes
B.	Yes	No
C.	No	Yes
D.	No	No

Fair Value Hedges

AICPA.090328FAR-SIM

709. On October 1, 2008, Buyco entered into a legally enforceable contract to acquire raw material inventory in 180 days for $20,000. In order to mitigate the risk of a change in the value of the raw materials, Buyco also entered into a qualified 180-day forward contract to hedge the fair value of the raw materials. At December 31, 2008, the value of the raw materials had decreased by $500, and the fair value of the futures contract had increased by $480. On March 29, 2009, the date the raw materials were delivered to Buyco, they had a fair value of $19,300, and the forward contract had a fair value of $700. Which one of the following is the amount by which the derivative is ineffective as a fair value hedge for 2008?

   A. $980
   B. $500
   C. $480
   D. $20

AICPA.090330FAR-SIM

710. On October 1, 2008, Buyco entered into a legally enforceable contract to acquire raw material inventory in 180 days for $20,000. In order to mitigate the risk of a change in the value of the raw materials, Buyco also entered into a qualified 180-day forward contract to hedge the fair value of the raw materials. At December 31, 2008, the value of the raw materials had decreased by $500, and the fair value of the futures contract had increased by $480. On March 29, 2009, the date the raw materials were delivered to Buyco, they had a fair value of $19,300, and the forward contract had a fair value of $700. Which one of the following is the net gain or loss that would be recognized on the raw material and related forward contract by Buyco in its 2009 net income?

   A. $ -0-
   B. $20
   C. $200
   D. $220

AICPA.090329FAR-SIM

711. On October 1, 2008, Buyco entered into a legally enforceable contract to acquire raw material inventory in 180 days for $20,000. In order to mitigate the risk of a change in the value of the raw materials, Buyco also entered into a qualified 180-day forward contract to hedge the fair value of the raw materials. At December 31, 2008, the value of the raw materials had decreased by $500, and the fair value of the futures contract had increased by $480. On March 29, 2009, the date the raw materials were delivered to Buyco, they had a fair value of $19,300, and the forward contract had a fair value of $700. Which one of the following is the amount of net gain or loss that would be recognized on the raw materials and related forward contract by Buyco in its 2008 net income?

   A. $500
   B. $480
   C. $20
   D. $ -0-

AICPA.090332FAR-SIM

712. Which one of the following is least likely to be a characteristic of a firm commitment?

   A. It is evidenced by a contractual obligation.
   B. It can be the hedged item in a fair value hedge.
   C. It has been recorded as an asset or liability.
   D. It is subject to the risk of change in fair value.

Cash Flow Hedges

AICPA.090333FAR-SIM

713. Which one of the following is not a characteristic of a cash flow hedge?

   A. Can be used to hedge the risk of variability in cash flow of a forecasted transaction.
   B. Measures the hedged item using the present value of expected cash flows.
   C. The derivative used as the hedging instrument is measured at fair value.
   D. All differences between the change in value of the hedged item and the change in value of the hedging instrument are recognized in current income.

AICPA.070742FAR

714. Qualified derivatives may be used to hedge the cash flow associated with a/an:

	Asset	Forecasted Transaction
A.	Yes	Yes
B.	Yes	No
C.	No	Yes
D.	No	No

assess.AICPA.FAR.cash.flow.hedg-0026

715. Which of the following items is included in accumulated other comprehensive income or loss?

   A. Unrealized gains and losses from the ineffective portion of a derivative properly designated as a cash flow hedge
   B. Unrealized holding gains or losses on securities classified as trading securities
   C. A reduction of shareholders' equity related to employee stock ownership plans
   D. Prior service costs not previously recognized as a component of net periodic pension costs

AICPA.090334FAR-SIM

716. Which one of the following is a characteristic of a forecasted transaction?

   A. Is evidenced by a contractual right or obligation.
   B. Can be a hedged item in a cash flow hedge.

   C. Is the same as a firm commitment.
   D. Is evidenced by a recorded asset or liability.

AICPA.090335FAR-SIM

717. In a cash flow hedge, the item being hedged is measured using:

   A. The nominal value of expected cash inflows.
   B. The present value of expected cash inflows.
   C. The nominal value of expected cash inflows or outflows.
   D. The present value of expected cash inflows or outflows.

Foreign Currency Hedges

AICPA.090359FAR-SIM

718. If a firm used a derivative to hedge the risk of exchange rate changes between the time a liability is recorded and the time it is settled in a foreign currency, which one of the following is being hedged?

   A. Unrecognized firm commitment.
   B. Forecasted transaction.
   C. Recognized liability.
   D. Net investment in a foreign entity.

AICPA.090357FAR-SIM

719. Which one of the following is not a characteristic of a foreign currency hedge?

   A. Hedges the risk due to change in foreign currency exchange rates.
   B. Can hedge net investments in a foreign entity.
   C. Are all treated as fair value hedges.
   D. Can be used to hedge forecasted intercompany transactions.

AICPA.090358FAR-SIM

720. Which of the following, if any, can be the risk being hedged in a foreign currency hedge?

	Fair Value	Cash Flows
A.	Yes	Yes
B.	Yes	No
C.	No	Yes
D.	No	No

AICPA.090360FAR-SIM

721. Which of the following statements concerning derivatives used as foreign currency hedges is/are correct?

   I. Can be used to hedge the risk of exchange rate changes on planned transactions.
   II. Can be used to hedge the risk of exchange rate changes on available-for-sale investments.

III. Can be used to hedge the risk of exchange rate changes on accounts receivable and accounts payable.

A. I only.
B. I and II only.
C. II and III only.
D. I, II, and III.

Effectiveness and Disclosure

AICPA.090364FAR-SIM

722. Which of the following statements concerning disclosure requirements for derivatives used as cash flow hedges is/are correct?

I. The net gain or loss recognized in earnings during the period must be disclosed.
II. The amount of gain or loss deferred in other comprehensive income must be disclosed.
III. A listing of derivatives used for cash flow hedges and the amount of each must be disclosed.

A. I only.
B. I and II only.
C. I and III only.
D. I, II, and III.

AICPA.090362FAR-SIM

723. Which one of the following is not a required disclosure for derivatives used as fair value hedges?

A. The amount of net gain or loss recognized in earnings during the period.
B. The location in the financial statements where any gain or loss is reported.
C. The net gain or loss in earnings from firm commitment hedges that no longer qualify for hedge treatment.
D. The amount of gain or loss arising during the period that was deferred.

AICPA.090361FAR-SIM

724. Specific disclosures are required for entities that:

	Issue Derivatives	Hold Derivatives
A.	Yes	Yes
B.	Yes	No
C.	No	Yes
D.	No	No

AICPA.090363FAR-SIM

725. Derivatives used for hedging purposes that require disclosure of reclassifications of accumulated other comprehensive income are most likely related to which of the following hedging purposes, if any?

I. Fair value hedges.
II. Cash flow hedges.

A. I only.
B. II only.
C. Both I and II.
D. Neither I nor II.

IFRS—Hedging

AICPA.121102FAR-SIM

726. Which of the following concepts is not part of the definition of a derivative under IFRS?

A. The instrument has one or more underlyings.
B. The instrument requires little or no initial net investment.
C. The instrument permits net settlement.
D. The instrument has a notional amount.

AICPA.101230FAR-SIM

727. Which of the following statements, if either, concerning differences between U.S. GAAP and IFRS in accounting for hedges is/are correct?

I. IFRS permits hedging a forecasted business combination that is subject to foreign exchange risk; U.S. GAAP does not permit hedging in that case.
II. IFRS permits hedging part of the life of a hedged item; U.S. GAAP does not permit hedging of part of the life of a hedged item.

A. I only.
B. II only.
C. Both I and II.
D. Neither I nor II.

Foreign Currency Denominated Transactions

Introduction and Definitions

AICPA.090161FAR-SIM

728. If $1.00 will buy 0.76 Euros, then how many dollars will one Euro buy (rounded)?

A. $0.24
B. $0.76
C. $1.00
D. $1.32

AICPA.090169FAR-SIM

729. On December 31, 20X8, the end of its fiscal year, Domco had a foreign currency account payable with a settlement amount greater than its previously recorded carrying amount. Which

one of the following would Domco recognize for 20X8?

A. No exchange gain or loss.
B. Exchange gain.
C. Exchange loss.
D. Deferred gain.

AICPA.090170FAR-SIM

730. Which of the following is not associated with the general principles of accounting for foreign currency operating transactions?

A. Transactions will be recorded in terms of the functional currency.
B. Gains and losses result from changes in currency exchange rates.
C. Gains and losses are deferred until transactions are settled.
D. Foreign currencies are converted using the current or spot exchange rate.

AICPA.090162FAR-SIM

731. Soco plans to buy 100,000 Euros with U.S. dollars. The exchange rate is $1.00 = 0.75 Euro. Assuming no transaction cost, how much will Soco have to pay in dollars (rounded) for 100,000 Euros?

A. $175,000
B. $133,333
C. $100,000
D. $75,000

AICPA.990516FAR-FA

732. In preparing consolidated financial statements of a U.S. parent company with a foreign subsidiary, the foreign subsidiary's functional currency is the currency:

A. In which the subsidiary maintains its accounting records.
B. Of the country in which the subsidiary is located.
C. Of the country in which the parent is located.
D. Of the environment in which the subsidiary primarily generates and expends cash.

Import Transaction

AICPA.090177FAR-SIM

733. RWB Co., a U.S. entity, purchased goods for resale from a Thai manufacturer. The purchase agreement provided that the U.S. entity would pay the Thai entity 500,000 baht, the Thai currency. The goods were delivered on July 1, 20X8, with payment due August 29, 20X8. The following exchange rates were determined for the number of baht to the dollar (i.e., B/$):

	Spot Rate	60-Day Forward Rate
July 1, 20X8	35.0B/$	36.5B/$
August 29, 20X8	37.0B/$	38.0B/$

Which one of the following is the amount (rounded) of exchange gain or loss, if any, that RWB Co. would recognize on the purchase of goods from the Thai manufacturer?

A. $-0-
B. $185
C. $541
D. $772

AICPA.110545FAR

734. Toigo Co. purchased merchandise from a vendor in England on November 20 for 500,000 British pounds. Payment was due in British pounds on January 20. The spot rates to purchase one pound were as follows:

November 20	$1.25
December 31	1.20
January 20	1.17

How should the foreign currency transaction gain be reported on Toigo's financial statements at December 31?

A. A gain of $40,000 as a separate component of stockholders' equity.
B. A gain of $40,000 in the income statement.
C. A gain of $25,000 as a separate component of stockholders' equity.
D. A gain of $25,000 in the income statement.

AICPA.090178FAR-SIM

735. A December 15, 20X8, purchase of goods was denominated in a currency other than the entity's functional currency. The transaction resulted in a payable that was fixed in terms of the amount of foreign currency and was paid on the settlement date, January 20, 20X9. The exchange rate of the currency in which the transaction was denominated changed at December 31, 20X8, resulting in a loss that should:

A. Not be reported until January 20, 20X9, the settlement date.
B. Be included as a component of comprehensive income for 20X8.
C. Be included as a deferred charge at December 31, 20X8.
D. Be included as a component of income from continuing operations for 20X8.

AICPA.090175FAR-SIM

736. Which one of the following is most likely a foreign currency import transaction by a U.S. company?

A. Sale of goods to be collected in dollars.
B. Purchase of goods to be paid in dollars.
C. Sale of goods to be collected in a foreign currency.
D. Purchase of goods to be paid in a foreign currency.

AICPA.950532FAR-FA

737. On September 22, 20X5, Yumi Corp. purchased merchandise from an unaffiliated foreign company for 10,000 units of the foreign company's local currency. On that date, the spot rate was $.55. Yumi paid the bill in full on March 20, 20X6, when the spot rate was $.65. The spot rate was $.70 on December 31, 20X5.

What amount should Yumi report as a foreign currency transaction loss in its income statement for the year ended December 31, 20X5?

A. $0
B. $500
C. $1,000
D. $1,500

Export Transaction

AICPA.120622FAR

738. On June 19, Don Co., a U.S. company, sold and delivered merchandise on a 30-day account to Cologne GmbH, a German corporation, for 200,000 euros. On July 19, Cologne paid Don in full. Relevant currency exchange rates were:

	June 19	July 19
Spot rate	$ .988	$ .995
30-day forward rate	.990	1.000

What amount should Don record on June 19 as an account receivable for its sale to Cologne?

A. $197,600
B. $198,000
C. $199,000
D. $200,000

AICPA.090180FAR-SIM

739. A sale of goods, denominated in a currency other than the entity's functional currency, resulted in a receivable that was fixed in terms of the amount of foreign currency that would be received. Exchange rates between the functional currency and the currency in which

the transaction was denominated changed. The resulting gain should be included as a:

A. Translation gain reported as a component of comprehensive income.
B. Translation gain reported as a component of income from continuing operations.
C. Transaction gain reported as a component of comprehensive income.
D. Transaction gain reported as a component of income from continuing operations.

AICPA.090183FAR-SIM

740. Which of the following is a foreign currency export transaction for a U.S. entity?

A. Sale of goods to be collected in dollars.
B. Purchase of goods to be paid in dollars.
C. Sale of goods to be collected in a foreign currency.
D. Purchase of goods to be paid in a foreign currency.

AICPA.090861FAR

741. On October 1 of the current year, a U.S. company sold merchandise on account to a British company for 2,000 pounds (exchange rate, 1 pound = $1.43). At the company's December 31 fiscal year-end, the exchange rate was 1 pound = $1.45. The exchange rate was $1.50 on collection in January of the subsequent year. What amount would the company recognize as a gain (loss) from foreign currency translation when the receivable is collected?

A. $-0-
B. $100
C. $140
D. $(140)

AICPA.911146FAR-P1-FA

742. On September 1, 20X5, Cano & Co., a U.S. corporation, sold merchandise to a foreign firm for 250,000 francs. Terms of the sale require payment in francs on February 1, 20X6. On September 1, 20X5, the spot exchange rate was $.20 per franc. At December 31, 20X5, Cano's year-end, the spot rate was $.19, but the rate increased to $.22 by February 1, 20X6, when payment was received.

How much should Cano report as a foreign exchange gain or loss in its 20X6 income statement?

A. $0
B. $2,500 loss
C. $5,000 gain
D. $7,500 gain

Foreign Currency Hedges

Introduction to Forward and Option Contracts

AICPA.090196FAR-SIM

743. Forward exchange contracts may be used to:

	Hedge Risk	Speculate
A.	No	No
B.	No	Yes
C.	Yes	No
D.	Yes	Yes

AICPA.090165FAR-SIM

744. Which of the following general types of transactions could be a foreign currency transaction?

	Operating Transactions	Forward Exchange Contract Transactions
A.	Yes	Yes
B.	Yes	No
C.	No	Yes
D.	No	No

AICPA.090163FAR-SIM

745. Which one of the following would be a foreign currency transaction for the U.S. entity?

A. A U.S. entity purchases goods from a Swiss entity to be settled in dollars.
B. A German entity purchases goods from a U.S. entity to be settled in dollars.
C. A U.S. entity purchases goods from a British entity to be settled in pounds sterling.
D. A U.S. entity sells goods to a Russian entity to be settled in dollars.

AICPA.090166FAR-SIM

746. Which of the following is not a characteristic associated with foreign currency transactions?

A. Are denominated in a foreign currency.
B. Can include contracts to exchange currencies.
C. Are affected by changes in currency exchange rates.
D. Occur only when initiated by a foreign entity.

Natural (Economic) Hedge

AICPA.090120FAR-SIM

747. Which one of the following is not a characteristic of hedging?

A. Typically involves offsetting transactions or positions.
B. Assures no gain or loss on the item being hedged.
C. Is a strategy for managing risks.
D. Can be used for obligations to be satisfied in a foreign currency.

AICPA.090203FAR-SIM

748. Even if the use of a forward contract for hedging prevents a loss (or gain) from exchange rate changes on the hedged item, which of the following may result in a cost to an entity that uses forward contracts for hedging purposes?

I. Fees imposed by the counterparty to the forward contract.
II. A difference between the spot rate and the forward rate when the forward exchange contract is executed.

A. I only.
B. II only.
C. Both I and II.
D. Neither I nor II.

AICPA.090201FAR-SIM

749. Which of the following exchange rates may be used in accounting for a forward contract hedging instrument?

	Spot Rate	Forward Rate
A.	Yes	Yes
B.	Yes	No
C.	No	Yes
D.	No	No

AICPA.090200FAR-SIM

750. Which one of the following sets identifies the correct relationship between a foreign currency hedged item and a hedging instrument?

	When the Hedged Item is	Then the Hedging Instrument is
I.	Receivable	Receivable
II.	Receivable	Payable

A. I only.
B. II only.
C. Either I or II.
D. Neither I nor II.

AICPA.09024FAR-SIM

751. The net effect of a change in value of a hedged item and its related hedging instrument may be:

I. A gain.
II. A loss.
III. Neither a gain nor a loss.

A. I only.
B. II only.
C. III only.
D. I, II, and III.

Hedging Forecasted Transactions and Firm Commitment

AICPA.090217FAR-SIM

752. Which one of the following is not a characteristic associated with hedging foreign currency firm commitments?

A. The hedged item is for purchase or sale to be recorded in the future.
B. The hedged item is for an already booked asset or liability.
C. The hedged item is evidenced by a contract or similar legal commitment.
D. The risk being hedged exists prior to an asset or liability being recognized.

AICPA.090212FAR-SIM

753. What general kind of hedge is the hedge of a forecasted transaction to be denominated in a foreign currency?

A. Fair value.
B. Cash flow.
C. Economic.
D. Income.

AICPA.090207FAR-SIM

754. A hedge to offset the risk of exchange rate changes on converting the financial statements of a foreign subsidiary to the domestic (functional) currency would be the hedge of:

A. A forecasted transaction.
B. A recognized asset.
C. A net investment in a foreign operation.
D. An available-for-sale investment.

AICPA.090218FAR-SIM

755. What kind of hedge can be used to hedge a foreign currency firm commitment?

	Cash Flow	Fair Value
A.	Yes	Yes
B.	Yes	No
C.	No	Yes
D.	No	No

AICPA.090210FAR-SIM

756. Which of the following types of planned transactions to be denominated in a foreign currency can be hedged?

	Planned Sale	Planned Purchase
A.	Yes	Yes
B.	Yes	No
C.	No	Yes
D.	No	No

Hedging Asset/Liability, Available-for-Sale, or Foreign Operations

AICPA.090223FAR-SIM

757. Hedging a recognized asset is intended to offset the risk of exchange rate changes between which of the following dates?

A. Between the dates a contractual right is established and when the right is fully satisfied.
B. Between the dates a contractual right is established and when the right is recognized.
C. Between the dates a transaction is planned and when the related asset is recognized.
D. Between the dates an asset is recognized and when the asset is fully satisfied.

AICPA.090224FAR-SIM

758. What general kind of hedge, if any, is the hedge of a recognized asset or liability?

I. Fair value.
II. Cash flow.

A. I only.
B. II only.
C. Either I or II.
D. Neither I nor II.

AICPA.090229FAR-SIM

759. Which of the following statements concerning the use of a forward contract to hedge a foreign currency investment held available-for-sale is/are correct?

I. The investment security must not be traded in the investor's functional currency.
II. The forward contract used as the hedging instrument must be highly effective in hedging the investment.

A. I only.
B. II only.
C. Both I and II.
D. Neither I nor II.

AICPA.090226FAR-SIM

760. On December 12, 20X8, Imp Co. entered into a forward exchange contract to hedge a purchase of inventory in November 2008, payable in March 20X9. The forward contract was to purchase 100,000 Euros in 90 days as a fair value hedge of the payable due in March. The relevant direct exchange rates were as follows:

	Spot Rate	Forward Rate (for 3/12/X9)
December 12, 20X8	$1.86	$1.80
December 31, 20X8	$1.96	$1.83

At December 31, 20X8, what amount of foreign currency transaction gain should Imp include in income from this forward contract only? (Ignore discount and present value considerations.)

A. $-0-
B. $3,000
C. $6,000
D. $10,000

AICPA.090234FAR-SIM

761. Which of the following actions would an entity most likely take to hedge an investment in a foreign operation?

A. Invest in the debt securities of the same foreign operation.
B. Invest in the equity securities of another foreign entity with the same foreign currency as the operation being hedged.
C. Invest in the debt securities of another foreign entity with the same foreign currency as the operation being hedged.
D. Borrow from another foreign entity with the same foreign currency as the operation being hedged.

Speculation and Summary

AICPA.090243FAR-SIM

762. In which of the following hedges using a forward contract will at least a portion of any currency exchange gain or loss on the hedging instrument be reported as a translation adjustment in other comprehensive income?

A. Forecasted transaction hedge.
B. Firm commitment hedge.
C. Investment in available-for-sale securities hedge.
D. Net investment in foreign operations hedge.

AICPA.020504FAR-FA

763. On November 2, 20X5, Platt Co. entered into a 90-day futures contract to purchase 50,000 Swiss francs when the contract quote was $.70. The purchase was for speculation in price movement. The following exchange rates existed during the contract period:

	30-Day Futures	Spot Rate
November 2, 20X5	$.62	$.63
December 31, 20X5	.65	.64
January 30, 20X6	.65	.68

What amount should Platt report as foreign currency exchange loss in its income

statement for the year ended December 31, 2005?

A. $2,500
B. $3,000
C. $3,500
D. $4,000

AICPA.930546FAR-P1-FA

764. On September 1, 2004, Brady Corp. entered into a foreign exchange contract for speculative purposes by purchasing 50,000 Euros for delivery in 60 days. The rates to exchange $1 for 1 Euro follow:

	9/1/04	9/30/04
Spot rate	.75	.70
30-day forward rate	.73	.72
60-day forward rate	.74	.73

In its September 30, 2004, income statement, what amount should Brady report as foreign exchange loss?

A. $2,500
B. $1,500
C. $1,000
D. $500

AICPA.090241FAR-SIM

765. A hedge to offset the risk of loss on a recognized asset or liability is which of the following types of hedge?

A. Cash flow hedge.
B. Fair value hedge.
C. Either a cash flow hedge or a fair value hedge, at management's discretion.
D. Neither a cash flow hedge nor a fair value hedge.

AICPA.090862FAR

766. On December 1 of the current year, Bann Co. entered into an option contract to purchase 2,000 shares of Norta Co. stock for $40 per share (the same as the current market price) by the end of the next two months. The time value of the option contract is $600. At the end of December, Norta's stock was selling for $43, and the time value of the option was now $400. If Bann does not exercise its option until January of the subsequent year, which of the following changes would reflect the proper accounting treatment for this transaction on Bann's December 31 year-end financial statements?

A. The option value will be disclosed in footnotes only.
B. Other comprehensive income will increase by $6,000.
C. Net income will increase by $5,800.
D. Current assets will decrease by $200.

Conversion of Foreign Financial Statements

Introduction to Conversion of Foreign Financial Statements

AICPA.090168FAR-SIM

767. Operating transactions denominated in a foreign currency are converted to the functional currency using the:

A. Historic exchange rate.
B. Current exchange rate.
C. Average exchange rate.
D. Forward exchange rate.

AICPA.090273FAR-SIM

768. Which of the following statements concerning the determination of a functional currency is/are correct?

I. The functional currency can be selected at management's discretion.
II. The functional currency could be the recording currency of the foreign entity.
III. The functional currency could be the reporting currency of a parent.

A. I only.
B. I and II only.
C. II and III only.
D. I, II, and III.

AICPA.090275FAR-SIM

769. Determining a foreign subsidiary's functional currency will take into account which of the following?

I. The extent to which the subsidiary operates, and generates and expends cash in the local foreign economy in which it is located.
II. The cumulative inflation rate in the local foreign economy in which it is located.

A. I only.
B. II only.
C. Both I and II.
D. Neither I nor II.

AICPA.090265FAR-SIM

770. The specific method to be used to convert financial statements of a subsidiary expressed in a foreign currency into the domestic currency of the parent depends primarily on:

A. The reporting currency of the subsidiary.
B. The reporting currency of the parent.
C. The functional currency of the subsidiary.
D. The functional currency of the parent.

AICPA.090262FAR-SIM

771. Which one of the following best describes the currency in which the final consolidated financial statements are presented?

A. The local currency.
B. The reporting currency.
C. The functional currency.
D. The temporal currency.

Conversion Using Translation

AICPA.090250FAR-SIM

772. Orr Corporation had a realized foreign exchange loss of $13,000 for the year ended December 31, 20X8, and must also determine whether the following items will require year-end adjustment.

1 Orr had a $7,000 gain resulting from the translation of the accounts of its wholly owned foreign subsidiary for the year ended December 31, 20X8.

2 Orr had an account payable to an unrelated foreign supplier payable in the supplier's local currency. The U.S. dollar equivalent of the payable was $60,000 on October 31, 20X8 and $64,000 on December 31, 20X8. The invoice is payable on January 30, 20X9.

In Orr's 20X8 consolidated income statement, what amount should be included as foreign exchange loss?

A. $6,000
B. $10,000
C. $13,000
D. $17,000

AICPA.090246FAR-SIM

773. A subsidiary's functional currency is the local currency that has not experienced significant inflation. The appropriate exchange rate for translating the depreciation on plant assets in the income statement of the foreign subsidiary is the:

A. Exit exchange rate.
B. Historical exchange rate.
C. Weighted average exchange rate over the economic life of each plant asset.
D. Weighted average exchange rate for the current year.

AICPA.090284FAR-SIM

774. Which one of the following would not be translated using the spot (or current) exchange rate as of the balance sheet date?

A. Cash.
B. Accounts payable.
C. Common stock.
D. Investments held-for-trading.

AICPA.090301AUD-SIM

775. Panco, a U.S. entity, has a subsidiary, Sanco, located in a foreign country. Sanco's operations are concentrated in the country in which it is located and are essentially independent of Panco. The economy of the foreign country is not highly inflationary. Sanco prepared the following shortened financial statements in its local currency, the FCU, for the fiscal year ended December 31, 20X8:

Statement of Net Income and Comprehensive Income (20X8)	FCUs (in 000)
Sales	12,000
COGS	(4,000)
Depreciation Expense	(1,000)
Other Expenses	(3,000)
Net Income	4,000
Other Comprehensive Income	0
Comprehensive Income	4,000
Retained Earnings (20X8)	
Beginning Retained Earnings (end 20X7)	6,000
Add: Net Income (20X8)	4,000
Deduct: Dividends (20X8)	(1,000)
Ending Retained Earnings	9,000
Balance Sheet (12/31/20X8)	
Cash and Account Receivable	2,000
Inventory	6,000
Fixed Assets	10,000
Total Assets	18,000
Liabilities	2,000
Common Stock	7,000
Retained Earnings	9,000
Subtotal	18,000
Accumulated Other Comprehensive Income	0
Total Liabilities + Equity	18,000

The following exchange rates were available:

Historic exchange rate when Sanco was established by Panco:	1 FCU = $1.200
Weighted average exchange rate for 20X8:	1 FCU = $1.300
Spot exchange rate at date dividend declared:	1 FCU = $1.290
Spot exchange rate at December 31, 20X8:	1 FCU = $1.310

Which one of the following is the amount (in 000) of Sanco's depreciation expense in U.S. dollars?

A. $1,000
B. $1,290
C. $1,300
D. $1,310

AICPA.090286FAR-SIM

776. In converting financial statements from a foreign currency to a reporting currency, which one of the following accounts would not be translated using an exchange rate?

A. Accounts receivable.
B. Bonds payable.
C. Common stock.
D. Retained earnings.

Conversion Using Remeasurement

AICPA.090291FAR-SIM

777. Which one of the following expenses would be remeasured using a historic exchange rate?

A. Rent expense.
B. Wage expense.
C. Depreciation expense.
D. Selling expenses.

AICPA.090289FAR-SIM

778. Remeasurement, based on the temporal method of conversion, converts foreign currency amounts to reporting currency amounts using different exchange rates for different accounts based on which of the following distinctions?

A. Current and non-current.
B. Monetary and non-monetary.
C. Asset and liability.
D. Income statement and balance sheet.

AICPA.090288FAR-SIM

779. Eagle, Inc. is a manufacturer and distributor of consumer products in the United States. It has a wholly owned foreign subsidiary, El Rio, which sells Eagle products in Mexico. El Rio receives all of its products from Eagle, sells those products, and remits the proceeds to Eagle. El Rio maintains its books and prepares its financial statements in the Mexican peso. Which one of the following methods will Eagle most likely use to convert El Rio's financial statements to dollar-based statements?

A. Translation.
B. Remeasurement.
C. Translation and then remeasurement.
D. Remeasurement and then translation.

AICPA.090296FAR-SIM

780. Papco, a U.S. entity, has a subsidiary, Sapco, located in a foreign country. Sapco is essentially a sales unit for Papco. Which one of the following processes should Papco use to convert Sapco's financial statements to dollar-based statements for consolidation purposes?

A. Translation.
B. Remeasurement.
C. Translation and then remeasurement.
D. Remeasurement and then translation.

AICPA.090290FAR-SIM

781. Which one of the following would not be remeasured using a historic exchange rate?

A. Cash.
B. Inventories carried at cost.
C. Property, plant, and equipment.
D. Common stock.

Remeasurement, Translation, and IFRS

AICPA.082044FAR-III.C.I

782. Gordon Ltd., a 100% owned British subsidiary of a U.S. parent company, reports its financial statement in local currency, the British pound. A local newspaper published the following U.S. exchange rates to the British pound at year end:

Current rate	$1.50
Historical rate (acquisition)	1.70
Average rate	1.55
Inventory (FIFO)	1.60

Which currency rate should Gordon use to convert its income statement to U.S. dollars at year end?

A. $1.50
B. $1.55
C. $1.60
D. $1.70

AICPA.090123FAR-SIM

783. Park Co.'s wholly-owned subsidiary, Schnell Corp., maintains its accounting records in pounds sterling. Because all of Schnell's branch offices are in Germany, its functional currency is the Euro. Remeasurement of Schnell's 20X8 financial statements resulted in a $7,600 gain, and translation of its financial statements resulted in an $8,100 gain. What amount should Park report as a foreign exchange gain

in its income statement for the year ended December 31, 20X8?

A. $-0-
B. $7,600
C. $8,100
D. $15,700

AICPA.090293FAR-SIM

784. Park Co.'s wholly-owned subsidiary, Schnell Corp., maintains its accounting records in pounds sterling. Because all of Schnell's branch offices are in Germany, its functional currency is the Euro. Remeasurement of Schnell's 20X8 financial statements resulted in a $7,600 gain, and translation of its financial statements resulted in an $8,100 gain. What amount should Park report as a foreign exchange gain in its other comprehensive income for the year ended December 31, 20X8?

A. $-0-
B. $7,600
C. $8,100
D. $15,700

AICPA.090295FAR-SIM

785. Which one of the following sets shows the correct reporting of an adjustment (gain or loss) that results from translation and one that results from remeasurement of financial statements from a foreign currency to a reporting currency?

	Translation Adjustment	Remeasurement Adjustment
A.	Net Income	Net Income
B.	Net Income	Other comprehensive income
C.	Other comprehensive income	Net Income
D.	Other comprehensive income	Other comprehensive income

AICPA.090294FAR-SIM

786. If the functional currency of a foreign subsidiary is a foreign currency other than the subsidiary's recording currency, which one of the following will be used to convert the subsidiary's financial statements to the final reporting currency?

A. Translation.
B. Remeasurement.
C. Translation and then remeasurement.
D. Remeasurement and then translation.

Leases

Background, Operating Leases

AICPA.921156FAR-P1-FA

787. On December 1, 20X4, Clark Co. leased office space for 5 years at a monthly rate of $60,000. On the same date, Clark paid the lessor the following amounts:

First month's rent	$60,000
Last month's rent	$60,000
Security deposit (refundable at lease expiration)	$80,000
Installation of new walls and offices	$360,000

What should be Clark's 20X4 expense relating to utilization of the office space?

A. $60,000
B. $66,000
C. $120,000
D. $140,000

AICPA.900548FAR-P1-FA

788. Rapp Co. leased a new machine to Lake Co. on January 1, Year 1. The lease expired on January 1, Year 6. The annual rental was $90,000.

Additionally, on January 1, Year 1, Lake paid $50,000 to Rapp as a lease bonus and $25,000 as a security deposit to be refunded upon expiration of the lease.

In Rapp's Year 1 income statement, the amount of rental revenue should be

A. $140,000.
B. $125,000.
C. $100,000.
D. $90,000.

AICPA.070785FAR

789. Main, a pharmaceutical company, leased office space from Ash. Main took possession and began to use the building on July 1, 20X0. Rent was due the first day of each month. Monthly lease payments escalated over the 5-year period of the lease as follows:

Period	Lease Payment $0–Rent Abatement during Move-In, Construction
July 1, 20X0–September 30, 20X0	
October 1, 20X0–June 30, 20X1	17,500
July, 1, 20X1–June 30, 20X2	19,000
July 1, 20X2–June 30, 20X3	20,500
July 1, 20X3–June 30, 20X4	23,000
July 1, 20X4–June 30, 20X5	24,500

What amount would Main show as deferred rent expense at December 31, 20X3?

A. $50,658
B. $52,580
C. $68,575
D. $71,550

AICPA.901114FAR-P1-FA

790. On January 1, 20X5, Glen Co. leased a building to Dix Corp. for a 10-year term at an annual rental of $50,000. At the inception of the lease, Glen received $200,000 covering the first 2 years' rent of $100,000 and a security deposit of $100,000.

This deposit will not be returned to Dix upon expiration of the lease but will be applied to payment of rent for the last two years of the lease.

What portions of the $200,000 should be shown as a current and long-term liability, respectively, in Glen's December 31, 20X5 balance sheet?

	Current Liability	Long-Term Liability
A.	$0	$200,000
B.	$50,000	$100,000
C.	$100,000	$100,000
D.	$100,000	$50,000

AICPA.920534FAR-TH-FA

791. On January 1, 20X5, Mollat Co. signed a 7-year lease for equipment having a 10-year economic life.

The present value of the monthly lease payments equaled 80% of the equipment's fair value. The lease agreement provides for neither a transfer of title to Mollat nor a bargain purchase option.

In its 20X5 income statement, Mollat should report

A. Rent expense equal to the 20X5 lease payments.
B. Rent expense equal to the 20X5 lease payments less interest expense.
C. Lease amortization equal to one-tenth of the equipment's fair value.
D. Lease amortization equal to one-seventh of 80% of the equipment's fair value.

Capital Lease Basics

AICPA.990519FAR-FA

792. Cott, Inc. prepared an interest amortization table for a 5-year lease payable with a bargain purchase option of $2,000, exercisable at the end of the lease. At the end of the 5 years, the balance in the leases payable column of the spreadsheet was zero. Cott has asked Grant,

CPA, to review the spreadsheet to determine the error. Only one error was made on the spreadsheet.

Which of the following statements represents the best explanation for this error?

A. The beginning present value of the lease did not include the present value of the bargain purchase option.
B. Cott subtracted the annual interest amount from the lease payable balance instead of adding it.
C. The present value of the bargain purchase option was subtracted from the present value of the annual payments.
D. Cott discounted the annual payments as an ordinary annuity, when the payments actually occurred at the beginning of each period.

AICPA.090667.FAR.III.J

793. Which of the following is a characteristic of a capital lease?

A. The lease term is substantially less than the estimated economic life of the leased property.
B. The lease contains a bargain purchase option.
C. The present value of the minimum lease payments at the beginning of the lease term is 75% or more of the fair value of the property at the inception of the lease.
D. The future obligation does not appear in the balance sheet of the lessee.

AICPA.921127FAR-TH-FA

794. Lease M does not contain a bargain purchase option, but the lease term is equal to 90% of the estimated economic life of the leased property.

Lease P does not transfer ownership of the property to the lessee at the end of the lease term, but the lease term is equal to 75% of the estimated economic life of the leased property.

How should the lessee classify these leases?

	Lease M	Lease P
A.	Capital lease	Operating lease
B.	Capital lease	Capital lease
C.	Operating lease	Capital lease
D.	Operating lease	Operating lease

AICPA.070782FAR

795. On January 1, year 1, Frost Co. entered into a 2-year lease agreement with Ananz Co. to lease 10 new computers. The lease term begins on January 1, year 1 and ends on December 31, year 2. The lease agreement requires Frost to pay Ananz two annual lease payments of $8,000. The present value of the minimum lease payments is $13,000. Which of the following circumstances

would require Frost to classify and account for the arrangement as a capital lease?

A. The economic life of the computers is 3 years.
B. The fair value of the computers on January 1, year 1 is $14,000.
C. Frost does not have the option of purchasing the computers at the end of the lease term.
D. Ownership of the computers remains with Ananz throughout the lease term and after the lease ends.

AICPA.061233FAR

796. Which of the following is a criterion for a lease to be classified as a capital lease in the books of a lessee?

A. The lease contains a bargain purchase option.
B. The lease does **not** transfer ownership of the property to the lessee.
C. The lease term is equal to 65% or more of the estimated useful life of the leased property.
D. The present value of the minimum lease payments is 70% or more of the fair value of the leased property.

Direct Financing Leases

AICPA.061209FAR

797. Koby Co. entered into a capital lease with a vendor for equipment on January 2 for 7 years. The equipment has no guaranteed residual value. The lease required Koby to pay $500,000 annually on January 2, beginning with the current year. The present value of an annuity due for 7 years was 5.35 at the inception of the lease.

What amount should Koby capitalize as leased equipment?

A. $500,000
B. $825,000
C. $2,675,000
D. $3,500,000

AICPA.110558FAR

798. What are the components of the lease receivable for a lessor involved in a direct-financing lease?

A. The minimum lease payments plus any executory costs
B. The minimum lease payments plus residual value
C. The minimum lease payments less residual value
D. The minimum lease payments less initial direct costs

AICPA.910545FAR-P1-FA

799. On January 1, 20X5, Blaugh Co. signed a long-term lease for an office building.

The terms of the lease required Blaugh to pay $10,000 annually, beginning December 30, 20X5 and continuing each year for 30 years. The lease qualifies as a capital lease. On January 1, 20X5, the present value of the lease payments is $112,500 at the 8% interest rate implicit in the lease.

In Blaugh's December 31, 20X5 balance sheet, the capital lease liability should be

A. $102,500.
B. $111,500.
C. $112,500.
D. $290,000.

AICPA.901121FAR-P1-FA

800. On December 31, 20X5, Neal, Inc. leased machinery with a fair value of $105,000 from Frey Rentals Co. The agreement is a 6-year noncancelable lease requiring annual payments of $20,000 beginning December 31, 20X5.

The lease is appropriately accounted for by Neal as a capital lease.

Neal's incremental borrowing rate is 11%. Neal knows the interest rate implicit in the lease payments is 10%.

1 The present value of an annuity due of $1 for 6 years at 10% is 4.7908.

2 The present value of an annuity due of $1 for 6 years at 11% is 4.6959.

In its December 31, 20X5 balance sheet, Neal should report a lease liability of

A. $75,816.
B. $85,000.
C. $93,918.
D. $95,816.

AICPA.911134FAR-TH-FA

801. Jay's lease payments are made at the end of each period. Jay's liability for a capital lease would be reduced periodically by the

A. Minimum lease payment less the portion of the minimum lease payment allocable to interest.
B. Minimum lease payment plus the amortization of the related asset.
C. Minimum lease payment less the amortization of the related asset.
D. Minimum lease payment.

Sales Type Leases, International

AICPA.901126FAR-TH-FA

802. In a lease that is recorded as a sales-type lease by the lessor, interest revenue

A. Should be recognized in full as revenue at the lease's inception.
B. Should be recognized over the period of the lease using the straight-line method.
C. Should be recognized over the period of the lease using the effective interest method.
D. Does not arise.

AICPA.911133FAR-P1-FA

803. On December 31, 20X5, Day Co. leased a new machine from Parr with the following pertinent information:

Lease Term	6 Years
Annual rental payable at beginning of each year	$50,000
Useful life of machine	8 years
Day's incremental borrowing rate	15%
Implicit interest rate in lease (known by Day)	12%
Present value of an annuity of one in advance for six periods at:	
12%	4.61
15%	4.35

The lease is not renewable, and the machine reverts to Parr at the termination of the lease. The cost of the machine on Parr's accounting records is $375,500. At the beginning of the lease term, Day should record a lease liability of

A. $375,500.
B. $230,500.
C. $217,500.
D. $0.

AICPA.900533FAR-P1-FA

804. On December 31, Year 1, Ball Co. leased a machine from Cook for a 10-year period expiring December 30, Year 10.

Annual payments of $100,000 are due on December 31. The first payment was made on December 31, Year 1, and the second payment was made on December 31, Year 2.

The present value at the inception of the lease for the 10 lease payments discounted at 10% was $676,000. The lease is appropriately accounted for as a capital lease by Ball.

In its December 31, Year 2 balance sheet, Ball should report a lease liability of

A. $643,600.
B. $608,400.
C. $533,600.
D. $518,400.

AICPA.921133FAR-P1-FA

805. On December 29, 20X4, Action Corp. signed a 7-year capital lease for an airplane to transport its sports team around the country. The airplane's fair value was $841,500. Action made the first annual lease payment of $153,000 on December 31, 20X4. Action's incremental borrowing rate was 12%, and the interest rate implicit in the lease, which was known by Action, was 9%.

The following are the rounded present value factors for an annuity due:

| 9% for 7 years | 5.5 |
| 12% for 7 years | 5.1 |

What amount should Action report as capital lease liability in its December 31, 20X4 balance sheet?

A. $841,500
B. $780,300
C. $688,500
D. $627,300

AICPA.951112FAR-FA

806. A 6-year capital lease entered into on December 31, 20X5 specified equal minimum annual lease payments due on December 31 of each year. The first minimum annual lease payment, paid on December 31, 20X5, consists of which of the following?

	Interest Expense	Lease Liability
A.	Yes	Yes
B.	Yes	No
C.	No	Yes
D.	No	No

Additional Aspects of Capital Leases

AICPA.931139FAR-P1-FA

807. Neal Corp. entered into a 9-year capital lease on a warehouse on December 31, 2003.

Lease payments of $52,000, which includes real estate taxes of $2,000, are due annually, beginning on December 31, 20X4 and every December 31 thereafter. Neal does not know the interest rate implicit in the lease; Neal's incremental borrowing rate is 9%. The rounded present value of an ordinary annuity for 9 years at 9% is 5.6.

What amount should Neal report as capitalized lease liability at December 31, 20X3?

A. $280,000
B. $291,200
C. $450,000
D. $468,000

AICPA.901133FAR-P1-FA

808. Winn Co. manufactures equipment that is sold or leased. On December 31, 20X5, Winn leased equipment to Bart for a 5-year period ending December 31, 201X, at which date ownership of the leased asset transferred to Bart.

Equal payments under the lease were $22,000 (including $2,000 executory costs) and were due on December 31 of each year.

The first payment was made on December 31, 20X5. Collectability of the remaining lease payments was reasonably assured, and Winn had no material cost uncertainties. The normal sales price of the equipment was $77,000, and cost was $60,000.

For the year ending December 31, 20X5, what amount of income should Winn realize from the lease transaction?

A. $17,000
B. $22,000
C. $23,000
D. $33,000

Depreciation, BPO, and Residuals

assess.AICPA.FAR.deprec.bpo-0009

809. On January 1 of the current year, Tree Co. enters into a five-year lease agreement for production equipment. The lease requires Tree to pay $12,500 per year in lease payments. At the end of the five-year lease term, Tree can purchase the equipment for $30,000. The fair value of the equipment is $75,000. The estimated useful life of the equipment is 10 years. The present value of the lease payments is $50,000. The present value of the purchase option is $20,000. Tree's controller believes the purchase option price is sufficiently below the expected fair value of the equipment at the date the option becomes exercisable to reasonably ensure its exercise. Tree would normally depreciate equipment of this type using the straight-line method. What amount is the carrying value of the asset related to this lease at December 31 of the current year?

A. $40,000
B. $45,000
C. $56,000
D. $63,000

AICPA.920533FAR-TH-FA

810. For a capital lease, the amount recorded initially by the lessee as a liability should normally

A. Exceed the total of the minimum lease payments.

B. Exceed the present value of the minimum lease payments at the beginning of the lease.

C. Equal the total of the minimum lease payments.

D. Equal the present value of the minimum lease payments at the beginning of the lease.

AICPA.941120FAR-FA

811. At the inception of a capital lease, the guaranteed residual value should be

A. Included as part of minimum lease payments at present value.

B. Included as part of minimum lease payments at future value.

C. Included as part of minimum lease payments only to the extent that guaranteed residual value is expected to exceed estimated residual value.

D. Excluded from minimum lease payments.

AICPA.020502FAR-FA

812. Douglas Co. leased machinery with an economic useful life of 6 years. For tax purposes, the depreciable life is 7 years. The lease is for 5 years, and Douglas can purchase the machinery at fair value at the end of the lease.

What is the depreciable life of the leased machinery for financial reporting?

A. Zero

B. 5 years

C. 6 years

D. 7 years

Capital Lease Examples

AICPA.921134FAR-P1-FA

813. On December 30, 2003, Ames Co. leased equipment under a capital lease for 10 years.

It contracted to pay $40,000 annual rent on December 31, 2003 and on December 31 of each of the next 9 years. The capital lease liability was recorded at $270,000 on December 30, 2003 before the first payment. The equipment's useful life is 12 years, and the interest rate implicit in the lease is 10%. Ames uses the straight-line method to depreciate all equipment.

In recording the December 31, 2004 payment, by what amount should Ames reduce the capital lease liability?

A. $27,000

B. $23,000

C. $22,500

D. $17,000

AICPA.911155FAR-P1-FA

814. On January 1, 20X5, Moul Mining Co. (lessee) entered into a 5-year lease for drilling equipment. Moul accounted for the acquisition as a capital lease for $120,000, which included a $5,000 bargain purchase option.

Moul expected to exercise the bargain purchase option at the end of the lease. Moul estimated that the equipment's fair value will be $10,000 at the end of its 8-year life. Moul regularly uses straight-line depreciation on similar equipment.

For the year ending December 31, 20X5, what amount should Moul recognize as depreciation expense on the leased asset?

A. $13,750

B. $15,000

C. $23,000

D. $24,000

AICPA.920534FAR-P1-FA

815. Robbins, Inc. leased a machine from Ready Leasing Co. The lease qualifies as a capital lease and requires 10 annual payments of $10,000 beginning immediately.

The lease specifies an interest rate of 12% and a purchase option of $10,000 at the end of the tenth year, even though the machine's estimated value on that date is $20,000. Robbins' incremental borrowing rate is 14%.

The present value of an annuity due of $1 at:

12% for 10 years is 6.328
14% for 10 years is 5.946

The present value of $1 at:

12% for 10 years is .322
14% for 10 years is .270

What amount should Robbins record as lease liability at the beginning of the lease term?

A. $62,160

B. $64,860

C. $66,500

D. $69,720

AICPA.921104FAR-P1-FA

816. On December 30, 2004, Rafferty Corp. leased equipment under a capital lease. Annual lease payments of $20,000 are due December 31 for 10 years.

The equipment's useful life is 10 years, and the interest rate implicit in the lease is 10%. The capital lease obligation was recorded on December 30, 2004 at $135,000, and the first lease payment was made on that date.

What amount should Rafferty include in current liabilities for this capital lease in its December 31, 2004 balance sheet?

A. $6,500
B. $8,500
C. $11,500
D. $20,000

AICPA.083756FAR-SIM

817. An asset with a market value of $100,000 is leased on 1/1/X1. The lease is a capital lease for both parties. Five annual lease payments are due each December 31 beginning 12/31/X1. The unguaranteed residual value on 12/31/X5, the last day of the lease term, is estimated at $40,000. The lessor's implicit interest rate is 8%. Compute the lessor's net lease receivable immediately after the first lease payment is received. Present value factors for 5 years at 8% are: 3.99271 and 0.68058.

A. $112,908
B. $57,073
C. $89,773
D. $92,000

Sale Leasebacks and Disclosures

AICPA.921135FAR-P1-FA

818. On June 30, 2004, Lang Co. sold equipment with an estimated useful life of 11 years and immediately leased it back for 10 years. The equipment's carrying amount was $450,000; the sales price was $430,000; and the present value of the lease payments, which is equal to the fair value of the equipment, was $465,000. In its June 30, 2004 balance sheet, what amount should Lang report as deferred loss?

A. $35,000
B. $20,000
C. $15,000
D. $0

AICPA.931142FAR-P1-FA

819. On July 1, 2003, South Co. entered into a 10-year operating lease for a warehouse facility.

The annual minimum lease payments are $100,000. In addition to the base rent, South pays a monthly allocation of the building's operating expenses, which amounted to $20,000 for the year ending June 30, 2004.

In the notes to South's June 30, 2004 financial statements, what amounts of subsequent years' lease payments should be disclosed?

A. $100,000 per annum for each of the next 5 years and $500,000 in the aggregate
B. $120,000 per annum for each of the next 5 years and $600,000 in the aggregate
C. $100,000 per annum for each of the next 5 years and $900,000 in the aggregate
D. $120,000 per annum for each of the next 5 years and $1,080,000 in the aggregate

AICPA.920532FAR-TH-FA

820. Rig Co. sold its factory at a gain and simultaneously leased it back for 10 years. The factory's remaining economic life is 20 years. The lease was reported as an operating lease.

At the time of sale, Rig should report the gain as

A. Part of income from continuing operations.
B. An asset valuation allowance.
C. A separate component of stockholders' equity.
D. A deferred credit.

AICPA.901124FAR-TH-FA

821. Able sold its headquarters building at a gain and simultaneously leased back the building. The lease was reported as a capital lease.

At the time of sale, the gain should be reported as

A. Operating income.
B. A gain, net of income tax.
C. A separate component of stockholders' equity.
D. An asset valuation allowance.

AICPA.930531FAR-P1-FA

822. On December 31, 2004, Dirk Corp. sold Smith Co. two airplanes and simultaneously leased them back. Additional information pertaining to the sale-leasebacks follows:

	Plane #1	Plane #2
Sales price	$600,000	$1,000,000
Carrying amount, 12/31/04	$100,000	$550,000
Remaining useful life, 12/31/04	10 years	35 years
Lease term	8 years	3 years
Annual lease payments	$100,000	$200,000

In its December 31, 2004 balance sheet, what amount should Dirk report as deferred gain on these transactions?

A. $950,000
B. $500,000
C. $450,000
D. $0

IV. State and Local Governments

Not-for-Profit Organizations

Introduction to Types of Not-For-Profit Entities and Standard Setting

AICPA.083787FAR-SIM

823. Nongovernmental not-for profit organizations that wish to follow generally accepted accounting principles in the preparation of their financial statements should follow

   A. FASB standards.
   B. GASB standards.
   C. Both FASB and GASB standards.
   D. Neither FASB nor GASB standards.

AICPA.083789FAR-SIM

824. Nongovernmental not-for-profit organizations are required to report their financial statements on

   A. A current financial resources measurement focus.
   B. An economic resources measurement focus.
   C. A cash measurement focus.
   D. None of the above.

AICPA.083791FAR-SIM

825. The primary standards-setting body for a public museum that receives the majority of its funding from local property taxes is the

   A. American Institute of CPAs (AICPA).
   B. Financial Accounting Standards Board (FASB).
   C. Government Accountability Office (GAO).
   D. Governmental Accounting Standards Board (GASB).

Financial Reporting

AICPA.0605231FAR-AR

826. An unrestricted cash contribution should be reported in a nongovernmental not-for-profit organization's Statement of Cash Flows as an inflow from

   A. Operating Activities.
   B. Investing Activities.
   C. Financing Activities.
   D. Capital and Related Financing Activities.

AICPA.060604FAR

827. A voluntary health and welfare organization received a $700,000 permanent endowment during the year. The donor stipulated that the income and investment appreciation be used to maintain its senior center. The endowment fund reported a net investment appreciation of $80,000 and investment income of $50,000. The organization spent $60,000 to maintain its senior center during the year.

What amount of change in temporarily restricted net assets should the organization report?

   A. $50,000
   B. $70,000
   C. $130,000
   D. $770,000

AICPA.060609FAR

828. A nongovernmental not-for-profit organization borrowed $5,000, which it used to purchase a truck. In which section of the organization's Statement of Cash Flows should the transaction be reported?

   A. In-cash inflow and cash outflow from investing activities
   B. In-cash inflow and cash outflow from financing activities
   C. In-cash inflow from financing activities and cash outflow from investing activities
   D. In-cash inflow from operating activities and cash outflow from investing activities

AICPA.060607FAR

829. Which of the following assets of a nongovernmental not-for-profit charitable organization must be depreciated?

   A. A freezer costing $150,000 for storing food for the soup kitchen
   B. Building costs of $500,000 for construction in progress for senior citizen housing
   C. Land valued at $1 million being used as the site of the new senior citizen home
   D. A bulk purchase of $20,000 of linens for its nursing home

AICPA.090820FAR

830. Arkin Corp. is a nongovernmental not-for-profit organization involved in research. Arkin's Statement of Functional Expenses should classify which of the following as support services?

   A. Salaries of staff researchers involved in research
   B. Salaries of fund-raisers for funds used in research
   C. Cost of equipment involved in research
   D. Cost of laboratory supplies used in research

Donations, Pledges, Contributions, and Net Assets

AICPA.130701FAR

831. Which of the following types of information would be included in total net assets in the statement of financial position for a nongovernmental not-for-profit organization?

   A. Total current net assets and total other assets.
   B. Total current assets and restricted assets.
   C. Unrestricted net assets, temporarily restricted net assets, and permanently restricted net assets.
   D. Unrestricted net assets, restricted net assets, and total current assets.

AICPA.090142FAR-SIM

832. Which of the following contributions would not have to be reported as an asset on the Statement of Financial Position of a not-for-profit organization?

   A. Land was donated to the Friends of the Forest Society for conversion into a nature trail.
   B. The original courthouse was donated to the Historical Preservation Society, which is converting the courthouse to a museum.
   C. An art collector donated a famous oil painting to a local nongovernmental art museum for display in its exhibit hall.
   D. None of the above donated assets would have to be reported on the statement of financial position of the not-for-profit organization.

AICPA.060610FAR

833. Janna Association, a nongovernmental not-for-profit organization, received a cash gift with the stipulation that the principal be held for at least 20 years.

   How should the cash gift be recorded?

   A. A temporarily restricted asset
   B. A permanently restricted asset
   C. An unrestricted asset
   D. A temporary liability

AICPA.110592FAR

834. A nongovernmental not-for-profit organization received a $2 million gift from a donor who specified it be used to create an endowment fund that would be invested in perpetuity. The income from the fund is to be used to support a specific program in the second year and beyond. An investment purchased with the gift earned $40,000 during the first year. At the end of the first year, the fair value of the investment was $2,010,000. What is the net effect on temporarily restricted net assets at year-end?

   A. $0
   B. $10,000 increase
   C. $40,000 increase
   D. $50,000 increase

AICPA.090819FAR

835. How should a nongovernmental not-for-profit organization report depreciation expense in its Statement of Activities?

   A. It should **not** be included.
   B. It should be included as a decrease in unrestricted net assets.
   C. It should be included as an increase in temporarily restricted net assets.
   D. It should be reclassified from unrestricted net assets to temporarily restricted net assets, depending on donor-imposed restrictions on the assets.

Special Issues—Recent Developments

AICPA.130710FAR

836. At which of the following amounts should a nongovernmental not-for-profit organization report investments in debt securities?

   A. Potential proceeds from liquidation sale.
   B. Discounted expected future cash flows.
   C. Quoted market prices.
   D. Historical cost.

AICPA.130709FAR

837. How should a nongovernmental not-for-profit organization classify gains and losses on investments purchased with permanently restricted assets?

   A. Gains may **not** be netted against losses in the statement of activities.
   B. Gains and losses can only be reported net of expenses in the statement of activities.
   C. Unless explicitly restricted by donor or law, gains and losses should be reported in the statement of activities as increases or decreases in unrestricted net assets.
   D. Unless explicitly restricted by donor or law, gains and losses should be reported in the statement of activities as increases or decreases in permanently restricted net assets.

AICPA.090141FAR-SIM

838. Investments in equity securities that have a readily determinable market value and all debt securities of a not-for-profit organization are reported at

   A. The lower of cost or market.
   B. Amortized cost.
   C. Fair value.
   D. Cost.

AICPA.101169FAR

839. A nongovernmental not-for-profit organization received the following donations of corporate stock during the year:

	Donation 1	Donation 2
Number of shares	2,000	3,000
Adjusted basis	$8,000	$5,500
Fair value at time of donation	8,500	6,000
Fair value at year-end	10,000	4,000

What net value of investments will the organization report at the end of the year?

A. $12,000
B. $13,500
C. $14,000
D. $14,500

AICPA.090139FAR-SIM

840. Which of the following terms is used to indicate that a donor provided a gift with explicit instructions that the gift is to be used for a specific purpose by the not-for-profit organization but the entire amount may be spent right away?

A. Board-designated net assets
B. Endowment assets
C. Permanently restricted net assets
D. Temporarily restricted net assets

State and Local Government Concepts

Introduction to Governmental Organizations

AICPA.083757FAR-SIM

841. Which of the following would not be considered a governmental or not-for-profit organization?

A. A church
B. A private foundation established for charitable purposes
C. A software company that sells educational software exclusively to public elementary schools
D. A public independent school district

AICPA.910551FAR-TH-AR

842. The primary authoritative body for determining the measurement focus and basis of accounting standards for governmental fund operating statements is the

A. Governmental Accounting Standards Board (GASB).
B. National Council on Governmental Accounting (NCGA).

C. Government Accounting and Auditing Committee of the AICPA (GAAC).
D. Financial Accounting Standards Board (FASB).

AICPA.083758FAR-SIM

843. Which of the following has the highest level of authority for setting GAAP for nongovernmental not-for-profit organizations?

A. GASB
B. FASB
C. FASAB
D. AICPA

AICPA.083759FAR-SIM

844. Which of the following sources of financial resources is unique to governmental entities?

A. Proceeds from bonds
B. Grant proceeds from the federal government
C. Charges for services
D. Proceeds from taxation

GASB Concept Statements

AICPA.130700FAR

845. Which of the following is the paramount objective of financial reporting by state and local governments?

A. Reliability
B. Consistency
C. Comparability
D. Accountability

AICPA.951159FAR-AR

846. Which event(s) is(are) supportive of interperiod equity as a financial reporting objective of a governmental unit?

I. A balanced budget is adopted.
II. Residual equity transfers out equal residual equity transfers in.

A. I only
B. II only
C. Both I and II
D. Neither I nor II

AICPA.110588FAR-SIM

847. The City of Palo Alto's Service Efforts and Accomplishments Report for Fiscal Year 2010 reported that the average response to fire calls within 8 minutes occurred on 90% of the fire calls in 2010. This rate met the benchmark target goal of 90%. According to GASB's conceptual framework, this information is classified as a measure of

A. Effort.
B. Output.

C. Outcome.
D. Efficiency.

AICPA.110585FAR-SIM
848. Which of the following is voluntary information within a general-purpose external financial report?

A. Basic financial statements
B. Notes to basic financial statements
C. Required supplemental information
D. Supplemental information

AICPA.921151FAR-TH-AR
849. Interperiod equity is an objective of financial reporting for governmental entities. According to the Governmental Accounting Standards Board, is interperiod equity fundamental to public administration, and is it a component of accountability?

	Fundamental to Public Administration	Component of Accountability
A.	Yes	No
B.	No	No
C.	No	Yes
D.	Yes	Yes

Fund Accounting

AICPA.951160FAR-AR
850. Fund accounting is used by governmental units with resources that must be

A. Composed of cash or cash equivalents.
B. Incorporated into combined or combining financial statements.
C. Segregated for the purpose of carrying on specific activities or attaining certain objectives.
D. Segregated physically according to various objectives.

AICPA.083760FAR-SIM
851. Which of the following funds is not a fiduciary fund type?

A. Police and fire pension trust fund
B. Motor pool fund
C. Historical society private-purpose trust fund
D. County and city tax collection fund

AICPA.120647FAR
852. Kenn City obtained a municipal landfill and passed a local ordinance that required the city to operate the landfill so that the costs of operating the landfill, as well as the capital costs, are to be recovered with charges to customers. Which of the following funds

should Kenn City use to report the activities of the landfill?

A. Enterprise
B. Permanent
C. Special revenue
D. Internal service

AICPA.130705FAR
853. Which of the following local government funds uses the accrual basis of accounting?

A. Enterprise
B. Debt service
C. Capital projects
D. Special revenue

AICPA.120645FAR
854. Which of the following funds would be reported as a fiduciary fund in Pine City's financial statements?

A. Special revenue
B. Permanent
C. Private-purpose trust
D. Internal service

Measurement Focus Basis of Accounting

AICPA.130703FAR
855. How should a city's general fund report the acquisition of a new police car in its governmental fund statement of revenues, expenditures and changes in fund balances?

A. Noncurrent asset
B. Expenditure
C. Expense
D. Property, plant, and equipment

AICPA.931154FAR-TH-AR
856. Which of the following funds of a governmental unit uses the modified accrual basis of accounting?

A. Internal service funds
B. Enterprise funds
C. Special revenue funds
D. Nonexpendable trust funds

AICPA.950551FAR-AR
857. For governmental fund types, which item is considered the primary measurement focus?

A. Income determination
B. Flows and balances of financial resources
C. Capital maintenance
D. Cash flows and balances

AICPA.941103FAR-AR

858. The orientation of accounting and reporting for all proprietary funds of governmental units is

A. Income determination.
B. Project.
C. Flow of funds.
D. Program.

AICPA.930555FAR-TH-AR

859. Which of the following funds of a governmental unit recognizes revenues in the accounting period in which they become available and measurable?

	General Fund	Enterprise Fund
A.	Yes	No
B.	No	Yes
C.	Yes	Yes
D.	No	No

Budgetary Accounting

AICPA.900554FAR-TH-AR

860. Todd City formally integrates budgetary accounts into its general fund. Todd uses an internal service fund to account for the operations of its data processing center, which provides services to Todd's other governmental units.

During the year ended December 31, Year 1, Todd received a state grant to buy a bus, and an additional grant for bus operation in Year 1. In Year 1, only 90% of the capital grant was used for the bus purchase, but 100% of the operating grant was disbursed.

Todd has incurred the following long-term obligations:

1. General obligation bonds issued for the water and sewer fund that will service the debt.
2. Revenue bonds to be repaid from admission fees collected from users of the municipal recreation center.

These bonds are expected to be paid from enterprise funds, and secured by Todd's full faith, credit, and taxing power as further assurance that the obligations will be paid.

Todd's Year 1 expenditures from the general fund include payments for structural alterations to a firehouse and furniture for the mayor's office.

When Todd records its annual budget, which of the following control accounts indicates the amount of the authorized spending limitation for the year ending December 31, Year 1?

A. Reserved for appropriations
B. Appropriations
C. Reserved for encumbrances
D. Encumbrances

AICPA.101176FAR

861. Assuming no outstanding encumbrances at year's end, closing entries for which of the following situations would increase the unassigned fund balance at year's end?

A. Actual revenues were **less** than estimated revenues.
B. Estimated revenues exceed actual appropriations.
C. Actual expenditures exceed appropriations.
D. Appropriations exceed actual expenditures.

AICPA.901157FAR-P2-AR

862. When Rolan County adopted its budget for the year ending June 30, Year 1, $20,000,000 was recorded for Estimated Revenues Control. Actual Revenues for the year ended June 30, Year 1 amounted to $17,000,000.

In closing the budgetary accounts at June 30, Year 1,

A. Revenues Control should be debited for $3,000,000.
B. Estimated Revenues Control should be debited for $3,000,000.
C. Revenues Control should be credited for $20,000,000.
D. Estimated Revenues Control should be credited for $20,000,000.

AICPA.120639FAR

863. On January 1, Fonk City approved the following general fund resources for the new fiscal period:

Property taxes	$5,000,000
Licenses and permits	400,000
Intergovernmental revenues	150,000
Transfers in from other funds	350,000

What amount should Fonk record as estimated revenues for the new fiscal year?

A. $5,400,000
B. $5,550,000
C. $5,750,000
D. $5,900,000

Encumbrance Accounting

AICPA.920523FAR-P2-AR

864. Park City uses encumbrance accounting and formally integrates its budget into the general fund's accounting records. For the year ending July 31, 2005, the following budget was adopted:

Estimated revenues	$30,000,000
Appropriations	27,000,000
Estimated transfer to debt service fund	900,000

When Park's budget is adopted and recorded, Park's budgetary fund balance would be a

- A. $3,000,000 credit balance.
- B. $3,000,000 debit balance.
- C. $2,100,000 credit balance.
- D. $2,100,000 debit balance.

AICPA.101177FAR

865. For state and local governmental units, generally accepted accounting principles typically require that encumbrances outstanding at year's end be reported as

- A. Expenditures.
- B. Assigned or committed fund balance.
- C. Deferred liabilities.
- D. Current liabilities.

AICPA.110594FAR

866. Encumbrances would not appear in which fund?

- A. Capital Projects.
- B. Special Revenue.
- C. General.
- D. Enterprise.

AICPA.101175FAR

867. Encumbrances outstanding at year's end in a state's general fund may be reported as a

- A. Liability in the general fund.
- B. Fund balance assigned in the general fund.
- C. Liability in the general long-term debt account group.
- D. Fund balance designation in the general fund.

Deferred Outflows and Deferred Inflows of Resources

AICPA.140406FAR-SIM

868. Taxes levied in the Debt Service Fund and due in the year 20X1 include $200,000 that is not expected to be collected within the first 60 days of the year 20X2. As of the end of year 20X1, the $200,000 would be reported as

- A. Revenue.
- B. A liability.
- C. A deferred inflow of resources.
- D. Another financing source.

AICPA.140409FAR-SIM

869. In Year 20X1 a local government levied $5,000,000 in special assessments. The assessments are due and payable in five equal installments at the beginning of each of the next five fiscal years, starting in year 20X2. Assume that all installments are collected four months (120 days) into the year that they are due. The Special Assessment Debt Service Fund would report revenues in year 20X2 in the amount of:

- A. $5,000,000
- B. $4,000,000
- C. $1,000,000
- D. $0

AICPA.140407FAR-SIM

870. In year 20X1 a local government levied $5,000,000 in special assessments. The assessments are due and payable in five equal installments at the beginning of each of the next five fiscal years, starting in year 20X2. Assume that all installments are collected four months (120 days) into the year that they are due. The Special Assessment Debt Service Fund would report revenue in year 20X1 in the amount of:

- A. $5,000,000
- B. $4,000,000
- C. $1,000,000
- D. $0

AICPA.140410FAR-SIM

871. In year 20X1 a local government levied $5,000,000 in special assessments. The assessments are due and payable in five equal installments at the beginning of each of the next five fiscal years, starting in year 20X2. Assume that all installments are collected four months (120 days) into the year that they are due. At the end of year 20X2, the Special Assessment Debt Service Fund would report the $4,000,000 remaining levy as:

- A. Revenues.
- B. Liabilities.
- C. Deferred inflow of resources.
- D. Deferred outflow of resources.

Net Position and Fund Balance

AICPA.101142FAR-SIM

872. Which of the following fund balance classifications is used for budgetary accounting but not for GAAP financial statement reporting?

A. Nonspendable Fund Balance.
B. Unreserved Fund Balance.
C. Committed Fund Balance.
D. Unassigned Fund Balance.

AICPA.101141FAR-SIM

873. As of the end of the fiscal year, a Capital Projects Fund has material balances of supplies inventory. Which fund balance classification would reflect the inventory of supplies?

A. Nonspendable.
B. Restricted.
C. Committed.
D. Assigned.

AICPA.101178FAR

874. At December 31, Year 1, Alto Township's committed appropriations that had not been expended in 2005 totaled $10,000. The commitment was made by the finance committee. These appropriations do not lapse at year-end. Alto reports on a calendar-year basis.

On its December 31, Year 1 Balance Sheet, the $10,000 should be reported as:

A. Vouchers Payable—prior year.
B. Deferred Expenditures.
C. Fund Balance Assigned.
D. Budgetary Fund balance—reserved for encumbrances.

AICPA.101143FAR-SIM

875. A Capital Projects Fund has outstanding encumbrances of $250,000 as of the end of the fiscal year. Assume that all resources in the Capital Projects Fund are considered to be committed due to the constraints established by the enabling legislation of the governing body of the government. How should the encumbrances be reported in the year-end external financial statements?

A. As a specific identifiable component of the restricted fund balance.
B. As a specific identifiable component of the committed fund balance.
C. As a specific identifiable component of the Assigned Fund balance.
D. The encumbrances would only be reported in the note disclosures.

AICPA.101140FAR-SIM

876. A Special Revenue Fund may report a positive amount in each of the following fund balance classifications *except:*

A. Restricted.
B. Committed.
C. Assigned.
D. Unassigned.

Governmental Funds

AICPA.083770FAR-SIM

877. Excel City received a donation of $400,000. The donor stipulated that the money be permanently invested, with the investment proceeds being used to provide funding for the community swimming pools. Which of the following best describes the reporting options for this transaction?

A. The city should record $400,000 as a capital contribution in a Permanent Fund.
B. The city should record $400,000 as revenue in a Permanent Fund.
C. The city should record $400,000 as another financing source in a Permanent Fund.
D. The city should record $400,000 as revenue in the General Fund.

AICPA.083771FAR-SIM

878. A local citizen donated land and an office complex to a city with the stipulation that net income from the office complex be used help finance the operations of a teenage alcohol and drug treatment center. At the time of donation, the property's fair market value was $800,000. The donor paid $500,000 for the land and house twenty years ago. The city spent $125,000 to upgrade the office complex. The city would capitalize the land and office complex in its permanent fund at:

A. $0
B. $500,000
C. $625,000
D. $925,000

AICPA.060601FAR

879. A Capital Projects Fund for a new city courthouse recorded a receivable of $300,000 for a state grant and a $450,000 transfer from the General Fund. What amount should be reported as revenue by the Capital Projects Fund?

A. $0
B. $300,000
C. $450,000
D. $750,000

AICPA.083769FAR-SIM

880. Excel City has $1,000,000 of 8%, 10-year general obligation bonds outstanding. The bonds were issue on October 1, 20X8 to finance construction of city park improvements. Interest is payable semiannually on October 1 and April 1. The bonds also require an annual principal payment of $100,000 each April 1. What amount of debt service expenditures should the government report in its Debt

Service Fund for the year ended December 31, 20X9?

A. $76,000
B. $80,000
C. $174,000
D. $176,000

Proprietary Funds

AICPA.900505FAR-P2-AR

881. Rock County has acquired equipment through a noncancelable lease-purchase agreement dated December 31, Year 1. This agreement requires no down payment and the following minimum lease payments:

December 31	Principal	Interest	Total
Year 2	$50,000	$15,000	$65,000
Year 3	$50,000	10,000	60,000
Year 4	$50,000	5,000	55,000

If the equipment is used in Enterprise Fund operations and the lease payments are to be financed with Enterprise Fund revenues, what account should be debited for $150,000 in the Enterprise Fund at inception of the lease?

A. Expenses Control.
B. Expenditures Control.
C. Other Financing Sources Control.
D. Equipment.

AICPA.900553FAR-TH-AR

882. Todd City formally integrates budgetary accounts into its General Fund. Todd uses an Internal Service Fund to account for the operations of its data processing center, which provides services to Todd's other governmental units.

During the year ended December 31, Year 1, Todd received a state grant to buy a bus and an additional grant for bus operation in Year 1. In Year 1, only 90% of the capital grant was used for the bus purchase, but 100% of the operating grant was disbursed.

Todd has incurred the following long-term obligations:

1. General obligation bonds issued for the Water and Sewer Fund, which will service the debt.
2. Revenue bonds to be repaid from admission fees collected from users of the municipal recreation center.

These bonds are expected to be paid from Enterprise Funds, and secured by Todd's full faith, credit, and taxing power as further assurance that the obligations will be paid.

Todd's Year 1 expenditures from the General Fund include payments for structural alterations to a firehouse and furniture for the mayor's office.

Which of Todd's long-term obligations should be accounted for in the general fund?

	General Obligation Bonds	Revenue Bonds
A.	Yes	Yes
B.	Yes	No
C.	No	Yes
D.	No	No

AICPA.120646FAR

883. At the beginning of the current year, Paxx County's enterprise fund had a $125,000 balance for accrued compensated absences. At the end of the year, the balance was $150,000. During the year, Paxx paid $400,000 for compensated absences. What amount of compensated absences expense should Paxx County's enterprise fund report for the year?

A. $375,000
B. $400,000
C. $425,000
D. $550,000

AICPA.901141FAR-P2-AR

884. Maple Township issued the following bonds during the year ended June 30, Year 1:

Bond issued for the Garbage Collection Enterprise Fund that will service the debt	$500,000
Revenue bonds to be repaid from admission fees collected by the Township Zoo Enterprise Fund	350,000

What amount of these bonds should be accounted for in Maple's Proprietary Funds?

A. $0
B. $350,000
C. $500,000
D. $850,000

AICPA.130704FAR

885. Which of the following statements is the most significant characteristic in determining the classification of an enterprise fund?

A. The predominant customer is the primary government.
B. The pricing policies of the activity establish fees and charges designed to recover its cost.

C. The activity is financed by debt that is secured partially by a pledge of the net revenues from fees and charges of the activity.

D. Laws or regulations require that the activity's costs of providing services including capital costs be recovered with taxes or similar revenues.

Fiduciary Funds

AICPA.060240FAR-AR

886. The City of New Hope Rotary Club, a private, not-for-profit organization, recently ended a fund drive that raised $500,000 to be used as a scholarship fund.

The $500,000 is to be used to create an endowment that will be invested and retained in perpetuity and the earnings used to provide college scholarships to outstanding local high school graduates selected by the Rotary Club. The City has agreed to manage the investment and disbursement of these monies on behalf of the Rotary Club.

The City should account for the $500,000 corpus of the endowment in a(n):

A. Agency Fund.
B. Private-Purpose Trust Fund.
C. Permanent Fund.
D. Special Revenue Fund.

AICPA.120641FAR

887. A government makes a contribution to its pension plan in the amount of $10,000 for year 1. The actuarially-determined annual required contribution for year 1 was $13,500. The pension plan paid benefits of $8,200 and refunded employee contributions of $800 for year 1. What is the pension expenditure for the general fund for year 1?

A. $8,200
B. $9,000
C. $10,000
D. $13,500

AICPA.090815FAR

888. Harland County received a $2,000,000 capital grant to be equally distributed among its five municipalities. The grant is to finance the construction of capital assets. Harland had no administrative or direct financial involvement in the construction. In which fund should Harland record the receipt of cash?

A. Agency Fund.
B. General Fund.
C. Special Revenue Fund.
D. Private-Purpose Trust Fund.

AICPA.060237FAR-AR

889. The City of Macon maintains a defined contribution pension plan for its employees. During the year, the city contributed $5,000,000 to the plan, which represented 100% of its required contribution for the year. City employees contributed $1,800,000 to the plan. In addition, plan assets earned $4,500,000.

What amount should the City report as Additions in its Pension Trust Fund?

A. $11,300,000
B. $9,500,000
C. $6,800,000
D. $4,500,000

AICPA.083774FAR-SIM

890. In a Tax Agency Fund, revenues must be recognized:

A. When measurable and available.
B. On the cash basis.
C. To extent fund expenditures.
D. None of the above. Revenues are not reported in Agency Funds.

Format and Content of Comprehensive Annual Financial Report (CAFR)

The Comprehensive Annual Financial Report

AICPA.090135FAR-SIM

891. The introductory section of a CAFR typically includes all of the following except:

A. The letter of transmittal.
B. An organizational chart.
C. The independent auditor's opinion.
D. The table of contents.

AICPA.060244FAR-AR

892. The Comprehensive Annual Financial Report (CAFR) of a state or local governmental unit should include fund-level statements for which of the following fund categories:

	Governmental Funds	Proprietary Funds	Fiduciary Funds
A.	No	No	No
B.	Yes	Yes	No
C.	Yes	No	No
D.	Yes	Yes	Yes

AICPA.090810FAR

893. Nack City received a donation of a valuable painting. Nack planned to add the painting to its collection and display it in the protected exhibition area of City Hall. Nack had a policy that if such donated art works were sold, the

proceeds would be used to acquire other items for its collections. Which of the following would be correct regarding the donated painting?

A. It must be capitalized and depreciated.

B. It must be capitalized but **not** depreciated.

C. It may be capitalized, but it is **not** required, and it must be depreciated.

D. It may be capitalized, but it is **not** required, and depreciation is **not** required.

AICPA.101171FAR

894. Which of the following statements are required to be presented for special-purpose governments engaged only in business-type activities (such as utilities)?

A. Statement of Net Position only.

B. Management's Discussion and Analysis (MD&A) and Required Supplementary Information (RSI) only.

C. The financial statements required for Governmental Funds, including MD&A.

D. The financial statements required for Enterprise Funds, including MD&A and RSI.

AICPA.110590FAR

895. Jonn City entered into a capital lease for equipment during the year. How should the asset obtained through the lease be reported in Jonn City's government-wide Statement of Net Position?

A. General Capital Asset.

B. Other Financing Use.

C. Expenditure.

D. Not reported.

Determining the Financial Reporting Entity

AICPA.090133FAR-SIM

896. The Metro Transportation Authority is governed by a seven-member board. Four of the board members are appointed by the town of Metro and the remaining three are appointed by the governing board of Metro County. Neither the town nor the county share in any profits, nor are they required to fund any deficits, of the Authority. The town, however, does approve the Authority's proposed budget. The county may make budgetary recommendations to the Authority, but they are not required to approve the proposed budget. The Authority should be reported as:

A. A jointly governed organization by both the town and the county.

B. Discrete component units of both the town and the county.

C. A blended component unit of the town.

D. A discretely presented component unit of the town.

AICPA.090132FAR-SIM

897. For general purpose external financial reporting, discrete component unit information:

A. Is not presented.

B. Is included in the government-wide statements only.

C. Is included in the fund financial statements only.

D. Is included in both the government-wide and the fund financial statements.

AICPA.110593FAR

898. If a city government is the primary reporting entity, which of the following is an acceptable method to present component units in its combined financial statements?

A. Consolidation.

B. Cost method.

C. Discrete presentation.

D. Government-wide presentation.

AICPA.090134FAR-SIM

899. The Excel City School District has a separate elected governing body that administers the public school system. The district's budget must be approved by the city council of Excel City. The school district's financial activity should be reported in the City's financial statements by:

A. Discrete presentation.

B. Blending.

C. Footnote.

D. Not at all.

Major Funds and Fund-Level Reporting

AICPA.021107FAR-AR

900. Nox City reported a $25,000 net increase in the fund balances for total Governmental Funds. Nox also reported an increase in Net Position for the following funds:

Motor pool Internal Service Fund	$9,000
Water Enterprise Fund	12,000
Employee pension fund	7,000

The motor pool Internal Service Fund provides service to the General Fund departments. What amount should Nox report as the Change in Net Position for governmental activities?

A. $25,000

B. $34,000

C. $41,000

D. $46,000

AICPA.021106FAR-AR

901. Tree City reported a $1,500 net increase in the fund balance for Governmental Funds. During the year, Tree purchased general capital assets totaling $9,000 and recorded a depreciation expense of $3,000.

    What amount should Tree report as the Change in Net Position for governmental activities in Tree's Statement of Activities?

    A. ($4,500)
    B. $1,500
    C. $7,500
    D. $10,500

AICPA.021109FAR-AR

902. According to GASB 34, Basic Financial Statements—and Management's Discussion and Analysis—for State and Local Governments, certain budgetary schedules require supplementary information.

    What is the minimum budgetary information required to be reported in those schedules?

    A. A schedule of unfavorable variances at the functional level.
    B. A schedule showing the final appropriations budget and actual expenditures on a budgetary basis.
    C. A schedule showing the original budget, the final appropriations budget, and actual inflows, outflows, and balances on a budgetary basis.
    D. A schedule showing the proposed budget, the approved budget, the final amended budget, actual inflows and outflows on a budgetary basis, and variances between budget and actual.

Typical Items and Specific Types of Transactions and Events

Interfund Transactions, Construction Projects, and Infrastructure

AICPA.140405FAR-SIM

903. If a local government reports eligible infrastructure assets using the modified approach,

    A. Maintenance and repair expenditures for the assets are capitalized.
    B. The assets are not being preserved at or above the established and disclosed condition level.

C. No depreciation expense is required to be recognized.
D. Complete condition assessments must be performed every year.

AICPA.090128FAR-SIM

904. A city's General Fund contributes $150,000 to its Debt Service Fund to meet upcoming debt service requirements for a general obligation serial bond. The General Fund should report this as a(n):

    A. Expenditure of $150,000.
    B. Capital Contribution of $150,000.
    C. Operating Transfer of $150,000.
    D. Interfund Loan of $150,000.

AICPA.140403FAR-SIM

905. Which of the following capital assets are least likely to be considered infrastructure assets of a local government?

    A. Roads.
    B. Buildings.
    C. Sewer system.
    D. Lighting system.

AICPA.901156FAR-TH-AR

906. On March 2, Year 1, Finch City issued 10-year general obligation bonds at face amount, with interest payable March 1 and September 1.

    The proceeds were to be used to finance the construction of a civic center over the period April 1, Year 1, to March 31, Year 2.

    During the fiscal year ended June 30, Year 1, no resources had been provided to the Debt Service Fund for the payment of principal and interest.

    The liability for the general obligation bonds should be recorded in the:

    A. General Fund.
    B. Capital Projects Fund.
    C. Government-wide financial statements.
    D. Debt Service Fund.

AICPA.101219FAR-SIM

907. In 2011, Kameron City received $4,000,000 from the sale of general obligation bonds to be used for major street and bridge renovations. $3,000,000 is expected to be spent in 2011, and the remainder will be spent in 2012. When will Kameron report bond proceeds as an other financing source in its Capital Projects Fund?

    A. $4,000,000 in 2011.
    B. $4,000,000 in 2012.
    C. $3,000,000 in 2011 and $1,000,000 in 2012.
    D. $0; the bond proceeds are not considered to be an other financing source.

Long-Term Liabilities Other Than Bonded Debt

AICPA.083779FAR-SIM

908. A government has the following debt:

1. Capital lease liabilities that mature in more than one year (General Fund department leases)—$2,000,000.
2. Net pension liability associated with general government employees—$4,000,000.
3. General government bonds that mature in the next fiscal year—$14,000,000.

What amount of debt should be reported in the long-term liabilities in the government-wide financial positions?

A. $2,000,000
B. $6,000,000
C. $18,000,000
D. $20,000,000

AICPA.083781FAR-SIM

909. Excel City's Water Utility Enterprise Fund issues $10,000,000 in 20-year serial revenue bonds to finance a major expansion of one of its water treatment plants. $500,000 in bonds mature each year. As a result of this transaction, the year-end long-term liability in the governmental activities section of the government-wide financial statements accounts will reflect:

A. $0.
B. An increase of $9,500,000.
C. An increase of $10,000,000.
D. A decrease of $500,000.

AICPA.101242FAR-SIM

910. Big City recently lost a lawsuit relating to an incident involving one of their police officers. A judgment was rendered against the city, and, immediately prior to the current fiscal year-end, the city was ordered to pay a total of $500,000. $100,000 is due immediately and the remaining is to be paid in installments of $100,000 per year for an additional four years. How will the external financial statements of the city be affected in the year the court case was settled?

A. The General Fund statements should report both expenditures and a claims and judgments liability of $500,000.
B. The General Long-Term Liabilities accounts should report a $500,000 liability.
C. The General Fund statements should report expenditures and a current liability of $100,000, and the Agency Fund should report a liability of $400,000.

D. The General Fund statements should report expenditures and a current liability of $100,000, and the government-wide statements should report a long-term liability of the present value of the $400,000.

Terminology and Non-Exchange Transactions

AICPA.900559FAR-TH-AR

911. Fixed assets donated to a governmental unit should be recorded:

A. As a memorandum entry only.
B. At the donor's carrying amount.
C. At estimated fair value when received.
D. At the lower of donor's carrying amount or estimated fair value when received.

AICPA.083765FAR-SIM

912. In which fund would Salaries Expense appear?

A. Water Utility Fund.
B. General Fund.
C. Pension Trust Fund.
D. Capital Projects Fund.

AICPA.083763FAR-SIM

913. Which account should Excel City credit when it issues a purchase order for supplies?

A. Appropriations Control.
B. Encumbrance Control.
C. Vouchers Payable.
D. Budgetary Fund Balance.

AICPA.060231FAR-AR

914. During the current year, Knoxx County levied property taxes of $2,000,000, of which 1% is expected to be uncollectible. The following amounts were collected during the current year:

Prior year taxes collected within 60 days of the current year	$ 50,000
Prior year taxes collected between 60 and 90 days into the current year	120,000
Current taxes collected in the current year	1,800,000
Current taxes collected within the first 60 days of the subsequent year	80,000

What amount of property tax revenue should Knoxx County report in its entity-wide Statement of Activities?

A. $1,800,000
B. $1,970,000
C. $1,980,000
D. $2,000,000

Special Items—Recent Developments

AICPA.083783FAR-SIM

915. In January 2010, Blue County acquired the right to draw water from a lake on the property of a privately owned ranch in exchange for a cash payment of $20 million. The annual volume of water that can be drawn is unlimited. The county's rights under the contract expire in 10 years; however, the contact provides the opportunity to renew the water rights for an additional 10 years for an additional payment of $10 million, if the county chooses . The county believes that it will request the renewal. The county expects the other party to agree to the renewal since the ranch is a significant user of the county's water supply and is a major employer of Blue County residents. The county operates on a calendar fiscal year. The county should recognize in its 2010 Government-Wide Financial Statements an annual amortization rate of:

   A. $20 million in its Statement of Activities.
   B. $2 million in its Statement of Activities.
   C. $1.5 million in its Statement of Activities.
   D. $30 million in its Statement of Activities.

AICPA.083785FAR-SIM

916. A government has an investment derivative instrument that is considered effective. The fair value of this derivative instrument has increased by $100,000 in the current period. The change in fair value should be reported as:

   A. Investment Revenue in the Statement of Activities.
   B. Deferred Credit in the Statement of Net Position.
   C. Holding Gain in Fund Balance.
   D. Should not be reported.

AICPA.083782FAR-SIM

917. In January 2010, Red County acquired the right to draw water from a lake on the property of a privately owned ranch in exchange for a cash payment of $20 million. The annual volume of water that can be drawn is unlimited. The county's rights under the contract expire in 10 years (2020); however, the contact provides the opportunity to renew the water rights for an additional 10 years (to 2030) for no additional payment, subject to the mutual agreement of the two parties. The county believes that it will request the renewal. The county expects the other party to agree to the renewal since the ranch is a significant user of the county's water supply and is a major employer of Red County residents. The county operates on a calendar

fiscal year. The county should recognize in its 2010 Government-Wide Financial Statements:

   A. $20 million expense in its Statement of Activities.
   B. $10 million expense in its Statement of Activities.
   C. $2 million amortization expense in its Statement of Activities.
   D. $1 million amortization expense in its Statement of Activities.

AICPA.083784FAR-SIM

918. Small County's tax assessment department identified the need for new property tax assessment and billing software. A project task force composed of county staff was assembled to address this need. The following outlays were incurred related to the project in 2015:

1. Task force interviews with operators of the software and users of the information to determine the needs of the users, evaluation of system hardware requirements, assessment of current in-house information technology resources and evaluation of commercially available software packages, and issuing requests for proposals from vendors. Outlays: $1.5 million.
2. The county awards a contract in the amount of $14.5 million to a vendor to acquire a perpetual license to use its property tax software as modified to meet the County's needs. The vendor is responsible for the installation and modification of the software, while four county employees are dedicated to the project full time until its completion at an additional cost of $0.5 million.
3. Outlays for data entry and for training software users and operators is $0.6 million.

How much should Small County capitalize related to the outlays associated to the project?

   A. $15.6 million
   B. $14.5 million
   C. $15 million
   D. $16.5 million

AICPA.083786FAR-SIM

919. Which of the following is not one of the five information classification sections that must be included in the Statistical Section of the CAFR?

   A. Operating information.
   B. Demographics information.
   C. Revenue Capacity information.
   D. Fund Balance information.

Special Industries: Health Care and Colleges

Health Care Organizations

AICPA.060233FAR-AR

920. Terry, an auditor, is performing test work for a not-for-profit hospital. Listed below are components of the Statement of Operations:

Revenue relating to charity care	$100,000
Bad debt expense	70,000
Net assets released from restrictions and used for operations	50,000
Other revenue	80,000
Net patient service revenue (includes revenue related to charity care)	500,000

What amount would be reported as total revenues, gains, and other support on the Statement of Operations?

A. $460,000
B. $530,000
C. $580,000
D. $630,000

AICPA.951175FAR-AR

921. Which of the following should normally be considered ongoing or central transactions for a not-for-profit hospital?

I. Room and board fees from patients.
II. Recovery room fees.

A. Neither I nor II.
B. Both I and II.
C. II only.
D. I only.

AICPA.941128FAR-AR

922. Which of the following normally would be included in Other Operating Revenues of a governmental hospital?

	Revenues from Educational Programs	Unrestricted Gifts
A.	No	No
B.	No	Yes
C.	Yes	No
D.	Yes	Yes

AICPA.940560FAR-AR

923. Valley's community hospital normally includes proceeds from the sale of cafeteria meals in:

A. Deductions from Dietary Service Expenses.
B. Ancillary Service Revenues.
C. Patient Service Revenues.
D. Other Revenues.

AICPA.950560FAR-AR

924. In April Year 1, Delta Hospital purchased medicines from Field Pharmaceutical Co. at a cost of $5,000. However, Field notified Delta that the invoice was being canceled and that the medicines were being donated to Delta.

Delta should record this donation of medicines as

A. A memorandum entry only.
B. A $5,000 credit to nonoperating expenses.
C. A $5,000 credit to operating expenses.
D. Other operating revenue of $5,000.

Colleges and Universities

AICPA.090144FAR-SIM

925. A college has a June 30 fiscal year-end. Assume that tuition revenue for the summer session that begins June 1, 20X8 and ends August 31, 20X8 totals $270,000. Tuition is billed and is due at the beginning of the session term. How much revenue should be reported as of the fiscal year ended June 30, 20X8?

A. $270,000
B. $90,000
C. $180,000
D. $135,000

AICPA.101163FAR

926. How should state appropriations to a state university choosing to report as engaged only in business-type activities be reported in its Statement of Revenues, Expenses, and Changes in Net Position?

A. Operating Revenues.
B. Nonoperating Revenues.
C. Capital Contributions.
D. Other Financing Sources.

AICPA.060602FAR

927. During the year, Public College received the following:

1. An unrestricted $50,000 pledge to be paid the following year.
2. A $25,000 cash gift restricted for scholarships.
3. A notice from a recent graduate that the college is named as a beneficiary of $10,000 in that graduate's will.

What amount of contribution revenue should Public College report in its Statement of Activities?

A. $25,000
B. $35,000
C. $75,000
D. $85,000

Answers and Explanations

1. **Answer: D**

   The FASB is currently the rule-making body for GAAP. The Board has codified well over 100 Statements of Financial Accounting Standards, and Interpretations of those standards. The FASB is a private-sector body, the third such body serving as the entity that creates GAAP for U.S. businesses. The FASB has no authority to enforce GAAP, however.

2. **Answer: A**

   The FASB has no official connection with the U.S. government although the SEC, an agency of the federal government, can modify or rescind an accounting standard adopted by the FASB.

3. **Answer: C**

   The SEC requires that all registrants provide financial statements that comply with GAAP and will sanction firms and individuals involved in financial reporting that does not comply with GAAP.

4. **Answer: C**

   One of the objectives of the FASB in setting standards is to develop rules that are unbiased. FASB statements generally do not reflect any reporting bias.

   For example, the requirement to expense all research and development costs is uniform across all firms and does not favor one firm over another.

5. **Answer: D**

   The purpose of financial reporting is to provide information relevant to the decision making of investors and creditors.

   These individuals and firms make decisions about allocating resources across thousands of firms. Investment and credit decisions are the primary focus of financial reporting.

6. **Answer: C**

   The approach on this question is to first calculate the cash-based operating expenses. Cash-based operating expenses are $150,000. The next step is to adjust the cash-based expense for the prepaid and accrued expenses. Beginning of the year prepaid expenses were paid in the prior year, but the expense was incurred (or consumed) in the current year, and end of the year prepaid expenses were paid this

year but will be consumed next year. Therefore, you add the beginning of the year prepaid and subtract the end of the year prepaid expenses from the cash-based number.

Cash-based expenses will also be adjusted for the accrued expense. Beginning of the year accrued expenses were not paid last year, but were last year's expense item paid this year. End of the year accrued expenses were not paid this year, but are this year's expense paid next year. Therefore, you subtract beginning of the year accrued expenses and add end of the year accrued expenses to the cash-based number.

Cash-based operating expenses	$150,000
Add the beginning of the year prepaid expenses	10,000
Subtract the end of the year prepaid expenses	(15,000)
Subtract the beginning of the year accrued expenses	(5,000)
Add the end of the year accrued expenses	25,000
Accrual-based operating expenses	$165,000

7. **Answer: B**

   An increase in prepaid expenses indicates that more cash was paid than expensed ($5,000). An increase in accrued liabilities indicates that more expense was accrued than paid ($12,000). The reconciliation of operating expense to cash paid is: $100,000 + $5,000 – $12,000 = $93,000.

8. **Answer: A**

   Revenue under the cash basis equals the amount of cash collected. The decrease in accounts receivable is $5,000 ($20,000 – $15,000).

Gross cash sales	$40,000
Less returns and allowances	(2,000)
Plus gross credit sales	60,000
Less discounts	(3,000)
Plus decrease in accounts receivable (More cash was collected than was recorded as sales when accounts receivable decreases)	5,000
Equals cash collected	$100,000

9. **Answer: C**

   Supplies expense for 20X1 under the accrual method is: supplies expense = beginning supplies + purchases – ending supplies. If beginning supplies cannot be determined, then it is assumed to be zero and supplies expense is understated, causing 20X1 income to be overstated. However, total supplies expense for the entire life of the business is unaffected by the inability to determine beginning supplies for 20X1. Total supplies expense for the life of the business is total purchases less ending inventory in 20X1. These two amounts are determinable, and thus, owners' equity at the end of 20X1 can be determined.

10. **Answer: C**

The general rule to convert from cash to accrual is to add the beginning liability balances and subtract the ending liability balances; also, subtract beginning asset balances and add ending asset balances.

11. **Answer: B**

Collection on a note receivable from a related party is an investing activity. The company is lending money to the related party and lending is not a primary business activity—the fact that the loan is in the form of a note implies that it is interest bearing.

12. **Answer: A**

Revenues are inflows of economic resources. The purchase discounts would be netted against purchases, not sales. The recovery of accounts written off is not revenue, it is an adjustment to the allowance for uncollectible accounts. Therefore the total revenue reported should be $250,000.

13. **Answer: A**

Net income is revenues less expenses, or $80,000 − $50,000 − $10,000 = $20,000. The foreign currency translation adjustment is part of comprehensive income.

14. **Answer: B**

Changes and updates to the Codification are accomplished through Accounting Standards Updates (ASUs).

15. **Answer: D**

IFRS are not U.S. GAAP and thus are not included in the Codification.

16. **Answer: B**

The Codification includes all authoritative GAAP for nongovernmental entities.

17. **Answer: D**

The question is asking which of the terms captures predictive value. Predictive value along with confirmatory value is a component of relevance.

18. **Answer: D**

Comparability is the quality of information that enables users to identify similarities and differences between sets of information. For information to be comparable, it must be both relevant (make a difference to a user) and faithfully represented.

19. **Answer: A**

Recognition is the process of formally recording and reporting an item as one of the elements of financial statements. It is the strongest application an item can receive.

Footnote disclosure may report an item, but it does not include the item in an account balance. When an item is recognized, it affects an account balance reported in the financial statements. The item may not be separately listed, but it will be reflected in one of the accounts in the statements.

20. **Answer: A**

Interim reporting emphasizes timeliness over faithful representation. Interim reports are generally more aggregate and reflect estimates that are of a more approximate nature than those found in annual reports. The objective is to provide reasonable information in a timely fashion, rather than exact information. The cost to provide the latter would often be prohibitive on a quarterly basis.

21. **Answer: D**

Predictive value is one of the ingredients of relevance, one of the primary characteristics of accounting information. The other ingredient of relevance is confirmatory value.

Predictive value is not an ingredient of faithful representation. Faithful representation is the other primary characteristic of accounting information. Its three main ingredients are completeness, being free from material error, and neutrality.

22. **Answer: D**

Consolidated financial statements are an example of trying to account for the economic entity that comprises more than one legal entity, making this the correct response.

23. **Answer: A**

Replacement cost is the amount to be paid for an item at the current time. This concept is used in the lower-of-cost-or-market inventory valuation procedure. Replacement cost is an example of an entry price—the amount required to be paid currently to obtain an asset already held.

24. **Answer: C**

When a firm is in liquidation, historical cost and entry values (replacement cost) are no longer relevant.

The going concern assumption supports the historical cost principle. The firm is no longer a going concern. The only amounts relevant are the amounts to be received on sale of the assets. Net realizable value is the net value to be received after the costs of getting the asset ready for sale are deducted.

25. **Answer: A**

LCM departs from historical cost because it provides an ending valuation below cost when market value is below cost. The inventory is actually written down to a value below what was originally paid. This is one of the few such departures.

26. **Answer: C**

The monetary unit assumption provides the basis for using the home-country currency as the reporting basis in the financial statements and also tends to imply that the unit of currency is stable (little or no inflation or deflation).

27. **Answer: A**

Gain contingencies are not recognized, but loss contingencies that are probable and estimable are recognized. This is a classic example of conservatism, which suppresses positive information under conditions of uncertainty but requires the reporting of negative information when the negative outcome is likely.

28. **Answer: B**

Cost-benefit is the only constraint among the four answer alternatives. When the cost of information exceeds its benefit, it should not be reported, even if it might be useful.

29. **Answer: A**

The framework for the use of fair value in GAAP is intended to achieve both increased consistency and increased comparability in fair value measurement and reporting.

30. **Answer: C**

Establishing new measurement requirements for financial instruments, or for any other asset or liability, is not one of the purposes of the fair value framework. Measurement requirements or elections are determined by other pronouncements; the "Fair Value Measurement" pronouncement establishes standards to be followed in determining (measuring) fair value when it is used.

31. **Answer: C**

In determining the fair value of a nonfinancial asset, how the reporting entity would use the asset would not be taken into account in assessing the highest and best use of the asset. The highest and best use is based on use of the asset by market participants, not by the reporting entity.

32. **Answer: A**

While the determination of fair value is for a particular (identified) asset or liability, that asset or liability, in fact, may be either a standalone asset or liability (e.g., a financial instrument or an operating asset) or a group of assets or liabilities taken as a unit (e.g., an asset group or a line of business).

33. **Answer: C**

The guidance for determining fair value provided in the fair value framework is not appropriate for determining the fair value of legal services received in exchange for an entity's common stock. ASC 820 specifically exempts share-based payment transactions (and inventory valuing and other minor items) from the purview of the fair value framework.

34. **Answer: A**

Papa should record the land and building on its books at the appropriately determined fair value at the date of the transaction. The prior carrying values on Sonny's books are not relevant to the amounts at which Papa should record the assets on its books, but are relevant to the amounts that should be reported in the consolidated financial statements.

35. **Answer: A**

Since Front market is the principal market, fair value would be based on the price at which Marco could sell the investment in that market, or $52/sh. The market selling price would not be adjusted for the related direct transaction cost.

36. **Answer: B**

The income approach to fair value measurement of an asset measures fair value by converting future amounts to a single present amount. Discounting future cash flows would be an income approach to determining fair value.

37. **Answer: A**

If an asset was acquired from the acquiring firm's majority shareholder, an auditor likely would be especially concerned as to whether the price paid to acquire the asset was fair value of the asset because an entity and its majority shareholder are related parties. Related party transactions may not be at arm's length and, therefore, may require special attention of an auditor and special disclosures related thereto.

38. **Answer: A**

If Able Co. intends to elect to implement the fair value option for its investment in Baker's debt, it must make its election on the date it first recognizes the investment, which is January 15, 2008.

39. **Answer: B**

An entity's assumptions may be used as inputs in determining fair value. Those assumptions would be level 3, unobservable inputs, but would be used when adequate observable inputs were not available to make fair value determinations.

40. **Answer: C**

In the fair value hierarchy, level 1 is the highest or most desirable level, and level 3 is the lowest or least desirable level.

41. **Answer: D**

Neither Statement I nor Statement II is correct. Quoted market prices should not be adjusted for a "blockage factor" when a firm holds a sizable portion of the asset being valued (Statement I). A "blockage factor" occurs when an entity holds a sizable portion of an asset (or liability) relative to the trading volume of the asset or liability in the market. Using a "blockage factor" would adjust the market value for the impact of such a large block of securities being sold, but is not permitted in determining fair value. Additionally, quoted market prices in markets that are not active because there are few relevant transactions can be used in determining fair value (Statement II). Such prices would be considered level 2 factors, observable inputs but not in active markets.

42. **Answer: C**

This response is a false statement—internally generated cash flow projections are not an observable input.

43. **Answer: C**

Quoted market prices on a stock exchange for identical assets would be level 1 inputs, the highest level in the hierarchy of inputs for valuation purposes, and the most reliable evidence of fair value.

44. **Answer: D**

Both Statements I and II are correct. The intended purposes of financial statement disclosures required of a firm that elects to use fair value measurement are to facilitate comparisons both across firms and for differently measured financial assets and liabilities of a single firm.

45. **Answer: A**

Fair value measurement disclosures require both that fair value amounts be disclosed separately for each level of the fair value hierarchy and that quantitative disclosures be provided in tabular format.

46. **Answer: C**

Disclosure requirements when fair value measurement is used are differentiated between items measured at fair value on a recurring basis and items measured at fair value on a non-recurring basis. Items measured at fair value on a recurring basis are adjusted to (measured at) fair value period after period; an example would be investments held-for-trading. Items measured at fair value on a non-recurring basis are adjusted to (measured at) fair value only when certain conditions are met; an example would be the impairment of an asset.

47. **Answer: C**

The disclosures required when the fair value option is used are not intended to replace the kind and amount of information that would have been provided if the fair value option had not been used. Rather, the intent is to provide the same kind and amount of information that would have been provided if the fair value option had not been elected.

48. **Answer: C**

Combined disclosures about fair value measurements required by all pronouncements are not required, but are encouraged.

49. **Answer: A**

The International Federation of Accountants (IFAC) is a global organization for the accounting profession. Its members are accounting and auditing organizations throughout the world. It is an independent organization not under the IFRS Foundation umbrella, but it does support the activities of the IFRS Foundation by encouraging high-quality practices by the world's accountants and auditors.

50. **Answer: C**

The IFRS Foundation, as the legal entity of the entire organization, has the responsibility to ensure that the operations are sufficiently funded in order to ensure the fulfillment of the standard-setting objectives without compromising the independence and objectivity of the standard-setting process.

51. **Answer: D**

The Trustees do not determine the agenda of the IASB. Rather, the Trustees annually review the strategy of the IFRS Foundation and the IASB and its effectiveness, including the consideration, but not the determination, of the IASB's agenda.

52. **Answer: D**

The Chair of the U.S. Securities and Exchange Commission is a member of the Monitoring Board. The Monitoring Board provides a formal link between the Trustees and public authorities. The U.S. Securities and Exchange Commission is the primary overseer and regulator of the U.S. securities markets. Its mission is to protect investors; maintain fair, orderly, and efficient markets; and facilitate capital formation.

53. **Answer: B**

The objective of the IFRS Foundation is to take account of, as appropriate, the needs of a range of sizes and types of entities in diverse economic settings.

54. **Answer: B**

There are two assumptions underlying the preparation and presentation of financial statements: accrual basis and going concern. IASB Framework, para 22–23.

55. **Answer: C**

Relevance and faithful representation are the two fundamental qualitative characteristics of financial information (IASB Framework 5–18).

56. **Answer: A**

According to the IASB's Framework, recognition is "the process of incorporating in the Balance Sheet or Income Statement an item that meets the definition of an element and satisfies the criteria for recognition." The element must be both probable that any future economic benefit will flow to or from the entity and have a cost or value that can be measured with reliability. IASB Framework, para. 82–83.

57. **Answer: A**

Recognition is the process of incorporating an item in the financial statements when it meets the definition of the element and satisfies the criteria for recognition. That criteria state that there is the probability of future economic benefit associated with the item that will flow to or from the entity and that the item has a cost or value that can be measured with reliability. IASB Framework, para. 82–83.

58. **Answer: D**

IFRS for SMEs is not an other comprehensive basis of accounting, but rather is one form of generally accepted accounting principles (GAAP). The cash basis of accounting, the modified cash basis, and the income tax basis are all regarded as an other comprehensive basis of accounting (OCBOA) systems.

59. **Answer: D**

Under IFRS for SMEs, neither earnings per share (EPS) nor information by segment is required in financial statements. Since financial statements prepared under IFRS for SMEs are those of entities not traded on exchanges or otherwise required to file with regulatory agencies, earnings per share and segment reporting are not considered important information for users. These are two of the simplifications in IFRS for SMEs that make the standards less burdensome than either U.S. GAAP or full IFRS.

60. **Answer: C**

Under IFRS for SMEs, goodwill is assumed to have a limited life and is amortized over that life, or a period not to exceed 10 years if the life cannot be reasonably estimated. Under U.S. GAAP, goodwill is assumed to have an unlimited life and is not amortized.

61. **Answer: A**

Under IFRS for SMEs, either the cost method or equity method may be used by an investor to account for an investment in another entity (called an "associate" in IFRS for SMEs) over which the investor has significant influence. Under U.S. GAAP, only the equity method may be used.

62. **Answer: D**

All of the items listed would appear on the Income Statement when using IFRS.

63. **Answer: D**

Under IFRS, the classified Statement of Financial Position has just two classifications: Current and Non-current. Both assets and liabilities are divided into these two classifications, with Non-current being the default category.

64. **Answer: D**

Reporting accounts receivable at net realizable value is a departure from the principle of historical cost. Accounts receivable is usually aged by some method and reported at net realizable value.

65. **Answer: A**

Accumulated depreciation is a contra account. The asset account Equipment is reported on the Balance Sheet as the net of accumulated depreciation. As such, the accumulated depreciation account has a credit balance, reducing the Equipment account from its historical cost balance to its carrying or book value.

66. **Answer: A**

Current assets are calculated as follows:

Cash	185,000
Accounts receivable, net	725,000
Reclassification of o/s receivable	(200,000)
Total current assets	710,000

67. **Answer: D**

Retained earnings are calculated as follows:

Revenue [4,500,000] – Expenses [3,750,000]	750,000
Income taxes = $0.30 \times 750,000$	(225,000)
Net income	525,000
Retained earnings, 1/1/Yr. 5	350,000
Retained earnings, 12/31/Yr. 5	875,000

68. **Answer: A**

Advertising	$150,000
Freight-out	80,000
Rent for office space ($220,000 × .50)	110,000
Sales salaries and commissions	140,000
Equals total selling expenses	$480,000

Advertising is part of the overall selling effort. Freight-out is delivery expense. Offering delivery service is also part of the overall sales effort. Only 1/2 the rent is included in selling expenses because the sales department occupies only 1/2 the premises.

69. **Answer: D**

Neither expense is normally included in general and administrative expenses because interest and advertising are expenses that result from very specific activities and are frequently material in amount. They should be separately identified.

70. **Answer: C**

All items are included in net income except the prior year adjustment to amortization expense and the unrealized gain on the AFS securities. The pre-tax income is $1,878,000 and after 30% taxes the net income is $1,314,600.

71. **Answer: A**

If the accountant forgets to record salary expense in the Statement of Income, then net income is too high. Salary expense would be a decrease from revenues, resulting in lower net income.

72. **Answer: B**

In a multi-step Income Statement, gross profit (margin), operating profit (margin), and pre-tax income from continuing operations are determined. The focus is on the determination of operating profit rather than simply income from continuing operations. Gross profit (margin) is shown as a separate item.

73. **Answer: C**

Foreign currency translation adjustments are reported in other comprehensive income.

74. **Answer: B**

The components of comprehensive income are: net income, unrealized gain/loss on AFS securities, foreign currency translation adjustment, unrecognized gain/loss on pension benefits, and deferred gain/loss on certain hedging transactions. Therefore, the comprehensive income of Palmyra Co is $11,000 – 3,000 + 2,000 = $10,000.

75. **Answer: D**

The components of comprehensive income are net income (or loss) plus/minus items of other comprehensive income, possibly including, for a period: (a) a minimum pension liability adjustment, (b) any unrealized gain or loss on available-for-sale investments, (c) a foreign currency translation adjustment and gain/loss on related hedge, and (d) the effective portion of cash flow hedges. U.S. GAAP requires that for-profit entities report comprehensive income and its components for a period (unless the entity has no items of other comprehensive income) in one of two statements:

1. as a separate "Statement of Comprehensive Income"
2. or combined with the Income Statement to provide a "Statement of Net Income and Comprehensive Income"

76. **Answer: B**

Comprehensive income reflects all changes from owner and nonowner sources. The other comprehensive income items are: unrealized G/L on AFS securities, unrealized G/L on pension costs, foreign currency translation adjustments, and unrealized G/L on certain derivative transactions.

77. **Answer: C**

Comprehensive income (CI) is the sum of net income (NI) and other comprehensive income (OCI). In this case, NI = $110,000 ($800,000 sales – $600,000 CGS – $90,000 expenses). The unrealized holding gain is an item of OCI. There are four types of OCI items in all. This firm has only one of them. Thus, CI = $110,000 NI + $30,000 OCI = $140,000.

78. **Answer: C**

All changes in items affecting equity on the Balance Sheet are reported in the Statement of Owner's Equity. Both treasury stock and retained earnings are equity items.

79. **Answer: D**

If the par value of the stock is $2, and the increase in the common stock account is $2,000, then $2,000/$2 = 1,000 shares issued. The average issue price is the sum of the par value ($2) and the additional paid-in capital ($10,000/1,000 shares, or $10), which totals $12.

80. **Answer: D**

The Statement of Changes in Equity reconciles all of the beginning and ending balances in the equity accounts. The statement shows the opening balance then details all changes in the accounts, ending with the closing balance.

81. **Answer: C**

This statement generally requires a significant amount of analysis to uncover the cash flows reported within. The adjusted trial balance presents ending account balances. The Statement of Cash Flows reports changes in cash by category. Cash flows are changes in cash and are categorized by type and reported in three categories: operating, investing, and financing.

82. **Answer: D**

The direct method Statement of Cash Flows must be supported by the supplemental disclosure of a reconciliation, but the reconciliation is of net income to net cash flow from operations, not retained earnings to net cash flow from operations. The ending retained earnings balance is not related to, and does not affect, operating cash flow.

83. **Answer: A**

Operating Activities come from adjustments to reconcile net income to net cash flows and through analyzing the change in current asset and liability accounts. Net income – increase in inventory – decrease in accounts payable $70,000 – $40,000 – $30,000 = $0

84. **Answer: C**

Cash flow per share is specifically prohibited from being disclosed unless it is based on contractual amounts.

The conversion of debt to equity is an example of a transaction that would appear in the supplemental noncash disclosure schedule.

85. **Answer: C**

This question provides an example of the need to read each answer alternative very carefully before choosing.

The Statement of Cash Flows is a listing of cash flows for a period in meaningful categories. Thus, it depicts the major cash receipts and disbursements during a period. Although such information may help a user to assess the ability of a firm to generate future cash flows, it does not, necessarily, say anything about the firm's ability to do so in the future.

Similarly, the cash flow statement does not directly indicate the firm's ability to meet future cash operating needs. The reconciliation of income and net operating cash flows does indicate the differences between income and operating cash flows, but this is not the primary purpose of the statement.

86. **Answer: C**

Cash flows from financing activities are those associated with how the company is financed such as with borrowing or equity. Therefore, the proceeds from the sale of the building would not be included in financing activities. The proceeds from the issuance of common stock (250), convertible bonds (100) and borrowing on the line of credit (200) are all cash inflows from financing activities. The payment of dividends (300) is a cash outflow from financing activities. 250 + 100 + 200 − 300 = 250.

87. **Answer: B**

Dividends paid to shareholders are a financing activity. The payment of interest on bonds is an operating activity, and payments to acquire shares of Marks Co. stock are investing activities.

88. **Answer: A**

Cash received from the customers and paid to employees are operating activities. Interest paid on a bank note is also an operating activity. Therefore, the cash for from operating activities is $25,000 − 3,000 − 8,000 = $14,000.

89. **Answer: C**

Financing cash flows are those between the firm and the parties providing it with debt and equity financing. Financing cash flows are the major sources of nonoperating cash inflows and repayments of those amounts to the providers. For example, borrowings and proceeds from stock issuance, retirements of debt, treasury stock purchases, and dividends paid are all

financing cash flows. Interest paid, however, is an operating cash flow.

90. **Answer: A**

The amounts paid to purchase plant assets and passive investments, such as stocks and bonds from other firms, are investing cash outflows. When part of the purchase price is financed, as in this question, only the cash amount paid is disclosed in the Statement of Cash Flows. The non-cash activity schedule would disclose the acquisition price and amount financed with the mortgage.

91. **Answer: B**

Cash paid to suppliers is determined by adjusting CGS for the effect of the accrual of accounts payable and the increase or decrease in inventory.

CGS	1,200,000
Subtract: Decrease in inventory	(50,000)—since inventory decreased, more goods were used than purchased
Add: Decrease in accounts payable	100,000—since AP decreased, more cash was paid than purchased on account
Cash paid to suppliers	1,250,000

92. **Answer: A**

Amount paid to suppliers	=	Cost of goods sold	−	Inventory decrease	−	AP increase
$490,000	=	Cost of goods sold	−	$30,000	−	$25,000
$545,000	=	Cost of goods sold				

The inventory decrease is subtracted from cost of goods sold because it is an inventory reduction included in cost of goods sold that was not paid for in the current period. The accounts payable increase is also subtracted because it represents an increase in inventory and, therefore, cost of goods sold that was not paid for in the current period.

93. **Answer: D**

When bond discount is amortized, a portion of the discount is recognized as expense. The result is that interest expense exceeds the amount of cash paid with each interest payment. The discount is gradually amortized over the bond term as additional interest expense because the firm received less than the amount due at maturity. The operating activity section of the indirect method begins with net income and ends with net cash flow from operations. Income is reduced by the interest expense that exceeds the cash interest paid by the amount of discount amortization. Therefore, the discount amortization is added back, yielding a reduction in net cash flow from operations equal to the amount of cash interest paid.

94. **Answer: A**

Proceeds from sale of securities	$135,000
Proceeds from sale of building	350,000
Purchase of other plant assets	(1,190,000)
Net cash used in investing activities	$(705,000)

The plant assets (gross) account increased $700,000. $700,000 increase = −$600,000 (sale of building) + $110,000 (equipment purchase) + X. X = additional purchases of plant assets. X = $1,190,000. The available long-term investments were sold at a gain. That is why the change in the account ($100,000) does not equal the cash inflow from the sale. The equipment purchased with long-term debt is not listed in the investing section because no cash was used on the purchase (it is disclosed in the supplemental information). The purchase of trading securities is an operating cash flow.

95. **Answer: C**

Net income	$150,000
Less increase in equity investment	(5,500)
Less amortization of bond premium	(1,400)
Plus increase in deferred income tax liability	1,800
Net cash flow from operating activities	$144,900

The increase in the equity method investment is Metro's share of the undistributed earnings of Videogold. This amount increases net income but causes no cash inflow and is subtracted. The amortization of bond premiums reduces interest expense relative to cash interest paid. Income, therefore, understates the cash outflow for interest. The subtraction of the premium adjusts income for the difference. The increase in the deferred tax liability increases income tax expense without any cash outflow. Therefore, the increase is added to income.

96. **Answer: C**

The summary of significant accounting policies requires that the methods of depreciation used by a firm be disclosed.

The composition of plant assets must also be disclosed, but not in the summary of significant accounting policies. The composition information typically is disclosed in another footnote.

97. **Answer: B**

The summary of significant accounting policies conveys information regarding the important accounting methods and policies chosen by the firm, when a choice is available.

Knowledge of the methods is critical to an understanding of the amounts disclosed in the financial statements. The method of accounting for long-term contracts may be the percentage of completion or completed contract method. Disclosure of this method assists the user in understanding the meaning of reported revenue and gross profit.

The other answer alternatives give data on specific accounts or the result of applying specific accounting principles. They do not indicate what choices the firm has made for accounting and reporting.

98. **Answer: D**

The accounting policy footnote discloses both the methods of accounting used by the firm and other information useful for understanding the bases under which the financial statements were prepared. How the firm classifies investments as cash equivalents is one such basis; it is disclosed in the policy footnote. The other answer alternatives are disclosures about specific aspects of particular accounts.

99. **Answer: D**

The summary of significant accounting policies footnote describes the important accounting choices made by the firm for financial reporting purposes. Such policies affect recognition, measurement, and disclosure.

For example, in some areas of revenue recognition, GAAP allows a choice from among several methods of recognition and measurement. This footnote discloses the choices made by the firm to help users understand the reported amounts of revenue and affected accounts in the Income Statement and Balance Sheet.

Different methods produce different reported amounts.

100. **Answer: A**

The summary of significant accounting policies footnote presents information that helps assist users in understanding the recognition, measurement, and disclosure decisions made by the firm.

GAAP allows many choices. In the long-term construction contracts area, GAAP allows both the completed contract and percentage of completion methods. The result of applying each method significantly affects both the Income Statement and Balance Sheet.

A user is much better equipped to evaluate the firm's financial performance and position with the knowledge of the revenue recognition method used by the firm.

101. **Answer: D**

Although diversification may be lacking in a firm's investment portfolio, passive investments are not one of the concentrations for which a firm is considered to be vulnerable. The fourth concentration (besides the three other answer alternatives) is concentration in the volume of business with a particular customer or supplier.

102. **Answer: B**

This is not one of the four sources noted in the applicable standard. It is specifically noted as a source not included in the accounting standard.

103. **Answer: D**

The actual numerical estimates typically are not disclosed. Rather, it is the effect of the change that is of interest to financial statement users.

104. **Answer: C**

Disclosures are required when the event is reasonably possible. The event is not required to be probable.

105. **Answer: C**

This is an internal policy matter and is not listed as a specific attribute for disclosure in the standard.

106. **Answer: C**

This is a subsequent event that did not exist at the balance sheet date but occurred before the financial statements were issued. The company is required to make a footnote disclosure describing the nature of the event and an estimate of the financial effect, or a statement that an estimate cannot be made. Recognition

is inappropriate because the condition existed after the balance sheet date.

107. **Answer: C**

Although bad debt expense has been recognized, it does not adequately account for the Botel loss, which is probable and estimable.

108. **Answer: A**

The Pernod acquisition occurred before the balance sheet and thus reflects a transaction or condition existing as of the balance sheet date. The Weynod acquisition, although also significant, is footnoted only because the transaction had not yet occurred as of the balance sheet date. The footnote description meets the full disclosure requirement for the transaction.

109. **Answer: D**

No transactions have taken place for either contract. Even though the French contract was signed before the balance sheet date, there is nothing to recognize. Footnotes will describe both contracts.

110. **Answer: B**

The firm faces a probable loss, and counsel has developed reasonable estimates. The condition leading to the future loss existed at the balance sheet date. Thus, the loss and liability should be recognized. Any difference between the estimated and actual loss is treated as a change in estimate in a future period. A footnote will describe the situation.

111. **Answer: C**

Cash is both a current and a quick asset (an asset immediately available to pay debts). Accounts payable is a current liability. Thus, the numerator and denominator of both ratios have decreased.

The current ratio was greater than 1.0 before the transaction. Therefore, the denominator decreased a greater percentage than the numerator causing the ratio to increase.

The quick ratio was less than 1.0 before the transaction. Therefore, the numerator decreased a greater percentage than the denominator causing the ratio to decrease.

112. **Answer: A**

The net cash sales are not involved in the accounts receivable turnover ratio, nor are inventory or purchases. Working backward from accounts receivable, net credit sales is found as:

Accounts receivable turnover = net credit sales/average accounts receivable.

5 = net credit sales/[($20,000 + $22,000)/2]

5($21,000) = net credit sales = $105,000

113. Answer: A

Inventory turnover is the ratio of cost of goods (CGS) sold to average inventory. First, calculate CGS = beginning inventory $100,000 + purchases $700,000 – ending inventory $300,000 = $500,000. Then, average inventory = (beginning inventory + ending inventory)/2 = ($100,000 + $300,000)/2 = $200,000. Turnover = $500,000/$200,000 = 2.5.

114. Answer: B

AR turnover is the ratio of sales to average AR or $1,400,000/[($120,000 + $100,000)/2] = $1,400,000/$110,000 = 12.73. Thus AR turns over 12.73 times per year. In days, AR turns over every 28.7 days = 365/12.73. If the year is divided into 12.73 parts, each part is 28.7 days long.

115. Answer: A

The current ratio is the ratio of current assets to current liabilities. Current assets for this firm include the first three items listed under assets: $300,000 + $350,000 + $600,000 = $1,250,000. Current liabilities are listed as $700,000. Their ratio is $1,250,000/$700,000 = 1.79.

116. Answer: D

Book value per share, for this basic situation, is total owners' equity divided by the number of shares outstanding: $2,200,000/45,000 = $49 rounded to the nearest dollar. The number of shares outstanding equals the number of shares issued (50,000) less the number in the treasury (5,000).

117. Answer: B

Rate of return on assets is the ratio of net income for a period to average total assets for the same period.

$150,000/[($2,000,000 + $3,000,000)/2] = 6%.

118. Answer: B

The defensive interval ratio is the ratio of quick assets to daily operating expenditures. Quick assets are current assets that are very readily converted to cash. They include cash, accounts receivable, and certain investments. The ratio indicates the length of time in days that the firm can operate with its present liquid resources. Thus, the measure is a liquidity measure.

The return on stockholders' equity is the ratio of income to average owners' equity. This ratio is a profitability ratio, not a liquidity ratio. A firm could have a strong return on equity ratio and not be particularly liquid.

119. Answer: B

First, we must compute the amount of debt. Since Assets = Liabilities + Stockholders' Equity, we have 760,000 = ? + (150,000 + 215,000). Thus, debt = $395,000. Debt to Equity is 395,000/(150,000 + 215,000) = 1.08.

120. Answer: D

The consolidating process takes place on worksheets and schedules, and the results are presented in the form of consolidated financial statements. Some of the worksheet and schedule data is carried forward from period end to period end to facilitate the recurring consolidating process.

121. Answer: C

Goodwill may be recognized by the entry that eliminates the parent's investment in the subsidiary against the parent's share of the subsidiary's shareholders' equity, but goodwill will not be eliminated through an eliminating entry.

122. Answer: A

A parent may use the cost method, the equity method, or any other method on its books to carry an investment in a subsidiary that it will consolidate. The method that is used on its books will affect the consolidating process, but the final consolidated financial statements will be the same regardless of the method the parent uses on its books.

123. Answer: B

Between 20% and 50% voting ownership of an investee normally is assumed to give the investor significant influence over the investee. Ownership of 20% to 50% of the voting stock of an investee may not give the investor significant influence over the investee if additional special circumstances exist, but normally it does.

124. Answer: C

Both book values and fair values of a subsidiary's assets and liabilities will need to be determined at the date of acquisition in order to prepare consolidated financial statements after a business combination.

125. **Answer: C**

The difference between fair market value and book value of inventories would be recognized by adjusting inventories to fair value on the consolidated balance sheet.

126. **Answer: A**

In an acquisition business combination, all assets and liabilities are revalued to fair value. Any excess of investment value over fair value of the revalued identifiable net assets is assigned to goodwill.

Book value of net assets was $220,000. Plant and Equipment needed to be written up by $60,000, making fair value of net assets $280,000. Since Penn paid $300,000 for Star, that leaves $20,000 in goodwill ($300,000–$280,000). Thus, this is the correct response.

127. **Answer: A**

First the fair value of the identifiable net assets must be determined:

Cash	$60,000
Inventory	$150,000
P&E (net)	$380,000
Liabilities	($120,000)
Net Assets	$470,000

Once this has been determined it is a simple matter of subtracting this amount from the purchase price to determine the goodwill ($620,000 – $470,000 = $150,000 goodwill).

128. **Answer: D**

On the date of a business combination using acquisition accounting, the consolidated stockholders' equity will exactly equal the parent company stockholders' equity. This will continue to be the case as long as the parent company uses a complete equity method of accounting for the subsidiary.

129. **Answer: B**

The excess of (fair) market value over book value of equipment would be recognized by writing up Plant and Equipment to fair value on the consolidated balance sheet.

130. **Answer: C**

Under the cost method of carrying an investment in a subsidiary, the parent does recognize its share of the subsidiary's dividends declared and, ultimately, the cash received in payment of the dividend. The dividend income (cr.) so recognized by the parent would be eliminated in the consolidating process against the retained earnings decrease (dr.) recognized by the subsidiary.

131. **Answer: A**

The purpose of the reciprocity is to bring the investment account (on the worksheet) in balance with the subsidiary's retained earnings **as of the beginning of the period being consolidated**. Therefore, only the undistributed income of the subsidiary since the business combination up to the beginning of the period being consolidated (January 1, 2009) will be the reciprocity entry at the end of 2009. The undistributed income from October 1 to December 31, 2008 (the beginning of 2009) is net income (+$3,000) less dividends declared and paid (–$1,000), or $2,000.

132. **Answer: A**

Although the cost of the investment was equal to book values, the cost of the investment was greater than the fair values, because the carrying amount of Scarp's building was more than its fair value. For consolidated statement purposes, the building would be written down to its lower fair value, and the excess of cost over fair values would be assigned to recognize goodwill. Since for consolidated purposes the building has a lower fair value than its carrying value, the depreciation expense taken on the carrying value would be greater than the depreciation expense for consolidated purposes. Thus, depreciation expense would be decreased in the consolidating process, and goodwill would be recognized.

133. **Answer: B**

When a parent company uses the cost method to account for its investment in a subsidiary, the parent will recognize its share of the subsidiary's dividends declared as income to the parent.

134. **Answer: B**

Under the equity method, when a subsidiary reports income, the parent recognizes its share as: DR: Investment and CR: Equity Income. Therefore, the subsidiary's reported income increases the investment account. In addition, when a subsidiary declares a dividend, the parent recognizes its share as: DR: Dividends Receivable/Cash and CR: Investment. Therefore, the subsidiary's dividends do not increase the investment account but rather decrease the investment account.

135. **Answer: A**

The investment-eliminating entry on the consolidating worksheet will write up (increasing on the worksheet) the value of depreciable asset, from book value to fair value on the date of the combination. The additional depreciable asset value recognized on the worksheet will then be depreciated on the worksheet, resulting in additional (increasing) depreciation expense.

136. **Answer: D**

Both accounts will be decreased. The investment-eliminating entry on the consolidating worksheet will write down (decreasing on the worksheet) the value of depreciable asset, from book value to the lower fair value on the date of the combination. The decrease in depreciable asset value recognized on the worksheet will mean that the depreciation expense on the worksheet, brought on by the subsidiary, will overstate depreciation expense to the parent, resulting in a reduction (decreasing) depreciation expense for consolidated statement purposes.

137. **Answer: D**

Noncontrolling interest at the date of the business combination should be the noncontrolling interest proportionate share of total fair value at that date, including goodwill. The total fair value of Shaw (including goodwill) at the date Ritt acquired 80% of Shaw's common stock would be $1,218,750 ($975,000/.80). The noncontrolling interest would be .20 × $1,218,750 = $243,750, the correct answer. The investment eliminating entry made immediately following the business combination would be:

DR: (Various) Identifiable Net Assets	$1,100,000	
Goodwill	118,750	
CR: Investment in Shaw		$975,000
Noncontrolling Interest (in Shaw)		243,750

138. **Answer: A**

When a parent uses the equity method to account for its investment in a subsidiary, the parent will recognize on its books during the year its share of the subsidiary's income (or loss) and its share of dividends declared by the subsidiary. Therefore, in the consolidating process, those entries (and any other equity-based entries made by the parent) must be reversed so that the elements that make up those entries (revenues, expenses, etc.) can be individually recognized on the consolidating worksheet and the consolidated financial statements.

139. **Answer: A**

Subsidiary dividends are never considered part of consolidated dividends. They are either eliminated in the consolidation entries or allocated to reducing noncontrolling interests. In this problem, 80% of Simba's dividends will be eliminated as intercompany, and 20% will be allocated to reducing noncontrolling interest.

In addition, since 10% of the dividends of Pride never go outside the consolidated entity, they are not considered dividends of the consolidated entity either.

140. **Answer: D**

Intercompany transactions between two subsidiaries that will be consolidated with the same parent do need to be eliminated. Intercompany transactions (i.e., transactions between affiliated firms) must be eliminated regardless of whether the transactions are between the parent and its subsidiaries or between two subsidiaries of the same parent. The consolidated financial statements must reflect accounts and amounts as though intercompany transactions never occurred.

141. **Answer: A**

When consolidated statements are prepared, 100% of all reciprocal accounts are eliminated regardless of the ownership fraction. Thus, the whole $400,000 must be eliminated.

142. **Answer: D**

A 90% owned subsidiary will be consolidated, and any intercompany receivables such as these are eliminated from both parties' books in the consolidating process.

Therefore, the $300,000 receivable from Winn will not appear on the consolidated balance sheet at all. The $200,000 from Carr is a receivable from an affiliate (20% owned) and will need to be reported as such.

143. **Answer: B**

The consolidated financial statements should reflect 100% of the assets and liabilities of the subsidiary less any intercompany balances. Therefore the balance on the consolidated balance sheet should be: $450,000 + 200,000 − 100,000 = $550,000.

144. **Answer: C**

Even though the intercompany inventory sale from Strawco to Pine was at no profit or loss (at Strawco's cost to manufacture), the intercompany sale and purchase, nevertheless, must be eliminated. Otherwise, consolidated sales and purchases (cost of goods sold) will be overstated. Therefore, the elimination related to the intercompany inventory transaction will be for $12,000, the cost of the sale from Strawco to Pine.

145. **Answer: B**

If an intercompany inventory transaction is not eliminated in the consolidating process, consolidated financial statements would show an overstatement of sales. Sales would be overstated by the amount of the intercompany sales reported by the selling affiliate. All intercompany sales and related purchases must be eliminated, even if they do not result in a profit or loss.

146. **Answer: A**

With a cost from non-affiliates of $18,000 and an intercompany selling price of $27,000, there is a $9,000 intercompany profit on the inventory transaction. Therefore, $9,000 profit/$27,000 cost to the buying affiliate results in a one third profit in ending inventory. Since the ending inventory at the buying affiliate's cost is $9,000, 1/3 × $9,000 = $3,000 is the intercompany profit in ending inventory and the amount that would have to be eliminated.

147. **Answer: A**

Since only the transaction between Papa and Sonnyco is an intercompany transaction, only the amount of that transaction, $27,000, will be eliminated. The purchase of inventory by Papa and the sale by Sonnyco are both with non-affiliates. Therefore, those transaction amounts would not be eliminated.

148. **Answer: A**

Either consolidated income or consolidated loss could be overstated on consolidated statements as a result of failure to eliminate intercompany inventory balances. An overstatement of income would result if the goods were sold by the selling affiliate at a price greater than the cost to the selling affiliate. An overstatement of loss would result if the goods were sold by the selling affiliate at a price less than the cost to the selling affiliate.

149. **Answer: C**

The amount of intercompany gain to be eliminated at the end of the year following the year of the intercompany fixed asset sale is $2,000. At the end of the year of the intercompany sale, depreciation taken by the buying affiliate on the $3,000 inter-company gain will be $1,000 ($3,000/3 years). As a consequence, $1,000 of the $3,000 intercompany gain will have been properly recognized, leaving only $2,000 to eliminate at the end of the second year. Depreciation expense taken on the intercompany gain for the second year will confirm another $1,000 of the intercompany gain, and depreciation expense taken on the intercompany gain for the third year will confirm the last $1,000 of the intercompany gain.

150. **Answer: D**

Either consolidated income or consolidated loss could be overstated on consolidated statements as a result of failure to eliminate intercompany fixed asset balances. An overstatement of income would result if the assets were sold by the selling affiliate at a price greater than the carrying value to the selling affiliate. An overstatement of loss would result if the assets were sold by the selling affiliate at a price less than the carrying value to the selling affiliate.

151. **Answer: C**

The individual books of Water and Fire would record this transaction as if they were independent companies. Fire would remove the asset and record a gain. Water would put the asset on its books at cost.

The problem is that they are not independent companies, and therefore, no real sale took place. The gain that was recorded must therefore be eliminated on the consolidated books. The net result is that the asset will be on the books at Water's original cost less Fire's recorded gain.

152. Answer: B

An intercompany sale of a fixed asset at a profit will result in the buying affiliate overstating depreciation expense by the amount of depreciation taken on the intercompany profit, and an intercompany sale at a loss will result in an understatement of depreciation expense taken by the buying affiliate. When an intercompany sale of a fixed asset results in a loss, the carrying value of the asset will be understated by the amount of the loss. As a result, depreciation expense taken by the buying affiliate will be understated by the amount of depreciation that would have been taken on the intercompany loss.

153. Answer: C

Consolidated depreciation expense will be less, not more, than the sum of depreciation expense of the separate companies being combined. Because the intercompany transaction resulted in a gain, the buying affiliate will have the asset on its books with the intercompany gain included in its carrying value and will depreciate that value on its books. For consolidated purposes, that depreciation on the intercompany gain will be eliminated, resulting in less depreciation expense than the sum of the depreciation expense of the separate companies.

154. Answer: A

Intercompany bonds exist when one affiliate to be consolidated owns the bonds of another affiliate to be consolidated. Thus, intercompany bonds would exist when a parent owns a subsidiary's bonds, when a subsidiary owns a parent's bonds, or when one subsidiary owns the bonds of another subsidiary that will be consolidated.

155. Answer: C

In the elimination of intercompany bonds, the intercompany bond liability at par will be eliminated against the intercompany bond investment at par. Therefore, the gain or loss recognized as a result of constructive retirement of intercompany bonds is the net of the premium or discount on the bond liability and the premium or discount on the bond investment. In this case, there is a total $100,000 premium on the bond liability, but because only one-fourth ($250,000/$1,000,000 = 1/4) of the bonds are intercompany, only one fourth of the premium is eliminated. Thus, $25,000 of premium on the bond liability (a credit) will be eliminated against the $50,000

discount on the bond investment (also a credit). As a result of eliminating the two credits ($25,000 + $50,000 = $75,000), a $75,000 gain on constructive retirement will be recognized.

156. Answer: D

A premium on a bond liability results from the sale of the bonds at a price in excess of par (face) value. Therefore, a premium would be added to par value to get net carrying value. Sico's premium on its bond liability ($100,000) should be added to the par (or face) value of its bond liability ($1,000,000) to determine the net carrying value of the liability. Thus, the answer should be $1,000,000 par value + $100,000 premium = $1,100,000 net carrying value.

157. Answer: D

The premium or discount on a bond investment is the difference between the par value of the bonds and the price paid for the bonds in the market. If the price paid is more than par value, there is a premium on the bond investment. If the price paid is less than par value, there is a discount on the bond investment. In this case, the price paid for the investment ($200,000) is less than the par value of the bonds ($250,000) by $50,000. Therefore, there is a $50,000 discount on Pico's investment.

158. Answer: D

The liability and investment related to intercompany bonds are eliminated only on the consolidating worksheet. They are not written off the books of either the issuing or the investing affiliate. From the perspective of the separate companies, the liability and investment related to the bonds continue to exist, but for consolidated purposes, they have been constructive retired.

159. Answer: A

Goodwill can only be recognized if it is acquired by purchase.

160. Answer: B

This answer is correct because it is not one of the three conditions required to exclude a subsidiary from consolidation. The three required conditions are: (1) it is wholly or partially owned and its other owners do not object to nonconsolidation; (2) it does not have any debt or equity instruments publicly traded; and (3) its parent prepares consolidated financial statements that comply with IFRS.

161. **Answer: D**

This answer is correct because IFRS permits recording noncontrolling interests at either fair value or the proportionate share of the value of identifiable net assets of the acquiree.

162. **Answer: B**

This answer is correct because IFRS disallows the use of push-down accounting.

163. **Answer: C**

Statement I and Statement III are correct; Statement II is not correct. Under IFRS, the guidelines for determining whether or not to consolidate an entity are more principles-based than are U.S. GAAP (Statement I). Under IFRS, the basic guideline is that an entity must be consolidated when another entity has the ability to govern the financial and operating policies of the entity to obtain benefits from it. U.S. GAAP has a specific two-tiered assessment process that must be followed to determine whether or not an entity should be consolidated. Under both U.S. GAAP and IFRS, there are circumstances under which a majority-owned subsidiary does not have to be consolidated (Statement III). U.S. GAAP does not require consolidation of a majority-owned subsidiary when the investor cannot exercise control of the subsidiary. IFRS does not require consolidation of a majority-owned subsidiary under certain conditions when the parent will be consolidated with a higher-level parent.

164. **Answer: A**

The amount at which Webb sold the inventory to Twill ($40,000 × 1.40 = $56,000) will be the amount of cost of goods sold to Twill and should be eliminated in combining the financial statements of Webb and Twill. The cost of goods to Webb ($40,000) is the cost from an unrelated entity and should be the cost of goods sold for the combined entity. Since both the $40,000 cost of goods to Webb and the $56,000 cost of goods to Twill will be on the combining worksheet, the cost of goods to Twill (from Webb) must be eliminated, leaving only the $40,000 cost from a nonaffiliate.

165. **Answer: B**

The correct answer is Astro's equity of $200,000 plus Bio's equity of $60,000, less Astro's investment in Bio of $8,000, or $200,000 + $60,000 − $8,000 = $252,000. Astro's investment in Bio must be eliminated to prevent double counting of the $8,000—once as an investment on Astro's books and again as

net assets (to which the investment has a claim) on Bio's books.

166. **Answer: C**

Since all the goods have been sold outside the combined entity, income recognition is correct.

However, sales and cost of goods sold have been recorded at two different points (i.e., the sale from Webb to Twill and the sale from Twill to outsiders). To the combined entity, Webb's cost of merchandise (the original cost to the combined entity) is what is needed for cost of goods sold, and Twill's sales (the amount the merchandise was sold for outside the combined entity) is needed for sales.

This means that the sale from Webb to Twill and the cost of goods recorded by Twill need to be eliminated. That amount is $56,000 (computed as $40,000 cost to Webb x transfer price to Twill of 140% of cost = $56,000).

167. **Answer: D**

According to ASC 810, if problems associated with minority interest, foreign operations, different fiscal periods, or income taxes occur in the preparation of combined financial statements, they should be treated in the same manner as in the preparation of consolidated financial statements. Therefore, all three items should be treated in the same manner as in consolidated statements.

168. **Answer: A**

The amount that should be included in sales is the amount of sales with unrelated parties. In this case, that is the $250,000 sales by Branch to unaffiliated entities.

169. **Answer: D**

Only an acquisition form of business combination will require the preparation of consolidated financial statements. In the merger and consolidation forms of business combination, only one firm will remain after the combination. Therefore, there will not be two (or more) sets of financial statements to consolidate.

170. **Answer: C**

When a subsidiary is in bankruptcy, it is under the control of the bankruptcy court and, therefore, not under the control of the parent. When a parent cannot exercise financial and/or operating control of a subsidiary, the subsidiary would not be consolidated, but would be reported as an unconsolidated subsidiary by the parent.

171. Answer: D

The consolidated statements would include not only Parco, but also all three of its subsidiaries, for a total of four.

172. Answer: A

The estimated disposal gain is $240 [($250 – $10) proceeds] – $200 book value, or $40. Estimated disposal gains are not recognized, only estimated losses. Next year, the actual disposal gain will be recognized. Nonfinancial assets are not written up in value.

173. Answer: A

The $600,000 total loss from discontinued operations is the sum of the operating loss ($120,000) and the loss on disposal ($480,000). The two amounts, $120,000 and $480,000, are disclosed separately but together comprise the total loss on the discontinued operation.

174. Answer: A

The after-tax net loss on the disposal of the division is the net asset value ($2,700,000 of assets – $1,700,000 of liabilities) $1,000,000, less the selling price of $800,000. The result is a net loss of $200,000 before tax. After 30% taxes, the net loss is $140,000.

175. Answer: D

There are two components for discontinued operations:

(1) The operating income or loss for the period in which the decision is made to dispose, and
(2) The disposal loss. Only actual operating income (or loss) is recognized, but estimated as well as actual disposal losses are recognized. The $350,000 estimated disposal loss is the difference between the $850,000 carrying value of the segment and its $500,000 estimated selling price. The operating loss for the period ($195,000) plus the estimated disposal loss ($350,000) equals the $545,000 total loss to be recognized for discontinued operations for Year 1.

176. Answer: B

To qualify for a discontinued operation, the component to be disposed of must be approved as a sale and represents a strategic shift in the entity's operations.

177. Answer: B

The mission of the SEC is to protect investors; maintain fair, orderly, and efficient markets; and facilitate capital formation. In order to carry out the mandates in the Securities Act of 1933, the SEC is ensuring that investors are provided with adequate information on which to base investment decisions.

178. Answer: B

The main pronouncements published by the SEC are the Financial Reporting Releases (FRR) and the Staff Accounting Bulletins (SAB).

179. Answer: A

The Division of Corporate Finance oversees the compliance with the securities acts and examines all filings made by publicly held companies.

180. Answer: A

Regulation S-X governs the form and content of financial statements and financial statement disclosures.

181. Answer: A

The market share of the company's product is not a required disclosure. The company may choose to voluntarily present this information, but it is not a required disclosure.

182. Answer: B

A large accelerated filer is a company with worldwide market value of outstanding voting and nonvoting common equity held by nonaffiliates of $700 million or more. A large accelerated filer must file its 10Q within 40 days after quarter-end.

183. Answer: D

Regulation S-X governs the form and content of financial statements and financial statement disclosures for publicly traded entities.

184. Answer: B

The SEC requires that the MD&A provide a "discussion and analysis" on operating results, liquidity, and capital resources, trends, and risks and uncertainties. Where there are significant increases in sales, management must discuss the extent that price, volume, or new products contributed to the increase.

185. Answer: A

Earnings per share is: (net income – preferred dividends)/common shares outstanding. Preferred stock dividends are $100 × 10% ×

20,000 shares = $200,000. Earnings per share is (2,000,000 – 200,000)/200,000 = $9 per share.

186. **Answer: C**

In general, the dividends subtracted in computing basic EPS are (1) the annual dividend commitment on cumulative preferred whether or not declared or paid, and (2) declared dividends on noncumulative preferred whether paid or not. The firm has negative income. This answer means that the dividends reduce the numerator further—beyond the loss. The final numerator amount is less than (more negative than) the loss. Also, arrear dividends are never included in EPS because they were subtracted in computing EPS in a previous year.

187. **Answer: B**

One year of preferred stock dividends is subtracted from income in the numerator of EPS because the stock is cumulative. The amount of dividends declared does not affect the calculation. The bonds are not relevant because basic EPS does not assume conversion of the bonds. The calculation is: Basic EPS = [$200,000 – (8,000 × $20 × .10)]/25,000 = ($200,000 – $16,000)/25,000 = $7.36.

188. **Answer: B**

The effect of the stock split is applied retroactively to all changes in the number of shares of common stock outstanding before the split.

The weighted average shares outstanding for this firm for Year 1 is: 45,000 = [20,000(2) + 10,000(1/2)]. The split affects only the shares issued before date of the split. The July 1 issuance is weighted only by 1/2 a year because the shares were outstanding only 1/2 a year. EPS is computed only on common stock outstanding. The preferred shares have no effect on the computation.

189. **Answer: B**

Basic EPS = Net Income – Preferred Dividends / Weighted shares outstanding. The numerator is $236,000 – preferred dividends [($60 × 10,000) × .04 = 24,000] = $212,000. The denominator is 50,000 (12/12) + 8,000 (9/12) = 56,000 shares. $212,000 / 56,000 = $3.786 or $3.79.

190. **Answer: B**

More than one approach is available to compute WA (each yields the same answer) but perhaps the easiest is to weight each item separately going forward to the end

of the year. This approach yields 139,008 = [100,000(12/12) + 30,000(9/12) + 36,000(7/12)] (1.05) – 35,000(4/12). The beginning shares are outstanding the entire year (12/12). The next two items are weighted for the fraction of the year they are outstanding. Stock dividends and splits are retroactively applied to all items before their issuance, hence the multiplication by 1.05. The treasury shares are removed from the average for 4/12 of the year—these shares already reflect the stock dividend.

191. **Answer: C**

Weighted average shares outstanding are weighted by the number of months the shares were outstanding during the year. The easiest way to do this is to take each change in common stock and multiply by the number of months remaining—add the shares that increased shares outstanding and subtract shares that reduced shares outstanding.

Shares	Months	Wtd avg
700,000	12/12	700,000
–20,000	9/12	–15,000
+40,000	6/12	+20,000
–36,000	1/12	–3,000
		702,000

192. **Answer: B**

For EPS purposes, stock dividends and splits are retroactively applied to all periods presented and to all share changes within the year of the split or dividend. This procedure ensures comparability.

The 2-for-1 split in Year 2 does not substantively change the value of any shares outstanding. Without retroactive application, EPS would be cut roughly in half in Year 2 compared to Year 1. Yet there was little substantive change in the performance of the firm. For reporting in Year 2:

Weighted average shares, Year 1 = 100,000(2) = 200,000.

EPS, Year 1 = $350,000/200,000 = $1.75.

Weighted average shares, 2006 = [100,000 + 20,000(9/12)]2 = 230,000

EPS, 2006 = $410,000/230,000 = $1.78.

Had the Year 1 shares not been adjusted for the split, Year 1 EPS would be $3.50 = $350,000/100,000, or roughly double the EPS of Year 2. Without retroactive application, it would appear that the firm had a drastic reduction in EPS in Year 2. The retroactive application of

Multiple Choice Answers and Explanations

the split ensures that the base on which EPS is computed uses the same measuring unit.

193. Answer: C

The stock dividend is considered to be outstanding since the beginning of the year. The weighted average is therefore:

100,000 + 24,000 + (5,000 × 6/12) = 126,500.

194. Answer: C

Firms may use the proceeds from the exercise of stock options for any purpose. However, to promote uniformity in reporting, and to reduce the dilution from exercise, the assumption is that the proceeds are used to purchase the firm's stock on the market. This reduces the net number of new shares outstanding from assumed exercise.

195. Answer: B

The options and convertible preferred stock are potential common stock (PCS). First compute basic EPS as the basis for diluted EPS, and also as a benchmark for determining whether the two potential common stock securities are dilutive. Basic EPS = ($30,000 − $4,500)/15,000 = $1.70. The preferred dividend is subtracted from income because the preferred is cumulative. Then determine the numerator and denominator effects of the PCS to enter them into diluted EPS in the order of lowest ratio of numerator to denominator effect (n/d) first. The option's numerator effect is zero; the denominator effect = 2,000 − (2,000)$12/$20 = 800. 2,000 shares would be issued upon exercise but under the treasury stock method the firm is assumed to apply the proceeds from exercise (2,000 × $12) and purchase shares of the firm's stock for $20 each. Thus, the n/d for options = 0/800 = 0. The n/d for the convertible preferred stock is the ratio of dividends that would not have been declared if the stock converted, to the common shares assumed issued on conversion. n/d = $4,500/2,900 = $1.55. Enter the options into diluted EPS first, because the options have the lower n/d. DEPS tentative = ($30,000 − $4,500)/(15,000 + 800) = $1.61. The convertible preferred is dilutive because its n/d ratio of $1.55 is less than $1.61, the tentative or first-pass amount for diluted EPS. DEPS final = ($30,000 − $4,500 + $4,500)/(15,000 + 800 + 2,900) = $1.60.

196. Answer: C

Earnings per share (EPS) is calculated on income before discontinued operations and net income.

197. Answer: C

Earnings per share (EPS) is calculated on net income available to the common stockholders, $130,000 − $20,000, or $110,000, divided by weighted average shares of common stock outstanding, 50,000. The EPS = $110,000/50,000 = $2.20.

198. Answer: A

Earnings per share is calculated by dividing earnings (profit) available to common stockholders by weighted average number of shares of common stock outstanding. If the denominator is decreased by purchasing treasury stock, then the EPS result is increased.

199. Answer: D

Earnings per share (EPS) is calculated on net income available to the common stockholders, divided by weighted average shares of common stock outstanding. The preferred dividends must be subtracted from the net income, as that amount is not available to the common stockholders.

200. Answer: D

Potential investors and current investors are interested in the future earnings potential of the entity. Thus, they are interested in the earnings per share on continuing income, which would be the $10.50 per share. The EPS attributed to discontinued operations cannot be used in predicting future earnings, as they are one-time events.

201. Answer: A

This is one of the disclosures required in FAS 131. The identity of the customer does not need to be disclosed, but the segment reporting the revenue must be identified. Such a segment would meet one of the three quantitative thresholds for reporting segment information. The three thresholds are 10% of revenue, income, and assets.

202. Answer: C

Using the three quantitative thresholds (tests) from FAS 131 (Disclosures about Segments), the five following segments are reportable operating segments:

A, B, C, and E meet the test: Reported revenue, including external and internal, is 10% or more of the combined revenue of all reported operating segments. 10% of $32,750,000 is $3,275,000. The revenues of A, B, C, and E all exceed this amount.

1103

D meets the test: Its assets (here $7,500,000 for D) are 10% or more of the combined assets of all operating segments (here $6,750,000 = .10 × $67,500,000).

F meets none of these tests.

Note: Some of the above segments meet more than one test. Only one needs to be met for a segment to be reportable.

203. **Answer: A**

There are three possible quantitative tests to determine if a segment is reportable. If one or more of the tests is met, the segment is reported. One of these tests is the revenue test. This test determines if the segment's revenue, which includes both sales to external (unaffiliated customers) and intersegment sales, is 10% or more of the combined revenue of all the company's operating segments. Therefore, both items are considered.

204. **Answer: D**

Under FAS 131, a segment is reportable if its sales (including intersegment sales) are at least 10% of total combined revenues (including intersegment sales) for all segments.

Total combined sales are $150,000. Thus, all three segments are reportable because the combined sales of each exceed $15,000.

205. **Answer: D**

FAS 131, issued in 1997, uses the term "operating segments" rather than business segments. All four meet at least one of the three criteria for a reportable segment. A segment needs to meet only one of these criteria to be reportable (that is, required to report income and other data separately).

The three criteria are (summarized):

1. Segment revenue is 10% or more of total revenue for all reported operating segments.
2. Segment profit or loss is 10% or more of total profit for those segments reporting a profit, or 10% of total loss for those segments reporting a loss, whichever is greater in absolute amount.
3. Segment assets are 10% or more of total assets of all operating segments. Thus, each segment meets at least one of the three criteria.

206. **Answer: A**

When interim period inventory market value declines are not considered temporary (not

expected to reverse), they are recognized in the quarter in which the decline occurs. Later recoveries are recognized as gains to the extent of previous losses only. The inventory may not be marked up above cost.

207. **Answer: C**

Discontinued operations are not related to any other interim period. Therefore, it would be erroneous to allocate their financial statement effects to more than one interim period.

208. **Answer: D**

Interim financial statements generally should reflect the same accounting principles used in preparing annual financial statements. Interim periods are considered an integral part of the annual period, with some exceptions.

209. **Answer: C**

Interim income tax expense equals the difference between (1) the total income tax through the end of the interim period at the estimated annual tax rate, and (2) the income tax expense recognized in previous interim periods of the same year. For the second quarter, income tax expense therefore is computed as ($10,000 + $20,000)(.25) − $1,500 = $6,000.

210. **Answer: D**

Unless temporary, declines in the market value of inventory should be recognized in full in the interim period in which they occur.

They should not be deferred to a later period. In this way, the quarterly financial statement reports a significant event for that quarter.

This is an example of an exception to the overall view adopted by the APB with regard to interim reports: that interim reports should be an integral part of the annual period.

211. **Answer: A**

The gain from discontinued operations should be recognized entirely in the second quarter. There is no meaningful basis on which to allocate the gain. It is a one-time occurrence. The cumulative effect is not recognized in income. The firm's treatment of the property tax cost is correct. The cost relates to the entire year. Therefore, each quarter should bear 1/4 of the cost.

Third quarter net income = $91,000 = $111,000 − $60,000/3.

212. **Answer: D**

Paragraph 14.d. of APB Opinion 28 states: "Purchase price variances or volume or capacity cost variances that are planned and expected to be absorbed by the end of the annual period should ordinarily be deferred at interim reporting dates."

The reason for the deferral is that, from the point of view of the entire reporting year, there will be no volume variance. The Opinion requires the integral view of interim reporting for most items—that an interim period is an integral part of the annual period. Recognizing, rather than deferring, the variance in the first quarter would cause the reporting of the first quarter results to be unrepresentative of the annual period of which it is a part.

213. **Answer: A**

Both nontaxable income items (e.g., life insurance proceeds from the death of an officer) and nondeductible expenses (e.g., premium cost of life insurance on an officer) would be recognized in financial statements prepared using an income tax basis of accounting.

214. **Answer: C**

The modified cash basis of accounting employs some elements of accrual accounting (Statement I) and the modifications to cash basis must have substantial support in practice (Statement II). Both statements are correct.

215. **Answer: C**

Pure accrual basis accounting is not an other comprehensive basis of accounting. The concept of "other comprehensive basis" means a comprehensive basis of accounting other than pure (or full) accrual accounting.

216. **Answer: C**

When the cash basis or the modified cash basis of accounting is used, the title Income Statement, which is appropriate when the accrual basis of accounting is used, should be replaced by the title Statement of Cash Receipts and Cash Disbursements. This helps distinguish that the statement is not based on full accrual accounting consistent with U.S. GAAP.

217. **Answer: C**

The amount of the rental expense error made in the tax return (and financial statements) of the prior period would be reported as a prior period adjustment in Alco's 2012 financial statements.

218. **Answer: A**

Liabilities are to be measured using existing GAAP and not written down based on expectations unless legally forgiven.

219. **Answer: B**

Adoption of a private company standard is done on a prospective basis.

220. **Answer: B**

The correct cash balance is the balance per the checkbook ($12,000) plus the $1,800 check written to the vendor, for a total of $13,800.

This check reduced the balance in the checkbook but was not mailed. Thus, the amount remains in Grey's cash balance at the end of the year. The bank statement balance is not the correct balance because information about transactions affecting cash near the end of the month, recorded by Grey, did not reach the bank by the cutoff date.

221. **Answer: C**

The first three items in the list are included in cash and cash equivalents. The total of these items is $1,400,000 ($350,000 + $250,000 + $800,000).

Money market accounts are included in cash equivalents because they maintain a $1 per share value, and are readily convertible to cash (there is no maturity date). The Treasury bill is a cash equivalent because it has an original maturity to the firm of three months or less (12/1/04, maturing 2/28/05).

The Treasury bond matures within two months from the balance sheet date but did not have an original maturity of less than three months. The original maturity is one year, far in excess of the three-month limit and thus the bond is not a cash equivalent.

The reason for the three-month rule is to minimize price fluctuations due to interest rate changes. A security with a fluctuating price is not "equivalent" to cash. One year is too long a time to expect interest rates to remain stable.

222. **Answer: A**

The accounts are with different banks. Thus, the accounts cannot be offset against one another.

The overdraft is a liability because the bank honored a check or withdrawal causing the account to be negative. The firm owes the bank this amount.

The regular corporate account is part of the cash account, a current asset. The segregated account is a long-term investment. The cash in this asset is set aside for a specific purpose. There is no intent to use the cash for ordinary operating purposes.

223. **Answer: D**

The cash balance is $20,200: the sum of the checking account balance and the petty cash. Because it has a maturity of less than three months, the only cash equivalent is the $7,000 of commercial paper. The final sum of these two accounts is $27,200.

224. **Answer: A**

Current assets are those assets expected to be consumed or realized in cash within one year of the balance sheet date. There is no overdraft because the checks were not sent as of the balance sheet date. Thus, the balance sheet should disclose $20,000 in cash ($30,000 − $10,000).

The land held for resale is a current asset because it is expected to be sold in the next year (and the corroboration of this expectation was known before the issuance of the financial statements).

Cash	$20,000
Net accounts receivable	35,000
Inventory	58,000
Prepaid expenses	12,000
Land held for resale	100,000
Total current assets	$225,000

225. **Answer: C**

There is no information about errors in the book's records, represented by the checkbook balance. The deposit in transit and outstanding checks have been recorded by the firm. The checkbook balance reflects these amounts. It is the bank balance that does not. The checkbook balance is the correct ending cash balance.

As a check, take the ending balance per bank + deposits in transit − outstanding checks; $10,000 + $5,000 − $1,000 = $14,000.

226. **Answer: A**

Only amounts adjusting the balance per books require an adjusting entry because only those amounts explain why the firm's recorded cash balance is not the same as the true cash balance. Common adjustments of this type include bank service charges, notes collected,

and interest. The firm cannot alter the bank balance.

227. **Answer: C**

The reconciling items that need to be adjusted to the bank balance are: checks outstanding (−1,500) and deposit in transit (+350). The net cash after the reconciliation is: Bank balance $54,200 − 1,500 + 350 = $53,050. The bank service charge and insufficient funds are already reflected in the bank balance. The error is on Hilltop's books, not on the bank statement, and therefore does not need to be included in the reconciliation.

228. **Answer: A**

Balance per bank statement	$18,050
Plus deposit in transit	3,250
Less outstanding checks	(2,750)
Equals ending cash balance	$18,550

The effects of the bank service charges and the insufficient funds check are already reflected in the balance per the bank statement. The bank was the source of that information.

229. **Answer: A**

Balance per books, 3/31	$44,200
Deposits per bank, April	$58,400
Less deposit in transit, 3/31	(10,300)
Equals deposits made by firm in April	48,100
Checks clearing bank in April	$49,700
Less outstanding checks, 3/31	(12,600)
Plus outstanding checks, 4/30	7,000
Equals checks written by firm in April	(44,100)
Balance per books, 4/30	$48,200

230. **Answer: C**

$5,000(1 − .30)(1 − .20)(.98) + $200 = $2,944.

The chain trade discounts are applied to each successive net amount as shown in the calculation, and the cash discount of 2% is then applied to the final invoice amount.

The cash discount applies because the payment was made within 15 days of purchase. The goods were shipped FOB shipping point. Therefore, title transferred to Burr at the shipping point, meaning Burr bears the shipping charges. Because Pitt prepaid them as an accommodation, Burr must reimburse Pitt for the $200, the last term in the calculation leading to $2,944.

231. Answer: A

The entry is:

Allowance for uncollectible accounts	xxxx
Accounts receivable	xxxx

The allowance is contra to accounts receivable and thus the entry does not affect net accounts receivable. The entry does not affect current assets, working capital, or income. However, the entry does reduce gross accounts receivable. Thus, the answer "affects neither net income nor working capital" is the only possible correct answer. The answer "affects neither net income nor accounts receivable" is incorrect if "accounts receivable" is interpreted as gross accounts receivable.

232. Answer: D

Under the allowance method for uncollectible accounts there is no impact on the balance sheet or net income when the receivable is written off. The estimated uncollectible is recognized at the time of the sale; therefore, when the account is written off, the allowance and the accounts receivable are both reduced, resulting in no effect on the income statement or balance sheet.

233. Answer: A

Under the cash basis of accounting, sales equals cash collected from customers. An equation or T account may be used to determine this amount:

AR, beginning	+	Sales	−	Write-offs	−	Customer collections	=	AR, ending
$500,000		$2,300,000		$10,000		?		= $650,000

Solving for the unknown (?) amount, customer collections equals $2,140,000.

This is the amount collected from customers, and is the amount that would be reported as sales under the cash basis method of accounting.

234. Answer: A

Under the direct write-off method, write-offs are credited directly to accounts receivable (AR). No allowance account is used. Under the terms of the question, accounts receivable increased during the year.

Increase in AR = sales − cash collections − write-offs

cash collections = sales − increase in AR − write-offs

235. Answer: D

Beginning allowance balance + uncollectible accounts expense − write-offs + recoveries = ending allowance balance

$28,000 + uncollectible accounts expense − $23,000 + $5,000 = ($270,000 − $250,000)

Uncollectible accounts expense = $10,000

Under the aging method, the ending allowance balance equals the difference between gross accounts receivable ($270,000) and net realizable value of accounts receivable ($250,000).

Write-offs decrease the allowance balance, and uncollectible accounts expense increases the allowance.

Recoveries also increase the allowance because the amount by which the allowance was decreased when the account was written off is reinstated on recovery.

236. Answer: B

This question requires a determination of the pre-adjustment balance in the allowance account, and the ending balance. The difference between these two amounts is the increase in the account needed, which is also the amount recognized as bad debt expense. The aging method first determines the required ending balance in the allowance account, and then places the amount needed to increase the account to this required balance into the allowance account.

The pre-adjustment allowance balance =

Beginning balance − Write-offs + Recoveries =

$30,000 − $18,000 + $2,000 = $14,000

The ending allowance balance =

$350,000 ending gross AR − $325,000 ending net value of AR = $25,000

Therefore, bad debt expense is the amount needed to bring the allowance balance up to the ending balance of $25,000. The increase needed is $11,000 ($25,000 − $14,000).

237. Answer: A

Beginning allowance balance	$24,000
Less write-off	(96,000)
Equals pre-adjustment allowance balance	(72,000) (debit)

The allowance balance normally is a credit. For the ending balance in the account after adjustment to be $100,000 credit, the account must be increased $172,000 by recognizing uncollectible accounts expense.

Under the aging method, uncollectible accounts expense equals the amount required to increase the allowance balance to the indicated total based on the aging of receivables.

238. **Answer: B**

The credit sales method does not adjust the allowance balance to a required ending amount, but rather simply places the appropriate percent of sales into uncollectible accounts expense and the allowance account. $2\% \times \$1,000,000 = \$20,000$.

239. **Answer: D**

The amount of the adjustment to get the $50,000 debit balance to a $90,000 ($3\% \times$ $3,000,000) credit balance is $140,000.

240. **Answer: D**

The correct answer, $30,000, is the ending balance in the allowance account and equals: $.03(\$1,000,000) = \$30,000$. The firm is basing its estimate on receivables. Therefore, the $30,000 is the target ending allowance balance.

The firm will recognize an amount of bad debt expense at the end of 2005 such that, after considering the beginning allowance balance and any write-offs during the year, the ending allowance balance will be $30,000.

The bad debt expense amount recognized will be affected by the $8,000 beginning balance, but the ending allowance balance will not.

241. **Answer: C**

The term "accrued interest receivable" refers to the cash amount of interest due. The cash amount of interest due is based on the contractual interest rate and face value. The loan origination fee is a way of increasing the effective interest but it does not affect the cash interest component. The $2,000 accrued interest = $(.12)(1/12)(\$200,000)$.

242. **Answer: C**

As of June 30, 2005, only one payment has been received (July 1, 2004). Thus, $100,000 of principal balance has been outstanding for an entire year as of the balance sheet date. Interest receivable on June 30, 2005 is thus $8,000 ($.08 \times$ $100,000).

243. **Answer: C**

The $610,000 net unearned fee revenue = $(21)(\$30,000) - \$20,000$. This amount includes the notes received, but does not include the one expected uncollectible note.

The notes receivable balance, recorded along with the unearned revenue, will not reflect the note expected to be uncollectible. Bad debt expense is not recorded for this note because there has been no revenue recognized against which to match the expense.

244. **Answer: C**

Because the last interest payment was made on November 1, the interest for November and December is unpaid as of December 31, 2005. Therefore, two months of interest is receivable, as of December 31, 2005, for a total receivable of $10,000 = $(2/12)(12\%)(\$500,000)$. No principal payments have yet been made as of this date.

245. **Answer: B**

Total interest revenue is the amount received over the term of the note less the present value of the note: $5(\$5,009) - \$19,485 = \$5,560$.

Leaf paid $19,485 for the note, and will receive $5(\$5,009)$ over the note term. The difference is interest revenue.

246. **Answer: C**

Total interest over the life of the note equals the total amount paid by Ace over the life of the note less the proceeds to Ace. The proceeds equal the present value of the payments at the 9% yield rate. The annual payment is found using the 8% rate because that rate is contractually set and determines the annual payment.

The annual payment P is found as: $20,000 = P(3.992). P = \$5,010$

Total interest revenue = total payments by Ace – proceeds to Ace

$= 5(\$5,010) - \$5,010(3.89) = \$5,560$.

247. **Answer: C**

Maturity value of the note: $500,000(1.08)	$540,000
Less discount to the bank: $540,000(.10)(6/12)	(27,000)
Equals proceeds to Roth	$513,000

The bank charges its discount on the maturity amount for the period it holds the note. In effect, it is charging interest on interest yet to accrue (for the last six months). This procedure is followed because the maturity value is the amount at risk.

248. **Answer: C**

Six months remain in the note term at the date of discounting.

Maturity value of note:	$200,000
Less discount: $200,000(.10)(6/12)	(10,000)
Equals proceeds on note	$190,000

249. **Answer: B**

Factoring is a sale of receivables. This allows Red Co. to sell the receivables and receive cash immediately upon sale.

250. **Answer: B**

The bank charges its discount (its fee) on the maturity value, which is the face value of the note plus 12% interest for 120 days. The bank charges 15% on this amount for the 80 remaining days in the note term. Thus, the proceeds equal the maturity value less its fee.

251. **Answer: C**

In a pledge arrangement, the title remains with the originator, in this case with Milton Co.

252. **Answer: A**

The net cash received when the receivables were factored was $80,000 × .85 (100% − 10% − 5%) = $68,000.

253. **Answer: D**

The firm is contingent for the maturity amount, which for a noninterest-bearing note is the face value. If the maker of the note fails to pay the bank or financial institution with whom Davis discounted the note, Davis would be called on to pay the entire maturity amount.

254. **Answer: D**

A CGU is the smallest group of assets that can be identified that generates cash flows independently of the cash flows from other assets.

255. **Answer: A**

A loan impairment is recorded by reducing the net book value of the receivable to the present value of probable future cash inflows, discounted at the original rate in the receivable. The original rate is used because the loan continues to exist. The loss to the firm is measured at the rate existing when the original loan was created. The difference between the book value and present value, at the date of recognizing the impairment, is recorded as an expense or loss. There is no reason to report overstated assets.

256. **Answer: D**

A note is considered to be impaired if the present value of remaining cash flows is less than book value, using the rate in the note. This is caused by an expected delay in timing of cash flows or reduction in amount of cash flows compared with the original agreement. The creditor makes the determination that the note is impaired and writes the note down to present value. A loss is recorded for the decline in carrying value to present value.

257. **Answer: A**

The interest method recognizes interest revenue each year until the note is collected because the note was written down to present value when the impairment was recorded. The estimated future cash flows to be received include interest, which is recognized over the remaining term of the note. The cost recovery method recognizes interest revenue only after cash equal to the new carrying value is collected. During Year 3, total collections surpassed the $25,000 new carrying value. $3,000 of interest revenue is recognized under this method in Year 3 ($28,000 − $25,000).

258. **Answer: B**

This is a chain discount and the correct recorded cost is $20,000(1 − .20)(1 − .10) = $14,400. Each successive discount in a chain discount is applied to the previous net amount.

259. **Answer: D**

Kerr will pay only $50,000 for the goods. None of the other costs listed are incurred by Kerr. Rather, the seller will incur those costs.

Even the shipping costs are borne by the seller because the terms are FOB destination. This means that title does not transfer to the buyer (Kerr) until the goods reach the destination. The seller owned the goods in transit and therefore incurred the transportation cost. Kerr's recorded cost is $50,000.

260. **Answer: D**

The correct ending inventory balance is $1,710,000 ($1,500,000 + $90,000 + $120,000).

The $90,000 of merchandise is included because it was shipped before year-end and the title was transferred to Herc at the shipping point (before year-end). The $120,000 also is included because the goods have not been shipped. The FOB designation is irrelevant because the goods have not yet reached a common carrier.

261. **Answer: D**

Consignment sales revenue is the revenue recognized on consignment sales.

In this case, total consignment revenue is $10 \times \$1,000 = \$10,000$. The commission and transportation costs are expenses that reduce earnings on consignment revenues, but they do not affect total revenues to be recognized.

262. **Answer: C**

Merchandise purchased for resale	$400,000
Freight-in	10,000
Purchase returns	(2,000)
Total inventoriable cost	$408,000

Freight-out is a delivery expense. It is not inventoried because the goods have reached salable condition before incurring this cost. Only costs that contribute to preparing inventory for sale are inventoried.

263. **Answer: B**

The correct answer is $910,000:

Raw materials purchased	$430,000
Plus decrease in raw materials	15,000*
Direct labor	200,000
Factory overhead	300,000
Less finished goods increase	(35,000)**
Cost of goods sold	$910,000

*The decrease in raw materials is added to the amount purchased, resulting in the cost of materials incorporated into production. In other words, $15,000 of materials purchased in 2005 were placed into production in 2005. The total cost of materials brought into production in 2005 equals $445,000.

** The increase in finished goods represents costs incurred in the current period to finish inventory that was not sold in the current period. Therefore, these costs must be removed in determining cost of goods sold.

Freight-out is not a manufacturing cost but rather is a distribution cost.

Therefore, freight-out is not inventoried.

There is no change in work-in-process inventory to affect the calculation.

264. **Answer: C**

Beginning inventory	$90,000
Plus purchases	124,000
Less write-off	(34,000)
Less ending inventory	(30,000)
Equals cost of goods sold	$150,000

The write-off cannot be counted in cost of goods sold because it is a decrease in inventory not associated with sales.

265. **Answer: B**

Cost of goods sold is determined (in a periodic inventory system) as:

Beginning Inventory

+ Net Purchases

= Goods Available for Sale

– Ending Inventory

= Cost of Goods Sold

Net Purchases includes any purchase discounts (or allowances) and other cost of getting the goods in place and condition for resale, including freight-in. Freight-out (to customers) is a selling cost. Therefore, Azur Co.'s cost of goods sold would be:

Beginning Inventory, $30,840

+ Purchases, $102,800

– Purchases Discounts, (10,280)

+ Freight-in, 15,420

+ Net Purchases, 107,940

= Goods Available for Sale, $138,780

– Ending Inventory, 20,560

= Cost of Goods Sold, $118,220

266. **Answer: B**

A periodic system does not record the cost of each item as it is sold; nor does it maintain a continuously current record of the inventory balance. Rather, cost of goods sold is the amount derived from the equation: Beginning inventory + Purchases = Ending inventory + Cost of goods sold. A count of ending inventory establishes the inventory remaining at the end of the period, but there is no recording of cost of goods sold during the period. Cost of goods sold is the amount that completes the equation. Thus, cost of goods sold is really the cost of inventory no longer with the firm at year-end—an amount that includes shrinkage. Inventory shrinkage refers to breakage, waste, and theft. Shrinkage cannot be identified directly with a periodic inventory system.

267. **Answer: A**

Under a perpetual inventory system, the cost of goods sold (COGS) is determined at the time of each sale. In a perpetual FIFO inventory system, the cost of each sale (COGS) would be based on the cost of the earliest acquired goods on hand at the time of the sales. The cost of the most recently acquired goods would remain in ending inventory. In a perpetual LIFO inventory system, the cost of each sale (COGS) would be based on the cost of goods acquired just prior to the sale. The cost of the earlier acquired goods would remain in inventory.

Under a periodic inventory system, the cost of goods sold (COGS) and ending inventory are determined only at the end of the period. In a periodic FIFO inventory system, the cost of sales for the period (COGS) would be based on the cost of the earliest acquired goods available during the period. The cost of the most recently acquired goods would remain in ending inventory. In a periodic LIFO inventory system, the cost of sales for the period (COGS) would be based on the last goods acquired during the period. The cost of the earliest acquired goods would remain in ending inventory. The above descriptions can be summarized as follows for determination of COGS:

Inventory System/ Method	Cost of Goods Sold Determined Using FIFO	Cost of Goods Sold Determined Using LIFO
Perpetual	Earliest goods acquired	Latest goods acquired prior to each sale
Periodic	Earliest goods acquired	Latest goods acquired during the period

Since cost of goods sold for the period would be the same under both perpetual FIFO and periodic FIFO, ending inventory would be the same under both perpetual FIFO and periodic FIFO. Cost of goods sold (and ending inventory) would not be the same under perpetual LIFO as under periodic LIFO because the perpetual system recognizes cost of goods sold based on the cost of goods acquired just prior to each sale, whereas the periodic system recognizes

cost of goods sold based on cost of goods acquired prior to the end of each period.

268. **Answer: C**

Units beginning inventory remaining at year-end (3,200 – 1,600)$8	= $12,800
Plus 1/22 purchase: 4,800($9.60)	= 46,080
Ending inventory	= $58,880
Ending unit cost: $58,880/6,400	= $9.20

The moving average method costs issues at the unit cost of goods on hand at that point. Thus, the issue was costed at $8.00 per unit. The cost per unit changes with each purchase.

269. **Answer: B**

Under the LIFO (last-in, first-out) inventory method, goods sold are assumed to be the most recently acquired goods (at their related costs). Therefore, goods remaining (ending inventory) are assumed to be the earliest acquired goods (at their related costs). If the perpetual LIFO inventory method is used, when goods are sold, they are assumed to be the goods acquired just prior to the sale.

Thus, Nest's sale of 1,800 units on 1/23 would have consisted of the 1,200 units acquired 1/8 and 600 units (of the 2,000) in beginning inventory. Ending inventory on January 31 would be:

1,400 units of beginning inventory @ $1 each	= $1,400
800 units purchased 1/28 @ $5 each	= 4,000
2,200 units in ending inventory reported @	= $5,400

If the periodic LIFO inventory method is used, ending inventory (and cost of goods sold) are determined only at the end of the period. Therefore, Nest's sale of 1,800 units on 1/23 would have consisted of (by assumption at the end of the period) 800 units acquired on 1/28 and 1,000 units (of the 1,200) acquired on 1/8. Ending inventory on January 31 would be:

200 units of the 1,200 purchased 1/8 @ $3	= $600
2,000 units (all) of beginning inventory @ $1	= 2,000
2,200 units in ending inventory reported @	= $2,600

270. **Answer: A**

FIFO produces the same results for periodic and perpetual systems. FIFO always assumes the sale of the earliest goods acquired. Therefore, unlike periodic LIFO, goods can never be assumed sold before they are acquired.

Cost of goods sold and ending inventory are the same under FIFO for both a periodic and a perpetual system.

271. **Answer: C**

Ending inventory would decrease because under LIFO, the latest items purchased (and therefore the most costly) are considered sold, leaving the earliest items purchased (and therefore the least costly) in inventory. This is opposite to the effect under FIFO.

The same is true for net income because now, under LIFO, cost of goods sold is increased relative to FIFO because the cost of the latest and most costly items are considered sold first.

272. **Answer: A**

FIFO assumes the sale of the earliest goods first. With rising prices, the earliest goods reflect the lowest prices. Therefore, cost of goods sold under FIFO is the lowest of the cost flow assumptions. With the lowest cost of goods sold, gross margin and income are the highest among the available cost flow assumptions (LIFO and average being the others).

273. **Answer: A**

LIFO assumes the sale of the most recent purchases first and thus results in cost of goods sold that is the most current value. FIFO assumes the sale of the earliest purchases first (and beginning inventory before any purchases) and thus results in ending inventory that is the most current value. FIFO is sometimes called LISH: last in still here.

274. **Answer: B**

Beginning inventory of $50,000 is at base-year dollars and the current-year increase of $30,000 is also at base-year dollars. The current-year layer must be converted to current-year costs ($30,000 × 1.10) = $33,000. Ending dollar value LIFO is the beginning dollar value LIFO (in this case it was adopted in January so the beginning inventory must be $50,000) plus the current-year layer of $33,000 or $83,000. Note that the sentence "The designated market value of Stitch's inventory exceeded its cost at year-end" is a distracter. It is simply stating that there is not an issue with the lower of cost or market since cost is lower.

275. **Answer: C**

The ending inventory is used to construct the internal price index. At the end of 2004, the ratio of current cost to base-year cost for ending inventory is $80,000/$60,000 = 1 1/3 or 4/3. This ratio is applied to the 2004 layer at base-year cost, yielding $20,000 ($15,000 × 4/3). This amount is the increase to DV LIFO. Therefore, ending 2004 DV LIFO is $66,000 ($46,000 + $20,000).

276. **Answer: C**

The price level index for 2006 is 1.1 ($440,000/$400,000). Ending 2006 DV LIFO inventory equals the beginning inventory DV LIFO plus the increase in inventory at base-year dollars converted to 2006 prices:

Ending DV LIFO = Beginning DV LIFO + (increase at base-year dollars)(1.1)

= $300,000 + ($400,000 – $300,000)(1.1) = $410,000.

277. **Answer: C**

The question provides the ending inventory for 2007 at current cost by layer. The sum of the current cost column ($200,000) is the current cost of the entire inventory at the end of 2007. The sum of the base-year cost for the three years is $150,000. Hence, under this assumption, the ratio of current cost for the total inventory at the end of 2007 to the base-year cost is 1.33 ($200,000/$150,000). This index is then multiplied by the 2007 layer in base-year dollars to derive the increment to DV LIFO ending inventory.

278. **Answer: B**

Lower of cost or net realizable value applies to inventories that are carried at FIFO or Average cost. Net realizable value is selling price less cost of disposal. In this case it is $408,000 – $20,000 = $388,00.

279. **Answer: C**

Inventory must be carried at lower of cost (such as LIFO, FIFO) or market. Market is replacement cost subject to a ceiling and floor. The ceiling for replacement cost is net realizable value (selling price less cost to complete) and the floor is net realizable value less normal profit margin. Use simple numbers to help solve this abstract question. In this question original cost (assume = 100) is greater than market ((replacement cost) assume = 80). Market (80) is greater than net realizable value (assume = 70). Market is subject to a ceiling of net realizable value (70).

In this case the inventory would be valued at net realizable value.

280. **Answer: B**

The "ceiling" for LCM (lower of cost or market) valuation is $261,000 net realizable value ($275,000 selling price less $14,000 disposal cost). The "floor" is net realizable value less normal profit margin or $251,000 ($261,000 – $10,000). Replacement cost of $230,000 is below the floor, so "market" value is the floor, or middle, of the three amounts ($251,000). This amount is less than cost of $258,000. Therefore, the lower of cost or market valuation is $251,000.

281. **Answer: C**

In LCM, market value is replacement cost if replacement cost is between the ceiling value (net realizable value) and the floor value (net realizable value less normal profit margin).

This is the situation in this question. The original cost is below the floor value. Thus, market exceeds cost and the item is recorded at cost (lower of cost or market).

282. **Answer: B**

The easiest way to answer a question like this is to make up simple numbers. The following simple numbers were made up to fit the abstract information in the question. Lower of cost or market states you record the inventory at the lower of original cost or market value (replacement cost) within the range of a ceiling and a floor. The numbers below show that replacement cost is lower than original cost and within the floor and ceiling. Replacement cost is the correct answer.

Original cost	$10
Net realizable value	9
Replacement cost	8
NRV less normal PM	7

283. **Answer: B**

The gross margin method applies the cost to sales ratio to sales in order to derive an estimate of cost of goods sold. Subtracting the resulting estimate of cost of goods sold from the cost of goods available for sale yields an estimate of ending inventory without counting the items. This firm determines the selling price to be 140% of cost because the markup is 40% of cost. Cost plus markup yields selling price. Therefore, the cost to sales ratio is 1.00/1.40 or .71.

284. **Answer: B**

The gross margin method estimates the cost of inventory at the time of the fire as follows: Beginning inventory $200,000 + $1,000,000 Purchases = Ending inventory + Cost of goods sold. The estimate of cost of goods sold is found by multiplying the cost to sales ratio and sales. The gross margin percentage plus the cost to sales ratio is 1; therefore, cost/sales is .60 (= 1 – .40). Estimated cost of goods sold is $720,000 (= .60($1,200,000)). The equation is Beginning inventory ($200,000) + Purchases ($1,000,000) = Ending inventory + Cost of goods sold ($720,000). Solving for ending inventory yields $480,000.

285. **Answer: C**

When items are purchased as a group, the total cost of the group is allocated to the individual items based on fair value. Replacement cost is the appropriate value to use in this case. The total replacement cost of the items is $1,100 ($400 + $700). Therefore, Item A is allocated 4/11 of the purchase cost, or $364 = ($400/$1,100)$1,000.

286. **Answer: A**

The gross margin method of estimating inventory is used to solve this problem. The cost of inventory lost cannot be identified by count but it can be estimated.

First, an estimate of cost of goods sold is subtracted from the cost of goods available on the date of the flood yielding the total amount of inventory that would have been present on May 1.

Second, the amount of inventory not lost is subtracted from the May 1 estimated total inventory. The result is an estimate of the amount lost.

With gross profit being 40% of sales, cost of goods sold must be 60% of sales, on average. Therefore, the estimate of cost of goods sold is $150,000 (.60 × $250,000). Beginning inventory ($35,000) + Purchases ($200,000) = Goods available = $235,000. Subtracting $150,000 of cost of goods sold yields $85,000 of inventory on May 1 ($235,000 – $150,000).

With $30,000 of inventory still accounted for, the amount of lost inventory at cost is $55,000 ($85,000 – $30,000).

287. **Answer: A**

The retail method measures beginning inventory and net purchases at both cost and retail. It then applies the average relationship between cost and retail (based on beginning inventory and purchases) to ending inventory at retail to determine ending inventory at cost.

Purchase returns reduce net purchases at both cost and retail because returns represent amounts included in gross purchases that are not available for sale.

288. **Answer: C**

Ending inventory at retail = $567 (= $467 + $2,000 + $100 − $300 − $1,700). The cost-to-retail ratio for FIFO LCM excludes both the beginning inventory amounts and net markdowns. C/R = $1,200/($2,000 + $100) = .57. Ending inventory at cost = $567(.57) = $323. Cost of goods sold = $300 + $1,200−$323 = $1,177. Note that cost of goods sold is based solely on cost.

289. **Answer: D**

Although the result is approximate, by excluding net markdowns from the denominator of the cost-to-retail ratio, the ratio is a smaller amount, resulting in a lower ending inventory valuation.

290. **Answer: A**

The cost-to-retail ratio under FIFO is: $60,000/($110,000 + $10,000 − $20,000) = .60.

Ending inventory at retail is $30,000 + $110,000 + $10,000 − $20,000 − $90,000 = $40,000.

Ending inventory at cost, therefore, is .60($40,000) = $24,000.

291. **Answer: C**

This is a two-step process. First, DV LIFO is applied to retail dollars to determine the layer added in current-year retail dollars. Then, the FIFO cost-to-retail ratio (C/R) is applied to convert that layer to cost. Finally, this layer is added to beginning inventory at cost to yield ending inventory at cost. The calculation is:

EI retail, current index = $2,000 + $40,000−$28,000 = $14,000

EI retail, base = $14,000/1.6 = $8,750

Increase in EI retail, base = $8,750−$1,600 = $7,150

Increase in EI retail, current = $7,150(1.6) = $11,440

C/R (use FIFO, not LCM) = $12,000/$40,000 = .30

Increase in EI, cost = .30($11,440) = $3,432

EI, cost = $800 + $3,432= $4,232

292. **Answer: A**

The DV LIFO retail process applies the DV LIFO method to retail dollars, and then deflates the retail layer added, now reflecting current prices, to cost, using the cost-to-retail ratio. The calculations are:

Ending inventory, retail, at base = $450(1.00/1.15) = $391

Increase in retail, current = $111(1.15/1.00) = $128

Increase in cost = $128(.42) = $54

Ending inventory at cost = ($80 + $30) + $54 = $164

293. **Answer: C**

DV LIFO retail uses the FIFO (not LCM) cost-to-retail ratio. Under LIFO, a layer added during a period should reflect only the cost and retail amounts pertaining to that period. Thus, beginning inventory amounts are not used in calculating the ratio. Also, because LIFO may contain inventory layers for several preceding periods, excluding net markdowns is not an effective way to accomplish the LCM valuation objective. Thus, net markdowns are included in the cost to retail computation.

294. **Answer: C**

The effect of the beginning-inventory error is to understate cost of goods sold $26,000. The effect of the ending-inventory error is to understate cost of goods sold $52,000. The total effect then is to understate cost of goods sold $78,000.

These effects are analyzed by using the equation:

Beginning inventory + Purchases − Ending inventory = Cost of goods sold

For example, if beginning inventory is understated, then the right-hand side of the equation (cost of goods sold) must also be understated by the same amount.

295. **Answer: D**

Counterbalancing simply means that the effect of the inventory error in the second year is opposite that of the first year. Discovery in year two provides an opportunity for the firm to correct year two beginning retained earnings, which is overstated by the error in year one. The overstatement of inventory in year one caused cost of goods sold to be understated and income overstated in year one. The prior period adjustment, dated as of the beginning of year two, is a debit to retained earnings for the after-tax effect of the income overstatement in year one. Inventory is credited for the amount of the overstatement. This allows year two to begin with corrected balances.

296. **Answer: D**

Use the equation BI + PUR = EI CGS. When EI is understated, CGS must be overstated to maintain the equation. Net income, therefore, is understated (20X5). Then next year, BI is also understated because BI for 20X6 is EI for 20X5. Using the equation, if BI is understated, CGS is also understated to maintain the equation.

297. **Answer: A**

The firm has committed to a purchase for a total cost of $26,000, but at year-end, the value of the item to be received is $3,000 less. The firm cannot postpone the loss and liability recognition because the reduction in the firm's earnings and net assets has already occurred. The economic events causing the loss have occurred as of the Balance Sheet date.

298. **Answer: C**

Both qualities are required for a loss to be recognized. The firm must honor a contract in a later period by paying more than current cost and, thus, is in a loss position at the end of the current year.

299. **Answer: B**

The maximum recorded value of the inventory is $60,000, which is the contractual amount and, also, the cost. If the firm can sell the inventory for more than $60,000, then gross margin will be recognized. The value of the inventory more than fully recovered, but gains are limited to the amount of previously recognized losses, which in this case is $8,000.

300. **Answer: A**

The firm has committed to a fixed price but must recognize the loss in the period the decline in price occurred, much like under lower-of-cost-or-market. Inventory is not reduced because the firm has not purchased the inventory under contract. There is no asset to reduce, but the decrease in net assets is accomplished by recording the liability for the portion of the purchase price that has no value.

301. **Answer: A**

Under IFRS, inventory is carried at the lower of cost or net realizable value. Recovery of

previous write-downs is allowed. Therefore, in year 2, the company can recover the previous write-down of $20 ($100 – 80) but cannot write the inventory above the original cost. The entry to record the recovery is a debit to inventory and credit to expense or cost of goods sold for $20.

302. **Answer: C**

IFRS reports inventory at lower of cost or net realizable value. Net realizable value is the selling price less the cost to complete or dispose of the inventory. The net realizable value is the selling price of $1,000 less the cost to complete of $100, or $900. Net realizable value is less than the cost ($910) so the inventory is reported at $900.

303. **Answer: D**

Only assets used in current operations are included in the category of property, plant, and equipment (PPE) on the balance sheet. Assets that are held for sale are reclassified from PPE to "assets held for sale" and are no longer depreciated. This questions is an example of a questions framed in the null form. That is, the question wants you to find the exception. This response states the asset will be valued at historical cost—that is false. An asset held for sale is reported at net realizable value.

304. **Answer: B**

A useful life of at least three years is NOT a requirement for classification of a plant asset. The plant asset must have a useful life extending more than one year beyond the Balance Sheet date.

305. **Answer: D**

All items listed are required disclosures: useful life, depreciation methods, and the accumulated depreciation of plant asset. Read through select disclosures of the financial statements of real companies—this will help reinforce the disclosure requirements and jog your memory because you will remember reading about the disclosure.

306. **Answer: A**

All three costs are included for a total of $155,000. Both the shipping and testing costs are necessary to place the asset into its intended location and condition for use. This is the criterion for capitalizing costs on acquisition of plant assets.

307. **Answer: C**

The gain or loss on the sale of an asset is part of continuing operations, as it is expected that a company will sell existing assets from time to time as the assets are replaced.

308. **Answer: C**

The correct answer, $332,000, equals: $300,000 + $25,000–$4,000 + $5,000 + $6,000.

The net cost to raze the old building ($21,000) is capitalized to land because it is a cost necessary to bring the land into its intended condition. The legal fees and title guarantee cost, likewise, must be incurred to avoid future legal problems, and thus contribute to the value of the land.

309. **Answer: D**

Every cost listed is a cost necessary to place the asset into its intended condition and location. This is the general rule for capitalizing costs to plant assets.

Thus, all four costs are capitalized to the machine yielding a final capitalized value of $138,000 ($126,000 + $3,000 + $4,000 + $5,000).

310. **Answer: D**

This response includes all the costs to get the equipment ready for use. The rearrangement costs and the wall removal costs were needed to put the equipment into use. The rearrangement costs made the production more efficient.

311. **Answer: B**

The more objective or readily determinable value is used for recording the building. If the number of shares is significant in relation to the total shares outstanding, the stock price will be affected by the increase in the shares outstanding resulting from the purchase. The more objective value is the appraised value of the building.

312. **Answer: C**

The sum of the four listed costs is $120,000, which exceeds fair value of $105,000. Therefore, the asset is capitalized at $105,000, the lesser of the two amounts. Subtracting the $10,000 residual value yields $95,000 depreciable cost— the total depreciation over the life of the asset.

313. **Answer: C**

The capitalized cost is the sum of the down payment, present value of the note payments,

and the shipping and installation charges: $4,000 + $6,000(2.58) $2,000 $3,500 = $24,980. The present value of the three payments required on the note is capitalized, which excludes the interest included in those payments. The two charges are capitalized because they were incurred to place the asset into its intended condition and location.

314. **Answer: C**

The amounts necessary to get the land ready for its intended purpose attach themselves as a part of the total cost of the land. This would be $2,500 + $625 + $135,000 + $16,000 = $154,125.

315. **Answer: A**

The interest expense recognized for the first year is .06($30,000) = $1,800. Although no interest is paid, interest is accrued, increasing the carrying value of the note. The asset is capitalized at $50,000, the sum of the cash down payment and present value of the note. The interest over the note term is not capitalized because it does not assist in the process of placing the asset into its intended condition and location.

316. **Answer: C**

First calculate the Average Accumulated Expenditures (AAE). This gives you the amount of borrowing from which to calculate avoidable interest ($625,000). Next calculate avoidable interest ($72,500) and actual interest (($500,000 × 12%) + ($800,000 × 10%) = $140,000). The amount that can be capitalized is the lesser of the avoidable interest or actual interest. The amount that can be capitalized is $72,500.

AAE		
200,000	12/12	200,000
600,000	8/12	400,000
300,000	1/12	25,000
		625,000

Avoidable interest			
500,000	12%	60,000
125,000	10%	12,500
		72,500

317. **Answer: C**

Neither debt issuances were identified as the construction loan. Therefore, the interest rate must be determined based on the weighted average of the interest on all of the debt outstanding during the year. The calculation is as follows:

	$6,0000,000 \times .08 =$	$480,000
	$8,000,000 \times .09 =$	$720,000
Totals	$14,000,000	$1,200,000
	$1,200,000 / $14,000,000 =	8.57%

318. **Answer: D**

Average accumulated expenditures is $156,000 = $40,000 + $120,000(10/12) + $96,000(2/12)$. This method uses the average interest rate on all interest bearing debt, weighted by principal. That rate is the quotient of the interest on all the debt divided by the principal on all the debt. The rate = ($3,600 + $3,600 + $5,400)/$240,000 = .0525$. Interest capitalized = $(.0525)$156,000 = $8,190$.

319. **Answer: D**

Interest during construction on assets constructed for a firm's own use is capitalized until construction is complete. Thus, only the interest incurred after completion is expensed.

Interest is capitalized on the construction of assets for sale only if the assets are large, individual, discrete projects, such as ships or real estate developments. The equipment constructed for sale does not appear to be a discrete item in that sense and, thus, none of the interest is capitalized. It is all expensed.

320. **Answer: A**

Interest on debt incurred when purchasing a plant asset is incurred after the asset has reached its intended condition and location. Therefore, it is expensed as incurred. Debt incurred during the construction of plant assets is considered avoidable and also incurred before the asset has reached its intended condition and location. Therefore, it is capitalized to the asset in the same way material, labor, and overhead are capitalized. The interest is expensed as part of depreciation during the service life of the asset.

321. **Answer: D**

Average accumulated expenditures is the amount of debt for the annual period that could have been avoided. In this case, the firm has $160,000 already invested in the project at the beginning of year six. That amount represents $160,000 in debt, that could have been avoided for year six if the firm had not been involved in the construction project. The expenditures

during year six were incurred evenly. Average accumulated expenditures therefore = $160,000(12/12) + $240,000/2 = $280,000$. Also, [$160,000 + ($160,000 + $240,000)]/2 = $280,000$.

322. **Answer: C**

Average accumulated expenditures for the second year = $400,000(12/12) + $240,000(10/12) + $600,000(3/12) = $750,000$. Interest capitalized = $.08($750,000) = $60,000$. Note that the interest capitalized in year one is compounded in year two because year one capitalized interest is included in average accumulated expenditures for the second year.

323. **Answer: A**

Interest is capitalized on the project's average expenditures times the interest during that period. Key here is to use the 5% annual interest over the three months (April, May, and June).

Average expenditures:	$\frac{500,000 + 800,000 + 1,500,000}{3}$	$= 933,333$
Interest rate for 3-month period:	$.05 \times 3/12$	$\times .0124998$
Capitalized interest:		$11,666$

324. **Answer: B**

The average accumulated expenditures for purposes of capitalizing interest during construction of the warehouse includes the land cost, but the interest is capitalized to the warehouse only. The land is not under construction.

325. **Answer: C**

When the cost and accumulated depreciation of a component or portion of a larger asset is identifiable, and that component or portion is replaced, the replacement is treated as two separate transactions:

(1) disposal of the old component (for zero proceeds in this case, due to the fire damage) and
(2) purchase of the new component.

Thus, a loss equal to the book value of the old component is recognized for (1) and the amount paid to purchase the new component is capitalized as a separate purchase for (2).

326. **Answer: D**

The disposal of the old boiler and purchase of the new boiler are separate transactions. The loss on disposal has no effect on the capitalized cost of the new boiler, which is recorded at its $100,000 purchase cost.

327. Answer: D

All four costs should be capitalized because they result in an increase in the productivity of the asset. Costs that increase EITHER the life OR productivity are capitalized. Either type of increase results in enhanced asset values. $160,000 is the sum of the four costs listed.

328. Answer: A

When the portion of an asset that is removed from a larger asset has identifiable costs and accumulated depreciation amounts, those amounts are removed from the books. The difference between these two amounts is the carrying value of the damaged portion of the larger asset. There is no insurance. Therefore, the carrying value of the damaged portion is written off as a loss. The replacement assets are capitalized at cost. The entries are:

Portion removed	New materials
Loss	Asset
Accumulated depreciation	Cash
Asset	

329. Answer: B

Post-acquisition expenditures, which increase the useful life (assuming normal maintenance) or the utility (usefulness or productivity) of the asset, are capitalized. Such expenditures provide value for more than one year. The original useful life of an asset assumes regular maintenance. Therefore, regular maintenance does not increase the intended useful life of the asset.

330. Answer: A

Without an estimate for total units to be produced, depreciation could not be computed. Annual depreciation under this method is:

[(Cost-salvage value)/(Total estimated production)](units produced year).

The quantity in square brackets is the rate of depreciation per unit.

331. Answer: A

This method is most appropriate when the service potential of an asset can be estimated reliably in terms of a physical variable, such as miles to be driven or number of units of output that can be produced by the asset.

Over time, as more units are produced, the service potential of the asset declines because the total number of units that can be produced is finite. Over time, the number of units that can be produced by the asset in the future declines. The primary causative agent for depreciation under the units of production method is, thus, the actual use of the asset in production.

332. Answer: A

The capitalized cost of the equipment is $110,000, not the total of the cash payments to be made. The latter amount includes interest.

Thus, annual depreciation is $10,500:

($110,000 – $5,000)/10.

333. Answer: C

The accumulated depreciation on the property sold was $10,000 ($50,000 cost less $40,000 carrying value). The sale of property requires that the accumulated depreciation on the property be removed from the accounts.

Thus, the $10,000 amount is a decrease in accumulated depreciation. With an overall increase of $200,000 in accumulated depreciation during the period ($800,000 – $600,000), depreciation must have been $210,000 ($200,000 + $10,000).

334. Answer: A

This is a change in estimate and is handled currently and prospectively by allocating the remaining book value at the beginning of 20X2 over the revised estimate of remaining years at that point. Through the beginning of 20X2, the asset has been used five years. Therefore, seven years remain in the original book value. The book value at the beginning of 20X2 is 7/12 × $48,000 or $28,000. The remaining useful life of seven years is extended to 10. Therefore, depreciation expense for 20X2 is $28,000 × 1/10 or $2,800.

335. Answer: A

Depreciation in 20X4 = $200,000 (1.50/5) =	$60,000
Depreciation in 20X5 = ($200,000 – $60,000)(1.50/5) =	42,000
Accumulated depreciation balance at the end of 20X5	$102,000

The declining balance class of depreciation method does not deduct salvage value when computing depreciation, although care must be taken not to depreciate the asset below salvage value. Also, the rate of depreciation applied to book value is the percentage of the method (150% in this case) divided by the useful life of the asset. Double-declining balance, for example, is 200%/n or 2/n where n = useful life.

336. Answer: B

$180,000, the correct answer, equals $300,000[(5 + 4)/(5 + 4 + 3 + 2 + 1)].

Two full years of depreciation have been recorded, and the SYD method uses the number of years left at the beginning of each year as the numerator of the fraction used in depreciation. At the beginning of the first and second years, five and four years of the asset's life remained, respectively. The denominator is the sum of the digits up to the asset's useful life (5).

337. Answer: C

The carrying amount (book value) of a depreciable asset is its original cost less accumulated depreciation. Under sum-of-the-years' digits method of calculating depreciation expense (and, therefore, accumulated depreciation), the net depreciable cost (original cost less estimated salvage value) is multiplied by a factor consisting of:

Numerator = the number of years the current year is from the end of the life of the asset

Denominator = the sum of numbers (digits) for each year in the life of the asset

For Spiro, the net depreciable cost is $20,000 – $2,000 = $18,000. Since the equipment has an estimated useful life of four years, the sum of the digits for each year would be 1 + 2 + 3 + 4 = 10, the denominator for calculating each year's depreciation. Depreciation for the four years would be:

338. Answer: B

The 200% declining balance depreciation method is also called the double-declining balance method or DDB. Because this is a declining balance method, the book value at the beginning of 20X3 must be computed, and that is affected by depreciation in 20X2. For 20X2, depreciation under DDB is 2/10 × $100,000 or $20,000. Note that salvage value is not subtracted when computing depreciation because the "declining balance" is book value. For 20X3, depreciation is 2/10 × ($100,000– $20,000) = $16,000 because the book value at the beginning of 20X3 is reduced by 20X2 depreciation.

339. Answer: B

Depreciation in 2004 = $240,000(2/10) = $48,000

Depreciation in 20X5 = ($240,000 – $48,000) (2/10) = $38,400

The DDB method's rate is always twice the straight-line rate, or 2/useful life. The method does not subtract salvage value when computing depreciation, but it also does not reduce book value below salvage value. The depreciation in any year is the rate times the beginning net book value of the asset.

340. Answer: D

The depletion rate = [$40 + (.25)($100) + $60]/20 = $6.25/ton. Depletion = 2,000,000($6.25/ton) = $12,500,000. Because all the ore removed was sold, cost of goods sold includes the entire amount of depletion and the extraction costs. Cost of goods sold = $12,500,000 $10,000,000 = $22,500,000. Note that extraction costs is included in inventory (and therefore, cost of goods sold), but not in the deposit (and therefore, not in depletion).

Year	Depreciable Cost	Factor	Annual Depreciation	Accumulated Depreciation	Carrying Value		
20X3	$18,000	× 4/10 =	$7,200	$7,200	$20,000 –	7,200 =	$12,800
20X4	18,000	× 3/10 =	5,400	12,600	20,000 –	12,600 =	7,400
20X5	18,000	× 2/10 =	3,600	16,200	20,000 –	16,200 =	3,800
20X6	18,000	× 1/10 =	1,800	18,000	20,000 –	18,000 =	2,000
Total	18,000	× 10/10 =	18,000	18,000			2,000

Thus, at the end of 20X5 the carrying amount is $3,800, which also can be calculated as salvage value 2,000 + (1/10 × $18,000) = $2,000 + $1,800 = $3,800.

341. **Answer: A**

The depletion rate = ($40 + $100 + $60)/20 = $10/ton. Depletion = 2,000,000($10/ton) = $20,000,000. Depletion for a period is the cost of the deposit allocated to the inventory removed for the period. In this case, the entire amount is included in cost of goods sold because there is no ending inventory. However, if there had been ore left at the end of the period, the $10/ton rate would have been applied to the units remaining. That would not change the answer to the question, however.

342. **Answer: D**

The successful efforts method capitalizes only the cost of exploration efforts that locate the resource. As such, only those efforts that yield a probable future benefit are capitalized. This is a direct application of the asset definition, which requires that an asset have a probable future benefit.

343. **Answer: B**

The sum of the carrying value ($520,000) and removal/cleanup cost ($10,000) is the amount to compare to the insurance proceeds when computing the loss. The fire caused the latter costs to be incurred; therefore, the cleanup costs should be included in the loss.

The fair value of the property would not figure into the recorded loss because the building account does not reflect this amount.

344. **Answer: B**

The gain of $300 is the difference between the insurance proceeds and the sum of the carrying value of the van plus the cost of the new engine. The repair cost is expensed. It does not increase the value of the van. $300 = $3,500 − $2,500 − $700.

345. **Answer: B**

The test for impairment for an asset in use is whether the carrying value (book value) is less than its recoverable cost. An asset's recoverable cost is the sum of its estimated net cash inflows projected for its remaining life.

When book value > recoverable cost, the carrying value is not recoverable. In other words, the asset is booked at more than the sum of its future net cash inflows.

For example, if an asset's carrying value is $100 and its recoverable cost is $80, then its carrying value is not recoverable (only $80 is recoverable). The AMOUNT of the loss

recognized is the difference between carrying value and fair value, but that difference is not used for TESTING whether an asset is impaired.

That difference is not the condition leading to the impairment loss.

346. **Answer: A**

Recovery of impairment losses is prohibited under U.S. GAAP.

347. **Answer: A**

The net book value of the asset at the time of impairment was $150,000: $250,000 cost less $100,000 accumulated depreciation (4 years of depreciation at $25,000 a year). After the impairment of $30,000, the net book value is $120,000 ($150,000 − 30,000). The remaining life is 6 years and annual depreciation is $20,000.

348. **Answer: C**

This response is the difference between carrying value and recoverable amount. According to IFRS the recoverable amount is the greater of fair value less cost to sell ($105,000) or value in use ($100,000). Value in use is the discounted cash flows. Therefore, this asset is has an impairment of $15,000 because the recoverable amount is $105,000 and the carrying value is $120,000.

349. **Answer: C**

The greater of fair value less cost to sell or value in use is the recoverable amount according to IFRS.

350. **Answer: A**

Under IFRS the impairment loss can be recovered if the asset is held for use or disposal.

351. **Answer: D**

Under IFRS the components of the asset must be depreciated over their estimated useful life. Therefore, the $100,000 cost is broken down into the following components:

Depreciable Value	Life	Depreciation
$72,000	10 yr.	$7,200
20,000	5 yr.	4,000
8,000	4 yr.	2,000
		$13,200

352. **Answer: A**

When remeasurement to fair value is used, it must be applied to the entire class or components of PPE.

353. **Answer: B**

Under component depreciation, the asset is separated into component parts, and each part is depreciated over its useful life. The bus would be separated into three parts and depreciated as follows:

Bus	65,000	÷ 20 years =	3,250
Engine	25,000	÷ 10 years =	2,500
Seats	10,000	÷ 8 years =	1,250
Total	100,000		7,000

354. **Answer: D**

Under IFRS an increase in an asset's fair value above original cost is recorded in a revaluation surplus account and any decreases in an asset's fair value below the original cost are recorded as losses to the income statement. Therefore, the $10,000 decrease in year 1 would have been recorded as a loss to the income statement and the $15,000 increase in year 2 would be recorded as a $10,000 gain to the income statement and $5,000 gain in revaluation surplus (OCI).

355. **Answer: C**

When there is commercial substance to the exchange, the acquired asset is measured at fair value. In this case, the value is $60,000 as given in the problem. This amount also equals the fair value of assets given up in the exchange. The implied fair value of the asset exchanged is $60,000 + $30,000 cash received, or $90,000. The fair value of assets given up is therefore $90,000 less $30,000 cash received, or $60,000. The full journal entry for the exchange is: dr. plant asset 60,000; dr. accumulated depreciation, 40,000; debit cash 30,000; credit plant asset 100,000; credit gain, 30,000. The gain equals the difference between the fair value of the asset exchanged (90,000) and its book value (60,000).

356. **Answer: D**

The book value of the delivery truck is $60,000 ($140,000 – $80,000). Its fair value is $90,000. A gain of $30,000 is therefore implied. Cash was paid and the exchange had commercial substance. Therefore, the gain is fully recognized. If the exchange lacked commercial substance, no gain would be recognized.

357. **Answer: A**

The loss recognized on the exchange equals the book value of the asset transferred less its fair value at the time of the exchange. The fair value is less than book value. The amount recorded for the asset acquired is its fair value, or the fair value of the asset transferred plus or minus cash paid or received, whichever is more reliably determinable. By using the lower fair value of the asset transferred to measure the value of the asset acquired, the asset acquired will not be overstated above its fair value.

358. **Answer: C**

Gains and losses from nonmonetary exchanges that have commercial substance are recognized immediately.

359. **Answer: C**

The gain on an exchange of nonmonetary assets is based on the fair value and book value of the asset exchanged. The land with a fair value of $50,000 is given for machinery. The company is using the land as legal tender. The gain will be the difference between the book value and the fair value of the asset given or $50,000 – $20,000 = $30,000.

360. **Answer: D**

Solen has an implied gain given that the fair value of its asset exceeds its book value. But when there is no commercial substance, such gains are recognized only when cash is received. Solen paid cash on the exchange.

361. **Answer: D**

There is an implied gain of $8,000, the difference between the $20,000 fair value of the old asset and its $12,000 book value. Because the proportion of cash received is 25% ($5,000/$20,000), the entire gain is recognized and the acquired asset is recognized at fair value ($15,000).

Note that the answer would be the same had there been commercial substance.

362. **Answer: A**

The fair value of the new asset equals the old asset's book value. Because cash was paid, the fair value of the old asset is less than the fair value of the new asset.

Therefore, the fair value of the old asset is also less than the old asset's book value, resulting in a loss.

Using dollar amounts, assume the fair value of the new asset is $10. The book value of the old asset is also $10 by assumption. Assume Transit paid $2 cash.

Then the fair value of the old asset is $8, implying a loss of $2, the amount of cash paid. Even without commercial substance, losses are recognized in full.

363. **Answer: B**

When commercial substance is lacking, gains are recognized in proportion to the amount of cash received.

364. **Answer: A**

The fair value of each asset is less than book value, implying that both firms have a loss. Losses are recognized in full regardless of whether there is commercial exchange.

365. **Answer: D**

The fair value of the advertising services provided can be reliably measured by reference to a nonbarter transaction for similar advertising with a different counterparty (SIC Interpretation 31, para 5).

366. **Answer: A**

When an investor owns more than 50% of the voting common stock of an investee, in the absence of constraining conditions (e.g., investee in bankruptcy), the investor has controlling interest in the investee.

367. **Answer: B**

The method of payment used to acquire an investment does not help determine the correct accounting treatment of the investment. While the method of payment determines what will be credited upon acquisition of the securities, it will not enter into the subsequent accounting treatment of the investment.

368. **Answer: D**

Although the acquisition of 18% of an entity's voting common stock is less than the 20% normally required to presume significant influence over the investee, the fact that the investor has material transactions with the investee (together with the 18% ownership) is presumed to give the investor

sufficient means for exercising significant influence.

369. **Answer: B**

North is the investee because it issued the bonds, but neither South nor East are investees. Since East owns the bonds on December 31, it is the investor. Since South did not issue the bonds and does not own the bonds on December 31, it is neither an investor nor an investee.

370. **Answer: A**

When an investor owns more than 50% of the voting common stock of an investee, in the absence of constraining conditions (e.g., investee in bankruptcy), the investor has controlling interest in the investee.

371. **Answer: C**

The amount paid by the buyer would have been more than the face amount of the bond because that amount would have included the amount of the premium and the amount of interest accrued since the last interest date.

372. **Answer: B**

When a bond is purchased at a discount, the price paid is less than face value. Any cash paid to the seller for accrued interest is debited to interest receivable, not to the bond investment. Thus, the carrying value is the portion of the total amount paid attributable to the total bond price, exclusive of accrued interest.

The carrying value must be less than the cash paid to the seller, which includes accrued interest.

373. **Answer: D**

For investments in debt securities other than those intended to be held to maturity, the fair value method is applied. $1,020,000 is the fair value of the investment in bonds and is the appropriate amount for reporting the investment.

374. **Answer: B**

The unrealized loss would be credited to the other comprehensive income account to reclassify the holding loss as a realized loss in the income statement for year 2. For purposes of illustration, assume the available for sale (AFS) securities were originally purchased for

$5 and that the loss during year 1 was $1. The related entries would be:

Purchase:	DR. AFS Securities	$5	
	CR. Cash		$5
Year 1 End:	DR. OCI (holding loss)	$1	
	CR. AFS Securities		$1
Year 2:	DR. Cash	$4	
	CR. AFS Securities		$4
	DR. Loss on AFS Securities	$1	(Income Statement)
	CR. OCI (holding loss)		$1 (B/S, Accumulated OCI)

The last entry (above) reclassifies the holding loss to recognize a realized loss on sale.

375. **Answer: B**

Securities classified as held-to-maturity are reported at amortized cost, which is the carrying amount of the securities. Further, securities classified as available-for-sale are reported at fair value.

376. **Answer: D**

Fair market value is the valuation basis used when investments are transferred between classifications. Conceptually, the existing carrying value is written off and the current fair value is written on in the new classification, with any difference being an unrealized gain or loss.

377. **Answer: A**

Both transfers from held-to-maturity to held-for-trading classifications and from held-for-trading to held-to-maturity classifications can occur in the accounting for investments where the investor does not have significant influence over the investee.

378. **Answer: A**

The securities were classified as available-for-sale at June 30, 20X2. The decline in market value from that date to December 31, 20X2 is $40,000 ($530,000 – $490,000).

That amount is reported in owners' equity because holding gains and losses on securities available-for-sale are not recognized in earnings.

379. **Answer: A**

Reclassifications between the two investment categories are always recorded at market value. The reclassification is treated as if the security in the old classification was sold and the security in the new classification was purchased.

Market value reflects a brand-new valuation and is treated as original cost from then on for the purpose of the annual year-end revaluation adjustment.

380. **Answer: A**

Statement I is correct; Statement II is not correct. Only investments in debt securities may be transferred between categories; equity securities may not be transferred between categories (Statement I). When investments are transferred between categories, financial statements of prior periods presented for comparative purposes must be restated (Statement II).

381. **Answer: B**

Under IFRS No. 9, investments in debt securities made under an entity's business model plan to make and hold such investments solely to receive cash from interest and principal repayment, and when there is no accounting mismatch, should be reported at amortized cost. Amortized cost is par value ($100,000) plus the unamortized premium ($3,500), or $100,000 + $3,500 = $103,500, the correct answer.

382. **Answer: A**

Under IFRS No. 9, investments in debt securities may be (1) transferred from amortized cost (when the investment originally meets both the business model test and the cash flow characteristic test) to fair value when the investment fails to continue to meet both the business model test and the cash flow characteristic test and (2) transferred from fair value to amortized cost when an investment that originally fails to meet both the business model test and the cash flow characteristic test subsequently meets both tests.

383. **Answer: A**

Under IFRS, changes in fair value may be reported in profit/loss or in other comprehensive income, depending on whether the investment is held for trading purposes or not. If an investment in equity securities is held-for-trading purposes (i.e., to make a profit on price appreciation), changes in fair value will be reported through profit/loss. If an investment in equity securities is not held-for-trading purposes, the investor may elect to report changes in fair value through other comprehensive income.

384. Answer: B

Statement II is correct; Statement I is not correct. The business model test used in evaluating debt instruments for classification purposes is concerned with the investor's intent. Specifically, did the investor make the investment to collect cash flows from interest and return of principal, rather than to make a profit on sale of the investment (Statement II)? While there is a single category for equity investments (at fair value), there are two categories for debt investments (at amortized cost and at fair value) (Statement I).

385. Answer: D

Under the equity method of accounting, changes in the market value of the investee's common stock are ignored. Further, cash dividends received by the investor from the investee are not recognized as investment income; rather they are recognized as a debit to cash and a reduction in (credit to) the investor's investment in investee account.

386. Answer: C

An investor that owns 25% of the voting stock of an investee, in the absence of evidence to the contrary, is presumed to be able to exercise significant influence over the investee. The fact that the investor and the investee are in different lines of business generally does not mitigate the influence the investor is able to exercise.

387. Answer: A

Anchor Co. would report 75% of Main's dividend on its noncumulative preferred stock as dividend income. That calculation would be: .75 × $100,000 = $75,000. Anchor Co. would not report 40% of Main's dividend on its common stock as dividend income because, since it can exercise significant influence over Main's operations, it must account for its common stock investment in Main using the equity method of accounting. Under the equity method, common stock dividends received from an investee are recognized as a reduction in the investment in the investee. So, Anchor's entry to recognize the $80,000 (.40 × $200,000) common stock dividend from Main would be:

DR:	Cash $80,000
	CR: Investment in Main $80,000

388. Answer: B

Grant uses the equity method because it has significant influence over South. Under the equity method, the investor recognizes its share of the investee earnings in its own income.

Thus, Grant will recognize $24,000 (.30 × $80,000) as equity in the earnings of South, in its own income.

389. Answer: C

Larkin's investment in Devon at year-end would be computed as the carrying amount of the investment at the beginning of the year ($200,000) + Larkin's share of Devon's reported net income for the year ($600,000 × .25 = $150,000) – Larkin's share of Devon's dividends paid during the year ($400,000 × .25 = $100,000), or $200,000 + $150,000 = $350,000 – $100,000 = $250,000, the correct answer.

390. Answer: B

If the investor has obligations or commitments to make payments on behalf of the associate, it may continue to recognize its share of losses to the extent of those obligations.

391. Answer: B

Under IFRS, the fair value option can only be applied by certain investors such as venture capitalists, mutual funds, or unit trusts.

392. Answer: A

Under IFRS, only certain investors can elect to measure the equity investee using the fair value option. Mutual fund investors are allowed to utilize the fair value option.

393. Answer: D

Stock dividends are not recognized in the accounts at receipt, at fair value, or any other value. Rather, they reduce the cost per share under both methods. The original cost is spread over more shares.

The investor's percentage of the firm has not changed as a result of the stock dividend, but the investor has more shares (as do all investors). When the shares received as a dividend are sold, the reduction in cost basis increases the gain or reduces the loss.

394. Answer: C

Cobb has 10,000 + 2,000 or 12,000 shares at the time of the dividend. The 2,000 shares were received from the stock dividend. Thus dividend income is 12,000($1.50) = $18,000. The stock dividend itself is not included in dividend income; rather, it decreases the cost per share of the investment. However, it does raise the number of shares that receive the cash dividend, which is recognized as income.

395. **Answer: D**

Only the $8,000 dividend is included in dividend revenue. The dividend on the Brill stock is accounted for under the equity method, which treats all dividends as a reduction in the investment account. The stock dividend is not revenue. Rather it reduces the per-share cost of the investment in Paul stock. No entry is recorded on receipt of a stock dividend.

396. **Answer: B**

Because Plack Co. owns only 2% of Ty Corp. stock, it does not have significant influence over Ty and will not use the equity method to account for its investment. Plank's dividend will be determined by the number of shares of Ty that it owns multiplied by the amount of dividend per share. The calculation is:

2/14 Purchase	10,000 shares
4/30 Stock dividend	2,000 shares
12/15 Total shares owned	12,000
Dividend rate	$2
Total dividend income	$24,000

The stock dividend would be recorded by Plack as a memorandum entry to adjust the per-share original cost, so it is based on the total 12,000 shares now owned.

397. **Answer: D**

Under any method used to account for an investment in common stock, the investor records a stock dividend received by a memorandum entry to increase the number of shares owned. Since the cost of the investment does not change, the per-share cost of the stock decreases.

398. **Answer: D**

When the entity has positive ability and intent to hold the impaired security and does not expect to recover the entire cost basis of the impaired security, the credit losses are recognized in earnings.

399. **Answer: B**

This is **not** a factor that is taken into consideration in determining whether the decline in fair value is OTTI.

400. **Answer: A**

When the decline in fair value is considered to be other-than-temporary, the unrealized losses in OCI are reclassified to earnings.

401. **Answer: A**

When the intangible asset can be renewed indefinitely, and the company has the positive ability and intent to continuously renew, then the intangible asset is an indefinite life intangible. Indefinite life intangibles are not amortized, but are tested for impairment on an annual basis.

402. **Answer: D**

The shorter of the lease term and useful life of the leasehold improvements is used for amortization because leasehold improvements revert to the lessor at the end of the lease term. A 10-year lease term is used because renewal is uncertain.

The leasehold improvements were capitalized at the beginning of 20X5. Annual amortization (and therefore amortization for 20X6) is $14,000 ($47,000 + $75,000 + $18,000)/10. Ten years is used for each asset because each has a useful life of at least 10 years and the lease term is 10 years as of the beginning of 20X6. The assets cannot be amortized over a period greater than 10 years because the lease will be concluded in 10 years.

403. **Answer: C**

Litigation costs can be capitalized only if the defense of the patent was successful.

404. **Answer: B**

The cash surrender value (CSV) is an asset that has been recorded previously and is considered paid when the firm decides to cash the policy in, or upon death of the insured. The remainder of the proceeds upon death of the insured is revenue. The surrender value has been built up over time, reducing insurance expense. Thus, the income effect of the surrender value has already been recognized.

405. **Answer: B**

This copyright has a definite life; the question is, what is the length of that life? The life assigned to the intangible asset is the shorter of its legal and useful life. The useful life is shorter than the legal life, so this copyright is amortized over 25 years.

406. Answer: C

This is a quantitative measure of the implied goodwill. The question asked which of the responses is not a qualitative factors used in the pre-step for goodwill impairment. This response is incorrect also because implied goodwill is determined by comparing the fair value of the reporting unit to the fair value of the identifiable assets—not by using a discount model.

407. Answer: C

The market value of Small's net assets is $6 ($9 – $3). Goodwill ($5) is the difference between the purchase price of $11 and the market value of Small's net assets of $6. Goodwill is the portion of the purchase price not attributable to identifiable assets.

408. Answer: D

In general, goodwill is impaired when factors and circumstances indicate that the fair value is less than the current recorded value. This generally occurs when the market value of the unit previously purchased has declined because of economic factors and events. In this question, the market value of B has declined significantly in one year. Goodwill is re-estimated the same way that it was when B was purchased, as the difference between unit market value and the market value of net identifiable assets. The new value for estimated goodwill is $1,200 (= $3,200 – $2,000). The goodwill originally recorded is $1,500 (= $4,000 – $2,000 – $500). The impairment loss is the decline in goodwill, or $300 (= $1,500 – $1,200).

409. Answer: C

Goodwill impairment testing permits a qualitative "pre-step" test to determine if it is more likely than not that the goodwill is impaired. This pre-step can result in considerable savings to companies who do not have to complete the quantitative tests associated with testing and measuring goodwill impairment.

410. Answer: A

When conducting goodwill impairment testing in a reporting unit, one must first determine the fair value of the identifiable net assets (assets minus liabilities). The fair value of the identifiable net assets is used to calculate implied goodwill to test recorded goodwill for impairment. Since the fair value of the identifiable assets is needed to determine implied goodwill. The measurement of the fair value of the identifiable net assets is essentially measuring (and recognizing) any impairment in that asset group before the impairment testing for goodwill is completed.

411. Answer: A

Under U.S. GAAP, all research and development costs are expensed as incurred.

412. Answer: C

R&D expense includes three of the four costs listed. Only routine design of tools, jigs, molds, and dies is excluded from R&D expense because it is not aimed at discovery of new knowledge or translation of knowledge into new products and processes or improvements in existing products and processes.

The other three costs meet this definition of R&D expense and sum to $1,015,000. R&D expense includes the cost of R&D services performed by other firms. The cost to Vest is conceptually the same whether Vest's employees perform the research on facilities acquired by Vest or another firm provides the service. Either way, Vest is paying for R&D.

413. Answer: B

The contract work performed for the government is not research and development expense to Ball but rather is normal contracting cost that will be applied against contract revenue in computing contract profit.

Research and development for Ball includes efforts aimed at discovering and translating new knowledge toward new products and services that Ball will produce and market. All four costs in the question are included in research and development.

The sum of $1,380,000 is the firm's research and development expense for 2005 ($300,000 + $700,000 + $200,000 + $180,000).

414. Answer: D

Each of the costs is appropriately included in research and development. The sum of the three costs is $460,000 ($150,000 + $125,000 + $185,000).

Each activity represented contributes either to the discovery of new knowledge or to the translation of that new knowledge. The last two costs listed are found verbatim in the ASC 730 list of items that are included in research and development. The first cost represents purchased services. When those services are for research and development, then they are included in this category of expense.

415. **Answer: D**

Only the first two costs are research and development costs. R&D involves the search for new knowledge and translation of that knowledge toward new products and processes and improvements in existing products and processes.

The first two items are listed in ASC 730 as being included in R&D.

The last two are listed as specifically being excluded from R&D because they are routine activities or do not involve essentially new products and processes. The total R&D expense is therefore $285,000 ($125,000 + $160,000).

416. **Answer: B**

Costs incurred (after technological feasibility has been established) in developing software for sale, lease, or licensing are capitalized and subsequently amortized. Annual amortization is the greater of:

1. The percentage of expected total revenues earned during the period multiplied by total capitalized amount, OR
2. Straight-line amortization based on expected life.

For reporting purposes, capitalized cost less accumulated amortization cannot exceed net realizable value. The calculation for Byte Co. for 2005 would be:

1. Percentage of expected total revenues = .10 × $600,000 =$60,000 amortization
2. Straight-line = 1 year/ 4years = .25 × $600,000 = $150,000 amortization

The greater is $150,000, the amount to amortize for 2005. For reporting purposes:

Capitalized cost = $600,000

Less: Amortization = 150,000

Net book value = $450,000 less than $480,000 net realizable value

Since amortized cost is less than net realizable value, no further write-down is required and Byte would report net capitalized cost at $450,000.

417. **Answer: B**

Only the last two costs in the list are inventoried. The software development is complete when the product masters are produced.

The duplication costs ($25,000) and packaging costs ($9,000) are debited to inventory for a total of $34,000. These are costs necessary to

bring the asset into salable condition. This cost is expensed when product is sold.

All the costs listed above the last two are aimed at developing the software. These costs are not debited to inventory. There is no product in which to inventory these costs until the development is complete.

418. **Answer: C**

Only software development costs incurred after the point of technological feasibility is reached are capitalized as an intangible and amortized.

Technological feasibility is the point at which the firm makes the decision to continue the product development with the expectation that a workable product is possible. Costs of duplication and packaging are all product costs and, although capitalized, are debited to inventory rather than to software development costs.

The capitalized software costs for this firm are:

Other coding costs after establishment of technological feasibility	$24,000
Other testing costs after establishment of technological feasibility	20,000
Costs of producing product masters for training materials	15,000
Total amount subject to amortization	$59,000

419. **Answer: D**

There are three expenses to be recognized:

(1) Software development costs incurred before the application development stage was reached, $4,000,000
(2) Amortization of capitalized software development costs incurred after the application development stage was reached, $8,000,000/4 = $2,000,000
(3) $50,000 training costs

The sum of these is $6,050,000.

Training costs are expensed as incurred. The application development stage is the point after which there is sufficient evidence of a product that software development costs are capitalized and amortized. Such costs will benefit future periods.

420. **Answer: C**

The cost of developing software for internal purposes is expensed up to the application development stage, at which point the effort appears to be leading to a useable application. After that point, costs are capitalized. With a three-year useful life and $10 million capitalized cost, the amortization expense is one-third, or $3.33 million.

The useful life of the product is used rather than the useful life of the equipment because new software can be developed after three years for use on that equipment.

421. **Answer: A**

Under IFRS goodwill, impairment is measured in a one-step process. The carrying value of the CGU is compared to the recoverable amount. If the CV > recoverable amount the goodwill is impaired. The impairment loss is the recoverable amount – the CV. In this case, $32,000 – $45,000 = ($13,000) loss.

422. **Answer: B**

An active market will provide a relevant and reliable reference to the asset's value. Therefore, just like with PPE, revaluation to fair value is permitted. IAS 38 defines an active market as one that the items traded in the market are homogeneous, there are willing buyers and sellers, and prices are available to the public.

423. **Answer: C**

The greater of fair value less cost to sell or value in use is the recoverable amount according to IFRS.

424. **Answer: B**

Under IFRS impairment losses associated with identifiable intangibles are recoverable. Impairment losses associated with goodwill are *not* recoverable.

425. **Answer: D**

IAS 38 defines an intangible asset as a nonmonetary asset without physical substance that is identifiable. Identifiable means that the asset is (1) separable or capable of being separated or divided from the entity and can be sold or transferred and (2) arises from contractual or other legal rights, regardless of whether those rights are transferable or separable from the entity. This definition is essentially the same as under U.S. GAAP.

426. **Answer: B**

All of the items are current liabilities. The computation is:

80,000 + (300,000 – 15,000) + 25,000 = $390,000.

427. **Answer: B**

Preadjusted balance in accounts payable	$900,000
Plus checks not sent to creditors until Jan. 10 (this amount was debited to accounts payable and must be reversed because the checks have not been sent— accounts payable has not been reduced as of December 31)	400,000
Plus goods received Dec. 28, at net: .98($153,061) (the firm records purchases at net of 2% discount)	150,000
Equals ending accounts payable	$1,450,000

There is no liability at December 31, 20X4 for the goods shipped FOB destination because title does not pass until the goods reach the destination, which did not occur until January.

The firm must include the December 28 receipt of goods in accounts payable because the firm has received the goods.

428. **Answer: D**

Accounts payable	$19,000
Bonds payable, due 20X6	34,000
Discount on bonds payable	(2,000)
Dividends payable on 2/15/X6	5,000
Income tax payable	9,000
Current liabilities at 12/31/X5	$65,000

The deferred tax liability could not be current because deferred tax liabilities are classified based on the underlying item, giving rise to the future temporary difference. The reversal of the temporary difference does not begin until 20X7, which is more than one year after the balance sheet date.

Therefore, the underlying accounts that give rise to the deferred tax liability must be noncurrent, which causes the deferred tax liability to be also noncurrent.

429. **Answer: C**

The $50,000 advance is not related to accounts payable, even though it was made to a supplier for which Acme would have accounts payable. It is a prepayment. Removing the $50,000 debit increases the accounts payable balance by that amount. The $45,000 shipment is not part of the inventory of Acme as of December 31 nor is it a liability (accounts payable) because title to the goods did not transfer to Acme until January 2.

FOB destination means that title does not transfer until goods reach their destination. Acme treated this item correctly because it was recorded January 2. Therefore, the correct accounts payable balance is $900,000 ($850,000 before adjustment + $50,000).

430. **Answer: C**

This question has three debt instruments that need to be categorized into current or long-term. The line of credit is due in one year so it is all current. The secured note is due in 5 annual installments so 1/5 is current and 4/5 is long-term. The balloon note is due in 3 years so it is all long term.

Instrument	Current	Long-Term
Line of credit	250,000	0
Secured	150,000	600,000
Balloon	0	300,000
Total	400,000	900,000

431. **Answer: A**

Both adjustments are included in compensation expense because they are costs of services rendered by employees in 20X4. The firm has incurred a liability and therefore an expense as of 12/31/92 for each of these items. $290,000 = $224,000 + $3,500 + $62,500.

432. **Answer: A**

The wage limit on unemployment tax is $10,000. Thus, the total accrued liability, which is also the unemployment tax amount, is 5($10,000)(.02) = $1,000.

433. **Answer: B**

Sales taxes payable at the end of 20X4 are .15($110,000 + $150,000) = $39,000 because November and December sales taxes were not yet paid as of 12/31/X4.

Occupancy taxes payable are $2(1,100 + 1,200 + 1,800) = $8,200 because the fourth quarter taxes were not paid as of 12/31/X4.

434. **Answer: A**

Only the bonus is a liability of the firm as of 12/31/Year 1. That amount was earned and granted in Year 1 and thus is recognized in the Year 1 balance sheet because it is not due for payment until Year 2. Dividends are not liabilities until declared. There is no unpaid declared dividend at 12/31/Year 1.

435. **Answer: D**

This question asks for the ending payroll tax liability. This amount is the employer's share of FICA at 7% and the unemployment tax at 3%. Both have maximum wage limits. The $6,200 ending payroll tax liability is computed as $80,000(.07) + $20,000(.03).

436. **Answer: B**

This question is testing your knowledge of what portion of a cash outlay should be recognized as an asset and what portion should be recognized as an expense. The entire cost of the service is $90,000 for 6 months; therefore, the monthly cost is $15,000 a month. On October 31, the company expensed the entire $90,000, but will receive future benefit over 4 months in the next year. The adjusting entry would be to reduce service expense for $60,000 (4 × $15,000) and increase prepaid services for $60,000.

437. **Answer: B**

This question has two costs that occurred during the year. You are asked how much of these costs would be recognized in year 1. The $15,000 of maintenance cost is for a 1 year period beginning March 1. The maintenance cost would be allocated 1/12 evenly over the life of the service period or $1,250 a month × 10 months in year 1 = 12,500. The $5,000 modification to the software has increased its functionality and therefore should be capitalized and amortized over the life of the software $5,000 / 5 years = $1,000/year. The total expense recognized in year 1 would be $12,500 + 1,000 = $13,500.

438. **Answer: B**

The September 30, 2005 liability balance equals the account's $3,000 beginning balance, plus the nine deposits of $2,500 received through September 1, 2005, less the three quarters of property tax installments paid in 2005 ($21,000 = .75 × $28,000). These installments were paid on January 1, April 1, and July 1.

The ending liability then is $4,500 = $3,000 + 9($2,500) − $21,000.

439. **Answer: B**

The total annual real estate tax is 2($12,000) or $24,000. Therefore, the tax per month is $2,000. Day assumed the taxes, already assessed on the property, for the full year.

The payment on November 1 covers the four months, July, August, September, and October, for a total cost of $8,000. This portion of the $12,000 payment is debited to real estate taxes payable, because the full annual property tax amount is already accrued on Day's books from the purchase of the property. Pre-paid real estate taxes are debited for the remaining $4,000 of the payment.

The $4,000 pre-pays the tax for the next two months (November and December). At the end of each of those two months, the payable is debited for $2,000 and the pre-paid is credited for $2,000. The cycle begins again when the second payment is made. In this jurisdiction, the tax is assessed for a year at the beginning of the year.

Therefore, payments are debited to pre-paid real estate taxes unless previously accrued, as was the case here.

440. Answer: C

The following equation is used to explain the changes in the escrow liability and the ending balance (31 December, 2004):

Beginning + Payments – Real estate + Interest – 10% (interest) = Ending

Balance received tax payments balance

$700,000 + $1.58mn – $1.72mn + $50,000 – $5,000 = $605,000

The interest increases the liability, because it is an amount owed to the mortgagee. This debt is extinguished by crediting the receivable from the mortgagee. The 10% fee reduces the portion of the liability owing to interest.

441. Answer: B

Only costs that are attributable to employee service already rendered can be accrued. The firm has received no benefit for services that employees have not yet rendered. The firm owes employees nothing for future services and therefore has no liability for these amounts and no cost or expense should be recognized.

442. Answer: B

Only Ryan's vacation rights vest or accumulate and cause a liability to be reported. This amount is $1,600 (two weeks' vacation × $800).

Todd's rights do not vest or accumulate and therefore fail to meet the criteria of FAS 43. These criteria require accrual of the liability if the benefits accumulate or vest, the benefits

are earned, and the payment is probable and estimable. Ryan's rights meet the criteria.

From the firm's point of view, because Todd's rights do not vest or accumulate (carry over to a future year), then Todd loses those rights. The firm has no obligation to pay those benefits, and therefore no liability or expense is accrued at the end of 2005 for Todd.

443. Answer: D

The liability must be accrued only for the vacation pay, because it is probable that paid vacations will be taken. Therefore, the liability is $15,000 (150 days × $100 per day).

The firm may, but is not required to, accrue a liability for sick days. If the employees were routinely paid for sick days not taken, then sick days would be required to be accrued. For this firm, there is no payment for sick days not taken, therefore there is no requirement to accrue this cost.

It may be argued that illness is the condition that mandates payment of sick pay. Illness cannot be predicted and therefore is not required to be accrued.

444. Answer: C

Under FAS 43, if compensated absences either accumulate OR vest, then the liability should be accrued. Benefits accumulate if they can be carried over to future years.

For example, assume an employee earns four weeks' vacation per year, but does not take a vacation for two years. If the employee can take an eight-week vacation in the third year, the benefits are said to accumulate (firms usually place restrictions on the total time that can be accumulated).

Benefits vest if they are no longer contingent on continued employment. This means that if an employee retires, he or she will receive their vested vacation pay.

Either way, through accumulation or vesting, it is probable that the vacation compensation will be paid. Therefore, a liability has been incurred as of the balance sheet date.

445. Answer: C

The total vacation pay expense for 2005 is $31,500. This is the sum of two amounts:

(1) The amount earned in 2005, plus
(2) The increase in cost from earlier periods owing to wage increases in 2005.

These two amounts are:

(1) $30,000 as given in the problem—this amount is already updated for the most current rate.

(2) $1,500 = ($35,000 − $20,000).10 = the amount of vacation pay yet to be disbursed on benefits earned before 2005; the liability for this amount is increased by the 10% pay increase.

The increase in pay rate on the pre-2005 benefits is treated as an estimate change. Therefore, it is handled in current and future years. Retroactive application does not apply in this case.

446. **Answer: C**

Under U.S. GAAP, impairment testing is a two-step process. The first step compares the assets' carry value (CV) to its undiscounted cash flows (UCF). In this problem the CV > UCF; therefore the asset is potentially impaired and we must go to the second step. The second step compares the assets CV to its fair value (FV). In this problem the FV < CV and the asset is written down to its FV. $170 million − $135 million = $35 million impairment loss.

447. **Answer: B**

Remote contingent losses may be disclosed in the footnotes, but there is no requirement to do so. Probable contingent losses are accrued. Certain losses are no longer contingent losses. When a loss is reasonably possible, it is footnoted. It is most likely that the loss is reasonably possible when a range of losses is disclosed.

448. **Answer: D**

A reasonably possible loss contingency is disclosed in the footnotes, but not recognized as a liability.

Only when the contingent loss is both probable and estimable is the loss accrued (recognized).

449. **Answer: D**

At the point of sale, Vadis has committed to service the products it sells. The firm has incurred a recognized obligation at that point because it is both probable and estimable (FAS 5).

The cost of the warranty, therefore, is recognized in the year of sale. The cost (expense) is the temporary account that measures the reduction in net assets from operations (earnings) caused by the increase in the obligation.

A less acceptable explanation is that the warranty cost or expense should be matched against the sales it helped to produce. Either explanation leads to the same result, however.

450. **Answer: D**

The contingent liability at the end of 2003 no longer exists.

It is not probable, given the facts in the question, that Halsey will be required to make any payment in the lawsuit. The favorable judgment indicates a contingent gain (asset). Contingent gains are not recognized in the accounts, but only footnoted.

451. **Answer: A**

In the interest of conservatism and disclosure, the guarantee should be disclosed. It is not required to be accrued because the probability is remote that the firm will have to pay the note.

452. **Answer: C**

This is a gain contingency. The possible gain is the difference between the compensation amount and the carrying value of the plant. However, the gain is contingent on receipt of the compensation. Gain contingencies are reported only in the notes and are not recognized in the financial statements.

453. **Answer: D**

Contingent gains are not recognized in the accounts. At most, footnote disclosure is considered acceptable reporting. This is the best answer because no amount in the range of possible values is more likely than any other. The $100,000 amount was not known when the financial statements were published.

454. **Answer: A**

The retooling costs are not part of the liability, but are rather a response to changing business conditions. They most likely would be capitalized and amortized over their useful life. The liability is a contingent liability.

The amount depends on the outcome of the bankruptcy proceedings. When a range of values is estimated with no one value being more probable than the others, the lowest amount is accrued. Thus, $250,000 is accrued as of the end of 2004.

455. **Answer: A**

When a contingent loss is both probable and estimable, it must be accrued. When only a range of amounts can be estimated, rather than a point estimate, the lowest amount in the range is accrued.

In this case, the low end of the range is $400,000, and that amount is accrued. The footnotes will describe the entire range to indicate the firm's maximum exposure to loss. The actual settlement offer amount was unknown before the statements were issued.

456. **Answer: A**

A probable (< 50%) outflow of benefits is implied, and the amount is estimable. This is a recognized liability for international accounting standards, not a contingent liability.

457. **Answer: A**

A provision is a present obligation. This is one of the ways a liability can be treated as a contingent liability under international standards. If the provision involved a probable outflow, then it would be recognized, but would not be a contingent liability.

458. **Answer: B**

International accounting standards recognize the midpoint, whereas U.S. standards recognize the low point.

459. **Answer: B**

For international accounting standards, this is a recognized provision. For U.S. standards, it is a recognized contingent liability.

460. **Answer: C**

Although the question is not completely clear, interest is paid at the time each principal payment is made. Thus, on 9/1/X4, after the principal payment of $450,000 (and interest as well) is made, the remaining note balance is $900,000 ($1,350,000 – $450,000). Note that only the principal payment reduces the note balance. Interest for four months to 12/31/X4 is recorded in accrued interest payable: $36,000 ($900,000 × .12 × 1/3 year).

461. **Answer: D**

The $30,000 answer is correct and equals ($1,200,000 – $400,000)(.15)(3/12).

On 10/1/Year 2, the first $400,000 principal payment was made. That left $800,000 of principal balance remaining on 10/1/Year 2. The interest on that amount is computed as shown above.

462. **Answer: C**

The first payment included interest of $22,500 (.09 × .25 × $1,000,000). Note that interest rates are always expressed for an annual period. Only 25% of year elapsed from September 30 to the end of the year. The rest of the payment ($241,700 = $264,200 – $22,500) is principal. The note payable balance at December 31 therefore is $758,300 ($1,000,000 – $241,700).

463. **Answer: A**

First loan:

Interest expense included in the $1,500 = $5,000(.12) = $600

Interest expense that should have been included in 20X5 interest expense = $5,000(.12)(10/12) = 500

Overstatement of 20X5 interest expense = $100

Second loan: (no error because the term is completely within 20X5 so the interest recognized equals the interest paid)

Third loan:

Interest expense included in the $1,500 = $0 (the loan and therefore the interest was not paid in 20X5) = 0

Interest expense that should have been included in 20X5 interest expense = $8,000(.12)(8/12) = 640

Understatement of 20X5 interest expense = $640

Net understatement = $540

464. **Answer: D**

The accrued interest covers the period from the borrowing to 12/31/X5 because no interest has yet been paid. The interest is also compounded (this is a stumbling point easily missed).

The 20X5 ending balance in accrued interest payable therefore includes interest on 20X4's accrued interest:

20X4: $10,000(.12)(10/12)	$1,000
20X5: ($10,000 + $1,000)(.12)(12/12)	1,320
Total accrued interest payable, December 31, 20X5	$2,320

465. **Answer: C**

The interest for three months on $1 million at 9% is $22,500: .09 × 3/12 × $1,000,000 = $22,500. This amount is part of the first payment; principal reduction of $241,700 is the other part.

No principal payment was made before the first payment, which occurred at year-end. There was no reduction in principal before the first payment.

466. Answer: C

When debt is issued at a discount from face value, the firm receives an amount less than face value but must pay the face value at issuance.

Interest is defined as amounts paid to service debt over and above the amount borrowed. For example, a $1,000 face value bond issued for $940 creates a $60 discount. The firm must pay the cash interest required over the bond term and $1,000 face value at the end of the term.

The $60 discount represents an additional amount that must be paid in excess of the amount borrowed ($940).

467. Answer: C

This problem requires the calculation of the amount of bond discount amortization through the end of the current year. Journal entries are the best way to do this. The two interest payment entries are as follows. June 30 entry: dr. Interest expense $2,307 ($46,139 × .05), cr. Discount $307, cr. Cash $2,000 ($50,000 × .04). The effective interest method is required (SL method is not mentioned). The discount amortization increases the carrying value of the liability because there is less discount remaining. Dec. 31 entry: dr. Interest expense $2,322 [($46,139 + $307) × .05], cr. Discount $322, cr. Cash $2,000 ($50,000 × .04). Carrying amount is now $46,139 $307 $322 = $46,768.

468. Answer: D

Serial bonds mature serially according to a schedule set in the bond contract. At each date, a portion of the bond issue is paid off (matures) until the entire face value of the issue is retired. Each portion is a percentage of the total face value of the issue. Serial bonds are designed to reduce the risk, to the bondholder, of default by the issuing firm.

469. Answer: A

The amount of interest paid each period on a bond issue is the product of the total face value and the contractual rate. A 4%, $1,000 bond pays $40 interest per year, for example. This answer is the same regardless of the amortization method used.

470. Answer: A

Interest expense is recognized only during the bond term, which began June 1 when the bonds were issued. The bonds were outstanding 7 months in 20X5. Seven months of interest is recognized in 20X5.

471. Answer: C

As of 12/31/Year 2, the first $300,000 principal installment has been paid, along with interest. This payment was made 9/1/Year 2. The remaining principal outstanding on that date is $600,000 ($900,000 – $300,000). Thus, accrued interest on 12/31/Year 2 is $24,000 = 600,000(.12)(4/12).

472. Answer: B

One month of accrued interest was collected from the bondholders at issuance for the period October 1–November 1, and interest for the next two months to December 31 was accrued.

Total accrued interest is $16,000 = $800,000(.08)(3/12).

473. Answer: D

The total proceeds on the bond issue equal the total bond price plus accrued interest. The latter amount is the cash interest between the bond issuance date (April 1, 20X4), and the most recent interest payment date before the bond issuance date (November 1, 20X3), a period of 5 months. The most recent interest payment date in this case is the bond date.

Total bond price: 200($1,000)(1.01)	$202,000
Plus accrued interest (5/12)($200,000)(.09)	7,500
Equals bond proceeds	$209,500

474. Answer: D

The bond term is 10 years. At 6/30/05, 8-1/2 years remain in the bond term. Thus, $212,500 [$250,000(8.5)/10] remain unamortized.

475. Answer: A

The fair value option for liabilities is limited to financial liabilities. Lease liabilities are excluded.

476. Answer: A

This question is a basic discount amortization scenario. The carrying amount of the bond will increase by the amount of the discount amortization each period until the carrying amount is $100,000 at maturity. Adding cells

E2+D3 together will add the discount amortized for the period to the carrying amount of the bond, giving the new carrying amount at the end of the period.

477. **Answer: C**

The $1,000,000 loan was successfully refinanced on a long-term basis and therefore was moved to the noncurrent liability category. The refinancing took place before the financial statements were issued, thus meeting the requirements for reclassification on a long-term basis. The remaining items are all current: $750,000 accounts payable + $400,000 short-term borrowings + $100,000 current portion of mortgage payable = $1,250,000 total current liabilities.

478. **Answer: B**

This is a short-term note that is scheduled to mature within one year. This type of note is excluded from current liabilities and shown as a long-term liability if both the following conditions are met:

1. The company intends to refinance.
2. The company demonstrates an ability to refinance.

The financial statements were issued after Paxton was informed that the financial institution would not be capable of honoring the commitment. Therefore, there is no intention or ability in existence when the financial statements were issued. As a result, this would be shown as a current liability.

479. **Answer: B**

There is no net use of current assets to liquidate the $400,000 amount of the liabilities because the stock issuance provided the necessary cash. Only the remaining $100,000 is classified as current.

480. **Answer: B**

This is a short-term note that is scheduled to mature within one year. This type of note is excluded from current liabilities and shown as a long-term liability if both the following conditions are met:

1. The company intends to refinance.
2. The company demonstrates an ability to refinance.

One way a company can demonstrate the ability to refinance is by entering into a financing agreement that permits the company to refinance on a long term basis. Taylor has entered into such an agreement.

481. **Answer: C**

The portion of the note paid between the balance sheet date and the date of issuing the financial statements is classified as current because current assets were used to retire that part of the note.

Even though proceeds from the bond issue may be used to replenish these funds, the $250,000 payment nonetheless reduced current assets. The remainder of the note is classified as noncurrent because the firm fully intends to refinance the remaining $500,000 with a long-term liability, and has shown its ability to do so by actually issuing bonds for the purpose of refinancing before issuing the financial statements.

Thus, the requirements for reclassifying the remaining $500,000 portion of the current note payable as noncurrent have been met.

482. **Answer: D**

The portion of the bond term that remains is 4-1/2 years as of July 1, year 6, because the bonds have been outstanding for 5-1/2 years as of that date. Therefore, the book value of the bonds on July 1, year 6 equals the face value of the bonds ($1,000,000) plus the unamortized bond premium of $18,000 = (4.5/10)$40,000, for a total of $1,018,000.

The gain on the bond extinguishment is the difference between the book value and the amount paid to extinguish the bonds: $1,018,000 − 1.01($1,000,000) = $8,000. The gain results because it cost Fox less to retire the bonds than the book value of the bonds.

483. **Answer: A**

The gain or loss on retirement of debt is included in income from continuing operations.

484. **Answer: C**

The journal entry for retirement:

Bonds payable	2,000,000	
Bond discount		70,000
Bond issue costs		20,000
Cash .94($2,000,000)		1,880,000
Gain		30,000

The gain is the difference between (1) the net bond liability less the unamortized bond issue costs and (2) the amount paid to retire the bonds:

Net bond liability: $2,000,000 – $70,000	$1,930,000	
Less unamortized bond issue costs	(20,000)	
Net carrying amount to use in computing gain or loss	$1,910,000	
Less amount paid to retire bonds	(1,880,000)	
Gain	$30,000	

The correct answer is $1,910,000.

485. Answer: C

The question asks for the book value amount to be compared to the price paid for the bonds retired when the gain or loss on retirement is computed.

The net book value includes the unamortized bond issue costs. The amount of unamortized issue costs relating to the portion of the bond issue retired increases the loss or decreases the gain. The remaining portion of the bond term for the portion of the bond issue retired is the period for which the bond issue costs were not amortized.

Number of semiannual periods in bond term:	15(2) = 30
Number of semiannual periods remaining at 6/2/Year 6 =	10(2) = 20
Remaining unamortized bond issue costs: $6,000(20/30)	= $4,000

Net amount to compare to price paid for bonds, to determine gain or loss on retirement, on one-half the bond issue: (1/2)($500,000 – $4,000) = $248,000. A journal entry recording the retirement of one-half the issue helps show why $248,000 is the correct answer.

Bonds payable	250,000	
Bond issue costs		2,000
Cash .98($250,000)		245,000
Gain		3,000

The gain equals the net value of two accounts removed from the books ($248,000) less the amount paid to retire the bonds.

486. Answer: B

This gain is included in income from continuing operations, as would other gains and losses such as on equipment disposal.

487. Answer: A

In a troubled debt restructuring involving only a modification of terms, the debtor will recognize a gain only if the total undiscounted future cash payments for principal and interest under the new terms are less than the current amount payable for principal and accrued interest.

When the future payments under the new terms are less than the current obligation, the debtor writes down the carrying amount of the liability by the amount of the difference and thus recognizes a gain.

488. Answer: B

The sum of restructured flows (2 × $196,270) exceeds $350,000, which requires that a new interest rate (m) be computed, as follows: $350,000 = $196,270(pva, m, 2). $350,000/$196,270 = (pva, m, 2) = 1.78326. The new rate (m) corresponds to 8%. Interest expense at the end of 20X2 is computed as .08($350,000) = $28,000.

489. Answer: B

This is one of the ways to determine if a restructuring is troubled. Under the terms of this answer, the creditor is receiving a stream of cash flows with a present value less than what is currently owed and is making a concession.

490. Answer: D

The gain on debt restructure recognized by the debtor Knob is the difference between the book value of the debt ($150,000) and the market value of the asset transferred in settlement ($90,000). Thus, the gain equals $60,000.

It represents the increase in net worth, measured at market value, from extinguishing debt at less than its carrying value. The carrying value of the asset transferred is not relevant to the determination of the restructuring gain.

491. Answer: A

The net loss listed is the difference between the carrying amount of the liability and the carrying amount of the machine. Nu has a gain of $9,000 on the note settlement, which is the difference between the liability carrying value ($105,000) and the fair value of the consideration given to extinguish the debt ($96,000). Nu also has a disposal loss on the machine. An ordinary loss of $13,000 is recognized and equals the difference between the machine's carrying value ($109,000) and its fair value ($96,000).

492. Answer: D

This transaction reduces total liabilities and increases OE by the same amount. The numerator of the ratio is reduced and the denominator is increased. Both factors cause the ratio to decrease below the maximum.

493. Answer: C

This transaction increases current liabilities, thus reducing the current ratio. The current ratio is current assets divided by current liabilities. There is no effect on current assets.

494. Answer: D

This accounting change would cause earnings to be reduced, possibly significantly. The successful efforts method expenses the cost of all unsuccessful exploration efforts immediately. Full costing capitalizes the cost of all efforts of expensing that take place when the resource is sold. Thus, the full costing method is the method of choice. This firm should use accounting methods that increase earnings. Higher earnings improve several quantitative measures used in debt covenants, including any measure of earnings, owners' equity balances, debt-to-equity ratio, and rates of return such as return on assets and return on equity.

495. Answer: C

It must be at least possible that the liability will be called in order for the classification to downgraded to current.

496. Answer: C

Both actions are appropriate. Refinancing current debt on a long-term basis reduces current liabilities (increases noncurrent debt) and increases the current ratio. Appropriating retained earnings is an action that typically signals a future reduction in dividends, albeit on a temporary basis. As a result, total retained earnings is maintained at a higher level.

497. Answer: C

The liability will be extinguished when the option is exercised or when it expires.

498. Answer: C

The total owners' equity increase of $20,000 (2,000 shares × $10) is recorded at signing. Of that amount, the common stock account will receive $10,000 (2,000 shares × $5 par). Therefore, the remainder ($10,000) is allocated to contributed capital in excess of par. Subsequent changes in stock price do not change the total amount of OE recorded.

499. Answer: A

Shifter paid $5,000 more for the treasury stock than its fair value: 1,000 shares × ($20 − $15). The $2,000 fee (1,000 × $2) offsets that loss yielding a net loss of $3,000.

500. Answer: B

The value of the stock to be issued is $20,000. At time of issuance, the stock price is $25. Therefore, 800 shares are issued ($20,000/$25). The par value of the stock is $2, requiring a credit of $1,600.

501. Answer: A

The value of the shares to be issued is the value of the contract or the agreed-upon value of the goods and services for the two parties. If the stock price changes between the time of contracting and the delivery of the goods or services, the number of shares changes in order to provide that fixed value.

502. Answer: A

Issued shares include outstanding shares and treasury shares. Treasury shares are issued but not outstanding. Stock splits are applied to all outstanding and treasury shares because a split reduces the par value of each share of issued stock, and increases the number of shares in inverse proportion.

Assume the stock has a par value of $3 before the split. After the 3-for-1 split in this question, the par value is $1, but the number of shares is tripled. Treasury shares must be adjusted for splits because treasury shares typically are reissued. No shares were retired.

Therefore, the number of issued shares at the end of the year is three times the number at the beginning of the year: 125,000(3) = 375,000 shares issued at December 31, 20X5.

Number of shares outstanding at December 31, 20X5 = (100,000 + 13,000)3 − 5,000 = 334,000.

Only 100,000 shares were outstanding at the beginning of the year because the 125,000 issued shares includes the 25,000 in the treasury. The split took effect after 13,000 of the 25,000 treasury shares at the beginning of the year were issued. The 5,000 treasury shares purchased at December 1 already reflect the split and are not adjusted further.

503. **Answer: A**

A 5% stock dividend increases outstanding shares by 5%, and a 2-for-1 split doubles outstanding shares. The number of outstanding shares at year-end therefore is 105,000 = 50,000(1.05)(2). Each subsequent dividend or split compounds the previous change.

504. **Answer: D**

This error reduces expenses because part of the holiday pay will be held back in ending inventory, which is a current asset. Thus, net income, and therefore OE, are overstated, as well as ending inventory, which is a current asset.

505. **Answer: C**

The change in total owners' equity for the year is $124,000, which equals the difference between the increase in assets and liabilities for the year ($178,000 – $54,000). Contributed capital increased $132,000 ($120,000 + $12,000). The firm paid dividends of $26,000. Thus:

$132,000 + net income – $26,000 = $124,000

net income = $124,000 – $132,000 + $26,000

= $18,000

506. **Answer: A**

Stock dividends and splits increase the number of shares outstanding on the date of distribution by the percentage effect implied by the dividend (10%) or split (100% or multiply by 2). The number of shares outstanding at 12/31/Year 1 = [300,000(1.10) – 100,000 + 50,000]2 = 560,000.

Treasury shares reduce the number of shares outstanding, and reissuance increases the number of shares outstanding. The total number of shares outstanding just before the split (280,000) is doubled in a 2-for-1 split.

507. **Answer: A**

Common stock: 5,000($1) = $5,000 (only par is recorded in common stock)

Preferred stock: 1,500($10) = $15,000 (only par is recorded in preferred stock)

Additional paid-in capital:

Common: 5,000($15 – $1) = $70,000

Preferred: 1,500($25 – $10) = 22,500

Total additional paid-in capital $92,500

508. **Answer: B**

The amount of the proceeds allocated to the stock is $70,000 ($110,000 – $40,000). When only one of the two securities has a known market value, that value is allocated to that security and the remaining proceeds are allocated to the security without a known market value.

The total par value of 1,000 shares of $5 par stock is $5,000. Therefore, $65,000 ($70,000 – $5,000) is recorded in additional paid-in capital on common stock.

509. **Answer: C**

The total proceeds are allocated to the two securities based on relative market values.

Market value of common: 1,000($36) =	$36,000
Market value of preferred: 2,000($27) =	54,000
Total market value	$90,000

Allocation of proceeds to preferred = ($54,000/$90,000)$80,000 = $48,000

510. **Answer: C**

The net effect of the transactions is to receive cash of $1,200 and issue stock for that amount at $15/share; $1,200/$15 = 80 shares fully paid. Required net changes in balances are (1) common stock, 80($10) = $800, (2) PIC-CS, 80($15 – $10) = $400, (3) cash $1,200. The share purchase contract receivable account is opened and then closed for the same amount. There is no ending balance in that account.

511. **Answer: A**

Common stock: 20,000($1) = $20,000. Only par value is credited to common stock.

Preferred stock: 6,000($10) = $60,000. Only par value is credited to preferred stock.

Additional paid-in capital (the amount received on issuance in excess of par):

Common: 20,000($30 – $1) = $580,000

Preferred: 6,000($50 – $10) = 240,000

Total $820,000

512. **Answer: C**

The journal entry for retirement:

Preferred stock $2,000(.25)($50)	$25,000
Additional paid-in capital, preferred stock $30,000(.25)	7,500
Additional paid-in capital from retirement of preferred stock	10,000
Cash	22,500

The additional paid-in capital from retirement of preferred stock is the net difference between the other amounts in the entry.

When preferred stock is retired, the par value of the stock retired is removed from the preferred stock account, and the pro-rata share of the additional paid-in capital from original issuance is removed. If the total of these two amounts exceeds the amount paid to redeem and retire the stock, as is the case here, additional paid-in capital from retirement of preferred stock is credited. The net effect on additional paid-in capital is an increase of $2,500 ($10,000 – $7,500).

Retained earnings is unaffected.

513. **Answer: A**

The $2 difference multiplied by 500 shares yields $1,000 paid-in capital kept by the firm. The journal entry is:

DR: Preferred stock 500($100)	50,000	
DR: PIC-preferred 500($103 – $100)	1,500	
CR: PIC-retirement of preferred		1,000
CR: Cash 500($101)		50,500

514. **Answer: B**

When a firm retires preferred stock, cash is paid to the shareholders reducing total owners' equity. Retained earnings can never be increased when shares are retired, redeemed, or converted into another class of stock.

515. **Answer: C**

The contributed capital accounts for the preferred are closed and the total amount is transferred to the common stock accounts resulting from issuance upon conversion. The total par value of common stock is first credited to the common stock account. If there is a credit remainder, it is recorded in paid-in capital in excess of par, common. If there is a debit remainder, retained earnings is debited. In this case, there is no remainder. The journal entry is:

DR: Preferred stock 500($100)	50,000	
DR: PIC-preferred 500($103 – $100)	1,500	
CR: Common stock 500(20)($5)		50,000
CR: PIC-common		1,500

516. **Answer: A**

Income is not affected by treasury stock transactions. When a firm transacts with its owners acting as owners, it cannot profit or report a negative income. In this case, the $3

difference between the $10 reissue price of the treasury stock and its $7 cost is credited to an owners' equity account as paid-in capital from treasury stock transactions. The firm's net worth has increased as a result of its treasury stock purchase and reissuance, but the "gain" is not recognized as earnings.

517. **Answer: B**

Under the par value method, when treasury stock is purchased and retired at a price exceeding the original issue price, the following entry is made. No additional paid-in capital from treasury stock transactions exists. Therefore, retained earnings is debited. Common stock par Additional paid-in capital original issue price – par Retained earnings acquisition price – original issuance price cash acquisition price. Thus, all three accounts listed in the question are decreased.

518. **Answer: C**

When treasury stock is cancelled (retired), the common stock account is reduced by the par value of the common stock cancelled. The ending common stock account balance is $415,000 = $540,000 – 50,000($2.50).

519. **Answer: C**

Under the cost method, additional paid-in capital from treasury stock transactions is credited when treasury stock is reissued at a price in excess of cost. This account is to be debited before retained earnings when the opposite occurs: reissue treasury stock at less than cost (as happened in the question).

However, only one treasury stock reissuance has occurred. Therefore, there is no additional paid-in capital from previous treasury stock transactions to draw on so the $4 difference between the purchase price and reissuance price is debited to retained earnings (a decrease). There is no effect on additional paid-in capital. The entry for reissuance is:

Cash $12(30,000)	360,000
Retained earnings	120,000
Treasury stock $16(30,000)	480,000

520. **Answer: C**

Additional paid-in capital is reduced when stock is retired because the additional paid-in capital from treasury stock transactions is closed.

The other three alternative answers cause income to change or retained earnings to increase. Retained earnings can never be increased through transactions with owners, nor can income be affected by such transactions.

521. **Answer: A**

The date of declaration is the date on which the firm has made the commitment to pay the dividend. The market value on this date is the value that was considered when the board made the decision to distribute a property dividend and thus is the appropriate measure of the sacrifice to the firm.

522. **Answer: A**

A legal liability comes into existence at declaration. The firm has committed itself to paying resources to shareholders from retained earnings on that date.

523. **Answer: D**

A liquidating dividend is a return of capital. Its source is not earnings, and, therefore, it is not retained earnings. The firm is liquidating part of its permanent capital. The usual account to debit for a liquidating dividend is additional paid-in capital.

524. **Answer: D**

The annual preferred stock dividend is $15,000 (3,000 × $100 × 5%). Total dividends in arrears at the end of 2005 are therefore $20,000 (2 years × $15,000 – $10,000 paid). Dividends in arrears are footnoted only. They are not recognized as a liability until they are declared.

525. **Answer: D**

It is at declaration that a dividend has its effect on the value of the firm and on working capital. Retained earnings are decreased (or a holding account called Dividends, which is closed to retained earnings, may be recorded), and dividends payable are increased. Dividends payable are a current liability, causing working capital to decrease.

Working capital equals current assets less current liabilities. The payment of a dividend does not affect working capital, because both cash and the dividend payable are reduced. Both current assets and current liabilities are reduced by the same amount.

526. **Answer: B**

Small stock dividends (less than 25%) are capitalized at the fair value of stock issued and large stock dividends (greater than 25%) are capitalized at the par value of stock issued.

The total amount capitalized (debited) to retained earnings, therefore, is $15,000 for the 10% stock dividend (fair value), plus $30,800 for the 28% stock dividend (par value) for a total of $45,800.

527. **Answer: C**

This is a large stock dividend (> 25%); therefore retained earnings is debited for par value. The amount is the par value of the shares distributed in the dividend, or 1,000(.30)($1) = $300. The credit is to common stock for the shares issued.

528. **Answer: C**

The annual preferred dividend commitment is $120,000 (20,000 × $100 × .06).

The amount paid in 20X5 ($240,000) covers both 20X5 and 20X4 (dividends in arrears). Wood owns 10% of Arlo's preferred stock and, therefore, received $24,000. This amount is recognized as revenue in 20X5.

Dividends in arrears are not recognized until received. The stock dividend is not treated as revenue, but rather reduces the cost per unit of Wood's investment in Arlo's common stock.

529. **Answer: B**

Total shares receiving a dividend equal 200,000, which is twice the number of shares at the beginning of the year.

The stock split doubled the number of shares outstanding. Therefore, the total cash dividend is $.50(200,000) = $100,000. This amount will appear in the statement of stockholders' equity as dividends declared.

530. **Answer: A**

This question is difficult, because authoritative sources and textbooks disagree as to the market value that should be used to value stock dividends. Small stock dividends (less than 25%) are measured at the market value of the stock issued. But the market value can be measured at declaration or at issuance.

The answer listed as correct uses the market value on the declaration date. The journal entry to record the dividend assuming the declaration and distribution occurred in the same fiscal period:

Retained earnings .10(3,000)($9)	2,700	
Common stock .10(3,000)($2)		600
Additional paid-in capital		2,100

531. **Answer: B**

Preferred represents one-fifth of total par value outstanding ($10,000/$50,000).

	To Preferred		To Common
Arrearage	.08(2)($10,000)	= $1,600	
Current year	.08($10,000)	= 800	
Matching			.08($40,000) = $3,200

Dividends remaining = $30,000 – $1,600 – $800 – $3,200 = $24,400, which is allocated according to total par value.

Participation	one-fifth($24,400) =	4,880	
	four-fifths($24,400)		= 19,520
Total		$7,280	$22,720

532. **Answer: C**

Participating dividends are allocated according to total par value after each class of stock receives the preferred dividend percentage.

Total par value of preferred stock outstanding is $300,000 (30,000 × $10), and total par value of common stock outstanding is $200,000 (200,000 × $1). Total par value of all stock outstanding is therefore $500,000. Preferred is three-fifths of total par value outstanding ($300,000/$500,000) and common is two-fifths ($200,000/$500,000) of total par value outstanding.

20X5 preferred requirement: 30,000(.05)($10) =	$15,000		
Preferred percentage to common: .05(200,000)($1) =	10,000	-->	$10,000
Subtotal	$25,000		

Remaining dividends: $100,000 – $25,000 = $75,000

Participation to preferred, based on total par value:

$75,000(3/5) = $45,000

Participation to common, based on total par value:

$75,000(2/5) = 30,000 -------------------->		30,000
Total common dividends		$40,000

533. **Answer: A**

Preferred represents one-fifth of total par value outstanding ($10,000/$50,000).

	To Preferred		To Common
Arrearage	.08(2)($10,000) = $1,600		
Current year	.08($10,000) = 800		
Matching			.08($40,000) = $3,200

Dividends remaining = $7,100 – $1,600 – $800 – $3,200 = $1,500, which is insufficient to provide 4% participation to both classes of stock [.04($50,000) = $2,000]. The remainder is allocated according to total par value.

Participation	1/5($1,500) =	300	
	4/5($1,500)		= 1,200
Total		$2,700	$4,400

534. Answer: C

Preferred represents one-fifth of total par value outstanding ($10,000/$50,000).

	To Preferred	To Common
Arrearage	.08(2)($10,000) = $1,600	
Current year	.08($10,000) = 800	
Matching		.08($40,000) = $3,200

Dividends remaining = $30,000 − $1,600 − $800 − $3,200 = $24,400, which exceeds .04($50,000), so there is enough for both classes of stock to participate at 4%.

	To Preferred	To Common
Participation	.04($10,000) = 400	
Remaining		$24,400 − $400 = 24,000
Total	$2,800	$27,200

535. Answer: A

Each item listed belongs in owners' equity. The treasury stock and net unrealized loss are negative items (debits), but the rest are positive items (credits).

Therefore, total owners' equity is $1.68mn = $600,000 + $800,000 − $50,000 − $20,000 + $150,000 + $200,000.

536. Answer: C

The dividend did not affect total OE, because no resources were expended or received. The payment of $0.10 per right reduces OE by a total of 120,000($0.10) = $12,000, because this amount of cash was paid.

537. Answer: D

The exercise is treated as would be any issuance of stock. The exercise price determines the total proceeds, the common stock account is credited for the total par of stock issued, and additional paid-in capital is credited for the remainder. The exercise price exceeds par value, so additional paid-in capital is increased. Retained earnings are unaffected.

538. Answer: D

The purpose of appropriations is to restrict dividends and communicate that restriction to users of the financial statements. It is merely a partitioning of retained earnings into two parts: (1) available for dividends, and (2) unavailable.

A firm need not record an appropriation in order to restrict dividends. However, it helps alert stockholders to the possibility that dividends may be curtailed, and informs them of the reason for that curtailment.

539. Answer: C

Retained earnings at December 31, 20X5 would be the sum of the beginning retained earnings of $630,000 and the net income. Net income is revenue ($3.6mn) − expense ($2.6mn) or $1mn.

However, this did not include taxes. Taxes on $1mn (at the 30% tax rate) are $300,000. This is exactly the same as the pre-paid taxes, so no additional liability exists. The pre-paid just need to be transferred to an expense category.

This makes income $700,000 and ending retained earnings $1.33mn. No adjustment need be made for the accounts receivable, unless Trey is handling this transaction differently for tax (installment method) than for book purposes, which is contrary to the facts presented in the problem.

540. Answer: C

The purchase of treasury stock at any price decreases total owners' equity under the cost method because treasury stock is a contra OE account. When the purchase price per share is less than book value per share, then the denominator decreases by a greater percentage than does the numerator, and book value per share increases.

For example, assume for simplicity that there is only common stock outstanding. Total owners' equity and number of shares before the treasury stock purchase is $40,000 and 4,000, respectively. Book value per share then is $10. The firm purchases 200 shares of treasury stock for $8 (less than book value). The new book value per share is:

($40,000 − $1,600)/(3,800) = $10.11. Book value per share has increased.

541. **Answer: C**

Reducing the par value to $5 creates $250,000 of additional paid-in capital: ($30 – $5)10,000 shares = $250,000. The common stock account is now $50,000: ($5)10,000.

Additional paid-in capital now stands at $400,000 ($150,000 + $250,000).

After absorbing the deficit in retained earnings, $190,000 remains in additional paid-in capital: ($400,000 – $210,000). Retained earnings are now zero.

542. **Answer: B**

Book value per share of common stock is common stockholders' equity per share of common stock. The portion of owners' equity allocated to preferred stock for this ratio is measured as the liquidation value per share. Therefore, the book value per share equals the net assets of the corporation per share that would be distributed to common shareholders on liquidation of the company, if the market value equaled book value for all assets and liabilities. The preferred shareholders would be paid the liquidation value per share first.

This firm has 1,000 shares of preferred stock outstanding: $100,000/$100 par; and 30,000 shares of common stock ($300,000/$10 par). It also has total owners' equity of $495,000 ($100,000 + $300,000 + $95,000).

For this firm, book value per share is $13.00 = [$495,000 – 1,000($105)]/30,000. Had there been dividends in arrears, they would also be subtracted from total owners' equity in the numerator. However, the preferred stock is non-cumulative, so there could be no dividends in arrears.

543. **Answer: D**

Assets and liabilities are revalued to market or fair value to provide a fresh-start valuation.

Usually, there are overvalued assets that have contributed to the operating losses and resulting retained-earnings deficit. The write-downs of overvalued assets further increase the retained-earnings deficit, but allow a new beginning for the firm. The contributed capital of the firm is reduced, permanently recording the losses, and retained earnings are increased to a zero balance.

544. **Answer: D**

Book value per share of common stock is the portion of owners' equity that would remain for common shareholders after the preferred claim was paid, divided by the number of common shares outstanding.

The preferred dividend claim includes the liquidation preference ($50,000 premium above par, plus par value) and the $25,000 dividends in arrears. All preferred stock dividends in arrears must be paid on liquidation before common shareholders receive any cash.

Total owners' equity is $1.025mn, the sum of the four items taken from the owners' equity section of the balance sheet ($250,000 + $350,000 + $125,000 + $300,000).

Book value per share of common stock = $7.00 = ($1.025 – $250,000 – $50,000 premium – $25,000 dividends in arrears)/100,000.

545. **Answer: C**

Deferred gross profit is the gross profit remaining on uncollected sales accounted for under the installment method. The gross profit percentage is 50% [($1mn – $500,000)/$1mn] on these sales.

Uncollected installment sales = $800,000 = $1mn – $200,000. Deferred gross profit = $400,000 = .50($800,000)

546. **Answer: C**

The cost recovery is the most conservative of the methods listed in the answer alternatives. It recognizes income slower than any other method listed.

This method recognizes no income until the cash collections exceed the cost of the equipment and would tend to overstate income the least. The cost recovery method is more conservative than the installment method, which recognizes profit on each dollar of cash collected.

547. **Answer: C**

The installment method of revenue recognition is used when the realizability criterion of revenue recognition is not met. In other words, there is significant uncertainty that the receivable will be collected. Until cash is collected (realizability is therefore assured for the amount collected), no gross profit is recognized. The cost-recovery method, which is even more conservative, may also be used in this situation.

548. **Answer: C**

The total gross profit to be recognized is $20,000 ($50,000 – $30,000). This is recognized over the length of the transaction at a rate of

$20,000/\$50,000 = 40\%$. The amount collected in year three multiplied by the gross profit rate is $\$15,000 \times 40\% = \$6,000$

549. **Answer: B**

Gross sales of $600,000, less 1% estimated returns = net sales of $594,000. Net sales × 10% = $59,400. The advance would have been unearned royalty revenue. This is earned based upon sales. Therefore, there is still a balance of $15,600 in the unearned account, as the $59,400 was earned in Year 1.

550. **Answer: A**

Before the franchisor (North) can recognize revenue, its activities pertaining to the franchise must be substantially complete. The earliest point at which substantial completion occurs is the commencement of operations by the franchisee. Operating activities will not begin until next year—therefore, North recognizes no fee revenue in the current year.

The $10,000 received is recorded in a liability account.

551. **Answer: C**

The unearned fees (current liability) balance is the sum of $40,000 cash received, plus the $48,000 present value of the note, for a total of $88,000. The remaining $12,000 (3 × $20,000 less the $48,000 present value) is interest to be recognized over the note term. No revenue is recognized until the service is performed.

552. **Answer: B**

The effect of estimated returns is recognized in the month of sale. Net sales to be reported for the current month equal $200,000 less the returns expected on those sales (5% or $10,000), or $190,000. The actual returns granted in the current month on previous months' sales were recognized as reductions in net sales in those previous months.

553. **Answer: C**

The $25,000 down payment, plus the $34,000 present value of remaining fee payments, is the appropriate amount of revenue to record. $59,000 is the cash equivalent amount accepted by the franchisor and therefore constitutes the amount received. Although the fee is listed at $65,000, the stronger evidence of value is the amount accepted. Also, the payments are non-refundable and the franchisor has no future performance. The revenue-recognition criteria are met.

554. **Answer: D**

The entire franchise fee is recognized as revenue when the franchisor has no significant responsibilities remaining under the contract. Also, the fee is not refundable. The installment nature of the payment plan has no bearing on the revenue recognition, because there is no uncertainty as to collection.

555. **Answer: C**

The project is 12.5% complete at the end of 20X5 ($2mn/$16mn). Total gross profit through the end of 20X5 is therefore $500,000 [= .125($20mn – $16mn)].

The $500,000 amount is the proportion of completion applied to the total contract profit of $4mn. 20X5 is the first year of construction; therefore no gross profit from previous years is subtracted. The entire $500,000 gross profit is recognized in 20X5.

556. **Answer: D**

The gross profit recognized for the first two years must be computed first. Then, the difference between the $500,000 final total gross profit on the project (= $2.5mn – $2mn), and the gross profit for the first two years, is the amount of gross profit recognized in the last (third) year. The percentage of completion at the end of the first two years is 70% (= $500,000 + $900,000)/$2mn). The gross profit recognized through the end of year two is $350,000 [= .70($2.5mn – $2mn)]. Therefore, gross profit for year three is $150,000 (= $500,000 total gross profit on project – $350,000).

557. **Answer: D**

The proportion of completion at the end of any year for a construction contract is the amount of work done, divided by the total amount of work required for the contract. Typically, cost is the measure of "work done." At the end of year three, the numerator is the cost incurred for all three years. The denominator is the total estimated cost of the project, which is the sum of

(1) the cost incurred for all three years so far, plus
(2) estimated costs to complete as of the end of year three.

The percentage of completion changes each year, because both the numerator and denominator change. The gross profit to be reported for year three is the profit for all three years (using the proportion of completion just computed), less the profit already reported in the first two years.

558. **Answer: B**

Total estimated project cost at the end of year 2 is $54,000 ($34,000 + $20,000). Note that this problem provides cumulative cost, rather than cost by year. There is an overall loss on this contract. Overall loss = $54,000 – $50,000 (contract price) = $4,000. Under the completed contract method, the overall loss is recognized immediately.

559. **Answer: A**

An overall loss is expected, because total estimated cost exceeds contract price. Under PC, the construction-in-progress account is increased by cost and gross profit. If the gross profit is negative (an overall loss), the loss is subtracted from construction in progress. The loss recognized in the year as overall loss becomes evident includes any previous profit. Therefore, the previously recognized gross profit is removed when the total loss is recognized. Under CC, the same idea applies, except that there is no gross profit from previous years to remove. The ending construction-in-progress balance is the same for both methods.

560. **Answer: B**

The damage deposit on all apartments is $500. Although it is likely that most tenants will be charged for some damages and cleaning, these reductions in the amount to be reimbursed cannot be anticipated. The damage to the apartments typically is not known until the end of the lease term.

The firm must maintain its $500 liability until the condition of each apartment becomes known at the end of the lease term. The conditions causing the need for repair or cleaning may not have occurred as of the balance sheet date.

561. **Answer: C**

The only liability (deferred revenue) to be recorded is the advance for 60% of the main contract price.

Dallas received this cash and has a liability for that amount until it performs on the contract. Dallas has no liability for the subcontracted production because no resources have been exchanged.

562. **Answer: A**

The redemption of the certificates would decrease deferred revenue and increase

revenue because the earnings process is completed once the store delivers the merchandise. If the gift certificates lapse, this will also decrease unearned revenue and recognize other income or a payable if the governing authorizes require these amounts to be remitted as unclaimed property.

563. **Answer: C**

The customer advances account is a liability. It represents amounts received from customers for orders not yet filled by the firm. Advances on cancelled orders may or may not be returned, but either way cancellation reduces the liability.

An analysis of the liability:

Beg. Balance	+ advances received	– advances applied	– advances cancelled	= End. Balance
$590,000	+ $920,000	– $820,000	– $250,000	= $440,000

When an order is filled, the advance is applied to the total purchase price. An advance is an amount already paid by the customer toward the total purchase price.

564. **Answer: B**

Included in the $20,000 received when the equipment was sold is $2,000 of unearned service revenue. Sales should have been recorded for $18,000. That amount will be earned over the two-year contract period. By the end of the current year (first year of the contract), some amount of that $2,000 revenue will be earned. Assume the SL basis—$1,000 of revenue is earned each year. Then for the current year, $19,000 of revenue in total is recognized, which is $1,000 less than the $20,000 of sales revenue recorded by the firm. Income is thus overstated for the current year.

565. **Answer: D**

No work has been performed at the time of sale. Unearned revenue is credited for the entire amount received. The unearned revenue is recognized as revenue over the term of the contract.

566. **Answer: B**

The $25,000 rent deposit is a noncurrent liability because it will be applied toward the rental of a tenant more than one year after the 200X4 balance sheet.

The ending liability for cans = $150,000 – (11,000,000 – 10,000,000).05 = $100,000.

When customers return cans, they are paid $.05 for each. Can returns reduce the liability. At sale, the deposit is collected and the liability increases. More cans were returned than were sold. Therefore, the deposit liability for cans decreased during the year. This is a current liability. Most customers do not keep cans for more than one year before returning them.

567. **Answer: C**

The beginning pension liability balance was $40mn ($200mn PBO – $160mn assets). With pension expense of $60mn and funding of $50mn, the pension liability increased an additional $10mn, yielding an ending pension-liability balance of $50mn ($40mn + $10mn). There is no information about amortization of PSC or net gain or loss, or difference between expected and actual return, or gain, loss or PSC during the period.

568. **Answer: B**

The reported pension liability for a defined benefit pension plan is the difference between projected benefit obligation ($68,100) and the fair value of plan assets ($62,000), or $6,100. The two underlying amounts are reported in the footnotes, but are not recognized in the balance sheet. Only their difference, which is also the underfunded amount, is reported in the balance sheet as a liability.

569. **Answer: D**

Accumulated benefit obligation is the present value of all unpaid future retirement benefits as of the balance sheet date based on (1) service rendered to that date, and (2) current salary levels.

Even if the pension benefit formula incorporates future salaries, accumulated benefit obligation uses current salary levels only to provide a more current measure of the pension liability.

570. **Answer: D**

Fair value represents the most representationally faithful amount to be applied to pension obligation. Fair value is the current amount available for payment of pension benefits.

571. **Answer: D**

The reported liability for defined benefit pension plans is the unfunded projected benefit obligation. This is the projected benefit obligation less pension plan assets at fair value. Projected benefit obligation is the fundamental

measure of a firm's pension liability, but is reported only in the footnotes.

572. **Answer: D**

The plan is currently underfunded and remains underfunded after the asset increase. Reported pension liability is the underfunded amount, the difference between PBO and plan assets. This firm's reported pension liability decreased from $800,000 to $300,000 ($800,000 – $500,000) owing to the asset increase.

573. **Answer: D**

When the actuarial gain is recognized, pension liability is debited, because PBO is reduced by the gain, and pension liability is the difference between PBO and assets. Pension gain/loss—OCI is credited, because the firm's pension costs have decreased. The pension gain/loss—OCI account causes other comprehensive income to be credited (increased).

574. **Answer: B**

The amortization decreases pension expense because the gain reduced the firm's pension costs. The amortization amount is the portion of the gain that is entered into pension expense (as a negative amount). The gain was recorded previously. At that time, pension liability was decreased, and other comprehensive income increased. The complete entry is: (dr.) Pension gain/loss—OCI $50, (cr.) Pension expense $50.

575. **Answer: A**

Pension plan assets are accumulated for the purpose of paying retiree benefits under the plan. In assessing the ability of the plan to pay benefit payments, fair value is the most relevant reporting attribute. The bulk of pension plan assets are invested in financial instruments whose value varies over time. Measurement of these investments is most appropriate at fair value and is consistent with reporting projected benefit obligation at present value—both are current values as of the reporting date.

576. **Answer: D**

Projected benefit obligation (PBO), January 1, 2005	$72,000
Plus interest cost (growth in PBO), .10($72,000)	$7,200
Plus service cost	$18,000
Less benefits paid in 2005	($15,000)
PBO, December 31, 2005	$82,200

577. **Answer: C**

Pension gains and losses are recognized immediately and in full in accumulated other comprehensive income. However, they are not subsequently amortized to earnings.

578. **Answer: C**

OCI is increased through the increase in pension gains/losses—OCI.

579. **Answer: C**

PSC is not recognized in other comprehensive income.

580. **Answer: A**

Until the specific accounting standard was adopted, firms often used the pay-as-you-go basis (cash basis) for the accounting, but now, firms must record the relevant expense in the period in which the benefits are earned by the employee, provided that the appropriate criteria are met.

581. **Answer: A**

This question requires you to work backward to solve for the amount paid during the year. Solving the following equation (or using a T account), the amount paid is $40,000. Equation: $67,000 + $34,000 – $5,000 – pmts = $56,000.

582. **Answer: C**

This answer is a description of vested benefits. Benefits need not vest for accrual to be mandatory.

583. **Answer: B**

Only 60% of the benefits earned are expected to be taken by the covered employees. The amount recognized as expense is limited to this amount, because the criteria for recognition require that payments be probable in order for accrual to take place. The following equation (or T-account) provides the solution: $112,000 + (.60)($48,000) – $38,000 = $102,800.

584. **Answer: B**

Accounting for post-retirement healthcare benefits is covered by a different standard, and involves a much different type of accounting, similar to accounting for defined-benefit pension plans. Such benefits include coverage for all or a portion of a retiree's healthcare costs for the rest of the retiree's life.

585. **Answer: A**

The per capita claims cost is the basis for computing the obligation reported for a post-retirement healthcare plan. These costs are estimated based on historical norms adjusted for estimated healthcare cost-trend rates and are affected by the estimated age of employees at retirement, their health, and other factors. Only post-retirement healthcare plans require this type of estimate. Pension benefits, for example, are based on variables such as age at retirement, number of years of service, and final salary. Both defined-benefit pension plans and post-retirement healthcare plans involve the other three answer alternatives. Both have service-cost and interest-cost components for their respective expenses, and both can incur prior-service cost.

586. **Answer: C**

The excess of plan assets over the benefit liability (accumulated postemployment benefit liability or APBO) is reported as an asset and is classified as noncurrent. The plan assets and APBO are not reported separately but rather are offset. Given the long-term nature of such plans, the asset is classified as a noncurrent asset.

587. **Answer: C**

The employee's full eligibility date occurs seven years from today. At that time, she is fully eligible for 75% coverage. The last three years of her service do not increase the level of her benefit. There is no additional service cost beyond that date, although interest cost will continue. If she were expected to work 15 years after today, her full eligibility would not occur until 15 years from now, at which time she would be fully eligible for 100% coverage and service cost would continue through that date.

588. **Answer: A**

Beginning post-retirement benefit liability equals $200mn ($300mn APBO – $100mn assets). Post-retirement benefit expense: $40mn SC + $15mn interest cost (.05 × $300mn) – $6mn expected return (.06 × $100mn) + $5mn amortization of PSC ($50mn/ten) – $2mn amortization of net gain ($20mn/10) = $52mn.

Entry: dr. post-retirement benefit expense 52, dr. postretirement gain/loss-OCI 2, cr. PSC-OCI 5, cr. post-retirement benefit liability 49. There is a $4mn asset gain = $10mn actual return – $6mn expected return.

Entry: dr. postretirement benefit liability 4, cr. postretirement gain/loss-OCI 4.

Entry for actuarial gain: dr. postretirement benefit liability 16, cr. post-retirement gain/loss-OCI 16.

Entry for funding: dr. post-retirement benefit liability 20, cr. cash 20.

From the entries: ending post-retirement benefit liability = 200 beginning + 49 – 4 – 16 – 20 = 209. Alternatively, ending post-retirement benefit liability = $200mn beginning post-retirement benefit + $40mn SC + $15mn interest cost – $10mn actual return – $16mn actuarial gain – $20mn funding = $209mn.

589. Answer: D

Post-retirement healthcare benefits often are provided in terms of percentage of total coverage. For example, an employee may have to work 20 years to attain 50% healthcare coverage during retirement, and 30 years to attain 100% coverage.

If the employee is expected to work 25 years, then the 50% coverage is the level built into the expense and liability computations, and the accrual period is the first 20 years of service. After serving 20 years, the employee earns no more benefit.

Therefore, the full eligibility date is the date by which the employee has served the required number of years to attain the level of benefits the employee is expected to attain.

590. Answer: C

The fair value of a fixed option plan at grant date is the fair value of the option. Typically the fair value of one option is given and that is multiplied by the number of options, but this problem provides the entire fair value. That total fair value is the total compensation expense to be recognized over the service period—the number of years from grant date to vesting. Once the options vest, no more compensation expense is recognized because the manager has provided the necessary service. Compensation expense per year is the total $300,000 compensation expense divided by 3 years, or $100,000 per year.

591. Answer: B

Expiration of stock options does not cause reversal of compensation expense because, at the grant date, the firm did provide value to the employee, given that the option had a fair value at that time.

The expense recognized for stock option plans is not based on the expected value of the employee services; rather, it is based on the value of what was given by the employer to the employee.

592. Answer: A

The fair value on the grant date is used for measuring compensation expense, because, on that date, the employer has given a resource of value to the employee.

593. Answer: C

Total compensation expense is the product of the fair value of one option at the grant date ($5) and the number of options granted (10,000). The result is $50,000 of total compensation expense. This total is allocated equally to each year in the service period. The service period is the period from grant date to vesting date (first exercisable date), or 4 years. Annual compensation expense is $50,000/4 = $12,500.

594. Answer: A

The fair value of the option sets the compensation expense to be recognized for each option expected to be vested. Applying the forfeiture rate ensures that only options expected to be vested will be entered into the calculation.

595. Answer: A

Total compensation expense is computed as the fair value of the stock awarded, and is allocated evenly over the vesting period. The fair value at award date is the fair value used for this computation. The two awards are treated as separate awards, each with four-year amortization periods. The total expense for year 2 is the sum of the compensation expense to be recognized for each plan for year 2 and is computed as 10,000($20)/4 + 20,000($25)/4 = $175,000. Total fair value is not updated after the award date.

596. Answer: D

Total compensation expense at grant date is $60,000 (3,000 × $20). The service period is four years (20X5 – 20X8). Annual expense recognized is $15,000 ($60,000/4).

Through 2006, a total of $30,000 of compensation expense is recognized. After the forfeit, only 2,900 shares remain to be awarded.

Annual compensation expense for the remaining two years before considering forfeited shares is therefore $14,500 [(2,900 × $20)/4].

The expense for the two years associated with the 100 shares forfeited is $1,000 [(100 × $20)/2].

For 2007, subtracting the reversal of the $1,000 yields $13,500 as the final amount of expense to be recognized.

Another way to calculate the $14,500 is: ($60,000 original total compensation expense – $30,000 expense for 2005 and 2006 – $1,000 expense for 2007 and 2008 on forfeited shares)/2.

597. Answer: C

The 2005 compensation expense for these stock-appreciation rights equals: (number of shares) × (ending market price – grant-date market price) = 20,000($45 – $30) = $300,000.

The rights are immediately vested, because they can be exercised immediately. Therefore, the entire $300,000 amount is recognized as expense in 2005. Changes in market price in future years, before the rights are exercised, are recognized on a current and prospective basis (change in estimate).

598. Answer: B

Total compensation expense is the product of the number of shares in the award and the market price of stock at the grant date. This amount is recognized over the service period required for the employee to receive or keep the shares.

599. Answer: D

The net amount of deferred tax expense or benefit is that amount that is not recognized in current period income.

A simple equation describes the total tax effects for a period: income tax expense or benefit + deferred income tax expense or benefit = current tax liability. The deferred income tax expense or benefit can further be described as the net change in both types of deferred tax accounts.

600. Answer: A

Total income tax expense is the sum of the current and deferred portions.

The current portion is the income tax liability for the year.

The deferred portion is the net sum of the changes in the deferred tax accounts.

Consider the tax-accrual entry for a year, assuming no estimated tax payments have been made:

Income tax expense	20	
Deferred tax asset	3	
Deferred tax liability		5
Income tax payable		18

$$\underset{\text{expense} = 20}{\text{Total income tax}} = \underset{\text{expense}}{\text{Current tax}} + \underset{\text{expense}}{\text{Deferred tax}}$$

Deferred tax asset = $18 + $2

The $2 deferred tax expense equals the increase in the deferred tax liability of $5, less the increase in the deferred tax asset of $3.

601. Answer: C

FAS 109 adopted the asset/liability approach. The deferred tax expense is the net change in the deferred tax accounts for the year. Deferred tax accounts are measured at the enacted tax rate for the period in which the future temporary differences reverse.

Rather than base income tax expense on accounting income adjusted for permanent differences, as was the case before 109, income tax expense is now the sum of current income tax expense (the income tax liability for the year) and the net change in deferred tax accounts. The expense is a residual amount, based on the changes in assets and liabilities. Matching is no longer the conceptual basis for measurement.

602. Answer: D

Both listed items are permanent differences. These are differences that never reverse and are not used in the determination of deferred tax accounts. Both income tax expense and income tax liability are affected the same way by these items.

A deferred income tax liability is based on future taxable differences at the end of the reporting year.

There are no such differences. Therefore, there is no deferred tax liability.

603. Answer: D

The future temporary difference at December 31, 20X4 is $9,500, the amount of insurance expense to be recognized for financial-reporting purposes.

The entire $19,000 deduction was taken for tax purposes in 20X4. Therefore, no further deduction will be taken beyond 20X4. The difference is taxable, because future taxable income exceeds future pre-tax accounting income from transactions through 20X4.

The deferred tax liability uses the future tax rate, because that is the rate at which the deferred taxes will be paid. The ending deferred tax liability for 20X4 = $2,375 = .25($9,500).

604. **Answer: B**

Deferred tax liabilities are the future tax effects of future taxable temporary differences. Such differences cause future taxable income to exceed future pre-tax accounting income.

I.   An increase in pre-paid insurance implies that future accounting insurance expense will exceed future tax insurance expense. Therefore, future taxable income will increase relative to future pre-tax accounting income. This increases the deferred tax liability.

II. An increase in rent receivable implies that future tax-rent revenue will exceed future accounting-rent revenue. A rent receivable is recorded when accounting-rent revenue is recognized before cash is received. Cash will be received in the future, which will be recognized as rent revenue for tax, but no revenue will be recognized for accounting. Therefore, again, future taxable income will increase relative to future pre-tax accounting income.

III. An increase in warranty obligations implies that future tax-warranty expense will exceed future accounting-warranty expense. Accounting has recognized the warranty expense in the year of sale, whereas tax-warranty expense is recognized in the year the repairs are made. This time, future taxable income will decrease relative to future pre-tax accounting income. This increases the deferred tax asset, rather than the deferred tax liability.

Therefore, only I and II increase the deferred tax liability.

605. **Answer: B**

This answer describes one category of temporary difference. In general, a temporary difference is one for which the item's recognition takes place at a different rate or time for financial reporting and the tax return. However, the total impact of the item is the same over its life, for both systems of reporting.

606. **Answer: A**

The tax liability is the tax rate times taxable income = .30($600,000 − $60,000 − $120,000 − $100,000) = $96,000.

The municipal bond interest is tax exempt, but included in pre-tax accounting income of $600,000 and therefore is subtracted when computing taxable income.

The excess depreciation is also subtracted, because pre-tax accounting income reflects only depreciation recorded for financial accounting purposes.

The proceeds on life insurance are included in pre-tax accounting income, but are not taxable and are therefore subtracted in computing taxable income.

607. **Answer: B**

More profit will be recognized under completed contract in year three for tax purposes than will be recognized under percentage-of-completion in year three for accounting purposes. The entire profit will be recognized under completed contract (tax purposes) in year three. But a portion of income has already been recognized for accounting purposes before year three. Therefore, less income will be recognized in year three for accounting purposes.

Consequently, at the end of year two, there is a future taxable difference because future taxable income will exceed future pre-tax accounting income. Taxable differences give rise to deferred tax liabilities.

608. **Answer: B**

The tax liability is 30% of taxable income.

Pre-tax accounting income	$90,000
Plus advance rent (taxable, but not included in pre-tax accounting income)	$16,000
Less municipal bond income (this is included in pre-tax accounting income, but is not taxable)	($20,000)
Less depreciation for tax in excess of depreciation for the books	(10,000)
Equals taxable income	$76,000
Times tax rate	× .30
Equals income tax liability	$22,800

609. **Answer: C**

Current income tax expense is the income tax liability for the year: .30($650,000) = $195,000.

The estimated tax payments do not alter the solution, as they are installment payments for the total tax liability.

610. Answer: C

The $5,000 difference (interest) is a permanent difference. Therefore, it is not considered in the computation of deferred tax account balances.

The $10,000 difference (loss accrual) is a deductible amount, because more loss is recognized in the current year for accounting purposes than for tax purposes. Therefore, in the future, a greater amount of loss will be deductible for tax purposes, when the difference reverses. This amount gives rise to a long-term deferred tax asset of $4,000 ($10,000 × .4).

The $25,000 difference (depreciation) is a taxable amount, because less depreciation will be recognized for tax purposes than for accounting purposes in the future. This amount gives rise to a long-term deferred tax liability of $10,000 ($25,000 × .4).

GAAP requires that one long-term deferred tax item be reported. Therefore, in the balance sheet, a net deferred tax liability of $6,000 ($10,000 – $4,000) will be reported.

611. Answer: D

The current portion of income tax expense is the amount currently due and is equal to the tax liability for the period. That amount is the product of the current tax rate and taxable income: .30 × $400,000 = $120,000.

612. Answer: C

Two of the three differences are temporary, and thus contribute to the deferral of tax. The uncollectible accounts expense gives rise to a future deductible difference of $30,000 ($250,000 – $220,000), causing the firm's deferred tax asset to increase $12,000 ($30,000 × .40). The future enacted tax rate is used to measure changes in deferred tax accounts. The depreciation difference gives rise to a future taxable difference of $290,000 ($860,000 – $570,000), causing the firm's deferred tax liability to increase $116,000 ($290,000 × .40). The net deferral is $104,000 ($116,000 – $12,000). The tax-exempt interest is a nontemporary difference. Therefore, it does not affect the deferral of tax.

613. Answer: D

Black will recognize a deferred tax asset, rather than a deferred liability, because its current taxable income is greater than its current pre-tax financial income.

This occurs because Black cannot deduct product warranty cost for tax purposes until the costs are incurred (paid), but, for financial reporting, it must recognize those estimated costs as an expense in the period of the related sales.

The result is an amount that will be deductible in the future for tax purposes: a deferred tax asset. Because it is deductible now for financial reporting and will be deductible in the future for tax purposes, it is a temporary difference.

The amount of deferred tax asset (or, in another case, deferred tax liability) on temporary differences is calculated by multiplying the amount of the temporary differences by the enacted tax rate for the period(s) during which the deferred asset (or liability) is expected to be realized.

Therefore, Black's deferred tax asset would be calculated as:

2005	$100,000 × .30 =	$30,000
20X6	$50,000 × .30 =	$15,000
20X7	$50,000 × .30 =	$15,000
20X8	$100,000 × .35 =	$35,000
Total deferred tax asset =		$95,000

Please note:

1. This was the first year of operation for Black. Therefore, there was no previously recorded tax asset or liability.
2. Since Black expects operating profits in future years, it implicitly expects to realize the benefit of the deferred tax asset and no valuation allowance is necessary.

A, B, and C are incorrect. The tax benefit (asset) is the amount to be recognized as deductible in each future year times (multiplied by) the enacted tax rate applicable to each future year.

614. Answer: D

The total future taxable difference at the end of 20X5 is $20,000.

Therefore, the balance in the deferred tax liability account is .40($20,000) = $8,000. Taxes payable in the future (after 20X5) will increase $8,000 as a result of transactions in 20X5 and earlier.

615. Answer: C

Total income for the three years under the two methods is:

Percentage-of-completion:	$1.75mn ($300,000 + $600,000 + $850,000)
Completed-contract:	$1,100,000 ($400,000 + $700,000)
Difference	$650,000

This difference is also the future difference in earnings to be recognized under the two methods, because both methods ultimately recognize the same total amount of income. Completed contract (for tax purposes) will recognize $650,000 more income than percentage of completion (for book purposes) after 20X5. Therefore, the difference is taxable and gives rise to a deferred tax liability of $162,500 ($650,000 × .25). The future enacted tax rate is applied, because that is the rate at which the deferred tax liability will be paid.

616. Answer: C

The $24,000 current tax liability is the current tax rate times taxable income: $24,000 = .30($100,000 − $20,000).

617. Answer: B

The current provision for income tax, also called the tax liability for the year, is the current tax rate multiplied by taxable income: .34 × $450,000 = $153,000.

618. Answer: A

A change in method of depreciation is treated as an estimate change. The remaining book value is allocated over the remaining useful life of the asset. Therefore, the total future difference between book and tax depreciation as of the beginning of 20X2 remains unchanged. That difference is $18,000, the difference between book and tax depreciation through the end of 20X1. The pattern of reversal of this difference in the future has changed owing to the change in method, but the total difference remains unchanged. Therefore, there is no reduction in the deferred tax asset at the beginning of 20X2.

619. Answer: D

The classification of deferred tax accounts is the same as the accounts giving rise to the deferred taxes.

The temporary differences referred to in the question are future taxable differences, which cause a deferred tax liability. The account giving rise to the difference is equipment, which is classified as long-term.

Therefore, the deferred tax liability is also classified as long-term (non-current).

620. Answer: D

Future taxable differences cause taxable income in the future to exceed pre-tax accounting income. Therefore, deferred tax liabilities are the result of taxable differences. Classification of deferred tax accounts is based on the item giving rise to the temporary differences. In this case, the underlying item is non-current. Therefore, the deferred tax liability is also classified as non-current.

621. Answer: B

The classification of deferred tax accounts is based on the underlying account to which they are related. The $15,000 income tax liability is related to a non-current asset. Therefore, that deferred tax liability is classified as non-current. Balance-sheet presentation of deferred tax accounts nets the non-current accounts and nets the current accounts, for a maximum of two net deferred accounts reported.

This firm would net the $15,000 non-current deferred tax liability with the $3,000 non-current deferred tax asset, to yield a net non-current deferred tax liability of $12,000.

622. Answer: D

Current and non-current deferred tax accounts are not netted together for balance sheet disclosure.

In this case, there is a non-current deferred tax liability, and a current deferred tax asset. Therefore, the full $75,000 of non-current deferred tax liability is separately disclosed in the balance sheet. Even though a portion of the liability is expected to reverse within one year of the balance sheet date, that does not change the classification of any of the deferred tax liability account.

It is the related asset classification that determines current or non-current classification. Because the deferred tax liability is related to a non-current asset, the entire amount is classified as non-current.

623. Answer: C

Income tax expense is the net sum of the income tax liability for the year, the changes in the deferred tax accounts, and the change in the valuation account for deferred tax assets.

Tax liability (current portion of income tax expense):	$13,000
Less increase in deferred tax asset: $20,000 – $15,000	($5,000)
Plus increase in valuation account: .10($20,000)	$2,000
Equals income tax expense	$10,000

The increase in the deferred tax asset causes income tax expense to decrease relative to the tax liability, because, as a result of transactions through the end of the current year, future taxable income will be reduced. This reduction is not realized in the current year as a reduction in the tax liability. Therefore, the anticipated future reduction is treated as an asset at the end of the current period. When realized, the asset is reduced in a future year.

The increase in the valuation allowance, which is contra to the deferred tax asset, reduces the deferred-tax-asset effect, because it is an amount of the deferred tax asset not likely to be realized.

624. **Answer: B**

This is the largest amount, which has at least a 50% probability of occurring. The cumulative probability through this amount is 60%. A liability is recognized for the $15,000 of the total $40,000, which has less than a 50% chance of occurring.

625. **Answer: A**

Income tax expense was reduced two years ago by $20,000, but the final benefit upon resolution is $22,000. The $2,000 increase in benefit is recognized in the year of resolution.

626. **Answer: B**

The unused net operating loss (NOL) at the beginning of the year is $20,000 (= $6,000/.3). The firm pays no tax for the current year, because $12,000 of the NOL is used to absorb the $12,000 of taxable income. $8,000 of the NOL remains to carry forward to the next year. Also, there is a future temporary difference of $20,000 from the future warranty deduction ($30,000 – $10,000 current-year claims). In total, then, the basis for the ending deferred tax asset is $28,000 (= $8,000 + $20,000). The ending deferred tax asset balance is $8,400 (= $28,000 × .3). The beginning deferred tax asset balance is $6,000. Therefore, the deferred tax asset is increased by $2,400 and income tax benefit of

that amount also is recorded (credited) in the tax-accrual entry.

627. **Answer: D**

Deferred income tax expense is the net change in deferred tax accounts for the year. Because the firm began the year without any deferred tax accounts, that change equals the net sum of the ending deferred tax accounts for 20X4. Enacted tax rates are used to compute the change in deferred tax accounts.

Ending deferred tax liability (from depreciation temporary differences): $2,000(.25) – $1,200(.30)	$140
Less ending deferred tax asset (from warranty temporary difference): $300(.25) + $100(.30)	($105)
Equals net change in deferred tax accounts, and deferred income tax expense	$35

The 20X5 temporary difference for depreciation is subtracted from the 20X6 difference, because the 20X5 difference is an originating difference, whereas the 20X6 difference is the reversing difference.

628. **Answer: B**

Deferred income tax accounts are not affected by permanent differences, because their effect on income tax is the same as their effect on income tax liability.

But temporary differences and operating loss and tax-credit carry-forwards produce deferred tax accounts. Temporary differences cause both deferred tax liabilities and assets to be recognized. Operating loss and tax credit carry-forwards generate only deferred tax assets.

To fully understand the nature of deferred tax accounts, the types and amounts of Statements I and III are reported in a detailed footnote. For example, depreciation differences are major causes of deferred tax liabilities.

629. **Answer: A**

The tax benefit of the carry-forward reduced taxes on Year 2 income from continuing operations, as indicated in the question. Therefore, the benefit is included in income from continuing operations.

630. **Answer: D**

Accounting-principle changes such as this one are recorded by retroactively restating prior-year financial statements. The entry to record the change results in an adjustment to the beginning balance of retained earnings in the year of the change.

631. **Answer: C**

The failure to accrue warranty expense is an accounting error. It gives rise to a Prior period adjustment in the year of discovery (2004).

Prior period adjustments are limited to corrections of errors affecting prior-year net income. They adjust the beginning balance of retained earnings in the year of correction. The change in depreciation method is an estimate change, which is reported in earnings. It is not a Prior period adjustment.

632. **Answer: C**

When an accounting principle change cannot be distinguished from an estimate change, it is accounted for as an estimate change. Changes in an accounting estimate are accounted for currently and prospectively and are reported in income from continuing operations. The relevant accounts affected by the change are adjusted for the current and future years. The change is not retroactively applied.

633. **Answer: D**

The accrual basis of accounting is required by GAAP. A change from an inappropriate method to the correct method is treated as an error correction. The procedure requires retrospective application, resulting in an after-tax cumulative adjustment to prior years' earnings (called a Prior period adjustment) to the beginning balance in retained earnings.

634. **Answer: A**

The cash basis of accounting is not acceptable under GAAP. Therefore, the change to the accrual basis is a change from an unacceptable method or basis of accounting to an acceptable method or basis. Such a change is treated as an error correction, which is reported as a Prior period adjustment. This adjustment is to the beginning balance in retained earnings for the current year.

635. **Answer: C**

$6,000 is the cumulative pre-tax income difference between the two methods as of January 1, 2005.

The after-tax difference is .70($6,000) or $4,200. Accounting changes are measured as of the beginning of the year of change. The $6,000 represents the total difference in cost of goods

sold between the two methods for the entire life of the firm, because under weighted-average, the firm has $6,000 more in inventory than under FIFO at January 1, 2005. This is the "ending" inventory for that firm, as of that date, for the firm's entire existence.

The $6,000 difference completely explains the pre-tax difference in income under the two methods for years up to January 1, 2005; the $4,200 is the after-tax difference.

Cumulative effects are reported net of tax as an adjustment to the beginning balance of retained earnings in the year of the change.

636. **Answer: B**

Accounting-principle changes are reported as an adjustment to retained earnings at the beginning of the year of change. Prior financial statements are retrospectively adjusted.

637. **Answer: A**

The cumulative effect is computed as of the beginning of the year of change (2005), because the new method (WA) is used in 2005 to compute cost of goods sold and ending inventory. The pre-tax effect of the change on the previous three years is the difference between ending 2004 inventory under the two methods. The only income account affected by the method change is cost of goods sold. The cumulative effect adjusts the beginning of 2005 retained earnings balance.

At the beginning of operations in 2002, there was no beginning inventory. Purchases are the same under either method. Therefore, the difference in cost of goods sold and therefore pre-tax income for the three years between the two methods is $5,000 = ($83,000 − $78,000). WA recognizes more cost of goods sold. Therefore, the cumulative effect reduces 2005 pre-tax income by $5,000.

638. **Answer: C**

This is an accounting-estimate change. These accounting changes are handled currently and prospectively by applying the new estimate to the current and future periods, if affected. The effect of the change on prior years' earnings is not computed, because the new information causing the estimate change was not known at that time.

Cumulative effects are reported for accounting principle changes, not estimate changes, because the effect of the change on prior years is computed and reported for accounting principle changes only.

639. **Answer: A**

This is a change in estimate. The new estimated useful life and salvage value are applied to the book value at the beginning of the year of the estimate change.

Accumulated depreciation, January 1, 2005 = $528,000(3/8) =	$198,000
Book value, January 1, 2005 = $528,000 – $198,000 = $330,000 Depreciation, 2005 = ($330,000 – $48,000)/(6 – 3) =	$94,000
Accumulated depreciation, 31 December 2005	$292,000

The denominator of the 2005 depreciation calculation (6 – 3) is the new total useful life of six years, less the three years for which the asset has been used as of January 1, 2005.

640. **Answer: A**

The book value at the beginning of the year of the change in estimated useful life is used as the base for subsequent depreciation. After four years, the book value remaining is one-fifth of its original cost, because there is no salvage value and the firm uses SL depreciation.

That remaining book value is spread equally over four more years, yielding $600 of depreciation in each of those years. Book value at the beginning of year five = $12,000 – 4($12,000/5) = $2,400. Depreciation expense for year five = $2,400/4 = $600. The four years remaining include year five.

641. **Answer: C**

When it is impossible to determine whether the change is an estimate or a change in accounting principle, the change should be considered a change in **estimate** and accounted for prospectively.

642. **Answer: D**

The asset has a depreciable base of $46,000 – $1,000 = $45,000. The depreciation expense for years one through four is $45,000/12 = $3,750.

Accumulated depreciation after four years is $3,750 × 4 = $15,000.

The carrying value after four years is $46,000 – $15,000 = $31,000.

Depreciation based on the new estimated useful life is $31,000 – $1,000 = $30,000 for the depreciable base. The remaining useful life is 10 – 4 = 6 years.

Depreciation for the current year is $30,000/6 = $5,000.

643. **Answer: B**

Accumulated depreciation is a pre-tax amount. The journal entry omitted in the past is:

dr. Depreciation expense, $40,000

cr. Accumulated depreciation, $40,000

The beginning balance of accumulated depreciation in the year the error was discovered is understated by $40,000 because that amount was not recorded in a prior year.

644. **Answer: B**

All publicly traded companies are required to report EPS information. However, only the current year is affected. Restatement of prior-year statements is not required.

645. **Answer: A**

This is an error correction. The correction of an error affecting the income of prior periods is accounted for as a Prior period adjustment. This adjustment corrects the beginning retained earnings balance in the period the error was discovered, thereby correcting the retained earnings carried forward from earlier periods.

646. **Answer: B**

The after-tax amount of the overstatement of 2004 earnings is $230,000 ($300,000 – $70,000 tax effect).

2004 income is overstated by this amount, because the expense and tax effect were not recorded. Ending 2004 retained earnings is overstated by $230,000. Therefore, beginning 2005 retained earnings must be decreased (debited) $230,000. This is accomplished by adjusting the beginning 2005 retained earnings balance with a Prior period adjustment of $230,000 (debit).

647. **Answer: A**

Neither of the changes listed are Prior period adjustments (PPA). A PPA is an adjustment to the beginning retained earnings balance that corrects the effect on retained earnings of errors in reporting prior-year income. A PPA is not a voluntary accounting change.

The change in inventory method is an accounting principle change, which requires the recording of a cumulative effect of accounting change as an adjustment to retained earnings. This account measures the effect of the change on prior-year net income. The change in depreciation method is treated as an estimate change. The remaining book value at the beginning of the year of change is allocated to the remaining useful life using the new depreciation method.

648. **Answer: B**

In a merger and a consolidation, at least one preexisting entity ceases to exist, but in an acquisition, no entity ceases to exist. In an acquisition, one preexisting entity acquires controlling interest in another preexisting entity, and both continue to exist as separate legal entities. In a legal merger, one preexisting entity is combined into another preexisting entity; one entity ceases to exist. In a legal consolidation, two or more existing entities are combined into one new entity; two or more entities cease to exist.

649. **Answer: C**

The correct amount is Alphaco's net income for January 200Y ($2,000) plus Betaco's net income for the period ($3,000), or $5,000. Income earned by the firms during 200X would not enter into 200Y income determination under any assumption.

650. **Answer: A**

Consolidated income for the year ended December 31, 200X, would consist of Parco's net income for the full year ($125,000 + $30,000 = $155,000) plus Setco's net loss for the period following its acquisition by Parco ($15,000 loss). Therefore, Parco's net income for the full year would be $155,000 – $15,000 = $140,000.

651. **Answer: C**

Only a legal consolidation results from the combination of two or more existing entities into one new entity. In a merger, one preexisting entity is combined into another preexisting entity; no new entity is formed. In an acquisition, one preexisting entity acquires controlling interest in another preexisting entity, and both continue to exist as separate legal entities; no new entity is formed.

652. **Answer: C**

In a merger and in a consolidation, the assets and liabilities of the acquired entity/entities are recorded on the books of the acquiring entity, but in an acquisition, the assets and liabilities of the acquired entity remain on the books of the acquired entity. In a merger and in a consolidation, at least one preexisting entity ceases to exist, and the assets and liabilities are recorded on the books of the surviving entity. In an acquisition, one preexisting entity acquires controlling interest in another preexisting entity, and both continue to exist as separate legal entities.

653. **Answer: C**

The recognition of additional identifiable assets would result in a decrease in the amount of goodwill initially recognized in a business combination. Since goodwill is basically the difference (residual) between the investment fair value and the fair value of the net identifiable assets acquired, an increase in the identifiable assets will result in a decrease in the amount of goodwill.

654. **Answer: D**

All three statements are correct. A business may be a group of assets (that constitute a business), a group of net assets (that constitute a business), or a separate legal entity (that is a business).

655. **Answer: D**

Determining the acquiring entity (Statement I), determining the acquisition date of the combination (Statement II), and determining the cost of the acquisition (Statement III), and other elements, are all requirements of the acquisition method of accounting for a business combination.

656. **Answer: D**

Because Company Z only paid cash and issued debt to effect the combination (no new equity was issued to effect the combination), Company Z is most likely the acquirer.

657. **Answer: C**

Generally, to be an acquirer, an entity must own, either directly or indirectly, more than 50% of the voting stock of another entity. In this case, Company A owns 35% of Company B directly and would control 20% indirectly, or a total of 55%. (Since Company A owns 60% of Company C, it has absolute control of C and could control C's 20% ownership of B.) Thus, Company A would control Company B and likely would be an acquirer in a business combination.

658. **Answer: B**

Statement I and Statement II are correct; Statement III is not correct. Most consideration used to effect a business combination should be measured at fair value (Statement I). The only exception is when the consideration transferred remains under the control of the acquirer. Contingent consideration should be included in the cost of an acquired business at fair value as of the acquisition date (Statement II). The cost of carrying out a business combination should not be included in the cost of an acquired business (Statement III); most such costs should be expensed.

659. **Answer: C**

Cost of legal fees (and other direct costs) to carry out the combination would not be included in the cost of an acquired business but would be expensed in the period incurred.

660. **Answer: D**

This question implies that the acquisition is a business combination. The costs associated with a business combination are expensed as incurred.

661. **Answer: A**

Acquisition-related costs incurred to carry out a business combination, including both direct costs of acquisition (e.g., finders' fees; legal, accounting, and consulting fees; etc.) and general expenses related to an acquisition (e.g., cost of acquisition department), are expensed when incurred and enter into the determination of income for the period.

662. **Answer: B**

Changes in the fair value of contingent consideration resulting from occurrences that occur after the acquisition date are recognized as gains or losses when the contingent consideration is classified as an asset or a liability. Contingent considerations classified as equity are not remeasured, and no gain or loss is recognized. The change in fair value of equity items is recognized as an adjustment within equity.

663. **Answer: D**

Neither Statement I nor Statement II is correct. The value assigned to a noncontrolling interest in an acquiree would not be based simply on the proportional share of that interest in the net assets of the acquiree (Statement I), but rather on the separately determined fair value of the noncontrolling interest. The fair value per share of the noncontrolling interest in an acquiree does not have to be the same as the fair value per share of the controlling interest (Statement II), because there is likely to be a premium in value associated with having control of an entity that the noncontrolling interest would not enjoy.

664. **Answer: D**

Generally, identifiable assets acquired, liabilities assumed, and any non-controlling interest in the acquiree are measured at fair value. A few exceptions exist for selected assets and liabilities.

665. **Answer: C**

Payment for a valid patent, even though not previously recognized by the acquiree, most likely would be a part of the business combination transaction. Since costs of developing a patentable item are expensed when incurred, the acquiree may not have recognized any asset associated with the patent, but the acquirer should record the patent acquired in a business combination at fair value.

666. **Answer: C**

In a business combination, an acquirer that obtains a lease contract should continue to classify the contract as established at the inception of the contract. The classification of a lease contract is established at the inception of the lease and would not change as a result of a transfer of ownership in a business combination.

667. **Answer: B**

Item I would be recognized; Item II would not be recognized. Contractual contingencies (contingencies related to existing contracts) are recognized by the acquirer and measured at fair value. Noncontractual contingencies (contingencies that do not result from an existing contract), including lawsuits, are recognized only if it is more likely than not that the contingency will give rise to a liability (or an asset). A probability of 20% that the suit will be lost is not more likely than not, and the lawsuit would not be recognized.

668. Answer: B

Damon should report a $70,000 gain, calculated as:

Fair value of net assets acquired:	
Assets ($350,000) – Liabilities ($70,000)	= $280,000
Cost of Investment:	
Stock (20,000 shares × $10/share)	= $200,000
Contingent consideration @ fair value	= 10,000
Total cost of investment	= 210,000
FV of net assets > Cost of investment = Gain	= $70,000

669. Answer: C

A bargain purchase gain is the excess of the fair value of the net assets acquired in a business combination over the fair value of the cost of the investment. The cost of investment to Pesto is $350,000, consisting of $200,000 cash and $150,000 fair value of stock issued (10,000 shares × $15 per share). The fair value of Nexto's net assets is $360,000 ($480,000 assets – $120,000 liabilities). Therefore, the fair value of the net assets exceeds the cost of the investment by $10,000, resulting in a bargain purchase gain.

670. Answer: A

A gain occurs in a business combination when the investment value in the acquired entity is less than the fair value of the entity's net assets. Thus, when the fair value of the identifiable net assets acquired exceeds the fair value of the investment by the acquirer and any noncontrolling interest in the acquiree, a bargain purchase gain will be recognized.

671. Answer: C

Goodwill is based on the excess of investment value over the fair value of net assets. Thus, an acquirer will recognize goodwill only when the fair value of its investment and that of any noncontrolling interest in the acquiree exceeds the fair value of the acquiree's net assets.

672. Answer: A

No gain will be recognized by Windco in connection with its acquisition of trace. Neither the cash transferred nor the common

stock issued had a carrying value less than (or different than) fair value. The carrying value and fair value of the cash are the same, $100,000. And, since the common stock was newly issued, it would be valued at the market price of the stock, with the excess over par value recognized as additional paid-in capital, not as a gain. Further, there was no bargain purchase amount to be recognized as a gain.

673. Answer: C

A bargain purchase means that the acquirer paid less than the fair market value of the identifiable net assets. The seller must have been under some sort of duress (perhaps eminent bankruptcy) and was willing to accept a price less than the value of the net assets. In this case the acquirer recognizes that gain on the date of the acquisition.

674. Answer: B

A reacquired right is a right granted by an acquirer to the acquiree prior to a business combination that is reacquired when the acquirer gains control of the acquiree or the asset in a business combination. For example, the acquiree may have acquired the right to use the acquirer's trade name as part of a franchise agreement. A reacquired right is an intangible asset that is amortized by the acquirer over the remaining contractual period of the contract that grants the right.

675. Answer: B

Statement I is correct. After an acquisition, a contingency that is a liability will be measured and reported at the higher of the amount reported on the acquisition date or the amount that would be recognized if the requirements of FASB #5 were followed. Thus, such a liability would not be measured at less than the fair value on the acquisition date (Statement I). Statement II is not correct. After an acquisition, a contingency that is an asset will be measured at the lower of the amount reported on the acquisition date or the best estimate of its future settlement amount. Thus, such an asset would be measured at no more than, not at no less than, the fair value reported on the acquisition date.

676. Answer: A

A contingent consideration liability is the obligation of an acquirer to transfer additional consideration, if specific conditions are met. Contingent consideration liabilities are initially recognized at fair value and adjusted to fair value each period until the contingency is resolved or expires. A change in fair value resulting from occurrences **after** the acquisition date would be recognized as a gain or loss in income in the period of the change, not as an adjustment to the consideration paid to acquire the acquiree. In this question, a $19,000 gain (reduction in liability) would be recognized ($28,000 − $9,000 = $19,000) and no change in the consideration paid will be recognized.

677. **Answer: B**

A contingent consideration liability is the obligation of an acquirer to transfer additional consideration, if specific conditions are met. Contingent consideration liabilities are initially recognized at fair value and adjusted to fair value each period until the contingency is resolved or expires. A change in fair value resulting from occurrences after the acquisition date would be recognized as a gain or loss in income in the period of the change. In this question, a $19,000 gain (reduction in liability) would be recognized ($28,000 − $9,000 = $19,000).

678. **Answer: D**

Statements I, II, and III are all required. When goodwill is recognized in a business combination, a quantitative description of the factors that make up the goodwill (Statement I), the amount of goodwill that is expected to be deductible for tax purposes (Statement II), and the amount of goodwill allocated to each reportable segment (Statement III) must all be disclosed.

679. **Answer: D**

All three statements identify required disclosures. When a bargain purchase occurs in a business combination, the amount of the gain (Statement I), the income statement line item that includes the gain (Statement II), and a description of the basis for the bargain purchase amount (Statement III) must be disclosed.

680. **Answer: A**

Statements I and II are correct. Statement III is not correct. If provisional amounts are reported for items recognized in a business combination, the reasons why the accounting is incomplete (i.e., the amounts are provisional) (Statement I) and the amounts of adjustment(s) made to the provisional amounts during the period (Statement II)—as well as the specific items for which the amounts are provisional—must be

disclosed. The date at which each provisional amount is expected to be resolved is not a required disclosure (Statement III).

681. **Answer: A**

Financial statement disclosures that enable users to evaluate the nature and financial effects of a business combination must be made both when the combination occurs during the reporting period and when the combination occurs after the reporting period but before the financial statements are released.

682. **Answer: D**

Statements I, II, and III are all required disclosures. The primary reason for a business combination (Statement I), how the acquirer gained control of the business (Statement II), and the acquisition date fair value of consideration transferred and each major class of asset acquired and liability assumed (Statement III) must all be disclosed.

683. **Answer: C**

The calculation is:

Fair value (200,000 sh. × $12/sh.)	$2,400,000
Par value (200,000 sh. × $5/sh)	(1,000,000)
Gross additional paid-in capital	$1,400,000
Less: Registration and issuance costs	35,000
Net additional paid-in capital	$1,365,000

The legal and consulting fees ($110,000) were paid in cash and would be expensed in the period incurred. The registration and issuance costs of the common stock are properly deducted from the additional paid-in capital derived from the issuance of the stock.

684. **Answer: B**

The entry that Plant will make to record its legal acquisition of Seed cannot include a debit to Goodwill. The entry Plant makes will debit (only) the Investment account and credit whatever form(s) of consideration is given (e.g., Cash, Bonds Payable, Common Stock, etc.). Goodwill cannot be debited at the time of the acquisition, though it may be recognized at the time of consolidation.

685. **Answer: A**

The cost of acquiring a company includes all cash and other assets distributed, liabilities incurred, and equity shares issued, all at fair value. Direct costs of carrying out a combination (such as accounting, legal, consulting, and finders' fees) are expensed in the period incurred; they are not included as part of the acquired entity. The cost of registering and issuing securities used to effect a business combination are charged against the fair value of the securities issued and, for equity securities, serve to reduce the amount of additional paid-in capital recognized. Thus, this correct answer ($3,600,000) was computed as 100,000 shares issued × $36 per share (fair market value) = $3,600,000. The $160,000 fees paid to a consultant would have been expensed, and the $80,000 cost of registering and issuing the common stock would have reduced the amount recognized from the sale of the stock.

686. **Answer: A**

Since Seashell's stock is newly issued to effect the consolidation, it has no prior market value. In the absence of a market value, the fair value of Seashell's stock is determined by the fair value of the net assets acquired in the consolidation. Therefore, the consideration given (common stock issued) is equal to the fair value of net assets acquired, and no goodwill is recognized.

687. **Answer: D**

Goodwill is recognized when the cost of the investment is greater than the fair value of net assets acquired (= the fair value of net assets acquired is less than the cost of the investment). In a legal merger, the goodwill would be recognized on the books of the surviving firm at the time of the business combination.

688. **Answer: A**

Under IFRS, contingent assets are not recognized. Under U.S. GAAP, contingent assets are recognized if the item meets the criteria of the definition of an asset.

689. **Answer: D**

All financial instruments do not have the same accounting requirements. Because financial instruments cover a variety of assets and liabilities, and are used for different purposes, there are different accounting requirements for different financial instruments, including derivatives.

690. **Answer: C**

When derivatives are used for speculative purposes, the intent is not to hedge an existing position, because there is no existing position

to hedge. Rather, when used for speculative purposes, the intent is to make a profit.

691. **Answer: B**

All derivative instruments do not have the same accounting requirements. The appropriate accounting requirements depend on the specific purpose of holding or issuing the derivative instrument.

692. **Answer: A**

Both contracts that result in the exchange of cash (debt securities—both investments and obligations) and evidence of ownership interest in an entity (equity securities) are financial instruments.

693. **Answer: C**

An "accounting mismatch" refers to a circumstance where related assets and liabilities are valued using different measures.

694. **Answer: A**

Financial assets classified as "Loans and Receivables" are measured at amortized cost, with interest and amortization related to the instrument recognized in current income. This treatment is the same as the treatment under U.S. GAAP for investments held to maturity.

695. **Answer: C**

Under IFRS, redeemable preferred stock would likely be treated in its entirety as a financial liability because the stock can be redeemed (repurchased) by the issuing corporation at its discretion. Since the preferred shares can be redeemed at the discretion of the issuing corporation, it is not treated as equity, but rather as a liability.

696. **Answer: C**

When it is not practicable for an entity to estimate the fair value of a financial instrument, both information pertinent to estimating the fair value of the instrument and the reasons it is not practicable to estimate fair value must be provided.

697. **Answer: A**

All entities must disclose all significant concentrations of credit risk arising from all financial instruments, whether from a single entity or a group of parties that engage in similar activities and that have similar economic characteristics.

698. Answer: A

Fair value disclosure of financial instruments may be made in either the body of the financial statements or in the footnotes to the financial statements. If in the footnotes, one note must show fair values and carrying amounts for all financial instruments.

699. Answer: D

When a concentration of credit risk exists, the maximum amount at risk must be disclosed. The maximum amount is measured as the gross fair value of all financial instruments that would be lost if the other parties fail completely to perform according to the terms of the contract(s) and assuming any collateral was of no value.

700. Answer: B

The intrinsic value of a call option is the difference between the exercise (strike) price and the market price. This call option has an exercise price of $9 / share and the market price is $10 / share. Therefore, there is a $1 / share intrinsic value (I can buy the stock at a price less than the market). The option is to purchase 100 shares so the total intrinsic value is $100.

701. Answer: B

A derivative does not require contractual satisfaction by delivery of the subject matter of the contract. Specifically, the terms of a derivative require or permit the contract to be settled with cash or an asset readily convertible to cash, in lieu of physical delivery of the subject matter of the contract. In addition, a derivative includes an underlying, a notional amount, and requires no initial net investment or one that is less than normally would be required.

702. Answer: A

Hedging is a risk management strategy that involves making an investment (the hedge) so as to offset (or counter) another investment (the hedged item) so that a loss on one investment (the hedged item) would be offset (at least in part) by a gain on the other investment (the hedge), and vice versa. A perfect hedge is achieved when the hedge investment has a 100% inverse correlation to the initial investment (hedged item) so that there is no possibility of future gain or loss. A perfect hedge rarely exists.

703. Answer: D

Stock options are derivatives; they derive their value from the value of the stock to which the option applies. The underlying of a derivative is a specified price, rate, or other monetary variable, in this case the (strike) price of each option, $50.00.

704. Answer: B

A contract that has its settlement value tied to an underlying notional amount best describes a derivative financial instrument. The value or settlement amount of a derivative is the amount determined by the multiplication (or other arithmetical calculation) of a notional amount and an underlying. Simply put, a derivative instrument is a special class of financial instrument that derives its value from the value of some other financial instrument or variable.

705. Answer: B

The fair value of an investment accounted for using the equity method of accounting is specifically excluded as being eligible to be hedged for accounting purposes under U.S. GAAP.

706. Answer: A

The risks associated with a foreign currency that can be hedged can be either the risk to fair value in the foreign currency or the risk to cash flows in the foreign currency.

707. Answer: D

Neither Statement I nor Statement II is correct. Derivative instruments can be used not only for hedging purposes (Statement I), but also for speculative purposes. In addition, derivative instruments can be used not only to hedge fair value (Statement II), but also to hedge cash flows.

708. Answer: A

The two basic kinds of risks that can be hedged for accounting purposes are fair value risks and cash flow risks.

709. Answer: D

Because Buyco entered into the forward contract (hedging instrument) to hedge the risk of change in the fair value of the raw materials (hedged item), the change in fair value of the forward contract offsets the change in the fair value of the raw materials. Since during 2008 the change in the value of the raw materials decreased more than the value of the forward contract increased, the difference is the amount by which the derivative is ineffective as a fair value hedge. Specifically, the decrease in the value of the raw materials, $500, was offset by the increase in the value of the forward contract of $480, so the hedge was ineffective by $500 − $480 = $20, which is the correct answer.

710. Answer: B

Because Buyco entered into the forward contract (hedging instrument) to hedge the risk of change in the fair value of the raw materials (hedged item), the change in fair value of the forward contract during 2009 offsets the change in the fair value of the raw materials. Specifically, the decrease in the value of the raw materials, $200 ($19,500 − $19,300 = $200), was offset by the increase in the value of the forward contract of $220 ($700 − $480 = $220), so the net gain recognized in 2009 was $220 − $200 = $20, which is the correct answer.

711. Answer: C

Because Buyco entered into the forward contract (hedging instrument) to hedge the risk of change in the fair value of the raw materials (hedged item), the change in fair value of the forward contract during 2008 offsets the change in the fair value of the raw materials. Specifically, the decrease in the value of the raw materials, $500, was offset by the increase in the value of the forward contract of $480, so the net loss recognized in 2008 was $500 − $480 = $20, which is the correct answer.

712. Answer: C

A firm commitment has not been recorded (yet) as an asset or liability. A firm commitment occurs when an entity has a contractual obligation or contractual right, but no transaction has been recorded (and no asset or liability recognized) because GAAP requirements for recognition have not yet been met. Nevertheless, the subject matter of the firm commitment is at risk of change in fair value and can be hedged.

713. Answer: D

All differences between the change in value of the hedged item and the change in value of the hedging instrument are not recognized in current income. To the extent the change in the fair value of the hedging instrument offsets the change in the fair value of the hedged item, the hedge is effective, and that amount is recognized in other comprehensive income, not current income. To the extent the change in the fair value of the hedging instrument is different than the change in the fair value of the hedged

item, the hedge is ineffective, and that amount is recognized in current income.

714. Answer: A

Derivative instruments may be used to hedge the cash flows associated with assets, liabilities, or forecasted transactions.

715. Answer: D

Prior service costs that have not been recognized in net periodic pension costs are included in accumulated other comprehensive income.

716. Answer: B

A forecasted transaction can be the hedged item in a cash flow hedge. A forecasted transaction is a planned or expected transaction that has not yet been recognized, but that is subject to the risk of changes in related cash flow. As such, the cash flow (inflow or outflow) associated with forecasted transactions can be hedged.

717. Answer: D

The item being hedged in a cash flow hedge is measured using the present value of expected cash inflows or cash outflows. The item being hedged in a cash flow hedge may be associated with an asset, a liability, or a forecasted transaction. The value of such items is measured using the present value of either cash inflows (e.g., receivable) or cash outflows (e.g., payable), depending on the nature of the item being hedged.

718. Answer: C

A foreign currency hedge of a recognized liability hedges the risk of exchange rate changes on the cash flow (or fair value) of a liability between the time it is recorded (recognized) and the time it is settled in a foreign currency.

719. Answer: C

All foreign currency hedges are not treated as fair value hedges. While foreign currency hedges of unrecognized firm commitments, investments in available-for-sale securities, and net investments in foreign operations are treated as fair value hedges, foreign currency hedges of forecasted transactions are treated as cash flow hedges, and foreign currency hedges of recognized assets or liabilities may be treated either as fair value hedges or cash flow hedges, depending on management's designation.

720. Answer: A

Foreign currency hedges may be either fair value or cash flow hedges. Foreign currency hedges of unrecognized firm commitments, investments in available-for-sale securities, and net investments in foreign operations are fair value hedges. Foreign currency hedges of forecasted transactions are cash flow hedges. Additionally, foreign currency hedges of recognized assets or liabilities may be treated either as fair value hedges or cash flow hedges, depending on management's designation.

721. Answer: D

Foreign currency hedges can be used to hedge the risk of exchange rate changes on planned (forecasted) transactions, available-for-sale investments, and accounts receivable/accounts payable (and unrecognized firm commitments and net investments in foreign operations).

722. Answer: B

Both the net gain or loss recognized in earnings during the period (Statement I) and the amount of gain or loss deferred in other comprehensive income (Statement II) must be disclosed. Statement III is not a required disclosure.

723. Answer: D

When derivatives are used for fair value hedges, the amount of gain or loss arising during the period that was deferred is not a required (or relevant) disclosure. When fair value hedges are used, any resulting gain or loss is recognized in current income, not deferred.

724. Answer: A

Entities that either issue or hold derivatives (or other contracts used for hedging) must disclose a considerable amount of information concerning their reasons for using derivatives and the outcomes (e.g., gains/losses) of their accounting for the derivatives. Generally, these disclosures must distinguish between instruments used for different purposes (e.g., fair value hedges, cash flow hedges, etc.).

725. Answer: B

When derivatives are used as cash flow hedges, an amount of gain or loss can be deferred in other comprehensive income and subsequently become part of accumulated other comprehensive income. Amounts of accumulated other comprehensive income (on the hedging instrument) will be reclassified to income when the hedged item affects income.

726. Answer: D

The definition of a derivative under IFRS does not include the concept of notional amount.

727. Answer: C

Both Statement I and Statement II are correct. IFRS permits (1) hedging a forecasted business combination that is subject to foreign exchange risk, and (2) hedging part of the life of a hedged item. U.S. GAAP does not permit hedging in either case.

728. Answer: D

If $1.00 will buy 0.76 Euro, then 0.76E = $1.00, and E = $1.00/0.76, or E = $1.32. So, one Euro will buy $1.32, the correct answer.

729. Answer: C

Since the foreign currency account payable had a settlement amount greater than its previously recorded carrying amount, Domco would have to recognize the change in settlement amounts in the period in which the settlement amount changed—20X8. Specifically, since the amount to settle the account payable increased during 20X8, Domco would have to recognize an exchange loss—it will take more dollars to acquire the foreign currency needed to settle the account.

730. Answer: C

Gains and losses on foreign currency operating transactions that result from changes in currency exchange rates are not deferred. Such gains and losses must be recognized in current income of the period in which the currency exchange rate changes.

731. Answer: B

If $1.00 will buy 0.75 Euro, then 0.75E = $1.00, and E = $1.00/0.75, or E = $1.33. So, one Euro will cost $1.33; therefore, 100,000 E × $1.33 = $133,333, the correct answer.

732. Answer: D

By definition (SFAS #52), an entity's functional currency is the currency of the primary economic environment in which the entity operates. Normally, that is the currency of the environment in which the entity primarily generates and expends cash.

733. Answer: D

Since the exchange rate changed between the date the obligation was incurred (July 1) and the date it was settled (August 29), the effects of the exchange rate change must be recognized as an exchange gain or loss. The correct answer would be the difference between the spot rate on July 1 and the spot rate on August 29, or (500,000B/35.0B per $ = $14,286) – (500,000B/37.0B per $ = $13,514) = $772.

734. **Answer: D**

A gain of $25,000 should be reported in the current income statement. The gain was computed as:

November 20	$1.25 × 500,000 British pounds = $625,000
December 31	$1.20 × 500,000 British pounds = $600,000
Gain	$25,000

And, gains (and losses) on foreign currency transactions should be reported in current income.

735. **Answer: D**

The foreign currency exchange loss that occurred as a result of the exchange rate change in 20X8 should be recognized in 20X8 as a component of income from continuing operations in the income statement. Gains and losses resulting from changes in exchange rates are recognized in current earnings in the period in which the exchange rate changes.

736. **Answer: D**

The purchase of goods by a U.S. entity would most likely reflect an import transaction and, since it is to be settled in a foreign currency, would be a foreign currency import transaction.

737. **Answer: D**

When a monetary obligation in a foreign currency exists, all gains and losses reflective of changes in exchange rates are recognized in current income.

The loss would be based on the rate at initiation and the rate at year-end. (The recovery in the next period would be treated as a gain in that period.) The loss is $1,500 [($.55 – $.70)10,000], making this response correct.

738. **Answer: A**

At the date Don Co. entered into the transaction, June 19, and agreed to accept euros in satisfaction of its account receivable, it should record the transaction (sale and account receivable) at the (then exiting or current) spot exchange rate of .988. Thus, the dollar amount of the account receivable (and sale) would be computed as 200,000 E × .988 = $197,600, which also is the dollar value that would be received if the transaction were settled at that date.

739. **Answer: D**

The event described is a foreign currency (FC) transaction, not FC translation, and the gain (or loss) would be reported as a component of income from continuing operations for the current period.

740. **Answer: C**

The sale of goods to be collected in a foreign currency would be a foreign currency export transaction. A foreign currency transaction occurs when a U.S. entity enters into a transaction that is denominated (to be settled) in a foreign currency, not in dollars.

741. **Answer: B**

A foreign currency exchange gain will be recognized for the change in exchange rate between December 31 and the January collection date. That gain is computed as $1.45 –> $1.50 = $0.05 × 2,000 pounds = $100 gain.

742. **Answer: D**

A foreign exchange gain or loss is recognized for any change in value of a monetary debt denominated in a foreign currency. This is true at balance sheet time as well as when it is realized.

Thus, a $2,500 loss would have been recognized at December 31, 20X5 (250,000 francs * [.20 – .19]). Then, in 20X6, the full difference between the $.19 and $.22 (250,000 francs * .03) would be realized for a total gain of $7,500.

743. **Answer: D**

Forward exchange contracts may be used both to hedge risk and to speculate. When used to hedge risk, the intent is to use the change in value of the forward exchange contract (hedging instrument) to offset, in part at least, an opposite change in value of whatever is being hedged (hedged item). When used to speculate, the forward exchange contract is entered into with the intent of making a profit on the change in its value.

744. Answer: A

Either operating transactions (export, import, lending, borrowing, investing, etc.) or forward exchange contract transactions (contracts to exchange currencies) could be foreign currency transactions. A foreign currency transaction occurs when a domestic entity (e.g., U.S. entity) agrees to settle a transaction (pay, receive, exchange, etc.) in a non-domestic (e.g., non-dollar) currency.

745. Answer: C

If a U.S. entity purchases goods from (or sells goods to) a British entity and the U.S. entity is to settle in a currency other than the dollar (pounds sterling), it is a foreign currency transaction to the U.S. entity (but would not be to the British entity). A foreign currency transaction occurs when a domestic entity agrees to settle a transaction in a foreign currency.

746. Answer: D

Foreign currency transactions do not occur only when initiated by a foreign entity. A foreign currency transaction occurs when a domestic entity (e.g., U.S. entity) agrees to settle a transaction (pay, receive, exchange, etc.) in a non-domestic (e.g., non-dollar) currency, regardless of whether the transaction is initiated by the domestic entity or the foreign entity.

747. Answer: B

While the intent of hedging is to mitigate the risk of loss (or gain) attributable to the item being hedged, hedging does not assure that no gain or loss will be incurred on the hedged item. Only in a perfect hedge does no gain or loss occur. In order to be a perfect hedge, the hedging instrument would need to have a 100% inverse correlation to the hedged item. Such an outcome is rare.

748. Answer: C

A firm that engages in a forward contract will both incur fees imposed by the counterparty and incur the cost of the difference between the spot rate and the forward rate at the time the forward contract is executed. The difference between the spot rate and the forward rate is the premium (or discount) on the forward contract and must be amortized over the life of the contract as a financing expense, not an exchange gain or loss.

749. Answer: A

Both the spot rate and the forward rate will be used in accounting for a forward contract used for hedging. The forward rate is used as the basis for determining the change in value of a forward contract. As the forward rate changes, so also will the carrying value of the forward contract, resulting in exchange gains and losses. The spot rate is used to determine the premium or discount on the forward contract. Specifically, the difference between the spot rate and the forward rate at the date of the forward contract is the premium (or discount) on the forward contract, which enters into the determination of income over the life of the contract.

750. Answer: B

Because a hedging instrument is intended to offset changes in the hedged item, when the hedged item is a receivable, the hedging instrument would have to be a payable.

751. Answer: D

The net effect of a change in value of a hedged item and its related hedging instrument may be a gain, a loss, or neither a gain nor a loss (a perfect hedge).

752. Answer: B

A firm commitment exists when an entity has a contractual obligation or right, but has not yet recorded the obligation or right because it does not meet the requirements of GAAP. Therefore, an asset or liability has not been booked (recognized) already.

753. Answer: B

The hedge of a forecasted transaction to be denominated in a foreign currency is a cash flow hedge. The risk being hedged is the variability in expected cash flows (inflows or outflows) on the planned transaction that would result from changes in the exchange rate.

754. Answer: C

A hedge to offset the risk of exchange rate changes on converting the financial statements of a foreign subsidiary to the domestic (functional) currency would be the hedge of a net investment in a foreign operation. Changes in exchange rates will result in changes in the amount of domestic (functional) currency that will result from converting (translating) financial statements from a foreign currency. Hedges of net investments in a foreign operation are intended to offset that risk.

755. Answer: A

A forward contract used to hedge a foreign currency firm commitment can be either a cash flow hedge (as permitted by the FASB's Derivatives Implementation Group) or a fair value hedge (as permitted by FASB #133).

756. Answer: A

Either a planned sale or a planned purchase would be a forecasted transaction and, if denominated in a foreign currency, could be hedged.

757. Answer: D

The time between when an asset is recognized and when the asset is fully satisfied would be intended to offset the risk of changes in the exchange rate on a recognized asset (or liability).

758. Answer: C

The hedge of a recognized asset or liability may be either a fair value hedge or a cash flow hedge, depending on management's designation. However, the hedge of a recognized asset or liability denominated in a foreign currency generally will be a cash flow hedge.

759. Answer: C

Both Statement I and Statement II are correct. In hedging a foreign currency investment held available-for-sale, the investment security must not be traded in the investor's functional currency, and the forward contract used as the hedging instrument must be highly effective in hedging the investment.

760. Answer: B

The gain (or loss) recognized on the contract will be computed as the number of Euros to be purchased (100,000E) multiplied by the change in the forward exchange rate between the date the contract was executed ($1.80) and the end of the fiscal period, December 31, 20X8 (1.83). Therefore, the gain recognized will be 100,000E × ($1.83 − $1.80 = $0.03) = $3,000. It is a gain because the forward contract increased in value as of December 31. The gain on the forward contract will partially offset the loss on the inventory for the period. A complete determination of the gain on the forward contract (only) would include amortization of the difference between the spot rate and forward rate at the initiation of the contract ($6,000) and discounting the nominal gain of

$3,000 for the period December 31 to the March settlement date.

761. Answer: D

Borrowing from another foreign entity with the same foreign currency as the operation being hedged would hedge the (equity) investment in the foreign operation. Since the equity investment in a foreign operation is an asset and the borrowing would be a liability, both in the same foreign currency, a change in the exchange rate would have offsetting effects. Thus, if an exchange rate change caused a decrease in the value of the investment (asset), it would cause an increase in the value of the borrowing (liability).

762. Answer: D

The hedge of a net investment in foreign operations is a fair value hedge, but changes in the fair value of the forward contract (hedging instrument) that are equal to or less than the change in the translated value of the financial statements of the foreign operation are reported as a translation adjustment in other comprehensive income. The change in the forward contract reported as a translation adjustment offsets the change in the value of the translated financial statements of the foreign operation, which also are reported as a translation adjustment.

763. Answer: A

A futures contract entered into for speculative purposes (not to hedge) is valued using futures rates, and any gain or loss as a result of changes in futures rates is recognized in net income in the period during which the rate changed. At initiation of Platt's contract, the 90-day futures rate was $.70, as quoted in the contract. On December 31, 20X5, 30 days before Platt's contract was to be settled, the 30-day futures rate was $.65. Platt's loss would be computed as follows:

November 2, 20X5, 50,000 Swiss francs × $.70 = $35,000

December 31, 20X5, 50,000 Swiss francs × $.65 = $32,500

Loss in dollar value of futures contract = $2,500

764. Answer: C

The correct answer is the difference between the 60-day forward rate on September 1 of $0.74 and the 30-day forward rate on September 30 of $0.72, or $0.02 × 50,000 Euros = $1,000, the correct amount of the loss.

765. **Answer: C**

A hedge to offset the risk of loss on a recognized asset or liability could be either a cash flow hedge or a fair value hedge, at management's discretion. If the risk of loss on the recognized asset or liability being hedged is from changes in exchange rates, the hedge would be classified as a cash flow hedge.

766. **Answer: C**

An option is a financial derivative and must be reported as either an asset or liability at fair value, with any change in fair value recognized in income of the period that the fair value changes (unless the option is used as a hedge). At the date the option contract was initiated, it had no intrinsic value (the strike price was the same as the current price), but had a time value of $600 (given). At December 31, the time value had decreased to $400, a decline of $200, but the intrinsic value had increased by $6,000, computed as the change in the market price from $40 per share to $43 per share, an increase of $3 × 2,000 shares (the option quantity) = $6,000. Thus, the net change in fair value, and the amount of gain that would be recognized in December 31 financial statements, is + $6,000 − $200 = $5,800, the correct answer.

767. **Answer: B**

Operating transactions denominated in a foreign currency are converted to the functional currency using the current (or spot) exchange rate. The current (or spot) exchange rate is the exchange rate in effect at the current time (or as close thereto as possible); that is, at the time of the transaction or revaluation.

768. **Answer: C**

The functional currency could be either the recording currency of the foreign entity (Statement II) or the reporting currency of a parent (Statement III) (or even another foreign currency). The functional currency will be the currency of the primary economic environment in which an entity operates and primarily generates and expends cash, not whatever currency management chooses (Statement I).

769. **Answer: C**

Determining a foreign subsidiary's functional currency will take into account both the extent to which the subsidiary operates, and generates and expends cash in the local foreign economy in which it is located and the cumulative inflation rate of that economy.

770. **Answer: C**

The method to be used to convert financial statements of a subsidiary from a foreign currency to the parent's currency depends primarily on the functional currency of the subsidiary. Whether the functional currency of the subsidiary is the local foreign currency, the parent's currency, or another foreign currency will determine the conversion method or methods to be used.

771. **Answer: B**

The reporting currency is the currency in which the final consolidated financial statements are presented (reported).

772. **Answer: D**

The correct amount of foreign exchange loss is $17,000. The $4,000 loss on the account payable ($64,000 − $60,000 = $4,000) would be included in net income. Therefore, the correct amount of foreign exchange loss is $13,000 + $4,000 = $17,000. The translation loss (or gain) would not be included in net income for the year, but rather would be reported as an item of other comprehensive income (outside net income) for the year.

773. **Answer: D**

The weighted average exchange rate for the current year is the correct rate to use to convert depreciation expense. Since the functional currency is the local currency, the income statement of the subsidiary would be converted using translation, which requires the use of the exchange rate when a revenue/gain was earned or expense/loss was incurred, or the weighted average exchange rate for the year. Since depreciation expense is incurred throughout the year, the weighted average exchange rate normally is the appropriate basis for conversion.

774. **Answer: C**

When converting financial statements from a foreign currency to a reporting currency using translation, paid-in capital accounts are translated using the historic exchange rate in effect when the account amount arose (or when the investment was made, if later). Therefore, common stock would not be translated using the spot (or current) exchange rate as of the balance sheet date, but the historic exchange rate for the common stock.

775. **Answer: C**

Since translation should be used to convert Sanco's financial statements expressed in FCUs to U.S. dollars, depreciation expense should be converted using the exchange rate in effect when depreciation was incurred during the year or the weighted average exchange rate for the period. In this case, the weighted average exchange rate for the period is given as 1 FCU = $1.300. Therefore, the correct dollar amount of Sanco's depreciation expense would be 1,000 FCUs $\times$ $1.300 = $1,300.

776. **Answer: D**

When converting financial statements from a foreign currency to a reporting currency using translation (or remeasurement), retained earnings is not translated using an exchange rate. Rather, retained earnings is calculated using already converted values. Specifically, beginning retained earnings in dollars + converted net income − converted dividends declared = ending retained earnings in dollars.

777. **Answer: C**

Under the remeasurement method of converting financial statements from a foreign currency to a reporting currency, most expenses (and revenues, gains, and losses) are converted using the current exchange rate. Expenses related to assets and liabilities converted at a historic rate are an exception—they are converted using a historic exchange rate. Therefore, since depreciation expense does result from an asset (property, plant, and equipment) measured using a historic exchange rate, depreciation expense would be remeasured using a historic exchange rate.

778. **Answer: B**

The distinction used for applying different exchange rates to different accounts when using remeasurement is based on whether the account is monetary or non-monetary.

779. **Answer: B**

Because El Rio's operations are a direct extension of Eagle, the peso is not El Rio's functional currency; Eagle's currency, the U.S. dollar, is El Rio's functional currency. Therefore, El Rio's financial statements will be converted to U.S. dollars using remeasurement.

780. **Answer: B**

Because Sapco's operations are a direct extension of Papco, Sapco's local foreign currency is not its functional currency. Rather, Papco's currency, the U.S. dollar, is Sapco's functional currency. Therefore, its financial statements expressed in the foreign currency

will be converted to U.S. dollars using remeasurement.

781. **Answer: A**

Under the remeasurement method of converting financial statements from a foreign currency to a reporting currency, monetary assets and liabilities are converted using the current exchange rate, not a historic exchange rate. Therefore, cash (the most monetary of assets) would be converted using the current exchange rate, not a historic exchange rate.

782. **Answer: B**

Since Gordon prepares its financial statements in its local currency, the British pound, and since the British economy has not been in hyperinflation, Gordon's functional currency would be the British pound, and its financial statements would be converted to U.S. dollars using translation, not remeasurement. Under the translation method of converting, income statement items are converted using the average exchange rate for the period.

783. **Answer: B**

Gains and losses from remeasurement enter into the determination of net income in the period in which the gains and losses occur. Gains and losses from translation do not enter into the determination of net income, but are recognized in other comprehensive income (outside of net income) in the period in which the gains and losses occur. Therefore, the correct answer is $7,600, the gain from remeasurement.

784. **Answer: C**

Gains and losses from translation are recognized in other comprehensive income (outside of net income) in the period in which the gains and losses occur; gains and losses from remeasurement enter into the determination of net income in the period in which the gains or losses occur. Therefore, the correct answer is $8,100, the gain from translation.

785. **Answer: C**

An adjustment resulting from translation of financial statements would be reported in other comprehensive income, and an adjustment resulting from remeasurement would be reported in net income.

786. **Answer: D**

Remeasurement and then translation would be used to convert to the reporting currency when a foreign currency other than the foreign subsidiary's recording currency is the functional currency. Specifically, the financial statements would be remeasured from the recording currency to the other foreign functional currency, and the remeasured financial statements would then be translated to the reporting currency.

787. Answer: B

Rent expense + Amortization of leasehold improvements = Total expense related to utilizing the office space. Rent expense ($60,000) + Amortization ($360,000/60) = $66,000.

Although the last month's rent was paid in 20X4, that amount is a prepayment of rent to be recognized as rent expense in the last month of the lease.

788. Answer: C

Rent revenue is recognized on a straight-line basis for operating leases unless information suggests a more appropriate method.

The $50,000 bonus is allocated to each year of the lease term because the bonus was paid to secure the lease. The $25,000 deposit is never recognized as a revenue because it is an amount that must be paid back to the lessee. The lease term was five years.

Thus, annual rent revenue was $90,000 + $50,000/5 = $100,000.

789. Answer: D

This is an operating lease. Thus, the rent expense should be recognized on a straight-line basis. Monthly rent expense would be

$(12 - 3) \times \$17,500 = \$157,500$

$12 \times \$19,000 = \$228,000$

$12 \times \$20,500 = \$246,000$

$12 \times \$23,000 = \$276,000$

$12 \times \$24,500 = \$294,000$

Total = $1,201,500

1,201,500/60 months = $20,025 rent expense each month. The deferred rent expense at 12/31/20X3 would be the difference between the monthly rent payment and the rent expense recognized each month multiplied by the number of months left on the lease. This would be

$(\$23,000 - \$20,025) \times 6$ months = $17,850

$(\$24,500 - \$20,025) \times 12$ months = $53,700

$17,850 + $53,700 = $71,550.

790. Answer: B

The ending total liability at 12/31/05 = $150,000

= $200,000 – $50,000 rent revenue earned in 20X5

also:

= $50,000 for 20X6 rent + $100,000 for last 2 years of rent in term

= current liability + noncurrent liability

The $50,000 liability for 20X6 rent will be earned by the end of 20X6 and thus is current as of 12/31/X5. The $100,000 liability will not be earned for many years and thus is noncurrent as of 12/31/X5.

791. Answer: A

The lease is an operating lease because title is not transferred to the lessee at the end of the lease term (this covers the first two lease capitalization criteria: title transfer and bargain purchase option), the lease term is not at least 75% of the useful life of the asset at inception, and the present value of the lease payments is not at least 90% of the fair value of the asset.

None of the four lease capitalization criteria is met. Therefore, the lessee records an operating lease and recognizes only rent expense for the lease term (no interest expense).

792. Answer: A

Cott, Inc. has a lease payable and is therefore the lessee. If the lease contains a bargain purchase option, the lessee records the lease obligation at the present value of minimum lease payments plus the present value of the bargain purchase option. If the present value of the bargain purchase option is included (as it should be), at the end of the lease period the amount of the bargain purchase will remain as an obligation until it is exercised/paid. If the present value of the bargain purchase option is not included (an error), at the end of the lease period the obligation will be zero, when it should show the amount of the bargain purchase option.

793. Answer: B

A bargain purchase option is one of the four capital lease criteria. The option allows the lessee to purchase the asset at the end of the term for significantly less than the estimated market value at that time. Thus, the lease arrangement is considered an installment purchase because the lessee is expected to exercise the option.

794. Answer: B

Both are capital leases. The relevant criterion for capitalizing leases in this question is:

If the lease term is equal to or greater than 75% of the remaining useful life of the asset at the inception of the lease, then the lease is a capital lease.

Only one of four criteria must be met for a lessee to account for the lease as a capital lease. Transfer of ownership is not required.

The rationale for this criterion is that if 75% of the useful life is used by the lessee, then substantially all of the rewards and obligations of ownership have been passed to the lessee.

795. Answer: B

There are four criteria for a capital lease. In summary, they are:

1. The lease agreement transfers ownership of the leased asset to the lessee at the conclusion of the lease term (title transfer).
2. There is a bargain purchase option.
3. The lease term is 75% or more of estimated economic life.
4. The present value of minimum lease payments is at least 90% of excess of fair value of leased property.

This answer meets item #4 above.

796. Answer: A

A bargain purchase option is one of the four criteria for lease capitalization by the lessee. Only one criterion needs to be met. A bargain purchase option implies that, at inception, the lessee will purchase the asset at the end of the lease term because the option price will be significantly below the market price of the asset at that time.

Under this circumstance, the lease is an installment purchase, thus justifying capitalization by the lessee who will receive all the benefits and bear all the costs of ownership.

797. Answer: C

The amount to be capitalized is the present value of the lease payments. This amount is $2,675,000 ($500,000 × 5.35) and should be equal to the market value of the equipment if the useful life is also 7 years.

Although $3,500,000 (7 × $500,000) will be paid by Koby over the lease term, the difference between that amount and $2,675,000 represents interest to be recognized over the term. The $2,675,000 amount is the current

sacrifice required to obtain the use of the equipment and should be close to the purchase price if the equipment is available by purchase.

If Koby invested that amount at the interest rate implied in the lease, the investment would be sufficient to cover all seven payments.

798. Answer: B

The net lease receivable initial balance is the present value of the minimum lease payments (payments expected to be received under the lease) plus the present value of the residual at the end of the lease term. The value used for the residual (before discounting) is the estimated fair value of the asset at the end of the lease term, not the end of the asset's useful life.

799. Answer: B

The entry at December 31, 20X5:

Interest expense ($112,500 × .08)	9,000	
Lease liability	1,000	
Cash		10,000

The ending lease liability for 20X5 is $111,500 ($112,500 – $1,000 from entry).

800. Answer: A

The $75,816 lease liability at December 31, 20X5 is the initial liability at inception less the first payment, which is completely a principal payment. The first payment occurs at inception and therefore could have no interest component. The initial liability at inception is the present value of an annuity due of six periods.

Ending 20X5 lease liability	= liability at inception – $20,000 first payment
	= $20,000(4.7908) – $20,000
	= $75,816

The lessee must use the lower of its incremental borrowing rate (11%) and the rate implicit in the lease (10%), hence the use of the 4.7908 present value factor.

801. Answer: A

Each lease payment includes interest based on the lease liability at the beginning of the period. The amount of each payment exceeding the interest component is the amount of principal reduction. This amount reduces the lease liability used to compute the interest portion of the next payment.

Thus, the interest component decreases with each payment as more principal is paid off.

802. **Answer: C**

For all capital leases, the lessor uses the effective interest method to compute interest over the period of the lease. The interest revenue recognized each period equals the interest rate implicit in the lease multiplied by the beginning net lease receivable.

The straight-line method is not used because each payment includes interest and principal. The distortion resulting from application of the straight-line method would be considerable.

803. **Answer: B**

The lease is a capital lease because the lease term of 6 years is 75% of the useful life of the machine (8 years). The lower of the two rates of interest must be used because Day knows the lessor's implicit interest rate. The $230,500 lease liability is the present value of the lease payments = (4.61)$50,000.

804. **Answer: C**

The ending Year 2 lease liability balance is the present value of remaining payments and also equals the initial lease liability amount less the principal portion of the first two payments.

The first payment is made at the inception and therefore is all principal. It reduces the lease liability by $100,000. The opening Year 2 lease liability balance is $676,000 – $100,000 or $576,000.

Interest expense .10($576,000)	57,600	
Lease liability	42,400	
Cash		100,000

Thus, the ending Year 2 lease liability balance is $533,600 = $676,000 – $100,000 – $42,400.

805. **Answer: C**

Action must use the 9% rate because it is the lower of the two and Action knows the lessor's implicit rate of 9%.

The initial capitalized value is $153,000 times the present value of a 7-year annuity due because the first payment is due at inception. Multiplying the 5.5 factor by $153,000 yields the fair value of $841,500, the initial capitalized value before the first payment.

After the first payment was made, which is all principal because it was made at the inception, the remaining lease liability is $688,500 ($841,500 – $153,000).

806. **Answer: C**

The first payment, which is made at inception, is completely a principal payment because no time has elapsed in the lease term. Thus, the entire payment is applied to principal and reduces the lease liability by the amount of the payment.

807. **Answer: A**

The executory costs of $2,000 must be subtracted from the annual lease payment before capitalizing. Otherwise, the problem is straightforward. The capitalized amount is: $50,000(5.6) = $280,000.

808. **Answer: A**

This is a capital lease to the lessor because ownership is transferred to the lessee. There is no interest revenue in 20X5 because the lease inception and the balance sheet date are the same. The first payment thus includes no interest.

The lease is a sales-type lease to the lessor because the normal selling price of $77,000 exceeds the cost of $60,000. The difference of $17,000 is the dealer profit to be recognized in 20X5. There is no other income to be recognized in 2005.

809. **Answer: D**

This is a capital lease because there is a bargain purchase option (BPO). The lessee can purchase the lease at the end of the term for significantly less than its expected fair value at that time. The amount of the BPO is considered a payment to be capitalized because it is expected to be paid (included in minimum lease payments). First, the amount capitalized for the lease is computed as the sum of the present values of the ordinary lease payments ($50,000) and the BPO ($20,000). The total capitalized leased asset (and liability) therefore is $70,000 at inception. Second, because the asset is expected to be purchased at the end of the term and used for the remaining five years of its total life, depreciation is computed over 10 years rather than the five-year lease term. Finally, annual depreciation is $7,000 (= $70,000/10-year life). At the end of the current year (first year of lease), the carrying value is $63,000 ($70,000 initial amount capitalized = $7,000 depreciation).

810. **Answer: D**

In most cases, the initial recorded value of the lease liability is the present value of the minimum lease payments (the payments expected to be made by the lessee under the lease).

Valuation at present value is required given the long-term nature of the lease liability. As payments are made over the lease term, the principal portion of each payment reduces the lease liability. At the end of the lease term the liability balance is zero.

811. **Answer: A**

Only minimum lease payments are considered when evaluating the fourth criterion of capital leases: "Is the present value of minimum lease payments equal to or greater than 90% of the leased asset's market value?"

A guaranteed residual value is always included in the minimum lease payments of the lessor and also in the lessee's if the lessee guarantees it. It is so included because it is a collection or payment that is expected to be made under the terms of the lease.

812. **Answer: B**

The lease will be treated as a capital lease for accounting purposes because the life of the lease (5 years) is at least 75% of the life of the asset (6 years) – 5 years/6 years = 83%.

Douglas will record the machinery as an asset (and related lease liability) and depreciate it over the periods benefited. Because Douglas neither obtains ownership of the machinery at the end of the lease nor has a written option to purchase the machinery at a bargain price, the equipment will be depreciated over the life of the lease, which is 5 years.

813. **Answer: D**

The lease liability balance at the beginning of 2004 is $230,000 ($270,000 – $40,000) because the first lease payment did not include any interest. It was paid at inception and thus consists completely of principal. The December 31, 2004 entry:

Lease liability	17,000	
Interest expense .10($230,000)	23,000	
Cash		40,000

The lease liability is reduced $17,000.

814. **Answer: A**

Depreciation expense = $13,750 = ($120,000 – $10,000)/8.

The bargain purchase option is included in the capitalized asset value because it is expected to

be paid. Given that the asset will be purchased, the 8-year total useful life is used by the lessee for depreciation. The salvage value at the end of the asset's useful life is used for depreciation.

815. **Answer: C**

The $66,500 beginning balance of the lease liability is the present value of the minimum lease payments, which includes the bargain purchase option.

The lower of the two rates should be used to capitalize the lease. $66,500 = $10,000(6.328) + $10,000(.322).

The bargain purchase option uses a single value present value factor.

816. **Answer: B**

The lease liability at the end of 2004 is $115,000 ($135,000 – $20,000) because the first payment has been made and it consisted only of principal.

The entry to be made at the end of 2005 will be:

Interest expense .10($115,000)	11,500	
Lease liability	8,500	
Cash		20,000

The amount of the lease liability to be extinguished in 2005 is $8,500 as shown in the entry. Therefore, as of December 31, 2004, the current portion of the lease liability is $8,500, the amount due within 1 year of the balance sheet date.

817. **Answer: C**

The lease payment (LP) is computed as: $100,000 = LP(3.99271) + $40,000(0.68058). Solving, LP = $18,227. The initial gross lease receivable balance is 5($18,227) $40,000 or $131,135. Unearned interest is recorded for $31,135 ($131,135 – $100,000) at inception. Interest revenue for the first year is $8,000 (= $100,000 × .08). The journal entry for the first lease payment is: dr. Cash $18,227, dr. unearned interest $8,000, cr. interest revenue $8,000, cr. lease receivable $18,227. The decrease in net lease receivable is $18,227 – $8,000 or $10,227. The ending net lease receivable at year-end is $100,000 – $10,227 = $89,773.

818. **Answer: B**

The loss on the sale is $20,000 ($450,000 carrying value – $430,000 sales price). But the fair value of the asset exceeds carrying value.

Thus, the firm has only an "artificial" loss. This loss will most likely be made up by lowering the lease payments on the leaseback. The entire loss is deferred. Whenever the market value exceeds carrying value, a true loss has not occurred on the sale and the loss is deferred.

819. **Answer: C**

The disclosure requirement is the amount of the minimum lease payment required for each of the next 5 years and the aggregate total future amount, including the payments for the first 5 years.

The expense payment of $20,000 is not a predictable amount and is not disclosed as part of the annual lease payment. It is an executory cost. There are 9 years left in the term as of the balance sheet data, thus 9 payments of $100,000 remain. The first 5 years' payments are separately disclosed, and there is a total of $900,000 of payments to be made in the aggregate over the remaining lease term.

820. **Answer: D**

The gain or loss on a sale-leaseback is deferred and amortized over the term of the lease for both operating and capital leases. There is no information about present value of lease payments or fair value of the asset.

Because this is an operating lease, the deferred gain is treated as a deferred credit. If it were a capital lease, it would be treated as an asset valuation allowance.

821. **Answer: D**

When an asset is sold and then leased back, the lessee defers the gain (subject to certain exceptions, which do not apply in this question). The deferred gain is recorded as a contra account to the leased asset in a capital lease.

822. **Answer: B**

Only the $500,000 gain ($600,000 – $100,000) on the sale-leaseback of plane #1 is deferred.

For both capital and operating leases, most gains and losses on the sale in a sale-leaseback are deferred. The gain or loss is an integral part of the transaction and should be recognized over the term of the lease. The exception is when the leaseback part of the transaction is minor. If the present value of the lease payments is 10% or less of the fair value of the property sold, then the leaseback part of the transaction is considered minor and the gain need not be deferred but rather is recognized immediately.

Given that the lease term is less than 10% of the useful life, in all probability the leaseback for plane #2 is a minor one.

823. **Answer: A**

The Financial Accounting Standards Board (FASB) sets accounting standards for not-for-profit and for-profit organizations.

824. **Answer: B**

Nongovernmental not-for-profit organizations use full accrual accounting and the flow of economic resources measurement focus.

825. **Answer: D**

A museum that receives the majority of its funding from property taxes is most likely a part of a city government and will be subject to accounting and reporting standards established by the Governmental Accounting Standards Board (GASB).

826. **Answer: A**

Unrestricted cash contributions should be included in the Operating Activities section of the Statement of Cash Flows, along with unrestricted investment earnings, revenue restricted for operating purposes (Program Restrictions), revenue from exchange transactions, and operating expenditures (salaries, supplies, interest expense), including grants to other organizations

827. **Answer: B**

Because of the donor stipulation, both the investment income and appreciation can be expended. Recognition of these resources increases temporarily restricted net assets by $130,000. The expenditure of $60,000 to maintain the senior center effectively reduces temporarily restricted net assets. The expenses themselves are paid out of unrestricted net assets; however, $60,000 of temporarily restricted net assets are released from restriction because of the payment, thus increasing unrestricted net assets and decreasing temporarily restricted net assets.

828. **Answer: C**

The structure of the Statement of Cash Flows for a not-for-profit organization is identical to that of a for-profit organization: debt proceeds are reported as cash inflows under financing activities, and purchases of capital assets are reported as cash outflows under investing activities.

829. Answer: A

The freezer is classified as equipment and therefore must be depreciated.

830. Answer: B

The Statement of Functional Expenses requires that expenses be reported by functional classification as either (a) program related or (b) support service related. Support expenses include management, general administrative, and fund-raising expenses required to operate. Program expenses are directly related to the program or mission of the organization. The salaries of researchers, cost of equipment used in research, and cost of laboratory supplies used in research are all examples of program expenses. The salaries of fund-raisers for funds used in research are support expenses because their efforts are not directly related to conducting the research itself.

831. Answer: C

ASC 958-22-45-9 requires three categories of net assets: (1) unrestricted net assets, (2) temporarily restricted net assets, and (3) permanently restricted net assets, which is the answer given here.

832. Answer: C

Collections (i.e., inexhaustible fixed assets) donated to a not-for-profit organization do not need to be capitalized. Three conditions must be met: (1) the asset is held for public exhibition, education, or research rather than financial gain; (2) the asset must be protected, unencumbered, cared for, and preserved; and (3) the asset is subject to a policy that requires proceeds from sales of collection items to be used to acquire other items for the collection. Only the famous painting donated for display appears to meet these three conditions.

833. Answer: A

Since the resources must be retained for 20 years, they must be reported under a restricted classification of net assets. However, because they are not permanently restricted but may ultimately be expended, they should be recorded as a temporarily restricted asset rather than a permanently restricted asset.

834. Answer: D

The $2,000,000 gift is permanently invested and will be reported as part of permanently restricted net assets. The income is dedicated to a specific program starting in year 2. Therefore,

in year 1 all the income and the change in fair value of the investment are temporarily restricted as to time, so $50,000 is temporarily restricted.

835. Answer: B

It should be included as a decrease in unrestricted net assets. ASC 958-360-35 requires depreciation of capital assets by not-for-profit organizations. Depreciation expense is allocated to programs and therefore is a decrease in unrestricted net assets. The first answer is incorrect because ASC 958-360-35 requires depreciation. The third and fourth answers are incorrect choices that are based on the option for a not-for-profit organization to adopt a policy of an implied time restriction on gifts of long-term assets. The question does not indicate that the capital assets were donated, and it does not mention that such a policy was adopted. Even if those two conditions exist, the third and fourth choices are still incorrect because the implied time restriction will result in depreciation reported in unrestricted assets and a reclassification of net assets to decrease temporarily restricted net assets and to increase unrestricted net assets for an amount equal to depreciation on the donated fixed assets.

836. Answer: C

Unlike for-profit entities, not-for-profit entities do not break debt securities into trading, available-for-sale, and held-to-maturity categories. Following ASC 958-320-35-1, not-for-profits value debt securities at fair value (quoted market price).

837. Answer: C

If the donor placed restrictions on the use of gains (purpose or time restrictions), the gains are temporarily restricted until the restriction is met. If there are no restrictions, the gains and losses are unrestricted. Revenues and expenses must be reported and should be reported separately but *gains and losses may be reported net*.

838. Answer: C

According to ASC 958-320-35-1, not-for-profit organizations report their investment in debt securities and equity securities at fair value.

839. Answer: C

ASC 958-650-30-2 requires donated securities to be initially recorded at their fair value on the date of the gift and to be reported at their market value at the financial reporting date (at the end of the year).

840. Answer: D

This is an example of a use restriction for which the gift will be recognized as an increase in temporarily restricted net assets at the time of the gift.

841. Answer: C

A vendor who specializes in offering goods and/or services exclusively to a governmental or not-for-profit organization is not considered a governmental or not-for-profit entity.

842. Answer: A

The Governmental Accounting Standards Board (GASB) was established in 1984 to promulgate standards of financial accounting and reporting for the activities and transactions of state and local governments. The GASB's authority includes determining the measurement focus and basis of accounting standards for governmental fund operating statements.

843. Answer: B

The Financial Accounting Standards Board (FASB) is the highest level of GAAP for all nongovernmental entities, which includes nongovernmental not-for-profit organizations.

844. Answer: D

One of the unique characteristics of government is its power to force involuntary financial resource contributions through taxation. No other form of organization has this power.

845. Answer: D

GASB Concept Statement No. 1 defines two paramount objectives for financial reporting in government: (1) accountability and (2) interperiod equity. Therefore, "Accountabilty" is the correct answer to this question. Concept Statement No. 1 describes six characteristics of effective financial reporting: (1) understandability, (2) reliability, (3) relevance, (4) timeliness, (5) consistency, and (6) comparability (TRUCCR).

846. Answer: A

The adoption of a balanced budget supports interperiod equity because it is an attempt to ensure that the current generation of citizens does not shift the burden of paying for current-year services to future-years' taxpayers (GASB Concepts Statement 1).

Residual equity transfers are nonrecurring or nonroutine transfers of equity between funds (GASB Codification 1800.102). These transfers occur within one accounting period and do not support interperiod equity as an objective of financial reporting.

847. Answer: C

The example in the question is an outcome measure. Outcome measures indicate the accomplishments or results that occur because of the services provided.

848. Answer: D

GASB Concepts Statement No. 3, basic financial statements, the accompanying notes to the basic financial statements, and required supplemental information are essential information and therefore required in general purpose external financial reporting. Supplemental information is useful but not required. Service efforts and accomplishment information are classified as supplemental information and are therefore voluntarily reported.

849. Answer: D

GASB Concepts Statement No. 1 states that interperiod equity is a basic component of accountability and fundamental to public administration.

850. Answer: C

Governmental accounting systems are organized and operated on a fund basis. A fund is a fiscal and accounting entity with a self-balancing set of accounts that record cash and other financial resources, along with the related liabilities and residual equities or balances, which are segregated for the purpose of carrying on specific activities or attaining certain objectives. GASB Codification 1100.102

851. Answer: B

A motor pool fund is a type of internal service fund that charges other parts of the government for services provided on a cost-reimbursement basis. An internal service fund is one of the two types of proprietary service funds. Recall the mnemonic PIPPA for fiduciary funds—pension trust funds, investment trust funds, private-purpose trust funds, and agency funds.

852. Answer: A

An Enterprise Fund is commonly used in situations where user fees are the primarily source of revenue and the fee charged is based on an amount sufficient to cover the costs of operations and to provide for capital maintenance, which is the case here. Note that the fee is for a service provided and that most of the users are external to the government.

853. Answer: A

Recall the acronym DRIP-CEG-PIPPA where the vowels in DRIP-CEG represent fund types that use accrual accounting and the consonants use modified accrual accounting. The "I" stands for Internal Service Fund and "E" for Enterprise Funds. This answer is correct.

854. Answer: C

Recall the acronym PIPPA for fiduciary funds. Fiduciary funds include the following four types of funds: **P**ension trust funds, **I**nvestment trust funds, **P**rivate-**P**urpose trust funds, and **A**gency funds.

855. Answer: B

Governmental fund types use the modified accrual basis of accounting, which focuses on the "flow of financial resources." Consequently, the use of financial resources is an expenditure rather than an expense without regard to the character of the expenditure (e.g., operating expense or capital expense). Therefore, as this answer states, the new police car (a long-term asset) is recorded as an expenditure in the period of acquisition because it represents an outflow of financial resources. Since it is an immediate expenditure, the General Fund does not list the car as a noncurrent asset. However, in the government-wide Statement of Net Position (not part of this question) the car would be included in the noncurrent assets and depreciated overtime.

856. Answer: C

All governmental funds, including special revenue funds, use the modified accrual basis of accounting.

857. Answer: B

The primary measurement focus for governmental fund types is on the flows and balances of financial resources (GASB Codification 1300.102).

858. Answer: A

Proprietary funds account for activities of the governmental unit that are similar to activities conducted by commercial enterprises. The orientation of accounting and reporting for proprietary funds is similar to that used in private businesses. The accrual basis of accounting is used, and the measurement focus

is on income determination, financial position, and cash flow (GASB Codification 1300.102).

859. Answer: A

The general fund uses the modified accrual basis of accounting. Under this basis, revenues are recognized in the accounting period when they become available and measurable.

An enterprise fund uses the accrual basis of accounting. Under this basis, revenues are recognized in the period in which they are earned and measurable.

860. Answer: B

The Appropriations Control account, a budgetary account, would be credited for the amount of the authorized spending limit.

861. Answer: D

Assuming that both actual and budgetary transactions are closed to the fund balance, closing appropriations, a credit balance account, would increase the fund balance whereas closing expenditures, a debit balance account, would decrease the fund balance.

Since appropriations were greater than expenditures, the net effect would be to increase the fund balance.

862. Answer: D

When the budgetary accounts are closed at the end of the fiscal year, the estimated revenues control account will be credited for the amount for which it was debited when the budget was recorded, $20,000,000.

863. Answer: B

Transfers in from other funds are classified as Other Financing Sources and are not revenues. The other three amounts are classified as revenues and, for budget purposes, should be included in determining estimated revenues. The total is $5,550,000.

864. Answer: C

Park would credit the budgetary fund balance for $2,100,000 when it makes the following entry to record the budget.

Estimated revenues	$30,000,000
Appropriations	$27,000,000
Estimated transfers to debt service fund	$900,000
Budgetary fund balance	$2,100,000

865. **Answer: B**

The fund balance classification is either restricted, committed, or assigned, depending on the level of authority behind the encumbrance. If the government intends to use the resources the specific purposes but is not a constraint imposed by external parties or enabling legislation (i.e., restricted) or by formal action of the government's highest decision making authority (i.e., committed). Assigned fund balances should be used to indicate that a portion of the fund balance is not available for expenditure. The use of a reserve for encumbrances indicates that a portion of the fund balance has been segregated for expenditure on vendor performance.

866. **Answer: D**

Encumbrance accounting is used for budgetary control and, therefore, is commonly used in governmental fund types, including the General, Special Revenue, and Capital Projects Funds. It is usually not used by Debt Service Funds since the terms of the debt control spending. It is rarely used by Proprietary Funds so the Enterprise Fund is the best choice for this question.

867. **Answer: B**

Encumbrances outstanding at year's-end represent outstanding purchase orders or unfilled contracts. The fund balance classification is either restricted, committed, or assigned depending on the level of authority behind the encumbrance. If the government intends to use the resources for specific purposes but is not a constraint imposed by external parties or enabling legislation (i.e., restricted) or by formal action of the government's highest decision making authority (i.e., committed) then a portion of the fund balance needs to be assigned for the outstanding encumbrances to indicate that a portion of the fund balance needs to be assigned for the outstanding encumbrances to indicate that a portion of the fund balance is not available for future appropriations.

868. **Answer: C**

Since the Debt Service Fund uses the modified accrual basis of accounting, revenues are recognized with measurable and available. The $200,000 is not expected to be available and hence should be reported as a deferred inflow or resources in Year 20X1.

869. **Answer: C**

The Debt Service Fund reports the amount that is measurable and available as revenue, which in Year 20X2 is the $1,000,000 collected.

870. **Answer: D**

The Debt Service Fund recognizes revenue when it is measurable and available. Since the first installment will be received 120 days into Year 20X2, no revenue is recognized in Year 20X1.

871. **Answer: C**

The remaining levy is measureable and available in Year 20X3 through Year 20X6 and is a deferred inflow of resources in Year 20X2.

872. **Answer: B**

GASB Statement No. 54 eliminated the use of "reserve" and "unreserved" fund balances. The appropriate fund balance classifications are Nonspendable, Restricted, Committed, Assigned, and Unassigned.

873. **Answer: A**

According to GASB Statement No. 54, a Nonspendable Fund Balance classification pertains to amounts that cannot be spent either because they are not in a spendable form (e.g., inventory) or are legally or contractually required to be maintained intact.

874. **Answer: C**

$10,000 of the fund balance should be assigned to show that those funds are not available for appropriation in the next fiscal year.

875. **Answer: D**

According to GASB Statement No. 54, outstanding encumbrances are no longer reported as Reserves in the fund balance section, which was the practice prior to Statement No. 54. Significant encumbrances should be disclosed in the notes to the financial statements.

876. **Answer: D**

Only the General Fund can report a positive amount in Unassigned Fund Balance. In all other Governmental Fund types (including a Special Revenue Fund), if expenditures exceed amounts restricted, committed, or assigned, it may be necessary to report a negative Unassigned Fund Balance. Should that occur, the Assigned Fund Balance is reduced to eliminate the deficit. If a deficit remains after eliminating Assigned Fund Balance, the negative residual should be classified Unassigned Fund Balance.

877. **Answer: B**

Permanent Funds account for the receipt of the endowment principal that is donated to a government and is to be held in trust for the benefit of the government (or of its citizenry as a whole) as revenue.

878. **Answer: D**

Permanent Funds account for the receipt of the endowment principal that is donated to a government and is to be held in trust for the benefit of the government (or of its citizenry as a whole) as revenue. The property should be capitalized at $925,000—fair market value at the time of donation ($800,000) plus the cost of improvements ($125,000) made by the city. Earnings from the office complex would usually be transferred to and expended through a Special Revenue Fund.

879. **Answer: B**

The $450,000 transfer from the General Fund is classified as an Other Financing Source—Transfer In, but the $300,000 state grant is recognized as Revenue. Though the grant has not yet been received in Cash, GASB #33 requires that it be recognized as Revenue in the Government-Wide Statements when the receivable is recognized, as long as there are no eligibility restrictions. It would also be recognized as Revenue in the fund statements as long as the cash was received within 60 days of the year end.

880. **Answer: D**

Both Interest Expenditures and Principal Expenditures are recognized in the Debt Service Fund. Debt Service Expenditures are usually not accrued at year-end but are recorded as Expenditures when due and payable. In 20X9 the Debt Service Fund paid a total of $176,000–$ $40,000 interest and $100,000 principal on April 1 (both expenditures of the fund) and $36,000 interest on October 1.

881. **Answer: D**

Enterprise Funds use accrual accounting and account for their fund-specific fixed assets. In accounting for capital leases an Enterprise Fund follows FASB ASC 840 – Leases, therefore the Equipment account should be debited for $150,000 at the inception of the lease.

882. **Answer: D**

Neither of the long-term obligations should be accounted for in Todd City's general fund. Bonds directly related to and expected to be paid from Proprietary Funds (Water and Sewer Fund and Municipal Recreation Fund) should be included in the accounts of such funds. These are specific fund liabilities, even though the full faith and credit of Todd City has been pledged as further assurance that the obligations will be paid.

883. **Answer: C**

Enterprise funds use accrual accounting. The amount of compensated absences expense for the current year can be computed as: ending accrued compensated absences ($150,000) plus compensated absences paid ($400,000) less beginning compensated absences ($125,000), which amounts to $425,000.

884. **Answer: D**

All of the long-term liabilities of these Enterprise Funds should be accounted for in the proprietary fund financial statements.

885. **Answer: B**

There are two types of proprietary funds: (1) internal service funds and (2) enterprise funds. Both use accrual accounting. They differ in terms of the primary user of their services and the pricing policy to set fees. Other governmental agencies/departments are the primary user of services provided by an internal service fund and the pricing policy is some portion of routine operating costs (e.g., from 50% to 100%). Motor pools, data processing, and self-insurance are some examples of Internal Service Funds. External users are the primary users of services provided by an enterprise fund and the pricing policy is to recover operating costs, depreciation, and to provide for capital maintenance. This answer is correct.

886. **Answer: B**

A Private-Purpose Trust Fund is used to account for resources, both expendable and non-expendable, which either must be used for a non-governmental purpose or the earnings from which have to be used for a non-governmental purpose.

As in this case, Private-Purpose Trust Funds usually disburse monies to individuals or organizations outside the governmental entity.

887. **Answer: C**

Because the question is about the General Fund, which uses the modified accrual basis of accounting, only the $10,000 contribution to the pension plan, which is a use of financial resources in year 1, is recognized as pension expenditure. The Pension Trust Fund would report the $10,000 received from the General Fund as an Addition and not as revenue.

888. **Answer: A**

Agency Funds are used to account for assets received on behalf of and paid to other funds, individuals, or organizations. The capital grant described in this question is an example of a pure pass-through grant in which Harland County acts as a conduit to distribute the funds to the five subrecipient municipalities. Hartland County will not record any revenues or expenditures related to the grant and will record a receivable and payable in the Agency Fund that acts as a clearinghouse for the funds.

889. **Answer: A**

In addition to the actual earnings on plan assets, both employer and employee contributions are recognized as Additions in the Pension Trust Fund.

890. **Answer: D**

Agency Funds act as intermediaries in the process of disbursing monies from one governmental entity to another. The government has no claim on the resources in the Agency Fund and does not recognize revenues when it receives the monies or recognize expenses when the monies are disbursed.

891. **Answer: C**

The auditor's report is not part of the introductory section of the CAFR. It is part of the financial section of the CAFR.

892. **Answer: D**

The CAFR includes fund statements from all three fund categories. The government-wide statements include data from the Governmental and Proprietary Funds only.

893. **Answer: D**

GASB Statement no. 34 para. 27–29, provides not-for-profit organizations with an option to not recognize contributions of donated works or art, historical treasures, or similar assets that are added to collections if the following conditions are met:

1. They are held for public exhibition, education, or research in furtherance of public service rather than financial gain;
2. They are protected, kept unencumbered, cared for, and preserved;
3. Or they are subject to a policy that requires the proceeds of items that are sold to be used to acquire other items for the collection.

Capitalized collections or individual items that are exhaustible, such as exhibits whose useful lives are diminished by display or educational or research applications, should be depreciated over their estimated useful lives. Depreciation is not required for collections or individual items that are inexhaustible. In this question, neither capitalization nor depreciation is required.

894. **Answer: D**

Special-purpose governments engaged in business-type activities follow the reporting standards required for enterprise funds, which are a Statement of Net Position; Statement of Revenues, Expenses, and Changes in Net Position; Statement of Cash Flows; and appropriate disclosures in MD&A, and RSI.

895. **Answer: A**

The Government-Wide Financial Statements will present both the asset and the liability associated with a capital lease asset.

896. **Answer: D**

The Authority is a component unit of the town because it is financially accountable to the town, as evidenced by the town approving the Authority's budget.

897. **Answer: B**

Discretely presented component units are presented in the Government-Wide Financial Statements only and not in the fund-level statements.

898. **Answer: C**

Two approaches are used for component units: (1) discrete presentation in a separate column of the Government-Wide Financial Statements and (2) blended with the primary government.

899. **Answer: A**

According to GASB Statement No. 61 (para 6), Excel City would have to appoint a voting majority of Excel ISD's governing body. The criteria for financial accountability require that, in addition to the primary government being able to impose its will on the component unit (e.g. approve the budget). at least 50% of the governing body of the component unit be appointed by the primary government. In this case, the governing body is independently elected and so does not meet the criteria for inclusion as a component unit.

900. **Answer: B**

GASB Statement #34 requires that Internal Service Funds be included in the Governmental Activities totals on the Government-Wide Statements since Internal Service Funds supply goods or services only to the government entity.

Therefore, the total fund balance for the Governmental Funds in the fund-based statements ($25,000) must be increased by the Net Position of the motor pool ($9,000) when the preparing the Governmental Activities column of the Government-Wide Statement of Net Position ($25,000 + 9,000 = $34,000).

901. **Answer: C**

The increase in the fund balance for Governmental Funds is measured on the modified accrual basis, while the Change in Net Position for governmental activities is measure on the full accrual basis. To convert the increase in fund balance to full accrual:

Increase in Fund Balance	+ $1,500
Add back the Expenditures related to the purchase of capital assets	+ 9,000
Deduct the depreciation expense not included in Fund Balance	– 3,000
Change in Net Position	$7,500

902. **Answer: C**

The Budgetary Comparison Schedule must report the original budget, the amended/final budget, and actual revenues and expenditures. The revenues and expenditures must be reported using the same basis used to prepare the budget: governmental budgets are frequently prepared on a cash or near-cash basis.

903. **Answer: C**

Under the modified approach, infrastructure assets that are part of a network or subsystem of a network need not be depreciated if the government uses an asset management system that documents that the assets are

being preserved approximately at (or above) a condition level established and disclosed by the government.

904. **Answer: C**

General Fund transfers to the Debt Service Fund to provide for the servicing of debt is an example of a regular, routine, recurring transfer of resources between funds to subsidize current activities that are classified as Operating Transfers.

905. **Answer: B**

Infrastructure assets are capital assets that are normally stationary and can be preserved for a longer time than most capital assets. Common infrastructure assets include roads, bridges, sewer systems, lighting systems, and drainage. Buildings are not infrastructure assets.

906. **Answer: C**

The government-wide financial statements are used to account for all unmatured long-term indebtedness of the government, except for that debt belonging to proprietary and similar trust funds. The liability for the general obligation bonds should be recorded in this account group.

907. **Answer: A**

The Capital Project Fund records the entire amount of the bond proceeds as an Other Financing Source in the year that the proceeds are received. Even though the expenditures are to occur over two years, under modified accrual accounting, the entire amount of the proceeds are recorded as a resource of the fund when received. Answer A is correct.

908. **Answer: D**

All of the items listed are Unmatured Long-Term Liabilities of the general government that will not be recorded in any of the Governmental funds but will appear as liabilities in the Government-Wide Statement of Net Position.

909. **Answer: A**

The Water Utility Enterprise Fund uses full accrual accounting and will account for and report on the bonds in the Enterprise Fund. Therefore, this liability appears in the business-type activity section of the government-wide financial statements and not in the governmental activity section.

910. **Answer: D**

The $100,000 portion of the judgment due in the current year is reported in the General Fund and will appear as expenditures in the fund-level statements. The unmatured $400,000 portion is reported in the Government-wide statements as a liability at present value. The long-term portion of the liability is RECORDED in the Schedule of General Long-term Debt.

911. **Answer: C**

Donated fixed assets should be recorded in the fund to which they relate or in the General Fixed Asset Account group, as appropriate, at their estimated fair value when received. GASB 1400.113

912. **Answer: A**

"Expense" is a term reserved for funds that use full accrual accounting. A Water Utility Fund is an Enterprise Fund type using full accrual accounting.

913. **Answer: D**

The entry to record a purchase order is a debit to Encumbrances and a credit to Budgetary Fund Balance.

914. **Answer: C**

The entity-wide statements are presented on the full accrual basis and hence used GASB #33 Revenue recognition rules.

GASB #33 requires that property taxes net of the estimated uncollectible taxes be recognized as Revenue in the year for which they were levied, regardless of when cash is actually collected.

915. **Answer: B**

The county would recognize in its Government-Wide Statement of Net Position a capital asset of $20 million for the acquisition of the water rights in 2010. A capital outlay expenditure of $20 million would be recorded in the county's Capital Projects Fund Statement of Revenues, Expenditures, and Changes in Net Position. Because the county would be required to make an additional payment to execute the 10-year renewal period, this period is not considered as part of the useful life acquired in exchange for the $20 million payment. The useful life of the water rights is 10 years. Using straight-line amortization, annual amortization expense of $2 million ($20 million over 10 years) would be recorded in the county's Government-Wide Statement of Activities starting in 2010.

916. **Answer: A**

GASB Statement No. 53 requires changes in the fair value of Derivative Instruments used for investment purposes to be reported within the Investment Income classification of the Statement of Activities. Changes in the fair value of Hedging Derivative Instruments are reported as Deferred Outflow or Deferred Inflow of Resources in the Statement of Net Position.

917. **Answer: D**

The county would recognize in its Government-Wide Statement of Net Position a capital asset of $20 million for the acquisition of the water rights in 2010. A capital outlay expenditure of $20 million would be recorded in the county's Capital Projects Fund Statement of Revenues, Expenditures, and Changes in Net Position. Since there is evidence that the county will seek and be able to acquire renewal of the water rights without incurring additional outlays, the useful life of the water rights is 20 years—the original 10-year term plus the 10-year renewal term. Using straight-line amortization, annual amortization expense of $1 million ($20 million over 20 years) would be recorded in the county's Government-Wide Statement of Activities, starting in 2010.

918. **Answer: C**

According to GASB Statement No. 51, the activities involved in developing and installing internally generated computer software can be grouped into the following three stages: (1) preliminary project stage, (2) application development stage, and (3) post-implementation/operation stage. Costs in the first and last stage are expensed as incurred. Costs related to the application development stage are capitalized in the Government-Wide Financial Statements. The $1.5 million spent to conduct interviews and evaluate various software programs is considered stage 1—preliminary project stage—and should be expensed as incurred. The $0.60 million in data entry and training is post-implementation/operation stage and should also be expensed as incurred. Both the $14.5 million outlay for commercial software and the $0.50 million for installation and testing of the software relate to the second stage-application and development-and should be capitalized ($15.0 million).

919. Answer: D

GASB Statement No. 44 requires that statistical information be presented in five categories—Financial Trends Information, Revenue Capacity Information, Debt Capacity Information, Demographic and Economic Information, and Operating Information. Fund balance information is not one of the five categories, but for Governmental Funds, Fund Balance Information is required as part of the financial trends information category.

920. Answer: B

Total revenues, gains, and other support on the Statement of Operations includes net patient revenue, premium revenues (e.g., HMO capitation fees), other revenue, and net assets released from restrictions. Net patient revenues are fees for patient services less contractual adjustments and charity care. How bad debt expense is treated differs between not-for-profit healthcare organizations and governmental healthcare organizations. Not-for-profit organizations report bad debt expense as part of operating expenses. Governmental organizations do not report bad debt expense; rather, revenues are reported "net" of bad debts. This choice is incorrect because it reduces revenues for the amount of bad debt expense ($70,000). The correct answer is $530,000; $500,000 (net patient revenues including charity care) less $100,000 (charity care) plus $50,000 (net assets released) plus $80,000 (other revenue).

921. Answer: B

Both room and board fees from patients and recovery room fees are normal, ongoing activities of a not-for-profit hospital.

922. Answer: C

Government hospitals classify revenues into three broad categories: Patient Service Revenues, Premium Fees, and Other Revenues. The Other Revenues category includes revenues generated by ongoing activities of the hospital other than patient care. Revenues from educational programs are included in this category.

Government hospitals record unrestricted gifts as Nonoperating Gains in the General Fund.

If we assume that the hospital is not a government entity, then it must conform with ASC 954-225-45. The revenues from educational programs would still be classified as Other Operating Revenues. The unrestricted gifts would be classified as Revenues from Contributions.

923. Answer: D

Government-affiliated hospitals normally have three broad categories of revenues:

1. Patient Service Revenues
2. Premium Fees
3. Other Revenues. Within the Other Revenues category is a variety of different activities including proceeds from the sale of cafeteria meals.

924. Answer: D

Medicine is considered essential to the major ongoing operation of the hospital, therefore the donation of medicine is recorded as other operating revenue at its fair value.

dr. Inventory of Medicine

   cr. Donated Revenues

ASC 958-605-30-9

925. Answer: B

Tuition revenue should be recognized proportionately in the two fiscal years. Since one-third of the semester is in the first fiscal year, $90,000 in revenue should be recognized ($270,000 × 1/3).

Journal Entry 6–1–20X8

Cash	270,000	
Revenue		$1/3 \times 270,000 = 90,000$
Deferred Revenue		$2/3 \times 270,000 = 180,000$

926. Answer: B

A state university is an example of a special purpose government. Since it is engaged only in business-type activities, it should report the financial statements required for Enterprise Funds. In that case, state appropriations to the university are Nonoperating Revenues.

927. Answer: C

Both the $50,000 pledge, which is not to be paid until the following year, and the $25,000 cash gift, which is restricted for scholarships, should be recognized as Revenue, albeit "Temporarily Restricted Revenue." The $50,000 pledge is restricted due to "Time Restrictions" (e.g. the money will not be received until a later time). The $25,000 gift is subject to a "Purpose Restriction." The $10,000 bequest is not recognized as revenue. It may be disclosed in the notes but should not be recognized as revenue until the amount is distributable.

Task-Based Simulations

Conceptual Framework and Financial Reporting

Financial Accounting Standards Board (FASB): Overview of U.S. GAAP

Accrual Accounting

Task-Based Simulation 1

The following information pertains to Baron Flowers, a calendar-year sole proprietorship, which maintained its books on the cash basis during the year.

Baron Flowers TRIAL BALANCE December 31, year 2		
	Dr.	**Cr.**
Cash	$25,600	
Accounts receivable, 12/31/Y1	16,200	
Inventory, 12/31/Y1	62,000	
Furniture & fixtures	118,200	
Land improvements	45,000	
Accumulated depreciation, 12/31/Y1		$32,400
Accounts payable, 12/31/Y1		17,000
Baron, Drawings		
Baron, Capital, 12/31/Y1		124,600
Sales		653,000
Purchases	305,100	
Salaries	174,000	
Payroll taxes	12,400	
Insurance	8,700	
Rent	34,200	
Utilities	12,600	
Living expenses	13,000	–
	$827,000	$827,000

Baron has developed plans to expand into the wholesale flower market and is in the process of negotiating a bank loan to finance the expansion. The bank is requesting year 2 financial statements prepared on the accrual basis of accounting from Baron. During the course of a review engagement, Muir, Baron's accountant, obtained the following additional information.

1. Amounts due from customers totaled $32,000 at December 31, year 2.
2. An analysis of the above receivables revealed that an allowance for uncollectible accounts of $3,800 should be provided.
3. Unpaid invoices for flower purchases totaled $30,500 and $17,000, at December 31, year 2, and December 31, year 1, respectively.

4. The inventory totaled $72,800 based on a physical count of the goods at December 31, year 2. The inventory was priced at cost, which approximates fair value.
5. On May 1, year 2, Baron paid $8,700 to renew its comprehensive insurance coverage for one year. The premium on the previous policy, which expired on April 30, year 2, was $7,800.
6. On January 2, year 2, Baron entered into a 25-year operating lease for the vacant lot adjacent to Baron's retail store for use as a parking lot. As agreed in the lease, Baron paved and fenced in the lot at a cost of $45,000. The improvements were completed on April 1, year 2, and have an estimated useful life of 15 years. No provision for depreciation or amortization has been recorded. Depreciation on furniture and fixtures was $12,000 for year 2.
7. Accrued expenses at December 31, year 1 and year 2, were as follows:

	Year 1	Year 2
Utilities	$900	$1,500
Payroll taxes	1,100	1,600
	$2,000	$3,100

8. Baron is being sued for $400,000. The coverage under the comprehensive insurance policy is limited to $250,000. Baron's attorney believes that an unfavorable outcome is probable and that a reasonable estimate of the settlement is $300,000.
9. The salaries account includes $4,000 per month paid to the proprietor. Baron also receives $250 per week for living expenses.

Using the worksheet below, prepare the adjustments necessary to convert the trial balance of Baron Flowers to the accrual basis of accounting for the year ended December 31, year 2. Formal journal entries are not required to support your adjustments. However, use the numbers given with the additional information to cross-reference the postings in the adjustment columns on the worksheet.

Baron Flowers
WORKSHEET TO CONVERT TRIAL BALANCE TO ACCRUAL BASIS
December 31, year 2

Account title	Cash basis Dr.	Cash basis Cr.	Adjustments Dr.	Adjustments Cr.	Accrual basis* Dr. *	Accrual basis* Cr. *
Cash	25,600					
Accounts receivable	16,200					
Inventory	62,000					
Furniture and fixtures	118,200					
Land improvements	45,000					
Accumulated depreciation and amortization		32,400				
Accounts payable		17,000				
Baron, Drawings						
Baron, Capital		124,600				
Sales		653,000				
Purchases	305,100					
Salaries	174,000					
Payroll taxes	12,400					
Insurance	8,700					
Rent	34,200					
Utilities	12,600					
Living expenses	13,000					
	827,000	827,000				

*Completion of these columns is not required.

Task-Based Simulations 1 Solution

Baron Flowers
WORKSHEET TO CONVERT TRIAL BALANCE TO ACCRUAL BASIS
December 31, year 2

Account title	Cash basis Dr.	Cash basis Cr.	Adjustments Dr.	Adjustments Cr.	Accrual basis* Dr. *	Accrual basis* Cr. *
Cash	25,600				25,600	
Accounts receivable	16,200		(1) 15,800		32,000	
Inventory	62,000		(4) 10,800		72,800	
Furniture and fixtures	118,200				118,200	
Land improvements	45,000				45,000	
Accumulated depreciation and amortization		32,400		(6) 14,250		46,650
Accounts payable		17,000		(3) 13,500		30,500
Baron, Drawings			(9) 61,000		61,000	
Baron, Capital		124,600	(7) 2,000	(5) 2,600		125,200
Allowance for uncollectible accounts				(2) 3,800		3,800
Prepaid insurance			(5) 2,900		2,900	
Accrued expenses				(7) 3,100		3,100
Estimated liability from lawsuit				(8) 50,000		50,000
Sales		653,000		(1) 15,800		668,800
Purchases	305,100		(3) 13,500		318,600	
Salaries	174,000			(9) 48,000	126,000	
Payroll taxes	12,400		(7) 500		12,900	
Insurance	8,700			(5) 300	8,400	
Rent	34,200				34,200	
Utilities	12,600		(7) 600		13,200	
Living expenses	13,000			(9) 13,000		
Income summary—inventory			(4) 62,000	(4) 72,800		10,800
Uncollectible accounts			(2) 3,800		3,800	
Depreciation and amortization			(6) 14,250		14,250	
Estimated loss from lawsuit			(8) 50,000		50,000	
	827,000	827,000	237,150	237,150	938,850	938,850

*Completion of these columns was not required.

Explanations of adjustments

[1] To convert year 2 sales to accrual basis.

Accounts receivable balances:

December 31, year 2	$32,000
December 31, year 1	16,200
Increase in sales	$15,800

[2] To record provision for uncollectible accounts.

[3] To convert year 2 purchases to accrual basis.

Accounts payable balances:

December 31, year 2	$30,500
December 31, year 1	17,000
Increase in purchases	$13,500

[4] To record increase in inventory from 12/31/Y1 to 12/31/Y2.

Inventory balances:

December 31, year 2	$72,800
December 31, year 1	62,000
Increase in inventory	$10,800

[5] To adjust prepaid insurance.

Prepaid balances:

December 31, year 2 ($8,700 × 4/12)	$2,900
December 31, year 1 ($7,800 × 4/12)	2,600
Decrease in insurance expense	$300

[6] To record year 2 depreciation and amortization expense.

Cost of leasehold improvement		$45,000
Estimated life	15 years	
Amortization ($45,000 × 1/15 × 9/12)		2,250
Depreciation expense on fixtures and equipment		12,000
		$14,250

[7] To convert expenses to accrual basis.

	Balances		
	December 31,		Increase
	Year 2	Year 1	in expenses
Utilities	$1,500	$900	$600
Payroll taxes	1,600	1,100	500
	$3,100	$2,000	$1,100

[8] To record lawsuit liability at 12/31/Y2.

Attorney's estimate of probable loss	$300,000
Amount covered by insurance	250,000
Baron's estimated liability	$50,000

[9] To record Baron's drawings for year 2.

Salary ($4,000 × 12)	$48,000
Living expenses	13,000
	$61,000

Task-Based Simulation 2

Adjusting Entries

Authoritative Literature

Help

Indicate whether each of the following adjusting entries is an accrual or a deferral type entry.

			Accrual	Deferral
1.	Depreciation expense	xx	○	○
	Accumulated depreciation	xx		
2.	Interest receivable	xx	○	○
	Interest revenue	xx		
3.	Rent expense	xx	○	○
	Prepaid rent	xx		
4.	Unearned revenue	xx	○	○
	Rent revenue	xx		
5.	Wage expense	xx	○	○
	Wages payable	xx		

Task-Based Simulations 2 Solution

Adjusting Entries

Authoritative Literature

Help

			Accrual	Deferral
1.	Depreciation expense	xx	○	●
	Accumulated depreciation	xx		
2.	Interest receivable	xx	●	○
	Interest revenue	xx		
3.	Rent expense	xx	○	●
	Prepaid rent	xx		
4.	Unearned revenue	xx	○	●
	Rent revenue	xx		
5.	Wage expense	xx	●	○
	Wages payable	xx		

General-Purpose Financial Statements

Balance Sheet/Statement of Financial Position

Task-Based Simulation 3

Account Classifications

Authoritative Literature

Help

Suppose Winston incorporated and had the following accounts. Indicate how each of the following is classified on the financial statements. Below is a list of classifications.

Balance sheet classification	Income statement classifications
A. Current asset	H. Revenue
B. Noncurrent asset	I. Expense
C. Current liability	J. Contra revenue
D. Noncurrent liability	
E. Owner's equity	
F. Contra asset	
G. Contra equity	

	Balance sheet classification							Income statement classification		
	(A)	(B)	(C)	(D)	(E)	(F)	(G)	(H)	(I)	(J)
1. Bonds payable, due in year 8	O	O	O	O	O	O	O	O	O	O
2. Treasury stock	O	O	O	O	O	O	O	O	O	O
3. Accounts payable	O	O	O	O	O	O	O	O	O	O
4. Sales discounts	O	O	O	O	O	O	O	O	O	O
5. Notes payable, due in nine months	O	O	O	O	O	O	O	O	O	O
6. Inventory	O	O	O	O	O	O	O	O	O	O
7. Accounts receivable	O	O	O	O	O	O	O	O	O	O
8. Common stock	O	O	O	O	O	O	O	O	O	O
9. Cost of goods sold	O	O	O	O	O	O	O	O	O	O
10. Allowance for uncollectible accounts	O	O	O	O	O	O	O	O	O	O

Task-Based Simulations 3 Solution

```
┌─────────────────────────────┐
│ Account Classifications     │
│   ┌─────────────────────────┴──┐
│   │ Authoritative Literature   │
│   │    ┌───────────────────────┴──┐
│   │    │ Help                     │
└───┴────┴──────────────────────────┘
```

	Balance sheet classification							Income statement classification		
	(A)	(B)	(C)	(D)	(E)	(F)	(G)	(H)	(I)	(J)
1. Bonds payable, due in year 8	○	○	○	●	○	○	○	○	○	○
2. Treasury stock	○	○	○	○	○	○	●	○	○	○
3. Accounts payable	○	○	●	○	○	○	○	○	○	○
4. Sales discounts	○	○	○	○	○	○	○	○	○	●
5. Notes payable, due in nine months	○	○	●	○	○	○	○	○	○	○
6. Inventory	●	○	○	○	○	○	○	○	○	○
7. Accounts receivable	●	○	○	○	○	○	○	○	○	○
8. Common stock	○	○	○	○	●	○	○	○	○	○
9. Cost of goods sold	○	○	○	○	○	○	○	○	●	○
10. Allowance for uncollectible accounts	○	○	○	○	○	●	○	○	○	○

Statement of Cash Flows

Operating, Investing, and Financing Activities

Task-Based Simulation 4

Assume that you are assigned to the audit of Health Corporation. The Controller of Health has asked you in which section of the statement of cash flows the proceeds from the sale of available-for-sale securities should be presented. Which section of the Professional Standards addresses this issue?

Enter your response in the answer fields below.

Task-Based Simulations 4 Solution

ASC	320	10	45	11

Task-Based Simulation 5

Concepts	
	Authoritative Literature
		Help

Indicate whether each of the following should be classified as an operating, investing, or financing activity on the statement of cash flows.

	Operating	Investing	Financing
1. Payment for inventory	○	○	○
2. Payment of dividend	○	○	○
3. Cash received from sale of equipment	○	○	○
4. Cash sales	○	○	○
5. Issuance of stock to investors	○	○	○
6. Payment of utility bill	○	○	○
7. Payment of interest on long-term note payable	○	○	○
8. Purchase of Treasury stock	○	○	○

Task-Based Simulations 5 Solution

Concepts	
	Authoritative Literature
		Help

	Operating	Investing	Financing
1. Payment for inventory	●	○	○
2. Payment of dividend	○	○	●
3. Cash received from sale of equipment	○	●	○
4. Cash sales	●	○	○
5. Issuance of stock to investors	○	○	●
6. Payment of utility bill	●	○	○
7. Payment of interest on long-term note payable	●	○	○
8. Purchase of treasury stock	○	○	●

Operating Cash Flows—Indirect Method

Task-Based Simulation 6

Situation

The following is a condensed trial balance of Clark Co., a publicly held company, after adjustments for income tax expense.

Clark Co.
CONDENSED TRIAL BALANCE

	12/31/Y10 BALANCES DR. (CR.)	12/31/Y9 BALANCES DR. (CR.)	NET CHANGE DR. (CR.)
Cash	$484,000	$817,000	$(333,000)
Accounts receivable, net	670,000	610,000	60,000
Property, plant, and equipment	1,070,000	995,000	75,000
Accumulated depreciation	(345,000)	(280,000)	(65,000)
Dividends payable	(25,000)	(10,000)	(15,000)
Income taxes payable	(60,000)	(150,000)	90,000
Deferred income tax liability	(63,000)	(42,000)	(21,000)
Bonds payable	(500,000)	(1,000,000)	500,000
Unamortized premium on bonds	(71,000)	(150,000)	79,000
Common stock	(350,000)	(150,000)	(200,000)
Additional paid-in capital	(430,000)	(375,000)	(55,000)
Retained earnings	(185,000)	(265,000)	80,000
Sales	(2,420,000)		
Cost of sales	1,863,000		
Selling and administrative expenses	220,000		
Interest income	(14,000)		
Interest expense	46,000		
Depreciation	88,000		
Loss on sale of equipment	7,000		
Gain on extinguishment of bonds	(90,000)		
Income tax expense	105,000		
	$0	$0	$300,000

Additional information

- During year 10 equipment with an original cost of $50,000 was sold for cash, and equipment costing $125,000 was purchased.
- On January 1, year 10, bonds with a par value of $500,000 and related premium of $75,000 were redeemed. The $1,000 face value, 10% par bonds had been issued on January 1, year 1, to yield 8%. Interest is payable annually every December 31 through year 19.

- Clark's tax payments during year 10 were debited to Income Taxes Payable. Clark recorded a deferred income tax liability of $42,000 based on temporary differences of $120,000 and an enacted tax rate of 35% at December 31, year 9; prior to year 9 there were no temporary differences. Clark's year 10 financial statement income before income taxes was greater than its year 10 taxable income, due entirely to temporary differences, by $60,000. Clark's cumulative net taxable temporary differences at December 31, year 10, were $180,000. The enacted tax rate for the current and future years is 35%.
- 60,000 shares of common stock, $2.50 par, were outstanding on December 31, year 9. Clark issued an additional 80,000 shares on April 1, year 10.
- There were no changes to retained earnings other than dividends declared.

For each transaction in items **1 through 7**

- Determine the amount to be reported in Clark's year 10 statement of cash flows prepared using the **direct method**.
- Select from the list the appropriate classification of the item on the statement of cash flows.
- Indicate whether the item is a cash inflow or cash outflow.

Calculate the amount, and select the classification and direction from the items shown below.

Classification of Activity	Direction of Cash Flow
Operating	Inflow
Investing	Outflow
Financing	
Supplementary information	
Not reported on Clark's statement of cash flows	

	Amount	Classification of Activity	Direction of Cash Flow
1. Cash paid for income taxes			
2. Cash paid for interest			
3. Redemption of bonds payable			
4. Issuance of common stock			
5. Cash dividends paid			
6. Proceeds from sale of equipment			
7. Cash collections from customers			

Task-Based Simulations 6 Solution

Item	Amount	Classification on Statement of Cash Flows	Cash Inflow/ Cash Outflow
1. Cash paid for income taxes	174,000	Operating Activity	Outflow
2. Cash paid for interest	50,000	Operating Activity	Outflow
3. Redemption of bonds payable	485,000	Financing Activity	Outflow

(Continued)

Item	Amount	Classification on Statement of Cash Flows	Cash Inflow/ Cash Outflow
4. Issuance of common stock	255,000	Financing Activity	Inflow
5. Cash dividends paid	65,000	Financing Activity	Outflow
6. Proceeds from sale of equipment	20,000	Investing	Inflow
7. Cash collections from customers	2,360,000	Operating Activity	Inflow

Explanations

1. **($174,000, O)** The payments for income taxes during the year were debited to the income taxes payable account. To arrive at the amount of payments, a T-account can be used as follows:

Income Taxes Payable

		150,000	12/31/Y9
Payments	174,000	84,000	Income Tax Accrual
		60,000	12/31/Y10

Note that the deferred tax liability account increased by $21,000 ($120,000 × 35%). Therefore, the entry for tax expense for year 10 would have been:

Tax Expense	105,000	
Deferred Tax Liability		21,000
Taxes Payable		84,000

Using the direct method, the payment of taxes would appear in the operating section of the cash flow statement.

2. **($50,000, O)** Interest paid on the bonds in year 10 would be $50,000 ($500,000 × 10%). Alternatively, the $46,000 plus the $4,000 premium amortization (see explanation for the next item below) also results in $50,000 as the amount paid for interest. The amount paid for interest would be included in the operating activities section of the cash flow statements if the direct method is used. (Note: The amount of cash paid for interest would be reported separately as supplementary information for a statement of cash flows using the indirect method.)

3. **($485,000, F)** Through the following T-account analyses, a journal entry for the redemption of the bonds payable can be determined:

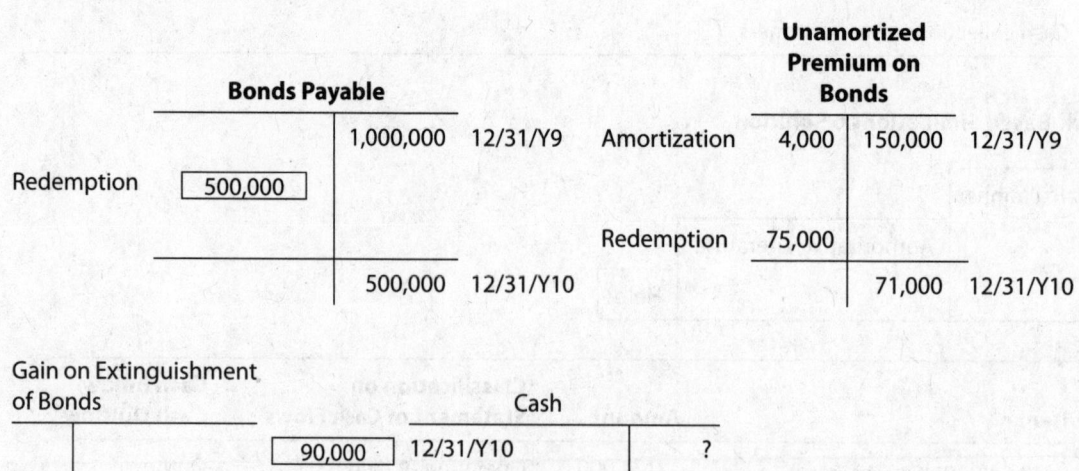

Journal entry for redemption:

Bonds payable	500,000	
Unamortized premium on bonds	75,000	
Gain on extinguishment of bonds		90,000
Cash		485,000

This amount paid for the redemption of the bonds would be separately reported in the financing section on the statement of cash flows prepared using the indirect method. Financing activities include obtaining resources from owners and returning the investment, as well as obtaining resources from creditors and **repaying the amounts borrowed**.

4. **($255,000, F)** An additional 80,000 shares of $2.50 par value common stock were issued during year 10. The following T-accounts depict the changes in the common stock and additional paid-in capital accounts:

Common Stock

	150,000	12/31Y9
	200,000	Issuance (80,000 × $2.50)
	350,000	12/31Y10

Additional Paid-in Capital

	375,000	12/31/Y9
	55,000	Issuance
	430,000	12/31/Y10

The journal entry for the issuance of the stock would have been

Cash	255,000	
Common stock		200,000
Additional paid-in capital		55,000

This amount received for the issuance of the common stock would be reported separately in the financing section of the statement of cash flows prepared using the indirect method. Financing activities include **obtaining resources from owners** and returning the investment, as well as obtaining resources from creditors and repaying the amounts borrowed.

5. **($65,000, F)** The problem states that there were no changes to retained earnings during the year other than dividends declared. Therefore, the following T-account analyses depict the dividend activity during the year:

Retained Earnings

	265,000	12/31/Y9
Dividends declared 80,000		
	185,000	12/31/Y10

	Dividends Payable					Cash	
		10,000	12/31/Y9			?	
Dividends paid	?	**80,000**	Accrual during year 10				
		25,000	12/31/Y10				

The following journal entry would have been made:

Retained earnings	80,000	
Dividends payable		80,000
Dividends payable	65,000	
Cash		**65,000**

This amount paid for the dividends would be reported separately in the financing section of the statement of cash flows prepared using the indirect method. Financing activities include obtaining resources from owners and **returning the investment**, as well as obtaining resources from creditors and repaying the amounts borrowed.

6. **($20,000, I)** The following T-account analyses depict the sale of the equipment during year 10:

Property, Plant, and Equipment

12/31/Y9	995,000		
		50,000	Sale
Purchase	125,000		
12/31/Y10	1,070,000		

Accumulated Depreciation

		280,000	12/31/Y9
Depreciation on sold asset	**23,000**	88,000	Depreciation expense
		345,000	12/31/Y10

Loss on Sale of Equipment		Cash	
12/31/Y10	**7,000**	?	

The following journal entry would have been made for the sale of the equipment:

Cash	**20,000**	
Accumulated depreciation	23,000	
Loss on sale of equipment	7,000	
Property, plant and equipment		50,000

The proceeds from the sale of equipment would be reported separately in the investing section of the statement of cash flows. Included in the investing section are the acquisition and disposition of long-term productive assets or securities (not considered cash equivalents), as well as the lending of money and collection of loans.

7. **($2,360,000, O)** The following T-account analysis depicts the cash received from customers. Assume all sales are made on account.

Accounts Receivable

12/31/Y10	610,000		
Sale on Account	2,420,000		
		2,360,000	Collections on account
12/31/Y2	670,000		

Therefore, the cash collections on account were 610,000 + 2,420,000 – 670,000 = 2,360,000.

Task-Based Simulation 7

Statement of Cash Flows—Indirect Method

Authoritative Literature

Help

Situation

The following is a condensed trial balance of Probe Co., a publicly held company, after adjustments for income tax expense.

Probe Co.
CONDENSED TRIAL BALANCE

	12/31/Y10 Balances Dr. (Cr.)	12/31/Y9 Balances Dr. (Cr.)	Net Change Dr. (Cr.)
Cash	$484,000	$817,000	$(333,000)
Accounts receivable, net	670,000	610,000	60,000
Property, plant, and equipment	1,070,000	995,000	75,000
Accumulated depreciation	(345,000)	(280,000)	(65,000)
Dividends payable	(25,000)	(10,000)	(15,000)
Income taxes payable	(60,000)	(150,000)	90,000
Deferred income tax liability	(63,000)	(42,000)	(21,000)
Bonds payable	(500,000)	(1,000,000)	500,000
Unamortized premium on bonds	(71,000)	(150,000)	79,000
Common stock	(350,000)	(150,000)	(200,000)
Additional paid-in capital	(430,000)	(375,000)	(55,000)
Retained earnings	(185,000)	(265,000)	80,000
Sales	(2,420,000)		
Cost of sales	1,863,000		
Selling and administrative expenses	220,000		
Interest income	(14,000)		
Interest expense	46,000		
Depreciation	88,000		
Loss on sale of equipment	7,000		
Gain on extinguishment of bonds	(90,000)		
Income tax expense	105,000		
	$ 0	$ 0	$300,000

Additional information

- During year 10 equipment with an original cost of $50,000 was sold for cash, and equipment costing $125,000 was purchased.
- On January 1, year 10, bonds with a par value of $500,000 and related premium of $75,000 were redeemed. The $1,000 face value, 10% par bonds had been issued on January 1, year 1, to yield 8%. Interest is payable annually every December 31 through year 20.
- Probe's tax payments during year 10 were debited to Income Taxes Payable. Probe recorded a deferred income tax liability of $42,000 based on temporary differences of $120,000 and an enacted tax rate of 35% at December 31, year 9; prior to year 9 there were no temporary differences. Probe's year 10 financial statement income before income taxes was greater than its year 10 taxable income, due entirely to temporary differences, by $60,000. Probe's cumulative net taxable temporary differences at December 31, year 10, were $180,000. Probe's enacted tax rate for the current and future years is 35%.
- 60,000 shares of common stock, $2.50 par, were outstanding on December 31, year 9. Probe issued an additional 80,000 shares on April 1, year 10.
- There were no changes to retained earnings other than dividends declared.

Prepare a statement of cash flows using the **indirect method**. Select the titles and the numbers from the lists provided. You may use a number more than once, if necessary. You should also enter the following amounts:

- Subtotals for each class of activity.
- Net change in cash for the year.
- Reconciliation to cash amounts.

Complete the following statement of cash flows using the **indirect method**. (Select from titles and amounts from the tables that follow.)

Probe Co.
STATEMENT OF CASH FLOWS
For the Year Ending 12/31/Y10

From Operating Activities	Cash Source (Use)
From Investing Activities	

From Financing Activities

Titles

Increase in accounts receivable	Decrease in bonds payable	Net income
Decrease in accounts receivable	Issue bonds	Net loss
Increase in property, plant, and equipment	Redeem bonds	Taxes paid
Decrease in property, plant, and equipment	Amortization of premium on bonds	Interest paid
Purchase of equipment	Gain on extinguishment of bonds	Depreciation expense
Sale of equipment	Payment of dividends	Cash collections from customers
Loss on sale of equipment	Increase in common stock	Cash paid for expenses
Increase in accumulated depreciation	Decrease in common stock	Net cash flows from operating activities
Decrease in accumulated depreciation	Issue common stock	Net cash flows from investing activities
Increase in income taxes payable	Repurchase common stock	Net cash flows from financing activities
Decrease in income taxes payable	Increase in additional paid-in capital	Other significant noncash transactions
Increase in deferred income tax liability	Decrease in additional paid-in capital	Net increase in cash
Decrease in deferred income tax liability	Increase in retained earnings	Net decrease in cash
Increase in bonds payable	Decrease in retained earnings	Cash at beginning of year
		Cash at end of year

Amounts				
4,000	46,000	88,000	255,000	610,000
7,000	50,000	90,000	300,000	670,000
10,000	55,000	95,000	333,000	780,000
13,000	60,000	120,000	350,000	817,000
14,000	63,000	125,000	410,000	1,000,000
15,000	65,000	150,000	484,000	2,360,000
20,000	74,000	174,000	485,000	2,420,000
21,000	75,000	185,000	500,000	2,480,000
23,000	79,000	195,000	515,000	3,030,000
25,000	80,000	200,000	575,000	
42,000	85,000	240,000	590,000	

Task-Based Simulation 7 Solution

Statement of Cash Flows—Indirect Method		
	Authoritative Literature	
		Help

Probe Co.
STATEMENT OF CASH FLOWS
For the Year Ending 12/31/Y10

	Cash Source (Use)
From Operating Activities	
Net income	195,000
Loss on sale of equipment	7,000
Gain on extinguishments of bonds	(90,000)
Depreciation Expense	88,000
Increase in Account Receivable	(60,000)
Decrease in Income Taxes Payable	(90,000)
Increase in Deferred Taxes Payable	21,000
Amortization of Premium on Bonds	(4,000)
Net cash flows from operating activities	67,000
From Investing Activities	
Sale of equipment	20,000
Purchase of equipment	(125,000)
Net cash flow from investing activities	(105,000)

	Cash Source (Use)
From Financing Activities	
Redeem bonds	(485,000)
Issue common stock	255,000)
Payment of dividends	(65,000)
Net cash flows from financing activities	(295,000)
Net decrease in cash	(333,000)
Cash at beginning of year	817,000
Cash at end of year	484,000

Task-Based Simulation 8

Concepts—Direct Method		
	Authoritative Literature	
		Help

Below is a list of accounts and transactions. Prepare the outline of a statement of cash flows using the **direct method** by placing the appropriate items in the correct location on the statement of cash flows. Indicate whether each item selected for use in the statement of cash flows would be a cash inflow or a cash outflow.

Amortization of patents	Dividends received on trading securities	Issue of common stock
Borrow on long-term note payable	Gain on sale of land	Loss on sale of equipment
Cash collected on account	Increase in accounts receivable	Net income
Cash paid for inventory	Increase in dividends payable	Payment of dividend
Cash paid for supplies	Increase in inventories	Purchase of held-to-maturity securities
Cash sales	Increase in taxes payable	Purchase of treasury stock
Decrease in accounts payable	Interest accrued at December 31	Redemption of bonds
Decrease in prepaid expenses	Interest expense	Sale of land
Depreciation expense	Interest paid on note	Taxes paid

Probe Co.
STATEMENT OF CASH FLOWS
For the Year Ending 12/31/Y2

	Cash Inflow or Cash Outflow
From Operating Activities	
From Investing Activities	
From Financing Activities	

Task-Based Simulation 8 Solution

Concepts—Direct Method

Authoritative Literature

Help

Probe Co.
STATEMENT OF CASH FLOWS
For the Year Ending 12/31/Y2

	Cash Inflow or Cash Outflow
From Operating Activities	
Cash paid for inventory	Outflow
Cash paid for supplies	Outflow
Cash collected on account	Inflow
Cash sales	Inflow
Dividends received on trading securities	Inflow

	Cash Inflow or Cash Outflow
From Operating Activities	
Interest paid on note	Outflow
Taxes paid	Outflow
From Investing Activities	
Purchase of held-to-maturity securities	Outflow
Sale of land	Inflow
From Financing Activities	
Borrow on long-term note payable	Inflow
Issue of common stock	Inflow
Payment of dividend	Outflow
Purchase of treasury stock	Outflow
Redemption of bonds	Outflow

Task-Based Simulation 9

Research

Authoritative Literature

Help

Easton Company purchased 4,000 shares of its own stock for $20 per share and immediately retired the shares. You have been asked to research the professional literature to determine how the item is presented in Easton's statement of cash flows, using the indirect method. Place the citation for the excerpt from the Professional Standards that provides this information in the answer box below.

Task-Based Simulation 9 Solution

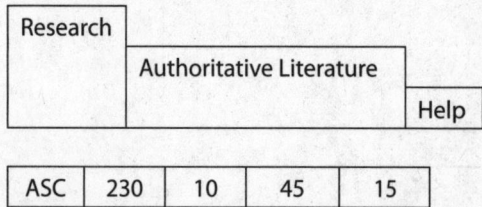

ASC	230	10	45	15

General-Purpose Financial Statements: Consolidated Financial Statements

Consolidating Process: Consolidation at Acquisition

Task-Based Simulation 10

Webster Corporation is acquiring Urton Company. You have been asked to research the professional literature to determine at what amounts the assets and liabilities of Urton should be recorded on the books of Webster Corporation. Place the citation for the excerpt from the Professional Standards that provides this information in the answer box below.

Task-Based Simulation 10 Solution

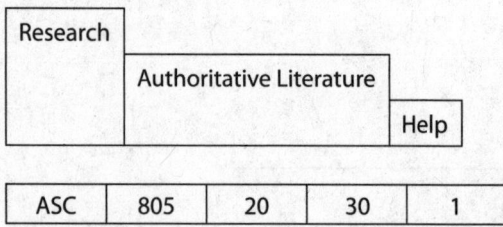

ASC	805	20	30	1

Task-Based Simulation 11

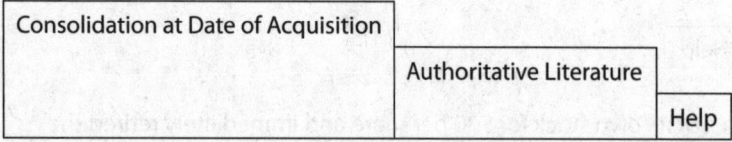

On January 1, year 2, Arcelia Corporation acquired Gavino Corporation by purchasing 100% of the stock of Gavino in exchange for 20,000 shares of Arcelia stock. On the date of acquisition Arcelia stock traded for $18 per share on the stock exchange. The fair value of Gavino's inventory is $10,000 higher than the book value.

The book values of each company on January 1, year 2, are shown below.

	Arcelia Corp.	Gavino Corp.
Current assets	$320,000	$70,000
Noncurrent assets	640,000	380,000
Current liabilities	210,000	50,000
Noncurrent liabilities	150,000	90,000
Owners' equity	600,000	310,000

Calculate each of the following balance sheet amounts for Arcelia Corporation immediately following the acquisition of Gavino.

Total current assets	
Total noncurrent assets	
Total current liabilities	
Total noncurrent liabilities	
Total owners' equity	

Task-Based Simulation 11 Solution

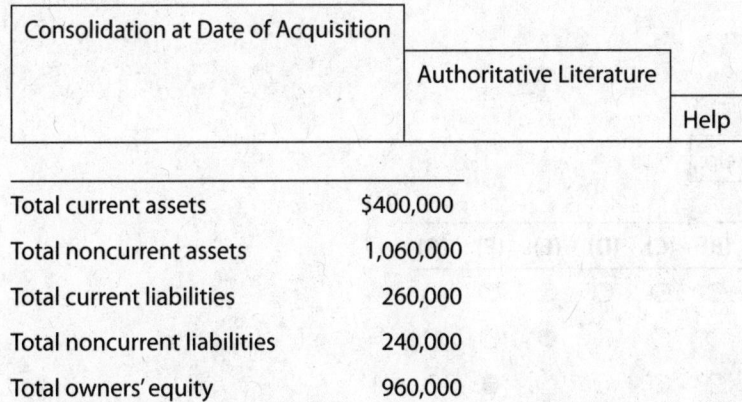

Total current assets	$400,000
Total noncurrent assets	1,060,000
Total current liabilities	260,000
Total noncurrent liabilities	240,000
Total owners' equity	960,000

Explanations

Current assets: $320,000 parent + $70,000 book value subsidiary + $10,000 inventory write-up = $400,000

Noncurrent assets: $640,000 parent + $380,000 book value subsidiary + $40,000 goodwill = $1,060,000

Total current liabilities: $210,000 parent + $50,000 subsidiary = $260,000

Noncurrent liabilities: $150,000 parent + $90,000 subsidiary = $240,000

Total owners' equity: $600,000 parent + $360,000 new stock of parent issued in acquisition = $960,000

Task-Based Simulation 12

On January 1, year 1, Rain acquires 90% of the stock in Snow in a transaction properly accounted for as a business combination. **Items 1 through 6** below refer to accounts that may or may not be included in

Rain and Snow's consolidated financial statements. The list below refers to the various possibilities of those amounts to be reported in Rain's consolidated financial statements for the year ended December 31, year 2. Both Rain and Snow paid dividends to investors. Ignore income tax considerations.

Responses to be selected

A. Sum of amounts on Rain and Snow's separate unconsolidated financial statements
B. Less than the sum of amounts on Rain and Snow's separate unconsolidated financial statements but not the same as the amount on either
C. Same as amount for Rain only
D. Same as amount for Snow only
E. Eliminated entirely in consolidation
F. Shown in consolidated financial statements but not in separate unconsolidated financial statements
G. Neither in consolidated nor in separate unconsolidated financial statements

	(A)	(B)	(C)	(D)	(E)	(F)
1. Cash	○	○	○	○	○	○
2. Investment in subsidiary	○	○	○	○	○	○
3. Noncontrolling interest	○	○	○	○	○	○
4. Common stock	○	○	○	○	○	○
5. Beginning retained earnings	○	○	○	○	○	○
6. Dividends paid	○	○	○	○	○	○

Task-Based Simulation 12 Solution

```
┌──────────┐
│ Concepts │
│     ┌──────────────────────┐
│     │ Authoritative Literature │
│     │            ┌──────┐
│     │            │ Help │
└─────┴────────────┴──────┘
```

	(A)	(B)	(C)	(D)	(E)	(F)	(G)
1. Cash	●	○	○	○	○	○	○
2. Investment in subsidiary	○	○	○	○	●	○	○
3. Noncontrolling interest	○	○	○	○	○	●	○
4. Common stock	○	○	●	○	○	○	○
5. Beginning retained earnings	○	○	●	○	○	○	○
6. Dividends paid	○	○	●	○	○	○	○

Explanations

1. **(A)** Consolidated statements are prepared as if the parent and subsidiaries are one economic entity. Therefore, cash is included in the consolidated balance sheet at their full amounts regardless of the percentage ownership held by the parent.
2. **(E)** In the consolidated balance sheet, the parent company's "Investment in subsidiary" should be eliminated completely and replaced by the net assets of the subsidiary.
3. **(F)** The percentage of the subsidiary's stockholders' equity not owned by the parent company represents the noncontrolling interest's share of the net assets of the subsidiary. This amount is only reported in the consolidated balance sheet in the equity section.
4. **(C)** In the consolidated balance sheet the subsidiary's common stock is not reported. Therefore, the parent's common stock equals the consolidated common stock.
5. **(C)** In the consolidated balance sheet, the subsidiary's beginning retained earnings is not reported. Therefore, the parent's beginning retained earnings equals the consolidated beginning retained earnings.
6. **(C)** The dividends paid by the subsidiary are eliminated in the consolidated financial statements. Ninety percent of the dividends paid are eliminated along with the "Investment in subsidiary" elimination. The

remaining 10% is reflected in "Noncontrolling Interest." Therefore, only the parent's dividends paid are included on the consolidated financial statements.

General-Purpose Financial Statements: Consolidated Financial Statements: Intercompany (I/C) Transactions and Balances

Intercompany (I/C) Transactions and Balances—Introduction

Task-Based Simulation 13

Wilson Corporation has several consolidated subsidiaries. You have been asked to research the professional literature to determine how intercompany transactions are treated for financial reporting purposes. Place the citation for the excerpt from the Professional Standards that provides this information in the answer box below.

Task-Based Simulation 13 Solution

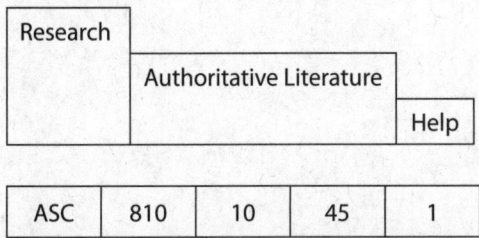

ASC	810	10	45	1

Intercompany (I/C) Bonds

Task-Based Simulation 14

On January 1, year 2, Near purchases 100% of the stock of Far in a transaction that was properly accounted for as a business combination. **Items 1 through 3** below represent transactions between Near and Far during year 2. Prepare the eliminating entries in general journal format for each of these transactions.

1. On January 3, year 2, Near sold equipment with an original cost of $30,000 and a carrying value of $15,000 to Far for $36,000. The equipment had a remaining life of three years and was depreciated using the straight-line method by both companies.

2. During year 2, Near sold merchandise to Far for $60,000, which included a profit of $20,000. At December 31, year 2, half of this merchandise remained in Far's inventory.

3. On December 31, year 2, Near paid $91,000 to purchase $100,000 of the outstanding bonds issued by Far. The bonds mature on December 31, year 6, and were originally issued at par ($100,000). The bonds pay interest annually on December 31 of each year, and the interest was paid to the prior investor immediately before Near's purchase of the bonds.

Task-Based Simulation 14 Solution

Journal Entries		
	Authoritative Literature	
		Help

1.

Gain on equipment	21,000	
Accumulated depreciation		15,000
Equipment		6,000
Accumulated depreciation	7,000	
Depreciation expense		7,000

2.

Sales	60,000	
Cost of goods sold		50,000
Ending inventory		10,000

3.

Bonds payable	100,000	
Discount on bonds	9,000	
Gain on retirement of bonds		9,000
Investment in bonds		100,000

Explanations

1. **($14,000)** When preparing consolidated financial statements, the objective is to restate the accounts as if the intercompany transactions had not occurred. Therefore, the year 2 gain on sale of equipment of $21,000 ($36,000 – $15,000) must be eliminated, since the consolidated entity has not realized any gain. In addition, for consolidated statement purposes, year 2 depreciation is based on the original cost of the equipment to Near. This elimination entry can be made in two separate entries. The first entry eliminated the gain, and restores the accumulated depreciation and equipment accounts as if the intercompany sale were never made. The second entry adjusts the current year depreciation expense to the amount that would have been recorded if the sale were never made. New depreciation is $36,000 ÷ 3 years = $12,000 for Far. Near's depreciation was book value $15,000 ÷ 3 years = $5,000 per year. Therefore, depreciation expense must be adjusted by $12,000 – $5,000 = $7,000.

2. **($10,000)** Unrealized profit in ending inventory arises when intercompany sales are made at prices above cost and the merchandise is not resold to third parties prior to year-end. The profit is unrealized because the inventory has not yet been sold outside the consolidated entity. In this case, one half of the merchandise was left in Far's inventory at year-end. For the consolidated entity, one half of the $20,000 profit has not been earned and must be eliminated.

3. **($9,000)** When Near purchased the bonds from an investor outside the consolidated entity, the bonds are viewed as retired from a consolidated viewpoint since there is no longer any obligation to an outside party. Therefore, the consolidated entity would recognize an ordinary gain of $9,000 ($100,000 carrying value of the bonds – $91,000 purchase price) on the retirement of the debt.

Task-Based Simulation 15

Presented below are selected amounts from the separate unconsolidated financial statements of Poe Corp. and its 90%-owned subsidiary, Shaw Co., at December 31, year 2. Additional information follows:

	Poe	Shaw
Selected income statement amounts		
Sales	$710,000	$530,000
Cost of goods sold	490,000	370,000
Gain on sale of equipment	–	21,000
Earnings from investment in subsidiary	63,000	–
Interest expense	–	16,000
Depreciation	25,000	20,000
Selected balance sheet amounts		
Cash	$50,000	$15,000
Inventories	229,000	150,000
Equipment	440,000	360,000
Accumulated depreciation	(200,000)	(120,000)
Investment in Shaw	191,000	–
Investment in Shaw bonds	100,000	–
Discount on bonds	(9,000)	–
Bonds payable	–	(200,000)
Common stock	(100,000)	(10,000)
Additional paid-in capital	(250,000)	(40,000)
Retained earnings	(404,000)	(140,000)

(Continued)

	Poe	Shaw
Selected statement of retained earnings amounts		
Beginning balance, December 31, year 1	$272,000	$100,000
Net income	212,000	70,000
Dividends paid	80,000	30,000

Additional information

- On January 2, year 2, Poe, Inc. purchased 90% of Shaw Co.'s 100,000 outstanding common stock for cash of $155,000. On that date, the fair value of the noncontrolling interest was $1.70 per share. On that date, Shaw's stockholders' equity equaled $150,000 and the fair values of Shaw's identifiable assets and liabilities equaled their carrying amounts. Poe has accounted for the purchase as an acquisition.
- On January 3, year 2, Poe sold equipment with an original cost of $30,000 and a carrying value of $15,000 to Shaw for $36,000. The equipment had a remaining life of three years and was depreciated using the straight-line method by both companies.
- During year 2, Poe sold merchandise to Shaw for $60,000, which included a profit of $20,000. At December 31, year 2, half of this merchandise remained in Shaw's inventory.
- On December 31, year 2, Poe paid $91,000 to purchase 50% of the outstanding bonds issued by Shaw. The bonds mature on December 31, 2015, and were originally issued at par. The bonds pay interest annually on December 31 of each year, and the interest was paid to the prior investor immediately before Poe's purchase of the bonds.
- On September 4, year 2, Shaw paid cash dividends of $30,000.
- On December 31, year 2, Poe recorded its equity in Shaw's earnings.

Calculate the amounts that will appear on Poe's consolidated financial statement on December 31, year 2.

1. Cash
2. Goodwill
3. Equipment
4. Common stock
5. Investment in Shaw
6. Dividends
7. Bonds payable
8. Noncontrolling interest

Task-Based Simulation 15 Solution

Financial Statement Amounts

Authoritative Literature

Help

Calculate the amounts that will appear on Poe's consolidated financial statement on December 31, year 2.

1.	Cash	$65,000
2.	Goodwill	$22,000
3.	Equipment	$794,000
4.	Common stock	$100,000
5.	Investment in Shaw	$0
6.	Dividends	$80,000
7.	Bonds payable	$100,000
8.	Noncontrolling interest	$21,000

Explanations

1. $50,000 + $15,000 = $65,000
2. The goodwill from Poe's 90% purchase of Shaw can be determined as follows:

Acquisition cost	$155,000
+ Fair value of noncontrolling interest (10,000 shares × $1.70)	17,000
Fair value of interests	172,000
– Fair value of net identifiable assets	(150,000)
Goodwill	$22,000

3. $440,000 + $360,000 – $6,000 = $794,000
4. $100,000, common stock of parent
5. The investment in Shaw account is eliminated.
6. Dividends paid of the subsidiary are eliminated.
7. $100,000: $200,000 bonds payable – $100,000 bonds payable eliminated
8. Noncontrolling interest

Fair value at acquisition date	$17,000
+ 10% net income	7,000
– 10% dividend	(3,000)
End of year noncontrolling interest	$21,000

General-Purpose Financial Statements

Exit or Disposal Activities and Discontinued Operations

Task-Based Simulation 16

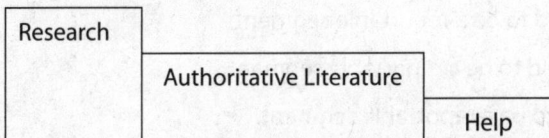

Assume that you are assigned to the audit of Lopez Corporation. Lopez has discontinued one of its business components, and the CFO of Lopez has asked you whether this should be reported as discontinued operations on the income statement. Which section of the Professional Standards provides the conditions that must exist for the component to be presented as discontinued operations?

Enter your response in the answer fields below.

Task-Based Simulation 16 Solution

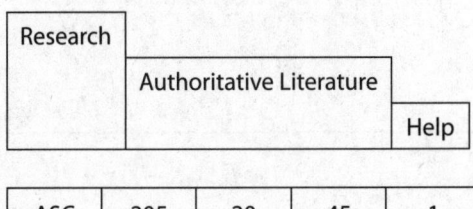

ASC	205	20	45	1

Public Company Reporting Topics (SEC, EPS, Interim, and Segment)

Segment Reporting

Task-Based Simulation 17

Income, Revenue, Asset, Reportable Segment Tests

Authoritative Literature

Help

Caslow Co. is a new manufacturing company located in the United States, with divisions that operate in Spain, Turkey, and Thailand.

Each division has several reporting units that report its activities and financial information to the chief operating decision maker. Below is a list of the units and information for each unit of the three divisions. All amounts are in thousands.

Division	Reporting unit	Total revenue	Total income	Total assets	External revenue	Affiliated revenue
Spain	A	$100,000	$20,000	$260,000	$60,000	$40,000
	B	45,000	6,000	110,000	20,000	25,000
Turkey	C	85,000	19,000	120,000	50,000	35,000
	D	65,000	11,000	150,000	50,000	15,000
	E	25,000	5,000	60,000	25,000	0
Thailand	F	38,000	7,000	90,000	30,000	8,000
	G	120,000	39,000	290,000	50,000	70,000

Identify which reporting units meet the income threshold to be a reportable segment.

Identify which reporting units meet the revenue threshold to be a reportable segment.

Identify which reporting units meet the asset threshold to be a reportable segment.

Which segments are reportable?

	Division	Reporting unit	Income threshold	Revenue threshold	Asset threshold	Reportable segment
1.	Spain	A	O	O	O	O
2.		B	O	O	O	O
3.	Turkey	C	O	O	O	O
4.		D	O	O	O	O
5.		E	O	O	O	O
6.	Thailand	F	O	O	O	O
7.		G	O	O	O	O

Task-Based Simulation 17 Solution

Income, Revenue, Asset, Reportable Segment Tests

Authoritative Literature

Help

Total income = $107,000

$107,000 × 10% = $10,700

Identify which reporting units meet the income threshold to be a reportable segment.

Total revenue = $478,000

$478,000 × 10% = $47,800

Identify which reporting units meet the revenue threshold to be a reportable segment.

Total assets = $1,060,000

$1,060,000 × 10% = $106,000

Identify which reporting units meet the asset threshold to be a reportable segment.

Which segments are reportable?

	Division	Reporting unit	Income threshold	Revenue threshold	Asset threshold	Reportable segment
1.	Spain	A	●	●	●	●
2.		B	○	○	●	●
3.	Turkey	C	●	●	●	●
4.		D	●	●	●	●
5.		E	○	○	○	○
6.	Thailand	F	○	○	○	○
7.		G	●	●	●	●

Task-Based Simulation 18

Assume that you are assigned to the audit of Whitman Corporation. The CFO of Whitman is working on developing the required information regarding business segments and has asked you to explain the tests to determine if a company must report information about a particular operating segment. Which section of the Professional Standards provides the tests that determine when a company must report information about an operating segment? Enter your response in the answer fields below.

Task-Based Simulation 18 Solution

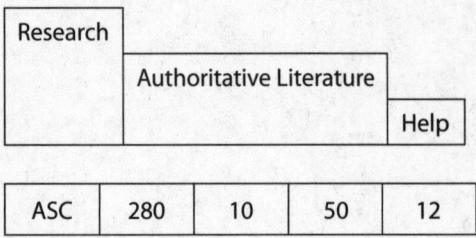

ASC	280	10	50	12

Task-Based Simulation 19

Indicate whether each of the following statements is True or False.

Statement	True	False
1. The method used for reporting segment information is the asset-liability approach.	○	○
2. If management judges that an operating segment is reportable in year 1 and is of continuing significance, information about that segment should be reported in year 2 even if it does not meet the requirements for reportability in year 2.	○	○
3. An enterprise must report separate information about an operating segment if its assets are 10% or more of the combined assets of all operating segments.	○	○
4. An enterprise must report separately the costs and expenses incurred by each segment.	○	○
5. One of the requirements of segment reporting is to report cash flows for each reportable segment.	○	○
6. An enterprise must report the interest revenue for each reportable segment if this information is normally reviewed by the chief operating decision maker.	○	○

Task-Based Simulation 19 Solution

Statement	True	False
1. The method used for reporting segment information is the asset-liability approach.	○	●
2. If management judges that an operating segment is reportable in year 1 and is of continuing significance, information about that segment should be reported in year 2 even if it does not meet the requirements for reportability in year 2.	●	○
3. An enterprise must report separate information about an operating segment if its assets are 10% or more of the combined assets of all operating segments.	●	○
4. An enterprise must report separately the costs and expenses incurred by each segment.	○	●
5. One of the requirements of segment reporting is to report cash flows for each reportable segment.	○	●
6. An enterprise must report the interest revenue for each reportable segment if this information is normally reviewed by the chief operating decision maker.	●	○

Task-Based Simulation 20

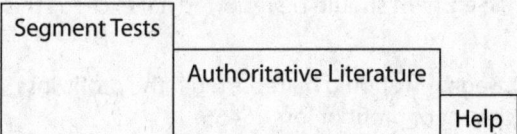

Barnet Co. has distinct operating units in its operations. Each of these components of the business reports its activities and its financial information to the chief operating decision maker. The company has no foreign operations, sales, or major individual customers. Below is information provided by Barnet's operating units (in millions).

Reporting unit	Total revenue	External revenue	Affiliated revenue	Income	Assets
A	4,200	3,000	1,200	1,200	15,900
B	500	200	300	(300)	6,700
C	800	650	150	250	4,420
D	1,400	800	600	510	7,800
E	2,300	1,200	1,100	(900)	6,500
F	5,000	4,000	1,000	2,600	28,600

Identify which of the segments meets the quantitative threshold for revenues, profits/losses, and assets.

	Reporting unit	Revenue threshold	Profits/losses threshold	Asset threshold	Reportable segment
1.	A	○	○	○	○
2.	B	○	○	○	○
3.	C	○	○	○	○
4.	D	○	○	○	○
5.	E	○	○	○	○
6.	F	○	○	○	○

Task-Based Simulation 20 Solution

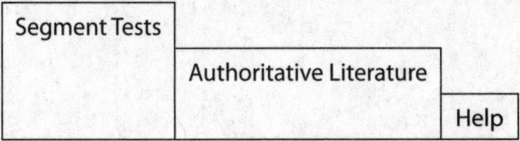

	Reporting unit	Revenue threshold	Profits/losses threshold	Asset threshold	Reportable segment
1.	A	●	●	●	●
2.	B	○	○	○	○
3.	C	○	○	○	○
4.	D	○	●	●	●
5.	E	●	●	○	●
6.	F	●	●	●	●

Explanations

Revenue threshold: Total revenues $14,200 × 10% = $1,420. Segment should be reported if it exceeds this revenue amount.

Income threshold: Total profit = $4,560. Total loss = $1,200. Segment should be reported if the profit/loss in absolute value is greater than 10% of $4,560 (the larger amount of profit or loss), $456.

Asset threshold: Total assets $69,920 × 10% = $6,992. Segment should be reported if it exceeds this asset amount.

Segment is reportable if it meets any one of the three threshold tests.

A meets all tests.
B and C do not meet any of the tests.
D meets the income and asset test.
E meets the revenue and income/loss test.
F meets all three tests.

Task-Based Simulation 21

Assume that you are assigned to the audit of Keger Corporation. The CFO of Keger has asked you to determine the information that must be disclosed about a reportable operating segment of the business. Which section of the Professional Standards provides guidance on the information that must be disclosed about a reportable segment? Enter your response in the answer fields below.

Task-Based Simulation 21 Solution

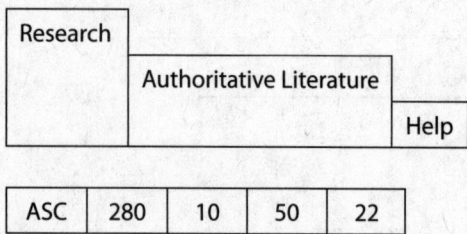

ASC	280	10	50	22

Select Financial Statement Accounts

Cash and Cash Equivalents

Cash

Task-Based Simulation 22

Concepts		
	Authoritative Literature	
		Help

Identify which of the following items are disclosed as cash or cash equivalents on the balance sheet.

	Cash	Not Cash
1. Checking accounts	○	○
2. Treasury stock	○	○
3. Treasury bills	○	○
4. Money market funds	○	○
5. Petty cash	○	○
6. Trading securities	○	○
7. Savings accounts	○	○
8. Sinking fund cash	○	○
9. Compensating balances against long-term borrowings	○	○
10. Cash restricted for new building	○	○
11. Postdated checks for customers	○	○
12. Available-for-sale securities	○	○

Task-Based Simulation 22 Solution

Concepts		
	Authoritative Literature	
		Help

	Cash	Not Cash
1. Checking accounts	●	○
2. Treasury stock	○	●
3. Treasury bills	●	○
4. Money market funds	●	○
5. Petty cash	●	○

(Continued)

	Cash	Not Cash
6. Trading securities	○	●
7. Savings accounts	●	○
8. Sinking fund cash	○	●
9. Compensating balances against long-term borrowings	○	●
10. Cash restricted for new building	○	●
11. Postdated checks for customers	○	●
12. Available-for-sale securities	○	●

Receivables

Uncollectible—Direct Write-Off and Allowance

Task-Based Simulation 23

Situation

Sigma Corp. has the following information regarding its allowance for uncollectible accounts.

Allowance for Uncollectible Accounts and Provision for Uncollectible Accounts

Balance December 31, year 1	$28,000
Write-offs during year 2	(27,000)
Recoveries during year 2	7,000
Balance before year 2 provision	8,000
Required allowance at December 31, year 2	39,000
Year 2 provision	$31,000

Prepare the journal entries for the write-offs and recoveries for year 2, and for the provision for uncollectible accounts expense at December 31, year 2.

Write-offs

Recoveries

Uncollectible accounts expense at December 31, year 2

Task-Based Simulation 23 Solution

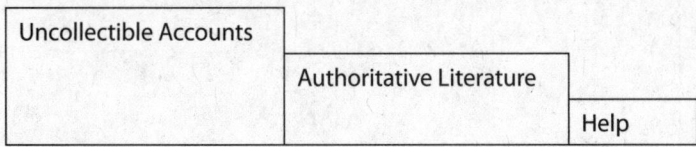

Write-offs

Allowance for uncollectible accounts	27,000	
Accounts receivable		27,000

Recoveries

Accounts receivable	7,000	
Allowance for uncollectible accounts		7,000

To reinstate the account receivable

Cash	7,000	
Accounts receivable		7,000

To show payment on the account

Uncollectible accounts expense at December 31, year 2

Uncollectible accounts expense	31,000	
Allowance for uncollectible accounts		31,000

Allowance—Income Statement and Balance Sheet Approach

Task-Based Simulation 24

Situation

Sigma Co. began operations on January 1, year 1. On December 31, year 1, Sigma provided for uncollectible accounts based on 1% of annual credit sales. On January 1, year 2, Sigma changed its method of determining its allowance for uncollectible accounts by applying certain percentages to the accounts receivable aging as follows:

Days Past Invoice Date	Percent Deemed to Be Uncollectible
0–30	1
31–90	5
91–180	20
Over 180	80

In addition, Sigma wrote off all accounts receivable that were over one year old. The following additional information relates to the years ended December 31, year 2, and year 1:

	Year 2	Year 1
Credit sales	$3,000,000	$2,800,000
Collections	2,915,000	2,400,000
Accounts written off	27,000	None
Recovery of accounts previously written off	7,000	None
Days past invoice date at 12/31		
0–30	300,000	250,000
31–90	80,000	90,000
91–180	60,000	45,000
Over 180	25,000	15,000

Complete the following schedules showing the calculation of the allowance for uncollectible accounts at December 31, year 2 and the calculation for uncollectible accounts expense for year 2.

Sigma Company
SCHEDULE OF CALCULATION OF ALLOWANCE FOR UNCOLLECTIBLE ACCOUNTS
December 31, Year 2

	Amounts of accounts receivable	Percentage of uncollectible accounts	Estimate of uncollectible accounts
0 to 30 days	_____	_____	_____
31 to 90 days	_____	_____	_____
91 to 180 days	_____	_____	_____
Over 180 days	_____	_____	_____
Total accounts receivable	_____		
Total allowance for uncollectible accounts			_____

Schedule of Uncollectible Accounts Expense

Balance December 31, year 1	
Write-offs during year 2	
Recoveries during year 2	
Balance before year 2 provision	
Required allowance at December 31, year 2	
Year 2 provision	

Task-Based Simulation 24 Solution

Uncollectible Accounts		
	Authoritative Literature	
		Help

Schedule to calculate allowance for uncollectible accounts.

Sigma Company
SCHEDULE OF CALCULATION OF ALLOWANCE FOR UNCOLLECTIBLE ACCOUNTS
December 31, Year 2

	Amounts of accounts receivable	Percentage of uncollectible accounts	Estimate of uncollectible accounts
0 to 30 days	$300,000	× 1%	$3,000
31 to 90 days	80,000	× 5%	4,000
91 to 180 days	60,000	× 20%	12,000
Over 180 days	25,000	× 80%	20,000
Total accounts receivable	$465,000		
Total allowance for uncollectible accounts			$39,000

Explanations

1. This problem consists of two related parts: part a requires a calculation of the allowance for uncollectible accounts at 12/31/Y2 using an aging approach, and part b requires a computation of the year 2 provision for uncollectible accounts (uncollectible accounts expense). The solutions approach is to quickly review the basics of accounting for uncollectible accounts, visualize the solution format, and begin. Some candidates may benefit from preparation of T-accounts (see item 4 below).
2. When using the aging approach, the **total** uncollectible accounts (in other words, the required ending balance in the allowance account) is estimated by applying a different percentage to the various age categories. The percentage increases as the age of the receivables increases because the older a receivable is, the less likely is its ultimate collection.
   2.1. In this case, Sigma estimates that 1% of its receivables in the 0 to 30 days age category will prove to be uncollectible. Therefore, of that $300,000 of accounts receivable, it is estimated that $3,000 (1% × $300,000) will be uncollectible. Similar computations are performed for the other age categories, resulting in an estimate that $39,000 of the $465,000 accounts receivable will prove to be uncollectible. This is the required 12/31/Y2 balance in the allowance account.
3. When using the aging approach, the first step is to compute the required ending balance in the allowance account (as discussed in items 2 and 2.1 above). The second step is to compute the uncollectible accounts expense necessary to bring the **unadjusted** allowance balance up to the **required** allowance balance.
   3.1. The only item affecting the allowance account in year 1 was the recording of uncollectible accounts expense of $28,000 (1% × $2,800,000 credit sales). Therefore, the 1/1/Y2 balance in this account is $28,000. No adjustment is necessary for the change in the method of estimating this expense (from percent of sales to aging schedule) because any such change is handled prospectively.

> **NOTE:**
> Using the aging percents given also results in a $28,000 balance at 1/1/Y2. Even if the result was different, though, no adjustment is necessary.

   3.2. During year 2, this $28,000 credit balance was decreased by write-offs of $27,000 (debit allowance, credit AR) and increased by $7,000 of recoveries (debit AR, credit allowance; and debit cash, credit AR). Therefore, the 12/31/Y2 balance in the allowance account, before adjustment, is $8,000 ($28,000 - $27,000 + $7,000).

3.3 To increase the allowance account from $8,000 (see 3.2 above) to $39,000 (see 2.1 above), a provision for uncollectible accounts (uncollectible accounts expense) of $31,000 must be recorded for year 2.

4. Some candidates may benefit from the preparation of T-accounts for the allowance account and accounts receivable. These T-accounts are provided below.

T-accounts for year 1

AR

Sales	2,800,000	2,400,000	Collections
12/31/Y1	400,000		

Allowance

		28,000	Provision
		28,000	12/31/Y1

Computation of year 2 provision

Balance December 31, year 1	$28,000
Write-offs during year 2	(27,000)
Recoveries during year 2	7,000
Balance before year 2 provision	8,000
Required allowance at December 31, year 2	39,000
Year 2 provision	$31,000

Criteria for Sale of Receivables

Task-Based Simulation 25

Transfer of Receivables		
	Authoritative Literature	
		Help

Jarvis enters into an agreement with First Finance Corporation to sell a group of receivables without recourse. The total face value of the receivables is $150,000. First Finance Corp. will charge 15% interest on the weighted-average time to maturity of the receivables of 45 days plus a 2% fee.

Prepare the journal entry to record the transfer of the receivables.

Task-Based Simulation 25 Solution

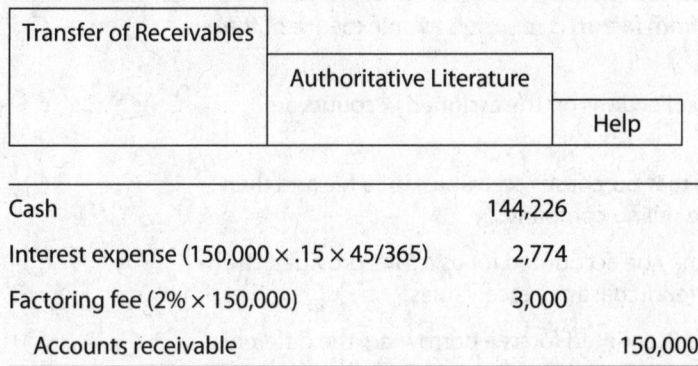

Cash	144,226
Interest expense (150,000 × .15 × 45/365)	2,774
Factoring fee (2% × 150,000)	3,000
Accounts receivable	150,000

Task-Based Simulation 26

Tammy Yee, the partner on the audit of Huber Corporation, has asked you to perform some research. The company has factored some accounts receivable. Tammy wants to know the criteria to determine when control has been surrendered in a transfer of receivables. Place the citation for the excerpt from the Professional Standards that provides this information in the answer fields below.

Task-Based Simulation 26 Solution

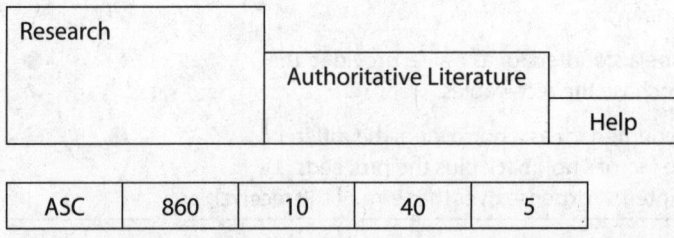

ASC	860	10	40	5

Factoring, Assignment, and Pledging

Task-Based Simulation 27

Chester Company has transactions involving current assets and current liabilities. Complete the various components of the simulation for Chester. Determine whether each statement is True or False.

	True	False
1. The balance in "factor's holdback" (due from factor) is reported as an expense of the period.	○	○
2. In a specific assignment of receivables, collections on the assigned accounts are generally remitted to the assignor.	○	○
3. Factors are banks or finance companies that purchase receivables for a fee and then collect the remittances directly from the selling company.	○	○
4. A transfer of receivables with recourse may be accounted for as a sale, provided the transferee can require the transferor to repurchase the receivables.	○	○
5. In a transfer of receivables with recourse accounted for as a borrowing, the difference between the receivables and the total of the factor's holdback plus the proceeds is a financing cost that should be amortized to interest expense over the term of the receivables.	○	○

Task-Based Simulation 27 Solution

```
┌─────────────┐
│ Concepts    │
│      ┌──────────────────────┐
│      │ Authoritative Literature │
│      │        ┌───────────┐
│      │        │ Help      │
└──────┴────────┴───────────┘
```

	True	False
1. The balance in "factor's holdback" (due from factor) is reported as an expense of the period.	○	●
2. In a specific assignment of receivables, collections on the assigned accounts are generally remitted to the assignor.	●	○
3. Factors are banks or finance companies that purchase receivables for a fee and then collect the remittances directly from the selling company.	○	●
4. A transfer of receivables with recourse may be accounted for as a sale, provided the transferee can require the transferor to repurchase the receivables.	○	●
5. In a transfer of receivables with recourse accounted for as a borrowing, the difference between the receivables and the total of the factor's holdback plus the proceeds is a financing cost that should be amortized to interest expense over the term of the receivables.	●	○

Explanations

1. (**F**) "Factor's holdback" accounts for the proceeds retained by the factor to cover estimated sales discounts, sales returns, and sales allowances. When all amounts have been collected by the factor, the balance in factor's margin is returned to the seller. Therefore, this account is a receivable reported as a current asset on the balance sheet.
2. (**T**) A specific assignment of receivables bestows more formal rights upon the assignee (lender) in that the AR do not simply collateralize the loan, but collections on the assigned accounts are actually remitted to the assignor who remits them to the assignee (lender).
3. (**F**) Once a company sells receivables to a factor it normally has no further involvement with the receivables. The factor usually collects the remittances directly from the **customer**.
4. (**F**) Transfers of receivables in which the transferee can require the transferor to repurchase the receivables may not be considered a sale.
5. (**T**) The difference between the amount of receivables sold to a factor in a borrowing transaction and the total of the factor's holdback plus the proceeds is recorded in a "Discount on Transferred AR" or interest expense account. This account represents interest cost and should be recognized over the term of the receivables. If interest expense is debited, an adjusting entry to defer some of the interest as "Discount" would be required if some of the discount pertains to a later period.

Task-Based Simulation 28

Journal Entries

Authoritative Literature

Help

Lake Company has the following items relating to the transfer of accounts and notes receivable. For each item, match the transaction with the appropriate journal entry. Entries may be used once, more than once, or not at all.

Journal entries

A. Cash   xxx
   Interest expense   xxx
       Liability on discounted NR   xxx
       Interest revenue   xxx

B. Cash   xxx
   Factor's holdback   xxx
   Interest expense (discount)   xxx
       Liability on transferred AR   xxx

C. Cash   xxx
   Finance charge   xxx
   AR assigned   xxx
       Note payable   xxx
       AR   xxx

D. Cash   xxx
   Factor's holdback   xxx
   Loss on sale of AR   xxx
       AR   xxx

E. Parenthetical or note disclosure only.

F. Cash   xxx
   Loss on sale of NR   xxx
       NR   xxx
       Interest revenue   xxx

	(A)	(B)	(C)	(D)	(E)	(F)
1. Lake transfers receivables by surrendering control. Collection is to be made by the purchaser (factor), who assumes risk of loss.	O	O	O	O	O	O
2. Lake specifically assigns a portion of its receivables as collateral for a loan. Collections from the assigned receivables will be used to repay the loan and interest.	O	O	O	O	O	O
3. Lake pledges its receivables as collateral to secure a loan and the debtor collects the proceeds.	O	O	O	O	O	O
4. Lake sells accounts receivable to a factor in a transaction considered a borrowing.	O	O	O	O	O	O
5. Lake transfers a note receivable by surrendering control over it. The transfer was on a without-recourse basis.	O	O	O	O	O	O
6. Lake pledges its accounts receivable as security for a loan.	O	O	O	O	O	O

Task-Based Simulation 28 Solution

Journal Entries		
	Authoritative Literature	
		Help

	(A)	(B)	(C)	(D)	(E)	(F)
1. Lake transfers receivables by surrendering control. Collection is to be made by the purchaser (factor), who assumes risk of loss.	○	○	○	●	○	○
2. Lake specifically assigns a portion of its receivables as collateral for a loan. Collections from the assigned receivables will be used to repay the loan and interest.	○	○	●	○	○	○
3. Lake pledges its receivables as collateral to secure a loan and the debtor collects the proceeds.	○	○	○	○	●	○
4. Lake sells accounts receivable to a factor in a transaction considered a borrowing.	○	●	○	○	○	○
5. Lake transfers a note receivable by surrendering control over it. The transfer was on a without-recourse basis.	○	○	○	○	○	●
6. Lake pledges its accounts receivable as security for a loan.	○	○	○	○	●	○

Explanations

1. (**D**) In this transaction, receivables are factored by surrendering control and without recourse. This constitutes an outright sale of the receivables in that title, risk of loss, and rights to future benefits are all transferred. Therefore, a loss on the transaction is recognized.
2. (**C**) In a specific assignment of receivables, AR assigned are identified by placing them in an AR assigned account. A finance charge is assessed on assignment transactions that are borrowings.
3. (**E**) When AR are pledged, the receivables serve as collateral for a loan but the proceeds are not remitted to the lender. In this case, the amount of AR pledged is reported at the balance sheet date either parenthetically or in the notes.
4. (**B**) In this transaction, considered a borrowing, receivables are considered to be factored with recourse. Thus, the transaction is viewed as a loan collateralized by AR and the amount of the proceeds plus the factor's holdback and interest charged should be reported as a liability.
5. (**F**) A note discounted on which control is surrendered and the terms include without recourse is considered a sales transaction upon which a loss should be recognized. Notes receivable should be credited.
6. (**E**) A general assignment of receivables is another term for pledging AR, and thus should be disclosed parenthetically or in the notes to the financial statements (no journal entry).

Inventory

Introduction to Inventory

Task-Based Simulation 29

Concepts		
	Authoritative Literature	
		Help

Indicate whether each of the following is included in the cost of inventory.

	Included	Not Included
1. Merchandise purchased for resale	○	○
2. Freight-out	○	○
3. Direct materials	○	○
4. Sales returns	○	○
5. Packaging for shipment to customer	○	○
6. Factory overhead	○	○
7. Interest on inventory loan	○	○
8. Purchase discounts not taken	○	○
9. Freight-in	○	○
10. Direct labor	○	○

Task-Based Simulation 29 Solution

Concepts

Authoritative Literature

Help

	Included	Not Included
1. Merchandise purchased for resale	●	○
2. Freight-out	○	●
3. Direct materials	●	○
4. Sales returns	○	●
5. Packaging for shipment to customer	○	●
6. Factory overhead	●	○
7. Interest on inventory loan	○	●
8. Purchase discounts not taken	○	●
9. Freight-in	●	○
10. Direct labor	●	○

Explanations

1. **(I)** Merchandise purchased for resale is a part of inventory.
2. **(N)** Freight-out is part of selling expense.
3. **(I)** Direct materials are part of work in process, which is an inventory account for manufacturers.
4. **(N)** Sales returns are a contra account to sales, and are not part of inventory.
5. **(N)** Packaging for shipment to customer is part of selling expenses.
6. **(I)** Factory overhead is part of work in process, which is an inventory account for manufacturing firms.
7. **(N)** Interest on inventory loan is an operating expense. Interest cost should not be capitalized for assets that are in use or ready for their intended use in the earnings activities of the enterprise.
8. **(N)** Purchase discounts lost are considered a financing expense and are excluded from the cost of inventory.
9. **(I)** Freight-in is part of getting the goods in place to sell and should be included in inventory.
10. **(I)** Direct labor is part of work in process, and is an inventory account for manufacturing firms.

Task-Based Simulation 30

Assume that you are assigned to the audit of the inventories of Litton Corporation. Research the Professional Standards for the section that provides guidance on the items that should be included in the cost of inventory. Enter your response in the answer fields below.

Task-Based Simulation 30 Solution

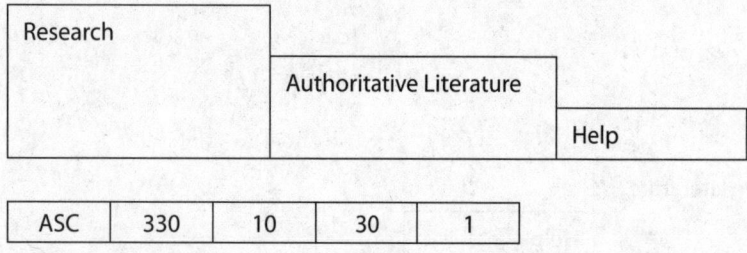

ASC	330	10	30	1

Periodic Inventory System and Cost-Flow Assumption

Task-Based Simulation 31

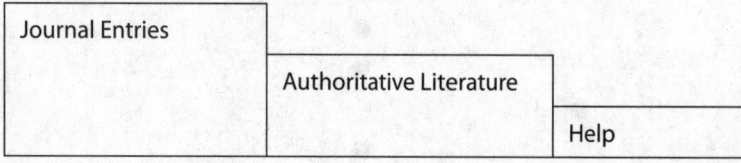

Blaedon uses the periodic inventory method for inventories. Prepare the journal entries for each of the following transactions. Blaedon uses the gross method for recording inventory transactions.

1. On January 5, year 2, purchased $17,000 of garden tillers on account from Bestbuilt Tillers, terms 2/10, n/30, FOB destination. Freight charges were $200.
2. On January 10, year 2, returned garden tillers worth $2,000 to Best-built Tillers due to defects.
3. On January 14, year 2, paid for the remaining tillers purchased in 1.
4. On January 28, year 2, purchased $30,000 of lawn mowers from Lawn Giant, terms 3/10, n/30, FOB shipping point. The freight charges were $820.
5. On February 6, year 2, paid for the lawn mowers purchased in 4. from Lawn Giant.

Task-Based Simulation 31 Solution

1. On January 5, year 2, purchased $17,000 of garden tillers on account from Bestbuilt Tillers, terms 2/10, n/30, FOB destination. Freight charges were $200.

Purchases	17,000	
Accounts payable		17,000

2. On January 10, year 2, returned garden tillers worth $2,000 to Bestbuilt Tillers due to defects.

Accounts payable	2,000	
Purchase returns		2,000

3. On January 14, year 2, paid for the remaining tillers purchased in 1.

Accounts payable	15,000	
Purchase discounts		300*
Cash		14,700

* $15,000 \times .02 = 300$

4. On January 28, year 2, purchased $30,000 of lawn mowers from Lawn Giant, terms 3/10, n/30, FOB shipping point. The freight charges were $820.

Purchases	30,000	
Freight-in	820	
Accounts payable		30,820

5. On February 6, year 2, paid for the lawn mowers purchased in 4. from Lawn Giant.

Accounts payable	30,000	
Purchase discounts		900
Cash		29,100

(This assumes the freight bill is paid separately to the freight company)

Dollar-Value LIFO

Task-Based Simulation 32

Below are statements describing inventory and cost flow methods. Identify which method matches each description by clicking on the correct term and placing it in the space provided. You may use a method once, more than once, or not at all.

Methods

Specific identification
Weighted-average
Simple average
Moving-average
First-in, first-out
Last-in, first-out
Dollar-value LIFO
Gross profit

	Method
1. During a period of rising prices, this method results in a higher net income.	_____
2. This method most closely matches the physical flow of inventory.	_____
3. Method that uses historical sales margins to estimate ending inventory.	_____
4. Method that is appropriate when there is a relatively small number of significant dollar value items in inventory.	_____
5. Average cost must be calculated each time additional inventory is purchased.	_____
6. Method that averages the cost of all items on hand and purchased during the period.	_____
7. This method results in the lowest ending inventory in a period of rising prices.	_____
8. Method that uses a price index to measure changes in inventory.	_____
9. If used for tax purposes, this method must also be used for financial reporting purposes.	_____
10. The cost of goods sold balance is the same whether a perpetual or periodic inventory system is used.	_____

Task-Based Simulation 32 Solution

Cost Flow Concepts		
	Authoritative Literature	
		Help

	Method
1. During a period of rising prices, this method results in a higher net income.	FIFO
2. This method most closely matches the physical flow of inventory.	FIFO
3. Method that uses historical sales margins to estimate ending inventory.	Gross Profit
4. Method that is appropriate when there is a relatively small number of significant dollar value items in inventory.	Specific identification
5. Average cost must be calculated each time additional inventory is purchased.	Moving-average
6. Method that averages the cost of all items on hand and purchased during the period.	Weighted-average
7. This method results in the lowest ending inventory in a period of rising prices.	LIFO
8. Method that uses a price index to measure changes in inventory.	Dollar-value LIFO
9. If used for tax purposes, this method must also be used for financial reporting purposes.	LIFO
10. The cost of goods sold balance is the same whether a perpetual or periodic inventory system is used.	FIFO

Property, Plant, and Equipment

Capitalized Costs

Task-Based Simulation 33

Concepts		
	Authoritative Literature	
		Help

For **items 1 through 6**, determine for each item whether the expenditure should be capitalized or expensed as a period cost.

	Capitalize	Expense
1. Freight charges paid for goods held for resale.	○	○
2. In-transit insurance on goods held for resale purchased FOB shipping point.	○	○
3. Interest on note payable for goods held for resale.	○	○
4. Installation of equipment.	○	○
5. Testing of newly purchased equipment.	○	○
6. Cost of current year service contract on equipment.	○	○

Task-Based Simulation 33 Solution

Concepts		
	Authoritative Literature	
		Help

	Capitalize	Expense
1. Freight charges paid for goods held for resale.	●	○
2. In-transit insurance on goods held for resale purchased FOB shipping point.	●	○
3. Interest on note payable for goods held for resale.	○	●
4. Installation of equipment.	●	○
5. Testing of newly purchased equipment.	●	○
6. Cost of current year service contract on equipment.	○	●

Explanations

Items 1 through 6 represent questions concerning expenditures for goods held for resale and equipment and whether these expenditures should be capitalized or expensed as a period cost. The general concept that determines whether expenditures should be product costs and, therefore, capitalized or expensed as period costs is whether or not these expenditures "attach" themselves to the assets of inventory or equipment. Costs that "attach" themselves to assets are those that are directly connected with bringing the goods or equipment to the place of business of the buyer and converting such goods to a salable (inventory) or usable (equipment) condition.

1. (**C**) Freight charges are directly connected with bringing the goods to the place of business of the buyer.
2. (**C**) Insurance charges are directly connected with bringing the goods to the place of business of the buyer.
3. (**E**) Only interest costs related to continued assets constructed for internal use or assets produced as discrete products for sale or lease should be capitalized. The informational benefit of capitalization does not justify the cost of the accounting for the interest as a product cost.

4. **(C)** Direct cost of bringing the equipment to the buyer.
5. **(C)** Direct cost of converting the equipment to a usable condition.
6. **(E)** Does not relate to bringing the equipment to the buyer or putting it into a usable condition.

Interest Capitalization Limits

Task-Based Simulation 34

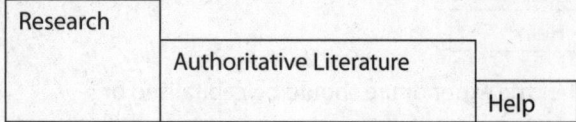

Assume that you are assigned to the audit of Dumas Corporation. Dumas has decided to self-construct a productive asset. Which section of the Professional Standards provides guidance on whether the asset qualifies for capitalization of interest?

Enter your response in the answer fields below.

Task-Based Simulation 34 Solution

ASC	835	20	15	5

Accelerated Depreciation Methods

Task-Based Simulation 35

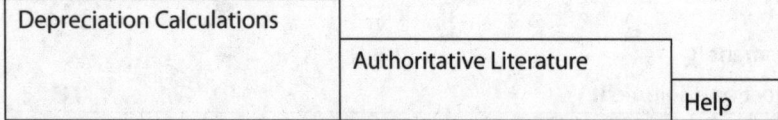

On January 2, year 3, Gray purchased a manufacturing machine for $864,000. The machine has an eight-year estimated life and a $144,000 estimated salvage value. Gray expects to manufacture 1,800,000 units over the life of the machine. During year 4, Gray manufactured 300,000 units.

Calculate depreciation expense on the manufacturing machine for year 4 for each method listed.

	Amount
1. Straight-line.	
2. Double-declining balance.	
3. Sum-of-the-years' digits.	
4. Units of production.	

Task-Based Simulation 35 Solution

1. **($90,000)** Under the straight-line method of depreciation, the depreciation expense would be calculated as follows:

$$\frac{\text{Cost-salvage value}}{\text{Estimated life}} = \frac{\$864{,}000 - 144{,}000}{8} = \$90{,}000$$

Depreciation expense would be $90,000 for all eight years, year 3–2016.

2. **($162,000)** The double-declining balance method is calculated by taking two times the straight-line rate times the net book value at the beginning of each year, but not below the salvage value. Furthermore the salvage value is not deducted to arrive at the depreciable base. The calculation would be as follows:

	NBV		Depreciation expense
Year 3	$864,000 × (1/8 × 2)	=	$216,000
Year 4	($864,000 − 216,000) × (1/8 × 2)	=	$162,000

3. **($140,000)** Under the sum-of-the-years' digits method, the depreciation expense is calculated as follows:

$$\text{Year 3} \quad 8 \div \frac{8(8+1)}{2} \times (\$864{,}000) - \$144{,}000 = \$160{,}000$$

$$\text{Year 4} \quad (7 \div 36) \times (\$864{,}000) - \$144{,}000 = \$140{,}000$$

4. **($120,000)** The units of production method is a type of physical usage depreciation that is based on activity. The formula is as follows:

$$\frac{\text{Current activity/output}}{\text{Total expected activity/output}} \times \text{Depreciable base} = \text{Annual depreciation}$$

Depreciation expense for year 4 is calculated as follows:

$$\frac{300{,}000 \text{ units}}{1{,}800{,}000 \text{ units}} \times (\$864{,}000 - \$144{,}000) = \$120{,}000$$

Impairment—Assets for Use and Held-for-Sale

Task-Based Simulation 36

Assume that you are assigned to the audit of Carson Corporation. Carson has determined that the value of a major productive asset has been impaired. Which section of the Professional Standards provides guidance on how the impairment loss should be presented in Carson's income statement?
Enter your response in the answer fields below.

Task-Based Simulation 36 Solution

ASC	360	10	45	4

Investments

No Significant Influence

Task-Based Simulation 37

Accounting Treatment		
	Accounting Treatment	
		Help

Determine whether each statement is True or False.

	True	False
1. Held-to-maturity securities are classified as current or noncurrent on an individual basis.	○	○
2. For trading securities, some realized gains/losses are excluded from earnings.	○	○
3. A premature sale of held-to-maturity securities may be considered at maturity if at least 80% of the principal has already been collected.	○	○
4. Dividends received on available-for-sale securities decrease the investment account.	○	○
5. A company that owns more than 50% of the outstanding shares of stock of another company must use the fair value method.	○	○

Task-Based Simulation 37 Solution

Accounting Treatment		
	Accounting Treatment	
		Help

	True	False
1. Held-to-maturity securities are classified as current or noncurrent on an individual basis.	●	○
2. For trading securities, some realized gains/losses are excluded from earnings.	●	○
3. A premature sale of held-to-maturity securities may be considered at maturity if at least 80% of the principal has already been collected.	○	●
4. Dividends received on available-for-sale securities decrease the investment account.	○	●
5. A company that owns more than 50% of the outstanding shares of stock of another company must use the fair value method.	○	●

Explanations

1. **(T)** Held-to-maturity securities are classified as current or noncurrent according to how soon they will mature (i.e., a security maturing within one year is classified as current, while one with a more distant maturity date is considered noncurrent).
2. **(T)** Some unrealized holding gains and losses on trading securities could have already been included in income as unrealized components. Thus, to recognize them again upon realization would result in an erroneous doubling of the actual gain/loss.
3. **(F)** Premature sale of held-to-maturity securities are considered at maturity if either (1) the sale occurs so close to maturity that interest rate risk is virtually eliminated, or (2) the sale occurs after at least 85% of the principal has been collected.
4. **(F)** Dividends received on available-for-sale securities are treated as dividend income on the income statement.
5. **(F)** A company that owns more than 50% of the outstanding shares of stock should use the equity method and prepare consolidated financial statements (assuming the company exercises control).

Task-Based Simulation 38

The following information pertains to Dayle, Inc.'s portfolio of marketable investments for the year ended December 31, year 2:

		Fair value	Year 2 activity		Fair value
	Cost	12/31/Y1	Purchases	Sales	12/31/Y2
Held-to-maturity securities					
Security ABC			$100,000		$95,000
Trading securities					
Security DEF	$150,000	$160,000			155,000
Available-for-sale securities					
Security GHI	190,000	165,000		$175,000	
Security JKL	170,000	175,000			160,000

Security ABC was purchased at par. All declines in fair value are considered to be temporary. Dayle does not elect the fair value option for any of its financial assets.

For the following questions, choose from the answer list below.

Answer List	
A.	$0
B.	$5,000
C.	$10,000
D.	$15,000
E.	$25,000
F.	$95,000
G.	$100,000
H.	$150,000
I.	$155,000
J.	$160,000
K.	$170,000

Items 1 through 6 describe amounts to be reported in Dayle's year 2 financial statements. For each item, select from the following list the correct numerical response. An amount may be selected once, more than once, or not at all. Ignore income tax considerations.

		(A)	(B)	(C)	(D)	(E)	(F)	(G)	(H)	(I)	(J)	(K)
						Amount						
1.	Carrying amount of security ABC at December 31, year 2.	○	○	○	○	○	○	○	○	○	○	○
2.	Carrying amount of security DEF at December 31, year 2.	○	○	○	○	○	○	○	○	○	○	○
3.	Carrying amount of security JKL at December 31, year 2.	○	○	○	○	○	○	○	○	○	○	○

Items 4 through 6 require a second response. For each item, indicate whether a gain or a loss is to be reported.

		(A)	(B)	(C)	(D)	(E)	(F)	(G)	(H)	(I)	(J)	(K)	GAIN	LOSS
							Amount							
4.	Recognized gain or loss on sale of security GHI.	○	○	○	○	○	○	○	○	○	○	○	○	○
5.	Unrealized gain or loss to be reported in year 2 net income.	○	○	○	○	○	○	○	○	○	○	○	○	○
6.	Unrealized gain or loss to be reported at December 31, year 2, as a separate component of stockholders' equity entitled "accumulated other comprehensive income."	○	○	○	○	○	○	○	○	○	○	○	○	○

Task-Based Simulation 38 Solution

> Financial Statement Disclosures
>
> Authoritative Literature
>
> Help

		(A)	(B)	(C)	(D)	(E)	(F)	(G)	(H)	(I)	(J)	(K)
							Amount					
1.	Carrying amount of security ABC at December 31, year 2.	○	○	○	○	○	○	●	○	○	○	○
2.	Carrying amount of security DEF at December 31, year 2.	○	○	○	○	○	○	○	○	●	○	○
3.	Carrying amount of security JKL at December 31, year 2.	○	○	○	○	○	○	○	○	○	●	○

					Amount									
		(A)	(B)	(C)	(D)	(E)	(F)	(G)	(H)	(I)	(J)	(K)	Gain	Loss
4.	Recognized gain or loss on sale of security GHI.	○	○	○	●	○	○	○	○	○	○	○	○	●
5.	Unrealized gain or loss to be reported in year 2 net income.	○	●	○	○	○	○	○	○	○	○	○	○	●
6.	Unrealized gain or loss to be reported at December 31, year 2, as a separate component of stockholders' equity entitled "accumulated other comprehensive income."	○	○	●	○	○	○	○	○	○	○	○	○	●

Explanations

1. **(G; $100,000)** Held-to-maturity securities shall be measured at amortized cost. Since this debt security was purchased at par, there is neither a discount nor a premium to amortize, therefore amortized cost equals par or $100,000. Ignore fair value.
2. **(I; $155,000)** Investments in securities that are not classified as held-to-maturity and that have readily determinable fair values shall be measured at fair value. $155,000 is fair value.
3. **(J; $160,000)** Same explanation as question 2. Since security JKL is not a debt security classified as held-to-maturity and since it has a readily determinable fair value it shall be measured at fair value.
4. **(D, L)** Recognized gains and losses on the sale of available-for-sale securities are measured as the difference between original cost ($190,000) and the selling price of the securities ($175,000). The unrealized loss that existed in accumulated other comprehensive income in the equity section prior to the sale ($25,000) will be reversed as a credit to unrealized loss and that reversal will be reported as other comprehensive income and closed to accumulated other comprehensive income that is reported in the equity section of the balance sheet (see question 10 below). The journal entry to record the sale would be

Cash	175,000	
Realized loss on sale of A-F-S securities	15,000	
A-F-S securities		165,000
Unrealized loss on A-F-S securities		25,000

5. **(B, L)** The only unrealized gains or losses on securities reported in the net income relate to value changes in trading securities. In this case the value of the JKL securities has decreased from $160,000 to $155,000.
6. **(C, L)** The 1/1/Y2 balance of the unrealized gain or loss on A-F-S securities reported in the equity section was $20,000, the difference between the 1/1/Y2 $25,000 unrealized loss of GHI ($190,000 – $165,000) and the 1/1/Y2 $5,000 unrealized gain of JKL ($175,000 – $170,000). The changes during the year were (1) the $25,000 reversal (credit) of the unrealized loss of GHI when it was sold and (2) the $15,000 loss ($175,000 – $160,000) in value during the year of JKL. The Other Comprehensive Income account would appear as follows:

	Other Comprehensive Income	
Beg. bal.	–	
12/31/Y2 JKL	15,000	12/31/Y2 Reverse GHI 25,000
Close to Accumulated Other Comprehensive Income	10,000	

The Accumulated Other Comprehensive Income account would appear as follows:

Accumulated Other Comprehensive Income	
1/1/Y2 20,000	
	10,000 12/31/Y2 Close from Other Comprehensive Income
12/31/Y2 Balance 10,000	

Task-Based Simulation 39

Assume that you are assigned to the audit of Millet Corporation. The CFO of Millet is trying to determine how to account for a transfer of investment securities between the trading portfolio and the available-for-sale portfolio. Which section of the Professional Standards addresses the issue of how to account for the transfer?

Enter your response in the answer fields below.

Task-Based Simulation 39 Solution

ASC	320	10	35	10

Task-Based Simulation 40

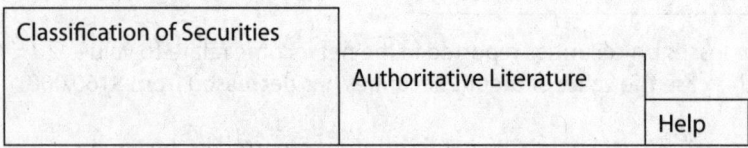

Items 1 through 4 are based on the following:

Cane Co. purchased various securities during year 1 to be classified as held-to-maturity securities (H), trading securities (A), or available-for-sale securities (A).

Items 1 through 4 describe various securities purchased by Cane. For each item, select from the following list the appropriate category for each security. A category may be used once, more than once, or not at all.

	Categories
H.	Held-to-maturity
T.	Trading
A.	Available-for-sale

		Category		
		(H)	**(T)**	**(A)**
1.	Debt securities bought and held for the purpose of selling in the near term.	○	○	○
2.	U.S. Treasury bonds that Cane has both the positive intent and the ability to hold to maturity.	○	○	○
3.	$3 million debt security bought and held for the purpose of selling in three years to finance payment of Cane's $2 million long-term note payable when it matures.	○	○	○
4.	Convertible preferred stock that Cane does not intend to sell in the near term.	○	○	○

Task-Based Simulation 40 Solution

Classification of Securities

Authoritative Literature

Help

		Category		
		(H)	**(T)**	**(A)**
1.	Debt securities bought and held for the purpose of selling in the near term.	○	●	○
2.	U.S. Treasury bonds that Cane has both the positive intent and the ability to hold to maturity.	●	○	○
3.	$3 million debt security bought and held for the purpose of selling in three years to finance payment of Cane's $2 million long-term note payable when it matures.	○	○	●
4.	Convertible preferred stock that Cane does not intend to sell in the near term.	○	○	●

Explanations

1. **(T)** Trading. Securities that are bought and held principally for the purpose of selling them in the near term (thus held for only a short period of time) shall be classified as **trading securities**.
2. **(H)** Held-to-maturity. Investments in debt securities shall be classified as **held-to-maturity** and measured at amortized cost only if the reporting enterprise has the positive intent and ability to hold those securities to maturity. Both conditions are met in this case.
3. **(A)** Available-for-sale. The company does not have the positive intent to hold this debt security to maturity, therefore the security cannot be classified as held-to-maturity. Also, since it will be sold beyond the "near term," it cannot be classified as "trading." Investments not classified as trading (nor as held-to-maturity securities) shall be classified as **available-for-sale securities**.
4. **(A)** Available-for-sale. Since this security is neither a debt security nor a security that will be sold in the near term, it is classified as available-for-sale.

Investments
Significant Influence—Equity Method

Equity Method

Task-Based Simulation 41

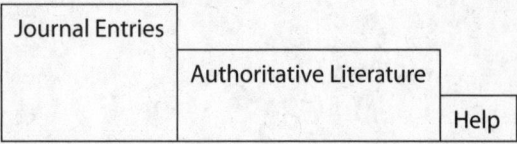

Situation

Harold Johnson, an investor in Acme Co., asked you for advice on the propriety of Acme's financial reporting for two of its investments. Assume that Acme does not elect the fair value option for reporting its financial assets and liabilities. You obtained the following information related to the investments from Acme's December 31, year 1 financial statements:

- 20% ownership interest in Kern Co., represented by 200,000 shares of outstanding common stock purchased on January 2, year 1, for $600,000.
- 20% ownership interest in Wand Co., represented by 20,000 shares of outstanding common stock purchased on January 2, year 1, for $300,000.
- On January 2, year 1, the carrying values of the acquired shares of both investments equaled their purchase price.
- Kern reported earnings of $400,000 for the year ended December 31, year 1, and declared and paid dividends of $100,000 during year 1.
- Wand reported earnings of $350,000 for the year ended December 31, year 1, and declared and paid dividends of $60,000 during year 1.
- On December 31, year 1, Kern's and Wand's common stock were trading over-the-counter at $18 and $20 per share, respectively.
- The investment in Kern is accounted for using the equity method.
- The investment in Wand is accounted for as available-for-sale securities.

You recalculated the amounts reported in Acme's December 31, year 1 financial statements, and determined that they were correct. Stressing that the information available in the financial statements was limited, you advised Johnson that, assuming Acme properly applied generally accepted accounting principles, Acme may have appropriately used two different methods to account for its investments in Kern and Wand, even though the investments represent equal ownership interests.

1. Prepare the journal entry for Acme's investment in Kern Co. on January 2, year 1.
2. Prepare the journal entry for the dividends received from Kern in year 1.
3. Prepare the journal entry required for Kern's reported income for the year ending on December 31, year 1.

Task-Based Simulation 41 Solution

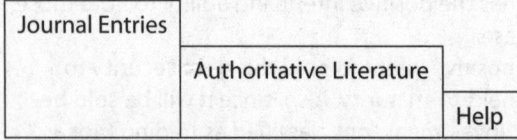

1. The journal entry for the investment in Kern Co. on January 2, year 1.

Investment in Kern	600,000	
Cash		600,000

2. The journal entry for the dividends received from Kern in year 1.

Cash	20,000	
Investment in Kern		20,000
[100,000 × 20% = 20,000]		

3. The journal entry required for Kern's reported income for the year ending December 31, year 1.

Investment in Kern	80,000	
Income from Kern		80,000
[400,000 × 20% = 80,000]		

Task-Based Simulation 42

Financial Statement Disclosures | Authoritative Literature | Help

Situation

Harold Johnson, an investor in Acme Co., asked you for advice on the propriety of Acme's financial reporting for two of its investments. Assume that Acme does not elect the fair value option for reporting its financial assets and liabilities. You obtained the following information related to the investments from Acme's December 31, year 1 financial statements:

- 20% ownership interest in Kern Co., represented by 200,000 shares of outstanding common stock purchased on January 2, year 1, for $600,000.
- 20% ownership interest in Wand Co., represented by 20,000 shares of outstanding common stock purchased on January 2, year 1, for $300,000.
- On January 2, year 1, the carrying values of the acquired shares of both investments equaled their purchase price.
- Kern reported earnings of $400,000 for the year ended December 31, year 1, and declared and paid dividends of $100,000 during year 1.
- Wand reported earnings of $350,000 for the year ended December 31, year 1, and declared and paid dividends of $60,000 during year 1.
- On December 31, year 1, Kern's and Wand's common stock were trading over-the-counter at $18 and $20 per share, respectively.
- The investment in Kern is accounted for using the equity method.
- The investment in Wand is accounted for as available-for-sale securities.

You recalculated the amounts reported in Acme's December 31, year 1 financial statements, and determined that they were correct. Stressing that the information available in the financial statements was limited, you advised Johnson that, assuming Acme properly applied generally accepted accounting principles, Acme may have appropriately used two different methods to account for its investments in Kern and Wand, even though the investments represent equal ownership interests.

Identify the following amounts on Acme's financial statements.

Carrying value of Kern investment	
Carrying value of Wand investment	
Income on Income Statement	
Kern investment	
Wand investment	
Other comprehensive income	
Kern investment	
Wand investment	

Task-Based Simulation 42 Solution

Carrying value of Kern investment	$660,000
Carrying value of Wand investment	$400,000
Income on Income Statement	
Kern investment	$80,000
Wand investment	$12,000
Other comprehensive income	
Kern investment	$ –
Wand investment	$100,000

Explanations

Carrying value of Kern.
Kern

Balance sheet—Acme reported its investment in Kern at a carrying amount of $660,000
Calculations:
Equity in earnings = $80,000 ($400,000 × 20%)
Dividend rec'd = $20,000 ($100,000 × 20%)
Carrying amount = $600,000 + $80,000 – $20,000 = $660,000

Carrying value of Wand.
Wand

Balance sheet—Acme reported its investment in Wand at a fair value of $400,000
Calculation:
20,000 shares × $20 per share = $400,000

Income Statement Amounts
Income from Kern $400,000 × 20% = $80,000
Income from Wand $12,000 dividend income
Dividend income $12,000
Calculation:
$60,000 × 20% = $12,000

Other Comprehensive Income
Kern investment $0
Wand investment unrealized gain $100,000
Calculation:
$400,000 – $300,000 = $100,000

Task-Based Simulation 43

Assume that you are assigned to the audit of Swartz Corporation. The Controller of Swartz has asked you to describe the guidance in the Professional Standards that indicate when the equity method of accounting for an investment is generally required. Which section of the Professional Standards provides guidance on percentage of ownership that generally results in the use of the equity method for the investment?

Enter your response in the answer fields below.

Task-Based Simulation 43 Solution

ASC	323	10	15	8

Task-Based Simulation 44

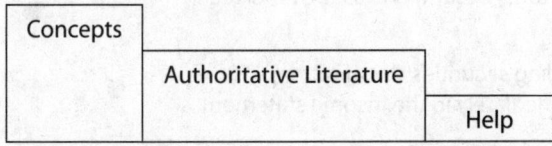

Identify whether each of the following statements is True or False. Assume the fair value option is not elected.

	True	False
1. Unrealized gains from trading securities are reported in other comprehensive income.	○	○
2. Investments in stocks and bonds may be classified as trading securities, available-for-sale securities, and held-to-maturity securities.	○	○
3. X Company has significant influence over Y Company and owns 35% of the voting stock of Y Company. X Company must use the equity method of accounting for the investment in Y Company.	○	○
4. Unrealized gains and losses from available-for-sale securities that result from the change in fair value during the period should be reported as other comprehensive income.	○	○
5. The temporary unrealized gain or loss from held-to-maturity securities must be reported in income for the current period.	○	○
6. If a security is transferred from available-for-sale to trading securities classification, unrealized holding gains and losses are recognized immediately in the income statement.	○	○
7. The equity method of accounting requires a company to include the percent of income of the investee in the investor company's net income for the period.	○	○
8. The equity method of accounting requires that a company adjust the cost of the investee to fair value at the end of each period.	○	○
9. A company that receives stock dividends records income equal to the fair value of the stock on the date the dividend is declared.	○	○
10. Held-to-maturity securities are carried at amortized cost using the effective interest method.	○	○

Task-Based Simulation 44 Solution

```
Concepts
        Authoritative Literature
                            Help
```

		True	False
1.	Unrealized gains from trading securities are reported in other comprehensive income.	○	●
2.	Investments in stocks and bonds may be classified as trading securities, available-for-sale securities, and held-to-maturity securities.	○	●
3.	X Company has significant influence over Y Company and owns 35% of the voting stock of Y Company. X Company must use the equity method of accounting for the investment in Y Company.	●	○
4.	Unrealized gains and losses from available-for-sale securities that result from the change in fair value during the period should be reported as other comprehensive income.	●	○
5.	The temporary unrealized gain or loss from held-to-maturity securities must be reported in income for the current period.	○	●
6.	If a security is transferred from available-for-sale to trading securities classification, unrealized holding gains and losses are recognized immediately in the income statement.	●	○
7.	The equity method of accounting requires a company to include the percent of income of the investee in the investor company's net income for the period.	●	○
8.	The equity method of accounting requires that a company adjust the cost of the investee to fair value at the end of each period.	○	●
9.	A company that receives stock dividends records income equal to the fair value of the stock on the date the dividend is declared.	○	●
10.	Held-to-maturity securities are carried at amortized cost using the effective interest method.	●	○

Explanations

1. **(F)** Unrealized gains from trading securities are reported in income for the period.
2. **(F)** Stocks cannot be classified as held-to-maturity because they have no maturity date.
3. **(T)** The equity method is required when an investor exercises significant influence over the investee.
4. **(T)** Unrealized gains and losses are reported as other comprehensive income.
5. **(F)** The temporary unrealized gain from held-to-maturity securities is excluded from earnings; instead, the held-to-maturities are reported at amortized cost.
6. **(T)** Unrealized gains or losses are recognized when transferred.
7. **(T)** The investor recognizes its share of income as earned.
8. **(F)** In the equity method, the investor does not revalue the stock to fair value. The equity method requires that the investor record the percentage share of net income and percentage share of dividends of the investee.
9. **(F)** Stock dividends require a memo entry to show receipt of additional shares of stock. The company then recomputes the cost per share based upon the new number of shares.
10. **(T)** Held-to-maturity securities are carried at amortized cost.

Intangible Assets—Goodwill and Other

Introduction to Intangible Assets

Task-Based Simulation 45

Indicate whether each of the following statements is True or False.

	True	False
1. An intangible asset that is determined to have an indefinite life should be amortized over 40 years.	○	○
2. If the carrying value of the intangible asset exceeds its fair value, an impairment loss must be recognized.	○	○
3. The impairment test for goodwill must be performed at the end of each fiscal year for each reporting unit.	○	○
4. When a company borrows funds to finance a construction project and temporarily invests this cash, the interest expense should be offset against the interest expense to be capitalized.	○	○
5. A company may capitalize interest on inventories it regularly produces for resale to customers.	○	○
6. Gains are never recognized when similar assets are exchanged.	○	○
7. In nonmonetary exchanges, losses are only recognized when cash is received in the transactions.	○	○
8. If the fair value of the asset is unknown in a nonmonetary exchange and no gain can be computed, the asset is recorded at the fair market value of the asset given up.	○	○
9. A capital expenditure is charged against income over the useful life of the asset.	○	○
10. Expenditures to improve the efficiency or extend the useful life of an asset should be capitalized.	○	○

Task-Based Simulation 45 Solution

Concepts | Authoritative Literature | Help

	True	False
1. An intangible asset that is determined to have an indefinite life should be amortized over 40 years.	○	●
2. If the carrying value of the intangible asset exceeds its fair value, an impairment loss must be recognized.	●	○
3. The impairment test for goodwill must be performed at the end of each fiscal year for each reporting unit.	○	●
4. When a company borrows funds to finance a construction project and temporarily invests this cash, the interest expense should be offset against the interest expense to be capitalized.	○	●

(Continued)

	True	False
5. A company may capitalize interest on inventories it regularly produces for resale to customers.	○	●
6. Gains are never recognized when similar assets are exchanged.	○	●
7. In nonmonetary exchanges, losses are only recognized when cash is received in the transactions.	○	●
8. If the fair value of the asset is unknown in a nonmonetary exchange and no gain can be computed, the asset is recorded at the fair market value of the asset given up.	○	●
9. A capital expenditure is charged against income over the useful life of the asset.	●	○
10. Expenditures to improve the efficiency or extend the useful life of an asset should be capitalized.	●	○

Explanations

1. **(F)** Intangible assets that have indefinite lives are not amortized.
2. **(T)** The recorded values of intangibles are impaired if they are above fair value.
3. **(F)** The impairment test for goodwill can be performed anytime during the year, but it must be performed at the same time every year.
4. **(F)** Interest earned on temporary investments from borrowed funds used to finance construction projects should be recognized as interest revenue and not netted against interest expense during the period.
5. **(F)** A company may not capitalize interest on funds borrowed to finance routinely produced inventory.
6. **(F)** Recognition of gain is required unless the transaction lacks commercial substance.
7. **(F)** Losses on nonmonetary exchanges are recognized.
8. **(F)** In a nonmonetary exchange, if the fair value is unknown and no gain can be computed, the asset is recorded at the book value of the asset given up.
9. **(T)** Capital expenditures are amortized over the useful life of the asset.
10. **(T)** Expenditures to improve capital assets should be capitalized.

Goodwill

Task-Based Simulation 46

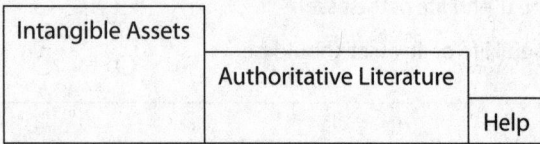

Situation

During year 4, Broca Co. had the following transactions:

- On January 2, Broca purchased the net assets of Amp Co. for $360,000. The fair value of Amp's identifiable net assets was $172,000. Broca believes that, due to the popularity of Amp's consumer products, the life of the resulting goodwill is unlimited.
- On February 1, Broca purchased a franchise to operate a ferry service from the state government for $60,000 and an annual fee of 1% of ferry revenues. The franchise expires after five years. Broca received $20,000 of ferry revenues in year 4.
- On April 5, Broca was granted a patent that had been applied for by Amp. During year 4, Broca incurred legal costs of $51,000 to register the patent and an additional $85,000 to successfully prosecute a patent infringement suit against a competitor. Broca estimates the patent's economic life to be 10 years.

Broca has determined that it is appropriate to amortize these intangibles on the straight-line basis over the maximum period permitted by generally accepted accounting principles, taking a full year's amortization in the year of acquisition.

Complete the following schedule for Broca's intangible assets and the related income statement expenses.

Broca Co.
SCHEDULE FOR INTANGIBLE ASSETS AND AMORTIZATION EXPENSE
December 31, Year 4

Item	Valuation before adjusting entries	Amortization expense for the year	Valuation on 12/31/Y4
Goodwill			
Franchise (net)			
Patent (net)			

Complete the following schedule for Broca's expenses.

Broca Co.
EXPENSES RESULTING FROM INTANGIBLES
For the Year Ended December 31, Year 4

Amortization:	
Franchise	
Patent	
Franchise fee	
Total expenses	

Task-Based Simulation 46 Solution

Intangible Assets

Authoritative Literature

Help

Broca Co.
SCHEDULE FOR INTANGIBLE ASSETS AND AMORTIZATION EXPENSE
December 31, Year 4

Item	Valuation before adjusting entries	Amortization expense for the year	Valuation on 12/31/Y4
Goodwill	188,000 [1]	–0–	188,000
Franchise (net)	60,000 [2]	12,000	48,000
Patent (net)	136,000 [3]	13,600	122,400

Broca Co.
EXPENSES RESULTING FROM INTANGIBLES
For the Year Ended December 31, Year 4

Amortization:	
Franchise	12,000
Patent	13,600
	$25,600
Franchise fee	200
($20,000 × 1%)	
Total expenses	$25,800

Explanations

Broca Co.
SUPPORTING CALCULATIONS FOR INTANGIBLES
December 31, Year 4

Goodwill	$188,000 [1]
Franchise, net of accumulated amortization of $12,000	48,000 [2]
Patent, net of accumulated amortization of $13,600	122,400 [3]

[1]	Cash paid	$360,000
	Value of net assets	(172,000)
	Goodwill	188,000
[2]	Franchise	$60,000
	Amortization over 5 years	(12,000)
	Balance	$48,000
[3]	Legal costs ($51,000 + $85,000)	$136,000
	Amortization over 10 years	(13,600)
	Balance	$122,400

[1] Goodwill calculation

In a purchase, the net assets acquired are recorded at their FV. The excess of the cost of the investment ($360,000) over the FV of the net assets acquired ($172,000) is allocated to goodwill ($360,000 – $172,000 = $188,000). Intangible assets with an indeterminate or unlimited life, such as this goodwill, are not amortized. The goodwill is reported in the 12/31/Y4 balance at its cost.

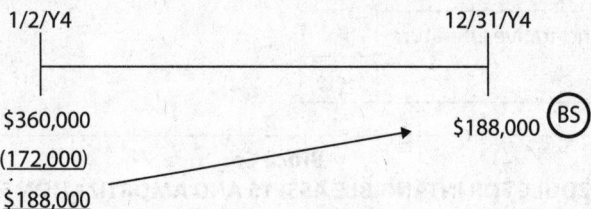

[2] Franchise fee

The franchise acquired on 2/1/Y4 is recorded at its cost of $60,000. Since Broca amortizes these intangibles on a straight-line basis, and takes a full year's amortization in the year of acquisition, year 4 amortization is $12,000 ($60,000 × 1/5), and the franchise is reported at cost less accumulated amortization at 12/31/Y4 ($60,000 – $12,000 = $48,000). In addition to the amortization expense, there is also an annual fee that must be expensed, equal to 1% of ferry revenues.

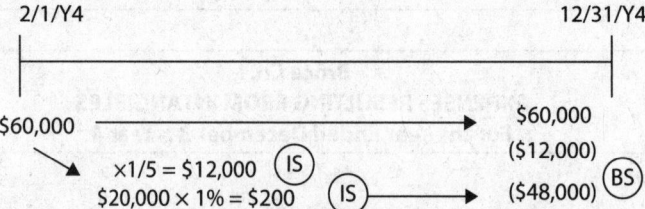

[3] Patents are initially recorded at cost of acquisition, which is purchase price for a purchased patent, or legal and other costs of registration ($51,000) for an internally generated patent. Legal fees incurred in **successfully** defending the patent ($85,000) are also capitalized because such fees help establish the legal right of the holder to any future benefits that will be derived from the patent. Therefore, this patent is capitalized at a total amount of $136,000 ($51,000 + $85,000). Since Broca amortizes these intangibles on a straight-line basis and takes a full-year's amortization in the year of acquisition,

amortization is $13,600 ($136,000 ×1/Y4). The patent is reported at cost less accumulated amortization at 12/31/Y4 ($136,000 − $13,600 = $122,400).

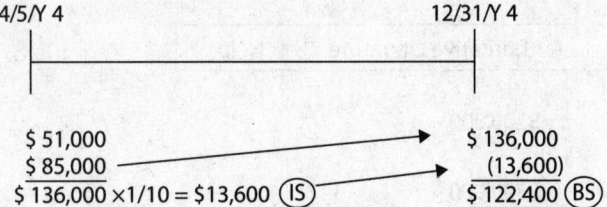

Task-Based Simulation 47

Goodwill Impairment		
	Authoritative Literature	
		Help

Jane Corporation is performing its annual test of the impairment of the goodwill related to its Technology reporting unit. The carrying value of goodwill allocated to the unit is $500,000. Using a multiple of revenue, Jane has determined the fair value of the Technology reporting unit to be $1,700,000 at 12/31/Y4, and the fair value and carrying value of the assets and liabilities were determined as follows:

	(In 000s)	
	Carrying value	**Fair value**
Cash	$200	$200
Accounts receivable	250	250
Inventory	350	400
Net equipment	700	700
Patents	400	450
Goodwill	500	?
Accounts payable	(200)	(200)
Long-term debt	(300)	(300)
	1,900	

1. Calculate the following amounts related to the impairment of goodwill.

   Implied Goodwill   [   ]

   Impairment of Goodwill   [   ]

2. Prepare the related journal entry if there is an impairment of goodwill for the Technology reporting unit.

Task-Based Simulation 47 Solution

Goodwill Impairment		
	Authoritative Literature	Help

1. Implied goodwill $200,000

      Impairment of goodwill $300,000

Explanations

1. Goodwill acquired through a business combination is the only type of goodwill that is recognized. Such goodwill is not amortized but is tested periodically for impairment. Internally generated goodwill is not recorded. Expenditures to develop, maintain, or enhance goodwill are expensed as incurred.

   Since the carrying value of the reporting unit ($1,900,000) exceeds the fair value of the unit ($1,700,000), the second step in the test of impairment should be performed.

   The implied value of goodwill is the difference between the fair value of the unit ($1,700,000) and the fair value of its assets and liabilities ($1,500,000). Therefore, the implied value of goodwill is $200,000. Since the carrying value of goodwill is $500,000, there is a $300,000 impairment that must be recognized as shown below.

2. Journal entry required for goodwill impairment

Impairment loss	$300,000
Goodwill	$300,000

   To recognize impairment of goodwill for the Technology reporting unit at 12/31/Y4.

Payables and Accrued Liabilities Contingencies, Commitments, and Guarantees (Provisions)

Examples of Contingent Liabilities and Additional Aspects

Task-Based Simulation 48

Reporting Requirements		
	Authoritative Literature	
		Help

Items 1 through 6 are based on the following:

Lorn Company is preparing its financial statements for the year ended December 31, year 2.

Items 1 through 6 represent various commitments and contingencies of Lorn at December 31, year 2, and events subsequent to December 31, year 2, but prior to the issuance of the year 2 financial statements. For each item, select from the following list the reporting requirement. A reporting requirement may be selected once, more than once, or not at all.

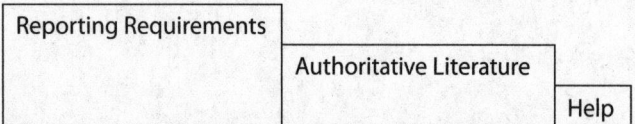

Reporting Requirement	
D. Disclosure only	B. Both accrual and disclosure
A. Accrual only	N. Neither accrual nor disclosure

	(D)	(A)	(B)	(N)
1. On December 1, year 2, Lorn was awarded damages of $75,000 in a patent infringement suit it brought against a competitor. The defendant did not appeal the verdict, and payment was received in January of year 3.	○	○	○	○
2. A former employee of Lorn has brought a wrongful-dismissal suit against Lorn. Lorn's lawyers believe the suit to be without merit.	○	○	○	○
3. At December 31, year 2, Lorn had outstanding purchase orders in the ordinary course of business for purchase of a raw material to be used in its manufacturing process. The market price is currently higher than the purchase price and is not anticipated to change within the next year.	○	○	○	○
4. A government contract completed during year 2 is subject to renegotiation. Although Lorn estimates that it is reasonably possible that a refund of approximately $200,000 – $300,000 may be required by the government, it does not wish to publicize this possibility.	○	○	○	○
5. Lorn has been notified by a governmental agency that it will be held responsible for the cleanup of toxic materials at a site where Lorn formerly conducted operations. Lorn estimates that it is probable that its share of remedial action will be approximately $500,000.	○	○	○	○
6. On January 5, year 3, Lorn redeemed its outstanding bonds and issued new bonds with a lower rate of interest. The reacquisition price was in excess of the carrying amount of the bonds.	○	○	○	○

Task-Based Simulation 48 Solution

Reporting Requirements		
	Authoritative Literature	
		Help

	(D)	(A)	(B)	(N)
1. On December 1, year 2, Lorn was awarded damages of $75,000 in a patent infringement suit it brought against a competitor. The defendant did not appeal the verdict, and payment was received in January of year 3.	○	○	●	○
2. A former employee of Lorn has brought a wrongful-dismissal suit against Lorn. Lorn's lawyers believe the suit to be without merit.	○	○	○	●
3. At December 31, year 2, Lorn had outstanding purchase orders in the ordinary course of business for purchase of a raw material to be used in its manufacturing process. The market price is currently higher than the purchase price and is not anticipated to change within the next year.	○	○	○	●
4. A government contract completed during year 2 is subject to renegotiation. Although Lorn estimates that it is reasonably possible that a refund of approximately $200,000 – $300,000 may be required by the government, it does not wish to publicize this possibility.	●	○	○	○
5. Lorn has been notified by a governmental agency that it will be held responsible for the cleanup of toxic materials at a site where Lorn formerly conducted operations. Lorn estimates that it is probable that its share of remedial action will be approximately $500,000.	○	○	●	○
6. On January 5, year 3, Lorn redeemed its outstanding bonds and issued new bonds with a lower rate of interest. The reacquisition price was in excess of the carrying amount of the bonds.	●	○	○	○

Explanations

1. **(B)** Contingencies that might result in gains usually are not reflected in the accounts since to do so might be to recognize revenue prior to its realization. Since this gain contingency was resolved before the issuance of the financial statements, it is handled similar to an ordinary transaction that occurred prior to the year-end and is accrued in the year of its occurrence.
   However, disclosure of the contingencies that might result in gains is made in the notes to financial statements.

2. **(N)** To accrue an estimated loss from a loss contingency it is necessary to show that it is probable that an asset has been impaired or a liability has been incurred and that the amount of loss can be reasonably estimated. Since Lorn's lawyers believe the suit to be without merit, neither condition has been met.
   Disclosure is also required of some loss contingencies that do not meet the accrual requirements if there is a **reasonable possibility** that a loss may be incurred. Again, this condition has not been met.

3. **(N)** The conditions described in this question would be considered general or unspecified business risks that do not meet the conditions for accrual or disclosure.

4. **(D)** The words "reasonably possible" require the disclosure of this item. No accrual need be made since the question does not state it is **probable** that an asset has been impaired or a liability incurred and that the amount of loss can be reasonably estimated.

5. **(B)** The word "probable" and the inclusion of the estimated amount of $500,000 mean that this situation meets the criteria of (1) a probable incurrence of a liability and (2) a reasonable estimate of an amount.

6. **(D)** Disclosure is made for commitments such as an obligation to reduce debts. Since the entire transaction took place in the next accounting period it does not meet the conditions for an accrual in the current period even though it would be disclosed in a footnote.

Long-Term Debt (Financial Liabilities)

Notes Payable

Task-Based Simulation 49

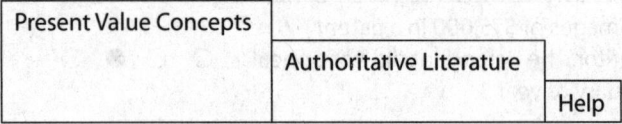

Assume that you are the accountant for Kern Corporation and are working on various debt accounting issues. Use the following responses to define the terms in the table that follows.

Responses to be selected

A. Effective interest rate × Net receivable or payable balance at the beginning of the period
B. Periodic interest is computed on principal balance and interest earned to date
C. Represents the debtor's incremental borrowing rate
D. Series of payments/receipts that occur at beginning of the period
E. The difference between the present value of the note and the cash exchanged when the market rate of interest < rate on note
F. Periodic interest is computed based on the principal balance only
G. Maturity value of note and interest payments discounted to the present value
H. This will result when face rate of the note < yield rate
I. The amount that will be available in the future as a result of consecutive payments/receipts at the end of each period—compounded at a specified interest rate
J. Series of payments/receipts which are made at the end of the period
K. No premium or discount exists

	(A)	(B)	(C)	(D)	(E)	(F)	(G)	(H)	(I)	(J)	(K)
1. Annuity due	O	O	O	O	O	O	O	O	O	O	O
2. Imputed interest rate	O	O	O	O	O	O	O	O	O	O	O
3. Fair value of note	O	O	O	O	O	O	O	O	O	O	O
4. Note issued at a discount	O	O	O	O	O	O	O	O	O	O	O
5. Premium on a note	O	O	O	O	O	O	O	O	O	O	O
6. Simple interest method	O	O	O	O	O	O	O	O	O	O	O
7. Interest revenue/expense	O	O	O	O	O	O	O	O	O	O	O
8. Future value of annuity	O	O	O	O	O	O	O	O	O	O	O
9. Face of note equals present value of the note	O	O	O	O	O	O	O	O	O	O	O

Task-Based Simulation 49 Solution

Present Value Concepts

Authoritative Literature

Help

	(A)	(B)	(C)	(D)	(E)	(F)	(G)	(H)	(I)	(J)	(K)
1. Annuity due	O	O	O	●	O	O	O	O	O	O	O
2. Imputed interest rate	O	O	●	O	O	O	O	O	O	O	O
3. Fair value of note	O	O	O	O	O	O	●	O	O	O	O
4. Note issued at a discount	O	O	O	O	O	O	O	●	O	O	O
5. Premium on a note	O	O	O	O	●	O	O	O	O	O	O
6. Simple interest method	O	O	O	O	O	●	O	O	O	O	O
7. Interest revenue/expense	●	O	O	O	O	O	O	O	O	O	O
8. Future value of annuity	O	O	O	O	O	O	O	O	●	O	O
9. Face of note equals present value of the note	O	O	O	O	O	O	O	O	O	O	●

Explanations

1. **(D)** An annuity due (annuity in advance) represents a series of payments made or received at the beginning of the period.
2. **(C)** An imputed interest rate is used when the rate on a note is not fair and the fair value of the items being exchanged is not readily determinable. An imputed interest rate represents the rate at which the debtor could obtain financing from a different source; this is known as the debtor's incremental borrowing rate.
3. **(G)** The fair value of a note is equal to the maturity value and the interest payments discounted to the present value. The present value represents the amount you would pay now for an amount to be received in the future. Thus, answer G is the correct response, as the present value equals the current fair value of the principal and interest amounts.
4. **(H)** When a note is exchanged for cash and no other rights or privileges exist, the present value of the note will equal the cash received if the stated rate on the note equals the market yield rate. However, if the stated rate is less than the market rate, then the note will be issued at a discount to compensate.
5. **(E)** A premium on a note occurs when the interest rate on a note is greater than the market yield rate. The market bids up the price of the bond above par until the effective interest rate on the note equals the market yield rate.
6. **(F)** The simple interest method computes interest based upon the amount of principal only. Interest is computed as Principal × Interest × Time. The compound interest method computes interest on principal and any interest earned and not withdrawn.
7. **(A)** The interest revenue or expense on a note is computed by taking the effective interest rate times the net receivable or payable balance.

8. **(I)** An annuity is a periodic payment or receipt made in consecutive intervals over time compounded at a stated interest rate. The future value of an annuity represents the total of the periodic payments and accumulated interest at some point in the future.

9. **(K)** When a note is exchanged for cash and no other rights or privileges exist, the present value of the note will be equal to the cash exchanged if the stated rate of interest equals the market yield rate. No premium or discount exists if the stated rate on the note equals the market yield rate.

Task-Based Simulation 50

Assume that you are assigned to the audit of Kern Corporation. On July 1, year 1, Kern borrows $100,000 on a noninterest-bearing, three-year note and receives $85,000 in proceeds. Which section of the Professional Standards provides guidance on how to determine the present value of the note?

Enter your response in the answer fields below.

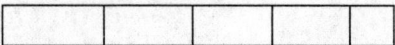

Task-Based Simulation 50 Solution

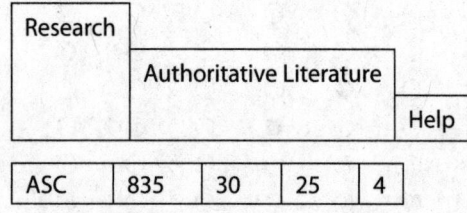

| ASC | 835 | 30 | 25 | 4 |

Task-Based Simulation 51

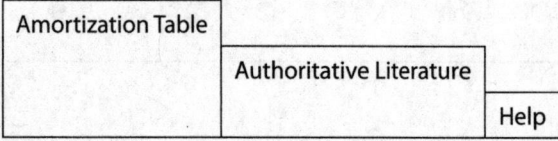

Situation

Assume that you are the CPA for Dawson Corporation. On January 1, year 1, Catrina Corporation sold to Dawson Corporation equipment that originally cost $320,000, with accumulated depreciation of $75,000 for a noninterest-bearing note with a face value of $300,000 due January 1, year 5. The fair value of the equipment is not readily determinable but the market rate for a note of this type is 6%. Dawson depreciates equipment over a five-year life with no residual value. The present value of the note is $237,630.

Prepare an amortization table and calculate the interest income and carrying value of the note for Catrina for year 1 and year 2. Indicate whether the note has a premium or discount by completing the correct columns in the schedule.

Year	Interest income	Premium on note	Discount on note	Carrying value

Task-Based Simulation 51 Solution

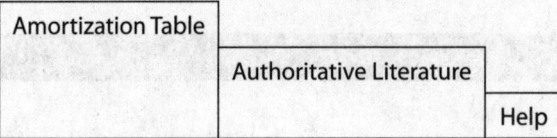

Amortization Table

Year	Interest income	Premium on note	Discount on note	Carrying value
1/1/Year 1			$62,370	$237,630
12/31/Year 1	$14,258		48,112	251,888
12/31/Year 2	15,113		32,999	267,001
12/31/Year 3	16,020		16,979	283,021
12/31/Year 4	16,981		(2)*	300,002

*due to rounding

Modification and Debt Retirement: Refinancing Short-Term Obligations

Task-Based Simulation 52

Sarah Young, the partner on the audit of Lee Company, has asked you to perform some research. Lee company intends to refinance a short-term note with a long-term note due in five years. Sarah wants to know the criteria to reclassify the short-term debt as long-term. Place the citation for the excerpt from the Professional Standards that provides this information in the answer box below.

Task-Based Simulation 52 Solution

ASC	470	10	45	14

Equity

Treasury Stock

Task-Based Simulation 53

Robar Corporation sold treasury shares at a price in excess of the shares' cost. You have been asked to research the professional literature to determine how this transaction is recorded. Place the citation for the excerpt from the Professional Standards that provides this information in the answer box below.

Task-Based Simulation 53 Solution

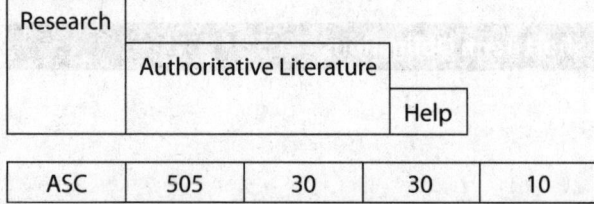

| ASC | 505 | 30 | 30 | 10 |

Dividends

Task-Based Simulation 54

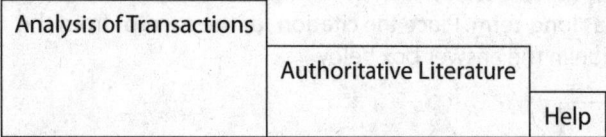

Situation

M Corporation was incorporated in year 1. During year 1, the company issued 100,000 shares of $1 par value common stock for $27 per share. During year 2, the company had the following transactions.

1/2/Y2	Issued 10,000 shares of $100 par value cumulative preferred stock at par. The preferred stock was convertible into five shares of common stock and had a dividend rate of 6%.
3/1/Y2	Issued 3,000 shares of common stock for legal service performed. The value of the legal services was $100,000. The stock was actively traded on a stock exchange and valued on 3/1/Y2 at $32 per share.
7/1/Y2	Issued 40,000 shares of common stock for $42 per share.
10/1/Y2	Repurchased 16,000 shares of treasury stock for $34 per share. M Corp. uses the cost method to account for treasury shares.
12/1/Y2	Sold 3,000 shares of treasury stock for $29 per share.
12/30/Y2	Declared and paid a dividend of $0.20 per share on common stock and a 6% dividend on the preferred stock.

During year 1, M Corporation had net income of $250,000 and paid dividends of $28,000. During year 2, M Corporation had net income of $380,000.

Indicate the impact that the transactions for M Company have on its owner equity accounts. Place the appropriate amounts in the table below. If an amount is negative, show the amount in parentheses.

Date	Transaction	Preferred stock	APIC—Preferred stock	Common stock	APIC—Common stock	Retained earnings	Treasury stock	APIC—Treasury stock
1/01	Beginning balance							
1/2/Y2	Issue preferred stock at par							
3/1/Y2	Issue common stock for services							
7/1/Y2	Issue common stock for cash							
10/1/Y2	Repurchase treasury stock							
12/1/Y2	Sell treasury stock							
12/30/Y2	Declare and pay dividends							
12/31/Y2	Net income							
12/31/Y2	Ending balance							

Task-Based Simulation 54 Solution

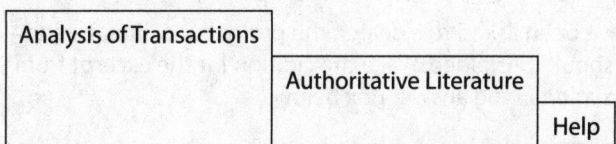

Date	Transaction	Preferred stock	APIC—Preferred stock	Common stock	APIC—Common stock	Retained earnings	Treasury stock	APIC—Treasury stock
1/01/Y2	Beginning balance			100,000	2,600,000	222,000		
1/2/Y2	Issue preferred stock at par	1,000,000						
3/1/Y2	Issue common stock for services			3,000	93,000			
7/1/Y2	Issue common stock for cash			40,000	1,640,000			
10/1/Y2	Repurchase treasury stock						(544,000)	
12/1/Y2	Sell treasury stock					(15,000)	102,000	
12/30/Y2	Declare and pay dividends					(86,000)		
12/31/Y2	Net income					380,000		
12/31/Y2	Ending balance	1,000,000	0	143,000	4,333,000	501,000	(442,000)	0

Explanations

- Preferred stock 10,000 × $100 = $1,000,000
- Value of services = Fair value of stock, which is more reliable since stock is traded on the open market. 3,000 shares × $32 per share = $96,000
- Common stock: 40,000 shares of common stock × $1 par = $40,000 to common stock account; $40,000 × 41 = $1,640,000 to APIC
- Treasury stock is recorded at cost: 16,000 shares × $34 per share = $544,000.
- Treasury stock is reduced by the cost paid 3,000 × $34 per share = $102,000. There is a $5 per share loss on the treasury shares which is debited to retained earnings: 3,000 shares × $5 = $15,000.
- Dividends to preferred shareholders = 10,000 × $100 par = $1,000,000 × 6% = $60,000 preferred dividends.
- Dividends to common shareholders. Number of common shares outstanding equals 100,000 shares + 3,000 shares issued + 40,000 shares issued – 16,000 treasury shares purchased + 3,000 treasury shares reissued = 130,000 outstanding shares × $0.20 = $26,000. Therefore, total dividend is $86,000.

Ending Balances

- Preferred stock: Issued at par. 10,000 shares × $100 = $1,000,000
- Common stock: $100,000 + $3,000 + $40,000 = $143,000
- Additional paid-in capital—Common stock: $2,600,000 + $93,000 + $1,640,000 = $4,333,000
- Retained earnings: $250,000 – $28,000 = $222,000 at end of year 1
- Retained earnings for year 2: $222,000 – $15,000 – $86,000 + $380,000 = $501,000
- Treasury stock: $544,000 – $102,000 = $442,000

Task-Based Simulation 55

Kerry Company issued a property dividend. You have been asked to research the professional literature to determine at what amount the property dividend should be valued. Place the citation for the excerpt from the Professional Standards that provides this information in the answer box below.

Task-Based Simulation 55 Solution

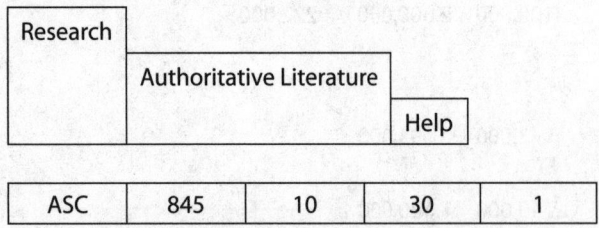

| ASC | 845 | 10 | 30 | 1 |

Book Value per Share

Task-Based Simulation 56

You have been asked to research the professional literature to determine how to calculate diluted earnings per share. Place the citation for the excerpt from the Professional Standards that provides this information in the answer box below.

Task-Based Simulation 56 Solution

Research

Authoritative Literature

Help

ASC	260	10	45	16

Task-Based Simulation 57

Calculation EPS

Authoritative Literature

Help

M Corporation was incorporated in year 1. During year 1, the company issued 100,000 shares of $1 par value common stock for $27 per share. During year 2, the company had the following transactions.

1/2/Y2	Issued 10,000 shares of $100 par value cumulative preferred stock at par. The preferred stock was convertible into five shares of common stock and had a dividend rate of 6%.
3/1/Y2	Issued 3,000 shares of common stock for legal service performed. The value of the legal services was $100,000. The stock was actively traded on a stock exchange and valued on 3/1/Y2 at $32 per share.
7/1/Y2	Issued 40,000 shares of common stock for $42 per share.
10/1/Y2	Repurchased 16,000 shares of treasury stock for $34 per share. M Corp. uses the cost method to account for treasury shares.
12/1/Y2	Sold 3,000 shares of treasury stock for $29 per share.
12/30/Y2	Declared and paid a dividend of $0.20 per share on common stock and a 6% dividend on the preferred stock.

During year 1, M Corporation had net income of $250,000 and paid dividends of $28,000. During year 2, M Corporation had net income of $380,000.

Calculate basic earnings per share. Show the components of your solution in the following table:

Numerator	
Denominator	
Basic earnings per share	

Calculate diluted earnings per share. Show the components of your solution in the following table:

Numerator	
Denominator	
Diluted earnings per share	

Task-Based Simulation 57 Solution

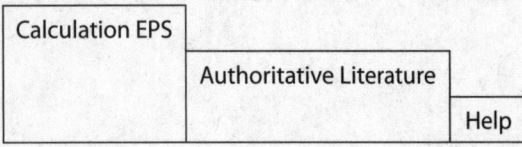

Basic earnings per share	
Numerator	320,000
Denominator	118,750
Basic earnings per share	2.6947

Diluted earnings per share	
Numerator	380,000
Denominator	168,750
Diluted earnings per share	2.2519

Explanations

Numerator: $380,000 net income – $60,000 in preferred dividends = $320,000. Denominator – Weighted-average common shares.

Date	# shares	Time outstanding	WACS
1/1	100,000	12/12	100,000
3/1	3,000	10/12	2,500
7/1	40,000	6/12	20,000
10/1	(16,000) treasury shares	3/12	(4,000)
12/1	3,000 treasury shares sold	1/12	250
	Total WACS outstanding		118,750

WACS outstanding: Basic EPS 118,750 + Convertible preferred (10,000 shares preferred × 5 shares common) 50,000 = 168,750.

Select Transactions

Revenue Recognition

Contract Accounting

Task-Based Simulation 58

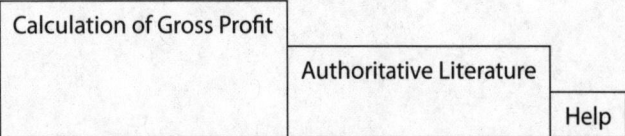

Situation

London, Inc. began operation of its construction division on October 1, year 1, and entered into contracts for two separate projects. The Beta project contract price was $600,000 and provided for penalties of $10,000 per week for late completion. Although during year 2 the Beta project had been on schedule for timely completion, it was completed four weeks late in August of year 3. The Gamma project's original contract price was $800,000. Change orders during year 3 added $40,000 to the original contract price.

The following data pertains to the separate long-term construction projects in progress:

	Beta	Gamma
As of September 30, year 2:		
Costs incurred to date	$360,000	$410,000
Estimated costs to complete	40,000	410,000
Billings	315,000	440,000
Cash collections	275,000	365,000
As of September 30, year 3:		
Costs incurred to date	450,000	720,000
Estimated costs to complete	–	180,000
Billings	560,000	710,000
Cash collections	560,000	625,000

Additional information

- London accounts for its long-term construction contracts using the percentage-of-completion method for financial reporting purposes and the completed-contract method for income tax purposes.
- Enacted income tax rates are 25% for year 2 and 30% for future years.
- London's income before income taxes from all divisions, before considering revenues from long-term construction projects, was $300,000 for the year ended September 30, year 2. There were no other temporary or permanent differences.

Prepare a schedule showing London's gross profit (loss) recognized for the years ended September 30, year 2, and year 3, under the percentage-of-completion method.

London Inc.

Schedule of Gross Profit (Loss)

	Beta	Gamma
For the Year Ended September 30, year 2:		
Estimated gross profit (loss):		
Contract price	_____	_____
Less total costs	_____	_____
Estimated gross profit (loss)	_____	_____
Percent complete:		
Costs incurred to date	_____	_____
Total costs	_____	_____
Percent complete	_____	_____
Gross profit (loss) recognized	_____	_____
For the Year Ended September 30, year 3:		
Estimated gross profit (loss):		
Contract price	_____	_____
Less total costs	_____	_____
Estimated gross profit (loss)	_____	_____

(Continued)

	Beta	Gamma
Percent complete:		
Costs incurred to date	_____	_____
Total costs	_____	_____
Percent complete	_____	_____
Gross profit (loss) recognized	_____	_____
Less gross profit (loss) recognized in prior year	_____	_____
Gross profit (loss) recognized	_____	_____

Task-Based Simulation 58 Solution

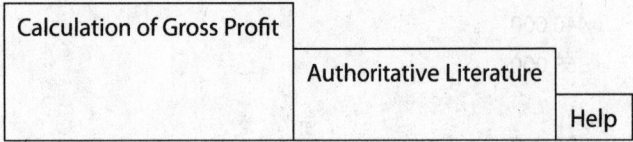

London Inc.
Schedule of Gross Profit (Loss)

	Beta	Gamma
For the Year Ended September 30, year 2:		
Estimated gross profit (loss):		
Contract price	$600,000	$800,000
Less total costs	400,000	820,000
Estimated gross profit (loss)	$200,000	$(20,000)
Percent complete:		
Costs incurred to date	$360,000	$410,000
Total costs	400,000	820,000
Percent complete	90%	50%
Gross profit (loss) recognized	$180,000	$(20,000)
For the Year Ended September 30, year 3:		
Estimated gross profit (loss):		
Contract price	$560,000	$840,000
Less total costs	450,000	900,000
Estimated gross profit (loss)	$110,000	$(60,000)
Percent complete:		
Costs incurred to date	$450,000	$720,000
Total costs	450,000	900,000
Percent complete	100%	80%
Gross profit (loss) recognized	110,000	(60,000)
Less gross profit (loss) recognized in prior year	180,000	(20,000)
Gross profit (loss) recognized	$(70,000)	$(40,000)

Explanations

- This problem consists of three related requirements concerning long-term construction contracts. The candidates must compute gross profit recognized for two years using the percentage-of-completion method, compute balances in various accounts, and reconcile financial statement income and taxable income.

- Using the percentage-of-completion method, gross profit is recognized periodically based on progress toward completion of the project using the following formula.

$$\frac{\text{Costs to date}}{\text{Total estimated costs}} \times \text{Estimated profit} = \text{Gross profit to date}$$

For the Beta project, London would recognize gross profit of $180,000 the first year.

$$\frac{\$360,000}{(\$360,000 + \$40,000)} \times [\$600,000 - (\$360,000 + \$40,000)] = \$180,000$$

The estimates available at 9/30/Y2 are used above.

- By the end of the second year, the Beta project is complete and has resulted in actual gross profit of $110,000 ($560,000 revenues less $450,000 costs). Since gross profit of $180,000 was recognized the first year, a loss of $70,000 must be recognized the second year [$110,000 – $180,000 = $(70,000)]. The loss of $70,000 is in effect an adjustment of the excessive gross profit recognized the first year. Instead of restating the prior period, the prior period misstatement is absorbed in the current period, as is appropriate for a change in estimate.
- Under both the percentage-of-completion method and the completed contract method, for financial accounting purposes, an expected **loss** on a contract must be recognized in full in the period in which the expected loss is discovered. At the end of the first year, London has an expected loss on the Gamma contract [$800,000 – ($410,000 + $410,000) = $(20,000)] that must be recognized immediately.
- By the end of the second year, the expected loss on the Gamma contract has increased to $60,000 [$840,000 – ($720,000 + $180,000)]. Since a loss of $20,000 was recognized the first year, an additional loss of $40,000 must be recognized in the second year to bring the cumulative loss recognized up to the new estimate of $60,000.
- Financial Statement Disclosures require the computation of the 9/30/Y2 balances of accounts receivable, costs and estimated earnings in excess of billings, and billings in excess of costs and estimated earnings. At 10/1/Y1, the balances in all three accounts were $0 since the construction division began operations on that date.

Task-Based Simulation 59

London, Inc. began operation of its construction division on October 1, year 1, and entered into contracts for two separate projects. The Beta project contract price was $600,000 and provided for penalties of $10,000 per week for late completion. Although during year 2 the Beta project had been on schedule for timely completion, it was completed four weeks late in August of year 3. The Gamma project's original contract price was $800,000. Change orders during year 3 added $40,000 to the original contract price.

The following data pertains to the separate long-term construction projects in progress:

	Beta	Gamma
As of September 30, year 2:		
Costs incurred to date	$360,000	$410,000
Estimated costs to complete	40,000	410,000
Billings	315,000	440,000
Cash collections	275,000	365,000
As of September 30, year 3:		
Costs incurred to date	450,000	720,000
Estimated costs to complete	–	180,000
Billings	560,000	710,000
Cash collections	560,000	625,000

Additional information

- London accounts for its long-term construction contracts using the percentage-of-completion method for financial reporting purposes and the completed-contract method for income tax purposes.
- Enacted income tax rates are 25% for year 2 and 30% for future years.
- London's income before income taxes from all divisions, before considering revenues from long-term construction projects, was $300,000 for the year ended September 30, year 2. There were no other temporary or permanent differences.

Prepare the following schedule showing London's balances in the following accounts at September 30, year 2, under the percentage-of-completion method:

- Accounts receivable
- Costs and estimated earnings in excess of billings
- Billings in excess of costs and estimated earnings

London Inc.
Schedule of Selected Balance Sheet Accounts

September 30, year 2:

Accounts receivable

Costs and estimated earnings in excess of billings:

    Construction in progress

    Less: Billings

    Costs and estimated earnings in excess of billings

Billings in excess of costs and estimated earnings

Estimated loss on contract

Task-Based Simulation 59 Solution

Financial Statement Disclosures		
	Authoritative Literature	
		Help

London Inc.
Schedule of Selected Balance Sheet Accounts

September 30, year 2:

Accounts receivable		$115,000
Costs and estimated earnings in excess of billings:		
Construction in progress	$540,000	
Less: Billings	315,000	
Costs and estimated earnings in excess of billings		225,000
Billings in excess of costs and estimated earnings		30,000
Estimated loss on contract		20,000

Explanations

- This problem consists of three related requirements concerning long-term construction contracts. The candidates must compute gross profit recognized for two years using the percentage-of-completion method, compute balances in various accounts, and reconcile financial statement income and taxable income.

- Using the percentage-of-completion method, gross profit is recognized periodically based on progress toward completion of the project using the following formula.

$$\frac{\text{Costs to date}}{\text{Total estimated costs}} \times \text{Estimated profit} = \text{Gross profit to date}$$

For the Beta project, London would recognize gross profit of $180,000 the first year.

$$\frac{\$360,000}{(\$360,000 + \$40,000)} \times [\$600,000 - (\$360,000 + \$40,000)] = \$180,000$$

$$\frac{\text{Costs to date}}{\text{Total estimated costs}} \times \text{Estimated profit} = \text{Gross profit to date}$$

The estimates available at 9/30/Y2 are used above.

- By the end of the second year, the Beta project is complete and has resulted in actual gross profit of $110,000 ($560,000 revenues less $450,000 costs). Since gross profit of $180,000 was recognized the first year, a loss of $70,000 must be recognized the second year [$110,000 − $180,000 = $(70,000)]. The loss of $70,000 is in effect an adjustment of the excessive gross profit recognized the first year. Instead of restating the prior period, the prior period misstatement is absorbed in the current period, as is appropriate for a change in estimate.
- Under both the percentage-of-completion method and the completed contract method, for financial accounting purposes, an expected **loss** on a contract must be recognized in full in the period in which the expected loss is discovered. At the end of the first year, London has an expected loss on the Gamma contract [$800,000 − ($410,000 + $410,000) = $(20,000)] that must be recognized immediately.
- By the end of the second year, the expected loss on the Gamma contract has increased to $60,000 [$840,000 − ($720,000 + $180,000)]. Since a loss of $20,000 was recognized the first year, an additional loss of $40,000 must be recognized in the second year to bring the cumulative loss recognized up to the new estimate of $60,000.
- Financial Statement Disclosures require the computation of the 9/30/Y2 balances of accounts receivable, costs and estimated earnings in excess of billings, and billings in excess of costs and estimated earnings. At 10/1/Y1, the balances in all three accounts were $0 since the construction division began operations on that date.
- **Accounts receivable** is increased by billings:

Accounts receivable
Billings on LT contracts

It is decreased by cash collections

Cash
Accounts receivable

Therefore, 9/30/Y2 AR is computed by adding the billings on the two projects ($315,000 + $440,000 = $755,000) and subtracting the collections on the two projects ($275,000 + $365,000 = $640,000). The 9/30/Y2 balance is $115,000 ($755,000 − $640,000).

- **Construction-in-progress** is debited for costs incurred and profit recognized. **Billings on LT contracts** is credited for billings made. In the balance sheet, the two accounts are netted on a project-by-project basis, resulting in a net current asset and/or a net current liability. At 9/30/Y2, the costs incurred on the Beta project ($360,000) and the estimated earnings ($180,000 from item 2 of this solution guide) exceed billings ($315,000) by $225,000.
- On the Gamma project billings ($440,000) exceed costs ($410,000) by $30,000. There is no estimated earnings on this project because it is expected, at 9/30/Y2, to result in a $20,000 loss. This estimated loss does not affect the excess of billings over costs and estimated earnings because it is reported separately as a current liability.

Task-Based Simulation 60

Assume that you are assigned to the audit of Cole Construction Company. Cole constructs buildings under long-term contracts using the completed contract basis of accounting. Cole has determined that a loss is anticipated on its contract with Hale corporation. Which section of the Professional Standards provides guidance on how this situation should affect Cole's financial statements? Enter your response in the answer fields below.

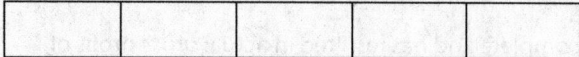

Task-Based Simulation 60 Solution

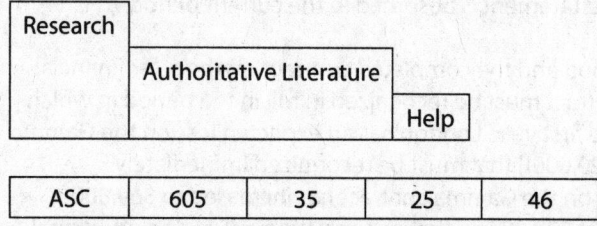

ASC	605	35	25	46

Specific Deferred Revenues

Task-Based Simulation 61

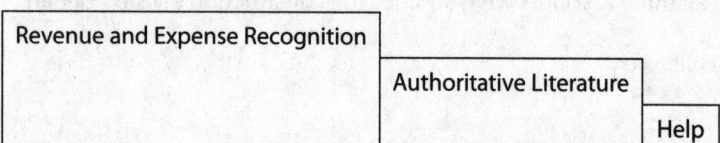

Emco has the following transactions in year 1. Indicate the amount of revenue or expense recognized in year 1, year 2, and year 3 for each of these items. You may show expense recognitions in parentheses (xx).

	Amounts to be recognized		
	Year 1	Year 2	Year 3

1. Emco sells $5,000 of goods to a customer, FOB shipping point on 12/30/Y1.

2. Emco sells three pieces of equipment on a contract over a three-year period. The sales price of each piece of equipment is $10,000. Delivery of each piece of equipment is on February 10 of each year. In year 1, the customer paid a $20,000 down payment, and paid $5,000 per year in year 2 and year 3. Collectibility is reasonably assured.

3. In 1/1/Y1, Emco pays $9,000 for a membership to Wholesalers Association for a two-year membership in the trade association.

4. On 6/1/Y1, Emco signs a contract for $20,000 for goods to be sold on account. Payment is to be made in two installments of $10,000 each on 12/1/Y2 and 12/1/Y3. The goods are delivered on 10/1/Y1. Collection is reasonably assured, and the goods may not be returned.

5. Emco sells goods to a customer on July 1, year 1, for $50,000. If the customer does not sell the goods to retail customers by December 31, year 2, the goods can be returned to Emco. The customer sells the goods to retail customers on October 1, year 2.

Task-Based Simulation 61 Solution

```
┌─────────────────────────────────────┐
│ Revenue and Expense Recognition      │
│          ┌──────────────────────────┐│
│          │ Authoritative Literature  ││
│          │             ┌──────┐      ││
│          │             │ Help │      ││
└──────────┴─────────────┴──────┴──────┘
```

		Amounts to be recognized		
		Year 1	Year 2	Year 3
1.	Emco sells $5,000 of goods to a customer, FOB shipping point on 12/30/Y1.	5,000	–	–
2.	Emco sells three pieces of equipment on a contract over a three-year period. The sales price of each piece of equipment is $10,000. Delivery of each piece of equipment is on February 10 of each year. In year 1, the customer paid a $20,000 down payment, and paid $5,000 per year in year 2 and year 3. Collectibility is reasonably assured.	10,000	10,000	10,000
3.	In 1/1/Y1, Emco pays $9,000 for a membership to Wholesalers Association for a two-year membership in the trade association.	(4,500)	(4,500)	–
4.	On 6/1/Y1, Emco signs a contract for $20,000 for goods to be sold on account. Payment is to be made in two installments of $10,000 each on 12/1/Y2 and 12/1/Y3. The goods are delivered on 10/1/Y1. Collection is reasonably assured, and the goods may not be returned.	20,000	–	–
5.	Emco sells goods to a customer on July 1, year 1, for $50,000. If the customer does not sell the goods to retail customers by December 31, year 2, the goods can be returned to Emco. The customer sells the goods to retail customers on October 1, year 2.	–	50,000	–

Explanations

1. When goods are sold FOB shipping point, title passes at the time the goods are shipped. Therefore, Emco may recognize revenue on 12/30/Y1 at the time the goods are shipped.
2. Revenue is recognized when earned and realizable. This sale is not complete until each piece of equipment is delivered. Therefore, Emco should recognize $10,000 each year as the equipment is delivered, regardless of payment terms.
3. Emco should match expenses to the year in which the benefits are received, which is over the two-year period.
4. Because Emco delivered the goods in year 1, and collectibility is reasonably assured, Emco should recognize all revenue in year 1.
5. Because there is a sale with a right of return, and the buyer may return the merchandise if it is not sold to a retail customer, recognition should be delayed until the right of return has expired.

Income Taxes °

Interperiod Tax Allocation Basics

Task-Based Simulation 62

Assume that you are assigned to the audit of Carson Corporation. The CFO of Carson is unsure of the tax rate that should be used to calculate deferred taxes. Which section of the Professional Standards provides guidance on the tax rate that should be used to calculate deferred taxes? Enter your response in the answer fields below.

Task-Based Simulation 62 Solution

ASC	740	10	30	8

Temporary Differences

Task-Based Simulation 63

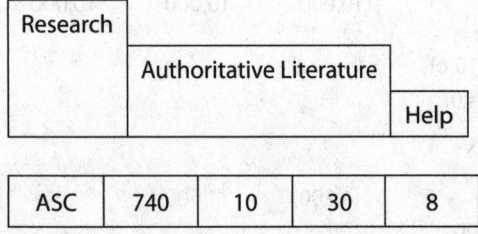

Items 1 through 7 describe circumstances resulting in differences between financial statement income and taxable income. For each numbered item, determine whether the difference is:

A. A temporary difference resulting in a deferred tax asset.

B. A temporary difference resulting in a deferred tax liability.

C. A permanent difference.

Indicate the classification of each item. An answer may be selected once, more than once, or not at all.

		A	B	C
1.	For plant assets, the depreciation expense deducted for tax purposes is in excess of the depreciation expense used for financial reporting purposes.	○	○	○
2.	A landlord collects some rents in advance. Rents received are taxable in the period in which they are received.	○	○	○
3.	Interest is received on an investment in tax-exempt municipal obligations.	○	○	○
4.	Costs of guarantees and warranties are estimated and accrued for financial reporting purposes.	○	○	○
5.	Life insurance proceeds are collected on the death of a key officer.	○	○	○
6.	Bad debts are estimated and expensed on the income statement. No bad debts were charged to the allowance account and written off during the year.	○	○	○
7.	Goodwill is deducted on the tax return.	○	○	○

Task-Based Simulation 63 Solution

```
┌─────────────────┐
│ Tax Differences │
│        ┌────────────────────────┐
│        │ Authoritative Literature │
│        │              ┌──────┐
│        │              │ Help │
└────────┴──────────────┴──────┘
```

		A	B	C
1.	For plant assets, the depreciation expense deducted for tax purposes is in excess of the depreciation expense used for financial reporting purposes.	○	●	○
2.	A landlord collects some rents in advance. Rents received are taxable in the period in which they are received.	●	○	○
3.	Interest is received on an investment in tax-exempt municipal obligations.	○	○	●
4.	Costs of guarantees and warranties are estimated and accrued for financial reporting purposes.	●	○	○
5.	Life insurance proceeds are collected on the death of a key officer.	○	○	●
6.	Bad debts are estimated and expensed on the income statement. No bad debts were charged to the allowance account and written off during the year.	●	○	○
7.	Goodwill is deducted on the tax return.	○	●	○

Explanations

1. (**B**) In cases in which tax depreciation is greater than accounting (book) depreciation, taxable income will be less than accounting income and a deferred tax liability results. The reason is that in future years tax depreciation will be less than book depreciation and taxable income will be greater than book income. This will result in future cash flows for the income tax liability shown on the firm's Form 1120

exceeding those that would occur based on pretax accounting income. Thus a deferred tax liability will result. The entry is

Deferred income tax expense	xx	
Deferred tax liability		xx

In the reversal year, the entry would be

Deferred tax liability	xx	
Deferred tax expense		xx

2. (**A**) Taxable income will exceed pretax accounting (book) income in the year in which the rents are received. In effect, income taxes on the portion of the rent that is unearned for financial reporting under GAAP must be prepaid under the Internal Revenue Code. Thus, a deferred tax asset would result because in future years when the rent received in advance is earned, no taxes will be payable on the amount earned, because the taxes were paid in the year rent was received. The entry is

Deferred tax asset	xx	
Deferred tax expense		xx

3. (**C**) Interest earned on a tax-exempt municipal obligation is a permanent difference. The interest is deducted in the year received from pretax accounting income to arrive at taxable income. However, it will never be reported as income on the firm's Form 1120. Therefore, such a difference does not result in deferred income taxes.

4. (**A**) Costs of guarantees and warranties are not deductible under the Internal Revenue Code until incurred. Under ASC Topic 450, however they are estimated and recorded as an expense (loss) and a liability in the period of sale. In effect, income taxes are prepaid because in later years a benefit is received when these costs are incurred and deducted on the tax return. The entry in the origination year is

Deferred tax asset	xx	
Deferred tax expense		xx

The entry when the warranty costs are deducted is

Deferred tax expense	xx	
Deferred tax asset		xx

5. (**C**) Life insurance proceeds are not taxable under the Internal Revenue Code. This gives rise to a permanent difference.

6. (**A**) The Internal Revenue Code requires the direct write-off method for bad debts. Therefore, bad debts cannot be deducted until the debt becomes uncollectible and is written off. Since no deduction is allowed in the current year, this leads to a future deductible amount and is a deferred tax asset.

7. (**B**) Goodwill is amortized for tax purposes and tested for impairment for GAAP purposes. Therefore, it results in a temporary difference.

Task-Based Simulation 64

Assume that you are assigned to the audit of Yee Corporation. The CFO has asked you to explain what is meant by a temporary difference with respect to deferred taxes. Which section of the Professional

Standards provides the definition of a temporary difference? Enter your response in the answer fields below.

Task-Based Simulation 64 Solution

ASC	740	10	05	7

Task-Based Simulation 65

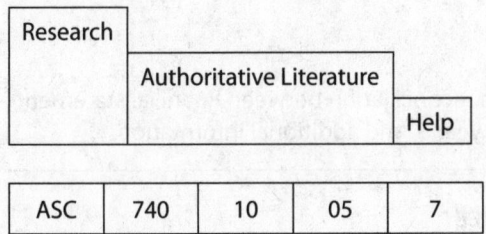

Lindy is a corporation with a calendar year-end for tax purposes. Identify for Lindy which of the following items create temporary differences and which create permanent differences.

	Temporary	Permanent
Premiums on life insurance of key officer	○	○
Depreciation	○	○
Interest on municipal bonds	○	○
Warranties	○	○
Bad debts	○	○
Rent received in advance from clients	○	○

Task-Based Simulation 65 Solution

	Temporary	Permanent
Premiums on life insurance of key officer	○	●
Depreciation	●	○
Interest on municipal bonds	○	●
Warranties	●	○
Bad debts	●	○
Rent received in advance from clients	●	○

Tax Allocation Process

Task-Based Simulation 66

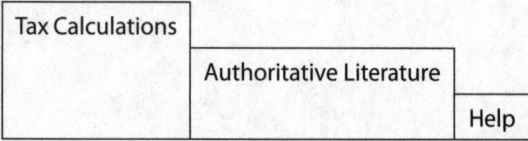

The following partially completed worksheet contain Lane Co.'s reconciliation between financial statement income and taxable income for the three years ended April 30, year 3, and additional information.

Lane Co.
INCOME TAX WORKSHEET
For the Three Years Ended April 30, Year 3

	April 30, Year 1	April 30, Year 2	April 30, Year 3
Pretax financial income	$900,000	$1,000,000	$1,200,000
Permanent differences	100,000	100,000	100,000
Temporary differences	200,000	100,000	150,000
Taxable income	$600,000	$800,000	$950,000
Cumulative temporary differences (future taxable amounts)	$200,000	$ (2)	$450,000
Tax rate	20%	25%	30%
Deferred tax liability	$40,000	$75,000	$ (4)
Deferred tax expense	—	$ (3)	—
Current tax expense	$ (1)	—	—

The tax rate changes were enacted at the beginning of each tax year and were not known to Lane at the end of the prior year.

Items 1 through 4 represent amounts omitted from the worksheet. For each item, determine the amount omitted from the worksheet. Select the amount from the following list. An answer may be used once, more than once, or not at all.

	Amount		
A.	$25,000	H.	$135,000
B.	$35,000	I.	$140,000
C.	$45,000	J.	$160,000
D.	$75,000	K.	$180,000
E.	$100,000	L.	$200,000
F.	$112,500	M.	$300,000
G.	$120,000	N.	$400,000

	Specific audit objective	(A)	(B)	(C)	(D)	(E)	(F)	(G)	(H)	(I)	(J)	(K)	(L)	(M)	(N)
1.	Current tax expense for the year ended April 30, year 1.	O	O	O	O	O	O	O	O	O	O	O	O	O	O
2.	Cumulative temporary differences at April 30, year 2.	O	O	O	O	O	O	O	O	O	O	O	O	O	O
3.	Deferred tax expense for the year ended April 30, year 2.	O	O	O	O	O	O	O	O	O	O	O	O	O	O
4.	Deferred tax liability at April 30, year 3.	O	O	O	O	O	O	O	O	O	O	O	O	O	O

Task-Based Simulation 66 Solution

Tax Calculations

Authoritative Literature

Help

Specific audit objective	(A)	(B)	(C)	(D)	(E)	(F)	(G)	(H)	(I)	(J)	(K)	(L)	(M)	(N)
1. Current tax expense for the year ended April 30, year 1.	○	○	○	○	○	○	●	○	○	○	○	○	○	○
2. Cumulative temporary differences at April 30, year 2.	○	○	○	○	○	○	○	○	○	○	○	○	●	○
3. Deferred tax expense for the year ended April 30, year 2.	○	●	○	○	○	○	○	○	○	○	○	○	○	○
4. Deferred tax liability at April 30, year 3.	○	○	○	○	○	○	○	●	○	○	○	○	○	○

Explanations

1. **(G)** Current tax expense for FY 1 is equal to taxable income (Form 1120) of $600,000 times 20% or $120,000.
2. **(M)** The $100,000 temporary difference for FY 2 is deducted from pretax financial income to arrive at taxable income. Therefore, cumulative temporary differences or future taxable amounts are increased. Thus, $300,000 ($200,000 + $100,000) will be added to pretax financial income in future reversal years.
3. **(B)** Deferred tax expense is equal to the increased rate on future taxable amounts outstanding at the beginning of FY 2 plus the amount related to the $100,000 of temporary differences that originated in FY 2. Thus, deferred tax expense is equal to $35,000 [$200,000 × (.25 − .20) + $100,000 × .25]. The entry is

Deferred tax expense	35,000	
Deferred tax liability		35,000

4. **(H)** In FY 3 cumulative temporary differences (future taxable amounts) increased by $150,000. The deferred tax liability account for three years is shown below.

Deferred Tax Liability

	Year 1	
40,000	(200,000 × .20)	
	Year 2	
10,000	[200,000 × (.25 − .20)]	
25,000	(100,000 × .25)	
	Year 3	
15,000	[300,000 × (.30 − .25)]	
45,000	(150,000 × .30)	
	Bal. 135,000	

The $135,000 is equal to the cumulative temporary differences of $450,000 × .30.

Business Combinations: Acquisition Method of Accounting

Post-Acquisition Issues

Task-Based Simulation 67

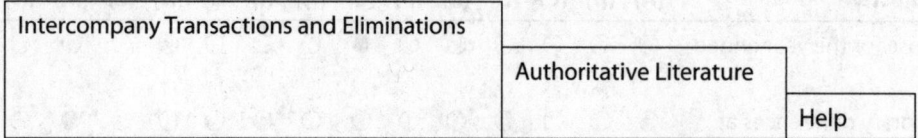

On January 1, year 4, Arcelia Corporation acquired Gavino Corporation by purchasing 100% of the stock of Gavino in exchange for 20,000 shares of Arcelia stock. On the date of acquisition Arcelia stock traded for $18 per share on the stock exchange. The fair value of Gavino's inventory is $10,000 higher than the book value.

The book values of each company on January 1, year 4, are shown below.

	Arcelia Corp.	Gavino Corp.
Current assets	$320,000	$70,000
Noncurrent assets	640,000	380,000
Current liabilities	210,000	50,000
Noncurrent liabilities	150,000	90,000
Owners' equity	600,000	310,000

Additional information

- During year 4, the following transactions occurred:
  1. Arcelia sold inventory to Gavino for $50,000 on account. The normal profit on sales for Arcelia is 40%. At December 31, year 4, Gavino had 20% of the goods remaining in ending inventory. At December 31, year 4, Gavino had not paid Arcelia for $8,000 of the inventory.
  2. On October 1, year 4, Gavino Corp. sold equipment to Arcelia for $24,000. The equipment was purchased by Gavino on 1/1/Y1 for $60,000 and was depreciated straight-line over five years with no salvage value. Arcelia depreciated the new equipment over three years with no salvage value.
- During year 4, Arcelia did not make entries to record the income of Gavino.
- At December 31, year 4, totals from the preclosing trial balances of both firms are as follows:

Arcelia Corporation and Subsidiaries UNADJUSTED TRIAL BALANCE December 31, Year 4		
	Arcelia Corp.	Gavino Corp.
Revenues	1,000,000	400,000
Expenses	780,000	335,000
Current assets	400,000	110,000
Noncurrent assets	1,260,000	420,000
Current liabilities	300,000	70,000
Noncurrent liabilities	180,000	85,000
Owners' equity	960,000	310,000

Below is a consolidation worksheet dated December 31, year 4 (before closing the books of Arcelia and Gavino). Prepare the following worksheet with working paper eliminations and entries.

Arcelia Corporation
CONSOLIDATION WORKSHEET
December 31, Year 4

	Arcelia Corp.	Gavino Corp.	Debit	Credit	End Balance
			Elimination Entries		
Revenues and gains	1,000,000	400,000			
Expenses	780,000	335,000			
Current assets	400,000	110,000			
Noncurrent assets	1,260,000	420,000			
Current liabilities	300,000	70,000			
Differential					
Noncurrent liabilities	180,000	85,000			
Owners' equity	960,000	310,000			

Task-Based Simulation 67 Solution

Intercompany Transactions and Eliminations		
	Authoritative Literature	
		Help

Arcelia Corporation
CONSOLIDATION WORKSHEET
December 31, Year 4

	Arcelia Corp.	Gavino Corp.		Debt	Credit		End Balance
				Elimination Entries			
Revenues and gains	1,000,000	400,000	(c)	50,000			1,341,000
			(e)	9,000			
Expenses	780,000	335,000	(f)	1,000	46,000	(c)	1,070,000
Current assets	400,000	110,000	(b)	10,000	4,000	(c)	508,000
					8,000	(d)	
Noncurrent assets	1,260,000	420,000	(b)	40,000	360,000	(a)	1,350,000
			(e)	36,000	45,000	(e)	
					1,000	(f)	
Differential			(a)	50,000	50,000	(b)	
Current liabilities	300,000	70,000	(d)	8,000			362,000
Noncurrent liabilities	180,000	85,000					265,000
Owners' equity	960,000	310,000	(a)	310,000			960,000

Elimination entries in journal entry form

a. Eliminate subsidiary equity accounts

Common stock and APIC	310,000	
Differential	50,000	
Investment in Gavino		360,000

b. To record asset write-up and goodwill. Goodwill = Acquisition cost $360,000 – FMV of net identifiable assets $320,000 ($460,000 – $140,000) = $40,000 goodwill.

Inventory	10,000	
Goodwill	40,000	
Differential		50,000

c. Eliminate the excess sales and costs of sales and profits in inventory not sold. The intercompany sales of $50,000 must be eliminated, along with the $50,000 in cost of sales reduced by the amount by which ending inventory is overstated. Ending inventory is carried on Gavino's books at $10,000. Ending inventory should be 20% × $30,000 cost to manufacture = $6,000. Therefore, inventory is overstated by $4,000 and cost of sales is overstated by $46,000 ($50,000 – $4,000).

Sales	50,000	
Cost of goods sold		46,000
Ending inventory		4,000

d. Eliminate intercompany receivable and payable

Accounts payable	8,000	
Accounts receivable		8,000

e. Eliminate sale of equipment

Gain on sale of equipment	9,000	
Equipment	36,000	
Accumulated depreciation		45,000

f. Restore depreciation expense as if equipment had not been sold. Normally Gavino depreciates equipment $60,000/5 years = $12,000 per year. Equipment sold on 10/1/Y4; therefore, Gavino recorded depreciation of 3/4 × $12,000 = $9,000. Arcelia's cost is $24,000 and depreciation is recorded straight-line over 3 years = $8,000 per year. However, Arcelia depreciated equipment 3/12 months = $2,000 per year. Total depreciation by both firms = $11,000. Total depreciation if the asset was not sold = $12,000. Therefore, an additional $1,000 depreciation must be recorded.

Depreciation expense	1,000	
Accumulated depreciation		1,000

Financial Instruments: Derivatives and Hedging

Derivatives Introduction

Task-Based Simulation 68

Select the **best** answer for each item from the terms listed in A–O. No answer should be used more than once.

A. An agreement with an unrelated party, binding on both, usually legally enforceable, specifying all significant terms and including a disincentive for nonperformance sufficient to make performance likely.

B. A call option where the price of the underlying is greater than the strike or exercise price of the underlying.

C. A feature on a financial instrument or other contract, which if the feature stood alone, would meet the definition of a derivative.

D. A forward-based contract or agreement generally between two counterparties to exchange streams of cash flows over a specified period in the future.

E. With regard to call options, it is the larger of zero or the spread between the stock price and the exercise price.

F. Provides the holder the right to acquire an underlying at an exercise or stock price, anytime during the option term.

G. An agreement between the two parties to buy and sell a specific quantity of a commodity, foreign currency, or financial instrument at an agreed-upon price, with delivery and/or settlement at a designated future date.

H. A call option where the strike or exercise price is greater than the price of the underlying.

I. The process of separating an embedded derivative from its host contract.

J. The referenced associated asset or liability, commonly a number of units.

K. A specified price or rate such as a stock price, interest rate, or commodity price.

L. An option where the price of the underlying is equal to the strike or exercise price.

M. The difference between an option's price and its intrinsic value.

N. Provides the holder the right to sell the underlying at an exercise or strike price, anytime during the option term.

O. A forward-based contract to make or take delivery of a designated financial instrument, foreign currency, or commodity during a designated period, at a specified price or yield.

	(A)	(B)	(C)	(D)	(E)	(F)	(G)	(H)	(I)	(J)	(K)	(L)	(M)	(N)	(O)
1. At the money	○	○	○	○	○	○	○	○	○	○	○	○	○	○	○
2. Bifurcation	○	○	○	○	○	○	○	○	○	○	○	○	○	○	○
3. Call option	○	○	○	○	○	○	○	○	○	○	○	○	○	○	○
4. Embedded derivative	○	○	○	○	○	○	○	○	○	○	○	○	○	○	○
5. Forward contract	○	○	○	○	○	○	○	○	○	○	○	○	○	○	○
6. Futures contract	○	○	○	○	○	○	○	○	○	○	○	○	○	○	○
7. In the money	○	○	○	○	○	○	○	○	○	○	○	○	○	○	○
8. Notional amount	○	○	○	○	○	○	○	○	○	○	○	○	○	○	○
9. Out of the money	○	○	○	○	○	○	○	○	○	○	○	○	○	○	○
10. Put option	○	○	○	○	○	○	○	○	○	○	○	○	○	○	○
11. Swap	○	○	○	○	○	○	○	○	○	○	○	○	○	○	○
12. Underlying	○	○	○	○	○	○	○	○	○	○	○	○	○	○	○

Task-Based Simulation 68 Solution

Terminology
Authoritative Literature
Help

	(A)	(B)	(C)	(D)	(E)	(F)	(G)	(H)	(I)	(J)	(K)	(L)	(M)	(N)	(O)
1. At the money	○	○	○	○	○	○	○	○	○	○	○	●	○	○	○
2. Bifurcation	○	○	○	○	○	○	○	○	●	○	○	○	○	○	○
3. Call option	○	○	○	○	○	●	○	○	○	○	○	○	○	○	○
4. Embedded derivative	○	○	●	○	○	○	○	○	○	○	○	○	○	○	○
5. Forward contract	○	○	○	○	○	○	●	○	○	○	○	○	○	○	○
6. Futures contract	○	○	○	○	○	○	○	○	○	○	○	○	○	○	●
7. In the money	○	●	○	○	○	○	○	○	○	○	○	○	○	○	○
8. Notional amount	○	○	○	○	○	○	○	○	○	●	○	○	○	○	○
9. Out of the money	○	○	○	○	○	○	○	●	○	○	○	○	○	○	○
10. Put option	○	○	○	○	○	○	○	○	○	○	○	○	○	●	○
11. Swap	○	○	○	●	○	○	○	○	○	○	○	○	○	○	○
12. Underlying	○	○	○	○	○	○	○	○	○	○	●	○	○	○	○

Explanations

1. **(L)** An at-the-money option is one in which the price of the underlying is equal to the strike or exercise price.
2. **(I)** Bifurcation is the process of separating an embedded derivative from its host contract. This process is necessary so that hybrid instruments (a financial instrument or other contract that contains an embedded derivative) can be separated into their component parts, each being accounted for using the appropriate valuation techniques.
3. **(F)** An American call option provides the holder the right to acquire an underlying at an exercise or strike price anytime during the option term. A premium is paid by the holder for the right to benefit from the appreciation in the underlying.
4. **(C)** An embedded derivative is a feature on a financial instrument or other contract which, if the feature stood alone, would meet the definition of a derivative.
5. **(G)** A forward contract is an agreement between two parties to buy and sell a specific quantity of a commodity, foreign currency, or financial instrument at an agreed-upon price, with delivery and/or settlement at a designated future date. Because a forward contract is not formally regulated by an organized exchange, each party to the contract is subject to the default of the other party.
6. **(O)** A futures contract is a forward-based contract to make or take delivery of a designated financial instrument, foreign currency, or commodity during a designated period, at a specified price or yield. The contract frequently has provisions for cash settlement. A futures contract is traded on a regulated exchange and, therefore, involves less credit risk than a forward contract.
7. **(B)** A call option is in the money if the price of the underlying is greater than the strike or exercise price of the underlying.
8. **(J)** The notional amount (or payment provision) is the referenced associated asset or liability. A notional amount is commonly a number of units such as shares of stock, principal amount, face value, stated value, basis points, barrels of oil, and so forth. It may be that amount plus a premium or minus a discount. The interaction of the price or rate (underlying) with the referenced associated asset or liability (notional amount) determines whether settlement is required and, if so, the amount.
9. **(H)** A call option is out of the money if the strike or exercise price is greater than the price of the underlying. A put option is out of the money if the price of the underlying is greater than the strike or exercise option.
10. **(N)** An American put option provides the holder the right to sell the underlying at an exercise or strike price, anytime during the option term. A gain accrues to the holder as the market price of the underlying falls below the strike price.
11. **(D)** A swap is a forward-based contract or agreement generally between two counterparties to exchange streams of cash flows over a specified period in the future.
12. **(K)** An underlying is commonly a specified price or rate such as a stock price, interest rate, currency rate, commodity price, or a related index. However, any variable (financial or physical) with (1) observable changes or (2) objectively verifiable changes such as a credit rating, insurance index, or climatic or geological condition (temperature, rainfall) qualifies. Unless it is specifically excluded, a

contract based on any qualifying variable is accounted for under the rules for derivatives if it has the distinguishing characteristics stated above.

Foreign Currency Hedges

Task-Based Simulation 69

Reston Corporation has a gain on a foreign currency fair value hedge. You have been asked to research the professional literature to determine where the gain should be reported in the financial statements.

Place the citation for the excerpt from the Professional Standards that provides this information in the answer box below.

Task-Based Simulation 69 Solution

ASC	815	25	35	16

Foreign Currency Denominated Transactions

Introduction and Definitions

Task-Based Simulation 70

Situation

Logan Corporation markets their products internationally. The company buys and sells goods in Great Britain, France, and Germany. Although Logan's functional currency is the U.S. dollar, the transactions are denominated in the currencies for each country as shown in the table below.

Country	Currency
Great Britain	£
France	€
Germany	€

The spot rates for various dates throughout the year are shown below.

Date	U.S. $ per £1	U.S. $ per €1
January 1, year 1	1.786	1.258
March 1, year 1	1.869	1.249
April 15, year 1	1.791	1.197
November 10, year 1	1.857	1.290
December 1, year 1	1.911	1.329
December 20, year 1	1.945	1.333
December 31, year 1	1.927	1.364
January 15, year 2	1.869	1.311
Average daily rate, year 1	1.886	1.279

The following transactions are denominated in each country's local currency.

On March 1, year 1, Logan sells goods on account to Lexington Corporation, located in London, for £370,000. The account is due in 60 days. Lexington pays the full balance due on April 15, year 1.

On November 10, year 1, Logan purchases supplies from Dietmar Corporation in Germany €190,000. On December 1, year 1, Logan pays Dietmar for the supplies.

On December 20, year 1, Logan sells goods on account to Cordier Corporation in France for €250,000. Cordier pays for the goods on January 15, year 2.

Prepare the following schedule outlining the foreign currency transaction gains and losses for year 1 and year 2 for Logan Corporation.

Logan Corporation
SCHEDULE OF FOREIGN CURRENCY TRANSACTION GAINS/LOSSES
Year 1 and Year 2

	Year 1 Gain/(Loss)	Year 2 Gain/(Loss)
Lexington Corporation		
Dietmar Corporation		
Cordier Corporation		
Total FC gain/(loss)		

Indicate from the list below where the foreign currency transaction gain or loss in year 1 will be disclosed on the financial statements.

A. Other gain/loss
B. Other comprehensive income
C. Revenue
D. Expense

	(A)	(B)	(C)	(D)
1. Foreign currency transaction gain/loss for year 1 will be disclosed where on the financial statement?	○	○	○	○

Task-Based Simulation 70 Solution

Logan Corporation		
SCHEDULE OF FOREIGN CURRENCY TRANSACTION GAINS/LOSSES		
Year 1 and Year 2		
	Year 1 Gain/(Loss)	**Year 2 Gain/(Loss)**
Lexington Corporation	(28,860)	0
Dietmar Corporation	(7410)	0
Cordier Corporation	7,750	(13,250)
Total FC gain/(loss)	(28,520)	(13,250)

	(A)	(B)	(C)	(D)
1. Foreign currency transaction gain/loss for year 1 will be disclosed where on the financial statement?	●	○	○	○

Export Transaction

Task-Based Simulation 71

Journal Entries

Authoritative Literature

Help

Situation

Logan Corporation markets their products internationally. The company buys and sells goods in Great Britain, France, and Germany. Although Logan's functional currency is the U.S. dollar, the transactions are denominated in the currencies for each country as shown in the table below.

Country	Currency
Great Britain	£
France	€
Germany	€

The spot rates for various dates throughout the year are shown below.

Date	U.S. $ per £1	U.S. $ per €1
January 1, year 1	1.786	1.258
March 1, year 1	1.869	1.249
April 15, year 1	1.791	1.197
November 10, year 1	1.857	1.290
December 1, year 1	1.911	1.329

(Continued)

Date	U.S. $ per £1	U.S. $ per €1
December 20, year 1	1.945	1.333
December 31, year 1	1.927	1.364
January 15, year 2	1.869	1.311
Average daily rate, year 1	1.886	1.279

The following transactions are denominated in each country's local currency.

On March 1, year 1, Logan sells goods on account to Lexington Corporation, located in London, for £370,000. The account is due in 60 days. Lexington pays the full balance due on April 15, year 1.

On November 10, year 1, Logan purchases supplies from Dietmar Corporation in Germany for €190,000. On December 1, year 1, Logan pays Dietmar for the supplies.

On December 20, year 1, Logan sells goods on account to Cordier Corporation in France for €250,000. Cordier pays for the goods on January 15, year 2.

1. Prepare the journal entry for the sale of goods to Lexington on March 1.

2. Prepare the journal entry on April 15, year 1, when Lexington pays for the goods.

3. Prepare the journal entry for the purchase of supplies from Dietmar Corporation on November 10, year 1.

4. Prepare the journal entry for the payment to Dietmar on December 1, year 1.

5. Prepare the journal entry for the sale of goods to Cordier Corporation.

6. Prepare any entries necessary on December 31, year 1, with regard to the foreign currency transactions with Lexington, Dietmar, and Cordier Corporation.

7. Prepare the journal entry for Cordier's payment of goods on January 15, year 2.

Task-Based Simulation 71 Solution

Journal Entries		
	Authoritative Literature	
		Help

---

1. Accounts receivable (£)   691,530

    Sales   691,530

£370,000 × 1.869 = $691,530

---

2. Cash   662,670

  Loss on FC transaction   28,860

    Accounts receivable (£)   691,530

£370,000 × 1.791 = $662,670

---

3. Supplies   245,100

    Accounts payable (€)   245,100

€190,000 × 1.290 = $245,100

---

4. Accounts payable (€)   245,100

  Loss on FC transaction   7,410

  Cash   252,510

€190,000 × 1.329 = $252,510

---

5. Accounts receivable (€)   333,250

  Sales   333,250

€250,000 × 1.333 = $333,250

---

6. Accounts receivable (€)   7,750

    Gain on FC transaction   7,750

Adjust to spot rate on balance sheet date
€250,000 × (1.364 − 1.333) = $7,750 gain

---

3. Cash   327,750

  Loss on FC transaction   13,250

    Accounts receivable (€)   341,000

€250,000 × 1.311 = $327,750

Original A/R of $333,250 + $7,750 gain = $341,000 balance in
  A/R as of 12/31/Y1

Loss is $341,000 − $327,750 = $13,250

Explanations

Foreign currency transactions are recorded at the spot rate on the date of the transaction. When the account is settled in the foreign currency, the currency is exchanged at the spot rate on the date of settlement, and any gain or loss is recognized as a transaction gain/loss.

If the account is outstanding at the balance sheet date, the account receivable or payable is adjusted to the spot rate on the balance sheet date and the gain/loss from foreign currency transaction is recognized as other income for the period.

Conversion Using Translation

Task-Based Simulation 72

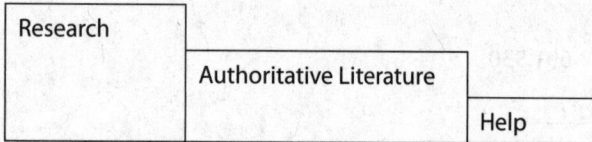

Emory Company has operations in the United States and Japan. You have been asked to research the professional literature to determine the exchange rate that should be used to translate a foreign currency transaction. Place the citation for the excerpt from the Professional Standards that provides this information in the answer box below.

Task-Based Simulation 72 Solution

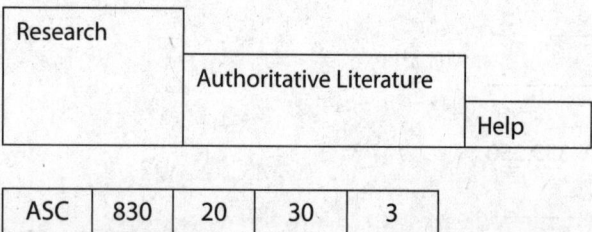

ASC	830	20	30	3

Leases

Capital Lease Examples

Task-Based Simulation 73

Situation

- Link Co. purchased an office building and the land on which it is located by paying $800,000 cash and assuming an existing mortgage of $200,000. The property is assessed at $960,000 for realty tax purposes, of which 60% is allocated to the building.

- Link leased construction equipment under a seven-year capital lease requiring annual year-end payments of $100,000. Link's incremental borrowing rate is 9%, while the lessor's implicit rate, which is not known to Link, is 8%. Present value factors for an ordinary annuity for seven periods are 5.21 at 8% and 5.04 at 9%. Fair value of the equipment is $515,000.
- Link paid $50,000 and gave a plot of undeveloped land with a carrying amount of $320,000 and a fair value of $450,000 to Club Co. in exchange for a plot of undeveloped land with a fair value of $500,000. The land was carried on Club's books at $350,000. This transaction is considered to lack commercial substance; the configuration of cash flows from the land acquired is not expected to be significantly different from the configuration of cash flows of the land exchanged.

Calculate the following amounts to be recorded by Link.

	Amount
1. Building.	
2. Leased equipment.	
3. Land received from Club on Link's books.	
4. Land received from Link on Club's books.	

Task-Based Simulation 73 Solution

Asset Valuation

Authoritative Literature

Help

1. (**$600,000**) Since the land and building were purchased together, the cost of each must be allocated based on the relative market value. The land and building were purchased together for a total cost of $1,000,000 ($800,000 cash + $200,000 mortgage assumption). For property tax purposes, the building is deemed to be 60% of the value of the land and building. Therefore, the cost of the building should be recorded at $600,000 ($1,000,000 × 60%).

2. (**$504,000**) As the lease is classified as a capital lease, Link must record an asset and liability based on the present value of the minimum lease payments. However, the leased assets cannot be recorded at an amount greater than the fair value. To determine the minimum value of the lease payments, Link should discount the future payments using the **lesser** of the lessee's (Link's) incremental borrowing rate (9%) or the lessor's implicit rate if **known** by the lessee. Therefore, since Link does not know the lessor's implicit rate, Link's rate of 9% should be used. The recorded value would be $100,000 × 5.04 = $504,000, which is less than the fair value.

3. (**$370,000**) In recording a nonmonetary exchange, if the transaction lacks commercial substance, the asset received is recorded at the book value of the asset given up plus any boot given when gains and losses are not recognized. The following fact pattern exists for Link:

	Boot	FV	BV	Gain (Loss)
Land given	50,000	450,000	320,000	130,000
Land received		500,000		

Link will record the land received from Club at the book value of the land given up plus the boot given ($320,000 + 50,000 = $370,000).

An alternative method to calculate the value to record the land at is to subtract the deferred gain from the fair value of the land received ($500,000 − 130,000 = $370,000).

4. **($315,000)** On Club's books the following situation exists:

	Boot	FV	BV	Gain (Loss)
Land given		500,000	350,000	150,000
Land received	50,000	450,000		

An exception to the nonrecognition of gain on similar assets exists when boot is received. The earnings process is considered complete for the portion related to the boot received, but not complete for the portion related to the asset received. A gain is recognized only for the portion related to the boot. The gain is computed as follows:

$$\frac{\text{Boot received}}{\text{Boot received} + \text{FMV of assets received}} \times \text{Total gain} = \text{Gain recognized}$$

$$\frac{50,000}{50,000 + 450,000} \times 150,000 = \$15,000$$

The land received will be recorded at its fair value less the gain deferred.

$$\$450,000 - (150,000 - 15,000) = \$315,000$$

An alternative method is to record the land received at the book value of the land given less the boot received plus the gain recognized, as follows:

$$\$350,000 - 50,000 + 15,000 = \$315,000$$

Index

A